MyDevelopmentLab

◄ The Video Series for *Human Sexuality* is available in MyDevelopmentLab, as well as through our web app for iPad and iPhone.

◄ The collection contains over 125 engaging clips, selected from a variety of sources. Students will find current video segments for each chapter of their text.

◄ Every video clip is accompanied by an introduction that identifies the main ideas. Many videos also have media assignments that allow instructors to assess student comprehension.

Why Do You Need This New Edition?

10 good reasons why you should buy this new edition of *Human Sexuality in a World of Diversity!*

1. Thorough updating of new scientific developments in the field throughout the text.

2. The new "*My Life, My Sexuality*" personalizes the study of human sexuality by encouraging students to reflect upon their own feelings, beliefs, and experiences and to think critically about topics discussed in the text.

3. Integration of print and digital media through use of QR codes in text that directly link students to online resources, including related videos and "*My Life, My Sexuality*" features.

4. New pedagogical features that support student learning and encourage critical thinking, including new learning objectives and a new review summary for each chapter.

5. Coverage of new topics such as surgical restoration of virginity prior to marriage, the relationship between intelligence and semen quality, the sexual appeal of the color red, and many others.

6. Updated coverage of topics such as gender differences (or, should we say, similarities?) in math ability, research reporting that boys and girls show visual preferences for gender-typed toys (trucks and dolls) at the ages of 3 to 8 months, and many others.

7. Twenty new "Closer Look" and "World of Diversity" boxed features.

8. New *Real Students—Real Questions* boxed features throughout the text.

9. New case studies, including Penn State child sexual abuse scandal involving Jerry Sandusky, Joe Paterno, and university officials, and 2012 Secret Service scandal involving prostitutes in Colombia.

10. This edition is accompanied by the new MyDevelopmentLab Video Series for Human Sexuality, which contains over 125 clips that the most recent research, science, and applications in human sexuality.

Human Sexuality

in a World of Diversity

Ninth Edition

Human Sexuality

in a World of Diversity

Spencer A. Rathus
The College of New Jersey

Jeffrey S. Nevid
St. John's University

Lois Fichner-Rathus
The College of New Jersey

PEARSON

Boston   Columbus   Indianapolis   New York   San Francisco   Upper Saddle River
Amsterdam   Cape Town   Dubai   London   Madrid   Milan   Munich   Paris   Montréal   Toronto
Delhi   Mexico City   São Paulo   Sydney   Hong Kong   Seoul   Singapore   Taipei   Tokyo

Editorial Director: *Craig Campanella*
Editor in Chief: *Jessica Mosher*
Acquisitions Editor: *Amber Chow*
Editorial Assistant: *Alexis Rodriguez*
VP, Director of Marketing: *Brandy Dawson*
Marketing Manager: *Jeremy Intal*
Marketing Assistant: *Frank Alarcon*
Director of Production: *Lisa Iarkowski*
Managing Editor: *Denise Forlow*
Project Manager, Production: *Shelly Kupperman*
Operations Supervisor: *Mary Fischer*
Operations Specialist: *Diane Peirano*

Creative Design Director: *Jodi Notowitz*
Interior/Cover Design: *Wanda Espana / Wee Design Group*
Digital Media Editor: *Amy Trudell*
Digital Media Project Manager: *Caitlin Smith*
Director of Development: *Sharon Geary*
Development Editor: *LeeAnn Doherty*
Full-Service Project Management: *GEX Publishing Services*
Printer/Binder: *Courier/Kendallville*
Cover Printer: *Lehigh-Phoenix Color/Hagerstown*
Cover Image: *Aleksandr Markin/Shutterstock*
Text Font: *Sabon LT Std 10.25/13*

Credits and acknowledgments borrowed from other sources and reproduced, with permission, in this textbook appear on the appropriate page of appearance.

10 9 8 7 6 5 4 3 2 1

ISBN-10:   0-205-94061-7
ISBN-13: 978-0-205-94061-5

Dedication

Dedicated with love to our children, Taylor Lane Rathus and Michael Zev Nevid, who were born at the time the first edition of this book was written.

Brief Contents

Contents

11 Conception, Pregnancy, and Childbirth 290

12 Contraception and Abortion 334

Feature Boxes

Self-Assessment

My Life, My Sexuality

Preface

There are more things in heaven and earth, Horatio,
Than are dreamt of
in your philosophy.

—Shakespeare, *Hamlet*

There are indeed more kinds of people in this world, and more ways in which people experience their sexuality, than most of us might imagine. Human sexuality may be intimately related to human biology, but it is embedded within the fabric of human cultures and societies. The approach that has separated *Human Sexuality in a World of Diversity* from other human sexuality textbooks is its full embrace of the richness of human diversity.

We would like to begin by discussing what has changed in the ninth edition, including new features. We will introduce the unique themes of our text, which represent continuing concerns in the realm of human sexuality. We will also review the supplements and media that accompany the text, which were carefully selected to engage students and enrich the learning process.

What's New in the Ninth Edition

The ninth edition of *Human Sexuality in a World of Diversity* embodies many exciting changes—changes that reflect the rapid developments in the behavioral and social sciences, and in biology and medicine. In addition to what is listed in the following sections, there are literally hundreds of new references throughout the text that reflect the newest research in the field of human sexuality. No part of the text has been left untouched by change. The following are just a few examples of updates within chapters.

CHAPTER 1

New: List of biblical sexual prohibitions of Leviticus

New: Results from the 2011 National Survey of Sexual Health

New: Update on erotic plasticity

New: My Life, My Sexuality: Talking Critically about Sexual Advice on the Internet–Are there any Quick Fixes?

CHAPTER 2

Updated: Coverage of National Surveys of Family Growth (NSFG)

Updated: Coverage of objective and subjective approaches to measurement of sexual arousal: "What Does a Woman Want?"

Updated: Coverage of effectiveness of Viagra with women

New: My Life, My Sexuality: Thinking about Research Methods in Human Sexuality

CHAPTER 3

Updated: Coverage of female genital mutilation

Updated: Coverage of cervical cancer, especially screening and treatment results at various stages

Updated: Coverage of risk factors for, and prevention of, endometrial cancer

Updated: Coverage of risk factors for ovarian cancer

Updated: Coverage of risk factors for breast cancer and the cost-benefit considerations of mammography

Updated: Coverage of menstrual problems

New: My Life, My Sexuality: Taking Charge of my Sexual Health

CHAPTER 4

Updated: Coverage of the controversies surrounding circumcision

Updated: Coverage of prostate cancer, including risk factors and new screening guidelines

New: My Life, My Sexuality: What do I Know about my Health Needs?

CHAPTER 5

Updated: Coverage of the role of body odor in sexual attraction

Updated: Coverage of use of alcohol and sexual response

Updated: Coverage of sex hormones and sexual response

New: Coverage of female orgasm in response to exercise ("coregasm")

New: My Life, My Sexuality: What Role do Vision and Smell Play in Sexually Arousing me?*

CHAPTER 6

New: Vignette about the experiences of a transgendered woman: Jayne Thomas

Updated: Coverage of factors in gender identity

Updated: Coverage of cognitive gender differences (and similarities)

New: My Life, My Sexuality: Feminine, Masculine or Androgyny? *

CHAPTER 7

New: Vignette about sexual attraction and the color red

Updated: Coverage of possible genetic contributions to gender differences in preferences for mates

Updated: Coverage of the attraction–similarity hypothesis

New: My Life, My Sexuality: What do you Think you Should be Thinking about when in the Market for a Long-Term Relationship?

CHAPTER 8

New: Coverage of online dating's role in matchmaking

Updated: Coverage of jealousy and evolutionary theory

New: Coverage of the cognitive perspective on jealousy

New: My Life, My Sexuality: Communication Skills for Enhancing Relationships and Sexual Relations—How To Do It

CHAPTER 9

New: Update on demographic factors and masturbation

New: Coverage of women's and men's beliefs about the use of vibrators

New: Coverage of demographic factors and frequency of marital sex

New: My Life, My Sexuality: What Would you do with Whom?

CHAPTER 10

Updated: Discussion of the classification of sexual orientation

Updated: Polls relating demographic factors to self-identification as LGBT

Updated: Discussion of biological factors—genetics, the brain, and hormonal influences—on sexual orientation

Updated: Discussion of the status of gay marriage around the world

Updated: Discussion of U.S. attitudes toward recognition of committed gay and lesbian relationships

New: Discussion of the end of "Don't ask—don't tell"

New: My Life, My Sexuality: Assessing your Attitudes toward Gay Males and Lesbians

CHAPTER 11

Updated: Discussion of attraction of sperm to odor resulting from changes in calcium ions

Updated: Discussion of male and female fertility problems, including causes and methods of treatment

New: Feature on LGBT family building

Updated: Discussion of the effects of use of marijuana, alcohol, and cigarettes during pregnancy

New: Update on the prevalence of C-sections

New: Discussion of global fertility rates

New: Update on factors in global maternal and infant mortality

New: Update on factors in, and benefits (and risks) of, breastfeeding

New: My Life, My Sexuality: Selecting an Obstetrician

CHAPTER 12

Updated: Information on the effectiveness, benefits, and risks associated with methods of contraception

New: Discussion of the revived interest in the IUD

New: Feature on errors in using condoms

Updated: Coverage of global sex selection through abortion of female embryos

Updated: Polls concerning U.S. attitudes toward abortion

New: My Life, My Sexuality: Talking with your Partner and Contraception

CHAPTER 13

Updated: Coverage of the effects of co-sleeping with children

Updated: Coverage of they ways in which children and adolescents learn about sex

Updated: Coverage of "sexting"

New: Update on the (declining) incidence of sexual intercourse among teenagers

Updated: Information on teenagers' use of contraception, attitudes toward their first sexual experience, and reasons for *not* having sex

New: Update on the declining incidence of teenage pregnancy—and why

New: Coverage of demographic factors and geographic location in teenage pregnancy

New: My Life, My Sexuality: Talking with your Children about Sex

CHAPTER 14

New: Update on median age at first marriage

New: Update on lifestyles associated with being single

New: Coverage of factors in "sexual hookups"

New: Update on increasing incidence of cohabitation *and* of high school seniors' attitudes toward cohabitation

New: Update on the declining incidence of marriage—and why

New: Coverage of high school seniors' attitudes toward marriage

New: Coverage of intermarriage—"marrying out" versus "marrying in"

Updated: Coverage of factors in marital satisfaction

Updated: Coverage of factors that increase and decrease the incidence of divorce

New: My Life, My Sexuality: Making Decisions about Your Style of Life

CHAPTER 15

Updated: Terminology and definitions for certain sexual dysfunctions, according to changes in the DSM (DSM-5)

Updated: Discussion of biological factors in sexual dysfunctions

Updated: Discussion of biological treatments for sexual dysfunctions

New: My Life, My Sexuality: Finding a Qualified Sex Therapist

CHAPTER 16

Updated: Discussion of trends in the incidence of sexually transmitted infections (STIs)— the latest findings from the CDC's STI Surveillance

Updated: Discussion of geographical factors in rates of syphilis, chlamydia, and other STIs

Updated: Discussion of ethnicity and infection by HIV

New: Diversity feature on whether use of hormonal methods of contraception is increasing the risk of being infected with HIV in sub-Saharan Africa

Updated: Discussion of human papilloma virus and its links to cancer in both women and men

New: My Life, My Sexuality: Talking with your Partner about STIs

CHAPTER 17

Updated: Discussion of the meaning of normal versus deviant sexual behavior

Updated: Discussion of cybersex addiction

New: Discussion of the new DSM-5 category, *hypersexual disorder*

New: My Life, My Sexuality: How to Respond to an Exhibitionist

CHAPTER 18

New: Vignette about the Penn State scandal involving Jerry Sandusky and Joe Paterno

Updated: Information on the incidence of rape

New: Information about violence committed by intimate partners

New: Update on the incidence of childhood sexual abuse

New: My Life, My Sexuality: Rape Prevention

CHAPTER 19

New: Vignette about the scandal involving secret service agents and prostitutes in Columbia

Updated: Information about the various kinds of prostitutes, female and male

New: Increased discussion of whether prostitution is harmful to prostitutes and whether prostitution should be legalized throughout the United States

New: My Life, My Sexuality: Developing Self Control to Avoid Use of Commercial Sex Outlets

The Themes of Human Sexuality in a World of Diversity

The ninth edition of *Human Sexuality in a World of Diversity* builds on the strong themes for which it has come to be known:

1. The rich diversity found in gender roles, sexual attitudes, and sexual behaviors and customs
2. Critical thinking
3. Making responsible sexual decisions
4. Sexual health

Theme 1: Human Diversity Colleges and universities are undertaking the mission of broadening students' perspectives so that they will appreciate and tolerate human diversity. The United States is a nation of hundreds of different ethnic and religious groups, many of which endorse culturally distinctive beliefs about appropriate gender roles for men and women, and distinctive sexual practices and customs. Diversity is even greater within the global village of the world's nearly 200 nations and the subcultures of those nations. *Human Sexuality in a World of Diversity* incorporates a multicultural, multiethnic perspective that reflects the diversity of sexual experience in our society and around the world. Our book thereby broadens students' understanding of the range of cultural differences in sexual attitudes and behavior worldwide and within our own society.

In addition, the "A World of Diversity" feature highlights the rich variety of human sexual customs and practices in our own society and in others around the world. Discussion of diversity encourages respect for people who hold diverse beliefs and attitudes. We also encourage students to question what is deemed appropriate for women and men in terms of social roles and sexual conduct in light of cultural traditions and standards.

Theme 2: Critical Thinking Colleges and universities in the new millennium are also encouraging students to become critical thinkers. Today's students are so inundated with information about gender and sexuality that it can be difficult to sort truth from fiction. Not only do politicians, theologians, and community leaders influence our gender- and sex-related attitudes and behaviors, but newspapers, TV programs, the Internet, and other media also brim with features about gender roles and issues concerning human sexuality.

Critical thinking means being skeptical of information that is presented in print or on the Internet, or uttered by authority figures or celebrities. Critical thinking requires thoughtful analysis and probing of the claims and arguments of others in light of evidence. Moreover, it requires a willingness to challenge conventional wisdom and common knowledge that many of us take for granted. It means scrutinizing definitions of terms, evaluating the premises or assumptions that underlie arguments, and examining the logic of arguments.

Throughout this book we raise issues that demand critical thinking. These issues are intended to stimulate student interest in analyzing and evaluating their beliefs and attitudes toward gender roles and sexuality in light of the accumulated scientific evidence. Moreover, this new edition fosters critical thinking through a section called "Thinking Critically about Human Sexuality" in Chapter 1, and by including "Critical Thinking" questions throughout each chapter.

Theme 3: Responsible Sexual Decision Making We also encourage students to make responsible sexual decisions. There are psychological and physical dangers in "going with the flow" or being passive about one's sexuality. Of course we do not encourage students to be sexually active (such a decision is personal). On the other hand, we do encourage students to make their own sexual decisions actively, on the basis of accurate information.

Decision making is deeply intertwined with individuals' sexual experiences. For example, each person needs to decide

- whom to date, and how and when to become sexually intimate
- whether to practice contraception and which methods to use
- how to protect himself or herself against HIV/AIDS and other STIs

Responsible sexual decision making is based not only on acquiring accurate information but also on carefully evaluating this information in the light of one's own moral values. We encourage students always to consider their own values, needs, and interests, rather than going along with the crowd or merely acceding to the wishes or demands of their partners. Throughout the text we provide students with the information they need to make responsible decisions about their physical health, the gender roles they will enact, sexual practices, birth control, and prevention of STIs. We also provide students with a unique opportunity to consider their feelings and think critically about their sexual philosophy with our new "My Life, My Sexuality feature." We have created a feature for every chapter, all of which can be accessed in MyDevelopmentLab and via QR code.

Theme 4: Sexual Health *Human Sexuality in a World of Diversity* places a strong emphasis on issues relating to sexual health, including extensive coverage of such topics as HIV/AIDS and other STIs, innovations in contraception and reproductive technologies, breast cancer, menstrual distress, sex and disabilities, and diseases that affect the reproductive tract. The text encourages students to take an active—in fact, a proactive—role in health promotion. For example, the book includes exercises and features that help students examine their bodies for abnormalities, reduce the risk of HIV infection, and cope with menstrual discomfort.

Features

Like earlier editions, the ninth edition of *Human Sexualitsy in a World of Diversity* contains various features that stimulate student interest and enhance understanding.

NEW! Learning Objectives Featured at the beginning of each chapter, new learning objectives help guide student reading by identifying main ideas and defining learning goals. These learning objectives appear again in the end of chapter summary, to help reinforce key information. They are also used to organize the Test Bank and Instructor Manual.

NEW! My Life, My Sexuality For every chapter, we have created a new online feature that encourages students to consider their feelings, think critically about their sexual philosophy, and apply what they have learned in the course. These features introduce topics and issues that students will likely face, like how to manage their sexual health or how to build effective communication skills with a partner. Each one of these online features is accompanied by a brief video clip that explores the issue further, as well as critical thinking questions that make it easy to assign. These features are available in MyDevelopmentLab and via QR code. To use QR codes, first download any free QR reader or bar code scanner app from your smartphone or tablet computer.

Real Students, Real Questions What do students know about human sexuality? What are they too embarrassed to ask of professors, peers, or parents? This feature highlights questions, collected from college students from across the country, on any human sexuality topic concerning them—big or small. We then answer their questions. Sample questions include the following:

- One of my breasts is bigger than the other. Is this normal?

- How do you tell someone the relationship is over?

- How can I keep my partner interested in sex? We've been together for five years.

A World of Diversity The "A World of Diversity" feature highlights the rich variety of human sexual customs and practices in our own society and in those throughout the world. Viewing human sexuality in a multicultural context helps students better understand how cultural beliefs, values, and attitudes can influence the expression of sexuality. Students may come to understand that their partners, who may not share the same ethnic or religious heritage as themselves, may feel differently than they do about sexual intimacy. Students will learn about cultural differences related to gender roles, sexual orientation, sexual jealousy, and premarital and extramarital sexual patterns.

A Closer Look The "A Closer Look" feature provides in-depth discussions of scientific techniques (for example, "Physiological Measures of Sexual Arousal") and skill-building exercises ("Breast Self-Examination," "Self-Examination of the Testes").

Self-Assessments Self-scoring questionnaires stimulate students' interest and provide self-insight by helping them satisfy their curiosity about themselves. These questionnaires also enhance the relevance of the text to students' lives. Examples include "Would You Tell an Interviewer the Truth on a Survey about Your Sexual Behavior? The Social-Desirability Scale" and "Sternberg's Triangular Love Scale" (which may help students decide whether they are "in love" and, if so, just what type of love they are in). Scoring rubrics are found in the appendix at the end of the text.

Truth or Fiction and Truth or Fiction Revisited These unique chapter-opening devices motivate students by challenging common sense, stereotypes, and folklore. "Truth or Fiction Revisited" sections are interspersed throughout each chapter and provide feedback to students regarding the accuracy of their assumptions in light of the evidence presented in the chapter.

Running Glossary Research shows that most students do not make use of glossaries at the end of books. Searching for the meanings of terms is a difficult task and distracts them from the subject matter. Therefore, *Human Sexuality in a World of Diversity* has a running glossary. Key terms are in bold type in the text and are defined in the margins near to where they appear. Students can readily find the meanings of key terms without breaking their concentration on the flow of the material.

A Comprehensive Supplements and Media Package

Human Sexuality in a World of Diversity presents instructors and students with a wide range of ancillaries and teaching aids.

INSTRUCTOR RESOURCES

MyDevelopmentLab for Human Sexuality NEW! MyDevelopmentLab for Human Sexuality combines proven learning applications with powerful assessment to engage students, assess their learning, and help them succeed.

Instructor's Manual Updated for the ninth edition, this online instructor's manual is a wonderful tool for classroom preparation and management. Organized by the same learning objectives that appear throughout the text, each chapter begins with an "at a glance" grid, which makes it easy for instructors to survey the available teaching tools and and find what they need. Each chapter contains a wealth of teaching tips, lecture launchers, discussion questions, activities, and references to online resources, and is hyperlinked to make navigation simple.

Test Bank A thoroughly revised and updated test bank helps instructors prepare for exams with challenging questions that target key concepts. Each chapter includes more than 100 questions, including multiple choice, true/false, short answer, and essay, each with a page reference, a difficulty rating, type designation, and reference to the textual learning objective it reinforces. This product is also available in MyTest and Black-Board/WebCT cartridges for ease in creating exams.

Powerpoint Presentation NEW for this edition, we are happy to offer highly visual, designed PowerPoint slides that support instructors in creating dynamic lectures. We also offer simple lecture PowerPoints that are easily modified to suit a variety of teaching styles.

MyDevelopmentLab Video Series for Human Sexuality The NEW MyDevelopmentLab Video Series for Human Sexuality engages students and brings course material to life through a wide range of videos, featuring over 125 carefully selected clips.

Drawn from a variety of sources including the Associated Press, ABC News, and Science Central, this video series contains the most recent research, science, and applications in human sexuality. This brief clips are ideal for display in lecture. Many of the videos are accompanied by media assignments in MyDevelopmentLab that allow instructors to assess student comprehension. For maximum flexibility, the videos are also available for viewing on iPad and iPhone.

STUDENT RESOURCES

MyDevelopmentLab™ NEW! MyDevelopmentLab for Human Sexuality combines proven learning applications with powerful assessment to engage students, assess their learning, and help them succeed.

An individualized study plan for each student, based on performance on chapter pre tests, helps students focus on the specific topics where they need the most support. The personalized study plan arranges content from less complex thinking, like remembering and understanding—to more complex critical thinking skills—like applying and analyzing and is based on Bloom's taxonomy. Every level of the study plan provides a formative assessment quiz.

Media Assignments for each chapter—including videos with assignable questions—feed directly into the gradebook, enabling instructors to track student progress automatically.

The Pearson eText lets students access their textbook anytime and anywhere, and any way they want, including listening online. With assessment tied to every chapter, students get immediate feedback, and instructors can see what their students know with just a few clicks. Instructors can also personalize MyDevelopmentLab to meet the needs of their students.

The NEW MyDevelopmentLab Video Series for Human Sexuality engages students and brings course material to life through a wide range of videos, featuring over 125 carefully selected clips. Drawn from a variety of sources including the Associated Press, ABC News, and Science Central, this video series contains the most recent research, science, and applications in human sexuality. Many of the videos are accompanied by media assignments in MyDevelopmentLab that allow instructors to assess student comprehension. For maximum flexibility, the videos are also available for viewing on iPad and iPhone.

Acknowledgments

We owe a great debt of gratitude to the many researchers and scholars whose contributions to the body of knowledge in the field of human sexuality are represented in these pages. Underscoring the interdisciplinary nature of the field, we have drawn on the work of scholars in such fields as psychology, sociology, medicine, anthropology, theology, and philosophy, to name a few. We are also indebted to the many researchers who have generously allowed us to quote from their work and reprint tabular material representing their findings. We also thank our professional colleagues who reviewed this text at various stages in its development:

Michael Bailey, Northwestern University; Keith E. Davis, University of South Carolina; Randy D. Fisher, University of Central Florida; Kam Majer, Glendale Community College; Patricia A. Tackett, San Diego State University; Michael L. Vinson, College of Charleston; and Mark A. Yarhouse, Regent University.

In addition, the following instructors provided invaluable feedback in their reviews. Their comments have contributed substantially to this edition. Several reviewers also supplied anonymous Real Students, Real Questions from their students, for which we are grateful:

Cindy Arem, Pima Community College; Rebecca L. Bosek, University of Alaska, Anchorage; Ted Coleman, California State University, San Bernadino; Ruth Conrad, Miami Dade College; Nancy P. Daley, The University of Texas at Austin; Darci Dance, Linn-Benton Community College; Dale Doty, Monroe Community College; Mary E. Doyle, Arizona State University; Laura Duvall, Heartland Community College; Steve Ellyson, Youngstown State University; Kathy Erickson, Pima Community College; Debra L. Golden, The Grossmont–Cuyamaca Community College; Jerry Green, Tarrant County College; Tawanda M. Greer, University of South Carolina; Chuck Hallock, University of Arizona; Mark L. Harmon, Reedley College–North Centers; Deborah Kindy, Sonoma State University; Amy Kolodji, Ithaca College; Gloria Lawrence, Wayne State College; Holly Lewis, University of Houston–Downtown; Sonya Lott-Harrison, Community College of Philadelphia; Ana Lucero-Liu, California State University, Northridge; Jason McCoy, Cape Fear Community College; Mary L. Meiners, San Diego Miramar College; Eva Mika, Loyola University Chicago; Ramona M. Noland, Sam Houston State University; Grace Pokorny, Long Beach City College; Jim Pond, Butler Community College; Marilyn Pugh, Texas Wesleyan University, North Texas; Rosalind Shorter, Jefferson Community College; Noam Shpancer, Otterbein University; Bette Speziale, Ohio State University; Virginia Sticinski, Delaware Technical Community College; Dana Stone, Virginia Tech; Virginia Totaro, Virginia Commonwealth University; Mixon Ware, Eastern Kentucky University; Mary Anne Watson, Metropolitan State College of Denver; O'Neal Weeks, Eastern Kentucky University; Steve Weinert, The Grossmont–Cuyamaca Community College; Lester Wright, Western Michigan University; and Brian Zamboni, Health University of Minnesota.

Last, we thank our long-time buddy David McPatchell, Associate Professor of Psychology, Compton Community College—and his students—for providing the heart of many of this edition's personal stories, including "Real Questions, Real Answers" features. It just would not have been the same without him—and them.

Spencer A. Rathus
Jeffrey S. Nevid
Lois Fichner-Rathus

1   What Is Human Sexuality?

Learning Objectives

THE SCIENCE OF HUMAN SEXUALITY

LO1   Define the science of human sexuality

SEXUALITY AND VALUES

LO2   Define the value systems people use in making sexual decisions

THINKING CRITICALLY ABOUT HUMAN SEXUALITY

LO3   Explain how you can become a critical thinker

PERSPECTIVES ON HUMAN SEXUALITY

LO4   Discuss the historical perspective on human sexuality
LO5   Describe the biological perspective on human sexuality
LO6   Describe the evolutionary perspective on human sexuality
LO7   Describe the cross-species perspective on human sexuality
LO8   Describe sociological perspectives on human sexuality
LO9   Describe psychological perspectives on human sexuality
LO10   Discuss feminist theory
LO11   Discuss queer theory
LO12   Explain why it is useful to look upon human sexuality from multiple perspectives

MY LIFE, MY SEXUALITY: THINKING CRITICALLY ABOUT SEXUAL ADVICE ON THE INTERNET: ARE THERE ANY QUICK FIXES?

sex, *n.*   **sex,** *v.*   **sex,** *adj.*

Adolescent Sexuality

Explore the video, **Adolescent Sexuality,** by scanning this QR code with your mobile device. If you don't already have one, you may download a free QR scanner for your device wherever smartphone apps are sold. You can also view this video in MyDevelopmentLab. For more videos related to this chapter's content, log into MyDevelopmentLab to view the entire Human Sexuality Video Series.

TRUTH OR FICTION?

Which of the following statements are the truth and which are fiction? You will find the answers as you read this chapter.

1 Scientific knowledge will enable you to make the right sexual decisions. **T F?**

2 In ancient Greece, a mature man would take a sexual interest in an adolescent boy, often with the blessing of the boy's parents. **T F?**

3 Throughout most of human history, women were considered to be the property of their husbands. **T F?**

4 The production of sex manuals originated in modern times. **T F?**

5 The graham cracker came into being as a means for helping young men control their sexual appetites. **T F?**

6 Female redback spiders eat their mates after the females have been inseminated. **T F?**

7 In our dreams, airplanes, bullets, snakes, sticks, and similar objects symbolize the male genitals. **T F?**

et's Google the islands off the coast of Europe and in the South Pacific—both in space and time. We go to Google Maps, find Inis Beag, click on the satellite image, further click on 1955 (no, you can't really do this—yet), and swoop in …

And suddenly we find ourselves visiting two islands that are a world apart—sexually as well as geographically. Our first stop is Inis Beag, which lies in the Atlantic, off the misty coast of Ireland. Our second stop will be Mangaia, which lifts languidly out of the blue waters of the Pacific.

The distant satellite image shows Inis Beag as a green jewel, fertile and inviting. The residents of this community do not believe that it is normal for women to experience orgasm. Anthropologists have reported that any woman who finds pleasure in sex—especially the intense waves of pleasure that can accompany orgasm—is viewed as deviant.

Premarital sex is all but unknown on Inis Beag. Prior to marriage, men and women socialize apart. Marriage comes late—usually in the middle 30s for men and the middle 20s for women. Mothers teach their daughters that they will have to submit to their husbands' animal cravings in order to obey God's injunction to "be fruitful and multiply."

But the women of Inis Beag need not be overly concerned about frequent sex, since the men of the island believe, erroneously, that sexual activity will drain their strength. Consequently, men avoid sex on the eve of sporting activity or strenuous work. Because of taboos against nudity, married couples have sex with their undergarments on. Intercourse takes place in the dark—literally as well as figuratively.

During intercourse, the man lies on top. He is always the initiator. Foreplay is brief. The man ejaculates as fast as he can, in the belief that he is the only partner with sexual needs and to spare his wife as best he can. Then he turns over and falls asleep. Once more the couple have done their duty.

On to Mangaia, which is a pearl of an island. It lies on the other side of the world from Inis Beag—in more ways than one. From an early age, Mangaian boys and girls are encouraged to get in touch with their own sexuality through sexual play and masturbation. At about the age of 13, Mangaian boys are initiated into manhood by adults who instruct them in sexual techniques.

Boys practice their new techniques with girlfriends on secluded beaches or beneath the listing fronds of palms. They may visit girlfriends in huts where they sleep with their families. Parents often listen for their daughters to laugh and gasp so that they will know that they have reached orgasm with a visiting young "sleepcrawler." Parents often pretend to be asleep so as not to interfere with courtship and impede their daughters' chances of finding a mate. Daughters may receive a nightly succession of sleepcrawlers and have multiple orgasms with each one.

Mangaians look on virginity with disdain, because virgins do not know how to provide sexual pleasure. Thus, the older male makes his contribution by initiating the girl.

Mangaians expressed concern when they learned that many Western women do not regularly experience orgasm. Orgasm is apparently universal among Mangaian women. Therefore, Mangaians could only assume that Western women suffered from some abnormality of the sex organs.

Mangaia. Perhaps they didn't wear coconut shells, but a generation or so ago, sex on Mangaia was free wheeling. In other places and at other times, sex has been seen as a necessary evil to follow God's command to "be fruitful and multiply."

The residents of Inis Beag and Mangaia have similar anatomical features but vastly different attitudes toward sex. Their cultural settings influence their patterns of sexual behavior and the pleasure they gain—or fail to gain—from sex. Sex may be a natural function, but few natural functions have been influenced so strongly by religious and moral beliefs, cultural tradition, folklore, and superstition.

We are about to embark on the study of human sexuality. But why study human sexuality? Isn't sex something to do rather than to talk about? Isn't sex a natural function? Don't we learn what we need to know from personal experience or from our parents or our friends?

Yes. And no. We can learn how our bodies respond to sexual stimulation through personal experience, but experience teaches us little about the biology of sexual response and orgasm. Nor does experience inform us about the variations in sexual behavior that exist around the world. Experience does not prepare us to recognize the signs of sexually transmitted infections (STIs) or to evaluate the risks of pregnancy. What many of us learned about sex from our parents can probably be summarized in a single word: "Don't." The information we received from our friends was probably riddled with exaggeration, even lies. Many young people today receive accurate information through sex education courses in the schools, but they are usually taught about STIs and contraception, not about sexual techniques.

You may know more about human sexuality than your parents or grandparents did at your age, or do today. But how much do you really know? What causes an erection or vaginal lubrication? What factors determine sexual orientation? What are sexual dysfunctions and what causes them? How do our sexual responsiveness and interests change as we age? Can you contract a sexually transmitted infection and not know it? If you have no symptoms, can you infect others?

These are just a few of the issues we will explore in this book. One feature of this text, "Real Students, Real Questions," illustrates some of the questions and erroneous ideas many of us have about sex. 👁

Watch the Video
Gender versus Sex:
Florence Denmark
on **MyDevelopmentLab**

Real Students, Real Questions

Q *I am 17 years old, and the topic of sex in my family is nonexistent. How do I begin a conversation with my family?*

A Most people find it difficult to talk about sex. You'll find ideas for initiating conversations about sex with family members and other people throughout this text—conversations about contraception, STIs, and problems in relationships. In all cases, think about selecting a good time and place to talk. Consider asking permission to talk about a sensitive topic, as in "I know that talking about birth control is a no-no in this house, but I have some questions. Can we talk about them?" Or, "I could use some help. Can we talk about it?" People who care about you might just surprise you by accepting the challenge of trying to communicate about topics that can be off-limits. If you desire parental help, you might think about catching the more receptive parent when he or she is alone.

The Science of Human Sexuality?

What is human sexuality? This is not a trick question. Consider the meaning, or rather meanings, of the word *sex*. One use of the term *sex* refers to our anatomic sex, male or female. The words *sex* or *sexual* are also used to refer to anatomic structures, called sex organs or sexual organs, that play a role in reproduction or sexual pleasure. We may also speak of sex when referring to physical activities involving our sex organs for purposes of reproduction or pleasure, as in *having sex*. Sex also relates to erotic feelings, experiences, or desires, such as sexual fantasies and thoughts, sexual urges, or feelings of sexual attraction.

Many researchers reserve the word *sex* for reference to anatomic or biological categories, but prefer the word **gender** when they are referring to social or cultural categories. For example, one might say that "reproductive anatomy appears to depend on the *sex* (not the *gender*) of the individual, but in so-called traditional societies, **gender roles** (not *sex roles*) are often seen as polar opposites."

The term **human sexuality** refers to the ways in which we experience and express ourselves as sexual beings. Our awareness of ourselves as females or males is part of our sexuality, as is the capacity we have for erotic experiences and responses. Our knowledge of the gender roles in our culture also has a profound influence on us. ◉

THE STUDY OF HUMAN SEXUALITY

The study of human sexuality draws on the scientific expertise of anthropologists, biologists, medical researchers, sociologists, and psychologists, to name some of the professional groups involved in the field. These disciplines all make contributions, because human sexuality reflects biological capabilities, psychological characteristics, and social and cultural influences. Biologists inform us about the physiological mechanisms of sexual arousal and response. Medical science teaches us about STIs and the biological bases of sexual dysfunctions. Psychologists examine how our sexual behavior and attitudes are shaped by perception, learning, thought, motivation and emotion, and personality. Sociocultural theorists examine relationships between sexual behavior and religion, race, and social class. Anthropologists focus on cross-cultural similarities and differences in sexual behavior.

TRUTH OR FICTION REVISITED: Although science provides us with information, it cannot make sexual decisions for us. In making sexual decisions, we also consider our **values**. The Declaration of Independence endorsed the fundamental values of "life, liberty, and the pursuit of happiness"—not a bad beginning. Our religious traditions also play a prominent role in shaping our values, as we see in the following section.

Sexuality and Values

Our society is pluralistic. It embraces a wide range of sexual attitudes and values. Some readers may be liberal in their sexual views and behavior. Others may be conservative. Some are pro-choice on abortion, others pro-life. Some approve of premarital sex for couples who know each other casually. Others hold the line at emotional commitment. Still others believe in waiting until marriage. People's sexual attitudes, experiences, and behaviors are shaped to a large extent by cultural traditions and beliefs. They influence how, where, and with whom we become sexually involved.

As noted by feminists, some of the variability in sexual behavior between males and females reflects power rather than choice (Smith & Konik, 2011). Throughout history and in many places, for example, women have been considered the property of men. Even today, women are often "given away" by their fathers to their husbands.

◉ **Watch** the **Video**
The Big Picture: The Power of Sex
on **MyDevelopmentLab**

1 Ⓣⓕ

Gender   The behavioral, cultural, or psychological traits typically associated with one sex.

Gender roles   Complex clusters of ways in which males and females are expected to behave within a given culture.

Human sexuality   The ways in which we experience and express ourselves as sexual beings.

Values   The qualities in life that are deemed important or unimportant, right or wrong, desirable or undesirable.

Let's consider the various value systems that people draw on in making sexual decisions. ◉

VALUE SYSTEMS FOR MAKING SEXUAL DECISIONS

◉▬Watch the Video
*Special Topics: Cultural Norms
and Sexual Behavior*
on **MyDevelopmentLab**

Although sex is a natural function, most of us choose how, where, and with whom to become sexually involved. We face a wide array of sexual decisions: Whom should I date? When should my partner and I become sexually intimate? Should I initiate sexual relations or wait for my partner to approach me? Should my partner and I practice contraception? If so, which method? Should I use a condom to protect against STIs, or insist that my partner does? Should I be tested for HIV (the virus that causes AIDS)? Should I insist that my partner be tested for HIV before we have sex?

Value systems provide a framework for judging the moral acceptability of sexual options. We often approach sexual decisions by determining whether the choices we face are compatible with our moral values. Our value systems—our sexual standards—have many sources: parents, peers, religious training, ethnic subcultures, the larger culture, and our appraisal of all these influences. Value systems include legalism, situational ethics, ethical relativism, hedonism, asceticism, utilitarianism, and rationalism.

Legalism The legalistic approach formulates ethical behavior on the basis of a code of moral laws derived from an external source, such as a religion. The Hebrew and Christian Bibles contain many examples of the moral code of the Jewish and Christian religions. In the Book of Leviticus (20:10–17) in the Hebrew Bible we find many of the prohibitions against adultery, incest, sexual activity with people of one's own gender, and bestiality:

10: And the man that committeth adultery with another man's wife, even he that committeth adultery with his neighbour's wife, the adulterer and the adulteress shall surely be put to death.

11: And the man that lieth with his father's wife hath uncovered his father's nakedness: both of them shall surely be put to death; their blood shall be upon them.

12: And if a man lie with his daughter in law, both of them shall surely be put to death: they have wrought confusion; their blood shall be upon them.

13: If a man also lie with mankind, as he lieth with a woman, both of them have committed an abomination: they shall surely be put to death; their blood shall be upon them.

14: And if a man take a wife and her mother, it is wickedness: they shall be burnt with fire, both he and they; that there be no wickedness among you.

15: And if a man lie with a beast, he shall surely be put to death: and ye shall slay the beast.

16: And if a woman approach unto any beast, and lie down thereto, thou shalt kill the woman, and the beast: they shall surely be put to death; their blood shall be upon them.

17: And if a man shall take his sister, his father's daughter, or his mother's daughter, and see her nakedness, and she see his nakedness; it is a wicked thing; and they shall be cut off in the sight of their people: he hath uncovered his sister's nakedness; he shall bear his iniquity.

18: And if a man shall lie with a woman having her sickness,[1] and shall uncover her nakedness; he hath discovered her fountain, and she hath uncovered the fountain of her blood: and both of them shall be cut off from among their people.

---

[1]That is, menstruation.

Many religious followers accept the moral codes of their religions as a matter of faith and commitment. Some people find it reassuring to be informed by religious authorities or scripture that a certain course of action is right or wrong. Others, however, take a more liberal view. They say that the Bible reflects the social setting of the time in which it was written, not just divine inspiration. Now that population growth is exploding in many parts of the world, biblical injunctions to be fruitful and multiply may no longer be socially and environmentally sound. Prohibitions, such as that against sexual relations during menstruation, may have been based on prescientific perceptions of danger. Some people thus view religious teachings as a general framework for decision making rather than as a set of absolute rules.

Situational Ethics Episcopal theologian Joseph Fletcher (1966, 1967) argued that ethical decision making should be guided by love for others rather than by rigid moral rules, and that sexual decision making should be based on the context of the situation that the person faces. For this reason, his view is termed *situational ethics*. According to Fletcher, a Roman Catholic woman will have been taught that abortion is the taking of a human life. Her situation, however—her love for her existing family and her recognition of her limited resources for providing for another child—might influence her to decide in favor of an abortion.

Fletcher argues that rules for conduct should be flexible. "The situationist is prepared in any concrete case to suspend, ignore, or violate any principle if by doing so he can effect more good than by following it" (1966, p. 34).

Ethical Relativism Ethical relativism assumes that diverse values are basic to human existence. Ethical relativists reject the idea that there is a single correct moral view about subjects as diverse as wearing revealing clothing, masturbation, premarital sex, oral sex, anal sex, contraception, and abortion. One person may believe that premarital sex is unacceptable under any circumstances, whereas another may hold that "being in love" makes it acceptable. Still another person may believe that sex is morally permissible without an emotional commitment. The ethical relativist

How do you make sexual decisions? What value system or systems do you employ?

believes that there is no objective way of justifying one set of moral values over another. In this view, the essence of human morality is to derive one's own principles and apply them according to one's own conscience. Opponents of ethical relativism argue that allowing people free rein to determine what is right or wrong may bring about social chaos and decay.

One form of ethical relativism is *cultural relativism*. From this perspective, what is right or wrong must be understood in terms of the cultural beliefs that affect sexual decision making. In some cultures, premarital sex is tolerated or even encouraged, whereas in others, it is considered immoral.

Hedonism The hedonist is guided by the pursuit of pleasure, not by whether a particular behavior is morally or situationally justified. "If it feels good, do it" expresses the hedonistic ethic. The hedonist believes that sexual desires, like hunger or thirst, do not invoke moral considerations.

Asceticism Religious celibates, such as Roman Catholic priests and Buddhist monks, choose *asceticism* (self-denial of material and sexual desires) in order to devote themselves to spiritual pursuits. Many ascetics in Eastern and Western religions seek to transcend physical and worldly desires.

Utilitarianism Ethical guidelines can be based on principles other than religious ones. The English philosopher John Stuart Mill (1806–1873) proposed an ethical system based on *utilitarianism*—the view that moral conduct is based on that which will bring about "the greatest good for the greatest number" (Mill, 1863). The utilitarian characterizes behavior as ethical when it does the greatest good and causes the least harm. This is not the same thing as freedom of action. Utilitarians may come down hard in opposition to premarital sex and bearing children out of wedlock, for example, if they believe that these behavior patterns jeopardize a nation's health and social fabric. Mill's ethics require that we treat one another justly and honestly, because it serves the greater good for people to be true to their word and just in their dealings with others.

Rationalism Rationalism is the use of reason to determine a course of action. The rationalist believes that decisions should be based on intellect and reason rather than emotions or faith. The rationalist assesses the facts in a sexual situation and then weighs the consequences of various courses of action to make a decision. The rationalist shares with the utilitarian the belief that reasoning can lead to ethical

---

Real Students, Real Questions

Q *Is a person who takes a vow of chastity, such as a nun, no longer considered a sexual being?*

A A person who takes a vow of chastity only promises not to be a sexually active being. The reason usually involves dedication to values in which self-denial of sexual desires plays a key role, as in a religious tradition. But this doesn't mean that the person is no longer a sexual being. The person remains female or male, and continues to be subject to the sexual drives, sexual health issues, and cultural expectations that affect females and males.

Table 1.1

Value Systems for Making Sexual Decisions

System	Core Belief	Example
Legalism	Ethical behavior is derived from an external source, such as a religion.	The Old Testament contains prohibitions against adultery, incest, sexual activity with people of one's own gender, and bestiality.
Situational Ethics	Ethical decision making should be guided by the situation and by genuine love for others.	A woman who has been taught that abortion is the taking of a human life may find herself with limited resources and decide in favor of an abortion.
Relativism	There is no objective way of justifying one set of moral values over another.	Cohabitation is tolerated in some cultures but considered immoral in others.
Hedonism	Pursuit of pleasure is the guide.	Hedonists might argue that sexual desires, like hunger or thirst, do not involve moral considerations.
Asceticism	One denies sexual desires to devote oneself to spiritual pursuits.	Many ascetics in Western and Eastern religions seek to transcend physical and worldly desires.
Utilitarianism	Moral conduct brings about the greatest good for the greatest number.	We should be honest and just because it serves the greater good for people to be true to their word and treat each other justly.
Rationalism	Sexual decisions should be based on intellect and reason, not blind obedience.	The rationalist might decide that the personal consequences of continuing an unhappy marriage outweigh the effects on the family or the community at large.

behavior but is not bound to the utilitarian code that makes choices on the basis of the greatest good for the greatest number. The utilitarian may decide, for example, to prolong an unhappy marriage because of the belief that the greater good of the family and the community is better served by maintaining an unhappy marriage than by dissolving it. The rationalist might decide that the personal consequences of continuing an unhappy marriage outweigh the consequences to the family or the community at large.

These ethical systems represent general frameworks of moral reasoning or pathways for judging the moral acceptability of sexual and nonsexual behavior. Whereas some of us may adopt one or another of these systems in their purest forms, others adopt a system of moral reasoning that involves some combination or variation of these ethical systems. Table 1.1 summarizes some of the value systems in use.

Many students will think critically about which values to apply to a given situation. They may also apply critical thinking to the claims and arguments about human sexuality they come across from authority figures, colleagues, friends, and advertisements. In the following section, we explore the nature of critical thinking.

Thinking Critically about Human Sexuality

We are flooded with so much information about sex that it is difficult to separate truth from fiction. Newspapers, TV shows, popular books and magazines, and the Internet contain one feature after another about sex. Many of them contradict one another, contain half-truths, or draw unsupported conclusions.

Most of us also tend to assume that authority figures such as doctors and government officials provide us with factual information and are qualified to make decisions that affect our lives. But when two doctors disagree on the need for breast surgery, or two officials disagree as to whether condoms should be distributed in public schools, how can both be correct? Critical thinkers never say, "This is true because so-and-so says that it is true."

To help students evaluate claims, arguments, and widely held beliefs, most colleges encourage critical thinking. The core of critical thinking is skepticism—taking nothing for granted. Critical thinking means being skeptical of things that are presented in print, uttered by authority figures or celebrities, or passed along by friends. Another aspect of critical thinking is thoughtful analysis and probing of claims and arguments. Critical thinking means scrutinizing definitions of terms and evaluating the premises of arguments and their logic. Critical thinkers maintain open minds. They suspend their beliefs until they have obtained and evaluated the evidence.

PRINCIPLES OF CRITICAL THINKING

Here are some principles of critical thinking:

1. *Be skeptical.* Politicians, religious leaders, and other authority figures attempt to convince you of their points of view. Even researchers and authors may hold certain biases. Accept no opinion as fact until you have personally weighed the evidence.

2. *Examine definitions of terms.* Some statements are true when a term is defined in one way but not in another. Consider the maxim, "Love is blind." If love is defined as head-over-heels infatuation, there may be substance to the statement. Infatuated people tend to idealize loved ones. But if love is defined as deep caring and commitment based on a more realistic (if still somewhat slanted) appraisal of the loved one, then love is not blind—just a bit nearsighted.

3. *Examine the assumptions or premises of arguments.* Consider the statement, "Abortion is murder." *Webster's New World Dictionary* defines murder as "the unlawful and malicious or premeditated killing of one human being by another." The statement is true, according to this dictionary, only if (a) the victim is a human being and (b) the act is unlawful and malicious or premeditated. Many pro-life advocates argue that embryos and fetuses are human beings from the moment of conception. Many pro-choice advocates argue that embryos and fetuses do not become human beings until various stages of development. Thus, the judgment that abortion is murder will rest in part on one's beliefs as to whether—and when—an embryo or fetus is a human being.

4. *Be cautious in drawing conclusions from evidence.* Research finds that teenagers who listen to rap, hip-hop, pop, and rock music with sexually explicit lyrics—or with lyrics that refer to women as sex objects—are more likely to initiate sexual activity at early ages (Martino et al., 2006). The popular media seem obsessed with the idea that "dirty" songs instigate sex, and lots of it. However, teens who choose to listen to these songs may differ from those who do not in their values, so that they not only spend hours with their iPods blasting sexual lyrics into their ears but also choose to have sex at early ages. The evidence of an association between listening to this music and having sex is open to various interpretations—which brings us to our next principle of critical thinking.

5. *Consider alternative interpretations of research evidence.* For example, teens who dwell on sexual song lyrics may also be more open to sexual activity because they are generally less traditional than teens who (literally) turn these songs off. Correlations or associations between events do not necessarily reveal cause and effect.

CRITICAL THINKING
What kinds of intellectual and interpersonal conflicts are likely to be encountered by people who decide that they would like to become critical thinkers?

A Closer Look

The National Survey of Sexual Health and Behavior: Who Does What with Whom?

You see surveys on sex all the time. They're in *Glamour* and *Cosmopolitan*. They're reported in newspapers and on talk shows. But what are you to believe?

One of the problems with most surveys on sex is the sampling. As we'll see in Chapter 2, if you're trying to report accurately on sex in the United States, you have to give everyone in the country an equal chance of participating. That never happens perfectly. What if you want to interview college students and use listed phone numbers to reach them? In doing so, you've just left out all students who use cell phones only. The researchers who published the National Survey of Sexual Health and Behavior (NSSHB) took measures to prevent that type of thing from happening (Reece et al., 2010), which we'll elaborate on in Chapter 2. All in all, they surveyed 5,865 adolescents and adults, aged 14 to 94, and derived what most researchers believe is a reasonably accurate snapshot of the American population—or at least a reasonably accurate picture of what people are willing to report.

You'll find a quick overview of some of the researchers' results in Table 1.2. The kinds of sexual behaviors they surveyed are shown across the top. The ages of the respondents are indicted in the column on the left. Respondents are broken down by gender (men and women) as well as by age. Let's take a look at the first sexual behavior in the list, masturbation, and see what we find. For every age group, men are more likely to report masturbating alone in the past year than women are. Why do you think that is so? Also, the incidence of masturbation alone generally rises through the late 20s and then begins to decline. How would you explain that? We'll consider possible explanations in the chapters to come.

The researchers also note the following about their results:

- American adults engage in an enormous variety of sexual behaviors.

- Many older people continue to have enjoyable sex lives.

- Men are most likely to reach orgasm when vaginal intercourse is involved; women are more likely to reach orgasm when a variety of sexual activities are used, including vaginal intercourse or oral sex.

- The percentage of people who have had experience with people of the same gender during their lives is nearly *double* that of people who identify themselves as being gay, lesbian, or bisexual.

- The percentage of adolescents who engage in vaginal intercourse has probably been exaggerated somewhat in the media.

You'll find more on all these topics in the chapters to come.

Table 1.2

Percentage of Americans Performing Certain Sexual Behaviors in the Past Year (N = 5865)

Age Groups		Masturbated Alone	Masturbated with Partner	Received Oral from Women	Received Oral from Men	Gave Oral to Women	Gave Oral to Men	Vaginal intercourse	Received Penis in Anus	Inserted Penis into Anus
14–15	Men	62%	5%	12%	1%	8%	1%	9%	1%	3%
	Women	40%	8%	1%	10%	2%	12%	11%	4%	
16–17	Men	75%	16%	31%	3%	18%	2%	30%	1%	6%
	Women	45%	19%	5%	24%	7%	22%	30%	5%	
18–19	Men	81%	42%	54%	6%	51%	4%	53%	4%	6%
	Women	60%	36%	4%	58%	2%	59%	62%	18%	
20–24	Men	83%	44%	63%	6%	55%	7%	63%	5%	11%
	Women	64%	36%	9%	70%	9%	74%	80%	23%	
25–29	Men	84%	49%	77%	5%	74%	5%	BS%	4%	27%
	Women	72%	48%	3%	72%	3%	76%	87%	21%	
30–39	Men	80%	45%	78%	6%	69%	5%	85%	3%	24%
	Women	63%	43%	5%	59%	4%	59%	74%	22%	
40–49	Men	76%	38%	62%	6%	57%	7%	74%	4%	21%
	Women	65%	35%	2%	52%	3%	53%	70%	12%	
50–59	Men	72%	28%	49%	8%	44%	8%	58%	5%	11%
	Women	54%	18%	1%	34%	1%	36%	51%	6%	
60–69	Men	61%	17%	38%	3%	34%	3%	54%	1%	6%
	Women	47%	13%	1%	25%	1%	23%	42%	4%	
70+	Men	46%	13%	19%	2%	24%	3%	43%	2%	2%
	Women	33%	5%	2%	8%	2%	7%	22%	1%	

Source: Center for Sexual Health Promotion. (2011). *National Survey of Sexual Health and Behavior (NSSHB)*. Indiana University, Bloomington: School of Health, Physical Education, and Recreation. http://www.nationalsexstudy.indiana.edu/graph.html (Accessed February 22, 2012)

6. *Consider the kinds of evidence on which conclusions are based.* Some conclusions, even seemingly "scientific" conclusions, are based on anecdotes and personal endorsements. They are not founded on sound research.

7. *Do not oversimplify.* Consider the statement, "Homosexuality is inborn." There is some evidence that sexual orientation may involve inborn predispositions, such as genetic influences. However, biology is not destiny in human sexuality. Gay male, lesbian, and heterosexual sexual orientations appear to develop as the result of a complex interaction of biological and environmental factors.

8. *Do not overgeneralize.* Consider the belief that gay males are effeminate and lesbians are masculine. Yes, some gay males and lesbians fit these stereotypes. However, many do not. Overgeneralizing makes us vulnerable to accepting stereotypes.

Perspectives on Human Sexuality

Human sexuality is a complex topic. No single theory or perspective can capture all its nuances. In this book we explore human sexuality from many perspectives. In this section we introduce a number of them—historical, biological, evolutionary, cross-species, cross-cultural, psychological, and sociocultural. We draw on these perspectives in subsequent chapters.

The "Venus of Willendorf." This ancient figurine is believed to be a fertility symbol.

THE HISTORICAL PERSPECTIVE

History places sexual attitudes and behavior in context. It informs us as to whether sexual behavior reflects trends that have been with us through the millennia or the customs of a particular culture and era. History shows little evidence of universal sexual trends. Attitudes and behaviors vary extensively from one time and place to another. Contemporary American society may be permissive when compared to the Victorian and post–World War II eras. Yet it looks staid when compared to the sexual excesses of some ancient societies, such as the ruling class of ancient Rome. History also shows how religion has been a major influence on sexual values and behavior. Let us trace some historical changes in attitudes toward sexuality. We begin by turning the clock back 20,000 to 30,000 years, to the days before written records were kept—that is, to prehistory.

Prehistoric Sexuality: From Female Idols to Phallic Worship Information about life among our Stone Age ancestors is drawn largely from cave drawings, stone artifacts, and the customs of modern-day preliterate peoples whose existence has changed little over the millennia. From such sources, historians and anthropologists infer a prehistoric division of labor. By and large, men hunted for game, and women tended to remain close to home. Women nurtured children and gathered edible plants and nuts, crabs, and other marine life that wandered along the shore or swam in shallow waters.

Art produced in the Stone Age suggests the worship of women's ability to bear children and perpetuate the species (Fichner-Rathus, 2013). Primitive statues and cave drawings portray women with large, pendulous breasts, rounded hips, and prominent sex organs. Most theorists regard the figurines as fertility symbols. Stone Age people may have been unaware of the male's contribution to reproduction.

As the glacial sheets of the last Ice Age retreated (about 11,000 BCE) and the climate warmed, human societies turned agrarian. Hunters and gatherers became farmers and herders. Villages sprang up around fields. Men tended livestock. Women farmed. As people grew aware of the male role in reproduction, **phallic worship** (worship of the penis) sprang into being. Knowledge of paternity is believed to have developed around 9000 BCE, resulting from observation of livestock. When people began to observe animals throughout the years, they also began to understand that a predictable period of time elapsed between copulation and the birth of offspring.

The penis became glorified in art as a plough, ax, or sword. **Phallic symbols** played roles in religious ceremonies in ancient Egypt. The ancient Greeks sometimes rendered phalluses as rings, sometimes as necklaces. In ancient Rome, a large phallus was carried like a float in a parade honoring Venus, the goddess of love.

The **incest taboo** may have been the first human taboo. All human societies apparently have some form of incest taboo, but societies have varied in terms of its strictness. Brother–sister marriages were permitted among the presumably divine rulers of ancient Egypt and among the royal families of the Incas and of Hawaii, even though they were generally prohibited among commoners. Father–daughter marriages were permitted among the aristocracy and royalty of ancient Egypt. Incestuous relationships in these royal blood lines may have kept wealth and power, as well as "divinity," in the family.

The Ancient Hebrews The ancient Hebrews viewed sex, at least in marriage, as a satisfying experience intended to fulfill the divine command to "be fruitful and multiply." The emphasis on the procreative function of sex led to some interesting social customs. For example, childlessness and the development of a repulsive abnormality, such as a boil, were grounds for divorce. Male–male and female–female sexual behavior were strongly condemned, as they threatened the perpetuation of the family.

The ancient Hebrews believed that sex helped strengthen marital bonds and solidify the family. But it would be inaccurate to ignore the fact that according to the Hebrew Bible, the prophet Abraham had several wives and concubines, and King Solomon had several hundred. In any event, Jewish law legislated the minimum frequency of marital relations, which varied according to the man's profession and the amount of time spent at home:

> Every day for those who have no occupation, twice a week for laborers, once a week for ass-drivers; once every thirty days for camel drivers; and once every six months for sailors.
>
> —Mishnah Ketubot 5:6; Ketubot 62b–62b

According to the Book of Proverbs, a good wife rises before dawn to tend to her family's needs, brings home food, instructs the servants, tends the vineyards, makes the clothes, keeps the ledger, helps the needy, and works well into the night. Even so, a wife was considered the property of her husband and could be divorced on a whim. A wife could also be stoned to death for adultery, but she might have to share her husband with secondary wives and concubines. Men who consorted with the wives of other men were considered to have violated the property rights of those men and might have to pay for "damages."

In case the notion that a woman is a man's property sounds ancient to you, we must note that in many cultures it remains current. For example, in Afghanistan some fathers have given other men their daughters as payment for gambling debts (Bearak, 2006). And Zambian judge Alfred Shilibwa ordered a hotel employee, Obert Siyankalanga, to pay a woman's husband $300 in compensation after he

Phallic worship Worship of the penis as a symbol of generative power.

Phallic symbol An image of the penis.

Incest taboo The prohibition against intercourse and reproduction among close blood relatives.

fondled her breasts ("Man pays victim's husband," 2000). The woman had been ironing at the time. She explained the scars on Obert's face and head: "I clobbered him on the head with the iron." Because Obert was the woman's supervisor, the judge also convicted him of sexual harassment.

The Ancient Greeks The classical or golden age of Greece lasted from about 500 to 300 BCE. Within this relatively short span lived the philosophers Socrates, Plato, and Aristotle; the playwrights Aristophanes, Aeschylus, and Sophocles; the natural scientist Archimedes; and the lawgiver Solon. Like the Hebrews, the Greeks valued family life, but Greek men also admired the well-developed male body and enjoyed nude wrestling in the arena. Erotic encounters and off-color jokes characterized the plays of Aristophanes and other playwrights. The Greeks held that the healthy mind must dwell in a healthy body. They cultivated muscle and movement along with mind.

The Greeks viewed their gods—Zeus, god of gods; Apollo, who inspired art and music; Aphrodite, the goddess of carnal love whose name is the basis of the word *aphrodisiac*; and others—as voracious seekers of sexual variety. Not only were they believed to have sexual adventures among themselves but they were also thought to have seduced mortals.

Three aspects of Greek sexuality are of particular interest to our study of sexual practices in the ancient world: male–male sexual behavior, pederasty, and

Many Ancient Greek Ceramics Depict Male–Male Sexual Activity. The ancient Greeks believed that males were bisexual. In Homer's *Iliad*, brought to the silver screen as *Troy*, Achilles is spurred to battle by the killing of his lover Patroclus. The film, however, glossed over this motive by emphasizing the family relationship between the two.

prostitution. The Greeks viewed people as **bisexual**. Male–male sex was deemed normal and tolerated so long as it did not threaten the institution of the family.

Pederasty means love of boys. Sex between men and prepubescent boys was illegal, but families were generally pleased if their adolescent sons attracted socially prominent mentors. **TRUTH OR FICTION** REVISITED: Men in ancient Greece might take on an adolescent male as a lover and pupil. Pederasty did not impede the boy's future male–female functioning, because the pederast himself was usually married, and Greeks believed people to be equally capable of male–female and male–male sexual activity.

Prostitution flourished at every level of society. Prostitutes ranged from refined **courtesans** to **concubines**, who were usually slaves. Courtesans could play musical instruments, dance, engage in witty repartee, and discuss politics. They were also skilled in the arts of love. No social stigma was attached to visiting a courtesan. At the lower rungs of society were streetwalkers and brothel prostitutes. The latter were not hard to find: A wooden or painted penis invariably stood by the door.

The women of Athens had no more rights than slaves. They were subject to the authority of their male next-of-kin before marriage and to their husbands afterwards. They received no formal education and were consigned mostly to women's quarters in their homes. They were chaperoned when they ventured out of doors. A husband could divorce his wife without cause and was obligated to do so if she committed adultery. **TRUTH OR FICTION** REVISITED: Women in the ancient world were treated as property.

The World of Ancient Rome Much is made of the sexual excesses of the Roman emperors and ruling families. Julius Caesar is reputed to have been bisexual—"a man to every woman and a woman to every man." Other emperors, such as Caligula, sponsored orgies at which guests engaged in sexual practices including **bestiality** and **sadism**. Sexual excesses were found more often among the upper classes of palace society than among average Romans, however.

Romans disapproved of male–male sexual behavior as a threat to the integrity of the Roman family. The family was viewed as the source of strength of the empire. Although Roman women were more likely than their Greek counterparts to share their husbands' social lives, they still were the property of their husbands.

Western society traces the roots of many of its sexual terms to Roman culture, as indicated by their Latin roots. **Fellatio**, for example, derives from the Latin *fellare*, meaning "to suck." **Cunnilingus** derives from *cunnus*, meaning "vulva," and *lingere*, "to lick." **Fornication** derives from *fornix*, an arch or vault. The term stems from Roman streetwalkers' practice of serving their customers in the shadows of archways near public buildings such as stadiums and theaters.

The Early Christians Christianity emerged within the Roman Empire during the centuries following the death of Jesus. Early Christian views on sexuality were largely shaped by Saint Paul and the church fathers in the first century and by Saint Augustine in the latter part of the fourth century. Adultery and fornication were rampant among the upper classes of Rome at the time, and early Christian leaders began to associate sexuality with sin (MacCulloch, 2011).

In replacing the pagan values of Rome, the early Christians, like the Hebrews, sought to restrict sex to marriage. They saw temptations of the flesh as distractions from spiritual devotion. Paul preached that celibacy was closer to the Christian ideal than marriage. He recognized that not everyone could achieve celibacy, however, so he said that it was "better to marry than to burn" (with passion, that is).

Christians, like Jews before them, demanded virginity of brides (MacCulloch, 2011). Prostitution was condemned. Christians taught that men should love their

Bisexual Sexually responsive to either gender.

Pederasty Sexual love of boys.

Courtesan A prostitute—especially the mistress of a noble or wealthy man.

Concubine A secondary wife, usually of inferior legal and social status.

Bestiality Sexual relations between a person and an animal.

Sadism The practice of achieving sexual gratification through hurting or humiliating others.

Fellatio A sexual activity involving oral contact with the penis.

Cunnilingus A sexual activity involving oral contact with the female genitals.

Fornication Sexual intercourse between people who are not married to one another.

wives with restraint, not passion. The goal of procreation should govern sexual behavior—the spirit should rule the flesh. Divorce was outlawed. Unhappiness with one's spouse might reflect sexual, thus sinful, restlessness. Dissolving a marriage might also jeopardize the social structure that supported the church. Masturbation, male–male sexual behavior, female–female sexual behavior, oral–genital contact, anal intercourse—all were viewed as abominations in the eyes of God, as in Leviticus.

Saint Augustine (353–430 CE) associated sexual lust with the original sin of Adam and Eve in the Garden of Eden. Lust and shame were passed down through the generations. Lust made any sexual expression, even in marriage, inherently evil. Only through celibacy, according to Augustine, could men and women attain a state of grace.

Islam

The Seraglio of the sultan of the Ottoman Empire housed about 1,600 virgins, each hoping to be chosen for one night of honor. The sultan makes [the Mormon] Brigham Young, who had only a few dozen wives, look like a piker. (Bentley, 2009)

Islam, the dominant religion in the Middle East, across North Africa and into parts of Southern Asia, was founded by the Prophet Muhammad. Muhammad was born in what is now Saudi Arabia, in about 570 CE. The Islamic tradition treasures marriage and sexual fulfillment in marriage. Premarital sex and adultery invite shame and social condemnation—and, in some fundamentalist Islamic states, the death penalty, by stoning.

Muhammad decreed that marriage represents the road to virtue. Islamic tradition permits a sexual double standard, however. Men under most circumstances may take up to four wives (we saw that the sultan of the Ottoman Empire had a few more), but women are permitted only one husband. Public social interactions between men and women are severely restricted in more conservative Islamic societies. Women are expected to keep their heads and faces veiled in public and to avoid all contact with men other than their husbands.

India Perhaps no culture has cultivated sexual pleasure as a spiritual ideal to the extent of the ancient Hindus of India. From the fifth century CE onward, temples show sculptures of gods, nymphs, and ordinary people in erotic poses. Hindu sexual practices were codified in a sex manual, the *Kama Sutra,* which illustrates sexual positions, some of which would challenge a contortionist. It also holds recipes for alleged aphrodisiacs. This manual is believed to have been written by the Hindu sage Vatsyayana sometime between the third and fifth centuries CE, at about the time that Christianity was ascending in the West.

In its graphic representations of sexual positions and practices, the *Kama Sutra* reflected the Hindu belief that sex was a religious duty, not a source of shame or guilt. Hindu deities were often portrayed as engaging in same-sex as well as male–female sexual activities. In the Hindu doctrine of karma (the passage of souls from one place to another), sexual fulfillment was regarded as one way to become reincarnated at a higher level of existence. Indian society grew more restrictive toward sexuality after about 1000 CE.

An Illustration from the *Kama Sutra*. The *Kama Sutra*, an Indian sex manual believed to have been written sometime between the third and fifth centuries CE, contained graphic illustrations of sexual techniques and pratices.

The Far East

> Second century sex manuals ... describe the beautiful bodies—"supple like grass"—of dancing girls, who "put forth all their charms so that one forgets life and death." (Bentley, 2009)

In the cultures of the Far East, sexuality was akin to spirituality. To the Taoist masters of China, who influenced Chinese culture for millennia, sex was a sacred duty—a form of worship that led toward harmony with nature and immortality. **TRUTH** OR **FICTION** REVISITED: It is not true that the production of sex manuals originated in modern times. The Chinese culture was the first to produce a detailed sex manual, which came into use about 200 years before the birth of Jesus. The man was expected to extend intercourse as long as possible to absorb more of his wife's natural essence, or yin. Yin would enhance his own masculine essence, or yang. Moreover, he was to help bring his partner to orgasm so as to increase the flow of energy that he might absorb.

Taoists believed that it was wasteful for a man to "spill his seed." Masturbation, acceptable for women, was ruled out for men. Sexual practices such as anal intercourse and oral–genital contact (fellatio and cunnilingus) were permissible, so long as the man did not squander yang through wasteful ejaculation. Same-sex activity was not prohibited by Taoist holy writings, but some Taoists frowned on exclusive homosexuality. A parallel to Western cultures was the role accorded women in traditional Chinese society. The "good wife," like her Western counterparts, was limited to domestic roles.

Christianity in the Middle Ages

The Middle Ages span the millennium of Western history from about 476 to 1450 CE. The attitudes of the Roman Catholic Church toward sexuality, largely unchanged since the time of Augustine, dominated medieval thought (Crawford et al., 2011). Yet some currents of change crept across medieval Europe in the social standing of women. The Church had long regarded all women as being tainted by the sin of Eve. But in the Eastern Empire of Byzantium, based in Constantinople, the cult of the Virgin Mary flourished. The ideal of womanhood was in the image of Mary: good, gracious, loving, and saintly. Imported by the Crusaders and others who returned from the East, the cult of the Virgin Mary swept European Christendom and helped elevate the status of women.

There were two conflicting concepts of woman: One was the woman as Eve, the temptress; the other was the woman as Mary, virtuous and pure. Contemporary Western images of women still show the schism between the good girl and the bad girl—the Madonna and the whore.

The Protestant Reformation

During the Reformation, Martin Luther (1483–1546) and other Christian reformers such as John Calvin (1509–1564) split off from the Roman Catholic Church and formed their own sects, which led to the development of the modern Protestant denominations. Luther disputed many Roman Catholic doctrines on sexuality. He believed that priests should be allowed to marry and rear children. To Luther, marriage was as much a part of human nature as eating or drinking. Calvin rejected the Roman church's position that sex in marriage was permissible only for procreation. He believed that sexual expression in marriage also strengthened the marriage bond and helped relieve the stresses of everyday life.

Coming to America

Early settlers brought to North America the religious teachings that had dominated Western thought and culture for centuries. Whatever their differences, each religion stressed the ideal of family life and viewed sex outside of marriage as immoral or sinful. A woman's place, by and large, was in the home and in the fields. Not until 1833, when Oberlin College opened its doors to women, were women permitted to attend college in the United States. (Not until 1920 did women gain the right to vote.)

The Victorian Period The middle and later parts of the nineteenth century are generally called the Victorian period, after Queen Victoria of England. Victoria assumed the throne in 1837 and ruled until her death in 1901. Her name has become virtually synonymous with sexual repression. Victorian society in Europe and the United States, on the surface at least, was prim and proper. Sex was not discussed in polite society. Even the legs of pianos were draped with cloth for the sake of modesty. Many women viewed sex as a marital duty to be performed for procreation or to satisfy their husbands' cravings. Consider the following quotation:

> I am happy now that Charles calls on my bed chamber less frequently than of old. As it is, I now endure but two calls a week and when I hear his steps outside my door I lie down on my bed, close my eyes, open my legs and think of England.
>
> —Attributed to Alice, Lady Hillingdon

Queen Victoria of England. Sexuality may not have been as repressed as advertised during the reign of Queen Victoria.

Women were assumed not to experience sexual desires or pleasures. "I would say," observed William Acton (1814–1875), an influential English physician, in 1857, "that the majority of women (happily for society) are not much troubled with sexual feeling of any kind."

It was widely believed among medical authorities in England and the United States that sex drains the man of his vitality. Physicians thus recommended that intercourse be practiced infrequently. The Reverend Sylvester Graham (1794–1851) preached that ejaculation depleted men of "vital fluids" they needed to maintain health and vitality. Graham preached against "wasting the seed" by masturbation or frequent marital intercourse (Haynes, 2012). (How frequent was "frequent"? In Graham's view, intercourse more than once a month could dangerously sap vital energies.) **TRUTH OR FICTION** REVISITED: Graham recommended that young men control their sexual appetites by a diet of simple foods based on whole-grain flours, and invented what we now call the Graham cracker to serve this purpose.

 5

But the behavior of Victorians was not as repressed as advertised. Despite Acton's beliefs, Victorian women did experience sexual pleasure and orgasm. Consider some findings from an early sex survey conducted in 1892 by a female physician, Clelia Duel Mosher. Although her sample was small and nonrandom, 35 of the 44 women who responded admitted to desiring sexual intercourse. And 34 of them reported experiencing orgasm. Women's diaries of the time also contained accounts of passionate love affairs.

Prostitution flourished during the Victorian era. Men apparently thought that they were doing their wives a favor by looking elsewhere. Accurate statistics are hard to come by, but there may have been as many as 1 prostitute for every 12 men in London during the nineteenth century; in Vienna, perhaps 1 for every 7 men.

Same-sex sexual behavior was considered indecent in Victorian society. The celebrated, gay Anglo-Irish novelist and playwright Oscar Wilde—author of *The Picture of Dorian Gray, An Ideal Husband,* and *The Importance of Being Earnest*—was imprisoned after being convicted of "gross indecency."

Foundations of the Scientific Study of Sexuality Against this backdrop of repression, scientists and scholars began to approach sexuality as an area of legitimate scientific study. The English physician Havelock Ellis (1859–1939) published a veritable encyclopedia of sexuality between 1897 and 1910, *Studies in the Psychology of Sex*. Ellis drew information from case histories, anthropological findings, and medical knowledge. He argued that sexual desires in women were natural and healthy. He wrote that many sexual problems had psychological rather than physical causes. Gay male or lesbian sexual orientation was a natural variation, Ellis argued, and not an aberration. He treated gay male and lesbian sexual orientations as inborn dispositions, not as vices or character flaws.

The influential German psychiatrist Richard von Krafft-Ebing (1840–1902) described case histories of people with sexual deviations in his book, *Psychopathia Sexualis* (1886). Cases included sadomasochism (sexual gratification through inflicting or receiving pain), bestiality, and necrophilia (intercourse with dead people). Krafft-Ebing viewed deviations as mental diseases that could be studied and perhaps treated by medical science.

At about the same time, a Viennese physician, Sigmund Freud (1856–1939), was developing a theory of personality that has had an enormous influence on modern culture and science. Freud believed that the sex drive was our principal motivating force.

Alfred Kinsey (1894–1956), an Indiana University zoologist, conducted the first large-scale studies of sexual behavior in the 1930s and 1940s. Kinsey conducted detailed interviews with nearly 12,000 people across the United States. The results of his surveys were published in two volumes, *Sexual Behavior in the Human Male* (Kinsey et al., 1948) and *Sexual Behavior in the Human Female* (Kinsey et al., 1953). These books represent the first scientific attempts to provide a comprehensive picture of sexual behavior in the United States.

The books made for dry reading. They were filled with statistical tables rather than racy pictures or vignettes. Nevertheless, they became best-sellers, exploding on a public that had not yet learned to discuss sex openly. Their publication unleashed the dogs of criticism. Kinsey's work had some methodological flaws—especially in its selection of participants—but much of the criticism branded it immoral and obscene. Many newspapers refused to report the results of his survey on female sexuality. A congressional committee in the 1950s claimed that Kinsey's work undermined the moral fiber of the nation, rendering it more vulnerable to a Communist takeover. Despite all the brouhaha, Kinsey and his colleagues made sex research a scientifically respectable field of study and helped lay the groundwork for discussing sexual behavior openly.

The Sexual Revolution The period of the mid-1960s to the mid-1970s is often referred to as the *sexual revolution*. Dramatic changes occurred in American sexual attitudes and practices during the "Swinging Sixties." Our society was on the threshold of major social upheaval, not only in sexual behavior but also in science, politics, fashion, music, art, and cinema. The so-called Woodstock generation, disheartened by commercialism and the Vietnam War, tuned in (to rock music on the radio), turned on (to drugs), and dropped out (of mainstream society). The heat was on between the hippies and the hardhats. Long hair became the mane of men. Bell-bottomed jeans flared out. Films became sexually explicit as censorship crumbled. Critics seriously contemplated whether the pornography "classic" *Deep Throat* had deep social implications. Hard rock music bellowed the message of rebellion and revolution.

The sexual revolution gained momentum from a timely interplay of scientific, social, political, and economic forces. The war (in Vietnam), the bomb (fear of the nuclear bomb), the pill (the introduction of the birth control pill), and the mass media (especially television) were four such forces. The pill lessened the risk of unwanted pregnancy, permitting young people to engage in recreational or casual sex. Pop psychology movements, such as the Human Potential Movement of the 1960s and 1970s (the "Me Decade"), spread the message that people should get in touch with and express their genuine feelings, including their sexual feelings. "Doing your own thing" became one catchphrase. "If it feels right, go with it" became another. The lamp was rubbed. Out popped the sexual genie.

The sexual revolution was tied to social permissiveness and political liberalism. The media dealt openly with sex. Popular books encouraged people to explore their sexuality. Film scenes of lovemaking became so commonplace that the movie rating system was introduced to alert parents.

Gay Activism Some say gay activism began in 1969, with the gay "rebellion" against police discrimination at the gay bar, the Stonewall Inn, in Manhattan. Gay activism mushroomed during the sexual revolution. Not only did gays become more voluble in demanding equal rights, but they also began gay parades in major cities, such as the annual parades in San Francisco and New York's Greenwich Village. In the early 1980s, gay people also built social institutions to tackle the problem of HIV/AIDS, which afflicted gay males disproportionately. Today gay activism is centered around the issue of gay marriage, which we will discuss further in Chapter 10.

Sex Research During the sexual revolution, sexually explicit questionnaires proliferated in popular magazines, interviewers posed sexually explicit questions by telephone and in person, and some pioneers, including William H. Masters and Virginia Johnson, observed people engaging in sexual activity in the laboratory. Shere Hite published controversial books based on magazine surveys, but her popularity fell when it became clear that 3,000 magazine readers did not represent the country, or even all readers of the magazine. Morton Hunt conducted a telephone survey financed by *Playboy* in the 1970s, and he claimed to find a populace more sexually liberal than in Kinsey's day. However, he, like Shere Hite, had a relatively low response rate. In the 1960s, Masters and Johnson were condemned by many as destroying the moral fabric of the nation—a complaint similar to those leveled earlier against Kinsey. Today, research on sexual behavior continues, with more valid methods of sampling the population and a largely jaded citizenry. 👁

CRITICAL THINKING
What, then, does history tell us about sex? Is there a universal standard for defining sexual values, or are there many standards?

◉ ⃞**Watch** the **Video**
Research Methods in Sexuality: Michael Bailey's Laboratory on **MyDevelopmentLab**

The Legacy of Stonewall. A month after Stonewall, the first gay-pride march was held. The Stonewall incident, in which police arrested gays for simply being at the Inn, unleashed a series of uprisings and mass actions. A provocative slogan came into use: "We're here. We're queer. Get used to it."

Are today's young people more or less liberal in the expression of their sexuality than people in earlier generations?

Recent Trends More teenagers are sexually active today, and at younger ages, than they were a couple of generations ago (Russell et al., 2012). In addition to premarital sex, two other features of the sexual revolution have become permanent parts of our social fabric: the liberation of female sexuality and a greater willingness to discuss sex openly. Countless pornography websites populate the Internet and can be accessed by children. As late as the early 1960s, men's magazines might reveal models' breasts, and nudist magazines might show some more. Today, however, with multiple websites offering the opportunity to download videos of celebrities such as Paris Hilton and Kim Kardashian engaging in sexual activity, pornography has nearly reached the status of wallpaper.

In sum, all societies have some form of an incest taboo. Most societies place a value on procreative sex within the context of an enduring relationship, usually in the form of marriage. Marriage provides security for children, maintains or increases the population, and institutionalizes the orderly transfer of property from generation to generation. Other sexual practices—masturbation, promiscuous sex, male–male sexual behavior, female–female sexual behavior, prostitution, polygamy, and so on—have been condemned in some societies, tolerated by others, and encouraged by still others.

THE BIOLOGICAL PERSPECTIVE

The biological perspective focuses on the roles of genes, hormones, the nervous system, and other biological factors in human sexuality. Sex, after all, serves the biological function of reproduction. We are biologically endowed with structures that make sexual behavior possible—and, for most people, pleasurable.

Study of the biology of sex informs us about the mechanisms of reproduction as well as of the mechanisms of sexual arousal and response. We learn that orgasm is a spinal reflex as well as a psychological event.

Biological researchers have made major strides in assisting infertile couples to conceive, for example, through laboratory-based methods of fertilization. Knowledge of biology has furthered our ability to overcome sexual problems.

THE EVOLUTIONARY PERSPECTIVE

Evolution The development of a species to its present state, which is believed to involve adaptations to its environment.

Species vary not only in their physical characteristics but also in their social behavior, including their mating behavior. Scientists look to **evolution** to help explain such variability (Buss & Schmitt, 2011). The English naturalist Charles Darwin (1809–1882) showed that current species of animals and plants evolved from other life-forms through **natural selection**, or "survival of the fittest." In each species, individuals vary, and some are better adapted to their environments than others. Better-adapted members are more likely to survive to reproduce and transmit their traits to succeeding generations. They are not necessarily the strongest or fleetest of foot, although these traits are adaptive for some species and enhance their reproductive success.

New variations in species can also be introduced through random genetic changes called **mutations**. Although mutations occur randomly, they are subject to natural selection. Adaptive mutations enhance reproductive success. As more members of the species come to possess these traits, the species changes.

Traits are transmitted by units of heredity called **genes**. Traits are determined by single genes or combinations of genes that offspring inherit from their parents. Genes are segments of **chromosomes**, which are composed of **deoxyribonucleic acid (DNA)**. Each human cell normally contains a complement of 46 chromosomes, which are arranged in 23 pairs. Each pair of chromosomes consists of 1,000 or so genes. A child normally inherits one member of each pair from each parent. Each child inherits half of his or her genes from each parent. The particular combinations of genes that one inherits account for whether one has blue eyes or brown eyes, light or dark hair, and arms or wings.

Some scientists suggest that there is also a genetic basis to social behavior, including sexual behavior, among humans and other animals (Buss & Schmitt, 2011). If so, we may carry traits that helped our prehistoric ancestors survive and reproduce successfully.

Does biology govern sexual behavior? Although the sexuality of other species is largely governed by biological processes, culture and experience also play vital roles in human sexuality (Petersen & Hyde, 2010). *Human* sexuality involves a complex web of biological, psychological, and cultural factors. ◉

The Evolutionary Perspective and Erotic Plasticity

Consider the concept of "erotic plasticity" (Baumeister, 2000), which addresses the fact that in response to various social and cultural forces, people show different levels of sex drive and express their sexual desires in a variety of ways. There is evidence that women show greater erotic plasticity than men do (Baumeister, 2000; Yost & Thomas, 2011). For example, (1) individual women show greater variation than men in sexual behavior over time; (2) women seem to be more responsive than men to most specific cultural factors, such as cultural permissiveness or restraint; and (3) men's sexual behavior is more consistent with their sexual attitudes than women's. Are evolutionary, biological forces an important factor in the greater female erotic plasticity?

Altruism

There is a tendency to think of adaptive traits as somehow more "worthy," "good," or "admirable" than less adaptive traits. But evolution is not a moralistic enterprise. A trait either does or does not enhance reproductive success. It is not good or bad in itself. It is apparently adaptive for the female of one species of insect to eat the male after mating. "Dad" then literally nourishes his offspring during the period of gestation. In evolutionary terms, his "altruism"—his personal sacrifice—is adaptive if it increases the chances that the offspring will survive and carry his genes. In other species, it may be adaptive for fathers to "love them and leave them"—that is, to mate with as many females as possible and abruptly abandon them to "plant their seed" elsewhere.

TRUTH OR FICTION REVISITED: Shortly after inseminating a female, the male redback spider does a somersault into the female's mouth and becomes her after-sex meal. Females pause in their sexual activity after "taking in" their partners. Thus, their partner's sacrifice improves the chance that his own sperm will fertilize her eggs before another male can have at her.

Natural selection The evolutionary process by which adaptive traits enable members of a species to survive to reproductive age and transmit these traits to future generations.

◉—**Watch the Video**
Evolution and Sex: Michael Bailey on **MyDevelopmentLab**

Mutation A random change in the molecular structure of DNA.

Genes The basic units of heredity, which consist of chromosomal segments of DNA.

Chromosomes The rodlike structures that reside in the nuclei of every living cell and carry the genetic code in the form of genes.

DNA Deoxyribonucleic acid—the chemical substance whose molecules make up genes and chromosomes.

 6

CRITICAL THINKING

The biological, evolutionary, and cross-species perspectives may offer some insights into what kinds of sexual behavior are "natural." If a sexual behavior pattern is judged to be natural, does that mean that it is right or good? Explain.

◉⊣**Watch** the **Video**
Mating Trick
on **MyDevelopmentLab**

Gender Differences in Preferred Number of Sex Partners Some evolutionary psychologists argue that men are naturally more promiscuous than women because they are the genetic heirs of ancestors whose reproductive success was related to the number of women they could impregnate (Buss & Schmitt, 2011). Women, by contrast, can produce only a few offspring in their lifetimes. Thus, the theory goes, they have to be more selective with respect to their mating partners. Women's reproductive success is enhanced by mating with the fittest males—not with any Tom, Dick, or Harry who happens by. From this perspective, the male's "roving eye" and the female's selectivity are embedded in their genes. ◉

THE CROSS-SPECIES PERSPECTIVE

The study of other animal species places human behavior in broader context. A surprising variety of sexual behaviors exists among nonhumans. There are animal examples, or analogues, of human male–male sexual behavior, female–female sexual behavior, oral–genital contact, and oral–oral behavior (i.e., kissing). Foreplay is also well known in the animal world. Turtles massage their mates' heads with their claws. Male mice nibble at their partner's necks. Most mammals use only a rear-entry position for copulation, but some animals, such as apes, use a variety of coital positions.

Cross-species research reveals an interesting pattern. Sexual behavior among "higher" mammals, such as primates, is less directly controlled by instinct than it is among the "lower" species, such as birds, fish, or lower mammals. Experience and learning play more important roles in sexuality as we travel up the evolutionary ladder.

SOCIOLOGICAL PERSPECTIVES

Sociological perspectives, like the historical perspective, provide insight into the ways in which cultural institutions and beliefs affect sexual behavior and people's sense of morality. Interest in the effects of culture on sexuality was spurred by the early-twentieth-century work of Margaret Mead (1901–1978) and Bronislaw Malinowski (1884–1942).

In *Sex and Temperament in Three Primitive Societies* (1935), Mead laid the groundwork for recent psychological and sociological research challenging gender-role stereotypes. In most cultures characterized by a gender division of labor, men typically go to business or to the hunt, and—when necessary—to war. In such cultures, men are perceived as strong, active, independent, and logical. Women are viewed as passive, dependent, nurturing, and emotional. Mead concluded that these stereotypes are not inherent in our genetic heritage. Rather, they are acquired through cultural expectations and socialization. That is, men and women learn to behave in ways that are expected of them in their particular culture.

In 1951, Clellan Ford, an anthropologist, and Frank Beach, a psychologist, reviewed sexual behavior in almost 200 preliterate societies around the world. They found great variety in sexual customs and beliefs. They also found some fairly common threads. Kissing was quite common although not universal. The Thonga of Africa did not practice kissing. When witnessing European visitors kissing each other, members of the tribe commented that they could not understand why Europeans "ate" each other's saliva and dirt. The frequency of sexual intercourse also varies from culture to culture, but intercourse is relatively more frequent among young people everywhere.

Societies differ in their attitudes toward childhood masturbation. Some societies, such as the Hopi Native Americans of the southwest United States, ignore it. Trobrianders encourage it. Other societies condemn it.

Societies differ widely in their sexual attitudes, customs, and practices. The members of all human societies share anatomic structures and physiological capacities for sexual pleasure, however. The same hormones flow through their arteries. Yet their sexual practices, and the pleasure they reap or fail to attain, may set them apart. If human sexuality were determined exclusively by biology, we might not find such diversity.

PSYCHOLOGICAL PERSPECTIVES

Psychological perspectives focus on the many psychological influences—perception, learning, motivation, emotion, personality, and so on—that affect our sexual behavior and our experience of ourselves as female or male. Some psychological theorists, such as Sigmund Freud, focus on the motivational role of sex in human personality. Others focus on how our experiences and mental representations of the world affect our sexual behavior.

Sigmund Freud and Psychoanalytic Theory Sigmund Freud, a Viennese physician, formulated a grand theory of personality termed **psychoanalysis**. Freud believed that we are all born with biologically based sex drives that must be channeled through socially approved outlets if family and social life are to carry on without undue conflict.

Freud proposed that the mind operates on conscious and unconscious levels. The conscious level corresponds to our state of present awareness. The unconscious mind refers to the darker reaches of the mind that lie outside our direct awareness. The ego shields the conscious mind from awareness of our baser sexual and aggressive urges by means of **defense mechanisms** such as **repression**, or motivated forgetting of traumatic experiences.

Although many sexual ideas and impulses are banished to the unconscious, they continue to seek expression. One avenue of expression is the dream, through which sexual impulses may be perceived in disguised, or symbolic, form. The therapists and scholars who follow in the Freudian tradition are quite interested in analyzing dreams, and the dream objects listed in Table 1.3 are often considered sex symbols.

Psychoanalysis   The theory of personality originated by Sigmund Freud, which proposes that human behavior represents the outcome of clashing inner forces.

Defense mechanisms   In psychoanalytic theory, automatic processes that protect the ego from anxiety by disguising or ejecting unacceptable ideas and urges.

Repression   The automatic ejection of anxiety-evoking ideas from consciousness.

Table 1.3

Dream Symbols in Psychoanalytic Theory

Symbols for the Male Genital Organs				
airplanes	fish	neckties	tools	weapons
bullets	hands	poles	trains	
feet	hoses	snakes	trees	
fire	knives	sticks	umbrellas	
Symbols for the Female Genital Organs				
bottles	caves	doors	ovens	ships
boxes	chests	hats	pockets	tunnels
cases	closets	jars	pots	
Symbols for Sexual Intercourse				
climbing a ladder		flying in an airplane		
climbing a staircase		riding a horse		
crossing a bridge		riding an elevator		
driving an automobile		riding a roller coaster		
entering a room		walking into a tunnel or down a hall		
Symbols for the Breasts				
apples		peaches		

Freud theorized that the content of dreams symbolized urges, wishes, and objects of fantasy that we would censor in the waking state.

How might a psychoanalyst interpret this dream image?

A World of Diversity

An "Honor Killing" in Germany

Hatun Surucu, 23, was killed on her way to a bus stop in Berlin-Tempelhof by several shots to the head and upper body, fired at point-blank range. Months before, she had reported one of her brothers to the police for threatening her. Three of her five brothers were tried for murder. According to the prosecutor, the oldest (age 25) acquired the weapon, the middle brother (age 24) lured his sister to the scene of the crime, and the youngest (age 18) shot her.

Hatun Surucu had "dishonored" her family. She grew up in Berlin as the daughter of Turkish Kurds. When she finished eighth grade, her parents took her out of school. Shortly after that she was taken to Turkey and married to a cousin. Later she separated from her husband and returned to Berlin, pregnant. At age 17 she gave birth to a son. She moved into a women's shelter and completed the work

Hatun Surucu

for her middle-school certificate. Later she finished a vocational-training program to become an electrician. She put on makeup, wore her hair unbound, went dancing, and adorned herself with rings, necklaces, and bracelets. Then her life was cut short.

Evidently, in the eyes of her brothers, Hatun Surucu's capital crime was that, living in Germany, she had begun living like a German. One brother noted that she had stopped wearing her head scarf, that she refused to go back to her family, and that she had declared her intent to "seek out her own circle of friends." Often in such cases it is the father of the family who decides about the punishment, but Seyran Ates, a Turkish-German lawyer, reports cases in which the mother has a leading role—mothers who were forced to marry forcing the same fate on their daughters. Necla Kelek, a Turkish-German author, explained, "The mothers are looking for solidarity by demanding that their daughters submit to the same hardship and suffering." By disobeying them, the daughter calls into question her mother's life—her silent submission to the ritual of forced marriage.

Many Germans were made aware of the parallel Muslim world arising in their midst primarily thanks to three women Muslim authors: Seyran Ates, Necla Kelek, and Serap Cileli. Ates and Kelek narrowly escaped Hatun Surucu's fate, and Serap Cileli, when she was 13 years old, tried to kill herself to escape her first forced marriage. Later she was taken to Turkey and married against her will, then she returned to Germany with two children from this marriage and took refuge in a women's shelter to escape her father's violence.

Seyran Ates estimates that perhaps half of young Turkish women living in Germany are forced into marriage every year. In the wake of these forced

marriages often come violence and rape; the bride has no choice but to fulfill the duties of the marriage arranged by her parents and her in-laws.

There have been 49 known "honor crimes" during the past nine years in Germany. Perhaps the murder of Hatun Surucu never would have made the headlines at all but for another piece of news that stirred up the press. Just a few hundred yards from where Surucu was killed, at the Thomas Morus High School, three Muslim students openly declared their approval of the murder. Shortly before that, the same students had bullied a fellow pupil because her clothing was "not in keeping with the religious regulations."

Politicians and religious scholars of all faiths are right in pointing out that there are many varieties of Islam, that Islamism and Islam should not be confused, and that there is no line in the *Koran* that would justify murder. However, disregard for women's rights—especially the right to sexual self-determination—is an integral component of almost all Islamic societies. Islam needs something like an Enlightenment—only by sticking hard to their own Enlightenment, with its separation of religion and state, can the Western democracies persuade their Muslim residents that human rights are universally valid. "We Western Muslim women," Seyran Ates says, "will set off the reform of traditional Islam, because we are its victims."

CRITICAL THINKING

The Muslim author Seyran Ates states that "human rights are universally valid." What human rights is she speaking about? Is she correct? Support your view.

Which institution has a greater right to govern people's attitudes and behavior: A nation or a religion? Explain your view.

 7   **TRUTH OR FICTION REVISITED:** To a psychoanalyst, dreams of airplanes, bullets, snakes, sticks, and similar objects may indeed symbolize the male genitals. But this is the case according to psychoanalytic theory, and not necessarily supported by research evidence. To his credit, Freud himself maintained skepticism about the importance of dream symbols. He once remarked, "Sometimes a cigar is just a cigar."

Freud introduced us to new and controversial ideas about ourselves as sexual beings. For example, he originated the concept of **erogenous zones**—the idea that many parts of the body, not just the genitals, are responsive to sexual stimulation.

One of Freud's most controversial beliefs was that children normally harbor erotic interests. He believed that the suckling by the infant in the oral stage was an erotic act, and he believed the same about the anal bodily experimentation through which 2-year-olds find pleasure in the control of their sphincter muscles in the process of elimination. He theorized that it was normal for children to progress through stages of development in which the erotic interest shifts from one erogenous zone to another, as, for example, from the mouth or oral cavity to the anal cavity. According to his theory of **psychosexual development**, children undergo five stages of development: oral, anal, phallic, latency, and genital, which are named according to the main erogenous zones of each stage.

Freud believed that it was normal for children to develop erotic feelings toward the parent of the other sex during the phallic stage. These incestuous urges lead to conflict with the parent of the same sex. In later chapters we will see that these developments, which Freud termed the **Oedipus complex**, have implications for the assumption of gender roles and sexual orientation.

Learning Theories To what extent does sexual behavior reflect experience? Would you hold the same sexual attitudes and do the same things if you had been reared in another culture? We think not. Even within the same society, family and personal experiences can shape unique sexual attitudes and behaviors.

Behaviorists such as John B. Watson (1878–1958) and B. F. Skinner (1904–1990) emphasized the importance of rewards and punishments in the learning process. Children left to explore their bodies without parental condemnation will learn what feels good and tend to repeat it. The Trobriand child who is rewarded for masturbation and premarital **coitus** through parental praise and encouragement will be more likely to repeat these behaviors than the child in a more sexually restrictive culture, who is punished for the same behavior. When sexual behavior (like masturbation) feels good, but parents connect it with feelings of guilt and shame, the child is placed in conflict and may vacillate between masturbating and swearing off it. If, as young children, we are severely punished for sexual exploration, we may come to associate sexual stimulation in general with feelings of guilt or anxiety. Can such early learning experiences set the stage for sexual problems or dysfunctions in adulthood?

Cognitive Views Cognitive psychologists emphasize the importance of cognitive activity (problem solving, decision making, expectations, and so on). They also recognize that people learn intentionally and by observing others. *Observational learning* refers to acquiring knowledge and skills through observing others. Observational learning includes seeing models in films or on television, hearing about them, and reading about them. According to **social–cognitive theory**, children acquire the gender roles deemed appropriate in a society through reinforcement of gender-appropriate

Erogenous zones   Parts of the body, including but not limited to the sex organs, that are responsive to sexual stimulation.

Psychosexual development   In psychoanalytic theory, the process by which sexual feelings shift from one erogenous zone to another.

Oedipus complex   In psychoanalytic theory, a conflict of the phallic stage in which the boy wishes to possess his mother sexually and perceives his father as a rival in love.

Behaviorists   Learning theorists who argue that a scientific approach to understanding behavior must refer only to observable and measurable behaviors.

Coitus (co-it-us or co-EET-us)   Sexual intercourse.

Social–cognitive theory   A cognitively oriented learning theory in which observational learning, values, and expectations play key roles in determining behavior.

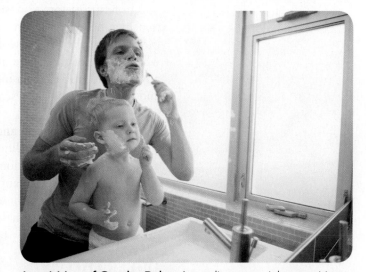

Acquisition of Gender Roles. According to social—cognitive theory, children learn gender roles by means of reinforcement of certain behavior patterns and by observing the gender-related behaviors of their parents, peers, and other role models in media such as TV, films, and books.

behavior and through observing the gender-role behavior of their parents, their peers, and other models on television, in films, in books, and so on.

FEMINIST THEORY

The Greek philosopher Aristotle is said to have described a female as a deformed male. We can only guess at the number of objectionable beliefs expressed in this description, such as seeing the male as the ideal, focusing on the differences rather than the similarities between men and women, and the implicit right of men to hold power over women.

Feminism and **feminist theory** are born of protest against ideas such as those of Aristotle's—ideas that remain with us today in many if not most parts of the world (Petersen & Hyde, 2010). Definitions of *feminism* and of *feminist theory* are controversial, but it is clear enough that feminist theory focuses on the subordination of women to men; analyzing the relationships between sexism, heterosexism (prejudice or discrimination against homosexuals by heterosexuals), racism, and class oppression; and exploring means of resistance—on individual and societal levels (Petersen & Hyde, 2010).

Among other things, feminist theory challenges:

- Traditional views of men as breadwinners and women as homemakers
- Traditional views of men as political policymakers, especially since those policies affect women and children
- Traditional views of men as sexual "aggressors" and women as sexual "gatekeepers"
- Traditional gender roles that view men as objective and rational, and women as emotional and irrational

Some feminists challenge the very concepts of femininity and masculinity because their existence tends to suggest that there is some sort of biological or "actual" basis to the distinction (Shields & Dicicco, 2011). They argue, instead, that femininity and masculinity might be purely social constructions that have the effect of giving women second-class citizenship—or, in many historic eras and parts of the world, no citizenship whatsoever.

In terms of topics most relevant to this book, we will find feminists asserting that men have no right to control women's bodies—for example, that abortion is the personal choice of a woman; that women have as much right as men to decide whether or not to engage in sexual activity, and with whom; that there are few if any gender differences in mental abilities, such as those used in math and science; and that most medical research has been conducted by men for men, with men as subjects.

Although the extent and nature of gender differences remain controversial, we can note that many traditions that subjugate women are falling by the wayside, at least in developed nations. Most Western women, for example, are now in the workforce. As a result, many men now share in child rearing and housekeeping with female partners. In the United States, as many women as men are pursuing careers in traditionally male domains, such as business, law, and medicine (Kimmel et al., 2012). Many women now feel free to initiate sex and relationships.

QUEER THEORY

The word *queer* was initially used as an insult to describe homosexuals. After approximately two centuries, the term became gradually replaced by the word *gay*. However, homosexuals have reappropriated the word *queer* as a sign of pride, as shown by the title of the former TV show, *Queer Eye for the Straight Guy*. As one

Feminist theory A theory that challenges acceptance of the male as the norm, traditional gender roles, and male oppression of females.

result of this reappropriation, a widely cited theory of the psychology and sociology of gender roles and sexual orientation is termed **queer theory** (Hegarty, 2011).

Queer theory challenges a number of commonly held assumptions about gender and sexuality, such as the assumptions that heterosexuality is normal and superior to homosexuality (Semp, 2011). Queer theory also challenges the assumption that people are naturally divided into heterosexuals and homosexuals (Downing & Gillett, 2011).

According to queer theory, the concepts of heterosexuality and homosexuality are social constructs that ignore commonly experienced mismatches among people's anatomic sex, society's gender roles, and individuals' sexual desires (Downing & Gillett, 2011). Queer theory asserts that human sexuality has always been more varied than those in power—particularly male heterosexuals—are willing to admit. They point to historical examples such as ancient Greek bisexuality and to current **homophobia** as evidence. We will revisit concepts of queer theory in later chapters, particularly the chapters on gender and sexual orientation. ◉

MULTIPLE PERSPECTIVES ON HUMAN SEXUALITY

Given the complexity and range of human sexual behavior, we need to consider multiple perspectives to understand sexuality. Each perspective—historical, biological, cross-species, sociological, psychological, feminist, and queer—has something to teach us. Let us venture a few conclusions based on our overview of these perspectives. First, human sexuality appears to reflect a combination of biological, social, cultural, and psychological factors that interact in complex ways. Second, there are few universal patterns of sexual behavior, and views on what is right and wrong show great diversity. Third, although our own cultural values and beliefs may be deeply meaningful to us, they may not indicate what is normal, natural, or moral in terms of sexual behavior. The complexity of human sexuality—a complexity that causes it to remain somewhat baffling even to scientists—adds to the wonder and richness of our sexual experience.

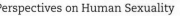

◉▸ **Watch** the **Video**
The Basics: Sex and Gender Differences
on **MyDevelopmentLab**

Queer theory A theory that challenges heteronormativity and heterosexism.

Homophobia Hatred of homosexuals.

Real Students, Real Questions

Q *If there are so many ways of looking at sex, how can you tell what is the right way of thinking about things? It makes it hard to make decisions.*

A Yes, it can be hard to make sexual decisions, but it doesn't have to be! If the decisions are informed decisions, if they are consistent with your values, and—most important—if they are *your* decisions, you can be quite comfortable with them. Do not allow yourself to be pressured by someone else; if you're pressured and you go along with the pressure, it's not you making the decision. This textbook will suggest things to consider when making decisions about dozens of sexual topics. But in the end, the decisions have to be your decisions. What is right for someone else might not be right for you. One more thing: We don't know anyone who makes the right decision about every issue all the time. Be stubborn about matters of sexual health, but if you err in a judgment about another person, know that you're not alone. We've "been there."

Chapter Review ✓—[Study and Review on MyDevelopmentLab

LO1 Define the science of human sexuality
Human sexuality concerns the ways in which we experience and express ourselves as sexual beings. The study of human sexuality draws on the expertise of anthropologists, biologists, medical researchers, sociologists, psychologists, and other scientists.

LO2 Define the value systems people use in making sexual decisions
Along with accurate knowledge about human sexuality, our values inform our sexual decisions. Value systems include legalism, situational ethics, ethical relativism, hedonism, asceticism, utilitarianism, and rationalism.

LO3 Explain how you can become a critical thinker
Critical thinking is a skeptical approach to evaluating arguments, widespread beliefs, and evidence. Critical thinkers examine definitions of terms and the premises of arguments.

LO4 Describe the historical perspective on human sexuality
The historical perspective suggests that there are few universal sexual trends. Ancient Hebrews, Greeks, and Romans dwelled in male-oriented societies that viewed women as property. Repressive Victorian sexual attitudes gave way to the sexual revolution of the 1960s and 1970s.

LO5 Describe the biological perspective on human sexuality
The biological perspective focuses on biological sexual processes such as genetic, hormonal, and neural factors. Evolutionary theory suggests that social behaviors that enhance reproductive success may be subject to natural selection. The cross-species perspective reveals the variety of sexual behaviors among nonhumans.

LO6 Describe the evolutionary perspective on human sexuality
Evolutionary theory has been active in studying the areas of mate selection and aggression—including sexual aggression. The evolutionary perspective suggests that social behaviors that enhance reproductive success may be subject to natural selection.

LO7 Describe the cross-species perspective on human sexuality
The cross-species perspective reveals the variety of sexual behaviors among nonhumans. Studying the behavior of other species may suggest that certain kinds of behaviors are "natural" in that other species do not plan and evaluate sexual behavior in the way that humans do. (Question: Can we equate "natural" with "good"—especially when it comes to humans?)

LO8 Describe sociological perspectives on human sexuality
The sociological perspective studies ways in which cultural beliefs affect sexual behavior and attitudes.

LO9 Describe psychological perspectives on human sexuality
Psychological perspectives focus on the processes of perception, learning, motivation, emotion, and personality that affect gender and sexual behavior. The theory of psychoanalysis proposes that biologically based sex drives come into conflict with social codes. Learning theories focus on factors such as rewards, punishments, and observational learning.

LO10 Discuss feminist theory
Feminist theory challenges traditional views of men as breadwinners and women as homemakers; of men as political policymakers, especially since those policies affect women and children; of men as sexual "aggressors" and women as sexual "gatekeepers"; and traditional gender roles that view men as objective and rational, and women as emotional and irrational.

LO11 Discuss queer theory
Queer theory challenges heteronormativity—the viewpoint that heterosexuality is normal. According to queer theory, *heterosexuality* and *homosexuality* are social constructs that ignore commonly experienced mismatches among people's anatomic sex, society's gender roles, and individuals' sexual desires.

LO12 Explain why it is useful to look upon human sexuality from multiple perspectives
Given the complexity and range of human sexual behavior, we need to consider multiple perspectives to understand sexuality. Based on our overview of these perspectives, we may conclude that human sexuality reflects a combination of biological, social, cultural, and psychological factors that interact in complex ways. Second, there are few universal patterns of sexual behavior, and views on what is right and wrong show great diversity.

Test Your Learning

1. Critical thinking involves all of the following *except*
   - (a) skepticism.
   - (b) challenging tradition.
   - (c) evaluating the premises of logic.
   - (d) blindly following authority figures.

2. Stone Age art suggests that people worshiped
   - (a) women's ability to bear children.
   - (b) a scientific approach to human sexuality.
   - (c) bisexuality in men.
   - (d) men's ability to father children.

3. The ancient _____ were first to produce a sex manual.
   - (a) Greeks
   - (b) Romans
   - (c) Chinese
   - (d) Indians

4. According to the text, _____ challenged the prevailing British view by arguing that sexual desires in women were natural and healthy.
   - (a) Havelock Ellis
   - (b) Sylvester Graham
   - (c) Sigmund Freud
   - (d) Richard von Krafft-Ebing

5. A controversial Freudian belief is that
   - (a) children normally harbor erotic interests.
   - (b) children ignore unacceptable impulses.
   - (c) childhood is an important time of life.
   - (d) children seek pain and avoid pleasure.

6. Masters and Johnson are best known for using _____ in their research on human sexual response.
   - (a) correlation coefficients
   - (b) cross-cultural methods
   - (c) the laboratory-observation method
   - (d) the survey

7. Queer theory opposes
   - (a) heterosexism.
   - (b) use of the word *queer*.
   - (c) activism.
   - (d) challenging prevailing views of gender and sexuality.

8. According to _____ theory, children acquire the gender roles deemed appropriate in a society through reinforcement and observational learning.
   - (a) evolutionary
   - (b) social–cognitive
   - (c) feminist
   - (d) psychoanalytic

9. *Psychopathia Sexualis* was written by
   - (a) Havelock Ellis.
   - (b) Sylvester Graham.
   - (c) Sigmund Freud.
   - (d) Richard von Krafft-Ebing.

10. According to queer theory,
    - (a) there is no such thing as homosexuality.
    - (b) all heterosexuals are prejudiced.
    - (c) everybody is bisexual.
    - (d) current categories of sexual orientation do not adequately describe all people.

Answers: 1. d; 2. a; 3. c; 4. a; 5. a; 6. c; 7. a; 8. b; 9. d; 10. d

My Life, My Sexuality

Thinking Critically about Sexual Advice on the Internet: Are There Any Quick Fixes?

*Explore this **My Life, My Sexuality** feature by scanning this QR code with your mobile device. If you don't already have one, you may download a free QR scanner for your device wherever smartphone apps are sold. You can also view this feature in MyDevelopmentLab, along with an accompanying critical thinking assignment*

The Internet would appear to have all the advice anyone would need on almost any topic. Sex is certainly no exception; sex, in fact, is the most commonly surfed topic on the Internet. But how can you safely bring sexual information on the Internet into your life? How can you enhance your life and at the same time protect your sexuality, your health, and your relationships? Scan the code to go online and find advice on how to sift the "chaff from the wheat" and make the most of what you find on the Internet—safely.

2 Research Methods in Human Sexuality

Learning Objectives

The Big Picture: How to Answer Psychological Questions

Explore the video, *The Big Picture: How to Answer Psychological Questions,* by scanning this QR code with your mobile device. If you don't already have one, you may download a free QR scanner for your device wherever smartphone apps are sold. You can also view this video in MyDevelopmentLab. For more videos related to this chapter's content, log into MyDevelopmentLab to view the entire Human Sexuality Video Series.

TRUTH OR FICTION?

Which of the following statements are the truth and which are fiction? Look for the Truth-or-Fiction icons on the pages that follow to find the answers.

1 The science of human sexuality tells people how they ought to behave. **T F?**

2 You could study the sexual behavior of millions of Americans and still not obtain an accurate picture of the sexual behavior of the general U.S. population. **T F?**

3 Case studies have been carried out on people who are dead. **T F?**

4 Only a small minority of adolescents and young adults are concerned about their sexual health. **T F?**

5 Some sex researchers have engaged in "swinging" with the people they have studied. **T F?**

6 Masters and Johnson created an artificial penis containing photographic equipment to study female sexual response. **T F?**

7 Viagra causes risky sexual behavior. **T F?**

8 People who attend church regularly tend to be more satisfied with their relationship. **T F?**

9 Researchers often publish the names of participants in sex research in professional journals. **T F?**

Wardell B. Pomeroy, one of Alfred Kinsey's core-researchers in the 1940s, was interviewing a man about his first ejaculation. He asked, "When?" The man answered, "Fourteen." Pomeroy then asked, "How?" and was surprised to hear: "With a horse."

In his biography, *Sex the Measure of All Things: A Life of Alfred C. Kinsey*, Jonathan Gathorne-Hardy records what happened next. Pomeroy asked the man, "How often were you having intercourse with animals at 14?"

The man looked confused and said, "Well, yes, it is true I had intercourse with a pony at 14." Pomeroy, it turned out, had misheard the man's previous answer. It was "with whores," not "with a horse." So the man was stunned that Pomeroy had had the insight to ask him the horse question out of the blue (Drucker, 2012).

The question was asked during the Kinsey studies of sexual behavior in the United States—the best-known surveys in the history of studying sexual behavior. The survey method typically gathers information about sexual attitudes and behaviors through questionnaires or interviews.

Research Interview. Interviewing is a commonly used method in surveys. Questionnaires are also used.

In this chapter we see how scientists who study human sexuality carry out research. Many of them, such as Wardell Pomeroy and other members of the Kinsey team, interview respondents. Interviews and questionnaires are examples of the survey method. But we will see that there are many other methods, including the case study, the field study, and the experiment. Then we will discuss ethical issues in sex research.

But let us begin by exploring the scientific method. Science is what separates research findings from opinion, superstition, folklore, and error.

A Scientific Approach to Human Sexuality

Scientists who study sex take an **empirical** approach. They base their knowledge on research evidence, rather than on intuition, faith, or superstition. Intuitions or religious beliefs may suggest topics to be studied scientifically. Yet once the topics are selected, answers are sought on the basis of the scientific method. 👁

THE SCIENTIFIC METHOD

Critical thinking and the scientific approach share the hallmark of skepticism. Scientists question prevailing assumptions and theories about sexual behavior. They are willing to dispute the assertions of authority figures such as political and religious leaders—even other scientists. They also recognize that they cannot gain perfect knowledge. One era's "truths" may become another era's ancient myths and fallacies. Scientists are involved in the continuous quest for truth, but they do not see themselves as experiencing revelations or defining final truths.

👁—**Watch** the **Video**
The Big Picture: How to Answer Psychological Questions
on **MyDevelopmentLab**

Empirical   Derived from or based on observation and experimentation.

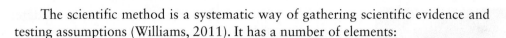

The scientific method is a systematic way of gathering scientific evidence and testing assumptions (Williams, 2011). It has a number of elements:

1. *Formulating a research question.* An example of a possible research question is "Does alcohol inspire or impair sexual response?" Scientists formulate research questions on the basis of their observations of, or theories about, events or behavior. They then seek answers to such questions by conducting empirical research.

2. *Framing the research question in the form of a hypothesis.* Experiments are usually undertaken with a **hypothesis** in mind—a precise prediction that is tested through research. For instance, a scientist might theorize that alcohol enhances sexual responsiveness either by directly stimulating sexual response or by reducing feelings of guilt associated with sex. He or she might then hypothesize that an intervention (called, in experimental terms, a "treatment"), such as drinking alcohol in a laboratory setting, will lead to heightened sexual arousal in the presence of sexually explicit films.

3. *Testing the hypothesis.* Scientists then test hypotheses through carefully controlled observation and experimentation. A specific hypothesis about alcohol and sexual arousal—that alcohol either increases or decreases sexual responsiveness—might be tested by administering a certain amount of alcohol to one group of people and then comparing their level of sexual arousal following specific types of sexual stimulation—such as exposure to sexually explicit films—to the level of sexual arousal of a group that was shown the films but not given any alcohol.

4. *Drawing conclusions.* Scientists then draw conclusions or inferences about the correctness of their hypotheses, based on their analyses of the results of their studies. If the results of well-designed research studies fail to bear out certain hypotheses, scientists can revise the theories that served as the frameworks for the hypotheses. Research findings often lead scientists to modify their theories, and in turn, generate new hypotheses.

GOALS OF THE SCIENCE OF HUMAN SEXUALITY

The goals of the science of human sexuality are congruent with those of other sciences: to describe, explain, predict, and control the events (in this case, the sexual behaviors) that are of interest. Scientists attempt to be clear, unbiased, and precise in their descriptions of events and behavior. The scientific approach to human sexuality describes sexual behavior through techniques as varied as the field study, the survey, the individual case study, and laboratory observation.

To underscore the importance of the need for unbiased description, consider the name of a tropical fish: the kissing gourami. These small, flat fish—particularly males—press their open mouths against one another. Yet the term *kissing* may be a misnomer if it is used to imply affection. Prolonged observations of the fish suggest that it is more likely that kissing in gouramis is a test of strength. The error in describing the behavior of gouramis as "kissing" involves confusing **inference** with description. It is, in fact, an **anthropomorphic** inference; it involves applying human standards to explain animal behavior. One of the challenges to scientists is the separation of description from inference.

Researchers attempt to relate their observations to other factors, or **variables**, that can help explain them. For example, researchers may attempt to explain variations in the frequency of sex by relating—or correlating—sexual frequency with **demographic** variables such as age, religious or social background, or cultural

Hypothesis A precise prediction about behavior that is tested through research.

Inference Conclusion or opinion.

Anthropomorphism The attributing of human characteristics to an animal.

Variables Quantities or qualities that vary or may vary.

Demographic Concerning the vital statistics (race, gender, age, religion, etc.) of human populations.

Kissing Gouramis. These fish obtain their moniker from pressing their open mouths against one another. Yet if the word kissing is meant to imply affection, think again. Prolonged observations of the fish suggest "kissing" is more likely to be a test of strength. Describing the behavior of the fish as "kissing" confuses inference (that is, drawing conclusions) with description. One of the challenges to scientists is to separate description from inference.

expectations. The variables that are commonly used to explain sexual behavior are biological (age, health), psychological (anxieties, skills), and sociological (educational level, socioeconomic status, ethnicity).

Theories provide frameworks within which scientists can explain what they observe and make predictions. Theories must allow us to make predictions. One test of the soundness of psychoanalytic and learning theories is whether or not they allow us to predict behavior. Sex researchers study factors that may predict various types of sexual behavior. Some researchers, for example, have examined childhood interests and behavior patterns that may predict the development of a gay male or lesbian sexual orientation. Others have explored factors, such as the age at which dating begins and the quality of the parent–adolescent relationship that may predict the likelihood of teenage pregnancy.

The concept of "controlling" human behavior does not mean coercing people to do the bidding of others. Rather, it means drawing from scientific knowledge to help people create their own goals and marshal their resources to meet them. Reputable scientists are held to ethical and professional standards that safeguard the rights of participants in research.

1 **TRUTH OR FICTION REVISITED:** The science of human sexuality does not tell people how they ought to behave. Rather, it furnishes information that people may use to help themselves or others make decisions. For instance, the science of human sexuality provides information that increases the chances that a couple who is having difficulty becoming pregnant will be able to conceive. At the same time, it develops and evaluates means of birth control that can be used to help couples regulate their reproductive choices.

Let's now look at the ways in which sexologists study human sexuality. Researchers must first identify whom or what they will study, which brings us to the topic of sampling.

Populations and Samples: Representing the World of Diversity

Researchers seek to learn about **populations**—complete groups of people or animals. Many researchers seek to learn about Americans, for example. Other researchers may identify American adults or American adolescents as their population. Still other researchers attempt to compare the sexual behavior of African Americans to that of Latin Americans and other Americans. These are termed the *populations of interest*, or *target populations*. These target populations are sizable; it would be expensive and difficult to try to study every individual in them. ◉

Because of the difficulty in studying all members of a population, scientists select individuals from the population and study them. The individuals who participate in research are said to compose a **sample**. However, that sample must *represent* the target population. If we wished to study the sexual behavior of Asian Americans, for example, our population would consist of all Asian Americans. If we used only Asian American college students as our sample, we could not **generalize** our findings to all Asian Americans.

◉┤**Watch** the **Video**
The Basics: Scientific Research Methods on **MyDevelopmentLab**

Population A complete group of organisms or events.

Sample Part of a population.

Generalize To go from the particular to the general.

SAMPLING METHODS: DOES SIZE MATTER?

Now and then, magazine editors boast that they have surveyed samples of 20,000 or 30,000 readers, but size alone does not mean that a sample is representative. *Psychology Today* and *Glamour* regularly poll readers, but their readers do not represent the general population. Readers of *Psychology Today* are "biased" in that they tend to be better educated and more liberal than the population at large (*Psychology Today*, 2006). Readers of *Glamour* are "biased" in that they are also better educated than the average American, and more likely to be concerned about their appearance and optimizing their sex lives. **TRUTH OR FICTION** REVISITED: You could study the sexual behavior of millions of Americans and still not obtain an accurate picture of the sexual behavior of the general American population. Researchers need to obtain samples that *represent* the target population.

One way of acquiring a representative sample is random sampling. A **random sample** is one in which every member of the target population has an equal chance of participating. In a **stratified random sample**, known subgroups of a population are represented in proportion to their numbers in the population. For instance, about 13% of the U.S. population is African American. Researchers could therefore decide that 13% of their sample must be African American if they are to represent the general U.S. population. The randomness of the sample would be preserved because the members of the subgroups would be selected randomly from their particular subgroups.

Random samples can be hard to come by, especially when it comes to asking people about their sexual attitudes or behavior. For instance, sexual research is almost invariably conducted with people who volunteer to participate. Volunteers tend to differ from people who refuse to participate (Quartaro & Spier, 2002; Zelenski et al., 2003). For example, volunteers tend to be more open about their sexuality than the general population.

Populations and Samples. To what populations do you belong? College students? Returning students? What of your gender? What about your ethnic background? How do researchers obtain samples that represent populations such as these? What problems do they encounter in attempting to do so?

One study attempted to assess the incidence of male–male sexual behavior that placed Hong Kong men at risk for contracting HIV/AIDS (for example, anal intercourse without use of condoms) by means of random telephone numbers generated by a computer (Lau et al., 2002). Eighty-five of 2,074 men contacted (4%) admitted to having sex with other men and described their sexual behavior. But how can we determine whether there were many others who had sex with men but denied doing so? How can we know whether the men who admitted to male–male sexual behavior accurately described their contacts? Another study assessed the usefulness of brief telephone interviews in a Boston neighborhood believed to have many lesbian residents (Meyer et al., 2002). There was a high (94%!) level of cooperation with the researchers, and 14% of respondents identified themselves as lesbians. But did all of the 94% who cooperated tell the truth? And what can we conclude about the incidence of a lesbian sexual orientation in the general population from such a survey?

The refusal of people who have been randomly selected to participate in the survey can ruin the representativeness of the sample, yet researchers cannot coerce people to participate in research. Therefore, researchers must use samples

Random sample A sample in which every member of a population has an equal chance of participating.

Stratified random sample A random sample in which known subgroups in a population are represented in proportion to their numbers in the population.

of volunteers, rather than true random samples. A low response rate to a voluntary survey is an indication that the responses do not represent the people for whom the survey was distributed.

Some samples are "samples of convenience." They consist of individuals who happen to be available to the researcher and share some characteristics with the target population, perhaps religious background or sexual orientation. Still, they do not truly represent the target group. Convenience samples often consist of European American, middle-class college students who volunteer for studies conducted at their schools. They may not be (and probably are not) representative of students in general.

Methods of Observation

Once scientists have chosen those they will study, they observe them. In this section, we consider several methods of observation: the case study method, the survey method, naturalistic observation, ethnographic observation, participant observation, and laboratory observation.

THE CASE-STUDY METHOD

A **case study** is a carefully drawn, in-depth biography of an individual or a small group. The focus is on understanding one or several individuals as fully as possible by unraveling the interplay of various factors in their backgrounds. In most case studies, the researcher comes to know the individual or group through interviews or other extended contacts. The interviewing pattern may build on itself with a good deal of freedom, as opposed to the printed set of questions used in survey questionnaires.

 Researchers also conduct case studies by interviewing people who have known the individuals or by examining public records. **TRUTH** OR **FICTION** REVISITED: It is true that some case studies have been carried out on people who are dead. Sigmund Freud, for example, drew on historical records in his case study of the Renaissance inventor and painter Leonardo da Vinci. Freud concluded that Leonardo's artistic productions represented the sublimating, or channeling, of an attraction to other men.

Reports of innovative treatments for sexual dysfunctions often appear as detailed case studies. A clinician may report the background of the client in depth, describe the treatment and the apparent outcomes, and suggest factors that might have contributed to the treatment's success or failure. Case studies or multiple case studies (reports concerning a few people) that hold promise may be subjected to experimental studies involving treatment and control groups.

Despite the richness of material that may be derived from case studies, they are not as rigorous a research design as an experiment. People often have gaps in memory, especially concerning childhood events. There is also the potential of observer bias; that is, clinicians and interviewers may unintentionally guide people into saying what they expect to hear. Researchers may even inadvertently color people's reports when they jot them down—shape them subtly in ways that reflect their own views.

THE SURVEY METHOD

Researchers may **survey** respondents by interviewing or administering questionnaires to thousands of people from particular population groups to learn about their sexual behavior and attitudes. Face-to-face interviews such as those used by Alfred Kinsey and his colleagues (1948, 1953) give the interviewer the opportunity

Case study A carefully drawn, in-depth biography of an individual or a small group of individuals that may be obtained through interviews, questionnaires, and historical records.

Survey A detailed study of a sample obtained by means such as interviews and questionnaires.

to probe—to follow up on answers that seem to lead toward useful information. A skilled interviewer may be able to establish a sense of trust or rapport that encourages self-disclosure (Drucker, 2012).

Questionnaires are less expensive than interviews. The major expenses in using questionnaires involve printing and distribution, posting the surveys online, or creating electronic instruments such as telephone-audio-computer-assisted self-interviewing (T-ACASI). If respondents are permitted to return questionnaires anonymously or are assured that interviews will be kept confidential, respondents may be more likely to disclose intimate information. One national random survey of 251 African American women and 544 European American women found that the African American women were more likely to rate themselves as being sexually attractive (Bancroft et al., 2011). One possible reason for the racial difference is that African American women are less likely to be driven by the contemporary desire to be extremely thin—a standard only a few can meet. Interviews can be used with people who cannot read or write, or who would not be motivated to complete a written questionnaire.

Some of the major surveys described in this book were conducted by Kinsey and his colleagues (1948, 1953), by the Monitoring the Future research group at the University of Michigan (Herbenick et al., 2010a, 2010b, 2010c; Reece et al., 2010), and by the U. S. Centers for Disease Control and Prevention (e.g., Martinez et al., 2011). These studies have reported the incidence and frequency of sexual activities among men and women, married and single—solitary, male–female, male–male, and female–female. Many surveys have something to contribute to our understanding of human sexuality, but none perfectly represents the American population at large. People who agree to be polled on political matters may resist participation in surveys about their sexual behavior. Even the best surveys suffer from **volunteer bias**.

Let us review the methods of some surveys of human sexuality, beginning with those used by Kinsey and his colleagues.

Volunteer bias A slanting of research data that is caused by the characteristics of individuals who volunteer to participate, such as willingness to discuss intimate behavior.

The Kinsey Reports Alfred Kinsey and his colleagues (1948, 1953) interviewed 5,300 males and 5,940 females in the United States between 1938 and 1949. They posed questions about sexual experiences, including masturbation, oral sex, and intercourse before and in marriage. Kinsey did not try to obtain a random sample (Drucker, 2012). He believed that a high refusal rate would wreck his chances of representing the general population. Instead, he used group sampling. He recruited participants from the organizations and community groups to which they belonged, such as college fraternities and sororities. He contacted representatives of groups in diverse communities and tried to persuade them to secure the cooperation of fellow group members. If he showed these individuals that they would not be subjected to embarrassment or discomfort, Kinsey hoped that they would persuade other members to participate. In some cases he obtained the full participation of a group.

Yet, people of color, people in rural areas, older people, poor people, and Catholics and Jews were underrepresented in Kinsey's interviews (Drucker, 2012). It is thus unlikely that Kinsey's results accurately mirrored the U.S. population at the time. But some relationships Kinsey uncovered, such as the positive link between level of education and participation in oral sex, are probably generalizable.

Alfred Kinsey. The "Kinsey Reports" shocked the United States of the 1950s. What kinds of surveys are there? How do researchers attempt to encourage people to participate? How do gaps in memory, volunteer bias, and social desirability distort the results of surveys?

Kinsey took measures to urge honest answers. Participants were assured of **confidentiality**. Interviewers were trained to behave nonjudgmentally; they held a "calm and steady eye" and tone of voice. On the other hand, all of Kinsey's interviewers were men, and women respondents might have felt freer to open up to female interviewers.

Kinsey checked the **reliability** of his data by reexamining hundreds of subjects after 18 months or more had passed. Their reports of the incidence of sexual activities (for example, whether or not they had ever engaged in premarital or extramarital coitus) were highly consistent, but reports of the frequency of sexual activities (such as the number of times one masturbates per week) were less consistent. People find it more difficult to estimate the frequencies of their activities than to answer whether or not they have ever engaged in them.

Kinsey knew that consistency of responses across time did not guarantee **validity**. That is, repeat interviews did not show whether the reported behaviors actually took place as described. However, he found high consistency in the reports of 706 pairs of spouses, suggesting that their self-reports were reasonably accurate.

The National Health and Social Life Survey (NHSLS) Study The NHSLS study was intended to provide general sexual information about people in the United States along with specific information that might be used to predict and prevent the spread of HIV/AIDS. It was conducted by Edward O. Laumann of the University of Chicago and three colleagues in the 1990s, and published as *The Social Organization of Sexuality: Sexual Practices in the United States* in 1994. The NHSLS was to be originally supported by government funds, but Senator Jesse Helms blocked federal financing on the grounds that it was inappropriate for the government to support sex research (Bronner, 1998). The research team managed to obtain private funding but had to trim the scope of the project.

The sample included 3,432 people. Of this number, 3,159 were drawn from English-speaking adults living in households (not dormitories, prisons, and so forth), ages 18 to 59. The other 273 were purposely obtained by oversampling African American and Latin American households, so that more information could be obtained about these ethnic groups. Although the sample probably represents the overall U.S. population quite well (or at least those of ages 18 to 59), there were too few Asian Americans, Native Americans, and Jews to offer much information about these groups.

The researchers identified samples of households in geographic areas—by addresses, not names. They sent a letter to each household, describing the purpose and methods of the study, and an interviewer visited each household one week

Confidentiality Ethics requires that sex researchers do not reveal the identities and behaviors of participants in research. Sometimes records are coded so that someone breaking into them would not be able to decipher the identity of participants. Records are also usually destroyed after all useful information has been gathered.

Reliability The consistency or accuracy of a measure.

Validity With respect to interviews, questionnaires, and tests, the degree to which an item measures what it is supposed to measure.

Real Students, Real Questions

Q *I saw the movie* Kinsey; *is it really true that he had sex with people other than his wife for purposes of research?*

A We won't join the gossip about Kinsey, but we'll note that the history of legitimate sex research is tainted by the occasional stories of abuse. However, a checkered past doesn't mean we should toss the research enterprise into the wastebasket. It has saved lives and given countless people pleasure.

later. Potential subjects were assured that the purposes of the study were important and that their identities would be kept confidential. Incentives of up to $100 were offered for cooperating. A high completion rate of close to 80% was obtained in this way.

The National Survey of Adolescents and Young Adults The Kaiser Family Foundation (2003) tried to obtain a nationally representative sample of 13- to 24-year-olds by selecting telephone numbers at random and conducting telephone interviews with 1,854 young people either in English or Spanish. They purposefully oversampled people in ethnic minority groups—African Americans, Latin Americans, and Asian Americans—because most studies do not generate enough information about them. Parents provided permission to interview minors (respondents younger than age 18). The response rate was 55%.

Note some of the study's major findings:

- **TRUTH** OR **FICTION** REVISITED: Four out of five respondents reported that they were concerned about their sexual health.
- About one adolescent in three reported being pressured into sex.
- Sixty percent of the sample agreed with the statement that "Waiting to have sex is a nice idea but nobody really does."
- One adolescent in three had engaged in oral sex, often to avoid intercourse. Many respondents underestimated the risk of contracting a sexually transmitted infection (STI) via oral sex.
- Seventy percent of sexually active young adults and 40% of sexually active adolescents reported that they or their partner had a pregnancy test.
- Four out of five adolescents reported that adolescents tend to drink or use drugs before sex. Many adolescents and young adults reported doing more than they had planned to do under the influence of alcohol or drugs, including "bareback sex" (sex without a condom).
- Many adolescents did not know the details of the transmission and consequences of many STIs.
- About 70% of adolescents erroneously believed that other forms of contraception provide better protection against STIs than condoms do.
- Although 90% of adolescents say that using condoms is a sign of respect and caring for one's partner, about half were reluctant to discuss condoms with their partners, fearing, for example, that raising the subject would be embarrassing or suggest that one is suspicious of one's partner.
- More than three out of four adolescents and young adults say they would like to have more information about STIs.

The National Surveys of Family Growth (NSFG) The National Surveys of Family Growth are conducted by the Centers for Disease Control and Prevention (CDC) as a means of assessing sexual behavior "relevant to demographic and public health concerns" (Mosher et al., 2005). One survey was run primarily in 2002, and results were published over the following years (Mosher, 2005). It involved face-to-face interviews in the homes of 12,571 people, including 4,928 men and 7,643 women aged 15 to 44. A more recent survey, published in 2011, reported the results of interviews with 22,682 face-to-face interviews of people aged 15 to 44, 12,279 with women and 10,403 with men over the years from 2006 to 2010 (Martinez et al., 2011). In the 2002 study, the interviewees responded to questions about their sexual behavior on laptop computers, to ensure their privacy and encourage honesty. The researchers who published in

2011 drew their sample from 110 locales across the United States and sampled randomly within those locales. All in all, the NHSLS and National Surveys of Family Growth may be the only surveys since Kinsey's day to offer a reasonably accurate—if not perfect—snapshot of the sexual behavior of the general population of the United States.

There were some interesting findings about male–male and female–female sexual behavior in the study published in 2005. For example, 5.7% of the males had had oral sex with another male, and 3.7% had had anal sex with another male. Among females, 11% said yes when asked "Have you ever had any sexual experience of any kind with another female?" In Chapter 10 we will see that smaller percentages of males and females identify themselves as homosexual or bisexual, adding more evidence that—as queer theorists suggest—there are discrepancies between sexual interests, sexual behavior, and self-identified sexual orientations. Ten percent of European American women reported having 15 or more sex partners, as compared with 9% of African American women and 5% of Latina American women.

Figure 2.1 is from the study published in 2011. It compares the sexual experience of single females and males aged 15 to 19 over four time periods when the survey was conducted. The percentage of people in this age group, and their marital status, who have engaged in sexual intercourse has been dropping steadily. The researchers admit that no survey method can yield perfect results. Therefore, they include bands referred to as "confidence intervals" in the figure. The researchers use statistical methods to estimate that the "real" numbers are 95% likely to fall within these intervals. We place the word *real* in quotes to further suggest that the relationship between these survey results and reality is somewhat open to debate. Even so, the downward trend is striking.

Why is the **incidence** of sexual intercourse decreasing among young people? We will be thinking about answers throughout the text, but here let us note that one possibility is more awareness of the potential of unwanted pregnancies and sexually transmitted infections. There is certainly no reason to suggest that today's teens are less healthy than yesterday's. Nor is there reason to believe that the media are less sexually stimulating than they were. Today we have sex-laden reality TV shows that did not exist in 1988 and 1995. Pornography is readily available over the Internet for anyone who wants it.

Incidence A measure of the occurrence or the degree of occurrence of an event.

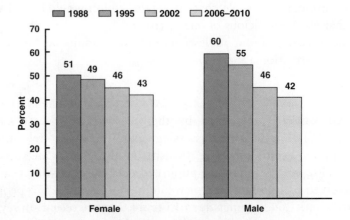

FIGURE 2.1 Single (Never-Married) Females and Males, Aged 15–19, Who Report Ever Having Had Sexual Intercourse: United States, 1988–2010.

Source: Martinez, G., Copen, C. E., & Abma, J. C. (2011). Teenagers in the United States: Sexual activity, contraceptive use, and childbearing, 2006–1010 National Survey of Family Growth. National Center for Health Statistics. *Vital Health Statistics, 23*(31), p. 6, Figure 1.

Magazine Surveys Readership surveys have also been conducted by popular magazines, such as *Psychology Today, Glamour, Ladies' Home Journal*, and *Cosmopolitan*. Although these surveys may obtain large numbers of respondents, their sampling techniques raise questions. Each sample represents, at best, the readers of the magazine in which the questionnaire appears. Moreover, we learn only about readers who volunteer to respond to these questionnaires, which is a small percentage of the overall readership. Finally, readers of these magazines are wealthier than the public at large, and readers of *Cosmopolitan, Psychology Today*, and *Glamour* tend to be more liberal (Cawley et al., 2011).

Limitations of the Survey Method One limitation of surveys involves the fact that they are self-reports of behavior and attitudes. Self-reports are subject to inaccuracies or biases because of factors such as faulty memory and tendencies to distort or conceal information due to embarrassment, shame, or guilt; or attempts to present a favorable image (Rosenbaum, 2006). People may not recall the age at which they first engaged in petting, or masturbated to orgasm. People may have difficulty recalling or calculating the **frequencies** of certain behaviors, such as the weekly frequency of marital intercourse. Survey data may also be drawn from haphazard or nonrepresentative samples and not represent the target population.

Participants in surveys of sexual behavior may feel pressured to answer questions in the direction of **social desirability**. Some try to ingratiate themselves with their interviewers by offering what they believe to be socially desirable answers. Even though interviewers may insist that participants will remain anonymous, respondents may fear their identities could be exposed someday.

One study asked 283 college students to record the incidence of their thoughts about sex, food, and sleep for a week. The men in the study reported signitifcantly more thoughts about sex than the women did. However, the women also evidenced more interest in answering in a socially desirable direction, as shown be responses to items similar to those you will find on the nearby social desirability scale (Fisher et al., 2012). So we can wonder whether women reported fewer thoughts about sex because frequent thoughts of sex are incompatible with the traditional feminine gender role (Fisher et al., 2012). You can assess your own tendency to provide socially desirable answers by taking the nearby self-assessment "Would You Tell an Interviewer the Truth on a Survey about Your Sexual Behavior?"

Frequency The number of times an action is repeated within a given period.

Social desirability A response bias to a questionnaire or interview in which the person provides a socially acceptable response.

Real Students, Real Questions

Q *How could I be part of a study on sexuality?*

A In general, responding to the typical questionnaire you find in a magazine or on a website isn't helpful to the study of sexuality. The sampling is probably biased and the "scientific" analysis of answers may not be all that scientific. Instead, you can check with your professor or a nearby medical school about useful studies that may be underway on campus or nearby. If a sexuality study comes your way, and you're satisfied that it is supported by a legitimate government agency or educational institution or private group, feel free to participate.

Would You Tell an Interviewer the Truth on a Survey about Your Sexual Behavior?

The Social-Desirability Scale

Researchers into human sexuality frequently encounter the problem of social desirability in their subjects. That is, many people being interviewed tell the researcher what they think he or she wants to hear, rather than divulge the truth about their sexual attitudes and behavior. The reason is often to earn the approval of the researcher. The tendency to respond in what people believe to be the socially desirable direction distorts the accuracy of the results in the case-study and survey methods.

What about you? Would you provide an interviewer with honest answers about your sexual attitudes and behaviors, or would you misrepresent your beliefs and behaviors to earn his or her approval?

You can complete the Social-Desirability Scale devised by Crowne and Marlowe to gain insight into whether you have a tendency to produce socially desirable responses.

Directions

Read each item and decide whether it is true (T) or false (F) for you. Try to work rapidly and answer each question by circling the T or the F. Then turn to the scoring key in the Appendix to interpret your answers.

T F 1. Before voting I thoroughly investigate the qualifications of all the candidates.

T F 2. I never hesitate to go out of my way to help someone in trouble.

T F 3. It is sometimes hard for me to go on with my work if I am not encouraged.

T F 4. I have never intensely disliked anyone.

T F 5. On occasions I have had doubts about my ability to succeed in life.

T F 6. I sometimes feel resentful when I don't get my way.

T F 7. I am always careful about my manner of dress.

T F 8. My table manners at home are as good as when I eat out in a restaurant.

T F 9. If I could get into a movie without paying and be sure I was not seen, I would probably do it.

T F 10. On a few occasions, I have given up something because I thought too little of my ability.

T F 11. I like to gossip at times.

T F 12. There have been times when I felt like rebelling against people in authority even though I knew they were right.

T F 13. No matter who I'm talking to, I'm always a good listener.

T F 14. I can remember "playing sick" to get out of something.

T F 15. There have been occasions when I have taken advantage of someone.

T F 16. I'm always willing to admit it when I make a mistake.

T F 17. I always try to practice what I preach.

T F 18. I don't find it particularly difficult to get along with loudmouthed, obnoxious people.

T F 19. I sometimes try to get even rather than forgive and forget.

T F 20. When I don't know something I don't mind at all admitting it.

T F 21. I am always courteous, even to people who are disagreeable.

T F 22. At times I have really insisted on having things my own way.

T F 23. There have been occasions when I felt like smashing things.

T F 24. I would never think of letting someone else be punished for my wrongdoings.

T F 25. I never resent being asked to return a favor.

T F 26. I have never been irked when people expressed ideas very different from my own.

T F 27. I never make a long trip without checking the safety of my car.

T F 28. There have been times when I was quite jealous of the good fortune of others.

T F 29. I have almost never felt the urge to tell someone off.

T F 30. I am sometimes irritated by people who ask favors of me.

T F 31. I have never felt that I was punished without cause.

T F 32. I sometimes think when people have a misfortune, they only got what they deserved.

T F 33. I have never deliberately said something that hurt someone's feelings.

Source: D. P. Crowne and D. A. Marlowe, A new scale of social desirability independent of pathology, *Journal of Consulting Psychology* 24 (1960): 351. Copyright 1960 by the American Psychological Association. Reprinted by permission.

Some respondents choose to exaggerate. In our culture, men may tend to exaggerate their sexual exploits, and women may tend to downplay them (Fisher et al., 2012). Some respondents exaggerate the bizarreness of their behavior or attitudes to draw attention to themselves or to foul up study results.

Because many people refuse to participate in surveys, samples are biased by large numbers of volunteers. Volunteers tend to be more sexually permissive and liberal-minded than nonvolunteers.

THE NATURALISTIC-OBSERVATION METHOD

In **naturalistic observation**, also called the *field study*, scientists directly observe the behavior of animals and humans where it happens. For example, biologists might observe the behavior of animals in the wild, sociologists might observe the street life of prostitutes, and psychologists might observe patterns of body language in romantic couples.

Scientists try to observe their subjects *unobtrusively*; that is, they try not to influence the behavior of the individuals they study. Naturalistic observers sometimes find themselves in ethical dilemmas. They have allowed sick or injured animals to die, rather than intervene, when medical assistance could have saved them. They have allowed substance abuse and illicit sexual behavior to go unreported to authorities. The ethical trade-off is that unobtrusive observation may yield data that will benefit large numbers of people—the greatest good for the greatest number.

THE ETHNOGRAPHIC-OBSERVATION METHOD

Ethnographic observation provides data concerning sexual behaviors and customs that occur among various ethnic groups—those that vary widely across cultures and those that are limited to one or few cultures. Anthropologists are the specialists who typically engage in ethnographic research. They have lived among societies of people in the four corners of the earth in order to observe and study human diversity. Margaret Mead (1935) reported on the social and sexual customs of various peoples of New Guinea. Bronislaw Malinowski (1929) studied the Trobriand Islanders, among others. Even so, ethnographic observation has its limits in the study of sexual behavior. Sexual activities are most commonly performed away from the watchful gaze of others, especially visitors from other cultures. Ethnographers may thus have to rely on methods such as interviewing.

The ethnographer who studies a particular culture or subgroup within a culture tries tries to do so unobtrusively, so as not to alter the behavior of the members of the group by focusing their attention on it. Falling prey to social desirability, some people may "straighten out their act" while the ethnographer is present. Other people may try to impress the ethnographer by acting in ways that are more aggressive or sexually provocative than usual. In either case, people supply distorted information.

THE PARTICIPANT-OBSERVATION METHOD

TRUTH OR **FICTION** REVISITED: It is true that some sex researchers have engaged in "swinging" with the people they studied. In **participant observation**, investigators learn about people's behavior by directly interacting with them (Boynton, 2008; Frank, 2007). Participant observation has been used in studies of male–male sexual behavior and mate-swapping. In effect, participation has been the "price of admission" for observation. In some cases, researchers have engaged in coitus with participants during "swinging parties," which raises questions as to what is permissible "for the sake of science."

Naturalistic observation
A method in which organisms are observed in their natural environments.

Ethnographic observation
A method of research that deals descriptively with specific cultures, especially preliterate societies.

 5

Participant observation
A method in which observers interact with the people they study as they collect data.

A World of Diversity

Gender Roles and Aggression

In our culture, aggressiveness is part of the masculine gender role stereotype. As we will see in Chapter 6, it is believed that the male sex hormone testosterone, which is more prevalent in males than females, plays an important role in aggressiveness. But can culture and social expectations also play roles?

In classic ethnographic research, anthropologist Margaret Mead (1935) found evidence that the stereotype of the aggressive male is not universal. Her research on the South Pacific island of New Guinea revealed that the sociocultural milieu influences motives such as aggression and nurturance. Among the Mundugumor, a tribe of headhunters and cannibals, both women and men were warlike and aggressive. The women felt that motherhood sidetracked them from more important activities, such as butchering inhabitants of neighboring villages. In contrast, both women and men of the Arapesh tribe were gentle and nurturing of children. Then there were the Tchambuli. In that tribe, the women earned a living while the men spent most of their time nurturing the children, primping, and gossiping.

There is a 99.9% overlap among diverse peoples in our genetic code. There is no reason to believe that significant differences in that other 0.1% account for differences in aggression among the Mundugumor, the Arapesh, and the Tchambuli. Isn't it more likely that the people within the various tribes had arrived at a consensus as to proper behavior over the generations and that they taught their children to behave accordingly?

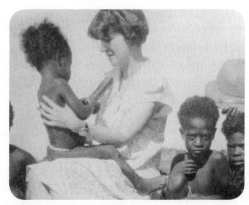

What Does Cross-Cultural Research Suggest about Aggression? Margaret Mead's anthropological research in New Guinea found wide variety in the incidence of aggression. Among a tribe of headhunters and cannibals, both women and men were warlike. In another tribe, both women and men were gentle and nurturant. A third tribe found reversal of the masculine and feminine stereotypes: Women earned a living while the men nurtured the children and spent time primping.

Katherine Frank. Frank worked as a stripper in graduate school, both to augment her income and to learn about men who frequented strip clubs.

Laboratory observation
A method in which subjects are studied in a laboratory setting.

We do not hear much anymore about "scientific swinging" with the public, but there are more current uses of participant observation. One area of interest has been strip clubs. There are some 4,000 strip clubs in the United States, with an income of about $15 billion a year (Deveruex, 2011). As a graduate student in anthropology, Katherine Frank worked as a stripper in a southeastern city "both as a means of earning extra cash for graduate school and as part of a feminism theory project investigating female objectification and body image" (Sternberg, 2004). In reports of her experiences, Frank (2002, 2003) notes that many men told her they attend the clubs because they "just want to relax." She writes that male customers may encounter some stigma for visiting the clubs, but not as much as the strippers do. Some men, moreover, do business in strip clubs and charge the expenses to their corporate accounts.

THE LABORATORY-OBSERVATION METHOD

Rather than study individuals in their natural settings, the **laboratory observation** brings them into the laboratory, where their behavior can be more carefully monitored. In *Human Sexual Response* (1966), William Masters and Virginia Johnson were among the first to report direct laboratory observations of individuals and couples engaged in sex acts. In all, 694 people (312 men and 382 women) participated in the research. The women ranged from ages 18 to 78; the men were from 21 to 80 years old. There were 276 married couples, 106 single women, and 36 single men. The married couples engaged in intercourse and manual and oral stimulation of the genitals. The unmarried people participated in studies that did not require intercourse, such as measurement of female sexual arousal in response to insertion of a penis-shaped probe, and male ejaculation during masturbation.

Direct laboratory observation of biological processes was not invented by Masters and Johnson, but they were confronting a society that was still unprepared to speak openly of sex, let alone observe people having sex. Masters and Johnson were accused of immorality and voyeurism. Nevertheless, their methods offered the first reliable set of data on what happens to the body during sexual response. Their instruments—the **penile strain gauge** and the **vaginal plethysmograph**—permitted them to directly measure **vasocongestion** (blood flow to the genitals), **myotonia** (muscle tension), and other physiological responses.

TRUTH OR FICTION REVISITED: Masters and Johnson created an artificial penis containing photographic equipment to study female sexual response. The transparent device enabled them to observe changes in women's internal sexual organs as they became sexually aroused. From these studies, they observed that it is useful to divide sexual response into four stages (Masters and Johnson's "sexual response cycle"): excitement, plateau, orgasm, and resolution (see Chapter 5).

One confounding factor in Masters and Johnson's research is that people who participate in laboratory observation know that they are being observed and that their responses are being measured. The problem of volunteer bias, troublesome for sex surveys, is even thornier in laboratory observation. How many of us would assent to performing sexual activities in full view of researchers while we were connected to monitoring equipment? Some of the women observed by Masters and Johnson were patients of Dr. Masters who felt indebted to him and agreed to participate. Many were able to persuade their husbands to participate as well. Some were medical students and graduate students who may have been motivated to earn extra money (participants were paid for their time) as well as by scientific curiosity.

Researchers have since developed more sophisticated physiological methods of measuring sexual arousal and response. The laboratory method is now used, with some variations but with less controversy, in research centers across the country. ◉▸

What Does a Woman Want? Using Objective and Subjective Measures to Find Out

> "The great question that has never been answered and which I have not yet been able to answer, despite my 30 years of research into the feminine soul, is, What does a woman want?"
>
> —Sigmund Freud

What sexually excites a man? What sexually excites a woman? Research using a variety of methods suggests that men's sexual responses are more predictable, and that what goes on in men's bodies is more likely to correlate with what they are thinking (Chivers et al., 2010). Consider some research by Meredith Chivers and her colleagues (Chivers & Bailey, 2007; Chivers et al., 2007). She showed men and women, both heterosexual and homosexual, erotic videos: male–female sex, male–male sex, female–female sex, a man masturbating, a woman masturbating, a muscled man walking nude on a beach, and a well-toned nude woman doing calisthenics. The subjects watched on recliners while Chivers measured their arousal objectively and subjectively. The objective measures were made possible by plethysmographs connected to the viewers' genitals. Men wore an apparatus on the penis

 6

A Penile Strain Gauge.
The gauge measures vasocongestion in the male genitals, providing an objective measure of sexual arousal.

◉▸ **Simulate** *Observational Research: Laboratory vs. Naturalistic* on **MyDevelopmentLab**

Penile strain gauge A device for measuring sexual arousal in men in terms of changes in the circumference of the penis.

Vaginal plethysmograph A tampon-like probe that is inserted in the vagina and suggests the level of vasocongestion by measuring the light reflected from the vaginal walls.

Vasocongestion Congestion from the flow of blood (from the Latin *vas*, meaning "vessel").

Myotonia Muscle tension.

A Closer Look

How to Show That Viagra Works for Women When It Doesn't Work for Women

The use of Viagra, and the related drugs Cialis and Levitra, has revolutionized the treatment of erectile disorder in men. Erections are made possible by the flow of blood into the penis. Viagra and the other drugs are phosphodiesterase type 5 (PDE5) inhibitors, which is a complicated way of saying that they prevent blood from flowing out the penis prematurely, keeping it sufficiently erect for sexual intercourse. We'll give you the full, unexpurgated explanation of thow these drugs work in Chapter 15.

Sexual arousal in women, like sexual arousal in men, involves the flow of blood into the genital region, which has a number of effects, including stiffening the clitoris and helping with the production of vaginal lubrication. Yet women who try these drugs to help with sexual arousal typically find them to be of little if any use.

Enter sex researchers Meredith Chivers and Raymond Rosen (2010).

They reviewed 16 studies that tested the effects of PDE5 inhibitors on women and determined that despite women's subjective reporting that the drugs were of little help, they increased genital vasocongestion as advertised.

How can we explain the disconnect between women's objective and subjective responses to PDE5 inhibitors? Chivers and Rosen suggest that the discrepancy is related to gender differences in the connectedness of the biological (objective) and psychological (subjective) components of sexual response. Genital response in women is less likely to mean that they want to engage in sexual activity than it is in men. For example, a woman who lacks sexual desire—or who lacks sexual desire with her usual partner—may see herself as having difficulty becoming sexually aroused, when sexual arousal—at least from a biological point of view—is not necessarily the problem. Men would unlikely seek professional help when they

A vaginal plethysmograph. The instrument provides an objective measure of sexual arousal.

lack desire, and women might not seek professional help when they have difficulty lubricating, because that particular difficulty can be aided with an artificial lubricant.

Watch the Video
Sexual Arousal in Women
on **MyDevelopmentLab**

that gauged its swelling (that is, erection). Women inserted a tampon-shaped probe in the vagina that bounced light off the vaginal walls, providing a gauge of genital blood flow. In men, genital engorgement with blood produces erection. In women, it spurs lubrication—the seeping of moisture through the vaginal walls. The participants could rate their subjective feelings of arousal with a keypad.

Self-labeled heterosexual ("straight") men achieved erection while watching male–female or female–female sex, and while gazing at the masturbating and the exercising women. They were generally unresponsive when they watched a man masturbating or male–male sex. Gay males showed the opposite pattern of sexual arousal. For both straight and gay males, the subjective ratings matched the numbers provided by the plethysmograph. The men's subjective rating were congruent with their body's responses.

Not so with the women. Regardless of whether the women labeled themselves as heterosexual or lesbian, they responded with genital arousal when they viewed male–male sex, female–female sex, and male–female sex. Their genitals were more responsive to the exercising woman than the nude man. However, their self-reported arousal did not particularly match their body's responses. Heterosexual women reported less arousal when they watched female–female sex than their bodies indicated. They reported less arousal than their bodies showed when they watched male–male sex, but they reported *more* arousal than their bodies showed when they watched male–female sex. Lesbians showed objective and subjective arousal in response to female–female sex, but they reported less arousal than their bodies showed when they viewed male–male sex.

Chivers (in Bergner, 2009) suggests that women are genitally aroused by a wider range of stimuli than men because these gender differences might reflect innate, evolutionary forces. Could female sexuality be divided into two systems: one physiological and the other subjective? According to this view, feminine lust would be a subjective phenomenon, and physiological genital arousal would not tell us much about desire—that is, what a woman cognitively "wants" might not always be the same as what her body responds to (Chivers et al., 2010). As another example, Chivers reports the results of a plethysmograph study showing surges of vaginal blood flow as women listened to descriptions of rape. Chivers uses an evolutionary hypothesis in a tentative explanation of female genital arousal in response to unwanted sex. Genital lubrication could be a reflexive response that reduces discomfort and the possibility of injury during intercourse. Ancestral females who did not lubricate in the presence of sexual cues might be more likely to sustain injuries that could lead to infertility and, possibly, death. They would thus be less likely to transmit this trait to their children. This is not to suggest that women desire to be forced into having sex—only that women, or some women, might have a built-in protective response in which they lubricate.

In the Chivers studies, both heterosexual and lesbian women showed greater sexual arousal in response to stimuli depicting female targets than to stimuli showing male targets. One possibility is that the women observers identify with the depicted female targets, imagining themselves in the place of the women receiving pleasure, whereas the men are more likely to attend to the physical attributes of the actors.

Sexologist Lisa Diamond suggests that the response of women to a wider range of sexual stimuli allows for quite a bit of plasticity in sexual response. She begins her 2008 book by noting that "The actress Anne Heche began a widely publicized romantic relationship with the openly lesbian comedian Ellen DeGeneres after having had no prior same-gender attractions or relationships. The relationship with DeGeneres ended after two years, and Heche went on to marry a man." Diamond went on to note that Julie Cypher was in a heterosexual marriage but left it for the musician Melissa Etheridge. But they separated after 12 years and Cypher returned to heterosexual relationships. She offers the possibility that many women's desires may be dictated more by intimacy or emotional connection than by the physical attractiveness—or even the gender—of one's partner.

Correlation

What are the relationships between age and frequency of sex among married couples? What is the connection between socioeconomic status and teenage pregnancy? How about listening to sexually explicit rap music? And what about the age of sexual initiation? In each case, variables are being related to one another The correlational method describes the relationship between variables in numerical terms, and as positive or negative.

A **correlation** is a statistical measure of the relationship between two variables. In correlational studies, two or more variables are related, or linked to, one another by statistical means. The strength and direction (positive or negative) of the relationship between any two variables is expressed with a statistic called a **correlation coefficient**.

Research has shown relationships (correlations) between satisfaction with a relationship and a host of variables: communication skills, shared values, flexibility, frequency of social interactions with friends, and churchgoing, to name a few (see Figure 2.2). Although such research may give us an idea of the factors associated

CRITICAL THINKING
Which strikes you as the truer measure of sexual arousal—the person's subjective reports of arousal or the levels shown on objective instruments such as the penile strain gauge or the vaginal photoplethysmograph? Support your answer. (*Hint*: Critical thinkers pay attention to definitions of terms. What does the word *truer* mean to you?)

CRITICAL THINKING
Would you expect that there would be a positive or negative correlation between satisfaction in a relationship and communication? Explain.

Correlation A statistical measure of the relationship between two variables.

Correlation coefficient A statistic that expresses the strength and direction (positive or negative) of the relationship between two variables.

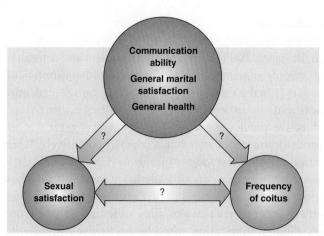

FIGURE 2.2 What Is the Relationship Between Frequency of Intercourse and Sexual Satisfaction? Couples in relationships who engage in more frequent sexual relations report higher levels of sexual satisfaction, but why? Because researchers have not manipulated the variables, we cannot conclude that sexual satisfaction causes high coital frequency. Nor can we say that frequent coitus causes greater sexual satisfaction. Perhaps both variables are affected by other factors, such as communication ability, health, and general satisfaction with the relationship.

with satisfaction in a relationship, the researchers have not manipulated the variables of interest. For this reason we cannot say which, if any, of the factors is causally related to happiness in the relationship.

Research has also shown relationships between the use of sildenafil (Viagra) to enhance sexual response and risky sexual behavior among gay and bisexual men (Kim et al., 2002). Men who use Viagra also report a greater number of sex partners and higher levels of anal sex without using a condom. **TRUTH** OR **FICTION** REVISITED: However, there is no evidence that Viagra *causes* risky sexual behavior. It is more likely that the effort to enhance sexual response explains both the use of Viagra and risky sex.

Correlations may be positive or negative. Two variables are positively correlated if one increases as the other increases. A Spanish study of 412 university students correlated sociodemographic, psychological, and interpersonal variables with sexual behavior and feelings of intimacy (Yela, 2000). It was found that commitment, feelings of intimacy, and frequency of sexual relations correlated positively with feelings of love and sexual satisfaction for both men and women. However, the researcher did not manipulate the variables. Therefore, we cannot conclude that sexual satisfaction causes high coital frequency. It could also be that frequent sexual activity contributes to greater sexual satisfaction. It is also possible that there is no causal relationship between the variables. Perhaps both coital frequency and sexual satisfaction are affected by other factors, such as communication ability, marital satisfaction, general health, and so on (see Figure 2.1). **TRUTH** OR **FICTION** REVISITED: Evidence suggests that people who attend church regularly tend to be more satisfied with their relationships. Does satisfaction with a relationship motivate churchgoing? Does churchgoing enhance relationships? Or does a quest for stability contribute to both?

7

8

Experiment A scientific method that seeks to confirm cause-and-effect relationships by manipulating independent variables and observing their effects on dependent variables.

The Experimental Method

The best method for studying cause and effect is the **experiment**. Experiments permit scientists to draw conclusions about cause-and-effect relationships because the experimenter directly manipulates the variables of interest and observes their effects.

In an experiment on the effects of alcohol on sexual arousal, for example, a group of participants would receive an intervention, called a **treatment**, such as a dose of alcohol. (In other experiments, the intervention or treatment might involve the administration of a drug, exposure to violent pornography, a program of sex education, etc.). The participants would then be carefully observed to learn whether this treatment made a difference in their behavior—in this case, their sexual arousal.

In an experiment, the variables (treatments) that are hypothesized to have a causal effect are manipulated or controlled by the researcher. Consider an experiment designed to determine whether or not alcohol stimulates sexual arousal. The design might involve giving one group of participants a certain dosage of alcohol, and then measuring its effects. In such an experimental arrangement, the dosage of alcohol is considered an **independent variable**, whose presence and quantity is manipulated by the researchers. The measured results are called **dependent variables** because changes in their values are believed to depend on the independent variable or variables. In this experiment, measures of sexual arousal would be the dependent variables. Dependent variables are outcomes; they are observed and measured by the researchers, but not manipulated. Sexual arousal might be measured by means such as physiological measurement (gauging the degree of erection in the male, for example) or self-report (asking participants to rate their sexual arousal on a scale).

In a study of the effects of sex education on teenage pregnancy, sex education would be the independent variable. The incidence of teenage pregnancy would be the dependent variable. Researchers would administer the experimental treatment (sex education) and track the participants for a period of time to determine their pregnancy rates. Ideally, the incidence of pregnancy among these subjects would be compared to that among subjects who do not receive sex education but are similar to the subjects in all other respects.

EXPERIMENTAL AND CONTROL GROUPS

True experiments randomly assign subjects to experimental and control groups. Subjects in **experimental groups** receive the treatment. Subjects in **control groups** do not. All other conditions are held constant for both groups. By using random assignment and holding other conditions constant, researchers can be reasonably confident that the independent variable (treatment), and not extraneous factors (such as the temperature of the room in which the treatment was administered or differences between subjects in the experimental and control groups), brought about the results.

Why do experimenters assign subjects to experimental or control groups at random? Consider a study conducted to determine the effects of alcohol on sexual arousal in response to sexually explicit material, such as pornography. If we permitted participants to choose whether or not they would drink alcohol, we might not know if it was the alcohol itself that accounted for the results. Some other factor, called a **selection factor**, might discriminate between people who would or would not choose to drink alcohol. One difference might be that people who chose to drink might also have more permissive attitudes toward sexually explicit material than the others. Their permissiveness rather than the alcohol could affect their sexual responsiveness to these stimuli.

Although scientists agree that the experimental method provides the best evidence of cause and effect, experimenters cannot manipulate many variables directly. For example, we cannot conduct experiments to determine the effects of cohabitation on college students. We cannot assign an experimental group to cohabitation and a control group to separate living quarters. We can only compare groups who have chosen to cohabit to groups who have not. Our research may thus inform us that cohabitors who get married are more likely to eventually get divorced than married couples who have never cohabited, but it cannot show that these problems

CRITICAL THINKING
Would it be possible to run an experiment to study the effects of rape on psychological health? Why or why not?

Treatment In experiments, an intervention that is administered to participants (e.g., a test, a drug, or sex-education program) so that its effects may be observed.

Independent variable A condition in a scientific study that is manipulated so that its effects may be observed.

Dependent variable The measured result of an experiment, which is believed to be a function of the independent variable.

Experimental group A group of study participants who receive a treatment.

Control group A group of study participants who do not receive the experimental treatment. However, other conditions are held comparable to those of individuals in the experimental group.

Selection factor A bias that may operate in research when people are allowed to determine whether or not they will receive a treatment.

CRITICAL THINKING
To run a true experiment on the effect of a new drug on people with HIV/AIDS, some people with HIV/AIDS would have to be assigned to a control group. To control for the effects of expectations, they might be told they are being given the real drug when they are really receiving "sugar pills" that look like the real thing. Can researchers justify withholding the real drug from people in the control group? What do you think?

👁—Watch the Video
Special Topics: Ethics and Psychological Research
on **MyDevelopmentLab**

CRITICAL THINKING
What types of harm could occur if a researcher disclosed the identity of an individual participating in a sex survey and his or her sexual behavior?

CRITICAL THINKING
In experiments on the effects of violent pornography on aggression, men are led to believe that they are shocking women by pressing a button when they actually are not. Do you believe that this deception is justified? Can you think of a more ethical way of measuring "aggression"?

👁—Watch the Video
Before Informed Consent: Robert Guthrie
on **MyDevelopmentLab**

are *caused* by cohabiting (see Chapter 14). Cohabitors and noncohabitors may differ on other factors—such as nontraditional versus traditional attitudes—that give rise to different outcomes of marriage.

Similarly, we cannot conduct experiments to determine the effects of pornography on children and adolescents. Societal prohibitions and ethical standards preclude experimenters from exposing children or adolescents to erotic materials.

Ethics in Sex Research

Sex researchers are required to protect the people being studied. People cannot be subjected to physical or psychological harm and must participate of their own free will. In colleges, universities, hospitals, and research institutions, ethics review committees help researchers weigh the potential harm of proposed studies in light of ethical guidelines. If the committee finds fault with a proposal, it may advise the researcher how to modify the research design to comply with ethical standards and withhold approval until the proposal has been modified. What kinds of ethical issues are raised concerning sex research? Let us consider a number of them: 👁

- *Exposing participants to harm.* Individuals may be harmed if they are exposed to pain or placed in stressful situations. For this reason, researchers do not expose children to erotic materials in order to determine the effects. Nor do researchers expose human fetuses to male or female sex hormones to learn whether they create predispositions toward tomboyishness, gay male or lesbian sexual orientations, and other variables of interest.

- *Confidentiality.* **TRUTH OR FICTION** REVISITED: It is not true that researchers publish the names of participants in sex research in professional journals. Sex researchers must keep the identities and responses of participants confidential to protect them from possible harm or embarrassment. In reports of research, enough information about participants' backgrounds can be given to make the studies useful (size of city of origin, region of country, religion, age group, race, educational level, and so on) without divulging their identities. Once the need for follow-up has passed and the results have been fully analyzed, the names and addresses of participants and their records can be destroyed.

- *Informed consent.* The principle of informed consent requires that people freely agree to participate after being given enough information about the procedures and purposes of the research, and its risks and benefits, to make an informed decision. Once the study has begun, participants must be free to withdraw at any time without penalty. 👁

- *The use of deception.* Ethical conflicts may emerge when experiments require that participants not know all about the experiment's purposes and methods. For example, in experiments on the effects of violent pornography on aggression against women, participants may be misled into believing that they are administering electric shocks to women (who are actually confederates of the experimenter), even though no shocks are actually delivered. The experimenter seeks to determine participants' willingness to hurt women following exposure to aggressive erotic films. Such studies could not be carried out if participants knew that no shocks would actually be delivered.

Research is the backbone of human sexuality as a science. This textbook focuses on scientific findings that can illuminate our understanding of sexuality, help enhance sexual experience, prevent and treat sexually transmitted infections (STIs), and build more rewarding relationships.

A World of Diversity

The Tuskegee Syphilis Study: Ethics Turned Upside Down in Research Gone Wrong

The Tuskegee Syphilis Study, carried out in Macon County, Alabama, from 1932 to 1972, is an example of medical research gone wrong. The United States Public Health Service, in trying to learn more about syphilis and justify treatment programs for blacks, withheld adequate treatment from a group of poor black men who had the disease, causing needless pain and suffering for the men and their loved ones.

In the wake of the Tuskegee Study and other studies, the federal government took a closer look at research involving human subjects and made changes to prevent the moral breaches that occurred in Tuskegee from happening again.

The Study Begins

In 1932, the Public Health Service, working with the Tuskegee Institute, began a study in Macon County, Alabama, to record the natural history of syphilis in hopes of justifying treatment programs for blacks. It was called the "Tuskegee Study of Untreated Syphilis in the Negro Male."

The study involved 600 black men—399 with syphilis and 201 who did not have the disease. Researchers told the men they were being treated for "bad blood," a local term used to describe

several ailments, including syphilis, anemia, and fatigue. In truth, the afflicted men did not receive the proper treatment needed to cure their illness. In exchange for taking part in the study, the men received free medical exams, free meals, and burial insurance. Although originally projected to last six months, the study actually went on for 40 years.

What Went Wrong?

In July 1972, a front-page *New York Times* story about the Tuskegee Study caused a public outcry that led the Assistant Secretary for Health and Scientific Affairs to appoint an ad hoc advisory panel to review the study. The panel had nine members from the fields of medicine, law, religion, labor, education, health administration, and public affairs.

The panel found that the men had agreed freely to be examined and treated. However, there was no evidence that researchers had informed them of the study or its real purpose. In fact, the men had been misled and had not been given all the facts required to provide informed consent.

The men were never given adequate treatment for their disease. Even when penicillin became the drug of choice for syphilis in 1947, researchers did not offer it

to the subjects. The advisory panel found nothing to show that subjects were ever given the choice of quitting the study, even when this new, highly effective treatment became widely used.

The Study Ends and Reparation Begins

The advisory panel concluded that the Tuskegee Study was "ethically unjustified"—the knowledge gained was sparse when compared with the risks the study posed for its subjects. In October 1972, the panel advised stopping the study at once. A month later, the Assistant Secretary for Health and Scientific Affairs announced the end of the Tuskegee Study.

In the summer of 1973, a class-action lawsuit filed by the National Association for the Advancement of Colored People (NAACP) ended in a settlement that gave more than $9 million to the study participants. As part of the settlement, the U.S. government promised to give free medical and burial services to all living participants. The Tuskegee Health Benefit Program was established to provide these services. It also gave health services to wives, widows, and children who had been infected because of the study. The Centers for Disease Control and Prevention was given responsibility for the program, where it remains today in the National Center for HIV, STD, and TB Prevention.

CRITICAL THINKING

What ethical principles were violated in the Tuskegee Study?

Source: Centers for Disease Control and Prevention. (2005, May 23). The Tuskegee Syphilis Study: A Hard Lesson Learned. www.cdc.gov/nchstp/od/tuskegee/time.htm

Chapter Review ✓●—⌐Study and Review on MyDevelopmentLab

LO1 **Explain the steps in the scientific method**
The scientific method tests assumptions through research. It entails formulating a research question, framing a hypothesis, testing the hypothesis, and drawing conclusions about the hypothesis.

LO2 **Describe the goals of the science of human sexuality**
The goals of the science of human sexuality are to describe, explain, predict, and control sexual behaviors. "Control" usually means to help people achieve their own goals in their sexual relationships and behavior.

LO3 **Explain the purpose of sampling and the methods of sampling**
A population is a complete group of people or animals that researchers target for study. A sample is a subgroup of a population that researchers select in order to study the population. Researchers use random sampling when possible, to assure that every member of a population has an equal chance of being selected to represent the population. The results are subject to "volunteer bias" when people choose whether or not to participate in the study.

LO4 **Describe the case-study method and its uses**
Case studies are carefully drawn biographies of individuals or small groups. Information can be gleaned from sources such as interviews, observation, and public records.

LO5 **Describe the survey method and its uses**
Surveys usually gather information about the behavior of large numbers of people through interviews or questionnaires. There are questions about the validity of surveys due to the truthfulness and accuracy of self-report.

LO6 **Describe the naturalistic-observation method and its uses**
In naturalistic observation, scientists directly observe the behavior of animals and humans where it happens—in the "field." Efforts are made not to interfere with—and therefore alter—the behavior being observed.

LO7 **Describe the ethnographic-observation method**
Ethnographic research provides us with data concerning sexual behaviors and customs that occur widely across cultures and those that are limited to one or few cultures.

LO8 **Describe the participant-observation method**
In participant-observation, investigators learn about people's behavior by personally interacting with them. A recent example involves interacting with customers in strip clubs.

LO9 **Describe the laboratory-observation method**
In the laboratory-observation method, people engage in the behavior under study in the laboratory setting. Masters and Johnson studied people involved in sexual activity in the laboratory to learn how their bodies respond to sexual stimulation.

LO10 **Describe the correlational method**
Correlational research reveals the strength and direction of the relationships between variables, such as communication ability and satisfaction with a relationship. However, they do not show cause and effect.

LO11 **Describe the ways in which experiments attempt to determine cause and effect**
Experiments allow scientists to draw conclusions about cause-and-effect relationships because they manipulate the variables of interest, control other variables, and observe their effects. Well-designed experiments randomly assign individuals to experimental and control groups to avoid the selection factor.

LO12 **Describe the ethical concerns that govern the ways in which professionals interact with study participants and clients in treatment**
Ethical standards require that potentially harmful research may be conducted only when the expected benefits clearly outweigh the risks to participants. Sex researchers keep the identities of participants confidential and obtain their informed consent, but they must now and then deceive people as to the purposes and methods of a study. The Tuskegee Syphilis Study was unethical because partcipants were harmed and deceived, and had not provided informed consent.

Test Your Learning

1. In a(n) _____ sample, every member of the target population has an equal chance of participating.
   - (a) distribution
   - (b) digitized
   - (c) egalitarian
   - (d) random

2. The _____ reports interviewed 5,300 males and 5,940 females between 1938 and 1949.
   - (a) Kaiser Family Foundation
   - (b) Kinsey
   - (c) Centers for Disease Control
   - (d) Masters & Johnson

3. Government studies of the sexual experience of single teenagers in the United States have found that the self-reported incidence of sexual intercourse
   - (a) increased from 1988 to 2005.
   - (b) increased from 2005 to 2010.
   - (c) remained about the the same from 1988 to 2010.
   - (d) decreased from 1988 through 2010.

4. Experimenters randomly assign subjects to experimental or _____ groups.
   - (a) placebo
   - (b) stratified
   - (c) control
   - (d) naturalistic

5. A scientific sample must be
   - (a) large.
   - (b) representative.
   - (c) natural.
   - (d) neutral.

6. Participants did not provide informed consent in the _____ Syphilis Study.
   - (a) Texarkana
   - (b) Tucson
   - (c) Tuskegee
   - (d) Tuckahoe

7. People who agree to participate in psychological research may not represent the general population because of
   - (a) obtrusive means of measurement.
   - (b) volunteer bias.
   - (c) dishonesty.
   - (d) level of education.

8. Most researchers agree that the best means of learning about cause and effect is
   - (a) the experiment.
   - (b) the correlational method.
   - (c) the survey.
   - (d) the case study.

9. Katherine Frank engaged in
   - (a) the experimental method.
   - (b) participant-observation.
   - (c) the case-study method.
   - (d) an online survey.

10. _____ conducted a case study of Leonardo da Vinci.
    - (a) Michelangelo
    - (b) Alfred Kinsey
    - (c) Sigmund Freud
    - (d) Katherine Frank

Answers: 1. d; 2. b; 3. d; 4. c; 5. b; 6. c; 7. b; 8. a; 9. b; 10. c

My Life, My Sexuality

Thinking about Research Methods in Human Sexuality

*Explore this **My Life, My Sexuality** feature by scanning this QR code with your mobile device. If you don't already have one, you may download a free QR scanner for your device wherever smartphone apps are sold. You can also view this feature in MyDevelopmentLab, along with an accompanying critical thinking assignment.*

Many students will have discussed sexual issues in high school, perhaps under the topic of "health," or in a unit on reproduction in a biology course. Such discussions usually involve avoiding pregnancy and sexually transmitted infections. But it may seem surprising that college-level courses in human sexuality also discuss social and religious attitudes toward human sexuality, sexual behavior, and matters such as sexual coercion and pornography. Scan the code to go online and learn more about the role of research into human sexuality in your life.

3 Female Sexual Anatomy and Physiology

Learning Objectives

EXTERNAL SEX ORGANS

LO1   Describe the external female sex organs and their functions

INTERNAL SEX ORGANS

LO2   Describe the internal female sex organs, their functions, and health probems that may affect them

THE BREASTS

LO3   Describe the composition and functions of the breasts
LO4   Discuss risk factors for and detection and treatment of breast cancer

THE MENSTRUAL CYCLE

LO5   Describe the regulation and the phases of the menstrual cycle
LO6   Define and discuss menopause, perimenopause, and the climacteric

MENSTRUAL PROBLEMS

LO7   Define menstrual problems and discuss what can be done about them

MY LIFE, MY SEXUALITY: TAKING CHARGE OF MY SEXUAL HEALTH

TRUTH OR FICTION?

1 Women, but not men, have a sex organ whose only known function is the experiencing of sexual pleasure.   **T   F**?

2 Women urinate and engage in sexual intercourse through the same bodily opening.   **T   F**?

3 One may determine whether or not a woman is a virgin by examining her hymen.   **T   F**?

4 Women with larger breasts produce more milk while nursing.   **T   F**?

5 Women who have had abortions are at greater risk of breast cancer.   **T   F**?

6 The American Cancer Society recommends that women engage in a breast self-examination once a month.   **T   F**?

7 The ancient Romans believed that menstrual blood soured wine and killed crops.   **T   F**?

8 Sex during menstruation is harmful.   **T   F**?

9 At menopause, women experience debilitating hot flashes.   **T   F**?

10 Menopause signals an end to women's sexual appetite.   **T   F**?

Despite hundreds of years of tradition, Hajia Zuwera Kassindja would not let it happen to her 17-year-old daughter, Fauziya. Hajia's own sister had died from it. So Hajia gave her daughter her inheritance from her deceased husband, amounting to only $3,500, which left Hajia a pauper. Fauziya used the money to buy a phony passport and flee to the United States from the African country of Togo.

On arrival in the United States, Fauziya requested asylum from persecution. However, she was imprisoned for more than a year due to her illegal entry into the country. But the Board of Immigration Appeals finally agreed that Fauziya was fleeing persecution, and she was allowed to remain in the United States.

From what had Hajia's sister died? From what was Fauziya escaping? *Clitoridectomy*, a form of female genital mutilation practiced in her home country. Some cultures in Africa and the Middle East ritually mutilate the female genitals, removing the clitoris and surrounding genital structures. Clitoridectomy—cutting out the clitoris—is a rite of initiation into womanhood in many Islamic cultures (World Health Organization, 2012). It is often performed as a puberty ritual in late childhood or early adolescence (not within a few days of birth, like male circumcision). In modern-day Egypt, the vast majority of female adolescents, aged 10 to 19, have the clitoris removed (World Health Organization, 2012).

The clitoris gives rise to feelings of sexual pleasure in women. Its destruction is an attempt to ensure the girl's chastity, because it is assumed that uncircumcised girls are consumed with sexual desires.

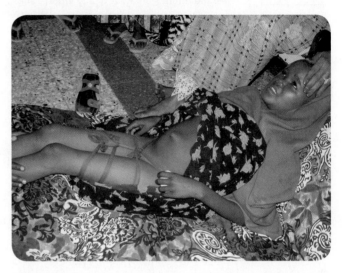

Clitoridectomy. Some predominantly Islamic cultures in Africa and the Middle East routinely cut out the clitoris as a rite of initiation into womanhood. Social critics point out the costs of girls' health and argue that the Koran—the Muslim holy book—does not call for such procedures.

The French have a saying, *"Vive la différence!"* ("Long live the difference!"). The well-known saying is a celebration of the differences between men and women. Given their possession of a clitoris, some might assert that women in particular have much to celebrate.

1 **TRUTH** OR **FICTION** REVISITED: The historic view of women as unresponsive to sexual stimulation is ironic because only women possess a sex organ—the clitoris—that is solely devoted to pleasurable sensations. The clitoris is the woman's most erotically charged organ; women most often masturbate through clitoral stimulation, not vaginal insertion.

This chapter explores women's sexual anatomy and physiology. We will locate and study the female sex organs. Even generally sophisticated students may fill in some gaps in their knowledge. For example, most of you know what a vagina is, but how many of you realized that only the female has an organ that is exclusively dedicated to pleasure? Or that a woman's passing of urine does not involve the vagina?

Chapter 4 describes the sexual anatomy and physiology of men. Despite the obvious differences, we will see that there may be more similarities in the sex organs than you would imagine. As women readers encounter the features of their sexual anatomy in their reading, they may wish to examine their own genitals with a mirror. By following the text and the illustrations, students may discover some new anatomic features. They will see that their genitals can resemble those in the illustrations yet also be unique.

External Sex Organs

Talking about one's sexual anatomy is often met with prejudice and misunderstanding. The derivation of the word *pudenda,* which refers to the external female genitals, speaks volumes about sexism in the ancient Mediterranean world.

Even today, this cultural heritage may lead women to develop negative attitudes toward their genitals. Girls and boys are both sometimes reared to regard their genitals with shame or disgust. Both may be reprimanded for expressing normal curiosity about them. They may be reared with a "hands-off" attitude, to keep their "private parts" private, even from themselves. This is unfortunate, because knowledge of one's sexual anatomy contributes both to sexual health and pleasure.

Taken collectively, the external sexual structures of the female are termed the **pudendum,** or the vulva. **Vulva** is a Latin word that means "wrapper" or "covering." The vulva consists of the *mons veneris,* the *labia majora* and *minora* (major and minor lips), the *clitoris,* and the vaginal opening (see Figure 3.1). Figure 3.2 shows variations in the appearance of women's genitals.

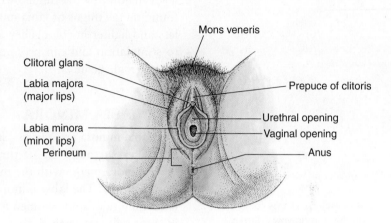

FIGURE 3.1 External Female Sex Organs. This figure shows the vulva with the labia opened to reveal the urethral and vaginal openings.

THE MONS VENERIS

The **mons veneris** consists of fatty tissue that covers the joint of the pubic bones in front of the body, below the abdomen and above the clitoris. At puberty, the mons becomes covered with pubic hair that may be thick and curly but varies from person to person in waviness, texture, and color. The pubic hair captures the chemical secretions that exude from the vagina during sexual arousal. Their scent may allure lovers. The mons cushions a woman's body during sexual intercourse, protecting her and her partner from the pressure against the pubic bone that stems from thrusting. There is an ample supply of nerve endings in the mons, so that caresses can produce pleasurable sensations.

Pudenda The external sexual structures of the female.

Vulva Another term for the external sexual structures of the female.

Mons veneris A mound of fatty tissue that covers the joint of the pubic bones in front of the body, below the abdomen and above the clitoris.

Real Students, Real Questions

Q *Are there any negative consequences to shaving (partly or in full) pubic hair?*

A Unless you cut yourself seriously, your downside is probably limited to some skin irritation and then to some itching as the hair grows back. But these effects are not fully predictable. "Bikini waxing" and laser hair removal are alternatives, but they can be painful. In addition, laser hair removal is expensive and irreversible. Some feminists will argue that your concern about shaving pubic hair—or even underarm hair—reflects an unhealthy need to conform to antifeminist cultural standards of beauty. Others will argue that you should do what makes you happy. It's your call and it's unlikely to usher in a health crisis.

THE LABIA MAJORA

The **labia majora** are large folds of skin that run downward from the mons along the sides of the vulva. In some women, the labia majora are thick and bulging. In others, they are thinner, flatter, and less noticeable. When close together, they hide the labia minora and the urethral and vaginal openings. The outer surfaces of the labia majora, by the thighs, are covered with pubic hair and darker skin than that found on the thighs or labia minora. The inner surfaces of the labia majora are hairless and lighter in color. They are amply supplied with nerve endings that respond to stimulation and can produce sexual pleasure. The labia majora also shield the inner female genitals.

THE LABIA MINORA

The **labia minora** are hairless, light-colored membranes, located between the major lips. They surround the urethral and vaginal openings. The outer surfaces of the labia minora merge with the major lips. At the top they join at the prepuce (hood) of the clitoris. The labia minora differ in appearance from woman to woman. The labia minora of some women form protruding flower shapes that are valued greatly in some cultures, such as that of the Khoikhoi people of Africa. (Khoikhoi women purposely elongate their labia minora by tugging at them.) Rich in blood vessels and nerve endings, the labia minora are highly sensitive to sexual stimulation. When stimulated, they darken and swell, engorging with blood.

THE CLITORIS

Worldwide, the clitoris is known by many names, from *bijou* (French for "jewel") to *pokhotnik* (Russian for "lust"). The Tuamotuan people of Polynesia have ten words for it, emblematic of their interest in female sexuality.

The word **clitoris** derives from the Greek word *kleitoris*, meaning "hill" or "slope." It receives its name from the manner in which it slopes upward in the shaft and forms a mound of spongy tissue at the glans (see Figure 3.1). The body of the clitoris—the clitoral shaft—is about 1 inch long and ¼ inch wide. The shaft consists of erectile tissue that contains two spongy masses called **corpora cavernosa** ("cavernous bodies") that fill with blood (become engorged) and become erect in response to sexual stimulation. The stiffening of the clitoris is less apparent than the erection of the penis, because the clitoris does not swing

Labia majora Large folds of skin that run downward from the mons along the sides of the vulva.

Labia minora Hairless, light-colored membranes, located between the labia majora.

Clitoris A female sex organ consisting of a shaft and glans located above the urethral opening. It is extremely sensitive to sexual sensations.

Corpora cavernosa Masses of spongy tissue in the clitoral shaft that become engorged with blood and stiffen in response to sexual stimulation.

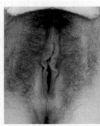

FIGURE 3.2 Normal Variations in the Vulva. The features of the vulva show a great deal of variation. A woman's attitude toward her genitals is likely to reflect her general self-concept and early childhood messages rather than the appearance of her vulva per se.

free from the body. The **prepuce** (meaning "before a swelling"), or hood, covers the clitoral shaft. It is a sheath of skin formed by the upper part of the labia minora. The clitoral glans is a smooth, round knob or lump of tissue above the urethral opening. The glans is revealed by gently separating the labia minora and retracting the hood. It is highly sensitive to touch because of the rich supply of nerve endings.

The size of the clitoris varies from woman to woman. Because the clitoral glans is highly sensitive to touch, women usually prefer to be stroked or stimulated on the mons, or on the clitoral hood, rather than directly on the glans.

In some respects, the clitoris is the female counterpart of the penis. Both organs—clitoris and penis—develop from the same embryonic tissue, which makes them similar in structure, or **homologous** (see Chapter 4). They are not fully similar in function, or **analogous**, however. Both organs receive and transmit sexual sensations, but the penis is directly involved in reproduction and excretion by serving as a conduit for sperm and urine, respectively.

Cutting out the clitoral hood—**clitoridectomy**—is common among Muslims in the Near East and Africa. As we see in the nearby World of Diversity feature, it is a "rite of passage" to womanhood that leaves scars—physical and emotional.

THE VESTIBULE

The word **vestibule**, which means "entranceway," refers to the area within the labia minora that contains the openings to the vagina and the urethra. The vestibule is richly supplied with nerve endings and is very sensitive to tactile or other sexual stimulation.

THE URETHRAL OPENING

Urine passes from the female's body through the **urethral opening** (see Figure 3.1), which is connected by a short tube (the urethra) to the bladder (see Figure 3.3). The urethral opening lies below the clitoral glans and above the vaginal opening. The urethral opening, urethra, and bladder are unrelated to the reproductive system.

TRUTH OR FICTION REVISITED: Many males (and even some females) believe erroneously that, for women, urination and coitus occur through the same bodily opening. The confusion may arise from the fact that urine and semen both pass through the penis of the male or because the urethral opening lies near the vaginal opening.

The proximity of the urethral opening to the external sex organs can pose hygienic problems for sexually active women (Belden, 2011). The urinary tract, which includes the urethra, bladder, and kidneys, may become infected by bacteria from the vagina or rectum. Disease organisms may pass from the partner's sex organs or hands to the urethral opening during sexual activity. Anal intercourse followed by vaginal intercourse may transfer disease organisms from the rectum to the bladder. For similar reasons, women should first wipe the vulva, then the anus, when using the toilet.

Cystitis is a bladder inflammation that may stem from any of these sources. Its symptoms include burning and frequent urination (also called *urinary urgency*). Pus or a bloody discharge is common, and there may be discomfort above the pubic bone. These

CRITICAL THINKING
Do you believe that disapproval of clitoridectomy by Americans and other Westerners shows cultural condescension or cultural insensitivity? Why or why not?

Prepuce The fold of skin covering the glans of the clitoris (or penis).

Homologous Similar in structure; developing from the same embryonic tissue.

Analogous Similar in function.

Clitoridectomy Surgical removal of the clitoris.

Vestibule The area in the labia minora that contains the openings to the vagina and the urethra.

Urethral opening The opening through which urine passes from the female's body.

Cystitis An inflammation of the urinary bladder.

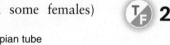

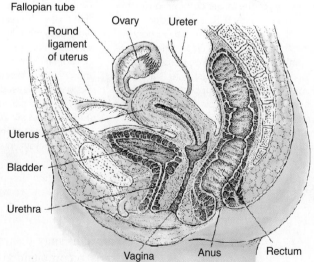

Fallopian tube
Round ligament of uterus
Ovary
Ureter
Uterus
Bladder
Urethra
Vagina
Anus
Rectum

FIGURE 3.3 The Female Reproductive System. This cross-section locates many of the internal sex organs that compose the female reproductive system. Note that the uterus is normally tipped forward.

A World of Diversity
Female Genital Mutilation

Dateline, Kafr al Manshi Abou Hamar, Egypt—The men in this poor farming community were seething. A 13-year-old girl was brought to a doctor's office to have her clitoris removed, a surgery considered necessary here to preserve chastity and honor. The girl died, but that was not the source of the outrage. After her death, the government shut down the clinic, and that got everyone stirred up.

—Slackman (2007)

According to the World Health Organization, approximately 140 million Muslim women and girls have undergone genital mutilation (World Health Organization, 2012). Despite the fact that people who practice it usually call it circumcision and compare it to male circumcision, social observers assert that female genital mutilation is an attempt by patriarchal societies to control the bodies and behavior of women (Amnesty International, 2012). In terms of their own perceptions, some groups in Egypt and in the Sudan simply perform clitoridectomies because it is a social custom that has been unchallenged in their own experience (Amnesty International, 2012). Because women tend to adopt the values of the larger cultures in which they dwell, nearly 80% of procedures are carried out by women who have undergone them themselves (World Health Organization, 2012). Some perceive it as part of their submission to Islam. However, there is no support for it in the Koran—the Islamic bible (Nour, 2000). The typical young woman in this culture—like the typical woman in most patriarchal cultures—does not grasp that she is a

victim (Amnesty International, 2012). She assumes that clitoridectomy is part of being female. As one young woman told gynecologist Nawal M. Nour (2000), the clitoridectomy hurt but was a good thing, because now she was a woman.

There are four major types of female genital mutilation (World Health Organization, 2012):

1. Clitoridectomy: partial or complete removal of the clitoris

2. Excision: partial or complete removal of the clitoris and the labia minora, with or without removal of the labia majora

3. Infibulation: narrowing of the vaginal opening by creating a seal formed by cutting and repositioning the inner, or outer, labia, with or without removal of the clitoris

4. Other: other procedures on the female genitalia that serve no medical purpose, such as pricking, piercing, scraping, and cauterizing (burning) the genital area

What effects does female genital mutilation have on women? A study of 250 female patients from the Maternal and Childhood Centers of Ismailia, Egypt, found that those who received the procedures were 80% more likely to complain of painful menstruation, 49% more likely to complain of vaginal dryness during intercourse, 45% more likely to lack sexual desire, 49% less likely to be pleased by sex, and 61% more likely to have difficulty reaching orgasm (El-Defrawi et al., 2001). Complications include severe bleeding, problems urinating, cysts, infections, infertility,

complications in childbirth, greater risk of newborn deaths, and psychological and emotional stress (Womenshealth.gov, 2009; World Health Organization, 2012).

Do not confuse male circumcision with the maiming inflicted on girls in the name of circumcision. Nour (2000) depicts the male equivalent of female genital mutilation as cutting off the penis. The Pulitzer Prize–winning, African American novelist Alice Walker drew attention to the practice in her novel *Possessing the Secret of Joy* and called for its abolition in her book and film *Warrior Marks*.

The United States has outlawed ritual genital mutilation within its borders and directed American representatives to world financial institutions to deny aid to countries that have not established educational programs to bring an end to the practice. Yet, calls from Westerners to ban the practice have sparked arguments that people in one culture cannot dictate the cultural traditions of another. For Alice Walker, however, "Torture is not culture."

The World health Organization summarizes its stand on the issue as follows:

[Female genital mutilation] is recognized internationally as a violation of the human rights of girls and women. It reflects deep-rooted inequality between the sexes, and constitutes an extreme form of discrimination against women. It is nearly always carried out on minors and is a violation of the rights of children. The practice also violates a person's rights to health, security and physical integrity, the right to be free from torture and cruel, inhuman or degrading treatment, and the right to life when the procedure results in death.

symptoms may disappear after several days, but consultation with a gynecologist is recommended because untreated cystitis can lead to kidney infections. "Honeymoon cystitis" is caused by the tugging on the bladder and urethral wall that occurs during vaginal intercourse. It may occur when beginning coital activity (although not necessarily on one's honeymoon) or when resuming coital activity after lengthy abstinence. Figure 3.3 shows the close proximity of the urethra and vagina.

A few precautions may help women prevent inflammation of the bladder:

- Drinking two quarts of water a day to flush the bladder.
- Drinking orange or cranberry juice to maintain an acid environment that discourages growth of infectious organisms.
- Decreasing use of alcohol and caffeine (from coffee, tea, or cola drinks) that may irritate the bladder.
- Washing the hands prior to masturbation or self-examination.
- Washing one's partner's and one's own genitals before and after intercourse.
- Preventing objects that have touched the anus (fingers, penis, toilet tissue) from subsequently coming into contact with the vulva.
- Urinating soon after intercourse to help wash away bacteria.

THE VAGINAL OPENING

> When I was five or six, my mother told me about sex. I remember that I was confused about what my mother said, because somehow I couldn't conceptualize what the female vagina looked like. I was curious to see an actual vagina and not just how it looked diagramed in a book.

One does not see an entire vagina, but rather the vaginal opening, or **introitus**, when one parts the labia minora. The introitus lies below and is larger than the urethral opening. Its shape resembles that of the hymen.

The **hymen** is a fold of tissue across the vaginal opening that is usually present at birth and may remain at least partly intact until a woman engages in coitus. For this reason the hymen has been called the "maidenhead." Its presence has been taken as proof of virginity, and its absence as evidence of coitus. However, some women are born with incomplete hymens, and other women's hymens are torn accidentally, such as during horseback riding, strenuous exercise or gymnastics, or even when bicycling. A punctured hymen is therefore poor evidence of coital experience. A flexible hymen may also withstand many coital experiences, so its presence does not guarantee virginity. Nevertheless, many Muslim women in Europe are having *hymenoplasty* prior to marriage—an operation that restores the hymen to provide the illusion of virginity on their wedding night (Ostrzenski, 2011). One woman having the operation remarked, "In my culture, not to be a virgin is to be dirt. Right now, virginity is more important to me than life" (cited in Sciolino & Mekhennet, 2008).

TRUTH OR **FICTION** REVISITED: Contrary to myth, it is not true that one may determine whether or not a woman is a virgin by examination of the hymen. Some people believe incorrectly that virgins cannot insert tampons or fingers into their vaginas, but most hymens will accommodate these intrusions.

Figure 3.4 illustrates various vaginal openings. The first three show common shapes of hymens among women who have not had coitus. The fifth drawing shows a *parous* ("passed through") vaginal opening, typical of a woman who has delivered a baby. Now and then the hymen consists of tough fibrous tissue and is closed, or *imperforate,* as in the fourth drawing. An imperforate hymen may not be discovered until after puberty, when menstrual discharges begin to accumulate in the vagina. In these rare cases, a surgical incision will perforate the hymen. A woman may also have a physician surgically perforate her hymen if she would rather forgo the tearing and discomfort that may accompany her initial coital experiences. A woman may also stretch the vaginal opening over several days in preparation for intercourse by inserting a finger and gently pressing downward toward the anus. After several repetitions, she may insert two fingers and repeat the process, spreading the fingers slightly after insertion.

Introitus The vaginal opening.

Hymen A fold of tissue across the vaginal opening that is usually present at birth and remains at least partly intact until a woman engages in coitus.

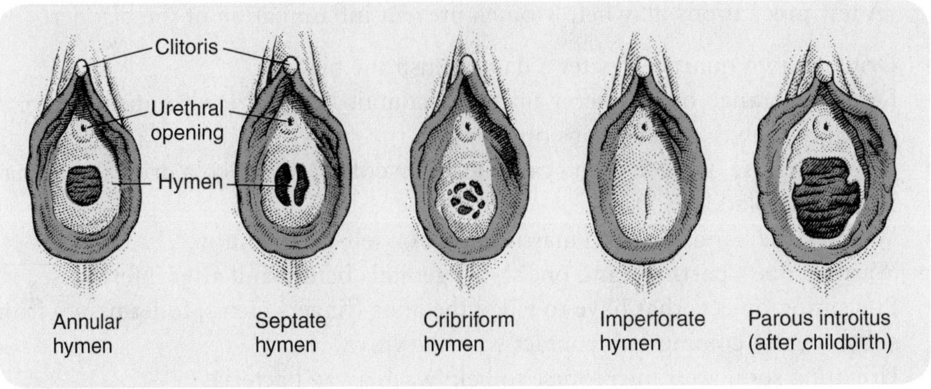

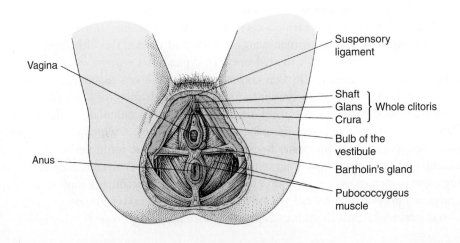

FIGURE 3.4 **Appearance of Various Types of Hymens and the Introitus (at right) as It Appears Following Delivery of a Baby**

[Figure labels: Clitoris, Urethral opening, Hymen; Annular hymen, Septate hymen, Cribriform hymen, Imperforate hymen, Parous introitus (after childbirth)]

The hymen is found only in female horses and humans. It is not present in animal species closest to humans on the evolutionary scale, such as chimps and gorillas. The hymen remains something of a biological mystery, because it serves no apparent biological function.

THE PERINEUM

The **perineum** incorporates the skin and underlying tissue between the vaginal opening and the anus. The perineum is rich in nerve endings. Stimulation of the area may heighten sexual arousal. Many physicians make a routine perineal incision during labor, called an *episiotomy*, to facilitate childbirth.

STRUCTURES THAT UNDERLIE THE EXTERNAL SEX ORGANS

Figure 3.5 shows what lies beneath the skin of the vulva. The *vestibular bulbs* and *Bartholin's glands* are active during sexual arousal and are found on both sides (shown on the right in Figure 3.5). Muscular rings (sphincters) that constrict bodily openings such as the vaginal and anal openings are also found on both sides.

The clitoral **crura** are wing-shaped, leglike structures that attach the clitoris to the pubic bone beneath. The crura contain corpora cavernosa, which engorge with blood and stiffen during sexual arousal.

The **vestibular bulbs** are attached to the clitoris at the top and extend downward along the sides of the vaginal opening. Blood congests them during sexual arousal, swelling the vulva and lengthening the vagina. This swelling contributes to coital sensations for both partners.

Perineum The skin and underlying tissue that lies between the vaginal opening and the anus.

Crura Anatomical structures resembling legs that attach the clitoris to the pubic bone.

Vestibular bulbs Cavernous structures that extend downward along the sides of the introitus and swell during sexual arousal.

FIGURE 3.5 **Structures That Underlie the Female External Sex Organs.** If we could see beneath the vulva, we would find muscle fibers that constrict the various body openings, plus the crura ("legs") of the clitoris, the vestibular bulbs, and Bartholin's glands.

[Figure labels: Vagina, Anus, Suspensory ligament, Shaft, Glans, Crura (Whole clitoris), Bulb of the vestibule, Bartholin's gland, Pubococcygeus muscle]

Bartholin's glands lie just inside the minor lips on each side of the vaginal opening. They secrete a couple of drops of lubrication just before orgasm. This lubrication is not essential for coitus. In fact, the fluid produced by the Bartholin's glands has no known purpose. If the glands become infected and clogged, however, a woman may notice swelling and local irritation. It is wise to consult a gynecologist if these symptoms do not fade within a few days.

It was once believed that the source of the vaginal lubrication or "wetness" that women experience during sexual arousal was produced by the Bartholin's glands. It is now known that engorgement of vaginal tissues during sexual excitement causes moisture from the many small blood vessels that lie in the vaginal wall to be forced out and to pass through the vaginal lining, forming the basis of the lubrication. In less time than it takes to read this sentence (generally within 10 to 30 seconds), beads of vaginal lubrication or "sweat" appear along the interior lining of the vagina in response to sexual stimulation, in much the same way that rising temperatures cause water to pass through the skin as perspiration.

Pelvic floor muscles permit women to constrict the vaginal and anal openings. They contract automatically, or involuntarily, during orgasm, and their tone may contribute to coital sensations.

Internal Sex Organs

The internal sex organs of the female include the innermost parts of the vagina, the cervix, the uterus, and two ovaries, each connected to the uterus by a fallopian tube (see Figures 3.3 and 3.6). These structures comprise the female reproductive system. 👁

THE VAGINA

The **vagina** extends back and upward from the vaginal opening (see Figure 3.3). It is usually 3 to 5 inches long at rest. Menstrual flow and babies pass from the uterus to the outer world through the vagina. During coitus, the penis is contained within the vagina.

The vagina is commonly pictured as a canal or barrel; but, when at rest, it is collapsed, like the inner tube of a bicycle tire. The vagina expands in length and width during sexual arousal. The vagina can also expand to allow insertion of a tampon, as well as the passage of a baby's head and shoulders during childbirth.

The vaginal walls have three layers. The inner lining, or vaginal mucosa, is made visible by opening the labia minora. It is a mucous membrane similar to the skin that lines the inside of the mouth. It feels fleshy, soft, and corrugated. It may vary from very dry to very wet. The middle layer of the vaginal wall is muscular. The outer or deeper layer is a fibrous covering that connects the vagina to other pelvic structures.

The vaginal walls are rich with blood vessels but poorly supplied with nerve endings. Unlike the sensitive outer third of the vaginal barrel, the inner two-thirds are so insensitive to touch that minor surgery may sometimes be performed on those portions without anesthesia. The entire vaginal barrel is sensitive to pressure, however, which can be experienced as pleasurable.

👁🗔**Watch** the **Video**
Female Reproductive Anatomy
on **MyDevelopmentLab**

Bartholin's glands Glands that lie just inside the minor lips and secrete fluid just before orgasm.

Vagina The tubular female sex organ that contains the penis during sexual intercourse and through which a baby is born.

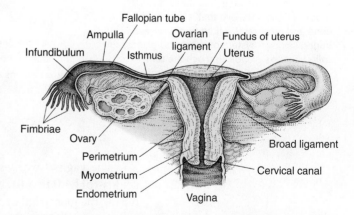

FIGURE 3.6 Female Internal Reproductive Organs. This drawing highlights the relationship of the uterus to the fallopian tubes and ovaries. Note the layers of the uterus, the ligaments that attach the ovaries to the uterus, and the relationship of the ovaries to the fimbriae of the fallopian tubes.

A Closer Look

The G Spot and Female Ejaculation: Realities or Myths?

The Grafenberg spot, or G spot, is theorized to be a part of the vagina—a bean-shaped area in the anterior (front) wall that may have special erotic significance. The G spot is believed to lie about 1 to 2 inches from the vaginal entrance and to consist of a soft mass of tissue that swells from the size of a dime to a half dollar when stimulated (see Figure 3.7). The name derives from the gynecologist Ernest Grafenberg, who first suggested the possible erotic import of the area. The spot can be directly stimulated by the woman's or her partner's fingers, or by penile thrusting in the rear entry or the female-superior positions. Some researchers suggest that stimulation of the spot produces intense erotic sensations and that, with prolonged stimulation, a distinct form of orgasm that is characterized by intense pleasure and, in some cases, a biological event formerly thought to be exclusively male: ejaculation. However, these claims are steeped in controversy (Dwyer, 2011; Kilchevsky et al., 2012).

Emmanuelle Jannini and her colleagues (2010) summarize much of the research on the G spot as follows: In experiments dating to the 1980s, some researchers claim to have found evidence that many women produce an ejaculate as a result of sexual stimulation. Some researchers believe that this fluid is urine that some women release involuntarily during orgasm. Others believe that it differs from urine and represents a fluid that is released during sex by a system of ducts and glands called *Skene's glands*, in much the same way that semen is released by the prostate gland in men. Some women, on the other hand, may expel urine during sex, perhaps because of urinary stress incontinence.

Even supporters of the existence of the G spot admit that it is difficult to locate because it is not apparent to the eye or touch (Jannini et al., 2010). Most women who are knowledgeable about sexuality in general seem to believe that they have a G spot, even if they cannot locate it with any certainty. Because of difficulties such as these, some researchers wonder whether the notion of a G spot is something of a myth (Dwyer, 2011; Kilchevsky et al., 2012).

CRITICAL THINKING

Some observers of the research on human sexuality suggest that the arguments over the existence of the G spot and female ejaculation have political as well as scientific implications. How do you think that the debates might relate to larger issues concerning female sexuality and male sexuality—namely, as to whether females or males are sexually superior, or more sexually active, or more sexually responsive? Explain.

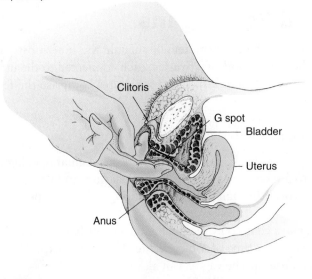

FIGURE 3.7 The Grafenberg Spot. It is theorized that the G spot can be stimulated by fingers or by intercourse in the rear entry or the female-superior positions. Does stimulation of the G spot produce intense erotic sensations and a distinct form of orgasm?

The vaginal walls secrete substances that help maintain the vagina's normal acidity (pH 4.0 to 5.0). Normally, they taste salty, but their odor and taste may vary during the menstrual cycle. The secretions may contain substances that act as sexual attractants. Women who frequently **douche** or use feminine deodorant sprays may remove or mask substances that arouse sex partners. Douching or spraying may also alter the natural chemical balance of the vagina, which can increase the risk of infections. Feminine deodorant sprays can also irritate the vagina and evoke allergic reactions. The normal, healthy vagina cleanses itself through regular chemical secretions that are evidenced by a mild white or yellowish discharge.

Douche Application of a jet of liquid to the vagina as a rinse.

Vaginitis refers to any vaginal inflammation, whether it is caused by an infection, birth control pills, antibiotics that alter natural body chemistry, an allergic reaction, chemical irritation, or lowered resistance as may be caused by fatigue or poor diet. Changes in body chemistry or lowered resistance permit microscopic organisms normally found in the vagina to multiply to infectious levels. Vaginitis may be recognized by abnormal discharge, itching, burning of the vulva, and urinary urgency. Women with vaginitis are advised to seek medical attention, but let us note some suggestions that may help prevent vaginitis:

- Wash your vulva and anus regularly with mild soap. Pat dry (taking care not to touch the vulva after dabbing the anus).
- Wear cotton panties. Nylon underwear retains heat and moisture that cause harmful bacteria to flourish.
- Avoid pants that are tight in the crotch.
- Be certain that sex partners are well washed. Condoms may also reduce the spread of infections from one's sex partner.
- Use a sterile, water-soluble jelly such as K-Y jelly if artificial lubrication is needed for intercourse. Do not use Vaseline. Birth control jellies can also be used for lubrication.
- Avoid intercourse that is painful or abrasive to the vagina.
- Avoid diets high in sugar and refined carbohydrates; they alter the normal acidity of the vagina.
- Women who are prone to vaginal infections may find it helpful to douche occasionally with plain water, a solution of 1 or 2 tablespoons of vinegar in a quart of warm water, or a solution of baking soda and water. Douches consisting of unpasteurized, plain (unflavored) yogurt may help replenish the "good" bacteria that are normally found in the vagina and that may be destroyed by use of antibiotics. Be careful when douching, and do not douche when pregnant or when you suspect you may be pregnant. Consult your physician before deciding to douche or applying any preparations to the vagina.
- Watch your general health. Eating poorly or getting insufficient rest will reduce your resistance to infection.

Vaginitis Vaginal inflammation.

Real Students, Real Questions

Q *I feel like I have an unpleasant odor from my vagina. Should I douche?*

A Most health-care providers will recommend regular superficial washing, as when taking a shower, and then, if you remain concerned, talking to your gynecologist about it. An unpleasant odor can be a sign of a health problem. If you're 18 years old, or younger but sexually active, you need to have a gynecologist and to see her or him regularly. Some vaginal odor is normal. If you are attending to your personal hygiene and are not diagnosed with a health problem, a partner is as likely—or more likely—to find normal vaginal odors attractive rather than repulsive.

THE CERVIX

When someone first said to me two years ago, "You can feel the end of your own cervix with your finger," I was interested but flustered. I had hardly ever put my finger in my vagina at all, and felt squeamish about touching myself there, in that place "reserved" for lovers and doctors. It took me two months to get up nerve to try it, and then one afternoon, pretty nervously, I squatted down in the bathroom and put my finger in deep, back into my vagina. There it was, feeling slippery and rounded, with an indentation at the center through which, I realized, my menstrual flow came. It was both very exciting and beautifully ordinary at the same time. Last week I bought a plastic speculum so I can look at my cervix. Will it take as long this time?

The **cervix** is the lower end of the uterus. Its walls, like those of the vagina, produce secretions that contribute to the chemical balance of the vagina (Belden, 2011). The opening in the middle of the cervix, or **os,** is normally about the width of a straw, although it expands to permit passage of a baby from the uterus to the vagina during childbirth. Sperm pass from the vagina to the uterus through the cervical canal.

Cervical Cancer Cervical cancer is relatively uncommon in the United States, although there are about 12,170 new cases a year as well as 4,220 deaths (American Cancer Society, 2012a). The primary cause of cervical cancer is infection with the human papilloma virus (HPV; see Chapter 16). A vaccine has been developed that makes most women immune to the form of HPV connected with cancer. The woman is best vaccinated before she becomes sexually active and may be exposed to the virus (American Cancer Society, 2012a). Cervical cancer is more common among women who have had many sex partners, became sexually active at a relatively early age, have sex with partners who have had many sex partners, and have sex with uncircumcized males (American Cancer Society, 2012a). The mortality rate is higher for African American women than for European American women, at least in part because HPV tends to be diagnosed later in African Americans. However, the death rate has been declining, especially for African American women (American Cancer Society, 2012a). ◉

A **Pap test** examines a sample of cervical cells that are smeared on a slide to screen for cervical cancer and other abnormalities. The HPV test is also appropriate because it finds infections that can lead to cancer. We'll note here and elsewhere in the text that HPV infections are common, and most clear up by themselves.

As of 2012, the American Cancer Society's recommendations for screening of cervical cancer were as follows:

- All women should begin screening at age 21.
- Women between the ages of 21 and 29 should have a Pap test every three years. They should only be tested for HPV if there is an abnormal Pap test result.
- Women between the ages of 30 and 65 should have both a Pap test and an HPV test every five years. A Pap test alone every three years is an alternative, but is not preferred.
- Women over age 65 who have a history of regular screenings with normal results need not be screened for cervical cancer, unless they have been previously diagnosed with cervical precancer.
- Women who have had their cervix removed as part of a hysterectomy and have no history of cervical cancer or precancer need not be screened.

◉—⌐**Watch** the **Video**
Cervical Cancer
on **MyDevelopmentLab**

Cervix The lower end of the uterus.

Os The opening in middle of the cervix.

Pap test A test of a sample of cervical cells that screens for cervical cancer and other abnormalities.

- Women who have had the HPV vaccine should still follow the screening recommendations for their age group.
- Women who are at high risk for cervical cancer may need to be screened more often. Women at high risk—because of factors such as HIV infection, organ transplant, or exposure to DES—may need more frequent screening.

Most cases of cervical cancer can be successfully treated by surgery and **radiotherapy** if they are detected early. For women diagnosed with localized cancer, the survival rate is nearly 100% (American Cancer Society, 2012a). Cervical cancer can also be prevented by removal or destruction of precancerous tissue. The five-year survival rate for the following situations is as follows:

- 92% for localized cancers
- 56% for cancers that have not spread beyond the region
- 17% for cancers that have metastasized (spread throughout the body) (University of Maryland, 2011)

THE UTERUS

The **uterus,** or womb (see Figures 3.3 and 3.6), is the organ in which a fertilized ovum implants and develops until birth. The uterus usually slants forward (*antroverted*), although about 10% of women have uteruses that tip backward (*retroverted*). In most instances a retroverted uterus causes no problems, but some women with one find certain positions of female–male coitus to be painful. A retroverted uterus normally tips forward during pregnancy. The uterus is suspended in the pelvis by flexible ligaments. In a woman who has not given birth, it is about 3 inches long, 3 inches wide, and 1 inch thick near the top. The uterus expands to house a fetus during pregnancy and shrinks after pregnancy, although not to its original size.

The uppermost part of the uterus is called the **fundus** (see Figure 3.6). The uterus is shaped like an inverted pear. If a ceramic model of a uterus were placed on a table, it would balance on the fundus. The central region of the uterus is called the *body*. The narrow lower region is the *cervix,* which leads downward to the vagina.

Like the vagina, the uterus has three layers (also shown in Figure 3.6). The innermost layer, or **endometrium,** is richly supplied with blood vessels and glands. Its structure varies according to a woman's age and phase of the menstrual cycle. Endometrial tissue is discharged through the cervix and vagina at menstruation. In some women, endometrial tissue may also grow in the abdominal cavity or elsewhere in the reproductive system. This condition is called **endometriosis,** and the most common symptom is menstrual pain. If untreated, it may lead to infertility.

The second layer of the uterus, the **myometrium,** is well muscled. It endows the uterus with flexibility and strength and creates the powerful contractions that propel a fetus outward during labor. The third or outermost layer, the **perimetrium,** provides an external cover.

Endometrial Cancer Cancer of the endometrial lining—the body of the uterus—is called *endometrial cancer.* There are about 47,130 new cases each year, and 8,010 deaths (American Cancer Society, 2012b). Endomretial cancer is rarer in women younger than 40. It is more common among European American women, but African American women are at greater risk of dying from it. Risk factors are as follows (American Cancer Society, 2012b):

- A shift in the balance between progesterone and estrogen toward higher estrogen levels
- Estrogen therapy (also called menopausal hormone therapy, or hormone replacement therapy)

Radiotherapy Treatment of a disease by X-rays or by emissions from a radioactive substance.

Uterus The hollow, muscular, pear-shaped organ in which a fertilized ovum implants and develops until birth.

Fundus The uppermost part of the uterus.

Endometrium The innermost layer of the uterus.

Endometriosis A condition caused by the growth of endometrial tissue in the abdominal cavity or elsewhere outside the uterus and characterized by menstrual pain.

Myometrium The middle, well-muscled layer of the uterus.

Perimetrium The outer layer of the uterus.

- Increased number of menstrual cycles during one's lifetime
- Obesity (fatty tissue can change other hormones into estrogen)
- Tamoxifen (a breast cancer–treatment drug, which acts like an antiestrogen medicine in breast tissue and like an estrogen in the uterus
- Ovarian tumors (sometimes produce estrogen)
- Increased age
- A high-fat diet
- Diabetes
- Family history of endometrial or colon cancer
- A personal history of breast or ovarian cancer

The following factors help protect *against* endometrial cancer (American Cancer Society, 2012b):

- Use of birth control pills
- Pregnancy
- Use of an intrauterine device (IUD)
- Exercise

Endometrial cancer is symptomized by abnormal uterine staining or bleeding, especially after menopause. The most common treatment is surgery (American Cancer Society, 2012b), but women may also be treated with radiation therapy, hormonal therapy, and chemotherapy. The five-year survival rate for endometrial cancer is 90% if it is discovered early and limited to the endometrium. (Endometrial cancer is usually diagnosed early because women tend to report postmenopausal bleeding to their doctors quickly.) The survival rate drops when the cancer invades surrounding tissues or metastasizes. (It drops to 15% when it has metastasized.)

THE FALLOPIAN TUBES

The **fallopian tubes** are about 4 inches in length and extend from the upper end of the uterus toward the ovaries (see Figure 3.6). The part of each tube nearest the uterus is the *isthmus,* which broadens into the *ampulla* as it approaches the ovary. The outer part, or *infundibulum,* has fringelike projections called *fimbriae* that extend toward, but are not attached to, the ovary. Ova pass through the fallopian tubes on their way to the uterus. The fallopian tubes are not just passageways. They help nourish and conduct ova. The tubes are lined with tiny hairlike projections termed *cilia* ("lashes") that help propel ova through the tube at about 1 inch per day. Because ova must be fertilized within a day or two after they are released from the ovaries, fertilization usually occurs in the infundibulum within a couple of inches of the ovaries. The form of sterilization called *tubal ligation* ties off the fallopian tubes, so that ova cannot pass through them or become fertilized.

About 2% of pregnancies are **ectopic**; that is, the fertilized ovum implants outside the uterus, most often in the fallopian tube where fertilization occurred. Ectopic pregnancies can eventually burst fallopian tubes, causing hemorrhaging and death, so such pregnancies are terminated before the tube ruptures. Ectopic pregnancies are not easily recognized, however, because their symptoms—missed menstrual period, abdominal pain, irregular bleeding—suggest many conditions. Any of these symptoms is an excellent reason to consult a gynecologist. Risk factors for ectopic pregnancy include a previous ectopic pregnancy, inflammation or infection of the fallopian tubes or uterus (as from the sexually transmitted infections gonorrhea or chlamydia), use of fertility drugs, or an unusually shaped fallopian tube (Mayo Clinic, 2012a).

Fallopian tubes Tubes that extend from the upper uterus toward the ovaries and that conduct ova to the uterus.

Ectopic pregnancy A pregnancy in which the fertilized ovum implants outside the uterus, usually in the fallopian tube.

THE OVARIES

The two **ovaries** are almond-shaped organs that are each about 1½ inches long. They lie on either side of the uterus, to which they are attached by ovarian ligaments. The ovaries produce ova (egg cells) and the female sex hormones estrogen and progesterone. **Estrogen** is a generic term for several hormones (such as estradiol, estriol, and estrone) that promote the changes of puberty and regulate the menstrual cycle. Estrogen also helps older women maintain cognitive functioning and feelings of psychological well-being (Sherwin, 2012). **Progesterone** is a hormone that also has multiple functions, including regulating the menstrual cycle and preparing the uterus for pregnancy by stimulating the development of the endometrium (uterine lining). Estrogen and progesterone levels vary with the phases of the menstrual cycle.

The human female is born with about 2 million ova, but they are immature in form. Of these, about 400,000 survive into puberty, each of which is contained in the ovary within a thin capsule, or **follicle**. During a woman's reproductive years, from puberty to menopause, only 400 or so ripened ova (typically 1 per month) will be released by their follicles for possible fertilization. How these ova are selected remains a mystery. 👁

Ovarian Cancer Each year some 22,280 women in the United States are diagnosed with ovarian cancer, and about 15,500 die from it (American Cancer Society, 2012c). Ovarian cancer most often strikes women between the ages of 40 and 70 and ranks as the fifth leading cancer killer of women, behind lung cancer, breast cancer, and colon cancer. It is more common in European American women that African American women.

Risk factors for ovarian cancer include (American Cancer Society, 2012c):

- Increased age (half of cases are found in women above the age of 63)
- Obesity
- Use of the fertility drug clomiphene citrate
- Use of androgens
- Use of estrogen therapy (espcially without progesterone)
- Family history of ovarian cancer, breast cancer, or colorectal cancer
- Personal history of breast cancer (especially if the woman is found to have an inherited mutation in the BRCA1 or BRCA2 genes)
- Use of talcum powder in the genital region

On the other hand, the following factors appear to lower the risk of ovarian cancer (American Cancer Society 2012c):

- Having had children
- Breast feeding
- Prolonged use of birth control pills
- Tubal ligation
- A low-fat diet
- Use of aspirin or acetaminophen

Early detection is the key to fighting ovarian cancer. When it is detected before spreading beyond the ovary, the five-year survival rate is 89% to 99%, depending on how aggressive the cancer is. When it has metastasized, the survival rate drops to as low as 18% (American Cancer Society, 2012c). Unfortunately, ovarian cancer is often "silent" in the early stages, showing no obvious signs or symptoms. The most common sign is enlargement of the abdomen, which is caused by the accumulation of fluid. Pelvic pressure or pain in the stomach, trouble eating of feeling full rapidly, and feeling the urge to urinate frequently

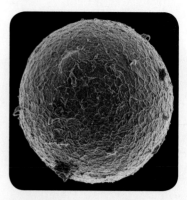

A Magnified Human Ovum (Egg Cell). The ripe human ovum is almost large enough to be seen with the naked eye. The ovum of a chicken is a couple of inches across, of course.

👁⎯**Watch** the **Video**
Female Anatomy: Ovaries and Ovulation
on **MyDevelopmentLab**

Ovaries Almond-shaped organs that produce ova and the hormones estrogen and progesterone.

Estrogen A generic term for female sex hormones or synthetic compounds that promote the development of female sex characteristics and regulate the menstrual cycle.

Progesterone A steroid hormone secreted by the corpus luteum or prepared synthetically that stimulates proliferation of the endometrium and is involved in regulation of the menstrual cycle.

Follicle A capsule within an ovary that contains an ovum.

are additional symptoms. The Pap test, which is useful in detecting cervical cancer, does not reveal ovarian cancer. Your gynecologist may detect the possibility of ovarian cancer during a regular pelvic examination. There is some success in using ultrasound and other imaging techniques (CT scans, MRI, PET scans), and blood tests. If ovarian cancer is suspected, the gynecologist usually does a biopsy—a minor surgical procedure in which the doctor obtains and then examines a sample or ovarian tissue.

Surgery, radiation therapy, and drug therapy are treatment options. One, two, or all of these methods may be recommended. Surgery usually includes the removal of one or both ovaries, the uterus, and the fallopian tubes.

Hysterectomy One in three women in the United States has a **hysterectomy** by the age of 60. Most women who obtain them do so between the ages of 35 and 45. The hysterectomy is the second most commonly performed operation on women in the United States. (Cesarean sections are the most common.) A hysterectomy may be performed when a woman develops cancer of the uterus, ovaries, or cervix, or another disease that causes pain or excessive uterine bleeding. A **complete hysterectomy** is the surgical removal of the ovaries, fallopian tubes, cervix, and uterus. It is usually performed to reduce the risk of cancer spreading throughout the reproductive system. A **partial hysterectomy** is the removal of the uterus, but the ovaries and fallopian tubes are spared; thus, the woman continues to ovulate and produce adequate quantities of female sex hormones.

The hysterectomy can relieve symptoms associated with various gynecological disorders and improve the quality of life for many women (Duru et al., 2012). However, many gynecologists believe that hysterectomies are recommended too often, before proper diagnostic steps are taken or when less radical interventions might alleviate the problem (Belden, 2011). We strongly suggest that women whose physicians advise a hysterectomy seek a second opinion before proceeding.

THE PELVIC EXAMINATION

Women are advised to have an internal (pelvic) examination at least once a year by the time they reach their late teens (or earlier if they become sexually active) and twice yearly if they are over age 35 or use birth control pills. The physician (usually a gynecologist) first examines the woman externally for irritations, swellings, abnormal vaginal discharges, and clitoral adhesions. The physician normally inserts a speculum to help inspect the cervix and vaginal walls for discharges (which can be signs of infection), discoloration, lesions, or growths. This examination is typically followed by a Pap test to detect cervical cancer. A sample of vaginal discharge may also be taken to test for the sexually transmitted infection (STI) gonorrhea (see Chapter 16).

To take a Pap test, or a Pap smear, the physician will hold open the vaginal walls with a plastic or (hopefully prewarmed!) metal speculum so that a sample of cells (a "smear") may be scraped from the cervix with a wooden spatula (see Figure 3.8). Women should not douche prior to Pap tests or schedule them during menstruation, because douches and blood confound analysis of the smear.

Hysterectomy   Surgical removal of the uterus.

Complete hysterectomy   Surgical removal of the ovaries, fallopian tubes, cervix, and uterus.

Partial hysterectomy   Surgical removal of the uterus but not the ovaries and fallopian tubes.

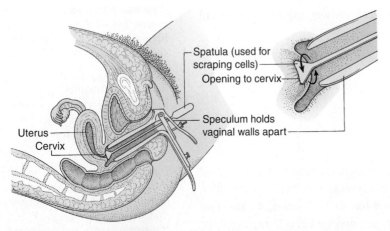

Spatula (used for scraping cells)
Opening to cervix
Speculum holds vaginal walls apart
Uterus
Cervix

FIGURE 3.8 Use of the Speculum and Spatula during a Pelvic Examination.   The speculum holds the vaginal walls apart while the spatula is used to gently scrape cells from the cervix. The Pap test screens for cervical cancer and other abnormalities.

The speculum exam is normally followed by a bimanual vaginal exam in which the index and middle fingers of one hand are inserted into the vagina while the lower part of the abdomen is palpated (touched) by the other hand from the outside. The physician uses this technique to examine the location, shape, size, and movability of the internal sex organs, searching for abnormal growths and symptoms of other problems. Palpation may be somewhat uncomfortable, but severe pain is a sign that something is wrong. A woman need not hide such discomfort from the examiner. She may only be masking a symptom (that is, depriving the physician of useful information). Physical discomfort is usually mild, however, and psychological discomfort is sometimes lessened by discussing it.

Finally, the physician should do a recto-vaginal examination in which one finger is inserted into the rectum while the other is inserted into the vagina. This procedure provides additional information about the ligaments of the uterus, the ovaries, and the fallopian tubes. The procedure also helps the physician evaluate the health of the rectum.

Although it may be somewhat uncomfortable, the pelvic examination is not ordinarily painful. It is normal for a woman who has not had one, or who is visiting a new doctor, to be anxious about the exam. The doctor should be reassuring if the woman expresses concern. If the doctor is not, the woman should feel free to consult another doctor. She should not forgo the pelvic examination itself, however. It is essential for early detection of problems.

The Breasts

A college woman recalls:

> I was very excited about my breast development. It was a big competition to see who was wearing a bra in elementary school. When I began wearing one, I also liked wearing see-through blouses so everyone would know…

> My breasts were very late in developing. This brought me a lot of grief from my male peers. I just dreaded situations like going to the beach or showering in the locker room…

Real Students, Real Questions

Q *Is there any way to make my breasts larger without having plastic surgery?*

A You'll come across advertisements for dietary supplements that supposedly do the job, but we advise you not to take anything without discussing it with your health-care provider. But think about why you are concerned about your breast size. Is it because you are succumbing to the popular idea that a sex partner will prefer a woman with large breasts? Some do, but many do not, and who you are as a person is more important than your cup size! If your partner doesn't agree with that, you need another partner, not larger breasts. In any case, small breasts are as sensitive to sexual stimulation as larger breasts, so show your partner what you want.

All through junior high and high school I felt unhappy about being "overendowed." I felt just too uncomfortable in sweaters—there was so much to reveal and I was always sure that the only reason boys liked me was because of my bustline....

By the time I was eleven I needed a bra...The girls in my gym class in sixth grade laughed at me because my breasts were pretty big and I still didn't have a bra. I tried to cover myself up when I dressed and undressed. On my eleventh birthday my mom gave me a sailor blouse and inside was my first bra.... (It) was the best present I could have received. The bra made me feel a lot better about myself, but I was still unsure of my femininity for a long time....

In some cultures the breasts are viewed merely as biological instruments for feeding infants. In American culture, however, breasts have such erotic significance that a woman's self-esteem may become linked to her bustline.

The breasts are **secondary sex characteristics**. That is, like the rounding of the hips, they distinguish women from men, but they are not directly involved in reproduction. Each breast contains 15 to 20 clusters of milk-producing **mammary glands** (see Figure 3.9). Each gland opens at the nipple through its own duct. The mammary glands are separated by soft, fatty tissue. It is the amount of this fatty tissue, not the amount of glandular tissue, that largely determines the size of the breasts (Dixson et al., 2011). **TRUTH** OR **FICTION** REVISITED: Women vary little in their amount of glandular tissue, so breast size does not determine the quantity of milk that can be produced.

The nipple, which lies in the center of the **areola**, contains smooth muscle fibers that erect the nipple when they contract. The areola, or area surrounding the nipple, darkens during pregnancy and remains darker after delivery (Dixson et al., 2011). Oil-producing glands in the areola help lubricate the nipples during breast feeding. Milk ducts conduct milk from the mammary glands through the nipples. Nipples are richly endowed with nerve endings, so that stimulation of the nipples heightens sexual arousal for many women. Male nipples are similar in sensitivity.

Figure 3.10 shows some of the normal variations in the size and shape of the breasts of adult women. The sensitivity of the breasts to sexual stimulation is unrelated to their size. Small breasts may have as many nerve endings as large breasts, but they will be more densely packed.

Women can prompt their partners to provide breast stimulation by informing them that their breasts are sensitive to stimulation. They can also guide a partner's hands in ways that provide the type of stimulation they desire. The breasts vary in sensitivity with the phases of the menstrual cycle, and some women appear less responsive to breast stimulation than others. However, some less sensitive women may learn to enjoy breast stimulation by focusing on breast sensations during lovemaking in a relaxed atmosphere.

BREAST CANCER

Susan contracted breast cancer in her 30s. A lump "suddenly" appeared in her **mammography**. She and her family dwelled in fear over the next couple of weeks as tissue from the tumor was biopsied, found to be malignant, and arrangements were made to remove the breast. Given the

Secondary sex characteristics Traits that distinguish the sexes from one another but are not directly involved in reproduction.

Mammary glands Milk-secreting glands.

Areola The dark ring on the breast that encircles the nipple.

Mammography A special type of X-ray test that detects cancerous lumps in the breast.

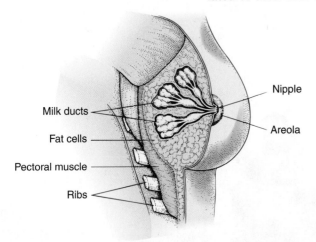

FIGURE 3.9 A Breast of an Adult Woman. This drawing reveals the structures underlying the breast, including milk ducts and fat cells.

Milk ducts
Fat cells
Pectoral muscle
Ribs
Nipple
Areola

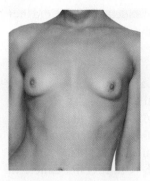

Figure 3.10 Normal Variations in the Size and Shape of the Breasts. The size and shape of the breasts have little bearing on ability to produce milk or on sensitivity to sexual stimulation. Breasts have become highly eroticized in our culture.

"aggressiveness" of the tumor—the rapidity with which it had grown—every physician she consulted recommended **mastectomy** (surgically removing the breast) rather than **lumpectomy** (surgically removing a lump from the breast). The question arose as to whether Susan should remove the healthy breast as a precautionary measure. A blood test determined that she did not possess genetic mutations in the BRCA1 or BRCA2 genes that are connected with early-onset breast cancer, so the healthy breast was preserved. There was additional anxiety following the removal of the breast as tissues were examined to determine whether the cancer had spread within the breast or to lymph nodes. Fortunately, it had apparently remained within a duct despite the rapidity of its growth.

Susan then dealt with the psychological issues of feeling unwhole, which were to some degree mitigated by attending a support group of women undergoing similar experiences. Reconstruction of the breast was an unexpected and lengthy process during which the muscles that normally underlie breasts were gradually ballooned out to surround and support a silicone implant. A new cosmetic nipple was

Mastectomy Surgical removal of the entire breast.

Lumpectomy Surgical removal of a lump from the breast.

Real Students, Real Questions

Q *One of my breasts is bigger than the other. Is this normal?*

A Sure. One hand is larger than the other, one foot, and, for men, one testicle. Unless there's a huge difference, don't worry about it. It is mostly the amount of fatty tissue in the breasts that accounts for differences in the size of the breasts among women. Moreover, breasts expand with pregnancy, and smaller breasts tend to increase more dramatically in size than larger breasts. And because production of milk depends on the amount of glandular tissue in the breasts, not fatty tissue, the size of your breasts has nothing to do with the amount of milk you can produce if you have children. On the other hand, if you have noticed a change in the size of one breast relative to the other, or in the texture of your breast tissue or in the nipple or areola, bring it to the attention of your health-care provider. It could mean nothing, but it's better to be sure.

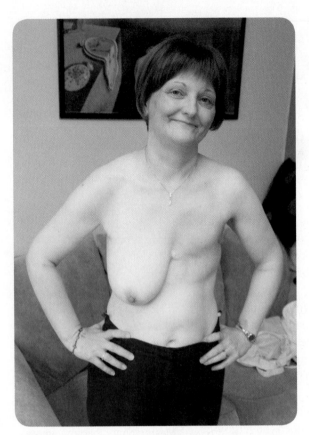

A Woman Following a Mastectomy. Today many surgeons begin breast reconstruction while the woman is still on the operating table.

constructed from thigh tissue. It was decided that she did not need chemotherapy or radiation, but she did go on tamoxifen, a drug that decreases the body's supply of estrogen—a factor in the development of cancerous tissue in the breast. There is no evidence of remaining malignant tissue as Susan approaches the "magical" five-year postsurgical survival date.

Breast cancer strikes nearly 230,000 women in the United States each year and takes about 39,500 lives (American Cancer Society, 2012d; National Cancer Institute, 2012). An estimated 410 men also die of breast cancer each year. It is not cancer in the breast that kills, but rather its spread to vital body parts, such as the brain, bones, lungs, or liver.

Physicians feel the breasts for lumps that may be breast cancer during clinical examination. Women with breast cancer have lumps in the breast, *but most lumps are not cancerous.* Most are either **cysts** or **benign** tumors called **fibroadenomas**. Breast cancer involves lumps in the breast that are **malignant**. Women can also detect lumps in their own breasts by means of breast self-examination (BSE), although some health professionals and organizations no longer recommend BSE, and BSE is not a substitute for regular clinical visits (National Cancer Society, 2012). **TRUTH OR FICTION REVISITED:** The American Cancer Society no longer recommends monthly breast self-examinations (BSEs). However, the "A Closer Look" feature provides instructions for women who choose to engage in breast self-examination.

More early cases of breast cancer are being detected because of an increased use of mammography, a kind of X-ray that detects cancerous lumps in the breast. Advances in early detection and treatment have led to increased rates of recovery among women from age 40 into their 70s (National Cancer Institute, 2012). On the other hand, health professionals admit that mammography has led to the detection and treatment of some localized cancers that might never have grown (National Cancer Institute, 2012). The American Cancer Society (2012d) counters that the majority of these small tumors would grow. In any event, the National Cancer Institute (2012) recommends that women aged 40 and above have mammograms every year or two, and that women in high-risk groups talk to their health-care providers about the possibility of more frequent mammograms. You can go to http://www.cancer.gov/cancertopics/factsheet/detection/mammograms for information on how much a mammogram costs, how low-income or uninsured women can obtaion free or low-cost mammograms, and where women can get good-quality mammograms, More on this later.

According to the National Cancer Institute (2012), the following factors increase the risk of breast cancer:

- Family history of breast cancer, especially if a mother, sister, or daughter has been diagnosed with it
- Inherited changes in certain genes, including the BRCA1 and BRCA2 genes (although this risk factor likely accounts for no more than 10% of cases)
- Higher breast density
- First menstrual period before the age of 12, menopause after age 55, delayed childbearing, and never having children—all of which increase lifetime exposure to estrogen
- Long-term use of menopausal hormone therapy (especially women who have used a combination of estrogen and progestin for more than five years)

5 Ⓣ🄵

Cysts Sac-like structures filled with fluid or diseased material.

Benign Doing little or no harm.

Fibroadenoma A benign, fibrous tumor.

Malignant Lethal; causing or likely to cause death.

A Closer Look

Breast Self-Examination

Regular visits to a physician and mammograms provide the best protection against breast cancer because they may lead to early detection and treatment. But many women find lumps themselves. It was once recommended that women conduct breast self-examinations (BSEs) at least once a month, but now the American Cancer Society considers BSEs to be optional. On the other hand, BSE may have psychological advantages for many women—empowering them to investigate their own bodies and to actively participate in their own disease prevention. Moreover, the American Cancer Society (2006) continues to recommend that women be *aware* of what is going on in their bodies. Breast self-exams would appear to be one way to cultivate awareness.

The following instructions for breast self-examination are based on American Cancer Society guidelines (see Figure 3.11). Additional material on breast self-examination may be obtained from the American Cancer Society by calling 1-800-ACS-2345. However, women are advised to initiate BSEs with a health professional in order to determine their baseline "lumpiness" and to learn the proper technique.

1. *In the shower.* Examine your breasts during your bath or shower; hands glide more easily over wet skin. Keep your fingers flat and move gently over every part of each breast. Use the right hand to examine the left breast and the left hand for the right breast. Check for any lump, hard knot, or thickening.

2. *Before a mirror:* Inspect your breasts with your arms at your sides. Next, raise your arms high overhead. Look for any changes in the contour of each breast, a swelling, dimpling of skin, or changes in the nipple. Then rest your palms on your hips and press down firmly to flex your chest muscles. Your left and right breasts will not exactly match. Few women's breasts are symmetrical. Regular inspection will allow you to determine what is normal for you and will give you confidence in your examination.

3. *Lying down.* To examine your right breast, put a pillow or folded towel under your right shoulder. Place your right arm behind your head. This position distributes breast tissue more evenly on the chest. With your left hand, fingers flat, press gently with the finger pads (the top thirds of the fingers) of the three middle fingers in small circular motions around an imaginary clock face. Begin at the outermost top of your right breast for 12 o'clock, then move to 1 o'clock, and so on around the circle back to 12 o'clock. A ridge of firm tissue in the lower curve of each breast is normal. Then move in 1 inch, toward the nipple. Keep circling to examine *every part of your breast,* including the nipple. This requires at least three more circles. Now slowly repeat the procedure on your left breast. Place the pillow beneath your left shoulder, place your left arm behind your head, and use the finger pads on your right hand.

After you examine your left breast fully, squeeze the nipple of each breast gently between your thumb and index finger. Any discharge, clear or bloody, should be reported to your doctor immediately.

CRITICAL THINKING

The American Cancer Society no longer recommends that women need to conduct breast self-examinations as a means of detecting breast cancer early. Do you believe that it is a good idea for women to do breast-self exams anyhow? Why or why not?

FIGURE 3.11 A Woman Examines Her Breast for Lumps

- Radiation therapy to the chest (as for Hodgkin lymphoma)
- Alcohol (the more you drink, the higher the risk)
- Use of DES (diethystilestrol)
- Being overweight or obese (fatty tissue produces estrogen)
- Physical *in*activity (exercise may reduce the risk of breast cancer by decreasing the amount of fatty tissue in the body)

In any event, the five-year survival rate for women whose breast cancers have not spread beyond the breast is about 93%, up from nearly 80% in the 1950s (American Cancer Society, 2012d). The five-year survival rate drops to about 80% if the cancer has spread to the surrounding region and to about 15% if it has spread to more distant sites.

 Does abortion increase a woman's risk of breast cancer? Some writers have speculated that because pregnancy decreases the risk of breast cancer, having an abortion will indirectly increase the risk (Malec, 2003). **TRUTH OR FICTION REVISITED:** However, an extensive review of carefully controlled studies does not find that abortion increases a woman's risk of breast cancer (Templeton & Grimes, 2011). Similarly, silicone breast implants have not been shown to increase the risk of breast cancer either—but they can lead to the development of scar tissue and obscure mammography readings (Lipworth et al., 2008).

Treatment Early detection of breast cancer offers many benefits. Smaller lumps are sometimes removed by lumpectomy, sparing the breast. More advanced cancers are likely to be treated by mastectomy.

A World of Diversity

African American Women and Breast Cancer

Overall, African Americans are more likely than European Americans to develop cancer. The case is somewhat different with breast cancer. As a group, African American women are somewhat less likely than European American women to develop breast cancer. However, when they do, they frequently do so at an earlier age (Simon, 2011). They tend to be diagnosed with the disease somewhat later, and they are also more likely to die from it (American Cancer Society, 2012d). Some aspects of the racial differences, such as the tendency to be diagnosed later, may reflect less access to health care. On the other hand, genetic factors are also likely to be involved. It is usually estrogen that causes the proliferation of breast cancer cells, and thus some drugs, such as tamoxifen, treat breast cancer by suppressing the body's supply of estrogen. However, African American are more likely to develop tumors that are "estrogen-receptor negative." That is, they develop rapidly even in the absence of estrogen (Simon, 2011). These tumors are highly aggressive—that is, they grow very rapidly—and are a major factor in the higher mortality rate for African American women (Simon, 2011).

African American Women and Breast Cancer. African American women are less likely than European American women to develop breast cancer, but when they do, the cancer tends to be more "aggressive" and lethal. Researchers generally believe that this racial difference is largely genetic.

Many drugs are also used to treat breast cancer, and others are in the research pipeline. For example, tamoxifen locks into the estrogen receptors of breast cancer cells, thereby blocking estrogen's stimulation of the cells to grow and proliferate. However, tamoxifen increases the risks of uterine cancer and of blood clots in the lungs, along with some other side effects. The risks of these side effects were lowest among women below the age of 50. The drug raloxifene has also been shown to reduce the risk of breast cancer (Cummings et al., 1999). Moreover, raloxifene does not appear to have the side effects associated with tamoxifen. Other drugs are also being studied for use against breast cancer. Ask your gynecologist for the latest research results and which drugs, if any, are right for you.

Many women who have had mastectomies have had surgical breast implants to replace the tissue that has been removed. Other women have breast implants to augment their breast size. Research suggests that breast implants probably have no effect on the probability of developing breast cancer, rheumatoid arthritis, and a number of other health problems, casting doubts on previous studies that had implicated them in the development of these problems. Again, consult your gynecologist for the latest findings.

The Menstrual Cycle

Menstruation is the cyclical bleeding that stems from the shedding of the uterine lining (endometrium). Menstruation takes place when a reproductive cycle has not led to the fertilization of an ovum. The word *menstruation* derives from the Latin *mensis*, meaning "month." The menstrual cycle averages 28 days.

The cycle is regulated by the hormones estrogen and progesterone and can be divided into four phases. The first phase, the *proliferative phase*, follows menstruation. During this phase, estrogen levels increase, causing the ripening of perhaps 10 to 20 ova (egg cells) within their follicles and the proliferation of endometrial tissue in the uterus. During the second phase of the cycle, estrogen reaches peak blood levels, and **ovulation** occurs. Normally only one ovum reaches maturity and is released by an ovary during ovulation. Then the third phase (the *secretory,* or *luteal,* phase) of the cycle begins. The luteal phase begins right after ovulation and continues through the beginning of the next cycle.

The term *luteal phase* is derived from **corpus luteum**, the name given to the follicle that releases an ovum. The corpus luteum functions as an **endocrine gland** and produces large amounts of progesterone and estrogen. Progesterone causes the endometrium to thicken, so that it will be able to support an embryo if fertilization occurs. If the ovum goes unfertilized, however, estrogen and progesterone levels plummet. The drops trigger the fourth phase, the *menstrual phase*, which leads to the beginning of a new cycle.

Ovulation may not occur in every menstrual cycle. *Anovulatory* ("without ovulation") cycles are most common in the years just after **menarche** (the first menstrual period). They may become frequent again in the years prior to menopause, but they may also occur irregularly at any age.

Although the menstrual cycle averages 28 days, variations among women, and in the same woman from month to month, are common. Girls' cycles are often irregular for a few years after menarche but later assume regular patterns. Variations from cycle to cycle tend to occur during the proliferative phase that precedes ovulation. Menstruation tends to reliably follow ovulation by about 14 days.

Hormones regulate the menstrual cycle, but psychological factors can affect the secretion of hormones. Stress can delay or halt menstruation. For example, many

Menstruation The cyclical bleeding that stems from the shedding of the uterine lining.

Ovulation The release of an ovum from an ovary.

Corpus luteum The follicle that has released an ovum and then produces copious amounts of progesterone and estrogen during the luteal phase of a woman's cycle.

Endocrine gland A ductless gland that releases its secretions directly into the bloodstream.

Menarche The first menstrual period.

Hypothalamus A structure near the center of the brain that is involved in regulating body temperature, motivation, and emotion.

Pituitary gland The gland that secretes growth hormone, prolactin, oxytocin, and others.

Hormone A substance secreted by an endocrine gland that regulates various body functions.

Testes The male gonads.

Testosterone The male sex hormone that fosters the development of male sex characteristics and is connected with the sex drive.

women in otherwise good health stopped menstruating during imprisonment in Nazi concentration camps during World War II (Ofer & Weitzman, 1998).

REGULATION OF THE MENSTRUAL CYCLE

The menstrual cycle involves finely tuned relationships between structures in the brain (the **hypothalamus** and the **pituitary gland**) and the ovaries and uterus. All these structures are parts of the endocrine system, which means that they secrete chemicals directly into the bloodstream (see Figure 3.12). The chemicals secreted by endocrine glands are called **hormones**. The ovaries and uterus are also reproductive organs.

The gonads—the ovaries in the female and the testes (or testicles) in the male—secrete sex hormones directly into the bloodstream. The female gonads, the ovaries, produce the sex hormones estrogen and progesterone. The male gonads, the **testes**, produce the male sex hormone **testosterone**. Males and females also produce relatively small amounts of the sex hormones of the other gender.

The hypothalamus is a pea-sized structure in the front part of the brain. It lies above the pituitary gland and below (hence the prefix *hypo-*, for "under") the thalamus. Despite its small size, it is involved in regulating many states of motivation, including hunger, thirst, aggression, and sex. For example, when the rear part of a male rat's hypothalamus is stimulated by an electric probe, the rat runs through its

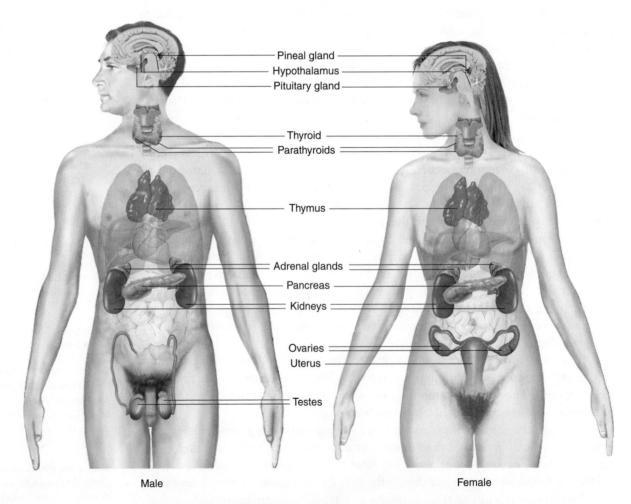

Male

Female

FIGURE 3.12 Major Glands of the Endocrine System. The endocrine system consists of glands that secrete chemicals called *hormones* directly into the bloodstream.

courting and mating sequence. It nibbles at a female's ears and at the back of her neck. When she responds, they copulate. Human sexuality is not so stereotyped or mechanical—although in the cases of people who have fallen into ruts, it may seem to be.

The pituitary gland, which is about the size of a pea, lies below the hypothalamus at the base of the brain. Because many pituitary secretions regulate other endocrine glands, the pituitary has also been called the *master gland*. Pituitary hormones regulate bone and muscle growth and urine production. Two pituitary hormones are active during pregnancy and motherhood: **prolactin**, which stimulates production of milk, and **oxytocin**, which stimulates uterine contractions in labor and the ejection of milk during nursing. The pituitary gland also produces **gonadotropins** (literally, "that which 'feeds' the gonads") that stimulate the ovaries: **follicle-stimulating hormone (FSH)** and **luteinizing hormone (LH)**. These hormones play key roles in regulating the menstrual cycle.

The hypothalamus receives information about bodily events through the nervous and circulatory systems. It monitors the blood levels of various hormones, including estrogen and progesterone, and releases a hormone called **gonadotropin-releasing hormone (Gn-RH)**, which stimulates the pituitary to release gonadotropins. Gonadotropins, in turn, regulate the activity of the gonads. It was once thought that the pituitary gland ran the show, but it is now known that the pituitary gland is regulated by the hypothalamus. Even the "master gland" must serve another.

PHASES OF THE MENSTRUAL CYCLE

The menstrual cycle has four stages or phases: proliferative, ovulatory, secretory, and menstrual (see Figure 3.13). It might seem logical that a new cycle begins with the first day of the menstrual flow, because this is the most clearly identifiable event of the cycle. Many women also count the days of the menstrual cycle beginning with the onset of menstruation. Biologically speaking, however, menstruation is really the culmination of the cycle. In fact, the cycle begins with the end of menstruation and the initiation of a series of biological events that lead to the maturation of an immature ovum in preparation for ovulation and possible fertilization.

The Proliferative Phase The first phase, or **proliferative phase**, begins with the end of menstruation and lasts about 9 or 10 days in an average 28-day cycle (see Figures 3.13 and 3.14). During this phase the endometrium develops, or "proliferates." This phase is also known as the *preovulatory* or *follicular* phase, because certain ovarian follicles mature and the ovaries prepare for ovulation.

Prolactin A pituitary hormone that stimulates production of milk.

Oxytocin A pituitary hormone that stimulates uterine contractions in labor and the ejection of milk during nursing.

Gonadotropins Pituitary hormones that stimulate the gonads.

Follicle-stimulating hormone (FSH) A gonadotropin that stimulates development of follicles in the ovaries.

Luteinizing hormone (LH) A gonadotropin that helps regulate the menstrual cycle by triggering ovulation.

Gonadotropin-releasing hormone (Gn-RH) A hormone secreted by the hypothalamus that stimulates the pituitary to release gonadotropins.

Proliferative phase The first phase of the menstrual cycle, which begins with the end of menstruation and lasts about nine or ten days. During this phase, the endometrium proliferates.

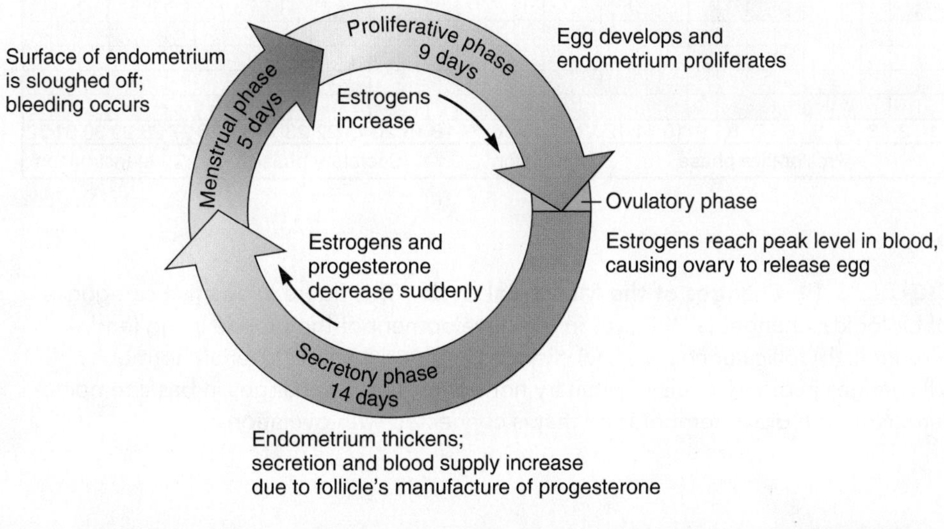

FIGURE 3.13 The Phases of the Menstrual Cycle. The menstrual cycle has proliferative, ovulatory, secretory (luteal), and menstrual phases.

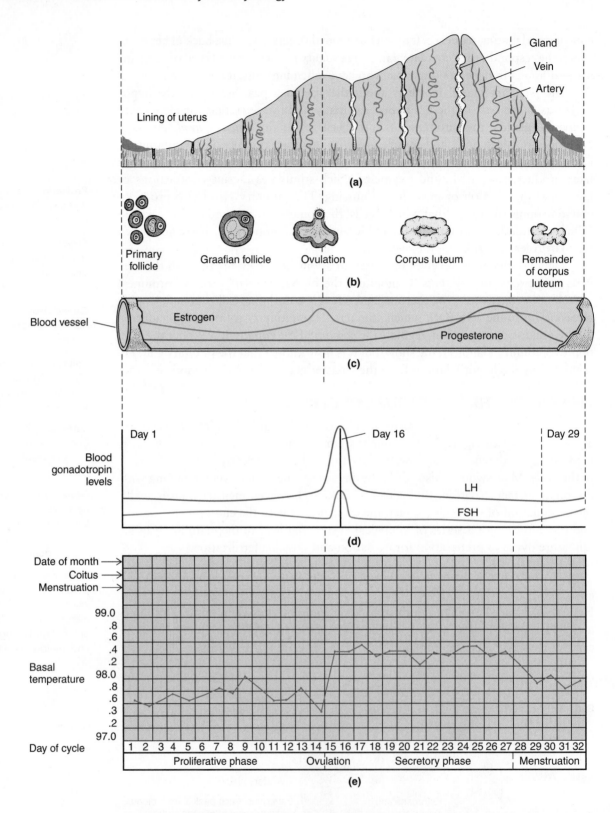

FIGURE 3.14 Changes of the Menstrual Cycle. This figure shows five categories of biological change: (a) changes in the development of the uterine lining (endometrium), (b) follicular changes, (c) changes in blood levels of ovarian hormones, (d) changes in blood levels of pituitary hormones, and (e) changes in basal temperature. Note the dip in temperature that is connected with ovulation.

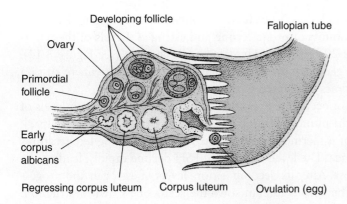

FIGURE 3.15 Maturation and Eventual Decomposition of an Ovarian Follicle. Many follicles develop and produce estrogen during the proliferative phase of the menstrual cycle. Usually only one, the graafian follicle, ruptures and releases an ovum. The graafian follicle then develops into the corpus luteum, which produces copious quantities of estrogen and progesterone. When fertilization does not occur, the corpus luteum decomposes.

Low levels of estrogen and progesterone are circulating in the blood as menstruation draws to an end. When the hypothalamus senses a low level of estrogen in the blood, it increases secretion of Gn-RH, which in turn triggers the pituitary gland to release a follicle-stimulating hormone (FSH). When FSH reaches the ovaries, it stimulates some follicles (perhaps 10 to 20) to begin to mature. As the follicles ripen, they begin to produce estrogen. Normally, however, only one of them—called the *graafian follicle*—will reach full maturity in the days just preceding ovulation. As the graafian follicle matures, it moves toward the surface of the ovary, where it will eventually rupture and release a mature egg (see Figures 3.14 and 3.15).

Estrogen causes the endometrium in the uterus to thicken to about 1/8 inch. Glands develop that would eventually nourish an embryo. Estrogen also stimulates the appearance of a thin cervical mucus. This mucus is alkaline and provides a hospitable, nutritious medium for sperm. The chances are thus increased that sperm that enter the female reproductive system at the time of ovulation will survive.

The Ovulatory Phase During ovulation, or the **ovulatory phase**, the graafian follicle ruptures and releases a mature ovum *near* a fallopian tube—not *into* a fallopian tube (see Figure 3.15). The other ripening follicles degenerate and are reabsorbed by the body. If two ova mature and are released during ovulation and both are fertilized, fraternal (nonidentical) twins will develop. Identical twins occur when one fertilized ovum divides into two separate **zygotes**.

Ovulation is set into motion when estrogen production reaches a critical level. The hypothalamus detects the high level of estrogen and triggers the pituitary to release copious amounts of FSH and LH (see Figures 3.14 and 3.15). The surge of LH triggers ovulation, which usually begins 12 to 24 hours after the level of LH in the body has reached its peak. The synthetic hormone *clomiphene* is chemically similar to LH and has been used by women who ovulate irregularly to induce reliable ovulation and thus increase the chances of conceiving.

A woman's *basal body temperature*, taken by oral or rectal thermometer, dips slightly at ovulation (see Figure 3.14) and rises by about 1°F on the day following ovulation. Many women use this information to help them conceive or avoid conceiving.

Some women have discomfort or cramping during ovulation, termed **mittelschmerz**. This condition is sometimes confused with appendicitis. Mittelschmerz, however, may occur on either side of the abdomen, depending on which ovary is releasing an ovum. A ruptured appendix always causes pain on the right side.

The Secretory Phase The phase following ovulation is called the *postovulatory* or **secretory phase**. Some people refer to it as the *luteal phase*, which reflects the name given to the ruptured (graafian) follicle—the *corpus luteum*. Figures 3.14 and 3.15 show the transformation of the graafian follicle into the corpus luteum.

Ovulatory phase The second stage of the menstrual cycle, during which a follicle ruptures and releases a mature ovum.

Zygote A fertilized ovum (egg cell).

Mittelschmerz Pain that occurs during ovulation, midway between menstrual periods. (German for "middle pain.")

Secretory phase The third phase of the menstrual cycle, which follows ovulation. Also referred to as the *luteal phase*, after the *corpus luteum*, which begins to secrete large amounts of progesterone and estrogen following ovulation.

Under the influence of LH, the corpus luteum, which has remained in the ovary, begins to produce large amounts of progesterone and estrogen. Levels of these hormones peak at around the 20th or 21st day of an average cycle (see Figure 3.14). These hormones cause the glands in the endometrium to secrete nutrients to sustain a fertilized ovum that becomes implanted in the uterine wall.

If implantation does not occur, the hypothalamus responds to the peak levels of progesterone by signaling the pituitary to stop producing LH and FSH. This feedback process is similar to that of a thermostat in a house reacting to rising temperatures by shutting down the furnace. The levels of LH and FSH decline rapidly, leading the corpus luteum to decompose. After its decomposition, levels of estrogen and progesterone fall precipitously. The corpus luteum sows the seeds of its own destruction: Its hormones signal the brain to shut down secretion of substances that maintain it.

The Menstrual Phase: An End and a Beginning The **menstrual phase** occurs when decreasing estrogen and progesterone levels can no longer sustain the uterine lining. The lining then disintegrates and is discharged from the body along with the menstrual flow.

The low estrogen levels of the menstrual phase signal the hypothalamus to release Gn-RH, which in turn stimulates the pituitary to secrete FSH. The follicle-stimulating hormone, in turn, prompts ovarian secretion of estrogen and the onset of another proliferative phase. Thus, a new cycle begins. The menstrual phase is a beginning as well as an end.

Menstrual flow contains blood from the endometrium (uterine lining), endometrial tissue, and cervical and vaginal mucus. Although the flow can appear persistent and last for five days or more, most women lose only a total of 2 or 3 ounces of blood (4 to 6 tablespoonfuls). A typical blood donor, by contrast, donates 16 ounces of blood at a sitting. Extremely heavy or prolonged (over a week) menstrual bleeding may reflect health problems and should be discussed with a health-care provider.

Menstrual phase The fourth phase of the menstrual cycle, during which the endometrium is sloughed off in the menstrual flow.

Real Students, Real Questions

Q *As a guy, I don't really know what girls go through day to day when they have their period. I also don't have a sister. Do they use more than one tampon a day? Do they leave the tampon in? Do all girls use tampons? I want to understand what they actually have to go through.*

A In developed nations today, many women use tampons or feminine napkins and change them several times a day. So-called superabsorbent tampons, which could be left in for much or most of a day, have gone out of fashion because of the risk of toxic shock syndrome. In most cases, there is probably also less blood than you would imagine. However, many females experience premenstrual or menstrual pain (especially cramping) and some irritability. Both are uncomfortable, but absolutely normal. At the time of the sexual revolution, sexologists and social critics minimized premenstrual syndrome (PMS) and other menstrual problems as a way of minimizing gender differences in general. Today, however, menstrual problems are accepted as widely occurring and reflective of female sexual anatomy and physiology. Now the question is, how can we help women who encounter such difficulties? It's not how can we pretend they don't exist.

Prior to 1933, women generally used external sanitary napkins or pads to absorb the menstrual flow. In that year, however, tampons were introduced. **Tampons** are inserted into the vagina and left in place to absorb menstrual fluid. Women who use tampons can swim without concern while menstruating, wear more revealing or comfortable apparel, and feel less burdened. Questions have arisen about whether or not tampons cause or exacerbate infections, such as *toxic shock syndrome (TSS)*, which is sometimes fatal. Signs of TSS include fever, headache, sore throat, vomiting, diarrhea, muscle aches, rash, and dizziness. Peeling skin, disorientation, and a plunge in blood pressure may follow. Toxic shock syndrome is caused by the *Staphylococcus aureus* ("staph") bacterium, which is most likely to overbreed when highly absorbent tampons are left in place for many hours. As a result, many women now use regular rather than superabsorbent tampons. Others change their tampons three or four times a day, or alternate them with sanitary napkins. Women are encouraged to consult their health-care providers about TSS.

SEX DURING MENSTRUATION

Many couples continue to have sex during menstruation; others abstain (Schneidewind-Skibbe et al., 2007). Some people abstain because of religious prohibitions. Others express concern about the "fuss" or the "mess" of the menstrual flow. **TRUTH** OR **FICTION** REVISITED: Despite traditional attitudes that associate menstruation with uncleanliness, there is no evidence that coitus during menstruation is physically harmful to either partner. Ironically, menstrual coitus may be helpful to the woman. The uterine contractions that occur during orgasm may help relieve cramping by dispelling blood congestion (Masters & Johnson, 1966). Orgasm from masturbation may have the same effect.

Women may be sexually aroused at any time during the menstrual cycle. The preponderance of the research evidence, however, points to a peak in sexual desire in women around the time of ovulation.

Human sexual patterns during the phases of the menstrual cycle reflect personal decisions and not just hormone fluctuations. Some couples may decide to increase their frequency of coitus at ovulation, in order to optimize the chances of conceiving, or to abstain during menstruation because of cultural or religious beliefs. Some may also increase their coital activity preceding menstruation to compensate for anticipated abstinence during menses, or to increase coital activity afterwards to make up for deprivation. In contrast, females of other species that are bound by the estrous cycle generally respond sexually only during **estrus**.

MENOPAUSE, PERIMENOPAUSE, AND THE CLIMACTERIC

Menopause, or the "change of life," is the cessation of menstruation. Menopause is a process that most commonly occurs between the ages of 46 and 50 and lasts for about two years. However, it may begin any time between the ages of 35 and 60.

Perimenopause refers to the beginning of menopause and is usually characterized by 3 to 11 months of amenorrhea (lack of menstruation) or irregular periods. Perimenopause ends with menopause. Menopause, in other words, is a specific event in a longer-term process known as the **climacteric** ("critical period"). The term *climacteric* specifically refers to the gradual decline in the reproductive capacity of the ovaries. The climacteric generally lasts about 15 years, from about ages 45 to 60. After age 35 or so, the menstrual cycles of many women shorten, from an average of 28 days to 25 days at age 40 and to 23 days by the mid-40s. By the end of her 40s, a woman's cycle may become erratic, with some periods close together and others missed. 👁

In menopause, the pituitary gland continues to pour normal levels of FSH and LH into the bloodstream; but, for reasons that are not well understood, the ovaries

👁⎯**Watch** the **Video**
Menopause
on **MyDevelopmentLab**

Tampon A plug made of cotton or a similar material that is inserted into the vagina to absorb the menstrual flow.

Estrus The period of time, as controlled by hormone levels, during which females in many species are most receptive to sexual activity.

Menopause The cessation of menstruation.

Perimenopause The beginning of menopause, as characterized by 3 to 11 months of amenorrhea or irregular periods.

Climacteric A long-term process, including menopause, that involves the gradual decline in the reproductive capacity of the ovaries.

A World of Diversity

Historical and Cross-Cultural Perspectives on Menstruation

In Peru, women speak of a "visit from Uncle Pepe," whereas in Samoa, menstruation is referred to as "the boogie man." One of the more common epithets for menstruation is "the curse." The Fulani of Upper Volta in Africa use a term that translates "to see dirt." Nationalism also rises to the call, with some nations blaming "the curse" on their historical enemies. The French once dubbed menstruation "the English" and its onset "the English are coming."

It is a common folk belief that menstruating women are contaminated. Men may thus avoid contact with menstruating women. To prevent their contaminating others, menstruating women in tribal societies have been dispatched to huts on the fringe of the village. In the traditional Navajo Native American culture, for instance, menstruating women would be consigned to huts that were set apart from other living quarters. In many Islamic societies, the menstrual flow is considered unclean, and menstruating women are not permitted to pray or enter a mosque.

Women in industrialized nations are not consigned to special huts, but throughout the history of Western culture, menstruation has been seen as unclean, contaminating, and sometimes even magical.

TRUTH OR FICTION **8**

REVISITED: The ancient Romans believed that menstrual blood soured wine and killed crops. In 77 CE, the Roman Pliny the Elder summed up Roman misbeliefs about menstrual blood in his *Natural History*:

> Contact with it turns new wine sour, crops touched by it become barren, grafts die, seeds in gardens are dried up, the fruit of trees falls off … [The] edge of steel and the gleam of ivory are dulled, hives of bees die, even bronze and iron are at once seized by rust, and a horrible smell fills the air; to taste it drives dogs mad and infects their bites with an incurable poison.

Ancient societies—and some contemporary ones—have limited understanding of bodily processes, or else they rely on tradition more than science. Science teaches that there is no medical basis for isolating menstruating women or avoiding sex during menstruation.

We might laugh off these misconceptions as folly and ignorance, if it were not for their profound effect on women. Women who believe the myths about menstruation may see themselves as unclean and endure anxiety, depression, and lowered self-esteem. Negative cultural beliefs concerning menstruation may also exacerbate menstrual distress.

---

gradually lose their capacity to respond. The ovaries no longer ripen egg cells or produce the sex hormones estrogen and progesterone.

The deficit in estrogen may lead to a number of unpleasant perimenopausal sensations, such as night sweats and hot flashes (suddenly feeling hot) and hot flushes (suddenly looking reddened) (Hunter, 2011). Hot flashes and flushes may alternate with cold sweats, in which a woman feels suddenly cold and clammy. Anyone who has experienced "cold feet" or hands from anxiety or fear will understand how dramatic the shifting patterns of blood flow can be. Hot flashes and flushes stem largely from "waves" of dilation of blood vessels across the face and upper body. All of these sensations reflect *vasomotor instability*. That is, there are disruptions in the body mechanisms that dilate or constrict the blood vessels to maintain an even body temperature. Additional signs of estrogen deficiency include dizziness, headaches, pains in the joints, sensations of tingling in the hands or feet, burning or itchy skin, and heart palpitations. The skin usually becomes drier. There is some loss of breast tissue and decreased vaginal lubrication during sexual arousal. Women may also encounter sleep problems, such as awakening more frequently at night and having difficulty falling back to sleep. Many perimenopausal women also experience migraine headaches (Nappi & Nappi, 2012).

Long-term estrogen deficiency has been linked to brittleness and porosity of the bones, known as **osteoporosis**. Bones break more readily, and some women develop "dowager's hump" (Lindsay, 2011). Osteoporosis can be handicapping, even life-threatening. The increased brittleness of the bones increases the risk of serious fractures, especially of the hip, and many older women never recover from them (Lindsay, 2011). Estrogen deficiency can also impair cognitive functioning and feelings of psychological well-being (Sherwin, 2012). 👁

Osteoporosis A condition caused by estrogen deficiency that is characterized by a decline in bone density, such that bones become porous and brittle.

👁 **Watch the Video**
Cognitive Changes Secondary to Menopause in Middle Adulthood on **MyDevelopmentLab**

HORMONE REPLACEMENT THERAPY: GOOD MEDICINE OR MENACE?

Candace tried almost everything to manage her discomforts of perimenopause: a chiropractor, acupuncture, anti-anxiety pills, soy tablets, and herbal remedies. Finally, she relented and followed her doctor's recommendation that she use **hormone replacement therapy (HRT)**. The doctor's believed that for Candace, age 51, the immediate benefits, outweighed the risks (Rabin, 2006).

Some women with severe physical symptoms, like Candace, have been helped by HRT medication, which typically consists of synthetic estrogen and progesterone. The hormones are used to offset the losses of their naturally occurring counterparts. Hormone replacement therapy may help reduce the hot flushes and other symptoms brought about by hormonal deficiencies during menopause (Hunter, 2011). There is also evidence that estrogen replacement lowers women's risks of osteoporosis (Lindsay, 2011). The connection between estrogen and colon cancer is unclear (Clendenen et al., 2009).

Yet, HRT is controversial. Although it has been helpful to many women, the Women's Health Initiative study of some 16,600 postmenopausal women aged 50 to 79 found that exposure to a combination of estrogen and progestin appears to increase the risk of breast cancer, strokes, and blot clots, and did not have a protective effect on the heart (Chlebowski et al., 2003). (Progestin is used along with estrogen because estrogen alone exposes women to a greater risk of uterine cancer.) In addition to stimulating the growth of breast cancer, the combination of hormones also makes the tumors harder to detect, causing dangerous delays in diagnosis (National Cancer Institute, 2012). During the course of the Chlebowski study, of 8,506 women on HRT, 199 developed invasive breast cancers, as compared with 150 cases among the 8,102 women taking a placebo (Chlebowski et al., 2003). Also, despite having yearly mammograms, 25.4% of the women who developed cancer while using HRT had cancers that had begun to metastasize, as compared with 16% of those taking the placebo.

Although estrogen stimulates proliferation of breast cancer cells, research suggests that women who have had hysterectomies might actually have a lower risk of breast cancer (Anderson et al., 2012). The researchers point out the importance of distinguishing between hormone therapy that is estrogen-only versus estrogen plus preogestin.

Hormone replacement therapy also appears to increase the risk of lung cancer in postmenopausal women who smoke or smoked (Chlebowski et al., 2009). Rowan Chlebowski, the first author of the study that detected this association, writes, "The clear message is don't smoke and take hormones."

Levels of LDL ("bad cholesterol") are known to rise among menopausal women, while levels of HDL ("good cholesterol") decrease (Altunkaynak et al., 2012). A number of studies suggest that HRT raises levels of HDL and lowers levels of LDL (Altunkaynak et al., 2012). Because high levels of LDL are connected with cardiovascular disease, it was believed that HRT would reduce the risk of heart disease in postmenopausal women. Although this view was supported in research following 120,000 nurses over the years, the women in the Hormone Replacement Therapy trial of the Women's Health Initiative apparently ran a slightly *greater* risk of heart attacks and strokes (Fletcher & Colditz, 2002).

Because of these concerns, the number of women using HRT has fallen. But more recent research from the Nurses Health Study (Grodstein et al., 2006) suggests that the women in the Women's Health Initiative trials might have been too old to profit from HRT—an average age of 64 when the average age of menopause is closer to 51. The arteries of women in their 50s are more elastic than those of women in their 60s, and estrogen might help them remain supple and reduce the buildup of plaque. But women in their 60s generally have less flexible arteries and

Osteoporosis: Not for Women Only. Men make up about one osteoporosis patient in five in the United States. Men are at lower risk for osteoporosis because they generally have larger, stronger bones than women do. Estrogen replacement lowers a woman's risk of osteoporosis, but there are some other risks in hormone replacement therapy (HRT).

Hormone replacement therapy (HRT) The administration of hormones such as estrogen and progestin to alleviate health problems associated with the loss of natural hormones.

A Closer Look

Myths about Menopause

Menopause is certainly a major life change for most women. For many women, menopause symbolizes the many midlife issues they face, including changes in appearance, sexuality, and health. And yet, exactly what types of changes do we find? Many of us harbor misleading ideas about menopause—ideas that can be harmful to women. Consider the following myths and the realities. To which myths have you fallen prey?

- *Menopause is abnormal.* Of course not. Menopause is a normal development in women's lives.

- *The medical establishment considers menopause a disease.* No longer. Menopause is described as a "deficiency syndrome" today, referring to the decline in secretion of estrogen and progesterone. Unfortunately, the term *deficiency* also has negative meanings.

- *After menopause, women need complete replacement of estrogen.* Not necessarily. Some estrogen continues to be produced by the adrenal glands, fatty tissue, and the brain.

- *Menopause is accompanied by depression and anxiety.* Sometimes but not necessarily. A number of reviews of the literature have found no consistent relationship between menopause and these psychological symptoms. A Dutch study followed 2,103 females aged 46 to 54 for five years. During this time, the number of women who reached postmenopausal status doubled, and the percentage of women reporting depression increased from 18.5 to 23.7% (Maartens et al., 2002). The increase is unlikely to be due to chance, but more than three out of four women in the study did not report significant levels of depression or anxiety at any time during the experience of menopause.

- *At menopause, women experience debilitating hot flashes.* **TRUTH** OR **FICTION** (T/F) **9** REVISITED: Sometimes but not necessarily. Many women do not have hot flashes at menopause.

Among those who do, the flashes are often mild. But let us recognize that some women do have disturbing hot flashes; we advise them to consult their gynecologists.

- *A woman who has had a hysterectomy will not undergo menopause afterward.* Actually, it depends on whether the ovaries (the major producers of estrogen) were also removed. If they were not, menopause should proceed normally.

- *Menopause signals an end to a woman's sexual appetite.* **TRUTH** OR **FICTION** (T/F) **10** REVISITED: It is not true that menopause signals an end to women's sexual appetite (Gass et al., 2011). In fact, some women feel newly sexually liberated because of the separation of sex from pregnancy.

- *A woman's general level of activity is lower after menopause.* Many postmenopausal women become peppier and more assertive.

CRITICAL THINKING

Why might a person be justified in complaining that she or he is confused about the evidence concerning the effects of HRT?

some plaque. Because estrogen can increase the clotting of blood, it might pose a risk to the older women, even if it helps the younger women.

What can we conclude? Research results on the benefits and dangers of HRT are mixed, and women considering HRT are well advised to explore the latest findings with their health-care providers. They might also consider alternatives. Selective serotonin reuptake inhibitors (SSRIs), such as Lexapro, Prozac, and Zocor are of help (Utian, 2012). Women using SSRIs to treat hot flashes usually take half the dose used to treat depression, which is their main usage, although they are also helpful with premenstrual syndrome (PMS), premenstrual dysphoric disorder (PMDD), eating disorders, and other problems.

Vaginal dryness can be treated with estrogens that are used locally—that is, placed in the vagina rather than the bloodstream, as hormones usually are. Creams (e.g., Estrace), suppositories (Vagifem), and a plastic ring (Estring) are available for this purpose.

Drinking milk, which is high in calcium, increases bone density among girls and is likely to help prevent against osteoporosis later in life. Calcium supplements and the bisphosphonates (Actonel or Fosamax) also help maintain bone strength.

Some women use HRT to help get through the years leading up to menopause and then stop it. At this time it appears that the one thing we can predict is that different health-care providers are likely to have different views on the matter.

Menstrual Problems

Although menstruation is a natural biological process, the majority of women experience some discomfort prior to or during menstruation (Studd & Nappi, 2012). The Self-Assessment on page 90 concerns common premenstrual symptoms. The problems we explore in this section include dysmenorrhea, mastalgia, menstrual migraine headaches, amenorrhea, premenstrual syndrome (PMS), and premenstrual dysphoric disorder (PMDD).

DYSMENORRHEA

Pain or discomfort during menstruation—**dysmenorrhea**—is the most common menstrual problem. Most women at some time have at least mild menstrual pain or discomfort, so it is perfectly normal, even if annoying. Pelvic cramps are the most common manifestation of dysmenorrhea. They may be accompanied by headache, backache, nausea, or bloated feelings. Women who develop severe cases usually do so within a few years of menarche. **Primary dysmenorrhea** refers to menstrual pain or discomfort in the absence of known organic pathology. Women with **secondary dysmenorrhea** have identified organic problems that are believed to cause their menstrual problems. Their pain or discomfort is caused by, or secondary to, these problems. Endometriosis, pelvic inflammatory disease, and ovarian cysts are just a few of the organic disorders that can give rise to secondary dysmenorrhea.

Evidence is accumulating, however, that supposed primary dysmenorrhea is often secondary to hormonal changes, although the precise causes have not been delineated. For example, menstrual cramps sometimes decrease dramatically after childbirth, as a result of the massive hormonal changes that occur with pregnancy. Women who have been pregnant report a lower incidence of menstrual pain but a higher incidence of premenstrual symptoms and menstrual discomfort.

Menstrual cramps appear to result from uterine spasms that may be brought about by copious secretion of hormones called **prostaglandins**. Prostaglandins apparently cause muscle fibers in the uterine wall to contract, as during labor. Most contractions go unnoticed, but powerful, persistent contractions are discomfiting in themselves and may temporarily deprive the uterus of oxygen, another source of distress. Women with more intense menstrual discomfort apparently produce higher quantities of prostaglandins. Prostaglandin-inhibiting drugs, such as ibuprofen, indomethacin, and aspirin, are often helpful. Menstrual pain may also be secondary to endometriosis.

Pelvic pressure and bloating may be traced to pelvic *edema* (Greek for "swelling")—the congestion of fluid in the pelvic region. Fluid retention can lead to a gain of several pounds, sensations of heaviness, and **mastalgia**—a swelling of the breasts that sometimes causes premenstrual discomfort. Masters and Johnson (1966) noted that orgasm can help relieve menstrual discomfort by reducing the pelvic congestion that spawns bloating and pressure. Orgasm may also increase the menstrual flow and shorten this phase of the cycle.

Headaches frequently accompany menstrual discomfort. Most headaches (in both females and males) stem from simple muscle tension, notably in the shoulders, the back of the neck, and the scalp. Pelvic discomfort may cause muscle contractions, therefore contributing to the tension that produces headaches. Women who are tense about their menstrual flow are thus candidates for muscle tension headaches. Migraine headaches may arise from changes in the blood flow in the brain, however. Migraines are typically limited to one side of the head and are often accompanied by visual difficulties.

Dysmenorrhea Pain or discomfort during menstruation.

Primary dysmenorrhea Menstrual pain or discomfort that occurs in the absence of known organic problems.

Secondary dysmenorrhea Menstrual pain or discomfort that is caused by identified organic problems.

Prostaglandins Hormones that cause muscle fibers in the uterine wall to contract, as during labor.

Mastalgia A swelling of the breasts that sometimes causes premenstrual discomfort.

AMENORRHEA

Amenorrhea is the absence of menstruation and is a primary sign of infertility. **Primary amenorrhea** describes the absence of menstruation in a woman who has not menstruated at all by about the age of 16 or 17. **Secondary amenorrhea** describes delayed or absent menstrual periods in women who have had regular periods in the past. Amenorrhea has various causes, including abnormalities in the structures of the reproductive system, hormonal abnormalities, growths such as cysts and tumors, and psychological problems, such as stress. Amenorrhea is normal during pregnancy and following menopause. Amenorrhea is also a symptom of **anorexia nervosa,** an eating disorder characterized by an intense fear of putting on weight and a refusal to eat enough to maintain a normal body weight, which often results in extreme (and sometimes life-threatening) weight loss. Hormonal changes that accompany emaciation are believed responsible for the cessation of menstruation. Amenorrhea may also occur in women who exercise strenuously, such as competitive long-distance runners (Berga & Naftolin, 2012). It is unclear whether the cessation of menstruation in female athletes is due to the effects of strenuous exercise itself, to related physical factors such as low body fat, to the stress of intensive training, or to a combination of factors.

PREMENSTRUAL SYNDROME (PMS) AND PREMENSTRUAL DYSPHORIC DISORDER (PMDD)

The term **premenstrual syndrome (PMS)** describes the combination of biological and psychological symptoms that may affect women during the 4- to 6-day interval that precedes their menses each month. For many women, premenstrual symptoms persist during menstruation. **Premenstrual dysphoric disorder (PMDD)** is a more technical term used as a diagnostic category by the American Psychiatric Association (2012) in its *Diagnostic and Statistical Manual (DSM)*. PMDD is more severe than PMS, and is characterized by the following symptoms:

- Depressed mood, as evidenced by crying and feelings of sadness, hopelessness, or worthlessness
- Withdrawal from activities that are usually sought out and enjoyed
- Difficulty concentrating and paying sustained attention to tasks
- Fatigue, lack of energy
- Feelings of tension and anxiety, being "on edge"
- Feelings of irritability or anger, possibly causing conflict with family members and others
- Feeling overwhelmed, that life is out of control
- Significant changes in appetite that can lead to binge eating or the craving of particular foods and often result in weight gain
- Problems in sleeping: sleeping too much (hypersomnia) or too little (insomnia)
- A variety of physical problems may also be present, such as swelling or tenderness of the breasts, pain in muscle, pain in joints, migraine headaches, and feeling bloated

Unlike PMS, PMDD is a persistent problem. The American Psychiatric Association does not apply the diagnosis unless the woman has experienced the problem during most menstrual cycles over a period of a year. Moreover, a number of the symptoms must be present. The Association also requires that the symptoms impair the woman's life, perhaps her functioning at work or in an academic pursuit, perhaps in her social or family relationships.

The term PMDD is not always used precisely, and some make the mistake of confusing it with PMS. But the diagnosis of PMDD requires that five or more of the following symptoms be present most of the time during the week before the period and end within a few days after the period begins. At least one symptom must be one of

Amenorrhea The absence of menstruation.

Primary amenorrhea Lack of menstruation in a woman who has never menstruated.

Secondary amenorrhea Lack of menstruation in a woman who has previously menstruated.

Anorexia nervosa A psychological disorder of eating characterized by intense fear of putting on weight and refusal to eat enough to maintain normal body weight.

Premenstrual syndrome (PMS) A combination of physical and psychological symptoms (e.g., anxiety, depression, irritability, weight gain from fluid retention, and abdominal discomfort) that regularly afflicts many women during the four- to six-day interval that precedes their menses each month.

Premenstrual dysphoric disorder (PMDD) A diagnosis used by the American Psychiatric Association to describe cases of PMS that are characterized by severe changes in mood and impairment of functioning at work, at school or in social relationships.

the first four. In addition, in order to diagnose PMDD, the DSM requires that symptoms have been present for most menstrual cycles over the past year and that they notably impair functioning at work or school or in social activities and relationships.

Nearly three women in four experience some premenstrual symptoms (Studd & Nappi, 2012). The most common symptoms of PMS are minor psychological discomfort, muscle tension, and aches or pains (Studd & Nappi, 2012). The great majority of cases involve mild to moderate discomfort. Only a small minority of women report menstrual symptoms severe enough to impair their social, academic, or occupational functioning. The causes of PMS and PMDD are unclear, but researchers are looking to possible relationships between menstrual problems, including PMS and PMDD, and chemical imbalances in the body. Researchers have yet to find differences in levels of estrogen or progesterone between women with PMDD and those with PMS or no symptoms (Bäckström et al., 2003), but who have possibly an abnormal response to these hormones (Schmidt et al., 1998). Also, PMS and PMDD appear to be linked with imbalances in neurotransmitters such as serotonin (Studd & Nappi, 2012). (Neurotransmitters are the chemical messengers in the nervous system.) Serotonin imbalances are also linked to changes in appetite. Women with PMS and PMDD show greater increases of appetite during the luteal phase than other women do. Another neurotransmitter, gamma-aminobutyric acid (GABA), also appears to be involved in premenstrual problems; medicines that affect the levels of GABA help many women with these problems (Bäckström et al., 2003). PMS and PMDD may well be caused by a complex interaction between ovarian hormones and neurotransmitters (Studd & Nappi, 2012).

A couple of generations ago, premenstrual disorders were seen as "a woman's lot"—something women must put up with. No longer. Today there are many treatment options. These include exercise; dietary control (for example, eating several small meals a day rather than two or three large meals, limiting salt and sugar, supplementing diet with vitamins); hormone treatments (usually progestin); and medications that reduce anxiety or increase the amount of serotonin in the nervous system. You can get in touch with whether you have PMS and how the symptoms affect you by completing the nearby Self-Assessment. If you have severe or disabling symptoms, you may be diagnosable with PMDD. What can women do about PMS or PMDD? Check with your gynecologist and consider the suggestions in the following section.

HOW TO HANDLE MENSTRUAL DISCOMFORT

Most women experience some menstrual discomfort. Women with persistent menstrual distress may profit from the suggestions listed here. Researchers are exploring the effectiveness of these techniques in controlled studies. You might consider trying the suggestions that sound right for you—all of them, if you wish. Try them for a few months to see if you reap any benefits.

- Don't blame yourself! Menstrual problems were once erroneously attributed to women's "hysterical" nature. This is nonsense. Menstrual problems appear, in large part, to reflect hormonal variations or chemical fluctuations in the brain during the menstrual cycle. Researchers have not yet fully identified all the causal elements and patterns, but their lack of knowledge does not mean that women who have menstrual problems are hysterical.
- Keep a menstrual calendar so that you can track your menstrual symptoms systematically and identify patterns.
- Develop strategies for dealing with days that you experience the greatest distress—strategies that will help enhance your pleasure and minimize the stress affecting you on those days. Activities that distract you from your menstrual discomfort may be helpful. Go see a movie or get into that novel you've been meaning to read.

CRITICAL THINKING
Critical thinkers avoid oversimplification. Explain how PMS and PMDD can have complex causes that involve both biological and psychological factors. Is there any significance in the fact that the research suggests that both medication and cognitive-behavioral therapy can be of help to women with PMS or PMDD?

Self-Assessment

Do You Experience PMS or PMDD?

Premenstrual syndrome (PMS) is a group of symptoms that may affect women for the period of about eight days prior to and during menstruation. Research evidence suggests that most women have some of these symptoms but that most often they are not severe enough to seriously impair daily functioning. When they do, these symptoms may qualify as premenstrual dysphoric disorder (PMDD). Women who have severe, even disabling, symptoms are advised to discuss them with their gynecologists.

Do you experience PMS or PMDD? Complete the following self-assessment to gain insight into whether you do.

Directions: Following is a list of psychological and physical symptoms of PMS and PMDD. Indicate whether you encounter these symptoms and how severe they are by checking the appropriate box. Then turn to the scoring key in the Appendix to assess your responses.

Part I: Psychological Symptoms of PMS	Do not have	Mild	Moderate	Severe	Disabling
Accident prone					
Depression					
Anxiety					
Panic					
Mood swings					
Crying spells					
Sudden anger					
Irritability					
Loss of interest in usual activities					
Difficulty concentrating					
Lack of energy					
Excessive use of alcohol					
Frustration					
Overeating or cravings for certain foods					
Insomnia or excessive sleeping					
Feelings of being out of control or over-whelmed					
Paranoia					

Part II: Physical Symptoms of PMS	Do not have	Mild	Moderate	Severe	Disabling
Migraines					
Breast tenderness					
Joint or muscle pain					
Stiffness					
Weight gain					
Feeling bloated					
Blurred vision					
Poor motor coordination					
Exhaustion					
Dark circles under the eyes					
Runny eyes					

- Consider whether you harbor self-defeating attitudes toward menstruation that might compound distress. Do close relatives or friends see menstruation as an illness, a time of "pollution," a "dirty thing"? Have you adopted any of these attitudes—if not verbally, then in ways that affect your behavior, such as by restricting your social activities during your period?

- See a gynecologist about your concerns, especially if you have severe symptoms. Severe menstrual symptoms can be secondary to medical disorders such as endometriosis and pelvic inflammatory disease (PID). Check it out.

- Ask your gynecologist about oral contraceptives that reduce the number of menstrual periods to four per year (Seasonale or Seasonique) or one per year (Lybrel). Still others shorten periods.

- Develop nutritious eating habits—and continue them throughout the entire cycle (that means always). Consider limiting intake of alcohol, caffeine, fats, salt, and sweets, especially during the days preceding menstruation. A low-fat, vegetarian diet may reduce the duration and intensity of premenstrual symptoms.

- Eat several smaller meals (or nutritious snacks) throughout the day, rather than a few highly filling meals.

- Some women find that vigorous exercise—jogging, swimming, bicycling, fast walking, dancing, skating, even jumping rope—helps relieve premenstrual and menstrual discomfort. Evidence suggests that exercise helps to relieve and possibly prevent menstrual discomfort (Daley, 2009).

- Check with your doctor about vitamin and mineral supplements (such as calcium and magnesium).

- Ibuprofen (brand names Medipren, Advil, Motrin, etc.) and other medicines available over the counter may be helpful for cramping. Prescription drugs such as anti-anxiety drugs (e.g., alprazolam) and anti-depressant drugs (selective serotonin reuptake inhibitors or SSRIs) may also be of help. Anti-depressants affect levels of neurotransmitters in a way that can be helpful for women with PMS or PMDD. Their benefits do not mean that women with PMS or PMDD are depressed. Ask your doctor for a recommendation.

- Remind yourself that menstrual problems are time limited. Don't worry about getting through life or a career. Just get through the next couple of days.

In this chapter we have explored female sexual anatomy and physiology. In the following chapter, we turn our attention to the male.

Seasonale. Women who use Seasonale have only four periods a year, thus reducing the incidence of any menstrual discomfort.

Exercise as a Strategy for Coping with Menstrual Discomfort. Some women find that vigorous exercise helps relieve menstrual discomfort. There are many other strategies; check with your doctor.

Chapter Review

✔•—[Study] and **Review** on **MyDevelopmentLab**

LO1 **Describe the external female sex organs and their functions**

The mons veneris is a mound of fatty tissue that covers the pubic area. The labia majora are large folds of skin that run downward from the mons along the sides of the vulva. The labia minora are hairless membranes that surround the urethral and vaginal openings. The clitoris is highly sensitive to sexual sensation but not directly involved in reproduction. The vestibule contains the openings to the vagina and the urethra. Urine passes from the female's body through the urethral opening. The vaginal opening, or introitus, lies below the urethral opening.

LO2 **Describe the internal female sex organs, their functions, and health problems that may affect them**

Menstrual flow and babies pass from the uterus to the outer world through the vagina. During coitus, the vagina contains the penis. The cervix contains an opening called the os. Cervical cancer is connected with HPV and detectable via a Pap test. The uterus is the pear-shaped organ in which a fertilized ovum implants and develops until birth. The uterine lining is called the endometrium. Ova pass through the fallopian tubes on their way to the uterus and are normally fertilized within these tubes. The ovaries produce ova and the sex hormones estrogen and progesterone.

LO3 **Describe the composition and functions of the breasts**

The breasts are secondary sex characteristics that contain mammary glands that make it possible for women to nurse children.

LO4 **Discuss risk factors for and detection and treatment of breast cancer**

Women with breast cancer have lumps in the breast, but most lumps are benign. Risk factors include family history, *BRCA1* or *BRCA2* mutations, exposure to estrogen, and alcohol.

LO5 **Describe the regulation and the phases of the menstrual cycle**

Menstruation is the cyclical bleeding that stems from the shedding of the endometrium when a reproductive cycle has not led to the fertilization of an ovum. The cycle has four phases: proliferative, ovulatory, secretory, and menstrual. During the first phase, ova ripen within their follicles and endometrial tissue proliferates. During the second phase, ovulation occurs. During the third phase, the corpus luteum produces copious amounts of progesterone and estrogen that cause the endometrium to thicken. If the ovum goes unfertilized, a plunge in estrogen and progesterone levels triggers the fourth, or menstrual, phase.

LO6 **Define and discuss menopause, perimenopause, and the climacteric**

Menopause is the cessation of menstruation. Perimenopause is the beginning of menopause and is characterized by irregular periods or amenorrhea. The climacteric is a multiyear process marked by declining levels of estrogen and ending in menopause. Hormone replacement therapy offsets losses of estrogen and progesterone and can help women with perimenopausal and postmenopausal symptoms, including night sweats, hot flashes, hot flushes, dry skin, loss of breast tissue, and decreased vaginal lubrication. But HRT has been linked to an increased risk of breast and endometrial cancers.

LO7 **Define menstrual problems and discuss what can be done about them**

Dysmenorrhea—painful menstruation—is the most common menstrual problem, and pelvic cramps are the most common symptom. Amenorrhea—the lack of menstruation—can be caused by abnormalities in the structures of the reproductive system, hormonal abnormalities, cysts, tumors, and stress. Premenstrual syndrome (PMS) can be characterized by depression and anxiety, irritability, difficulty concentrating, migraines, breast tenderness, and bloating. Premenstrual dysphoric disorder (PMDD) is like a severe case of PMS, said to occur when symptoms are extreme and impair functioning in school, at work, or in relationships.

Test Your Learning

1. HPV is connected with
   (a) cervical cancer.
   (b) endometrial cancer.
   (c) breast cancer.
   (d) ovarian cancer.

2. Urine passes through the
   (a) uterus.
   (b) urethra.
   (c) cervix.
   (d) introitus.

3. Menstrual cramps are thought to be caused by
   (a) estrogen.
   (b) progesterone.
   (c) prostaglandins.
   (d) testosterone.

4. Hot flashes and flushes stem largely from waves of dilation of
   (a) the cervix.
   (b) blood vessels.
   (c) ovarian follicles.
   (d) muscles.

5. The endometrium develops during the _____ phase of the menstrual cycle.
   (a) ovulatory
   (b) menstrual
   (c) secretory
   (d) proliferative

6. A surge of _____ triggers ovulation.
   (a) follicle stimulating hormone
   (b) luteinizing hormone

   (c) oxytocin
   (d) prolactin

7. The _____ is the only organ whose only known purpose is the experiencing of sexual pleasure.
   (a) cervix
   (b) vagina
   (c) breast
   (d) clitoris

8. For women who obtain HRT, combining estrogen with _____ lessens the risk of endometrial cancer.
   (a) progestin
   (b) prolactin
   (c) oxytocin
   (d) prostaglandins

9. Skeptics concerning the G spot are most likely to argue that
   (a) the anterior vaginal wall is not sensitive to erotic stimulation.
   (b) the G spot is not a discrete sex organ.
   (c) no research has been done into the existence of the G spot.
   (d) *G spot* is a silly name for a sex organ.

10. When the hypothalamus senses a low level of estrogen in the blood, it increases secretion of Gn-RH, which in turn triggers the pituitary gland to release
    (a) FSH.
    (b) LH.
    (c) the graafian follicle.
    (d) prolactin.

Answers: 1. a; 2. b; 3. c; 4. b; 5. d; 6. b; 7. d; 8. a; 9. b; 10. a

My Life, My Sexuality

Taking Charge of My Sexual Health

*Explore this **My Life, My Sexuality** feature by scanning this QR code with your mobile device. If you don't already have one, you may download a free QR scanner for your device wherever smartphone apps are sold. You can also view this feature in MyDevelopmentLab, along with an accompanying critical thinking assignment.*

You may think that your health—including your sexual health—should be taken care of by your doctor, and in many ways it should. Yet it is best for you to see yourself as being in charge of your sexual health. You're your own best expert about yourself, and you have the capacity to digest the knowledge in this book and other sources to decide how you will use it to obtain and maintain maximum sexual health. Scan the code to go online for specific advice as to how you can maximize your sexual health.

4 Male Sexual Anatomy and Physiology

Learning Objectives

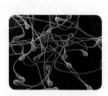

EXTERNAL SEX ORGANS

LO1 Describe the external male sex organs and their functions
LO2 Discuss the pros and cons of circumcision

INTERNAL SEX ORGANS

LO3 Describe the internal male sex organs and their functions

HEALTH PROBLEMS OF THE UROGENITAL SYSTEM

LO4 Discuss urethritis
LO5 Discuss testicular cancer
LO6 Discuss benign prostate hyperplasia
LO7 Discuss prostatitis
LO8 Discuss prostate cancer

MALE SEXUAL FUNCTIONS

LO9 Explain how erection occurs
LO10 Explain how ejaculation occurs

MY LIFE, MY SEXUALITY: WHAT DO I DO ABOUT MY HEALTH NEEDS?

TRUTH OR FICTION?

Which of the following statements are the truth, and which are fiction? Look for the Truth-or-Fiction icons on the pages that follow to find the answers.

1 The penis contains bone and muscle. **T F**?

2 The father determines the baby's sex. **T F**?

3 *Semen* is a synonym for *sperm*. **T F**?

4 Morning erections reflect the need to urinate. **T F**?

5 Men can will themselves to have erections. **T F**?

6 The penis has a mind of its own. **T F**?

7 Many men who are paralyzed below the waist can attain erection, engage in sexual intercourse, and ejaculate. **T F**?

8 Men can have orgasms without ejaculating. **T F**?

A 34-year-old Chinese man, H. K. F., felt the need to urinate while at the movies. In the bathroom, he suddenly lost feeling in his genital region and developed fear that his penis was going to retract into his body. He went into a panic and his legs gave way. He sat on the floor, holding onto his penis to prevent it from retracting and waited a half hour, until the attack was over. He visited a health professional who assured him that his penis would not retract into his body, and H. K. F. has not suffered another attack since.

H. K. F. had experienced Koro, otherwise known as *genital retraction syndrome*, a syndrome found in Malaysia, Indonesia, and China, in which men mistakenly believe that their penises will shrink and retract into their bodies (Crozier, 2012; Stewart et al., 2010). The anxiety they experience during an attack does cause the penis to shrink somewhat, but it does not retract into the body—an anatomical impossibility. Koro is most likely to occur when a man attempts to urinate in the cold, is guilty over masturbating or visiting prostitutes, is worried about his sexual performance, or has argued with his wife.

The man will typically grab his genitals to prevent them from retracting. He may use mechanical devices like cords, chopsticks, clamps, or small weights to prevent retraction until he can find help. Koro is not all that common, but an "epidemic" of the problem, a sort of mass hysteria, occurred among men in Singapore a few years back.

Many men who experience Koro attacks, like H. K. F., profit from anatomical information and reassurance, as given by a health professional. In a couple of recent cases, men with attacks have also been treated effectively with antidepressant medications, which also have the effect of reducing tendencies to obsess about one's concerns (Fang & Hofmann, 2010).

Koro is a Chinese "culture-bound syndrome" that is believed to reflect loss (or fear of loss) of *yang*, a form of positive male energy that is balanced in nature by *yin*, or female energy. However, as contemporary health information becomes more widely spread, we will probably have fewer rather than more cases of Koro.

The experience of H. K. F. informs us about the perceived importance of the size of the male genitalia in the eyes of men, and of the folklore that has grown around it. In the murky predawn light of Western civilization, people engaged in phallic worship. Phallic symbols became glorified in art in the form of plows, axes, and swords. The ancient Greeks carried over-sized images of fish as phallic symbols in their Dionysian processions, which celebrated the wilder and more frenzied aspects of human sexuality. The Greeks also adorned themselves with phallic rings and necklaces.

The ancient Romans honored Venus by outfitting a float in the shape of a large phallus and parading it through the streets. Men in Roman courts often swore to tell the truth with their hands on their genitals—as we swear to tell the truth by placing our hands on the Bible. The words *testes* and *testicles* derive from the same Latin word as "testify." The Latin *testis* means "a witness."

Even today, men with large genitals are accorded respect from male peers and sometimes adoration from admirers (Crozier, 2012). Given these cultural attitudes, it is not surprising that young men (and some not-so-young men) belittle themselves if they feel they do not measure up. Boys who mature late may be ridiculed by their peers. Adult men, too, may wonder whether their penises are large enough to satisfy lovers. Or they may fear that their partners' earlier lovers had larger genitals.

Real Students, Real Questions

Q *Are men really that obsessed with their penises? Why?*

A Not necessarily. There are individual differences. A large penis is generally considered a plus in our culture. But males with average or somewhat smaller penises tend to become less concerned with size so long as their sex partner or partners are adequately aroused by them.

In this chapter we examine male sexual anatomy and physiology, and we attempt to sort out truth from fiction. As in our exploration of female sexual physiology and anatomy, we begin with the external genitalia and then move inward. Once inside, we focus on the route of sperm through the male reproductive system.

External Sex Organs

The external male sex organs include the penis and the scrotum (see Figures 4.1 and 4.2). 👁

Watch the **Video**
Male Reproductive Anatomy
on **MyDevelopmentLab**

THE PENIS

> *The penis mightier than the sword.*
> —Mark Twain

> *Is that a gun in your pocket, or are you just glad to see me?*
> —Mae West

At first glance the penis may seem simple and obvious in its structures, particularly when compared to women's organs. Yet, as Figure 4.1 shows, the apparent simplicity of the penis is misleading. Much goes on below the surface.

The penis, like the vagina, is the sex organ used in sexual intercourse. But unlike the vagina, the penis serves as a conduit for urine. Both semen and urine pass through the urethral opening, or urethral *meatus* (pronounced me-ATE-us). The urethra is connected to the bladder, which is unrelated to reproduction, and to those parts of the reproductive system that transport semen.

TRUTH OR **FICTION** REVISITED: Many mammals, including dogs, have penile bones that stiffen the penis to facilitate copulation. But despite the slang term *boner*, the human penis has no bones. Nor, despite another slang term, *muscle*, does the penis contain muscle tissue. However, muscles at the base of the penis, like the muscles surrounding the vaginal and urethral openings in women, are involved in urination and ejaculation.

Rather than bones or muscles, the penis contains three cylinders of spongy material that run its length and swell (become "engorged") with blood during sexual arousal, causing erection. The larger two, the **corpora cavernosa** (see Figures 4.1 and 4.2), lie side by side and function like the cavernous bodies in the clitoris. They fill with blood and stiffen when the male is aroused. In addition, a **corpus spongiosum** (spongy body) runs along the bottom, or ventral, surface of the penis. It contains the penile urethra that conducts urine to the urinary opening (urethral meatus) at the tip. Also at the tip, the spongy body enlarges into the glans, or head, of the penis.

 1

Corpora cavernosa Cylinders of spongy tissue in the penis that become congested with blood and stiffen during sexual arousal.

Corpus spongiosum The spongy body that runs along the bottom of the penis, contains the penile urethra, and enlarges at the tip of the penis to form the glans.

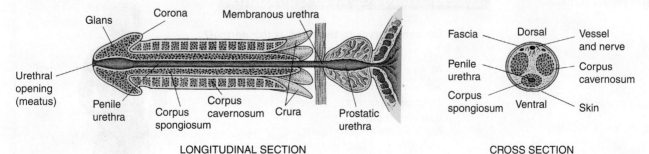

LONGITUDINAL SECTION

CROSS SECTION

FIGURE 4.1 The Penis. During sexual arousal, the copora cavernosa and corpus spongiosum become congested with blood, causing the penis to enlarge and stiffen.

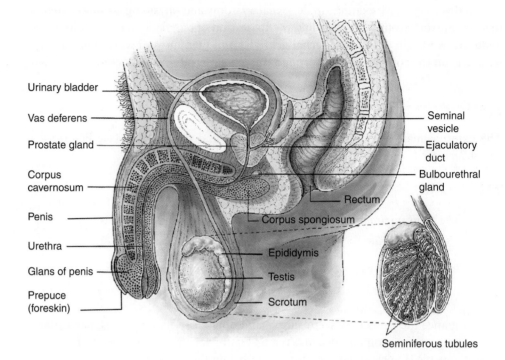

Urinary bladder

Vas deferens

Prostate gland

Corpus
cavernosum

Penis

Urethra

Glans of penis

Prepuce
(foreskin)

Seminal
vesicle

Ejaculatory
duct

Bulbourethral
gland

Rectum

Corpus spongiosum

Epididymis

Testis

Scrotum

Seminiferous tubules

FIGURE 4.2 The Male Reproductive System. The external male sex organs include the penis and the scrotum.

Corona The ridge that separates the glans from the body of the penis.

Frenulum The sensitive strip of tissue that connects the underside of the penile glans to the shaft.

Root The base of the penis, which extends into the pelvis.

Shaft The body of the penis, which expands as a result of vasocongestion.

Foreskin The loose skin that covers the penile glans. Also referred to as the *prepuce*.

◉—|Watch the **Video**
Male Genital Exam
on **MyDevelopmentLab**

The penile glans, like the clitoral glans, is highly sensitive to sexual stimulation, but direct, prolonged stimulation can become irritating. Most men prefer to masturbate by stroking the penile shaft rather than the glans. The **corona**, or coronal ridge, separates the glans from the body of the penis. It is also quite sensitive to sexual stimulation. The **frenulum**, a thin strip of tissue that connects the underside of the glans to the shaft, is also very sensitive. Most men find the top of the penis to be least sensitive.

The base of the penis, or **root**, extends into the pelvis. It is attached to the pelvic bone by leglike structures, called *crura*, similar to those that anchor the female's clitoris. The body of the penis is called the penile **shaft**. Unlike the clitoral shaft, it is free-swinging. Thus, the result of engorgement, erection, is obvious.

The skin of the penis is hairless and loose, allowing expansion during erection. It is fixed to the penile shaft just behind the glans. Some of it, however, like the labia minora in the female, folds over to partially cover the glans. This covering is the prepuce, or **foreskin**. It covers part or all of the penile glans just as the clitoral prepuce (hood) covers the clitoral shaft. The prepuce consists of loose skin that freely moves over the glans. However, *smegma*—a cheeselike, foul-smelling secretion—may accumulate below the foreskin, causing it to adhere to the glans. ◉

Real Students, Real Questions

Q *My penis curves to the right. Is this normal?*

A Sure. Penises do not tend to hang straight. As noted in the text, one testicle—usually the left testicle—tends to hang lower than the other because of the differential lengths of the spermatic cords.

Circumcision As told by Roni Rabin (2011), Allison had her first son at the age of 37. Prior to the delivery, she focused on many issues. Was she going to use anesthesia during the delivery? (No.) Was she going to use disposable diapers or cloth diapers? (Cloth.) And was she going to breast feed? (A resounding yes!) But she hadn't really thought about circumcision, so when her obstetrician recommended it, she just did it. ◉

Which is not to say the she regrets the decision, but just that circumcision isn't quite as common as it was in the United States. Male **circumcision** is surgical removal of the prepuce (see Figure 4.3). It has a long history as a religious rite. Jews traditionally carry out male circumcision shortly after a baby is born. Circumcision is performed as a sign of the covenant between God and the people of Abraham. Muslims also circumcise for religious reasons, although they tend do so some years later.

But the great majority of Americans are neither Jews nor Muslims, so circumcision has no religious meaning for them. For that reason, most American parents who decide to circumcise their sons do so for health reasons. And in recent years, opponents of circumcision have argued that it is a form of genital mutilation that is carried out without the consent of the person receiving it, who is usually a newborn baby (Tobian & Gray, 2011). Moreover, circumcision is demonstrably painful, even if the boy does not remember the operation. There is also some evidence that circumcision might reduce male sexual sensations because the foreskin is rich in nerve endings (Smith et al., 2010). Circumcision rates consequently vary widely in the United States, from the majority of boys in the Midwest to about one in three in the West. Overall, the American rate is about 57%, down from about 62.5% a decade ago (McMillen, 2011). Circumcision is uncommon in many other parts of the world, and is rare in Latin America. Latin American immigration accounts for some of the disparity in circumcision rates across the United States (*Medical News Today,* 2008). The rate is about 17% in Canada and 5% in England. Figure 4.4 shows that the world's highest circumcision rates are found in countries where the population is largely or exclusively Muslim.

Although Allison's obstetrician recommended circumcision, the American Academy of Pediatrics issued statements that circumcision was unnecessary in 1999 and then again in 2005. For that reason, many health insurance companies stopped covering the cost of circumcision and many parents doubted its effectiveness. On the other hand, after much "obsessing" and a careful review of the research literature, the Academy reversed its position in 2012—sort of. The Academy admitted that circumcision may protect heterosexual men, and their sex partners, against HIV (the virus that causes AIDS) and stated that the health benefits of circumcision were likely to outweigh any risks (American Academy of Pediatrics Task Force on

◉⎯│**Watch** the **Video**
San Francisco to Vote on Circumcision Ban
on **MyDevelopmentLab**

Circumcision Surgical removal of the foreskin of the penis.

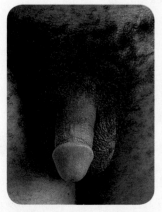  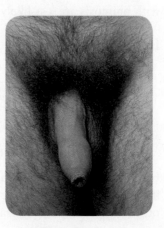

FIGURE 4.3 Normal Variations in the Male Genitals. The penis and scrotum vary a good deal in appearance from one man to another. The penis in the photo to the right is uncircumcised.

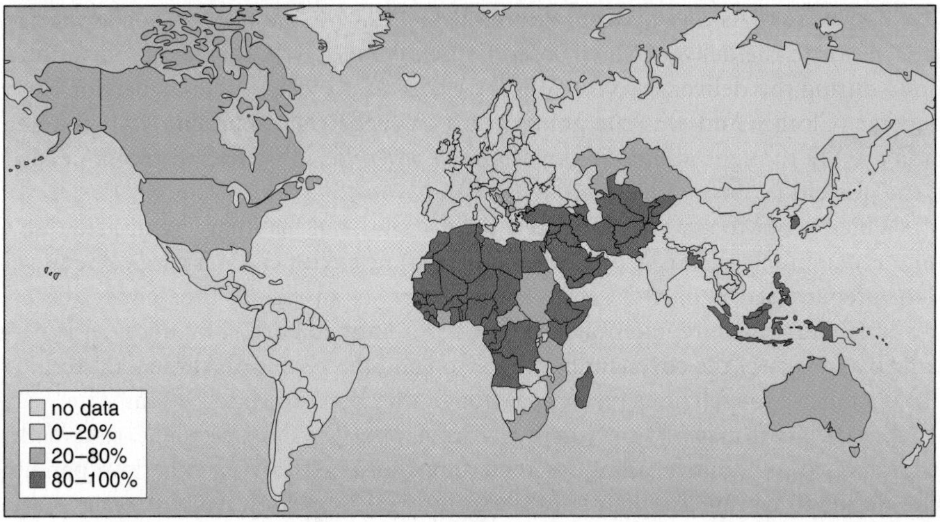

FIGURE 4.4 Prevalence of Circumcision around the Globe. Circumcision is most prevalent in Islamic countries and in Israel. It is a religious rite in both places.

no data
0–20%
20–80%
80–100%

Circumcision, 2012). But they still characterized circumcision as a family decision rather than wholeheartedly recommending it.

In fact, the evidence seems overwhelming that circumcision has many, many health benefits (Tobian & Gray, 2011; Wright et al., 2012). Circumcision lessens the risk of infections of the urinary tract, including infections by the human papilloma virus (HPV) and by HIV, and even the risk of prostate cancer, whose development appears to be facilitated by infections. Randomized trials in Africa have shown that men who are circumcised are 51% to 60% less likely to be infected with HIV (Tobian & Gray, 2011). The protective effects of circumcision are likely to reflect a lower incidence of local inflammation and genital ulcers, both of which provide ports of entry for HIV, and the removal of cells in the foreskin—Langerhans cells—that are receptive to infection by HIV. Other studies have found that circumcised males are about 30% less likely to contract genital herpes (Tobian & Gray, 2011). In a study of 4,000 men, men who had been circumcised were 15% less likely to develop prostate cancer than those who had not (Wright et al., 2012).

Circumcision also has notable health benefits for *women*—that is, for the sex partners of circumcised men. Generally speaking, if a woman's male partner is less likely to have sexually transmitted infections, so is she. But more specifically, the female partners of circumcised men are 28% less likely to be infected with HPV, the virus that is connected with cervical cancer, 40% less likely to develop bacterial vaginosis, and 48% less likely to develop trichomoniasis (Tobian & Gray, 2011).

Physicians once agreed that circumcision is the treatment for **phimosis**, a condition in which is it difficult to retract the foreskin from the glans. But today, men with phimosis are less likely to be circumcised for that reason.

Penis Size

> IRAS: *Am I not an inch of fortune better than she?*
>
> CHARMIAN: *Well, if you were but an inch of fortune better than I, where would you choose it?*
>
> IRAS: *Not in my husband's nose.*
>
> —William Shakespeare, *Antony and Cleopatra*

In our culture, the size of the penis is often seen as a measure of a man's masculinity and his ability to please his sex partner (Lever et al., 2006). Shakespeare and other writers inform us that men have looked down at themselves for centuries,

CRITICAL THINKING
What are the similarities and differences between male circumcision and female circumcision (clitoridectomy), as described in Chapter 3? Can one logically favor one of these practices but oppose the other?

Phimosis An abnormal condition in which the foreskin is so tight that it cannot be withdrawn from the glans.

sometimes in delight but more often in chagrin. Men who are heralded for their sexual or reproductive feats are presumed to have more prominent "testaments" to their manhood. Clinical experience with dysfunctional couples suggests that women are more likely to complain about their partner's communication ability or the feeling or tone of their relationship rather than the size of his penis (Zilbergeld, 1999). Nevertheless, surveys show that a minority of women are dissatisfied with the size of their partner's penis (Lever et al., 2006; Štulhofer, 2006).

An Internet survey of some 52,000 heterosexual men and women found that two-thirds of the men (66%) rated their penises as average in size, 22% rated them as large, and 12% rated them as small (Lever et al., 2006). Self-reported penis size was correlated negatively with the amount of body fat, consistent with other studies, reported in Chapter 15, that connect male sexual functioning negatively with levels of low-density ("bad") cholesterol. Most women (85%) were content with the size of their partner's penis, as compared with only 55% of the men. Forty-five percent of the men desired larger penises, and hardly any (only 0.2%) wanted smaller penises.

Penises generally range in length from 3 inches to a little more than 4 inches when flaccid, or soft (Masters & Johnson, 1966). The average erection ranges from 5 to 7 inches in length. Erect penises differ less in size than flaccid penises do. Penises that are small when soft tend to gain more size when they become erect.

Even when flaccid, the same penis can vary in size. Factors such as cold air or water or emotions of fear or anxiety can cause the penis (along with the scrotum and testicles) to draw closer to the body, reducing its size. These factors can trigger Koro syndrome in Chinese culture, as we saw at the beginning of the chapter. The flaccid penis may expand in warm water or when the man is relaxed.

THE SCROTUM

The **scrotum** is a pouch of loose skin below the base of the penis that becomes covered lightly with hair at puberty. It has two compartments that hold the testes. Each testicle is held in place by a **spermatic cord**, a structure that contains the **vas deferens**, blood vessels and nerves, and the cremaster muscle. The **cremaster muscle** raises and lowers the testicle within the scrotum in response to temperature changes and sexual stimulation. (Sexual arousal draws the testes closer to the body.)

Sperm production is optimal at slightly below the 98.6°F that is normal for most of the body. Scrotal temperature tends to be from 5 to 6°F lower than body temperature. The scrotum is loose-hanging and flexible. It permits the testes and nearby structures to escape the higher body heat, especially in warm weather. In the middle layer of the scrotum is the **dartos muscle**, which, like the cremaster, contracts and relaxes reflexively in response to temperature changes. In cold weather, or when a man jumps into a body of cold water, the dartos muscle contracts and brings the testes closer to the body. In warm weather, it relaxes, allowing the testes to hang farther from the body. The dartos muscle also increases or decreases the surface area of the scrotum in response to temperature changes. Smoothing allows greater dissipation of heat in hot weather. Constricting the skin surface helps retain heat and wrinkles the scrotum in the cold.

The scrotum is developed from the same embryonic tissue that becomes the labia majora of the female. Thus, like the labia majora, it is quite sensitive to sexual stimulation.

Scrotum The pouch of loose skin that contains the testes.

Spermatic cord The cord that suspends a testicle within the scrotum and contains a vas deferens, blood vessels, nerves, and the cremaster muscle.

Vas deferens A tube that conducts sperm from the testicle to the ejaculatory duct of the penis.

Cremaster muscle The muscle that raises and lowers the testicle in response to temperature changes and sexual stimulation.

Dartos muscle The muscle in the middle layer of the scrotum that contracts and relaxes in response to temperature changes.

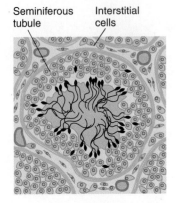

Seminiferous tubule   Interstitial cells

FIGURE 4.5 Interstitial Cells. Testosterone is produced by the interstitial cells, which lay between the seminiferous tubules in each testis. Sperm (see in the middle of the diagram) are produced within the seminiferous tubules.

Germ cell A cell from which a new organism develops.

Sperm The male germ cell.

Androgens Male sex hormones.

Testosterone A male steroid sex hormone.

Interstitial cells Cells that lie between the seminiferous tubules and secrete testosterone.

Leydig's cells Another term for *interstitial cells.*

Secondary sex characteristics Traits that distinguish the genders but are not directly involved in reproduction.

Seminiferous tubules Tiny, winding, sperm-producing tubes within the lobes of the testes.

Spermatogenesis The process by which sperm cells are produced and developed.

Spermatocyte An early stage in the development of sperm cells, in which each parent cell has 46 chromosomes, including one X and one Y sex chromosome.

Spermatids Cells formed by the division of spermatocytes. Each spermatid has 23 chromosomes.

Internal Sex Organs

The male internal sex organs include the testes, the organs that manufacture sperm and testosterone; the system of tubes and ducts that conduct sperm through the male reproductive system; and the organs that help nourish and activate sperm and neutralize some of the acidity that sperm encounter in the vagina (see Figure 4.2).

THE TESTES

The testes are the male gonads (*gonad* derives from the Greek *gone,* meaning "seed"). In slang, the testes are frequently referred to as "balls" or "nuts." These terms are considered vulgar, but they are reasonably descriptive.

The testes serve two functions analogous to those of the ovaries. They secrete sex hormones and produce mature **germ cells**. In the case of the testes, the germ cells are **sperm** and the sex hormones are **androgens**. The most important androgen is **testosterone**.

Testosterone Testosterone is secreted by **interstitial cells**, which are also known as **Leydig's cells**. Interstitial cells lie between the seminiferous tubules and release testosterone into the bloodstream (see Figure 4.5). Testosterone stimulates prenatal differentiation of male sex organs, sperm production, and development of **secondary sex characteristics**, such as the beard, a deep voice, and muscle mass.

In men, several endocrine glands—a feedback loop among the hypothalamus, pituitary gland, and testes (see Figure 4.6)—keep blood testosterone levels at a more or less even level, although there are slight variations with stress, time of day or month, and other factors. This contrasts with the peaks and valleys in levels of female sex hormones during the phases of the menstrual cycle.

The pituitary hormones, FSH and LH, which regulate the activity of the ovaries, also regulate the activity of the testes. FSH regulates the production of sperm. LH stimulates secretion of testosterone by interstitial cells. Low testosterone levels signal the hypothalamus to secrete the hormone, LH-releasing hormone (LH–RH). Like dominoes falling in a line, LH–RH causes the pituitary gland to secrete LH, which in turn stimulates the testes to secrete testosterone. LH is also known as *interstitial-cell-stimulating-hormone* (ICSH).

When the level of testosterone in the blood system reaches a peak, the hypothalamus directs the pituitary gland *not* to secrete LH. This system for circling information around these three endocrine glands is called a *feedback loop*. This feedback loop is *negative*. That is, it increases in hormone levels in one part of the system trigger another part to shut down and vice versa.

The testes usually range between 1 and 1¾ inches in length. They are about half as wide and deep. The left testicle usually hangs lower, because the left spermatic cord tends to be somewhat longer.

Sperm Each testicle is divided into many lobes, which are filled with winding **seminiferous tubules** (see Figure 4.2). Although packed into a tiny space, these tubules, placed end to end, would span the length of several football fields. Through **spermatogenesis**, these threadlike structures produce and store hundreds of billions of sperm over a lifetime.

Sperm cells develop through several stages. It takes about 72 days for the testes to manufacture a mature sperm cell. In an early stage, sperm cells are called **spermatocytes**. Each one contains 46 chromosomes, including one X and one Y sex chromosome. Each spermatocyte divides into two **spermatids**, each of which has

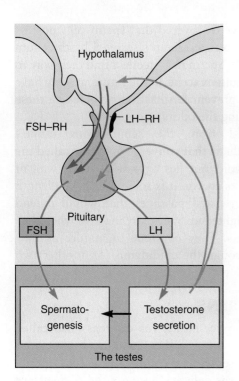

FIGURE 4.6 Hormonal Control of the Testes. Several endocrine glands—the hypothalamus, the pituitary gland, and the testes—keep blood testosterone levels at a more or less constant level. Low testosterone levels signal the hypothalamus to secrete LH-releasing hormone (LH–RH). Like dominoes falling in line, LH–RH causes the pituitary gland to secrete LH, which in turn stimulates the testes to release testosterone. Follicle-stimulating hormone releasing hormone (FSH–RH) from the hypothalamus causes the pituitary to secrete FSH, which, in turn, causes the testes to produce sperm cells.

23 chromosomes. Half the spermatids have X sex chromosomes, and the other half have Y sex chromosomes. Looking something like tadpoles when examined under a microscope, mature sperm cells, called **spermatozoa**, each have a head, a cone-shaped midpiece, and a tail. The head is about 5 microns (1/50,000 of an inch) long and contains the cell nucleus that houses the chromosomes. The midpiece contains structures that provide the energy that the tail needs to lash back and forth as it swims. Each sperm cell is about 50 microns (1/5,000 of an inch) long, one of the smallest cells in the body.

During fertilization, the 23 chromosomes from the father's sperm cell combine with the 23 chromosomes from the mother's ovum, furnishing the standard ensemble of 46 in the offspring. Among the 23 chromosomes borne by sperm cells is one sex chromosome—an X sex chromosome or a Y sex chromosome. Ova contain X sex chromosomes only. The union of an X sex chromosome and a Y sex chromosome leads to the development of male offspring. Two X sex chromosomes combine to yield female offspring.

TRUTH OR **FICTION** REVISITED: It is true that the father determines the baby's sex through the presence of an X or Y sex chromosome.

The testes churn out about 1,000 sperms per second or 30 *billion* per year. Mathematically speaking, 10 to 20 ejaculations hold enough sperm to populate the Earth. (Men are always so taken with themselves, notes the third author.)

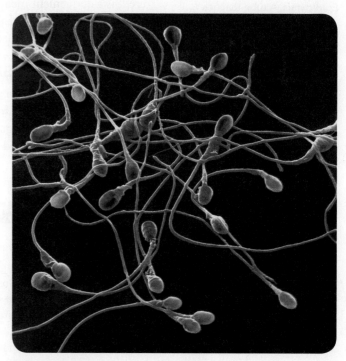

Human Sperm Cells Magnified Many Times.

 2

Spermatozoa Mature sperm cells.

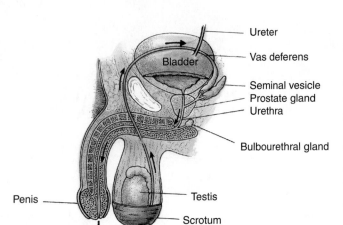

FIGURE 4.7 Passage of Spermatozoa. Each testicle is divided into lobes that contain threadlike seminiferous tubules. Through spermatogenesis, the tubules produce and store hundreds of billions of sperm over the course of a lifetime. During ejaculation, sperm cells travel through the vas deferens, up and over the bladder, into the ejaculatory duct, and then through the urethra. Secretions from the seminal vesicles and the bulbourethral glands join with sperm to compose semen.

Epididymis A tube that lies against the back wall of each testicle and stores sperm.

Vasectomy Severing of the vas deferens, preventing sperm from reaching the ejaculatory duct.

Seminal vesicles Small glands that lie behind the bladder and secrete fluids that combine with sperm in the ejaculatory ducts.

Ejaculatory duct A duct formed by the convergence of a vas deferens with a seminal vesicle through which sperm pass through the prostate gland and into the urethra.

Researchers have discovered that sperm cells possess the receptors that detect attractants secreted by the ovum (Alvarez et al., 2012). Sperm may in effect find their way to an egg cell by detecting its scent. In the future we may have contraceptives that prevent fertilization by blocking these receptors from sensing the odors of egg cells.

Sperm proceed from the seminiferous tubules through a maze of ducts that converge in a tube called the **epididymis.** The epididymis lies against the back wall of the testicle and stores sperm. It is some 2 inches in length and it consists of twisted passages that would extend 10 to 20 feet if straightened. Sperm are inactive when they enter the epididymis. They continue to mature as they make their way through the epididymis for another two to four weeks.

THE VAS DEFERENS

Each epididymis empties into a vas deferens (also called *ductus deferens*). The vas is a thin, cylindrical tube about 16 inches long that serves as a conduit for mature sperm. In the scrotum, the vas deferens lies near the skin surface within the spermatic cord. Therefore, a **vasectomy,** an operation in which the right and left vas deferens are severed, is a convenient means of sterilization. The tube leaves the scrotum and follows a circuitous path up into the abdominal cavity. Then it loops back along the rear surface of the bladder (see Figure 4.7).

THE SEMINAL VESICLES

The two **seminal vesicles** are small glands, each about 2 inches long. They lie behind the bladder and open into the **ejaculatory ducts,** where the fluids they secrete combine with sperm (see Figure 4.7). The seminal vesicles were so named because they were mistakenly believed to be reservoirs for semen, rather than glands.

Real Students, Real Answers

Q *What does ejaculate taste like, and is it harmful to ingest?*

A In a word, salty. Some people like the taste, others find it unpleasant, and still others are simply indifferent to it. Some find the taste to be sexually arousing. It is not clear as to how much of the response reflects natural individual differences and how much reflects what people expect as a result of cultural reasons and tales from friends.

The substances in the ejaculate are absolutely harmless. It is vaguely conceivable (no pun intended) that the fluid of the ejaculate could go down "the wrong pipe" and cause choking, but this possibility exists with the ingestion of any fluid, even water. By the way, the ejaculate is a low-calorie food—largely protein—when ingested.

A Closer Look

Andropause: When Hormones Rage No More

Most of us are familiar enough with the phrase "raging hormones" when it comes to the alleged irritability shown by some women prior to menstruation and apparently related to the fluctuations of sex hormones. Yet men, too, can be said to be prey to "raging hormones." The male sex hormone testosterone is related to tendencies to dominate other people. There is research evidence that aggressive boys, college students, and men have higher testosterone levels than their peers (Crofoot & Wrangham, 2010; Peterson & Harmon-Jones, 2011; Pradhan et al., 2010). High levels of testosterone also appear to reduce fear of the consequences of aggression (King et al., 2005). For reasons such as these, social commentator Anna Quindlen wrote an article, "Is Testosterone Toxic?" We will see that the answer to Anna Quindlen's question might be yes—that is, testosterone might well be toxic—but not for reasons that she was writing about. 👁

Historically speaking, more research has been done with men's health problems than women's. Yet the problems related to low levels of sex hormones in men do not yet even have an agreed-upon name. *Andropause* suggests

👁—**Watch** the **Video** *Male Menopause* on **MyDevelopmentLab**

a falloff in androgens (male sex hormones). *Viropause* suggests a decline in virility, which is not a scientific term and suggests a general loss of ability. *Manopause* is a widely used but unscientific knockoff of the scientific term *menopause*. A more scientific term is *androgen decline*.

For women, menopause is a time of relatively distinct age-related declines in sex hormones and fertility. In men, the decline in the production of male sex hormones and fertility is more gradual (Yamaguchi et al., 2011). It therefore is not surprising to find a man in his 70s or older fathering a child. However, many men in their 50s and 60s experience problems in achieving and maintaining erections, which may reflect circulatory problems or hormone deficiencies.

Sexual performance is one part of the story. Between the ages of 40 and 70, the typical American male loses 12 to 20 pounds of muscle, about 2 inches in height, and 15% of his bone mass. (Men as well as women are at risk for osteoporosis [Yeap, 2009].) The percent of fat in the body nearly doubles. There is some loss in hearing and vision. There is loss of endurance as the cardiovascular system and lungs become less capable of adapting to exertion.

Some of these changes can be slowed or reversed. Exercise helps maintain muscle tone, keeps the growth of fatty tissue in check, and helps combat osteoporosis. A diet rich in calcium and vitamin D also wards off bone loss. Hormone replacement therapy may help but is controversial.

U.S. physicians also write more than one million prescriptions for testosterone and related drugs for men each year, even though it has been suspected that testosterone replacement therapy may heighten the risks of prostate cancer and cardiovascular disorders. However, research to date relies mainly on findings that suppression of naturally occurring testosterone decreases the risk of prostate cancer and its rate of growth (Gould & Kirby, 2006). Research that has actually followed the effects of testosterone replacement has so far shown no clear evidence that testosterone replacement leads to prostate cancer or other major diseases such as heart problems or diabetes (e.g., Ginzburg et al., 2010; Gould & Kirby, 2006).

CRITICAL THINKING

Does the evidence suggest that men undergo an "andropause" that is similar to menopause? Explain.

Real Students, Real Questions

Q *Is it possible to urinate with a full erection?*

A No and yes. The ductwork of the male is constructed such that urination and ejaculation tend to be mutually exclusive. On the other hand, if a male with an erection makes an effort to relax his bladder fully (that is, to allow himself to urinate), he may well be able to do so, even if the flow of urine is delayed.

The fluid produced by the seminal vesicles is rich in fructose, a form of sugar, which nourishes sperm and helps them become active, or motile. Sperm motility is a major factor in male fertility. Before reaching the ejaculatory ducts, sperm are propelled along by contractions of the epididymis and vas deferens and by **cilia** that line the walls of the vas deferens. Once they become motile, they propel themselves by whipping their tails.

At the base of the bladder, each vas deferens joins a seminal vesicle to form a short ejaculatory duct that runs through the middle of the prostate gland (see Figure 4.7). In the prostate, the ejaculatory duct opens into the urethra, which carries sperm and urine out through the tip of the penis.

THE PROSTATE GLAND

The **prostate gland** lies beneath the bladder and approximates a chestnut in shape and size (about 3/4 inch in diameter). It contains muscle fibers and glandular tissue that secrete prostatic fluid. Prostatic fluid is milky and alkaline. It provides the characteristic texture and odor of the seminal fluid. The alkalinity neutralizes some of the acidity of the vaginal tract, prolonging the life span of sperm as seminal fluid spreads through the female reproductive system. The prostate is continually active in mature males, but sexual arousal further stimulates secretions. Secretions are conveyed into the urethra by a sieve-like duct system. There the secretions combine with sperm and fluid from the seminal vesicles.

A vasectomy prevents sperm from reaching the urethra but does not cut off fluids from the seminal vesicles or prostate gland. A man who has had a vasectomy thus emits an ejaculate that appears normal but contains no sperm.

COWPER'S GLANDS

The two **Cowper's glands** are also known as the **bulbourethral glands,** in recognition of their shape and location. They lie below the prostate and empty their secretions into the urethra. During sexual arousal they secrete a drop or so of clear, slippery fluid that appears at the tip of the penis. The fluid may help buffer the acidity of the male's urethra and lubricate the urethral passageway, but not enough is produced to lubricate the vagina during intercourse.

Fluid from the Cowper's glands precedes the ejaculate and often contains sperm. Thus, male–female coitus may lead to pregnancy even if the penis is withdrawn before ejaculation. For this reason, people who practice the "withdrawal method" of birth control are often called "parents."

SEMEN

TRUTH OR **FICTION** REVISITED: Semen is *not* a synonym for sperm. Sperm and the fluids contributed by the seminal vesicles, the prostate gland, and the Cowper's glands make up **semen,** or whitish seminal fluid, which is expelled through the tip of the penis during ejaculation. The seminal vesicles secrete about 70% of the fluid that constitutes the ejaculate. The remaining 30% of seminal fluid consists of sperm and fluids produced by the prostate gland and the Cowper's gland. Sperm themselves account for only about 1% of the volume of semen. This is why men with vasectomies ejaculate nearly as much semen as before the operation.

Semen carries sperm through the male's reproductive system and the reproductive tract of the female. Semen contains water, mucus, sugar (fructose), acids, and bases. It activates and nourishes sperm, and the bases help shield sperm from vaginal acidity. The typical ejaculate contains between 200 and 400 million sperm and ranges between 3 and 5 milliliters in volume. (Five milliliters is equal to about one tablespoon.)

Cilia Hairlike projections from cells that beat rhythmically to produce locomotion or currents.

Cowper's glands Structures that lie below the prostate and empty their secretions into the urethra during sexual arousal.

Bulbourethral glands Another term for *Cowper's glands.*

Prostate gland The gland that lies beneath the bladder and secretes prostatic fluid, which gives semen its characteristic odor and texture.

Semen The whitish fluid that constitutes the ejaculate, consisting of sperm and secretions from the seminal vesicles, prostate, and Cowper's glands.

The quantity of semen decreases with age and frequency of ejaculation. On the other hand, there appears to be a relationship between the quality of semen and intelligence. Arand Pierce and his colleagues (2009) used standardized intelligence tests to assess the intelligence of several hundred U.S. army veterans and found that intelligence was related to the concentration of sperm in semen ($r = +0.15$), the sperm count ($r = +.19$), and the motility of the sperm ($r = +0.14$). No correlation equals a correlation of 0.00, and a perfect correlation equals +1.00. The correlations found in the study are too small to make meaningful predictions about intelligence and semen quality, but they are large enough to be unlikely due to chance fluctuation. The authors suggest that biological factors might be at work such that the overall long-term trend could be toward greater intelligence, but this interpretation of the findings might be a "reach."

Health Problems of the Urogenital System

Because the organs that comprise the urinary and reproductive systems are near each other and share some "piping," they are referred to as the *urinogenital* or *urogenital* system. A number of health problems affect the urogenital system. The type of physician who specializes in their diagnosis and treatment is a urologist.

URETHRITIS

Men, like women, are subject to bladder and urethral inflammations, which are generally referred to as **urethritis**. The symptoms include frequent urination (urinary frequency), a strong need to urinate (urinary urgency), burning during urination, and a penile discharge. People with symptoms of urinary frequency and urinary urgency feel the pressing need to urinate repeatedly, even though they may have just done so and may have but another drop or two to expel. The discharge may dry on the urethral opening, in which case it may have to be peeled off or wiped away before it is possible to urinate. The urethra also may become constricted when it is inflamed, slowing or halting urination.

Preventive measures for urethritis parallel those suggested for cystitis (bladder infection):

- Drink more water
- Drink cranberry juice (4 ounces, two or three times a day). Cranberry juice is highly acidic, and acid tends to eliminate many of the bacteria that can give rise to urethritis.
- Lower your intake of alcohol and caffeine.

Urethritis is usually treated with antibiotics.

CANCER OF THE TESTES

Cancer of the testicles remains a relatively rare form of cancer, accounting for about 8,290 new cases annually, and about 350 men will die from it every year (American Cancer Society, 2012f). It is the most common form of solid-tumor cancer to strike men between the ages of 20 and 34, accounting for nearly 10% of all deaths from cancer among men in that age group. ◉

There is no evidence that testicular cancer results from sexual overactivity or masturbation. About 14% of men with testicular cancer had **cryptorchidism** as children, a condition in which one or both testicles fail to descend from the abdomen into the scrotum (American Cancer Society, 2012f). Family history also increases

◉—◗ **Watch** the **Video**
Testicular Cancer
on **MyDevelopmentLab**

Urethritis An inflammation of the bladder or urethra.

Cryptorchidism A condition in which one or two testicles fails to descend from the abdomen into the scrotum.

the risk. European Americans are 5 to 10 times more likely than African Americans to develop cancer of the testes, and more than twice as likely as Asian Americans (American Cancer Society, 2012f).

Although testicular cancer was generally fatal in earlier years, the prognosis today is quite favorable, especially when detected early. Treatments include surgical removal of the diseased testis, radiation, and chemotherapy. The five-year survival rate among cases that are detected before the cancer has spread beyond the testes is about 99% (American Cancer Society, 2012f). If it has spread to nearby lymph nodes, the five-year survival rate is 96%. If it has spread beyond the lymph nodes, the five-year survival rate drops to about 71%.

The surgical removal of a testicle may have profound psychological implications. Some men who have lost a testicle feel less "manly." Also, fears related to sexual performance can engender sexual dysfunctions. From a physiological standpoint, sexual functioning may remain unimpaired, as adequate testosterone may be produced by the remaining testis. There are a couple of caveats. One is that surgery to remove the lymph nodes behind the belly can accidentally damage nearby nerves that control ejaculation, causing sperm to be ejaculated into the urinary bladder. (Check on the success rate of potential surgeons!) This condition can render the man infertile. If both testes are removed, the man is infertile. However, with testosterone replacement therapy, he can usually obtain an erection and have sex. Since only a small amount of semen consists of sperm, sex can remain satisfying.

The early stages of testicular cancer usually produce no symptoms, other than the mass itself. Because early detection is crucial to survival, men are advised to examine themselves monthly following puberty and to have regular medical checkups. Self-examination may also reveal evidence of sexually transmitted infections (STIs) and other problems.

Self-Examination of the Testes Self-examination (see Figure 4.8) is best performed shortly after a warm shower or bath, when the skin of the scrotum is most relaxed. The man should examine the scrotum for evidence of pea-sized lumps. Each testicle can be rolled gently between the thumb and the fingers. Lumps are generally found on the side or front of the testicle. The presence of a lump is not necessarily a sign of cancer, but it should be promptly reported to a physician for further evaluation. The American Cancer Society (2012) lists these warning signals:

- A lump on a testicle
- Enlargement or swelling of a testicle
- Change in the consistency of a testicle
- Dull ache in the lower abdomen or groin (pain may be absent in cancer of the testes, however)
- Sensation of dragging and heaviness in a testicle

Less common symptoms are:

- Growth of breast tissue; tender or swollen breasts
- Loss of the sex drive
- Premature (prior to puberty) growth of hair on the face and body

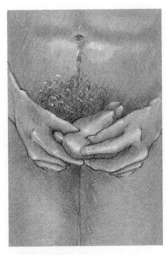

FIGURE 4.8
Self-Examination
of the Testes

Benign prostatic hyperplasia
Enlargement of the prostate due to hormonal changes of aging and symptomized by urinary frequency, urinary urgency, and difficulty starting the flow of urine.

BENIGN PROSTATIC HYPERPLASIA (BPH)

The prostate gland is tiny at birth and grows rapidly at puberty. It may shrink during adulthood, but usually becomes enlarged past the age of 50. The prostate gland becomes enlarged in about half the men past the age of 50 and 80% of men by age 80 (www.prostatecare.com, 2006). **Benign prostatic hyperplasia (BPH)** is noncancerous enlargement of the prostate gland due to hormonal changes associated with aging rather than other causes, such as inflammation from sexually transmitted infections. Because the prostate surrounds the upper part of the urethra (see Figure 4.2), enlargement constricts the urethra, causing urinary frequency (including increased frequency of nocturnal urination), urinary urgency, and difficulty starting the flow of urine. Several treatments are available to relieve the pressure on the urethra and increase the flow of urine. Two types of drugs help men with BPH. The first type, 5-ARIs (5-alpha reductase inhibitors), inhibits the production of the hormone DHT (a form of testosterone), which causes enlargement of the prostate. The 5-ARIs shrink the prostate, provide long-term improvement of symptoms, and reduce the risk of severe urinary retention and the need for surgery. The second type is alpha-blockers, which act by relaxing the muscles of the bladder to improve the flow of urine, providing symptom relief. Part of the prostate is also sometimes surgically removed (www.prostatecare.com, 2006).

PROSTATITIS

Prostatitis is inflammation of the prostate, which can be caused by various infectious agents. The chief symptoms are an ache or pain between the scrotum and anal opening and painful ejaculation. Prostatitis is usually treated with antibiotics. Although aspirin and ibuprofen may relieve the pain, men with these symptoms should consult a physician. Painful ejaculation may discourage masturbation or coitus, which is ironic, because regular flushing of the prostate through ejaculation may be helpful in the treatment of the inflammation. Prostatitis is usually treated with antibiotics, most commonly ciproflaxin.

CANCER OF THE PROSTATE

Prostate cancer is a serious and life-threatening problem. About one man in six in the United States will develop prostate cancer (American Cancer Society, 2012e). It is the second most common form of cancer among men, after skin cancer, and the second leading cause of cancer deaths in men, after lung cancer. There are about 241,740 new cases of prostate cancer in the United States each year, and about 28,170 deaths (American Cancer Society, 2012e). Prostate cancer involves the growth of malignant prostate tumors that can metastasize to bones and lymph nodes if not detected and treated early.

Risk Factors The American Cancer Society (2012e) and the National Cancer Institute (2012) at the National Institutes of Health agree on the following risk factors:

- Age. Prostate cancer is rare below the age of 45. The risk rises rapidly after the age of 50, and most men with the disorder are 65 or older.
- Family history. The risk is higher for men who have a father, brother, or son who has had the disease.
- Mutations of the BRCA1 or BRCA2 genes. Mutations in these genes are why breast and ovarian cancers are significantly more common in some families. It is believed that mutations in these genes may also heighten the risk of prostate cancer in men
- Race. Prostate cancer is more common among African American men than among European American or Latin American men. It is least prevalent among Asian Americans and Native Americans. African American men are 50 to 60% more likely than European American men to develop prostate cancer. In general, African American men have less access to health care than European American men do, so prostate cancer tends to be diagnosed later among them, and they are twice as likely to die from it (American Cancer Society, 2012e).

CRITICAL THINKING

If a man has a strong family history of prostate cancer, is there any point to his making an effort to watch his diet? Explain.

Prostatitis Inflammation of the prostate gland.

The American Cancer Society (2012e) notes that prostate cancer is most common in North America, northwestern Europe, Australia, and the Caribbean islands, but less common in Africa, Asia, and Central and South America. It has been speculated that these national differences may be related to dietary differences, such as a higher intake of red meat and high-fat dairy products in the nations where prostate cancer is more prevalent. In fact, the American Cancer Society (2012e) writes that a diet rich in red meat and high-fat dairy products appears to increase risk of prostate cancer, but it should be noted that the National Cancer Institute (2012) writes "the chance of getting prostate cancer is not increased" by such a diet. We will not get involved in the issue as to which of these organizations is more likely to be correct. However, we will note that diets high in red meat and fatty dairy products have been shown to add on the pounds and increase the risk of cardiovascular disorders; therefore, there is certainly nothing wrong with watching one's intake of these foods.

The American Cancer Society (2012e) and National Cancer Institute (2012) both state that there is no clear connection between prostate cancer and the following:

- Obesity. However, the American Cancer Society (2012e) notes that obese men may have less risk of developing a "less dangerous" form of cancer but a greater risk of developing a "more aggressive" form of cancer.
- Sexually transmitted infections.
- Vasectomy.

The National Cancer Institute (2012) adds that there are *no* clear connections between prostate cancer and the following:

- Smoking. But note that smoking is the number 1 cause of lung cancer and many respiratory diseases.
- Prostatitis (benign inflammation of the prostate gland).
- Use of alcohol.
- Lack of exercise (that is, a sedentary life style). Do not interpret this particular lack of connection as a license to become a couch potato; there are many good health reasons for exercising.

Symptoms The early symptoms of cancer of the prostate may mimic those of benign prostate enlargement: trouble obtaining or maintaining an erection, urinary frequency and difficulty in urinating, blood in the urine, pain or burning when urinating, and pain in the lower back, pelvis, or upper thighs, weakness or numbness in the legs or feet, and loss of control of the bladder or bowels (American Cancer Society, 2012e). Most cases occur without noticeable symptoms in the early stages; therefore, screening for prostate cancer is an important topic of discussion for a man and his doctor.

Diagnosis and Screening Health professionals detect and assess prostate cancer by a combination of tests. One of these is the digital rectal examination (DRE; see Figure 4.9). In this case, digital means "finger" and has nothing to do with computers or our "digital age." In the DRE, the physician inserts a finger into the rectum and feels for bumps or hard spots in the prostate gland. Unfortunately, many men are reluctant to have a rectal examination, even though it is only mildly uncomfortable and may save their lives. Some are embarrassed or reluctant to discuss urinary problems with their physicians. Some may resist the rectal examination because they associate rectal insertion with male–male sex. Some, of course, fear they may have cancer and choose to remain ignorant. Failure to have regular exams is a major contributor to the death rate from prostate cancer.

These include a PSA test, which is a blood test for *prostate-specific antigen,* recommended once a year for men aged 50 and over, and beginning at a younger age for men at greater risk. African American men are advised to begin at age 45. Results under 4 nanograms per milliliter are normal. A result above 10 is considered high; results between 4 and 10 are borderline. PSA is a protein that helps transform a gel-like substance in the prostate gland to a liquid that transports sperm during ejaculation. In the diseased or enlarged prostate, PSA seeps into the blood at higher levels, yielding higher test scores.

Ultrasound may also be used. We will see throughout this book that ultrasound is too high in pitch to be heard by the human ear. However, ultrasound wave can be bounced off the interior of the body from an instrument held outside the body. Computer software converts the reflections (or bouncing back) of the sound waves into a "picture" of interior organs.

If cancer is suspected from any or a combination of these tests, the doctor performs a biopsy. That is, the doctor uses a needle to take a sample of prostate tissue and sometimes of lymph nodes in the area. If a tumor is found, pathologists grade two samples of tissue and rate them from 1 to 5 on the socalled Gleason scale to provide a measure of the cancer's aggressiveness. The scores are added. Sums of 2 through 4 are considered low in aggressiveness (slow growing), 5 and 6 are intermediate, and 7 to 10 are high, with the worst prognoses. Doctors may do other tests such as bone scans, CAT scans, and MRIs to see if the cancer has spread.

Early detection permits treatment before the cancer has metastasized. If it has, the survival rate drops dramatically. Still, the overall survival rate has improved from 50% in the 1960s to well above 80% (American Cancer Society, 2012e). Yet the value of screening—especially PSA screening—has been questioned.

Two results of two major studies on the effectiveness of PSA screening for prostate cancer were reported in the *New England Journal of Medicine* in 2009. The American study found no statistically significant difference in the death rates due to prostate cancer in men from the experimental group who were screened annually, and in men in the control group who were left to their own judgment as to whether or not to obtain PSA tests (Andriole et al., 2009). The European study found that screening every four years as opposed to screening at the individual's discretion was associated with a 20% lower risk of dying from prostate cancer (Schröder et al., 2009). But if we place the European results in perspective, we find that the average risk of dying from prostate cancer for an unscreened man is about 3%, and the reduced rate for screened men is about 2.4%.

Prostate cancer is not necessarily lethal, and men over age 75 are usually advised not to be screened for PSA. Therefore, in both the United States and Europe, a positive PSA result (one that is indicative of prostate cancer) exposes many men to "aggressive and unnecessary treatments" (Parker-Pope, 2009a) that can cause erectile dysfunction (difficulty achieving an erection) and incontinence. According to Otis Brawley (2009) of the American Cancer Society, the European results suggest that "the [PSA] test is about 50 times more likely to ruin your life than it is to save your life." Yet surgeon Gerald L. Andriole (2009), the lead author of the U.S. study, believes that middle-aged or older men whose life expectancy is ten years or more "need to be informed about the potential pros and harms of screening. If they want to embark on it, that's fine. I'm still open to accepting that we learn a lot about a man's prostate and about the probability of him getting or having prostate cancer by measuring PSA." 👁

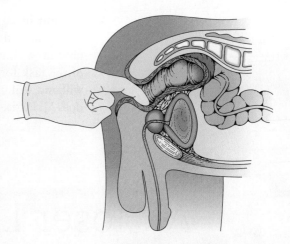

FIGURE 4.9 Digital Rectal Examination for Prostate Cancer

Source: American Cancer Society, 2006.

👁⊦Watch the Video
Male Rectal Exam
on **MyDevelopmentLab**

But in 2011, the United States Preventive Services Task Force (Harris, 2011) recommended against the use of routine PSA tests. "Unfortunately, the evidence now shows that this test does not save men's lives," Dr. Virginia Moyer, chairwoman of the task force, noted. "This test cannot tell the difference between cancers that will and will not affect a man during his natural lifetime. We need to find one that does" (Harris, 2011).

A Closer Look

Screening for Prostate Cancer: What the American Cancer Society Recommends[1]

The American Cancer Society recommends that men make an informed decision with their health care provider about whether to be screened for prostate cancer. They should first get information about what is known and what is not known about the risks and possible benefits of prostate cancer screening. Men should not be screened unless they have received this information.

- The talk about screening should take place at age 50 for men who are at average risk of prostate cancer.
- This talk should take place starting at age 45 for men at high risk of getting prostate cancer. This includes African American men and men who have a father, brother, or son found to have prostate cancer at an early age (younger than age 65).
- This talk should take place at age 40 for men at even higher risk (those with more than one close family member [father, brothers, sons] who had prostate cancer at an early age).
- After this discussion, men who want to be screened should be tested with the PSA blood test. The DRE may also be done as a part of screening.
- If, after this talk, a man is not able to decide whether testing is right for him, the screening decision can be made by the health care provider, who should take into account the patient's overall health and values.
- If no prostate cancer is found as a result of screening, the time between future

Who Is at Higher Risk of Prostate Cancer? The African American man is, possibly for genetic reasons. Health professionals usually recommend that African Americans begin screening for prostate cancer at earlier ages.

screenings depends on the results of the PSA blood test:

Men who have a PSA of less than 2.5 ng/ml (see below) may only need to be retested every 2 years. Screening should be done yearly for men whose PSA level is 2.5 ng/ml or higher.

- Because prostate cancer often grows slowly, men without symptoms of prostate cancer who aren't likely to live ten more

years should not be offered testing since they are not likely to benefit.

Even after a decision about testing has been made, men and their doctors should keep on talking about the pros and cons of testing as new information about the benefits and risks of testing becomes known. The patient's health, values, and choices can change as well.

[1]American Cancer Society. (2012, March 9). What the American Cancer Society Recommends. http://www.cancer.org/Cancer/ProstateCancer/OverviewGuide/prostate-cancer-overview-diagnosed

Treatment The most widely used treatment for prostate cancer is surgical removal of the prostate gland. However, the surgery may damage surrounding nerves, leading to problems in urinary and sexual functions. Surgeons attempt to spare surrounding nerves, but cannot guarantee elimination of the risk of complications. Other treatments include radiation, hormone treatment, and anti-cancer drugs. Hormone treatment in the form of androgen (testosterone) suppression therapy and anti-cancer drugs may shrink the size of the tumor and relieve pain. Men who obtain surgery are more likely to have urinary incontinence (loss of control over urination) and sexual dysfunction (trouble attaining erection) than men who use radiation (American Cancer Society, 2012e). But many physicians argue that surgery remains the better choice in terms of survival rates. Among older men with slow-growing prostate cancer, physicians may prefer "watchful waiting" to surgery. The men may live long enough to die from causes other than cancer. Treatment choices are explored further in the nearby "A Closer Look."

The five-year survival rate for (local) prostate cancer (cancer that has remained within the prostate gland) is nearly 100%. If it is "regional"—that is, it has spread to nearby lymph nodes, the five-year survival rate is also at nearly 100%. The significant problem rears its head when prostate cancer has spread to distant sites—that is, to distant lymph nodes, bone, or other organs. The five-year survival rate then drops to 29% (American Cancer Society, 2012e). This is why it is so essential that men talk to their doctors about screening and make informed decisions.

Male Sexual Functions

The male sexual functions of erection and ejaculation provide the means for sperm to travel from the male's reproductive tract to the female's. There the sperm cell and ovum unite to conceive a new human being. Of course, the natural endowment of reproduction with sensations of pleasure help ensure that reproduction will take place with or without knowledge of these biological facts. ◉

ERECTION

Erection is caused by the engorgement of the penis with blood, such that the penis expands and stiffens. The erect penis is an efficient funnel for depositing sperm deep within the vagina.

Erection is a hydraulic event. The spongy, cavernous masses of the penis fill with blood, causing the penis to enlarge, much like a sponge swells when it absorbs water. Erection involves both the vascular (circulatory) system and the nervous system.

In a few moments—10 or 15 seconds—the penis can double in length and firmness, and will shift from a funnel for passing urine to one that expels semen. Muscles close off the bladder when the male becomes sexually aroused, preventing the mixture of semen and urine.

The corpora cavernosa are surrounded by a tough, fibrous covering. Just as the rubber of a balloon resists the pressure of pumpedin air, this covering resists expansion, stiffening the penis. The corpus spongiosum, which contains the urethra, also engorges with blood during erection. It does not become hard, however, because it lacks the fibrous casing. The penile glans, which is formed by the crowning of the spongiosum at the tip of the penis, turns a dark purplish hue as it becomes engorged, but it too does not stiffen.

Erection is reversed when more blood flows out of erectile tissue than flows in, restoring the prearousal circulatory balance and shrinking the spongy masses. Loss of erection occurs when sexual stimulation ceases, or when the body returns to a (sexual) resting state following orgasm. Loss of erection can also occur in

◉ Watch the Video
Anatomy of the Male Erection
on **MyDevelopmentLab**

Erection Enlargement and stiffening of the penis caused by engorgement with blood.

A Closer Look

Prostate Cancer: Treat It or Wait It Out?

Each year more than 240,000 men are diagnosed with prostate cancer, but nobody can inform them what kind of treatment will most likely save their lives. Such are the findings of a report from the Agency for Healthcare Research and Quality (Parker-Pope, 2008), which analyzed 592 published studies to try to advise men about the most successful treatments. The agency compared the successes and risks of eight treatments, from prostate

Former Mayor Rudolph Giuliani of New York.
Giuliani decided to treat his prostate cancer with radioactive seed implants in an outpatient procedure. There are many treatments for prostate cancer, and people with the disease need to weigh the benefits and risks of each.

removal to radioactive implants to rapid freezing and thawing to watchful waiting—monitoring the disease and doing nothing unless it progresses. The treatments also included minimally invasive surgery (laparoscopic or robotic-assisted prostatectomy); hormone therapy or testicle removal, both of which deprive the cancer of androgens; high-intensity ultrasound; and radiation therapy. None of the treatments emerged as more successful than watchful waiting.

The study, published in the *Annals of Internal Medicine*, affords men little guidance. Prostate cancer is usually slow growing, and many live with it for years and die from something else. But for some men, prostate cancer is more aggressive, and in 2012, over 28,000 men were expected to die from it.

Other findings are as follows:

- All treatments have side effects such as urinary incontinence, bowel problems, and erectile dysfunction (Parker-Pope, 2011). The chances of sexual dysfunction and bowel problems are similar for surgery and radiation, but urine leakage is much more likely among surgery patients than patients treated with external radiation.

- External-beam radiation therapy and androgen deprivation each led to a higher frequency of bowel urgency (3%) than prostate removal (1%).

- Erectile dysfunction was more likely to be associated with androgen deprivation (86%) and radical prostatectomy (58%) than with watchful waiting (33%).

- One study concluded that men who were treated with surgery were less likely

to have their cancer metastasize or to die than those who waited watchfully, but another study reported no difference in survival between the two.

- Hormone therapy before prostatectomy did not enhance survival rates or decrease recurrence rates.

- Combining radiation with hormone treatments may decrease mortality, but when compared to radiation alone, the combination appears to increase the rates of impotence and abnormal breast development.

New treatments come along. One is a therapeutic prostate cancer vaccine, Provenge (American Cancer Society, 2012e). Therapeutic vaccines do not prevent a disease as childhood vaccines do. Instead, they are meant to trigger the body's immune system to attack a disease that is already in progress.

The American Cancer Society (2012e) advises that the treatment a man chooses should depend on the following:

- His age and how long he can expect to live
- Other health problems
- The stage and grade of his cancer (whether it has metastasized and how aggressive it is)
- His feelings—and his doctor's—about whether the cancer needs to be treated
- The probability that a given treatment will cure the cancer
- His feelings about the treatment's side effects ◉

Check with your doctor about the latest findings for the various treatments.

◉⊙ **Watch** the **Video** *Prostate Cancer* on **MyDevelopmentLab**

Performance anxiety Feelings of dread and foreboding experienced in connection with sexual activity (or any other activity that might be judged by another person).

response to anxiety or perceived threats (Cuzin et al., 2011). Such loss can be abrupt, as when a man in the "throes of passion" suddenly hears a noise suggestive of an intruder. A man who fears that he will be unable to perform successfully may experience **performance anxiety**, which can prevent him from obtaining or maintaining an erection.

Men have nocturnal erections every 90 minutes or so as they sleep. They generally occur during REM (rapid eye movement) sleep, which is associated with dreaming. It is so named because the sleeper's eyes dart about rapidly under the closed eyelids during this stage.

The mechanism of nocturnal erection is physiological. That is, dreams may not have erotic content. Morning erections are actually nocturnal erections. They occur when the man awakens during REM sleep. **TRUTH** OR **FICTION** REVISITED: Morning erections do not reflect the need to urinate.

 4

SPINAL REFLEXES AND SEXUAL RESPONSE

Men may become sexually aroused by a range of stimuli, including tactile stimulation provided by their partners, visual stimulation (as from scanning photos of nudes on the Internet), or sexual fantasies. Regardless of the source of stimulation, the man's sexual responses, erection, and ejaculation occur by reflex.

Sexual reflexes are automatic, unlearned responses to sexual stimulation. Examples in women include vaginal lubrication and orgasm. We need not try to become aroused. We need only expose ourselves to sexual stimulation and allow reflexes to do the job for us.

TRUTH OR **FICTION** REVISITED: Men cannot will themselves to have erections. People do not control sexual reflexes voluntarily, as they might lift an arm, but they can set the stage for them to occur by seeking sexual stimulation. Efforts to control sexual responses consciously by "force of will" can backfire and make it more difficult to become aroused (for example, to attain erection or vaginal lubrication).

 5

The reflexes governing erection and ejaculation are controlled in the spinal cord. They are thus called *spinal reflexes*. Erectile responses to direct stimulation such as touching or licking involve a simple spinal reflex that does not require the direct participation of the brain (see Figure 4.10). Erections can also be initiated by the brain, such as when a man has sexual fantasies or catches a glimpse of an attractive person. In such cases, stimulation from the brain travels to the spinal cord, where the erectile reflex is triggered.

Tactile stimulation (touching) of the penis or nearby areas (lower abdomen, scrotum, inner thighs) causes sensory neurons to transmit nerve messages (signals) to an erection center in the lower back, in an area of the spinal cord called the **sacrum**. The sacral erection center controls reflexive erections—that is, erections

Sacrum The thick, triangular bone located near the bottom of the spinal column.

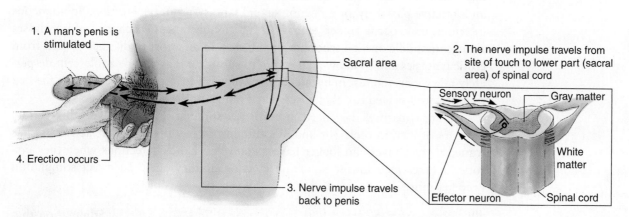

FIGURE 4.10 Reflexes. Reflexes need not involve the brain, although messages to the brain may make us aware when reflexes are occurring. Reflexes are the product of "local government" in the spine.

CRITICAL THINKING
Since erection and ejaculation
are reflexes, how is it that
people can consciously cause
them to happen?

occurring in response to direct stimulation of the penis and nearby areas. When direct penile stimulation occurs, messages in the form of nerve impulses are received by this erection center, which in turn sends impulses to the genitalia via nerves that serve the penis. These impulses cause arteries carrying blood to the corpora cavernosa and corpus spongiosum to dilate, so that more blood flows into them, causing erection.

The sacral erection center makes it possible for men whose spinal cords have been injured or severed above the center to achieve erections (and ejaculate) in response to direct tactile stimulation of the penis. Erection occurs even though their injuries prevent nerve signals from reaching their brains. Because of the lack of communication between the genital organs and the brain, there are no sensations, but many spinal-injured men report that sex remains psychologically pleasurable because they can observe the responses of their partners.

The Role of the Brain If direct penile stimulation triggers erection at the spinal level, what is the role of the brain? Although it may seem that the penis sometimes has "a mind of its own," the brain plays an important role in regulating sexual responses.

Tactile (touch) stimulation of the penis may trigger erection through the spinal cord, but sexual sensations are then normally relayed to the brain, which generally results in pleasure and perhaps in a decision to focus on erotic stimulation. The sight of one's partner, erotic fantasies, memories, and so forth can result in messages being sent by the brain through the spinal cord to the arteries servicing the penis, maintaining or strengthening the erection.

When the brain originates messages that trigger the erectile reflex, it transmits nerve impulses to a second and higher erection center located in the upper back in the lumbar region of the spinal cord. This higher spinal erection center serves as a "switch board" between the brain and the penis, allowing perceptual, cognitive, and emotional responses to make their contributions. When the nerve pathways between the brain and the upper spinal cord are blocked or severed, men cannot achieve erections in response to mental stimulation alone.

The brain can also stifle sexual response. A man who is highly anxious about his sexual abilities may be unable to achieve an erection even with intense penile stimulation. Or a man who believes that sexual pleasure is sinful or dirty may be filled with anxiety and guilt and be unable to achieve erection with a partner.

In some males, especially adolescents, the erectile reflex is so easily tripped that incidental rubbing of the genitals against his own undergarments, the sight of an attractive passer-by, or a fleeting sexual fantasy produces erection. Spontaneous erections may occur under embarrassing circumstances, such as before classes change in middle or high school or on a beach. In an effort to distract himself from erotic fantasies and to allow an erection to subside, many a male adolescent desperately renews his interest in his algebra or language textbook in class before the bell rings. (A well-placed towel may serve in a pinch on the beach.)

As men mature, they need more penile stimulation to achieve full erection. Partners of men in their 30s and 40s should not feel that their attractiveness has waned if their lovers no longer have instant "no-hands" erections when they disrobe. It takes men longer to obtain erection as they age, and direct stimulation becomes more important.

The Role of the Autonomic Nervous System (ANS) Stimulation that brings about an erection can originate in the brain, but erection is not a voluntary response, like raising your arm. Whatever the original or dominant source of stimulation—direct penile stimulation or sexual fantasy—erection remains an unlearned, automatic reflex.

Automatic responses, such as erection, involve the division of the nervous system called the **autonomic nervous system (ANS)**. *Autonomic* means "automatic." The ANS controls automatic bodily processes such as heartbeat, pupil dilation, respiration, and digestion. In contrast, voluntary movement (like raising an arm) is under the control of the *somatic* division of the nervous system.

The ANS has two branches: the sympathetic and the parasympathetic. These branches have largely opposing effects; when they are activated at the same time, their effects become balanced out to some degree. In general, the **sympathetic** branch is in command during processes that involve a release of bodily energy from stored reserves, such as during running, performing some other athletic task, or being gripped by fear or anxiety. The sympathetic branch also governs the general mobilization of the body, such as by increasing the heart rate and respiration rate in response to a threat.

The **parasympathetic** branch is most active during processes that restore reserves of energy, such as digestion. When we experience fear or anxiety, the sympathetic branch of the ANS quickens the heart rate. When we relax, the parasympathetic branch curbs the heart rate. It also activates digestive processes, but inhibits digestive activity. Because the sympathetic branch is in command when we feel fear or anxiety, such stimuli can inhibit the activity of the parasympathetic system, possibly causing indigestion.

The divisions of the ANS play different roles in sexual arousal and response. The nerves that cause penile arteries to dilate during erection belong to the parasympathetic branch of the ANS. The parasympathetic system largely governs erection. The nerves governing ejaculation belong to the sympathetic branch, however. One implication of this division of neural responsibility is that intense fear or anxiety, which involves sympathetic nervous system activity, may inhibit erection by counteracting the activity of the parasympathetic nervous system. Since sympathetic arousal helps trigger ejaculation, anxiety or fear may also accelerate ejaculation, causing *premature ejaculation* (Graziottin & Althof, 2011; see Chapter 15).

The connection between emotions, sympathetic activity, and ejaculation can set up a vicious cycle. Anxiety in a sexual encounter may trigger premature ejaculation. During a subsequent sexual encounter, the man might fear recurrence of premature ejaculation. The fear may bring on the reality. He may face further sexual encounters with yet greater fear, perhaps further hastening ejaculation—but possibly inhibiting erection. Methods for helping men with erectile dysfunction and premature ejaculation aim at reducing their levels of anxiety and thereby lessening sympathetic activity.

TRUTH OR FICTION REVISITED: Because erections seem spontaneous at times and often occur when the man would rather not have them, it may seem to men that the penis has a mind of its own. But despite this common folk belief, the penis possesses no guiding intelligence. It consists of spongy masses of erectile tissue, not the lovely dense gray matter that renders your thought processes so incisive.

Erectile Abnormalities Some men find that their erect penises are slightly curved or bent. Some degree of curvature is normal, but men with **Peyronie's disease** have excessive curvature that can make erections painful. The condition is caused by buildup of fibrous tissue in the penile shaft. Although some cases of Peyronie's disease appear to clear up on their own, most require medical attention.

Some men experience erections that persist for hours or days. This condition is called *priapism*, after Priapus of Greek myth, the son of Dionysus and Aphrodite

Autonomic nervous system (ANS) The division of the nervous system that regulates automatic bodily processes, such as heartbeat, pupil dilation, respiration, and digestion.

Sympathetic The branch of the ANS most active during emotional responses that spend energy, such as fear and anxiety. The sympathetic ANS largely controls ejaculation.

Parasympathetic The branch of the ANS most active during processes that restore energy, like digestion. The parasympathetic ANS largely controls erection.

Peyronie's disease Excessive curvature of the penis that can make erections painful.

who personified male procreative power. Priapism is often caused by leukemia, sickle cell anemia, or diseases of the spinal cord, although in some cases the cause remains unknown. Priapism occurs when the mechanisms that drain the blood that erects the penis are damaged and cannot readily return the blood to the circulatory system. Priapism may become a medical emergency, because erection prolonged beyond six hours can starve penile tissues of oxygen, leading to tissue deterioration. Medical intervention in the form of drugs or surgery may be required to reverse the condition.

EJACULATION

Ejaculation, like erection, is a spinal reflex. It is triggered when sexual stimulation reaches a critical point or threshold. Ejaculation generally occurs together with **orgasm,** the sudden muscle contractions that occur at the peak of sexual excitement and result in the abrupt release of sexual tension that had built up during sexual arousal. Orgasm is generally pleasurable. *Ejaculation,* however, refers only to the expulsion of semen from the tip of the penis. Orgasm and ejaculation are *not* synonymous, however. For example, **paraplegics** can ejaculate if the area of the lower spinal cord that controls ejaculation is intact. They do not experience the subjective aspects of orgasm, however, since the sensations of orgasm do not reach the brain.

TRUTH OR FICTION REVISITED: Many men who are paralyzed below the waist can attain erection, engage in sexual intercourse, and ejaculate, if the spinal centers controlling erection and ejaculation remain intact.

TRUTH OR FICTION REVISITED: Prepubertal boys may also experience orgasms even though they emit no ejaculate (so-called *dry orgasms*). Boys do not begin to produce seminal fluid (and sperm) until puberty. Mature men can also experience dry orgasms. These take the form of "little orgasms" preceding a larger orgasm, or they can follow "wet orgasms" when sexual stimulation is continued but seminal fluids have not been replenished.

Ejaculation occurs in two stages. The first phase, often called the **emission stage,** involves contractions of the prostate, seminal vesicles, and the upper part of the vas deferens (the **ampulla**). The force of these contractions propels seminal fluid into the prostatic part of the urethral tract—a small tube called the **urethral bulb**—which balloons as muscles close at either end, trapping the semen. It is at this point that the man perceives orgasm as inevitable. The man feels that nothing can prevent ejaculation.

In the second or **expulsion stage,** seminal fluid is propelled through the urethra and out of the urethral opening at the tip of the penis. In this stage, muscles at the base of the penis and elsewhere contract rhythmically, expelling semen. The second stage is generally accompanied by the sensations of orgasm.

In ejaculation, seminal fluid is released from the urethral bulb and expelled by contractions of the pelvic muscles that surround the urethral channel and the crura of the penis. The first few contractions are most intense and occur at 0.8-second intervals. Subsequent contractions weaken. The interval between them increases. Seminal fluid is expelled in spurts during the first few contractions. In young men, seminal fluid may be propelled 12 to 24 inches. But in some men, semen travels but a few inches, or oozes from the penile opening. The force of the expulsion varies with the condition of the man's prostate, his general health, and his age. More intense orgasms tend to accompany more forceful ejaculations.

Like erection, ejaculation is regulated by two centers in the spinal cord, one in the sacral region and one in the higher lumbar region. When sexual arousal reaches the point of ejaculatory inevitability, the lumbar ejaculatory center triggers the first stage of ejaculation, seminal emission. The lower, or sacral, ejaculatory center triggers the second stage of orgasm.

Orgasm The climax of sexual excitement.

Paraplegic A person with sensory and motor paralysis of the lower half of the body.

Emission stage The first phase of ejaculation, which involves contractions of the prostate gland, seminal vesicles, and the upper part of the vas deferens.

Ampulla A sac or dilated part of a tube or canal.

Urethral bulb The small tube that makes up the prostatic part of the urethral tract and balloons out as muscles close at either end, trapping semen prior to ejaculation.

Expulsion stage The second stage of ejaculation, during which muscles at the base of the penis and elsewhere contract rhythmically, forcefully expelling semen and providing pleasurable sensations.

Although ejaculation occurs by reflex, a man can delay ejaculation by maintaining the level of sexual stimulation below the critical threshold, or "the point of no return." Men who ejaculate prematurely have been successfully treated in programs that train them to learn to recognize their "point of no return" and maintain sexual stimulation below it. (Issues concerning the definition and treatment of premature ejaculation are explored in Chapter 15 on sexual dysfunction.) Recognizing the point of no return and keeping stimulation beneath the critical level can also prolong coitus and enhance sexual pleasure for couples even when the man does not experience premature ejaculation.

Retrograde Ejaculation In **retrograde ejaculation**, the ejaculate empties into the bladder rather than being expelled from the body. During normal ejaculation, an external sphincter opens, allowing seminal fluid to pass out of the body. Another sphincter, this one internal, closes off the opening to the bladder, preventing the seminal fluid from backing up into the bladder. In retrograde ejaculation, the actions of these sphincters are reversed. The external sphincter remains closed, preventing the expulsion of the seminal fluid, while the internal sphincter opens, allowing the ejaculate to empty into the bladder. The result is an apparently dry orgasm. Retrograde ejaculation may be caused by prostate surgery (less so now than in former years), drugs such as tranquilizers, certain illnesses, and accidents. Retrograde ejaculation is usually harmless in itself, because the seminal fluid is later discharged with urine. But infertility can result, and there may be changes in the sensations associated with orgasm. Persistent dry orgasms should be medically evaluated.

Male sexual functions, like female sexual functions, are complex. They involve the cooperation of the nervous system, the endocrine system, the cardiovascular system, and the musculoskeletal system. In Chapter 5 we learn more about how the female and male sex organs respond to sexual stimulation. In Chapter 6 we examine the similarities and differences between females and males with respect to sexual differentiation, behavior, and personality.

Retrograde ejaculation
Ejaculation in which the ejaculate empties into the bladder.

Chapter Review ✔●⌐Study and Review on MyDevelopmentLab

LO1 **Describe the external male sex organs and their functions**

The external male sex organs include the penis and the scrotum, both of which are sensitive to sexual stimulation. Semen and urine pass out of the penis through the urethral opening. The scrotum is the pouch that contains the testes.

LO2 **Discuss the pros and cons of circumcision**

Circumcision has been carried out for religious and hygienic reasons. Research shows that circumcision makes a male less vulnerable to certain health problems but decreases sexual sensations.

LO3 **Describe the internal male sex organs and their functions**

The internal male sex organs consist of the testes, tubes and ducts that conduct sperm, and organs that nourish and activate sperm. Testes secrete male sex hormones and produce sperm. The hypothalamus, pituitary gland, and testes keep blood testosterone levels at more or less even levels through a negative feedback loop. Each epididymis empties into a vas deferens that conducts sperm over the bladder. The seminal vesicles open into the ejaculatory ducts where their fluids nourish sperm. Semen is made up of sperm and fluids contributed by the seminal vesicles, prostate gland, and Cowper's glands.

LO4 **Discuss urethritis**

Men, like women, are subject to bladder and urethral inflammations, which are generally referred to as urethritis.

LO5 **Discuss testicular cancer**

Cancer of the testes is the most common form of solid-tumor cancer to strike young men between the ages of 20 and 34. Treatment is typically removal of the cancerous testis.

LO6 **Discuss benign prostate hyperplasia**

Benign prostate hyperplagia (BPH) is noncancerous enlargement of the prostate, which is caused by testosterone and connected with aging.

LO7 **Discuss prostatitis**

Prostatitis is an inflammation of the prostate gland that is typically symptomized by discomfort between the legs, behind the testes, and, sometimes, by visible blood in the urine. It is treated with antibiotics.

LO8 **Discuss prostate cancer**

Risk factors for prostate cancer include genetics, aging, and race (African American men are at higher risk). Treatments include surgery, chemotherapy, radiation, and watchful waiting.

LO9 **Explain how erection occurs**

The penis erects when caverns within it become engorged with blood, expanding and stiffening it. Erection occurs in response to sexual stimulation but is also common during REM sleep. There are two erection centers in the spinal cord. Although erection is a reflex, penile sensations are relayed to the brain, where they generally result in pleasure.

LO10 **Explain how ejaculation occurs**

The parasympathetic branch of the autonomic nervous system largely governs erection, whereas the sympathetic branch largely controls ejaculation. Ejaculation, like erection, is a reflex. It is triggered when sexual stimulation reaches a threshold. The emission phase of ejaculation involves contractions of the prostate, seminal vesicles, and the upper part of the vas deferens. In the expulsion stage, muscles propel semen out of the penis.

Test Your Learning

1. _____ is characterized by prolonged erection.
   - (a) Phimosis
   - (b) Peyronie's disease
   - (c) Ejaculation
   - (d) Priapism

2. During the emission stage of ejaculation, semen is propelled into the
   - (a) urethral bulb.
   - (b) prostate gland.
   - (c) sacrum.
   - (d) bladder.

3. Both males and females have
   - (a) sperm.
   - (b) semen.
   - (c) vas deferens.
   - (d) corpora cavernosa.

4. Male circumcision removes the
   - (a) frenulum.
   - (b) prepuce.
   - (c) glans.
   - (d) corona.

5. Scrotal temperature tends to be _____ body temperature.
   - (a) 5 to 6°F higher than
   - (b) 5 to 6°F lower than
   - (c) the same as
   - (d) an unpredictable

6. _____ stimulates secretion of testosterone by interstitial cells.
   - (a) Progestin
   - (b) Prolactin
   - (c) Luteinizing hormone
   - (d) Follicle-stimulating hormone

7. _____ nanograms of prostate specific antigen per milliliter of blood are considered normal.
   - (a) Under 4
   - (b) 4–10
   - (c) 10–20
   - (d) Over 20

8. Both semen and urine pass through the
   - (a) vas deferens.
   - (b) bladder.
   - (c) urethral meatus.
   - (d) intestines.

9. Men have erections every _____ minutes or so while they sleep.
   - (a) 30
   - (b) 60
   - (c) 90
   - (d) 120

10. The human penis contains
    - (a) corpora cavernosa.
    - (b) bone.
    - (c) muscle.
    - (d) interstitial tissue.

Answers: 1. d; 2. a; 3. d; 4. b; 5. b; 6. c; 7. a; 8. c; 9. c; 10. a

My Life, My Sexuality

What Do I Do about My Health Needs?

*Explore this **My Life, My Sexuality** feature by scanning this QR code with your mobile device. f you don't already have one, you may download a free QR scanner for your device wherever smartphone apps are sold. You can also view this feature in MyDevelopmentLab, along with an accompanying critical thinking assignment.*

Men are less willing than women to see the doctor when they have health questions or symptoms, such as discomfort in the prostate (experienced as discomfort a bit behind the testes) or visible blood in the urine. Women in our society have an "advantage" in that they are encouraged to see the doctor annually once they have become sexually active, or else beginning in young adulthood. Scan the code to go online to learn more about sexual health issues for men, even if you are in your late teens or early 20s. Doing so may help you lead a longer and healthier sex life.

5 Sexual Arousal and Response

Learning Objectives

TRUTH OR FICTION?

Which of the following statements are the truth, and which are fiction? Look for the Truth-or-Fiction icons on the pages that follow to find the answers.

1 The ancient Romans were so obsessed with offensive odors that they perfumed their horses. **T F?**

2 The menstrual cycles of women who live together tend to become synchronized. **T F?**

3 The primary erogenous zone is the brain. **T F?**

4 Strippers earn higher tips when they are ovulating. **T F?**

5 "Spanish fly" will not turn your date on, but it may cure his or her warts. **T F?**

6 Electrical stimulation of certain areas in the human brain can yield sensations similar to those of sexual pleasure and gratification. **T F?**

7 Normal men produce estrogen, and normal women produce androgens. **T F?**

8 Written descriptions of men's and women's experiences during orgasm cannot be differentiated. **T F?**

9 Orgasms attained through sexual intercourse are more intense than those attained through masturbation. **T F?**

Y ou have probably heard about the birds and the bees. How about the buds and the bees?

It may be that we should cover our children's eyes when bees are at work in the yard. Researchers at the Australian National University have learned that bees who land on certain flowers are seeking something other than pollen. It turns out that some plants emit chemical secretions that mimic chemical signals secreted by female bees ("Australia scientists," 2000). As a result, male bees try to mate with these plants. As a side effect, the bees transfer pollen from one plant to another, facilitating fertilization and the survival of these species of plants.

In case you are wondering, there is no evidence that these plants are "trying" to dupe the bees. Plants do not think, after all. It just happens, evolutionarily speaking, that whatever genes contribute to the development of these chemical secretions are likely to be transmitted to the next generation.

The kinds of plants that are "in on" the signal scam are orchids. One type is found in Europe, and nine types are found in Australia, where the bees are apparently especially active. These orchids produce the same hydrocarbon compounds that are found in chemicals secreted by the female bee.

These chemicals are called **pheromones**; they are odorless chemicals that are nevertheless detected in the same way that animals detect odors—by sampling molecules of substances in the air. Lower animals use pheromones to stimulate sexual response, organize food gathering, maintain pecking orders, sound alarms, and mark territories (Mostafa et al., 2012; Shackelford & Goetz, 2012). Pheromones induce mating behavior in insects such as bees. In the case of the orchids, the power of the pheromones apparently overrides bees' vision. Even so, one of the researchers noted that

"the bees will… only try mating with the flowers a few times each" (cited in "Australia scientists," 2000). Better to learn late than never.

A Pheromonal Scam. Australian researchers have discovered that certain orchids emit pheromones that mimic those of female bees. As a result, male bees attempt to mate with them (the flowers, that is). In the process, they pick up pollen and transfer it to other orchids, helping the orchids reproduce.

W hat turns you on? What springs your heart into your mouth, tightens your throat, and opens the floodgates into your genitals? The sight of your lover undressing, a photo of George Clooney or Emily Blunt, a sniff of musky perfume, a sip of wine?

Many factors contribute to sexual arousal. Some people are aroused by magazines with photographs of nude or seminude models that have been airbrushed to perfection. Some need only to imagine Hollywood's latest sex symbol. Some become aroused by remembrances of past lovers. Some are stimulated by sexual fantasies of flings with strangers.

People vary greatly in the cues that excite them sexually and in the frequency with which they experience sexual thoughts and feelings. Some young people seem perpetually aroused or arousable. Some people rarely or never entertain sexual thoughts or fantasies.

In this chapter we look at factors that contribute to sexual arousal and the processes that relate to sexual response. Because our experience of the world is initiated by our senses, we begin the chapter by asking: What are the roles of the senses in sexual arousal? In our discussion, we will explore the possible role of pheromones.

Pheromones Chemical substances secreted externally by certain animals, which convey information to, or produce specific responses in, other members of the same species.

Making Sense of Sex

We come to apprehend the world around us through our senses—vision, hearing, smell, taste, and the skin senses, which include that all-important sense of touch. Each of the senses plays a role in our sexual experience, but some senses play larger roles than others.

VISION: THE BETTER TO SEE YOU WITH

Visual cues can be sexual turn-ons. We may be turned on by the sight of a lover in the nude, disrobing, or dressed in evening wear. Lingerie enhances women's sex appeal by strategically concealing and revealing body parts. Men appear to be more responsive to visual stimuli than women, although women are also clearly attuned to appealing eyefuls—and what they mean to them (Chivers, 2010; Thompson, 2011).

Evolutionary psychologists note that it would make sense for males and females to be more attracted to one another when the woman is ovulating: that is, capable of conceiving a child. It would be likely that women might act somewhat differently or that men would pick up on certain cues—perhaps unconsciously—that would communicate a woman's phase of the menstrual cycle (Haselton & Gildersleeve, 2011). One study found that women tend to dress and ornament themselves in more appealing ways when they are in the fertile phase of their ovulatory cycle (Haselton et al., 2007). Forty-two judges selected photos of women as "trying to look more attractive" in their fertile (59.5%) phase as compared with their luteal phase (40.5%). Other research shows that men's "mate-retention efforts" increase as their partners are approaching ovulation, and perhaps the men perceive subtle changes in their partners' appearance that make them more attractive (Haselton & Gildersleeve, 2011).

Science has endorsed what lingerie companies have known for centuries—that women seeking male interest might do well to clothe themselves in red. Research shows that men are more likely to consider women dressed in red as more sexually desirable and attractive, although men seem to be unaware of this colorful effect (Elliot & Niesta, 2008; Kayser et al., 2010). Women, interestingly, also find men dressed in red to be more attractive, although men are much less likely to wear this color (Elliot et al., 2010). But participants in these research studies do not rate people dressed in red as kinder, more intelligent, or more likeable.

Some couples find it arousing to observe themselves making love in an overhead mirror or on videotape. Some people find sexually explicit movies arousing. Others are bored or offended by them. Although both males and females can be sexually aroused by visually mediated erotica (a technical term for "porn flicks"), men are more interested in them (Petersen & Hyde, 2011).

SMELL: DOES THE NOSE KNOW BEST?

Although the sense of smell plays a lesser role in governing sexual arousal in humans than in lower mammals, research shows that humans can detect literally millions of different odors (Hoover, 2010). Odors can be powerful sexual turn-ons or turn-offs. Perfume companies, for example, bottle fragrances purported to be sexually arousing.

Most Westerners prefer their lovers to be clean and fresh smelling (Boston Women's Health Book Collective, 2005). People in the United States have learned to remove or mask odors by the use of soaps, deodorants, and perfumes or colognes. The ancient Egyptians invented scented bathing to rid themselves of offensive odors (Illes, 2000).

Real Students, Real Questions

Q *My boyfriend has to watch pornography to get aroused. Is this normal?*

A No and yes. The no is that he should be able to get aroused without watching pornography. It could be that you don't turn him on (ouch!) and for some reason he's prolonging a relationship that isn't working for him. Or maybe he's checking to see what you'll put up with. In either case, the situation may not be a good one for you and you may want to evaluate whether you want to remain in it. We're not casting value judgments on porn per se here, unless it's degrading to women, in which case we're completely opposed. But if your boyfriend is selecting stuff that's violent or otherwise degrading to women, there could be lots of messages for you in what he's doing. It's probably not just a question of something to help him get aroused. Now, the "normal" part is that many males and females use sexual fantasies of some kind to heighten arousal. But again, he shouldn't *have* to have porn to get going, even if he might enjoy it.

 1 **TRUTH OR FICTION REVISITED:** The ancient Romans of the upper classes also had a passion for perfume. They would bathe in fragrances and even dab their horses and household pets.

Inclinations to find underarm or genital odors offensive may reflect cultural conditioning rather than biological predispositions. In some societies, genital secretions are considered aphrodisiacs. And the underarms? Check out the nearby "A Closer Look" (on page 128) on pheromones for possible answers.

Menstrual Synchrony Exposure to other women's sweat can modify a woman's menstrual cycle (Pause, 2012). How does this phenomenon happen? Let us examine some research on the subject and see.

In one study, women exposed to underarm secretions from other women, which contain steroids that may function as pheromones, showed converging shifts in their menstrual cycles (Preti et al., 1986). Similar synchronization of menstrual cycles has also been observed among women who share dormitory rooms. In another study, 80% of the women who dabbed their upper lips with an extract of perspiration from other women began to menstruate in sync with the cycles of the donors after about three menstrual cycles (Cutler, 1999). A control group, women who dabbed their lips with alcohol, showed no changes in their menstrual cycles. In yet another study from this research group, the length of the cycles of women with unusually short or long cycles began to normalize when they were **2** exposed to an extract of male underarm perspiration (Preti et al., 1986). **TRUTH OR FICTION REVISITED:** Therefore, it is true that the menstrual cycles of women who live together tend to become synchronized—so long as the women's cycles are not being regulated by birth control pills.

Attraction to—or Dislike of—Body Odors of Heterosexual Males and Females versus Gay Males and Lesbians There is reason to believe that body odors play a role in the selection of sex partners (Moshkin et al., 2011; Preti et al., 2003). Yolanda Martins and her colleagues (2005) hypothesized that preferences for axillary (underarm) odors would be related to people's sexual orientation: heterosexual male or female, and gay male or lesbian. They collected samples of axillary odors from 24 volunteers—6 exclusively male heterosexual, 6 exclusively female heterosexual, 6 exclusively gay male, and 6 exclusively lesbian, according to the Kinsey heterosexuality–homosexuality scale described in Figure 10.1.

A study of 46 male and 19 female college students compared the pleasantness or unpleasantness of male and female armpit odors as related to the phases of women's menstrual cycles (Moshkin et al., 2011). Men rated women's armpit odors as more pleasant when women were in the ovulatory phases of their cycles. The women were less likely to rate intense male body odor as unpleasant when they were in the ovulatory phase.

The researchers had a number of interesting findings. For example,

What Does the Nose Know about Sexual Orientation? Research by Yolanda Martins, George Preti, Charles Wysocki, and their colleagues (2005) suggests that gay males prefer the body odors of other gay males to those of heterosexuals and lesbians. Heterosexual males, however, seem least likely to prefer the body odors of gay males as compared to heterosexual males and to females, both heterosexual and lesbian.

- Heterosexual males and females and lesbians preferred axillary odors taken from heterosexual males over those taken from gay males.
- Gay males preferred axillary odors taken from other gay males.
- Heterosexual males and females and lesbians aged 25 and above preferred axillary odors taken from lesbians to those from gay males.
- When axillary odors of heterosexual females were compared to those of lesbians, all groups except for heterosexual males preferred the odors from heterosexual females.
- Heterosexual males preferred the odor from lesbians over the odor taken from gay male donors.

The researchers suggest that the data show that gay males and lesbians may produce axillary odors that can be distinguished from those of heterosexuals. It would also appear that gay males may perceive these typical odorants differently from the way in which heterosexual males do. We can note, at least in the few studies that have investigated the relationships between body odor and sexual orientation, that gay males are most likely to be attracted to the body odors of other gay males, and that heterosexual males are least likely to prefer the body odors of gay males.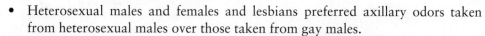

THE SKIN SENSES: SEX AS A TOUCHING EXPERIENCE

Our skin senses enable us to sense pain, changes in temperature, and pressure (or touch). Whatever the roles of vision and smell in sexual attraction and arousal, the sense of touch has the most direct effects on sexual arousal and response. Any region

CRITICAL THINKING

As critical thinkers read the study by Martins and her colleagues (2005), they will recognize the importance of remaining open-minded about the interpretation of the study's results. For example, does the study show that preferences for body odors *cause* sexual attraction or sexual orientation? Could it also be that sexual experiences give rise to preferences for certain body odors? Or is it possible that sexual orientation gives rise both to patterns of sexual attraction and preferences for body odors? Final question: Might the results of the study have any implications for the origins of homophobia?

◉ **Watch** the **Video**
Scent of a Man
on **MyDevelopmentLab**

A Closer Look

The Search for a "Magic" Love Potion: On the Threshold?

Pheromones have been found across the animal kingdom, sending messages between courting lobsters, alarmed aphids, suckling rabbit pups, mound-building termites and trail-following ants.

—T. D. Wyatt (2009)

For centuries, people have searched for a love potion—a magical formula that could make other people fall in love with you or be strongly attracted to you. But some scientists suggest that such potions may already exist in the form of chemical secretions known as pheromones. Pheromones may enhance people's moods, have effects on fertility, and provide a basis for sexual communication below the level of conscious awareness (T. Wyatt, 2009).

Pheromones are odorless chemicals that in many animals are detected through a "sixth sense"—the *vomeronasal organ (VNO)*. People possess VNOs in the mucous lining of the nose (Touhara & Vosshall, 2009; T. Wyatt, 2009). During prenatal development, the VNO shuttles sex hormones into the brain, aiding in the sexual differentiation of

the embryo (Rodriguez et al., 2000). But before birth, the human VNO shrinks, and some researchers suggest that it stops working (Kouros-Mehr et al., 2001). But if it does continue to work, it might detect pheromones and direct information about them to the hypothalamus, where they might affect sexual response (T. Wyatt, 2003). Infants apparently use pheromones to recognize their mothers, and adults might respond to them in seeking a mate (Martins et al., 2005). Male rodents such as mice are extremely sensitive to several kinds of pheromones (Leinders-Zufall et al., 2000). Male rodents show less sexual arousal when their sense of smell is blocked, but the role of pheromones in sexual behavior becomes less vital as one moves upward through the ranks of the animal kingdom.

Only a few years ago, most researchers did not believe that pheromones played a role in human behavior, but today the issue has attracted new interest. In a typical study, Winnifred Cutler and her colleagues (1998) had heterosexual men wear a suspected male pheromone, whereas a control group wore a placebo. The men using the pheromone increased

their frequency of sexual intercourse with their female partners but did not increase the frequency of masturbation. The researchers conclude that the substance increased the sexual attractiveness of the men to their partners, although they do not claim that it directly stimulated sexual behavior.

Experiments that expose men and women to suspected pheromones (*androstadienone* produced by males and *estratetraenol* produced by females) find that they enhance the moods of women but not of men; the substances also apparently reduce feelings of nervousness and tension in women, but again, not in men (Jacob et al., 2001; Jacob & McClintock, 2000). The findings about estratetraenol are not surprising. This substance is related to estrogen, and women tend to function best during the time of the month when estrogen levels are highest (Ross et al., 2000). The fact that the women responded positively to the androstadienone is of greater interest. Women may thus generally feel somewhat better when they are around men, even if male chemicals have not been shown to have direct sexual effects. Of course, being in a good mood can indirectly contribute to a woman's interest in sex.

Male perspiration primes women's emotional responses (Hummer & McClintock, 2009; Preti et al., 2003). It induces feelings of relaxation and helps lessen stress (Preti et al., 2003). It even affects the menstrual cycle. Researchers extracted samples from the underarms of men who avoided using deodorant for a month. The samples were blended and applied to the upper lips of 18 women, aged 25 to 45. The women did not know the source or makeup of the chemicals on the swabs. The women then rated their moods over a six-hour period and reported feeling more relaxed and in better moods. Analysis of their blood revealed a rise in levels of luteinizing hormone (LH), which surges before ovulation. There was no indication that the women were sexually aroused, but it might be that men's perspiration provides "chemical communication"

How Much Sexual Communication Is Occurring below the Level of Conscious Awareness? Research suggests that underarm secretions may make people more sexually attractive, even when others are unaware of sensing them. Are they drawn to each other's personal traits or to their pheromones?

when they meet women, allowing them to coordinate reproductive efforts below the level of awareness. These substances do not directly stimulate behavior, as pheromones do with lower animals.

In a double-blind experiment, 36 university women were randomly assigned to wear a perfume laced with a suspected pheromone extracted from their underarm secretions or a placebo (McCoy & Pitino, 2002). The women recorded their sexual behaviors over three menstrual cycles (12 weeks). Three-quarters (74%) of the women who used the suspected pheromone showed significant increases in their frequency of sexual intercourse, sleeping next to a partner, formal dates, and kissing, petting, and other displays of affection, as compared with one-quarter (23%) of the users of the placebo. Perhaps the suspected pheromone increased the women's attractiveness to men.

of that sensitive layer we refer to as skin can become eroticized. The touch of your lover's hand on your cheek, or your lover's gentle massage of your shoulders or back, can be sexually stimulating.

Erogenous Zones **Erogenous zones** are parts of the body that are especially sensitive to tactile sexual stimulation—to strokes and other caresses. **Primary erogenous zones** are erotically sensitive because they are richly endowed with nerve endings. **Secondary erogenous zones** are parts of the body that become erotically sensitized through experience.

Primary erogenous zones include the genitals; the inner thighs, perineum, buttocks, and anus; the breasts (especially the nipples); the ears (particularly the earlobes); the mouth, lips, and tongue; the neck; the navel; and, yes, the armpits. Preferences vary somewhat from person to person, reflecting possible biological, attitudinal, and experiential differences. Areas that are exquisitely sensitive for some people may produce virtually no reaction, or discomfort, in others. Many women, for example, report little sensation when their breasts are stroked or kissed. Many men are uncomfortable when their nipples are caressed. On the other hand (or foot), many people find the areas between their toes sensitive to erotic stimulation and enjoy keeping a toehold on their partners during coitus.

Secondary erogenous zones become eroticized through association with sexual stimulation. For example, a woman might become sexually aroused when her lover gently caresses her shoulders, because such caresses have been incorporated into the couple's lovemaking. A few of the women observed by Masters and Johnson (1966) reached orgasm when the smalls of their backs were rubbed.

People are also highly responsive to images and fantasies. This is why the brain is sometimes referred to as the primary sexual organ or an erogenous zone. Some women reported reaching orgasm through fantasy alone to interviewers in the Kinsey studies (Kinsey et al., 1953). Men regularly experience erection and nocturnal emissions ("wet dreams") without direct stimulation of the genitals.

TRUTH OR **FICTION** REVISITED: The brain is not an erogenous zone, because it is not stimulated directly by touch. The brain processes tactile information from the skin, but it does not have sensory neurons to directly gather this information itself. However, the brain can certainly pave the path toward erotic sensations through the production of fantasy, erotic memories, and other thoughts.

TASTE: ON SAVORY SEX

Taste appears to play a minor role in sexual arousal and response. Some people are sexually aroused by the taste of genital secretions, such as vaginal secretions or seminal fluid. We do not know, however, whether these secretions are laced

A Touching Experience. The sense of touch is intimately connected with sexual experience. The touch of a lover's hand on the cheek, or a gentle massage, can be sexually stimulating. Certain parts of the body—called erogenous zones—have special sexual significance because of their response to erotic stimulation.

Erogenous zones Parts of the body that are especially sensitive to tactile sexual stimulation.

 3

Primary erogenous zones Erogenous zones that are particularly sensitive because they are richly endowed with nerve endings.

Secondary erogenous zones Erogenous zones that become especially sensitive through experience.

A Closer Look

Strippers: A Treat for the Eyes or the Nose?

Many patrons of bars and strip clubs say they go "just to see what's going on" (or off?). But it could also be that many of them go to titillate their senses of smell, especially during lap dances. A study published in *Evolution and Human Behavior* (Miller et al., 2007) found that strippers' tips were related to their "time of month."

TRUTH OR FICTION REVISITED: As you can see in Figure 5.1, when strippers were ovulating, they made twice as much money in tips as when they were menstruating—and one and one-half the amount of money they

made when they were neither ovulating nor menstruating. When women are ovulating, they are usually somewhat more interested in sex, and it is possible that they subtly communicated their interest through their movements. However, it is also possible that they emitted olfactory cues that were more arousing to their patrons, who, in turn, showed their enhanced appreciation via their wallets (Haselton & Gildersleeve, 2011). It could also be that subliminal menstrual odors—which, in biological terms, are a sign of an infertile period of time—communicated unavailability at some fundamental sexual level.

Strippers and the Time of the Month. Strippers earn higher tips when they are ovulating. It is possible that male customers sense their time of the month through the sense of smell. But as critical thinkers, can you think of alternate explanations?

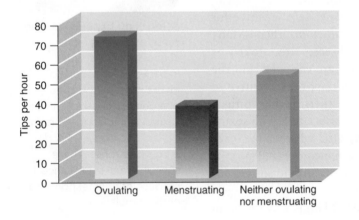

FIGURE 5.1 Strippers' Time of the Month and Amount of Tips. Strippers earned twice as much when they were ovulating as compared to when they were menstruating. It is possible that male customers sense their time of the month through the sense of smell. But as critical thinkers, can you think of alternate explanations?

Source: Data from G. Miller, J. Tybur, & B. D. Jordan. (2007). *Evolution and Human Behavior, 28* (6), 375–381.

with chemicals that have biologically arousing effects or whether arousal reflects the meaning that these secretions have to the individual. That is, we may learn to become aroused by, or to seek out, flavors or odors that have been associated with sexual pleasure. Others are turned off by them.

HEARING: THE BETTER TO HEAR YOU WITH

The sense of hearing also provides an important medium for sexual arousal and response. Like visual and olfactory cues, sounds can be turn-ons or turn-offs. The sounds of one's lover, whether whispers, indications of pleasure, or animated sounds that may attend orgasm, may be arousing during the heat of passion. For some people, key words or vocal intonations may become as arousing as direct stimulation of an erogenous zone. Many people are aroused when their lovers "talk dirty." Spoken vulgarities spur their sexual arousal. Others find vulgar language offensive.

Music can contribute to sexual arousal. Music can relax us and put us "in the mood" or have associations ("They're playing our song!"). Many couples find background music "atmospheric"—a vital accouterment of lovemaking.

Sounds can also be sexual turn-offs. Most of us would find funeral music a damper on sexual arousal. We may also be inhibited by scratchy, unnerving voices. Heavy metal rock might be a sexual turn-off to many (are your authors showing their age?), but it could help set the right tone for others.

Aphrodisiacs: of Spanish Flies and Rhino Horns

The only known aphrodisiac is variety.
—Marc Connolly

An **aphrodisiac** arouses or increases one's capacity for sexual pleasure or response. You may have heard of "spanish fly," an alleged aphrodisiac once extracted from a spanish beetle. (The beetle from which it was taken, *lytta vesicatoria*, is near extinction.) A few drops in a date's drink were believed to make you irresistible. Spanish fly is but one of many purported aphrodisiacs. It is toxic, however, not sexually arousing. Spanish fly is now synthesized—but not as an aphrodisiac.

 5

TRUTH OR FICTION REVISITED: It is true that Spanish fly will not turn your date on but it might cure his or her warts. Spanish fly contains *cantharidin*, a skin irritant that is used medically to burn off warts. If it can burn off warts, consider the damage it can do when taken internally. It irritates the urinary tract and can damage tissue or cause death (Bengoa Vallejo et al., 2008). It inflames the urethra, producing a burning sensation in the penis that is sometimes misinterpreted as sexual feelings.

Foods that in some way resemble male genitals have now and then been considered aphrodisiacs. They include oysters, clams, bull's testicles ("prairie oysters"), tomatoes, and "phallic" items such as celery stalks, bananas, and even ground-up rhinoceros, reindeer, and elephant horns (which is one derivation of the slang term *horny*). Even potatoes—both white and sweet—have been held to be aphrodisiacs. None of these foods or substances has been shown to be sexually stimulating, however. Sadly, myths about the sexually arousing properties of substances drawn from rhinoceroses or elephants may be contributing to the rapidly diminishing numbers of these animals (Ascher, 2006).

Other drugs and psychoactive substances may have certain effects on sexual arousal and response. The drug arginine, an amino acid extracted from the African yohimbe tree, does stimulate blood flow to the genitals. However, its effects are limited and unreliable (Downs & Nazario, 2003).

Amyl nitrate (in the form of "snappers" or "poppers") has been used mostly by gay men (and by some heterosexuals) in the belief that it heightens sensations of arousal and orgasm. Poppers dilate blood vessels in the brain and genitals, producing sensations of warmth in the pelvis and possibly facilitating erection and prolonging orgasm. Amyl nitrate does have some legitimate medical uses, such as helping reduce heart pain (angina) among cardiac patients. It is inhaled from ampules that "pop" open for rapid use when heart pain occurs. Poppers can cause dizziness,

Aphrodisiacs Drugs or other agents that are sexually arousing or that increase sexual desire.

A Closer Look

YSEX—That Is, Why Do People Engage in Sexual Intercourse? Is the Answer (Always) Obvious?

Do you see yourself as engaging in sexual intercourse to get a job or a raise? To be "used" or degraded? Because you lost a bet? Or to feel closer to God? These are infrequent reasons for having sex, but some people have engaged in intercourse because of them.

Cindy Meston and David Buss (2007) sought to learn about the most common—and least common—reasons for sex, to see if they were consistent with pervasive gender roles and what they might suggest about theories of human sexuality. To do so, they created a questionnaire with the intriguing title, "YSEX ('Why Sex?')" and administered it to college students.

The researchers had 1,549 students take the questionnaire in exchange for course credit. The sample was 62%

European American, 15% Asian American, 15% Latin American, 4% African American, and 1% Native American.

The following nine themes characterized the most common reasons among both men and women for having sex: (1) feelings of attraction, (2) desire for physical pleasure, (3) expression of feelings of love, (4) feeling desired by the other person, (5) desire to deepen the relationship, (6) novel experience, (7) celebration of special occasion, (8) opportunity, and (9) seeming to "just happen." People were least likely to have sex to hurt their partners (that is, cheating on them), to get a job or a promotion, to be more popular, to get rid of a headache or cramps, or because of pressure or a sense of duty.

Some reasons were unexpected, to put it mildly: "I wanted to feel closer to God."

There were some gender differences: Men were significantly more likely than women to have sex for physical reasons (physical appearance, an attractive face) and because of sheer opportunity. Men's greater emphasis on physical reasons seems to support the view that men are more responsive to visual cues. Men were also more interested in sex for bragging rights, purposes of "conquest," and enhancing their social status among other men. Women exceeded men on having sex to express love. All in all, the responses were consistent with traditional gender roles that portray men as sexual initiators and women as "gate keepers."

---

fainting, and migraine-type headaches, however. They should be taken only under a doctor's care for a legitimate medical need, not to intensify sexual sensations.

The drug Viagra was originally developed as a treatment for angina (heart pain) because it increases the blood flow to the heart—modestly. However, it also dilates blood vessels in the genital organs, thereby facilitating vasocongestion and erection—and, according to some reports, sexual response in women as well (Slovenko, 2001). Viagra and similar drugs—Levitra and Cialis—are treatments for erectile dysfunction (once termed *impotence*). Is Viagra also an aphrodisiac? Apparently not. Although Viagra facilitates erection, it still takes a sexual turn-on for erection to occur.

But certain drugs do appear to have aphrodisiac effects, apparently because they act on the brain mechanisms controlling the sex drive. For example, drugs that affect brain receptors for the neurotransmitter dopamine, such as the antidepressant drug bupropion (trade name Wellbutrin) and the drug L-dopa used in the treatment of Parkinson's disease, can increase the sex drive (Saks, 2008).

The most potent chemical "aphrodisiac" may be a naturally occurring substance in the body, the male sex hormone testosterone. It is the basic fuel of sexual desire in both males and females (Basson et al., 2009).

The safest and perhaps most effective method for increasing the sex drive may not be a drug or substance but proper diet and exercise. Regular exercise not only enhances general health but it also boosts energy and increases the sex drive in both sexes. Perhaps the strongest aphrodisiac is novelty. Partners can invent new ways of sexually discovering one another. They can make love in novel places, experiment with different techniques, wear provocative clothing, share or enact fantasies, or whatever their imaginations inspire.

ANAPHRODISIACS

Aphrodisiacs are thought to stimulate a sexual response. **Anaphrodisiacs** would have the opposite effect. These include substances such as potassium nitrate (saltpeter), which have been considered inhibitors of sexual response, or anaphrodisiacs. Saltpeter, however, only indirectly dampens sexual arousal. As a diuretic that can increase the need for urination, it may make the thought of sex unappealing, but it does not directly dampen sexual response.

Other chemicals do dampen sexual arousal and response. Tranquilizers and central nervous system depressants, such as barbiturates, can lessen sexual desire and impair sexual performance. These drugs may paradoxically enhance sexual arousal in some people, however, by lessening sexual inhibitions or the fear of possible repercussions from sexual activity. Anti-hypertensive drugs, which are used in the treatment of high blood pressure, may produce erectile and ejaculatory difficulties in men and reduction of sexual desire in men and women. Certain anti-depressant drugs, such as fluoxetine (brand name Prozac), amitriptyline (brand name Elavil), and imipramine (brand name Tofranil), appear to dampen the sex drive (Kennedy & Rizvi, 2009). Anti-depressants may also impair erectile response and delay ejaculation in men and orgasmic responsiveness in women (Kennedy & Rizvi, 2009). (Because they delay ejaculation, some of these drugs are used to treat premature ejaculation.)

Nicotine, the stimulant in tobacco smoke, constricts the blood vessels. Thus, it can impede sexual arousal by reducing the capacity of the genitals to become engorged with blood. Chronic smoking can also reduce the blood levels of testosterone in men, which, in turn, can lessen sex drive or motivation.

Antiandrogen drugs may have anaphrodisiac effects. They have been used in the treatment of deviant behavior patterns such as sexual violence and sexual interest in children, with some promising results (e.g., Roesler & Witztum, 2000).

PSYCHOACTIVE DRUGS

Psychoactive drugs, such as alcohol and cocaine, are widely believed to have aphrodisiac effects. Do any psychoactive drugs stimulate a sexual response? Perhaps some do, but their effects may also reflect our expectations of them, or their effects on sexual inhibitions, rather than direct stimulation of sexual response.

Alcohol Small amounts of alcohol are stimulating, but large amounts curb sexual response. This fact should not be surprising because alcohol is a depressant; it reduces central nervous system activity. Large amounts of alcohol can severely impair sexual performance in both men and women.

People who drink moderate amounts of alcohol may feel more sexually aroused because of their expectations about alcohol, not because of its chemical properties (Davis, 2010; Gil-Rivas, 2012). That is, people who expect alcohol to enhance sexual responsiveness may act the part. Expectations that alcohol serves as an aphrodisiac may lead men with problems achieving erection to turn to alcohol as a cure. The fact is that alcohol is a depressant, and a few drinks can reduce sexual potency rather than restore it.

Alcohol may also lower sexual inhibitions, because it allows us to ascribe our behavior to the effects of the alcohol rather than to ourselves. Alcohol is connected with a liberated social role and thus provides an excuse for dubious behavior. "It was the alcohol," people can say, "not me." People may express their sexual desires and do things when drinking that they would not do when sober. For example, a person who feels guilty about sex may become sexually active when drinking because he or she can later blame the alcohol.

CRITICAL THINKING
Agree or disagree with the following statement and support your answer: Alcohol stimulates sexual desire and behavior.

Anaphrodisiacs Drugs or other agents whose effects are antagonistic to sexual arousal or sexual desire.

Antiandrogen A substance that decreases the levels of androgens in the bloodstream.

What Are the Effects of Alcohol on Sexual Behavior?
Small doses of alcohol can be stimulating, induce feelings of euphoria, and lower inhibitions, all of which could be connected with sexual interest and could facilitate social and sexual behavior. Alcohol also reduces fear of consequences of engaging in risky behavior—sexual and otherwise, and it provides an excuse for otherwise unacceptable behavior, such as sexual intercourse on the first date (or upon a casual meeting). That is, drinkers can say, "It was the alcohol, not me." Alcohol is also expected to be sexually liberating, and people often live up to social and cultural expectations. Yet, as a depressant drug, large amounts of alcohol will biochemically dampen sexual response.

Binge drinking—having five or more drinks in a row for a male, or four or more for a female—is connected with high-risk sexual behavior, sexual promiscuity, and sexual assault (Ragsdale et al., 2012; Scott-Sheldon et al., 2010). Nevertheless, more than two out of five college students binge at least twice a month, and half this number binge three or more times every two weeks (Patrick & Schulenberg, 2011; Squeglia et al., 2012).

Alcohol can also induce feelings of euphoria. Euphoric feelings may enhance sexual arousal and also wash away qualms about expressing sexual desires. Alcohol also appears to impair the ability to weigh information ("information processing") that might otherwise inhibit sexual impulses (Orchowski et al., 2012; Purdie et al., 2011). When people drink, they may be less able to foresee the consequences of misconduct and less likely to ponder their standards of conduct.

Hallucinogenics There is no evidence that marijuana and other hallucinogenic drugs directly stimulate sexual response, yet marijuana use is connected with increased sexual activity and engaging in unprotected sex (Anderson & Stein, 2011). However, fairly to strongly intoxicated marijuana users claim to have more empathy with others, to be more aware of bodily sensations, and to experience time as passing more slowly. These sensations can heighten subjective feelings of sexual response and apparently contribute to women's sexual enjoyment and physical responsiveness, but marijuana use, especially at high doses, may decrease testosterone levels in males and have an inhibitory effect on erection (Gorzalka et al., 2010).

Other hallucinogenics, such as LSD and mescaline, have also been reported by some users to enhance sexual response. Again, these effects may reflect dosage level, as well as expectations, user experiences, attitudes toward the drugs, and altered perceptions.

Stimulants Stimulants such as amphetamines ("speed," "uppers," "bennies," "dexies") and methamphetamine ("meth") are reputed to heighten arousal and sensations of orgasm (Frohmader et al., 2010). The drugs can also elevate the mood, and sexual pleasure may be in part heightened by general elation. But overdoses of

135

these drugs can give rise to irritability, restlessness, hallucinations, paranoid delusions, insomnia, loss of appetite—and, at their worst, cardiac problems. Moreover, methamphetamine is highly addictive. ◉

Cocaine is a natural stimulant that is extracted from the leaves of the coca plant—the plant from which the soft drink Coca-Cola obtained its name. In fact, Coke—Coca-Cola, that is—contained cocaine as part of its original formula. Cocaine was removed from the secret formula in 1906 and replaced with extra caffeine. The drug is ingested in various forms, snorted as a powder, smoked in hardened rock form ("crack" cocaine) or in a freebase form, or injected directly into the bloodstream in liquid form. Cocaine produces a euphoric rush, which tends to ebb quickly. Physically, cocaine constricts blood vessels (reducing the oxygen supply to the heart), elevates blood pressure, and boosts heart rate. There is also evidence that cocaine has complicated effects on hormone levels in mammals, which may induce feelings of anxiety and inhibit sexual response (Kohtz et al., 2010).

Despite any effects on sexual arousal, high doses of stimulants can cause irritability, restlessness, hallucinations, paranoid delusions, insomnia, loss of appetite—and in high doses, cardiac arrest. Use of crack cocaine is connected with a higher number of sex partners (Maranda et al., 2004).

Sexual Response and the Brain: Cerebral Sex?

The brain may not be an erogenous zone, but it plays a central role in sexual functioning (fisher, 2000). Direct genital stimulation may trigger spinal reflexes that produce erection in the male and vaginal lubrication in the female without the direct involvement of the brain. The same reflexes, however, may also be triggered by sexual stimulation that originates in the brain in the form of erotic memories, fantasies, visual images, and thoughts. The brain may also inhibit sexual responsiveness, as when we experience guilt or anxiety in a sexual situation, or when we suddenly realize in the midst of a sexual encounter that we have left the car lights turned on. Let us explore the brain mechanisms involved in sexual functioning.

Parts of the brain, in particular the cerebral cortex and the limbic system, play key roles in sexual functioning (see Figure 5.2). Cells in the cerebral cortex fire (transmit messages) when we experience sexual thoughts, images, wishes, fantasies, and the like. Cells in the cerebral cortex interpret sensory information as sexual turn-ons or turn-offs. The sight of your lover disrobing, the anticipation of a romantic kiss, a passing sexual fantasy, or an erotic photo can trigger the firing of cortical cells. These cells, in turn, transmit messages through the spinal cord that send blood rushing to the genitals, causing erection or vaginal lubrication. The cortex also provides the conscious sense of self. The cortex judges sexual behavior to be proper or improper, moral or immoral, relaxing or anxiety- or guilt-provoking. ◉

◉ Watch the Video
Addicted to Love
on **MyDevelopmentLab**

CRITICAL THINKING

Critical thinkers are cautious in their interpretation of research findings. There is evidence that use of crack cocaine is connected with having more sex partners. Does this connection mean that the relationship is causal? Can you think of other possible explanations of the relationship?

◉ Watch the Video
Sex in the Brain
on **MyDevelopmentLab**

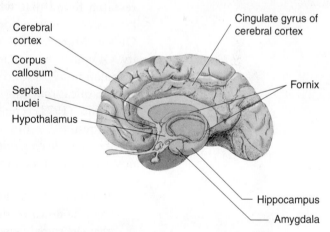

FIGURE 5.2 Parts of the Brain Involved in Sexual Functioning. A view of the brain, split from top to bottom. Cells in the cerebral cortex transmit messages when we experience sexual thoughts and mental images. Cells in the cortex interpret sensory information as sexual turn-ons or turn-offs. The cerebral cortex may then transmit messages through the spinal cord that send blood coursing to the sex organs, leading to erection or vaginal lubrication. The limbic system lies along the inner edge of the cerebrum. When part of a male rat's hypothalamus is electrically stimulated, the rat engages in its courting and mounting routine. Klüver and Bucy (1939) found that destruction of areas of the limbic system triggered continuous sexual behavior in monkeys. Electrical stimulation of the hippocampus and septal nuclei produces erections in monkeys.

CRITICAL THINKING

If you electrically stimulate part of a rat's brain, it mechanically runs through a mating routine. Does it seem useful or wise to attempt to apply this research finding to humans?

Areas of the brain below the cortex, especially the limbic system, also play roles in sexual processes (Kimble, 1992). For example, when the rear part of a male rat's hypothalamus is stimulated by an electrical probe, the animal mechanically runs through its courting and mounting routine. It nibbles at the ears and the back of the neck of a female rat and mounts her when she responds. People, of course, are influenced by learning, fantasy, and values as well as simple brain (or spinal) stimulation.

The importance of the limbic system in the sexual behavior in animals was demonstrated in experiments by Heinrich Klüver and Paul Bucy of the University of Chicago in 1939. Klüver and Bucy reported that destruction of areas of the limbic system triggered persistent sexual behaviors that included masturbation and male–female and male–male mounting attempts. The monkeys even tried to mount the experimenters. For obvious ethical reasons, researchers have not injured or destroyed parts of people's brains to observe the effects on humans.

Electrical stimulation of the hippocampus and septum of the limbic system can produce erections in laboratory monkeys (Ferris et al., 2004). Electrical stimulation of a pathway in the thalamus, moreover, can produce a seminal discharge in these monkeys—without erection. Stimulation of certain areas in the thalamus and hypothalamus may induce ejaculation. It remains to be seen how these findings will be useful with humans.

ON PUSHING THE RIGHT BUTTONS: ARE THERE PLEASURE CENTERS IN THE BRAIN?

Research with electrical probes suggests that "pleasure centers" may exist in and near the hypothalamus in other animals and perhaps even in people. Classic research found that when electrodes are implanted in certain parts of the limbic system, investigators find that laboratory animals such as rats (Olds, 1956; Olds & Milner, 1954) will repeatedly press controls to receive bursts of electricity. Of course we cannot know what the rats experience, but people report that stimulation of these so-called pleasure centers leads to feelings of sexual arousal and gratification.

Heath (1972) found that electrical stimulation of the septal region of the limbic system resulted in orgasm-like sensations in two people. Delgado (1969) reported that two female epileptic patients who received limbic stimulation as part of a diagnostic evaluation became sexually aroused by the stimulation:

> [One] reported a pleasant tingling sensation in the left side of her body "from my face down to the bottom of my legs." She started giggling and [stated] that she enjoyed the sensation "very much." Repetition of these stimulations made the patient more communicative and flirtatious, and she ended by openly expressing her desire to marry the therapist. [The other patient reported] a pleasant sensation of relaxation and considerably increased her verbal output, which took on a more intimate character. [She] expressed her fondness for the therapist [whom she had just met], kissed his hands, and talked about her immense gratitude. (p. 145)

TRUTH OR **FICTION** REVISITED: It is apparently true that electrical stimulation of certain areas in the human brain can yield sensations similar to those of sexual pleasure and gratification. We might wonder whether we would bother to develop sexual relationships if such centers could be stimulated directly. But before you run to the store for electrodes, consider that few researchers suggest that we will someday replace lovers with electronic kits.

Sex Hormones and Sexual Behavior

In a tv situation comedy, a male adolescent was described as a "hormone with feet." Ask parents why teenagers act the way they do, and you are likely to hear a one-word answer: hormones!

Hormones are chemicals that are secreted by the ductless glands of the endocrine system directly into the bloodstream. The word *hormone* derives from the Greek *horman,* meaning "to stimulate" or "to goad." We could say that hormones very much goad us into sexual activity. Hormones also regulate various bodily functions, including growth and resistance to stress as well as sexual functions.

The hypothalamus and pituitary gland regulate gonadal secretion of sex hormones, specifically testosterone in males and estrogen and progesterone in females. At puberty, a surge of sex hormones causes the blossoming of reproductive maturation: the sperm-producing ability of the testes in males and the maturation of ova and ovulation in females. Sex hormones released at puberty also cause the flowering of secondary sex characteristics. In males, the vocal cords lengthen (and the voice consequently lowers), and facial and pubic hair grow. In females, the breasts and hips become rounded with fatty tissue, and pubic hair grows.

Hormone A chemical that is secreted directly into the bloodstream by a ductless gland, and which influences the functions of the body and/or behavior.

ORGANIZING AND ACTIVATING INFLUENCES

Sex hormones have organizing and activating effects on behavior. That is, they exert an influence on the type of behavior that is expressed (an organizing effect) and the frequency or intensity of the drive that motivates the behavior and the ability to perform the behavior (activating effects). For example, sex hormones predispose lower animals and possibly people toward stereotypical masculine or feminine mating behaviors (an organizing effect). They also facilitate sexual response and influence sexual desire (activating effects).

Although sex hormones clearly determine the sex of the sex partners that many lower animals will seek, their roles in human sexual behavior may be relatively more subtle and are not as well understood. Much of our knowledge of the organizing and activating effects of sex hormones comes from research with other species in which hormone levels were manipulated by castration or injection. Ethical standards prohibit such research with human infants, for obvious reasons.

The activating effects of testosterone can be clearly observed among male rats. For example, males who are castrated in adulthood and thus deprived of testosterone discontinue sexual behavior. If they are given injections of testosterone, however, they resume stereotypical male sexual behaviors, such as mounting females.

In rats, testosterone apparently organizes or differentiates the brain in the masculine direction such that adult male rats display stereotypical masculine behaviors—including sniffing (especially sniffing of females), and mounting females—upon activation by testosterone. Male fetuses and newborns normally have sufficient amounts of testosterone in their blood systems to organize their brains in the masculine direction. Female fetuses and newborns normally have lesser amounts of testosterone. Their brains

Are Adolescents "Hormones with Feet"? Research shows that levels of androgens are connected with sexual interest in both male and female adolescents. Hormone levels are more likely to predict sexual behavior in adolescent males, however, perhaps because society places greater restraints on female sexuality.

thus become organized in a feminine direction. When female rodents are prenatally exposed to large doses of testosterone, their sexual organs become somewhat masculinized, and they are predisposed toward masculine mating behaviors in adulthood (Banszegi et al., 2010).

In rats and other rodents, sexual differentiation of the brain is not complete at birth. Female rodents and monkeys who are given testosterone injections shortly before or shortly following birth (depending on the species) show typical masculine sexual patterns in adulthood, mounting other females and resisting mounting by males (Phoenix, 2009).

Questions remain about the organizing effects of sex hormones on human sexual behavior. Prenatal sex hormones play a role in the sexual differentiation of the genitalia and of the brain structures, such as the hypothalamus. Their role in patterning sexual behavior in adulthood remains unclear, however. It has been speculated that prenatal sexual differentiation of the brain may also be connected with sexual orientation.

What of the activating effects of sex hormones on human sex drive and behavior? Although the countless attempts to extract or synthesize aphrodisiacs have failed to produce the real thing, men and women normally produce a genuine aphrodisiac—testosterone. Testosterone activates the sex drives of both men and women (Guzick & Hoeger, 2000). 👁

👁—|Watch the **Video**
*Study Finds Tears Are
a Sexual Turnoff*
on **MyDevelopmentLab**

SEX HORMONES AND MALE SEXUAL BEHAVIOR

Male sex hormones are known to influence the sex drive and sexual response in nonhuman animals and men (Maggi et al., 2012). Evidence of the role for hormones in the sex drive is found among men who have declines in testosterone levels as the result of chemical or surgical castration. Surgical castration (removal of the testes) is sometimes performed as a medical treatment for cancer of the prostate or other diseases of the male reproductive tract, such as genital tuberculosis. But some convicted sex offenders have voluntarily undergone castration as a condition of release.

Men who are surgically or chemically castrated usually exhibit a gradual decrease in the incidence of sexual fantasies and loss of sexual desire (Barbaree & Blanchard, 2008). They also gradually tend to lose the capacities to attain erection and to ejaculate—an indication that testosterone is important in maintaining sexual functioning as well as drive, at least in males. Castrated men show great variation in their sexual interest and functioning, however. Some continue to experience sexual desires and are able to function sexually for years, even decades. Learning appears to play a large role in determining continued sexual response following castration. Males who were sexually experienced before castration show a more gradual decline in sexual activity. Those who were sexually inexperienced at the time show relatively little or no interest in sex. Male sexual motivation and functioning thus involve interplay of hormonal influences and experience.

Further evidence of the relationship between hormonal levels and male sexuality is found in studies of men with hypogonadism, a condition marked by abnormally low levels of testosterone production. Hypogonadal men generally suffer loss of sexual desire and a decline in sexual activity (Maggi, 2012). Here again, hormones do not tell the whole story. Hypogonadal men are capable of erection, at least for a while, even though their sex drives may wane. The role of testosterone as an activator of sex drives in men is further supported by evidence of the effects of testosterone replacement in hypogonadal men. When such men receive testosterone injections, their sex drives, fantasies, and activity are often restored to former levels (Maggi, 2012).

Although minimal levels of androgens are critical to male sexuality, there is no one-to-one correspondence between hormone levels and the sex drive or sexual performance in adults. In men who have ample supplies of testosterone, sexual interest and functioning depend more on learning, fantasies, attitudes, memories, and other psychosocial factors than on hormone levels. At puberty, however, hormonal variations may play a more direct role in stimulating sexual interest and activity in males. Udry (2001) found, for example, that testosterone levels predicted sexual interest, masturbation rates, and the likelihood of engaging in sexual intercourse among teenage boys. A positive relationship also has been found between testosterone levels in adult men and frequency of sexual intercourse (Maggi, 2012). Moreover, drugs that reduce the levels of androgen in the blood system, called *antiandrogens,* lead to reductions in the sex drive and in sexual fantasies (Maggi, 2012).

  7

TRUTH OR **FICTION** REVISITED: Men and women produce small amounts of the sex hormones of the other sex. Testosterone, the major form of androgen, or male sex hormone, is secreted in small amounts by the adrenal glands (located above the kidneys) in both sexes, but in much larger amounts by the testes. The ovaries produce small amounts of androgens but much larger amounts of the female sex hormones, estrogen and progesterone. The testes similarly produce small amounts of estrogen and progesterone.

SEX HORMONES AND FEMALE SEXUAL BEHAVIOR

The female sex hormones estrogen and progesterone play prominent roles in promoting the changes that occur during puberty and in regulating the menstrual cycle. Female sex hormones do not appear to play a direct role in determining sexual motivation or response in human females, however.

In most mammals, females are sexually receptive only during **estrus**. Estrus is a brief period of fertility that corresponds to time of ovulation; during estrus, females are said to be "in heat." Estrus occurs once a year in some species; in others, it occurs periodically during the year in mating seasons. Estrogen peaks at time of ovulation, so there is a close relationship between fertility and sexual receptivity in most female mammals. Human females' sexuality is not clearly linked to hormonal fluctuations, however. Unlike females of most other species of mammals, the human female is sexually responsive during all phases of the reproductive (menstrual) cycle—even during menstruation, when ovarian hormone levels are low—and after menopause.

Estrus   A brief period of fertility that corresponds to ovulation.

Real Students, Real Questions

Q *I don't get an erection as quickly as I used to. What is wrong with me?*

A Could be nothing. After the later teens, it's all downhill, physiologically speaking, but it's a very, very long slope—and a very gradual one. Also, in your middle teens you'll have an erection in just a few seconds, so what does it matter if it takes a few more seconds, or a minute or two? Even when you're in your 50s and older, when it can take a few minutes and manual or oral stimulation to become erect, it's the quality of the overall experience that ought to matter and not the stopwatch. So many of our sexual problems are actually problems with our "oughts" and our "shoulds," or with our partner's "oughts" and "shoulds," and not with our bodies. Keep in mind that sex is not a race.

There is some evidence, however, that sexual responsiveness in women is influenced by the presence of circulating androgens, or male sex hormones, in their bodies. The adrenal glands of women produce small amounts of androgens, just as they do in males (Davis & Braunstein, 2012). The fact that women normally produce smaller amounts of androgens than men does not mean that they necessarily have weaker sex drives. Rather, women appear to be more sensitive to smaller amounts of androgens. Even so, women's sexual activity increases at points in the menstrual cycle when levels of androgens in the bloodstream are high.

Women who have **ovariectomies**, which are sometimes carried out when a hysterectomy is performed, no longer produce female sex hormones. Nevertheless, they may continue to experience sex drives and interest as before. Loss of the ovarian hormone estradiol may cause vaginal dryness and make coitus painful, but it does not necessarily reduce sexual desire. (The dryness can be alleviated by a lubricating jelly or by estrogen-replacement therapy.) However, women whose adrenal glands and ovaries have been removed, so that they no longer produce androgens, gradually lose sexual desire (Davis & Braunstein, 2012). An active and enjoyable sexual history seems to ward off this loss, however, suggestive of the impact of cognitive and experiential factors on human sexual response.

Research provides further evidence on the links between testosterone levels and women's sex drives. Androgen levels predict sexual interest among teenage girls. In contrast to boys, however, girls' androgen levels were unrelated to the likelihood of coital experience. Androgens apparently affect sexual desire in both sexes, but sexual interest may be more likely to be directly translated into sexual activity in men than in women (Carvalho & Nobre, 2010; Petersen & Hyde, 2011). This sex difference may be explained by society's placement of greater restraints on female sexuality.

Androgens thus play a prominent role in activating and maintaining women's sex drives. As with men, however, women's sexuality is too complex to be explained fully by hormone levels. For example, an active and enjoyable sexual history seems to ward off the loss of sexual interest that generally follows the surgical removal of the adrenal glands and ovaries.

Sexual Response

Although we may be culturally attuned to focus on sex differences rather than similarities, Masters and Johnson (1966) found that the physiological responses of men and women to sexual stimulation (whether from coitus, masturbation, or other sources) are quite alike. The sequence of changes in the body that takes place as men and women become progressively more aroused is referred to as the *sexual response cycle*. ✳

THE FOUR-PHASE MASTERS AND JOHNSON SEXUAL RESPONSE CYCLE

Masters and Johnson divided the **sexual response cycle** into four phases: excitement, plateau, orgasm, and resolution. Figure 5.3 suggests the levels of sexual arousal associated with each phase. Both males and females experience vasocongestion and myotonia early in the response cycle. **Vasocongestion** is the swelling of the genital tissues with blood, which causes erection of the penis and engorgement of the area surrounding the vaginal opening. The testes, nipples, and even earlobes become engorged as blood vessels in these areas dilate.

Ovariectomy Surgical removal of the ovaries.

✳ ⌐Explore the **Concept**
The Sexual Response Cycle
on **MyDevelopmentLab**

Sexual response cycle Masters and Johnson's model of sexual response, which consists of four phases.

Vasocongestion The swelling of the genital tissues with blood, which causes erection of the penis and engorgement of the area surrounding the vaginal opening.

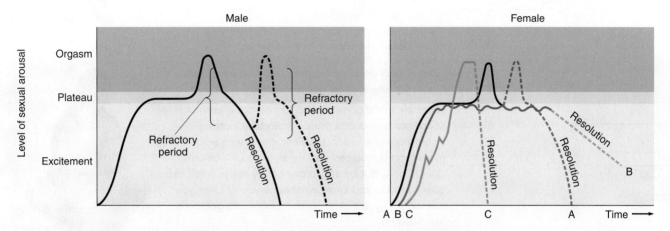

FIGURE 5.3 Levels of Sexual Arousal during the Phases of the Sexual Response Cycle. Masters and Johnson (1966) divide the sexual response cycle into four phases: excitement, plateau, orgasm, and resolution. During the resolution phase, the level of sexual arousal returns to the prearoused state. For men, there is a refractory period after orgasm. As shown by the broken line, however, men can become rearoused to orgasm after the refractory period has passed and their level of sexual arousal returns to preplateau levels. Pattern A for women shows a typical response cycle, with the broken line suggesting multiple orgasms. Pattern B shows the cycle of a woman who reaches the plateau phase, but for whom arousal is "resolved" without reaching the orgasmic phase. Pattern C shows the possibility of orgasm in a highly aroused woman who passes quickly through the plateau phase.

Myotonia refers to muscle tension. Myotonia causes voluntary and involuntary muscle contractions, which produce facial grimaces, spasms in the hands and feet, and eventually, the spasms of orgasm. Let us follow these and the other bodily changes that constitute the sexual response cycle.

Excitement Phase In younger men, vasocongestion during the **excitement phase** produces penile erection as early as 3 to 8 seconds after stimulation begins. Erection may occur more slowly in older men, but the responses are essentially the same. Erection may subside and return as stimulation varies. The scrotal skin thickens, losing its baggy appearance. The testes increase in size. The testes and scrotum become elevated.

In the female, vaginal lubrication may start 10 to 30 seconds after stimulation begins. Vasocongestion swells the clitoris, flattens the labia majora and spreads them apart, and increases the size of the labia minora. The inner two-thirds of the vagina expand. The vaginal walls thicken and, because of the inflow of blood, turn from their normal pink to a deeper hue. The uterus becomes engorged and elevated. The breasts enlarge, and blood vessels near the surface become more prominent.

The skin may take on a rosy **sex flush** late in this phase. It varies with intensity of arousal and is more pronounced in women. The nipples may become erect in both sexes, especially in response to direct stimulation. Men and women show some increase in myotonia, heart rate, and blood pressure.

Plateau Phase A plateau is a level region, and the level of arousal remains somewhat constant during the plateau phase of sexual response. Nevertheless, the **plateau phase** is an advanced state of arousal that precedes orgasm. Men in this phase show a slight increase in the circumference of the coronal ridge of the penis. The penile glans turns a purplish hue, a sign of vasocongestion. The testes are elevated further

Myotonia Muscle tension.

Excitement phase The first phase of the sexual response cycle, which is characterized by erection in the male, vaginal lubrication in the female, and muscle tension and increases in heart rate in both males and females.

Sex flush A reddish rash that appears on the chest or breasts late in the excitement phase of the sexual response cycle.

Plateau phase The second phase of the sexual response cycle, which is characterized by increases in vasocongestion, muscle tension, heart rate, and blood pressure in preparation for orgasm.

Real Students, Real Questions

Q *Sometimes I don't get lubricated, and intercourse is painful. why don't I get lubricated?*

A There are many possibilities. Sometimes a woman needs more time or a more comfortable setting. If you suspect a health problem, check with your gynecologist. You can also try an artificial lubricant, like K-Y jelly. But by and large, simply ask yourself two questions: Do you know what turns you on? Are you making sure you get it? Maybe this means getting a new partner!

into position for ejaculation and may reach one and one-half times their unaroused size. The Cowper's glands secrete a few droplets of fluid that are found at the tip of the penis (see Figure 5.4).

In women, vasocongestion swells the tissues of the outer third of the vagina, contracting the vaginal opening (thus preparing it to "grasp" the penis) and building the orgasmic platform (see Figure 5.5 on page 144). The inner part of the vagina expands fully. The uterus becomes fully elevated. The clitoris withdraws beneath the clitoral hood and shortens. Thus, a woman (or her partner) may feel that the clitoris has become lost. This may be mistaken as a sign that the woman's sexual arousal is waning, although it is actually increasing.

Coloration of the labia minora appears, which is referred to as the **sex skin**. The labia minora become a deep wine color in women who have borne children and bright red in women who have not. Further engorgement of the areolas of the breasts may make it seem that the nipples have lost part of their erection (see Figure 5.6 on page 145). The Bartholin's glands secrete a fluid that resembles mucus.

About one man in four and about three women in four show a sex flush, which often does not appear until the plateau phase. Myotonia may cause spasmodic contractions in the hands and feet and facial grimaces. Breathing becomes rapid, like panting, and the heart rate may increase to 100 to 160 beats per minute. Blood pressure continues to rise. The increase in heart rate is usually less dramatic with masturbation than during coitus.

Orgasmic Phase The **orgasmic phase** in the male consists of two stages of muscular contractions. In the first stage, contractions of the vas deferens, the seminal vesicles, the ejaculatory duct, and the prostate gland cause seminal fluid to collect in the urethral bulb at the base of the penis (see Figure 5.4). The bulb expands to accommodate the fluid. The internal sphincter of the urinary bladder contracts, preventing seminal fluid from entering the bladder in a backward, retrograde ejaculation. The normal closing off of the bladder also serves to prevent urine from mixing with semen. The collection of semen in the urethral bulb produces feelings of ejaculatory inevitability—the sensation that nothing will stop the ejaculate from "coming." This sensation lasts for about 2 to 3 seconds.

In the second stage, the external sphincter of the bladder relaxes, allowing the passage of semen. Contractions of muscles surrounding the urethra and urethral bulb and the base of the penis propel the ejaculate through the urethra and out of

Sex skin Reddening of the labia minora that occurs during the plateau phase.

Orgasmic phase The phase of the sexual response cycle that is characterized by a rapid succession of muscular contractions in the genital regions of both males and females, and also by ejaculation by the male.

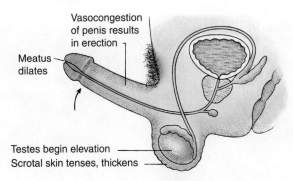

1. EXCITEMENT PHASE

Vasocongestion of penis results in erection

Meatus dilates

Testes begin elevation

Scrotal skin tenses, thickens

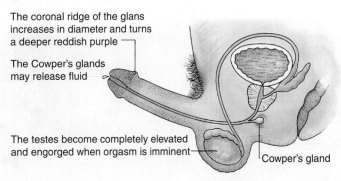

2. PLATEAU PHASE

The coronal ridge of the glans increases in diameter and turns a deeper reddish purple

The Cowper's glands may release fluid

The testes become completely elevated and engorged when orgasm is imminent

Cowper's gland

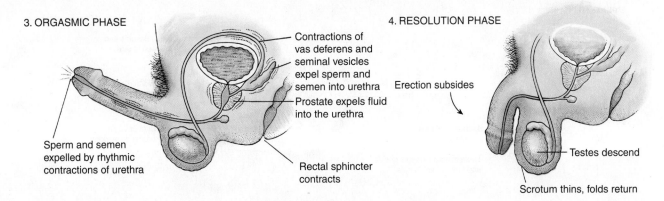

3. ORGASMIC PHASE

Contractions of vas deferens and seminal vesicles expel sperm and semen into urethra

Prostate expels fluid into the urethra

Sperm and semen expelled by rhythmic contractions of urethra

Rectal sphincter contracts

4. RESOLUTION PHASE

Erection subsides

Testes descend

Scrotum thins, folds return

FIGURE 5.4 The Male Genitals during the Phases of the Sexual Response Cycle

the body. Sensations of pleasure tend to be related to the strength of the contractions and the amount of seminal fluid. The first three or four contractions are generally most intense and occur at 0.8-second intervals (five contractions every 4 seconds). Another two to four contractions occur at a somewhat slower pace. Rates and patterns vary somewhat from man to man.

Orgasm in the female is manifested by 3 to 15 contractions of the pelvic muscles that surround the vaginal barrel. The contractions first occur at 0.8-second intervals, producing, as in the male, a release of sexual tension. Another three to six weaker and slower contractions follow. The spacing of these contractions is generally more variable in women than in men. The uterus and the anal sphincter also contract rhythmically. Uterine contractions occur in waves from the top to the cervix. In both sexes, muscles go into spasm throughout the body. Blood pressure and heart rate reach a peak, with the heart beating up to 180 times per minute. Respiration may increase to 40 breaths per minute.

Subjective Experience of Orgasm The sensations of orgasm have challenged the descriptive powers of poets. Words like *rush*, *warmth*, *explosion*, and *release* do not adequately capture them. We may assume (rightly or wrongly) that others of our sex experience pretty much what we do, but can we understand the sensations of the other sex?

TRUTH OR **FICTION** REVISITED: Several studies suggest that written descriptions of women's and men's orgasms cannot be told apart. The orgasms of both may feel quite similar. In one study, 48 men and women provided written descriptions of orgasms. The researchers (Proctor et al., 1974) modified the language (for example,

1. EXCITEMENT PHASE

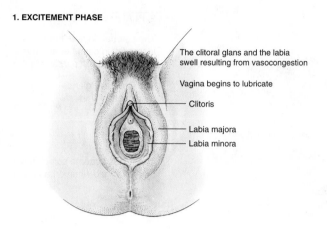

The clitoral glans and the labia swell resulting from vasocongestion

Vagina begins to lubricate

Clitoris

Labia majora

Labia minora

2. PLATEAU PHASE

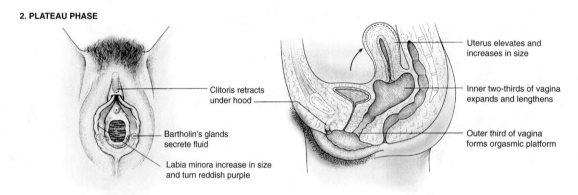

Clitoris retracts under hood

Bartholin's glands secrete fluid

Labia minora increase in size and turn reddish purple

Uterus elevates and increases in size

Inner two-thirds of vagina expands and lengthens

Outer third of vagina forms orgasmic platform

3. ORGASMIC PHASE

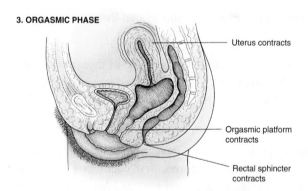

Uterus contracts

Orgasmic platform contracts

Rectal sphincter contracts

4. RESOLUTION PHASE

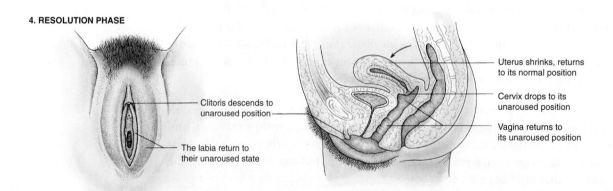

Clitoris descends to unaroused position

The labia return to their unaroused state

Uterus shrinks, returns to its normal position

Cervix drops to its unaroused position

Vagina returns to its unaroused position

FIGURE 5.5 The Female Genitals during the Phases of the Sexual Response Cycle

1. EXCITEMENT PHASE

Breast increases in size

Nipple becomes erect

Veins become more visible

2. PLATEAU AND ORGASMIC PHASES

Vasocongestion of areola makes nipple seem less erect

Breast increases still more in size

Rashlike sex flush may appear

3. RESOLUTION PHASE

Reduction of areola causes increased prominence of nipple

Breast size is reduced to normal in 5–10 minutes

Sex flush disappears rapidly

FIGURE 5.6 The Breasts during the Phases of the Sexual Response Cycle

---

Real Students, Real Questions

Q *Is there such thing as a female ejaculation? How does it occur? Where does the fluid come from?*

A The notion of female ejaculation is controversial. Some researchers argue that evidence has been found for an ejaculate in some women (Korda et al., 2010). They also point to ancient Asian, Greek, and Roman texts that tell of a female ejaculate. But the nature of the fluid remains unclear. It might be urine or it might be released by a system called Skene's glands. It might be none of the above. The only thing we're certain of is that women usually have nothing to worry about if they expel a little liquid during orgasm.

---

changing "penis" to "genitals") so that the authors' sexes would not be apparent. They then asked 70 "experts" (psychologists, gynecologists, etc.) to indicate the sex of each author. The ratings were no more reliable than guesswork—at least when they were altered to exclude language that gives away exactly which anatomic features are involved. (Thus, this Truth-or-Fiction item is only qualifiedly "true." Listen: Life is complex. Be tolerant.)

Resolution Phase The period following orgasm, in which the body returns to its prearoused state, is called the **resolution phase**. Following ejaculation, the man loses his erection in two stages. The first occurs in about a minute. Half the volume of the erection is lost as blood from the corpora cavernosa empties into the other parts of the body. The second stage occurs over a period of several minutes: The remaining tumescence subsides as the corpus spongiosum empties. The testes and scrotum return to normal size, and the scrotum regains its wrinkled appearance.

In women, orgasm also triggers release of blood from engorged areas. In the absence of continued stimulation, swelling of the areolas decreases; then the nipples return to normal size. The sex flush lightens rapidly. In about five to ten seconds the clitoris descends to its normal position. The clitoris, vaginal barrel, uterus, and labia gradually shrink to their prearoused sizes. The labia minora turn lighter (the "sex skin" disappears) in about 10 to 15 seconds.

Resolution phase The fourth phase of the sexual response cycle, during which the body gradually returns to its prearoused state.

Most muscle tension (myotonia) tends to dissipate within five minutes after orgasm in both men and women. Blood pressure, heart rate, and respiration may also return to their prearousal levels within a few minutes. About 30 to 40% of men and women find their palms, the soles of their feet, or their entire bodies covered with a sheen of perspiration. Both men and women may feel relaxed and satiated. However,...

Although the processes by which the body returns to its prearousal state are similar in men and women, there is an important sex difference during the resolution phase. Unlike women, men enter a **refractory period** during which they are physiologically incapable of experiencing another orgasm or ejaculation. The refractory period of adolescent males may last only minutes, whereas that of men age 50 and above may last from several minutes (yes, it could happen) to a day. Women do not undergo a refractory period and so can become quickly rearoused to the point of repeated (multiple) orgasms if they desire and receive continued sexual stimulation (see Figure 5.3).

Myotonia and vasocongestion may take an hour or more to dissipate in people who are aroused but who do not reach orgasm. Persistent pelvic vasocongestion may cause "blue balls" in males—the slang term for a throbbing ache. Some men insist that their dates should consent to coitus because it is unfair to stimulate them to the point where they have this condition. This condition can be relieved through masturbation as well as coitus, however—or allowed to dissipate naturally. Although it may be uncomfortable, it is not dangerous and should not be an excuse to pressure or coerce another person into any sexual activity. "Blue" sensations are not limited to men. Women, too, may experience unpleasant pelvic throbbing if they have become highly aroused and do not find release. Women, too, can relieve the throbbing through masturbation.

TRUTH OR **FICTION** REVISITED: Masters and Johnson (1966) did find that orgasms experienced during masturbation were generally more physiologically intense than those experienced during intercourse. Perhaps masturbation allows one to focus only on one's own pleasure and ensure that one receives effective stimulation to climax. This does not mean that orgasms during masturbation are more enjoyable or gratifying than those experienced through coitus. Given the sexual attraction and emotional connectedness we may feel toward our lovers, we are unlikely to break off relationships in favor of masturbation. "Physiological intensity" does not directly translate into subjective pleasure or fulfillment.

KAPLAN'S THREE STAGES OF SEXUAL RESPONSE: AN ALTERNATIVE MODEL

Perhaps the only alternative view of the sexual response cycle that has received continued attention is the one proposed by Helen Singer Kaplan. Kaplan was a prominent sex therapist and author of several professional books (1974, 1987) on sex therapy. Whereas Masters and Johnson had proposed a four-stage model of sexual response, Kaplan developed a three-stage model consisting of (1) desire, (2) excitement, and (3) orgasm. Kaplan's model is an outgrowth of her clinical experience in working with people with sexual dysfunctions. She believes that their problems can best be classified according to these three phases. Kaplan's model makes it convenient for clinicians to classify sexual dysfunctions involving desire (low or absent desire), excitement (such as problems with erection in the male or lubrication in the female), and orgasm (such as premature ejaculation in the male or orgasmic dysfunction in the female).

Masters and Johnson view sexual response as composed of successive stages; the order is crucial and invariant. Kaplan treats her phases as relatively independent

Refractory period A period of time following a response (e.g., orgasm) during which an individual is no longer responsive to stimulation (e.g., sexual stimulation).

A World of Diversity

"Coregasm"?—When Women's Exercise Leads to More Than Flexibility and Strength

Coregasm is the term that is sometimes used to describe exercise-induced orgasms (EIO) in women. The appellation reflects the relationship between orgasm and exercises for core abdominal muscles, which has been reported among women but not men (sorry, guys).

Debby Herbenick and J. Dennis Fortenberry (2011) ran an Internet survey on the subject that did not address the incidence of EIO, but delved more deeply into questions about the kinds of exercise that led to EIO or exercise-induced sexual pleasure (EISP). The following lists some of their findings:

- Of women who experienced EIO or EISP, about 40% had done so on ten or more occasions.

- Somewhat more than half of these women were engaging in abdominal exercises at the time—especially the "captain's chair" exercise.

- Women also experienced EIO or EISP while lifting weights, doing yoga, bicycling, running, and walking or hiking.

- Most women who experienced EIO said they were not engaging in sexual fantasies or thinking about an attractive person at the time.

- Not surprisingly, EIO made many of the women self-conscious.

The authors make no attempt to explain the bodily mechanisms that might lead to EIO or EISP, but we can note that the exercises reported tend to rub the upper legs together. Similar experiences were reported among women using pedal-powered sewing machines in the late nineteenth and early twentieth centuries.

Abdominal exercises are most likely to induce orgasms or sexual pleasure in women who report exercise-induced orgasms (EIO) or exercise-induced sexual pleasure (EISP).

components of sexual response whose sequence is somewhat variable. For example, a person may experience sexual excitement and even orgasm, even though sexual desire remains low.

Kaplan's model is noteworthy for designating desire as a separate phase of sexual response. Problems in lack of sexual interest or desire are among the most common brought to the attention of sex therapists.

CONTROVERSIES ABOUT ORGASM

Few other topics in human sexuality have aroused more controversies over the years than orgasm. We do not have all the answers, but some intriguing research findings have shed light on some lingering controversies. For example, are women capable of having multiple orgasms? Are men?

Multiple Orgasms Kinsey and colleagues (1953) reported that 14% of his female respondents regularly had **multiple orgasms**, surprising fellow scientists as well as the community at large. Many people were aghast that women could have more than one orgasm at a time. There were comments (mostly by men, of course!)

Multiple orgasms One or more additional orgasms following the first, which occur within a short period of time and before the body has returned to a preplateau level of arousal.

that the women in the Kinsey surveys must be "nymphomaniacs" who were incapable of being satisfied with the "normal" complement of one orgasm per occasion. However, only 13 years later, Masters and Johnson (1966) reported that most if not all women are capable of multiple orgasms. Although all women may have a biological capability for multiple orgasms, not all women report them. A survey of 720 nurses showed that 43% reported experiencing multiple orgasms (Darling et al., 1991). Nearly half of them experienced multiple orgasms when they used a vibrator. They generally applied the vibrator to the clitoris and reported that orgasms experienced with the vibrator were more intense than other kinds. Two-thirds of the women, by the way, used the vibrators in conjunction with sexual activity with their husbands.

By Masters and Johnson's definition, men are not capable of achieving multiple orgasms because they enter a refractory period following ejaculation. Men who want more than one orgasm during one session may have to pause for a while. Women, however, can maintain a high level of arousal between multiple orgasms and have them in rapid succession because women do not have a refractory period. Women can continue to have orgasms if they continue to receive effective stimulation (and, of course, are interested in continuing). Some men thus refrain from reaching orgasm until their partners have had the desired number. The differential capacity for multiple orgasms is one of the major sex differences in sexual response.

Some men have two or more orgasms without ejaculation ("dry orgasms") preceding a final ejaculatory orgasm. These men may not enter a refractory period following their initial dry orgasms and may therefore be able to maintain their level of stimulation at near-peak levels.

Masters and Johnson (1966) found that some women experienced 20 or more orgasms by masturbating. Still, few women have multiple orgasms during most sexual encounters, and many are satisfied with just one per occasion. Some women who have read or heard about female orgasmic capacity wonder what is "wrong" with them if they are content with just one. Nothing is wrong with them, of course: A biological capacity does not create a behavioral requirement.

Do Orgasms Increase the Likelihood of Conception? The evolutionary perspective has some interesting suggestions about women's orgasm—or at least the circumstances under which she is likely to have an orgasm. Notes William McKibbin of the University of Michigan:

> It's almost like an arms race, with women maybe evolving the orgasm to select high-quality sperm, men counter-evolving an interest in orgasms to help ensure paternity, and women perhaps evolving the tendency to fake, obscuring paternity (in Dingfelder, 2011, p. 44).

The point is that orgasms apparently increase the probability that a sexual act will lead to conception by holding the sperm within their bodies, increasing the likelihood that one of them will fertilize an ovum (Puts et al., 2011). It has even been speculated that a woman can choose or choose not to have an orgasm as a "subconscious last-minute call" as to whether they wish their partner to fertilize them (Dingfelder, 2011).

How Many Kinds of Orgasms Do Women Have? One, Two, or Three?
Until Masters and Johnson published their laboratory findings, many people believed that there were two types of female orgasm, as proposed by the psychoanalyst Sigmund Freud: the clitoral orgasm and the vaginal orgasm. *Clitoral orgasms*

were achieved through direct clitoral stimulation, such as by masturbation. Clitoral orgasms were seen by psychoanalysts (mostly male psychoanalysts, naturally) as emblematic of a childhood fixation—a throwback to an erogenous pattern acquired during childhood masturbation.

The term *vaginal orgasm* referred to an orgasm achieved through coitus and was theorized to be a sign of mature sexuality. Freud argued that women achieve sexual maturity when they forsake clitoral stimulation for vaginal stimulation. This view would be little more than an academic footnote but for the fact that some adult women who continue to require direct clitoral stimulation to reach orgasm, even during coitus, have been led by traditional (generally male) psychoanalysts to believe that they are sexually "fixated" at an immature stage or are sexually inadequate.

Despite Freudian theory, Masters and Johnson (1966) were able to find only one kind of orgasm, physiologically speaking, regardless of the source of stimulation (manual–clitoral or penile–vaginal). By monitoring physiological responses to sexual stimulation, they found that the female orgasm involves the same biological events whether it is reached through masturbation, petting, coitus, or even stimulation of the breasts. In men, also, it does not matter how orgasm is achieved—through masturbation, petting, oral sex, coitus, or by fantasizing about a fellow student in chem lab. Orgasm still involves the same physiological processes: Involuntary contractions of the pelvic muscles at the base of the penis expel semen and release sexual tension. A woman or a man might prefer one source of orgasm to another— with a lover rather than by masturbation, or with one person rather than another, but the biological events that define orgasm remain the same.

The purported distinction between clitoral and vaginal orgasms also rests on an assumption that the clitoris is not stimulated during coitus. Masters and Johnson showed this assumption to be false. Penile coital thrusting draws the clitoral hood back and forth against the clitoris. Vaginal pressure also heightens blood flow in the clitoris, helping set the stage for orgasm (Cai et al., 2008).

One might think that Masters and Johnson's research settled the question of whether or not there are different types of female orgasm. Other investigators, however, have proposed that there are distinct forms of female orgasm, yet not those suggested by psychoanalytic theory. For example, Singer and Singer (1972) suggested that there are three types of female orgasm: vulval, uterine, and blended. According to the Singers, the vulval orgasm represents the type of orgasm described by Masters and Johnson (1966). It involves vulval contractions—that is, contractions of the vaginal barrel. Consistent with the findings of Masters and Johnson (1966), they accept that a vulval orgasm remains the same regardless of the source of stimulation, clitoral or vaginal.

Chapter Review ✓●—⎡Study and Review on MyDevelopmentLab

LO1 **Discuss the roles of the senses of vision, smell, touch, taste, and hearing in sexual arousal**

Visual cues, particular odors, and sounds can be sexual turn-ons or turn-offs. The sense of touch has the most direct effects on sexual arousal and response. Taste appears to play only a minor role. Many organisms are sexually aroused by pheromones, but their role in human sexual behavior remains unclear. Underarm secretions may make men and women more sexually attractive, and male underarm secretions have a positive effect on the moods of women. Exposure to the odor of other women's sweat appears to synchronize the menstrual cycles of women who live together. Gay males may be drawn to the body odors of other gay males. Heterosexual males prefer the body odors of females and of heterosexual males to those of gay males. Primary erogenous zones are richly endowed with nerve endings. Secondary erogenous zones become erotically sensitized through experience.

LO2 **Define aphrodisiac and discuss research on the aphrodisiacal qualities of various substances**

An aphrodisiac is a substance that is sexually arousing. Alleged aphrodisiacs such as Spanish fly and foods that resemble the genitals have not been shown to contribute to sexual arousal. The male sex hormone testosterone heightens the sex drive in both males and females. Anaphrodisiacs include amyl nitrate and antiandrogens. The alleged aphrodisiac effects of psychoactive drugs, such as alcohol and cocaine, may reflect our expectations or their effects on sexual inhibitions, rather than direct stimulation of sexual response. Some people report initial increased sexual pleasure with cocaine use, but frequent use can lead to sexual dysfunctions. Wellbutrin and L-dopa may have aphrodisiacal properties.

LO3 **Describe the role of the brain in sexual arousal and response**

The cerebral cortex interprets sensory information as sexual turn-ons or turn-offs. It transmits messages through the spinal cord that cause vasocongestion. Stimulation of parts of the limbic system causes sexual arousal and sensations similar to those of orgasm.

LO4 **Discuss the organizing and activating influences of sex hormones**

Sex hormones have organizing and activating effects. Men and women normally produce one genuine aphrodisiac: testosterone.

LO5 **Describe the sexual response cycle, according to Masters and Johnson**

Masters and Johnson found that the physiological responses of men and women to sexual stimulation are similar, including vasocongestion and myotonia. Sexual excitement is characterized by erection in the male and vaginal lubrication in the female. The plateau phase is an advanced state of arousal that precedes orgasm. The third phase of the sexual response cycle is characterized by orgasmic contractions of the pelvic musculature. During the resolution phase, the body returns to its prearoused state.

LO6 **Discuss other views of sexual response**

Kaplan developed a three-stage model of sexual response consisting of desire, excitement, and orgasm.

LO7 **Discuss controversies about orgasm**

Multiple orgasm is the occurrence of one or more additional orgasms following the first, within a short period of time and before the body has returned to a preplateau level of arousal. Freud theorized two types of female orgasm: clitoral and vaginal. Masters and Johnson found only one kind of orgasm among women. Singer and Singer suggested that there are three types of female orgasm: vulval, uterine, and blended.

Test Your Learning

1. The effects of Spanish fly are due to _____ in the urinary tract.
   (a) a burning sensation
   (b) moisture
   (c) a burst of cerebral neurons
   (d) ethanol

2. Alcohol is known to have
   (a) depressing effects only.
   (b) stimulating effects only.
   (c) both stimulating and depressing effects.
   (d) neither stimulating nor depressing effects.

3. Cells in the _____ cortex transmit messages when we experience sexual thoughts and fantasies.
   (a) reticular
   (b) avuncular
   (c) sexual
   (d) cerebral

4. When the rear part of a male rat's _____ is stimulated by electricity, the animal runs through its sexual routine mechanically.
   (a) thalamus
   (b) hypothalamus
   (c) occipital lobe
   (d) larynx

5. According to Masters and Johnson, sexual arousal is characterized by vasocongestion and
   (a) myotonia.
   (b) blurry vision.
   (c) cramping.
   (d) constriction of blood vessels.

6. According to Masters and Johnson, erection and lubrication occur during the _____ phase of the sexual response cycle.
   (a) orgasmic
   (b) excitement
   (c) plateau
   (d) resolution

7. Men enter a refractory period following the _____ phase of the sexual response cycle.
   (a) excitement
   (b) plateau
   (c) resolution
   (d) orgasmic

8. The hormone _____ activates the sex drives of both men and women.
   (a) prolactin
   (b) oxytocin
   (c) progesterone
   (d) testosterone

9. Foods such as oysters and bananas have been considered aphrodisiacs because they
   (a) are chemically similar to compounds secreted by the male genitals.
   (b) are enjoyed by women.
   (c) are popular among the upper classes.
   (d) resemble the male genitals.

10. In many animals, the vomeronasal organ detects
    (a) pheromones.
    (b) contractions of the orgasmic platform.
    (c) pituitary secretions.
    (d) cerebral activity.

Answers: 1. a; 2. c; 3. d; 4. b; 5. a; 6. b; 7. d; 8. d; 9. d; 10. a

My Life, My Sexuality

Making Sense of Sex?

*Explore this **My Life, My Sexuality** feature by scanning this QR code with your mobile device. If you don't already have one, you may download a free QR scanner for your device wherever smartphone apps are sold. You can also view this feature in MyDevelopmentLab, along with an accompanying critical thinking assignment.*

What roles do vision and smell play in sexually arousing me? How important is the way someone looks? What about his or her odors? Do I have body odor? Scan the code to go online and learn more about the role of the senses in sexual arousal, and how they affect you.

6 Gender Identity, Gender Roles, and Gender Differences

Learning Objectives

PRENATAL SEXUAL DIFFERENTIATION

LO1 Describe the processes of prenatal sexual differentiation

LO2 Discuss sex chromosomal abnormalities that may affect sexual differentiation

GENDER IDENTITY

LO3 Define gender identity and the roles of nature and nurture in gender identity

LO4 Discuss transgenderism

GENDER ROLES AND STEREOTYPES

LO5 Discuss gender roles and stereotypes

LO6 Explain the relationship between gender roles and sexual behavior

GENDER DIFFERENCES

LO7 Discuss gender differences in cognitive abilities

LO8 Discuss gender differences in personality

LO9 Discuss gender differences in social behavior

ON BECOMING A MAN OR A WOMAN: GENDER TYPING

LO10 Discuss biological and psychological perspectives on gender typing

PSYCHOLOGICAL ANDROGYNY AND THE RECONSTRUCTION OF MASCULINITY–FEMININITY: THE MORE TRAITS, THE MERRIER?

LO11 Define psychological androgyny and discuss its possible advantages

MY LIFE, MY SEXUALITY: DO YOU FIT THE MASCULINE OR FEMININE GENDER-ROLE STEREOTYPE? (DO YOU WANT TO FIT ONE OF THEM?)

The Basics: Sex and Gender Differences

Explore the video, **The Basics: Sex and Gender Differences,** by scanning this QR code with your mobile device. If you don't already have one, you may download a free QR scanner for your device wherever smartphone apps are sold. You can also view this video in MyDevelopmentLab. For more videos related to this chapter's content, log into MyDevelopmentLab to view the entire Human Sexuality Video Series.

TRUTH OR FICTION?

Which of the following statements are the truth, and which are fiction? Look for the Truth-or-Fiction icons on the pages that follow to find the answers.

1 If male sex hormones were not present during critical stages of prenatal development, we would all develop external female sexual organs. **T F?**

2 A woman with Turner syndrome cannot become pregnant, but she can carry and deliver a baby. **T F?**

3 Seventeen of 18 boys who appeared to have female external sex organs suddenly developed male sex organs at puberty, when male sex hormones went to work. **T F?**

4 The gender of a baby crocodile is determined by the temperature at which the egg develops. **T F?**

5 Thousands of people have changed their anatomic sexes through gender-reassignment surgery. **T F?**

6 Men act more aggressively than women do. **T F?**

7 A 2½-year-old child may know that he is a boy but might think that he can grow up to be a mommy. **T F?**

Jayne Thomas, Ph.D.—In Her Own Words

"The 'Glass Ceiling,' male bashing, domestic violence, nagging, PMS, Viagra—these are but a few of the important issues examined in the Human Sexuality classes I instruct. As a participant-observer in my field, I see many of these topics aligning themselves as masculine/feminine or male/female. Ironically, I can both see and not see such distinctions. Certainly women have bumped up against, smudged (and in some cases even polished) this metaphorical limitation of women's advancement in the workplace (i.e., that 'Glass Ceiling'). And most assuredly men have often found themselves 'bashed' by angry women intent upon extracting a pound of flesh for centuries of felt unjust treatment. As previously mentioned, these distinctions between masculine and feminine, for me often become blurred; I must add that, having lived my life in both the roles of man and woman, I offer a rather unique perspective on masculinity and femininity.

"All of my life, I harbored the strongest conviction that I was in appropriately assigned to the wrong gender—that of a man—when inside I knew myself to be a woman. Even so I continued a life-long struggle with this deeply felt mistake; I was successful in school, became a national swimming champion, received my college degrees, married twice (fathering children in both marriages) and was respected as a competent and good man in the workplace. However, the persistently unrelenting wrongfulness of my life continued. Not until my fourth decade was I truly able to address my gender issue.

"Jay Thomas, Ph.D., underwent gender reassignment and officially became Jayne Thomas, Ph.D., in November of 1985, and what has transpired in the ensuing years has been the most enlightening of glimpses into the plight of humankind. As teachers we are constantly being taught by those we purport to instruct. My students, knowing my background (I share who I am when it is appropriate to do so), find me accessible in ways that many professors are not. Granted, I am continually asked the titillating questions that one watching *Geraldo* might ask and we do have fun with the answers (several years ago I even appeared on a few of the *Geraldo* shows). My students, however, are able to take our discussions beyond the sensational and superficial, and we enter into meaningful dialogue regarding sex differences in society and the workplace, sexual harassment, power and control issues in relationships, and what it really means to be a man or a woman.

Challenging both the Masculine and the Feminine

"Iconoclastically, I try to challenge both the masculine and feminine. 'I know something none of you women know or will ever know in your lifetime,' I can provocatively address the females in my audiences as Jayne. 'I once lived as a man and have been treated as an equal. You never have nor will you experience such equality.' Or, when a male student once came to my assistance in a classroom, fixing an errant video playback device and then strutting peacock

like back to his seat as only a satisfied male can, I teasingly commented to a nearby female student,' I used to be able to do that.'

"Having once lived as a man and now as a woman, I can honestly state that I see profound differences in our social/psychological/biological being as man and woman. I have now experienced many of the ways in which women are treated as less than men. Jay worked as a consultant to a large banking firm in Los Angeles and continued in that capacity as a woman following her gender shift. Amazingly the world presented itself in a different perspective. As Jay, technical presentations to management had generally been received in a positive manner and credit for my work fully acknowledged. Jayne now found management less accessible, credit for her efforts less forthcoming and, in general, found herself working harder to be well prepared for each meeting than she ever had as a male. As a man, her forceful and impassioned presentations were an asset; as a woman they definitely seemed a liability. On one occasion, as Jayne, when I passionately asserted my position regarding what I felt to be an important issue, my emotion and disappointment in not getting my point across (my voice showed my frustration) was met with a nearby colleague (a man) reaching to touch my arm with words of reassurance,' There, there, take it easy, it will be all right.' Believe me; that never happened to Jay. There was also an occasion when I had worked most diligently on a presentation to management only to find the company vice president more interested in the fragrance of my cologne than my technical agenda.

"Certainly there are significant differences in the treatment of men and women, and yet I continue to be impressed with how similar we two genders really are. Although I have made this seemingly enormous change in lifestyle (and it is immense in so many ways), I continue as the same human being, perceiving the same world through these same sensory neurons. The difference—I now find myself a more comfortable and serene being, than the paradoxical woman in a man's body, with anatomy and gender that have attained congruence."

This chapter addresses the biological, psychological, and sociological aspects of gender. First we define **gender** as the psychological sense of being female or being male and the roles society ascribes to gender. Anatomic sex is based on, well, anatomy. But gender is a complex concept that is based partly on anatomy, partly on the psychology of the individual, and partly on culture and tradition.

Next we focus on **sexual differentiation**—the process by which males and females develop distinct reproductive anatomy. We then turn to gender roles—the clusters of behavior that are deemed "masculine" or "feminine" in a particular culture. The chapter examines research findings on gender differences. We next consider gender typing—the processes by which boys come to behave in line with what is expected of men (most of the time) and girls behave in accordance with what is expected of women (most of the time). We will also explore the concept of psychological androgyny, which applies to people who display characteristics associated with both gender roles in our culture.

Prenatal Sexual Differentiation

Over the years, many ideas have been proposed to account for sexual differentiation. Aristotle believed that the anatomic difference between males and females was due to the heat of semen during sexual relations. Hot semen generated males, whereas cold semen made females (National Center for Biotechnology Information, 2006). Aristotle may have given in to stereotyping—the stereotypes of "hot-blooded male" and the "frigid female." Others believed that sperm from the right testicle made females, and sperm from the left testicle made males.

When a sperm cell fertilizes an ovum, 23 **chromosomes** from the male parent normally combine with 23 chromosomes from the female parent. The *zygote,* the beginning of a new human being, is only 1/175 of an inch long. Yet, on this tiny stage, one's stamp as a unique individual has already been ensured—whether one will have black or blond hair, grow bald or develop a widow's peak, or become female or male.

The chromosomes from each parent combine to form 23 pairs. The 23rd pair makes up the sex chromosomes. An ovum carries an X sex chromosome, but a sperm cell can carry either an X or a Y sex chromosome. The denotation of *X* and *Y* refers to the shapes of the chromosomes. If a sperm cell with an X sex chromosome fertilizes the ovum, the newly conceived individual will have an XX sex chromosomal structure and normally develop as a female. If the sperm cell carries a Y sex chromosome, the child will normally develop as a male (XY).

After fertilization, the zygote divides repeatedly. After a few short weeks, one cell has become billions of cells. At about three weeks a primitive heart begins to drive blood through the embryonic bloodstream. At about five to six weeks, when the **embryo** is only ¼- to ½-inch long, primitive gonads, ducts, and external genitals whose anatomic sex cannot be distinguished visually have formed (see Figures 6.1 and 6.2). Each embryo possesses primitive external genitals, a pair of sexually undifferentiated gonads, and two sets of primitive duct structures, the Müllerian (female) ducts and the Wolffian (male) ducts.

During the first six weeks or so of prenatal development, embryonic structures of females and males develop along similar lines and resemble primitive female structures. At about the seventh week after conception, the genetic code (XX or XY) begins to assert itself, causing changes in the gonads, genital ducts, and external genitals. Genetic activity on the Y sex chromosome causes the testes to begin to differentiate (National Center for Biotechnology Information, 2006). Ovaries begin to differentiate if the Y chromosome is absent. The reproductive organs of some rare individuals who have only one X sex chromosome instead of the typical XY or XX arrangement also become female in appearance, because they too lack the Y sex chromosome. One could

Gender The psychological state of being female or being male, as influenced by cultural concepts of gender-appropriate behavior. Compare and contrast the concept of gender with *anatomic sex,* which is based on the physical differences between females and males.

Sexual differentiation The process by which males and females develop distinct reproductive anatomy.

Chromosome One of the rodlike structures found in the nucleus of every living cell that carries the genetic code in the form of genes.

Embryo The stage of prenatal development that begins with implantation of a fertilized ovum in the uterus and concludes with development of the major organ systems at about two months after conception.

thus say that the basic blueprint of the human embryo is female (De Vries et al., 2002; Steinemann & Steinemann, 2005). The genetic instructions in the Y sex chromosome cause the embryo to deviate from the female developmental course.

By about the seventh week of prenatal development, strands of tissue begin to organize into seminiferous tubules. Female gonads begin to develop somewhat later than male gonads. The forerunners of follicles that will bear ova are not found until the fetal stage of development, about ten weeks after conception. Ovaries begin to form at 11 or 12 weeks.

GENETIC FACTORS IN SEXUAL DIFFERENTIATION

What roles do genes play in sexual differentiation? Some of the answers to this question are fascinating. Animal studies suggest a role for genes in the determination of mating and other behavior patterns in humans. For example, the interaction of a number of genes has led to the development of three different types of males in a crustacean as well as to a quite complex mating strategy (Benvenuto & Weeks, 2012). One anatomic-sex-determining gene called *transformer (tra)* is needed in the development of female fruit flies. Chromosomal (XX) females with inactive tra attempt to mate with other females but they are attractive to males because they still emit female pheromones (Dauwalder, 2011). Researchers conclude that among fruit flies, sexual differentiation, sexual orientation, and sexual behavior are all determined by the interactions of genes (Meissner et al., 2011).

The SRY gene—which stands for *sex-determining region Y* gene—is also connected with sexual differentiation. In an article that could have been entitled "The Mouse That Roared," researcher Stephen Maxson (1998) reported that a number of genes that are involved in determining maleness in mice, including SRY, are connected with aggressiveness. SRY is also involved in anatomic sex determination in humans (Savic et al., 2010), leading to formation of the testes. Another gene involved in anatomic sex determination has also been researched in mice: *Sox* 9. Sox 9 appears to regulate the expression of SRY (Czech et al., 2012). Females with XX sex chromosomal structure normally suppress the action of their own Sox 9, which in turn prevents the expression of SRY. However, when these XX mice are chemically prevented from turning off Sox 9, they develop as males—albeit sterile males.

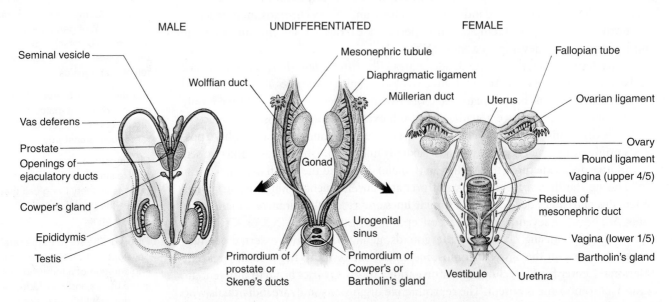

FIGURE 6.1 Development of the Internal Sex Organs from an Undifferentiated Stage at about Five or Six Weeks after Conception

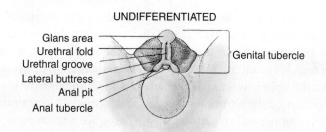

UNDIFFERENTIATED

Glans area
Urethral fold
Urethral groove
Lateral buttress
Anal pit
Anal tubercle

Genital tubercle

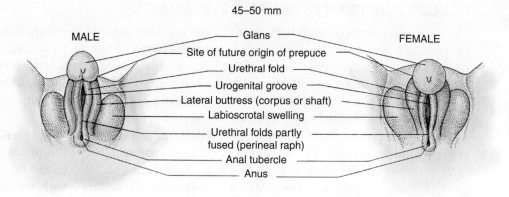

45–50 mm

MALE   FEMALE

Glans
Site of future origin of prepuce
Urethral fold
Urogenital groove
Lateral buttress (corpus or shaft)
Labioscrotal swelling
Urethral folds partly
fused (perineal raph)
Anal tubercle
Anus

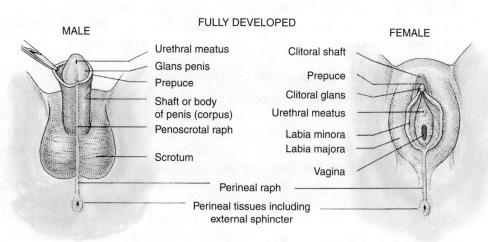

FULLY DEVELOPED

MALE   FEMALE

Urethral meatus   Clitoral shaft
Glans penis
Prepuce   Prepuce
                                         Clitoral glans
Shaft or body
of penis (corpus)   Urethral meatus
Penoscrotal raph
                                         Labia minora
                                         Labia majora
Scrotum
                                         Vagina

Perineal raph

Perineal tissues including
external sphincter

FIGURE 6.2 Development of the External Sex Organs from an Undifferentiated Stage at about Five or Six Weeks after Conception

THE ROLE OF SEX HORMONES IN SEXUAL DIFFERENTIATION

Once genes have done their work and testes develop in the embryo, they begin to produce male sex hormones, or androgens. Without androgens, we would all develop female external reproductive organs. The most important androgen, testosterone, spurs differentiation of the male (Wolffian) duct system (see Figure 6.1). Each Wolffian duct develops into an epididymis, vas deferens, and seminal vesicle. The external genitals, including the penis, begin to take shape at about the eighth week of development under the influence of another androgen, dihydrotestosterone (DHT). **TRUTH** OR **FICTION** REVISITED: It is true that without male sex hormones, or androgens, we would all develop female external reproductive organs. However, *Müllerian inhibiting substance (MIS),* a testicular hormone that is secreted during the fetal stage, prevents the Müllerian ducts from developing into the female duct system.

 1

CRITICAL THINKING

Critical thinkers do not oversimplify or overgeneralize. Consider this statement: *In the absence of prenatal male sex hormones we would all develop as females.* Question: Would we all develop as fertile females? In what way would we all develop as females?

Small amounts of androgens are produced in female fetuses, but they are not normally sufficient to cause male sexual differentiation. In female fetuses, the relative absence of androgens causes degeneration of the Wolffian ducts and prompts development of female sexual organs. The Müllerian ducts evolve into fallopian tubes, the uterus, and the upper two-thirds of the vagina. Although female sex hormones are crucial in puberty, they are not involved in fetal sexual differentiation. If a fetus with an XY sex chromosomal structure failed to produce testosterone, it would develop external female sexual organs, but be infertile.

DESCENT OF THE TESTES AND THE OVARIES

The testes and ovaries develop from slender structures high in the abdominal cavity. By about ten weeks after conception, they have descended so that they are almost even with the upper edge of the pelvis. The ovaries remain there for the rest of the prenatal period. Later they rotate and descend farther to their adult position in the pelvis. About four months after conception, the testes normally descend into the scrotal sac via the **inguinal canal.** Then the passageway closes.

In a small percentage of males, one or both testes do not descend and remain in the abdomen at birth. The condition is termed **cryptorchidism.** In most cases of cryptorchidism, the testes migrate to the scrotum during infancy. In still other cases, the testes descend by puberty. Men with undescended testes are usually treated through surgery or hormonal therapy, because they are at higher risk for cancer of the testes. Sperm production is also impaired because the undescended testes are subjected to a higher-than-optimal body temperature, causing sterility.

SEX CHROMOSOMAL ABNORMALITIES

Abnormalities of the sex chromosomes can have profound effects on sexual characteristics, physical health, and psychological development. **Klinefelter syndrome,** a condition that affects about 1 in 500 males, is caused by an extra X sex chromosome, so the man has an XXY rather than an XY pattern. Men with this pattern fail to develop appropriate secondary sex characteristics. They have enlarged breasts, poor muscular development, and, because they fail to produce sperm, they are infertile. They may be mildly retarded.

Turner syndrome occurs in about 1 of every 2,500 females and is a consequence of having one rather than two X sex chromosomes. Individuals with this abnormality are at risk of developing heart disease, short arms and legs, kidney problems, hypothyroidism (producing too little thyroid hormone), and diabetes. Turner syndrome does not cause general cognitive impairment, but women may have specific problems in spatial relationships and math. Females with the syndrome may not naturally undergo puberty, so hormone treatments are usually begun when pubertal changes would start to spur growth of secondary sex characteristics. Nevertheless, nearly all women with the syndrome are infertile.

TRUTH OR **FICTION** REVISITED: Interestingly, however, if another woman donates an ovum (egg cell), and it is fertilized in a laboratory dish, it can usually be implanted in a woman with Turner syndrome and the embryo can develop normally to term.

The brain, like the genital organs, undergoes prenatal sexual differentiation. Testosterone causes cells in the hypothalamus of male fetuses to become insensitive to the female sex hormone estrogen. In female fetuses the hypothalamus develops sensitivity to estrogen.

Sensitivity to estrogen is important in the regulation of the menstrual cycle after puberty. The hypothalamus detects low levels of estrogen in the blood at the end of each cycle and initiates a new cycle by stimulating the pituitary gland to secrete follicle-stimulating hormone (FSH). FSH, in turn, stimulates estrogen production by the ovaries and the ripening of an immature follicle in an ovary.

Inguinal canal A fetal canal that connects the scrotum and the testes, allowing their descent.

Cryptorchidism The condition defined by undescended testes.

Klinefelter syndrome A sex-chromosomal disorder caused by an extra X sex chromosome.

Turner syndrome A genetically determined condition associated with the presence of only one complete X chromosome and with characteristics including usually infertile ovaries, absence of menstruation, and short stature.

Gender Identity

Our **gender identity** is our psychological awareness or sense of being male or being female, and it's one of the most obvious and important aspects of our self-concepts. **Sex assignment** (also called *gender assignment*) reflects the child's anatomic sex and usually occurs at birth. A child's anatomic sex is so important to parents that they usually want to know "Is it a boy or a girl?" before they count fingers and toes.

Most children first become aware of their anatomic sex by about the age of 18 months. By 36 months, most children have acquired a firm sense of gender identity (Rathus, 2014).

NATURE AND NURTURE IN GENDER IDENTITY

What determines gender identity? Are our brains biologically programmed along masculine or feminine lines by prenatal sex hormones? Does the environment, in the form of postnatal learning experiences, shape our self-concepts as males or females? Or does gender identity reflect an intermingling of biological and environmental influences?

Gender identity is almost always consistent with chromosomal sex, but such consistency does not certify that gender identity is biologically determined. Caregivers also rear us as males or females, according to our anatomic sex. How, then, might we sort out the roles of nature and nurture, of biology and the environment?

Investigators have found clues in the experiences of rare individuals, **intersexuals**, who possess the gonads of one anatomic sex but external genitalia that are ambiguous or typical of the other anatomic sex. Intersexuals are sometimes reared as members of the other sex (the sex other than their chromosomal sex). Researchers have wondered whether the gender identity of these children reflects their chromosomal and gonadal sex or the gender to which they were assigned at birth, and according to which they were reared. Before going further, let us distinguish between true hermaphrodites and intersexuals.

Hermaphrodites and Intersexuals Hormonal factors during prenatal development produce various congenital outcomes. Some individuals are born with both ovarian and testicular tissue. They are called **hermaphrodites**, after the Greek myth of the son of Hermes and Aphrodite, whose body became united with that of a nymph while he was bathing. True hermaphrodites may have one gonad of each anatomic sex (a testicle and an ovary), or gonads that combine testicular and ovarian tissue.

Regardless of their genetic sex, hermaphrodites often assume the gender identity and gender role of the gender assigned at birth. Figure 6.3 shows a genetic female (XX) with a right testicle and left ovary. This person married and became a stepfather with a firm male identity. The roles of biology and environment remain tangled, however, because true hermaphrodites have gonadal tissue of females and males.

Intersexualism True hermaphroditism is quite rare. Less rare is intersexualism, which occurs in perhaps 1 infant in 5,000 or so (Intersex Society of North America [www.isna.org], 2012). Intersexuals have testes or ovaries, but not both. Unlike hermaphrodites, their gonads (testes or ovaries) match their chromosomal sex. Because of prenatal hormonal factors, however, their external genitals and sometimes their internal reproductive anatomy are ambiguous or resemble those of the other anatomic sex. Intersexualism has given scientists an opportunity to examine the roles of nature (biology) and nurture (environmental influences) in the shaping of gender identity. ◉

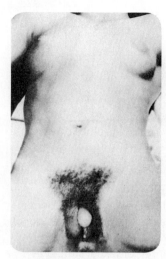

FIGURE 6.3
A Hermaphrodite. This genetic (XX) female has one testicle and one ovary and the gender identity of a male.

Gender identity One's belief that one is male or female.

Sex assignment The labeling of a newborn as a male or female. Also termed *gender assignment*.

Intersexual A person who possesses the gonads of one anatomic sex but external genitalia that are ambiguous or typical of the other anatomic sex. Also termed *pseudohermaphrodite*.

Hermaphrodite A person who possesses both ovarian and testicular tissue.

◉—**Watch** the **Video**
Intersexuals
on **MyDevelopmentLab**

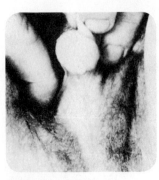

FIGURE 6.4
Intersexualism. In congenital adrenal hyperplasia, a genetic (XX) female has female internal sexual structures (ovaries) but masculinized external genitals.

Congenital adrenal hyperplasia A form of intersexualism in which a genetic female has internal female sexual structures but masculinized external genitals.

Androgen-insensitivity syndrome A form of intersexualism in which a genetic male is prenatally insensitive to androgens such that his genitals are not normally masculinized.

Dominican Republic syndrome A form of intersexualism in which a genetic enzyme disorder prevents testosterone from masculinizing the external genitalia.

The most common form of female intersexualism is **congenital adrenal hyperplasia (CAH)**, in which a genetic (XX) female has female internal sexual structures (ovaries), but masculinized external genitals (www.congenitaladrenalhyperplasia.org, 2012; see Figure 6.4). The clitoris is enlarged and may resemble a small penis. CAH is caused by high levels of androgens, which are usually produced by the fetus's own adrenal glands. In other cases, mothers may have received synthetic androgens during their pregnancies. In the 1950s and 1960s, before these side effects were known, synthetic androgens were sometimes prescribed to help prevent miscarriages in women with histories of miscarriage.

Swedish investigator Anna Servin and her colleagues (2003) studied gender-typed behaviors and interests in 26 girls aged 2 to 10 who had CAH and in 26 girls without CAH who were matched for age. Girls with CAH showed more interest in masculine-typed toys, such as transportation toys, and less interest in feminine-typed toys, such as dolls. The girls with CAH were also more likely to have boys as play-mates and to desire masculine-typed careers. Parents rated the behavior of daughters with CAH as being more "boy-like" in choice of toys and aggressiveness. Servin and her colleagues interpret the results as supporting a hormonal contribution to styles of play between girls with and without CAH, although other researchers also find a role for socialization (Wong et al., 2012).

There are several varieties of **androgen-insensitivity syndrome**, which is another type of intersexualism. One involves genetic (XY) males who, due to a mutated gene, have lower-than-normal prenatal sensitivity to androgens. As a result, their genitals do not become normally masculinized. At birth their external genitals are feminized, including a small vagina, and their testes are undescended. Because of insensitivity to androgens, the male duct system (epididymis, vas deferens, seminal vesicles, and ejaculatory ducts) fails to develop. Nevertheless, the fetal testes produce Müllerian inhibiting substance (MIS), preventing the development of a uterus or fallopian tubes. Genetic males with androgen-insensitivity syndrome usually have no or sparse pubic and axillary (underarm) hair, because the development of hair in these locations is dependent on androgens.

Girls with *partial androgen-insensitivity syndrome (PAIS)* or *complete androgen-insensitivity syndrome (CAIS)* are also intersexuals. PAIS and CAIS occur in 1 in 2,000 to 5,000 girls with a single X sex chromosome and in girls with XX chromosomal structure who lose some X sex chromosomal material. Girls with CAIS develop typical external genital organs, but their internal reproductive organs do not develop or function normally. By contrast, girls with PAIS develop masculinized external genitals and are sometimes raised as boys, sometimes as girls. A study by Melissa Hines and her colleagues (2003) compared 22 women with CAIS and single X sex chromosomal structure with 22 women who had the normal XX sex chromosomal structure. They found no differences between the women with CAIS and controls in self-esteem, general psychological well-being, gender identity, sexual orientation, gender-typed behavior patterns, marital status, personality traits, or hand preferences. The researchers conclude that two X sex chromosomes and ovaries are not essential to the development of feminine-typed behavior patterns in humans.

Dominican Republic syndrome is a form of intersexualism that was first documented in a group of 18 boys in two villages in the Dominican Republic (Lang & Kuhnle, 2008; Newman, 2012). Dominican Republic syndrome is a genetic enzyme disorder that prevents testosterone from masculinizing the external genitalia. The boys were born with normal testes and internal male reproductive organs, but their external genitals were malformed. Their penises were stunted and resembled clitorises. Their scrotums were incompletely formed and resembled female labia. They also had partially formed vaginas. Because the boys resembled girls at birth, they were reared as females. At puberty, however, their testes swung into normal testosterone production, causing startling changes: Their testes descended, their voices deepened, their musculature filled out, and their "clitorises" expanded into penises.

TRUTH OR **FICTION** REVISITED: Of the 18 Dominican Republic boys who were reared as girls, 17 shifted to a male gender identity. Sixteen of the 18 assumed a stereotypical masculine gender role. Of the remaining 2, 1 identified himself as a male but continued to maintain a feminine gender role, including wearing dresses. The 18th continued to see herself/himself as female and later sought gender-reassignment surgery to counter the pubertal masculinization. Despite being reared as girls, 16 of the 18 made the transition to the male role without problems, suggesting the importance of biology in gender identity (Bailey, 2003b).

Many scientists conclude that gender identity is influenced by complex interactions of biological and psychosocial factors. But could the "complex-interaction" approach be a way of avoiding the hot-potato issue as to whether nature (biological factors) or nurture (psychosocial factors) is more important? To place the emphasis on nature is to lessen the role of personal choice and thus has major political consequences. Although some place relatively greater emphasis on psychosocial factors (Bradley et al., 1998; Money, 1994), others emphasize the role of biological factors (Diamond, 2011; Savic et al., 2010). However, as noted in the nearby "A Closer Look" titled "Boys Who Are Reared as Girls," the theory that newborns are psychosexually neutral and that gender identity depends mainly on environmental factors has had rough sledding in recent years.

In case you have had enough discussion of the complex issues surrounding the origins of anatomic sex and gender identity in human beings, consider the crocodile. Crocodile eggs do not carry sex chromosomes. **TRUTH** OR **FICTION** REVISITED: The crocodile offspring's anatomic sex is determined by the temperature at which the eggs develop (Ackerman, 1991). Some (males) like it hot (at least in the mid-90s F), and some (females) like it cooler, under the mid-80s F.

TRANSGENDERISM

In 1953, an ex-GI who journeyed to Denmark for a "sex-change operation" made headlines. She became known as Christine (formerly George) Jorgensen. Since then, thousands of transgendered individuals have undergone gender-reassignment surgery.

In **transgenderism**, the individual wishes to possess the anatomic features of people of the other sex and to live as a person of the other gender. The term *transsexualism* was earlier used for transgenderism.

Many transgendered individuals undergo hormone treatments and surgery to create the appearance of the external genitals typical of the other anatomic sex. This can be done more precisely with male-to-female than female-to-male transgendered individuals. After surgery, people can participate in sexual activity and even attain orgasm. One survey found that 85% of transgendered women attained orgasm during sexual activity (Lawrence, 2005). They cannot, however, conceive or bear children.

CRITICAL THINKING
How do intersexuals provide researchers with a special opportunity to explore the origins of gender identity?

Transgenderism A condition in which people strongly desire to be of the other anatomic sex and live the gender roles of the other anatomic sex.

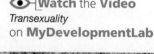
Watch the **Video**
Transexuality
on **MyDevelopmentLab**

Is It a Boy or a Girl? We haven't checked, but the answer has to do with the temperature at which the egg was incubated. Clue: Some like it hot.

Real Students, Real Questions

Q *Can a man who has sex reassignment surgery get pregnant, or is that option futuristic?*

A No, he can't. Getting pregnant in the future is also unlikely. However—there's often a however in these matters—she could provide sperm prior to the change, use it to fertilize an egg from a donor, and the donor or another woman might carry the embryo to term.

TRUTH OR **FICTION** REVISITED: Gender-reassignment surgery cannot implant the internal reproductive organs of the other anatomic sex. Therefore, it is not accurate to say that people have actually changed their sexes through gender-reassignment surgery. Instead, surgery creates the appearance of the external genitals typical of the other anatomic sex.

What motivates transgendered people to wish to live as people of the other anatomic sex? It appears that they experience incongruity between their genital anatomy and their gender identity. Although they have the anatomic sex of a male or a female, they *feel* that they are members of the other anatomic sex. The discrepancy motivates them to wish to be rid of their own primary sex characteristics (their external genitals and internal sex organs) and to live as members of the other anatomic sex. A male-to-female transgendered individual perceives himself to be a female who, through some quirk of fate, was born with the wrong genital equipment. A female-to-male transgendered individual perceives herself as a man trapped in a woman's body.

But some researchers contend that many men who seek to become women tend to fall into other categories: either men who are extremely feminine or men who are sexually aroused by the idea of becoming a woman. The first category includes **homosexual transgendered men**—men who are extremely feminine gays and not fully satisfied by sexual activity with other males (Blanchard, 1989; Cantor, 2011). The second category refers to males who are **autogynephilic,** or sexually stimulated by fantasies of their own bodies as being female (Moser, 2010; Nuttbrock et al., 2011).

Although the prevalence of transgenderism remains unknown, it is thought to be relatively rare. The number of transgendered people in the United States is estimated to be below 50,000. Of these, only a minority have undergone gender-reassignment surgery (Jones & Hill, 2002).

Homosexual transgendered males usually show cross-gender preferences in play and dress in early childhood. Some report that they felt they belonged to the other anatomic sex as long as they can remember (Zucker, 2005a, 2005b). Some male-to-female transgendered men recall that, as children, they preferred playing with dolls, enjoyed wearing frilly dresses, and disliked rough-and-tumble play. They were often perceived by their peers as "sissy boys." Some female-to-male transgendered people report that as children they disliked dresses and acted like "tomboys." They preferred playing

Homosexual transgendered men Extremely feminine gay males who seek gender reassignment.

Autogynephilic Descriptive of transgendered men who are sexually stimulated by fantasies that their own bodies are female.

A Closer Look

Boys Who Are Reared as Girls

Are children "psychosexually neutral" at birth? Can you surgically reassign a boy as a female, rear him as a girl, and have him feel that he is truly a girl as the years go on? Will cosmetic surgery, female sex hormone treatments, and laces and ribbons do it? Or will he be maladjusted and his male gender identity sort of "break through"? No one has sought to answer these questions by randomly selecting male babies and reassigning their genders. Evidence on the matter derives from studies of children who have lost their penises or failed to develop them through accidents or unusual medical conditions.

Getting Down to Cases

For example, one of a pair of male twins, David Reimer, lost much of his penis as a result of a circumcision accident. As this case study is related by Colapinto (2000), the parents wondered what to do. Johns Hopkins sexologist John Money believed that gender identity was sufficiently malleable that the boy could undergo sex-reassignment surgery (have his testes removed and an artificial vagina constructed) and female hormone treatments and be successfully reared as a girl.

For a number of years, the case seemed to supply evidence for the view that children may be psychosexually neutral at birth. The sex-reassigned twin, unlike his brother, seemed to develop like a "real girl," albeit with a number of "tomboyish" traits. But at the age of 14, when "she" was informed about the circumcision accident and the process of sex reassignment, David immediately decided to pursue life as a male. As an adult, he recalled that he had never felt quite comfortable as a girl—a view confirmed by the recollections of his mother. At the age of 25, he married a woman and adopted her children. He reported being sexually attracted to women only. According to researchers such as Milton Diamond (1996), this outcome would appear to support the view that gender identity may be determined to a considerable extent in the uterus, as the fetal brain is being exposed to androgens.

Reimer committed suicide with a sawed-off shotgun in 2004, at the age of 38. When Colapinto received the news from David's father, he wrote, "I was shocked, but I cannot say I was surprised. Anyone familiar with David's life—as a baby, after a botched circumcision, [after] an operation to change him from boy to girl—would have understood that the real mystery was how he managed to stay alive for 38 years, given the physical and mental torments he suffered in childhood and that haunted him the rest of his life" (2004).

Another Case Study

Susan Bradley and her colleagues (1998) report on the development of another boy who suffered a circumcision accident in infancy. Again, John Money recommended sex reassignment, and the surgery was carried out at the age of 21 months. In this case, as Money found out in a follow-up at the age of 9, the individual was also tomboyish in behavior and personality traits but considered herself to be a girl.

She was interviewed subsequently at the ages of 16 and 26, and her situation had grown more complex. She considered herself to be bisexual and had sexual relationships with both men and women. However, when last interviewed, she had begun living with a woman in what the authors label a "lesbian" relationship. Of course, if one remembers that the individual has XY sex chromosomal structure, the relationship with the woman is not with a person of the same sex at all. On the other hand, the individual did retain the self-concept of being female.

A Larger Study

These celebrated cases are far from the only ones. On May 12, 2000, researchers from the Johns Hopkins Hospital, including

David Reimer

William G. Reiner, a psychiatrist and urologist, presented a paper on the subject to the Lawson Wilkins Pediatric Endocrine Society Meeting in Boston. They recounted the development of 27 children who had been born without penises due to a rare condition called cloacal exstrophy. However, the children had normal testicles, male sex chromosomal structure, and male sex hormones.

Nevertheless, the sex of 25 of the 27 children was reassigned shortly after birth. They were surgically castrated and reared as girls by their parents. As the years went on, all 25—now 5 to 16 years old—showed the rough-and-tumble play considered stereotypical of males. Of the 25, 14 declared themselves to be males. Reiner (2000) suggests that "with time and age, children may well know what their gender is, regardless of any and all information and child-rearing to the contrary," he said. "They seem to be quite capable of telling us who they are." Reiner also noted that 2 of the 27 children who were not sex-reassigned fit in with male peers and appeared to be better adjusted than the children who were reassigned.

Swedish neuroscientists Ivanka Savic and her colleagues (2010) report evidence that gender identity and sexual orientation (heterosexual or homosexual) can develop during the intrauterine period. However, sexual differentiation of the sex organs occurs during the first two months of pregnancy, whereas sexual differentiation of

(continued on next page)

(continued from page 163)

the brain begins later, during the second half of pregnancy. Sexual differentiation of the genitals and the brain both depend on surges of testosterone, but because they happen at different times, they occur independently. Therefore, it is possible that an individual's sex organs can develop in one direction while his or her brain develops in the other direction. And, as in the case of David Reimer, it is possible that sexual differentiation can be ambiguous although sexual differentiation of the brain occurs more precisely later on.

As Marianne J. Legato (2000), a professor of medicine at Columbia University, describes it, "When the brain has been masculinized by exposure to testosterone, it is kind of useless to say to this individual, 'You're a girl.' It is this impact of testosterone that gives males the feelings that they are men." The view that newborns are psychosexually neutral and that gender identity depends mainly on nurture has become increasingly criticized in recent years.

Phalloplasty The surgical creation of an artificial penis.

Watch the Video
Gender Roles: Charlotte Anjelica, Transsexual
on **MyDevelopmentLab**

Chaz Bono's Transition. Chastity ("Chaz") Bono, 40, daughter of singers Cher (seen here on the left) and the late Sony Bono, announced in 2009 that she was undergoing the initial stages of gender reassignment surgery from female to male. Chaz expressed through a spokesperson the hope that this transition would open the "hearts and minds" of people toward transgendered individuals.

"boys' games" and playing them with boys. Female-to-male transgendered individuals appear to have an easier time adjusting than male-to-female transgendered individuals. Even in adulthood, it may be easier for a female transsexual to don men's clothes and pass as a slightly built man than it is for a brawny man to pass for a tall woman.

Gender Reassignment Surgery is one element of gender reassignment. Because the surgery is irreversible, health professionals conduct careful evaluations to determine that people seeking reassignment are competent to make such decisions and that they have thought through the consequences (Bockting & Fung, 2006). They usually require that the transsexual live openly as a member of the other sex for an extended trial period before surgery.

After the decision is reached, a lifetime of hormone treatments is begun. Male-to-female transsexuals receive estrogen, which fosters the development of female secondary sex characteristics. It causes fatty deposits to develop in the breasts and hips, softens the skin, and inhibits growth of the beard. Female-to-male transsexuals receive androgens, which promote male secondary sex characteristics. The voice deepens, hair becomes distributed according to the male pattern, muscles enlarge, and the fatty deposits in the breasts and hips are lost. The clitoris may also grow more prominent. In the case of male-to-female transsexuals, "phonosurgery" can raise the pitch of the voice (Bockting & Fung, 2006).

Despite its complexity and intimacy, sex-reassignment surgery is largely cosmetic. Medical science cannot construct internal genital organs or gonads. Male-to-female surgery is generally more successful. The penis and testicles are first removed. Tissue from the penis is placed in an artificial vagina so that sensitive nerve endings will provide sexual sensations. A penis-shaped form of plastic or balsa wood is used to keep the vagina distended during healing.

In female-to-male transsexuals, the internal sex organs (ovaries, fallopian tubes, uterus) are removed, along with the fatty tissue in the breasts. Some female-to-male transsexuals engage in a series of operations, termed **phalloplasty**, to construct an artificial penis, but the penises don't work very well, and the procedures are costly. Therefore, most female-to-male transsexuals are content to have hysterectomies, mastectomies, and testosterone treatments (Bailey, 2003b).

Some transsexuals hesitate to undertake surgery because they are repulsed by the prospect of extreme medical intervention. Others forgo surgery so as not to jeopardize high-status careers or family relationships. Such people continue to think of themselves as members of the other sex, even without surgery.

Q *Does an artificial penis get an erection? Can it ejaculate?*

A Yes and no. Female-to-male transsexuals who undergo phalloplasty (construction of an artificial penis) can have a pump installed that enables them to get erections, but medical science cannot create the glands that make ejaculation of seminal fluid possible.

Outcomes of Sex-Reassignment Surgery Most reports of the postoperative adjustment of transsexuals are positive (Smith et al., 2005). A Canadian follow-up study of 116 transsexuals at least one year after surgery found that most were content with the results and were reasonably well adjusted (Blanchard et al., 1985). Positive results for surgery were also reported in a study of 141 Dutch transsexuals (Kuiper & Cohen-Kettenis, 1988). ◉

A study of 326 Dutch candidates for sex-reassignment surgery found that about two-thirds (222) began hormone treatment, whereas 103 did not (Smith et al., 2005). Of the 222, about 15% dropped out before surgery. Generally speaking, after surgery the group was no longer gender dysphoric and most individuals functioned well sexually, psychologically, and socially. Only two male-to-female transsexuals regretted their decision. Male-to-female transsexuals outnumbered female-to-males, but postoperative adjustment was more favorable for female-to-males. One reason may be that society is more accepting of women who desire to become men (Smith et al., 2005). Female-to-male transsexuals tend to be better adjusted socially before surgery as well so their superior postoperative adjustment may be nothing more than a selection factor.

Gender Roles and Stereotypes

"Why can't a woman be more like a man?" This is the title of a song in the musical *My Fair Lady*. In the song, Professor Henry Higgins laments that women are emotional and fickle, whereas men are logical and dependable. The "emotional woman" is a stereotype. The "logical man" is also a stereotype—albeit more generous. Even emotions are stereotyped. People assume that women are more likely to experience feelings of fear, sadness, and sympathy, whereas men are more likely to experience anger and pride (Plant et al., 2000). A **stereotype** is a fixed, conventional—and often distorted—idea about a group of people. Sex assignment—our identification of ourselves as female or male—does not determine the roles or behaviors that are deemed masculine or feminine in our culture. Cultures have broad expectations for the personalities and behaviors of men and women, and these are termed **gender roles**. A survey of 30 countries confirmed that these gender-role stereotypes are widespread (Williams & Best, 1994; see Table 6.1).

One of the effects of stereotyping is sexism, as we see in the following section.

SEXISM ◉

We have all encountered the effects of **sexism**—the prejudgment that because of her or his sex, a person will possess certain negative traits. These negative traits are assumed to disqualify the person for certain vocations or prevent him or her from performing adequately in these jobs or in some social situations.

Watch the **Video**
Lisa Feldman Barrett: What is the difference in emotions in terms of males and females?
on **MyDevelopmentLab**

CRITICAL THINKING
Why would a researcher bother to study whether traditional gender-role stereotypes are found around the world?

Stereotype A fixed, conventional idea about a group of people.

Gender roles Complex clusters of behavioral expectations for males and females.

Sexism The prejudgment that, because of her or his sex, a person will possess negative traits.

Watch the **Video**
Adults' Perceptions of Boys and Girls
on **MyDevelopmentLab**

Table 6.1

Gender-Role Stereotypes in 30 Nations

Stereotypes of Males		Stereotypes of Females	
Active	Opinionated	Affectionate	Nervous
Adventurous	Pleasure seeking	Appreciative	Patient
Aggressive	Precise	Cautious	Pleasant
Arrogant	Quick	Changeable	Prudish
Autocratic	Rational	Charming	Self-pitying
Capable	Realistic	Complaining	Sensitive
Coarse	Reckless	Complicated	Sentimental
Conceited	Resourceful	Confused	Sexy
Confident	Rigid	Dependent	Shy
Courageous	Robust	Dreamy	Softhearted
Cruel	Sharp witted	Emotional	Sophisticated
Determined	Show-off	Excitable	Submissive
Disorderly	Steady	Fault finding	Suggestible
Enterprising	Stern	Fearful	Superstitious
Hardheaded	Stingy	Fickle	Talkative
Individualistic	Stolid	Foolish	Timid
Inventive	Tough	Forgiving	Touchy
Loud	Unscrupulous	Frivolous	Unambitious
Obnoxious		Fussy	Understanding
		Gentle	Unstable
		Imaginative	Warm
		Kind	Weak
		Mild	Worrying
		Modest	

Note: Psychologists John Williams and Deborah Best (1994) found that people in 30 countries largely agreed on what constituted masculine and feminine gender-role stereotypes.
Source: Data from Williams and Best (1994, p. 193, Table 1).

Sexism may lead us to interpret the same behavior in prejudicial ways when performed by women or by men. A "sensitive" woman is simply sensitive, but a sensitive man may be seen as a "sissy." We may see a man as "self-assertive," but a woman who behaves in the same way is often seen as "pushy." 👁

Children develop stereotypes about the differences between "man's work" and "woman's work" (Rathus, 2014). Women have been historically excluded from "male occupations," and stereotypical expectations concerning "men's work" and "women's work" filter down to the primary grades. For example, according to traditional stereotypes, women are not expected to excel in math. Exposure to such negative expectations may discourage women from careers in science and technology. Even when they choose a career in science or technology, women are often subject to discrimination in hiring, promotions, allocation of facilities for research, and funds

👁 **Watch the Video**
Sexism in Education
on **MyDevelopmentLab**

A World of Diversity
Third Gender/Third Sex

The terms *third gender* and *third sex* describe people who are considered to be neither women nor men, along with the social category in societies that recognize three or more sexes. Being neither male nor female has ramifications not only in terms of the person's sex but also in terms of the person's gender role, gender identity, and sexual orientation. In some cultures or to some individuals, a third sex or gender may represent an intermediate state between men and women, or it may represent a state of being both, as in the case of "the spirit of a man in the body of a woman." It may also represent the state of being neither (neuter), the ability to cross or swap sexes and gender roles, or another category that is independent of being male or being female. This last definition is favored by those who argue for a strict interpretation of the "third gender" concept.

The term *third gender* has been used to describe the Hijras of India and Pakistan, the Fa'afafine of Polynesia, and the Sworn virgins of the Balkans. In the Western world, lesbian, gay, transgender, and intersex people have also been described as belonging to a third sex or gender, although many object to being so categorized.

Third Sex in Biology

A small number of individuals within a population will not differentiate sexually into typical male or female bodies. They are sometimes called *hermaphrodites* or (especially among humans) *intersexuals*. Biologist and gender theorist Anne Fausto-Sterling (1993) proposed that five sexes may be more adequate than just two for describing human bodies. In addition to the physical morphology of sex, transgender biologist Joan Roughgarden argues that in some nonhuman animal species, there may be more than two *genders* (understood in terms of behavior and identity). She argues that there might be multiple behavior patterns available to individuals with a given biological sex.

Feminists distinguish between (biological) sex and (social/psychological) gender. Contemporary gender theorists usually argue that that a two-gender system is neither inborn nor universal. A sex/gender system that recognizes only the following two social norms has been labeled "heteronormativity," but feminists and queer theorists consider it to be too limited to describe the variety of sexual interests and behaviors we find in the real world:

- Female genitalia, female gender identity, feminine behavior, desire male partner
- Male genitalia, male gender identity, masculine behavior, desire female partner

Let's have a look at some *non-heteronormative* patterns around the world.

South-Central Asia

The Hijra of India, Pakistan, and Bangladesh are probably the most well known and populous third sex type in the modern world. The Mumbai-based community health organization called The Humsafar Trust estimates there are between 5 and 6 million hijras in India. In different areas they are known as Aravani/Aruvani or Jogappa. British photographer Dayanita Singh writes about her friendship with a Hijra, Mona Ahmed, and their two different society's beliefs about gender: "When I once asked her if she would like to go to Singapore for a sex change operation, she told me, 'You really do not understand. I am the third sex, not a man trying to be a woman. It is your society's problem that you only recognize two sexes'" (Singh et al., 1999). Hijra social movements have campaigned for recognition as a third sex, and in 2005, Indian passport application forms were updated with three gender options: M, F, and E.

The "Ladyboys" of Thailand

Also commonly referred to as a third sex are the *kathoeys* (or *"ladyboys"*) of Thailand. However, although a significant number of Thais perceive kathoeys as belonging to a third gender, including many kathoeys themselves, others see them as either a kind of man or a kind of woman. Researcher Sam Winter (2003) writes:

We asked our 190 [kathoeys] to say whether they thought of themselves as

men, women, *sao praphet song* ["a second kind of woman"] or *kathoey*. None thought of themselves as male, and only 11% saw themselves as kathoey (i.e., "non-male"). By contrast 45% thought of themselves as women, with another 36% as *sao praphet song*.... Unfortunately we did not include the category *phet tee sam* (third sex/gender); conceivably if we had done so there may have been many respondents who would have chosen that term.... Around 50% [of non-transgender Thais] see them as males with the mistaken minds, but the other half see them as either women born into the wrong body (around 15%) or as a third sex/gender (35%).

In 2004, the Chiang Mai Technology School allocated a separate restroom for kathoeys, with an intertwined male and female symbol on the door. The 15 kathoey students are required to wear male clothing at school but are allowed to sport feminine hairdos. The restroom features four stalls, but no urinals.

The Western World

Some writers suggest that a third gender emerged around 1700 in England: the male sodomite. According to these writers, this was marked by the emergence of a subculture of effeminate males and meeting places (molly houses), as well as a marked increase in hostility toward effeminate and/or homosexual males. People described themselves as members of a third sex in Europe from at least the 1860s with the writings of Karl Heinrich Ulrichs and continuing in the late nineteenth century with Magnus Hirschfeld, John Addington Symonds, Edward Carpenter, Aimée Duc, and others. These writers described themselves and those like them as being of an "inverted" or "intermediate" sex and experiencing homosexual desire, and their writing argued for social acceptance of such sexual intermediates.

Throughout much of the twentieth century, the term *third sex* was a popular descriptor for homosexuals and gender nonconformists, but after the gay liberation movement of the 1970s and a growing separation of the concepts of sexual orientation and gender identity, the term

(continued on next page)

(continued from page 167)

fell out of favor among LGBT (lesbian-gay-bisexual-transgender) communities and the wider public. With the renewed exploration of gender that feminism, the modern transgender movement, and queer theory has fostered, some in the contemporary West have begun again to describe themselves as a third sex. One well-known social movement of male-bodied people that identify as neither men nor women is the *Radical Faeries*. Other modern identities that cover similar ground include *pangender, bigender, genderqueer, androgyne, other gender,* and *differently gendered*.

The term *transgender*, which often refers to those who change their gender, is increasingly being used to signify a gendered subjectivity that is neither male nor female. One recent example is on a form for the Harvard Business School, which has three gender options: male, female, and transgender.

Indigenous Cultures of North America: "Two Spirits"

Native American cultures are also very much associated with multiple genders. They often contain social gender categories that are collectively known as "berdache" or Two-Spirit. Individual examples include the Winkte of Lakota culture, the ninauposkitzipxpe ("manly-hearted woman") of the North Piegan (Blackfoot) community, and the Zapotec Muxe. Various scholars have debated the nature of such categories, as well as the definition of the term *third gender*. Different researchers may characterize the berdache as a gender-crosser, a mixed gender, an

intermediate gender, or distinct third and fourth genders that are not dependent on male and female as primary categories. Those (such as Will Roscoe) who have argued for the latter interpretation also argue that mixed-, intermediate-, cross-, or non-gendered social roles should not be understood as truly representing a third gender. According to Jean-Guy Goulet (2006):

"Berdache" may signify a category of male human beings who fill an established social status other than that of man or woman; a category of male and female human beings who behave and dress "like a member of the opposite sex"; or categories of male and female human beings who occupy well established third or fourth genders. Scheffler, however, sees Native American cases of "berdache" and "amazon" as "situations in which some men (less often women) are permitted to act, in some degree, as though they were women (or men), and may be spoken of as though they were women (or men), or as anomalous 'he-she' or 'she-he.'" In Scheffler's view,

"Ethnographic data … provide definitive evidence that such persons were not regarded as having somehow moved from one sex category to the other, but were only metaphorically 'women' (or 'men')." In other words, according to Scheffler, we need not imagine a multiple gender system. Individuals who appeared in the dress and/or occupation of the opposite sex were only metaphorically spoken of as members of that sex or gender.

Sources: This feature is adapted from the Wikipedia entry on Third Gender and obtains information from Agrawal (1997), Fausto-Sterling (1993), Goulet (2006), Hester (2005), Murray and Roscoe (1997), Roscoe (2000), Roughgarden (2004), Stockett (2005), Totman (2004), and Winter (2003).

Thai "Ladyboys"

to conduct research (Loder, 2000). Similarly, only recently have men begun to enter occupational domains previously restricted largely to women, such as secretarial work, nursing, and teaching in the primary grades.

Sexism is psychologically damaging. One experiment found that women who were led to believe that sexism was pervasive reported lower self-esteem than women who were led to think that sexism was rare (Schmitt et al., 2003). In another experiment, men and women were led to believe that they were rejected from taking a course either due to sexism or personal reasons (Major et al., 2003). Attributing the rejection to prejudice rather than to personal deservingness had the effect of protecting their self-esteem ("It's not me; it's society").

Fortunately, it appears that education can modify sexist attitudes. One study reported on the degree to which women's studies courses can help individuals become more aware of sexism and develop more egalitarian attitudes (Stake & Hoffman, 2001).

In the study, 548 women's studies students completed questionnaires prior to and following the courses in areas such as openness to women's studies, egalitarian attitudes toward females and gender issues, and awareness of sexism and discrimination against females. As compared with students who did not take women's studies, the students in the courses reported increased awareness of sexism and other kinds of prejudice, more egalitarian attitudes toward women and other stigmatized groups, and more interest in engaging in activism for social causes.

A Nurse and a Patient. If you think there is something wrong with this picture, could it be because you have fallen prey to traditional gender-role stereotypes? Tradition has prevented many women from seeking jobs in "male" preserves such as construction work and the military. Tradition has also prevented many men from obtaining work in "female" domains such as secretarial work, nursing, and teaching at the elementary level.

GENDER ROLES AND SEXUAL BEHAVIOR

Gender roles affect relationships and sexual behavior. Children learn at an early age that men usually approach women and initiate sexual interactions, whereas women usually serve as the "gatekeepers" in romantic relationships. In their traditional role as gatekeepers, women are expected to wait to be approached and to screen suitors. Men are expected to make the first (sexual) move, and women are to determine how far they will go.

The cultural expectation that men are initiators and women are gatekeepers is embedded within the larger stereotype that men are sexually aggressive and women are sexually passive. Men are expected to have a higher number of sexual partners than women do (Fisher et al., 2012; Schmitt et al., 2012). Men not only initiate sexual encounters; they are also expected to dictate all the "moves" thereafter, just as they are expected to take the lead on the dance floor. People who adhere to the masculine gender-role stereotype, whether male or female, are more likely to engage in risky (unprotected) sexual behavior (Belgrave et al., 2000). According to the stereotype, women are supposed to let male partners determine the choice, timing, and sequence of sexual positions and techniques. Unfortunately, the stereotype favors men's sexual preferences, denying women the opportunity to give and receive their preferred kinds of stimulation.

According to another stereotype, men become sexually aroused at puberty and remain at the ready throughout adulthood. Women, however, do not share men's natural interests in sex, and a woman discovers her own sexuality only when a man ignites her sexual flame. Despite the stereotype, it is not clear that women are biologically less arousable than men; however, they are more likely to desire to limit sexual activity to intimate, committed relationships (Schmitt et al., 2012). On the other hand, researchers (Fisher et al., 2012) find consistent empirical support for the view that men generally have more sexual desire than women.

Questions remain as to the extent to which the gender differences associated with gender-role stereotypes reflect nature or the influences of culture and tradition.

CRITICAL THINKING
Why do you think some writers suggest that it is "politically correct" to minimize gender differences in cognitive abilities?

Watch the **Video**
Gender Differences:
Robert Sternberg
on **MyDevelopmentLab**

Gender differences are also vastly more pervasive than those involving sexual behavior, as we see next.

Gender Differences

If females and males were not anatomically different, this book would never have been written. But how do females and males differ in cognitive abilities, personality, and social behavior, if at all? ◉

DIFFERENCES IN COGNITIVE ABILITIES

Although females and males do not differ noticeably in overall intelligence (Halpern & LaMay, 2000), beginning in childhood, gender differences appear in certain cognitive abilities. Females are somewhat superior to males in verbal ability. Males seem somewhat superior in visual–spatial skills. The picture for mathematics appears to be much more complex, with females excelling in some areas and males in others.

Verbal Ability Verbal abilities include reading, spelling, grammar, oral comprehension, and word fluency. As a group, females surpass males in verbal ability throughout their lives (Andreano & Cahill, 2009; Lohman & Lakin, 2009). These differences show up early. Girls seem to acquire language faster than boys. They make more prelinguistic vocalizations, utter their first word sooner, and develop larger vocabularies. Boys in the United States are more likely than girls to have reading problems, ranging from reading below grade level to learning disorders (Brun et al., 2009).

Why do females excel in verbal abilities? Biological factors such as the organization of the brain may play a role, but do not discount cultural factors—whether a culture stamps a skill as gender-neutral, masculine, or feminine (Goldstein, 2005). In Nigeria and England, reading is looked on as a masculine activity, and boys traditionally surpass girls in reading ability. But in the United States and Canada, reading tends to be stereotyped as feminine, and girls tend to excel.

Visual–Spatial Abilities Visual–spatial ability refers to the ability to visualize objects or shapes and to mentally manipulate and rotate them. This ability is important in such fields as art, architecture, and engineering. Boys begin to outperform girls on many types of visual–spatial tasks starting at age 8 or 9, and the difference persists into adulthood (Andreano & Cahill, 2009; Yazzie, 2010). The gender difference is particularly notable on tasks that require imagining how objects will look if they are rotated in space (see Figure 6.5).

Some researchers link visual–spatial performance to evolutionary theory and sex hormones. It may be related to a genetic tendency to create and defend a territory (Ecuyer-Dab & Robert, 2004). An environmental theory is that gender stereotypes influence the spatial experiences of children. Gender-stereotyped "boys' toys," such as blocks, Legos, and Erector sets, provide more practice with spatial skills than gender-stereotyped "girls' toys." Boys are also more likely to engage in sports, which involve moving balls and other objects through space (Leaper & Bigler, 2011).

Mathematical Abilities For half a century or more, it has been believed that male adolescents generally outperform females in mathematics, and research has tended to support that belief (Collaer & Hill, 2006; Halpern et al., 2007). But a study by Janet Hyde and her colleagues (2008) of some 7 million children in second through eleventh grade found no overall gender difference for performance in mathematics on standardized tests.

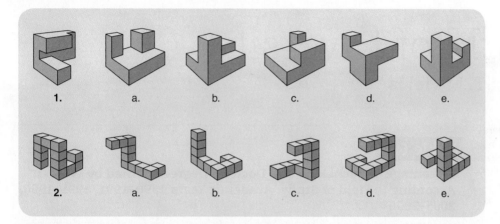

FIGURE 6.5 Rotating Geometric Figures in Space. Visual–spatial skills—for example, the ability to rotate geometric figures in space—are considered part of the male gender-role stereotype. But such gender differences are small and can be modified by training.

Regarding differences in verbal abilities and spatial-relations skills, note that the reported gender differences are group differences. There is greater variation in these skills among individuals within the groups than between males and females (Halpern, 2003). Millions of females outdistance the "average" male in math and spatial abilities. Men have produced their verbally adept Shakespeares. Moreover, in most cases, differences in cognitive skills are small in societies in which women are empowered, including most parts of the United States, Canada, Europe, Japan, and South Korea (Else-Quest et al., 2010; Else-Quest & Grabe, 2012).

DIFFERENCES IN PERSONALITY

There are also many gender differences in personality. According to a meta-analysis of the research literature, females exceed males in extraversion, anxiety, trust, and nurturance (Feingold, 1994). Overall, however, differences in personality tend to be small (Bailey, 2003b). Males do tend to exceed females in assertiveness, tough-mindedness, and self-esteem. Two factors may largely account for the relatively lower self-esteem of females:

- Parents, on average, prefer to have boys.
- Society has created an unlevel playing field in which females have to perform better than males to be seen as doing equally well.

DIFFERENCES IN SOCIAL BEHAVIOR

There are important gender differences in social behavior, particularly in matters concerning sex and aggression. Consider communication styles. Research shows that males tend to dominate classroom discussions unless teachers take steps to encourage gender equity in the classroom (McHugh & Hambaugh, 2010). As girls mature, it appears that they often learn to "take a backseat" to boys and let the boys do most of

Are There Gender Differences in Cognitive Abilities? The physical differences between females and males are well established—and well celebrated! But are there cognitive differences between females and males? If so, what are they? How large are they? Are they the result of nature (heredity) or nurture (environmental influences such as educational experiences and cultural expectations)?

A World of Diversity

Women in STEM Fields

Despite research findings that there is no overall gender difference in performance on standardized mathematics achievement tests, most Americans continue to have different expectations for boys and girls, and these expectations may still dissuade some math-proficient girls from entering so-called STEM (science, technology, engineering, and mathematics) fields (Hyde & Mertz, 2009).

Thus, there is reason to believe that women have the capacity to be entering STEM fields in greater numbers. So why, in the twenty-first century in the United States, do women remain underrepresented in STEM fields? According to psychologists Stephen Ceci, Wendy Williams, and Susan Barnett (2009), the reasons are likely as follows:

- Women who are proficient in math are more likely than math-proficient men to prefer careers that do not require skills in math.
- More males than females obtain extremely high scores on the SAT mathematics test and the quantitative reasons sections of the Graduate Record Exam.
- Women who are proficient in math are more likely than men with this proficiency to have high verbal competence as well, which encourages many such women to choose careers other than those in STEM fields.
- In some STEM fields, women with children find themselves penalized in terms of promotions.

Women's preferences may well be a key reason that there are more men entering and remaining in STEM fields today. However, we need to note two caveats: First, women are in fact entering STEM fields in increasing numbers (see Table 6.2 and Figure 6.6). Second, women's preferences cannot be fully divorced from society's expectations. As long as gender stereotypes about who belongs in STEM fields remain, at least some women will be discouraged from entering them.

FIGURE 6.6 Women Flood Professions Once Populated Almost Exclusively by Men

Source: As appeared in "Scientists Are Made, Not Born" by W. Michael Cox and Richard Alm, *The New York Times*, February 28, 2005. Reprinted by permission of Management Design.

Table 6.2

Percentage of Bachelor's and Doctoral Degrees Earned by Women, According to Field of Study: Academic Years 1990–1991, 1995–1996, 2005–2006

	1990–1991	1995–1996	2005–2006
BACHELOR'S DEGREES			
Health professions & related clinical sciences	83.9	81.5	86.0
Biological & biomedical sciences	50.8	52.6	61.5
Physical sciences & science technologies	31.6	36.0	41.8
Mathematics & statistics	47.3	46.1	45.1
Engineering & engineering technologies	14.1	16.2	17.9
DOCTORAL DEGREES			
Health professions & related clinical sciences	57.7	60.3	72.5
Biological & biomedical sciences	36.9	41.8	49.2
Physical sciences & science technologies	19.6	22.9	30.0
Mathematics & statistics	19.2	20.6	29.5
Engineering & engineering technologies	9.3	12.6	20.2

Source: U.S. Department of Education, National Center for Education Statistics (NCES). Digest of Education Statistics, 2007 (NCES 2008-022), tables 258, 286, 288, 290–301, 303, 305, and 307, data from U.S. Department of Education, NCES, 1990–91, 1995–96, and 2005–06. Integrated Postsecondary Education Data System, "Completions Survey" (IPEDS-C91-96), and IPEDS, Fall 2006. Table 27.I.

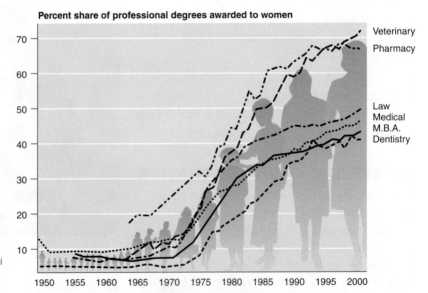

Percent share of professional degrees awarded to women

the talking when they are in mixed-gender groups, especially if they are reared in "traditional" communities or regions of the nation. Women are more willing than men to disclose their feelings and personal experiences, however (Valkenburg et al., 2011). The stereotype of the "strong and silent" male may not discourage men from hogging the conversation, but it may inhibit them from expressing their personal feelings.

Differences in Sexuality According to almost any measure that is used, men show more interest in sex than women do, although the gender difference may not be as large as is generally believed and may also be influenced by sex-role expectations (Fisher et al., 2012). Women are more likely to want to combine sex with a romantic relationship (Thompson & O'Sullivan, 2011). Men also report being more interested than women in casual sex and in multiple sex partners (Schmitt et al., 2012).

Differences in Aggressiveness **TRUTH** OR **FICTION** REVISITED: It is true that males tend to behave more aggressively than females, and that this gender difference emerges early (Hay et al., 2011). In almost all cultures, it is the males who march off to war and who battle for fame and glory (and shaving-cream-commercial contracts in stadiums and arenas). As we will see, the key question is: Why?

 6

Differences in Willingness to Seek Health Care Men's life expectancies are seven years shorter, on average, than women's. Female and male anatomy and physiology predispose them to different health issues, but part of the difference, according to surveys of physicians and of the general population, is women's greater willingness to seek health care (Glaesmer et al., 2012). Men often let symptoms go until a problem that could have been prevented or readily treated becomes serious or life-threatening. Women, for example, are much more likely to check themselves for breast cancer than men are to even recognize the symptoms of prostate cancer. Many men have a "bullet-proof mentality." They are too strong to see the doctor in their 20s, too busy in their 30s, and too frightened later on.

On Becoming a Man or a Woman: Gender Typing

We have chronicled the biological processes of sexual differentiation, and we have explored gender differences in cognitive abilities, personality, and social behavior. In this section we consider various explanations of gender typing, the process by which males and females come to develop personality traits and behavior patterns that society considers to be consistent with their gender, male or female—at least most of the time. Researchers who investigate people's perceptions of gender differences in personality traits tend to find groups of "masculine" and "feminine" traits such as those shown in Table 6.1.

One study using the "Big Five Inventory" investigated gender differences in personality in 55 nations, with a sample size of 17,637 (Schmitt et al., 2008). Responses revealed that women reported higher levels of anxiety, extraversion (outgoingness), agreeableness, and conscientiousness than men did in most nations.

BIOLOGICAL PERSPECTIVES: IT'S ONLY NATURAL

Biological views on gender typing tend to focus on the roles of hormones, genetics, and brain structures in predisposing men and women to gender-linked behavior patterns. It is largely assumed that a major mechanism by which heredity expresses itself in this realm is through prenatal sex hormones.

Hormones Researchers suggest that the development of gender differences in personality, along with the development of anatomic gender differences, may be related to prenatal levels of sex hormones. Although results of many studies attempting to correlate prenatal sex hormone levels with subsequent gender-typed play have been mixed, a study of 212 pregnant women conducted by Bonnie Auyeung and her colleagues (2009) found that fetal testosterone was related to masculine or feminine-typed play at the age of 8½ years. Other studies show that children display gender-typed preferences—with boys preferring transportation toys and girls preferring dolls—as early as the age of 13 months (Knickmeyer et al., 2005). Another study investigated the gender-typed visual preferences of 30 human infants at the early ages of 3 to 8 months (Alexander et al., 2009). The researchers assessed interest in a toy truck and a doll by using eye-tracking technology to indicate the direction of visual attention. Girls showed a visual preference for the doll over the truck (that is, they made a greater number of visual fixations on the doll), and boys showed a visual preference for the truck.

The Evolutionary Perspective From the evolutionary perspective, the story of the survival of our ancient ancestors is etched in our genes. Genes that bestow attributes that increase an organism's chances of surviving to produce viable offspring are most likely to be transmitted to future generations. We thus possess the genetic remnants of traits that helped our ancestors survive and reproduce (Buss, 2009). This heritage influences our social and sexual behavior as well as our anatomic features.

According to the evolutionary perspective, men's traditional roles as hunters and warriors and women's roles as caregivers and gatherers of fruits and vegetables are bequeathed to us in our genes. Men are better suited to war and the hunt because of physical attributes passed along since ancestral times. Upper-body strength, for example, would have enabled them to throw spears and overpower adversaries. Men also possess perceptual–cognitive advantages, such as superior visual–motor skills that favor aggression. Visual–motor skills would have enabled men to aim spears or bows and arrows.

Women, it is argued, are genetically predisposed to be empathic and nurturant because these traits enabled ancestral women to respond to children's needs and to enhance the likelihood that their children would flourish and eventually reproduce, thereby transmitting their own genetic legacy to future generations. Prehistoric women thus tended to stay close to home, care for the children, and gather edible plants, whereas men ventured from home to hunt and raid their neighbors' storehouses.

The evolutionary perspective is steeped in controversy. Although scientists do not dispute the importance of evolution in determining physical attributes, many are reluctant to attribute complex social behaviors, such as aggression and gender roles, to heredity. The evolutionary perspective implies that stereotypical gender roles—men as breadwinners and women as homemakers, for example—reflect the natural order of things. Critics contend that, among humans, biology is not destiny, and behavior is not dictated by genes.

Prenatal Brain Organization Researchers have sought the origins of gender-typed behavior in the organization of the brain. Is it possible that the cornerstone of gender-typed behavior is laid in the brain before the first breath is taken?

The hemispheres of the brain are specialized to carry out certain functions (Shaywitz et al., 1995). In most people, the right hemisphere ("right brain") appears to be specialized to perform visual–spatial tasks. The "left brain" appears to be more essential to verbal functions, such as speech, in most people.

We know that sex hormones are responsible for prenatal sexual differentiation of the genitals and for the gender-related structural differences in the hypothalamus of the developing prenatal brain. Sexual differentiation of the brain may also partly explain

CRITICAL THINKING
Why do you think many feminists and queer theorists argue that evolutionary theory is little more than a sophisticated excuse for maintaining the status quo in the centers of power in society?

A World of Diversity

The Eye That Roves Around the World?

One of the more controversial gender differences is the suggestion that males are naturally polygamous and females are naturally monogamous (Schmitt, 2008). If this were so, it would place a greater burden on societies in which men are expected to remain loyal to their mates. If the man strayed, after all, he could have the attitude, "Don't blame me. It's in my genes." Women, moreover, might wonder how realistic it is to expect that their partners will remain faithful.

Evolutionary psychologists have hypothesized *sexual strategies theory*, which holds that men and women differ in their long-term and short-term mating strategies, with men more interested in sexual variety in the short term (Cohen & Belsky, 2008; Njus & Bane, 2009). In the long term, both males and females may seek a heavy investment in a relationship, and feelings of love, companionship, and a sharing of resources. Even so, men are hypothesized to place more value on signals of fertility and reproductive value, as found in a woman's youth and physical appearance. But women are hypothesized to place relatively more value on a man's social status, maturity, and resources—cues that are relevant to his ability to provide over the long term. The qualities that men and women seek are believed to help solve adaptive problems that humans have faced over their evolutionary history.

But in the short term, men are more interested in one-night stands and relatively brief affairs. Women, evolutionarily speaking, would have little to gain from such encounters. Impregnation requires a long-term commitment to childrearing, and evolutionary forces would favor the survival of the children of women who created a long-term nurturing environment. But men would have a greater chance of contributing their genes to future generations by impregnating as many women as possible.

Because a "universal" form of behavior is more likely to be embedded in people's genes, the evolutionary theory of different sexual strategies would find support if males and females from various cultures showed similar gender differences

in short-term mating strategies. In seeking just such evidence, David Schmitt (2003) supervised a survey of 16,288 people across ten major regions of the world, including North America, South America, Western Europe, Eastern Europe, Southern Europe, Middle East, Africa, Oceania, South/Southeast Asia, and East Asia. He found that, indeed, gender differences in the desire for sexual variety were culturally universal.

Table 6.3 and Figure 6.7 reveal Schmitt's findings concerning desire for variety in short-term and long-term relationships. When asked whether they would like to have more than one sex partner in the next month, men from all ten areas of the world were significantly more likely than women to say that they would. For example, 23.1% of North American men would like more than one partner, as compared with just 2.9% of North American women (see Table 6.3). When asked about the mean (average) number of sex partners they would like to have over the next 30 years, men from every area said they would like to have significantly more sex partners than did the women (see Figure 6.7).

We cannot conclude that these research findings, intriguing as they are, "prove" the validity of the evolutionary approach to understanding gender differences in "sexual strategies." For example, we could point to details in Figure 6.7, such as the fact that Oceanic women reported that they wanted more sex partners in the long term than did African men. We can also accept the universality of the finding but consider rival explanations for the data. For example, in a world with common global communication, it might not be surprising that there is world-wide overlap in gender roles. This overlap might affect the ways in which parents and cultural institutions influence children around the world.

Do Men around the World Have Roving Eyes? A study of ten different areas of the world found that in every culture surveyed, men were more likely than women to desire multiple sex partners. According to the sexual strategies theory, this gender difference reflects human adaptation to environmental forces. Here's a question for critical thinking: Does this research finding mean that it is "unnatural" to expect men to remain faithful to their partners?

CRITICAL THINKING

According to evolutionary theory, men have inherited a tendency to be interested in having multiple sex partners. Does this mean that it is "unnatural" for society to promote monogamous relationships?

men's superiority at spatial-relations tasks, such as interpreting road maps and visualizing objects in space. Testosterone in the brains of male fetuses spurs greater growth of the right hemisphere and slows the rate of growth of the left hemisphere (Cohen-Bendahan et al., 2005; Siegel-Hinson & McKeever, 2002). This difference may be connected with the ability to accomplish spatial-relations tasks, and with preferences for childhood toys.

Might boys' inclinations toward aggression and rough-and-tumble play also be prenatally imprinted in the brain? Some theorists argue that prenatal sex hormones may masculinize or feminize the brain by creating predispositions that are consistent with gender-role stereotypes, such as rough-and-tumble play and aggressive behavior in males (Cohen-Bendahan et al., 2005).

The gender differences in activity preferences of children are also found in rhesus monkeys. For example, male rhesus juveniles and boys are more likely than female rhesus juveniles and girls to engage in rough-and-tumble play (Wallen & Hassett, 2009). Researchers also introduced wheeled toys and plush toys into a 135-member rhesus monkey troop and found that male monkeys, like boys, showed consistent, strong preferences for the wheeled toys, whereas female monkeys, like girls, showed greater flexibility in preferences, sometimes playing with the plush toys and sometimes playing with the wheeled toys (Hassett et al., 2008). Do these cross-species findings suggest that such preferences in humans can develop without human gender-typed socialization experiences?

Another study investigated the gender-typed visual preferences of human infants at the early ages of 3 to 8 months (Alexander et al., 2009). The researchers hypothesized that preferences for gender-typed toys might be at least in part inborn and would therefore emerge in children before they were self-aware of their gender identity. The researchers assessed interest in a toy truck and doll in 30 infants by using eye-tracking technology to indicate the direction of visual attention. They did find the hypothesized gender differences in visual interest: Girls showed a visual preference for the doll over the truck, and boys showed a higher number of visual fixations on the truck than on the doll. As noted, these gender differences emerge much earlier than self-awareness of one's sex, and there has been relatively little time for social influences to take effect.

PSYCHOLOGICAL PERSPECTIVES

Developmentally speaking, children acquire awareness of gender-role stereotypes by the tender ages of 2½ to 3½ (Rathus, 2014). When asked to describe gender differences, boys and girls generally agree that boys build things, play with transportation

Real Students, Real Questions

Q *Aren't there cultures in which women do the hunting/gathering and men take care of the children?*

A There certainly have been some. In her 1935 book *Sex and Temperament in Three Primitive Societies*, anthropologist Margaret Mead described the Tchambuli of New Guinea as follows: "The men 'primped' and spent their time decorating themselves while the women worked and were the practical ones—the opposite of how it seemed in early 20th century America." But, frankly, what makes this finding notable is its rarity.

Table 6.3

Gender Differences in the Percentage of Men and Women Who Desire More Than One Sex Partner "in the Next Month" across 10 World Regions

World Region	Percentage of Men Wanting More Than One Sexual Partner	Percentage of Women Wanting More Than One Sexual Partner
North America	23.1	2.9
South America	35.0	6.1
Western Europe	22.6	5.5
Eastern Europe	31.7	7.1
Southern Europe	31.0	6.0
Middle East	33.1	5.9
Africa	18.2	4.2
Oceania	25.3	5.8
South/Southeast Asia	32.4	6.4
East Asia	17.9	2.6

Note: The chances that any gender differences within a given region are the result of chance is less than 1 in 1,000 (p < 0.001).

Source: David P. Schmitt (2003). Universal sex differences in the desire for sexual variety: Tests from 52 nations, 6 continents, and 13 islands. *Journal of Personality and Social Psychology, 85*(1), 85–104, Table 5. Copyright © 2003 by the American Psychological Association. Reprinted with permission.

toys such as cars and fire trucks, enjoy helping their fathers, and hit other children. Both boys and girls also agree that girls enjoy playing with dolls, help their mothers cook and clean, and are talkative, dependent on others for help, and nonviolent. They perceive the label "cruel" to be a masculine trait, whereas "cries a lot" is perceived as feminine. By the time they are age 3, most children have become aware of the stereotypical ways in which men and women dress and the types of occupations that are considered appropriate for each (Rathus, 2014).

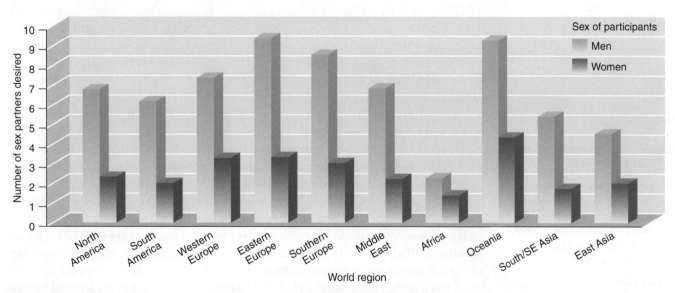

FIGURE 6.7 Mean Number of Sexual Partners Desired by Men and Women in the Next 30 Years, across 10 World Regions

Source: David P. Schmitt (2003). Universal sex differences in the desire for sexual variety: Tests from 52 nations, 6 continents, and 13 islands. *Journal of Personality and Social Psychology,* 85(1), 85–104. Copyright © 2003 by the American Psychological Association. Reprinted with permission.

Many psychologists have attempted to explain how children acquire such knowledge and adopt stereotypical behavior patterns in terms of psychoanalytic, social–cognitive, or cognitive–developmental theories.

Psychoanalytic Theory Sigmund Freud explained gender typing in terms of identification. Appropriate gender typing, in Freud's view, requires that boys come to identify with their fathers and girls with their mothers. **Identification** is completed, in Freud's view, as children resolve the **Oedipus complex** (sometimes called the *Electra complex* in girls).

According to Freud, the Oedipus complex occurs during the phallic period of psychosexual development, from the ages of 3 to 5. During this period the child develops incestuous wishes for the parent of the other sex and comes to perceive the parent of the same sex as a rival. The complex is resolved by the child's forsaking incestuous wishes for the parent of the other sex and identifying with the parent of the same sex. Through identification with the same-sex parent, the child comes to develop preferences and behavior patterns that are typically associated with that sex. But children display stereotypical gender-typed behaviors earlier than Freud would have predicted. Babies show visual preferences for sex-typed toys at 3 to 8 months (Alexander et al., 2009). During the first year, boys are more independent than girls. Girls are more quiet and restrained. Because of their lack of empirical support, many researchers believe that Freud's views are now of historic interest only.

Social–Cognitive Theory Social–cognitive theorists explain the development of gender-typed behavior in terms of processes such as observational learning, identification, and socialization (Golombok et al., 2008; Zosuls et al., 2009). In social–cognitive theory, identification is seen as a continuous learning process in which rewards and punishments influence children to imitate adult models of the same sex. In identification, the child not only imitates the behavior of the model but tries to become broadly like the model.

Socialization is thought to play a role in gender typing (Golombok et al., 2008; Zosuls et al., 2009). Almost from the moment a baby comes into the world, she or he is treated in ways that are consistent with gender stereotypes. Parents tend to talk more to baby girls, and fathers especially engage in more roughhousing with boys. When children are old enough to speak, caregivers and even other children begin to tell them how they are expected to behave. Parents may reward children for behavior they consider gender appropriate and punish (or fail to reinforce) them for behavior they consider inappropriate for their gender. Girls are encouraged to practice caregiving behaviors, which are intended to prepare them for traditional feminine adult roles. Boys are handed Legos or doctor sets to help prepare them for traditional masculine adult roles.

Fathers generally encourage their sons to develop assertive, instrumental behavior (that is, behavior that gets things done or accomplishes something) and their daughters to develop nurturant, cooperative behavior. Fathers are likely to cuddle their daughters gently. They are likely to carry their sons like footballs or toss them into the air. Fathers also tend to use heartier and harsher language with their sons, such as "How're yuh doin', Tiger?" and "Hey you, get your keester over here." Being a nontraditionalist, your first author made sure to toss his young daughters into the air, which raised immediate objections from the relatives, who chastised him for being too rough. This, of course, led him to modify his behavior. He learned to toss his daughters into the air when the relatives were not around.

In traditional households, boys are more likely to receive toy cars and guns and athletic equipment and to be encouraged to compete aggressively from an early age.

Identification In psychoanalytic theory, the process of incorporating within ourselves our perceptions of the behaviors, thoughts, and feelings of others.

Oedipus complex According to psychoanalytic theory, a conflict of the phallic stage in which the boy wishes to possess his mother sexually and perceives his father as a rival in love.

Socialization The process of guiding people into socially acceptable behavior patterns by means of information, rewards, and punishments.

Girls are spoken to more often, whereas boys are handled more frequently and more roughly.

Parental roles in gender typing are apparently changing. With more mothers working outside the home in our society, daughters are exposed to more women who represent career-minded role models than was the case in earlier generations. More parents today are encouraging their daughters to become career minded and to engage in strenuous physical activities, such as organized sports. Many boys today are exposed to fathers who take a larger role than men used to in child care and household responsibilities.

Social–cognitive theorists believe that aggression is largely influenced by learning. Boys are permitted, even encouraged, to engage in more aggressive behavior than girls.

Cognitive theorists address ways in which children integrate gender-role expectations within their self-concepts. Let us consider two cognitive approaches to gender typing: cognitive–developmental theory and gender schema theory.

Gender Typing through Observational Learning. According to social–cognitive theory, people learn about the gender roles that are available to them—and expected of them—at an early age. Gender schema theory adds that once children have learned the expected gender roles (i.e., the gender schema of their culture), they blend these roles with their self-concepts. Their self-esteem comes to be dependent on their adherence to the expected gender roles.

Cognitive–Developmental Theory Psychologist Lawrence Kohlberg (1966) proposed a cognitive–developmental view of gender typing. Children form concepts, or **schemas**, about gender and then conform their behavior to their gender concepts. These developments occur in stages and are entwined with general cognitive development.

According to Kohlberg, gender typing entails the emergence of three concepts: *gender identity, gender stability,* and *gender constancy.* Gender identity is usually acquired by the age of 3. By the age of 4 or 5, most children develop a concept of **gender stability**—the recognition that people retain their genders for a lifetime.

TRUTH OR FICTION REVISITED: Prior to the age of 4 or 5 or so, children may have not developed the concept of gender stability. As a result, boys may think that they will become mommies when they grow up, and girls may believe that they can become daddies.

The more sophisticated concept of **gender constancy** develops in most children by the age of 7 or 8. They recognize that gender does not change, even if people alter their dress or behavior. So gender remains constant even when appearances change. A woman who wears her hair short (or shaves it off) remains a woman. A man who dons an apron and cooks dinner remains a man.

According to cognitive–developmental theory, children are motivated to behave in gender-appropriate ways once they have established the concepts of gender stability and gender constancy. Boys and girls who come to recognize that their genders will remain a fixed part of their identity will show preferences for "masculine" and "feminine" activities, respectively. Researchers find, for instance, that boys who had achieved gender constancy played with an uninteresting gender-typed toy for a longer period of time than did boys who hadn't yet achieved gender constancy (Frey & Ruble, 1992). Both groups of boys played with an interesting gender-typed toy for about an equal length of time.

Cross-cultural studies of the United States, Samoa, Nepal, Belize, and Kenya find that the concepts of gender identity, gender stability, and gender constancy emerge in the order predicted by Kohlberg. However, gender-typed play often emerges at an

Schema Concept; way of interpreting experience or processing information.

Gender stability The concept that people retain their genders for a lifetime.

Gender constancy The concept that people's genders do not change, even if they alter their dress or behavior.

earlier age than would be predicted by the cognitive–developmental theory. Many infants show visual preferences for gender-typed toys by 3 to 8 months (Alexander et al., 2009).

Gender Schema Theory Gender schema theory proposes that children develop a **gender schema** as a means of organizing their perceptions of the world (Bem, 1993). A gender schema is a cluster of mental representations about masculine and feminine physical qualities, behaviors, and personality traits. Gender gains prominence as a schema for organizing experience because of society's emphasis on it.

Children's gender schemas determine how important gender-typed traits are to them. Consider the dimension of *strength–weakness*. Children may learn that strength is connected with maleness and weakness with femaleness. (Other dimensions, such as *light–dark*, are not gender-typed and thus may fall outside children's gender schemas.) Children also gather that some dimensions, such as *strong–weak*, are more important to one sex (in this case, the male) than the other.

Once children acquire a gender schema, they begin to judge themselves according to traits considered appropriate to their sex (Fagot et al., 2000; Grace et al., 2008). In doing so, they blend their developing self-concepts with the prominent gender schema of their culture. Children with self-concepts that are consistent with the prominent gender schema of their culture are likely to develop higher self-esteem than children whose self-concepts are inconsistent. Jack learns that muscle strength is a characteristic associated with "manliness." He is likely to think more highly of himself if he perceives himself as embodying this attribute than if he does not. Jill is likely to discover that the dimension of kindness–cruelty is more crucial than strength–weakness to the way in which women are perceived in society.

According to gender schema theory, gender identity itself is sufficient to inspire gender-appropriate behavior. Once children develop a concept of gender identity, they begin to seek information concerning gender-typed traits and try to live up to them. Jack will retaliate when provoked, because boys are expected to do so. Jill will be "sugary and sweet" if such is expected of little girls. Thus, gender-typed behavior would emerge earlier than would be proposed by cognitive–developmental theory. But even gender-schema theory cannot explain why boys and girls tend to show visual preferences for gender-typed toys before they are 1 year old.

In the following section, we see that some people have traits that are stereotypical of both males and females and that they promote psychological adjustment to a complex society.

Psychological Androgyny and the Reconstruction of Masculinity–Femininity: The More Traits, the Merrier?

Most people think of masculinity and femininity as opposite ends of one continuum. People tend to assume that the more masculine a person is, the less feminine he or she must be, and vice versa. So a man who exhibits stereotypical feminine traits of nurturance, tenderness, and emotionality is often considered less masculine than other men. Women who compete with men in business are perceived not only as more masculine but also as less feminine than other women.

Some investigators, such as Sandra Bem, argue that masculinity and femininity comprise separate personality dimensions (DiDonato & Berenbaum, 2011). A person who is highly masculine, whether male or female, may also possess feminine traits—and vice versa. People who exhibit "masculine" assertiveness and instrumental skills

Gender schema A cluster of mental representations about male and female physical qualities, behaviors, and personality traits.

(skills in the sciences and business, for example) along with "feminine" nurturance and cooperation fit both the masculine and feminine gender-role stereotypes. They are said to show **psychological androgyny.** Assertiveness and instrumental skills are consistent with the masculine stereotype. Nurturance and cooperation are consistent with the feminine stereotype. People low in the stereotypical masculine and feminine traits are "undifferentiated," according to gender-role stereotypes.

People who are psychologically androgynous may be capable of summoning a wider range of masculine and feminine traits to meet the demands of various situations and to express their desires and talents (Cooper et al., 2011; Prakash et al., 2010). Researchers, for example, have found psychologically androgynous persons of both genders to show "masculine" independence under group pressures to conform and "feminine" nurturance in interactions with children (DiDonato & Berenbaum, 2011). Psychologically androgynous adolescents are less likely to stereotype occupations as masculine or feminine (Kulik, 2000).

Many people who oppose the constraints of traditional gender roles may perceive psychological androgyny as a desirable goal. Some feminist writers, however, have criticized psychological androgyny on grounds that the concept is defined in terms of, and thereby perpetuates, belief in the existence of masculine and feminine gender roles (Denmark et al., 2008).

Other critics suggest that some benefits of psychological androgyny are actually confounded with masculinity. For example, psychologically androgynous people tend to have higher self-esteem and to be generally better adjusted psychologically than people who are feminine or undifferentiated (DiDonato & Berenbaum, 2011; Parent et al., 2011). Does this mean that masculine traits such as assertiveness and independence may be related to psychological well-being, whether or not they are combined with feminine traits such as warmth, nurturance, and cooperation?

In any event, not all males are extremely "masculine," and not all females are overwhelmingly "feminine." Perhaps it is fortunate that few of us are completely masculine or feminine, despite our anatomic sex.

In this chapter we have explored what it means to be female, male, or another sex within a cultural setting such as ours. In the following chapter we consider how feelings of attraction and love develop in females, males, and others.

CRITICAL THINKING
Explain why feminists have criticized the concept of psychological androgyny.

Psychological androgyny A state characterized by possession of both stereotypical masculine traits and stereotypical feminine traits.

Real Students, Real Questions

Q *Are there more similarities or differences between men and women?*

A Here's a shocking answer: It depends on how you look at it. We are used to focusing on the differences, but we'll take a flyer and say there are more similarities. For example, men and women share well over 99% of their genetic material. They both walk upright, use language, think, perform in the sciences and the arts, play tennis and golf, have iPods and cell phones attached to their ears, and on and on. And, sadly, they both pay taxes and carry mortgages.

Chapter Review

✓•┌**Study** and **Review** on **MyDevelopmentLab**

LO1 **Describe the processes of prenatal sexual differentiation**

During the first six weeks or so of prenatal development, embryonic structures of both sexes resemble female structures. At about the seventh week, the genetic code (XX or XY) begins to cause changes in the gonads, genital ducts, and external genitals. Testosterone spurs differentiation of the male (Wolffian) duct system. In the absence of testosterone, the Wolffian ducts degenerate, and female sex organs develop. The testes and ovaries develop in the abdominal cavity. A few months after conception, the ovaries descend to the pelvic region, and the testes descend into the scrotal sac.

LO2 **Discuss sex chromosomal abnormalities that may affect sexual differentiation**

These abnormalities include Klinefelter syndrome (in which a male has an XXY sex chromosomal structure) and Turner syndrome (in which a woman has just one X sex chromosome).

LO3 **Define gender identity and the roles of nature and nurture in gender identity**

Gender identity is almost always consistent with anatomic sex. However, research with intersexuals suggests that prenatal exposure to androgens may masculinize the brain as well as the sex organs.

LO4 **Discuss transgenderism**

Transgenderism is the desire to have the genital organs of, and to live as, a member of the other sex. The third gender area addresses matters that have to do with people whose anatomy and/or patterns of sexual behavior or sexual desire do not fit "heteronormativity."

LO5 **Discuss gender roles and stereotypes**

Cultures have broad expectations of men and women that are termed *gender roles*. In our culture the stereotypical female is seen as nurturant, gentle, dependent, kind, helpful, patient, and submissive. The stereotypical male is self-assertive, tough, competitive, gentlemanly, and protective. Sexism is the prejudgment that because of gender, a person will possess negative traits.

LO6 **Explain the relationship between gender roles and sexual behavior**

Gender roles encourage many males to take the initiative in matters of sex.

LO7 **Discuss gender differences in cognitive abilities**

Females excel somewhat in verbal skills, and males somewhat in spatial-relations skills. Recent research challenges the view that males perform better in math, showing no overall differences on math achievement tests.

LO8 **Discuss gender differences in personality**

Females are usually more extraverted and nurturing. Males are usually more aggressive and tough minded.

LO9 **Discuss gender differences in social behavior**

Males often dominate classroom discussions, and females are usually more likely to share their feelings. Men are relatively more interested in sex with multiple partners, and women are usually more interested in combining sex with romance.

LO10 **Discuss biological and psychological perspectives on gender typing**

Evolutionary theory explains gender differences in terms of adaptation to environmental forces. Testosterone in the brains of male fetuses spurs greater growth of the right hemisphere, which may be connected with spatial-relations tasks. Freud explained gender typing in terms of identification with the parent of the same sex. Social–cognitive theorists explain the development of gender-typed behavior in terms of processes such as observational learning, identification, and socialization. According to Kohlberg, gender typing entails the emergence of gender identity, gender stability, and gender constancy. Gender schema theory proposes that children blend their developing self-concepts with the prominent gender schema of their culture.

LO11 **Define psychological androgyny and discuss its possible advantages**

There is a question as to whether masculinity and femininity comprise two independent personality dimensions or a single bipolar dimension. People who combine stereotypical masculine and feminine behavior patterns are termed *psychologically androgynous*.

Test Your Learning

1. Müllerian inhibiting substance prevents the Müllerian ducts from developing into
   (a) the female duct system.
   (b) the male duct system.
   (c) interstitial cells.
   (d) external genital organs.

2. Congenital adrenal hyperplasia is caused by excessive levels of
   (a) androgens.
   (b) estradiol.
   (c) pheromones.
   (d) Müllerian inhibiting substance.

3. Transgendered people are most likely to have
   (a) an extra X chromosome.
   (b) androgen insensitivity syndrome.
   (c) aggressive tendencies.
   (d) gender dysphoria.

4. The masculine gender-role stereotype is seen as all of the following *except*
   (a) sensitive.
   (b) tough.
   (c) protective.
   (d) gentlemanly.

5. Which gender difference is supported by evidence?
   (a) Males are better writers.
   (b) Females are better in math and science.
   (c) Females are more aggressive.
   (d) Males have more reading problems.

6. According to sexual strategies theory,
   (a) women choose the best-looking men.
   (b) only humans have long-term mates.
   (c) men are more interested in short-term sexual variety.
   (d) women seek sex without commitment.

7. According to Kohlberg, gender _____ develops last.
   (a) stability
   (b) identity
   (c) exclusivity
   (d) constancy

8. The concept of the third gender challenges
   (a) feminist theory.
   (b) queer theory.
   (c) heteronormativity.
   (d) transgender activism.

9. Research shows that following sex reassignment, most male-to-female transsexuals
   (a) are orgasmic during sexual intercourse.
   (b) regret their decision to have the operation.
   (c) develop psychological disorders they did not show evidence of previously.
   (d) eventually discontinue hormone treatments.

10. The most common form of female intersexualism is
    (a) Dominican Republic syndrome.
    (b) congenital adrenal hyperplasia.
    (c) transgenderism.
    (d) gender instability.

Answers: 1. a; 2. a; 3. d; 4. a; 5. d; 6. c; 7. d; 8. c; 9. a; 10. b

My Life, My Sexuality

Do You Fit the Masculine or Feminine Gender-Role Stereotype? (Do You Want to Fit One of Them?)

*Explore this **My Life, My Sexuality** feature by scanning this QR code with your mobile device. If you don't already have one, you may download a free QR scanner for your device wherever smartphone apps are sold. You can also view this feature in MyDevelopmentLab, along with an accompanying critical thinking assignment.*

Would you like to see whether you generally fit the feminine or masculine gender-role stereotype, or whether you tend more toward psychological androgyny? Scan the QR code to check it out with our online self-assessment. Then, of course, regardless of the results, you can think about what it all means—or ask your professor for ideas. Also remember that these are stereotypes, and researchers are not in agreement as to what it means to be masculine or feminine, or as to how people develop "masculinity" or "femininity."

7 Attraction and Love— Binding Forces

Learning Objectives

PHYSICAL ATTRACTIVENESS: HOW IMPORTANT IS LOOKING GOOD?

LO1 Describe cultural standards for physical attractiveness

LO2 Describe nonphysical traits that affect perceptions of physical attractiveness

THE ATTRACTION–SIMILARITY HYPOTHESIS: WHO IS "RIGHT" FOR YOU?

LO3 Explain the role of similarity in the formation of romantic relationships

LOVE: "THE MORNING AND THE EVENING STAR"?

LO4 Discuss the meaning of love

ROMANTIC LOVE

LO5 Discuss the meaning of romantic love

CONTEMPORARY MODELS OF LOVE: DARE SCIENCE INTRUDE?

LO6 Discuss theories of love

LO7 Explain how people's preferences for partners differ for short-term and long-term relationships

MY LIFE, MY SEXUALITY: WHAT DO YOU THINK YOU SHOULD BE THINKING ABOUT WHEN YOU'RE IN THE MARKET FOR A LONG-TERM RELATIONSHIP?

TRUTH OR FICTION?

Which of the following statements are the truth, and which are fiction? Look for the
Truth-or-Fiction icons on the pages that follow to find the answers.

1 Beauty is in the eye of the beholder.   T   F?

2 Women find men with deeper voices to be more attractive.   T   F?

3 People are regarded as more attractive when they are smiling.   T   F?

4 Women who are randomly assigned names like Kathy and
Jennifer are rated as more attractive than women assigned
names like Harriet and Gertrude.   T   F?

5 "Opposites attract." That is, we are more apt to be
attracted to people who disagree with our views and
tastes than to people who share them.   T   F?

6 It is possible to be in love with someone who is not
also a friend.   T   F?

7 Committed couples can remain in love even after
passion fades.   T   F?

8 Physical appeal is the most important trait
we seek in partners for long-term
relationships.   T   F?

When you go to buy a box of Valentine's Day candy, what color will the box be? Green? Blue? The answer, of course, is red. What is the most popular color of women's lipstick? Yellow? Brown? Again, the answer is red (Elliot et al., 2007). Red has been the most popular lipstick color since the hot days that saw the construction of the pyramids in ancient Egypt (Elliot & Niesta, 2008). Red is similarly the most popular color for women's lingerie.

At a traffic light, the color red means stop. But when it comes to sexual attraction, the color red is more likely to mean go.

But why is the color red associated with feelings of attraction? Could the answer be cultural conditioning? Anthropologists have found evidence that females used red ochre as a face and body paint in rituals carried out before the dawn of history (Lee, 2006). We find red used in ancient myths and folklore as a symbol of passion and fertility (Elliot & Pazda, 2012; Hutchings, 2004). Red has been associated with lust in literature, most notably in Nathaniel Hawthorne's novel of illicit romance and consequences—*The Scarlet Letter*. Red has been used as a symbol of prostitution for centuries, as in the term *red-light district* (Moore, 2010).

The link between red and physical attraction may also be rooted in our biological heritage. Many nonhuman female primates, including baboons, chimpanzees, gorillas, and rhesus monkeys, show reddened genital regions and sometimes reddened chests and faces when they are nearing ovulation—the time of the month when they are fertile (Barelli et al., 2008; Engelhardt et al., 2012). Reddening of the skin is caused by elevated estrogen levels (relative to progesterone), which increase the flow of blood under the surface of the skin. It is widely believed that reddish skin tones are a sexual signal that attracts mates (Huchard et al., 2009). Research has found that male primates are in fact especially attracted to females when they display red, as shown by attempts at sexual relations (Waitt et al., 2006).

As in the case of other female primates, women's estrogen levels relative to progesterone are elevated near ovulation, enhancing the flow of blood beneath the surface of the skin (Lynn et al., 2007). At this time of the month, women also tend to choose clothing that leaves more skin visible (Durante et al., 2008), use sexier gaits and walk more slowly ahead of men (Gueguen, 2012), and are more readily sexually aroused (Rupp et al., 2009). For men, then, as with other male primates, the reddening of a woman's skin at the time of ovulation may be a sexual signal.

Andrew Elliot and Daniela Niesta (2008) ran a series of experiments in which men did, indeed, rate the same woman as more attractive when her photograph was shown against a red background compared with a variety of other background colors. One experiment revealed

that the red-related difference in attractiveness was found in male raters but not in female raters. As you can see in Figure 7.1, male raters found women more attractive when they were shown with red backgrounds as opposed to white, but female raters did not show the same preference.

Andrew Elliot and his colleagues (2010) also ran experiments with women and found that they rated photos of men as being more attractive when the photos were bordered in red or the men were wearing red clothing. Women are more interested in the status of potential partners than men are, and it seems that they connect the color red with status in males. Cross-cultural research links the color red in males with power and social dominance, and the Elliot group found that women rated males in red as having more status than males in white, blue, or green. The color red had no effect on women's ratings of males as being likeable, agreeable, or outgoing—status was the lone association. But, as with men viewing women, red is "sexy."

A biological possibility as to why women are more attracted to males who are associated with the color red is that testosterone is involved in oxygenating blood and increasing its flow to the skin (giving off a reddish hue) and to the genitals, leading to sexual excitement. Red coloration

Why did they deck her out in red? The answers may lie in our cultural conditioning and our genetic heritage.

can also be an indicator of health, because highly oxygenated blood levels can be maintained only by organisms in good health (Elliot et al., 2010).

Reddening of the skin, then, is a cue that is connected with attraction. Body odor—or scent—is another cue. We noted in Chapter 5 that female strippers and lap dancers earn higher tips when they are ovulating (Haselton & Gildersleeve, 2011). We may wonder if the "mechanism" connected with attraction was indeed body odor, however. A critical thinker might ask whether ovulation might have in some way prompted the women to behave in a manner that was more appealing to men.

Attraction and one of its possible consequences, love, are the subjects of this chapter. Investigators define feelings of attraction as psychological forces that draw people together. We will see that many factors enter into personal attraction. The first of these that we consider is physical appearance.

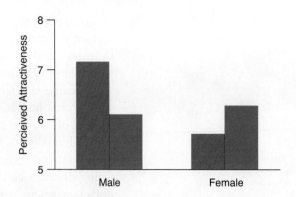

FIGURE 7.1 Rated Attractiveness as a Woman Shown in a Photograph, as Related to the Color of the Background and the Gender of the Rater.

Source: Elliot, A. J., & Niesta, D. (2008). Romantic red: Red enhances men's attraction to women. *Journal of Personality and Social Psychology, 95*(5), 1150–1164.

Physical Attractiveness: How Important Is Looking Good?

We might like to think of ourselves as so sophisticated that physical attractiveness does not move us. We might like to claim that sensitivity, warmth, and intelligence are more important to us. However, we may never learn about other people's personalities if they do not meet our minimal standards for physical attractiveness. Research shows that physical attractiveness is a major determinant of interpersonal and sexual attraction (Lippa, 2012; Little et al., 2011). Some researchers, in fact, contend that physical appearance is the key factor in consideration of partners for dates, sex, and long-term relationships (Wilson et al., 2005). ◉

◉ **Watch** the **Video**
Secrets of Beauty
on **MyDevelopmentLab**

IS BEAUTY IN THE EYE OF THE BEHOLDER?

Are our standards fully subjective, or is there broad agreement on what is attractive? Cross-cultural studies of preliterate societies have found that people universally want physically appealing partners (Ford & Beach, 1951). However, is that which appeals in one culture repulsive in others?

In certain African tribes, as among the Khoikhoi, long necks and round, disk-like lips are signs of feminine beauty. Women thus stretch their necks and lips to make themselves more appealing. Women of the Nama tribe persistently tug at their labia majora to make them "beautiful"—that is, prominent and elongated (Ford & Beach, 1951). **TRUTH** OR **FICTION** REVISITED: Beauty may not be completely in the eye of the beholder. As noted in the "A World of Diversity" feature, "Wide-Eyed with . . . Beauty?" some aspects of beauty seem to be largely cross-cultural.

In our culture, taller men are considered to be more attractive by women (Furnham, 2009; Kurzban & Weeden, 2005). Height plays a key role in choice of a mate because it suggests social dominance, status, access to resources, and a positive heritable trait (Salska, 2008). Undergraduate women prefer their dates to be about 6 inches taller than they are. Undergraduate men, on the average, prefer women who are about 4 to 5 inches shorter (Furnham, 2009; Kurzban & Weeden, 2005). Because of gender roles, tall women are not viewed so positively. In a Polish survey of 2,000 personal ads and about 400 undergraduates, only 23% of men and 4% of women indicated that they would accept a date in which the woman was taller. But short men and tall women were more flexible; otherwise their potential dating pool would have been much smaller.

Because shorter men are discouraged from asking them out, some tall women walk with a hunch, as if to minimize their height. A neighbor of the first and third authors of this text refers to herself—humorously, of course—as 5 feet 13 inches tall.

"Thin is in" is the dominant European American culture of the United States. Some young women are so affected by the cultural ideal that they suffer from the eating disorder called **anorexia nervosa,** in which they literally starve themselves. Both females and males find slenderness (though not anorexic thinness) attractive, especially for females (Furnham, 2009; Glasser et al., 2009; Wilson et al., 2005).

An examination of the Internet dating profiles of 5,810 Yahoo personal ads shows that "thin" is more "the in thing" in the expressed preferences for partners of European Americans and males (Glasser et al., 2009). European American males are more likely than African American and Latino males to want to date slender and buffed women. African American and Latino men are significantly more likely to be interested in women with large or thick bodies. Although being a heavy woman is connected with a negative body image in our culture, African American and Latina women are significantly more likely than European American women with similar body shapes to be satisfied with their bodies (Glasser et al., 2009; La Rocque & Cloe, 2011). Moreover, women who are displeased with their bodies are more likely to avoid sexual activity, although women with a history of sexual satisfaction and with strong sexual desire are more likely to engage in sexual activity despite their body images (La Rocque & Cloe, 2011).

The dominant culture also prefers the hourglass figure. Studies find that women of average weight with a waist-to-hip ratio of 0.7 to 0.8 are rated as most attractive and desirable for relationships (Furnham et al., 2005; Weeden & Sabini, 2005). Neither gaunt nor obese women were found to be as attractive, regardless of their waist-to-hip ratio. ◉

LESBIANS' PREFERENCES CONCERNING WAIST-TO-HIP RATIO

Cohen and Tannenbaum (2001) conducted an Internet study in which they posted various women's body shapes and asked lesbian and bisexual women to indicate which were most sexually attractive to them. Respondents included 209 women self-identified as lesbian and 141 women self-identified as bisexual. The women, like heterosexual men, found women with a 0.7 waist-to-hip body ratio to be the most sexually attractive. However, they differed from the men in that their first choice was for heavy women with a 0.7 waist-to-hip body ratio and large breasts. Their second choice was for heavy women with the same waist-to-hip body ratio but with small breasts. The authors of the study suggest that lesbians rejected societal emphasis on excessive slenderness.

People who are attractive know it. In one study, men and women rated each other for attractiveness and also rated themselves (Marcus & Miller, 2003). By and large, the individuals' self-ratings meshed with those by others, both female and male. Women's judgments were most closely related to how men perceived them, suggesting that they were reflecting men's opinions of them more so than women's.

The voice is another physical feature in attraction. An experiment manipulated men's voices and asked women to rate them for attractiveness. Heterosexual women at the fertile (late-follicular) phase of the menstrual cycle found men with more "masculine"—that is, deeper—voices to be more attractive (Feinberg et al., 2006).

◉⊦**Watch** the **Video**
What's in It for Me?:
on **MyDevelopmentLab**

Anorexia nervosa A potentially life-threatening eating disorder characterized by refusal to maintain a healthy body weight, intense fear of becoming overweight, a distorted body image, and, in females, lack of menstruation (amenorrhea).

CRITICAL THINKING
Do you think the study that concluded that heterosexual women find men with deeper voices to be more attractive during the late follicular phase of the menstrual cycle is consistent with evolutionary theory? Explain.

A Closer Look

Thin May Be In, But Not with Bust Size

Which size breasts do men prefer? How would you assess the answer?

It is generally believed that men prefer women with large breasts. For this reason, as well as dissatisfaction with their own body image, many women with small breasts decide to obtain breast implants (Moser & Alken, 2011). *Do* men prefer women with large breasts?

One study assessed men's interest in women of various breast sizes by tracking their eye movements when they were viewing images of various breast sizes (Dixson et al, 2011). The researchers predicted that the men would have a greater number of visual fixations on larger breasts, and also rate them as more attractive. They predicted that the coloration of the areolae would also play a role. Lightly pigmented areolae are suggestive of youth, so the researchers also expected that the men would prefer lighter areolae.

The men in the study rated women with medium-sized or large breasts as more attractive than small breasts, as predicted. Contrary to expectations, the men rated the breasts with the darker areolae as being more attractive than the breasts with the lightly pigmented areolae. But—and this may be a huge but—the rated preferences of the men did not correlate with their visual fixation times on breast size or areolar pigmentation. Does this finding suggest that the men had no "real" preferences? Does it suggest that the men are "out of touch" with their "real" feelings? What would a critical thinker have to say?

CRITICAL THINKING

Critical thinkers will be skeptical of the use of the word *real*. Critical thinkers also look for rival explanations for research findings. For example, could it be that in our visual culture, with its ubiquitous sexual and anatomic images, that the men were just scanning the breasts and the areolae for differences, but they had no particular arousing quality? Can you think of other rival explanations for the results?

The study did not assess possible differences between heterosexual and lesbian women. **TRUTH** OR **FICTION** REVISITED: It is only partly true that women preferred men with deeper voices. First of all, the finding was true for heterosexual women only. Second it was true for heterosexual women only during the time of the month when they were fertile.

 2

A World of Diversity
Wide-Eyed with . . . Beauty?

Research suggests that European Americans, African Americans, Asian Americans, and Latin Americans tend to agree on the facial features that they find to be attractive (Cunningham et al., 1995). They all prefer female faces with large eyes; greater distance between the eyes; small noses; narrower faces with smaller chins; high, expressive eyebrows; larger lower lips; and a well-groomed, full head of hair.

Consider the methodology of a study that compared the facial preferences of people in Japan and England. Perrett (cited in Brody, 1994) created computer composites of the faces of 60 women. Part A of Figure 7.2 is a composite of the 15 women who were rated the most attractive. He then used computer enhancement to exaggerate the differences between the composite of the 60—that is, the average face—and the composite of the 15 most attractive women. Perret found that both Japanese and British men deemed women with

large eyes, high cheekbones, and narrow jaws to be the most attractive. Computer enhancement resulted in the image shown in Part B of Figure 7.2. The enhanced composite has still higher cheekbones and a narrower jaw than Part A. Part B was then rated as the most attractive image. Similar results were found for the image of a Japanese woman.

Cunningham and his colleagues (1995) reported historical anecdotes that suggest that the facial preferences of people as diverse as Europeans, Black Africans, Native Americans, Indians (in India, that is), and Chinese are quite consistent. They quoted from Charles Darwin's 1871 treatise, *The Descent of Man*, and *Selection in Relation to Sex*:

> Mr. Winwood Reade . . . who has had ample opportunities for observation [with Black Africans] who have never associated with Europeans is convinced that their ideas of beauty are, on the whole, the same as ours;

and Dr. Rohlfs writes to me the same effect with respect to Borneo and the countries inhabited by the Pullo tribes. . . . Capt. Burton believes that a woman whom we consider beautiful is admired throughout the world.

Darwin believed that our physical preferences were largely inborn and related to survival of our species. What do you think? Do you believe that "their ideas of beauty are, on the whole, the same as ours"? Or do you think that research hasn't yet ferreted out significant cultural or ethnic differences that might exist? If there is ethnic consistency in these preferences, how would you explain them? For example, do you believe

- that they are coincidental?
- that there has been more exchange of ideas among cultures than has been believed?
- that there is something instinctive about them?

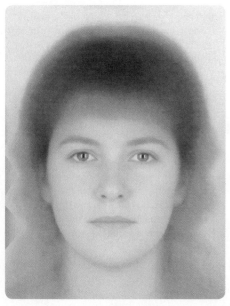

A

B

FIGURE 7.2 What Features Contribute to Facial Attractiveness? In both England and Japan, features such as large eyes, high cheekbones, and narrow jaws contribute to perceptions of the attractiveness of women. View A is a computer composite of the faces of 15 women rated as the most attractive of a group of 60. View B is a computer composite that exaggerates the features of these 15 women. That is, they are developed further in the direction that separates them from the average of the full group.

NONPHYSICAL TRAITS AFFECT PERCEPTIONS OF PHYSICAL BEAUTY

Although there are physical standards for beauty in our culture, nonphysical traits also affect our perceptions of beauty. For example, the perceived beauty of a partner is likely to be enhanced by nonphysical traits such as familiarity, liking, respect, and sharing of values and goals (Morry et al., 2011; Reis et al., 2011; Sprecher & Fair, 2011). **TRUTH** OR **FICTION** REVISITED: Females and males also rate the attractiveness of faces higher when they are smiling than when they are not smiling (O'Doherty et al., 2003). So there is reason to "put on a happy face" when you meet people.

 3

A World of Diversity

Gender Differences in Preferences in Mates across 37 Cultures

What do men in Nigeria, Japan, Brazil, Canada, and the United States have in common? For one thing, men in these countries report that they prefer mates who are younger than themselves. Buss (1994) reviewed survey evidence on the preferred age difference between oneself and one's mate in 37 cultures (representing 33 countries) in Europe, Africa, Asia, Australia, New Zealand, and North and South America. In every culture men preferred younger mates (the range was from 0.38 year to 6.45 years). Women, however, preferred older mates (the range was from 1.82 years to 5.1 years).

Gender differences in the preferred age of mates paralleled actual differences in age of men and women at the time of marriage. Men were between two and five years older, on average, than their wives at the time of marriage. The smallest average age difference at marriage, 2.1 years, was found in Poland. The largest average difference, 4.92 years, was found in Greece. Men in the mainland United States averaged 2.71 years older than women at the time of marriage. In Canada, men were 2.51 years older than their mates, on average.

Buss found that in all 37 cultures, men placed greater value on a prospective partner's "good looks" than did women. On the other hand, women in 36 of 37 cultures placed greater value on "good earning capacity" of prospective mates.

The consistency of Buss's findings lends credence to the notion that there are widespread gender differences in preferences with respect to age, physical characteristics, and financial status of prospective mates. Generally speaking, men place greater value on the physical attractiveness and relative youth of prospective mates. Women place relatively greater value on the earning capacity of prospective mates. Buss interpreted women's preferences for relatively older mates as additional evidence that women appraise future mates on the basis of their ability to provide for a wife and family, because age and income tend to be linked among men.

Despite these gender differences in preferences for mates, Buss found that both men and women placed greater emphasis on personal qualities than on looks or income potential of prospective mates. In all 37 cultures, the characteristics "kind," "understanding," and "intelligent" were rated higher than earning power or physical attractiveness.

Who Is Mr. or Ms. Right? Are your judgments of attractiveness based on universal standards or on your cultural experiences? Evolutionary psychologist David Buss found some nearly universal standards for beauty in his study of 37 cultures.

HOW BEHAVIOR AND NAMES AFFECT PERCEPTIONS OF PHYSICAL ATTRACTIVENESS: ON THE IMPORTANCE OF *NOT* BEING EARNEST

Gender-role expectations may affect perceptions of attractiveness. For example, women are more likely to be attracted to socially dominant men than men are to be attracted to socially dominant women (Graziano & Bruce, 2008). Women who viewed videos of prospective dates found men who acted outgoing and self-expressive more appealing than men who were passive (Riggio & Woll, 1984). Another study found that highly feminine women are more likely to be attracted to dominant "macho" men than less feminine women are (Maybach & Gold, 1994). And yet, men who viewed videos in the Riggio and Woll (1984) study were put off by outgoing, self-expressive behavior in women. In still another study, women rated videos of dominant college men (defined in this study as social control over a troublesome interaction with an instructor) as more appealing than submissive men. Again, male viewers were put off by similarly dominant women (Sadalla et al., 1987). Men are more likely to be jealous of socially dominant men, whereas women are more likely to be jealous of physically attractive women (Dijkstra & Buunk, 2002). **TRUTH OR FICTION** REVISITED: Names can also affect perceptions of attractiveness. In one study, women who were randomly assigned names like Kathy, Jennifer, and Christine were rated more attractive than women assigned the names Harriet, Gertrude, and Ethel (Garwood et al., 1980). Seems silly, does it not? After all, our parents name us, and there need be no relationship between our names and our physical appeal. On the other hand, we may choose to keep our names or to use nicknames. So if you are unhappy with your name, why not assume a more popular nickname? Beginning college or a new job is an ideal time for doing so. Men, too, can doff their Sylvesters and Ernests, if they prefer. If you have an unusual name and are content with it, be yourself, however.

Are Preferences Concerning Attractiveness Inherited? On the surface, gender differences in perceptions of attractiveness seem unbearably sexist—and perhaps they are. But some evolutionary psychologists believe that evolutionary forces

---

Real Students, Real Questions

Q *I keep attracting the same kind of guy—one that is not good for me. Why do I do this?*

A We don't know you well enough to give you a precise answer, but your complaint sounds familiar enough. Try listing the traits you want in a guy. Seriously—write them down. Then write down how you go about meeting guys and how you decide to get intimate with them, or whether you just let it happen.

Should you meet guys in other places, in other ways? Should you get to know them better before getting intimate? Should you end things early on if things aren't going the way you want them to? Just be honest with yourself and figure it out. It's more likely because of poor choices, lack of self-confidence, low self-esteem (if you think you're not worth very much, maybe you allow people to treat you as if you aren't), or—gulp—laziness, rather than something like a deep unconscious desire to punish yourself.

Real Students, Real Questions

Q *What do you do if you're attracted to your best friend's boyfriend (or girlfriend)?*

A Generally speaking, flirting with or "messing around with" your friend's boyfriend or girlfriend is a no-no. You may win the boyfriend or girlfriend, but you'll probably lose the friend, and, possibly, the respect of people who know both of you. Having said that, the reality of the situation must also accept the fact that what you are essentially doing is making a decision regarding who is more important to you—your friend or his or her partner. You probably can't have both. This also goes for "exes." Even if the relationship between your friend and his or her partner comes to an end, seeing the ex-partner may still be a sore point, so you may still be unable to have both.

favor the continuation of gender differences in preferences for mates because certain preferred traits provide reproductive advantages (Buss, 2005, 2009; Schmitt et al., 2012). Some physical features, such as cleanliness, good complexion, clear eyes, good teeth, good hair, firm muscle tone, and a steady gait, are universally appealing to both females and males. Perhaps they are markers of reproductive potential (Buss, 2005). Age and health may be relatively more important to a woman's appeal, because these characteristics tend to be associated with her reproductive capacity (the "biological clock" limits her reproductive potential). Physical characteristics associated with a woman's youthfulness, such as smooth skin, firm muscle tone, and lustrous hair, may thus have become more closely linked to a woman's appeal (Buss, 2005). A man's reproductive value, however, may depend more on how well he can provide for his family than on his age or physical appeal. The value of men as reproducers, therefore, is more intertwined with factors that contribute to a stable environment for childrearing—such as economic status and reliability. Evolutionary psychologists argue that these gender differences in mate preferences may have been passed down through the generations as part of our genetic heritage (Buss, 2009).

The Attraction–Similarity Hypothesis: Who Is "Right" for You?

Do not despair if you are less than exquisite in appearance, along with most of us mere mortals. You may be saved from permanently blending in with the wallpaper by the effects of the attraction–similarity hypothesis. 👁

The **attraction–similarity hypothesis** holds that people tend to develop romantic relationships with people who are similar to themselves in physical attractiveness and other traits (Morry et al., 2011; Sprecher & Fair, 2011). There are some gender differences: Research shows that men are more likely than women to communicate positive feelings and present themselves in a positive light when they are conversing with a woman who is similar in physical attractiveness (van Straaten et al., 2009). Women did not show the same selectivity in talking with men. These findings are consistent with research showing that physical attractiveness is a more important

CRITICAL THINKING
Do your own preferences in a romantic partner appear to support or contradict evolutionary theory? Explain.

👁 **Watch** the **Video**
Finding a Mate
on **MyDevelopmentLab**

Attraction–similarity hypothesis
The view that people tend to develop romantic relationships with people who are similar to themselves in factors such as physical attractiveness, cultural background, personality traits, and interests.

Who Is Right for You? Research shows that people tend to pair off with others who are similar in physical characteristics and personality traits.

criterion for men than women in mate selection. Yet, as we will see in the following chapter, women can be as direct as men in signaling interest when they begin conversations.

People who are involved in committed relationships are most likely to be similar to their partners in their attitudes and cultural attributes (Morry et al., 2011). People are more often than not similar to their mates in height, weight, personality traits, intelligence, educational level, religion, and even in use of alcohol and tobacco (DeCuyper et al., 2012; Montoya et al., 2008; van Straaten et al., 2009). Nearly 95% of marriages and 80% to 90% of cohabiting unions were between partners of the same race at the time of the 2010 U.S. census (U.S. Census Bureau, 2011). The concept of "like marrying like" is termed **homogamy**. Research shows that marriages between people from similar backgrounds tend to be more stable (DeCuyper et al., 2012), perhaps because partners are more likely to share values and attitudes (Willetts, 2006).

Most people also tend to follow *age homogamy*—to select a partner who falls in their own age range, with husbands 2 to 5 years older than wives (Skopek et al., 2011; Zhang et al., 2011). But age homogamy reflects the tendency to marry in early adulthood. Persons who marry late or who remarry tend not to select partners so close in age because they are "out in the world"—rather than in school or fresh out of school—and tend to work with or otherwise meet people from different age groups.

ATTITUDES: DO "OPPOSITES ATTRACT" OR DO "BIRDS OF A FEATHER FLOCK TOGETHER"?

In their mate selection, it could be said that the females of many species face a complex decision: Do they—as many finches and cichlids (an African fresh-water fish) do—choose a very closely related mate? Doing so will lead to inbreeding. On the other hand, choosing a very dissimilar mate risks destroying local genetic adaptations. Many species therefore choose a mate somewhere in between similarity and difference (Gow, 2008). Some species, however, select mates that are genetically extremely similar to themselves. An example is the spotted salamander, who apparently prefers a look-alike (or smell-alike?), unless he is small (Chandler & Zamudio, 2008). **TRUTH** OR **FICTION** REVISITED: With humans, as with salamanders, it is usually not true that "opposites attract." But here we are talking about specifically human traits such as attitudes, level of education, and preferences in taste, as well as physical features. In other words, we are actually less apt to be

5 (T/F)

Homogamy Like marrying like.

Real Students, Real Questions

Q *Is it okay to be attracted to your stepbrother (or stepsister)?*

A It is not unusual to be attracted to one's stepbrother or stepsister. Stepbrothers and stepsisters are not blood relations, and many excellent partnerships have developed between them. However, if they are raised together, a change from a fraternal to a romantic relationship may raise conflicting feelings or issues that they will need to sort through.

attracted to people who disagree with our views and tastes than to people who share them.

Why do the great majority of us have partners from our own backgrounds? One reason is **propinquity**; that is, relationships are made in the neighborhood and not in heaven. Although mobility has increased in Western societies in recent decades, we tend to live among people who are reasonably similar to us in background and thus come into contact with them. Another is that we are drawn to people who are similar in their attitudes. People similar in background are more likely to be similar in their attitudes. Similarity in attitudes and tastes is a key contributor to attraction, friendships, and love relationships (Brown et al., 2003; Morry & Gaines, 2005).

Let us also note a gender difference. Evidence shows that women place greater emphasis on attitude similarity as a determinant of attraction to a stranger of the other gender than do men, whereas men place more value on physical attractiveness (Furnham, 2008). We also tend to assume that people we find attractive share our attitudes (Montoya et al., 2009). A powerful physical attraction can motivate them to pretend that their preferences, tastes, and opinions coincide. When sexual attraction is strong, perhaps we want to think that we can iron out all the kinks in the relationship. Although similarity may be important in determining initial attraction, compatibility appears to be a stronger predictor of maintaining an intimate relationship (Amodio & Showers, 2005).

RECIPROCITY: IF YOU LIKE ME, YOU MUST HAVE EXCELLENT JUDGMENT

Has anyone told you that you are good looking, brilliant, and emotionally mature to boot? That your taste is elegant? Ah, what superb judgment! 👁

When we feel admired and complimented, we tend to return these feelings and behaviors. This is called **reciprocity**. Reciprocity is a potent determinant of attraction (Levine, 2000; Sprecher, 1998). We tend to be much more warm, helpful, and candid when we are with strangers who we believe like us (Sprecher, 1998). We even tend to welcome positive comments from others when we know them to be inaccurate (Levine, 2000).

Perhaps the power of reciprocity has enabled many couples to become happy with one another and reasonably well adjusted. By reciprocating positive words and

👁️⃝ **Watch** the **Video**
Interpersonal Attraction
on **MyDevelopmentLab**

Propinquity Nearness.

Reciprocity Mutual exchange.

actions, a person can perhaps stoke neutral or mild feelings into robust, affirmative feelings of attraction.

Attraction can lead to feelings of love. Let us now turn to that most fascinating topic.

Love: "The Morning and the Evening Star"?

For thousands of years, poets have sought to capture love in words. A seventeenth-century poet wrote that his love was like "a red, red rose." The novelist Sinclair Lewis wrote of love as "the morning and the evening star." Love is beautiful and elusive. It shines, brilliant and heavenly. Passion and romantic love are also earthy and sexy, brimming with sexual desire.

Our culture idealizes the concept of romantic love (Aron et al., 2008). Thus, we readily identify with the plight of the "star-crossed" lovers in *Romeo and Juliet* and *West Side Story*, who sacrificed for love. We learn that "love makes the world go round" and that "love is everything." Like other aspects of sexual and social behavior among humans, the concept of love must be understood within a cultural context.

We can trace the concept of love at least as far back as the classical age of Greece. The Greeks distinguished four concepts related to the modern meanings of love:

- Storge: loving attachment, deep friendship, or nonsexual affection
- Agape: selfless giving
- Philia: friendship
- Eros: passion

Storge is the emotion that binds friends and parents and children. Some scholars believe that even romantic love is a form of attachment that is similar to the types of attachments infants have to their mothers (Gonzaga et al., 2006; Moore & Leung, 2002).

Agape is similar to generosity and charity. It implies the wish to share one's bounty and is epitomized by anonymous donations of money. Agape, according to Lee's (2006) research, is the kind of love least frequently found between adults in committed relationships.

Philia is based on liking and respect, rather than sexual desire. It involves the desire to do and enjoy things with the other person and to see him or her when one is lonely or bored.

Eros was a character in Greek mythology (transformed by the Romans into Cupid) who would shoot the unsuspecting with love arrows, causing them to fall madly in love with whomever was nearby at the time. Erotic love embraces sudden passionate desire: "love at first sight" and "falling head over heels in love." Younger college students are more likely to believe in love at first sight and that "love conquers all" than older (and wiser?) college students (Knox et al., 1999a). Passion can be so gripping that one is convinced that life has been changed forever (Aron et al., 2008). This feeling of sudden transformation was captured by the Italian poet Dante Alighieri (1265–1321), who exclaimed upon first beholding his beloved Beatrice, "Incipit vita nuova," which can be translated as "My life begins anew." Unlike the ancient Greeks, we tend to use the word *love* to describe everything from feelings of affection toward another to romantic ardor to sexual intercourse ("making love"). Still, different types or styles of love are recognized in our own culture, as we will see.

Agape (AH-gah-pay) Selfless love; a kind of loving that is similar to generosity and charity.

Philia (FEEL-yuh) Friendship love, which is based on liking and respect rather than sexual desire.

Eros The kind of love that is closest in meaning to the modern-day concept of passion.

Storge (STORE-gay) Loving attachment and nonsexual affection; the type of emotion that binds parents to children.

A Closer Look

Watching New Love as It Sears the Brain

New love can look for all the world like mental illness, a blend of mania, dementia, and obsession that cuts people off from friends and family and prompts out-of-character behavior—compulsive phone calling, serenades, yelling from rooftops—that could almost be mistaken for psychosis.

Now neuroscientists have produced brain scan images of this fevered activity, before it settles into the wine and roses phase of romance or the joint holiday card routines of long-term commitment. In an analysis of the images in *The Journal of Neurophysiology*, researchers in New York and New Jersey argue that romantic love is a biological urge distinct from sexual arousal.

The researchers assert that romantic love is closer in its neural profile to drives like hunger, thirst, or drug craving than to emotional states like excitement or affection. As a relationship deepens, the brain scans suggest, the neural activity associated with romantic love alters slightly, and in some cases primes areas deep in the primitive brain that are involved in long-term attachment.

The research helps explain why love produces such disparate emotions, from euphoria to anger to anxiety, and why it seems to become even more intense when it is withdrawn. In a separate, continuing

Anthropologist Helen Fisher of Rutgers University. Dr. Fisher has investigated the biochemical aspects of attraction and love in human sexuality.

experiment, the researchers are analyzing brain images from people who have been rejected by their lovers.

"When you're in the throes of this romantic love it's overwhelming, you're out of control, you're irrational, you're going to the gym at 6 a.m. every day—why? Because she's there," said Dr. Helen Fisher, an anthropologist at Rutgers University and the co-author of the analysis. "And when rejected, some people contemplate stalking, homicide, suicide. This drive for romantic love can be stronger than the will to live."

Brain imaging technology cannot read people's minds, experts caution, and a phenomenon as many sided and socially influenced as love transcends simple computer graphics, like those produced by the technique used in the study, called functional M.R.I.

Still, said Dr. Hans Breiter, director of the Motivation and Emotion Neuroscience Collaboration at Massachusetts General Hospital, "I distrust about 95% of the M.R.I. literature and I would give this study an 'A'; it really moves the ball in terms of understanding infatuation."

He added: "The findings fit nicely with a large, growing body of literature describing a generalized reward and aversion system in the brain, and put this intellectual construct of love directly onto the same axis as homeostatic rewards such as food, warmth, craving for drugs."

In the study, Dr. Fisher, Dr. Lucy Brown of Albert Einstein College of Medicine, and Dr. Arthur Aron of the State University of New York at Stony Brook led a team that analyzed about 2,500 brain images from 17 college students who were in the first weeks or months of new love. The students looked at a picture of their beloved while an M.R.I. machine scanned their brains. The researchers then compared the images with others taken while the students looked at a picture of an acquaintance.

Functional M.R.I. technology detects increases or decreases of blood flow in the brain, which reflect changes in neural activity. In the study, a computer-generated map of particularly active areas showed hot spots deep in the brain, below conscious awareness, in areas called the *caudate nucleus* and the *ventral tegmental* (see Figure 7.3), which communicate

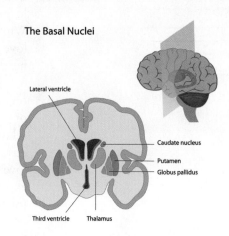

The Basal Nuclei

Lateral ventricle

Caudate nucleus
Putamen
Globus pallidus

Third ventricle   Thalamus

FIGURE 7.3 The Caudate Nucleus. A part of the brain that is particularly active when we undergo the throes of a new romantic love.

with each other as part of a circuit. These areas are dense with cells that produce or receive a brain chemical called *dopamine*, which circulates actively when people desire or anticipate a reward. In studies of gamblers, cocaine users, and even people playing computer games for small amounts of money, these dopamine sites become extremely active as people score or win.

Yet, falling in love is among the most irrational of human behaviors, not merely a matter of satisfying a simple pleasure or winning a reward. And the researchers found that one particular spot in the M.R.I. images, in the caudate nucleus, was especially active in people who scored highly on a questionnaire measuring passionate love. This passion-related region was on the opposite side of the brain from another area that registers physical attractiveness and appeared to be involved in longing, desire, and the unexplainable tug that people feel toward one person, among many attractive alternative partners.

Source: Reprinted by permission from Benedict Carey. (2005, May 31). Watching New Love as It Sears the Brain. *New York Times.*

Romantic Love

The experience of romantic love, as opposed to loving attachment or sexual arousal per se, occurs within a cultural context in which the concept is idealized (Aron et al., 2008). Western culture has a long tradition of idealizing the concept of romantic love, as represented, for instance, by romantic fairy tales that have been passed down through the generations. In fact, our exposure to the concept of romantic love may begin with hearing the fairy tales of Sleeping Beauty, Cinderella, and Snow White—along with their princes charming. Later, perhaps, the concept of romantic love blossoms with exposure to romantic novels, television and film scripts, and the heady tales of friends and relatives.

During adolescence, strong sexual arousal along with an idealized image of the object of our desires leads us to label our feelings as love. We may learn to speak of "love" rather than "lust," because sexual desire in the absence of a committed relationship might be viewed as primitive or animalistic. Being "in love" ennobles attraction and sexual arousal, not only to society but also to oneself. Unlike lust, love can be discussed even at the dinner table. If others think we are too young to experience "the real thing"—which presumably includes knowledge of and respect for the other person's personality traits—our feelings may be called "puppy love" or a "crush."

Western society maintains much of the double standard toward sexuality. Thus, women are more often expected to justify sexual experiences as involving someone they love. Young men usually need not attribute sexual urges to love. So men are more apt to deem love a "mushy" concept. The vast majority of people in the United States nonetheless believe romantic love is a prerequisite for marriage or another kind of long-term or permanent relationship. Romantic love is rated by young people as the single-most important reason for marriage (Hatfield et al., 2012; Reis & Aron, 2008). You can explore your self-perceptions of being a romantic or a realist when it comes to love by completing the Triangular Love Scale on page 203.

When reciprocated, romantic love is usually a source of deep fulfillment and ecstasy (Hatfield et al., 2012). How wonderful when love meets its match! When love is unrequited, however, it can lead to emptiness, anxiety, or despair. Romantic love can thus teeter between states of ecstasy and misery. Perhaps no other feature of our lives can lift us up as high or plunge us as low as romantic love. 👁

INFATUATION VERSUS "TRUE LOVE": WILL TIME TELL?

Perhaps you first noticed each other when your eyes met across a classroom. Or perhaps you met when you were both assigned to the same Bunsen burner in chemistry lab—less romantic but closer to the flame. However it happened, the meeting triggered such an electric charge through your body that you could not get him (or her) out of your mind. But were you truly in love, or was it merely a passing fancy? Was it infatuation or the "real thing"—a "true," lasting, and mutual love? How do you tell them apart?

Perhaps you don't, at least not at first. **Infatuation** is a state of intense absorption in or focusing on another person (Aloni & Bernieri, 2004). It is usually accompanied by sexual desire, elation, and general physiological arousal or excitement. Some refer to passion as infatuation. Others dub it a "crush." Both monikers suggest that it is a passing fancy. In infatuation, your heart may pound whenever the other person draws near or enters your fantasies.

For the first month or two, infatuation and the more enduring forms of romantic love are hard to differentiate. At first, both may be characterized by intense focusing or absorption. Infatuated people may become so absorbed that they cannot

👁⎯**Watch** the **Video**
Hungry for Love
on **MyDevelopmentLab**

Infatuation A state of intense absorption in or focus on another person, which is usually accompanied by sexual desire, elation, and general physiological arousal or excitement; passion.

sleep, work, or carry out routine chores. Logic and reason are swept aside (Aron et al., 2008; Hatfield et al., 2012). Infatuated people hold idealized images of their love objects and overlook the faults of their loved one. Caution may be cast to the winds. In some cases, couples in the throes of infatuation rush to the altar, only to find a few weeks or months later that they are not well suited.

As time goes on, signs that distinguish infatuation from a lasting romantic love begin to emerge. The partners begin to view each other more realistically and determine whether or not the relationship should continue. Although the tendency to idealize one's lover is strongest at the outset of a relationship, we should note that a so-called positive illusion tends to persist in relationships (Aron et al., 2008). That is, people maintain some tendency to differentiate their partners from the average and also to differentiate the value of their relationships from the average.

Infatuation is based on feelings of passion but not on the deeper feelings of attachment and caring that typify a more lasting mutual love (Hatfield et al., 2012). Although infatuation may be a passing fancy, it can be supplanted by the deeper feelings of attachment and caring that characterize enduring love relationships.

Contemporary Models of Love: Dare Science Intrude?

Despite the importance of love, scientists have historically paid little attention to it. Some people believe that love cannot be analyzed scientifically. Love, they maintain, should be left to the poets, philosophers, and theologians. Others think that love is sort of a silly topic for the purview of science.

Yet, researchers today are applying the scientific method to the study of love. They recognize that love is a complex concept, involving many areas of experience—biological, emotional, cognitive, and motivational (Berscheid, 2010). Let us begin with some biological comments and then move on to some psychological approaches.

BIOLOGICAL MECHANISMS

Some researchers focus on the bodily changes that occur when we experience feelings of romantic love. There are many. Some of the research focuses on the search for distinct neural pathways (roadmaps in the brain) that define feelings of love (Ackerman, 2012). Others involve chemistry, with special focus on

- monoamines and neuropeptides—including dopamine and naturally produced opium look-alikes we call *endorphins*—that are involved in the brain's pleasure system.
- the hormones oxytocin and vasopressin, which we come across repeatedly in this book.

There are always interesting new studies arriving on our desks. For example, we tend to have heightened levels of nerve growth factor (Ackerman, 2012), which partly explains—at least on a biological level—why new lovers are so acutely aware of everything going on around them and why everything seems so bathed in a luxurious light. (How's that for a sad attempt at poetry in a textbook?)

As we noted in an earlier "Closer Look," fMRI research (research using functional magnetic resonance imaging) shows heightened activity in a part of the brain called the caudate nucleus. What is perhaps of interest here is that the caudate

CRITICAL THINKING

The student of psychology or sociology might wonder what all of this biological research *means*. Does it mean, for example, that students of human sexuality must memorize every corner of the brain and every neurological activity? Or does it call, rather, for a more general appreciation that thoughts and emotions are based in the body—and particularly in the brain—and that these scientific facts are not to be ignored when we discuss the nature of human beings? How can you best make use of this information?

nucleus is part of the brain's "limbic system," which is intimately connected with emotional arousal.

Let us now consider several psychologically oriented views of love. They may touch indirectly on things that happen in the body, but as we will see, they do so almost apologetically.

LOVE AS APPRAISAL OF AROUSAL

Social psychologists Ellen Berscheid and Elaine Hatfield (Berscheid, 2010; Graham, 2011) defined romantic love in terms of a state of intense physiological arousal, and the cognitive appraisal of that arousal as love. The physiological arousal may be experienced as a pounding heart, sweaty palms, and butterflies in the stomach when one is in the presence of or thinking about one's love interest. Cognitive appraisal of the arousal means attributing it to some cause, such as fear or love. The perception that one has fallen in love is thus derived from several simultaneous events: (1) a state of intense physiological arousal that is connected with an appropriate love object (that is, a person, not an event like a rock concert), (2) a cultural setting that idealizes romantic love, and (3) the attribution of the arousal to feelings of love toward the person.

STYLES OF LOVE

Some researchers speak in terms of styles of love. Susan and Clyde Hendrick and their colleagues speak of love as a positive emotion that contributes to happiness, feelings of psychological well-being, and optimism about the future (Hatfield et al., 2012). The Hendricks developed a Love Attitude Scale that suggests the existence of six styles of love. The following is a list of the styles. Each one is exemplified by statements similar to those on the original scale. As you can see, the styles owe a debt to the Greeks:

- *Romantic love (eros):* "My lover fits my ideal." "My lover and I were attracted to one another immediately."
- *Game-playing love (ludus):* "I keep my lover up in the air about my commitment." "I get over love affairs pretty easily."
- *Friendship (storge, philia):* "The best love grows out of an enduring friendship."
- *Logical love (pragma):* "I consider a lover's potential in life before committing myself." "I consider whether my lover will be a good parent."
- *Possessive, excited love (mania):* "I get so excited about my love that I cannot sleep." "When my lover ignores me, I get sick all over."
- *Selfless love (agape):* "I would do anything I can to help my lover." "My lover's needs and wishes are more important than my own."

Most people who are "in love" experience a number of these styles, but the Hendricks found some interesting gender differences in styles of love. College men are significantly more likely than college women to develop game-playing and romantic love styles. College women are more apt than college men to develop friendly, logical, and possessive love styles. (There were no gender differences in selfless love.) The Hendricks have also found that romantically involved couples tend to experience the same kinds of love styles. They also found evidence that couples with romantic and selfless styles of love are more likely to remain together. A game-playing love style leads to unhappiness, however, and is one reason that relationships come to an end.

Real Students, Real Questions

Q *I am in love with two people at the same time. Can this continue or must I choose?*

A You can probably continue until you want to settle down, one of them gets fed up with it, or you conclude it's immoral. We'll add this to the mix: It's not abnormal to be in love with two people at the same time. There's no reason to think there's just one perfect person for you. But given the realities of life in our culture today, the situation will probably eventually become unstable. In the meantime, we'll be jealous of you.

STERNBERG'S TRIANGULAR THEORY OF LOVE

Robert Sternberg (1988) offers a "triangular theory" of love that organizes the relationships among kinds of love discussed by many theorists, including passionate love, romantic love, and companionate love (Hatfield et al., 2012). The three building blocks, or components, of loving experiences are as follows:

1. **Intimacy:** The experience of warmth toward another person that arises from feelings of closeness and connectedness to the other. Intimacy also involves the desire to give and receive emotional support and to share one's innermost thoughts with the other.
2. **Passion:** An intense romantic or sexual desire for another person, which is accompanied by physiological arousal.
3. **Commitment:** A component of love that involves commitment to maintain the relationship through good times and bad.

Intimacy Closeness, characterized by deep knowledge and understanding of another person.

Passion A powerful, compelling emotion.

Commitment A pledge, promise, or decision to maintain a relationship.

👁️⎡**Watch** the **Video**
Triangluar Theory of Love: Robert Sternberg
on **MyDevelopmentLab**

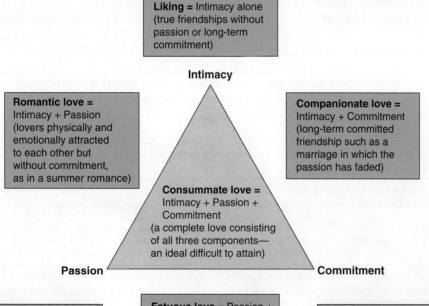

Liking = Intimacy alone (true friendships without passion or long-term commitment)

Intimacy

Romantic love = Intimacy + Passion (lovers physically and emotionally attracted to each other but without commitment, as in a summer romance)

Companionate love = Intimacy + Commitment (long-term committed friendship such as a marriage in which the passion has faded)

Consummate love = Intimacy + Passion + Commitment (a complete love consisting of all three components— an ideal difficult to attain)

Passion   **Commitment**

Infatuation = Passion alone (passionate, obsessive love at first sight without intimacy or commitment)

Fatuous love = Passion + Commitment (commitment based on passion but without time for intimacy to develop— shallow relationship such as a whirlwind courtship)

Empty love = Commitment alone (commitment to remain together without intimacy or passion)

FIGURE 7.4 The Triangular Model of Love. According to psychologist Robert Sternberg, love consists of three components, as shown by the vertices of this triangle. Various kinds of love consist of different combinations of these components. Romantic love, for example, consists of passion and intimacy. Consummate love— the cultural ideal—consists of all three.

FIGURE 7.5 Compatibility and Incompatibility, According to the Triangular Model of Love. Compatibility in terms of Sternberg's types of love can be represented as triangles. View A shows a perfect match in which triangles are congruent. View B depicts a good match; the partners are similar according to the three dimensions. View C shows a mismatch; major differences exist between the partners on all three components.

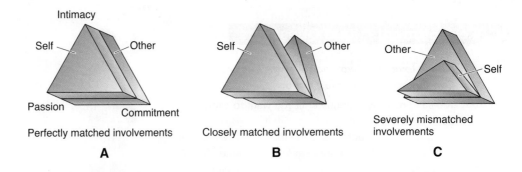

Sternberg's model is triangular in that various kinds of love can be conceptualized in terms of a triangle in which each vertex (corner?) represents one of the building blocks (see Figure 7.4). The strength of each component can be represented by the shape of the triangle. For example, a love in which all three components were equally balanced—as in consummate love—would be represented by an equilateral triangle, as in Figure 7.5.

The Hendricks noted that couples who are romantically involved tend to share similar love styles. In terms of Sternberg's model, couples are well matched if they possess corresponding levels of passion, intimacy, and commitment. Compatibility can be represented visually in terms of the congruence (fit) of the love triangles (see Figure 7.5). Figure 7.5A shows a perfect match, in which the triangles are congruent. Figure 7.5B depicts a good match; the partners are similar in the three building blocks of love. Figure 7.5C shows a mismatch; major differences exist between the partners on all three components. Relationships may run aground when partners are mismatched. A relationship may fizzle, rather than sizzle, when one partner experiences more passion than the other, or when one wants a long-term commitment when the other's idea of commitment is to stay the night.

Various combinations of the three elements of love characterize different types of love relationships (see Figures 7.4 and 7.6). For example, infatuation (passionate love) is typified by strong sexual desire but not by intimacy and commitment. The

FIGURE 7.6 Types of Love, According to Sternberg's Triangular Model

1. Nonlove	A relationship in which all three components of love are absent. Most of our personal relationships are of this type—casual interactions or acquaintances that do not involve any elements of love.
2. Liking	An experience with another person such as a friendship in which intimacy is present, but passion and commitment are lacking.
3. Infatuation	A kind of "love at first sight," in which one experiences a passionate desire for another person in the absence of intimacy and commitment.
4. Empty love	A kind of love characterized by commitment (to maintain the relationship) in the absence of either passion or intimacy. Stagnant relationships that no longer involve the emotional intimacy or physical attraction that once characterized them are of this type.
5. Romantic love	A loving experience characterized by the combination of passion and intimacy but without commitment.
6. Companionate love	A kind of love characterized by intimacy and commitment. It often occurs in long-term relationships in which passionate attraction has waned and has been replaced by a kind of committed friendship.
7. Fatuous love	The type of love associated with whirlwind romances and "quickie marriages" in which passion and commitment are present, but intimacy is not.
8. Consummate love	The full or complete measure of love involving the combination of passion, intimacy, and commitment. Many of us strive for consummate love.

Source: Adapted from Sternberg (1988).

Sternberg's Triangular Love Scale

Which are the strongest components of your love relationship? Intimacy? Passion? Commitment? All three components? Two of them?

   To complete the following scale, fill in the blank spaces with the name of one person you love or care about deeply. Then rate your agreement with each of the items by using a 9-point scale in which 1 = "not at all," 5 = "moderately," and 9 = "extremely." Use points in between to indicate intermediate levels of agreement between these values. Then consult the scoring key in the Appendix.

Intimacy Component

____ 1. I am actively supportive of _____'s well-being.

____ 2. I have a warm relationship with _____.

____ 3. I am able to count on _____ in times of need.

____ 4. _____ is able to count on me in times of need.

____ 5. I am willing to share myself and my possessions with _____.

____ 6. I receive considerable emotional support from _____.

____ 7. I give considerable emotional support to _____.

____ 8. I communicate well with _____.

____ 9. I value _____ greatly in my life.

____ 10. I feel close to _____.

____ 11. I have a comfortable relationship with _____.

____ 12. I feel that I really understand _____.

____ 13. I feel that _____ really understands me.

____ 14. I feel that I can really trust _____.

____ 15. I share deeply personal information about myself with _____.

Passion Component

____ 16. Just seeing _____ excites me.

____ 17. I find myself thinking about _____ frequently during the day.

____ 18. My relationship with _____ is very romantic.

____ 19. I find _____ to be very personally attractive.

____ 20. I idealize _____.

____ 21. I cannot imagine another person making me as happy as _____ does.

____ 22. I would rather be with _____ than anyone else.

____ 23. There is nothing more important to me than my relationship with _____.

____ 24. I especially like physical contact with _____.

____ 25. There is something almost "magical" about my relationship with _____.

____ 26. I adore _____.

____ 27. I cannot imagine life without _____.

____ 28. My relationship with _____ is passionate.

____ 29. When I see romantic movies and read romantic books, I think of _____.

____ 30. I fantasize about _____.

Commitment Component

____ 31. I know that I care about _____.

____ 32. I am committed to maintaining my relationship with _____.

____ 33. Because of my commitment to _____, I would not let other people come between us.

____ 34. I have confidence in the stability of my relationship with _____.

____ 35. I could not let anything get in the way of my commitment to _____.

____ 36. I expect my love for _____ to last for the rest of my life.

____ 37. I will always feel a strong responsibility for _____.

____ 38. I view my commitment to _____ as a solid one.

____ 39. I cannot imagine ending my relationship with _____.

____ 40. I am certain of my love for _____.

____ 41. I view my relationship with _____ as permanent.

____ 42. I view my relationship with _____ as a good decision.

____ 43. I feel a sense of responsibility toward _____.

____ 44. I plan to continue my relationship with _____.

____ 45. Even when _____ is hard to deal with, I remain committed to our relationship.

Source: Sternberg, 1988. The triangle of love: Intimacy, passion, commitment. By permission of Robert Sternberg.

partners may each feel passionate love for the other, or, as in the case of Tom, such feelings may go unrequited:

> Tom sat behind Lisa in physics class. Tom hated physics, but he could not say the same for Lisa. One look at her was enough to change his life. He had fallen madly in love with her. Instead of listening to the teacher or looking at the blackboard, he would gaze at Lisa throughout the class. Lisa was aware of this and was not happy about it. She did not much care for Tom, and when he tried to start a conversation with her, she moved on as quickly as possible. Tom's staring and his awkwardness in talking to her made her feel uncomfortable. Tom, on the other hand, could think of little else besides Lisa, and his grades began to suffer as he spent the time he should have been devoting to his homework thinking about her. He was a man obsessed. The obsession might have gone on for quite some time had not both Tom and Lisa graduated that June and gone to different colleges. Tom never saw Lisa again, and after several unanswered love letters, he finally gave up on her. (Sternberg, 1988, p. 123)

Liking is a basis for friendship. It consists of feelings of closeness and emotional warmth without passion or commitment. Liking is not felt toward passing acquaintances. It is reserved for people to whom one feels close enough to share one's innermost feelings and thoughts. We sometimes develop these intimate relationships without making the commitment to maintaining a long-term relationship that typifies other types of love, however. Liking may develop into a passionate love or into a more committed form of love called companionate love by many writers, including Sternberg (Hatfield et al., 2012).

Should lovers also be friends, or are lovers and friends part of the twain that never meet? Some couples lack the quality most often associated with true friendship: the willingness to share confidences. Despite their physical intimacy, their relationships remain superficial. **TRUTH** OR **FICTION** Revisited: It is possible to be in love with someone who is not also a friend. Being in love can refer to states of passion or infatuation, whereas friendship is usually based on shared interests, liking, and respect. Friendship and passionate love do not necessarily overlap. There is nothing that prevents people in love from becoming good friends, however—perhaps even the best of friends. Sternberg's model recognizes that the intimacy we find in true friendships and the passion we find in love are blended in two forms of love—romantic love and consummate love. These love types differ along the dimension of commitment, however.

Romantic love has both passion and intimacy but lacks commitment. Romantic love may burn brightly and then flicker out. Or it may develop into a more complete love (consummate love) in which all three components flower. Desire is accompanied by a deeper intimacy and commitment. The flames of passion can be stoked across the years, even if they do not burn quite as brightly as they once did. Consummate love is most special and certainly an ideal toward which many Westerners strive.

In empty love, by contrast, there is little else than commitment. Neither the warm emotional embrace of intimacy nor the flame of passion exists. With empty love, one's lover is a person whom one tolerates and remains with because of a sense of duty. Remaining in an empty-love relationship is often based either on the belief that one should persist in a relationship or that one's community or family members believe that it is right to persist in a relationship.

Sometimes a love relationship has both passion and commitment but lacks intimacy. Sternberg calls this fatuous (foolish) love. Fatuous love is associated with

6

CRITICAL THINKING
Why do you think that most people in the United States believe that people should get married only when they experience romantic love?

whirlwind courtships that burn brightly but briefly as the partners come to the realization that they are not well matched. Intimacy can develop in such relationships, but couples who rush into promises of marriage often find that the realities of their relationships give the lie to their expectations. **TRUTH** OR **FICTION** REVISITED: It is true that couples can remain "in love" after passion fades; for example, they can experience companionate love. Companionate love need not be lacking in romance, however. Although passion may have ebbed, sexual pleasure can help strengthen bonds. In companionate love, intimacy and commitment are strong, but passion is lacking. This form of love typifies long-term (so-called platonic) relationships and marriages in which passion has ebbed but a deep and abiding friendship remains for those with whom our lives are entwined (Hatfield et al., 2012; Hendrick & Hendrick, 2003).

The balance among Sternberg's three aspects of love is likely to shift through the course of a relationship (Hatfield et al., 2012). A strong dose of all three components—found in consummate love—typifies, for many of us, an ideal relationship. At the outset of a relationship, passions may be strong but intimacy weak. Couples may only first be getting to know each other's innermost thoughts and feelings. Time alone does not cause intimacy and commitment to grow, however. Some couples are able to peer into each other's deeper selves and form meaningful commitments at relatively early stages in their relationships. Yet some couples who have been together for many years may remain distant or waver in their commitment. Some couples experience only a faint flickering of passion early in the relationship. Then it becomes quickly extinguished. For some, the flames of passion burn ever brightly. Many couples, though, find that passion tends to fade while intimacy and commitment grow stronger.

Knowledge of the components of love can help couples avoid pitfalls. Couples who recognize that passion exerts a strong pull early in a relationship may be less likely to let passion rush them into a premature long-term legal commitment. Couples who recognize that it is normal for passion to fade may avoid assuming that their love is at an end when it may, in fact, be changing into a deeper, more intimate and committed form of love. This knowledge may also encourage couples to focus on finding ways of rekindling the embers of romance, rather than looking to escape at the first signs that the fires may be cooling. ◉

Watch the **Video**
Relationships and Love
on **MyDevelopmentLab**

Real Students, Real Questions

Q *What is the secret to a loving relationship?*

A Here are a few secrets: First is honesty—that is, being honest about your likes and dislikes, your feelings, and your values. Another is sharing interests and values with your partner. You can't expect a relationship to endure if you're only pretending to agree with your partner about your likes and dislikes. A third is respect. You probably cannot truly love your partner if you do not respect him or her as a person.

Chapter Review

✓●—[Study and **Review** on **MyDevelopmentLab**

LO1 Describe cultural standards for physical attractiveness

Physical appearance is a key determinant of sexual attraction. In our culture, slenderness is in style. Men prefer medium to large breasts. Women prefer taller men.

LO2 Describe nonphysical traits that affect perceptions of physical attractiveness

Females and males both consider smiling faces more attractive. Socially dominant men, but not dominant women, are usually found attractive. Women place relatively greater emphasis on traits like vocational status and earning potential, whereas men give relatively more consideration to physical attractiveness. Some evolutionary psychologists believe that evolutionary forces favor such gender differences in preferred traits because these traits provide reproductive advantages.

LO3 Explain the role of similarity in the formation of romantic relationships

Despite the adage "opposites attract," research tends to support the attraction–similarity hypothesis, which holds that people tend to develop romantic relationships with people who are similar to themselves in attractiveness, cultural background, and interests. Our feelings are warmer toward people who appear to like us. Through reciprocation of positive words and actions, neutral or mild feelings may be stoked into strong feelings of attraction.

LO4 Discuss the meaning of love

The ancient Greeks had four concepts related to the modern meanings of love: storge (loving attachment, as between parents and children), agape (generosity and charity), philia (friendship, liking, respect), and eros (passion).

LO5 Discuss the meaning of romantic love

Western culture has a tradition of idealizing the concept of romantic love. Most people in the United States see romantic love as a prerequisite to marriage. At first, infatuation and more enduring forms of romantic love may be indistinguishable.

LO6 Discuss theories of love

Berscheid and Hatfield define romantic love in terms of intense physiological arousal and cognitive appraisal of that arousal as love. Cultural belief in romantic love contributes to that labeling of arousal. Hendrick and Hendrick suggest that there are six styles of love among college students: romantic love, game-playing love, friendship, logical love, possessive love, and selfless love. Sternberg suggests that there are three distinct components of love: intimacy, passion, and commitment. Romantic love is characterized by the combination of passion and intimacy. Consummate love—the cultural ideal—is described by all three components.

LO7 Explain how people's preferences differ for short-term and long-term relationships

People may pay more attention to superficial characteristics such as physical attractiveness when they are selecting partners for short-term relationships.

Test Your Learning

1. _____ is found to be universally attractive in women.
   - (a) A good complexion
   - (b) Slenderness
   - (c) Plumpness
   - (d) Socially dominant behavior

2. Susan Sprecher and her colleagues found that women are more willing than men to marry someone who is
   - (a) six or more years younger than they are.
   - (b) not good looking.
   - (c) less well educated than they are.
   - (d) not likely to hold a steady job.

3. Loving attachment, deep friendship, or nonsexual affection describe the ancient Greek concept of

   (a) agape.
   (b) storge.
   (c) eros.
   (d) philia.

4. People who say "I keep my lover up in the air about my commitment," or "I get over love affairs pretty easily" appear to be in the _____ style of love.

   (a) logical
   (b) romantic
   (c) game-playing
   (d) possessive

5. According to Sternberg, romantic love involves

   (a) passion and intimacy.
   (b) passion and commitment.
   (c) intimacy and commitment.
   (d) passion alone.

6. According to the NHSLS, the sex partners of nearly _____% of single European American men are European American women.

   (a) 34
   (b) 54
   (c) 74
   (d) 94

7. In his study on gender differences in preferences for mates across 37 cultures, Buss found that

   (a) men preferred women who earned more money than they did.

   (b) women preferred men who were older than they were.
   (c) only European men expressed an interest in marriage.
   (d) evolutionary forces contributed to preferences in some cultures but not in others.

8. Helen Fisher and her colleagues found that the _____ is highly active when we experience a new romantic love.

   (a) reticular activating system
   (b) prefrontal cortex
   (c) metatarsal-phalangeal joint
   (d) caudate nucleus

9. In his study on gender differences in preferences for mates, Buss found that both men and women placed greatest emphasis on

   (a) intelligence.
   (b) income potential.
   (c) facial features.
   (d) complexion.

10. The Hendricks found that college men were significantly more likely than college women to develop a _____ love style.

    (a) friendly
    (b) logical
    (c) romantic
    (d) possessive

Answers: 1. a; 2. b; 3. d; 4. c; 5. a; 6. d; 7. b; 8. d; 9. a; 10. c

---

My Life, My Sexuality

What Do You Think You Should Be Thinking about When You're in the Market for a Long-Term Relationship?

Explore this **My Life, My Sexuality** *feature by scanning this QR code with your mobile device. If you don't already have one, you may download a free QR scanner for your device wherever smartphone apps are sold. You can also view this feature in MyDevelopmentLab, along with an accompanying critical thinking assignment.*

Physical attractiveness may win out as the single most important factor in looking for short-term partners, but is physical appeal also the most important trait we seek in partners for long-term relationships? Scan the code to go online and learn more about what women and men want in enduring relationships. Do women and men look for the same things, or are their approaches different?

8 Relationships and Communication

Learning Objectives

THE ABC(DE)'S OF ROMANTIC RELATIONSHIPS

LO1   Describe the development of relationships

JEALOUSY: IS THE WORLD A REAL-LIFE *TEMPTATION ISLAND*?

LO2   Discuss the effects of jealousy on a relationship

DETERIORATION OF RELATIONSHIPS

LO3   Discuss the deterioration of relationships and ways to cope

LONELINESS: "ALL THE LONELY PEOPLE, WHERE DO THEY ALL COME FROM?"

LO4   Discuss the causes and effects of loneliness

SATISFACTION IN RELATIONSHIPS: COMMUNICATION AS KEY

LO5   Describe ways to find satisfaction in a relationship

MY LIFE, MY SEXUALITY: COMMUNICATION SKILLS FOR ENHANCING RELATIONSHIPS AND SEXUAL RELATIONS: HOW TO DO IT

TRUTH OR FICTION?

Which of the following statements are the truth, and which are fiction? Look for the Truth-or Fiction icons on the pages that follow to find the answers.

1 Small talk is an insincere method of opening a relationship. **T F?**

2 Only phonies practice opening lines. **T F?**

3 Swift self-disclosure of intimate information is the best way to deepen a new relationship. **T F?**

4 People can have intimate relationships without being sexually intimate. **T F?**

5 Many people remain lonely because they fear being rejected by others. **T F?**

6 Conflict is destructive to a relationship. **T F?**

7 "Love is all you need." That is, when partners truly love one another, they instinctively know how to satisfy each other sexually. **T F?**

" **O**ne, two. One, two." A great opening line? In the film *Play It Again, Sam*, Woody Allen plays Allan Felix, a nerd who has just been divorced. Diane Keaton plays his platonic friend Linda. At a bar one evening with Linda and her husband, Allan Felix spots a young woman on the dance floor who is so attractive that he wishes he could have her children.

The thing to do, Linda prompts him, is to begin dancing, then dance over to her and "Say something." With a bit more prodding, Linda convinces Allan to dance. It's so simple, she tells him. He need only keep time—"One, two, one, two."

"One, two," repeats Allan. Linda shoves him off to his dream woman.

Hesitantly, Allan dances up to her. Working up courage, he says, "One, two. One, two, one, two." He is ignored and finds his way back to Linda.

"Allan, try something more meaningful," Linda implores.

Once more, Allan dances nervously back toward the woman of his dreams. He stammers, "Three, four, three, four."

"Speak to her, Allan," Linda insists.

He dances up to her again and tries, "You interested in dancing at all?"

"Get lost, creep," she replies.

Allan dances rapidly back toward Linda. "What'd she say?" Linda asks.

"She'd rather not," he shrugs.

So much for "One, two, one two" and, for that matter, "Three, four, three, four." Striking up a relationship requires some social skills, and the first few conversational steps can be big ones.

In this chapter we define the stages that lead to intimate relationships. We define intimacy and see that not all relationships—not even all long-term, committed relationships—achieve this level of interrelatedness. Moreover, some of us remain alone, and, perhaps, lonely. However, there are steps that people can take to overcome loneliness, as we illustrate in the pages ahead. Finally, we discuss satisfaction in relationships and enumerate ways of increasing satisfaction by enhancing communication skills.

The ABC(DE)'s of Romantic Relationships

Romantic relationships, like people, undergo stages of development. According to **social-exchange theory,** the development reflects the unfolding of social exchanges, which involve the rewards and costs of maintaining the relationship as opposed to dissolving it (Allen & de Tormes Eby, 2012). During each stage, positive factors sway partners toward maintaining and enhancing their relationship. Negative factors incline them toward letting it deteriorate and end.

Numerous investigators have viewed the development of romantic relationships in terms of phases or stages (Allen & de Tormes Eby, 2012; Dindia & Timmerman, 2003; Hendrick & Hendrick, 2000). From their work, we can build a five-stage **ABCDE model** of romantic relationships: (1) attraction, (2) building, (3) continuation, (4) deterioration, and (5) termination (or ending).

Attraction occurs when two people become aware of each other and find one another appealing or enticing. We may find ourselves attracted to an enchanting

Social-exchange theory The view that the development of a relationship reflects the unfolding of social exchanges—that is, the rewards and costs of maintaining the relationship as opposed to ending it.

ABCDE model The view that romantic relationships encompass five stages or phases: attraction, building, continuation, deterioration, and ending.

person "across a crowded room," in a nearby office, or in a new class. We may meet others through blind dates, through introductions by mutual friends, by way of computer match-ups, or by "accident." According to the NHSLS study (Michael et al., 1994), married people are most likely to have met their spouses through mutual friends (35%) or self-introductions (32%) (see Figure 8.1). Other sources of introductions are family members (15%) and coworkers, classmates, or neighbors (13%). Unmarried couples also most commonly report meeting through mutual friends and self-introductions (Michael et al., 1994).

Being in a good mood apparently heightens feelings of attraction. George Levinger and his colleagues (Forgas et al., 1994) exposed 128 male and female moviegoers to either a happy or a sad film. Those shown the happy film reported more positive feelings about their partners and their relationships. (Think twice about what you take your date to see.)

Factors that motivate us to build relationships include similarity in physical attractiveness, similarity in attitudes, and mutual liking. Factors that deter building of relationships include lack of physical appeal, dissimilar attitudes, and lack of liking.

Many studies show that males tend to be more "romantic" (meaning passionate) than women in choosing whether to build relationships. For example, men are more likely than women to focus on sex and fun, whereas women are more likely to focus on issues such as communication ability and reciprocity (Hassebrauck, 2003; Holmberg et al., 2009). Thus, in male–male relationships, both partners are likely to entertain sexual behavior relatively early. In female–female relationships, both partners are likely to be relatively cautious, unless they are revolting against female stereotypes. These findings fit with the evolutionary view that the male is more likely to be the initiator of sexual activity and that the female is more likely to be contemplating the value of the male as a reliable provider.

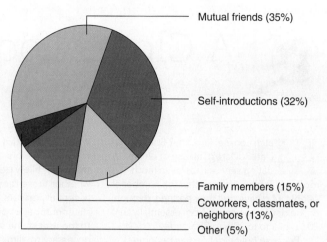

FIGURE 8.1 **How People Meet Their Partners.** According to the NHSLS study (Michael et al., 1994), carried out two decades ago, two-thirds of married people met their partners through either mutual friends or self-introductions. But today, one in four to one in five people meet their partners through online dating.

NOT-SO-SMALL TALK: AN AUDITION FOR BUILDING A RELATIONSHIP

TRUTH OR FICTION REVISITED: Small talk is not an insincere method of opening a relationship. It is a useful way of seeking common ground (Cunningham & Barbee, 2008). Successful small talk encourages a couple to venture beneath the surface. At a get-together or a club, individuals may flit about from person to person, exchanging small talk, but now and then a couple finds common ground and pairs off. ◉

Small talk enables people to probe one another during the early stages of building a relationship. It helps people find an overlapping of attitudes and interests—and to check out feelings of attraction (Knapp & Vangelista, 2000). Small talk stresses breadth of topic coverage rather than in-depth discussion. Engaging in small talk may have a "phony" ring to it, but it is a legitimate trial balloon for a relationship. Moreover, the ability to make small talk is a valuable social skill.

"OPENING LINES": HOW DO YOU GET THINGS STARTED?

One kind of small talk is the greeting, or opening line (Cunningham & Barbee, 2008). We usually precede greetings with eye contact and decide to try talking if eye contact is reciprocated. Avoidance of eye contact may mean that the person is shy, but it can also signify lack of interest. If you are interested in somebody, try a smile and eye contact.

◉━▌Watch the Video
Dating and Finding a Mate: Stephanie, 31 Years Old
on **MyDevelopmentLab**

Small talk A superficial kind of conversation that allows exchange of information but stresses breadth of topic coverage, rather than in-depth discussion.

A Closer Look

Online Dating—A Revolution in Matchmaking?

Match.com? eHarmony? Speed-Date? JDate? The use of online dating services has been mushrooming. Table 8.1 shows that the number of people who have met their partners through online dating has grown from essentially zero 20 years ago to 20% to 25% today.

Because online dating has become such an important way of finding prospective partners, Eli Finkel and his colleagues—Paul Eastwick, Benjamin Karney, Harry Reis, and Susan Sprecher (2012)—take an incisive look at online dating to answer two key questions: Is online dating different from offline (that is, traditional) dating? Are there better outcomes for online dating, as claimed by online dating services?

The investigators note that online dating sites offer users three things:

1. They provide access to other people who are also seeking potential dating partners—people they would be unlikely to meet in their everyday lives.

2. They facilitate communication between potential partners, enabling them to explore each other online before they have a face-to-face meeting.

3. They make some attempt to match potential partners according to demographic variables such as (desired) race, religion, and age; and according to personality traits (see Table 8.1). Potential partners thereby obtain a great deal of factual information about potential partners before meeting them

Yet the investigators note certain pitfalls related to these services. First, three-dimensional flesh-and-blood people tend to be reduced to a photograph and a pack of statistics, eliminating the subtle factors of interaction that often allow people to judge whether those they meet could be potential partners. Moreover, the sheer number of people displayed to the user of the service makes it necessary to eliminate people who might have worked out just fine if they had met offline.

Online meetings provide opportunities for extended communication before offline meetings. While such communication allows people to probe beneath the surface, it may also display too much too soon. Overly rapid self-disclosure can turn other people "off" (Park et al., 2011).

Concerning matching according to personality traits, the authors simply remark that they have not found any "compelling" evidence that such computer matching provides benefits that lead to greater satisfaction in relationships. Many dating sites say they use "scientific" matching techniques. One can question the variables the sites use. One can also question whether it is useful to seek complementarity in various traits—that is, a blending of opposites.

There is also reason to believe that when sites do not have enough respondents, they "stretch" the limits of the variables that are supposed to match. That is, if you're looking for someone who is at least 6'2" tall, but the website has hardly anyone who reaches even 6', you may wind up with "matches" who are 5'7" tall.

The authors conclude that "matching sites promise to identify potential mates who are uniquely compatible with their users, and this is a promise unlikely to have a great deal of empirical support. … Research on intimate relationships suggests that there are inherent limits to how well the success of a relationship between two individuals can be predicted in advance of their awareness of each other" (Finkel et al, 2012, p. 47).

Let us conclude that online dating has revolutionized the ways in which couples seek partners and start relationships. Using the power of the Internet has enabled many

people who lack other significant means for finding potential partners to explore the universe of possibly compatible individuals who are also seeking partners. It even offers shy people a safer way to initiate a relationship; people who might be somewhat tongue-tied in person may find it easier to type messages at a keyboard. Knowing in advance that there are certain common backgrounds and common interests can give an individual a running start in developing a relationship if and when a couple does choose to meet in person. On the other hand, online dating sites remove the advantage of being able to "play it cool" because registering on the site means that one is looking for a partner. That disadvantage might be a small price to pay for those who desire relatively safe awareness of and access to the "universe" of potential partners.

Table 8.1	
Americans Who Have Met Their Partners Online (Percents)	
1970–1980	0–1%
1980–1990	1–3%
1990–2000	5–10%
2000–2010	20–25%

Data: Adapted from link Finkel et al., 2012

If the eye contact is reciprocated, try an opening line, or greeting. These include the following:

- Verbal salutes, such as "Good morning."
- Personal inquiries, such as "How are you doing?"
- Compliments, such as "I like your outfit."
- References to your mutual surroundings, such as "What do you think of that painting?" or "This is a nice apartment house, isn't it?"
- References to people or events outside the immediate setting, such as "Have you been following the [local athletic team]?"
- References to the other person's behavior, such as "I couldn't help noticing you were sitting alone" or "I see you out on this track every Saturday morning."
- References to your own behavior, or to yourself, such as "Hi, my name is Allan Felix" (feel free to use your own name, if you prefer).

A simple "Hi" or "Hello" is very useful. A friendly glance followed by a cheerful hello ought to give you some idea of whether the attraction is reciprocated. If the hello is returned with a friendly smile and inviting eye contact, follow it up with another greeting, such as a reference to your surroundings, the other person's behavior, or your name.

TRUTH OR FICTION REVISITED: It is not true that only phonies practice opening lines. It can be helpful for everyone to practice opening lines.

What Do You Say When You're Meeting Someone New? Do you make small talk? About what? Do you use an opening line? Which one? Are you genuine? Are you phony? Are you tense? At ease? Small talk actually isn't so small at all. People use it to search for common ground and test possible feelings of attraction.

 2

Exchanging "Name, Rank, and Serial Number" Early exchanges are likely to include name, occupation, marital status, and hometown. This has been likened to exchanging "name, rank, and serial number" with the other person. Each person seeks a sociological profile of the other to discover common ground that may provide a basis for pursuing the conversation (Cunningham & Barbee, 2008). An unspoken rule seems to be at work: "If I provide you with some information about myself, you will reciprocate by giving me an equal amount of information about yourself. Or . . . I'll tell you my home town if you tell me yours" (Knapp & Vangelista, 2000). If the other person is unresponsive, she or he may not be attracted to you. But you may also be awkward in your approach or perhaps turn the other person off by disclosing too much about yourself at the outset.

A generation or two ago, women rarely approached men to signal romantic interest or initiate relationships. Today, however, many women in developed nations do precisely that (Wade et al., 2009). Moreover, both women and men rate direct opening lines—lines that signal interest—as most effective in launching relationships (Wade et al, 2009).

SELF-DISCLOSURE: YOU TELL ME AND I'LL TELL YOU . . . CAREFULLY

Self-disclosure, or opening up, is central to building intimate relationships (Uysal et al., 2012). But what sort of information is safe to disclose when meeting someone? If you refuse to go beyond name, rank, and serial number, you may look

Self-disclosure The revelation of personal, perhaps intimate, information.

Surface contact A probing phase of building a relationship in which people seek common ground and check out feelings of attraction.

uninterested or as though you are trying to keep things under wraps. But if you spill out the fact that you have a painful rash on your thigh, you may have disclosed too much too soon.

TRUTH OR **FICTION** REVISITED: Research suggests that we should refrain from disclosing intimate information too rapidly (Anderson et al., 2011). In a classic experiment, confederates of the researchers (Wortman et al., 1976) engaged in ten-minute conversations with study participants. Some confederates were "early disclosers," who shared intimate information early. Others, "late disclosers," shared intimate information toward the end of the conversation only. In both cases, the information was identical. Study participants then rated the disclosers. The early disclosers in this study were rated less mature, secure, well adjusted, and genuine than the late disclosers.

Self-Disclosure, Social Networking, and Privacy Settings Online

On the other hand, rapid self-disclosure seems to be more common when people meet online (Park et al., 2011; Special & Li-Barber, 2012). Depending on the nature of the site, cyberspace may allow for relative anonymity and enables people to control what they want to reveal—to safeguard their privacy even as they increase their emotional closeness and openness.

Research suggests that people who disclose more information on social networking sites, such as Facebook, are not necessarily more satisfied with their networking experience (Special & Li-Barber, 2012). Moreover, despite the generalization that females are more likely than males to engage in self-disclosure, the same "rule" does not hold for social networking sites. Because of concern with their safety, females are likely to use higher privacy settings on these sites than males are (Special & Li-Barber, 2012).

If the **surface contact** provided by small talk and initial self-disclosure has been mutually rewarding, partners in a relationship tend to develop feelings of liking for each other (Abell et al., 2006; Collins & Miller, 1994). Self-disclosure may build through the course of a relationship as partners come to trust each other enough to share intimate feelings.

Working on the Relationship. When one partner works on the relationship, the other partner is more motivated to reciprocate. Why did one partner give this gift? "Just because."

A Closer Look

They Say You Can't Hurry Love … But How about Speed Dating?

This is a short story about two cable news network reporters who tried speed dating in the line of duty. But of course they also thought that it wouldn't hurt if they found someone spectacular along the way.

Allie, age 25, is a fresh field reporter from the Midwest who is looking for someone who is a professional, a bit older but not too much older, who loves animals, who likes traveling, who is well groomed, who speaks well, and who meets her minimal physical standards. He doesn't have to be celebrity Daniel Craig, but he has to take care of himself, Allie says.

Michael is a 24-year-old news editor from Delaware who would like to find someone who knows a good bottle of wine, likes the theater, reads, and is good looking.

Allie and Michael tried speed dating so they could do a story about it. The idea behind speed dating is that singles without a lot of time to spare can meet a whole bunch of people in a short amount of time (Eastwick & Finkel, 2008). Using HurryDate, the Manhattan dating service, Allie and Michael talked to potential soul mates for only four minutes each.

They paid HurryDate a fee, signed up for an event, posted their profiles on the HurryDate website, and attended the event at a conveniently located bar where they were matched with other single people who were each assigned a number—no names.

Then the men played musical chairs, with a switch taking place every four minutes, except that no chairs were pulled out of the bunch. A part of the bar was cordoned off and the men sat down across from the women, with just four minutes to chat them up, back and forth. Then a whistle blew—literally!—and the men moved over a seat, and the process continued, couple by couple. After each conversation, both parties jot down quick notes on a sheet provided by HurryDate next to their current partner's number so they can remember how they reacted to them later on.

Once the event is over and the participants have returned home, they can log on to the HurryDate website and search for the numbers of the people they met at the event. They can indicate whether they

would like to hear from them by entering a "yes" or a "no." Then the yesses are matched and participants can send messages through HurryDate to their matches.

What happened with Allie and Michael? Keep reading.

Allie

I did this for a story and I didn't expect much from it. To be honest, I got from it what I expected—very little. I thought it might be amusing, and sometimes it was, but it was also sort of hectic, and if I didn't distance myself from it a bit, I think I would have found it sort of emotionally churning, if you know what I mean. I didn't think for a minute there would be a chance of meeting Mr. Right, and I was right about that. Twenty faces in an hour and a half were sort of tough-going if you take this sort of thing too seriously, I guess.

Almost all the guys told me what they did for a living, though I didn't ask. Maybe they thought that was strange, but when I saw them, I guess I really didn't feel like I had to know. Some said they were into finance with some sort of emphasis as if that was supposed to mean millions. There were a couple of teachers, no college professors. No doctors. Oh, yes—"sales," generic. Some said they lived in Manhattan, again emphasizing Manhattan, like to say they could afford it.

They asked me what I did, as if I was supposed to contribute to the rent or the mortgage. They also wanted to know where I lived and what I liked to do in my spare time.

I did ask them if they traveled or liked foreign films.

I wound up with 15 guys saying "yes" on the website. Truth is I'm going to find Mr. Right another way.

Michael

Allie told me about her experience, and, frankly, I guess mine was a bit better than hers. She's sort of outgoing and guys sort of flock to her, if you know what I mean. I'm outgoing when I know people, but people don't flock to me the way they flock to Allie, so the idea of meeting 20 people in

an hour and a half isn't a negative for me. In fact, six of them said "yes," meaning that they're willing to have more contact with me, and of that six, I find two attractive enough in one way or another. Now, you could say that's low odds, right? One in ten. I mean I met 20 women and something could happen with 2 of them. But that's not bad at all. If I were out with my friends at a bar on the weekend, I might wind up talking with one woman, and the chances of her having an interest in seeing me again might be, what, one in five?

I'll say this about the four minutes. It may sound like very little, but it's more than you think. I mean you say, like, "What do you do?" and "What do you like?" and stuff, and she asks you "What do you do?" and "What do you like?" and a couple more questions, and if the answers are pretty short, you can be done in pretty much two minutes. Well, let me put it this way: If you're both kind of shy and you're both not long-winded, you might run out of stuff to say fairly quickly. Well, that's one of my problems, looking at someone and wondering what to say next.

Anyhow, and don't ask me how, with one of the women who said yes, my favorite, somehow we wound up talking about Gilbert and Sullivan and all sorts of mutual cultural interests. I guess she's the one who did it. I'm really looking forward to seeing her again!

Watch the **Video**
Sexuality in Adulthood: Paula, Owner of Three-Minute Dating
on **MyDevelopmentLab**

Allie and Michael, Scouting Out a Location in a Park

CRITICAL THINKING
Do you believe it is possible for a person to maintain complete individuality while at the same time investing in mutuality with another person? Explain.

Gender Differences in Self-Disclosure A woman complains to a friend, "He never opens up to me. It's like living with a stone wall." Women commonly declare that men are loath to express their feelings. Researchers find that masculine-typed individuals, whether male or female, tend to be less willing to disclose their feelings, perhaps in adherence to the traditional "strong and silent" masculine stereotype (Derlega et al., 2008). Susan Basow and Kimberly Rubenfeld (2003) found that feminine-typed individuals are more likely to be empathic and to listen to other people's troubles than masculine-typed individuals, regardless of their anatomic sex.

Factors that encourage continuation of relationships include seeking ways to introduce variety and maintain interest (such as trying out new sexual practices and social activities), showing evidence of caring and positive evaluation (such as sending birthday or Valentine's Day cards), trusting one's partner, perceiving fairness in the relationship, and experiencing feelings of general satisfaction. One of the developments in a continuing relationship is that of **mutuality,** which leads a couple to regard themselves as "we," not just two "I's" who happen to be in the same place at the same time (Avivi et al., 2009; Deci et al., 2006). Mutuality favors continuation and further deepening of the relationship. It also implies cognitive interdependence. Planning for the future, both in little ways (What will I do this weekend?) and in big ways (What will I do about my education and my career?), includes consideration of the needs and desires of one's partner. Cognitive interdependence is related to intimacy, as we will see in the following section.

INTIMACY: SHARING INNERMOST THOUGHTS AND FEELINGS

Intimacy consists of feelings of emotional connectedness with another person and the desire to share innermost thoughts and feelings (Burke & Young, 2012). Partners in the throes of romantic love usually want to disclose everything to, and know everything about, one another (Kito, 2005; Vaculík & Hudecek, 2005). Along with sex, intimacy is one of the key ingredients in passionate relationships (Burke & Young, 2012). Feelings of intimacy and affection tend to grow as romantic relationships develop (Perlman & Sprecher, 2012; Rubin & Campbell, 2012). Relationships also develop from being more casual and superficial to being relatively committed. As couples age, intimacy becomes one of the most valued—if not the most valued—components of the relationship (Villar et al., 2005). Intimate relationships are also characterized by trust, caring, and acceptance.

Sternberg's (2007) triangular theory of love regards intimacy as a basic component of romantic love, but people can be intimate and not in love, at least not in romantic love. Close friends and family members become emotionally intimate when they care deeply for each other and share their feelings and experiences.

TRUTH OR FICTION REVISITED: People need not be *sexually* intimate to be emotionally intimate. Nor does sexual intimacy automatically create emotional intimacy. Often, people who are sexually involved may not achieve emotional closeness. They can be more emotionally intimate with friends than with lovers.

Since intimacy involves the sharing of innermost thoughts and feelings, honesty is a core feature of intimacy. A person need not be an "open book" to develop and maintain intimacy, however. Some aspects of experience are better kept even from one's most intimate partners, especially when they are embarrassing or threatening (Anderson et al., 2011). We would not expect partners to disclose every passing sexual fantasy. Nor should we expect intimate partners to divulge the details of

Mutuality A phase in building a relationship in which members of a couple come to regard themselves as "we," no longer as two "I's" who happen to be in the same place at the same time.

4

Intimacy Feelings of closeness and connectedness that are marked by sharing of innermost thoughts and feelings.

past sexual experiences. Honesty means *saying what one means,* not providing hurtful details.

Intimacy is important not only to interpersonal relationships but also to one's health. Researchers have found that intimacy fosters well-being and that its absence can be psychologically and physically harmful (Rubin & Campbell, 2012; Perlman & Sprecher, 2012).

Intimacy and Self-Esteem Some social scientists suggest that getting to know and like yourself is an initial step toward intimacy with others. By coming to know and value yourself, you identify your own feelings and needs and develop the security to share them. Research suggests that partners with low self-esteem are more likely to harbor self-doubts that can interfere with the development and maintenance of romantic relationships (Leary & Tangney, 2012). For example, experiments show that when their partner is in a "bad mood," people with low self-esteem tend to feel more responsible for that mood, to feel more rejected, and, consequently, to behave in a more hostile manner (Bellavia & Murray, 2003). Yet, people with high self-esteem seem to be more likely to use their partners' acceptance and approval as a way of maintaining their self-esteem when self-doubts arise (Murray et al., 2001). That is, even when we feel rather good about ourselves, we can come to rely on our partners' impressions of us.

Too much self-esteem can also be detrimental to a relationship if it takes the form of narcissism, or being wrapped up in oneself. Research shows that narcissists tend to play love games with their partners; they show less commitment and are more likely to have alternatives handy if relationships do not work out (Campbell et al., 2002). The same researchers found that self-esteem, as opposed to narcissism, was positively linked to romantic love.

Two other ingredients of an intimate relationship are trust and caring. *Trust* enables partners to feel confident that disclosing intimate feelings will not lead to ridicule or rejection. Trust usually builds gradually, as partners learn whether it is safe to share confidences.

A German study of 72 adolescents who were followed from the ages of 14 through 20 found that the quality of their relationships with their parents contributed to their ability to trust romantic partners (Seiffge-Krenke & Kuehnemund, 2001). Research also shows that people come to trust their partners when they see that their partners have made sincere investments in the relationship, as evidenced, for example, by making sacrifices to be with them, such as incurring the disapproval of their family (Van Lange & Rusbult, 2012). Commitment and trust in a relationship can be seen as developing according to a model of **mutual cyclical growth:**

- Feelings that one needs one's partner promote commitment to and dependence on the relationship.
- Commitment to the relationship encourages the partners to do things that are good for the relationship (that is, to perform "pro-relationship acts").
- One's partner perceives the pro-relationship acts.
- Perception of the pro-relationship acts enhances the partner's trust in the other partner and in the relationship.
- Feelings of trust increase the partners' willingness to depend on the relationship.

Caring is an emotional bond that allows intimacy to develop. Caring means that partners try to satisfy each other's needs, gratify each other's interests, and make sacrifices, if necessary. Research shows that willingness to sacrifice is

Mutual cyclical growth The view that the need for one's partner promotes commitment; commitment promotes acts that enhance the relationship; and these acts build trust, increasing one's partner's commitment to the relationship.

Real Students, Real Questions

Q *When is the best time in a relationship to tell someone you love him or her? When is it too early? Too late?*

A Wait until you've gotten to know the person—at least a few weeks. Let it be "true love" and not merely infatuation, which you can feel pretty quickly, even immediately. You can say the other person is "wow" or something like that right away, but save the word *love* until you've had a while to show your head is screwed on right. When is it too late? We don't hear that question very often, but it could be too late if your partner has concluded that your feelings are too shallow or that you're not the kind of person who can make the commitment he or she is looking for. But that's not likely to happen out of the blue. You're likely to get lots of hints, like "So where is this relationship going?"

connected with commitment to the relationship, level of satisfaction in the relationship, and, interestingly, poor alternatives to the relationship (Rusbult et al., 2012; Van Lange & Rusbult, 2012). In other words, it may not be easy to find partners if one does not sacrifice for relationships (Katz & Tirone, 2009). Is self-sacrifice thus self-serving?

Because intimacy involves the sharing of innermost thoughts and feelings, honesty is a core feature of intimacy. But must a person be an "open book" to develop and maintain intimacy? Should some embarrassing or threatening experiences be kept from even one's most intimate partner? Perhaps. We would not expect partners to disclose every passing sexual fantasy. Nor would it be reasonable to expect intimate partners to divulge the details of past sexual experiences. Honesty means saying what one means, not providing hurtful details. Nor is intimacy established by frank but brutal criticism, even if it is honest.

Making a Commitment People may open up to strangers on airplanes or trains, or to health care providers, and still find it hard to talk openly with people to whom they are closest. This phenomenon is true even though we know that we will not see the strangers again, or that the health professionals are required to keep our personal matters confidential. Truly intimate relationships are marked by commitment to maintain the relationship through thick and thin (Sternberg, 2004).

Numerous studies find that men tend to be more reluctant than women to make commitments. David Popenoe, co-director of the National Marriage Project at Rutgers University in New Jersey, conducted a study with 60 unmarried heterosexual men and found that the commonness of cohabitation is one reason why they are reluctant to make a commitment. In cohabitation, sex—traditionally a key reason for men to marry—is readily available. Popenoe notes, "In a sense, with cohabitation he gets a quasi-wife without having to commit" (Hussain, 2002).

In committed relationships, a delicate balance exists between individuality and mutuality. In healthy unions, a strong sense of togetherness does not eradicate individuality. Partners in such relationships remain free to be themselves. Neither seeks to dominate or submerge himself or herself into the personality of the other. Each partner maintains individual interests, likes and dislikes, and needs and goals.

Factors that can throw continuing relationships into a downward spiral include boredom, as in falling into a rut in leisure activities or sexual practices. Yet, boredom does not always end relationships. Consider a study of 12 men who admitted to experiencing sexual boredom in long-term heterosexual relationships (Tunariu & Reavey, 2003). The men were not happy with sexual boredom, particularly in a culture in which men are viewed as highly sexual, and romantic love is supposed to remain passionate. On the other hand, they viewed their boredom as a normal trade-off for so-called true love and long-term companionship.

Other factors that contribute to the discontinuation of a relationship include evidence of negative evaluation (such as bickering, and forgetting anniversaries and other important dates or pretending that they do not exist), lack of fairness in the relationship (such as one partner's always deciding how the couple will spend their free time), jealousy, and general dissatisfaction. Question: How does jealousy affect relationships?

Jealousy: Is the World a Real-Life Temptation Island?

O! beware, my lord, of jealousy;
It is the green-ey'd monster ...

        —William Shakespeare, *Othello*

Thus was Othello, the Moor of Venice, warned of jealousy in the Shakespearean play that bears his name. Othello could not control his feelings, however, and killed his beloved wife, Desdemona. The English poet John Dryden labeled jealousy a "tyrant of the mind." Anthropologists find evidence of jealousy in all cultures, although it may vary in amount and intensity across and within cultures. It appears to be more common and intense among cultures with a stronger machismo tradition, in which men are expected to display their virility. It is also powerful in cultures in which men view a woman's infidelity as a threat to their honor. But jealousy is found among gay males and lesbians as well as among heterosexuals (Peluso, 2008).

The emotion of jealousy accounted in part for the popularity of the reality TV show *Temptation Island*. On this show, people in committed relationships were exposed to attractive others, and the audience was apparently intrigued by the question of how much temptation the contestant on the show could withstand. No doubt, members of the audience also speculated on how much temptation they themselves could withstand.

Sexual jealousy is aroused when we suspect that an intimate relationship is threatened by a rival. Lovers can become jealous when others show sexual interest in their partners or when their partners show an interest (even a casual or nonsexual interest) in another. Jealousy can lead to loss of feelings of affection, feelings of insecurity and rejection, anxiety and loss of self-esteem, and feelings of mistrust of one's partner and potential rivals (Guerrero et al., 2011). It is one of the commonly mentioned reasons why relationships fail. Feelings of possessiveness, related to jealousy, also place stress on a relationship. In extreme cases, jealousy can cause depression or give rise to spouse abuse, suicide, or, as with Othello, murder (Harmon-Jones et al., 2009). But milder forms of jealousy are not necessarily destructive to a relationship. They may even serve the positive function of revealing how much one cares for one's partner. For this reason,

Jealousy. How do we explain feelings of jealousy? What does jealousy do to an intimate relationship?

we can distinguish between *normal jealousy*, which reflects occasional self-doubts and the belief that one's partner is attractive, and *obsessional jealousy*, in which the individual, like Othello, is consumed by his or her fears of interference in the relationship.

What causes jealousy? Experience and personality variables play roles. People may become mistrustful of their partners because former partners had cheated. People with low self-esteem may experience sexual jealousy because they become overly dependent on their partners. They may fear that they will not be able to find another partner if their present partner leaves.

JEALOUSY AND EVOLUTIONARY THEORY

Researchers (e.g., Buss, 2009; Sagarin et al., 2012, Shackelford et al., 2005) note that gender differences in jealousy appear to support evolutionary theory. Males seem to be more upset by sexual infidelity, females by emotional infidelity (Buss, 2009; Sagarin et al., 2012). That is, males are made more insecure and angry when their partners have sexual relations with someone else. Females are made more insecure and angry when their partners become emotionally attached to someone else. Why? Evolutionary theory hypothesizes that sexual jealousy was shaped by natural selection as a method of ensuring males that their female partner's offspring are their own, and of ensuring females that their male partners will continue to provide resources to facilitate childrearing (Buss, 2009).

LACK OF GENDER DIFFERENCES IN RESPONSES TO AFFAIRS AMONG GAY MALES AND LESBIANS

Interestingly, the hypothesized gender difference in reactions to infidelity disappear when one's partner has an affair with someone of his or her own gender (Sagarin et al., 2003). Is it because the affair carries no threat of impregnation (a view that would be consistent with evolutionary theory)? Or is it because the victim consoles

Real Students, Real Questions

Q *My boyfriend wants me to move in with him, but I am not sure if I am ready. How can I decide? Also, how do you know when you are ready to marry someone?*

A If you're not sure you're ready, don't do it. If he cares about you, he'll wait until you're ready. If he won't wait, you haven't lost anything you need to worry about. (We can talk tough when we have to.) How do you know when you are ready to marry someone? One thing we're rather sure of is that you'll know when it's time. You'll probably know who you are, where you're going, who he is, where he's going, and whether you want to go there together.

himself or herself by thinking that he or she really isn't competing in the same arena with the intruder? Are both explanations and other explanations possible?

A COGNITIVE PERSPECTIVE

In recent years, cognitive theory has gained importance in many areas of the behavioral sciences, and sexual jealousy is no exception. In two studies, Stacie Bauerle and her colleagues (2002) presented 156 college undergraduates and 128 members of the general population with various scenarios in which their partners were unfaithful. By and large, jealousy increased when the individuals attributed their partner's infidelity to internal causes, such as clear personal choice. When they attributed the infidelity to external causes, such as alcohol or social pressure, the individuals in the study reported feeling significantly less jealous. ("Don't blame me; it was the alcohol.")

Many lovers—including many college students—play jealousy games. They let their partners know that they are attracted to other people. They flirt openly or manufacture tales to make their partners pay more attention to them, to test the relationship, to inflict pain, or to take revenge for a partner's disloyalty.

COMMUNICATIVE RESPONSES TO JEALOUSY

Researchers have found four types of communicative responses to situations that create feelings of jealousy (Guerrero et al., 2012):

1. Destructive communication. Such communications include insults, threats, and, in the worst case, violence. They also tend to bring relationships to an end.
2. Constructive communication. Such communication involves discussing the context of feelings of jealousy and exploring ways to restore and strengthen the relationship. Constructive communication tends to increase satisfaction with the relationship.
3. Avoidance. Avoidance means remaining silent and acting as if the events that led to feelings of jealousy had not happened.
4. Rival-focused communication. Such communications involve claims that one possesses one's partner, following or stalking one's partner, derogating one's rival, and, sometimes, directly contacting and confronting one's rival. Rival-focused communication, like destructive communication, is extremely harmful to the relationship.

> ◉ Watch the Video
> *Love in the 21st Century*
> on **MyDevelopmentLab**

Deterioration of Relationships

Here's a fact of modern life: In our society, where people make personal choices about the people with whom they will develop relationships, and when marriage is delayed, and when divorce is an option, most relationships will deteriorate. The deterioration of a relationship is not always a bad thing, but it can be difficult and painful. ◉

RESPONSES TO DETERIORATION OF A RELATIONSHIP

A relationship begins to fail when it becomes less rewarding than it was. Couples can respond to deterioration in active or passive ways. Active means of response include doing something

How Will She Get Rid of Him? Perhaps she will give him a phony e-mail address. Some women now use e-mail as a method of avoiding seeing people they do not want to go out with. They may give out their actual e-mail addresses but never respond, or they may give out seldom-used or erroneous e-mail addresses. It's like giving out the wrong phone number. (Bye-bye.)

that may enhance the relationship (such as working on improving communication skills, negotiating differences, or seeking professional help) or deciding to end the relationship. Passive methods of responding include merely waiting for something to happen, doing little or nothing. People can sit back and wait for the relationship to improve on its own (occasionally it does) or for the relationship to deteriorate to the point where it ends. ("Hey, these things happen.")

It is irrational (and damaging to a relationship) to assume that good relationships require no investment of time and effort (Stephanou, 2012). No two people are matched perfectly. When problems arise, it is better to work to resolve them than to act as though they don't exist and hope that they will just disappear.

BREAKING UP: "BREAKING UP IS [OFTEN] HARD TO DO"

According to social exchange theory, relationships draw to a close when the partners find little satisfaction in the affiliation, when the barriers to leaving the relationship are low (that is, the social, religious, and financial constraints are manageable), and especially when alternative partners are available. Problems in jealousy and communication are common reasons for ending a relationship. The availability of alternatives decreases one's commitment to a relationship (Rusbult et al., 2012; Van Lange & Rusbult, 2012). This fact has been widely recognized throughout the ages, which is one reason why patriarchal cultures like to keep their women locked up—or, in the Middle East, literally "under wraps"—as much as possible.

Breaking up, as the song goes, can be hard to do—both for the person terminating the relationship and for the other party. A study of more than 5,000 people, who responded to a survey on the Internet, found that anxious people were more likely to be highly preoccupied with the lost partner, to suffer more physical and emotional distress, to attempt to reestablish the relationship, and to be angry and vengeful (Davis et al., 2003). Emotionally secure individuals were most likely to seek social support among their friends and their families. Insecure individuals were most likely to turn to alcohol and drugs. A survey of 92 college undergraduates found that many believed they would grow from the experience of breaking up (Tashiro & Frazier, 2003). Individuals' "attributional styles" entered the picture: People who blamed themselves for the breakup experienced more stress than those who blamed external factors, such as the situation.

Breaking up is sometimes followed by **stalking**, or other "unwanted pursuit behaviors" (UPBs), such as unwelcome phone calls, e-mails, or texting, asking third parties about the person who dissolved the

Stalking Following or observing a person persistently, especially because of obsession with the person. Stalking can occur online as well as in person, as when a person breaks into someone else's e-mail.

People Who Have Been Rejected Sometimes Stalk Their Former Partners. Stalking includes behaviors such as breaking into their e-mail. (Hint: Change your passwords from time to time.)

relationship, and following, threatening, or attacking that person or new partners of that person (De Smet et al., 2012; Norris et al., 2011). Jealousy, abusiveness, and physical violence in relationships are key predictors of unwanted pursuit (Norris et al., 2011). Stalkers and violent individuals also tend to have a strong need to control others (Dye & Davis, 2003). We will see in the chapter on sexual coercion that a need to control other people is also connected with the violent crime of rape.

Various factors can save a deteriorating relationship. For example, people who continue to find some sources of satisfaction, who are committed to maintaining the relationship, or who believe that they will eventually be able to overcome their problems are more likely to invest what they must to prevent the collapse.

Breaking up is often associated with psychological distress and a decrease in life satisfaction, especially for a partner who wanted to maintain a deteriorating relationship (Rhoades et al., 2011). On the other hand, sometimes the swan song of a relationship—moving on—is a sign of healthful decision making, not a sign of failure. When people are highly incompatible, and when genuine attempts to preserve the relationship have failed, ending the relationship can offer each partner a chance for happiness with someone else.

Loneliness: "All the Lonely People, Where Do They All Come From?"

Many people start relationships because of loneliness. Loneliness and solitude (being alone) are not synonymous. **Loneliness** is a state of painful isolation, of feeling cut off from others. **Solitude**, however, can be quite positive. Inner-directed solitude can

Loneliness Painful isolation.

Solitude Characterized by self-discovery, inner peace, reflection, and spirituality.

Loneliness or Solitude? Solitude can be a positive experience, allowing us to think or read or write. But loneliness is painful social isolation that can be detrimental to both our psychological and our physical health.

Real Students, Real Questions

Q *How do you tell someone the relationship is over?*

A It's never easy. Nor should it be. The other person has invested in you, and losing someone a person cares about hurts. A lot. But once you've made up your mind, do it as quickly as possible to give the other person as much time as possible to rebuild his or her life. In the "old days," people would pick public places, so the person who was "dumped" was unlikely to make a scene. Now people often use e-mail or texting. (We know someone who sent an indirect message by changing her status on Facebook!) The most decent thing to do is to tell the person face to face in private. Just say that it no longer works for you—not that the other person is somehow bad or a loser. And don't be surprised if the other person has suspected something was wrong. After all, how good an actor can you be?

be characterized by self-discovery and inner peace. Outer-directed solitude can refer to spirituality or allow us to reflect on the world around us. Solitude is usually a matter of choice; loneliness is not.

Lonely people tend to spend a lot of time by themselves, eat dinner alone, spend weekends alone, and participate in few social activities. They are unlikely to date. Some lonely people report having many friends, but a closer look suggests that these "friendships" are shallow. Lonely people are unlikely to share confidences. Loneliness tends to peak during adolescence, when peer relationships begin to supplant family ties.

EFFECTS OF LONELINESS

Loneliness is associated with a host of problems in psychological adjustment (Pak et al., 2012). A study of 90 adolescents aged 16 to 18 found that feelings of loneliness were connected with low self-confidence, introversion, unhappiness, and emotional instability (Cheng & Furnham, 2002). Loneliness is also often connected with feelings of depression. A study of 101 dating couples with a mean age of 21 found that poor relationships contributed to feelings of loneliness and to depression—even though the individuals had partners (Segrin et al., 2003).

Loneliness is connected with physical health problems as well as with psychological problems such as depression. One study, for example, found that lonely people had higher blood pressure than people who were not lonely (Hawkley et al., 2003). Lonely people also found stressful experiences to be more discomfiting, an observation that suggests the value of social support when we are undergoing stress (Hawkley et al., 2003). Social isolation has also been shown to predict cancer, cardiovascular disease, various other diseases, eating disorders such as anorexia nervosa and bulimia nervosa, and a higher mortality rate (Hawkley & Cacioppo, 2003; Levine, 2012). It appears that one causal pathway between loneliness and illness involves stress. Stress impairs the functioning of the immune system, and lonely people perceive stress to be more aversive (Cacioppo et al., 2003).

The causes of loneliness are many and complex. Lonely people tend to have several of the following characteristics:

- Lack of social skills. Lonely people often lack the interpersonal skills to make friends or cope with disagreements.
- Lack of interest in other people.
- Lack of empathy. Empathy is a key aspect of satisfaction in romantic relationships.
- **TRUTH** OR **FICTION** REVISITED: It is true that many people remain lonely because of fear of rejection. This fear is often connected with self-criticism of social skills and expectations of failure in relating to others (Gable, 2012).
- Failure to disclose personal information to potential friends.
- Cynicism about human nature (for example, seeing people as only out for themselves).
- Demanding too much too soon. The lonely perceive other people as cold and unfriendly in the early stages of a relationship.
- General pessimism. When we expect the worst, we often get … you guessed it.
- An external locus of control. That is, lonely people do not see themselves as capable of taking their lives into their own hands and achieving their goals.

Satisfaction in Relationships: Communication as Key

Some relationships work out. Others don't. In Western culture, where people tend to form relationships with more than one partner as they develop, perhaps the majority of relationships draw to an end. Termination of a relationship is not always a bad thing. As people spend time together, they learn more about whether they are well matched or poorly matched. Most also learn how to compromise to help build relationships and how to approach resolving conflicts in a constructive way (Rosenblatt & Rieks, 2009).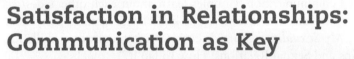

 Watch the **Video**
Marital Fix
on **MyDevelopmentLab**

CONFLICT RESOLUTION

Some researchers, such as John M. Gottman (Cleary Bradley et al., 2011; Madhyastha et al., 2011), have focused on the ways in which couples resolve conflicts. Gottman has videotaped couples as they do so and also monitored their physiological responses, including their heart rates, sweating, and large motor movement. He found that deterioration of satisfaction in the relationship could be predicted by physiological measures, particularly on the part of the male. The calmer the couple's bodily responses, the more their relationship improved as time went on. On the other hand, couples whose heart rates were more rapid, who sweated more, and who moved about agitatedly had relationships that deteriorated over the next three years.

TRUTH OR **FICTION** REVISITED: Gottman also found that conflict itself is not necessarily destructive to a relationship (Gottman & Gottman, 2008). The important thing is the way in which the couple attempts to resolve it. Couples who were open and calm during the conflict tended to improve their satisfaction. Couples who were defensive experienced deterioration in the relationship. A notable trait that contributed to deterioration was stonewalling by the male. *Stonewalling* means that there is little movement of the head, few if any nods, and few of the verbal acknowledgments made by listeners who are participating in a discussion.

Deterioration of the relationship was also predicted by excessively agreeable, compliant behavior on the part of the female or by her verbalizing feelings of contempt. Facial expressions predicted deterioration, especially facial expressions that suggested disgust on the part of the female, fear on the face of the male, and then miserable smiles by both parties. These nonverbal behaviors were accompanied by more defensiveness, excuses, and denial of responsibility.

Stonewallers suffer not only in terms of their relationships. Stonewalling predicted loneliness after the relationship ended, and loneliness, in turn, was connected with deteriorating health.

Good outcomes for relationships could also be predicted by positive attributes during conflict, such as displays of humor, empathy, and affection; by mutual effort to solve problems; and by determination to listen to one's partner nondefensively. These positive elements kept physiological responses in check as well.

Other researchers have generally found evidence in support of Gottman's conclusions about couples in conflict (Caughlin et al., 2012; Noller, 2012). For example, the ways in which couples communicate to resolve conflicts are the key to the survival or termination of a relationship. Couples who validated each other's feelings in a respectful and helpful manner were most satisfied with their relationships. Couples who were hostile or explosive, or who attempted to avoid conflict, were less satisfied with their relationships.

TRUTH OR **FICTION** REVISITED: Despite the Beatles' song lyrics, love is not all you need. You also need communication. Couples learn about each other's desires and needs through communication. Otherwise, this knowledge remains a mystery. The chapter's *My Life, My Sexuality* feature discusses "Communication Skills for Enhancing Relationships and Sexual Relations: How to Do It."

A World of Diversity

Relationships between Heterosexuals, Gay Males, Lesbians, Bisexuals, and Transgendered Individuals

Numerous researchers have studied the factors that predict satisfaction in a relationship or the deterioration and ending of a relationship (Holmberg et al., 2009). Much of this research has sought to determine whether there are differences in the factors that satisfy heterosexual and homosexual couples, and the interesting finding is that we are hard-pressed to find differences (Holmstrom, 2009). One difference that stands out favors the gay and lesbian couples: They tend to distribute household chores evenly and not in terms of gender-role stereotypes (Kurdek, 2005, 2006; Wong, 2012). Now for the similarities: Sexual satisfaction is tied to satisfaction with the relationship in both heterosexual and lesbian women (Wong, 2012). Gay, lesbian, and male–female couples are all more satisfied when they receive social support from their partners, there is sharing of power in the relationship, they fight fair, and they perceive their partners to be committed to the relationship. But there are a couple of differences that favor stability in the relationships of the male–female couples: They are more likely to have the support of their families and less likely to be stigmatized by society at large.

Couples therapists who work with gays, lesbians, bisexuals, and transgendered individuals and couples will find problems akin to those in heterosexual couples, such as infidelity, and many that need special sensitivity to these commonly stigmatized subpopulations (Schwartz & Young, 2009):

- Lesbian-gay-bisexual (LGB) identity development and how it affects the functioning of the couple
- Parenting and its impact on the couple
- LGB individuals as members of families
- The kinds of stressors that impact individuals who are underrepresented in the LGB literature, including older LGB people, LGB individuals who are members of ethnic minority groups, and LGB individuals who are members of religious groups
- Legal issues and their impact on the couple

Working with Lesbians, Gays, and Bisexuals. Couples therapists who work with LGBs (lesbian, gays, and bisexual couples) will find many problems akin to those of heterosexual couples, but some will reflect the sexual orientations of the members of the couple; for example, LGB identity development, gays as parents, and so on.

- Workplace issues and their impact on the couple

Chapter Review

✓•⎯[**Study** and **Review** on **MyDevelopmentLab**

LO1 **Describe the development of relationships**

According to the ABCDE model, relationships develop through five stages: attraction, building, continuation, deterioration, and ending. Small talk enables people to learn whether they share interests, attitudes, and feelings of attraction. The opening line—or greeting—enables individuals to begin surface contact. Self-disclosure allows people to get below surface contact to determine whether they have things in common. Too little self-disclosure prevents development of intimacy; too much may appear to be socially inappropriate. Intimacy involves feelings of emotional closeness with another person and the desire to share each other's innermost thoughts and feelings. Intimacy involves trust, caring, tenderness, honesty, and commitment.

LO2 **Discuss the effects of jealousy on a relationship**

Jealousy can harm or end relationships, especially when there is destructive or rival-directed communication. According to evolutionary theory, males are more jealous when their partners have sexual relations with an outsider, whereas females are more concerned when their partners develop emotional closeness with an outsider.

LO3 **Discuss the deterioration of relationships and ways to cope**

Relationships may fail when they become less rewarding. Active responses to deterioration include working on improving communication, negotiating differences, seeking help, or deciding to end the relationship.

LO4 **Discuss the causes and effects of loneliness**

Loneliness is a state of painful isolation, of feeling cut off from others. Causes of loneliness include lack of social skills, lack of interest in other people, lack of empathy, fear of rejection, lack of self-disclosure, cynicism about people, demanding too much too soon, pessimism, and an external locus of control. People can overcome loneliness by challenging self-defeating attitudes, developing social skills, and placing themselves among others.

LO5 **Describe ways to find satisfaction in a relationship**

Factors such as caring, lack of excessive jealousy, perceived fairness, mutual respect, and ability to communicate are connected with satisfaction in relationships. Lesbians, gay males, bisexuals, and transgendered people have problems in relationships similar to those of heterosexuals, but also unique problems such as those associated with LGB identity development, LGB parenting, and LGB issues with the law and in the workforce.

Test Your Learning

1. Sexual satisfaction for lesbians is connected with
   (a) their sexual orientation.
   (b) their relationship.
   (c) social stigmatization.
   (d) issues in the workplace.

2. Evolutionary theory predicts that _____ will be most jealous about their partners' sexual infidelity.
   (a) heterosexual males
   (b) heterosexual females

   (c) gay males
   (d) lesbians

3. About _____% of couples today meet their partners through online dating services.
   (a) 1–5
   (b) 5–10
   (c) 10–20
   (d) 20–25

4. Which of the following is not part of an intimate relationship?

(a) narcissism
(b) trust
(c) caring
(d) honesty

5. "Small talk"

(a) is a phony way to begin a relationship.
(b) is an in-depth discussion of issues.
(c) promotes premature self-disclosure.
(d) stresses breadth of topic coverage.

6. It is not true that

(a) good relationships require no work.
(b) jealousy harms a relationship.
(c) partners need to work to keep relationships strong.
(d) communication skills are important to relationships.

7. Which statement is accurate?

(a) People need to be sexually intimate to have an emotionally intimate relationship.
(b) People need not be sexually intimate to have an emotionally intimate relationship.
(c) Love is necessary for intimacy.
(d) Intimacy requires total honesty.

8. According to the text, _____ are most reluctant to make commitments in relationships.

(a) men
(b) heterosexual women
(c) lesbians
(d) transgendered individuals

9. Kurdek finds that LGB couples tend to differ from heterosexual couples in that they

(a) distribute household chores more evenly.
(b) avoid conflict at all costs.
(c) do not consider sexual activity per se to be an important aspect of their relationship.
(d) believe that love conquers all and that it is not necessary to work on relationships.

10. Which of the following is accurate about self-disclosure?

(a) Females tend to set higher privacy setting than males do on Facebook.
(b) Men are more likely to self-disclose than are women.
(c) Couples should disclose their sexual histories to promote intimacy.
(d) Self-disclosure is the same online and offline.

Answers: 1. b; 2. a; 3. d; 4. a; 5. d; 6. a; 7. b; 8. a; 9. a; 10. a

My Life, My Sexuality

Communication Skills for Enhancing Relationships and Sexual Relations: How to Do It

*Explore this **My Life, My Sexuality** feature by scanning this QR code with your mobile device. If you don't already have one, you may download a free QR scanner for your device wherever smartphone apps are sold. You can also view this feature in MyDevelopmentLab, along with an accompanying critical thinking assignment.*

Many couples are troubled by poor communication skills, especially when it comes to sexual matters. Scan the code to learn how to develop your communication skills. Topics covered include:

■ Understanding obstacles to sexual communication
■ Getting started communicating
■ Learning about your partner's sexual needs
■ Communicating your own sexual needs
■ Making requests
■ Delivering criticism (uh, oh)
■ Receiving criticism
■ Negotiating differences
■ When communication is not enough: handling impasses

9 Sexual Behaviors and Fantasies

Learning Objectives

TRUTH OR FICTION?

Which of the following statements are the truth, and which are fiction? Look for the Truth-or-Fiction icons on the pages that follow to find the answers.

1 Married people rarely if ever masturbate. **T F?**

2 Women who masturbate during adolescence are less likely to find gratification in marital coitus than women who do not. **T F?**

3 Women are more likely to reach orgasm through sexual intercourse than through masturbation. **T F?**

4 Most women masturbate by inserting a finger or other object into the vagina. **T F?**

5 Statistically speaking, oral sex is the norm for today's young couples. **T F?**

6 Lesbian couples commonly strap on dildos and engage in sexual intercourse with their partner. **T F?**

7 Anal sex is more common among less well-educated people. **T F?**

8 Sexual fantasies are abnormal. **T F?**

9 When lovers fantasize about other people, the relationship is in trouble. **T F?**

231

Rachel Maines's intentions were innocent enough. She was going to write a book about needlework in the late nineteenth and early twentieth centuries. (Yawn.) But in the course of her research, she noticed advertisements for vibrators—100 years ago! Being a scholar with a free-ranging mind, she turned her attention to the meaning and use of vibrators in U.S. history and wound up writing a book called *The Technology of Orgasm: "Hysteria," the Vibrator, and Women's Sexual Satisfaction.*

It turns out that genital massage to orgasm—often using a vibrator—was once a standard treatment for "hysteria," a health problem considered common in women (Starr & Aron, 2011). (After all, a man would never be hysterical, would he?) The treatment was usually carried out by a physician or a midwife. Genital massage would be used to bring the woman to "hysterical paroxysm" (another name for orgasm, at least in women). The introduction of the vibrator in the 1880s made treatment more efficient.

Hysteria? What's that? In earlier centuries the diagnosis of hysteria would be made on the basis of symptoms such as anxiety, irritability, nervousness, pelvic swelling, heaviness in the abdomen (bloating), and fainting. There were other symptoms as well, including sexual fantasies and vaginal lubrication. The word *hysteria* derives from the Greek word for "uterus." The medical establishment believed that the uterus caused these symptoms by choking the patient because of sexual deprivation. Pregnancy would help; so would coitus. Single women were encouraged to get married, and married women were encouraged to get pregnant. Women without men might try horseback riding, use rocking chairs (yes, rocking chairs), or obtain genital massage. Maines found no evidence that physicians delighted in the task. Rather, they apparently relegated it to midwives whenever they could. Women, by the way, were not encouraged to masturbate as a way of achieving, uh, "hysterical paroxysm." Masturbation was seen as deviant and unhealthful. Use of the vibrator in the hands of the physician or midwife was seen

In the late nineteenth and early twentieth centuries, vibrators came into use as means of helping women with "hysterical" health problems—as they were conceptualized by the health establishment at the time. At most times and in most places, women's sexuality has taken a back seat to that of men.

CRITICAL THINKING

An—shall we say—easily upset male character in the musical comedy *A Funny Thing Happened on the Way to the Forum*, set in ancient Rome, is named "Hysterium." What's funny about that?

as a medical treatment, not a sexual act (Starr & Aron, 2011). An orgasm was a "hysterical crisis," not an orgasm.

It is obvious that the "symptoms of hysteria" are related to menstruation. Today we recognize that menstrual and premenstrual symptoms are associated with the secretion of sex hormones, but even as late as the mid-twentieth century, health professionals attributed a wide variety of mental disorders to hysteria. Therefore, the behaviors connected with the disorders—such as the development of physical symptoms in response to stress—were expected in women but surprising in men.

This is the chapter that discusses sexual techniques and gives statistical breakdowns of "who does what with whom." There is great variety in human sexual expression today; vibrators are still in use, but we do not hear of them resulting in hysterical paroxysms anymore.

Readers of this book are as varied in their sexual values, preferences, and attitudes as is society in general. Some of the techniques discussed may thus strike some readers as indecent. Our aim is to provide information about the diversity of sexual expression. We are not seeking unanimity on what is acceptable. Nor do we pass judgments or encourage readers to expand their sexual repertoires.

The human body is sensitive to many forms of sexual stimulation. Biology is not destiny, however: A biological capacity does not impose a behavioral requirement. Cultural expectations, personal values, and individual experience—not only our biological capacities—determine our sexual behavior. What is right for you is right for you—and not necessarily for your neighbor.

We begin by reviewing the techniques that people practice on their own to derive sexual pleasure. We then consider techniques that involve a partner.

Sex Without a Partner

> In solitude he pollutes himself, and with his own hand blights all his prospects for both this world and the next. Even after being solemnly warned, he will often continue this worse than beastly practice, deliberately forfeiting his right to health and happiness for a moment's mad sensuality.
>
> —J. H. Kellogg, M.D., *Plain Facts for Old and Young*, 1888

Various forms of sexual expression do not require a partner or are not generally practiced in the presence of a partner. Masturbation is one of the principal forms of one-person sexual expression. Masturbation involves direct stimulation of the genitals. Other forms of individual sexual experience, such as sexual fantasy, may or may not be accompanied by genital stimulation.

The word *masturbation* is not simply a descriptive term. It derives from the Latin *masturbari,* from the roots for "hand" and "to defile." The derivation provides clues to historical cultural attitudes toward the practice (Polansky, 2006). **Masturbation** may be practiced by manual stimulation of the genitals, perhaps with the aid of artificial stimulation, such as a vibrator. It may employ an object, such as a pillow or a **dildo** that touches the genitals. Even before we conceive of sexual experiences with others, we may learn early in childhood that touching our genitals can produce pleasure.

Pleasure is not the only reason that people masturbate. Table 9.1 lists reasons reported for masturbation, according to the findings of the National Health and Social Life Survey (NHSLS).

Within the Judeo-Christian tradition, masturbation has been condemned as sinful (Kaestle & Allen, 2011). Early Judeo-Christian attitudes toward masturbation reflected the censure that was applied toward nonprocreative sex. Masturbation has also been referred to as "onanism" or "onania," names derived from the biblical story of Onan (Obald, 2012). According to the book of Genesis (38:9–11), Onan was the second-born son of Judah. Judah's first son, Er, died without an heir. Biblical law required that if a man died without a male heir, his brother must take the widow as a wife and rear their first son as his brother's heir. Judah thus directed Onan to "Go in unto thy brother's wife, and perform the duty of a husband's brother unto her, and

Masturbation Sexual self-stimulation.

Dildo A penis-shaped object used in sexual activity.

Table 9.1

Reasons for Masturbation (Percentage of Respondents Who Report Reason), According to the NHSLS

Reasons for Masturbation	Men	Women
To relax	26	32
To relieve sexual tension	73	63
Partners are unavailable	32	32
Partner does not want to engage in sexual activity	16	6
Boredom	11	5
To obtain physical pleasure	40	42
To help get to sleep	16	12
Fear of HIV/AIDS and other STIs	7	5
Other reasons	5	5

Source: Adapted by permission from E. O. Laumann, J. H. Gagnon, R. T. Michael, & S. Michaels (1994). *The social organization of sexuality: Sexual practices in the United States.* Chicago: University of Chicago Press, Table 3.3, p. 86.

raise up seed to thy brother." But Onan "spilled [his seed] upon the ground" during relations with his deceased brother's wife and was struck down by God for his deed.

Although "onanism" has come to be associated with masturbation, scholars have noted that Onan's act was **coitus interruptus**, not masturbation. Both acts, however, involve nonprocreative sex—"spilling the seed." Whatever its biblical origins, masturbation is prohibited under Jewish law. St. Augustine was influenced by ancient Persian beliefs, which condemned all nonprocreative sex as sinful (van Oort, 2012). Historians suspect that people in ancient times condemned sex that did not lead to pregnancy because of the need for an increase in their numbers. The need for progeny is also linked to the widespread view that marital intercourse is the only morally acceptable avenue of sexual expression.

HISTORICAL MEDICAL VIEWS OF MASTURBATION

St. Augustine's views were carried into medicine in the eighteenth century, and the medical profession "translated" sin into disease (van Oort, 2012). Thus, until recent times, masturbation was thought to be physically and mentally harmful, as well as degrading. The eighteenth-century physician Benjamin Rush, a signer of the Declaration of Independence, believed that masturbation caused tuberculosis, "nervous diseases," poor eyesight, memory loss, and epilepsy.

Many clergy and medical authorities of the nineteenth century were persuaded that certain foods had a stimulating effect on the sex organs. They therefore advised parents to modify their children's diets to eliminate foods that were believed to excite the sexual organs—notably meat, coffee, tea, and chocolate. Rather, parents should substitute "unstimulating" foods, primarily grain products. In the 1830s, the Reverend Sylvester Graham developed a cracker, since called the graham cracker, to help people control their sexual impulses (Ley, 2012).

Another household name belongs to a man who made his mark by introducing a bland diet that was also intended to help people, especially youngsters, control sexual impulses. One of the more influential medical writers of the nineteenth century was the superintendent of the Battle Creek Sanatorium in Michigan, Dr. J. H. Kellogg (1852–1943), better known now as the creator of the modern breakfast cereal. Kellogg identified 39 "signs of masturbation," including acne, paleness, heart palpitations, rounded shoulders, weak backs, and convulsions. Kellogg, like Graham, believed that sexual desires could be controlled by a diet of simple foods, especially grains, including the corn flakes that have since borne his name (Ley, 2012).

Coitus interruptus The practice of withdrawing the penis prior to ejaculation during sexual intercourse. Also called *withdrawal method*.

Many nineteenth-century physicians also advised parents to take measures to prevent their children from masturbating. Kellogg suggested that parents bandage or cage their children's genitals, or tie their hands. Some contraptions devised to prevent masturbation were barbarous (see Figure 9.1).

Several nineteenth-century scholars of sexuality joined the crusade against masturbation. Richard von Krafft-Ebing (in *Psychopathia Sexualis*, 1886) and Havelock Ellis (in *Studies in the Psychology of Sex*, 1900) condemned masturbation as psychologically dangerous. Krafft-Ebing linked masturbation to sexual orientation. Male masturbation, or so it was mistakenly believed, arrested the development of normal erotic instincts and led to erectile dysfunction with women. Thus, it encouraged male–male sexual activity.

Despite this history, there is no scientific evidence that masturbation is harmful. It doesn't cause insanity, grow hair on the hands, or cause warts or any of the other ills once ascribed to it, except for rare injuries to the genitals due to rough stimulation. Nor is masturbation

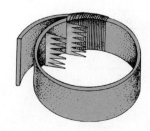

FIGURE 9.1 Devices Designed to Curb Masturbation. Because of widespread beliefs that masturbation was harmful, various contraptions were introduced during the nineteenth century to prevent the practice in children. Some of the devices were barbarous.

A Closer Look

St. Augustine's Influential Views on Sex

Grant me chastity and continence, but not yet (da mihi castitatem et continentiam, sed noli modo).

—St. Augustine, prior to his conversion to Christianity

Augustine (354–430 CE) was a philosopher and a theologian. He was of Berber descent and spent most of his life in what is now Algeria in North Africa. His mother was a devout Roman Catholic, but his father was a pagan. At school he came under pagan influences but also became immersed in Latin literature. At age 17 a sponsor arranged to support his studies in Carthage. At this time he was attracted to the polytheistic Manichaean religion, which had originated in Persia and spread as far as Rome to the West and China to the East. Augustine followed a hedonistic lifestyle in Carthage, taking a woman as concubine for more than 13 years, during which time they had a son. Augustine moved to Rome and then to Milan, where he converted to Christianity in 387. He chronicled his spiritual journey in his *Confessions*. But it is thought that Manichaeism contributed to his views on the nature of good and evil, hell, predestination, and his hostility toward the flesh and sexual activity.

Following his conversion and his denunciation of the flesh, Augustine became a priest and then a bishop in Hippo in North Africa, and eventually one of the Latin Church Fathers. He developed the concepts of original sin and the just war. Augustine was a prolific author; among his works are *Confessions, The City of God,* and *On the Trinity*. He tackled "heresies," such as the idea that people could become virtuous enough to merit salvation without the intervention of Jesus.

Augustine wrote that original sin, the guilt of Adam for eating the forbidden fruit, is inherited by all humans. Humans are depraved and incapable of doing good without divine grace. Augustine associated sexual desire with original sin. He did not see the sexual act itself as evil, but rather the lustful emotions that can accompany it. Although there is a tendency to blame the victim when women are raped, Augustine offered comfort to virgins raped during the sack of Rome: "Another's lust cannot pollute thee." On the other hand, virtue is lost when a person intends to sin, even if the act is not carried out.

Augustine condemned the practice of abortion, as did other church fathers. Yet, in his mind, the seriousness of abortion depended on the ensoulment status of

An Early Renaissance Fresco Depicting St. Augustine, Florence, Italy

the fetus—that is, whether or not it has received its soul at the time. He believed that male fetuses receive a soul at 40 days of gestation, and female fetuses at 90 days (Coles, 2010).

in itself psychologically harmful, although it may suggest an adjustment problem if people use masturbation as an exclusive sexual outlet when they have opportunities for sexual relationships. Sex therapists have used masturbation as a treatment for individuals with low sexual desire and for women who have difficulty reaching orgasm (Kaestle & Allen, 2011; ter Kuile et al., 2012; see Chapter 15).

Of course, people who consider masturbation wrong, harmful, or sinful may experience anxiety or guilt about it (Zuckerman, 2012). But these negative reactions are linked to their beliefs about masturbation, not masturbation per se. Nevertheless, feelings of guilt can lower the incidence and frequency of masturbation (Ortega et al., 2005).

Surveys indicate that most people in our society masturbate at some time. But individuals are now masturbating at earlier ages than in Kinsey's day (Dekker & Schmidt, 2002). The incidence of masturbation is generally greater among men than women. The nearby "A World of Diversity" feature elaborates on masturbation among different demographic groups.

A World of Diversity
Demographic Factors and Masturbation

Few "forbidden" activities have been as widespread as masturbation. Nearly all of the adult men and about two-thirds of the adult women in the classic Kinsey studies (Kinsey et al., 1948, 1953) reported that they had masturbated at some time. Research also finds a gender gap in the incidence of masturbation. For example, among 14- to 17-year-olds in the United States, 74% of males report that they have masturbated, as compared with 48% of females (Robbins et al., 2011). The NHSLS study also found a gender gap in reported frequencies of masturbation (Laumann et al., 1994). Within every social category, men reported masturbating more frequently than women. Despite the sexual revolution, women may be less motivated to masturbate than men are (Chivers et al., 2007; McAnulty, 2012). Traditional women may still be subject to socialization pressures that teach that sexual activity for pleasure's sake is more of a taboo for women than men (McAnulty, 2012). Then, too, women are more likely to pursue sexual activity within the context of a relationship.

TRUTH OR FICTION **1**
REVISITED: Married people are less likely to have masturbated during the past 12 months than never-married and formerly married people.

Nevertheless, only 43% of the married men and 63% of the married women sampled in the NHSLS study said that they did not masturbate at all during the past year. Therefore, many married people do masturbate.

Females and males with more education reported more frequent masturbation. Perhaps people with more schooling are more likely to learn that masturbation itself is harmless or are less likely to follow traditional social restrictions. Traditional religious beliefs appear to restrain masturbation. Conservative Protestants are less likely to masturbate than liberal and moderate Protestants.

2 There appears to be a link between masturbation and orgasm during sex with others. **TRUTH OR FICTION** REVISITED: Women who have masturbated during adolescence are more likely, not less likely, to find gratification in sex with others in adulthood than women who had not (Hogarth & Ingham, 2009).

The evidence does not suggest that adolescents should be encouraged to masturbate to foster sexual fulfillment in adulthood. A selection factor may explain the link (see Figure 9.2). That is, people who masturbate early may be more open to exploring their sexuality. These attitudes would carry over into adulthood and increase the likelihood that women would seek the stimulation they need to obtain sexual gratification. Adolescent masturbation may also set the stage for sexual satisfaction in adulthood by providing information about the types of stimulation **3** that lead to sexual gratification. **TRUTH OR FICTION** REVISITED: Researchers also find that women achieve orgasm more reliably through masturbation than through sexual intercourse (Hogarth & Ingham, 2009; ter Kuile et al., 2012).

FIGURE 9.2 What Are the Connections between Masturbation during Adolescence and Sexual Satisfaction during Marriage? There is a positive correlation between masturbation during adolescence and sexual satisfaction during marriage. What hypotheses can we make about the causal connections? Does experience with masturbation teach people about their sexual needs so that they are more likely to obtain adequate sexual stimulation during marriage? Are people who masturbate early generally more open to exploring their sexuality and learning about the types of stimulation that arouse them? Such attitudes might also increase the likelihood that people would seek the coital stimulation they need to achieve sexual gratification during marriage.

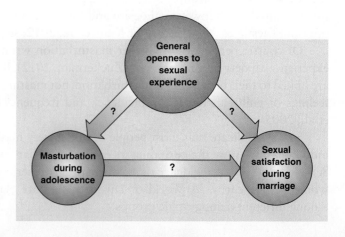

In our efforts to correct misinformation about masturbation, let us not suggest that there is anything wrong with choosing *not* to masturbate. Readers are encouraged to make their own choices on the basis of their own values.

Masturbation Techniques

Sex is like bridge—if you don't have a good partner, you'd better have a good hand.

　　—Bathroom graffiti

The comment observed once upon a time on bathroom walls may be humorous, but in terms of masturbation techniques, it is only part of the story.

TECHNIQUES USED BY MALES

Although masturbation techniques vary widely, most men do report that they masturbate by manual manipulation of the penis (see Figure 9.3). Kinsey and his colleagues (1948) reported that they typically take one or two minutes to reach orgasm. Men tend to grip the penile shaft with one hand, jerking it up and down in a milking motion. Some men move the whole hand up and down the penis, while others use just two fingers, generally the thumb and index finger. Men usually shift from a gentler rubbing action during the flaccid or semi-erect state of arousal to a more vigorous milking motion once full erection takes place. Men are also likely to stroke the glans and frenulum lightly at the outset, but their grip tightens and their motions speed up as orgasm nears. At orgasm, the penile shaft may be gripped tightly, but the glans has become sensitive, and contact with it is usually avoided. (Likewise, women usually avoid stimulating the clitoris directly during orgasm because of increased sensitivity.)

Some men use soapsuds (which may become irritating) as a lubricant for masturbation during baths or showers. Other lubricants, such as petroleum jelly or K-Y jelly, are less irritating and also more effective at reducing friction and simulating the moist conditions of coitus.

A few men prefer to masturbate by rubbing the penis and testicles against clothing or bedding. A few men rub their genitals against inflatable dolls sold in

FIGURE 9.3 Male Masturbation. Masturbation techniques vary widely, but most men report that they masturbate by manual manipulation of the penis. They tend to grip the penile shaft with one hand and jerk it up and down in a milking motion.

sex shops. These dolls may come with artificial mouths or vaginas that can be filled with liquid to mimic the sensations of coitus. Artificial vaginas are also for sale.

Some men strap vibrators to the backs of their hands (Reece et al., 2009). Electrical vibrators save labor but do not simulate the type of up-and-down motions of the penis that men favor. Hence, they are not used very often. Most men use fantasy, photos, videos, or the Internet, but not sex-shop devices. With the exception of a real-life partner—a notable exception, indeed—the Internet offers one-stop sex shopping for millions.

TECHNIQUES USED BY FEMALES

Techniques of female masturbation also vary widely, but some general trends have been noted. Most women masturbate by massaging the mons, labia minora, and clitoral region with circular or back-and-forth motions. They may also straddle the clitoris with their fingers, stroking the shaft rather than the glans (see Figure 9.4). The glans may be lightly touched early during arousal, but because of its exquisite sensitivity, it is rarely stroked for any length of time during masturbation. Women typically achieve clitoral stimulation by rubbing or stroking the clitoral shaft or pulling or tugging on the vaginal lips. Some women also massage other sensitive areas, such as their breasts or nipples, with the free hand. Many women, like men, fantasize during masturbation.

4　**TRUTH OR FICTION** REVISITED: In contrast to the male myth that women usually masturbate by simulating penile thrusting through the insertion of fingers or phallic objects into their vaginas, relatively few women actually do. Kinsey and his colleagues (1953) reported that only one in five women inserted objects into the vagina during masturbation. Some women experimented with vaginal insertion but gave it up as they became more familiar with their sexual anatomy and capabilities. Others practiced the technique because their male partners found it sexually stimulating to watch them. Still, some women reported erotic pleasure from deep vaginal penetration.

Even when women use insertion, they usually precede or combine it with clitoral stimulation. Sex shops sell dildos, which women can use to rub their vulvas or to insert. Penis-shaped vibrators may be used in the same way. Many women masturbate during baths; some spray their genitals with jets of water.

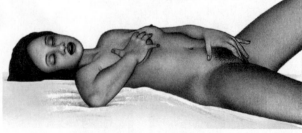

FIGURE 9.4 Female Masturbation. Techniques of female masturbation vary so widely that Masters and Johnson reported never observing two women masturbating in precisely the same way. Most women masturbate by massaging the mons, labia minora, and clitoral region, however, either with circular or back-and-forth motions.

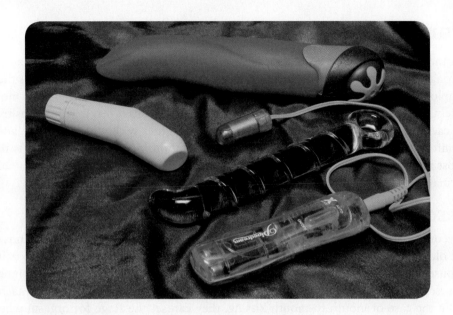

FIGURE 9.5 Electric Vibrators and Other Sex Toys. Both females and males use devices like these in the place of real penises, to try to increase the volume of the penis, or for other sexual ends. If they are to be used at all, they should be used with extreme caution.

Handheld electrical vibrators (see Figure 9.5) massage the genitals in a way that can be erotic (Herbenick et al., 2009; Shick et al., 2011). But some women find this type of stimulation too intense and favor vibrators that strap to the back of the hand, helping the fingers to vibrate during manual stimulation of the genitals. But this type of vibration may numb the hand attached to the vibrator. Women experiment with different vibrators to find one with the shape and intensity of vibration that suits them. Women who have sex with women seem more likely than women who have sex with men to use vibrators when they are masturbating or having partnered sex (Shick et al., 2011).

Women may stimulate their nipples during masturbation or seek nipple stimulation from their partners during partnered sex. fMRI research (functional magnetic resonance imaging research) has shown the stimulation of the nipples not only activates the parts of the brain that represent the chest, but also those parts of the brain that indicate arousal in the genital reason (Komisaruk et al., 2011). Thus, there is a clear neurological basis for women's reporting that stimulation of the nipples is sexually arousing. We suspect that stimulation of men's nipples is also connected to the genitals in the male brain, but we have yet to see evidence supporting this suspicion.

Real Students, Real Questions

Q *Are vibrators bad for your health in any way?*

A Could be. Use some common sense. As a rule of thumb, vibrators that penetrate the body are more potentially harmful than vibrators that strap onto the back of the hand (or foot, or whatever). And vibrators that have sharp or pointed edges, even if they're called something apparently harmless, like "ticklers," are more potentially dangerous than those that have smooth edges or those that don't directly touch the body at all. If you're going to use a vibrator, start by seeing how it affects a nongenital area of the body. When you move it to the genital region, apply it gently at first. You may also have a partner use a vibrator to provide you with sexual stimulation, but be very specific and cautious in showing him or her what to do. When in doubt, stop, or at least slow down.

Partnered Sex

Partners' feelings for one another, and the quality of their relationships, may be stronger determinants of their sexual arousal and response than the techniques they employ (Chivers & Timmers, 2012; Stephenson et al., 2012). Partners are most likely to experience mutually enjoyable sexual interactions when they are sensitive to each other's sexual needs and incorporate techniques with which they are both comfortable. As with other aspects of sharing relationships, communication is the most important "sexual" technique. Let us begin our discussion of sex with others as many sexual episodes begin—with a discussion of foreplay.

PRECOITAL AND NONCOITAL PARTNERED SEX

Precoital partnered sex is also known as "foreplay." The term *foreplay* sounds a bit old-fashioned. It implies that the kinds of methods that partners use to sexually arouse one another—and themselves, of course—are intended to culminate in intercourse. Not necessarily. Most of the methods we will discuss can lead to orgasm, or in the case of mouth-to-mouth kissing, they can set the stage for orgasm when another technique is applied. In fact, many people prefer one or more of these methods to intercourse, at least some of the time. Females having sex with females, of course, will not be having penile–vaginal intercourse, although they may choose to simulate intercourse manually or with the use of a sex toy.

But various forms of noncoital sex, such as cuddling, kissing, petting, and oral–genital contact, are in fact used as **foreplay**. The pattern and duration of foreplay vary widely within and across cultures.

There is a general assumption in the United States and Canada that women in heterosexual relationships want more foreplay than men do, which may be more or less the case. But a side effect of this stereotype is that men often wind up receiving less foreplay than they would actually like (Miller & Byers, 2004). Since women usually require a longer period of stimulation during sex with a partner to reach orgasm, increasing the duration of foreplay may increase female coital responsiveness. On the other hand, men have become more aware of this since Kinsey's day, and women sometimes want men to "get on with it" (Miller & Byers, 2004).

A telephone survey with more than 1,000 French subjects in heterosexual relationships found that simultaneous orgasms and feelings of closeness were highly important for about 36% of the respondents (Colson et al., 2006). Foreplay, by contrast, was mentioned as being crucial by only about 13%, which, of course, begs the question as to whether the couple would reach simultaneous orgasm and closeness without some form of foreplay.

Although, as noted, kissing, genital touching, and oral–genital contact may all be experienced as ends in themselves and not as preludes to coitus, some people object to petting for petting's sake, equating it with masturbation or at least as a form of sexual activity without a "product" or "result." Many people behave as though all sexual contact must lead to coitus, perhaps because of the importance that our culture places on it and because of some people's traditional idea that purely recreational (nonprocreative) sex is of questionable moral value.

KISSING

Kissing is almost universal in our culture, but it is unknown in some cultures, such as among the Thonga of Africa and the Siriono of Bolivia. Variations in styles of kissing also exist across cultures (Ford & Beach, 1951). Kissing is now practiced in Japan because of the influence of Western culture but was previously unknown there. Instead of kissing, the Balinese of Indonesia used to bring their faces close

Foreplay Physical interactions that are sexually stimulating and set the stage for intercourse.

enough to each other to smell each other's perfume and feel the warmth of each other's skin. This practice has been dubbed "rubbing noses" by Europeans. Among some preliterate societies, kissing consists of sucking the partner's lips and tongue and allowing saliva to pass from one mouth to the other.

Couples may kiss for their own enjoyment or as a prelude to intercourse, in which case it is a part of foreplay. In *simple kissing,* the partners keep their mouths closed. Simple kissing may develop into caresses of the lips with the tongue, or into nibbling of the lower lip. In what Kinsey called *deep kissing,* which is also called *French* or *soul kissing,* the partners part their lips and insert their tongues into each other's mouths. Some prefer the lips parted slightly. Others open their mouths widely.

Kissing may also be an affectionate gesture without erotic significance, as in kissing someone good night. Some people kiss relatives and close friends affectionately on the lips. Others limit kissing relatives to the cheek. Sustained kissing on the lips and deep kissing are almost always erotic gestures.

Kissing is not limited to the partner's mouth. Kinsey found that more than nine husbands in ten kissed their wives' breasts. Women may prefer several minutes of body contact and gentle caresses before desiring to have their partner kiss their breasts, or lick or suck their nipples. Women also usually do not prefer sucking until they are highly aroused. Many women are reluctant to tell their partners that sucking hurts because they do not want to interfere with their partner's pleasure. 👁

TOUCHING

Hugging or holding another person can feel good. Touching or caressing erogenous zones with the hands or other parts of the body can be highly arousing. Even simple handholding can be sexually stimulating for couples who are sexually attracted to one another. The hands are rich in nerve endings.

Touching is a common form of foreplay. Both men and women generally prefer manual or oral stimulation of the genitals as a prelude to intercourse. Women generally prefer that direct caressing of the genitals be focused

Watch the **Video**
With Valentine's Day Approaching, Celebrities Tell the Story Behind Their First Kiss
on **MyDevelopmentLab**

Kissing. Kissing is a nearly universal part of lovemaking. Nonerotic kissing may also be used with relatives and friends.

How Touching? Touching is a common form of foreplay. Most people like manual or oral stimulation of the genital organs as a prelude to sexual intercourse.

around the clitoris but not directly on the extremely sensitive clitoral glans. Men sometimes assume (often mistakenly) that their partners want them to insert their finger or fingers into the vagina as a form of foreplay. But not all women enjoy this form of stimulation. Some women go along with it because it's what their partners want or something they think their partners want.

Masters and Johnson (1979) noted sex differences with respect to preferences in foreplay. Men typically prefer direct stroking of their genitals by their partner early in lovemaking. Women, however, tend to prefer that their partners caress their genitals after a period of general body contact that includes holding, hugging, and nongenital massage. This is not a hard and fast (or slow) rule, but it concurs with other observations that men tend to be more genitally oriented than women. Women are more likely to view sex within a broader framework of affection and love.

Techniques of Manual Stimulation of the Genitals Here again, variability in technique is the rule, so partners need to communicate their preferences. The man's partner may use two hands to stimulate his genitals. One may be used to fondle the scrotum, by gently squeezing the skin between the fingers (taking care not to apply pressure to the testes themselves). The other hand may circle the coronal ridge and engage in gentle stroking of the penis, followed by more vigorous up and down movements as the man becomes more aroused.

The penis may also be gently rolled back and forth between the palms as if one were making a ball of clay into a sausage—increasing pressure as arousal progresses. Note that men who are highly aroused or who have just had an orgasm may find direct stimulation of the penile glans uncomfortable.

The woman may prefer that her partner approach genital stimulation gradually, following stimulation of other body parts. Genital stimulation may begin with light, stroking motions of the inner thighs and move on to the vaginal lips (labia) and the clitoral area. Women may enjoy pressure against the mons pubis from the heel of the hand, or tactile stimulation of the labia, which are sensitive to stroking motions. Clitoral stimulation can focus on the clitoral shaft or the region surrounding the shaft, rather than the clitoris itself, because of the extreme sensitivity of the clitoral glans to touch.

Moreover, the clitoris should not be stroked if it is dry, lest it become irritated. Since it produces no lubrication of its own, a finger may enter the outer portion of the vagina to apply some vaginal lubrication to the clitoral region.

Some, but not all, women enjoy having a finger inserted into the vagina, which can stroke the vaginal walls or simulate thrusting of the penis. Vaginal insertion is usually not preferred, if at all, until the woman has become highly aroused. Many women desire that their partners discontinue stroking motions while they are experiencing orgasm, but others wish stimulation to continue. Men and women may physically guide their partners' hands or otherwise express their preferences as to the types of strokes they find most pleasurable.

If a finger is to be inserted into the vagina, it should be clean. Fingernails should be well trimmed. Inserting fingers that have been in the anus into the vagina is dangerous. The fingers may transfer microbes from the woman's digestive tract, where they do no harm, to the woman's reproductive tract, where they can cause serious infections.

Fisting Some individuals engage in "fisting," which is the insertion of the fist or hand into the rectum, usually after the bowels have been evacuated with an enema. Fisting is more common among male–male than male–female couples, and it carries the risk of infection or injury to the rectum or anus. A survey of 75 gay men in Australia found that fisting was usually done with gloves, although fingering was not (Richters et al., 2003).

STIMULATION OF THE BREASTS

Men are more likely to stimulate women's breasts than to have their own breasts fondled, even though the breasts (and especially the nipples) are erotically sensitive in both females and males. Most, but not all, women enjoy stimulation of the breasts (see Figure 9.6). Masters and Johnson (1966) report that some women are capable of achieving orgasm from stimulation of the breasts alone.

The hands and the mouth can be used to stimulate the breasts and the nipples. Since the desired type and intensity of stimulation of the breasts varies from person to person, partners need to communicate their preferences.

ORAL–GENITAL STIMULATION

Oral stimulation of the male genitals is called **fellatio**. Fellatio is referred to by slang terms such as "a blow job," "sucking," "sucking off," and "giving head." Oral stimulation of the female genitals is called **cunnilingus**, which is referred to by slang expressions such as "eating" (a woman) and "going down" on her.

The popularity of oral–genital stimulation has increased dramatically since Kinsey's day, especially among young married couples. Kinsey and his colleagues (1948, 1953) found that at least 60% of married, *college-educated* couples had experienced oral–genital contact. Such experiences were reported by only about 20% of couples who had only a high school education and 10% who had only a grade-school education. The more recent National Survey of Sexual Health and Behavior, from the Center for Sexual Health Promotion (2011) founded by Kinsey, shows that within any given recent year, upward of 70% of men and women will have given and received oral sex. The numbers are especially high in the 20s and the 30s, when the sex drive is high, people are sexually experienced, and, presumably, the body remains relatively physically attractive.

Among married couples, 80% of the men and 71% of the women have performed oral sex. Similarly, 80% of the men and 74% of the women have received oral sex (Laumann et al., 1994). **TRUTH OR FICTION REVISITED:** Oral sex is in fact the norm for today's young couples, statistically speaking. A majority of young couples report participating in this form of sexual expression.

As with touching, oral–genital stimulation can be used as a prelude to intercourse or as a sexual end in itself. If orgasm is reached through oral–genital stimulation, a partner may be concerned about tasting or swallowing the ejaculate. There is no evidence that swallowing semen is harmful to one's health unless the man has an infection that can be transmitted through oral contact with semen. Oral contact with the genitals of an infected partner, even without semen, may transmit harmful organisms. Couples are therefore advised to practice "safer sex" techniques (see Chapter 16) unless they know that they and their partners are free of sexually transmitted infections. 👁

Techniques of Fellatio Although the word *fellatio* is derived from a Latin root meaning "to suck," sucking is generally not highly arousing. The up-and-down movements of the penis in the partner's mouth, or the licking of the penis, are generally the most stimulating (see Figure 9.7 on page 244). Gentle licking of the scrotum may also be highly arousing.

The mouth stimulates the penis because it contains warm, moist mucous membranes, as does the vagina. Muscles of the mouth and jaw can vary pressure and movements. Erection may be stimulated by gently pulling the penis with the mouth

FIGURE 9.6 Erotic Touch. Erotic touch is a pleasurable, intimate behavior by itself and need not necessarily lead to other sexual activities.

 5

▶ Watch the Video
Sexually Transmissible Infections: Ken, STI Counselor
on **MyDevelopmentLab**

Fellatio Oral stimulation of the male genitals.

Cunnilingus Oral stimulation of the female genitals.

A World of Diversity

Gay Males, Lesbians, and Partnered Sex

Gay men apparently make more use of stimulation of their partner's nipples than heterosexual women do. Gay male couples tend to engage in sexual activities such as kissing, hugging, petting, mutual masturbation, fellatio, and anal intercourse. Laboratory observations of sexual relations between gay males by Masters and Johnson (1979) showed that gay males spent a good deal of time caressing their partners' bodies before approaching the genitals. After hugging and kissing, 31 of 42 gay male couples observed by Masters and Johnson used oral or manual nipple stimulation.

Although some heterosexual men enjoy having their breasts and nipples stimulated by their partners, many, perhaps most, do not. Many men are unaware that their breasts are erotically sensitive. Others may feel uncomfortable receiving a form of stimulation that they have learned to associate with the stereotypical feminine sexual role.

Sexual techniques practiced by lesbians vary. Lesbian couples report kissing, manual and oral breast stimulation, and manual and oral stimulation of the genitals (Kinsey et al., 1953). Manual genital stimulation is the most common and frequent sexual activity among lesbian couples (Bell & Weinberg, 1978). Most lesbian couples also engage in genital apposition. That is, they position themselves so as to rub their genitals together rhythmically (Kinsey et al., 1953). Like gay males, lesbians spend a good deal of time holding, kissing, and caressing each other's bodies before they approach the breasts and genitals By contrast, heterosexual males tend to move quickly to stimulate their partners' breasts or start directly with genital stimulation (Masters & Johnson, 1979).

Like heterosexual women, lesbians are less genitally oriented and less fixated on orgasm than men. Lesbians generally begin stimulating their partners with more general genital stimulation rather than direct clitoral stimulation, whereas heterosexual males often begin by stimulating the clitoris (Masters & Johnson, 1979). Nor do lesbian couples generally engage in deep penetration of the vagina with fingers. Rather, they may use more shallow vaginal penetration, focusing stimulation on the vaginal lips and entrance.

TRUTH OR FICTION REVISITED: 6
Images of lesbians strapping on dildos for vaginal penetration exist more in the imagination of uninformed heterosexual people than in the sexual repertoire of lesbian couples (Masters & Johnson, 1979). The emotional components of lovemaking—gentle touching, cuddling, and hugging—are important elements of sexual sharing in lesbian relationships.

(being careful not to touch the penis with the teeth) and simultaneously providing manual stimulation.

Higher levels of sexual arousal or orgasm can be promoted by thrusting the penis in and out of the mouth. The speed of the motions can be varied, and manual stimulation near the base of the penis (firmly encircling the lower portion of the penis or providing pressure behind the scrotum) can also be stimulating.

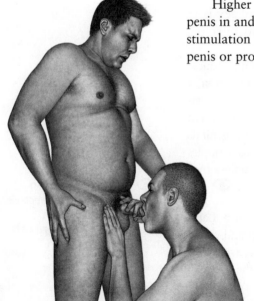

FIGURE 9.7 Fellatio. Fellatio involves stimulation of the male penis and surrounding genital area with the mouth, lips, and tongue.

A World of Diversity
Demographic Factors and Oral Sex

What are the roles of education and race/ethnicity in the incidence of oral sex? Some answers reported by people in the NHSLS are suggested in Table 9.2. As with masturbation, the incidence of oral sex correlates with level of education. That is, more highly educated individuals are more likely to have practiced oral sex. Why? Perhaps education encourages experimentation. Perhaps education dispels myths that nontraditional behavior patterns are necessarily harmful. Note also that African American men and women are less likely to have engaged in oral sex than people from other racial/ethnic backgrounds. African American men and women were also less likely than other ethnic groups to report

masturbating during the past 12 months. African Americans may adhere more strictly to traditional ideas as to what kinds of sexual behavior are and are not proper.

Findings from a national survey of more than 3,000 sexually active men between the ages of 20 and 39 conducted by the Battelle Human Affairs Research Center in Seattle are consistent with the NHSLS findings. Seventy-five percent of the men reported performing oral sex. Seventy-nine percent reported receiving oral sex (Billy et al., 1993). Mirroring the racial differences observed by Laumann and his colleagues (1994), African Americans in other surveys are also less likely than European Americans to have performed or received oral sex (Ompad et al., 2006).

Some people may gag during fellatio, a reflex that is triggered by pressure of the penis against the back of the tongue or against the throat. Gagging may be avoided if the man's partner grasps the shaft of the penis with one hand and controls the depth of penetration. Gagging is less likely to occur if the partner performing fellatio is on the top, rather than below, or if there is verbal communication about how deep the man may comfortably penetrate. Gagging may also be overcome by allowing gradually deeper penetration of the penis on successive occasions while keeping the throat muscles relaxed.

Techniques of Cunnilingus Women can be highly aroused by their partner's tongue because it is soft, warm, and well lubricated (see Figure 9.8 on page 246). In contrast to a finger, the tongue can almost never be used too harshly. A woman may thus be more receptive to direct clitoral contact by a tongue. Cunnilingus provides such intense stimulation that many women find it to be the best means for achieving orgasm.

Table 9.2

Percent of NHSLS Respondents Who Report Experience with Oral Sex

Demographic Factor	Performed Oral Sex		Received Oral Sex	
	Men	Women	Men	Women
Education				
Less than high school	59.2	42.1	60.7	49.6
High school graduate	75.3	59.6	76.6	67.1
Some college	80.0	78.2	84.0	81.6
College graduate	83.7	78.9	84.6	83.1
Advanced college degree	80.5	79.0	81.4	81.9
Race/Ethnicity				
European American	81.4	75.3	81.4	78.9
African American	50.5	34.4	66.3	48.9
Latin American	70.7	59.7	73.2	63.7
Asian American	63.6	—*	72.7	—*

*There were not enough Asian American women in the sample to report meaningful findings.

Source: Adapted by permission from E. O. Laumann, J. H. Gagnon, R. T. Michael, & S. Michaels (1994). *The social organization of sexuality: Sexual practices in the United States.* Chicago: University of Chicago Press, Table 3.6, p. 98.

FIGURE 9.8 Cunnilingus.
Cunnilingus is the stimulation of the vulva with the mouth, lips, and tongue.

👁️‍🗨️ **Watch** the **Video**
Vaccine Debate: Cervical Cancer
on **MyDevelopmentLab**

In performing cunnilingus, the partner may begin by kissing and licking the woman's abdomen and inner thighs, gradually nearing the vulva. Gentle tugging at or sucking of the labia minora can be stimulating, but the partner should take care not to bite. Many women enjoy licking of the clitoral region, and others desire sucking of the clitoris itself. The tongue may also be inserted into the vagina where it may imitate thrusting.

We should note here that there has been a recent rise in oropharyngeal cancer (cancer of the throat) among men who have engaged in cunnilingus with women who are infected with the human papilloma virus (HPV) (Chaturvedi et al., 2011). In Chapter 3 we had noted that HPV is also connected with cancer of the cervix. Researchers also point out, however, that despite the incidence of throat cancer, there are fewer than 10,000 cases per year, and that most people infected with HPV do not develop cancer (Gillison, 2011). Even so, health professionals are wondering whether it would be worthwhile to vaccinate boys with Gardasil or Cervarix, one of the vaccinations used with girls to help prevent development of cervical cancer (Cullen, 2011). 👁️‍🗨️

"69" The term *sixty-nine* describes simultaneous oral–genital stimulation. The numerals 6 and 9 are used because they resemble two partners who are upside-down and facing each other.

The "69" position has the psychologically positive feature of allowing couples to experience simultaneous stimulation, but it can be awkward if two people are not similar in size. Some couples avoid "69" because it deprives each partner of the opportunity to focus fully on receiving or providing sexual pleasure.

The "69" technique may be practiced side by side or with one partner on top of the other. There are no strict rules, and couples often alternate positions.

Abstaining from Oral Sex Despite the popularity of oral sex among couples today, many people choose to abstain. Some people object on grounds of cleanliness. They view the genitals as "dirty" because of their proximity to the urinary and anal openings. Concerns about offensive odors or cleanliness may be relieved by thoroughly washing the genitals beforehand. Some abstain because they are concerned or embarrassed about providing (or receiving) a direct view of parts of the body we have been reared to keep private.

Some prefer not to taste or swallow semen because they find it to be dirty, sinful, or repulsive. Others are put off by the taste or texture. Semen has a salty taste and a texture similar to the white of an egg. If couples are to engage in unprotected oral sex, open discussion of feelings can enhance pleasure and diminish anxiety. For

A Closer Look

Good Vibes

The use of vibrators during sexual activity is one of the more apparent examples of the old General Electric slogan, "Better living through electricity." Surveys with nationally representative samples reveal that half of U.S. residents use vibrators, slightly less than half of men (Reece et al., 2009) and more than half of women (Herbenick et al., 2009). Vibrators are incorporated into both solo and partnered sexual activities (Herbenick et al., 2011). These include—but are not limited to!—clitoral stimulation, (attempted) stimulation of the G-spot (we say "attempted" because, as noted in Chapter 3, the existence of a G-spot remains controversial), securing of the base of a condom (to prevent leakage), anal stimulation (eternal and internal), the simulation of cunnilingus, and couples sex play (Herbenick et al., 2011).

Given these varied usages, and the penetration (excuse the pun) of the vibrator into sexual activity in the United States, we must consider the vibrator to be a normal (at least statistically normal) aid in the achievement of sexual pleasure. Looking at vibrator use a bit more deeply, the survey of 1,047 men aged 18–60 found that 45% had incorporated a vibrator into their sexual activities over the course of their lifetime, and 10% had done so in the past month (Reece et al., 2009). Responses of 2,056 women aged 18–60 to a survey found that 52.5% had incorporated vibrators into their sexual activities over their lifetime (Herbenick et al., 2009).

What do we know about the men and women who used vibrators? Responses to other survey questions showed that men who used vibrators were more likely to pay attention to their sexual health, such as being more likely to engage in testicular self-exams. Men who had used vibrators also reported more positively on their erectile functioning, their satisfaction with intercourse, their ability to reach orgasm, and

their sexual desire. As with the men, use of a vibrator among women was connected with more healthful behaviors such as obtaining gynecological exams and doing self-genital exams. And as with the men, vibrator use was positively correlated with sexual desire and arousal and orgasm, and negatively correlated with sexual pain. More than 70% of the women reported that they had never had negative side effects from vibrator use.

We also have a study of beliefs about the use of vibrators by women (Herbenick et al., 2011; Table 9.3). Participants included a nationally representative sample of both women and men. The only way to sum up the results is to say that the great majority of both genders agreed with the positive statements about women's usage of vibrators, and that the great majority *disagreed* with the *negative* statements. It would appear that today, the general public favors, or is not concerned about, women's use of vibrators.

Table 9.3

Women's and Men's Beliefs about Women's Use of Vibrators

Belief items	Female respondents		Male respondents	
	Disagree or strongly disagree	Agree or strongly agree	Disagree or strongly disagree	Agree or strongly agree
POSITIVE BELIEFS				
Makes it easier for a woman to have an orgasm	27%	73%	18.7%	81.3%
Can enhance a woman's sexual relationship with her partner	25.6%	74.4%	18.1%	81.9%
Helps women to become more sexually independent	33.5%	66.4%	39.2%	60.8%
Can take the pressure off a woman's partner to give her an orgasm	32.2%	67.8%	32.4%	67.5%
Is a healthy part of many women's sex lives	23.4%	76.6%	19.8%	80.2%
Can make sex with a partner more exciting	24.8%	75.2%	19.6%	80.4%
NEGATIVE BELIEFS				
Makes women too dependent on them for pleasure	66.3%	33.7%	65%	35%
Is embarrassing for women	71.7%	28.3%	76.6%	23.4%
Is something that only women who are lonely do	84.7%	15.3%	85.4%	14.6%
Is intimidating to women's partners	63.3%	36.7%	70.4%	29.6%

Source: Adapted from Debra Herbenick, Michael Reece, Vanessa Schick, Kristen N. Jozkowski, Susan E. Middelstadt, Stephanie A. Sanders, Brian S. Dodge, Annahita Ghassemi & J. Dennis Fortenberry (2011): Beliefs About Women's Vibrator Use: Results From a Nationally Representative Probability Survey in the United States, *Journal of Sex & Marital Therapy*, *37*(5), 329–345, p. 339, Table 4. Journal of sex & marital therapy by ROUTLEDGE. Reproduced with permission of ROUTLEDGE in the format republish in a book/textbook via Copyright Clearance Center.

example, a man can be encouraged to warn his partner or remove his penis from her or his mouth when he is nearing ejaculation.

Let us dispel a couple of myths about semen. For one thing, it is impossible to become pregnant by swallowing semen. For another, semen is not fattening. The average ejaculate contains about five calories. On the other hand, it is not our intention to encourage swallowing of semen. The aesthetics of swallowing semen have little or nothing to do with concerns about pregnancy or weight. They involve the preferences of the individual.

Sexual Intercourse: Positions and Techniques

Sexual intercourse, or *coitus* (from the Latin *coire*, meaning "to go together"), is sexual activity in which the penis is inserted into the vagina. Each position of sexual intercourse must allow the genitals to be aligned so that the penis is contained by the vagina. In addition to varying positions, couples also vary the depth and rate of thrusting (in-and-out motions) and additional sexual stimulation.

Table 9.4 shows the monthly frequency of sexual intercourse reported by heterosexual men and women aged 25 to 45 (Eisenberg et al., 2010). Overall, younger people within the age group were more likely than older people to engage in sexual intercourse. Married people had a higher monthly frequency than unmarried people. Latin Americans were most likely to report having sex and Asian Americans least likely. People with less education had a higher frequency of coitus (but don't drop out of college!). There was also a relationship between frequency of coitus and body mass index (BMI). People with a BMI above 25 are considered overweight, and those with a BMI over 30 are labeled obese. Men of normal weight were more sexually active than overweight people, but, strangely, obese people had a higher frequency of sexual activity than people in the overweight category. The thinnest women reported the lowest frequency of sexual activity, suggesting, perhaps, that women's efforts to meet the very thin cultural ideal are having a negative effect on their health. Pregnant women had less frequent sex than women who were not pregnant, but notice that pregnant women still had sex on about a weekly basis.

Although the number of possible coital positions is virtually endless, we will focus on four of the most commonly used positions: the male-superior (man-on-top) position, the female-superior (woman-on-top) position, the lateral-entry (side-entry) position, and the rear-entry position. We discuss anal intercourse as well, a sexual technique used by both male–female and male–male couples. ◉

THE MALE-SUPERIOR (MAN-ON-TOP) POSITION

The male-superior position ("superiority" is used purely in relation to body position, but has sometimes been taken as a symbol of male domination) has also been called the **missionary position**. In this position, the partners face one another. The man lies above the woman, perhaps supporting himself on his hands and knees rather than applying his full weight against his partner (see Figure 9.9). Still, movement is easier for the man than for the woman, which suggests that he is responsible for directing their activity.

Many students of human sexuality suggest that it is preferable for the woman to guide the penis into the vagina, rather than having the man do so. The idea is that the woman can feel the location of the vaginal opening and determine the proper angle of entry. It is easier to accomplish this if the woman feels comfortable "taking charge" of lovemaking. With the breaking down of the traditional stereotype of the female as passive, women are feeling more comfortable assuming this role. On

◉—▭ **Watch** the **Video**
Women, Sex, and Satisfaction
on **MyDevelopmentLab**

Missionary position The coital position in which the man is on top. Also termed the *male-superior position.*

Table 9.4

Heterosexual Monthly Coital Frequency among Men and Women Aged 25–45 Years

Characteristic		Men	Women
Age	25–29	6.81	6.92
	30–34	6.30	6.17
	35–39	5.11	6.22
	40–45	4.83	6.22
Married	No	5.31	5.46
	Yes	5.81	6.27
Race	European American	5.23	6.39
	African American	5.70	5.74
	Latin American	7.40	7.27
	Asian American	4.05	5.12
Education	Less than high school	6.91	6.72
	High School	5.70	6.70
	More than high school	5.13	5.42
Body Mass Index (BMI)	18 or less	7.00	5.00
	19–24	6.12	6.54
	25–29[1]	5.35	6.59
	30 or above[2]	5.68	6.16
Currently pregnant	No	6.17	6.43
	Yes	4.11	5.05

[1]Overweight
[2]Obese

Source: Adapted from Eisenberg, M., Shindel, A. W., Smith, J. F., Breyer, B. N., and Lipshultz, L. I. (2010). Socioeconomic, anthropomorphic, and demographic predictors of adult sexual activity in the United States: Data from the national survey of family growth. *Journal of Sexual Medicine 7*, 50–58, Tables 1 and 3.

the other hand, if the couple prefers that the man guide his penis into his partner's vagina, the slight loss of efficiency need not trouble them, as long as he moves prudently to avoid hurting his partner.

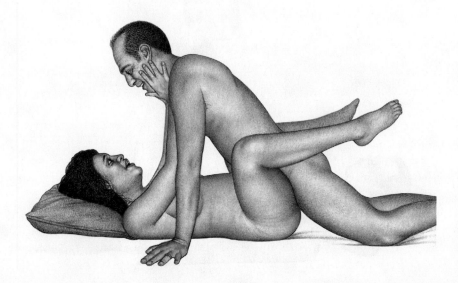

FIGURE 9.9 The Male-Superior (Man-on-Top) Coital Position. The man-on-top position requires somewhat more physical effort on the part of the male; it is the most common position for coitus in Western cultures.

The male-superior position has the advantage of permitting the couple to face one another so that kissing is easier. The woman may run her hands along her partner's body, stroking his buttocks and perhaps cupping a hand beneath his scrotum to increase stimulation as he reaches orgasm.

But the male-superior position makes it difficult for the man to caress his partner while simultaneously supporting himself with his hands. So the position may not be favored by women who enjoy having their partners provide manual clitoral stimulation during coitus. This position can be highly stimulating to the man, which can make it difficult for him to delay ejaculation. The position also limits the opportunity for the woman to control the angle, rate, and depth of penetration. It may thus be more difficult for her to attain the type of stimulation she may need to achieve orgasm, especially if she favors combining penile thrusting with manual clitoral stimulation. Finally, this position is not advisable during the late stages of pregnancy. At that time the woman's distended abdomen would force the man to arch severely above her, lest he place undue pressure on her abdomen.

THE FEMALE-SUPERIOR (WOMAN-ON-TOP) POSITION

In the female-superior position, the couple face one another with the woman on top. The woman straddles the male from above, controlling the angle of penile entry and the depth of thrusting (see Figure 9.10). Some women maintain a sitting position; others lie on top of their partners. Many women vary their position.

In the female-superior position the woman is psychologically, and to some degree physically, in charge. She can move as rapidly or as slowly as she wishes with little effort, adjusting her body so as to vary the angle and depth of penetration. She can reach behind her to stroke her partner's scrotum, or lean down to kiss him.

As in the male-superior position, kissing is relatively easy. This position has additional advantages. The man may readily reach the woman's buttocks or clitoris in order to provide manual stimulation. Assuming that the woman is shorter than he is, it is rather easy for him to stimulate her breasts orally (a pillow tucked behind his head may help). The woman can, in effect, guarantee that she receives adequate clitoral stimulation, either by the penis or manually by his hand or her own. This position thus facilitates orgasm in the woman. As it tends to be less stimulating for the male, it may help him to control ejaculation. For these reasons, this position is commonly used by couples who are learning to overcome sexual difficulties.

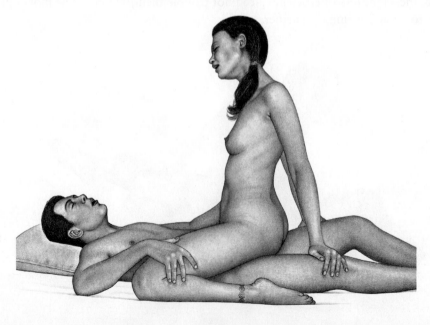

FIGURE 9.10 The Female-Superior (Woman-on-Top) Coital Position. The female-superior position allows the woman more control over angle and depth of penetration and the greater control over the orgasm.

FIGURE 9.11 The Lateral-Entry (Side-by-Side) Coital Position. The side-by-side position requires less physical effort for both partners and allows more freedom of movement for mutual caressing during intercourse.

THE LATERAL-ENTRY (SIDE-ENTRY) POSITION

In the lateral-entry position, the man and woman lie side by side, facing one another (see Figure 9.11). This position has the advantages of allowing each partner relatively free movement and easy access to the other. The man and woman may kiss freely, and they can stroke each other's bodies with a free arm. The position is not physically taxing, because both partners are resting easily on the bedding. Thus, it is an excellent position for prolonged coitus or for coitus when couples are somewhat fatigued.

Let us note some disadvantages to this position. First, inserting the penis into the vagina while lying side by side may be awkward. Many couples thus begin coitus in another position and then change into the lateral-entry position—often because they wish to prolong coitus. Second, one or both partners may have an arm lying beneath the other that will "fall asleep" or become numb because of the constricted blood supply. Third, women may not receive adequate clitoral stimulation from the penis in this position. Of course, such stimulation may be provided manually (by hand) or by switching to another position after a while. Fourth, it may be difficult to achieve deeper penetration of the penis. The lateral position is useful during pregnancy (at least until the final stages, when the distension of the woman's abdomen may make lateral entry difficult).

THE REAR-ENTRY POSITION

In the rear-entry position, the man faces the woman's rear. In one variation (Figure 9.12), the woman supports herself on her hands and knees while the man supports himself on his knees, entering her from behind. In another, the couple lie alongside one another and the woman lifts one leg, draping it backward over her partner's thigh. The latter position is particularly useful during the later stages of pregnancy.

The rear-entry position may be highly stimulating for both partners. The man may enjoy viewing and pressing his abdomen against his partner's buttocks. He man can reach around or underneath to provide additional stimulation of the clitoris or breasts, and she may reach behind (if she is on her hands and knees) to stroke or grasp her partner's testicles.

Potential disadvantages to this position include the following: First, this position is the mating position used by most other mammals, which is why it is sometimes referred to as *doggy style*. Some couples may feel uncomfortable about using the position because of its association with animal mating patterns. The position is also impersonal in the sense that the partners do not face one another, which may create a sense of emotional distance. Since the man is at the woman's back, the couple may feel that he is very much in charge—he can see her, but she cannot readily see him.

FIGURE 9.12 Rear-Entry Coital Position.
Some people enjoy the sensations provided
by the rear-entry position; it may also be more
comfortable if the woman is pregnant.

Physically, the penis does not provide adequate stimulation to the clitoris. The penis also tends to pop out of the vagina from time to time. Finally, air tends to enter the vagina during rear-entry coitus. When it is expelled, it can sound as though the woman has passed air through the anus—a possibly embarrassing though harmless occurrence.

ANAL INTERCOURSE

Anal intercourse is insertion of the penis into the rectum. It is practiced by male–female couples and male–male couples. The rectum is richly endowed with nerve endings and highly sensitive to sexual stimulation. Both partners may reach orgasm through anal sex. Anal intercourse is also referred to as "Greek culture," or lovemaking in the "Greek style" because of male bisexuality in ancient Greece. It is also the major act that comes under the legal definition of sodomy.

In anal intercourse, the penetrator can situate himself behind his partner, or lie above or below his partner face to face. The receiving partner can supplement anal stimulation with manual stimulation of the clitoral region or penis to reach orgasm. Since the rectum produces no natural lubrication, couples are advised to use an artificial lubricant, such as K-Y jelly.

People often want their partner's fingers in the anus at the height of passion or at the moment of orgasm. A finger in the rectum can heighten sexual sensation because the anal sphincters contract during orgasm.

Many couples are repulsed by the idea of anal intercourse. They view it as unnatural, immoral, or risky. Others find anal sex to be an enjoyable sexual variation, though perhaps not a regular feature of their sexual diet.

The NHSLS found that one man in four (26%) and one woman in five (20%) reported having engaged in anal sex at some time (Laumann et al., 1994). But only about one person in ten (10% of the men and 9% of the women) had engaged in anal sex in the past year. The more recent National Survey of Sexual Health and Behavior (Center for Sexual Health Promotion, 2011) found that some 21% to 27% of people in their 20s and 30s had engaged in anal intercourse in the past year—something of a jump upward. Other surveys report numbers in the same ballpark (e.g., Ompad et al., 2006). As with oral sex, there is a higher incidence of anal sex among more highly educated people. Education appears to be a liberating influence on sexual experimentation. **TRUTH** OR **FICTION** REVISITED: Anal intercourse is more common among better-educated men.

Religion appears to be a restraint on anal sex. About 34% of the men and 36% of the women in the NHSLS who said they had no religion reported engaging in anal sex at some time. Figures for male Christians ranged from the lower to upper 20s, and for female Christians, from the midteens to the lower 20s (Laumann et al., 1994, p. 99).

Many couples kiss or lick the anus in their foreplay. This practice is called **anilingus.** Oral–anal sex carries a health risk because microorganisms causing intestinal diseases and many sexually transmitted infections (STIs) can be spread through oral–anal contact.

Many couples today hesitate to engage in anal intercourse because of the fear of HIV/AIDS and other STIs. HIV and microorganisms causing STIs such as gonorrhea, syphilis, and hepatitis can be spread by anal intercourse (Koblin et al., 2006; Lane et al., 2006). Cells in the rectum are especially susceptible to infection by some organisms, and small tears in the rectal tissues may allow other microbes to enter the recipient's blood system (see Chapter 16). However, if both partners are infection free, they are at no risk of contracting STIs.

Anilingus Oral stimulation of the anus. Slang: *rimming, rim job.*

Not all gay males enjoy or practice anal intercourse. Of those who do, most alternate between being the inserter and the insertee. The incidence of anal intercourse—especially without using condoms—among gay males declined as gays became aware of the connection between anal sex and transmission of HIV. However, now that highly active antiretroviral therapy (HAART) is prolonging the lives of many people with HIV/AIDS, some gay males are again forgoing use of condoms in anal intercourse (Dilley et al., 2003). Men report that they prefer to forgo condoms because condoms reduce sexual sensations and emotional connectedness with a partner (Bancroft et al., 2005a; Crosby et al., 2005). Moreover, gays—like heterosexuals—are more likely to forgo condoms with strangers when they are under the influence of alcohol and drugs (Irwin et al., 2006; Semple et al., 2003).

Sexual Fantasies

People may use sexual fantasies either when they are alone or to heighten sexual excitement with a partner. Some couples find it sexually arousing to share fantasies or to enact them. Sexual fantasies may also be experienced without sexual behavior, as in erotic dreams or daydreams. Masturbators often require some form of cognitive stimulation, such as fantasy or viewing erotica, to reach orgasm.

There are many theories about sexual fantasies. One view that apparently has little, if any, research evidence behind it is that people who fantasize about sex are less likely to have enjoyable sex lives. That is, the fantasy takes the place of life. But fantasies can also enhance sexual arousal, providing greater pleasure.

TRUTH OR FICTION REVISITED: Research suggests that sexual fantasies are normal. Most people have them—even during sex with another person. Fantasies heighten their sexual arousal during activity with their partners (Dawson et al., 2012). Males seem to engage in sexual fantasies more often than females, but most females do so also—at least within our American culture. A survey of 349 university students and employees, aged 18 to 70, who were involved in heterosexual relationships found that the great majority—98% of the men and 80% of the women—reported sexual fantasies about someone *other* than their sex partner (Hicks & Leitenberg, 2001).

 8

Real Students, Real Questions

Q *If you have anal sex, is there any way that the sperm can get to the egg once they are inside?*

A No and yes. When the penis is withdrawn from the anus, there will be some sperm at the tip. Or there will be sperm all along the shaft if thrusting continues after ejaculation. Some of the sperm may find their way along the outside of the woman's body to the vaginal opening (introitus), and from there, into the vagina. So the "no" refers to the fact that there's no direct internal passage between the rectum and the vagina. The "yes" refers to the off chance that fertilization could occur through a much more indirect route. Highly improbable, but not completely impossible.

These fantasies were more common among people who had been in their relationships longer, perhaps providing sexual novelty. Women were more likely than men to fantasize about *prior* sex partners, suggesting, perhaps, that they had less need to mentally stray from familiar relationships. According to a *New York Times* poll, men are somewhat more likely than women—52% versus 40%—to think it is acceptable to fantasize about sex with someone other than their partner (Eggers, 2000).

Evolutionary theorists conjecture that women are relatively more likely to fantasize about the images of familiar lovers because female reproductive success in ancestral times was more likely to depend on a protective relationship with a reliable partner (Buss, 2009; Symons, 1995). Women can bear and rear relatively few offspring. Thus, they would have a relatively greater genetic investment in each reproductive opportunity.

In keeping with genderrole stereotypes, studies also find that males are more likely to fantasize about forcing women into sexual activity. Women are more likely to fantasize about being victimized (Critelli & Bivona, 2008; Dawson et al., 2012).

Research also shows that women are more likely to report that they have more frequent and arousing sexual fantasies at time of ovulation (Dawson et al., 2012). In this study, heterosexual women kept diaries in which they recorded their fantasies, and ovulation was assessed by means of self-administered urine tests. The number of males in their fantasies increases during ovulation, but not the number of females. Fantasies during ovulation are also more likely to emphasize sex within a relationship rather than explicit sexual content.

Researchers, by the way, use the frequency and variety of sexual fantasies as one measure of the sex drive (Fisher et al., 2012). The sex drive—and the frequency of sexual fantasizing—is related to testosterone levels in both males and females. One study surveyed the frequency of sexual activity and sexual fantasies among women who had had their ovaries and uteruses surgically removed (Shifren et al., 2000). The women were then administered various doses of testosterone or a placebo via skin patches. Women given higher doses of testosterone doubled or tripled their reported incidence of sexual fantasies, masturbation, and sexual intercourse.

Studies suggest that most of us consider sexual fantasies normal. One study surveyed 178 university students and staff and found that 84% of them reported having sexual fantasies at least occasionally during sexual intercourse (Cado & Leitenberg, 1990). Most of these individuals said that they believed that such fantasies were common, normal, moral, socially acceptable, and more beneficial than harmful. Still, about one-quarter of the sample reported feeling guilty about the fantasies. Those who felt most guilty were also most likely to experience sexual dissatisfaction and problems in their actual lives.

There are also "deviant" sexual fantasies, such as sadistic rape fantasies. Research evidence with personality tests suggests that men with frequent deviant sexual fantasies are more likely to be socially isolated and emotionally unstable (Bartels & Gannon, 2011; Maniglio, 2011). Yet, the extent to which deviant sexual fantasies contribute to crimes involving sex and aggression remained clouded. Nevertheless, many helping professionals work with men who have deviant sexual fantasies in the hope that by changing their fantasies the men will be less likely to commit crimes of violence (Schmidt et al., 2012). And when it comes to fantasies about being victimized, Nancy Friday (2008) reports the following from a woman she interviewed:

> My fantasies are so personal, and the pleasure I get from them derives so much,
> I think, from the fact that they are private and locked away in my imagination,
> that I wouldn't dream of trying to make them come true.... But act my fantasies

out? Make them come true? No, absolutely not. My real life's not what they're about; I don't want those things to really happen to me, I simply want to imagine what it would be like. So that's where they'll stay.

As with masturbation, mental excursions into fantasy during coitus may be used to enhance sexual arousal and response (Murray & Milhausen, 2012). Fantasies enable couples to inject sexual variety into their sexual activity without being unfaithful. Researchers find that most married people have coital fantasies (Bader, 2003; Murray & Milhausen, 2012). A survey of a sample of 178 students, faculty, and staff members at a college in Vermont found that 84% reported fantasizing at least occasionally during intercourse (Cado & Leitenberg, 1990).

TRUTH OR FICTION REVISITED: There does not appear to be any connection between sexual dissatisfaction with one's relationship and the use of coital fantasies (Davidson & Hoffman, 1986). Thus, coital fantasies are not a form of compensation for an unrewarding sexual relationship.

Coital fantasies, like masturbation fantasies, run a gamut of themes. They include making love to another partner, group sex, orgies, images of past lovers or special erotic experiences, and making love in fantastic and wonderful places, among others. Heterosexual men are likely to fantasize about women, and gay men are more likely to fantasize about men (Chivers et al., 2004). Heterosexual women and lesbians are more flexible in their selection of the gender of the objects of their fantasies (Chivers et al., 2004; Chivers & Timmers, 2012).

Partners may be reluctant to share their fantasies, or even to admit to them, especially when the fantasy includes people other than the partner. The fantasizer might fear being accused of disloyalty or that the partner will interpret fantasies as a sign of rejection: "What's the matter? Don't I turn you on anymore?"

SEXUAL FANTASIES OF LESBIAN, GAY, AND BISEXUAL INDIVIDUALS

If you just change the gender of the person being fantasized about, most fantasies of lesbian, gay, and bisexual people would appear to be familiar enough. For example, a survey of 129 women (85 lesbian, 44 bisexual) who were in same-gender relationships that had lasted from five to ten years found connections between satisfaction in the relationship and the nature of sexual fantasies (Robinson & Parks, 2003). By and large, the happier the women were with their relationships, the more likely they were to fantasize about common activities with their partners. If their relationships were not going so well, they were relatively more likely to fantasize about things they used to do with their partners or things they did with former partners. In this regard, the patterns were quite similar to those for heterosexual women.

A study in India compared the sexual fantasies of 30 heterosexual males to those of 30 gay males (Bhugra et al., 2006). The heterosexual males appeared to be more limited in the sphere of their fantasies, restricting them more to standard sexual activities with females. The gay males were more open to fantasizing about exploratory techniques, and with both male and female partners. Fantasy apparently mirrored behavior. The authors suggested that the heterosexual males were more "inhibited" or "restricted" in both their sex lives and their fantasies, but a simpler explanation of the findings might be that both groups—heterosexual and gay—were simply fantasizing about the people and activities that enticed them.

In this chapter, we have observed many of the variations in human sexual expression. People show diversity not only in sexual behavior but also in sexual orientation—which is the focus of the following chapter.

Chapter Review ✓●—[Study and Review on MyDevelopmentLab

LO1 Discuss attitudes toward masturbation
Masturbation is self-stimulation of the genitals for purposes such as relieving sexual tension and obtaining sexual pleasure. Within the Judeo-Christian tradition, masturbation has been condemned as sinful, as have been many other nonprocreative sexual acts. Masturbation itself is rarely if ever physically harmful, although people whose values oppose masturbation may experience guilt and anxiety if they masturbate. Surveys indicate that most people have masturbated. Males are more likely than females to masturbate.

LO2 Describe ways in which people masturbate
Males tend to masturbate by using a manual milking motion. Females tend to stroke the mons and the area around the clitoral shaft. Males and females may both use vibrators or other sex toys. Females do not necessarily insert vibrators or other sex toys into the vagina.

LO3 Discuss purposes and methods of precoital and noncoital partnered sex
Foreplay involves kissing, touching, and other activities that heighten sexual arousal prior to coitus. Women have traditionally desired longer periods of foreplay than men do.

LO4 Discuss kinds of kissing
Kissing signals intimacy and can be sexually arousing.

LO5 Discuss the uses of touching in partnered sex
Touching or caressing erogenous zones can be highly arousing. Men typically prefer manual stroking of their genitals by their partner earlier than women do. Women do not necessarily enjoy insertion of fingers into the vagina, and when they do, it is usually after the have received whole body and external genital stimulation.

LO6 Describe ways of stimulating the breasts
Most, but not all, women enjoy stimulation of the breasts by the hands and mouth. Gay males and lesbians both tend to spend more time focusing on their partner's breasts and nipples than do heterosexuals.

LO7 Describe methods of oral–genital stimulation
The majority of young couples use oral–genital stimulation. Kissing, licking, or sucking the male genitals is called fellatio. Kissing or licking or sucking the female genitals is called cunnilingus.

LO8 Describe various methods of sexual intercourse
Four of the most commonly used coital positions are the male-superior position, the female-superior position, the lateral-entry position, and the rear-entry position. The female-superior position allows the female to better obtain the stimulation needed to reach orgasm. Anal intercourse may be carried out in male–female and male–male sex. Artificial lubrication facilitates anal intercourse.

LO9 Discuss kinds and uses of sexual fantasies
Sexual fantasies are often incorporated with masturbation or with partnered sex to heighten sexual response. Sexual fantasies range from the realistic to flights of fancy. Many people fantasize about sexual activities that they would not actually engage in. Sexual fantasies can also heighten sexual excitement during coitus. Sexual fantasies are normal in that most people have them and that they are not signs of psychological disorders or troubled relationships.

Test Your Learning

1. What is the connection between education and masturbation?

   (a) There is no connection.
   (b) More educated people are more likely to masturbate.
   (c) Education causes masturbation.
   (d) Education is a pack of lies that distorts the truth about masturbation.

2. Which of the following is connected with cancer of the throat?

   (a) Human papilloma virus
   (b) Bacterial vaginosis
   (c) Hepatitis
   (d) Herpes

3. _____ American men report the highest monthly frequency of coitus.

   (a) African
   (b) Asian
   (c) European
   (d) Latin

4. According to the NHSLS, the most common reason for masturbating is to

   (a) relax.
   (b) get to sleep.
   (c) relieve sexual tension.
   (d) obtain physical pleasure.

5. Research shows that sexual fantasies are

   (a) sent in from evil spirits.
   (b) a sign of masturbation.
   (c) bad for the health.
   (d) normal.

6. _____ are most likely to report having performed oral sex.

   (a) African American men
   (b) African American women
   (c) European American men
   (d) European American women

7. A woman is most likely to reach orgasm in the _____ coital position.

   (a) male-superior
   (b) female-superior
   (c) lateral-entry
   (d) rear-entry

8. Couples are least likely to report engaging in

   (a) fellatio.
   (b) cunnilingus.
   (c) penile–vaginal intercourse.
   (d) anal intercourse.

9. According to Kinsey, women who masturbated during adolescence

   (a) grew hair in the palms of their hands.
   (b) had difficulty forming social relationships in adulthood.
   (c) were more likely to find sexual gratification with others in adulthood.
   (d) were less likely to find sexual gratification with others in adulthood.

10. Which is true of approval of U.S. women's use of vibrators?

    (a) Most women and most men disapprove.
    (b) Most men and most women approve.
    (c) Most women approve and most men disapprove.
    (d) Most men approve and most women disapprove.

Answers: 1. b; 2. a; 3. a; 4. d; 5. d; 6. c; 7. b; 8. d; 9. c; 10. b

My Life, My Sexuality

What Would You Do with Whom?

*Explore this **My Life, My Sexuality** feature by scanning this QR code with your mobile device. If you don't already have one, you may download a free QR scanner for your device wherever smartphone apps are sold. You can also view this feature in MyDevelopmentLab, along with an accompanying critical thinking assignment.*

This is the chapter that described the kinds of sexual behavior people engage in—whether alone or with partners. Scan the code to go online and indicate which of these behaviors seems to be normal to you, and to get in touch with your reasoning.

10 Sexual Orientation

Learning Objectives

GETTING ORIENTED TOWARD SEXUAL ORIENTATION

LO1   Describe the various sexual orientations and discuss controversies in defining them

PERSPECTIVES ON GAY MALE AND LESBIAN SEXUAL ORIENTATIONS

LO2   Explain how homosexuality been viewed historically and scientifically

SEXUAL ORIENTATION IN CONTEMPORARY SOCIETY

LO3   Discuss contemporary American attitudes toward homosexuals

ADJUSTMENT OF GAY MALES AND LESBIANS

LO4   Discuss the adjustment of homosexuals

COMING OUT: COMING TO TERMS WITH BEING GAY

LO5   Describe what is meant by "coming out"

MY LIFE, MY SEXUALITY: ASSESSING YOUR ATTITUDES TOWARD GAY MALES AND LESBIANS

TRUTH OR FICTION?

Which of the following statements are the truth, and which are
fiction? Look for the Truth-or-Fiction icons on the pages that
follow to find the answers.

1 Gay males and lesbians would prefer to be members of the
other sex. **T F?**

2 Members of ethnic minority groups in the United States
are more tolerant of homosexuals than are European
Americans. **T F?**

3 Gay males unconsciously fear women's genitals because they
associate them with castration. **T F?**

4 A majority of Americans would prefer that gay people be
allowed to get married to one another. **T F?**

5 Most Americans believe that gay people are born gay. **T F?**

The movie *Brokeback Mountain*, with Heath Ledger as Ennis Del Mar and Jake Gyllenhaal as Jack Twist, won four Golden Globe awards, including the coveted award for best drama. What made the movie remarkable? Not the fact that it was about a love affair between gay men. *Entertainment Weekly* counted nine movies debuting in the same year, including *Capote* and *Rent,* which had gay characters in major roles. Nor was it the fact that some lovemaking appeared on the screen. There are many more sexually explicit movies with gay males, including those produced by the pornography factories.

Nor was it remarkable that the movie's characters got married to women and had children. Many gay people do just that.

Nor was it notable that the film was set in the past. There have been many movies about gay characters in ancient Greece and Rome.

But perhaps there has been no movie about gay sheepherders in the mountains of Wyoming in 1963. *Brokeback Mountain* took place in a time and a setting in which gay people had few words—or no words—to describe their emotions or who they were. As columnist Frank Rich noted, the heroes of Brokeback Mountain are "neither midnight

Brokeback Mountain. In the film *Brokeback Mountain*, Jake Gyllenhaal and Heath Ledger portray two cowboys who begin a love affair in Wyoming in 1963. Because of the time and the geographic setting of the story, neither understands what it means to have a gay sexual orientation.

cowboys, drugstore cowboys nor Village People cowboys." Instead, they're high school dropouts in the country, brought up to work hard for little reward.

Sexual orientation The directionality of one's sexual interests—toward members of the same gender, the other gender, or both.

Heterosexual orientation Erotic attraction to, preference for, and developing romantic relationships with members of the other gender.

Homosexual orientation Erotic attraction to, preference for, and developing romantic relationships with members of the same gender. (From the Greek *homos,* meaning "same," not the Latin *homo,* which means "man").

Gay males Males who are erotically attracted to and desire to form romantic relationships with other males.

👁‍🗨 **Watch the Video**
Thinking Like a Psychologist: Sexual Orientation
on **MyDevelopmentLab**

This chapter is about sexual orientation. Sexual orientation concerns the *direction* of one's romantic interests and erotic attractions—toward members of the same gender, the other gender, or both. We will see that homosexual people, like heterosexual people, struggle to incorporate their sexuality within their personal identity, to find lovers, and to establish satisfying lifestyles. In fact, gay marriages are now permitted in a number of states. Unlike heterosexual people, gay people in our culture face a backdrop of social intolerance, even if they commit themselves to long-term relationships.

Getting Oriented toward Sexual Orientation

Sexual orientation refers to one's erotic attractions toward, and interests in developing romantic relationships with, members of one's own gender or the other gender. A **heterosexual orientation** refers to an erotic attraction to, and preference for developing romantic relationships with, members of the other gender. (Many homosexual people refer to heterosexual people as being *straight,* or as *straights.*)

A **homosexual orientation** refers to an erotic attraction to, and interest in forming romantic relationships with, members of one's own gender. The term *homosexuality* denotes sexual interest in members of one's own anatomic sex and applies to both men and women. Homosexual men are often referred to as **gay males.** Homosexual women are often called **lesbians.** Gay males and lesbians may also be referred to collectively as "gays" or "gay people." The term **bisexuality** describes an orientation in which one is sexually attracted to, and interested in forming romantic relationships with, both males and females. 👁‍🗨

Real Students, Real Questions

Q *Are some people so unsuccessful with the opposite sex they become gay?*

A No. Sexual orientation has nothing to do with success or failure with one gender or the other.

COMING TO TERMS WITH TERMS

Now that we have defined homosexuality, let us note that the term is somewhat controversial. Some gay people object to it because they feel that it draws attention to sexual behavior. Moreover, the term bears a social stigma and has been historically associated with concepts of deviance and mental illness. Also, the term is often used to refer to men only. It thus renders lesbians "invisible." Thus, many people would prefer terms such as *gay male* or *lesbian sexual orientation*. Then, too, the word *homosexual* is ambiguous in meaning. Does it refer to sexual behavior or to sexual orientation? In this book, your authors speak of male–female sexual behavior (not *heterosexual* behavior), male–male sexual behavior, and female–female sexual behavior to help distinguish sexual behavior from sexual orientation.

SEXUAL ORIENTATION AND GENDER IDENTITY

Since gay people are attracted to members of their own gender, some people assume that they would prefer to be members of the other gender. **TRUTH OR FICTION REVISITED:** Like heterosexuals, most gay people have a gender identity that is consistent with their anatomic sex. J. Michael Bailey (2003b) writes that some "extremely gay" people become transgendered—that is, adopt the lifestyle of people of the other gender within our culture. But feeling "trapped" in the body of the other gender is *not* part of the definition of homosexuality.

When heterosexuals think about homosexuals, they tend to focus almost exclusively on sexual aspects of male–male and female–female relationships. But the relationships of homosexuals, like those of heterosexuals, involve more than sex. Homosexuals, like heterosexuals, spend only a small amount of time in sexual activity. More basic to a gay male or lesbian sexual orientation is the formation of romantic attachments with members of one's own gender. These attachments, like male–female attachments, provide a framework for love and intimacy. Sexual orientations are not defined by sexual activity per se, but rather by the *direction* of one's romantic interests and erotic attractions (Savin-Williams, 2012).

CLASSIFICATION OF SEXUAL ORIENTATION: IS YES OR NO ENOUGH?

Determining a person's sexual orientation might seem to be a clear-cut task. Some people are exclusively gay and limit their sexual activities to partners of their own gender. Others are strictly heterosexual and limit their sexual activities to partners of the other gender. Some people fall in between.

CRITICAL THINKING
Critical thinkers pay close attention to the meanings—and implications—of terms. Why do some writers prefer to use the terms *male–male sexual behavior* or *female–female sexual behavior* rather than *homosexual behavior*?

 1

Many heterosexual people have had sexual experiences with people of their own gender (Savin-Williams et al., 2012). In the absence of heterosexual outlets, adolescents and isolated populations such as prison inmates may have sexual experiences with people of their own gender while they maintain their heterosexual identities.

Gay males and lesbians, too, may engage in male–female sexual activity while maintaining a gay sexual orientation. Some gay males and lesbians marry members of the other gender but harbor unfulfilled desires for members of their own gender. Then, too, some people are bisexual but may not act on their attraction to members of their own gender (Rosenthal et al., 2012).

Sexual orientation is not necessarily expressed in sexual behavior. Many people see themselves as gay or heterosexual long before they ever have sex with members of their own gender (Thompson & Morgan, 2008; Savin-Williams & Diamond, 2000). Some people, gay and heterosexual alike, adopt a celibate lifestyle for religious or ascetic reasons.

People's erotic interests and fantasies may also shift over time. Men who consider themselves to be "100% heterosexual" are least likely to change their sexual orientation (Savin-Williams et al., 2012). Gay males and lesbians may experience sporadic **heteroerotic** interests. Heterosexual people may have occasional **homoerotic** interests. To some extent, women's sexual orientations are more flexible or plastic than men's, with women being somewhat more dependent on social experience (Savin-Williams et al., 2012). Lisa M. Diamond (2003b) conducted a survey of lesbian and bisexual women that involved three interviews over a five-year period. She found that more than 25% of the women relinquished their lesbian or bisexual orientation as time went on. Half of these relabeled themselves as heterosexual, and the other half renounced any effort at self-labeling. Some heterosexual people report fantasies about sexual activity with people of their own gender.

Attraction to people of the other gender and people of one's own gender may therefore not always be mutually exclusive. People may have various degrees of sexual interest in, and sexual experience with, people of either gender (Vrangalova & Savin-Williams, 2012). Kinsey and his colleagues recognized that the boundaries between gay male and lesbian sexual orientations, on the one hand, and a heterosexual orientation, on the other, are sometimes blurry. As Kinsey and his colleagues noted,

> The world is not to be divided into sheep and goats.... Only the human mind invents categories and tries to force facts into separated pigeonholes. The living world is a continuum in each and every one of its aspects. (1948, p. 639)

Kinsey and his colleagues (1948, 1953) found evidence of a continuum of sexual orientation among the people they surveyed, with bisexuality representing a midpoint between exclusively heterosexual and exclusively homosexual sexual orientations (see Figure 10.1). People are located on the continuum according to their patterns of sexual attraction and behavior. People in category 0 are considered exclusively heterosexual. People in category 6 are considered exclusively gay.

Although the research by Kinsey and his colleagues is old, more current researchers also find a kind of continuum in sexual orientation. One research group studied the responses of 1,784 individuals to an online survey advertised on Facebook. The respondents provided information about three aspects of their sex lives: their self-reported sexual orientation, the people to whom they were sexually attracted, and their actual sexual experiences (Vrangalova & Savin-Williams, 2012). Their findings were consistent with a five-point continuum of sexual identity: heterosexual, "mostly" heterosexual, bisexual, "mostly" gay/lesbian, and gay/lesbian.

Heteroeroticâ€ƒOf an erotic nature and involving members of the other gender.

Homoeroticâ€ƒOf an erotic nature and involving members of one's own gender.

The "mostly" participants, whether mostly heterosexual or mostly gay/lesbian, generally reported patterns of sexual attraction and sex partners at odds with their self-reported sexual orientation (which is also referred to as one's *sexual identity*). But in contrast to the Kinsey view, their findings also supported the two-dimensional view of same- and other-gender sexuality shown in Figure 10.2. That is, having more other-gender sexuality did not necessarily imply less same-gender sexuality, and vice versa.

Kinsey and his colleagues reported that about 4% of men and 1 to 3% of women in their samples were exclusively gay (category 6 on their scale). A larger percentage of people were considered predominantly gay (4 or 5 on their scale) or predominantly heterosexual (1 or 2 on their scale). All in all, Kinsey's data suggested that close to 10% of the U.S. population was gay or predominantly gay, a number that dramatically exceeds current estimates. Some were classified as equally gay and heterosexual in orientation and could be labeled bisexual (scale point 3). Most people were classified as exclusively heterosexual (scale point 0).

Statistics concerning *past* sexual activity with a member of one's own gender can be misleading. They may represent a single episode or a brief period of adolescent experimentation. Half of the men who reported male–male sexual activity in Kinsey's sample limited it to the ages of 12 to 14. Another third had male–male sexual experience by the age of 18, but not again.

Kinsey's research, consistent with more recent research, also showed that sexual behavior patterns can change, sometimes dramatically so. Sexual experiences or feelings involving people of one's own gender are common, especially in adolescence, and do not necessarily mean that one will engage in sexual activity exclusively with people of one's own gender in adulthood (Savin-Williams et al., 2012).

The controversy over how many people are gay continues. About 7% of American women and men define themselves as being "other than heterosexual," but the behavior of the other 93% doesn't exactly match up with the way in which people label themselves. For example, nearly twice as many people—about 14%—say they

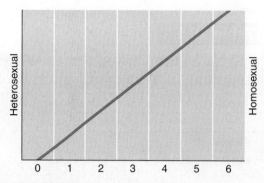

FIGURE 10.1 The Kinsey Continuum. Kinsey and his colleagues conceived of a 7-point heterosexual—homosexual continuum that classifies people according to their homosexual behavior and the magnitude of their attraction to members of their own gender. People in category 0, who accounted for most of Kinsey's study participants, were considered exclusively heterosexual. People in category 6 were considered exclusively homosexual.

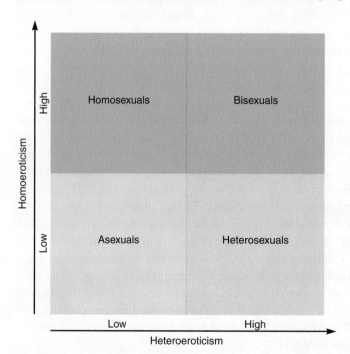

FIGURE 10.2 Heterosexuality and Homosexuality as Separate Dimensions. According to this model, homosexuality and heterosexuality are independent dimensions. One can thus be high or low on both dimensions at the same time. Most people are high on one dimension. Bisexuals are high on both dimensions. People who are extremely low on both may be considered to be *asexual*.

Table 10.1

People in the United States Who Identify Themselves as LGBT (Lesbian, Gay, Bisexual, or Transgender), in Percents

Racial/Ethnic Group	African American	Asian American	European American	Latin American
Ages 18–29				
Female	9.6	8.0	8.6	6.6
Male	6.1	4.8	3.9	5.8
Ages 30–49				
Female	3.4	2.7	3.3	3.4
Male	3.6	4.1	3.1	3.6
Ages 50–64				
Female	2.6	1.2	2.3	2.0
Male	2.3	1.7	3.0	3.3
Ages 65+				
Female	2.0	0.4	1.5	1.5
Male	4.1	5.2	2.4	1.4

Source of data: Based on Gallup organization and the Williams Institute at the law school of UCLA, October 18, 2012. Based on telephone interviews June 1–September 30, 2012 of 121,290 Americans.

Gates, G. J., & Newport, F. (2012, October). Gallup special report: The LGBT vote in the 2012 presidential election. The Williams Institute. http://williamsinstitute.law.ucla.edu/research/census-lgbt-demographics-studies/gallup-special-report-lgbt-vote-18oct-2012/(Accessed October 20, 2012).

have had oral sex with a person of the same gender (Herbenick et al., 2010a, 2010b, 2010c; Reece et al., 2010).

The most recent, and possibly the most accurate, survey of sexual orientation in the United States was conducted by the Gallup organization as part of the Gallup Daily tracking survey leading up to the 2012 presidential election (Gates & Newport, 2012). The Gallup organization used random telephone dialing and asked about sexual orientation as one among many questions having to do with political preferences. The findings were compiled and organized by the Gallup organization along with the Williams Institute at the law school of the University of California at Los Angeles, and the main findings are shown in Table 10.1.

It is clear that 18–29-year-olds are most likely to identify themselves as lesbian, gay, bisexual, or transgender. Note the systematic falloff for females in every racial/ethnic group in the survey. There is also a falloff for males, but a "rebound" among African American and Asian American males aged 65 and above. Why do we see these dropoffs? If one assumes that biological factors are the major contributor to sexual orientation, one has to ask how biology would have changed over the years in these various age cohorts, or else why older cohorts, beginning in their 30s, are less likely to identify themselves as LGBT. Perhaps, in our more liberated times, young adults are more likely to feel free to identify themselves as LGBT, or more likely to be in touch with their sexual orientations? These inferences are speculative.

Why do we see the "rebound" among older African American and Asian American males, when the same age cohort, for women, shows relatively rare self-identification as LGBT? It is tempting to think that males of the age cohort are possibly more outspoken and of an age at which they might be thinking, "Why does it matter anymore to admit to the truth?" But perhaps women from that cohort (across all racial/ethnic groups) are less likely to have examined their sexual orientations across the years? We must admit that we don't have the answers and are not comfortable with our speculations.

In the youngest age cohort, we must also note that females are significantly more likely than males to identify themselves as being LGBT. Is the gender difference due to more common presence of biological factors that influence a lesbian, bisexual, or transgender orientation in females? Does the difference reflect greater erotic plasticity in females? Or more willingness to admit to a lesbian, bisexual, or transgender orientation? (Females, presumably, more so than males, would *not* be influenced by a desire to be masculine or "tough.")

Interestingly, 18–29-year-old African Americans are most likely to label themselves as lesbian, gay, bisexual, transgender (LGBT). Among African Americans, males in the 50–64-year-old age cohort are least likely to label themselves as gay, bisexual, or transgender. Might one reason be that this was the group most likely to be devastated by the HIV/AIDS epidemic?

The Gallup/UCLA survey would appear to provide the most accurate information to date about sexual orientation. However, it raises more questions than it answers (Blow, 2012).

Keep in mind that the following factors affect survey results:

- The ways in which the questions are phrased (for example, do they look into sexual identity, sexual behavior, or sexual attraction—and over what period of time?)
- The social desirability of the professed behavior
- The gender of the interviewer
- The manner in which the questions were administered, such as by face-to-face interviews, by phone calls, or in written form
- Possible biases of respondents, such as volunteer bias

Challenges to the Kinsey Continuum Alfred Kinsey believed that exclusive heterosexual and gay sexual orientations lay at opposite poles of one continuum. Therefore, the more heterosexual a person is, the less gay that person is, and vice versa. Viewing gay and heterosexual orientations as opposite poles of one continuum is akin to the traditional view of masculinity and femininity as opposite poles of one continuum, such that the more masculine one is, the less feminine, and vice versa.

We may also regard masculinity and femininity as independent personality dimensions. But it may be that these sexual orientations are in fact separate dimensions, rather than polar opposites (Vrangalova & Savin-Williams, 2012). There are apparently separate dimensions of responsiveness to male–female sexual stimulation (heteroeroticism) and sexual stimulation that involves someone of the same gender (homoeroticism), as shown in Figure 10.2. According to this model, bisexuals are high in both dimensions, whereas people who are low in both are essentially asexual (Bogaert, 2006). According to Kinsey, bisexual individuals would be *less* responsive to stimulation by people of the other gender than heterosexual people are, but *more* responsive to stimulation by people of their own gender. However, the two-dimensional model allows for people to be as responsive to stimulation by people of the other gender as heterosexual people are, and as responsive to stimulation by people of their own gender as gay people are.

Chivers and Bailey (2005) exposed men and women to visual male and female sexual stimuli. They measured the subjects' genital responses as well as their self-reports of sexual arousal. Male heterosexuals responded genitally only to the female stimuli, and gay males showed the reverse pattern. Their genital responses bore out their verbal reports. The women, both heterosexual and lesbian, were more likely to be aroused by both male and female sexual stimuli.

Chivers and Bailey's findings are consistent with research showing that women's sexual orientations are more flexible than men's and apparently more intertwined

Table 10.2

Factors in Males' and Females' Sexual Behaviors and Attitudes

Males	Females
Bipolar sexual orientation	Homosexuality
Emotional commitment	Heterosexuality
Sex drive	Emotional commitment
Sexual fantasy	Sex drive

Source: "The structure of sexual orientation and its relation to masculinity, femininity, and gender diagnosticity: Different for men and women" by Richard Lippa and Sara Arad, *Sex Roles*, 1997, 37(3–4), 187–208, with kind permission from Springer Science and Business Media.

with their social experience (Diamond, 2000, 2002, 2003a; Mock & Elbach, 2012). When we discuss **homophobia,** or hatred of homosexuals, we will see that men tend to be more homophobic than women. Homophobia is connected with traditional "tough" masculine attitudes (Davies, 2004). However, it may also be that part of the reason for this gender difference in homophobia is that heterosexual men have a more difficult time than heterosexual women understanding how any man could be attracted to a person of the same gender (see Table 10.2).

BISEXUALITY

To me, I never felt like I had a stronger attraction to men or women. I didn't have a problem identifying myself as gay, but I knew that wasn't the whole picture.

—A 29-year-old social worker from North Carolina who fell in love with a woman and then had a sexual relationship with his male roommate*

I don't limit myself to a guy or a girl. Whoever comes into my life, if we hit it off, great. That's happened with a lot of people I know. They'll say, "Guess what happened last night." It's very accepted.

—A 22-year-old political science major*

She finally came out of the closet and said, "Mom, there's this girl and she's the most gorgeous girl you've ever seen." I said, "You're only for girls?" She said, "No, it's not just the girls. I can see a really good-looking guy, too."

—The mother of a 19-year-old woman who uses a computer bulletin board to meet other bisexuals*

Bisexual people are sexually attracted to both males and females. They are sometimes said to "swing both ways," or to be "A/C–D/C" (as in "alternating current" and "direct current"). Yet, many have a somewhat stronger attraction to people of one gender than the other. In fact, Weinrich and Klein (2002) speak of bisexuals as being "bi-gay," "bi-straight," or "bi-bi," meaning that some have a stronger leaning toward people of their own gender (bi-gays), some toward people of the other gender (bi-straights), and still others appears to be equally attracted to people of their own gender and the other gender (bi-bi's). Depending on how one defines bisexuality, perhaps 1% to 4% of the population is bisexual. About 1% of the people (0.8% of the

Homophobia A cluster of negative attitudes and feelings toward gay people, including intolerance, hatred, and fear.

*The three quotes are extracted from Gabriel (1995).

men and 0.9% of the women) surveyed in the NHSLS study (Laumann et al., 1994) reported having a bisexual *identity*. However, about 4% said they were sexually attracted to both women and men.

Some gay people (and some heterosexual people) believe that claims to bisexuality are a "cop-out" that people use to deny being gay. Perhaps they fear leaving their spouses or "coming out" (declaring their gay male or lesbian sexual orientation publicly). Others view bisexuality as a form of sexual experimentation with people of one's own gender by people who are mostly heterosexual. Surveys of more than 600 college undergraduates confirm that **biphobia**, or hatred of bisexuals, can be found in both the heterosexual and homosexual populations (Mulick & Wright, 2002).

But many avowed bisexuals and researchers assert that bisexuals can maintain erotic interests in, and romantic relationships with, members of both genders. They insist that bisexuality is an authentic sexual orientation with its own developmental patterns, and not just a "cover" for a gay male or lesbian sexual orientation (Savin-Williams et al., 2012).

Some bisexual people follow lifestyles that permit them to satisfy their dual inclinations. Others feel pressured by heterosexual and gay people alike to commit themselves one way or the other (Savin-Williams et al., 2012). Some gay people also mask their sexual orientation by adopting a bisexual lifestyle. That is, they get married but also enter into clandestine sexual liaisons with members of their own gender.

Still, it appears that many bisexual men remain reasonably comfortable in committed heterosexual relationships, such as marriages. An in-depth study of 20 married men who scored as bisexual on the Kinsey Scale found that they encountered some anxiety, some feelings of guilt, and some sense of loss, but not to the point where they experienced high levels of stress (Edser & Shea, 2002). By and large, the men were psychologically stable and most of their marriages were in what the authors call "relatively good condition." The authors conclude that long-term committed relationships with women are a "viable option" for bisexual men. The authors were not moralistic; that is, they were not suggesting that bisexual men *should* seek committed relationships with women. They merely pointed out that such relationships can work.

Perspectives on Gay Male and Lesbian Sexual Orientations

Gay male and lesbian sexual orientations have existed throughout history. Attitudes toward them have varied widely. They have been tolerated in some societies, openly encouraged in others, but condemned in most. In this section we review historical and other perspectives on gay male and lesbian sexual orientations.

HISTORICAL PERSPECTIVES

In Western culture, few sexual practices have met with such widespread censure as sexual activities with members of one's own sex. But it was not always that way. In ancient Greece, for example, established men frequently formed sexual relationships with adolescent males at about the age of first growing a beard. The main sexual activity depicted on Greek vases is of the older male inserting his penis between the boy's thighs (not in the anus) and thrusting until he ejaculates.

A few centuries later, the Romans described highly feminine gay men who dressed flamboyantly, had showy hair styles and mannerisms, and cruised certain neighborhoods, searching for partners. The Apostle Paul commented on this

Biphobia Negative attitudes and feelings toward bisexual people, including intolerance, hatred, and fear.

behavior as the key sign of the decadence of Rome, and the Christian Church assumed a strongly negative attitude toward homosexuality.

In the fifteenth century, Florence, a Christian city, was reputed to house numerous "sodomites." (Jews and Christians have traditionally referred to male–male sexual activity as the sin of Sodom—hence the origins of the term *sodomy*, which generally alludes to anal intercourse, and sometimes to oral–genital contact. According to the book of Genesis, the city of Sodom was destroyed by God. Yet it is unclear what behavior incurred God's wrath. Pope Gregory III was not ambiguous, however, in his eighth-century account of the city's obliteration as a punishment for sexual activity with members of the same gender.) Sodomy was so common in Florence, and (theoretically) so disturbing to the city's governors, that they created the "Office of the Night" in 1432, which enabled the populace to anonymously accuse individuals of sodomy. During the 70 years that the office was in operation, some 17,000 men were investigated as possible sodomites, nearly half of the male population of Florence throughout that period! Fewer than 3,000 were actually convicted, however, and those who were convicted were required to pay a fine rather than tossed into prison (Bailey, 2003b).

The book of Leviticus was also clear in its condemnation:

> If a man lies with a man as with a woman, both of them have committed an abomination; they shall be put to death, their blood is upon them. (Leviticus 20:13)

Sexual activity with members of one's own gender was not the only sexual act considered sinful by the early Christians. Any nonprocreative sexual act was considered sinful, even within marriage. With the fall of the Roman Empire, the influence of Christianity spread across Western Europe. Christian beliefs were eventually encoded into secular law. By the late Middle Ages, most civil statutes throughout Western Europe contained penalties for nonprocreative sexual acts involving the discharge of semen, including oral or anal sex, masturbation, male–male sexual behavior, and bestiality. Male–male and female–female sexual practices continue to be condemned by most Christian and Jewish denominations, and by Islam.

Our legal system, grounded in this religious tradition, maintains criminal penalties for sexual practices commonly associated with male–male and female–female sex, such as anal and oral sex. But much of the criminalization of male–male and female–female sex has been directed against men.

CROSS-CULTURAL PERSPECTIVES

Male–male sexual behavior has been practiced in many preliterate societies. In their review of the literature on 76 preliterate societies, Ford and Beach (1951) found that in 49 societies (64%), male–male sexual interactions were viewed as normal and deemed socially acceptable for some members of the group. The other 27 societies (36%) had sanctions against male–male sexual behavior. Nevertheless, male–male sexual activity persisted. In another cross-cultural analysis, Broude and Greene (1976) found that male–male sexual behavior was present but uncommon in 41% of a sample of 70 of the world's non-European societies. It was rare or absent in 59% of these societies. Broude and Greene also found evidence of societal disapproval and punishment of male–male sexual activity in 41% of a sample of 42 societies for which information was available.

Sexual activities between males are sometimes limited to rites that mark the young male's initiation into manhood. In some preliterate societies, semen is believed to boost strength and virility. Older males thus transmit semen to younger

A World of Diversity

Ethnicity and Sexual Orientation: A Matter of Belonging

Lesbians and gay males frequently suffer the slings and arrows of an outraged society. Because of societal prejudices, it is difficult for many young people to come to terms with an emerging lesbian or gay male sexual orientation. You might assume that people who have been subjected to prejudice and discrimination—members of ethnic minority groups in the United States—would be more tolerant of a lesbian or gay male sexual orientation. **TRUTH OR FICTION** **2** REVISITED: However, members of ethnic minority groups in the United States tend to be less tolerant of homosexuals than European Americans are (Chisholm & Greene, 2008; Herek & Gonzalez-Rivera, 2006).

Within traditional Latin American culture, the family is the primary social unit. Men are expected to support and defend the family, and women are expected to be submissive, respectable, and deferential to men. Because women are expected to remain virgins until marriage, men sometimes engage in male–male sexual behavior without considering themselves gay (Barrett et al., 2005). Latin American culture frequently denies the sexuality of women. Thus, women who label themselves lesbians are doubly condemned—because they are lesbians and because they are confronting others with their sexuality. Because lesbians are independent of men, most Latin American heterosexual people view Latina American lesbians as threats to the tradition of male dominance (Barrett et al., 2005).

Asian American cultures emphasize respect for elders, obedience to parents, and sharp distinctions in gender roles (Kumashiro, 2004). The topic of sex is generally taboo within the family. Asian Americans, like Latin Americans, tend to assume that sex is unimportant to women. Women are also considered less important than men. Open admission of a lesbian or gay male sexual orientation is seen as rejection of traditional cultural roles and a threat to the continuity of the family line (Collins, 2004).

Ethnicity and Sexual Orientation. The experiences of lesbians and gay men can differ according to their ethnicity. For example, traditional Latin American culture supports strong differences in gender roles. Men are expected to support and defend the family. Women are expected to be submissive, respectable, and deferential to men.

Because many African American men have had difficulty finding jobs, gender roles among African Americans have been more flexible than those found among European Americans and most other ethnic minority groups (Chisholm & Greene, 2008). Nevertheless, the African American community appears to strongly reject gay men and lesbians, pressuring them to remain secretive about their sexual orientations. Greene (2000) hypothesizes a number of factors that influence African Americans to be hostile toward lesbians and gay men. One is allegiance to Christianity and Biblical scripture. Another is internalization of the dominant culture's stereotyping of African Americans as highly sexual beings. That is, many African Americans may wish to assert their sexual "normalcy."

Prior to European colonization, sex may not have been discussed openly by Native Americans, but sex was generally seen as a natural part of life. Individuals who incorporated both traditional feminine and masculine styles were generally accepted and even admired. The influence of the religions of colonists led to greater rejection of lesbians and gay men, and pressure to move off the reservation to the big city (Adams & Phillips, 2006; Balsam et al., 2004). Native American lesbians and gay men, like Asian American lesbians and gay men, thus often feel doubly removed from their families.

If any generalization is possible, it may be that lesbians and gay men find more of a sense of belonging in the gay community than in their ethnic communities.

males through oral or anal sexual activities. Among the Sambian people of New Guinea, a tribe of warlike headhunters, 7- to 10-year-old males leave their parents' households and live in a "clubhouse" with other prepubertal and adolescent males. There they undergo sexual rites of passage. To acquire the fierce manhood of the headhunter, they fellate older males and drink semen (Bailey, 2003b). They are encouraged to take in as much semen as they can, as if it were mother's milk. Ingestion of semen is believed to give rise to puberty. Following puberty, adolescents are fellated by younger males. In their late teens or early twenties, however, young men are expected to take brides and enter into exclusively male–female sexual relationships.

These practices of Sambian culture might seem to suggest that the sexual orientations of males are fluid and malleable. But the practices involve *behavior* and not *sexual orientation*. Male–male sexual behavior among Sambians takes place within a cultural context that bears little resemblance to consensual male–male sexual activity in Western society. The prepubertal Sambian male does not *seek* sexual liaisons with other males. He is removed from his home and thrust into male–male sexual encounters by older males.

Little is known about female–female sexual activity in non-Western cultures. Evidence of female–female sexual behavior was found by Ford and Beach in only 17 of the 76 societies they studied. Perhaps female sexual behavior in general, not just sexual activity with other females, was more likely to be repressed. Perhaps women are less likely than men to develop sexual interests in, or romantic relationships with, members of their own gender. Whatever the reasons, this cross-cultural evidence is consistent with data from our own culture. Here, too, males are more likely than females to develop sexual interests in, or romantic relationships with, members of their own gender.

CROSS-SPECIES PERSPECTIVES

Biologists have observed male–male and female–female sexual behavior in at least 450 different animal species in every part of the world (Hird, 2006). Rare it's not.

On the other hand, what you see isn't always what you get. A male baboon may present his rear and allow himself to be mounted by another male. This behavior may resemble anal intercourse among gay men. Is the behavior sexually motivated, however? Mounting behavior among male baboons may represent a type of dominance ritual in which lower-ranking males adopt a submissive (feminine) posture to ward off attack from dominant males. (Some male–male acts among people also involve themes of dominance, as in the case of a dominant male prisoner forcing a less dominant one to submit to anal intercourse.) In other cases, male baboons may be seeking favors or protection from more dominant males. Among juvenile animals, male–male behaviors may also be a form of play. Females may also attempt to mount other females, but here too, the motives may not be the same as those of humans.

Sexual motivation appears to play a role in some, but not all, male–male and female–female sexual interactions among animals. Fellatio and anal intercourse to ejaculation among juvenile male orangutans may be a case in point, as may be thrusting by one adult female gorilla against another.

BIOLOGICAL PERSPECTIVES

Biological perspectives focus on the possible roles of evolution, genetics, and hormonal influences in shaping sexual orientation.

The Evolutionary Perspective It might seem odd that evolutionary theorists have endeavored to explain gay male and lesbian sexual orientations. After all, gay males and lesbians are not motivated to engage in sexual activity with members of the other gender. How, then, can gay and lesbian sexual orientations confer any evolutionary advantage?

To answer the question, we must look to the group or the species rather than the individual. Kirkpatrick (2000) suggests that male–male and female–female sexual behavior derive from individual selection for reciprocal *altruism*. That is, strong male–male and female–female alliances have advantages for group survival in that they bind group members together emotionally. This hypothesis remains quite speculative.

However, researchers have also compared the family trees of homosexuals with those of heterosexuals and found that there is a significant increase in fecundity in the women related to the homosexuals in the maternal line but not in women in the paternal line (Iemmola & Ciani, 2009). These findings suggest the possibility that genetic factors that are linked to the X sex chromosome and might influence homosexual orientation in males are not eliminated by natural selection because they also increase fecundity in women carriers. That is, the women related to gay males apparently bear more children, compensating for the lesser likelihood that homosexuals will reproduce.

Genetics, the Brain, and Sexual Orientation Considerable evidence exists that gay male and lesbian sexual orientations run in families (Jannini et al., 2010). Twin studies shed light on the possible role of heredity (Bailey, 2003b). **Monozygotic (MZ) twins**, or identical twins, develop from a single fertilized ovum and share 100% of their heredity. **Dizygotic (DZ) twins**, or fraternal twins, develop from two fertilized ova. Like other brothers and sisters, DZ twins share only 50% of their heredity. Thus, if a gay male or lesbian sexual orientation were transmitted genetically, it should be found about twice as often among identical twins of gay people as among fraternal twins. Since MZ and DZ twins who are reared together share similar environmental influences, differences in the degree of **concordance** for a given trait between the types of twin pairs are further indicative of genetic origins. Several studies have identified gay men who had either identical (MZ) or fraternal (DZ) twin brothers in order to examine the prevalence of a gay male sexual orientation in their twin brothers. In one of the most carefully conducted twin studies, about 52% of identical (MZ) twin pairs were found to be "concordant" (in agreement) for a gay male sexual orientation, as compared with 22% of fraternal (DZ) twins and only 11% of adoptive brothers (Bailey, 2003a; Bailey & Pillard, 1991). Bear in mind that MZ twins are more likely to be dressed alike and treated alike than DZ twins. Thus, their greater concordance for a gay sexual orientation may at least in part reflect environmental factors (Hines, 2011; Jannini et al., 2010).

Researchers have found evidence linking a region on the X sex chromosome to a gay male sexual orientation (Bailey et al., 1999). One group of researchers (Hamer et al., 1993) found that gay males in a sample of 114 gay men were more likely to have gay male relatives on their mothers' side of the family than would be expected, based on the prevalence of a gay male sexual orientation in the general population. However, they did not have a greater than expected number of gay male relatives on the paternal side of the family. This pattern of inheritance is consistent with genetic traits, such as hemophilia, that are linked to the X sex chromosome, which men receive from their mothers.

Watch the **Video**
Gay Brains
on **MyDevelopmentLab**

Monozygotic (MZ) twins Twins who develop from the same fertilized ovum; identical twins.

Dizygotic (DZ) twins Twins who develop from different fertilized ova; fraternal twins.

Concordance Agreement.

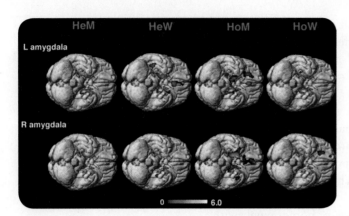

FIGURE 10.3 PET Scans of the Amygdalas of Heterosexuals and Homosexuals. The amygdalas of gay men (HoM) and heterosexual women (HeW) appear to have similar patterns of blood flow, as shown by PET scanning. Moreover, the patterns of blood flow of the amygdalas of lesbians (HoW) and heterosexual men (HeM) also appear to be similar.

Source: I. Savic, and P. Lindström. (2008). PET and MRI show differences in cerebral asymmetry and functional connectivity between homo- and heterosexual subjects. Published online on June 16, 2008. *Proceedings of the National Academy of Sciences.* USA, 10.1073/pnas.0801566105.

The researchers then examined the X sex chromosome in 40 pairs of gay male, nontwin brothers. In 33 of the pairs, the brothers had identical DNA markers on the end tip of the X chromosome. For brothers overall in the general population, about half would be expected to have inherited this chromosomal structure. It is suspected, therefore, that this chromosomal region may hold a gene that predisposes men to a gay male sexual orientation.

The researchers cautioned that they had not found a particular gene linked to sexual orientation, just a general location of where the gene may be found. Nor do scientists know how such a gene, or combination of genes, might account for sexual orientation. Perhaps a particular gene or gene combination governs the development of proteins that sculpt parts of the brain in ways that favor the development of a gay male sexual orientation. On the other hand, a number of the gay brothers, 7 of the 40 pairs, did *not* share the chromosomal marker.

In a search for possible differences in the brain among heterosexuals, gay men, and lesbians, Swedish researchers (Savic & Lindström, 2008) conducted MRI scans of the brains of 90 subjects—25 heterosexual men (HeM) and women (HeW), and 20 gay men (HoM) and lesbians (HoW). They found that the brains of the heterosexual men and the lesbians were slightly asymmetrical; the right hemisphere was slightly larger than the left hemisphere. This difference was not found among the brains of gay men and heterosexual women. The researchers also measured the blood flow to the amygdala, an area of the brain involved in the emotional response to threats, and they found that it was wired similarly in gay men and heterosexual women, and also in lesbians and heterosexual men (see Figure 10.3). The researchers admitted that their methodology cannot show whether the differences in brain shape and interconnectivity are inherited or due to environmental factors such as exposure to testosterone in the womb. Nor can they conclude that the differences in the brain are responsible for sexual orientation. But even at this stage in the research, it would appear that the brains of heterosexuals and homosexuals *might* be different in ways that are consistent with their sexual orientations.

Hormonal Influences and Sexual Orientation Sex hormones strongly influence the mating behavior of other species (Crews, 1994). Researchers have thus looked into possible hormonal factors in determining sexual orientation in humans.

Testosterone is essential to male sexual differentiation. Thus, levels of testosterone and its by-products in the blood and urine have been studied as possible influences on sexual orientation. Research has failed to connect sexual orientation in either gender with differences in the levels of either male or female sex hormones in adulthood (Hines, 2011). In adulthood, testosterone appears to have **activating effects**. That is, it affects the intensity of sexual desire, but not the preference for partners of the same or the other gender.

But can sex hormones influence the developing human embryo and fetus (Garcia-Falgueras & Swaab, 2010)? Swedish neuroscientists Ivanka Savic and her colleagues (2010) report evidence that one's gender identity as being male or being female and one's sexual orientation (heterosexual, homosexual, or bisexual) can develop during the intrauterine period. They point out that sexual differentiation of the sex organs

Activating effects Those effects of sex hormones that influence the level of the sex drive but not sexual orientation.

occurs during the first two months of pregnancy, whereas sexual differentiation of the brain begins later, during the second half of pregnancy. Sexual differentiation of the genitals and the brain both depend on surges of testosterone, but because they happen at different times, they can occur independently. Therefore, it is possible that an individual's sex organs can develop in one direction while the biological factors that may underlie one's sexual orientation develop in another direction.

Pregnant rats in experiments were given anti-androgen drugs that block the effects of testosterone. When the drugs were given during critical periods in which the fetuses' brains were becoming sexually differentiated, male offspring were likely to show feminine mating patterns as adults (Ellis & Ames, 1987). The adult males became receptive to mounting attempts by other males and failed to mount females.

The Structure of the Brain Evidence suggests that there may be structural differences between the brains of heterosexual and gay men. In 1991, Simon LeVay, a neurobiologist at the Salk Institute in La Jolla, California, carried out autopsies on the brains of 35 AIDS victims—19 gay men and 16 (presumably) heterosexual men. He found that a segment of the hypothalamus (specifically, the *third interstitial nucleus of the anterior hypothalamus*) in the brains of the gay men was less than half the size of the same segment in the heterosexual men. The same brain segment was larger in the brain tissues of heterosexual men than in brain tissues obtained from a comparison group of six presumably heterosexual women. No significant differences in size were found between the brain tissues of the gay men and the women, however.

LeVay's findings are intriguing but preliminary. We do not know, for example, whether the structural differences found by LeVay are innate. Nor do the findings prove that biology is destiny.

The belief that sexual orientation is innate or inborn has many adherents—both in the scientific and general communities. Support for the possible influences of prenatal hormonal factors in "sculpting" the brain in a masculine or feminine direction is based largely on animal studies, however. Direct evidence with people is lacking. We must also be careful in generalizing results from other species to our own.

PSYCHOLOGICAL PERSPECTIVES

Psychoanalytic theory and learning theory provide two of the major psychological approaches to understanding the origins of sexual orientation.

Psychoanalytic Views We are going to make you aware of the psychoanalytic approach to the origins of homosexuality, but let us make it clear at the outset that there is no adequate scientific evidence to support this view. Why, then, you may ask, do we bother discussing it at all? The answer is that many people still believe in it, so it may be useful to know "where they are coming from"—especially if you are a gay male or a lesbian.

In any event, Sigmund Freud, the originator of psychoanalytic theory, believed that children are naturally open to all forms of sexual stimulation. However, through proper resolution of the Oedipus complex, a boy will forsake his incestuous desires for his mother and come to identify with his father. As a result, his erotic attraction to his mother will eventually be transferred to more appropriate *female* partners. A girl, through proper resolution of her Electra complex, will identify with her mother and seek erotic stimulation from men when she becomes sexually mature.

In Freud's view, a gay male or lesbian sexual orientation results from failure to successfully resolve the Oedipus complex by identifying with the parent of the same gender. In men, faulty resolution of the Oedipus complex is most likely to result

CRITICAL THINKING
Some people believe that sexual orientation is inborn; others believe that it represents the choice of the individual. Why are people who believe sexual orientation is inborn more tolerant of homosexuals?

A Closer Look

Pheromones and Sexual Orientation

In the film *Scent of a Woman*, Al Pacino played a blind man who was drawn to women by their odor. Are there odors that are characteristic of the other gender? If so, does one's response to these odors play a role in one's sexual orientation?

Some answers are suggested by a study by Swedish researchers (Savic et al., 2005) who used PET scans to show that gay and heterosexual men respond differently to smelling chemicals that may affect sexual arousal, and that the gay men respond similarly to heterosexual women (see Figure 10.4). The Swedish study investigated the effects of two chemicals: a testosterone derivative produced in men's sweat and an estrogen-like compound found in women's urine. Most odors activate neurons in specific regions

of the brain, increasing the blood flow to these regions and causing them to "light up" when imaged by the PET scan. The estrogen-like compound activated the usual smell-related areas in women, but it lit up the hypothalamus—a structure involved in sexual behavior—in heterosexual men. The chemical extracted from male sweat, in contrast, did the opposite; it activated the hypothalamus in women and the usual smell-related areas in men. Each chemical seemed to be just another odor with one gender but a pheromone with the other. However, gay men in the study responded to the chemicals as women did. That is, their hypothalamus was lit up by the chemical drawn from male sweat.

It must be noted that the Swedish study does not reveal cause and effect. A

"snapshot" was taken of brain functioning at a point in time. The snapshot did not show how the brain's responses develop. Were the activity patterns in heterosexual and gay men a cause of their sexual orientation or an effect of their sexual orientation? If sexual orientation has a genetic basis or is influenced by hormones in the womb or at puberty, it might be that the neurons in the hypothalamus become hardwired in a way that shapes sexual orientation. Conversely, the findings could mean that experience leads straight and gay men to respond in different ways. In any event, the study does suggest a role for pheromones in human sexual response and lays the groundwork for further research.

FIGURE 10.4 Who Lights Up Your Hypothalamus? Certain areas of the hypothalamus "light up" when heterosexual males smell an estrogen-like compound ("estratetraenol") found in women's urine, when heterosexual women smell an androgen-like compound ("androstadienone"), and when gay males smell the androstadienone. The hypothalamus of gay males responds similarly to that of heterosexual women when the person is presented with the odor of androstadienone.

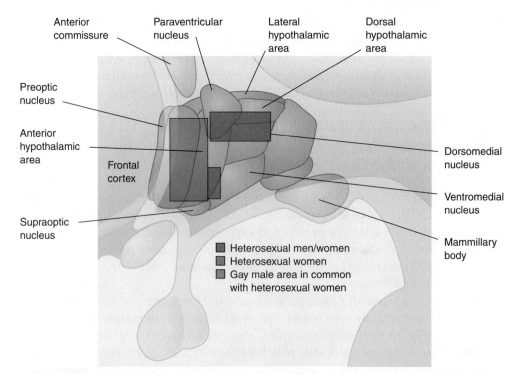

Source: Adapted with permission from I. Savic, H. Berglund, and P. Lindström (2005). Brain response to putative pheromones in homosexual men. *Proceedings of the National Academy of Sciences*, Vol. 102, pp. 7356–7361, 7539. Copyright © 2005 National Academy of Sciences, U.S.A.

from the so-called classic pattern of an emotionally "close-binding" mother and a "detached–hostile" father. A boy reared in such a family may come to identify with his mother and even to "transform himself into her" (Freud, 1922/1959, p. 40). He may thus become effeminate and develop sexual interests in men.

Freud believed that unresolved **castration anxiety** plays a role in a gay male sexual orientation. By the time the Oedipus complex takes effect, the boy will have learned from self-stimulation that he can obtain sexual pleasure from his penis. In his youthful fantasies, he associates this pleasure with mental images of his mother. Similarly, he is likely to have learned that females do not possess a penis. Somewhere along the line, the psychoanalyst theorizes that the boy may also have been warned that his penis will be removed if he plays with himself. From all this, the boy may surmise that females—including his mother—once had penises, but that they were removed.

During the throes of the Oedipus complex, the boy unconsciously comes to fear that his father, his rival in love for the mother, will retaliate by removing the organ that the boy has come to associate with sexual pleasure. His fear causes him to repress his sexual desire for his mother and to identify with the potential aggressor—his father. The boy thus overcomes his castration anxiety and is headed along the path of adult heterosexuality.

If the Oedipus complex is not successfully resolved, castration anxiety may persist. When sexually mature, the man will not be able to tolerate sex with women. His lack of a penis will arouse unconscious castration anxiety within himself.

The Electra complex in little girls follows a somewhat different course. Freud believed that little girls become envious of boys' penises, since they lack their own. Jealousy leads little girls to resent their mothers, whom they blame for their anatomic "deficiency," and to turn from their mothers to their fathers as sexual objects. They now desire to possess the father, because the father's penis provides what they lack. But incestuous desires bring the girl into competition with her mother. Motivated by fear that her mother will withdraw her love if the desires persist, the girl normally represses them and identifies with her mother. She supplants her childhood desire for a penis with a desire to marry a man and bear children. The baby, emitted from between her legs, serves as the ultimate penis substitute.

A nagging problem for Freudian theory is that many of its concepts, such as castration anxiety and penis envy, are believed to operate at an unconscious level. As such, they lie beyond the scope of scientific observation and measurement. Moreover, viewing childhood sexuality from the vantage point of adulthood, as happens in psychoanalysis, can provide a distorted view of what really took place—especially when the analyst is motivated to find support for his or her theory (Hergenhahn, 2013).

TRUTH OR **FICTION** REVISITED: Therefore, the idea that "castration anxiety" in gay males is aroused by knowledge of male–female intercourse has not been scientifically demonstrated. Moreover, gender nonconformity and gender preferences in gays all occur earlier than Freudian theory would suggest.

Learning Theories Learning theorists agree with Freud that early experiences play an important role in the development of sexual orientation. But they focus on the role of reinforcement of early patterns of sexual behavior, rather than on the resolution of unconscious conflicts. People generally repeat pleasurable activities and discontinue painful ones. Thus, people may learn to engage in sexual activity with people of their own gender if childhood sexual experimentation with them is connected with sexual pleasure.

If sexual motivation is high, as it tends to be during adolescence, and the only outlets are with others of one's own gender, adolescents may experiment sexually with them. If these encounters are pleasurable and heterosexual experiences are

Castration anxiety In psychoanalytic theory, a man's fear that his genitals will be removed. Castration anxiety is an element of the Oedipus complex and is implicated in the directionality of erotic interests.

unpleasant, a firmer gay male or lesbian sexual orientation may develop (Gagnon & Simon, 1973). Conversely, pain, anxiety, or social disapproval may be connected with early contacts with people of one's own gender. In such cases, the child may learn to inhibit feelings of attraction to people of one's own gender and develop a firmer heterosexual orientation.

Although learning may play a role in the development of a gay male or lesbian sexual orientation, learning theorists have not identified specific learning experiences that would lead to these orientations. Moreover, most adolescent encounters with people of the same gender, even if pleasurable, do not lead to an adult gay male or lesbian sexual orientation. Many heterosexual people have had adolescent encounters with members of their own gender without swaying their adult orientations. This is true even of people whose early sexual interactions with the other gender were fumbling and frustrating. Moreover, the overwhelming majority of gay males and lesbians were aware of sexual interest in people of their own gender *before* they had sexual encounters with them, pleasurable or otherwise (Savin-Williams & Diamond, 2000).

GENDER NONCONFORMITY

Gender nonconformity means not behaving in a way that is consistent with the gender-role stereotype associated with one's anatomic sex in a given culture. On average, gay males tend to be somewhat feminine and lesbians to be somewhat masculine, but there is a good deal of variation within each group (Dawood et al., 2009; Rieger et al., 2008). Gender nonconformity begins in childhood. Gay males and lesbians are more likely than heterosexuals to report childhood behavior stereotypical of the other gender (Green, 2008; Lippa, 2008). Many gay males and lesbians recall acting and feeling "different" from their childhood peers. Many gay males from a variety of groups, such as college students, prisoners, psychiatric patients, and activists, report that they avoided participating in competitive sports as children, were more fearful of physical injury, and were more likely to avoid getting into fights than heterosexual males (Dawood et al., 2009; Green, 2008). Some gay males recall feeling different as early as the age 3 or 4, a feeling that was related to behavior that is stereotypical of the other gender.

Gay males are also more likely to recall feeling more sensitive than their heterosexual peers during childhood (Green, 2008; Lippa, 2008). They cried more easily. Their feelings were more readily hurt. They had more artistic interests. They had fewer male buddies and more female playmates (Bos et al., 2008). Gay males were more likely than their heterosexual counterparts to have preferred "girls' toys." They preferred playing with girls to playing with trucks or guns or engaging in rough-and-tumble play (Dawood et al., 2009). Their preferences often led to their being called "sissies." Gay men also recall more cross-dressing during childhood. They preferred the company of older women to older men and engaged in childhood sex play with other boys rather than with girls.

Gender Nonconformity and the Butch–Femme Dimension There is also evidence of masculine-typed behavior among lesbians as children (Lippa, 2008). Lesbians as a group were more likely than heterosexual women to perceive themselves as having been "tomboys." They were more likely to prefer rough-and-tumble games to playing with dolls, and they enjoyed wearing boys' clothing rather than "cutesy" dresses.

A study by Devendra Singh and colleagues (1999) relates gender nonconformity in lesbians to the butch–femme dimension and biological factors. The investigators compared self-identified **butch** and **femme** lesbians on various personality,

Butch A lesbian who assumes a traditional masculine gender role.

Femme A lesbian who assumes a traditional feminine gender role.

behavioral, and biological measures. They found that butch lesbians were significantly more likely than femme lesbians to recall gender-atypical behavioral preferences in childhood. Butch lesbians also had higher waist-to-hip ratios and higher testosterone levels in their saliva, both of which are more typical of males. The Singh group suggests that their findings support the validity of the butch–femme distinction, and that the distinction may be caused by differences in exposure to prenatal androgens (male sex hormones).

Childhood Effeminacy and a Gay Male Sexual Orientation How might extreme childhood effeminacy lead to a gay male sexual orientation? Those who support an environmental view speculate that the social detachment of these boys from male peers and role models (especially fathers) creates strong, unfulfilled cravings for male affection. This craving then leads them to seek males as partners in sex and love relationships in adolescence and adulthood (Green, 2008).

Of course, there is another possibility (Green, 2008; Dawood et al., 2009): Gender nonconformity appears to be somewhat inheritable. Moreover, if a tendency toward homosexuality is inherited, gender nonconformity could also be an expression of that tendency.

All in all, the origins of a gay male or lesbian sexual orientation remain mysterious and complex. In reviewing theories and research, we are left with the impression that sexual orientation appears to spring from multiple origins, including biological and psychosocial factors. Genetic and biochemical factors (such as hormone levels) may affect the prenatal organization of the brain. These factors may predispose people to a certain sexual orientation. But it may be that early socialization experiences also play a role. The precise influences and interactions of these factors have so far eluded researchers.

The New Look of *Bride's Magazine*? Many newspapers and magazines regularly report stories and photos of gay couples who are getting engaged or married.

Sexual Orientation in Contemporary Society

The General Social Survey (National Science Foundation, 2007) found that the percentage of people saying intercourse between people of the same gender is "always wrong" had dropped by 21 points over the ten years between studies, from 77% to 56%. Although opposition remains high, the director of the study said the decline

Real Students, Real Questions

Q *Can parents know if their child will be homosexual by a certain age? Are there attributes they should look for?*

A Children who become gay or lesbian often but not always show gender nonconformity. That is, the boy may not be very interested in sports. The girl may not want to play with dolls. A word to the wise parent: Pushing sports and dolls on a child will not affect his or her sexual orientation. It might make the child miserable if he or she wants something else.

"is as large a social change as any ever." Much survey data suggest that greater acceptance has come from more people knowing someone who is gay.

"It's the same as racial equality," the director said. "The point is to think of them as individuals, who are also co-workers, neighbors, someone who supports the local charity drive—to see people as people, except in this one little way they're different" (National Science Foundation, 2007).

Gay "civil unions" have been with us for several years now, and as this book goes to press, many states allow gay marriage (see Table 10.3). Table 10.4 on page 279 reports the results of a nationally representative 2012 *New York Times* news poll and compares them to those of polls since 2004. In 2004, only a little over one-fifth of respondents (22%) supported gay marriage; 33% supported civil unions, but two people in five (40%) wanted no legal recognition of gay relationships. Eight years later, in 2012, the percentage of people supporting gay marriage almost doubled to 40%; a smaller percentage (23%) supported civil unions because of the increased number in favor of permitting marriage. And fewer than one in three respondents, 31%—down from 40% in 2004—favored no legal recognition of gay marriage.

TRUTH OR **FICTION** REVISITED: The majority of Americans apparently continue to oppose gay marriage, according to the poll; however, when we combine support for gay marriage with support for gay civil unions, we see nearly two people in three (63%) supporting legal recognition of gay relationships.

There is further evidence of a trend toward support of gay marriage. In one study (Nagourney, 2009), 31% of the respondents older than age 40 said they supported gay marriage, but 57% of those younger than 40 said they favored it—a 26 percentage–point difference. Moreover, in May of 2012, the President of the United States, Barack Obama, endorsed gay marriage (Calmes & Baker, 2012). "At a certain point, I've just concluded that for me personally it is important for me to go ahead and affirm that I think same-gender couples should be able to get married,"

4 (T/F)

👁️ Watch the **Video**
A Family with Two Fathers
on **MyDevelopmentLab**

Real Students, Real Questions

Q *I don't understand why people can be supportive of gays/lesbians, but not supportive of marriage for gays/lesbians. Can you explain?*

A *Marriage* seems to be the trip word. Many people who are otherwise tolerant of gay males and lesbians see marriage as something defined by scripture to apply only to a man and a woman. Of course, one could ask whether one can be truly tolerant of gays and lesbians if one restricts marriage to males and females? On the other hand, let's not minimize the struggle that many well-meaning people experience when they attempt to reconcile social trends and their own feelings with religious dogma. The Book of Leviticus and other parts of the Old Testament, and the writings of early Christian theologians such as St. Augustine proscribe many sexual acts other than male–male and female–female acts, for example, masturbation and sex without being married. Gay marriage is just one of the sources of internal conflict for many people. On the other hand, polls show that Americans are in fact becoming more tolerant of gay marriage.

Table 10.3

Status of Gay Marriage around the World as of November 2012

Countries in Which Gay Marriage Is Legal	Countries in Which Gay Marriage Is Being Debated	States in the United States in Which Gay Marriage Is Legal*
Belgium	Australia	Connecticut
Brazil	China	Iowa
Canada	Colombia	Maine
Iceland	Denmark	Maryland
Israel	Finland	Massachusetts
Mexico	France	New Hampshire
The Netherlands	Germany	New York
Norway	Luxembourg	Vermont
Portugal	Nepal	Washington**
South Africa	New Zealand	
Spain	Nigeria	
Sweden	United Kingdom	

*Many other states and countries have legalized civil unions between gay couples and lesbian couples.

**This list is growing and may be outdated by the time you are reading this page. Search online for a current list.

Mr. Obama said. "I had hesitated on gay marriage in part because I thought that civil unions would be sufficient," Mr. Obama continued. "I was sensitive to the fact that for a lot of people, the word *marriage* was something that invokes very powerful traditions and religious beliefs." Obama also supported repeal of the federal Defense of Marriage Act.

TRUTH OR FICTION REVISITED: Most Americans assume that gay people choose to be gay, despite the accumulation of research evidence that inborn biological factors play a strong role in the development of sexual orientation. For example, a nationwide poll con ducted in 1977 found that only 13% of Americans believed that gay people were "born with" their sexual orientation, compared to 56% who favored environmental causes. An Associated Press poll, conducted in 2000, found that 30% of Americans believe that gay people are born that way, as compared to 46% who say they "choose" to be gay. More people are coming to look on sexual orientation as something that one is born with. And so, fewer people are likely to believe that young people can be "seduced" into one sexual orientation or another.

Table 10.4

U.S. Attitudes toward Recognition of Committed Gay and Lesbian Relationships

- In 2004, approximately 40% of Americans would allow no legal recognition whatsoever

- In 2006 through 2009, that percentage of Americans who would not recognize gay and lesbian unions dropped to about 36%

- In 2010 through 2012, only some 30% of Americans still refused to recognize gay unions

- In 2012, 40% of Americans were willing to recognize gay and lesbian marriage, and another 23% were willing to recognize gay and lesbian civil unions

Source: New York Times, Feb. 8-13, 2012.

A World of Diversity

Latin American Attitudes toward Gay Males and Lesbians

A survey by Herek and Gonzalez-Rivera (2006) examined attitudes toward gay males and lesbians among a sample of California residents of Mexican origin. It was found that men's attitudes toward homosexual men were significantly more negative than women's. Women expressed relatively more negative attitudes toward lesbians. When compared with respondents reporting positive attitudes, respondents reporting negative attitudes

- endorsed more traditional gender attitudes.

- tended to be older and less educated.

- had more children.

- were more likely to belong to a fundamentalist religious denomination and to attend religious services religiously.

- were more conservative politically.

- were less likely to have personal contact with gay people.

A more recent study of Latina mothers toward Latina lesbian parents (Rincon & Lam, 2011) found that the women considered that Latina lesbians' parenting of children was actually normal. But they did have some concerns. For example,

they felt that raising children in a household without a male figure could lead to some difficulties in adjustment. They also noted that the children might be teased by other children and that they could become confused about their own sexual orientation as they developed. Let us note, parenthetically, that there is no scientific evidence that being reared by gay or lesbian parents has an effect on the children's sexual orientation. ◉

◉ Watch the Video
Gay Kiss Protest in Barcelona
on **MyDevelopmentLab**

SEXUAL ORIENTATION AND THE LAW

During the past generation, gay people have organized effective political groups to fight discrimination and to overturn the sodomy laws that have traditionally targeted them. Despite their success, sodomy laws are still on the books in many states. Sodomy laws prohibit "unnatural" sexual acts, even between consenting adults. Certain sexual acts that many gay people (and heterosexual people) practice, such as anal intercourse and oral–genital contact, fall under the legal definition of sodomy in many states. Although sodomy laws are usually written to apply equally to all adults, the vast majority of prosecutions have been directed against gay people.

A 1986 Supreme Court decision (*Hardwick v. Bowers*) let stand a Georgia sodomy law that makes oral–genital or anal–genital sexual contact crimes punishable by up to 20 years in prison, even when engaged in by consenting adults. The decision was a blow to gay rights organizations, which had looked to the Supreme Court to overturn state sodomy laws.

However, in 2003, by a vote of 6 to 3, the Supreme Court reversed that decision by striking down a Texas law against "deviant sexual intercourse with another individual of the same sex." The Texas law "demeans the lives of homosexual persons," wrote Justice Anthony M. Kennedy, explaining the majority vote. Over the years, the Constitution's right to privacy has been in conflict with laws against same-gender sexual behavior. Gay people "are entitled to respect for their private lives," Kennedy wrote further. In an interview, he added that "the state cannot demean their existence or control their destiny by making their private sexual conduct a crime."

GAY ACTIVISM

Like many other young people in the 1960s, Frank Rich was involved in the civil rights movement. He was shocked by the violent confrontation between protesters and police in Selma, Alabama, in 1965 and in Chicago in 1968. But he had never heard about the days of rioting that rocked Greenwich Village when the police raided the Stonewall Inn, a gay bar, in the wee hours of the morning. Looking back, Rich (2009) realizes that in the 1960s he did not know one gay friend, student, or teacher throughout his high school and college career. The *New York Times*, the paper for which he now writes, did not allow journalists to use the word *gay* until 1987. Nobody he knew had come out as gay, and, as he puts it, the "issue of gay civil rights wasn't on our radar screen."

After the Stonewall incident, all of that changed. Gay activism is now front and center in the nation's civil rights movement. Nowhere in the United States have gay people been more politically effective than in San Francisco. They are well represented on the city police force and in other public agencies. The coming out of many gay people, and their flocking to more tolerant urban centers, has rendered them formidable political forces in these locales and throughout the nation.

During the 1980s and 1990s, HIV/AIDS was a key topic for gays. Gay rights organizations worked to combat the HIV/AIDS epidemic on several fronts:

- To increase funding for HIV/AIDS research and treatment
- To educate the gay and wider communities of the dangers of high-risk sexual behavior
- To encourage gay men and others to adopt safer sex practices, including use of condoms
- To protect the civil rights of people with HIV/AIDS with respect to employment, housing, and medical and dental treatment
- To provide counseling and support services for people with HIV/AIDS

Gay activism has also focused on ending discrimination against gays on all fronts. Notable among these are obtaining partner job benefits (health plan, retirement, and so on), serving openly in the military, and having governments permit gays to get married. Two of the largest issues gays face today are gay marriage and the repeal of Defense of Marriage Acts, which define marriage as taking place between a man and a woman, wherever they are found. In the previous edition of this book, replacement of the Don't Ask–Don't Tell order in the military—instituted by President Bill Clinton in 1993 and considered a "cop-out" by most gays—with the right to serve openly was a key concern. However, in 2011, President Barack Obama gave gay males and lesbians the right to serve their country openly (Dao, 2011). ◉

◉⌐**Watch** the **Video**
Gay in the Military
on **MyDevelopmentLab**

What Is the Sexual Orientation of These Soldiers? During Bill Clinton's presidency, a "Don't Ask–Don't Tell" policy was adopted toward gay people in the military. If they divulged their sexual orientation, they could be removed from the military, but superiors were not allowed to ask them about it.

👁—|**Watch** the **Video**
Sexual Orientation and Gender:
Michael Bailey
on **MyDevelopmentLab**

STEREOTYPES AND SEXUAL BEHAVIOR

Among heterosexuals, sexual aggressiveness is linked to the masculine gender role. Sexual passivity is linked to the feminine role. Some heterosexual people assume (often erroneously) that in gay male and lesbian relationships, one partner consistently assumes the masculine role in sexual relations, and the other assumes the feminine. 👁

Many gay couples vary the active and passive roles, however. Among gay male couples, for example, roles in anal intercourse (*inserter* versus *insertee*) and in fellatio are often reversed. Contrary to popular assumptions, sexual behavior between lesbians seldom reflects distinct butch–femme gender roles. Most lesbians report providing and receiving oral–genital stimulation, alternating roles or simultaneously. Many gay people claim that the labels of *masculine* and *feminine* only represent the "straight community's" efforts to pigeonhole them in terms "straights" can understand.

Adjustment of Gay Males and Lesbians

Are homosexuals more likely than heterosexuals to suffer from mental disorders? Michael King and his colleagues (2008) identified 13,706 research articles on the mental health of gay males, lesbians, and bisexuals. Of these, 476 were selected for analysis. The researchers ultimately compared the mental health of 214,344 heterosexuals and 11,971 nonheterosexuals. A sophisticated statistical averaging technique found that lesbian, gay, and bisexual people were more than twice as likely as heterosexuals to attempt suicide. Lesbian, gay, and bisexual people were 1.5 Times as likely to be diagnosed with depression, anxiety, and dependence on alcohol and other substances. 👁

👁—|**Watch** the **Video**
Being Gay in the US
on **MyDevelopmentLab**

Many observers believe that societal oppression might cause the greater incidence of these mental disorders that we find among gay males, lesbians, and bisexuals. "Surely," writes psychologist J. Michael Bailey (1999), "it must be difficult for young people to come to grips with their homosexuality in a world where homosexual people are often scorned, mocked, mourned, and feared."

There are also connections between lifestyle and health—physical and psychological—among gay males and lesbians, and among heterosexual people. Gay men and lesbians occupy all socioeconomic and vocational levels and follow a variety of lifestyles. In their classic research, Bell and Weinberg (1978) found variations in adjustment in the gay community that seem to mirror the variations in the heterosexual community. Gay people who lived with partners in stable, intimate relationships—so-called close couples—were about as well adjusted as married heterosexual couples. Older gay people who lived alone and had few sexual contacts were more poorly adjusted. So, too, are many heterosexual people who have similar lifestyles. All in all, Bell and Weinberg found that differences in adjustment were more likely to reflect the lifestyle of the individual than his or her sexual orientation.

Most gay males and lesbians who share close relationships with their partners are satisfied with the overall quality of their relationships. Researchers find that heterosexual and gay couples report similar levels of satisfaction with their relationships (Henderson et al., 2009; Kurdek, 2005). Moreover, gay males and lesbians in enduring relationships generally report high levels of love, attachment, closeness, caring, and intimacy.

As with heterosexual people, not all the relationships of gay people are satisfying. Among both groups, satisfaction is higher when both partners feel that the benefits they receive from the relationship outweigh the costs (Henderson et al.,

2009). Like heterosexual people, gay men and lesbians are happier in relationships in which they share power and make joint decisions.

HOMOPHOBIA

Jacob Robida, age 18, entered the Puzzles Lounge, a gay bar in New Bedford, Massachusetts, with a hatchet and a handgun beneath his clothing. He would soon be charged with three counts of assault with intent to murder, assault with a dangerous weapon, and hate crimes.

Robida ordered a shot of liquor. Then he asked the bartender whether the lounge was intended for gay or straight patrons. The bartender told Robida it was usually patronized by gays. Robida had another shot of liquor and then pulled out the hatchet and struck a patron in the head. He then struck a man who tried to help the first victim. Robida also pulled out his gun and shot the man who tried to assist the first hatchet victim. Before fleeing, he shot another patron.

Robida had also aimed the gun at the bartender, but it failed to fire. "I heard a click, and his eyes were just squinted," the bartender told a reporter (Zezima, 2006).

Before it was all over, Robida would shoot a police officer to death at a traffic stop. He is also believed to have killed a woman in West Virginia. He was finally felled during a shootout with Arkansas police officers (Belluck, 2006).

Robida's hatred of gay males was an extreme example of homophobia, but certainly not the only one. Clearly homophobia is the greatest challenge to the adjustment of gay males and lesbians, and it takes many forms, including the following:

- Using derogatory names (such as *queer*, *faggot*, and *dyke*)
- Telling disparaging "queer jokes"
- Barring gay people from housing, employment, or social opportunities
- Taunting (verbal abuse)
- **Gay bashing** (physical, sometimes lethal, abuse)

Gay bashing Violence against homosexuals.

Homophobia. A bartender, right, at Puzzles Lounge, is consoled by a friend after the homophobic assaults by Jacob Robida.

Homophobia derives from root words meaning "fear of homosexuals." Although some psychologists link homophobia to fears of a gay male or lesbian sexual orientation within oneself, homophobic attitudes may also be embedded within a cluster of stereotypical gender-role attitudes toward family life (Rosky, 2009; Lewis & White, 2009). These attitudes support male dominance and the belief that it is natural and appropriate for women to sacrifice for their husbands and children. People who have a strong stake in maintaining stereotypical gender roles may feel more readily threatened by homosexuals, since gay people appear to confuse or reverse these roles. Men have more at stake in maintaining the tradition of male dominance, so perhaps it is not surprising that college men are more intolerant of gay males than college women (Rosky, 2009; Lewis & White, 2009).

Homophobic attitudes are more common among males who identify with a traditional tough male gender role, a conservative political orientation (Rosky, 2009; Lewis & White, 2009), those who hold a fundamentalist religious orientation (Davies, 2004), and those who identify with Nazi beliefs and regalia (Zezima, 2006). But those who actually engage in violence against gay males, and especially those who kill, tend to be criminal psychopaths (Parrot et al., 2006). That is, they are in frequent conflict with the law and do not feel guilt or shame when they inflict pain (Parrott et al., 2006).

Although strides toward social acceptance of gay people have been made since Kinsey's day, the advent of HIV/AIDS has added fuel to the fires of homophobia (Herek et al., 2005). When HIV/AIDS first appeared, it primarily struck the gay male community. Some homophobes in the larger society believed that the epidemic was a God-sent plague intended to punish gay people for sinful behavior. Perhaps the epidemic serves as a pretext for some people to attack gay males, whom they blame for spreading the disease.

"TREATMENT" OF GAY MALE AND LESBIAN SEXUAL ORIENTATIONS

Since the great majority of individuals are heterosexual, let us assume that most readers of this book will also be heterosexual. We have a question for you: Would you be interested in changing your sexual orientation? Does the idea of obtaining some sort of treatment that would cause you to prefer having romantic and sexual relationships with people of your own gender appeal to you? The answer is likely to be no, and the great (great!) majority of gay males and lesbians would also not be interested in changing their sexual orientations. ◉

Yet some gay males and lesbians do express an interest in changing their orientations, for such reasons as religious beliefs or the desire to create a typical family life. But many helping professionals believe that gay males and lesbians would not wish to change their sexual orientation if it were not for social pressure and prejudice. Green (2003) adds that most gay people who seek to change their sexual orientations are ambivalent. Haldeman (2002) notes that the very existence of "conversion therapy" contributes to the social devaluation of homosexuals and bisexuals. Let us note that the American Psychological Association has taken the position that it is unethical to attempt conversion therapy. Their rational is that gay males and lesbians would not seek to change their sexual orientation if homophobia did not exist in society. Therefore, the real issue is to change social and cultural prejudices against individuals with minority sexual orientations.

Nonetheless, a few therapists have reported changing the sexual orientations of some individuals. Among the best known of these, Masters and Johnson (1979) employed methods used to treat sexual dysfunctions (see Chapter 15) to "reverse" clients' gay male or lesbian sexual orientations. For example, they involved gay males in a graded series of pleasurable activities with women, such as massage and

◉ **Watch the Video**
Straightening Out Homosexuals
on **MyDevelopmentLab**

genital stimulation. Masters and Johnson reported a failure rate of 20% for the gay men and 23% for the lesbians they treated in their therapy program. However, these patients do not represent the general gay population:

- Most of the patients were bisexuals. Only about one in five engaged exclusively in male–male or female–female sexual activities.
- More than half were married.
- All were highly motivated to switch their sexual orientations.

Also remember that sexual behavior is *not* the equivalent of sexual orientation. There is no evidence that Masters and Johnson changed anyone's sexual *orientation*.

Coming Out: Coming to Terms with Being Gay

Because of the backdrop of social condemnation and discrimination, gay males and lesbians in our culture often struggle to come to terms with their sexual orientation (Legate et al., 2012). Homosexuals usually speak of the process of accepting their sexual orientation as "coming out" or as "coming out of the closet." Coming out is a two-pronged process: coming out to oneself (recognizing one's sexual orientation) and coming out to others (declaring one's orientation to the world). Coming out can create a sense of pride in one's sexual orientation and foster the ability to form emotionally and sexually satisfying relationships with gay male or lesbian partners (Legate et al., 2012). ◉

COMING OUT TO ONESELF

Many gay people have a difficult time coming to recognize, let alone accept, their sexual orientation:

> Youths with emerging identities that are gay, lesbian, or bisexual, living in generally hostile climates, face particular dilemmas. They are well aware that in many secondary schools the words "fag" and "dyke" are terms of denigration and that anyone who is openly gay, lesbian, or bisexual is open to social exclusion and psychological and physical persecution. Some of their families too will express negative feelings about people who are gay, lesbian, or bisexual; youths in such families may be victimized if they disclose that they are not heterosexual. (Bagley & D'Augelli, 2000)

According to Ritch Savin-Williams and Lisa Diamond (2000), the development of sexual identity in gay males and lesbians involves four steps or features:

- Attraction to members of the same gender
- Self-labeling as gay or lesbian
- Sexual contact with members of the same gender
- Disclosure of one's sexual orientation to other people

The researchers by and large found a ten-year gap between initial attraction to members of one's own gender, which tended to occur at about the age of 8 or 9, and disclosure of one's orientation to other people, which usually occurred at about age 18. In keeping with gender differences noted in Chapter 4, females were more likely to focus on the emotional or romantic aspects of their budding feelings. Males were more likely to focus on the sexual aspects. Males—who are generally more open than females to sexual experimentation—were likely to become involved

CRITICAL THINKING
We live in a society that is generally prejudiced against homosexuals. Therefore, is it possible to know whether a homosexual who asks for help in changing his or her sexual orientation is acting of his or her own free will?

◉ **Watch** the **Video**
Video Essay: Gay College Runner Comes Out
on **MyDevelopmentLab**

in sexual activity with other males before they labeled themselves as being gay. Females, on the other hand, were more likely to label themselves as lesbians before pursuing relationships with other females. Males also tend to form their sexual identity and come out about two years earlier than females (Grov et al., 2006).

Younger cohorts (people ages 18 to 24) in New York and Los Angeles also came out earlier than older cohorts (Grov et al., 2006). Factors such as the current greater acceptance of gay males and lesbians and also the more common portrayal of gay males and lesbians in the media contribute to greater willingness to come out.

For some people, coming to recognize and accept a gay male or lesbian sexual orientation involves gradually stripping away layers of denial. For others, it may be a sudden awakening. Longstanding sexual interests in members of one's own gender may rush into focus on a particular person, as happened with a graduate student named David:

> In college [David's] closest friend was gay. Although this friend had wanted to have sex with David and the attraction was mutual, David still could not associate this attraction with a sexuality that was not acceptable to him. In his first year of graduate school, when he was about 23, he fell in love and then suddenly and with a great sense of relief recognized and acknowledged to himself that he was homosexual. He then had sex for the first time and has subsequently been ... open about his sexuality. (Isay, 1990, p. 295)

CRITICAL THINKING
How do you account for the gender differences in the processes of coming out in males and females?

COMING OUT TO OTHERS

There are different patterns of coming out to others. Coming out occasionally means an open declaration to the world. More often, a person may inform only one or a few select people. For example, the person might tell friends but not family members.

Many gay men and lesbians remain reluctant to declare their sexual orientation, even to friends and family. Disclosure is fraught with the risk of loss of jobs, friendships, and social standing (Legate et al., 2012; Rosario et al., 2009). On the other hand, if the organization at which the individual works is generally supportive of gays, coming out can be related to greater job satisfaction and less anxiety (Legate et al., 2012). Also, "butch" lesbians are more comfortable with coming out to others than "femme" lesbians (Rosario et al., 2009).

Gay men and lesbians often anticipate negative reactions from informing family members, including denial, anger, and rejection (Legate et al., 2012). Family members and loved ones may refuse to hear or be unwilling to accept reality, as noted in *Invisible Lives,* which chronicles the lives of a sample of lesbians in the United States:

> Parents, children, neighbors, and friends of lesbians deny, or compartmentalize, or struggle with their knowledge in the same way the women themselves do. "My parents know I've lived with my partner for six years. She goes home with me. We sleep in the same bed there. The word *lesbian* has never been mentioned." "I told my mother and she said, 'Well, now that's over with. We don't need to mention it again.' She never has, and that was ten years ago. I don't know if she ever told my father." (Barrett, 1990, p. 52)

Some families are more accepting. They may have had suspicions and prepared themselves for such news. Other families are initially rejecting but eventually come to a grudging acceptance that a family member is gay.

Coming Out. Coming out to one's parents can be a scary thing, and many lesbians and gay males avoid it for years, or even for a lifetime. On the other hand, some parents have suspected or known about their children's sexual orientation for quite some time, and even though they may have initially had deep concerns, they may be more accepting than the "children" (who may already be in their thirties or forties) expect.

Christian Grov and his colleagues (2006) found no racial differences in the ages at which European Americans and African Americans came out to themselves and others. However, African Americans were less likely than European Americans to come out to their parents, which is consistent with findings that African American families tend to have more conservative views than European American families.

Real Students, Real Questions

Q *Are there studies that show the effects of being raised by homosexual parents?*

A Loads of them, and they do not show that having one or two gay parents affects a child's sexual orientation. Children of gay parents do develop more egalitarian attitudes; that is, they are less fixated on the tunnel vision of traditional gender-role stereotypes. Overall, the adjustment of the children of gay parents does not differ from the adjustment of the children of heterosexual parents.

Chapter Review ✓•⌐Study and Review on MyDevelopmentLab

LO1 **Describe the various sexual orientations and discuss controversies in defining them**
Heterosexuals are attracted to members of the other gender. Homosexuals are attracted to members of the same gender. Bisexuals are attracted to both males and females. Most homosexuals are content with their anatomic sex. Researchers find that men tend to be bipolar in their erotic interests, but for women, heterosexuality and homosexuality may be independent dimensions. The best evidence we have suggests that about 3% of American males are exclusively gay, and about 2% of American women are exclusively lesbian.

LO2 **Explain how homosexuality been viewed historically and scientifically**
The Judeo-Christian and Islamic traditions frown on homosexuality and other forms of nonprocreative sex. Ancient Greek men often had sexual relationships with adolescent males. Research with MZ and DZ twins suggests a role for genetic factors in the development of sexual orientation. Prenatal sex hormones are also believed to play a role; female embryos exposed to androgens tend to develop more masculine behavior patterns. Early experience with parents and early sexual experience do not appear to sway sexual orientation. Many homosexuals showed gender nonconformity in childhood.

LO3 **Discuss contemporary American attitudes toward homosexuals**
Most Americans are growing more tolerant of homosexuals. A majority would now support either gay marriage or civil unions. Most would grant gay people equal rights to jobs and housing. Men are more likely than women to be homophobic. Sodomy laws have been enforced against gay males more often than against male–female couples.

LO4 **Discuss the adjustment of homosexuals**
Homosexuals are more likely than heterosexuals to encounter anxiety and depression and to have suicidal thoughts, probably because of social prejudice. Most professionals agree that homosexuals who seek to change their sexual orientation are influenced by social prejudice.

LO5 **Describe what is meant by "coming out"**
Coming out to oneself is a gradual process in which the individual eventually comes to accept his or her homosexual orientation. Coming out to others is for many an anxiety-evoking process characterized by fear of social disapproval, loss of a job, and the like.

Test Your Learning

1. In ancient _____, men often had sexual relationships with adolescent males.
   - (a) Egypt
   - (b) Greece
   - (c) Rome
   - (d) Macedonia

2. _____ are most likely to share a homosexual orientation.
   - (a) Monozygotic twins
   - (b) Dizygotic twins
   - (c) Parents and their biological children
   - (d) Adoptive parents and their adopted children

3. Psychoanalytic theory ties male homosexuality to faulty resolution of the _____ complex.
   - (a) inferiority
   - (b) Electra
   - (c) whore–Madonna
   - (d) Oedipus

4. The hypothalamus of gay males responds similarly to that of _____ when gay males are presented with the odor of a testosterone derivative.
   - (a) heterosexual men
   - (b) heterosexual women
   - (c) lesbians
   - (d) bisexuals

5. Homosexuals differ from transgendered people in that homosexuals

(a) are satisfied with their anatomic sex.
(b) are dissatisfied with their anatomic sex.
(c) are confused about their gender identity.
(d) seek therapy to change their sexual orientation.

6. Ivanka Savic and her colleagues suggest that sexual differentiation and sexual identity may reflect the timing of prenatal surges of

(a) dopamine.
(b) serotonin.
(c) estrogen.
(d) testosterone.

7. According to Savin-Williams and Diamond, the first step in the development of sexual identity in homosexuals is

(a) sex with members of the same gender.
(b) attraction to members of the same gender.
(c) acceptance of one's sexual orientation.
(d) self-labeling as gay or lesbian.

8. _____ tried to develop methods to "reverse" a homosexual orientation.

(a) Masters and Johnson
(b) Laumann
(c) Freud
(d) Kinsey

9. In contrast to Kinsey and his colleagues, Vrangalova and Savin-Williams (2012) see sexual attraction to people of one's own gender or the other gender as

(a) one-dimensional.
(b) two-dimensional.
(c) three-dimensional.
(d) four-dimensional.

10. The behavior of adolescent Sambian males provides evidence that

(a) some cultures are superior to others.
(b) sexual orientation is genetic.
(c) homosexuality is normal.
(d) culture influences sexual practices.

Answers: 1. b; 2. a; 3. d; 4. b; 5. a; 6. d; 7. b; 8. a; 9. b; 10. d

My Life, My Sexuality

Assessing Your Attitudes toward Gay Males and Lesbians

*Explore this **My Life, My Sexuality** feature by scanning this QR code with your mobile device. If you don't already have one, you may download a free QR scanner for your device wherever smartphone apps are sold. You can also view this feature in MyDevelopmentLab, along with an accompanying critical thinking assignment.*

Here is another self-assessment that is designed to help you get in touch with your feelings. Scan the code to go online and learn more about whether you are generally accepting or unaccepting of gay males and lesbians. We'll also ask you how you feel about what you find?

11 Conception, Pregnancy, and Childbirth

Learning Objectives

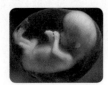

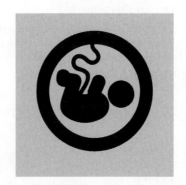

TRUTH OR FICTION?

Which of the following statements are the truth, and which are fiction? Look for the Truth-or-Fiction icons on the pages that follow to find the answers.

1 Prolonged athletic activity may decrease fertility in the male. **T F?**

2 A "test-tube baby" is grown in a laboratory dish throughout the nine-month gestation period. **T F?**

3 Morning sickness is a sign that a pregnancy is progressing normally. **T F?**

4 For the first week after conception, a fertilized egg cell is not attached to its mother's body. **T F?**

5 Pregnant women can have one or two alcoholic beverages a day without harming their babies. **T F?**

6 The way that the umbilical cord is cut determines whether the baby will have an "inny" or an "outy." **T F?**

7 In the United States, nearly 3 births in 10 are by cesarean section. **T F?**

8 Couples should abstain from sexual activity for at least six weeks after childbirth. **T F?**

On a balmy day in October, Marta and her partner Jorge rush to catch the train to their jobs in the city. Marta's workday is outwardly the same as any other. Within her body, however, a drama is unfolding. Yesterday, hormones had caused an ovarian follicle to rupture, releasing its egg cell, or ovum. How this particular follicle was selected to ripen and release its ovum this month remains a mystery. But for the next day or so, Marta will be capable of conceiving.

The previous morning Marta had used her ovulation-timing kit, which showed that she was about to ovulate. So later that night, Marta and Jorge had made love, hoping that Marta would conceive. Jorge ejaculated hundreds of millions of sperm within Marta's vagina. Only a few thousand survived the journey through the cervix and uterus to the fallopian tube that contained the ovum, released just hours earlier. Of these, a few hundred remained to bombard the ovum. One succeeded in penetrating the ovum's covering, resulting in conception. From a single cell formed by the union of sperm and ovum, a new life begins to form. The **zygote** is but 1/175 of an inch across—a tiny beginning for the drama about to occur.

Marta is age 37. Four months into her pregnancy, Marta obtains **amniocentesis** in order to check for the presence of chromosomal abnormalities, such as **Down syndrome**. (Down syndrome is more common among children born to women in their late 30s and older.) Amniocentesis also indicates the sex of the fetus. Although many parents prefer to know the sex of their baby before it is born, Marta and Jorge ask their doctor not to inform them. "Why ruin the surprise?" Jorge tells his friends. So Marta and Jorge are left to debate boys' names and girls' names for the next few months.

Zygote   A fertilized ovum.

Amniocentesis   A procedure for drawing off and examining fetal cells in the amniotic fluid to determine the presence of various disorders in the fetus.

◉┤**Watch** the **Video**
Challenges of Becoming a New Parent
on **MyDevelopmentLab**

Down syndrome   A chromosomal abnormality that leads to mental retardation, caused by an extra chromosome on the twenty-first pair.

Spontaneous abortion   The sudden, involuntary expulsion of the embryo or fetus from the uterus before it is capable of independent life. Also termed *miscarriage*.

Conception: Against All Odds

Conception is the union of a sperm cell and an ovum. On the one hand, conception is the beginning of a new human life. It is also the end of a fantastic voyage, however, in which a viable ovum, one of only several hundred that will mature and ripen during a woman's lifetime, unites with one of several hundred *million* sperm produced by the man in the average ejaculate. ◉

Ova carry X sex chromosomes. Sperm carry either X or Y sex chromosomes. Girls are conceived from the union of an ovum and an X-bearing sperm, boys from the union of an ovum and a Y-bearing sperm. Sperm that bear Y sex chromosomes appear to be faster swimmers than those bearing X sex chromosomes. This is one of the reasons that between 120 and 150 boys are conceived for every 100 girls. What seem to be natural balancing factors favor the survival of female fetuses, however. Male fetuses are more likely to be lost in a **spontaneous abortion,** which often occurs during the first month of pregnancy. In many cases of early spontaneous abortion, the woman never realizes that she had been pregnant. Despite spontaneous abortions, boys still outnumber girls at birth. Boys suffer from a higher incidence of infant mortality, however. Thus, the numbers of boys and girls in the population are further equalized by the time they mature to the point of pairing off.

The 200 to 400 million sperms in an average ejaculate may seem excessive, since only 1 can fertilize an egg. Only 1 in 1,000 will ever arrive in the vicinity of an ovum, however. Millions deposited in the vagina simply flow out of the woman's body because of gravity, unless she remains prone for quite some time. Normal vaginal acidity kills many more. Many surviving sperm swim against the current of fluid coming from the cervix, through the os and into the uterus. Surviving sperm may reach the fallopian tubes 60 to 90 minutes after ejaculation. About half the sperm end up in the wrong tube—that is, the one not containing the egg. Perhaps some 2,000 sperm find their way into the right tube. Fewer still manage to swim the final two inches against the currents generated by the cilia that line the tube.

The journey of sperm may be blind but it is not random. Sperm cells are apparently attracted by the odor of a chemical secreted by ova. They seem to be "egged on" (pardon the pun) by a change in calcium ions that occurs when an ovum is released (Olson et al., 2011).

Fertilization normally occurs in a fallopian tube. (Figure 11.1 shows sperm swarming around an egg in a fallopian tube.) Ova contain chromosomes, proteins, fats, and nutritious fluid and are surrounded by a gelatinous layer called the **zona pellucida**. This layer must be penetrated if fertilization is to occur. Sperm that have completed their journey secrete the enzyme **hyaluronidase,** which briefly thins the zona pellucida, enabling one sperm to penetrate. Once a sperm has entered, the zona pellucida thickens, locking other sperm out. The corresponding chromosomes in the sperm and ovum line up opposite each other. Conception occurs as the chromosomes from the sperm and ovum combine to form 23 new pairs, which carry a unique set of genetic instructions.

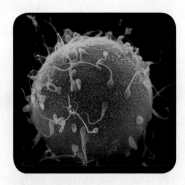

FIGURE 11.1 Human Sperm Swarming around an Ovum in a Fallopian Tube. Fertilization normally occurs in a fallopian tube, not in the uterus. Sperm secrete the enzyme hyaluronidase, which thins the layer surrounding the ovum, allowing one sperm cell to penetrate.

OPTIMIZING THE CHANCES OF CONCEPTION

Couples may wish to optimize their chances of conceiving during a particular month so that birth occurs at a certain time. Others may have trouble conceiving and want to maximize their chances for a few months before seeing a fertility specialist. Fairly simple procedures can increase the chances of conceiving for couples without serious fertility problems.

The ovum can be fertilized for about 4 to 20 hours after ovulation. Sperm are most active within 48 hours after ejaculation. So one way to optimize the chances of conception is to engage in coitus within a few hours of ovulation. There are several ways to predict ovulation.

Using the Basal Body Temperature Chart Few women have perfectly regular cycles, so they can only guess when they are ovulating. A basal body temperature (BBT) chart (see Figure 11.2) can provide a more reliable estimate.

Body temperature is fairly even before ovulation. Early-morning temperature is usually below 98.6°F. But just before ovulation, basal temperature dips slightly. Then, on the day after ovulation, temperature tends to rise by about 0.4 to 0.8°F and to remain higher until menstruation. A woman can detect these changes by tracking her temperature after awakening in the morning but before rising from bed. Thermometers that provide finely graded readings, such as electronic digital thermometers, best detect the minor changes. The couple records the woman's temperature and the day of the cycle (as well as the day of the month) and indicates whether they have engaged in coitus. With regular charting for six months, the woman may learn to predict the day of ovulation more accurately—assuming that her cycles are fairly regular.

Opinion is divided as to whether it is better for couples to have coitus every 24 hours or every 36 to 48 hours for the several-day period during which ovulation

Zona pellucida A gelatinous layer that surrounds an ovum.

Hyaluronidase An enzyme that briefly thins the zona pellucida, enabling one sperm to penetrate.

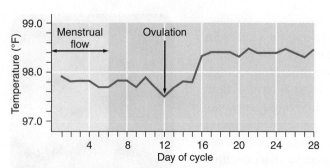

FIGURE 11.2 **A Basal Body Temperature (BBT) Chart.** Because most women have somewhat irregular menstrual cycles, they may not be able to predict ovulation perfectly. The BBT chart helps them to do so. Body temperature is fairly even before ovulation but dips slightly just before ovulation. On the day after ovulation, a woman's body temperature increases about 0.4 to 0.8°F above the level before ovulation.

is expected. More frequent coitus around the time of ovulation may increase the chances of conception. Relatively less frequent (that is, every 36 to 48 hours) coitus leads to a higher sperm count during each ejaculation. Most fertility specialists recommend that couples seeking to conceive a baby have intercourse once every day or two during the week in which the woman expects to ovulate. Men with lower than normal sperm counts may be advised to wait 48 hours between ejaculations.

Analyzing Urine or Saliva for Luteinizing Hormone
Over-the-counter kits are more accurate than the basal body temperature method and predict ovulation by analyzing the woman's urine or saliva for the surge in luteinizing hormone (LH) that precedes ovulation by about 12 to 24 hours.

Tracking Vaginal Mucus Women can track the thickness of their vaginal mucus during the menstrual cycle by rolling it between their fingers and noting changes in texture. The mucus is thick, white, and cloudy during most phases of the cycle but turns thin, slippery, and clear for a few days before ovulation. A day or so after ovulation the mucus again thickens and becomes opaque.

Additional Considerations Coitus in the male-superior position allows sperm to be deposited deeper in the vagina and minimizes leakage of sperm out of the vagina due to gravity. Women may improve their chances of conceiving by lying on their backs and drawing their knees close to their breasts after ejaculation. This position, perhaps aided by use of a pillow to support the buttocks, may prevent sperm from dripping out and will elevate the pool of semen in relation to the cervix. Gravity will therefore work for, rather than against, conception. Women may lie still for about 30 to 60 minutes after ejaculation.

Women with severely retroverted or "tipped" uteruses may profit from supporting themselves on their elbows and knees and having their partners enter them from behind. Again, this position helps prevent semen from dripping out.

The man should penetrate as deeply as possible just before ejaculation, hold still during ejaculation, then withdraw slowly in a straight line to avoid dispersing the pool of semen.

SELECTING THE SEX OF YOUR CHILD

Parents have wished that they could select the sex of their children for thousands of years. In many cultures, one sex—usually male—has been preferred over the other. In other cases, parents who already have girls (or boys) would like to be able to "balance" their family by having a boy (or girl). Then, too, there are sex-linked diseases that show up only in sons. In such cases, parents would feel safer if they could choose to have daughters.

Folklore is replete with methods. Some cultures advised coitus under the full moon to conceive boys. The Greek philosopher Aristotle suggested that making love during a north wind will beget sons. A south wind would produce daughters. Sour foods were once suggested for parents desirous of having boys. Those who wanted girls were advised to consume sweets. Husbands who yearned to have boys might be advised to wear their boots to bed. It goes without saying that none of these methods worked (but we will say it anyhow).

These methods, or nonmethods, would supposedly lead to the conception of children of the desired sex. However, methods after conception have also been used, such as the abortion of fetuses because of their sex. There are also many cultures in which infanticide has been used. Because boys have usually been considered more desirable than girls, female infanticide has been more common than male infanticide.

Today, there is a reliable method for selecting the sex of your child prior to implantation: preimplantation genetic diagnosis (PGD). PGD was developed to detect genetic disorders, but it also allows health professionals to learn of the sex of the embryo (Puri & Nachtigall, 2009). In PGD, ova are fertilized in vitro, leading to conception of perhaps six to eight embryos. After a few days of cell division, a cell is extracted from each. The sex chromosomal structure of the cell is examined microscopically to determine whether the embryo is female or male. Embryos of the desired sex are implanted in the woman's uterus, where one or more can grow to term. PGD is a foolproof sex-selection method, but it is medically invasive and expensive, and implantation cannot be guaranteed. Yet, when implantation occurs, the sex of the embryo is known.

Preimplantation Genetic Diagnosis. PGD is the only perfectly reliable method for selecting the sex of one's child prior to implantation.

Infertility and Assisted Reproductive Technology

For couples who want children, few problems are more frustrating than the inability to conceive. Physicians often recommend that heterosexual couples try to conceive on their own for six months before seeking medical assistance. The term **infertility** is usually not applied until the couple has tried to get pregnant for more than a year, but women above the age of 35 are advised to seek help within six months of attempts (American Fertility Association, 2012a).

Because the incidence of infertility increases with age, it is partially the result of a rise in couples who postpone childbearing until their 30s and 40s. About one American couple in six or seven has fertility problems (American Fertility Association, 2012a). However, about half of them eventually succeed in conceiving a child. Many treatment options are available, as we will see.

MALE FERTILITY PROBLEMS

The fertility lies with the man in about 40% of cases. In about 20% of cases, problems are found in both partners.

The following fertility problems are found in men (American Fertility Association, 2012a):

- Low sperm count
- Irregularly shaped sperm— for example, malformed heads or tails
- Low sperm **motility**
- Chronic diseases such as diabetes, as well as infectious diseases such as sexually transmitted infections
- Injury to the testes
- An **autoimmune response,** in which antibodies produced by the man deactivate his own sperm
- A pituitary imbalance and/or thyroid disease

Problems in producing normal, abundant sperm may be caused by genetic factors, advanced age, hormonal problems, diabetes, injuries to the testes, varicose veins in the scrotum, drugs (alcohol, narcotics, marijuana, tobacco), blood pressure medications, environmental toxins, excess heat, and stress. Sperm production gradually declines with age, but normal aging does not necessarily produce infertility. Men in late adulthood have fathered children.

CRITICAL THINKING
Sex selection raises many moral and ethical questions. Many people wonder whether people have the "right" to select the sex of their children. Where do you stand on the issue? Why?

Infertility Inability to conceive a child.

Motility Self-propulsion. A measure of the viability of sperm cells.

Autoimmune response The production of antibodies that attack naturally occurring substances that are (incorrectly) recognized as being foreign or harmful.

Low sperm count (or no sperm) is the most common problem. Sperm counts of 40 million to 150 million sperm per milliliter of semen are considered normal. A count of fewer than 20 million is regarded as low. Sperm production may be low among men with undescended testes that were not surgically corrected before puberty. Also, frequent ejaculation can reduce sperm counts. Sperm production may be impaired in men whose testicles are consistently one or two degrees above the typical scrotal temperature of 94° to 95°F. Frequent hot baths and tight-fitting underwear may also be responsible for low sperm production, at least temporarily.

TRUTH OR **FICTION** REVISITED: Some men may encounter fertility problems from prolonged athletic activity, use of electric blankets, or even long, hot baths. In such cases the problem can be readily corrected. Male runners with fertility problems are often advised to take time off to increase sperm counts. Pressure, which can be caused by certain bicycle seats, may also impair fertility; have your doctor recommend a comfortable, safe seat. Aging and certain prescription and illicit drugs are other causes (American Fertility Association, 2012a).

Sometimes the sperm count is adequate, but prostate, hormonal, or other factors deprive sperm of motility or deform them. Motility can also be hampered by scar tissue from infections. Scarring may prevent sperm from passing through parts of the male reproductive system, such as the vas deferens. To be considered normal, sperm must be able to swim for at least two hours after coitus and most (60% or more) must be normal in shape.

Sperm counts have been increased by surgical repair of the varicose veins in the scrotum. Microsurgery can also open blocked passageways that prevent the outflow of sperm. Researchers are also investigating the effects on sperm production of special cooling undergarments. Most men whose infertility is due to higher-than-normal scrotal temperatures show increased sperm count and quality when they wear such undergarments.

Artificial Insemination The sperm of men with low sperm counts can be collected and frozen. The sperm from multiple ejaculations can then be injected into a woman's uterus at the time of ovulation. This is one kind of **artificial insemination.** Also, the sperm of men with low sperm motility can be injected into their partners' uteruses, so that the sperm begin their journey closer to the fallopian tubes. Sperm from a donor can be used to artificially inseminate a woman whose male partner is infertile. The child then bears the genes of one of the parents (the mother). A donor can be chosen who resembles the partner in physical traits and ethnic background.

A variation of artificial insemination has been used with some men with very low (or zero!) sperm counts in the semen, immature sperm, or immotile sperm. Immature sperm can be removed from a testicle by a thin needle and then directly injected into an egg in a laboratory dish. The method has even been successful with a few men who only have tailless spermatids in the testes.

FEMALE FERTILITY PROBLEMS

Women encounter the following major fertility problems (American Fertility Association, 2012a):

- Irregular ovulation, including failure to ovulate
- Obstructions or malfunctions of the reproductive tract, which are often caused by infections or diseases involving the reproductive tract
- Endometriosis
- Declining hormone levels of estrogen and progesterone that occur with aging and may prevent the ovum from becoming fertilized or remaining implanted in the uterus

Artificial insemination The introduction of sperm in the reproductive tract through means other than sexual intercourse.

From 10% to 15% of female infertility problems stem from failure to ovulate. Many factors can play a role in failure to ovulate, including hormonal irregularities, malnutrition, genetic factors, stress, and chronic disease. Failure to ovulate may occur in response to low levels of body fat, as in the cases of women athletes and women who have eating disorders (Frisch, 2002).

Ovulation may often be induced by the use of fertility drugs such as *clomiphene* (Clomid). Clomiphene stimulates the pituitary gland to secrete FSH and LH, which in turn stimulate the maturation of ova. Clomiphene leads to conception in most cases of infertility that are due *solely* to irregular or absent ovulation. But since infertility can have multiple causes, only about half of the women who use clomiphene become pregnant. Another infertility drug, Pergonal, contains a high concentration of FSH, which directly stimulates maturation of ovarian follicles. Like clomiphene, Pergonal has high success rates with women whose infertility is due to lack of ovulation. These drugs may cause multiple births by stimulating more than one ovum to ripen during a month (McClamrock, 2012).

Local infections that scar the fallopian tubes and other organs impede the passage of sperm or ova. Such infections include pelvic inflammatory disease, which is an inflammation of the woman's internal reproductive tract that can be caused by various infectious agents, such as the bacteria responsible for gonorrhea and chlamydia (see Chapter 16).

In **endometriosis,** cells break away from the uterine lining (the endometrium) and become implanted and grow elsewhere. When they develop on the surface of the ovaries or fallopian tubes, they may block the passage of ova or impair conception. About one case in six of female sterility is believed to be due to endometriosis. Hormone treatments and surgery sometimes reduce the blockage to the point that women can conceive. A physician may suspect endometriosis during a pelvic exam, but it is diagnosed with certainty by **laparoscopy.** A long, narrow tube is inserted through an incision in the navel, permitting the physician to inspect the organs in the pelvic cavity visually. (The incision is all but undetectable.)

Suspected blockage of the fallopian tubes may also be checked by a **Rubin test** or a **hysterosalpingogram** (or "hysterogram"). In a Rubin test, carbon dioxide gas is blown through the cervix. Its pressure is then monitored to determine whether it flows freely through the fallopian tubes into the abdomen or is trapped in the uterus. In the common hysterosalpingogram, the movement of an injected dye is monitored by X-rays. This procedure may be uncomfortable. Several methods help many couples with problems such as blocked fallopian tubes bear children.

In Vitro Fertilization When Louise Brown was born in England after being conceived by the method of **in vitro fertilization (IVF),** the event made headlines around the world. Louise was dubbed the world's first "test-tube baby." **TRUTH OR FICTION REVISITED:** But with a so-called test-tube baby, conception actually takes place in a laboratory dish (not a test tube), and the embryo is implanted in the mother's uterus, where it develops to term. Before in vitro fertilization, fertility drugs stimulate ripening of ova. Ripe ova are then surgically removed from an ovary and placed in a laboratory dish along with the father's sperm. Fertilized ova are then injected into the mother's uterus to become implanted in the uterine wall.

Several attempts may be needed to achieve a pregnancy because only a minority of attempts leads to births. Yet several embryos may be injected into the uterus at once, heightening the odds. IVF remains costly but is otherwise routine—if not guaranteed.

Laura Schieve and her colleagues (1999) studied nearly 10,000 births from IVF and found that the greatest success rates were achieved when professionals

Endometriosis An abnormal condition in which endometrial tissue is sloughed off into the abdominal cavity rather than out of the body during menstruation. The condition is characterized by abdominal pain and may cause infertility.

Laparoscopy A medical procedure in which a long, narrow tube (laparoscope) is inserted through an incision in the navel, permitting the visual inspection of organs in the pelvic cavity.

Rubin test A test in which carbon dioxide gas is blown through the cervix and its progress through the reproductive tract is tracked to determine whether or not the fallopian tubes are blocked.

Hysterosalpingogram A test in which a dye is injected into the reproductive tract and its progress is tracked by X-rays to determine whether or not the fallopian tubes are blocked.

In vitro fertilization (IVF) A method of conception in which mature ova are surgically removed from an ovary and placed in a laboratory dish along with sperm.

A World of Diversity

LGBT Family Building

Not only heterosexual couples want children. So do heterosexual (and gay and lesbian) singles. And so do couples who belong to the gay, lesbian, bisexual, transgendered community.

Some gay and lesbian couples, of course, bring children from previous marriages or other kinds of relationships. But if they want children, they have to make decisions as to who the children will be and how to make it happen. Transgendered individuals who have had genital surgery are also sterilize, so they cannot father or bear offspring.

Lesbians, of course, can conceive through sexual intercourse with a friend or confidant, but many prefer not to do so. The American Fertility Association (2012b) notes that they can also conceive through assisted productive technologies such as at-home insemination, intrauterine insemination (IUI), in vitro fertilization (IVF),

and reciprocal in vitro fertilization (RIVF). All these methods require obtaining donor sperm, from either a known or anonymous source. IUI, known better perhaps as artificial insemination, is a low-technology method in which washed sperm are inserted directly into the uterus through a catheter. If IUI does not work, a woman may consider IVF. When both members of a lesbian couple are fertile, they sometimes choose to harvest the eggs from one partner, have them fertilized with donor sperm, and then insert the resulting embryos in the other partner, who may become pregnant through this process. The other partner may do the same. That's why this method is called *reciprocal* IVF. It permits both partners to play a role in bearing the child.

Gay males will need a surrogate mother to become impregnated by their sperm and carry the embryo and fetus to

term. The two potential fathers' sperm is analyzed, and either the sperm with the strongest likelihood to impregnate the surrogate are selected, or the sperm may be mixed so that the fathers do not know which partner actually fathered the child. On the other hand, actual fatherhood usually becomes clear enough in terms of the child's appearance and behavior as time goes on. DNA testing can also be used to make the determination. But both men played a role in the process and as long as their relationship remains stable, they usually make no effort to precisely determine paternity.

The American Fertility Association (www.theafa.org) invites all individuals who have fertility questions or issues to be in touch with them—heterosexual couples; would-be single parents; and lesbian, gay, bisexual, and transgendered couples.

---

attempted to implant two embryos: 43% success among 20- to 29-year-olds and 36% success among 30- to 34-year-olds. For each age group, multiple births (of DZ twins) occurred in about half of the cases. In vitro fertilization is associated with some greater risks for mother and child, such as high blood pressure in the mother and spontaneous abortion. Discuss the risks and rewards with your gynecologist.

GIFT In **gamete intrafallopian transfer (GIFT)**, sperm and ova are inserted together into a fallopian tube for fertilization. Unlike in vitro fertilization, conception occurs in a fallopian tube rather than a laboratory dish.

ZIFT Zygote intrafallopian transfer (ZIFT) involves a combination of IVF and GIFT. Sperm and ova are combined in a laboratory dish. After fertilization, the zygote is placed in the mother's fallopian tube to begin its journey to the uterus for implantation. ZIFT has an advantage over GIFT in that the fertility specialists can ascertain that fertilization has occurred before insertion is performed.

Donor IVF Donor IVF is a variation of IVF. It is used when a woman does not produce ova of her own but when her uterus is apparently capable of providing an adequate environment to bring a baby to term. An ovum is harvested from another woman—the donor. It is fertilized in vitro, often by sperm from the partner of the recipient. Then, as in other cases of IVF, the fertilized ovum is placed directly into the uterus of the recipient. The embryo becomes implanted and undergoes the remainder of prenatal development in the recipient's uterus. This procedure is known as an *embryonic transplant*.

Gamete intrafallopian transfer (GIFT) A method of conception in which sperm and ova are inserted into a fallopian tube to encourage conception.

Zygote intrafallopian transfer (ZIFT) A method of conception in which an ovum is fertilized in a laboratory dish and then placed in a fallopian tube.

Donor IVF A variation of in vitro fertilization in which the ovum is taken from one woman, fertilized, and then injected into the uterus or fallopian tube of another woman.

Embryonic Transfer **Embryonic transfer** can be used with women who do not produce ova of their own. A woman volunteer is artificially inseminated by the male partner of the infertile woman, or by donor sperm. Five days later the embryo is removed from the volunteer and inserted within the uterus of the mother-to-be, where it is hoped that it will become implanted.

Intracytoplasmic Sperm Injection **Intracytoplasmic sperm injection (ICSI)** can be used when a man has too few sperm for IVF, or when IVF fails. ICSI injects a sperm cell directly into an ovum. However, these methods may be associated with an increase in birth defects, such as heart, stomach, kidney, and bladder problems; cleft palate; hernia; and, in boys, malformation of the penis.

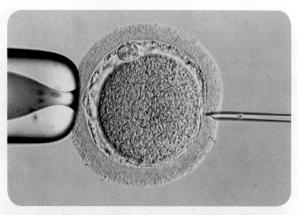

Intracytoplasmic Sperm Injection (ICSI). ICSI is sometimes used when the man has too few sperm for IVF, or when IVF fails. As shown in the photograph, a thin (very thin!) needle injects a single sperm directly into an ovum.

Surrogate Motherhood **Surrogate mothers** bring babies to term for other women who are infertile. (The word *surrogate* means "substitute.") Surrogate mothers may be artificially inseminated by the partners of infertile women, in which case the baby thus carries the genes of the father. But sometimes—as with 53-year-old singer-songwriter James Taylor and his 47-year-old wife—ova are surgically extracted from the biological mother, fertilized in vitro by the biological father, and then implanted in another woman's uterus, where the baby is brought to term. Surrogate mothers are usually paid fees and sign agreements to surrender the baby. (These contracts have been annulled in some states, however, so surrogate mothers cannot be forced to hand over their babies.) In the case of Taylor and his wife, the surrogate mother was a friend of the family, and she delivered twins.

Biologically, surrogate motherhood might seem the mirror image of the more common artificial insemination technique in which a fertile woman is artificially inseminated with sperm from a donor. But the methods are psychologically very different. For example, sperm donors usually do not know the identity of the women who have received their sperm, nor do they follow the child's prenatal development. Surrogate mothers, however, are involved throughout the course of prenatal development.

Ethical and legal dilemmas revolve around the fact that artificially inseminated surrogate mothers have a genetic link to their babies. If they change their minds and do not want to hand the babies over to the contractual parents, there can be legal struggles.

Adoption Adoption is another way for people to obtain children. Despite occasional conflicts that pit adoptive parents against biological parents who change their minds about giving up their children, most adoptions result in the formation of loving new families. 👁

Many Americans find it easier to adopt infants from other countries or infants/children with special needs. Until the past generation, most adopted children were European American babies adopted within a few days of birth. But the more widespread use of contraception and the decisions by many unwed mothers to keep their babies has contributed to a scarcity of European American babies. Today, however, greater numbers of adopted children are older, have spent some time in foster care, are of other races, have special needs, or were born in other countries (Gauthier et al., 2011; Schwam-Harris, 2008). Similarly, a generation or so ago, most adoptive parents were infertile married European American couples of secure socioeconomic status. However, today many adoption agencies allow more diversity in their pool of adopting people: single people, older people, and gay males and lesbians.

Embryonic transfer A method of conception in which a woman volunteer is artificially inseminated by the male partner of the intended mother, after which the embryo is removed from the volunteer and inserted within the uterus of the intended mother.

Intracytoplasmic sperm injection (ICSI) A method of conception in which a single sperm is injected directly into an ovum.

👁 **Watch** the **Video**
Juan and Tracey: Adoptive Parents, Part 1
on **MyDevelopmentLab**

Surrogate mother A woman who is impregnated, through artificial insemination, with the sperm of a prospective father, carries the embryo and fetus to term, and then gives the child to the prospective parents.

Angelina Jolie and Brad Pitt with Their Adopted and Natural Children. Film actors Angelina Jolie and Brad Pitt derive satisfaction from adopting children even though they are fertile.

 Watch the Video
Juan and Tracey: Adoptive Parents, Part 2
on **MyDevelopmentLab**

Most adopted children and adoptive parents fare well, but everything is relative. Adopted children are apparently less likely to be secure with their caregivers than biological children are (Gilmore, 2008). Everything else being equal, the younger the child at the time of adoption, the more smoothly the adoption seems to go (Klahr et al., 2011). Although adoptive parents of children from other races and ethnic backgrounds may make strong efforts to "expose" their adoptive children to their cultures of origin, children adopted at younger ages acquire the language and customs of their adoptive parents more readily (Gauthier et al., 2011). Insecurities and anxiety are most likely to emerge in middle childhood, when they do at all, because of increased understanding of what adoption means. One aspect of coping with adoption is that it often seems to be an inexplicable rejection by the birth mother, which has detrimental effects on the development of the child's self-esteem (Gilmore, 2008; MacCallum & Keeley, 2008). Institutionalization prior to adoption, which can be a form of social deprivation, can heighten problems. Postinstitutionalized children are at still greater risk of being insecure with the adoptive parents, and the insecurity can be found early (Chatham, 2008). One study found such children to show higher cortisol (a stress hormone) levels than noninstitutionalized children in the presence of their mothers (Wismer Fries et al., 2008).

An aspect of adoption that is often not considered is its effects on the relinquishing mother (Aloi, 2009). These mothers often encounter senses of loss and guilt, along with wondering how their child is developing and adjusting. ◉

Pregnancy

Women react to pregnancy in different ways. For those who are psychologically and economically prepared, pregnancy may be greeted with joyous celebration. But an unwanted pregnancy may evoke feelings of fear and hopelessness.

In this section we examine biological and psychological aspects of pregnancy: signs of pregnancy, prenatal development, complications, effects of drugs and sex, and the psychological experiences of pregnant women and fathers.

EARLY SIGNS OF PREGNANCY

For many women the first sign of pregnancy is missing a period. But some women have irregular menstrual cycles or miss a period because of stress. Missing a period, then, is not a fully reliable indicator. Some women experience cyclic bleeding or spotting during pregnancy, although the blood flow is usually lighter than normal. If a woman's BBT remains high for about three weeks after ovulation, there is reason to suspect pregnancy even if she spots two weeks after ovulation.

PREGNANCY TESTS

You may have heard your parents say that they learned your mother was pregnant by means of the "rabbit test," in which a sample of the woman's urine was injected into a laboratory animal. This procedure, which was once commonly used to confirm

pregnancy, relied on the fact that women produce **human chorionic gonadotropin (HCG)** shortly after conception. HCG causes rabbits, mice, or rats to ovulate.

Today, pregnancy can be confirmed in minutes by tests that directly detect HCG in the urine as early as the third week of pregnancy. A blood test—the *beta subunit HCG radioimmunoassay (RIA)*—can detect HCG in the woman's blood as early as the eighth day of pregnancy, about five days preceding her expected period.

Over-the-counter home pregnancy tests are also available. They too test the woman's urine for HCG and are intended to be used as early as one day after a missed period. Laboratory-based tests are considered 98 to 99% accurate. Home-based tests performed by laypeople are somewhat less accurate. Women are advised to consult their physicians if they suspect that they are pregnant or wish to confirm a home pregnancy test result.

EARLY EFFECTS OF PREGNANCY

Just a few days after conception, a woman may note tenderness of the breasts. Hormonal stimulation of the mammary glands may make the breasts more sensitive and cause sensations of tingling and fullness.

Morning sickness, which can actually occur throughout the day, refers to the nausea, food aversions, and vomiting that many women experience during pregnancy. Women carrying more than one child usually experience more nausea. Although called morning sickness, it is not a "sickness" at all, but rather a perfectly normal part of pregnancy (Flaxman & Sherman, 2000). There is some evidence that the nausea and vomiting experienced by pregnant women reflect bodily changes that promote the development of the placenta (Huxley, 2000). **TRUTH** OR **FICTION REVISITED:** Biologists Samuel Flaxman and Paul Sherman (2000) reviewed records of some 20,000 pregnancies and found that morning sickness was associated with a healthy outcome, including lower incidences of miscarriage and stillbirth. The researchers suggest that the food aversions protect the mother and fetus from likely sources of toxins and disease-causing agents, which are most commonly found in spoiled meat. Although it may have provided an evolutionary advantage, the usefulness of morning sickness has waned over the millennia, especially with the advent of refrigeration to help safely store foods.

All this may be of little consolation to pregnant women. In some cases, morning sickness is so severe that the woman cannot eat regularly and must be hospitalized to ensure that she and the fetus receive adequate nutrition. In milder cases, having small amounts of food throughout the day is of help. Many women find that eating a few crackers at bedtime and before getting out of bed in the morning are of help. Other women profit from medication. Women are advised to discuss the situation with their obstetricians rather than assume that they have to tough it out. Morning sickness usually—but not always—subsides by about the twelfth week of pregnancy.

Pregnant women may experience greater-than-normal fatigue during the early weeks, so that they sleep longer and fall asleep more readily than usual. Frequent urination, which may also be experienced, is caused by pressure from the swelling uterus on the bladder.

MISCARRIAGE

Miscarriages have many causes, including chromosomal defects in the fetus and abnormalities of the placenta and uterus. Miscarriage is more common among older mothers (Stein & Susser, 2000). About three in four miscarriages occur in the first 16 weeks of pregnancy, and most of these occur in the first 7 weeks. Some miscarriages occur so early that the woman does not know she was pregnant.

Human chorionic gonadotropin (HCG) A hormone produced by women shortly after conception, which stimulates the corpus luteum to continue to produce progesterone. The presence of HCG in a woman's urine indicates that she is pregnant.

Morning sickness Symptoms of pregnancy, including nausea, aversions to specific foods, and vomiting.

Miscarriage A spontaneous abortion.

After a miscarriage, the mother or couple may feel a deep sense of loss and undergo a period of mourning. Emotional support from friends and family often help the mother or couple cope with the loss. In most cases women who miscarry can carry subsequent pregnancies to term.

SEX DURING PREGNANCY

Most health professionals agree that coitus is safe for pregnant women until labor begins, provided that the pregnancy is proceeding normally and the woman has no history of miscarriages. Women who experience bleeding or cramps during pregnancy may be advised by their obstetricians not to engage in coitus.

A study of 188 women showed a decline in sexual activity as pregnancy progresses (Pauleta et al., 2010). The frequency of sexual intercourse was greatest during the first trimester, followed by the second and then the third trimester. Nearly one in four of the women (23.4%) reported having fear of sexual intercourse during the pregnancy. About 10% said they feared intercourse could harm the baby. A few were concerned that sex would be painful.

About one in four (24.5%) said they experienced loss of sexual desire on the part of their partners. Two of five (41.5%) of the women said that they themselves felt less sensual or attractive. Nearly all (98%) of the women reported having vaginal intercourse during pregnancy. Nearly two in five (38%) reported having oral sex. Smaller numbers masturbated (20%) or had anal sex (7%).

In another study, three women in five (61%) reported having intercourse at least once a month during the third trimester (Fox et al., 2008); 24% reported intercourse at least once a week. During the two weeks prior to delivery, 40% reported having intercourse, and almost one woman in five (17%) reported having intercourse during the two days prior to delivery.

As the woman's abdominal region swells, the male-superior position becomes unwieldy. For heterosexual couples, the female-superior, lateral-entry, and rear-entry positions are common alternatives. Manual and oral sex can continue as usual. Some women are concerned that the uterine contractions of orgasm may dislodge an embryo, but such concerns are usually unfounded. Still, women and their partners are advised to ask their obstetricians about sex during pregnancy.

PSYCHOLOGICAL CHANGES DURING PREGNANCY

A woman's psychological response to pregnancy reflects her desire to be pregnant, her physical changes, and her attitudes toward these changes. Women with the financial, social, and psychological resources to meet the needs of pregnancy and childrearing may welcome pregnancy. Some describe it as the most wondrous experience of their lives. Some women question their ability to handle pregnancy and childbirth. Or they fear that pregnancy will impair their careers or their partner's feelings about them. In general, women who choose to become pregnant are better adjusted during their pregnancies.

The first trimester may be difficult for women who are ambivalent about pregnancy. At that stage symptoms such as morning sickness are most pronounced, and women must come to terms with being pregnant. The second trimester is generally smoother. Morning sickness and other symptoms largely vanish. It is not yet difficult to move about, and childbirth remains a while off. Women first note fetal movement during the second trimester, and for many the experience is stirring:

> I was lying on my stomach and felt— something, like someone lightly touching my deep insides. Then I just sat very still and … felt the hugeness of having something living growing in me. Then I said, No, it's not possible, it's too early yet, and then I started to cry…. That one moment was my first body awareness of another living thing inside me. (Boston Women's Health Book Collective, 2005)

CRITICAL THINKING
How would you explain the relationship between a woman's experience of the physical aspects of pregnancy and her desire to have a child? Why might some women consider "morning sickness" to be a blessing and other women consider it a curse?

A Closer Look

Advice for Expectant Fathers

I got hungry while we were waiting for the contractions to get more frequent, and I made the mistake of bringing a tuna sandwich into the birthing room. My wife gave me a horrible look and threatened to throw up on me—and much worse—if I didn't get it out of there immediately.

> —A former expectant father, now a father

First piece of advice: Unless your will is made out and your passage in this world has become weary, don't bring a tuna sandwich into the delivery room.

It's women who get pregnant, but these days it's often politically correct to say things like "We're pregnant"—especially if a father doesn't want to be left out of the process. But expectant fathers may sometimes feel that pregnancy is not a "we" proposition; in fact, they can feel left out of the process. They can also have many concerns about a pregnancy, and some fears (Eriksson et al., 2007). Following are some concerns expressed by expectant fathers, and thoughts about responding to them.

1. *Will I be a good father? How will I know what to do?* "Women seem to take to motherhood naturally, but is fatherhood 'natural'?" One might counter, "Is motherhood really so natural for women, or has it been a learned role because typically women have been thrust into caregiving roles with dolls and with other people's children since early childhood (Golombok et al., 2008)?" Think of parenthood as a set of skills that can be learned, and if the father is motivated, those skills can be acquired straightforwardly and rapidly.

2. *What if I die when they need me?* "I realized I was no longer the kid," said one expectant father. "I was going to have one. Suddenly my life didn't seem as open-ended." It's always good to think about our responsibilities toward others. Expectant fathers may be exaggerating the threats in their lives, but taking out an insurance policy is a good idea. A young father may find that a term insurance policy fits into his financial picture quite well.

3. *Will she love the baby more than she loves me?* Perhaps, but that doesn't mean she'll love the father less. Having a baby creates a totally new configuration of attachments and emotions in a family. At the very least, it expands the potential for feelings of love. Many new fathers say things like "I never knew I had that much love in me." Your baby will form an attachment to you as well as to his or her mother, and the sum total of positive feelings you will be experiencing will most likely increase. Moreover, your partner may also be wondering if you will prefer the baby to her, especially if it's a daughter.

4. *How can I help during the pregnancy when I don't particularly understand women's medical issues?* A vast knowledge gap can emerge as the mother becomes very educated about pregnancy, childbirth, and parenting, and the father feels left out. The father can support the mother by trying to remain involved (Locock & Alexander, 2005). For example, he can attend as many clinical visits as he can fit into his schedule, but he should not, perhaps, blow things out of proportion if he must miss some. He can also generally help by listening when his partner expresses her concerns, trying to understand them and offering to help.

5. *Will I do what I'm supposed to do at the birth? Does she even really want me at the birth, or is she just being "politically correct" by including me?* Back to the tuna fish: You may have attended clinical visits and childbirth lessons with your partner, but you won't be the only person there to assist (Premberg & Lundgren, 2006).

6. *But I don't even particularly like kids, so how am I going to feel about this one?* Since *this* one is, as the expression goes, "your own flesh and blood," you'll probably have rather positive feelings (Goodman, 2006). Does that mean you'll never be annoyed when

the baby cries at night or when your partner dotes on the baby? Not at all, but you'll likely put these concerns into perspective.

7. *What do I do if it's a girl (boy)?* Many fathers worry that they won't provide a masculine enough role model for sons and that they won't have any idea what to do if it's a girl. "The fact of the matter is that I wanted a boy because I didn't know what I would do with a girl. But even so, I wasn't sure I wanted to have to toss around a football or a baseball with a boy. I never threw a football all that well, in truth. When we had a girl, I bonded with her immediately—she was very cute—and I found myself prepared to hug her. And I learned quickly enough that a large part of fatherhood is really about changing diapers, no matter how bad the smell."

Expectant fathers tend to worry—about whether the mother will prefer the baby to them, whether they might die and leave the mother and baby to their own devices, how they'll feel about the baby. This father at least already knows that his wife has delivered a healthy baby.

During the third trimester it is normal, especially for first-time mothers, to worry about the mechanics of delivery and whether the child will be normal. The woman becomes increasingly heavy and literally "bent out of shape." It may become difficult to get up from a chair or out of bed. She must sit farther from the steering wheel when driving. Muscle tension from supporting the extra weight in her abdomen may cause backaches. She may feel impatient in the days and weeks just before delivery.

Men, like women, respond to pregnancy according to the degree to which they want the child. Many men are proud and look forward to the child with great anticipation. In such cases, pregnancy may bring parents closer together. But fathers who are financially or emotionally unprepared may consider the pregnancy a "trap."

Real Students, Real Questions

Q *How often do pregnant women have to go to the doctor during the pregnancy, assuming everything is going okay, and what kinds of things happen during the visits?*

A If you think you're pregnant, arrange for prenatal care as soon as possible. If you're not sure how to do that, check in with your college health center or Planned Parenthood. If you're young, 18 to 35 years old, you'll probably have a low-risk pregnancy and will be asked to see the doctor once a month for the first seven months, then every two to three weeks from the 28th through the 36th weeks, and then every week from the 35th week until delivery. If you're older or at high risk, your doctor will arrange to see you more often. The first visit is usually longest. You'll provide a full medical history and have a thorough physical exam, including measurements of height and weight, respiration rate (breathing), blood pressure, and pulse rate. You'll have a breast exam, Pap test, and tests for chlamydia and gonorrhea. Your state might require testing for HIV/AIDS. You may have blood, skin, and urine tests to check for anemia, blood type, cystic fibrosis, Gaucher's disease, hepatitis, rubella, sickle-cell anemia, Tay–Sachs disease, thalassemias, tuberculosis, and diabetes.

At follow-ups the doctor will check your urine, blood pressure, fluid retention (swollen hands, face, feet), as well as check the growth of your uterus, examine your abdomen for the position of the fetus, and listen for the fetal heartbeat. At some point ultrasound may be used to show the size and position of the fetus, check the placenta, confirm the due date, detect multiple pregnancies and certain abnormalities, and even check the sex of the fetus. Between 10 and 18 weeks chorionic villus sampling (CVS), a "triple test," and amniocentesis may be offered to screen for various abnormalities.

During the third trimester the doctor will usually perform a biophysical profile, which combines ultrasound with a fetal monitor to check out the fetal heartbeat and movement more closely.

Prenatal Development

We can date pregnancy from the onset of the last menstrual cycle before conception, which makes the normal gestation period 280 days. We can also date pregnancy from the date at which fertilization was assumed to have taken place, which normally corresponds to two weeks after the beginning of the woman's last menstrual cycle. In this case, the normal gestation period is 266 days.

Once pregnancy has been confirmed, the delivery date may be calculated by *Nagele's rule:*

- Jot down the date of the first day of the last menstrual period.
- Add seven days.
- Subtract three months.
- Add one year.

For example, if the last period began on November 12, 2009, adding seven days yields November 19, 2009. Then subtracting three months yields August 19, 2009. Adding one year gives a "due date" of August 19, 2010. Few babies are born exactly when they are due,* but the great majority is delivered during a ten-day period that spans the date.

STAGES OF PRENATAL DEVELOPMENT

Shortly after conception, the single cell that results from the union of sperm and egg begins to multiply—becoming 2 cells, then 4, then 8, and so on. During the weeks and months that follow, tissues, structures, and organs begin to form, and the fetus gradually takes on the shape of a human being. By the time the fetus is born, it consists of hundreds of billions of cells—more cells than there are stars in the Milky Way galaxy. Prenatal development can be divided into three periods: the *germinal stage,* which corresponds to about the first two weeks; the *embryonic stage,* which coincides with the first two months; and the *fetal stage.* We also commonly speak of prenatal development in terms of three trimesters of three months each.

The Germinal Stage Within 36 hours after conception, the zygote divides into two cells. It then divides repeatedly, becoming 32 cells within another 36 hours as it continues its journey to the uterus. **TRUTH OR FICTION** REVISITED: For the first week after conception, a fertilized egg cell is not attached to its mother's body. It takes the zygote perhaps three or four days to reach the uterus. This mass of dividing cells then wanders about the uterus for perhaps another three or four days before it begins to become implanted in the uterine wall. Implantation takes about another week. This period from conception to implantation is termed the **germinal stage,** or the **period of the ovum** (see Figure 11.3).

Several days into the germinal stage, the cell mass takes the form of a fluid-filled ball of cells, which is called a **blastocyst.** Already some cell differentiation has begun. Cells begin to separate into groups that will eventually become different structures. Within a thickened mass of cells that is called the **embryonic disk,** two distinct inner layers of cells are beginning to form. These cells will become the embryo and eventually the fetus. The outer part of the blastocyst, called the **trophoblast,** consists of several membranes from which the amniotic sac, placenta, and umbilical cord eventually develop.

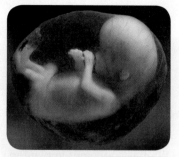

Prenatal Development. Developmental changes are most rapid and dramatic during prenatal development. Within a few months, a human embryo, and then fetus, advances from weighing a fraction of an ounce to several pounds, and from one cell to billions of cells. Development is cephalocaudal and proximodistal. Growth of the head takes precedence over the growth of the lower parts of the body.

Germinal stage   The period of prenatal development before implantation in the uterus.

Period of the ovum   Germinal stage.

Blastocyst   A stage within the germinal stage of prenatal development, at which the embryo is a sphere of cells surrounding a cavity of fluid.

T/F 4

Watch the Video
Period of the Zygote
on **MyDevelopmentLab**

Embryonic disk   The platelike inner part of the blastocyst, which differentiates into the ectoderm, mesoderm, and endoderm of the embryo.

Trophoblast   The outer part of the blastocyst, from which the amniotic sac, placenta, and umbilical cord develop.

---

*The Rathi wish to boast, however, that their daughters Allyn and Jordan were born precisely on their due dates. At least one of them has been just as compulsive ever since. Nevid adds that he and his wife Judy had their son Michael within one day of the due date. (Close—but no cigar.)

FIGURE 11.3 The Ovarian Cycle, Conception, and the Early Days of the Germinal Stage. The zygote first divides about 36 hours after conception. Continuing division creates the hollow sphere of cells termed the blastocyst. The blastocyst normally becomes implanted in the wall of the uterus.

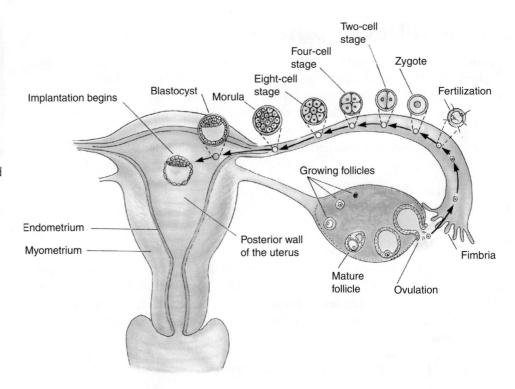

Implantation may be accompanied by some bleeding, which results from the usual rupturing of some small blood vessels that line the uterus. Bleeding can also be a sign of a miscarriage—although most women who experience implantation bleeding do not miscarry but go on to have normal pregnancies and deliver healthy babies.

The Embryonic Stage The period from implantation to about the eighth week of development is called the **embryonic stage.** The major organ systems of the body begin to differentiate during this stage.

Development of the embryo follows two trends: **cephalocaudal** and **proximodistal** (see Figure 11.4). Growth of the head (the cephalic region) takes precedence over the growth of the lower parts of the body. You can also think of the body as containing a central axis that coincides with the spinal cord. The growth of the organ systems that lie close to this axis (that is, *proximal* to the axis) takes precedence over the growth of those that lie farther away toward the extremities (that is, *distal* to the axis). Relatively early maturation of the brain and organ systems that lie near the central axis allows these organs to facilitate further development of the embryo and fetus.

As the embryonic stage unfolds, the nervous system, sensory organs, hair, nails, teeth, and the outer layer of skin begin to develop from the outer layer of cells, or **ectoderm,** of the embryonic disk. By about three weeks after conception, two ridges appear in the embryo. The ridges fold together to form the **neural tube.** This tube develops into the nervous system. The inner layer of the embryonic disk is called the **endoderm.** From this layer develop the respiratory and digestive systems, and organs such as the liver and the pancreas. A short time later in the embryonic stage, the middle layer of cells, or **mesoderm,** differentiates and develops into the reproductive, excretory, and circulatory systems, as well as the skeleton, muscles, and the inner layer of the skin.

During the third week of development, the head and blood vessels begin to form. By the fourth week, a primitive heart begins to beat and pump blood in an embryo that measures but a fifth of an inch in length. The heart will normally continue to beat without rest for every minute of every day for the better part of a century. By

Embryonic stage The stage of prenatal development that lasts from implantation through the eighth week and is characterized by the differentiation of the major organ systems.

Cephalocaudal From the head downward.

Proximodistal From the central axis of the body outward.

Ectoderm The outermost cell layer of the newly formed embryo, from which the skin and nervous system develop.

Neural tube A hollow area in the blastocyst from which the nervous system will develop.

Endoderm The inner layer of the newly formed embryo, from which the lungs and digestive system develop.

Mesoderm The central layer of the embryo, from which the bones and muscles develop.

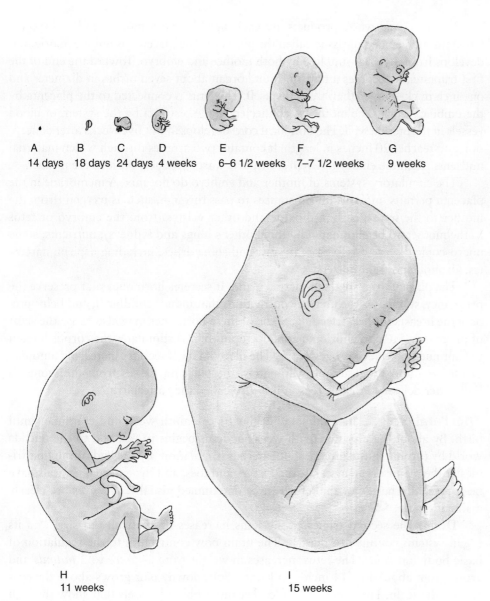

A · | 14 days   B ⌀ 18 days   C 🦐 24 days   D 🦐 4 weeks   E 6–6 1/2 weeks   F 7–7 1/2 weeks   G 9 weeks

H
11 weeks

I
15 weeks

FIGURE 11.4 Human Embryos and Fetuses. Development is cephalocaudal and proximodistal. Growth of the head takes precedence over the growth of the lower parts of the body.

the end of the first month of development we can see the beginnings of the arms and legs—"arm buds" and "leg buds." The mouth, eyes, ears, and nose begin to take shape. The brain and other parts of the nervous system begin to develop.

The arms and legs develop in accordance with the proximodistal principle. First the upper arms and legs develop. Then the forearms and lower legs appear. Next the hands and feet form, followed by webbed fingers and toes by about six to eight weeks into development. The webbing is gone by the end of the second month. By this time the head has become rounded, and the limbs have elongated and separated. Facial features are visible. All this has occurred in an embryo that is about 1 inch long and weighs 1/30th of an ounce. During the second month, nervous impulses also begin to travel through the developing nervous system.

The embryo—and later, the fetus—develop within a protective environment in the mother's uterus called the **amniotic sac,** which is surrounded by a clear membrane. The embryo and fetus are suspended within the sac in **amniotic fluid.** The amniotic fluid acts like a shock absorber. It cushions the embryo from damage that might result from the mother's movements. The fluid also helps maintain a steady temperature.

Amniotic sac The sac containing the fetus.

Amniotic fluid Fluid within the amniotic sac that suspends and protects the fetus.

Nutrients and waste products are exchanged between mother and embryo (or fetus) through a mass of tissue called the **placenta.** The placenta is unique in origin. It develops from material supplied by both mother and embryo. Toward the end of the first trimester, it becomes a flattish, round organ about seven inches in diameter and one inch thick—larger than the fetus itself. The fetus is connected to the placenta by the **umbilical cord.** The mother is connected to the placenta by the system of blood vessels in the uterine wall. The umbilical cord develops about five weeks after conception and reaches 20 inches in length. It contains two arteries through which maternal nutrients reach the embryo. A vein transports waste products back to the mother.

The circulatory systems of mother and embryo do not mix. A membrane in the placenta permits only certain substances to pass through, such as oxygen (from the mother to the fetus); carbon dioxide and other wastes (from the embryo or fetus to the mother, to be eliminated by the mother's lungs and kidneys); nutrients; some microscopic disease-causing organisms; and some drugs, including aspirin, narcotics, alcohol, and tranquilizers.

The placenta is also an endocrine gland. It secretes hormones that preserve the pregnancy, stimulates the uterine contractions that induce childbirth, and helps prepare the breasts for breastfeeding. Some of these hormones may also cause the signs of pregnancy. Human chorionic gonadotropin (HCG) stimulates the corpus luteum to continue to produce progesterone. The placenta itself secretes increasing amounts of estrogen and progesterone. Ultimately, the placenta passes from the woman's body after delivery. For this reason it is also called the "afterbirth."

The Fetal Stage The fetal stage begins by the ninth week and continues until birth. By about the ninth or tenth week the fetus begins to respond to the outside world by turning in the direction of external stimulation. By the end of the first trimester the major organ systems, the fingers and toes, and the external genitals have been formed. The sex of the fetus can be determined visually. The eyes are clearly distinguishable. 👁

During the second trimester the fetus increases dramatically in size, and its organ systems continue to mature. The brain now contributes to the regulation of basic body functions. The fetus increases in weight from 1 *ounce* to 2 *pounds* and grows from about 4 to 14 inches in length. Soft, downy hair grows above the eyes and on the scalp. The skin turns ruddy because of blood vessels that show through the surface. (During the third trimester layers of fat beneath the skin will give the red a pinkish hue.)

Usually by the middle of the fourth month the mother can feel the first fetal movements. By the end of the second trimester the fetus moves its limbs so vigorously that the mother may complain of being kicked—often at 4:00 a.m. It opens and shuts its eyes, sucks its thumb, alternates between periods of wakefulness and sleep, and perceives lights and sounds. The fetus also does somersaults, which the mother will definitely feel. Fortunately, the umbilical cord will not break or strangle the fetus, no matter what acrobatic feats the fetus performs.

Near the end of the second trimester the fetus approaches the **age of viability.** Still, only a minority of babies born at the end of the second trimester who weigh under two pounds will survive—even with intense medical efforts.

During the third trimester, the organ systems continue to mature and enlarge. The heart and lungs become increasingly capable of maintaining independent life. Typically, during the seventh month the fetus turns upside down in the uterus so that it will be head first, or in a **cephalic presentation,** for delivery. But some fetuses do not turn during this month. If such a fetus is born prematurely it can have either a **breech presentation** (bottom first) or a shoulder-first presentation, which can complicate

👁 **Watch the Video**
Fetal Development
on **MyDevelopmentLab**

Placenta An organ connected to the fetus by the umbilical cord. The placenta serves as a relay station between mother and fetus, allowing the exchange of nutrients and wastes.

Umbilical cord A tube that connects the fetus to the placenta.

Age of viability The age at which a fetus can sustain independent life.

Cephalic presentation Emergence of the baby head first from the womb.

Breech presentation Emergence of the baby bottom or feet first from the womb.

problems of prematurity. The closer to term (the full nine months) the baby is born, the more likely it is that the presentation will be cephalic. If birth occurs at the end of the eighth month, the odds are overwhelmingly in favor of survival.

During the final months of pregnancy, the mother may become concerned that the fetus seems to be less active than before. Generally, the change in activity level is normal. The fetus has grown so large that it is cramped, and its movements are restricted.

ENVIRONMENTAL INFLUENCES ON PRENATAL DEVELOPMENT

Advances in scientific knowledge have made us more aware of the changes that take place during prenatal development. They have also heightened our awareness of the problems that can occur and what might be done to prevent them. These include the mother's diet, maternal diseases and disorders, and the mother's use of drugs.

The Mother's Diet It is a common misconception that the fetus will take what it needs from its mother. Actually, malnutrition in the mother can adversely affect fetal development. Women who are too slender risk preterm deliveries and having babies who are low in birth weight (Cnattingius et al., 1998). Pregnant women who are adequately nourished are more likely to deliver babies of average or above-average size. Their infants are also less likely to develop colds and serious respiratory disorders. However, maternal *obesity* is linked with a higher risk of stillbirth (Cnattingius et al., 1998).

The slimmer a woman is prior to pregnancy, the more weight she is advised to gain during pregnancy. For example, a woman with a body mass index (BMI)* of less than 18.5 is advised to gain 28 to 40 pounds (Rasmussen et al., 2009; see Table 11.1). Normal-weight women, those with a BMI of 24.9 or less, are advised to gain 25 to 35 pounds. However, 55% of pregnant women in the United States are overweight or obese (Parker-Pope, 2009). Women who are overweight, with a BMI of 25 to 29.9 are advised to gain 15 to 25 pounds. And obese women, those with a BMI over 30, are advised to limit their weight gain to 11 to 20 pounds. Regular weight gains are most desirable.

Table 11.1

Body Mass Index (BMI) and Weight Status

BMI	Weight Status
Below 18.5	Underweight
18.5–24.9	Normal
25.0–29.9	Overweight
30.0 and Above	Obese

Maternal Diseases and Disorders Environmental influences or agents that can harm the embryo or fetus are called **teratogens.** These include drugs taken by the mother, such as alcohol and even aspirin, as well as substances produced by the mother's body, such as Rh-positive antibodies. Other teratogens include the metals lead and mercury, radiation, and disease-causing organisms such as viruses and bacteria. Although many disease-causing organisms cannot pass through the placenta to infect the embryo or fetus, some extremely small organisms, such as those causing syphilis, measles, mumps, and chicken pox, can. Some disorders such as toxemia are not transmitted to the embryo or fetus but can adversely affect the environment in which it develops.

Critical Periods of Vulnerability The times at which exposure to particular teratogens can cause the greatest harm are termed **critical periods of vulnerability.** Critical periods correspond to the times at which the structures most affected by the teratogens are developing (see Figure 11.5). The heart, for example, develops rapidly from the third to the fifth week after conception. It may be most vulnerable to certain teratogens at this time. The arms and legs, which develop later, are most vulnerable from the fourth through the eighth week of development. Since the

Teratogens Environmental influences or agents that can damage an embryo or fetus.

Critical period of vulnerability A period of time during which an embryo or fetus is vulnerable to the effects of a teratogen.

---

*The formula for calculating your BMI is: weight (lb) / [[height (in)]]² × 703. That is, divide your weight in pounds (lbs) by your height in inches (in.) squared, and multiply by a conversion factor of 703. For example:
Weight = 150 lbs, Height = 5′5″ (65′)
Calculation: [[150 ÷ (65)²]] × 703 = 24.96.

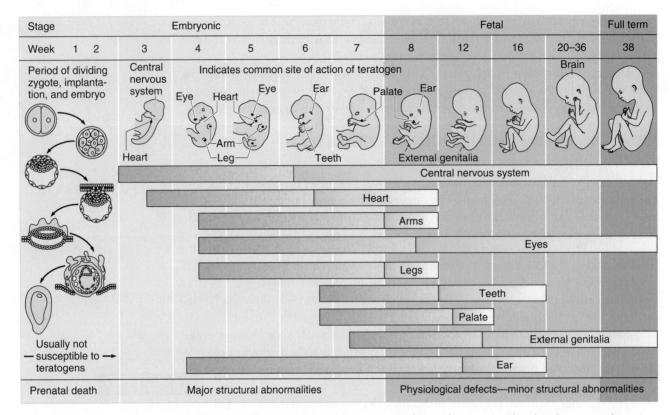

Stage	Embryonic							Fetal				Full term
Week	1 2	3	4	5	6	7	8	12	16	20–36	38

FIGURE 11.5 Critical Periods in Prenatal Development. The developing embryo is most vulnerable to teratogens when the organ systems are taking shape. The periods of greatest vulnerability of organ systems are shown in gray. Periods of lesser vulnerability are shown in yellow.

major organ systems differentiate during the embryonic stage, the embryo is most vulnerable to the effects of teratogens. Let us now consider some of the most damaging effects of specific maternal diseases and disorders.

Rubella (German Measles) **Rubella** is a viral infection. Women who contract rubella during the first month or two of pregnancy, when rapid differentiation of major organ systems is taking place, may bear children who are deaf or who develop mental retardation, heart disease, or cataracts. Risk of these defects declines as pregnancy progresses.

Nearly 85% of women in the United States had rubella as children and so acquired immunity. Women who do not know whether they have had rubella may be tested. If they are not immune, they can be vaccinated *before pregnancy.* Inoculation during pregnancy is considered risky because the vaccine causes a mild case of the disease in the mother, which can affect the embryo or fetus. Increased awareness of the dangers of rubella during pregnancy and of the protective effects of inoculation has led to a dramatic decline in the number of children born in the United States with defects caused by rubella, from about 20,000 cases in 1964–1965 to 28 in year 2000 (Centers for Disease Control and Prevention, 2001).

Syphilis Maternal **syphilis** may cause miscarriage or **stillbirth,** or be passed along to the child in the form of congenital syphilis. Congenital syphilis can impair the vision and hearing, damage the liver, or deform the bones and teeth.

Routine blood tests early in pregnancy can diagnose syphilis and other problems. Because the bacteria that cause syphilis do not readily cross the placental

Rubella A viral infection that can cause mental retardation and heart disease in an embryo. Also called *German measles.*

Syphilis A sexually transmitted bacterial infection.

Stillbirth The birth of a dead fetus.

membrane during the first months of pregnancy, the fetus will probably not contract syphilis if an infected mother is treated successfully with antibiotics before the fourth month of pregnancy.

HIV/AIDS Acquired immunodeficiency syndrome (**AIDS**) is caused by the *human immunodeficiency virus (HIV)*. HIV is blood-borne and is sometimes transmitted through the placenta to infect the fetus. The rupturing of blood vessels in mother and baby during childbirth provides another opportunity for transmission of HIV. *However, the majority of babies born to mothers who are infected with HIV do not become infected themselves.* Using antiviral medication can also minimize the probability of transmission (see the A Closer Look on p. 303). HIV can also be transmitted to children by breastfeeding. Research suggests that about half of infected newborns are infected while in the uterus, and half are infected during childbirth (Mofenson, 2000; Wood et al., 2000).

African American children account for more than half of the pediatric cases of HIV/AIDS, and Latino and Latina Americans account for almost one quarter. Inner-city neighborhoods, where there is widespread intravenous drug use, have been hard hit (Centers for Disease Control and Prevention, 2003).

Toxemia Toxemia is a life-threatening condition characterized by high blood pressure. It may afflict women late in the second or early in the third trimester of pregnancy. The first stage is termed *preeclampsia*. It is diagnosed by protein in the urine, swelling from fluid retention, and high blood pressure, and the condition may be mild. As preeclampsia worsens, the mother may have headaches and visual problems from high blood pressure, along with abdominal pain. If left untreated, the disease may progress to the final stage, *eclampsia*. Eclampsia can lead to maternal or fetal death. Babies born to women with toxemia are often undersized or premature.

Toxemia appears to be linked to malnutrition. Ironically, undernourished women may gain weight rapidly through fluid retention, but their swollen appearance may discourage them from eating. Pregnant women who gain weight rapidly but have not increased their food intake should consult their obstetricians.

Ectopic Pregnancy In an **ectopic pregnancy**, the fertilized ovum implants itself someplace other than the uterus. Most ectopic pregnancies occur in a fallopian tube ("tubal pregnancies") when the ovum is prevented from moving into the uterus because of obstructions caused by infections. Ectopic pregnancies are more common among older women. If ectopic pregnancies do not abort spontaneously, they must be removed by surgery or aborted by use of medications such as methotrexate, since the fetus cannot develop to term. Delay in removal may cause hemorrhaging and the death of the mother. A woman with a tubal pregnancy will not menstruate, but may notice spotty bleeding and abdominal pain.

Rh Incompatibility In **Rh incompatibility**, antibodies produced by the mother are transmitted to the fetus or newborn infant. *Rh* is a blood protein found in some people's red blood cells. Rh incompatibility occurs when a woman who does not have this blood factor, and is thus *Rh-negative,* is carrying an *Rh-positive* fetus, which can happen if the father is Rh-positive. The negative–positive combination is found in about 10% of U.S. marriages. However, it becomes a problem only in a minority of the resulting pregnancies. In such cases the mother's antibodies attack the red blood cells of the fetus, which can cause brain damage or death. Rh incompatibility does not usually adversely affect a first child because women will usually not yet have formed antibodies to the Rh factor.

Since mother and fetus have separate circulatory systems, it is unlikely that Rh-positive fetal red blood cells will enter the Rh-negative mother's body. The

Acquired immunodeficiency syndrome (AIDS) A condition caused by HIV that destroys white blood cells in the immune system, leaving the body vulnerable to various "opportunistic" diseases.

Toxemia A life-threatening condition that is characterized by high blood pressure.

Ectopic pregnancy A pregnancy in which the fertilized ovum becomes implanted someplace other than the uterus.

Rh incompatibility A condition in which antibodies produced by a pregnant woman are transmitted to the fetus and may cause brain damage or death.

A Closer Look

Preventing Your Baby from Being Infected with HIV

Pregnant women with HIV/AIDS or other sexually transmitted infections (STIs) should discuss these conditions with their doctors. Physicians can take measures to help protect infected babies. For example, the medication zidovudine reduces the amount of HIV in the mother's bloodstream. Infected women who use zidovudine during pregnancy reduce the rate of HIV infection in their neonates by two-thirds (Mofenson, 2000). In one study, 8% of the babies born to women who obtained zidovudine became infected with HIV, as compared to 25% of babies whose mothers did not obtain zidovudine (Connor et al., 1994).

The European Mode of Delivery Collaboration Trial of 400 mothers infected with HIV compared the use of C-section versus vaginal delivery as a means of decreasing the risk of transmission of HIV to the baby (Ricci et al., 2000). All mothers received zidovudine during pregnancy. Half were randomly assigned to deliver vaginally, and the other half by C-section. The rate of HIV infection among the babies was 10.6% for those delivered vaginally as compared with 1.7% for those delivered by C-section. Thus, the combination of zidovudine and C-section cut the chance that an infected mother will transmit HIV to her baby to about 1 in 50.

For up-to-date information on HIV/AIDS, call the National AIDS Hotline at 1-800-342-AIDS. If you want to receive information in Spanish, call 1-800-344-SIDA.

---

probability of an exchange of blood increases during childbirth, however, especially when the placenta becomes detached from the uterine wall. If an exchange of blood occurs, the mother will then produce antibodies to the baby's Rh-positive blood. The mother's antibodies may enter the fetal bloodstream and cause a condition called *fetal erythroblastosis*, which can result in anemia, mental deficiency, or even the death of the fetus or newborn infant.

Fortunately, blood-typing of pregnant women significantly decreases the threat of uncontrolled erythroblastosis. If an Rh-negative mother is injected with the vaccine Rhogan within 72 hours after delivery of an Rh-positive baby, she will not develop the dangerous antibodies and thus will not pass them on to the fetus in a subsequent pregnancy. A fetus or newborn child at risk for erythroblastosis may also receive a preventive blood transfusion, in order to remove the mother's Rh-positive antibodies from its blood.

Drugs Taken By the Mother (or the Father) Some widely used drugs, including nonprescription drugs, are linked with birth abnormalities. In the 1960s, the drug thalidomide was marketed to pregnant women as a presumably safe treatment for nausea and insomnia. However, the drug caused birth deformities, including stunted or missing limbs. Maternal use of illegal drugs such as cocaine and marijuana may also place the fetus at risk.

Paternal use of certain drugs also may endanger the fetus. One question is whether drugs alter the genetic material in the father's sperm. The use of certain substances by those who come into contact with a pregnant woman can harm the fetus. For example, the mother's inhalation of secondhand tobacco or marijuana smoke can hurt the fetus.

Several antibiotics may harm a fetus, especially if they are taken during certain periods of fetal development. Tetracycline may yellow the teeth and deform the bones (Koren et al., 1998). Other antibiotics have been implicated in deafness and jaundice. Acne drugs such as Accutane can cause physical and mental handicaps in the children of women who use them during pregnancy. Antihistamines, used commonly for allergies, may deform the fetus.

If you are pregnant, or suspect that you are, it is advisable to consult your obstetrician before taking any and all drugs, not just prescription drugs. Your obstetrician can usually direct you to a safe and effective substitute for a drug that could harm a fetus.

Hormones The hormones progestin and DES have sometimes been used to help women at risk of miscarriage maintain their pregnancies. When taken at about the time that sex organs differentiate, progestin (which is similar in composition to male sex hormones) can masculinize the external sex organs of embryos with female (XX) sex chromosomal structures. Progestin taken during the first trimester has also been linked to increased levels of aggressive behavior during childhood.

DES (short for *diethylstilbestrol*), a powerful estrogen, was given to many women at risk for miscarriage from the 1940s through the 1960s to help maintain their pregnancies. DES is suspected of causing cervical and testicular cancer in some of the children whose mothers used it when pregnant (Centers for Disease Control and Prevention, 2005b). Other problems have been reported as well. Daughters whose mothers used DES during their pregnancies have a higher-than-expected rate of miscarriages and premature deliveries. It was once suspected that men who were exposed prenatally to DES had higher than expected rates of infertility. However, research reveals no connection between in utero exposure to DES and male infertility. DES users themselves appear to be at high risk of some serious medical problems, such as breast cancer (Centers for Disease Control and Prevention, 2005b).

Vitamins Many pregnant women are prescribed daily doses of multivitamins to maintain their own health and to promote the development of a healthy pregnancy. "Too much of a good thing" may be hazardous, however. High doses of vitamins such as A, B_6, D, and K have been linked to birth defects. Vitamin A excesses have been linked with cleft palate and eye damage, whereas excesses of vitamin D are linked to mental retardation.

Narcotics Narcotics such as heroin and methadone can readily pass from mother to fetus through the placental membrane. Narcotics are addictive. Fetuses of mothers who use them regularly during pregnancy can become addicted in utero. At birth, such babies may undergo withdrawal and show muscle tension and agitation. Women who use narcotics are advised to notify their obstetricians so that measures can be taken to aid the infants before and after delivery.

Tranquilizers and Sedatives The tranquilizers Librium and Valium cross the placental membrane and may cause birth defects such as harelip. Sedatives, such as the barbiturate *phenobarbital,* are suspected of decreasing testosterone production and causing reproductive problems in the sons of women who use them during pregnancy.

Marijuana The active ingredient in marijuana, THC, readily crosses the placenta. Research into the cognitive effects of maternal prenatal use of marijuana suggests that there may be no impairment in global intellectual functioning per se (Fried & Smith, 2001). However, there may be increased hyperactivity and impulsivity. Researchers also find a connection between prenatal exposure to marijuana and anxiety and depression later on (LaGasse et al., 2012).

Alcohol Mothers who drink heavily during pregnancy expose the fetus to greater risk of birth defects, infant mortality, sensory and motor problems, and mental retardation (Paintner et al., 2012). Nearly 40% of children whose mothers drank

DES (Diethylstilbestrol) An estrogen that was once given to women at risk for miscarriage to help maintain pregnancy.

◉—|**Watch** the **Video**
Fetal Alcohol Syndrome: Sidney
on **MyDevelopmentLab**

5 (T/F)

heavily during pregnancy develop **fetal alcohol syndrome (FAS)**. FAS is a cluster of symptoms typified by developmental lags and characteristic facial features, such as an underdeveloped upper jaw, flattened nose, and widely spaced eyes. Infants with FAS are often smaller than average and have smaller than average brains. They may be mentally retarded, lack coordination, and have deformed limbs and heart problems. They are more susceptible to developing conduct disorders in middle childhood (Disney et al., 2008). ◉

TRUTH OR **FICTION** REVISITED: It has *not* been shown that pregnant women can have one or two alcoholic beverages a day without harming their babies. Although research suggests that light drinking is unlikely to harm the fetus in most cases, FAS has been found even among the children of mothers who drank only two ounces of alcohol a day during the first trimester (Astley & Clarren, 2001). Moreover, individual sensitivities to alcohol may vary widely. The critical period for the development of the facial features associated with FAS seems to be the first two months of prenatal development, when the head is taking shape.

Cigarette Smoking Cigarette smoke contains chemicals such as carbon monoxide and the stimulant nicotine that are transmitted to the fetus. It also lessens the amount of oxygen received by the fetus. Maternal smoking increases the risk of spontaneous abortion and complications during pregnancy such as premature rupturing of the amniotic sac, stillbirth, premature birth, low birth weight, and early infant mortality (Beyerlein et al., 2011). Maternal smoking may also lead to attention deficit hyperactivity disorder and impair the child's intellectual development (Thapar et al., 2012). In one study, women who smoked during pregnancy were 50% more likely than women who did not smoke to have children whose intelligence test scores placed them in the mentally retarded range (that is, beneath an IQ score of 70) when the children were 10 years old (Drews et al., 1996).

Low birth weight is a common risk factor for infant disease, mortality, and problems in learning in school (O'Keeffe et al., 2003). The combination of smoking and drinking alcohol places the child at greater risk of low birth weight than either practice alone (Spencer, 2006). Maternal smoking affects the fetal heart rate and increases the risk of sudden infant death syndrome (SIDS) (Gordon et al., 2002; Pollack, 2001). Maternal smoking has also been linked to reduced lung function in newborns (Sasaki et al., 2008) and asthma in childhood (Goodwin et al., 2009). Evidence also points to reduced attention spans, hyperactivity, and lower IQs and achievement test scores in children exposed to maternal smoking during and after pregnancy.

Smoking by the father (or other household members) may be dangerous to a fetus because secondary smoke (smoke exhaled by the smoker or emitted from the tip of a lit cigarette) may be absorbed by the mother and passed along to the fetus. Passive exposure to secondhand smoke during infancy is also linked to increased risk of SIDS (Gordon et al., 2002).

Most American women of reproductive age drink alcohol, at least occasionally. Nearly one in five smokes (D'Angelo et al., 2007). Many do not suspend drug use until they learn that they are pregnant, which may not occur until weeks into the pregnancy. Some women are unwilling or unable to change their drug use habits even after learning they are pregnant (Cnattingius, 2004).

Our clinical experience suggests that it may be easier for women to quit if they consider quitting as limited to the terms of their pregnancies rather than as permanent. Then, of course, if they should remain abstinent after delivery, perhaps they will not be disappointed.

Fetal alcohol syndrome (FAS)
A cluster of symptoms caused by maternal drinking, in which the child shows developmental lags and characteristic facial features such as an underdeveloped upper jaw, flattened nose, and widely spaced eyes.

Methamphetamine Prenatal exposure to methamphetamine is associated with increased emotional reactivity, anxiety, and hyperactivity by the age of 5 (LaGasse et al., 2012).

Other Agents X-rays increase the risk of malformed organs in the fetus, especially within a month and a half after conception. (Ultrasound has *not* been shown to harm the embryo or fetus.)

CHROMOSOMAL AND GENETIC ABNORMALITIES

Not all of us have the normal complement of chromosomes. Some of us have genes that threaten our health or our existence (see Table 11.2).

Down Syndrome Children with Down syndrome have characteristic round faces; wide, flat noses; protruding tongues; and a downward sloping crease of skin in the inner corners of the eyes. They often suffer from respiratory problems and heart malformations; these problems tend to claim their lives by middle age—the "prime of life" for most people. The individuals with Down syndrome are also moderately mentally retarded, but they usually can learn to read and write. With a little help from family and social agencies, they may hold jobs and lead largely independent lives.

The risk of giving birth to a child with Down syndrome increases with the mother's age (see Table 11.3). Down syndrome is usually caused by an extra chromosome on the 21st pair ("Trisomy 21"). In most cases, Down syndrome is transmitted by the mother.

Sickle-Cell Anemia and Tay-Sachs Disease Sickle-cell anemia and Tay-Sachs disease are genetic disorders that are most likely to afflict certain racial and ethnic groups. Sickle-cell anemia is most prevalent in the United States among African

Don't Do It! Smoking cigarettes and pregnancy do not mix. Maternal smoking has been shown to increase the risk of spontaneous abortion and complications during pregnancy. It is connected with premature rupturing of the amniotic sac, stillbirth, premature birth, low birth weight, infant mortality, and delayed intellectual development in the child.

Table 11.2

Some Chromosomal and Genetic Abnormalities

Health Problem	Comments
Cystic fibrosis	A genetic disease in which the pancreas and lungs become clogged with mucus, which impairs the processes of respiration and digestion.
Down syndrome	A condition characterized by a third chromosome on the 21st pair. The child with Down syndrome is mentally retarded and has a characteristic fold of skin over each eye and mental retardation. The risk of having a child with the syndrome increases as parents increase in age.
Hemophilia	A sex-linked disorder in which blood does not clot properly.
Huntington disease	A fatal neurological disorder with an onset that occurs in middle adulthood.
Neural tube defects	Disorders of the brain or spine, such as *anencephaly*, in which part of the brain is missing, and *spina bifida*, in which part of the spine is exposed or missing. Anencephaly is fatal shortly after birth, but some spina bifida victims survive for a number of years, albeit with severe handicaps.
Phenylketonuria	A disorder in which children cannot metabolize phenylalanine, which builds up in the form of phenylpyruvic acid and causes mental retardation. The disorder can be diagnosed at birth and controlled by diet.
Retinal blastoma	A form of blindness caused by a dominant gene.
Sickle-cell anemia	A blood disorder that mostly afflicts African Americans, in which deformed blood cells obstruct small blood vessels, decreasing their capacity to carry oxygen and heightening the risk of occasionally fatal infections
Tay-Sachs disease	A fatal neurological disorder that primarily afflicts Jews of European origin.

Table 11.3

Risk of Giving Birth to an Infant with Down Syndrome, According to Age of the Mother

Age of Mother	Probability of Down Syndrome in the Child
20	1 in 1,667
30	1 in 953
40	1 in 106
49	1 in 11

Source: American Fertility Association, 2012. [Online]. www.theafa.org.

Americans. One of every 375 African Americans is affected by the disease, and 8% are carriers of the sickle-cell trait (Ashley-Koch et al., 2000). In sickle-cell anemia, the red blood cells assume a sickle shape—hence the name—and they form clumps that obstruct narrow blood vessels and diminish the supply of oxygen. As a result, victims can suffer problems ranging from swollen, painful joints to potentially lethal problems such as pneumonia and heart and kidney failure. Infections are a leading cause of death among those with the disease.

Tay-Sachs disease is a fatal neurological disease of young children. Only 1 in 100,000 people in the United States is affected, but among Jews of Eastern European background the figure rises steeply to 1 in 3,600 (Bodurtha & Strauss, 2012). The disease is characterized by degeneration of the central nervous system and gives rise to retardation, loss of muscle control, paralysis, blindness, and deafness. Victims seldom live beyond the age of 5.

Sex-Linked Genetic Abnormalities Some genetic defects, such as hemophilia, are sex linked, in that they are carried only on the X sex chromosome. They are transmitted from generation to generation as **recessive traits.** Females, each of whom has two X sex chromosomes, are less likely than males to be afflicted by sex-linked disorders, because the genes that carry the disorder would have to be present on both of their sex chromosomes for the disorder to be expressed. Sex-linked disorders are more likely to afflict sons of female carriers because they have only one X sex chromosome, which they inherit from their mothers. England's Queen Victoria was a hemophilia carrier and transmitted the condition to many of her children, who in turn carried it into several ruling families of Europe. For this reason hemophilia has been dubbed the "royal disease."

CRITICAL THINKING

Why do some women aged 35 and older decide to have amniocentesis, and others decide not to do so? Where do you stand on the issue? Explain.

Averting Chromosomal and Genetic Abnormalities Based on information about a couple's medical background and family history of genetic defects, genetic counselors help couples appraise the risks of passing along genetic defects to their children. Some couples facing a high risk of passing along genetic defects to their children decide to adopt. Other couples decide to have an abortion if the fetus is determined to have certain abnormalities.

Various medical procedures are used to detect the presence of these disorders in the fetus. *Amniocentesis* is usually performed about four months into pregnancy but is sometimes done earlier. Fluid is drawn from the amniotic sac (or "bag of waters") with a syringe. Fetal cells in the fluid are grown in a culture and examined under a microscope for the presence of biochemical and chromosomal abnormalities. *Chorionic villus sampling (CVS)* is performed at about ten weeks. A narrow tube is used to snip off material from the chorion, which is a membrane that contains the amniotic sac and fetus. The material is analyzed. The risks of amniocentesis and CVS are comparable (Bauland et al., 2012; Simpson, 2000). The tests detect Down syndrome, sickle-cell anemia, Tay-Sachs disease, spina bifida, muscular dystrophy, Rh incompatibility, and other conditions. The tests also identify the sex of the fetus.

In ultrasound, high-pitched sound waves are bounced off the fetus, like radar, revealing a picture of the fetus on a TV monitor and allowing the obstetrician to detect certain abnormalities. Obstetricians also use ultrasound to locate the fetus during amniocentesis in order to lower the probability of injuring it with the syringe.

Parental blood tests can suggest the presence of problems such as sickle-cell anemia, Tay-Sachs disease, and neural tube defects. Still other tests examine fetal DNA and can indicate the presence of Huntington's chorea, cystic fibrosis, and

Recessive trait A trait that is not expressed when the gene or genes involved have been paired with dominant genes. Recessive traits are transmitted to future generations, however, and are expressed if they are paired with other recessive genes.

A Closer Look

The Effects of Parents' Age on Children—Do Men Really Have All the Time in the World?

What if 30-year-old women started looking at 50-year-old men as damaged goods, what with their washed-up sperm, meaning those 50-year-olds might actually have to date (gasp!) women their own age? What if men, as the years passed, began to look with new eyes at Ms. Almost Right?

—Lisa Belkin

The artist Pablo Picasso fathered children in his 70s. Former Senator Strom Thurmond fathered a child in his 90s. It has been widely known that women's chances of conceiving children decline as they age. As noted by Belkin (2009), the traditional message has been "Women: You'd better hurry up. Men: You have all the time in the world."

Not so, apparently. True: From a biological vantage point, the 20s may be the ideal age for women to bear children. Teenage mothers have a higher incidence of infant mortality and children with low birth weight (Martin et al., 2008; Save the Children, 2011). Early teens who become pregnant may place a burden on bodies that may not have adequately matured to facilitate pregnancy and childbirth. Teenage mothers also are less educated and less likely to obtain prenatal care.

What about women older than 30 years old? Women's fertility declines gradually until the mid-30s, after which it declines more rapidly. Women beyond their middle-30s may have passed the point at which their reproductive systems function most efficiently. Women possess their ova in immature form at birth. Over 30 years, these cells are exposed to the slings and arrows of an outrageous environment of toxic wastes, chemical pollutants, and radiation, thus increasing the

risk of chromosomal abnormalities such as Down syndrome (Sartorius & Nieschlag, 2009). Women who wait until their 30s or 40s to have children also increase the likelihood of having stillborn or preterm babies, or children with autism (Martin et al., 2008; Sandin et al., 2012). But with adequate prenatal care, the risk of bearing a premature or unhealthy baby still is relatively small, even for older first-time mothers (Martin et al., 2008). This news should be encouraging for women who have delayed, or plan to delay, bearing children until their 30s or 40s.

Older fathers are more likely to produce abnormal sperm, leading to fertility problems (Parner et al., 2012). But that's only the

Chance of autism spectrum disorder among 132,271 subjects, by paternal age:

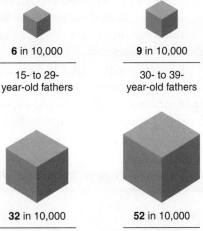

6 in 10,000
15- to 29-year-old fathers

9 in 10,000
30- to 39-year-old fathers

32 in 10,000
40- to 49-year-old fathers

52 in 10,000
50-year-old fathers and older

FIGURE 11.6 Risky Business? Chance of autism spectrum disorder among 132,271 subjects, by paternal age.
Source: Archives of General Psychiatry, September 2006.

Pablo Picasso with His Son Claude. This photo, from 1955, shows the older Picasso playing with his son. Is it safe for men to father children at advanced ages?

tip of the iceberg. University of Queensland researchers analyzed data from some 33,000 U.S. children and found that the older the father is at conception, the lower a child's score may be on tests of reading skills, reasoning, memory, and concentration. The ages of 29 and 30 are something of a turning point for men, because children conceived past these ages are at greater risk for the psychological disorders of schizophrenia and bipolar disorder (Perrin et al., 2007). Children born to men past the age of 40 also have a greater risk of autism and **schizophrenia** (Callaway, 2012; Reichenberg et al., 2006). (See Figure 11.6).

These findings do not mean that the majority of children born to men past their reproductive "prime" will develop these problems, but it does mean that men's age, as women's, is related to risks for their children. As noted by one of the researchers in schizophrenia, "It turns out the optimal age for being a mother is the same as the optimal age for being a father" (Malaspina, 2009).

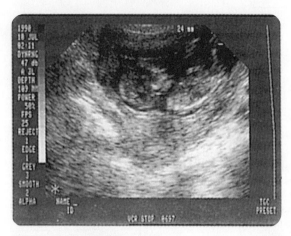

An Ultrasound Image. An ultrasound image of Jeff Nevid's son, Michael, at 12 weeks after conception. The head and upper torso (facing upward) can be seen by those of you willing to look for many hours in the upper middle section of the photo. Michael was handsome even then, his father points out. The first and third author note that they did not insist on including their own boring ultrasound photos in this text.

👁 Watch the **Video**
Conception, Pregnancy, and Childbirth: Dr. Holly Casele, Obstetrician
on **MyDevelopmentLab**

Schizophrenia A severe psychological disorder characterized by problems in thought, language, and perception.

Braxton-Hicks contractions So-called false labor contractions that are relatively painless.

Prostaglandins Uterine hormones that stimulate uterine contractions.

Oxytocin A pituitary hormone that stimulates uterine contractions.

other disorders. Blood tests also now allow detection of Down syndrome during the first trimester. Blood tests also allow determination of the gender of the fetus as early as seven weeks into pregnancy (Bodurtha & Strauss, 2012).

Childbirth

Early in the ninth month of pregnancy, the fetus's head settles in the pelvis. This shift is called *dropping* or *lightening*. The woman may actually feel lighter because of lessened pressure on the diaphragm. About a day or so before the beginning of labor, the woman may notice blood in her vaginal secretions because fetal pressure on the pelvis may rupture superficial blood vessels in the birth canal. Tissue that had plugged the cervix, possibly preventing entry of infectious agents from the vagina, becomes dislodged. There is a resultant discharge of bloody mucus. At about this time one woman in ten also has a rush of warm "water" from the vagina. The "water" is amniotic fluid, and it means that the amniotic sac has burst. Labor usually begins within a day after rupture of the amniotic sac. For most women the amniotic sac does not burst until the end of the first stage of childbirth. Other signs of impending labor include indigestion, diarrhea, abdominal cramps, and an ache in the small of the back. Labor begins with the onset of regular uterine contractions.

The first uterine contractions are relatively painless and are called **Braxton-Hicks contractions,** or *false labor contractions.* They are false because they do not widen the cervix or advance the baby through the birth canal. They tend to increase in frequency but are less regular than labor contractions. Real labor contractions, by contrast, become more intense when the woman moves around or walks.

The initiation of labor may involve the secretion of hormones by the fetal adrenal and pituitary glands that stimulate the placenta and mother's uterus to secrete **prostaglandins.** Prostaglandins stimulate the uterine musculature to contract. It would make sense for the fetus to have a mechanism for signaling the mother that it is mature enough to sustain independent life. The mechanisms that initiate and maintain labor are not fully understood, however. Later in labor the pituitary gland releases **oxytocin,** a hormone that stimulates contractions strong enough to expel the baby. 👁

Real Students, Real Questions

Q *What triggers childbirth? Why does it trigger premature births?*

A It is speculated that hormones secreted by the fetus may stimulate the placenta and the mother's uterus to secrete prostaglandins that, in turn, cause uterine muscles to contract. These contractions might feel similar to premenstrual cramping. Thus, it could be that the fetus has a mechanism for signaling the mother that it is ready to sustain independent life. Other possible triggers include the possible "urge" of the uterus to empty itself when it reaches a certain fullness or aging of the placenta. Later, during labor, the mother's pituitary gland releases oxytocin, the hormone that stimulates contractions strong enough to expel the baby. Some common causes of prematurity include infection, inflammation, and maternal smoking.

STAGES OF CHILDBIRTH

Childbirth begins with the onset of labor and has three stages. In the first stage uterine contractions **efface** and **dilate** the cervix to about 4 inches (10 cm) in diameter, so that the baby may pass. Stretching of the cervix causes most of the pain of childbirth. A woman may experience little or no pain if her cervix dilates easily and quickly. The first stage may last from a couple of hours to more than a day. About 12 to 24 hours of labor is considered average for a first pregnancy. In later pregnancies labor takes about half this time.

The initial contractions are usually mild and spaced widely, at intervals of 10 to 20 minutes. They may last 20 to 40 seconds. As time passes, contractions become more frequent, long, strong, and regular.

Transition is the process that occurs when the cervix becomes nearly fully dilated and the baby's head begins to move into the vagina, or birth canal. Contractions usually come quickly during transition. Transition usually lasts about 30 minutes or less and is often accompanied by feelings of nausea, chills, and intense pain.

The second stage of childbirth follows transition and begins when the cervix has become fully dilated and the baby begins to move into the vagina and first appears at the opening of the birth canal (see Figure 11.7). The woman may be taken to a delivery room for the second stage of childbirth. The second stage is shorter than the first stage. It lasts from a few minutes to a few hours and ends with the birth of the baby. 👁

Efface To become thin.

Dilate To open or widen.

Transition The process during which the cervix becomes nearly fully dilated and the head of the fetus begins to move into the birth canal.

👁⃞ Watch the Video
Labor
on **MyDevelopmentLab**

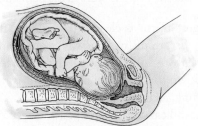

1. The second stage of labor begins

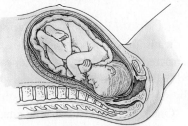

2. Further descent and rotation

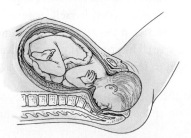

3. The crowning of the head

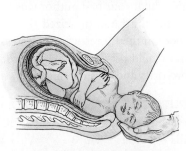

4. Anterior shoulder delivered

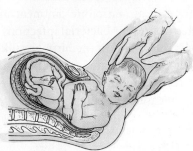

5. Posterior shoulder delivered

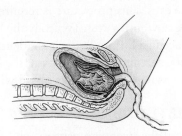

6. The third stage of labor begins with separation of the placenta from the uterine wall

FIGURE 11.7 The Stages of Childbirth. During the first stage, uterine contractions efface and dilate the cervix to about four inches so that the baby may pass through. The second stage begins with movement of the baby into the birth canal and ends with the birth of the baby. During the third stage, the placenta separates from the uterine wall and is expelled through the birth canal.

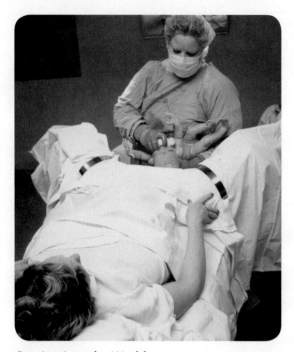

Coming into the World.
Childbirth progresses through three stages. During the first stage, uterine contractions efface and dilate the cervix so that the baby may pass. The second stage lasts from a few minutes to a few hours and ends with the birth of the baby. During the third stage, the placenta is expelled.

6 (T/F)

Episiotomy A surgical incision in the perineum that widens the birth canal, preventing random tearing during childbirth.

Perineum The area between the vulva and the anus.

Each contraction of the second stage propels the baby farther along the birth canal (vagina). When the baby's head becomes visible at the vaginal opening, it is said to have *crowned*. The baby typically emerges fully a few minutes after crowning.

An **episiotomy** may be performed on the mother when the baby's head has crowned. The purpose is to prevent random tearing of the **perineum** that can occur if it becomes extremely effaced. Episiotomies are controversial, however. The incision can cause infection and pain, and create discomfort and itching as it heals. In some cases the discomfort interferes with coitus for months. A national survey reported in *Obstetrics & Gynecology* found that the overall episiotomy rate dropped from nearly 70% to about 19% over the past two decades (Goldberg et al., 2002). Don't hesitate to ask prospective obstetricians about their views on episiotomies.

With or without an episiotomy, the baby's passageway to the external world is a tight fit. As a result, the baby's facial features and the shape of its head may be temporarily distended. The baby may look as if it has been through a prizefight. Its head may be elongated, its nose flattened, and its ears bent. Although parents may be concerned about whether the baby's features will assume a more typical shape, they almost always do.

The third, or placental, stage of childbirth may last from a few minutes to an hour or more. During this stage, the placenta is expelled. Detachment of the placenta from the uterine wall may cause some bleeding. The uterus begins the process of contracting to a smaller size. The attending physician sews up the episiotomy or any tears in the perineum.

In the New World As the baby's head emerges, mucus is cleared from its mouth by means of suction aspiration to prevent the breathing passageway from being obstructed. Aspiration is often repeated once the baby is fully delivered. (Newly delivered babies are no longer routinely held upside down to help expel mucus. Nor is the baby slapped on the buttocks to stimulate breathing, as in old films.)

Once the baby is breathing adequately, the umbilical cord is clamped and severed about three inches from the baby's body. (After the birth of your first and third authors' third child, your first author was invited by the obstetrician to cut the umbilical cord— but the third author seized the scissors and cut the umbilical cord herself, squirting blood on the obstetrician's glasses. "Who gave the obstetrician the right to determine who would cut the umbilical cord!" she wanted to know.) The stump of the umbilical cord dries and falls off in its own time, usually in seven to ten days.

TRUTH OR **FICTION** REVISITED: It is *not* true that the cutting of the umbilical cord determines whether the baby will have an "inny" or an "outy." The cord dries and falls off on its own.

While the mother is in the third stage of labor, a nurse may perform procedures on the baby, such as placing drops of silver nitrate or an antibiotic ointment into the eyes. This procedure is required by most states to prevent bacterial infections in the newborn's eyes. Typically the baby is also footprinted and (if the birth has taken place in a hospital) given an identification bracelet. Since neonates do not manufacture vitamin K on their own, the baby may also receive an injection of the vitamin to ensure that her or his blood will clot normally in case of bleeding.

METHODS OF CHILDBIRTH

Until the twentieth century, childbirth usually occurred at home and involved the mother, a midwife, family, and friends. These days, women in the United States and Canada typically give birth in hospitals attended by obstetricians who use surgical instruments and anesthetics to protect mothers and children from infection, complications, and severe pain. Medical procedures save lives but also make childbearing more impersonal. Social critics argue that these procedures have medicalized a natural process: They have usurped control over women's bodies and, through the use of drugs, denied many women the experience of giving birth.

Anesthetized Childbirth During the past two centuries, science and medicine have led to the expectation that women should experience minimal discomfort during childbirth. Today only about 10% of American women use no anesthesia (Jameson, 2000).

General anesthesia first became popular when Queen Victoria of England delivered her eighth child under chloroform in 1853. General anesthesia, like the chloroform of old, induces unconsciousness. The drug sodium pentothal, a barbiturate, induces general anesthesia when it is injected into a vein. Barbiturates may also be taken orally to reduce anxiety while the woman remains awake. Women may also receive tranquilizers such as Valium or narcotics such as Demerol to help them relax and to blunt pain without inducing sleep.

Anesthetic drugs, as well as tranquilizers and narcotics, decrease the strength of uterine contractions during delivery. They may therefore delay the process of cervical dilation and prolong labor. They also weaken the woman's ability to push the baby through the birth canal. Because these drugs cross the placental membrane, they also lower the newborn's overall responsiveness.

Regional or **local anesthetics** block pain in parts of the body without generally depressing the mother's alertness or putting her to sleep. In a *pudendal block,* the external genitals are numbed by local injection. In an *epidural block* and a *spinal block,* an anesthetic is injected into the spinal canal, which temporarily numbs the mother's body below the waist. To prevent injury, the needles used for these injections do not come into contact with the spinal cord itself. Although local anesthesia decreases the responsiveness of the newborn baby, there is little evidence that medicated childbirth has serious, long-term consequences on children.

Prepared Childbirth: The Lamaze Method The French obstetrician Fernand Lamaze visited the Soviet Union in 1951 and found that many Russian women bore babies without anesthetics and without reporting a great deal of pain. Lamaze returned to Western Europe with some of the techniques the women used; they are now termed the **Lamaze method,** or *prepared childbirth.* Lamaze (1981) argued that women can learn to conserve energy during childbirth and reduce the pain of uterine contractions by associating the contractions with other responses, such as thinking of pleasant mental images such as beach scenes, or engaging in breathing and relaxation exercises.

A pregnant woman typically attends Lamaze classes with a "coach"—usually the father or partner—who will aid her in the delivery room by timing contractions, offering emotional support, and coaching her in the breathing and relaxation exercises. The woman and her partner also receive general information about childbirth. The partner is integrated into the process, and many couples report that their relationships are strengthened as a result.

The Lamaze method is flexible about the use of anesthetics. Many women report some pain during delivery and obtain anesthetics. However, the Lamaze method appears to help women to gain a greater sense of control over the delivery process.

Cesarean Section In a **cesarean section,** the baby is delivered through surgery rather than through the vagina. The term *section* is derived from the Latin for "to cut." Julius Caesar is said to have been delivered in this way, but health

General anesthesia The use of drugs to put people to sleep and eliminate pain, as during childbirth.

Local anesthesia A type of anesthesia that eliminates pain in a specific area of the body, as during childbirth.

Lamaze method A childbirth method in which women learn about childbirth, learn to relax and to breathe in patterns that conserve energy and lessen pain, and have a coach (usually the father) present at childbirth. Also termed *prepared childbirth.*

Cesarean section A method of childbirth in which the fetus is delivered through a surgical incision in the abdomen.

professionals believe this unlikely. In a cesarean section ("C-section" for short) the woman is anesthetized, and incisions are made in the abdomen and uterus so that the surgeon can remove the baby. The incisions are then sewn up and the mother can begin walking, often on the same day, although generally with some discomfort for a while. Although most C-sections are without complications, some cause urinary tract infections, inflammation of the wall of the uterus, blood clots, or hemorrhaging.

C-sections are most likely to be advised when normal delivery is difficult or threatening to the health of the mother or child. Vaginal deliveries can become difficult if the baby is large, the mother's pelvis is small or misshapen, the mother is tired or weakened, or the mother is aging. Herpes and HIV infections in the birth canal can be bypassed by C-section. Cesarean sections are also likely to be performed if the baby presents for delivery in the breech position (feet downward) or the **transverse position** (lying crosswise), or if the baby is in distress.

Use of the C-section has mushroomed. **TRUTH** OR **FICTION** REVISITED: One birth in three (33%) in the United States is currently by C-section (National Center for Health Statistics, 2012; see also Figure 11.8). Compare this figure to about 1 in 20 births in 1965. Much of the increase in the rate of C-sections reflects advances in medical technology, such as use of fetal monitors that allow doctors to detect fetal distress, concern about malpractice suits, and, simply, current medical practice patterns. Yet, some women request C-sections to avoid the discomforts of vaginal delivery or to control the timing of the delivery. Women are also having children at more advanced ages, when there is more risk to the urogenital system from vaginal delivery.

Medical opinion once held that once a woman had a C-section, subsequent deliveries also had to be by C-section. Otherwise, uterine scars might rupture during labor. Research has shown that the rate of uterine rupture during a vaginal delivery following a C-section is about 5% (Peaceman et al, 2009), which is about twice the risk of uterine rupture among women delivering vaginally who have not

Transverse position   A crosswise birth position.

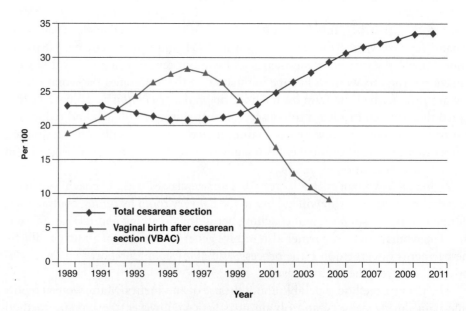

FIGURE 11.8 The Increase in C-Sections. Since 1996, the percentage of American women undergoing C-sections has mushroomed from 21% to 33%. The percentage of women having a vaginal delivery after a C-section has declined, owing largely to fear that the healed uterine incision for the earlier C-section might rupture.

Source: U.S. National Center for Health Statistics (2012).

A World of Diversity

Birth Rates around the World

Let's have a look at some history and some prehistory—that is, some guesstimates of events that might have occurred before records were made. According to the U.S. Census Bureau, which was *not* distributing questionnaires at the time, some 5 million humans walked the Earth about 10,000 years ago. It took another 5,000 years for that number to expand to 14 million. Skipping ahead 2,000 years to the year 1, humans gained a stronger foothold on the planet and the number increased tenfold, to some 170 million. By 1900, the population increased tenfold again, to about 1.7 billion. In 1950, estimates placed the number at about 2.5 billion, and today—with the increase in the food supply, sanitary water supplies, and vaccinations—the number is estimated to be close to 7 billion.

Therefore, we are in the middle of a population explosion, are we not?

The answer depends on where you look. Parents need to have slightly in excess of two children to reproduce themselves because some children are lost to illness, accidents, or violence. Table 11.4 shows you that in countries such as Spain, Greece, Italy, Japan, Canada, Russia, and the United Kingdom, parents are not reproducing themselves.

Table 11.4	Fertility Rates and Related Factors around the World					
Nation	**Fertility Rates**	**Rate of Usage of Modern Methods of Contraception (%)**	**Literacy Rates (%)**		**Years of Education**	
			Men	**Women**	**Men**	**Women**
Afghanistan	5.97	15	**	**	10	6
Brazil	1.80	77	90	90	14	14
Canada	1.69	72	**	**	15	16
China	1.56	84	97	91	11	12
Congo	4.44	13	**	**	11	10
Cuba	1.45	72	100	100	15	17
France	1.99	75	**	**	16	16
Germany	1.46	66	**	**	**	**
Greece	1.54	46	98	96	16	16
India	2.54	49	75	51	11	10
Iran	1.59	59	89	81	13	13
Iraq	4.54	33	86	70	11	9
Israel	2.91	52	**	**	15	16
Italy	1.48	41	99	99	16	17
Jamaica	2.26	66	81	91	13	14
Japan	1.42	44	**	**	15	15
Kenya	4.62	39	91	84	11	11
Mexico	2.23	67	95	92	13	14
Pakistan	3.20	19	69	40	8	6
Philippines	3.05	34	95	96	11	12
Russia	1.53	65	100	99	14	15
Saudi Arabia	2.64	**	90	81	15	14
Spain	1.50	62	98	97	16	17
United Kingdom	1.87	84	**	**	16	17
U.S.A.	2.08	73	**	**	16	17

**Missing information

Sources: United Nations. (2012). Department of Economic and Social Affairs. Economic and Social Development. Social Indicators.

had a previous C-section. However, maternal deaths due to uterine rupture during delivery are rare. In any event, only a small minority of women who have previously had a C-section deliver subsequent babies vaginally.

Consumer advocates advise pregnant women who would like to deliver vaginally, if possible, to ask about the rates of C-sections when they are choosing a physician and a hospital. Women can try to choose obstetricians who have lower rates or who are open to a second opinion for elective surgery. But it should not be forgotten that there are excellent reasons for having C-sections. It makes no sense to avoid a C-section if vaginal delivery might put the mother or the baby at risk.

BIRTH PROBLEMS

Most deliveries are uncomplicated, or "unremarkable," in the medical sense—although childbirth is the most remarkable experience of many parents' lives. Problems can and do occur, however. Some of the most common birth problems are anoxia and the birth of preterm and low–birth weight babies.

Anoxia Prenatal **anoxia** can cause various problems in the neonate and affect later development. It leads to complications such as brain damage and mental retardation. Prolonged anoxia during delivery can also result in cerebral palsy and possibly death.

The baby is supplied with oxygen through the umbilical cord. Passage through the birth canal squeezes the umbilical cord. Temporary squeezing, like holding one's breath for a moment, is unlikely to cause problems. (In fact, slight oxygen deprivation at birth is not unusual because the transition from receiving oxygen through the umbilical cord to breathing on its own may not happen immediately after the baby emerges.) Anoxia can result if constriction of the cord is prolonged, however. Prolonged constriction is more likely to occur with a breech presentation, because the baby's head presses the umbilical cord against the birth canal during delivery. Fetal monitoring can help detect anoxia early, however, before damage occurs. A C-section can be performed if the fetus appears to be in distress.

Preterm and Low–Birth Weight Children A neonate is considered to be premature, or **preterm,** if it is born before 37 weeks of gestation. The normal period of gestation is 40 weeks. Prematurity is generally linked with low birth weight, since the fetus normally makes dramatic gains in weight during the last weeks of pregnancy.

Regardless of the length of its gestation period, a newborn baby is considered to have a low birth weight if it weighs less than 5 pounds (about 2,500 grams). Preterm and low–birth weight babies face a heightened risk of infant mortality from causes ranging from asphyxia and infections to sudden infant death syndrome (SIDS) (Berger, 2000; Kramer et al., 2000). Neurological and developmental problems are also common among preterm infants, especially those born at or prior to 25 weeks of gestation (Saigal et al., 2006; Wood et al., 2000).

Twins and other multiple birth groupings are more likely to be of low birth weight than individual births (Blickstein et al., 2000). There is also a relationship between prematurity and the spacing of babies. Women who have babies less than 18 months or more than 59 months apart have the highest risk of giving birth to premature infants (Fuentes-Afflick & Hessol, 2000). On the other hand, it is common for women carrying more than one child to deliver prematurely, apparently because the babies are running out of space.

CRITICAL THINKING
Critical thinkers tackle controversial issues. What are the pros and cons of the following aspects of childbirth: Episiotomy? Use of anesthesia? C-section?

Anoxia Oxygen deprivation.

Preterm Born before 37 weeks of gestation.

A World of Diversity
Maternal and Infant Mortality around the World

Modern medicine has made vast strides in decreasing the rates of maternal and infant mortality, but the advances are not equally spread throughout the world. Save the Children, a nonprofit relief and development organization, tracks the likelihood that a woman will die in childbirth and that an infant will die during its first year. The likelihood of maternal and infant mortality is connected with factors such as the percentage of births that are attended by trained people, the literacy rate of adult women (which is one measure of the level of education of women), and the participation of women in national government (which is one measure of the extent to which a society empowers women). Figure 11.9 shows the various reasons why children die, according to a recent edition of "State of the World's Mothers" (Save the Children, 2011).

The safest place for a woman to deliver and for her baby to survive is Greece, where the chances of the woman dying are about 1 in 31,800, and where only 3 infants in 1,000 die during the first five years after birth (see Table 11.5). Female life expectancy at birth in Greece is 82, and the average number of years of schooling is 17. In Afghanistan, 1 woman in 11 will die as a result of pregnancy, and 199 children of 1,000 will die during their first five years. In Afghan society, only 14% of births are attended by trained personnel, and female life expectancy at birth is 45. European countries in general are safest. One out of 2100 women die in pregnancy or childbirth in the United States.

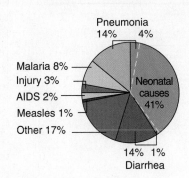

FIGURE 11.9 Global Causes of Infant Mortality.

Source: Data from Save the Children, 2011.

Table 11.5	Maternal and Child Mortality around the World as Related to Women's Life Expectancy and Years of Education			
Country	Lifetime Risk of Maternal Mortality	Female Life Expectancy at Birth	Expected Number of Years of Formal Female Schooling	Child Mortality Rate (Birth To 5 Years of Age) Per 1,000 Live Births
Greece	31,800	82	17	3
Ireland	17,800	83	18	4
Italy	15,200	84	17	4
Poland	13,300	80	16	7
Japan	12,200	87	15	3
Spain	11,400	84	18	4
Sweden	11,400	83	16	3
Canada	5,600	83	16	6
United Kingdom	4,700	82	17	6
United States	2,100	82	17	8
Russia	1,900	74	15	12
China	1,500	75	12	19
Cuba	1,400	81	19	6
Egypt	380	72	11	21
India	140	66	10	66
Afghanistan	11	45	5	199

Source: Save the Children (2011).

Preterm babies are relatively thin because they have not yet formed the layer of fat that accounts for the round, robust appearance of most full-term babies. Their muscles are immature, weakening their sucking and breathing reflexes. Also, in the last weeks of pregnancy fetuses secrete **surfactant,** which prevents the walls of their airways from sticking together. Muscle weakness and incomplete lining of the airways with surfactant can cause a cluster of problems known as **respiratory distress syndrome,** which is responsible for many neonatal deaths. (Today, surfactant replacement therapy is extending the possibilities of survival in preterm infants [Cole, 2000].) Preterm babies may also suffer from underdeveloped immune systems, which leave them more vulnerable to infections.

Preterm infants usually remain in the hospital for a time. There, they can be monitored and placed in incubators that provide a temperature-controlled environment and offer some protection from disease. If necessary, they may also receive oxygen. Although remarkable advances are being made in the medical field's ability to help preterm babies survive, the likelihood of developmental disabilities continues to increase dramatically for babies who are born at 25 weeks of gestation or earlier (Cole, 2000).

Stillbirth Stillbirth, in which the baby is born dead, is the gravest of birth problems. Stillbirth is no surprise. The baby is "silent" prior to birth—no heartbeat is heard and no movement is felt (Trulsson & Rådestad, 2004). Stillbirth is connected with fetal abnormalities, infection, medical conditions of the mother, and pregnancy complications such as preeclampsia and problems with the placenta (Pasupathy & Smith, 2005). However, the majority of cases have no clear cause and are considered unexplained. Even so, many "unexplained" deaths are connected with restriction of growth of the fetus. Growth restriction, in turn, may be associated with the mother's age and smoking (Cnattingius, 2004). The risk of stillbirth is also connected with the functioning of the placenta early in the pregnancy. Pregnancies at risk must be carefully monitored. Sometimes corrective actions can be taken to improve placental circulation.

Stillbirth has a deep psychological impact on parents. In many cases it leads to posttraumatic stress disorder (PTSD), which is characterized by ruminating about the loss, experiencing intrusive thoughts, and having nightmares (Born et al., 2006). When a baby still within the mother is declared dead, she may need a few hours before labor is induced to adjust to the fact (Trulsson & Rådestad, 2004). During this period, the woman may seek as much medical information as possible, or be silent herself. Afterward, she may encounter what Brin (2004) refers to as a "grief storm," which can find some outlet through social ritual or speaking with a compassionate therapist.

Subsequent pregnancies are likely to be experienced with extreme anxiety by both parents (Brisch et al., 2005; Turton et al., 2006). In the case of a miscarriage, parents may feel that they have to get safely through the first trimester for the subsequent pregnancy to be valid. In the case of a stillbirth, they are likely to have misgivings for the entire gestation period, and through labor. This is a painful process, but it is to be expected.

The Postpartum Period

The weeks after delivery are called the **postpartum** period. The first few days of postpartum are frequently happy ones. The long wait is over, as are the discomforts of childbirth. However, about 70% of new mothers have periods of tearfulness, sadness,

Surfactant   Substances that prevent the walls of the airways from sticking together.

Respiratory distress syndrome A cluster of breathing problems, including weak and irregular breathing, to which preterm babies are especially vulnerable.

Postpartum   Following birth.

and irritability that the American Psychiatric Association (2000) refers to as "baby blues." Baby blues and other postpartum mood problems are so common that they are statistically normal (Gavin et al., 2005).

These problems include the baby blues and more serious mood disorders ("postpartum-onset mood episodes"), which occasionally include "psychotic features" (Grigoriadis & Romans, 2006; American Psychiatric Association, 2000). These problems are far-flung; researchers find them in China, Turkey, Guyana, Australia, and South Africa—occurring with similar frequency (Bloch et al., 2006; Cohen et al., 2006).

Baby blues affect the majority of women in the weeks after delivery. Researchers believe they are common because they are caused by the hormonal changes that accompany and follow delivery (Bloch et al., 2006; Morris, 2000). They last for about ten days and are not severe enough to impair the mother's functioning. Don't misunderstand: The baby blues are seriously discomforting and not to be ignored. (Don't say, "Oh, you're just experiencing what most women experience.") The point is that most women tolerate the baby blues, even though with great difficulty at times, partly because they know that the mood problems are transient.

As many as one in five to ten women encounter a more serious mood disorder called **postpartum depression (PPD)**. This disorder begins within four weeks after delivery and may linger for weeks or months. PPD is symptomized by serious sadness, feelings of hopelessness and helplessness, feelings of worthlessness, difficulty concentrating, and major changes in appetite (usually loss of appetite) and sleep patterns (frequently insomnia). There can also be severe fluctuations in mood, with women sometimes feeling elated. Some women show obsessive concern with the well-being of their babies at this time.

Some researchers suggest that PPD is caused by the interactions of biological (mainly hormonal) factors, including that precipitous drop-off in estrogen (Johnstone et al., 2001), and psychological factors, such as the following:

- Concerns about the life changes that motherhood creates
- Concerns about whether one will be a good mother
- Marital problems
- Having a sick or unwanted baby

But the focus today is on the biological factors because there are major changes in body chemistry during and after pregnancy, and because women around the world seem to experience similar disturbances in mood, even when their life experiences and support systems are very different from those we find in the United States (Cohen et al., 2006).

According to the American Psychiatric Association (2000), postpartum mood episodes are accompanied by "psychotic features" (loss of touch with reality) in 1 woman in 500 to 1,000. Very rarely, women experience delusions that the infant is possessed by the devil or that they must kill the infant.

Women who experience PPD may profit from psychotherapy or drugs. Drugs that increase estrogen levels or antidepressants may help. Most women get over PPD on their own. At the very least, women need to know that the problem is not unusual and does not necessarily mean that there is something seriously wrong with them or that they are not living up to their obligations.

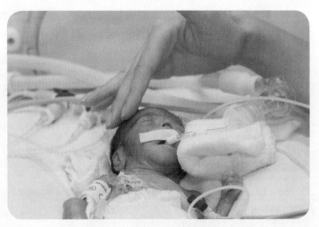

Too Early. A baby is considered premature if it is born before 37 weeks of gestation. Premature babies are vulnerable to various developmental problems.

Postpartum depression (PPD) Persistent and severe mood changes during the postpartum period, involving feelings of despair and apathy and characterized by changes in appetite and sleep, low self-esteem, and difficulty concentrating.

Brooke Shields Testifies at Hearing on Postpartum Depression. Since suffering PPD herself, actress Brooke Shields has been promoting means of prescreening for the disorder and treating it.

CRITICAL THINKING

How have women you know reacted emotionally in the hours, days, and weeks following childbirth?

Breastfeeding Seems to Be the "Gold Standard" for Mothers in the United States and Canada Today. Why? Is it always possible? Under what circumstances should women not breastfeed their children?

BREASTFEEDING VERSUS BOTTLE-FEEDING

In many developing nations, women have no choice: If their infants are going to be nourished, they will have to breastfeed. Yet even in developed nations, where formula is readily available, breast milk today is considered by most health professionals to be the "medical gold standard," and by many (perhaps most) mothers to be the "moral gold standard" (Walker, 2010). Largely for this reason, the majority of mothers in the United States and Canada today breastfeed their children (see Figure 11.10). The American Academy of Pediatrics (2012) recommends that women exclusively breastfeed infants for the first six months, gradually introduce complementary foods over the next six months, and continue breastfeeding as long as the mother and infant wish to do so.

Breastfeeding is, of course, the "natural" way to nourish a baby. Infant formulas were developed in the 1930s. Over the next several decades, the incidence of breastfeeding declined because women were entering the workforce, bottle feeding was seen as "scientific," and the women's movement encouraged women to become liberated from traditional roles (Weaver, 2012). Breastfeeding thus has political and social aspects as well as nutritional aspects. Much of the decision of whether or not to breastfeed has to do with domestic and occupational arrangements, day care, social support, reactions to public breastfeeding, and beliefs about mother–infant bonding (Weaver, 2012).

A survey of 35 African American and Latina mothers or pregnant adolescents (ages 12 to 19) found that those who recognized the benefits of breastfeeding were more likely to use it (Hannon et al., 2000). They reported benefits such as promoting mother–infant bonding and the infant's health. A survey of 349 Latina American mothers found that younger mothers and mothers born in the United States were more likely to breastfeed (Newton, 2009). Barriers to breastfeeding include fear of pain, embarrassment by public exposure, and unease with the act itself. However, an influential person—such as the woman's partner or mother—often encourages the mother to breastfeed (Sloan et al., 2006). Community support through volunteer workers ("Birth Sisters"), visiting nurses, and community clinics also encourages women to breastfeed (Frick et al., 2012; Wambach et al., 2011). Better-educated women are more likely to breastfeed, even among low-income women (Wambach et al., 2011).

In any event, breastfeeding has become more popular during the past generation, largely because of increased knowledge of its health benefits, even among women at the lower end of the socioeconomic spectrum (Weaver, 2012). Most American mothers—more than 70%—breastfeed their children, at least for a while. However, only about two women in five continue to breastfeed after six months, and only one in five are still breastfeeding at one year (Breastfeeding, 2006). The American Academy of Pediatrics (2012) recommends that women breastfeed for a year or longer.

Breastfeeding reduces the risk of infectious diseases to the baby by transmitting the mother's antibodies to the baby. Breastfeeding also reduces the incidence of allergies in babies, sudden infant death syndrome, diabetes, and many other health problems, both in developed and developing countries (American Academy of Pediatrics, 2005). Uterine contractions that occur during breastfeeding help return the uterus to its typical size. Breastfeeding similarly promotes a return to prepregnancy body

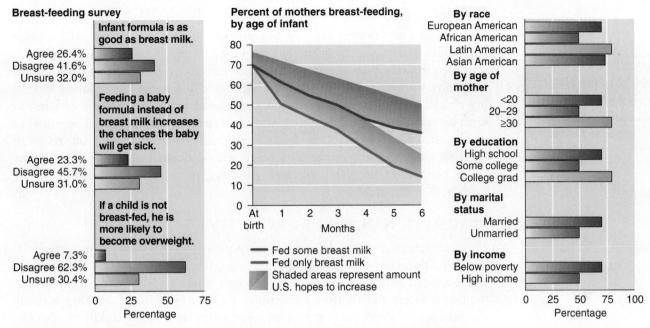

FIGURE 11.10 Who Breastfeeds? Although the majority of mothers breastfeed, many are unsure of its benefits over baby formula.

Source: CDC, Healthy Styles Survey, 2010.

weight (Baker et al., 2008). In addition, breastfeeding delays resumption of normal menstrual cycles but is not a perfectly reliable birth-control method.

There are also some downsides to breastfeeding. For example, breast milk is one of the bodily fluids that transmit HIV (the virus that causes AIDS). Researchers estimate that as many as one-third of the world's infants who have HIV/AIDS were infected in this manner (UNICEF, 2012). Alcohol, many drugs taken by the mother, and environmental hazards such as polychlorinated biphenyls (PCBs) can also be transmitted to infants through breast milk. Therefore, breast milk is not always as pure as it would seem to be. Moreover, in order for breast milk to contain the necessary nutrients, the mother must be adequately nourished herself. In many cases, mothers in developing countries do not eat sufficiently well to pass along proper nutrition to their infants.

Other negatives to breastfeeding include the mother's assumptions of the sole responsibility for nighttime feedings. She also encounters the physical demands of producing and expelling milk, a tendency for soreness in the breasts, and the inconvenience of being continually available to meet the infant's feeding needs.

The hormones prolactin and oxytocin are involved in breastfeeding. **Prolactin** stimulates production of milk, or **lactation,** two to three days after delivery. Oxytocin causes the breasts to eject milk and is secreted in response to suckling. When an infant is weaned, secretion of prolactin and oxytocin is discontinued, and lactation comes to an end.

Advantages to breast milk are summarized in Table 11.6. *Should* a woman breastfeed her baby? The issue is largely political. Much of the literature on breast-feeding has little to do with the advantages of breast milk or formula, but with occupational and domestic arrangements, child day care, mother–infant bonding, and the politics of domestic decision making. Although breastfeeding benefits both mother and infant, the outcomes for bottle-feeding in the developed world do not show that the relative risks are unacceptable. Each woman is advised to weigh the pluses and minuses for herself.

Prolactin A pituitary hormone that stimulates production of milk.

Lactation Production of milk by the mammary glands.

RESUMPTION OF OVULATION AND MENSTRUATION

For close to a month after delivery, women experience a reddish vaginal discharge called **lochia**. A nonnursing mother does not resume actual menstrual periods until two to three months postpartum. The first few cycles are likely to be irregular. Many women incorrectly assume that they will resume menstruating following childbirth by having a menstrual period and ovulating two weeks later. In most cases the opposite is true. Ovulation precedes the first menstrual period after childbirth. Thus, a woman may become pregnant before the menstrual phase of her first postpartum cycle. Some women who suffered premenstrual syndrome before their pregnancies find that their periods give them less discomfort after the birth of their children.

RESUMPTION OF SEXUAL ACTIVITY

The resumption of coitus depends on a couple's level of sexual interest, the healing of episiotomies or other injuries, fatigue, the recommendations of obstetricians, and, of course, tradition. Obstetricians usually advise a six-week waiting period for safety and comfort. One study of 570 women found that they actually resumed sexual intercourse at an average of seven weeks after childbirth (Byrd et al., 1998).

TRUTH OR **FICTION** REVISITED: It is true that couples should abstain from coitus for at least six weeks following childbirth. However, many other kinds of sexual activities are safe and do not cause discomfort. (Check with your obstetrician.)

Women will typically prefer to delay coitus until it becomes physically comfortable, generally when the episiotomy or other lacerations have healed and the lochia has ended. This may take several weeks. Women who breastfeed may also find they have less vaginal lubrication, and the dryness can cause discomfort during coitus. K-Y jelly or other lubricants may help in such cases.

The return of sexual interest and resumption of sexual activity may take longer for some couples than for others. Sexual interest depends more on psychological than on physical factors. Many couples encounter declining sexual interest and activity in the first year following childbirth, generally because child care can sap energy and limit free time. Not surprisingly, couples whose sexual relationships were satisfying before the baby arrived tend to show greater sexual interest and to resume sexual activity earlier than those who had less satisfying relationships beforehand.

CRITICAL THINKING

What are the "political" issues involved in breastfeeding versus bottle-feeding?

 8

CRITICAL THINKING

What inaccurate ideas did you have about conception or pregnancy before you read this chapter? In what way did those ideas change?

Lochia　A reddish vaginal discharge that may persist for a month after delivery.

Table 11.6

Advantages of Breast Milk over Formula

There are numerous advantages to breast milk (American Academy of Pediatrics, 2012; Breastfeeding, 2010):

- Breast milk conforms to human digestion processes (i.e., it is unlikely to upset the infant's stomach).
- Breast milk alone is adequate for the first six months after birth. Other foods can merely supplement breast milk through the first year.
- As the infant matures, the composition of breast milk changes to help meet the infant's changing needs.
- Breast milk contains the mother's antibodies and helps the infant ward off health problems ranging from ear infections, pneumonia, wheezing, bronchiolitis, and tetanus to chicken pox, bacterial meningitis, and typhoid fever.
- Breast milk helps protect against the form of cancer known as childhood lymphoma (a cancer of the lymph glands).
- Breast milk decreases the likelihood of developing serious cases of diarrhea.
- Infants who are nourished by breast milk are less likely to develop allergic responses and constipation.
- Breastfed infants are less likely to develop obesity later in life.
- Breastfeeding is associated with better neural and behavioral organization in the infant.

Source: Breastfeeding, 2010

Chapter Review ✓–[Study and Review on MyDevelopmentLab

LO1 Describe the process of conception
Conception is the union of a sperm cell and an ovum, which normally occurs in a fallopian tube. Male fetuses have a higher rate of miscarriage. Chromosomes from the sperm cells combine to form 23 new pairs.

LO2 Discuss fertility problems and ways in which people with such problems can become parents
Male fertility problems mainly involve low sperm count and motility. Female fertility problems include failure to ovulate, infections, endometriosis, and obstructions in the reproductive tract. Fertility drugs stimulate ovulation. Artificial insemination may use sperm from a donor. In vitro fertilization (IVF) may be used when the fallopian tubes are blocked. Some couples adopt.

LO3 Discuss signs of pregnancy and sex during pregnancy
Early signs of pregnancy include a missed period and the presence of human chorionic gonadotropin (HCG) in the blood or urine. "Morning sickness" is believed to be linked with a healthy pregnancy. Miscarriages have many causes, including chromosomal defects in the fetus. Most health professionals agree that sexual intercourse is normally safe until the start of labor.

LO4 Discuss the key events of the stages of prenatal development
During the germinal stage, the dividing mass of cells travels to the uterus, where it becomes implanted. The embryo and fetus exchange nutrients and wastes with the mother through the placenta and umbilical cord. Major organ systems develop during the embryonic period. The fetal stage is mainly characterized by maturation of organs and gains in size.

LO5 Discuss the effects of environmental hazards on the child
Maternal malnutrition is linked with low birth weight, prematurity, and cognitive problems. Maternal diseases and disorders can harm the embryo and are called *teratogens*. Syphilis can cause miscarriage or stillbirth. Babies born to HIV-infected mothers may become infected by childbirth. In Rh incompatibility, antibodies produced by the mother can kill the fetus or cause brain damage. Maternal use of alcohol is linked to fetal alcohol syndrome (FAS). Maternal cigarette smoking deprives the fetus of oxygen and is linked with low birth weight, stillbirth, and learning problems.

LO6 Discuss the effects of genetic abnormalities on the child
Chromosomal abnormalities such as Down syndrome become more likely as parents age. Amniocentesis cultures fetal cells found in amniotic fluid to detect genetic abnormalities. Parental blood tests can reveal genes and markers for many disorders.

LO7 Discuss the stages of childbirth
Before labor begins, blood typically appears in the birth canal. Some women have a rush of amniotic fluid. Oxytocin stimulates contractions strong enough to expel the baby. Childbirth begins with the onset of regular contractions of the uterus, which efface and dilate the cervix, causing most of the discomfort of childbirth. The second stage begins when the baby appears and ends with birth. The third stage expels the placenta.

LO8 Describe various methods of childbirth
General anesthesia puts the woman to sleep. Local anesthetics deaden pain without putting the mother to sleep. A C-section delivers a baby surgically through the abdomen.

LO9 Discuss various birth problems
Prenatal oxygen deprivation can damage the nervous system and kill the baby.

LO10 Discuss events of the postpartum period, including breastfeeding versus bottle-feeding
Women may encounter baby blues and more severe postpartum depression. These problems apparently reflect hormonal changes following birth. Breastfeeding is connected with fewer infections and allergic reactions in the baby. Obstetricians usually advise waiting six weeks following childbirth before resuming sexual intercourse.

Test Your Learning

1. The enzyme hyaluronidase
   - (a) stimulates production of milk.
   - (b) passes through the placenta.
   - (c) stimulates contractions of labor.
   - (d) thins the zona pellucida.

2. The most common cause of male infertility is
   - (a) low sperm motility.
   - (b) low sperm count.
   - (c) injury to the testes.
   - (d) higher-than-normal scrotal temperature.

3. The presence of human chorionic gonadotropin is assessed to determine
   - (a) blocked fallopian tubes.
   - (b) sickle-cell anemia.
   - (c) pregnancy.
   - (d) Down syndrome.

4. If we date pregnancy from the onset of the last menstrual cycle before conception, the normal gestation period is _____ days.
   - (a) 266
   - (b) 272
   - (c) 280
   - (d) 288

5. A breech presentation is
   - (a) bottom or feet first.
   - (b) head first.
   - (c) sideways.
   - (d) shoulder first.

6. The critical period for the development of the facial features associated with FAS seems to be the first _____ of prenatal development.
   - (a) week
   - (b) two weeks
   - (c) month
   - (d) two months

7. The pudendal block is an example of
   - (a) general anesthesia.
   - (b) local anesthesia.
   - (c) a birth problem.
   - (d) anoxia.

8. Which of the following is most likely to afflict African Americans?
   - (a) Tay-Sachs disease
   - (b) Hemophilia
   - (c) Sickle-cell disease
   - (d) Retinal blatoma

9. An underdeveloped upper jaw is characteristic of
   - (a) children whose mothers smoked during pregnancy.
   - (b) fetal alcohol syndrome.
   - (c) prenatal exposure to PCBs.
   - (d) prenatal exposure to stress.

10. Mothers in _____ are most likely to die in childbirth.
    - (a) Denmark
    - (b) Austria
    - (c) Pakistan
    - (d) Afghanistan

Answers: 1. d; 2. b; 3. c; 4. c; 5. a; 6. d; 7. b; 8. c; 9. b; 10. d

My Life, My Sexuality

Selecting an Obstetrician

*Explore this **My Life, My Sexuality** feature by scanning this QR code with your mobile device. If you don't already have one, you may download a free QR scanner for your device wherever smartphone apps are sold. You can also view this feature in MyDevelopmentLab, along with an accompanying critical thinking assignment.*

A healthy pregnancy can make the difference between a joyous experience and a lifetime of regrets. One way to help ensure a healthy pregnancy is to obtain adequate prenatal health care. The physician who provides prenatal care is called an obstetrician. How do you find the obstetrician who is right for you? Scan the code to learn more about selecting an obstetrician.

12 Contraception and Abortion

Learning Objectives

TRUTH OR FICTION?

Which of the following statements are the truth, and which are fiction? Look for the Truth-or-Fiction icons on the pages that follow to find the answers.

1 Ancient Egyptians used crocodile dung as a contraceptive. **T F?**

2 There is an oral contraceptive that can be taken the morning after unprotected intercourse. **T F?**

3 Sterilization operations can be surgically reversed. **T F?**

4 Contraceptives not only prevent conception, they also provide protection against sexually transmitted infections. **T F?**

5 Douching quickly after unprotected intercourse is a reasonably good contraceptive method. **T F?**

6 Abortions were legal in the newly founded United States. **T F?**

7 The D&C is the most widely used abortion method in the United States. **T F?**

It was a stifling day in July 1912. Margaret Sanger (1883–1966), a nurse practitioner, was summoned to the house of a woman near death from a botched self-induced abortion. Her husband had called a doctor, and the doctor sent for Sanger. Together, doctor and nurse worked feverishly through the days and nights that followed to stem an infection that had taken hold in the woman. Sanger later commented,

> Never had I worked so fast, never so concentratedly. The sultry days and nights were melted into a torpid inferno. It did not seem possible there could be such heat, and every bit of food, ice, and drugs had to be carried up three flights of stairs.... (Sanger, 1938)

After two interminable weeks, the woman began to recover. Her neighbors, who had feared the worst, came to express their joy. But the woman, who smiled wanly at those who came to see her, appeared more depressed and anxious than would be expected of someone who was recovering from a grave illness. By the end of the third week, when Sanger prepared to leave her patient, the woman, Mrs. Sachs, voiced the fear that was haunting her. Her face registered deep despair as she explained to Sanger that she dreaded becoming pregnant again and facing a choice between attempting another abortion, which she feared might kill her, and bearing a baby whose care it was beyond her means to support. She pleaded for information about contraception but Sanger could offer none. In 1912, it was a crime even for health professionals like Margaret Sanger to dispense information about contraceptives. Abortions, too, were illegal. Sanger tried to comfort her and promised to return to talk again (Engelman, 2011).

Three months later Sanger received another urgent call. It was Mr. Sachs. His wife was sick again—from the same cause. Sanger recalled,

Margaret Sanger Testifying before a Senate Committee

> For a wild moment I thought of sending someone else, but actually, of course, I hurried into my uniform, caught up my bag, and started out. All the way I longed for a subway wreck, an explosion, anything to keep me from having to enter that home again. But nothing happened, even to delay me. I turned into the dingy doorway and climbed the familiar stairs once more. The children were there, young little things.
>
> Mrs. Sachs was in a coma and died within ten minutes. I folded her still hands across her breast, remembering how they had pleaded with me, begging so humbly for the knowledge which was her right. I drew a sheet over her pallid face. Jake was sobbing, running his hands through his hair and pulling it out like an insane person. Over and over again he wailed, "My God! My God! My God!" (Sanger, 1938)

Today, partly because of the work of Margaret Sanger, who went on to become a key advocate for birth control, information about contraceptives is disseminated freely throughout the United States.

Methods of birth control include contraception and abortion. The term *contraception* refers to techniques that prevent conception. The term *abortion* refers to the termination of a pregnancy before the embryo or fetus is capable of surviving outside the womb, as we see later in the chapter. ◉

👁**Watch** the **Video**
Cost of Birth Control
on **MyDevelopmentLab**

Coitus interruptus A method of contraception in which the penis is withdrawn from the vagina prior to ejaculation. Also known as the *withdrawal method.*

Contraception

People have been devising means of contraception since they became aware of the relationship between coitus and conception. Ironically, the safest and most effective method of contraception is also the least popular: abstinence. The bible contains many references to contraceptive techniques, including vaginal sponges and contraceptive concoctions. It also refers to **coitus interruptus,** or withdrawal. The story of onan, for example, implies knowledge of the withdrawal method.

Ancient Egyptian methods of birth control included douching with wine and garlic after coitus, and soaking crocodile dung in sour milk and stuffing the mixture deep within the vagina. The dung blocked the passage of many—if not all—sperm through the cervix and also soaked up sperm. The dung may also have done its job through a social mechanism. It may have discouraged all but the most ardent suitors. **TRUTH** OR **FICTION** REVISITED: It is true that ancient Egyptians used crocodile dung as a contraceptive. (No comment.)

 1

Ancient Greek and Roman women placed absorbent materials within the vagina to absorb semen. The use of sheaths or coverings for the penis has a long history. Sheaths worn over the penis as decorative covers can be traced to ancient Egypt (1350 BCE). Sheaths of linen were first described in European writings in 1564 by the Italian anatomist Fallopius (from whom the name of the fallopian tube is derived). Linen sheaths were used, without success, as a barrier against syphilis. The term **condom** was not used to describe penile sheaths until the eighteenth century. At that time, sheaths made of animal intestines became popular as a means of preventing sexually transmitted infections and unwanted pregnancies. Among the early advocates of condoms as a method of contraception was the Italian adventurer and writer Giovanni Casanova (1725–1798). We now associate his name with men who are known for their amorous adventures. James Boswell (1740–1795), the biographer of Samuel Johnson, described his use of "armor," or condoms, in his graphic *London Journal*. On one occasion, however, he was so enamored with a street prostitute that he neglected to use his armor and contracted gonorrhea. Condoms made of rubber (hence the slang "rubbers") were introduced shortly after Charles Goodyear invented vulcanization of rubber in 1843. Many other forms of contraception were also used widely in the nineteenth century, including withdrawal, vaginal sponges, and douching.

CRITICAL THINKING
Critical thinkers pay attention to definitions of terms. The Roman Catholic Church opposes the use of artificial contraception. What is meant by *artificial* contraception?

Contraception in the United States: The Political Battle

As methods of contraception grew more popular in the nineteenth century, opponents waged a battle to make contraception illegal. One powerful opponent of contraception was Anthony Comstock, who served for a time as the secretary of the new york society for the suppression of vice. Comstock lobbied successfully for passage of a federal law in 1873—the Comstock law—that prohibited the dissemination of birth-control information through the mail on the grounds that it was "obscene and indecent." Many states passed even more restrictive laws. They outlawed passage of information from one person to another, even from physician to patient.

Consider the resistance that Margaret Sanger met when she challenged the laws restricting information about contraception (Engelman, 2011). In 1914, she established the National Birth Control League, which published the magazine *The Woman Rebel*. *Rebel* did not publish birth-control information but challenged the view that it was obscene. Nevertheless, charges were brought against Sanger, and she fled to Europe before her trial. During her self-imposed exile, she visited birth-control clinics in the Netherlands. When the charges against her in the United States were dropped in 1916, Sanger returned and established a birth-control clinic in Brooklyn, New York. The clinic was closed by the police, and Sanger was arrested. Released on bail, she reopened the clinic and was thereupon sentenced to 30 days in jail. She successfully appealed the sentence. In 1918, the courts ruled that physicians must be allowed to disseminate information that might aid in the cure and prevention of disease. Dismantling of the Comstock law had begun. With the financial support of

Condom A sheath made of animal membrane or latex that covers the penis and serves as a barrier to sperm.

Real Students, Real Questions

Q *If my druggist refuses to fill my birth-control pills, can I sue?*

A Cases on suits involving pharmacists who refuse to provide patients with prescribed birth-control pills, Plan B medications, and RU-486 are currently in courts and legislatures around the country. The answer to your question really depends on where you are and what legislation applies. By and large, a pharmacist is more likely to be compelled to supply birth-control pills than abortion pills. There are ways in many states, including California, for pharmacists to "opt out" of supplying abortion pills based on their conscience, or to pass the job to a fellow pharmacist without such objections. Right now the trend is for pharmacists to be fired for refusal to fill certain prescriptions and then to sue to get their jobs back based on the view that their freedom to practice their religion was abridged by their loss of job. Sometimes they succeed; sometimes they don't. The long and short of it is this: Check with a local attorney.

a wealthy friend, Katherine Dexter McCormack, Sanger spurred research into the use of hormones as one approach to contraception. In 1960, only six years before Sanger's death, oral contraception—"the pill"—was finally marketed in the United States. In 1965, the Supreme Court struck down the last impediment to free use of contraception: a law preventing the sale of contraceptives in Connecticut (*Griswold v. Connecticut,* 1965). In 1973, abortion was, in effect, legalized by the Supreme Court in the case of *Roe v. Wade,* permitting women to terminate unwanted pregnancies.

Today, contraceptives are advertised in popular magazines and sold through vending machines in college dormitories. U.S. history is not a one-way road to unrestricted use of birth control, however. Recent Supreme Court decisions have set aside bits and pieces of *Roe v. Wade,* giving the states more discretion over the regulation of abortion and restricting access to abortions for minors.

Even the use of artificial contraception continues to be opposed by many groups, including the Roman Catholic Church. In 2012 a brief battle emerged during the run-up to the presidential election when the Obama administration required

Table 12.1

Some Results on a Poll as to Whether Religious Institutions Should Include Contraception as Part of Their Health Benefits for Employees

	Support	Do Not Support
U.S. voters in general	56%	37%
Independents	55%	36%
Women	63%	29%
Catholics	53%	44%

*Public Policy Polling. (2012, February 10). Our polling on the birth control issue. http://www.publicpolicypolling.com/main/2012/02/our-polling-on-the-birth-control-issue.html. (Accessed June 23, 2012)

Catholic institutions to include birth control as one of the health benefits for female employees (Pear, 2012). Republicans for a while condemned the administration's stance as interfering with separation of church and state. However, the great majority of women in the country and many men expressed support for the administration's point of view (see Table 12.1), which claimed that such benefits were essential to women's health. Even the majority of the nation's Catholics supported the administration, and the political conflict was dropped. ◉

Methods of Contraception

There are many methods of contraception, including hormonal methods (the pill, the contraceptive patch, and injectable contraceptives), intrauterine devices (IUDs), diaphragms, cervical caps, spermicides, condoms, douching, withdrawal (coitus interruptus), and timing of ovulation (rhythm methods).

HORMONAL METHODS

Hormonal methods include "the pill," the contraceptive patch, and injectable contraceptives.

Oral Contraceptives ("The Pill") An **oral contraceptive** is commonly referred to as a birth-control pill, or simply "the pill." However, there are many kinds of birth-control pills that vary in the type and dosages of hormones they contain. Birth-control pills fall into two major categories: combination pills and mini-pills. Available only by prescription, birth-control pills are the most popular form of contraception among single women of reproductive age (Hatcher et al., 2011).

Combination pills (such as Ortho-Novum, Ovcon, and Loestrin) contain a combination of synthetic forms of the hormones estrogen and progesterone (progestin). Most combination pills provide a steady dose of synthetic estrogen and progesterone. Other combination pills, called *multiphasic* pills, vary the dosage of these hormones across the menstrual cycle to reduce the overall dosages to which the woman is exposed as well as reduce possible side effects. The **mini-pill** contains synthetic progesterone (progestin) only. ◉

How They Work Women cannot conceive when they are already pregnant because their bodies suppress maturation of egg follicles and ovulation. The combination pill fools the brain into acting as though the woman is already pregnant, so that no additional ova mature or are released. If ovulation does not take place, a woman cannot become pregnant.

In a normal menstrual cycle, low levels of estrogen during and just after the menstrual phase stimulate the pituitary gland to secrete FSH, which in turn stimulates the maturation of ovarian follicles. The estrogen in the combination pill inhibits FSH production, so that follicles do not mature. The progesterone (progestin) inhibits the pituitary's secretion of LH, which would otherwise lead to ovulation. The woman continues to have menstrual periods, but there is no unfertilized ovum to be sloughed off in the menstrual flow.

The combination pill is taken for 21 days of the typical 28-day cycle. Then, for seven days, the woman either takes no pill at all or an inert placebo pill to maintain the habit of taking a pill a day. The sudden drop in hormone levels causes the endometrium to disintegrate and menstruation to follow three or four days after the last pill has been taken. Then the cycle is repeated.

The progestin in the combination pill also increases the thickness and acidity of the cervical mucus. The mucus thus becomes a more resistant barrier to sperm and

---

Watch the Video
Pope Benedict XVI Condom Remarks Mark Significant Change in Vatican Attitude
on **MyDevelopmentLab**

CRITICAL THINKING
Is the use of the mini-pill or of the IUD a method of contraception or of abortion? Does it matter? Explain your views.

Watch the Video
The Pill Turns 50
on **MyDevelopmentLab**

Oral contraceptive
A contraceptive consisting of sex hormones and taken by mouth.

Combination pill
A birth-control pill that contains estrogen and progesterone.

Mini-pill A birth-control pill that contains progesterone only.

inhibits development of the endometrium. Therefore, even if an egg were somehow to mature and become fertilized in a fallopian tube, sperm would not be likely to survive the passage through the cervix. Even if sperm were somehow to succeed in fertilizing an egg, the failure of the endometrium to develop would mean that the fertilized ovum could not become implanted in the uterus. Progestin may also impede the progress of ova through the fallopian tubes and make it more difficult for sperm to penetrate ova.

The mini-pill contains progestin but no estrogen. Mini-pills are taken daily through the menstrual cycle, even during menstruation. They act in two ways. They thicken the cervical mucus to impede the passage of sperm through the cervix, and they render the inner lining of the uterus that is less receptive to a fertilized egg. Thus, even if the woman does conceive, the fertilized egg will pass from the body rather than becoming implanted in the uterine wall.

In Chapter 3 we noted that hormonal preparations such as Seasonique and Lybrel provide birth control as well as decrease the number of periods a woman has.

Effectiveness The failure rate of the birth-control pill associated with perfect use is very low—0.5% or less depending on the type of pill (see Table 12.2). The failure rate increases to 3% in typical use. Failures can occur when women forget to take the pill for two days or more, when they do not use backup methods when they first go on the pill, and when they switch from one brand to another. But forgetting to take the pill for a day or two might allow ovulation—and fertilization.

Reversibility Oral contraceptives may temporarily reduce fertility after they are stopped but they are not associated with permanent infertility. Nearly all women begin ovulating regularly within three months of suspending use (Hatcher et al., 2011). When a woman appears not to be ovulating after going off the pill, a drug such as clomiphene is often used to induce ovulation.

Advantages and Disadvantages The great advantage of oral contraception is that when used properly it is nearly 100% effective. Unlike many other forms of contraception, such as the condom or diaphragm, its use does not interfere with sexual spontaneity or diminish sexual sensations. The sex act need not be interrupted, as it would be by use of a condom.

Birth-control pills may also have some *healthful* side effects. They appear to reduce the risk of pelvic inflammatory disease (PID), benign ovarian cysts, and fibrocystic (benign) breast growths. The pill regularizes menstrual cycles and reduces menstrual cramping and premenstrual discomfort. The pill may also be helpful in the treatment of iron-deficiency anemia and facial acne. The combination pill reduces the risks of ovarian and endometrial cancer, even for a number of years after the woman has stopped taking it (Hatcher et al., 2011; Phipps et al., 2011).

The pill does have some disadvantages. It provides no protection against STIs. Moreover, it may reduce the effectiveness of antibiotics used to treat STIs. Going on the pill requires medical consultation, so a woman must plan to begin using the pill at least several weeks before becoming sexually active or before discontinuing the use of other contraceptives, and she must incur the expense of medical visits. Marchbanks and her colleagues (2002) compared 4,575 women with breast cancer with 4,682 controls and found no increased risk for breast cancer among women who were using or had used oral contraceptives. Moreover, the pill did not increase the risk of breast cancer in women with a family history of the disorder.

The main drawbacks of birth-control pills are potential side effects and possible health risks. Although a good deal of research suggests that the pill is safe for healthy women, many researchers (e.g., the American College of Obstetricians and

Table 12.2

Failure Rates, Reversibility, and Protection Provided against Sexually Transmitted Infections by Various Methods of Birth Control (in Percent of Women Who Become Pregnant within the First Year of Use)

Method	Percent (%) of Women Who Have an Unplanned Pregnancy within the First Year of Use		Is It Reversible?	Does It Protect Against Sexually Transmitted Infections (STIs)?
	Typical Use[1]	Consistent, Correct Use		
None	85	85	yes	no
Spermicides	29	18	yes	no
Rhythm Methods	20		yes	no
Calendar		9		
Ovulation Method		3		
Basal Body Temperature		2		
Post-Ovulation		3		
Withdrawal	27	4	yes	no
Cervical Cap[2]	20–40	10–30	yes	some
Diaphragm[2]	16	6	yes	some
Condom alone				
Female condom	21	5	yes	(scarce information)
Male condom	15	2	yes	yes
The Pill	8	0.3	yes	no, but may *reduce* the risk of pelvic inflammatory disease
Progestin Only		0.5		
Combined		0.1		
IUD	0.2–0.8	0.2–0.6	yes, except if fertility is impaired	no
Depo-Provera	3	0.3	yes	no
Injectable Contraceptives	0.5	0.5	yes	no
Female Sterilization	0.5	0.5	questionable	no
Male Sterilization	0.15	0.10	questionable	no

[1]Accidental pregnancies among typical couples.
[2]With spermicide.

Sources: American Academy of Family Physicians (2012), Cleland et al., 2012; Hatcher et al. (2011).

Gynecologists, 2006; Sun & Ren, 2012) suggest caution among women with medical conditions such as hypertension, diabetes, migraine headaches, fibrocystic breast tissue, uterine fibroids, or elevated cholesterol.

The estrogen in combination pills may produce side effects such as nausea and vomiting, fluid retention (feeling bloated), weight gain, increased vaginal discharge, headaches, tenderness in the breasts, and dizziness. Many of these are temporary. When they persist, women may be switched from one pill to another, perhaps to one with lower doses of hormones. Pregnant women produce high estrogen levels in the corpus luteum and placenta. The combination pill artificially raises levels of estrogen, so it is not surprising that some women who use it have side effects that mimic the early signs of pregnancy, such as weight gain or nausea ("morning sickness").

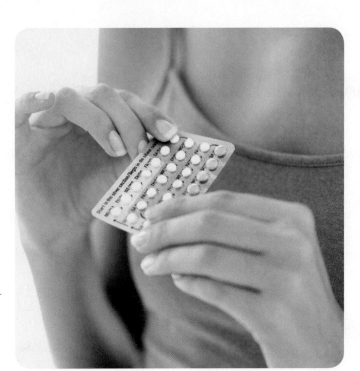

Taking the Pill. What are the advantages and disadvantages of the birth control pill? Will there ever be a birth control pill for men?

Weight gain can result from estrogen (through fluid retention) or progestin (through increased appetite and development of muscle). Oral contraceptives may also increase blood pressure in some women, but clinically significant elevations are rare in women using the low-dose pills that are available today (Hatcher et al., 2011). Still, it is wise for women who use the pill to have their blood pressure checked regularly. Women who encounter problems with high blood pressure from taking the pill are usually advised to switch to another form of contraception.

Hormone withdrawal symptoms are experienced by many women when they discontinue the pill (Spencer & Bonnema, 2011). These include headaches, pelvic pain, bloating, and breast tenderness.

Many women have avoided using the pill because of the risk of blood clots. The lower dosages of estrogen found in most types of birth-control pills today are associated with much lower risk of blood clots than was the case in the 1960s and 1970s when higher dosages were used (Hatcher et al., 2011). Still, women who are at increased risk for blood clotting, such as women with a history of circulatory problems or stroke, are typically advised not to use the pill.

Women who are considering using the pill need to weigh the benefits and risks with their health-care providers. For the great majority of young, healthy women in their 20s and early 30s, the pill is unlikely to cause blood clots or other cardiovascular problems (Hatcher et al., 2011; Spencer & Bonnema, 2011). Although research has found the pill to be safe for most women who do not smoke and are younger than age 35, pill users may have a slightly higher chance than nonusers of developing blood clots in the veins and lungs, stroke, and heart attack.

Some women should not be on the pill at all: women who have had circulatory problems or blood clots; women who have suffered a heart attack or stroke; or women who have a history of coronary disease, breast, or uterine cancer, genital bleeding, liver tumors, or sickle cell anemia (because of associated blood-clotting problems). Because of their increased risk of cardiovascular problems, caution should be exercised when the combination pill is used with women over 35 years of age who smoke (Hatcher et al., 2011). Nursing mothers should also avoid using the pill, as the hormones may be passed to the baby in the mother's milk.

Since the risks of cardiovascular complications generally increase with age, many women over the age of 35 have been encouraged by their gynecologists to use other forms of birth control. However, the American College of Obstetricians and Gynecologists believes that healthy nonsmokers can use the pill safely at least until the age of 45. This number keeps expanding, with many women now being advised to continue using pills to regulate their periods into their 50s.

The pill may also have psychological effects. Some users report depression or irritability. Switching brands or altering doses may help. Evidence is lacking concerning the effects of lower-estrogen pills on sexual desire.

Progestin fosters male secondary sex characteristics, so women who take the mini-pill may develop acne, facial hair, thinning of scalp hair, reduction in breast size, vaginal dryness, and missed or shorter periods. Irregular bleeding, or so-called breakthrough bleeding, between menstrual periods is a common side effect of the mini-pill. Irregular bleeding should be brought to the attention of a health professional. Because they can produce vaginal dryness, mini-pills can hinder vaginal lubrication during intercourse, decreasing sexual sensations and rendering sex painful.

Researchers have also examined suspected links between the use of the pill and certain forms of cancer, especially breast cancer. Results from several large-scale studies show no overall increase in the rates of breast cancer among pill users, but it remains possible that some subgroups of women who use the pill may be at increased risk (Crandall et la., 2012; Hatcher et al., 2011). The evidence linking use of the pill with cervical cancer is mixed, with some studies showing a link and others showing none (Hatcher et al., 2011).

Women considering the pill are advised to have a thorough medical evaluation to rule out conditions that might make usage unsafe. The evaluation should include a detailed medical and family history, and a physical exam including a Pap smear, assessment of blood pressure, screening for STIs, urinalysis, breast and pelvic exam, and possibly an EKG (electrocardio-

Plan B. Plan B—the "morning-after pill"—is available over the counter for women age 18 and over, and by prescription for those who are younger.

gram). Women who begin to use the pill, regardless of their age or risk status, should pay attention to changes in their physical condition, have regular checkups, and promptly report any physical complaints or unusual symptoms to their physicians.

The "Morning-After" Pill The so-called morning-after pill, or postcoital contraceptive, refers to several types of pills that have high doses of estrogen and progestin. Since they are not taken regularly, they do not prevent ovulation. Instead, they prevent fertilization or prevent the fertilized egg from implanting in the uterus. As of 2009, the morning-after pill, Plan B, became available to women aged 17 and older without prescription.

Morning-after pills are most effective when taken within 72 hours after ovulation. Women who wait to see whether they have missed a period are no longer candidates for the morning-after pill.

Morning-after pills have a higher hormone content than most birth-control pills. For this reason, nausea is a common side effect. Nausea is usually mild and passes within a day or two after treatment, but it can be treated with anti-nausea medication.

TRUTH OR FICTION REVISITED: The morning-after pill is certainly not recommended as a regular form of birth control. They are *one-time* forms of emergency protection, which may be most appropriate to use following rape or when regular contraceptive devices fail (for example, if a condom breaks or a diaphragm becomes dislodged). The morning-after pill generally prevents implantation, but if it fails, the fetus may be damaged by exposure to the hormones. 👁

T/F **2**

The Contraceptive Patch The contraceptive patch is another method of delivering estrogen and progestin to prevent ovulation and implantation. The patch is thin and measures about two inches by two inches. It is worn on the abdomen, buttocks, upper arm, or upper torso. The patch contains a week's worth of hormones and releases them gradually into the bloodstream.

👁🗎**Watch** the **Video**
Morning After Pill
on **MyDevelopmentLab**

Like the birth-control pill, when used correctly, the patch is more than 99% effective. Women who use the patch need not think about contraception daily. Also, like the pill, the patch doesn't interrupt sex. Its side effects and potential hazards are similar to those of the pill.

Injectable Contraceptives Injectable hormone preparations such as Lunelle and Depo-Provera are available by prescription. Lunelle is similar to the combination pill in that it contains estrogen and progestin. It is injected monthly. Like the mini-pill, Depo-Provera contains progestin only. It prevents pregnancy for three months. Injectables have become the second-most popular contraceptive method after the pill, accounting for 18% of users (Frost & Frohwirth, 2005).

Lunelle prevents ovulation; thickens cervical mucus, which prevents the sperm from reaching the egg; and changes the lining of the uterus to prevent implantation. Depo-Provera prevents ovulation. Lunelle, like oral contraceptives, has a failure rate of less than 1% when used properly.

Injectable contraceptives have the advantages of being highly effective, which permits spontaneous sex, and of remaining effective without being taken every day. They have side effects similar to those of other types of hormonal contraceptives, including oral contraceptives. These include vaginal bleeding, headaches, tenderness in the breasts, irregular menstrual cycles, weight gain, bloating, nausea, and vomiting. Injectable contraceptives are usually not recommended for women who smoke, have elevated blood pressure, have breast or uterine cancer, have a history of blood clots, have a history of heart attack or stroke, have diabetes, have liver disease, or are allergic to hormones.

The effects of Lunelle and Depo-Provera are reversible, but ovulation may take a few months to return. Neither contraceptive affords protection against STIs.

INTRAUTERINE DEVICES (IUDS)

Camel drivers setting out on long desert journeys once placed round stones in the uteruses of female camels to prevent them from becoming pregnant and lost to service. The stones may have acted as primitive **intrauterine devices (IUDs)**. IUDs are small objects of various shapes that are inserted into the uterus. They have been used by humans since ancient Greek times. Today, they are inserted into the uterus by a physician or nurse practitioner and usually left in place for a year or more. Fine plastic threads or strings hang down from the IUD into the vagina, so that the woman can check to see that it remains in place.

Intrauterine devices are used by more than 100 million women around the world (Hatcher et al., 2011). Most of them live in China, where nearly one in three married women uses an IUD during her childbearing years. By contrast, IUDs are used by only about 3% of women in committed relationships in the United States (Hatcher et al., 2011).

IUDs achieved their greatest popularity in the United States in the 1960s and 1970s. Then there was a sharp drop off in their use during the 1980s after use of a popular model, the Dalkon Shield, was linked to a high incidence of pelvic infections and tubal infertility.

Two IUDs are available in the United States: ParaGard, which releases small amounts of copper; and Mirena, which releases tiny amounts of the progestin levonorgestrel (Hatcher et al., 2011).

After all the fears that attended use of IUDs were shown to be exaggerated or baseless, IUDs began to make a comeback in popularity in the United States (Brody, 2012). Many now see the UID as safe, convenient, and effective, and the number of women using the IUD has tripled over the past 10 years, such that they now account

Intrauterine device (IUD) An object inserted into the uterus and left in place to prevent conception.

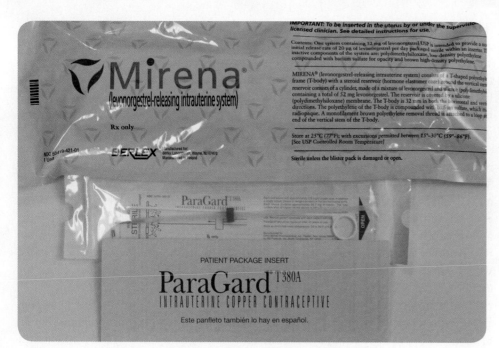

for 10% of prescribed contraceptives. (Keep in mind that many contraceptives, such as condoms and the sponge, do not require a prescription.) The IUD is 99% effective in preventing pregnancy, and if inserted soon following coitus without a condom, it may be as useful in preventing implantation as the morning-after pill, acting by preventing the uterine lining changes that permit implantation (Cleland, 2012). The IUD may even help protect against cervical cancer (Castellsague, 2012).

Effectiveness The failure rate associated with typical use of the IUD is 1% to 2% (see Table 12.2). Most failures occur within three months of insertion, often because the device shifts position or is expelled. ParaGard is the most effective IUD. The first-year failure rate in typical use is 0.8% (Hatcher et al., 2011).

The IUD may irritate the muscular layer of the uterine wall, causing contractions that expel it through the vagina. The device is most likely to be expelled during menstruation, so users are advised to check their sanitary napkins or tampons before discarding them. Women who use IUDs are advised to check the string several times a month to ensure that the IUD is in place. Spontaneous expulsions occur in 2% to 10% of users within a year of use (Hatcher et al., 2011). Some family-planning clinics advise women to supplement their use of IUDs with other devices for the first three months, when the risks of a shift in position or expulsion are greatest.

Reversibility IUDs may be removed readily by professionals. Nine out of ten former IUD users who try to become pregnant do so within a year (Hatcher et al., 2011).

Advantages and Disadvantages The IUD's advantages are it is highly effective, it does not diminish sexual spontaneity or sexual sensations, and, once in place, the woman need not do anything more to prevent pregnancy. The IUD also does not interfere with the woman's normal hormonal production. Users continue to produce pituitary hormones that stimulate ovarian follicles to mature and rupture, thereby releasing mature ova and producing female sex hormones.

A disadvantage is that insertion can be painful. Another disadvantage is side effects. The most common side effects are excessive menstrual cramping, irregular bleeding (spotting) between periods, and heavier than usual menstrual bleeding

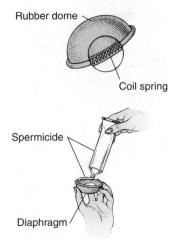

FIGURE 12.1 A Diaphragm.
The diaphragm is a shallow cup or dome made of latex. Diaphragms must be fitted to the contour of the vagina by a health professional. The diaphragm forms a barrier to sperm but should be used in conjunction with a spermicidal cream or jelly.

(Hatcher et al., 2011). These usually occur shortly following insertion and are among the primary reasons women ask to have the device removed. A more serious concern is the possible risk of pelvic inflammatory disease (PID), a serious disease that can become life threatening if left untreated. Women who use the IUD may have an increased risk of PID. The risk of infection is associated more with the insertion of the device (bacteria may enter the woman's reproductive tract during insertion) than with use of the device itself.

Pelvic inflammatory disease can produce scar tissue that blocks the fallopian tubes, causing infertility. Women with pelvic infections should not use an IUD. Women who have risk factors for PID may also wish to consider the advisability of an IUD. Risk factors include a recent episode of gonorrhea or chlamydia, recurrent episodes of these STIs, sexual contact with multiple partners, or sexual contact with a partner who has had multiple partners.

Another risk is that the IUD may perforate (tear) the uterine or cervical walls, which can cause bleeding, pain, and adhesions. Perforations are not common but can be serious when they occur (Hatcher et al., 2011). IUD users are also at greater risk for ectopic pregnancies, both during and after usage, and for miscarriage. Ectopic pregnancies occur in about 5% of women who become pregnant while using an IUD (Hatcher et al., 2011). The IUD is not recommended for women with a history of ectopic pregnancy. Women who become pregnant while using the IUD stand about a 50–50 chance of miscarriage (Hatcher et al., 2011).

Another drawback to the IUD is its cost. The typical cost of an IUD insertion in a family-planning clinic is a few hundred dollars. But users can think of the cost as being averaged out over the years that the device is in use. Moreover, the IUD, like the pill, offers no protection against STIs. Finally, like the pill, IUDs place the burden of contraception entirely on the woman.

BARRIER METHODS

Barrier methods such as the diaphragm prevent sperm from reaching ova. However, as we'll see, many of them are best used with chemicals that kill sperm (spermicides).

The Diaphragm **Diaphragms** were once used by about one-third of American couples who practiced birth control. When invented in 1882, they were a breakthrough. Their popularity declined only in the 1960s with the advent of the pill and the IUD.

The diaphragm is a shallow cup or dome made of thin latex rubber (see Figure 12.1). The rim is a flexible metal ring covered with rubber. Diaphragms come in different sizes to allow a precise fit.

Diaphragms are available by prescription and must be fitted to the contour of the vagina by a health professional. Several sizes and types of diaphragms may be tried during a fitting. Women practice insertion in a health professional's office so they can be guided as needed.

How It Works The diaphragm is inserted and removed by the woman, much like a tampon. It is akin to a condom in that it forms a barrier against sperm when placed snugly over the cervical opening. Yet it is unreliable as a barrier alone. Thus, the diaphragm should be used in conjunction with a spermicidal cream or jelly. One might even say that the diaphragm's main function is to keep the spermicide in place.

How It Is Used The diaphragm should be inserted no more than two hours before coitus, since the spermicides that are used may begin to lose effectiveness beyond this time. Some health professionals, however, suggest that the diaphragm may be inserted up to six hours preceding intercourse. (It seems reasonable to err on the side of caution and assume that there is a two-hour time limit.) The woman or

Diaphragm   A rubber cup or dome, fitted to the contour of a woman's vagina, coated with a spermicide and inserted prior to coitus to prevent conception.

her partner places a tablespoonful of spermicidal cream or jelly on the inside of the cup and spreads it inside the rim. (Cream spread outside the rim might cause the diaphragm to slip.) The woman opens the inner lips of the vagina with one hand and folds the diaphragm with the other by squeezing the ring. She inserts the diaphragm against the cervix, with the inner side facing upward (see Figure 12.2). Her partner can help insert the diaphragm, but the woman is advised to check its placement. Some women prefer a plastic insertion device, but most find it easier to insert the diaphragm without it. The diaphragm should be left in place *at least six hours* to allow the spermicide to kill sperm remaining in the vagina (Hatcher et al., 2011). It should not be left in place for longer than 24 hours, to guard against toxic shock syndrome (TSS).

After use, the diaphragm should be washed with mild soap and warm water and stored in a dry, cool place. When cared for properly, a diaphragm can last about two years. Women may need to be refitted after pregnancy or a change in weight of about ten pounds or more.

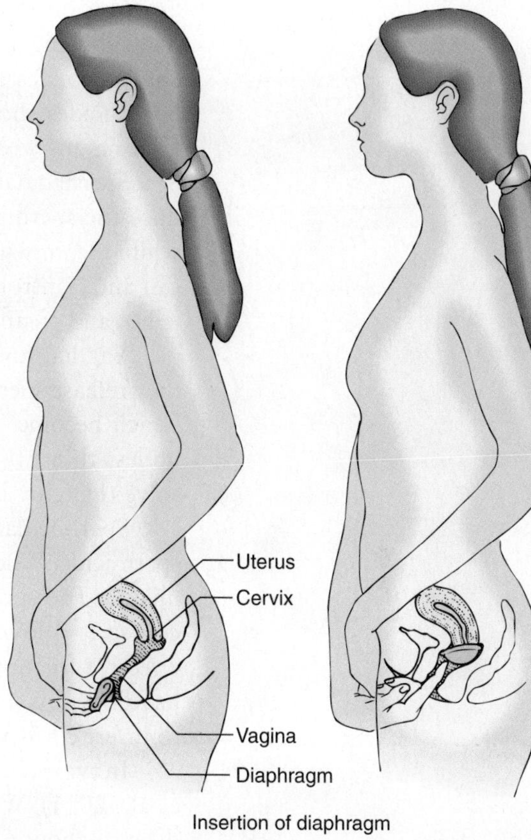

Effectiveness If used consistently and correctly, the failure rate of the diaphragm is estimated at 6% during a year of use (see Table 12.2) In typical use, however, the failure rate is believed to be three times as high—18%. Some women become pregnant because they do not use the diaphragm during every coital experience. Others may insert it too early or not leave it in long enough. The diaphragm may not fit well, or it may slip—especially if the couple is acrobatic. A diaphragm may develop tiny holes or cracks. Women are advised to inspect the diaphragm for signs of wear and consult their health professionals when in doubt. Effectiveness also is seriously compromised when the diaphragm is not used along with a correctly applied spermicide.

Reversibility The effects of the diaphragm are fully reversible. In order to become pregnant, the woman simply stops using it. The diaphragm has not been shown to influence subsequent fertility.

Advantages and Disadvantages When used correctly, the diaphragm is a safe and effective means of birth control and does not alter the woman's hormone production or reproductive cycle. The diaphragm can be used as needed, whereas the pill must be used daily and the IUD remains in place whether or not the woman engages in coitus. Another advantage is the virtual absence of side effects. The few women who are allergic to the rubber in the diaphragm can switch to a plastic model.

The major disadvantage is the high failure rate of typical users. Nearly one in five typical users (18%), who also uses a spermicide, becomes pregnant during a year of use (Hatcher et al., 2011). Another disadvantage is the need to insert the diaphragm prior to intercourse, which the couple may find disruptive. The woman's partner may find the taste of the spermicide unpleasant during oral sex. The pressure exerted by the diaphragm against the vaginal and cervical walls may also irritate the urinary tract and cause urinary or vaginal infections. Switching to a different size diaphragm or one with a different type of rim may alleviate this problem. About 1 woman or man in 20 may develop allergies to the particular spermicide that is used, which can lead to irritation of the genitals. This problem may be alleviated by switching to another brand.

Uterus
Cervix
Vagina
Diaphragm

Insertion of diaphragm

FIGURE 12.2 Insertion and Checking of the Diaphragm. Women are instructed in insertion of the diaphragm by a health professional. In practice, a woman and her partner may find joint insertion an erotic experience.

Spermicides Spermicides are agents that kill sperm. They coat the cervical opening, blocking the passage of sperm and killing sperm by chemical action. They come as jellies and creams, suppositories, aerosol foam, and a contraceptive film. Spermicides should be left in place in the vagina (no douching) for several hours after having sex (Hatcher et al., 2011).

Spermicidal jellies and creams come in tubes with plastic applicators that introduce the spermicide into the vagina (see Figure 12.3). Spermicidal foam is a fluffy white cream with the consistency of shaving cream. It is contained in a pressurized can and is introduced with a plastic applicator in much the same way as spermicidal jellies and creams.

Vaginal suppositories are inserted into the upper vagina, near the cervix, where they release spermicide as they dissolve. Unlike spermicidal jellies, creams, and foam, which become effective immediately when applied, suppositories must be inserted no less than 10 to 15 minutes before coitus so that they have sufficient time to dissolve (Hatcher et al., 2011).

Spermicidal film consists of thin, two-inch-square sheets that are saturated with spermicide. When placed in the vagina, they dissolve into a gel and release the spermicide. The spermicidal film should be inserted at least five minutes before intercourse to allow it time to melt and for the spermicide to be dispersed. It remains effective for upwards of one hour. One disadvantage of the film that some users have noted is a tendency for it to adhere to the fingertips, which makes it difficult to insert correctly.

In typical use, the yearly failure rate of spermicides used alone is 21% (Hatcher et al., 2011). When used correctly and consistently, the failure rate is estimated to drop to about 6%. Spermicides are more effective when combined with other forms of contraception, such as the condom or diaphragm.

The major advantages of spermicides are that they do not alter the woman's natural biological processes and are applied only as needed. Spermicides have not been linked with any changes in reproductive potential. So couples who wish to become pregnant simply stop using them. They do not require a doctor's prescription or a fitting, and can be bought in virtually any drugstore.

The major disadvantage is the high failure rate among typical users. Foam often fails when the can is not shaken enough, when too little is used, when it is not applied deeply enough within the vagina near the cervix, or when it is used after coitus has begun.

Spermicides are generally free of side effects but occasionally can irritate the vagina or penis. Irritation is sometimes alleviated by changing brands. Partners may find the taste of spermicides unpleasant.

It was once thought that spermicides that contain nonoxynol-9 might afford protection against STIs such as HIV/AIDS, genital herpes, trichomoniasis ("trich"), syphilis, and chlamydia. Yet researchers have found that nonoxynol-9 provides no

FIGURE 12.3 The Application of Spermicidal Foam. Spermicidal jellies and creams come in tubes with plastic applicators. Spermicidal foam comes in a pressurized can and is applied with a plastic applicator in much the same way as spermicidal jellies and creams.

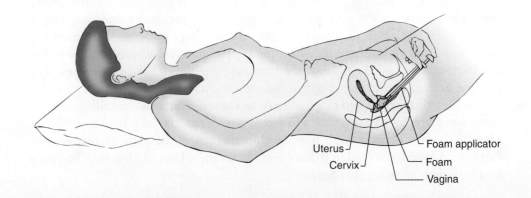

Uterus
Cervix
Foam applicator
Foam
Vagina

protection against STIs (Zalenskaya et al., 2011). In a study of the effectiveness of the spermicide as a means of preventing HIV infection among African and Thai prostitutes, the group using nonoxynol-9 actually had a significantly higher rate of HIV infection (15%) than the group using the placebo (10%) (Stephenson, 2000). Commentators suggest that local irritation caused by nonoxynol-9 might have made the vaginal tract an easier port of entry for HIV (e.g., Weiss et al., 2008).

The Contraceptive Sponge The contraceptive sponge is a soft, disposable device. Unlike the diaphragm, the sponge does not need to be fitted. Like the diaphragm, it provides a barrier that holds a spermicide, but the spermicide is built in. The sponge can also be inserted into the vagina several hours before coitus and has the additional advantage of absorbing sperm. It is odorless and tasteless, and users found it less drippy than the diaphragm. On the negative side, about 1 user in 20 (male and female) is mildly irritated by the spermicide. There is also a remote chance of toxic shock syndrome (TSS): one case arose for every four *million* days of use.

The Cervical Cap The cervical cap, like the diaphragm, is a dome-shaped cup. It comes in different sizes and must be fitted by a health professional. It is smaller than the diaphragm—about the size of a thimble—and is meant to fit snugly over the cervical opening.

Like the diaphragm, the cap is intended to be used with a spermicide applied inside it. When inserting it, the woman (or her partner) fills the cap about a third full of spermicide. Then, squeezing the edges together, she inserts the cap high in the vagina, so that it presses firmly against the cervix. The woman can test the fit by running a finger around the cap to ensure that the cervical opening is covered. It should be left in place for at least eight hours after intercourse. The cap provides continuous protection for about 48 hours without the need for additional spermicide. To reduce the risk of toxic shock syndrome, the cap should not be left in place longer than 48 hours. Like the diaphragm, the cervical cap forms a barrier and also holds spermicide in place. It prevents sperm from passing into the uterus and fallopian tubes and kills sperm by chemical action. The cap should be cleaned after use and checked for wear and tear. When cared for properly, it can last upward of three years.

The failure rate in typical use is estimated to be high, ranging from 18% in women who have not borne children to 36% in women who have (Hatcher et al., 2011). Failures may be attributed, at least in part, to the cap becoming dislodged and to changes in the cervix during the menstrual cycle, which can cause the cap to cover the cervix less snugly.

Similar to the diaphragm, the cap is a mechanical device that does not affect the woman's hormonal production or reproductive cycle. The cap may be especially suited to women who cannot support a diaphragm because of lack of vaginal muscle tone. Because of concern that the cap may irritate cervical tissue, however, users are advised to have regular Pap tests.

Some women find the cervical cap uncomfortable. It can also become dislodged during sex or lose its fit as the cervix changes over the menstrual cycle. Side effects include urinary tract infections and sensitivities to the rubber or spermicide. Other disadvantages include the expense and inconvenience of being fitted by a health professional. Moreover, some women are shaped so that the cap does not remain in place. For these reasons, and because they may be difficult to obtain, cervical caps are not very popular in the United States.

The Condom Condoms are also called "rubbers," "safes," **prophylactics** (because latex condoms protect against STIs), and "skins" (referring to those that are made from lamb intestines). Condoms lost popularity with the advent of the pill and the

Prophylactic An agent that protects against disease.

FIGURE 12.4 Condoms. Some condoms are plain tipped, whereas others have nipples or reservoirs that catch semen and may help prevent the condom from bursting during ejaculation. Latex condoms form effective barriers to HIV (the AIDS virus).

👁️—**Watch** the **Video**
Male Condom Demonstration
on **MyDevelopmentLab**

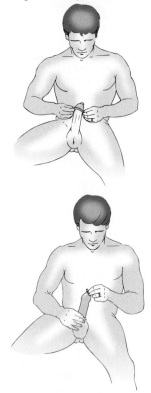

FIGURE 12.5 Applying a Condom. First the rolled-up condom is placed on the head of the penis, and then it is rolled down the shaft of the penis. If a condom without a reservoir tip is used, a one-half-inch space should be left at the tip for the ejaculate to accumulate.

IUD. They are less effective than either of them, may disrupt sexual spontaneity, and can lessen sexual sensations because they prevent contact between the penis and the vaginal wall.

Condoms have regained popularity, however, because latex condoms can help prevent the spread of HIV/AIDS and other STIs and, to a lesser extent, because of concerns about side effects of the pill and the IUD. The current popularity of condoms has been spurred by the increased assertiveness of women. By using a condom, the man assumes much of the responsibility for contraception. Condoms are the only contraceptive device worn by men, and the only readily reversible method of contraception that is available to men. Condoms are inexpensive and can be obtained without prescription from pharmacies, family-planning clinics, and vending machines.

Some condoms are made of latex rubber. Thinner, more expensive condoms ("skins") are made from the intestinal membranes of lambs. The latter allow greater sexual sensation, but only latex condoms are effective against HIV. Condoms made of animal intestines have pores large enough to permit HIV and other viruses, such as the one that causes hepatitis B, to slip through (Hatcher et al., 2011). A few condoms are made from other materials, such as plastic (polyurethane). Questions remain about the effectiveness of polyurethane condoms. Some condoms have plain ends. Others have nipples or reservoirs (see Figure 12.4) that catch semen and may help prevent the condom from bursting during ejaculation. 👁️

How They Work A condom serves as a barrier, preventing the passage of sperm and disease-carrying microorganisms.

How They Are Used The condom is rolled onto the penis once erection is achieved and before contact between the penis and the vagina (see Figure 12.5). If the condom is *not* used until moments before the point of ejaculation, sperm-carrying fluid from the Cowper's glands or from preorgasmic spasms may already have passed into the vagina. Nor does the condom afford protection against STIs if it is fitted after penetration.

Between 1 and 2% of condoms break or fall off during intercourse or when withdrawing the penis afterward (Hatcher et al., 2011). Condoms also sometimes slip down the shaft of the penis without falling off. To use a condom most effectively and to help prevent it from either breaking or falling off, a couple should observe the following guidelines (which are adapted from the Centers for Disease Control pamphlet, *Condoms and Sexually Transmitted Diseases ... Especially AIDS* [HHS Publication FDA 90-4329] as well as other sources):

- Use a condom each and every time you have intercourse.
- Handle the condom carefully, making sure not to damage it with your fingernail, teeth, or sharp objects.
- Place the condom on the erect penis before it touches the vulva.
- Uncircumcised men should pull back the foreskin before putting on the condom.
- If you use a spermicide, place some inside the tip of the condom before placing the condom on the penis. (The couple may apply additional spermicide inside the vagina to provide extra protection.)
- Do not pull the condom tightly against the tip of the penis.
- For a condom without a reservoir tip, leave a small empty space—about a half-inch—at the tip for semen, but do not allow air to get trapped at the tip.
- Unroll the condom all the way to the bottom of the penis.

A Closer Look

Errors in Using Condoms

All right, you're going to be using condoms because they have no side effects (other than some decrease in sexual sensations) and are the one method that places the responsibility squarely on the shoulders of the man. Condoms are highly effective—when used properly. However, the authors of a review of the literature (Sanders et al., 2012) found that many couples experience problems such as the following in using condoms:

- Breakage: From 1% to 41% of condom users report discovering that the condom they were using was broken. In fact, 2% to 11% of users say they have used sharp objects to open the condom package, clearly exposing the condom to cutting.
- Slippage: From 13% to 19% of users reported that a condom had slipped, allowing semen to leak.
- Leakage: Condoms can also leak when they do not slip, with 8% of men and 13% of women reporting at least one such experience.
- Late application: In perhaps the most common error, 17% to 51% of users report putting on the condom after they have begun sexual intercourse. Better late than never? Perhaps, but …
- Early removal: At least as problematic as late application is removing a condom before the couple has finished having sexual intercourse—an error that is nevertheless reported by 14% to 45% of users.
- Unrolling a condom before putting it on: Manufacturers intend for condoms to be unrolled onto the penis, yet 2% to 25% of users unroll them first

and then struggle to put them on—increasing the chances of breakage and leakage.

- No space at the tip: Space should be left at the tip of the condom to collect semen without placing undue pressure on the condom, yet from 24% to 46% of users fail to leave such a reservoir for semen.
- Failing to remove air: Users should squeeze out air from the tip of the condom to help make room for semen, but 48% of women and 42% of men admit to failing to do so.
- Inside-out condoms: No, condoms are not manufactured inside out, but 4% to 30% of users report rolling condoms on inside out, and then removing them and applying them the correct way, but exposing the woman to semen during the process.
- Failing to unroll all the way: Condoms should be completely unrolled, but 11% of women and 28% of men have begun intercourse before the condom was completely unrolled.
- Assuming the condom is not damaged: 83% of women and 75% of men admit to having sex without checking whether or not the condom is damaged.
- Lack of lubrication: From 16% to 26% of users use condoms with no lubrication, increasing friction and the risk of breakage. Meanwhile, from 3% to 5% of users use the wrong lubrication with latex condoms, such as an oil-based lubrication that can degrade the rubber, increasing the risk of breakage.
- Incorrect withdrawal: Then there are users—perhaps as many as half!—who do not withdraw the penis promptly

The Condom. Many single women carry condoms in case their partners are not prepared.

and carefully after ejaculating, increasing the possibility of leakage.

- Condom reuse: Condoms are meant to be used once, but a few people admit to re-using the same condom during a given sexual encounter—increasing the probabilities of leakage and breakage.
- Incorrect storage: Finally, from 3% to 19% of users store condoms in ways that will promote degradation, such as exposing them to high temperatures, bending, and so on.

- Ensure that adequate vaginal lubrication during intercourse is present, using lubricants if necessary. But use only water-based lubricants such as contraceptive jelly or K-Y jelly. Never use oil-based lubricants, which can weaken the latex material, such as petroleum jelly (Vaseline), cold cream, baby oil or lotion, mineral oil, massage oil, vegetable oil, Crisco, hand or body lotions, and most skin creams.
- If the condom breaks during intercourse, withdraw the penis immediately and use a spermicide.

- After ejaculation, carefully withdraw the penis while it remains erect.
- Hold the rim of the condom against the base of the penis as the condom is withdrawn to prevent slippage.
- Check the removed condom for tears or cracks. If any are found, use a spermicide.

Since condoms can be eroded by exposure to body heat or other sources of heat, they should not be kept for any length of time in a pocket or the glove compartment of a car. The nearby "Closer Look" feature describes condom use errors that will compromise their effectiveness.

Effectiveness In typical use, the failure rate of the male condom is estimated at 15% (see Table 12.2). In other words, 12 women out of 100 whose partners rely on condoms alone can expect to become pregnant during a year of use. The rate drops dramatically if the condom is used with a spermicide (Hatcher et al., 2011). The effectiveness of a condom and spermicide combined rivals that of the pill when used correctly.

Reversibility The condom is simply a mechanical barrier to sperm and does not compromise fertility. Therefore, a couple who wish to conceive a child simply discontinue its use.

Advantages and Disadvantages Condoms have the advantage of being readily available. They can be purchased without prescription. They require no fitting and can remain in sealed packages until needed. They are readily discarded after use. The combination of condoms and spermicides increases effectiveness. Some condoms contain a spermicide as a lubricant. When in doubt, ask a pharmacist.

Condoms do not affect production of hormones, ova, or sperm. Women whose partners use condoms ovulate normally. Men who use them produce sperm and ejaculate normally. With all these advantages, why are condoms not more popular?

One reason is that it may render sex less spontaneous. The couple must interrupt lovemaking to apply the condom. Condoms also lessen sexual sensations, especially for the man. Latex condoms do so more than animal membrane sheaths. Condoms also sometimes slip or tear, allowing sperm to leak through.

On the other hand, condoms are almost entirely free of side effects. They offer protection against STIs that is unparalleled among contraceptive devices. They can be used without prior medical consultation. Both partners can share putting on the condom, which makes it an erotic part of their lovemaking. The use of textured or ultrathin condoms may increase sensitivity, especially for the male. Sex in the age of HIV/AIDS has given condoms a new respectability, even a certain trendiness. Advertisers now also target women in their ads, suggesting that women, like men, can come prepared with condoms.

It is tempting to claim that the condom never has side effects. Let us settle for "close to never." Some people have allergic reactions to the spermicides with which some lubricated condoms are coated or that the woman may apply. Some people are allergic to latex.

Women have a right to insist that their male sex partners wear latex condoms if their partners are not latex-sensitive. STIs such as gonorrhea and chlamydia (see Chapter 16) do more damage to a woman's reproductive tract than to a man's. Condoms can help protect women from vaginitis, pelvic inflammatory disease (PID), infections that can harm a fetus or cause infertility, and HIV (Hatcher et al., 2011).

FERTILITY AWARENESS METHODS

There are several fertility awareness methods, which are also referred to as *rhythm methods*. They all rely on awareness of the occurrence of the fertile segments of the woman's menstrual cycle. You will also hear them referred to as *natural birth control* or *natural family planning*. Each of them aims to avoid coitus on days when conception is likely. Fertility awareness methods are used by a small minority of women, more so by women in committed relationships. Since the rhythm method does not employ artificial devices, it is acceptable to the Roman Catholic Church.

A number of rhythm methods are used to predict the likelihood of conception. They are the mirror images of the methods that couples use to increase their chances of conceiving (see Chapter 11). Methods for enhancing the chances of conception seek to predict time of ovulation so the couple can arrange to have sperm present in the woman's reproductive tract at about that time. As methods of *birth control,* rhythm methods predict ovulation so that the couple can *abstain* from coitus when the woman is fertile.

Recording Basal Body Temperature

The Calendar Method

The **calendar method** assumes that ovulation occurs 14 days prior to menstruation. The couple abstains from intercourse during the period that begins three days prior to day 13 (because sperm are unlikely to survive for more than 72 hours in the female reproductive tract) and ends two days after day 15 (because an unfertilized ovum is unlikely to remain receptive to fertilization for longer than 48 hours). The period of abstention thus covers days 10 to 17 of the woman's cycle.

When a woman has regular 28-day cycles, predicting the period of abstention is relatively straightforward. Women with irregular cycles are generally advised to chart their cycles for 10 to 12 months to determine their shortest and longest cycles. The first day of menstruation counts as day 1 of the cycle. The last day of the cycle is the day preceding the onset of menstruation.

Consider a woman whose cycles vary from 23 to 33 days. In theory she will ovulate 14 days before menstruation begins. (To be safe she should assume that ovulation will take place anywhere from 13 to 15 days before her period.) Applying the rule of "three days before" and "two days after," she should avoid coitus from day 5 of her cycle, which corresponds to three days before her earliest expected ovulation (computed by subtracting 15 days from the 23 days of her shortest cycle and then subtracting 3 days), through day 22, which corresponds to two days after her latest expected ovulation (computed by subtracting 13 days from the 33 days of her longest cycle and then adding 2 days). Another way of determining this period of abstention would be to subtract 18 days from the woman's shortest cycle to determine the start of the "unsafe" period and 11 days from her longest cycle to determine the last "unsafe" day. The woman in the example has irregular cycles. She thus faces an 18-day abstention period each month—quite a burden for a sexually active couple.

Most women who follow the calendar method need to abstain from coitus for at least ten days during the middle of each cycle. Moreover, the calendar method cannot ensure that the woman's longest or shortest menstrual cycles will occur during the 10- to 12-month period of baseline tracking. Some women, too, have such irregular cycles that the range of "unsafe" days cannot be predicted reliably even if baseline tracking is extended.

The Basal Body Temperature (BBT) Method

In the **basal body temperature (BBT) method**, the woman tracks her body temperature upon awakening each morning to detect the small changes that occur directly before and after ovulation. A woman's basal body temperature sometimes dips slightly just before ovulation and then tends to rise between 0.4 and 0.8 degree Fahrenheit just before, during, and after ovulation. It remains elevated until the onset of menstruation. (The rise in temperature is caused by the increased production of progesterone by the corpus

Calendar method A fertility awareness (rhythm) method of contraception that relies on prediction of ovulation by tracking menstrual cycles, typically for a 10- to 12-month period, and assuming that ovulation occurs 14 days prior to menstruation.

Basal body temperature (BBT) method A fertility awareness method of contraception that relies on prediction of ovulation by tracking the woman's temperature over the menstrual cycle.

luteum during the luteal phase of the cycle.) Thermometers that provide finely graded readings, such as electronic thermometers, are best suited for determining minor changes. A major problem with the BBT method is that it does not indicate the several *unsafe* preovulatory days during which sperm deposited in the vagina may remain viable. Rather, the BBT method indicates when a woman *has* ovulated. Thus, many women use the calendar method to predict the number of "safe" days prior to ovulation and use the BBT method to determine the number of "unsafe" days after. A woman would avoid coitus during the "unsafe" preovulatory period (as determined by the calendar method) and then for three days when her temperature rises and remains elevated. A drawback of the BBT method is that changes in body temperature may also result from factors unrelated to ovulation, such as infections, sleeplessness, or stress. So, some women triple-check themselves by also tracking their cervical mucus.

The Cervical Mucus (Ovulation) Method The **ovulation method** tracks changes in the **viscosity** of the cervical mucus. Following menstruation, the vagina feels rather dry. There is also little or no discharge from the cervix. These dry days are relatively safe. Then a mucous discharge appears in the vagina that is first thick and sticky, and white or cloudy in color. Coitus (or unprotected coitus) should be avoided at the first sign of any mucous. As the cycle progresses, the mucus discharge thins and clears, becoming slippery or stringy, like raw egg white. These are the **peak days.** This mucus discharge, called the *ovulatory mucus,* may be accompanied by a feeling of vaginal lubrication or wetness. Ovulation takes place about a day after the last peak day (about four days after this ovulatory mucus first appears). Then the mucus becomes cloudy and tacky once more. Intercourse may resume four days following the last peak day. However, many women have difficulty detecting changes in the mucus discharge. Such changes may also result from infections, certain medications, or contraceptive creams, jellies, or foam. Sexual arousal may also induce changes in viscosity.

Ovulation-Prediction Kits Predicting ovulation is more accurate with an ovulation-prediction kit. Kits allow women to test their urine regularly for the presence of luteinizing hormone (LH). LH levels surge about 12 to 24 hours prior to ovulation. Kits can be used to help couples conceive or avoid pregnancy. Ovulation kits can be costly, however.

Effectiveness The estimated first-year failure rate of rhythm methods is 20%, which reminds us of the joke: "What do you call people who use the rhythm method? Parents!" *But*—and this is a big "but"—fewer failures occur when these methods are applied conscientiously, when a combination of rhythm methods is used, and when the woman's cycles are regular. Restricting coitus to the postovulatory period can reduce the pregnancy rate to 1% (Hatcher et al., 2011). The trick is to determine when ovulation occurs.

Advantages and Disadvantages Because they are a natural form of birth control, rhythm methods appeal to many people who, for religious or other reasons, prefer not to use artificial means. Since no devices or chemicals are used, there are no side effects. Nor do they cause loss of sensation, as condoms do. Nor is there disruption of sex, as with condoms, diaphragms, or foam—although sex could be said to be quite "disrupted" during the period of abstention. Rhythm methods are inexpensive, except for ovulation-prediction kits. Both partners may share the responsibility for rhythm methods. The man, for example, can take his partner's temperature or assist with charting. All rhythm methods are fully reversible.

Ovulation method A fertility awareness method of contraception that relies on prediction of ovulation by tracking the viscosity of cervical mucus.

Viscosity Stickiness, consistency.

Peak days The days during the menstrual cycle during which a woman is most likely to be fertile.

Rhythm methods may be unsuitable for women with irregular cycles. Moreover, the rhythm method requires abstaining for many days, perhaps weeks, each month. Rhythm methods also require that records of the menstrual cycle be kept for many months prior to implementation. Rhythm methods cannot be used spontaneously. Nor do rhythm methods afford protection against STIs.

STERILIZATION

Sterilization permanently makes the individual incapable of fertilizing a partner or of conceiving. Many people decide to be sterilized when they plan to have no children or no more children. With the exception of abstinence, sterilization is the most effective form of contraception. Yet the prospect of sterilization arouses strong feelings because a person is transformed all at once, and presumably permanently, from someone who might be capable of bearing children to someone who cannot. This transformation involves a change in self-concept, which may disturb people who link fertility to their self-identity. Still, sterilization is the most widely used form of birth control among couples in committed relationships aged 30 and above.

Male Sterilization The male sterilization procedure used today is the **vasectomy**. About one man in six in the United States has had a vasectomy.

A vasectomy is usually carried out in a doctor's office, under local anesthesia, in 15 to 20 minutes. Small incisions are made in the scrotum. Each vas is cut, a small segment is removed, and then the ends are tied off or cauterized to prevent them from growing back together (see Figure 12.6). Sperm no longer reach the urethra and are reabsorbed harmlessly by the body.

The man can usually resume sexual relations within a few days. However, health-care providers recommend follow-ups to check for the presence of sperm in the ejaculate, since sperm can be found for many weeks and sometimes months even when operations have been successful. And rarely—in about 1 case in 500—the vas

Sterilization Surgical procedures that render people incapable of reproduction without affecting sexual activity.

Vasectomy The surgical method of male sterilization in which sperm are prevented from reaching the urethra by cutting each vas deferens and tying it back or cauterizing it.

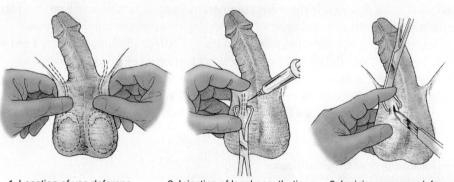

1. Location of vas deferens

2. Injection of local anesthetic

3. Incision over vas deferens

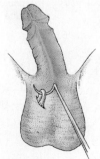
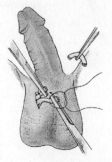
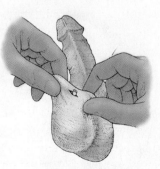

4. Isolation of vas from surrounding tissue

5. Removal of segment of vas; tying of ends

6. Return of vas to position; incision is closed and process is repeated on the other side

FIGURE 12.6 Vasectomy. The male sterilization procedure is usually carried out in a doctor's office, using local anesthesia. Small incisions are made in the scrotum. Each vas deferens is cut, and the ends are tied off or cauterized to prevent sperm from reaching the urethra. Sperm are harmlessly reabsorbed by the body after the operation.

"recanalizes," meaning that the severed ends rejoin spontaneously (Jayaraman & Mann, 2012).

Vasectomy does not diminish sex drive or result in any change in sexual arousal, erectile or ejaculatory ability, or sensations of ejaculation. Male sex hormones and sperm are still produced by the testes. Without a passageway to the urethra, however, sperm are no longer expelled with the ejaculate. Since sperm account for only about 1% of the ejaculate, the volume of the ejaculate is not noticeably different.

Over the years there has been some concern as to whether or not vasectomy raises the risk of prostate cancer. A New Zealand study comparing the incidence of vasectomy among 923 men who had had prostate cancer and a matched group of 1,224 who had not (Cox et al., 2006) found no connection between the two. Individuals considering vasectomy should discuss the most recent available findings with their physicians.

Reversibility is simple in concept but not in practice. Thus, vasectomies should be considered permanent. In an operation to reverse a vasectomy, called a **vasovasotomy**, the ends of the vas deferens are sewn together, and in a few days they grow together. Estimates of success at reversal, as measured by subsequent pregnancies, are quite variable and have been reported to range from 16 to 79% (Brechin & Bigrigg, 2006; Hatcher et al., 2011). Even so, the man still produces viable sperm and they can be harvested, if with some difficulty, and used to fertilize ova via methods such as intracytoplasmic sperm injection (Karpman et al., 2006).

Few serious complications from vasectomies have been reported, but minor complications are not uncommon. They typically involve temporary local inflammation or swelling after the operation. Ice packs and anti-inflammatory drugs, such as aspirin, may help reduce swelling and discomfort.

Female Sterilization About 21% of American women between the ages of 15 and 44 have been surgically sterilized (U.S. Bureau of the Census, 2006). The percentages are higher among older women in committed relationships. **Tubal sterilization**, also called *tubal ligation,* is the most common method of female sterilization. Tubal sterilization prevents ova and sperm from passing through the fallopian tubes.

The surgical procedures for tubal sterilization occlude fallopian tubes. The two main methods of doing so are *mini-laparotomy* and *laparoscopy.* In a **mini-laparotomy**, a small incision is made in the abdomen, just above the pubic hairline, to provide access to the fallopian tubes. Each tube is cut and tied back or clamped. In a **laparoscopy** (see Figure 12.7), sometimes called "belly button surgery,"

Vasovasotomy The surgical reversal of vasectomy in which the cut or cauterized ends of the vas deferens are sewn together.

Tubal sterilization The method of female sterilization in which the fallopian tubes are surgically blocked. Also called *tubal ligation.*

Mini-laparotomy A kind of tubal sterilization in which an incision is made in the abdomen to access the fallopian tubes.

Laparoscopy Tubal sterilization by means of a *laparoscope,* which is inserted through a small incision just below the navel and used to cauterize, cut, or clamp the fallopian tubes.

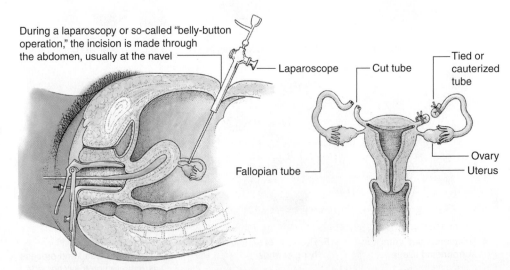

FIGURE 12.7 Laparoscopy. During this method of female sterilization, the surgeon approaches the fallopian tubes through a small incision in the abdomen just below the navel. A narrow instrument called a *laparoscope* is inserted through the incision, and a small section of each fallopian tube is cauterized, cut, or clamped to prevent ova from joining with sperm.

During a laparoscopy or so-called "belly-button operation," the incision is made through the abdomen, usually at the navel

Laparoscope

Cut tube

Tied or cauterized tube

Fallopian tube

Ovary

Uterus

the fallopian tubes are approached through a small incision in the abdomen just below the navel. The surgeon uses a narrow, lighted instrument called a *laparoscope* to view the tubes. A small section of each of the tubes is cauterized, cut, or clamped. The woman usually returns to her daily routine in a few days and can resume sex when it becomes comfortable. In an alternative sterilization procedure, a **culpotomy**, the fallopian tubes are approached through an incision in the back wall of the vagina.

None of these methods disrupts the sex drive or sexual response. Surgical sterilization does not induce premature menopause or alter the woman's production of sex hormones. The menstrual cycle is undisturbed. The unfertilized egg is reabsorbed by the body rather than sloughed off in the menstrual flow.

A **hysterectomy** also sterilizes a woman, but a hysterectomy is a major operation that is commonly performed because of cancer or other diseases of the reproductive tract; it is inappropriate as a method of sterilization.

Overall, about 1 woman in 200 (0.4%) is likely to become pregnant in the first year following a tubal sterilization (Hatcher et al., 2011), most likely the result of a failed surgical procedure or an undetected pregnancy at the time of the procedure. Like vasectomy, tubal ligation should be considered irreversible. Reversals are successful, as measured by subsequent pregnancies, in 43% to 88% of cases (Hatcher et al., 2011). Reversal is difficult and costly, however.

TRUTH OR **FICTION** REVISITED: Not all sterilization operations can be surgically reversed. Therefore, sterilization is not advised for individuals who believe they might change their minds. Nevertheless, the woman continues to ovulate, and even if the tubes cannot be rejoined, it may be possible to harvest the ova, fertilize them in vitro, and insert them into the uterus for implantation.

Some women have medical complications, such as abdominal infections, excessive bleeding, punctures of nearby organs, and scarring. The use of general anesthesia (typical in laparoscopies and in some mini-laparotomies) poses additional risks, as in any major operation. (Most of the deaths that are attributed to tubal sterilization actually result from the anesthesia. But there are only 2 to 5 deaths per 100,000 operations.)

Advantages and Disadvantages of Sterilization

The major advantages of sterilization are effectiveness and permanence. Sterilization is nearly 100% effective. The permanence is also its major drawback, however. People sometimes change their minds about wanting to have children.

Sterilization procedures create varying risks of complications following surgery, with women generally incurring greater risks than men. Sterilization affords no protection against STIs.

Culpotomy A kind of tubal sterilization in which the fallopian tubes are approached through an incision in the back wall of the vagina.

Hysterectomy Surgical removal of the uterus.

Real Students, Real Questions

Q *I was watching Grey's Anatomy the other night, and a patient wanted to have her tubes tied without her husband knowing. Is there a law that says that spouses need to talk to each other before a procedure is done?*

A By and large, medical procedures requested by competent adults are protected by patient–physician confidentiality. Women, therefore, need not discuss sterilization with their husbands or anyone else—other than their health care providers, of course.

A Closer Look

Selecting a Method of Contraception

If you believe that you and your partner should use contraception, how will you determine which method is right for you? There is no simple answer. What is right for your peers may be wrong for you. You and your partner will make your own selections, but there are some issues you may want to consider:

1. *Convenience.* Is the method convenient? Does it require a device that must be purchased in advance? If so, is a prescription required? Will the method work at a moment's notice, or, as with the birth-control pill, will it require time to reach maximum effectiveness?

2. *Moral acceptability.* A method that is morally acceptable to one person may be objectionable to another. For example, those who strictly follow the teachings of the Roman Catholic Church may find any artificial means of contraception to be objectionable.

3. *Cost.* Methods vary in cost. Some more costly methods involve devices (such as the diaphragm, the cervical cap, and the IUD) or hormones that require medical visits in addition to the cost of the devices themselves.

4. *Sharing responsibility.* Most forms of birth control place the burden of responsibility largely, if not entirely, on the woman. The woman must consult with her doctor to obtain birth-control pills or other prescription devices such as diaphragms, cervical caps, and IUDs. The woman must take birth-control pills reliably or check to see that her IUD remains in place.

Some couples prefer methods that allow for greater sharing of responsibility, such as alternating use of the condom and diaphragm. A man can also share the responsibility for the birth-control pill by accompanying his partner on her medical visits and sharing the expense.

5. *Safety.* How safe is the method? What are the side effects?

6. *Reversibility.* In most cases the effects of birth-control methods can be fully reversed by discontinuing their use. In other cases reversibility may not occur immediately, as with oral contraceptives. It's most cautious to consider sterilization irreversible.

7. *Protection against sexually transmitted infections (STIs).* **TRUTH OR FICTION REVISITED:** The truth is that only some contraceptives, like the condom, prevent STIs as well as conception. **T/F 4**

8. *Effectiveness.* Techniques and devices vary widely in their effectiveness in actual use. The failure rate for a particular method refers to the percentage of women who become pregnant when using the method for a given period of time, such as during the first year of use. Most contraceptive methods are not used correctly much or even all of the time. Failure rates among typical users are often considerably higher because of incorrect, unreliable, or inconsistent use. Table 12.2 shows the failure rates, reversibility, and degree of protection against STIs associated with various contraceptive methods.

Selecting a Method of Contraception. Should you and your partner use contraception? If so, how can you determine which method is right for you? Issues you may want to consider include convenience, effectiveness, moral acceptability, safety, reversibility, and cost. Other issues include whether the method allows you and your partner to share the responsibility and whether it also affords protection from STIs.

"NONMETHODS" OF CONTRACEPTION

Nonmethods may sound like an ironic lead-in to this topic, but we use the term because many people think that the following methods work. If they do, they work occasionally, and, frankly, sometimes because of luck. "Luck" isn't all that dependable if you're trying to prevent a pregnancy.

Douching Many couples believe that if a woman **douches** shortly after coitus, she will not become pregnant. Women who douche for contraceptive purposes often use syringes to flush the vagina with water or a spermicidal agent. **TRUTH** OR **FICTION** REVISITED: Douching is ineffective, however, because large numbers of sperm move beyond the range of the douche seconds after ejaculation. In addition, squirting a liquid into the vagina may even propel sperm *toward* the uterus. Regular douching may also alter the natural chemistry of the vagina, increasing the risk of vaginal infection. In short, douching is a nonmethod of contraception.

The Withdrawal Method Withdrawal means that the man removes his penis from the vagina before ejaculating. Withdrawal—also referred to as *coitus interruptus*—has a first-year failure rate among typical users of about 20% (Hatcher et al., 2011). There are several reasons for these failures. The man may not withdraw in time. Even if the penis is withdrawn just before ejaculation, some ejaculate may still fall on the vaginal lips, and sperm may find their way to the fallopian tubes. Sperm may also be present in the *pre*ejaculatory secretions of fluid from the Cowper's glands. Because of its unreliability and high failure rate, withdrawal is *not* a viable method of contraception.

Abortion

"When I was young, I felt it myself, that it was wrong to kill a baby," said Maria, a 17-year-old Latina high school student who lives in Houston. She is waiting to be seen at an abortion clinic. "But when I got to be a teenager, and started having sex, things looked different. It's more complicated when it's your own life. I want to go to college, and I know that having a baby now, without a husband or anything, would make that very hard" (Lewin, 1998a)

Maria is not all that unusual for young people in the United States today. Abortion has little to do with politics to her. The *Roe v. Wade* decision occurred a decade before Maria was born. Like many adults in the United States, Maria believes that abortion is murder, but like many of those, Maria also believes that abortion is an acceptable solution to a bad situation.

In common usage, the term *abortion* usually refers to an **induced abortion** (in contrast to a spontaneous abortion, or miscarriage)—that is, the purposeful termination of a pregnancy. Perhaps more than any other contemporary social issue, induced abortion (hereafter referred to simply as *abortion*) has divided neighbors and family members into opposing camps.

In the United States, the abortion rate increased steadily from the early 1970s through 1980, leveled off somewhat in the 1980s, reached a peak in

Douche To rinse or wash the vaginal canal by inserting a liquid and allowing it to drain out.

Induced abortion The purposeful termination of a pregnancy before the embryo or fetus is capable of sustaining independent life.

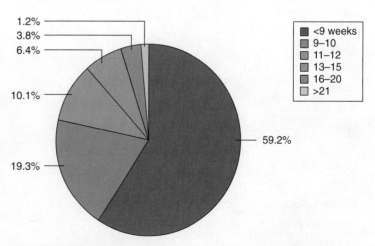

FIGURE 12.8 When Women Have Abortions (in Weeks). Eighty-eight percent of abortions occur during the first 12 weeks of pregnancy.

Source: Guttmacher Institute, Facts on induced abortion in the United States. *In Brief.* New York: Guttmacher Institute, 2006. www.guttmacher.org/pubs/fb_induced_abortion.html (Accessed 9/16/06).

A World of Diversity

Where Are the Missing Chinese Girls?

It is no secret that most people in most cultures would prefer that their child, or at least their first child, be a boy. According to traditional gender roles, boys carry on the business of the family and represent continuity of the lineage (Russo et al., 2012). They pass on the family name. In less developed nations such as China and India, especially in rural areas, sons also represent protection from neglect and poverty in the later years. These attitudes are reflected in verses from the ancient Chinese *Book of Songs*, written some 3,000 years ago:

> When a son is born,
> Let him sleep on the bed,
> Clothe him with fine clothes,
> And give him jade with which to play …
> When a daughter is born,
> Let her sleep on the ground,
> Wrap her in common wrappings,
> And give broken tiles with which to play …

When Mao Zedong took power in 1949, his Communist government replaced family support in old age with state support and also rejected male superiority. There remained a balance in the numbers of males and females in the population throughout most of the 1970s. But beginning in 1979, China attempted to gain control of its mushrooming population of more than a billion by enforcing strict limits on family size. One child per family is allowed in urban areas. A second child is usually allowed in rural areas after five years have passed, especially if the first child is a girl. Because Chinese families, like the families of old, continue to prefer boys, the ratio of boys to girls began to change with the limitations on family size (Zhang et al., 2012).

As noted in Table 12.3, the desirability of having small families has generally caught on in the Chinese population. That is, the great majority of women

interviewed in a recent survey expressed the desire to have either one or two children. However, there were some differences according to the woman's age, her area of residence, and her level of education. How would you account for them?

Since more boys than girls die in infancy, a "normal" ratio of boys to girls is about 104 to 100, which characterized China in the 1970s. The ratio was about 108.5 boys to 100 girls under the age of 15 in the early 80s, then 111 to 100 in 1990, and has been 117 to 100 since the year 2000 (CIA, 2012).

Note the ratios in a few other countries (under the age of 15) according to the CIA (2012):

	Boys	Girls
Argentina	1.05	1
Australia	1.05	1
Brazil	1.04	1
Canada	1.05	1
France	1.05	1
Germany	1.05	1
India*	1.13	1
United Kingdom	1.05	1
United States	1.04	1

*In India, like China, there is a powerful preference for boys. Vans with ultrasound machines make it possible for women, even in rural areas, to determine the gender of their fetuses and to abort girls.

Therefore, a great shortage of Chinese women is being created, which may not be much of a problem for parents but which will certainly be a problem for men seeking mates in future years. Chinese officials are concerned that the shortfall means that millions of men will have no prospect of getting married and settling down when they are of age. Thus, there will be an increased likelihood of social unrest, which can become political dissent as well as ordinary crime (Zhang et al., 2012).

Prenatal Gender Selection

How do the Chinese have so many more sons than daughters? Once upon a time in places like China and India, much of the

Table 12.3

Preferred Number of Children among Chinese Women (Percent Expressing Preference)

Preferred Number of Children	0	1	2	3 or more
Age of Woman				
15–19	2.1	49	45	1.9
20–29	1.3	47	48	2.1
30–39	0.8	32	60	6.1
40–49	1.0	27	62	11.0
Area of Residence				
Urban	3.1	52	43	1.5
Rural	0.4	30	61	7.5
Level of Education				
Illiterate or semi-literate	0.4	17	67	14.0
Primary school	0.3	25	65	8.5
Secondary school	2.1	46	47	2.5
College	4.0	49	44	2.2

Note: Number of women interviewed: 39,344

Source: National Family Planning and Reproductive Health Survey. Q. J. Ding and T. Hesketh (2006). Family size, fertility preferences, and gender ratio in China in the era of the one child family policy: Results from National Family Planning and Reproductive Health Survey. *British Medical Journal, 333*(7564), 371–373.

An Endangered Gender? Chinese people show a preference for boys and, because they usually have just one chance to have a child, often use gender selection techniques to guarantee having a child of the preferred gender.

answer lay in infanticide—that is, in the killing of unwanted female babies. Today, according to the International Planned Parenthood Federation, the main answer is the selective abortion of female fetuses, as identified by inexpensive, portable ultrasound scanners and backstreet abortion clinics. It is estimated that there are some seven million abortions in China each year, and that 70% percent of them are of females (Hesketh & Xing, 2006; LaFraniere, 2009). The director of China's National Population and Family Planning Commission admitted that the gender gap created by the country's population policy has created a very serious challenge for the country. However, the country does not intend to loosen its constraints on population growth. Instead, the government will experiment with educational campaigns, penalties for gender-selective abortions, and bonuses for parents who have girls (Sullum, 2007).

about 1990, when there were about 1.4 million abortions, and has declined to about 1.2 million abortions per year (U.S. Abortion Statistics, 2012). The great majority of abortions in the United States occur during the first trimester (see Figure 12.8). This is when they are safest to the woman and least costly.

About 40% to 45% of U.S. women have an abortion at some time (Guttmacher Institute, 2011):

- 18% are teenagers
- More than half (57%) of women who have abortion are in their 20s
- European American women account for 36%; African American women for 30%; Latinas for 25%
- Single women account for 45% of abortions
- Two women in five (42%) who have abortions live below the federal poverty level
- 28% of them are Roman Catholic; 37% are Protestant
- Most women who have abortions (75%) say they cannot afford a child, or that having a child would interfere with school work, and/or ability to care for existing family members

Abortion is practiced widely in Canada, Japan, Russia, and many European nations. It is less common in developing nations, largely because of sparse medical facilities. Abortion is rarely used as a primary means of birth control. It usually comes into play when other methods have failed.

There are many reasons why women have abortions, including psychological factors as well as external circumstances. Abortion is often motivated by a desire to reduce the risk of physical, economic, psychological, and social disadvantages that the woman perceives for herself and her present and future children should she take the pregnancy to term.

The national debate over abortion has been played out in recent years against a backdrop of demonstrations, marches, and occasional acts of violence, such as firebombing of abortion clinics, even murder. Most who label themselves pro-life believe that human life begins at conception and view abortion as the killing of an unborn child. Some pro-life people brook no exception to their opposition to abortion, but most would permit abortion to save the mother's life or when a pregnancy results from rape or incest.

Self-Assessment

Pro-Choice or Pro-Life? Where Do You Stand?

What does it mean to be "pro-life" on the abortion issue? What does it mean to be "pro-choice"? Which position is closer to your own views on abortion?

The *Reasoning about Abortion Questionnaire (RAQ)* (Parsons et al., 1990) assesses agreement with pro-life or pro-choice lines of reasoning about abortion. To find out which position is closer to your own, indicate your level of agreement or disagreement with each of the following items by circling the

number that most closely represents your feelings. Then refer to the key in the appendix to interpret your score.

5 = Strongly Agree

4 = Agree

3 = Mixed Feelings

2 = Disagree

1 = Strongly Disagree

1. Abortion is a matter of personal choice.	5 4 3 2 1
2. Abortion is a threat to our society.	5 4 3 2 1
3. A woman should have control over what is happening to her own body by having the option to choose abortion.	5 4 3 2 1
4. Only God, not people, can decide if a fetus should live.	5 4 3 2 1
5. Even if one believes that there may be some exceptions, abortion is still basically wrong.	5 4 3 2 1
6. Abortion violates an unborn person's fundamental right to life.	5 4 3 2 1
7. A woman should be able to exercise her rights to self-determination by choosing to have an abortion.	5 4 3 2 1
8. Outlawing abortion could take away a woman's sense of self and personal autonomy.	5 4 3 2 1
9. Outlawing abortion violates a woman's civil rights.	5 4 3 2 1
10. Abortion is morally unacceptable and unjustified.	5 4 3 2 1
11. In my reasoning, the notion that an unborn fetus may be a human life is not a deciding issue in considering abortion.	5 4 3 2 1
12. Abortion can be described as taking a life unjustly.	5 4 3 2 1
13. A woman should have the right to decide to have an abortion based on her own life circumstances.	5 4 3 2 1
14. If a woman feels that having a child might ruin her life, she should consider an abortion.	5 4 3 2 1
15. Abortion could destroy the sanctity of motherhood.	5 4 3 2 1
16. An unborn fetus is a viable human being with rights.	5 4 3 2 1
17. If a woman feels she can't care for a baby, she should be able to have an abortion.	5 4 3 2 1
18. Abortion is the destruction of one life for the convenience of another.	5 4 3 2 1
19. Abortion is the same as murder.	5 4 3 2 1
20. Even if one believes that there are times when abortion is immoral, it is still basically the woman's own choice.	5 4 3 2 1

Source: Parsons, N. K., Richards, H. C., & Kanter, G. D. (1990).Validation of a scale to measure reasoning about abortion. Journal of Counseling Psychology, 37, 107–112.

The pro-choice movement contends that abortion is a matter of personal choice and that the government has no right to interfere with a woman's right to terminate a pregnancy. Pro-choice advocates argue that women are free to control what happens within their bodies, including pregnancies.

Perspectives on Abortion

Attitudes toward abortion have varied across cultures and eras. Abortion was permitted in ancient greece and rome, but women in ancient assyria were impaled on stakes for attempting abortion. The Bible does not specifically prohibit abortion (sagan & dryan, 1990). For much of its history, the Roman Catholic Church held to thomas aquinas's belief that ensoulment of the fetus did not occur until 40 days after conception for boys and 90 days for girls. In 1869, Pope Pius IX declared that human life begins at conception. Thus, an abortion at any stage of pregnancy became murder in the eyes of the church and grounds for excommunication.

 6

TRUTH OR **FICTION** REVISITED: It is true that abortions were legal in the United States prior to the Civil War. In fact, abortion was legal in the United States from 1607 to 1828 (Calabresi et al., 2012; Hitt, 1998). Women were permitted to terminate a pregnancy until "quickening" occurred (the point at which the woman was first able to feel the fetus stirring within her). More restrictive abortion laws emerged because of a national desire to increase the population and because of concerns voiced by physicians about protecting women from botched abortions. By 1900, virtually all states in the union had enacted legislation banning abortion *at any point* during pregnancy, except when necessary to save the woman's life (Calabresi et al., 2012).

Abortion laws remained essentially unchanged until the late 1960s, when some states liberalized their abortion laws under mounting public pressure. Then, in 1973, the U.S. Supreme Court, in effect, legalized abortion nationwide in the landmark *Roe v. Wade* decision. *Roe v. Wade* held that a woman's right to an abortion was protected under the right to privacy guaranteed by the Constitution. The decision legalized abortions for any reason during the first trimester. In its ruling, the Court also noted that a fetus is not considered a person and is thus not entitled to constitutional protection. The Court ruled that states may regulate a woman's right to have an abortion during the second trimester to protect her health, as in requiring her to obtain an abortion in a hospital rather than a doctor's office. The Supreme Court also held that when a fetus becomes viable, its rights override the mother's right to privacy. Because the fetus may become viable early in the third trimester, states may prohibit third-trimester abortions, except when an abortion is necessary to protect a woman's health.

Since *Roe v. Wade,* most states have also enacted laws requiring parental consent or notification before a minor may have an abortion. According to a CBS News Poll taken in 2005, 80% of adults in the United States say that at least one parent should be notified before minor girls can have abortions. Yet, with or without such rules, most girls seeking abortion do consult their parents. On the other hand, a survey reported in the *Journal of the American Medical Association* found that 48% of a sample of 950 girls visiting Planned Parenthood said that they would stop using all of the organization's services if their parents were notified of the visits (Reddy et al., 2002).

Let's look at why the controversy over abortion has existed. Many opponents of abortion argue that abortion is the taking of a human life—tantamount to murder. Therefore, it is useful to discuss the issue as to when human life begins. ◉

👁-**Watch** the **Video**
Annie: Anti-Abortion Activist
on **MyDevelopmentLab**

CRITICAL THINKING

One of the issues concerning abortion is whether it is the taking of a human life. How do *you* define *human life*? When do *you* believe human life begins? At conception? When the embryo becomes implanted in the uterus? When the fetus begins to assume a human shape or develops human facial features? When the fetus is capable of sustaining independent life? Do your beliefs have anything to do with the concept of ensoulment? Explain.

👁 Watch the **Video**
Family Planning Services
on **MyDevelopmentLab**

CRITICAL THINKING

Are your beliefs about abortion the result of being exposed to certain authority figures, or do they reflect your own critical thinking?

WHEN DOES HUMAN LIFE BEGIN?

The issue as to when human life begins is at the heart of the abortion controversy. It is a question that you will have to answer for yourself. We can only note that moral concerns about abortion often turn on the question of when human life begins. For some Christians, the matter revolves around when they believe the fetus obtains a soul.

In his thesis on *ensoulment*, the thirteenth-century Christian theologian Saint Thomas Aquinas wrote that a male fetus does not acquire a human soul until 40 days after conception. A female fetus does not acquire a soul until after 80 days. Scientists, too, have attempted to define when human life can be said to begin. Astronomer Carl Sagan, for example, wrote that fetal brain activity can be considered a scientific marker of human life (Sagan & Druyan, 1990). Brain activity is needed for thought, the quality that is considered most "human" by many. Brainwave patterns typical of children do not begin until about the thirtieth week of pregnancy. But opponents argue that a newly fertilized ovum carries the *potential* for human thought in the same way that the embryonic or fetal brain does. It could even be argued that sperm cells and ova are living things in that they carry out the biological processes characteristic of cellular life. All in all, the question of when *human* life begins is apparently not going to be resolved by science. 👁

ATTITUDES TOWARD LEGALIZED ABORTION: A NATION DIVIDED

National public opinion polls taken since *Roe v. Wade,* including the Gallup Poll taken in May 2012 (Saad, 2012), have consistently shown that a majority of people in the United States support a woman's right to have an abortion *under at least some circumstances* (see Figures 12.9 and 12.10). Reduced support for legal abortion is associated with religious commitment, conservative attitudes on premarital sex, and belief in having large families. Democrats are significantly more likely than Republicans to label themselves as pro-choice and favor abortion either under all or some circumstances (Saad, 2012).

FIGURE 12.9 Response to the Question, "With Respect to the Abortion Issue, Would You Consider Yourself to Be Pro-Choice or Pro-Life?"

Source: Gallup Poll, 2012.

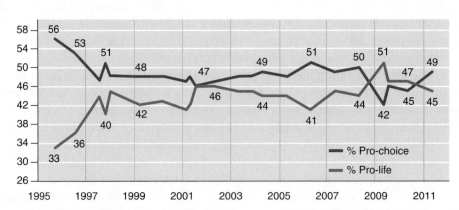

FIGURE 12.10 Responses to the Question, "Do You Think Abortions Should Be Legal under Any Circumstances, Legal Only under Certain Circumstances, or Illegal in All Circumstances?" The majority of American still prefer that abortion be legal under some (or all) circumstances.

Source: Gallup Poll, 2012.

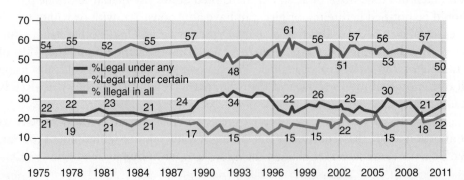

A Closer Look
A Death in Wichita

Occasionally the pro-choice–pro-life battle turns deadly. At least four physicians who practice abortions have been killed. The latest to die, as of this writing, was George Tiller of Wichita, Kansas. He was gunned down in his church in 2009. Tiller was one of the few remaining doctors who are willing to practice late-term abortions. Despite Dr. Tiller's death, pro-life groups are still demonstrating in the area of his office.

How do pro-life people feel about the killing of Tiller? We can only note what some of them say. Troy Newman (2009), president of Operation Rescue, a well-known anti-abortion organization headquartered in Wichita, said, "This idiot"—referring to Tiller's killer—"did more to damage the pro-life movement than you can imagine."

Mark S. Gietzen (2009), president of the Kansas Coalition for Life, noted, "You can't be pro-life and go around killing people, but some people are really mad at me for saying that."

The protests against Wichita's abortion provider continued after Dr. George R. Tiller's death, including at his funeral.

Source: Steve Hebert/Atlas Press for the *New York Times*

Many people in the pro-choice movement argue that if abortions were to be made illegal again, thousands of women, especially poor women, would die or suffer serious physical consequences from botched or nonsterile abortions. People in the pro-life movement counter that alternatives to abortion, such as adoption, are available. Pro-choice advocates argue that the debate about abortion should be framed not only by notions of the mother's right to privacy but also by the issue of the quality of life of an unwanted child. They argue that minority and physically or mentally disabled children are often hard to place for adoption. These children often spend their childhoods being shuffled from one foster home to another. Pro-life advocates counter that killing a fetus eliminates any potential that it might have, despite hardships, of living a fruitful and meaningful life.

Figure 12.9 shows the breakdown of Americans who have considered themselves to be pro-life and pro-choice according to national surveys done from 1995 to 2012 (Saad, 2012). You can see that the percentage of people who label themselves pro-life has been growing and that the percentage of people who label themselves pro-choice dropped dramatically in one year from 49% to 41%. One might wonder whether the strong emphasis on "social issues" such as birth control and abortion during the early months of the 2012 election exerted an influence on these attitudes. In 2012, 72% of Republicans self-identified as pro-life compared to 22% who labeled themselves pro-choice. Among Democrats, the picture was quite different:

58% self-identified as pro-choice and 34% as pro-life. On the other hand, looking at all American adults, including Independents, only a minority of respondents—22% in the 2012 poll—would restrict abortion under all circumstances (see Figure 12.10). But there is yet another caveat: Of those who would permit abortion under certain circumstances, the majority would permit it in only a few circumstances. Such few circumstances might include rape, incest, and deformity in the fetus.

Despite polls such as these, *Roe v. Wade* is not in the personal memories of most women who choose to have abortions in the United States today. Many of them have a hard time recognizing that abortion was ever illegal, and cannot imagine what it would mean if abortion were to be made illegal again.

Says a 19-year-old woman from Chicago who is waiting in an abortion clinic: "I've never heard anything about *Roe vs. Wade*. I know there is tension between different groups and that there are people who are really, really against abortion. My mom is totally against it. If she knew I was here, Wow! I can't even imagine what it was like when abortion was illegal. I just opened up the phone book. People definitely take it for granted today. I think of the movie *Dirty Dancing*. I never understood why she was so sick, but it was because she got an illegal abortion" (Lewin, 1998a).

So, are we a nation divided? Do people divide themselves into two camps, pro-life and pro-choice? Yes, but only a minority of people are at the extremes—either favoring or restricting abortion under all circumstances (Saad, 2009).

Methods of Abortion

Regardless of the moral, legal, and political issues that surround abortion, there are many abortion methods. Let us explain what they are, and why a woman might choose one rather than another.

VACUUM ASPIRATION

TRUTH OR **FICTION** REVISITED: It is not true that the D&C is the most widely used type of abortion method; **vacuum aspiration**—also called *suction curettage*—accounts for more than 90% of abortions in the United States. It is relatively painless and inexpensive. It can be done with little or no anesthesia in a medical office or clinic, but only during the first trimester. Later, thinning of the uterine walls increases the risks of perforation and bleeding.

In the procedure the cervix is usually dilated first by insertion of progressively larger curved metal rods, or "dilators," or by insertion, hours earlier, of a stick of seaweed called *Laminaria digitata*. *Laminaria* expands as it absorbs cervical moisture, providing a gentler means of opening the os. Then a tube connected to an aspirator (suction machine) is inserted into the uterus. The uterine contents are evacuated (emptied) by suction (see Figure 12.11). Possible complications include perforation of the uterus, infection, cervical lacerations, and hemorrhaging, but these are not common.

DILATION AND CURETTAGE (D&C)

The **D&C** was once the customary method of performing abortions. It now accounts for only a small number of abortions in the United States. It is usually performed 8 to 20 weeks following the last menstrual period (LMP). Once the cervix has been dilated, the uterine contents are scraped from the uterine lining with a blunt scraping tool.

D&Cs are carried out in a hospital, usually under general anesthesia. The scraping increases the chances of hemorrhaging, infection, and perforation. Because

Vacuum aspiration Removal of the uterine contents by suction; an abortion method used early in pregnancy.

D&C Abbreviation for *dilation and curettage*, an operation in which the cervix is dilated and uterine contents are then gently scraped away.

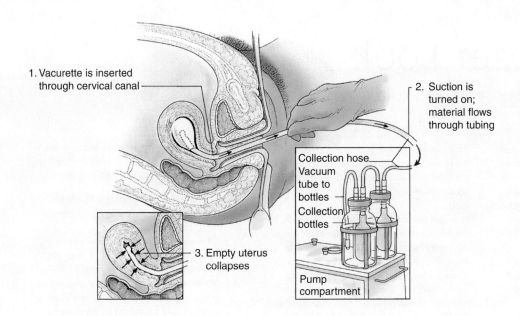

1. Vacurette is inserted through cervical canal

2. Suction is turned on; material flows through tubing

Collection hose
Vacuum tube to bottles
Collection bottles

3. Empty uterus collapses

Pump compartment

FIGURE 12.11 Vacuum Aspiration. This is the safest and most common method of abortion, but it can be performed only during the first trimester. An angled tube is inserted through the cervix into the uterus, and the uterine contents are then evacuated (emptied) by suction.

of these risks, D&Cs have largely been replaced by the vacuum aspiration method. D&Cs are still used to treat various gynecological problems, however, such as abnormally heavy menstrual bleeding.

DILATION AND EVACUATION (D&E)

The **D&E** is used most commonly during the second trimester, when vacuum aspiration alone would be too risky. The D&E combines suction and the D&C. First, the cervix is dilated. The cervix must also be dilated more fully than with vacuum aspiration to allow for passage of the larger fetus. Second, a suction tube is inserted to remove some of the contents of the uterus. But suction alone cannot safely remove all uterine contents. So the remaining contents are removed with forceps. A blunt scraper may also be used to scrape the uterine wall to make sure that the lining has been removed fully. Like the D&C, the D&E is usually performed in the hospital under general anesthesia. Most women recover quickly and relatively painlessly. In rare instances, however, complications such as excessive bleeding, infection, and perforation of the uterine lining arise.

D&E Abbreviation for *dilation and evacuation*, an abortion method in which the cervix is dilated prior to vacuum aspiration.

Real Students, Real Questions

Q *Will having an abortion make it difficult for me to get pregnant again?*

A There is usually no connection between having an abortion and getting pregnant again, as long as the abortion is carried out *competently* by a licensed physician. If you are contemplating having an abortion, ask the doctor where she or he studied medicine, where he or she is licensed to practice, and inquire about her or his experience. The diploma and license should be displayed on the wall of her or his office.

A Closer Look

The Political Battle over Partial-Birth Abortion

Most Americans believe that early abortions should be permitted, but there is great concern over the late-term surgical abortion method generally known as *partial-birth abortion* and referred to, medically, as an *intact dilation and extraction,* or *intact D and X.* In this method, the cervix is dilated and a fetus that may be ten inches long is extracted through the birth canal. Brain tissue is destroyed to rapidly terminate any life functions in the fetus.

Support of abortion rights drops off rapidly as the stages of pregnancy progress. Most people who support early first-trimester abortions oppose partial-birth abortion because of its timing. Others oppose it because of the nature of the disposal of the fetus. However, many pro-choice people argue in favor of partial-birth abortions for at least two reasons. One is that they are relatively rare and usually performed when the health of the mother is at stake. Another is the

"slippery-slope" argument, or fear that surrendering a woman's right to have a partial-birth abortion could eventually lead to surrendering other rights to her own body.

The general attitudes of the medical profession toward the partial-birth abortion may be expressed in the fact that the procedure is rarely found in medical books. Many states have passed bills to outlaw partial-birth abortion, and a number of them have been struck down by the courts on the grounds that the bans do not provide for a health exception— that is, an exception in the case where the mother's life is at stake. The battle will likely continue.

In the year 2000, the U.S. Supreme Court struck down a Nebraska statute *(Stenberg v. Carhart)* that banned partial-birth abortion on two grounds. One was that the definition of partial-birth abortion was too vague. The second was that the law did not make an exception for the

case in which the procedure was necessary to protect the mother's health. Today the national picture looks something like this:

- The great majority of the 50 states have passed laws preventing partial-birth abortion.
- Of these, the majority have been blocked by courts because they do not have health exceptions.
- Most of the remainder of these continue to be unchallenged, but they will presumably be found to be unenforceable on the grounds that they lack health exceptions.
- A relatively small number of states have bans that specifically allow for a health exception.

CRITICAL THINKING

What are the political consequences of labeling this abortion method "partial-birth abortion" as opposed to "intact D&X"?

INDUCING LABOR BY INTRA-AMNIOTIC INFUSION

Second-trimester abortions are sometimes performed by chemically inducing premature labor and delivery. The procedure, which must be performed in a hospital, is called *instillation,* or **intra-amniotic infusion**. It is usually performed when fetal development has progressed beyond the point at which other methods are deemed safe. A saline (salt) solution or a solution of prostaglandins (hormones that stimulate uterine contractions during labor) is injected into the amniotic sac. Prostaglandins may also be administered by vaginal suppository. Uterine contractions (labor) begin within a few hours after infusion. The fetus and placenta are expelled from the uterus within the next 24 or 48 hours.

Intra-amniotic infusion accounts for only a small number of abortions. Medical complications, risks, and costs are greater with this procedure than with other methods of abortion. Overly rapid labor can tear the cervix, but previous dilation of the cervix with *Laminaria* lessens the risk. Perforation, infection, and hemorrhaging are rare if prostaglandins are used, but about half the recipients experience nausea and vomiting, diarrhea, or headaches. Saline infusion can cause shock and even death if the solution is carelessly introduced into the bloodstream.

Intra-amniotic infusion An abortion method in which a substance is injected into the amniotic sac to induce premature labor. Also called *instillation*.

HYSTEROTOMY

The **hysterotomy** is, in effect, a cesarean section. Incisions are made in the abdomen and uterus, and the fetus and uterine contents are removed. Hysterotomy may be performed during the late second trimester, between the 16th and 24th weeks following the last menstrual period. It is performed very rarely, usually only when intra-amniotic infusion is not advised. A hysterotomy is major surgery that must be carried out under general anesthesia in a hospital. Hysterotomy involves risks of complications from the anesthesia and the surgery itself.

ABORTION DRUGS

RU-486 (mifepristone) induces early abortion by blocking the effects of progesterone. Progesterone is the hormone that stimulates proliferation of the endometrium, allowing implantation and development of the placenta. The typical course is for the woman to take three mifepristone pills. Two days later, she is given a second oral drug, misoprostol, that causes uterine contractions to expel the embryo.

As the abortion debate continues, so does research into the use of other drugs. A combination of the cancer drug methotrexate and misoprostol can also be used to terminate early pregnancy. Methotrexate is toxic to the trophoblastic tissue of the embryo, and—as in combination with RU-486—misoprostol causes the uterus to expel the embryo.

Hysterotomy Abortion of the fetus by cesarean section.

Real Students, Real Questions

Q *I had an abortion. Should I tell the father—even if we are not seeing each other?*

A Complicated question. What would be your motive? To show him what he lost? To punish him? We are doubtful that he would fully understand the extent of *your* loss. So if your motive is to make him understand, you might be headed down a blind alley. Looking at it from another point of view, we can't think of any reason you would be *obligated* to tell him. After all, it was, and is, your body. Have an honest talk with yourself about your motives, and maybe your answer will develop from that.

Chapter Review ✔●⌐Study and Review on MyDevelopmentLab

LO1 Define contraception

Contraception is a technique that prevents a sperm cell and ovum from uniting.

LO2 Discuss historic issues concerning the legalization of contraception in the United States

Anthony Comstock lobbied for passage of a federal law in 1873 that prohibited the dissemination of birth-control information through the mail on the grounds that it was obscene and indecent. In 1918, the courts ruled that physicians must be allowed to disseminate information that might aid in the cure and prevention of diseases. Dismantling of the Comstock law had begun.

LO3 Explain how hormonal methods of contraception work, and discuss their advantages and disadvantages

Hormone methods supply estrogen and progestin, or just the latter. Birth-control pills include combination pills (estrogen and progestin) and mini-pills (progestin). Combination pills fool the brain into acting as though the woman is already pregnant, so no additional ova are released. Mini-pills contain progestin, thicken the cervical mucus to impede the passage of sperm through the cervix, and render the inner lining of the uterus less receptive to a fertilized egg. Other methods of supplying these hormones include skin patches and injections. "Morning-after" pills have high hormone content that prevents fertilization or implantation of a fertilized ovum.

LO4 Explain how intrauterine devices (IUDs) work, and discuss their advantages and disadvantages

The intrauterine device (IUD) thickens cervical mucus and apparently irritates the uterine lining, causing inflammation and the production of antibodies that may prevent ova from becoming implanted. As with "the pill," the woman need do nothing after the IUD is inserted.

LO5 Explain how barrier methods of contraception work, and discuss their advantages and disadvantages

The diaphragm covers the cervix and should be used with a spermicide. The contraceptive sponge absorbs sperm and also contains a spermicide. The cervical cap covers the cervix. Latex condoms afford protection against STIs as well as conception.

LO6 Explain how fertility awareness methods of contraception work, and discuss their advantages and disadvantages

Rhythm methods of contraception rely on awareness of the occurrence of fertile segments of the menstrual cycle. The calendar method informs women with regular cycles when they are likely to ovulate. Ovulation detection kits and body temperature methods provide similar estimates.

LO7 Describe methods of sterilization, and discuss the prospects of reversibility

Sterilization is considered permanent, although it may be reversed in many cases. The male vasectomy consists of cutting the vas deferens. Female sterilization methods prevent ova and sperm from passing through the fallopian tubes.

LO8 Identify "nonmethods" of contraception, and explain why they are not dependable

Douching is ineffective because sperm may pass beyond the range of the douche within seconds after ejaculation. Withdrawal has a high failure rate.

LO9 Define spontaneous abortion versus induced abortion

Spontaneous abortion is another term for miscarriage. Induced abortion is the intentional removal of an embryo or fetus prior to viability of the fetus.

LO10 Discuss the history of abortion in the United States and controversies concerning abortion

In 1973, the U.S. Supreme Court, in effect, legalized abortion nationwide in the landmark *Roe v. Wade* decision. Opinions regarding the law vary across cultures and eras. Some pro-life activists have been challenging the extent of the *Roe v. Wade* decision; some would like it completely overturned. Others are strong supporters of the law. The abortion controversy is largely about when human life begins. Some argue that it begins at conception; others say it begins when the fetus becomes viable; and still others are somewhere in between, as, for example, when they maintain that life begins when neural activity begins in the fetal brain.

LO11 Discuss various methods of abortion

Abortion methods in use today include vacuum aspiration, D&C, D&E, induction of labor by intra-amniotic infusion, hysterotomy, and drugs such as RU-486. Partial-birth abortion (intact D&X) is the most controversial method because it occurs closest to the age of viability, and sometimes when the fetus might be viable with contemporary medical procedures.

Test Your Learning

1. Which of the following is termed a *nonmethod* of birth control in the text?

    (a) Sterilization
    (b) The condom
    (c) Withdrawal
    (d) Fertility awareness techniques

2. Which of the following is the most effective method of birth control?

    (a) The female condom
    (b) Oral contraceptives
    (c) The contraceptive sponge
    (d) Douching

3. Which of the following methods of birth control has the most side effects?

    (a) The intrauterine device (IUD)
    (b) The male condom
    (c) The diaphragm
    (d) The mini-laparotomy

4. Which is true of attitudes toward abortion in the United States?

    (a) Most people would allow abortion under some circumstances.
    (b) Most people would allow abortion for women who cannot afford to raise children.
    (c) All Roman Catholics oppose abortion.
    (d) Few parents want to be notified if an underage daughter is seeking an abortion.

5. The most common method of abortion practiced in the United States today is

    (a) the D&C.
    (b) the D&E.
    (c) vacuum aspiration.
    (d) ectopic pregnancy.

6. _____ is/are the most widely used contraceptive.

    (a) Injectable contraceptives
    (b) The contraceptive sponge
    (c) The diaphragm
    (d) The pill

7. The most controversial abortion method is the

    (a) mini-pill.
    (b) D&C.
    (c) hysterotomy.
    (d) intact D&X.

8. Rhythm methods rely on

    (a) fertility awareness.
    (b) hormonal preparations.
    (c) barriers.
    (d) spermicides.

9. Research with African and Thai prostitutes shows that nonoxynol-9 _____ the chances of being infected with HIV.

    (a) decreases
    (b) increases
    (c) has no measurable effect on
    (d) has mixed effects on

10. The Supreme Court struck down a Nebraska statute (*Stenberg v. Carhart*) that banned partial-birth abortion because

    (a) partial-birth abortion was politically popular.
    (b) partial-birth abortion was a medical issue and not a legal issue.
    (c) the Court was conservative.
    (d) the law did not make an exception when the procedure was necessary to protect the mother's health.

Answers: 1. c; 2. b; 3. a; 4. a; 5. c; 6. d; 7. d; 8. a; 9. b; 10. d

My Life, My Sexuality

Talking with Your Partner about Contraception

*Explore this **My Life, My Sexuality** feature by scanning this QR code with your mobile device. If you don't already have one, you may download a free QR scanner for your device wherever smartphone apps are sold. You can also view this feature in MyDevelopmentLab, along with an accompanying critical thinking assignment.*

When is the right time to discuss contraception? On a first date? When you are invited to meet your partner's family? When you are lost in amorous embraces? Broaching the topic can be awkward, but *not* broaching it can be disastrous. Scan the code for ideas on how to handle this tricky situation.

13 Sexuality in Childhood and Adolescence

Learning Objectives

Adolescent
Sexual
Behavior

Explore the video, **Adolescent Sexual Behavior**, by scanning this QR code with your mobile device. If you don't already have one, you may download a free QR scanner for your device wherever smartphone apps are sold. You can also view this video in MyDevelopmentLab. For more videos related to this chapter's content, log into MyDevelopmentLab to view the entire Human Sexuality Video Series.

TRUTH OR FICTION?

Which of the following statements are the truth, and which are fiction? Look for the Truth-or-Fiction icons on the pages that follow to find the answers.

1 Many boys are born with erections.   T F?

2 Infants often engage in pelvic thrusting at 8 to 10 months of age.   T F?

3 Most children do not talk with their parents about sex.   T F?

4 Sex education encourages sexual activity among children and adolescents.   T F?

5 Nocturnal emissions in boys accompany erotic dreams.   T F?

6 Petting is practically universal among adolescents in the United States.   T F?

7 About 700,000 adolescent girls in the United States become pregnant each year.   T F?

hildren tend to play at sex for many years before they are ready for "real" sex. In this and the following chapter, we will see that our sexuality remains—or can remain—an integral part of our lives for all our days.

We begin long before children are capable of understanding anything about menstruation. However, let us note that reliable information about children's sexuality is hard to come by. Few empirical studies on the sexual behavior of children are available (Kenny & Wurtele, 2012; Thigpen, 2009). Few studies ask children about their sexual behavior. We tend to rely either on retrospective reports by adults or on observations by caregivers (Kenny & Wurtele, 2012).

Infancy (0 to 2 Years): The Search for the Origins of Human Sexuality

Infants—and fetuses—engage in a variety of sexual behaviors, although the "meaning" of these behaviors, if there is one, is a matter of speculation. Imaging techniques such as ultrasound have shown, for example, that male fetuses have erections. Fetuses of both sexes suck their fingers. The sucking reflex allows babies to obtain nourishment, but infants also appear to reap pleasure from sucking fingers, pacifiers, nipples, or whatever else fits into the mouth. None of this is surprising, given the sensitivity of the mouth's mucous lining.

Stimulation of the genitals in infancy can also produce pleasure. Parents who touch their infants' genitals while changing or washing them may discover the infants smiling or becoming excited. Infants discover the pleasure of self-stimulation ("masturbation") for themselves when they gain the ability to manipulate their genitals with their hands.

CRITICAL THINKING
What are the scientific problems in attempting to explain or interpret the meaning of pelvic thrusting in infants? Is it possible that pelvic thrusting in infants can have no meaning? (What does *meaning* mean?)

THE INFANT'S CAPACITY FOR SEXUAL RESPONSE

1 Boys have erections in utero. **TRUTH** OR **FICTION** REVISITED: In fact, many boys are born with erections. Erection is a reflex that begins to operate early in life. Most boys have erections during the first few weeks. Signs of sexual arousal in infant girls, such as vaginal lubrication, are less readily detected. However, evidence of lubrication and genital swelling has been reported (Mazur, 2006).

But do not interpret children's reflexes according to adult concepts of sexuality. The reflexes of lubrication and erection do not necessarily signify "interest" in sex. We cannot say what, if anything, infants' sexual reflexes "mean" to them.

2 **Pelvic Thrusting** Pelvic thrusting is observed in infant monkeys, apes, and humans. These observations led ethologist John Bowlby (1969) to suggest that infantile sexual behavior may be the rule in mammals, not the exception. **TRUTH** OR **FICTION** REVISITED: Thrusting has been observed in humans at eight to ten months of age and may be an expression of excitement, affection, or both. Typically, the infant clings to the parent, nuzzles, and thrusts and rotates the pelvis for several seconds.

Orgasm At least some infants seem capable of involuntary muscular contractions that resemble orgasm. Kinsey and his colleagues (1953) noted that baby boys show behaviors that resemble orgasm as early as five months, and baby girls as early as four months. Orgasms in boys are similar to those in men in terms of muscular contraction, but there is no ejaculation. Ejaculation occurs only after puberty.

MASTURBATION

Masturbation is typical for infants and young children and may start as early as five months of age (Narchi, 2003; Zhu et al., 2011). Infants may masturbate by rubbing their genitals against a soft object, such as a towel, bedding, or a doll. As they mature and develop sensorimotor coordination, infants may engage in manual stimulation of the genitals.

Masturbation to orgasm is rare until the second year (Reinisch, 1990). Some children begin masturbating to orgasm later. Some never do. All in all, however, orgasm from masturbation is found frequently among children, as among adults (Reinisch, 1990).

SEXUAL CURIOSITY

Children frequently develop sexual curiosity as early as 12 to 15 months of age. Later on they play "Doctor" and show their curiosity about the sexual anatomy of other people in other ways, such as wanting to watch a parent take a shower or bath (de Graaf & Rademakers, 2011).

GENITAL PLAY

Children in the United States typically do not engage in genital play with others until about the age of 2. Then, as an expression of their curiosity about their environment and other people, they may investigate other children's genitals or may hug, cuddle, kiss, or climb on top of them. None of this need cause concern. Spiro (1965) describes 2-year-olds at play in an Israeli kibbutz:

> Ofer [a boy] and Pnina [a girl] sit side by side on chamber pots.... Ofer puts his foot on Pnina's foot, she then does the same—this happens several times. ... Finally, Pnina shifts her pot away, then moves back, then away ... they laugh.... Pnina stands up, lies on the table on her stomach, ... Ofer pats her buttocks.... Ofer kicks Pnina gently, and they laugh.... Pnina touches and caresses Ofer's leg with her foot [and] says "more more."... Ofer stands, then Pnina stands, both bounce up and down ... both children are excited, bounce, laugh together.... Pnina grabs Ofer's penis, and he pushes her away ... she repeats, he pushes her away, and turns around.... Pnina touches his buttocks. (p. 225)

There is no reason to infer that Ofer and Pnina were seeking sexual gratification. Rough-and-tumble play, including touching the genitals, is common among children.

CO-SLEEPING

An issue that causes concern among many parents is whether it is "safe" for infants to share their beds. Parents have several motives for doing so, including the fact that infants are more likely to get back to sleep in their parents' beds when they awaken in the night. Co-sleeping also simplifies breastfeeding at odd hours. But the American Academy of Pediatrics does not recommend co-sleeping (Ratnayake, 2011) for fear that parents may accidentally suffocate children. There is also concern that allowing infants to spend the night with parents may have adverse effects on their sexual development. Despite any concerns, it seems that the majority of American mothers have slept at least occasionally with their infants, and perhaps one in five mothers are given information about co-sleeping by their physicians (Krouse et al., 2012).

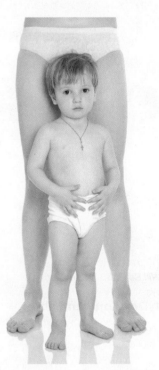

At What Age Does Curiosity about Sex Develop? Children are naturally inquisitive about sexual anatomy and sexual behavior. Much curiosity is triggered when they become aware that males and females differ in anatomy.

But research does not reveal harmful effects for co-sleeping. For example, an Austrian study found no significant connections between children's sleeping arrangements and their social development (Rothrauff et al., 2004). Another research group followed the development of children in 205 families from infancy to 18 years of age (Okami et al., 2002). They found that the children who shared beds with their parents during infancy showed superior intellectual development at the age of 6, as compared with children who did not co-sleep. The advantage of bed-sharing essentially disappeared by the age of 18. Most instructive is the finding that no sexual problems were connected with bed-sharing, at any age.

SEXUAL ORIENTATION OF PARENTS

There are apparently few, if any, differences in the psychological adjustment of children reared by parents in heterosexual or in gay or lesbian relationships (Regnerus, 2012). For example, a Scandinavian research group analyzed the findings of 23 studies of 615 children reared from infancy by gay and lesbian parents and 387 control children reared by heterosexual parents (Anderssen et al., 2002). Outcome measures included emotional stability, sexual orientation, gender-typed behavior, adjustment, gender identity, and intellectual functioning. The children reared by homosexual parents did not differ from controls on any of the variables, including sexual orientation and gender-typed behavior patterns.

Early Childhood (3 to 8 Years)

Susan: Once my younger sister and I were over at a girl friend's house playing in her bedroom. For some reason she pulled her pants down and exposed her rear to us. We were amazed to see she had an extra opening down there we didn't know about. My sister reciprocated by pulling her pants down so we could see if she had the same extra opening. We were amazed at our discovery, our mothers not having mentioned to us that we had a vagina!

Christopher: Nancy was a willing playmate, and we spent many hours together examining each other's bodies as doctor and nurse. We even once figured out a pact that we would continue these examinations and watch each other develop. That was before we had started school. (Morrison, E. S., et al. (1980). Growing up sexual. New York: Van Nostrand Reinhold. p. 19)

These recollections from early childhood illustrate children's interest in sexual anatomy and behavior. Children in early childhood often show each other their bodies (Pike, 2011). The unwritten rule seems to be "I'll show you mine if you'll show me yours." ◉

MASTURBATION

Kim: I began to masturbate when I was 3 years old. My parents . . . tried long and hard to discourage me. They told me it wasn't nice for a young lady to have her hand between her legs.

When I was five I remember my mother discovering that I masturbated with a rag doll I slept with. She was upset, but she didn't make a big deal about it. She just told me in a matter-of-fact way, "Do you know that what you're doing is called masturbating?" That didn't make much sense to me, except I got the impression she didn't want me to do it. (Morrison et al., 1980, pp. 4–5)

◉ **Watch the Video**
Girls Will Be Girls and Boys Will Be Boys
on **MyDevelopmentLab**

A Closer Look

How Should Parents React When Children Masturbate?

Few parents in developed nations still believe that childhood masturbation sets the stage for physical and mental maladies. And yet, some parents react to childhood masturbation with concern, disgust, or shock.

Parents who are unaware that masturbation is commonplace among children may erroneously think that children who masturbate are oversexed or abnormal. They may pull a child's hands away and scold her or him. Some may slap the child's hand. Once the child is capable of understanding speech, the parent may say things like, "Don't touch down there! That's a bad thing to do. Stop doing that." Parents may use threats and punishments. Or parents may verbally "ignore" the behavior but move the child's hands away from the genitals or pick up the child when he or she is found masturbating.

Sex educators argue that punishment may cause children to become secretive and guilty about masturbation (University of Michigan, 2009). Sex guilt tends to persist and may impede sexual pleasure in marriage. June Reinisch (1990) of the Kinsey Institute noted:

> Parents who scowl, scold, or punish in response to a child's exploring his or her genitals may be teaching the child that this kind of pleasure is wrong and that the *child* is "bad" for engaging in this kind of behavior. This message may hinder the ability to give and receive erotic pleasures as an adult and ultimately interfere with the ability to establish a loving and intimate relationship. (p. 248)

But most sex educators agree that children need to learn that public masturbation is not acceptable in our culture. The child who masturbates publicly can be told something like this by the age of 4: "It's okay in your room but not in the grocery store."

Not all authorities, and certainly not all parents, endorse tolerance. Some object to masturbation on religious or moral grounds. Others feel uncomfortable or conflicted about masturbation themselves. We must also recognize that some religious leaders sincerely believe that it does a child—and a parent—little good to be relaxed about bodily pleasures if the payoff is going to hell. From their point of view, there is nothing new about the body's capacity to respond to sexual stimulation with pleasure, and certainly nothing new about the necessity to make sometimes self-denying and painful choices. Parents must examine their own values and decide for themselves how to react when they discover their children masturbating.

Real Students, Real Questions

Q *Will masturbating earlier make you develop sooner?*

A Physically? No. Emotionally or mentally? Let's simply say that masturbation will help one get in touch with one's sexuality—with what feels good and what happens when it feels good—at whatever age one masturbates.

Because of the difficulties in conducting research into childhood sexuality, statistics on masturbation and other sexual activities are largely speculative (de Graaf & Rademakers, 2011). Parents may not wish to answer questions about their children's sexual behavior. Or they may want to present their children as little "gentlemen" and "ladies" by underreporting their sexual activity. Their biases may lead

CRITICAL THINKING
Why is it difficult to obtain accurate information about sexual behavior in children?

them not to perceive genital touching as masturbation. Many parents will not even allow their adolescents, let alone their younger children, to be interviewed about sex. And when we try to look back as adults, our memories may be cloudy.

A study by William Friedrich and colleagues (1998) of the Mayo Institute relied on interviews with the mothers of more than 1,100 children. The goal of the study was to establish what kinds of sexual behaviors can normally be expected in childhood, in order to help educators and other professionals determine when sexual behavior might be suggestive of childhood sexual abuse. The study did not provide data about masturbation per se, but, as shown in Table 13.1, it offered some insight into how many children touch their "private parts." Friedrich suggests that behavior that occurs in at least 20% of children is normal from a statistical point of view.

Table 13.1

Some Common Sexual Behaviors during Childhood

	Boys	Girls
Ages 2–5		
Touches or tries to touch mother's or other women's breasts	42.4%	43.7%
Touches private parts when at home	60.2%	43.8%
Tries to look at people when they are nude or undressing	26.8%	26.9%
Ages 6–9		
Touches private parts when at home	39.8%	20.7%
Tries to look at people when they are nude or undressing	20.2%	20.5%
Ages 10–12		
Is very interested in the opposite sex	24.1%	28.7%

Source: Data from W. M. Friedrich, J. Fisher, D. Broughton, M. Houston, and C. R. Shafran (1998). Normative sexual behavior in children: A contemporary sample. *Pediatrics, 101*(4) e9.

MALE–FEMALE SEXUAL BEHAVIOR

Alicia: On my birthday when I was in the second grade, I remember a classmate, Tim, walked home with a friend and me. He kept chasing me to give me kisses all over my face, and I acted like I didn't want him to do it, yet I knew I liked it a lot; when he would stop, I thought he didn't like me anymore. (Morrison et al., 1980, pp. 21, 29)

It is quite common for 3- and 4-year-olds to express affection through kissing. Curiosity about the genitals increases in this stage. Sex games like "show" and "playing doctor" may begin earlier, but they become common between the ages of 3 and 7 (de Graaf & Rademakers, 2011). Much of this sexual activity takes place in same-sex groups, although mixed-sex sex games are not uncommon. Children may show their genitals to each other, touch each other's genitals, or masturbate together.

MALE–MALE AND FEMALE–FEMALE SEXUAL BEHAVIOR

Arnold: When I was about 5, my cousin and I . . . went into the basement and dropped our pants. We touched each other's penises, and that was it. I guess I didn't realize the total significance of the secrecy in which we carried out this act. For later . . . my parents questioned me . . . and I told them exactly what we had done. They were horrified and told me that that was definitely forbidden. (Morrison et al., 1980, p. 24)

Real Students, Real Questions

Q *How can you tell the difference between normal child-hood sex play or exploration and signs of sexual abuse?*

A It's not always easy. Children often know or suspect when something is wrong. Abuse most often comes from someone older and close to the child—not a stranger—so parents need to be open to listening to the child, even when he or she implicates a family member or close friend. Children who are abused often act depressed—withdrawn, listless—or, at the other extreme, aggressively. They may not have the concept of abuse or the words to talk about it. Or they may fear *they* have done something wrong. Children need to be taught the difference between "good touching" and "bad touching." They need to know they can tell you what's on their mind without being judged or scolded. By and large, a good deal of abuse can be avoided simply by having children play with children who are pretty much their own age. They may play "doctor" or "show," but such games are usually not abusive.

Despite Arnold's parents' "horror," same-sex sexual play in childhood does not foreshadow adult sexual orientation (Reinisch, 1990). It may, in fact, be more common than heterosexual play. It typically involves handling the other child's genitals, although it may include oral or anal contact. It may also include an outdoor variation of the game of "show" in which boys urinate together and see who can reach farthest or highest.

Preadolescence (9 to 13 Years)

Some preadolescent behaviors are sexually related rather than sexual per se. For example, preadolescents typically form relationships with a "best friend" of the same sex that enable them to share secrets and confidences. Preadolescents also tend to socialize with larger networks of friends in sex-segregated groups. At this stage, boys are likely to think that girls are "dorks." To girls at this stage, *dork* is too nice an epithet to apply to most boys.

Preadolescents grow increasingly preoccupied with, and self-conscious about, their bodies. Peers pressure preadolescents to conform to dress codes, the "proper" slang, and group norms concerning sex and drugs. Peer disapproval can be an intense punishment.

Sexual urges are experienced by many preadolescents but may not emerge until adolescence. Sigmund Freud had theorized that sexual impulses are hidden (latent) during preadolescence, but many preadolescents are quite active sexually.

MASTURBATION

Paul: When I was about 10, stories about masturbation got me worried. A friend and I went to a friend's older brother whom we respected and asked, "Is it really bad?" His reply stuck in my mind for years. "Well, it's like a bottle of olives—every time you take one out, there is one less in there." We were very worried because we thought we'd run out before we got to girls. (Morrison et al., 1980, pp. 6–8)

Kinsey and his colleagues (1948, 1953) reported that masturbation is the primary means of achieving orgasm during preadolescence for both boys and girls. They found that 45% of males and 15% of females masturbated by age 13. Although the frequencies of masturbation reported by Kinsey and his colleagues are suspect, other studies agree that adolescent males are more likely to masturbate than adolescent females (Petersen & Hyde, 2011; Robbins et al., 2011).

MALE–FEMALE SEXUAL BEHAVIOR

Preadolescent sex play often involves mutual display of the genitals, with or without touching. Such sexual experiences are quite common and do not appear to affect future sexual adjustment (Martinez et al., 2011).

Although preadolescents tend to socialize in same-sex groups, interest in the other sex among heterosexuals tends to gradually increase as they approach puberty. Group activities and mixed-sex parties often provide preadolescents with their first exposure to heterosexual activities (Connolly et al., 2004). But couples may not begin to pair off until middle adolescence.

MALE–MALE AND FEMALE–FEMALE SEXUAL BEHAVIOR

Much preadolescent sexual behavior among members of the same sex is simply exploration. Some incidents reflect lack of availability of partners of the other sex. As with younger children, preadolescent experiences with children of the same sex may be more common than heterosexual experiences (Martinez et al., 2011). These activities are usually limited to touching each other's genitals or mutually masturbating. Since preadolescents generally socialize with peers of their own sex, their sexual explorations are also often with peers of their own sex. Most same-sex sexual experiences involve single episodes or short-lived relationships and do not reflect one's sexual orientation.

 Watch the **Video**
Sexual Education
on **MyDevelopmentLab**

Sex Education

Sex Education. Despite the availability of sex education in most schools, many young people still learn about sex from their peers. Survey data show that most parents want sex education to cover abstinence, avoiding pregnancy, sexually transmitted infections, abortion, and sexual orientation. However, we may do a poorer job of teaching our children about sex than most European nations do.

Sixty or seventy years ago in the United States, people did not generally talk openly about sex. Sure, there were dirty jokes. Friends confided in one another, or asked for opinions. Mothers may have "warned" their daughters about the onset of menstruation or about the aggressive "advances" of boys, but there was little if any formal discussion about human anatomy, sexually transmitted infections, and methods of preventing unwanted pregnancies. In fact, many young people weren't sure exactly how females got pregnant, and there were myths such as the (wrong!) belief that a female cannot get pregnant the first time she has sex. The message from mother and church was simple: "Don't." And hundreds of thousands of teenage girls became pregnant each year, and many youngsters would up infected with the sexually transmitted infections of the day, such as gonorrhea and syphilis.

Since that time, the numbers of teenagers getting pregnant showed some increase and the threat of HIV/AIDS emerged. Even so, many parents felt that sex education should not be taught outside the home or the church, and some still felt that sex should not be discussed at all. ◉

It is interesting, then, that some kind of formal sex education for children or adolescents is nearly universal in the United States today (Figure 13.1). There is more than discussion; adolescents practice unrolling condoms on bananas and the like. There is more than warnings about pregnancy and illness; some adolescents are told how to engage in oral sex and other sexual activities.

Figure 13.2 shows the results of a survey run by the government National Survey of Family Growth (Martinez et al., 2010) that recruited some 7,000 females and 6,000 males. The question answers in Figure 13.2 was whether or not they had received—or were receiving—any formal sex education between the ages of 15 and 19. "Formal" meant at a school, church, community center, or a similar setting rather than from parents, friends, books, or the Internet. Ninety-seven percent of males and 96% of females had received at least some formal sex education. That information was most likely to be about the nature and prevention of sexually transmitted infections. A strong runner-up was learning "how to say no to sex." The teenagers were less likely to be taught about methods of birth control, but even so, 70% of females and 62% of males received that information. Of course, the primary method of preventing disease is by using condoms, so recognizing their usefulness to prevent pregnancy would be a "side effect."

TRUTH OR **FICTION** REVISITED: Figure 13.2 shows that the majority of teenagers aged 15 to 19 actually have talked with a parent about sex. Females were more likely to do so than males, and nearly four out of five (79%) reported doing so. Therefore, in the United States today, the incidence of parent–child communication about sex is quite common. *What* they talked about is suggested in Figure 13.3.

Generally speaking, parents were most likely to talk to their children and adolescents about abstinence—how to say no to sex—although females (63%) were much more likely than males (42%) to discuss that issue. About half of the children and adolescents (55% of females and 50% of males) reported discussing sexually transmitted infections with their parents. More than half of females (51%) were told

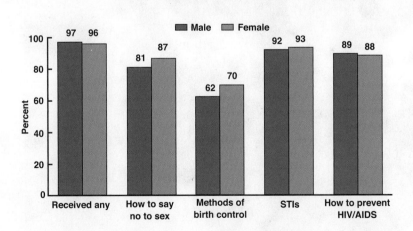

FIGURE 13.1 Teenagers Aged 15–19 Who Reported Receiving Formal Sex Education Prior to the Age of 18

Source: Martinez, G., Abma, J., & Copen, C. (2010). Educating teenagers about sex in the United States. NCHS data brief, no. 44. Hyattsville, MD: National Center for Health Statistics, Figure 1.

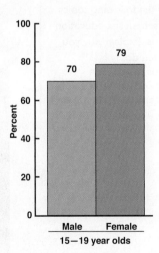

FIGURE: 13.2 Teenagers 15–19 Who Talked with a Parent about Sex

Source: Martinez, G., Abma, J., & Copen, C. (2010). Educating teenagers about sex in the United States. NCHS data brief, no. 44. Hyattsville, MD: National Center for Health Statistics, from Figure 3.

FIGURE: 13.3 Teenagers 15–19 Who Talked with a Parent about Sex by Topic and Gender

Source: Martinez, G., Abma, J., & Copen, C. (2010). Educating teenagers about sex in the United States. NCHS data brief, no. 44. Hyattsville, MD: National Center for Health Statistics, Figure 4.

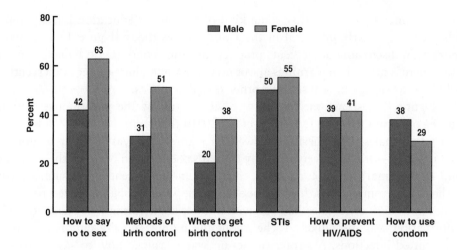

about birth control, as compared with fewer than one-third (31%) of males; and nearly twice as many females (38%) as males (20%) were told where to get birth control. In other words, many youngsters were told "Don't get pregnant" and "Don't get sick," but not all of them were given the specifics as to how to avoid these problems.

Some people argue that sex education ought to be left to parents and religious authorities. But the data suggest that adolescents will all too often learn about sex from peers and the Internet. Many parents worry that teaching about sexual techniques and contraception encourages sexual activity, but research does not support this concern (Kirby, 2011; Kraft et al., 2012). **TRUTH** OR **FICTION** REVISITED: There is actually no evidence that sex education encourages sexual activity among children and adolescents.

4

CRITICAL THINKING

What is your view concerning each of the following topics in high school sex education programs. Explain why you feel as you do.
• Methods of abortion
• How to obtain methods of contraception without parental knowledge or permission
• How to use condoms

Adolescence. Adolescence begins with puberty. Many adults see adolescents as impulsive, as needing to be controlled for "their own good." However, adolescents have a sex drive that is heightened by surges of sex hormones, and they are flooded with sexual themes in the media. Therefore, it is not surprising that many of them are in conflict with their families about issues of autonomy and sexual behavior.

Adolescence

Adolescence is bounded by the onset of puberty at the lower end and the capacity to take on adult responsibilities at the upper end. In our society adolescents are "neither fish nor fowl," as the saying goes—neither children nor adults. Adolescents may be able to reproduce and be taller than their parents, but they may not be allowed to get driver's licenses or attend R-rated films. They are prevented from working long hours and must usually stay in school until age 16. They cannot marry until they reach the "age of consent." The message is clear: Adults see adolescents as impulsive, and needing to be restricted for "their own good." Given these restrictions, a sex drive that is heightened by surges of sex hormones, and media inundation with sexual themes, it is not surprising that many adolescents are in conflict with their families about going around with certain friends, sex, and using the family car. 👁

👁▸│**Watch** the **Video**
Adolescent Sexual Behavior
on **MyDevelopmentLab**

PUBERTY

Puberty begins with the appearance of **secondary sex characteristics** and ends when the long bones make no further gains in length. The appearance of pubic hair is often the first visible sign of puberty. Puberty also involves changes in **primary sex characteristics**. Most major changes occur within three years in girls and within four years in boys.

Reproduction becomes possible toward the end of puberty. The two principal markers of reproductive potential are **menarche** in the girl and the first ejaculation in the boy. But these events may not signify immediate fertility.

Pubertal Changes in Females In girls, the pituitary gland signals the ovaries to vastly increase estrogen production at puberty. Estrogen may stimulate the growth of breast tissue ("breast buds") as early as the age of 8 or 9, but the breasts usually begin to enlarge during the tenth year. The development of fatty tissue and ducts elevates the areas of the breasts surrounding the nipples and causes the nipples themselves to protrude. The breasts typically reach full size in about three years, but the mammary glands do not mature fully until a woman has a baby. Events of puberty for girls are shown in Table 13.2.

Estrogen also promotes the growth of the fatty and supporting tissue in the hips and buttocks, which, along with the widening of the pelvis, causes the hips to become rounded. Growth of fatty deposits and connective tissue varies considerably. For this reason, development of breasts and hips differs.

Beginning at about the age of 11, girls' adrenal glands produce small amounts of androgens, which, along with estrogen, stimulate the growth of pubic and underarm hair. Excessive androgen production can darken or increase the amount of facial hair. Androgens and estrogen have other functions as well.

Estrogen causes the labia, vagina, and uterus to develop during puberty, and androgens cause the clitoris to develop. The vaginal lining varies in thickness according to the amount of estrogen in the bloodstream.

Estrogen typically brakes the female growth spurt some years before testosterone brakes that of males. Girls deficient in estrogen during their late teens may grow quite tall, but most girls reach their heights because of normal, genetically determined variations.

Menarche (first menstruation) commonly occurs between the ages of 11 and 14. But it is quite normal for menarche to occur as early as age 9 or as late as age 16 (Natsuaki et al., 2011). In the middle 1800s, European girls first menstruated at about the age of 16, as shown in Figure 13.4. During the past century and a half, however, the processes of puberty have occurred at progressively earlier ages in Western

Puberty The biological stage of development during which reproduction first becomes possible. Puberty begins with the appearance of secondary sex characteristics and ends when the long bones make no further gains in length.

Secondary sex characteristics Physical characteristics that differentiate males and females and that usually appear at puberty but are not directly involved in reproduction, such as the bodily distribution of hair and fat, development of the muscle mass, and deepening of the voice.

Primary sex characteristics Physical characteristics that differentiate males and females and are directly involved in reproduction, such as the sex organs.

Menarche The onset of menstruation; first menstruation.

Table 13.2

Five Stages of Pubertal Development for Females

Girls usually start to show the physical changes of puberty between the ages of 9 and 13, which is slightly sooner than boys. The female sex hormone called estrogen and other hormones cause the physical changes.

Many girls are fully developed by the age of 16. Some girls will continue to develop through age 18.

Here are the five stages and what happens:

Stage	Characteristics
Stage 1: Between ages 8 and 12	▪ No visible signs of physical development, but the ovaries are enlarging and hormone production is beginning.
Stage 2: May begin anywhere from ages 8 to 14.	▪ Height and weight increase rapidly. ▪ Fine hair growth begins close to the pubic area and underarms. ▪ Breast buds appear; nipples become raised and this area may be tender. ▪ Sweat and oil glands become more active, which can result in acne.
Stage 3: May begin anywhere from ages 9 to 15.	▪ Breasts become rounder and fuller. ▪ Hips may start to widen in relation to waist. ▪ Vagina begins secreting a clear or whitish fluid. ▪ Pubic hair becomes darker, thicker, and curlier. ▪ Height and weight continue to increase. ▪ For some girls, ovulation and menstruation (periods) begin but may be irregular.
Stage 4: May begin anywhere from ages 10 to 16.	▪ Underarm hair becomes darker. ▪ Pubic hair starts to form a triangular patch in front and around sides of genital area. ▪ The nipple and the dark area around the breast (areola) may stick out from the rest of the breast. ▪ For many girls, ovulation and menstruation (periods) begin, but may be irregular.
Stage 5: May begin anywhere from ages 12 to 19.	▪ Adult height is probably reached. ▪ Breast development is complete. ▪ Pubic hair forms a thick, curly, triangular patch. ▪ Ovulation and menstruation (periods) usually occur regularly. ▪ Overall look is that of a young adult woman.

Source: U.S. Department of Health and Human Services. *Sexual development of girls.* http://www.4parents.gov/sexdevt/girlswomen/girls_sexdevt/index.html (Accessed June 22, 2012).

nations, an example of the secular trend in development. By the 1960s, the average age of menarche in the United States had plummeted to its current figure of 12½.

No single theory of the onset of puberty has found wide acceptance. In any event, the average age of the advent of puberty for girls and boys appears to have leveled off in recent years. The precipitous drop suggested in Figure 13.4 has come to an end.

A World of Diversity

The Many Meanings of Menarche

In different times, in different places, menarche has had different meanings. The Manus of New Guinea greet menarche with elaborate ceremony (Lohmann, 2004). The other girls of the village sleep in the menstruating girl's hut. They feast and have parties. In the West, menstruation has historically received a mixed response. The menstrual flow itself has generally been seen, erroneously, as polluting, and the frequent discomforts of menstruation have led menstruating women to be stereotyped as irrational (Hubbard, 2009). Menarche itself has generally been perceived as the event in which a girl suddenly develops into a woman, but because of taboos and prejudice against menstruating women, girls historically matured in ignorance of menarche.

Girls' attitudes toward menarche reflect their level of education as well as certain physical realities. A Hong Kong study of 1,573 Chinese high school students found a mixed response to the onset of menstruation (Tang et al., 2003). The average age of menarche was 11.67 years. Although most of the girls reported that menstruation was annoying (it involved some discomfort for them, along with the need to dispose of the menstrual flow), two in three reported feeling more "grown up" and four in ten felt that they had become more feminine. Girls who felt positive about menarche were more likely to be educationally prepared to welcome it as a natural event, have a positive body image, and reject traditional negative attitudes. On the other hand, the circulating hormones connected with menarche may make the girl more vulnerable to stress (Allison & Hyde, 2011).

Most American girls currently receive advance information about menstruation, not only from family and girlfriends but also from school health classes. The old horror stories are pretty much gone, at least in societies in developed countries. However, most girls experience at least some menstrual discomfort and need to discreetly dispose of the menstrual flow (Harel, 2008). Most girls can separate pride in "becoming women" from the realities of some discomfort and the fact that menarche usually means that the girl will not be growing much taller because of the braking effects of estrogen. 👁

👁 **Watch** the **Video**
Girls Maturing Faster
on **MyDevelopmentLab**

What accounts for the earlier age of puberty? One hypothesis is that girls must reach a certain body weight to trigger pubertal changes such as menarche (Terasawa et al., 2012; Wagner et al., 2012). Body fat could trigger the changes because fat cells secrete the protein leptin (Terasawa et al., 2012). Leptin would then signal the brain to secrete a cascade of hormones that raise estrogen levels in the body. Menarche comes later to girls who have a lower percentage of body fat, such as athletes or those with eating disorders (Schtscherbyna et al., 2009; Novotny et al., 2011).

The average body weight for triggering menarche depends on the girl's height (Novotny et al., 2011). Today's girls are larger than those of the early twentieth century, probably because of improved nutrition and health care. It seems that the age threshold for reaching menarche may have been attained because the average age has leveled off in recent years.

The age at menarche has been shown to be related to adverse health outcomes later in life. For example, earlier menarche has been associated with higher risk of breast cancer and possibly a higher risk of endometrial cancer, adult obesity, and menstrual problems (Mishra et al., 2009).

Estrogen production becomes cyclical in puberty and regulates the menstrual cycle. A girl's initial menstrual cycles are typically **anovulatory**. Girls cannot become pregnant until ovulation occurs, which may lag menarche by a year or two. However, some teenagers are highly fertile soon after menarche (Frisch, 2002). 👁

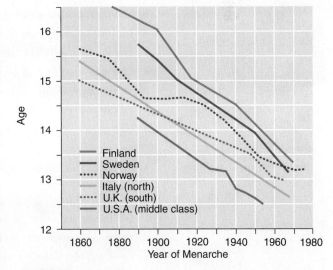

FIGURE 13.4 Age at Menarche. The age at menarche has been declining since the mid-1800s among girls in Western nations, apparently because of improved nutrition and health care. Menarche may be triggered by the accumulation of a critical percentage of body fat.

Anovulatory Without ovulation.

👁 **Watch** the **Video**
Adolescent Sexuality:
Deborah L. Tolman
on **MyDevelopmentLab**

Pubertal Changes in Males At puberty the hypothalamus signals the pituitary to increase production of FSH and LH. These hormones stimulate the testes to increase their output of testosterone. Testosterone prompts growth of the male genitals: the testes, scrotum, and penis (see Table 13.3). It fosters differentiation of male

Table 13.3

Five Stages of Pubertal Development for Males

Boys usually start to show the physical change of puberty between the ages of 11 and 14, which is slightly older than when girls start puberty. The male sex hormone called testosterone and other hormones cause the physical changes.
Here are the five stages and what happens:

Stage	Characteristics
Stage 1: May begin as early as age 9 and continue until 14.	■ No sign of physical development, but hormone production is beginning.
Stage 2: May begin anywhere from ages 11 to 13.	■ Height and weight increase rapidly. ■ Testicles become larger and scrotum hangs lower. ■ Scrotum becomes darker in color. ■ Fine hair growth begins at the base of the penis. ■ Hair growth may begin on the legs and underarms.
Stage 3: May begin anywhere from ages 12 to 14.	■ The penis, scrotum, and testicles grow. ■ Pubic hair becomes darker, thicker, and curlier. ■ Muscles become larger and shoulders become broader. ■ Sweat and oil glands become more active, which can result in acne. ■ Sperm production may begin. ■ Temporary swelling and tenderness may occur around nipples. ■ Height and weight continue to increase. ■ Hair growth on the legs and underarms continues.
Stage 4: May begin anywhere from ages 13 to 16.	■ Sperm production has usually begun. ■ The larynx (Adam's apple) increases in size. Vocal chords become longer and thicker, and the voice begins to break or crack, then becomes low. ■ Height and weight continue to increase. ■ Penis and testicles continue to grow. ■ Pubic hair increases in amount and becomes darker, coarser, and curly.
Stage 5: May begin anywhere from ages 14 to 18.	■ Growth of facial hair begins. ■ Chest hair growth may begin (not all males get much chest hair). ■ Adult height is reached. ■ Penis and testicles have reached full adult size. ■ Pubic, underarm, and leg hair are adult color, texture, and distribution. ■ Overall look is that of a young adult man.

Source: U.S. Department of Health and Human Services. *Sexual development of boys.* http://www.4parents.gov/sexdevt/boysmen/boys_sexdevt/index.html (Accessed June 22, 2012)

A Closer Look

Sexting: Of Cell Phones, Sex, and Death

Jessica Logan was 18 years old when she committed suicide. She had used her cell phone to snap and send nude photos of herself to her boyfriend. After they broke up, he forwarded the photos to other girls at their high school. The girls taunted Jessica mercilessly, calling her a whore and a slut. Jessica told her depressing tale in a local TV interview, and two months later—finding no peace—she hanged herself in her bedroom.

Jessica's sending of her photos to her boyfriend is an example of what is now called "sexting"—short for *sex texting*. It refers to sending or receiving text messages with sexual content. However, it's also used to describe what Jessica did—sending nude or otherwise provocative still images or videos by cell phone. Sexting can be used to titillate the recipient, to highlight the intimacy of one's relationship, to humiliate someone—or to ask or arrange for a sexual encounter (Dake et al., 2012; Judge, 2012).

In other "case studies," a 15-year-old Pennsylvania girl has been charged with producing and sending child pornography after sending nude photos of herself to other adolescents. A 19-year-old Florida college student was expelled and ordered to register as a sex offender for the next 25 years because he shared nude photos of his girlfriend with others. These instances are anything but rare, although the penalties are high.

A recent survey of high school students in Texas found that 28% said they had transmitted a nude photo of themselves in a text message or an email (Temple et al., 2012). Three in ten (31%) had requested a "sext" message, and more than half (57%) had asked someone else to send them a sexual text or email. Girls who had engaged in sexting were

significantly more like than those who had not to begin dating early and to engage in risky sexual behavior.

On the *TODAY Show*, attorney Larry Walters noted that the same sexting that is a crime for teenagers is legal for adults. He continued, "These teens don't see themselves as children. They see themselves as teens. They don't see what they're doing as child pornography. Teens believe it is normal. It is normal for them. To use child porn laws to punish teens for behavior the law was never designed to address is overkill . . . and it dilutes the effectiveness of child pornography laws for everyone else" (Celizic, 2009).

Five Things to Think about Before Pressing "Send"

- **Don't believe that anything you post or send will remain private.** Forty percent of teens say they have received a sexually suggestive message that was meant to be private, and 20% admit they shared this kind of message with someone other than the intended recipient.
- **Whatever you post or send may never go away.** Potential employers, college recruiters, teachers and coaches, parents, friends, enemies, and total strangers may be able to access your posts, even after you have deleted them.
- **Don't give in to peer pressure to post or send something that makes you uncomfortable.** Forty-seven percent of teens say that "pressure from guys" is a reason that girls post and send sexually suggestive pictures and messages. Twenty-four percent of teens say boys also send and post sexually suggestive messages and images because of peer pressure.
- **Consider the recipient's reaction before you press send.** You may intend for a message to be fun but the recipient may not perceive it that way. Forty percent of teen girls who send sexually suggestive content do so for a "joke," but 29% of boys think that girls who send this content are expected to date or "hook up" with the recipient in real life.
- **Nothing you post or send will necessarily remain anonymous.** Fifteen percent of teens send sexually suggestive pictures and messages to people they have "met" only online. Those people can often track you down on the basis of your screen name and the other information you have provided.

Source: Sex & Tech. (2009). A survey commissioned by The National Campaign to Prevent Teen and Unplanned Pregnancy and *CosmoGirl.com*. For additional data, please visit www.TheNationalCampaign.org/sextech or contact The National Campaign at 1-202-478-8500.

secondary sex characteristics: the growth of facial, body, and pubic hair; and the deepening of the voice. Testicle growth, in turn, accelerates testosterone production and pubertal changes. The testes continue to grow, and the scrotal sac becomes larger and hangs loosely from the body. The penis widens and lengthens, and pubic hair appears.

By age 13 or 14, erections become common. Many middle school boys dread that they may be caught between classes with erections, or asked to stand before the class. Testosterone causes the prostate and seminal vesicles—the organs that produce semen—to grow and produce semen. Boys typically experience their first ejaculation by age 13 or 14, often through masturbation. But there is much variation. Mature sperm are not usually found in the ejaculate until about a year after the first ejaculation, at age 14 on average. But sperm may be present in the first ejaculate, so pubertal boys should not assume that they have an infertile "grace period" following first ejaculation. About a year after first ejaculation, boys may also begin to experience **nocturnal emissions**, which are also called "wet dreams" because of the belief that nocturnal emissions accompany erotic dreams—which need not be so. **TRUTH** OR **FICTION** REVISITED: Despite the term *wet dreams*, nocturnal emissions need not accompany boys' erotic dreams.

Underarm hair appears at about age 15. Facial hair is at first a fuzz on the upper lip. A beard does not appear for another two or three years. Only half of U.S. boys shave (of necessity) by age 17. The beard and chest hair continue to develop past the age of 20. At age 14 or 15 the voice deepens because of the growth of the voice box and the lengthening of the vocal cords. Development is gradual, and the voices of adolescent boys sometimes crack embarrassingly.

Boys and girls undergo general growth spurts during puberty. Girls usually shoot up before boys. Individuals differ, however, and some boys spurt sooner than some girls.

Increases in muscle mass increase body weight. The shoulders and the circumference of the chest widen. At the age of 18 or so, men stop growing taller because estrogen prevents the long bones from making further gains in length. (Males normally produce some estrogen in the adrenal glands and testes.) Nearly one in two boys experiences temporary enlargement of the breasts, or **gynecomastia**, during puberty, which is also caused by estrogen.

In both females and males, sex hormones course through the bloodstream in copious amounts, giving rise to a relatively strong sex drive. Thus, many adolescents seek sexual outlets, such as masturbation.

TYPES OF SEXUAL BEHAVIORS IN ADOLESCENCE

Adolescents are generally pressed by high levels of sex hormones and interested in seeking sex outlets. These outlets include masturbation and sex with others, including members of the other sex and the same sex.

Masturbation　Masturbation—sexual self-stimulation—is the most common sexual outlet in adolescence. Even before children imagine sexual experiences with others, they may learn that touching their own genitals can produce pleasure.

Surveys indicate that most adolescents masturbate at some time. The well-known Kinsey studies, published in the mid-twentieth century (Kinsey et al., 1948, 1953), suggested that masturbation was nearly universal among male adolescents but less common among adolescent females. This gender difference is confirmed in nearly every survey (Kaestle & Allen, 2011; Schmitt et al., 2012). Boys who masturbate may do so several times a week, on average, much more frequently than most girls who masturbate. It is unclear whether this gender difference reflects a stronger sex drive in boys, greater social constraints on girls, or both. Beliefs that masturbation is harmful and guilt about masturbation tend to lessen the incidence of masturbation, although masturbation has not been shown to be physically harmful (Kaestle & Allen, 2011).

Nocturnal emission　Involuntary ejaculation of seminal fluid while asleep. Also referred to as a "wet dream," although the individual need not be dreaming about sex, or dreaming at all, at the time.

Gynecomastia　Overdevelopment of a male's breasts.

Male–Female Sexual Behavior Adolescents today start dating and going out earlier than in past generations. Teens who date earlier are more likely to engage in sexual activity during high school (Temple et al., 2012; Waylen et al., 2010). Teens who initiate sexual activity earlier are also less likely to use contraception and more likely to become pregnant (Temple et al., 2012). But early dating does not always lead to early sex, and early sex does not always lead to unwanted pregnancies. Still, some young women find their options in adulthood restricted by a chain of events that began in early adolescence.

TRUTH OR FICTION REVISITED: It is true that petting is practically universal among American adolescents and has been for many generations. Adolescents use petting to express affection, satisfy their curiosities, heighten their sexual arousal, and reach orgasm while avoiding pregnancy and maintaining virginity. Many adolescents do not think that they have had sex if they stop short of vaginal intercourse. Girls are more likely than boys to be coerced into petting and to feel guilty about it (Gavin et al., 2009).

Since the early 1990s, the percentage of high school students who have engaged in sexual intercourse has been gradually declining. The incidences of kissing, "making out," oral sex, and sexual intercourse all increase with age. Figure 13.5 summarizes some findings about teenage male–female sexual behavior with results from the National Survey of Family Growth (Martinez et al., 2011). Despite a gradual decline in the incidence of sexual intercourse over the past 25 years, the incidence of never-married teenagers between the ages of 15 and 19 who have had sex remains between 40% and 45%. Note from Figure 13.6 that in recent years, teenagers have also become more careful to use contraception—even the first time they are having sex. Some two out of three teens used a condom and about one out of six females were using birth control pills. That does not mean that these girls were using the pill to prevent pregnancy. You have to plan ahead to use the pill for that purpose. Many teenage females use the pill to regularize their menstrual periods or to help cope with menstrual discomfort.

Some teenagers do not intend for their first sexual experience to happen. Rather, they perceive it as simply happening to them (Martinez et al., 2011). According to the National Survey of Family Growth, females were more likely than males to say they didn't want it to happen (see Table 13.4). In fact, the largest number of females had mixed feelings about it. But the great majority of males were likely to report that they really wanted it to happen (Martinez et al., 2011).

Table 13.5 on page 391 shows why teenagers say they have abstained from having sex. Overall, the main reason for abstaining for females is that having sex is against their religious beliefs or moral values. For males, religious or moral beliefs

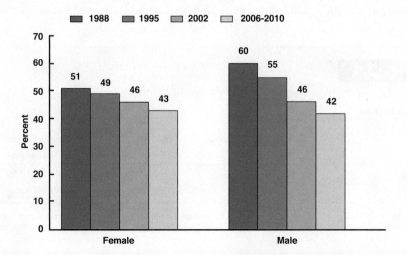

FIGURE: 13.5 Never-Married Teenagers, Aged 15–19, Who Have Had Sexual Intercourse

Source: Martinez, G., Copen, C. E., & Abma, J. C. (2011). Teenagers in the United States: Sexual activity, contraceptive use, and childbearing, 2006–2010. National Survey of Family Growth. National Center for Health Statistics. *Vital and Health Statistics, 23*(31), Figure 1.

FIGURE 13.6 Use of Contraception at First Sexual Intercourse

Source: Martinez, G., Copen, C. E., & Abma, J. C. (2011). Teenagers in the United States: Sexual activity, contraceptive use, and childbearing, 2006–2010. National Survey of Family Growth. National Center for Health Statistics. *Vital Health Statistics, 23*(31), Figure 2.

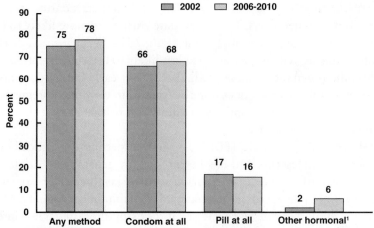

¹Includes Lunelle injectable, emergency contraception, and contraceptive patch in 2002; adds contraceptive ring (Nuva-Ring) and implant in 2006-2010.

and not having found the right person are somewhat of a tie. European Americans were much less likely than Latin Americans or African Americans to be worried about pregnancy or sexually transmitted infections. In terms of socioeconomic status, it is possible that European Americans have greater access to preventive measures.

The incidences of kissing, petting, oral sex, and sexual intercourse all increase with age (McLeod & Knight 2010). For example, according to a CDC survey, 42% of girls aged 15 to 17 reported engaging in oral sex as compared to 72% of girls aged 18 to 19 (Mosher et al., 2005). Among adolescents who have not engaged in sexual intercourse, the lowest rates of oral sex—about 19%—were for adolescents who cited moral or religious reasons for abstaining from sexual intercourse. Some adolescent couples use oral sex as a means of maintaining virginity and preventing pregnancy.

Motives for Intercourse Premarital intercourse is motivated by a number of factors. The pubertal surge of sex hormones directly activates sexual arousal, at least among boys (Petersen & Hyde, 2011). But about half of the men (51%) and one-quarter of the women (24%) in the National Health and Social Life Survey (NHSLS) reported that the main reason for their first experience was curiosity, or "readiness for sex" (Michael et al., 1994, p. 93). Hormonal changes stoke the development of secondary sex characteristics. Some early maturers are pressured into dating or sex—ready or not.

Motives including love, desire for pleasure, conformity to peer norms, peer recognition, even the desire to dominate someone are involved in sexual activity (Browning et al., 2000; O'Donnell et al., 2003). The NHSLS found that affection for

Table 13.4

Attitudes of Teenagers Ages 15–19 Toward Their First Sexual Intercourse

	Didn't Want It to Happen	Had Mixed Feelings	Really Wanted It to Happen
Females	10.8%	48%	41.2%
Males	5%	32.5%	62.5%

Source: Martinez, G., Copen, C. E., & Abma, J. C. (2011). Teenagers in the United States: Sexual activity, contraceptive use, and childbearing, 2006–2010. National Survey of Family Growth. National Center for Health Statistics. *Vital Health Statistics, 23*(31).

Table 13.5

Main Reason for Never Having Had Sex, Ages 15–19

Gender and Reason	Latin American	European American	African American
Female			
Against religion or morals	28.2%	48.3%	28.7%
Don't want to get pregnant	22.4	13.6	21.5
Don't want to get a sexually transmitted infection	10.1	5.5	13.9
Haven't found the right person yet	20.6	20.2	15.4
In a relationship, but waiting for the right time	8.1	4.7	7.4
Other reason	10.7	7.6	13.2
Male			
Against religion or morals	27.2	33.3	20.9
Don't want to get (a female) pregnant	16.8	11.1	13.4
Don't want to get a sexually transmitted infection	7.0	4.7	16.3
Haven't found the right person yet	31.8	29.0	25.9
In a relationship, but waiting for the right time	7.5	12.0	12.7
Other reason	9.7	9.8	10.6

Source: Martinez, G., Copen, C. E., & Abma, J. C. (2011). Teenagers in the United States: Sexual activity, contraceptive use, and childbearing, 2006–2010. National Survey of Family Growth. National Center for Health Statistics. *Vital Health Statistics, 23*(31), Table 15.

the partner was the primary reason for first intercourse among nearly half (48%) of the women and one-quarter (25%) of the men sampled (Michael et al., 1994). Betsy believed she was in love:

> I was 17 when I had my first sexual experience. I had been going out with my boyfriend for about five months, during which time he had been continually pressuring me to have sex. He made it seem as though I had to comply or he would end the relationship. Because I was deeply in love with him (or so I thought), I allowed it to happen. (McIntyre et al., 1991, p. 64)*

Adolescents may consider intercourse a sign of maturity, a way for girls to reward a loyal boyfriend, or a way to punish parents (McBride et al., 2003; O'Donnell et al., 2003). Adolescents whose friends have had sex are more likely to have sex themselves (Fava & Bay-Cheng, 2012). Sometimes the pressure comes from partners. About one-quarter (24%) of the women sampled in the NHSLS study said that they agreed to sex only for their partner's sake (Michael et al., 1994):

> *Megan* (18, California): I have felt pressure before. My first boyfriend pressured me because he knew I loved him and that he could take advantage of my feelings. I was blinded by my feelings and I had sex with him. I hated it.

---

*Copyright © 1991 by McIntyre, Formichella, Osterhout, and Green by arrangement with AVON BOOKS.

Amy (18, Washington, D.C.): I was sexually pressured by my second boyfriend. He didn't love me, but he did want to have sex. I helped him sneak into my room in the middle of the night. Just before we were about to have sex, I realized that it wasn't something I wanted to do. I wanted my first time to be with someone I loved and who loved me. I stopped him, although he tried everything to get me to say yes. The next day we broke up, and I couldn't have been happier. (McIntyre et al., 1991, pp. 4–6)*

About 8% of the men in the NHSLS study say they went along with intercourse for the sake of their partners (Michael et al., 1994). As one young man describes it:

Matt (18, New York): My girlfriend pressured me and I didn't handle it very well. I submitted so she wouldn't be mad or disappointed. (McIntyre et al., 1991, p. 65)*

The relationship between teens and their parents is a factor (Belgrave et al., 2000; Langille & Curtis, 2002). Adolescents whose parents are permissive are more likely to have premarital intercourse (Mundy, 2000). Parents who show interest in their children's behavior and communicate their expectations with understanding and respect often influence their children to show sexual restraint (National Campaign to Prevent Teen and Unplanned Pregnancy, 2012).

Male–Male and Female–Female Sexual Behavior About 4.5% of the male adolescents and 10.6% of the female adolescents in the National Survey of Family Growth (Mosher et al., 2005) report ever having "same-sex sexual contact." Among all respondents aged 15 to 44, the percentages grow to 6% for males and 11.2% for females. But again, among all respondents, the percentages drop to 2.9% for males and 4.4% for females when asked about the incidence of same-sex sexual activity in the past year. Same-sex sexual activity in adolescence can reflect limited availability of partners and not sexual orientation. Seduction of adolescents by gay male and lesbian adults is relatively rare.

Many gay males and lesbians, of course, develop a firm sense of being gay during adolescence. Coming to terms with adolescence is often a struggle in itself, but it is usually more intense for people who are gay (see Chapter 10). Adolescents can be particularly cruel in their stigmatization, referring to gay peers as "homos," "queers," "faggots," and other derogatory names. Many adolescent gays therefore feel isolated and cloak their sexual orientation.

TEENAGE PREGNANCY

The title of this section is "loaded": It suggests that there is a problem with teenage pregnancy. So let's toss in a couple of caveats at the beginning. First, throughout most of history, even most of the history of the United States, girls first became pregnant in their teens. Second, throughout most cultures in the world today, girls are first becoming pregnant in their teens (Save the Children, 2011). Why, then, do we bother with a section on this topic? The answer is that in the United States today, nine of ten adolescents who become pregnant do so accidentally and without committed partners (Guttmacher Institute, 2012). Most young women in developed nations defer pregnancy until after they have completed some or all of their education. Many defer pregnancy until they are well into their careers—in their late 20s, their 30s, even their 40s. So it is in our place and time that we have a topic called "Teenage Pregnancy," implying that there might be a problem with it. 👁

👁 **Watch** the **Video**
Teen Pregnancy
on **MyDevelopmentLab**

---

*Ibid.

So in our culture, today, why do teenage girls become pregnant? For one thing, adolescent girls typically get little advice in school or at home about how to deal with boys' sexual advances. Another reason is failure to use contraception. Some initiate sex at very early ages, when they are least likely to use contraception (Ali & Dwyer, 2011). Many adolescent girls, especially younger adolescents, do not have access to contraceptive devices. Among those who do, fewer than half use them reliably (Teen Pregnancy Prevention and United States Students, 2011).

Some teenage girls purposefully get pregnant to try to force their partners to make a commitment to them. Some are rebelling against their parents or the moral standards of their communities. But most girls are impregnated because they and their partners do not know as much about reproduction and contraception as they think they do or because they miscalculate the odds of getting pregnant (National Campaign to Prevent Teen and Unplanned Pregnancy, 2012). Even those who have been to all the sex education classes and who have access to family-planning clinics slip up now and then, especially if their partners push them or do not want to use condoms.

TRUTH OR **FICTION** REVISITED: For all these reasons, it is true that about 700,000 teenage girls in the United States were impregnated in 2010, the most recent year for which the government has been able to collect data. The pregnancies in 2010 resulted in about 368,000 births (Figure 13.7) and somewhat fewer abortions. However large this number may sound, it is the same number that we see from the mid-1940s. Keep in mind that in the 1940s, the population of the United States was less than 130 million. We have the same number of births today with a population of some 310 million—about two and one-half times as many people! There is also a drop of 10% from 2009 to 2010. Therefore, the current pregnancy rate for girls aged 15 to 19 may be seen as (relatively) good news. The drop-off may reflect findings that sexual activity among teenagers has leveled off and that relatively more adolescents are using condoms (Guttmacher Institute, 2012; Martinez et al., 2011). Researchers at the Centers for Disease Control and Prevention also attribute the drop-off in careless sex to educational efforts by schools, the media, religious institutions, and communities (National Campaign to Prevent Teen and Unplanned Pregnancy, 2012).

Let us now consider the ethnic/racial breakdown of these numbers. Figure 13.8 compares the teenage pregnancy rates from four years: 1991, 2005, 2007, and 2010. The figure shows that Latina teenagers currently have the highest pregnancy rates (55.7 per 1,000 girls aged 15 to 19), and Asian Americans have the lowest teenage pregnancy rates (10.9 per 1,000 girls of the same age range). How do we interpret these findings? We could say that Latin American and African American teenagers have the highest pregnancy rates, and that would be accurate (Khurana et al., 2011).

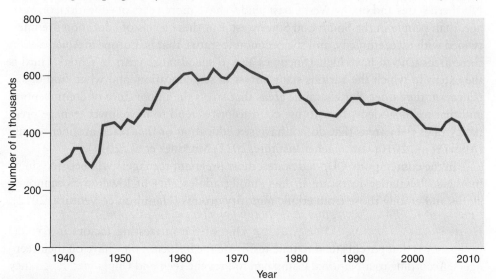

FIGURE 13.7 Number of Births for Women Aged 15–19: United States, 1940–2010

Source: Hamilton, B. E., & Ventura, S. J. (2012). Birth rates for U.S. teenagers reach historic lows for all age and ethnic groups. NCHS data brief, No. 89. Hyattsville, MD. National Center for Health Statistics, Figure 2.

FIGURE: 13.8 Birth Rates for Women Aged 15–19, by Race and Ethnicity

Source: Hamilton, B. E., & Ventura, S. J. (2012). Birth rates for U.S. teenagers reach historic lows for all age and ethnic groups. NCHS data brief, No. 89. Hyattsville, MD. National Center for Health Statistics, Figure 3.

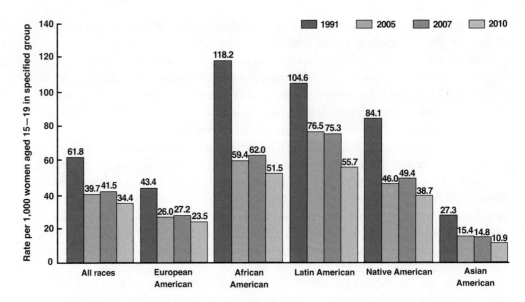

On the other hand, we can focus on the fact that the overall teenage pregnancy rate for all races has dropped by about half since 1991. We can also note that the teenage pregnancy rate from African Americans has dropped by more than half since 1991 (from 118.2 per 1,000 women to 51.5 per 1,000 women), and that the rate for Latin Americans has dropped by nearly half (from 104.6 per 1,000 women to 55.7 per 1,000 women)! According to the National Center for Health Statistics (Hamilton & Ventura, 2012), if the overall birth rates for teenagers had remained as they were in 1991, we would have had another *3.4 million* children born to them by today.

Now let us consider differences in teenage birth rates among the states, as shown in Figure 13.9. If we look at broad regions of the United States, we see that teenage birth rates are lowest in the New England states. The birth rates are generally highest in the South and the Southwest. According to the National Center for Health Statistics (Hamilton & Ventura, 2012), there are a number of factors to consider—for example, the racial and ethnic makeup of the various states. New England, for example, is one of the areas of the country most densely population by European Americans. The South and the Southwest tend to have higher percentages of Latin Americans and African Americans in the population, and these groups continue to have the highest teenage birth rates, although, as noted earlier, the numbers have dropped by half over the past couple of decades. Second is the general level of education. Americans in the Northern states and on the West Coast tend to have more years of education, on average, than people in the South and Southwest. But these levels of education are intertwined with race, ethnicity, and socioeconomic status; that is, European Americans in these areas tend to have higher incomes and to spend more years in school. Third is the extent to which the various states invest in sex education, and what kind of sex education they offer. For example, areas that stress the importance of contraception and that teach students how to use contraceptives tend to have lower teenage pregnancy rates than areas that do not have sex education or that teach abstinence only (Abma et al., 2010; Guttmacher Institute, 2012; Martinez et al., 2011).

In the contemporary United States, most pregnant teenagers will become single mothers. Pregnancy rates are higher among adolescents of lower socioeconomic status and among those from ethnic minority groups (Hamilton & Ventura, 2012).

Combating Teenage Pregnancy One of the interesting factors in teenage pregnancy is that parents tend to underestimate the influence they have on their teenagers. According to a National Campaign to Prevent Teen and Unplanned Pregnancy

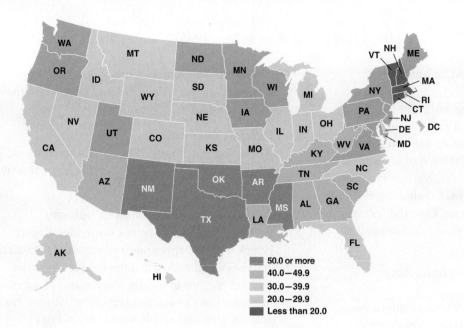

FIGURE: 13.9 Birth Rates for Women Aged 15–19, by State, United States

Source: Hamilton, B. E., & Ventura, S. J. (2012). Birth rates for U.S. teenagers reach historic lows for all age and ethnic groups. NCHS data brief, No. 89. Hyattsville, MD. National Center for Health Statistics, Figure 6.

Legend:
- 50.0 or more
- 40.0—49.9
- 30.0—39.9
- 20.0—29.9
- Less than 20.0

(2003) poll of several thousand teenagers, 88% said it would be easier for them to postpone sex and avoid pregnancy if they could have more open discussions with their parents! Yet nearly one teen in four (23%) said that they had never discussed sex, contraception, or pregnancy with their parents. *PARENTS: Talk to your kids!*

Other means for combating teenage pregnancy include sex education and free contraceptive services. Given the effects of sex education in other industrialized countries, many helping professionals believe that the rate of teenage pregnancy and the spread of STIs in the United States could be curtailed through education and provision of contraceptives. 👁

Pregnancy prevention programs in the schools range from encouraging teens to delay sex ("Just say no.") to providing information about contraception to distributing condoms or referring students to contraceptive clinics (Jemmott et al., 2010). Abstinence is the best way to prevent pregnancy and HIV/AIDS, but does sex education that advises "abstinence only" work? States most likely to teach "abstinence only" are also those with the highest rates of teenage pregnancy. However, one study with 662 African American children (mean age = 12.2 years) reduced the incidence of sexual intercourse over the next two years through an eight-hour program that discussed the practical problems rather than the moral issues associated with teenage pregnancy (Jemmott et al., 2010). About one-third of youngsters in the program reported engaging in intercourse over the next two years, as opposed to nearly half of those who were in a control group in which there was a general discussion of health. "Moralistic" programs that promote abstinence until marriage are less effective (Rodriguez, 2010). In any event, three out of four large school districts in the United States also provide instruction about methods of contraception and prevention of STIs.

Blake and her colleagues (2003) surveyed more than 4,000 high school students in Massachusetts. About 20% of their schools made condoms available to students. Distributing condoms did not increase the percentage of students who were sexually active; however, it led to more consistent use of condoms among students who were already sexually active. In sum:

> Studies consistently show that making condoms available to students does not increase any measure of their sexual behavior—whether the teens have sex, how frequently they have it, or the number of partners they have. And some studies show that the percentage of teens having sex declined after condoms were made available to them. (Kirchheimer & Smith, 2003)

👁─Watch the Video
Debate Over Abstinence Only Education
on **MyDevelopmentLab**

CRITICAL THINKING
Where do you stand on the issue as to whether school districts should make contraceptive devices available to students? On what do you base your views? Moral values? Research findings? Explain. As an intellectual exercise, can you argue a point of view opposed to your own?

Chapter Review
✓ Study and Review on MyDevelopmentLab

LO1 Describe sexually-related behaviors in infancy

Male fetuses have erections; male and female fetuses suck their fingers. Stimulation of the genitals in infancy may produce sensations of pleasure. Pelvic thrusting has been observed as early as eight months of age. Masturbation may begin at 6 to 12 months. Co-sleeping does not affect sexual development. Gay and lesbian parents are no more likely than heterosexuals to have gay or lesbian children.

LO2 Describe sexually-related behaviors in early childhood

Statistics concerning the incidence of masturbation at ages 3 to 8 is speculative. In early childhood, children show curiosity about the genitals and may play "doctor." Same-sex sexual activity play may be more common than heterosexual play and does not foreshadow sexual orientation.

LO3 Describe sexual behaviors in preadolescence

Preadolescents tend to socialize with same-sex peers and to become self-conscious about their bodies. Masturbation is the primary means of obtaining orgasm in preadolescence. Preadolescent sex play often involves mutual display of the genitals, with or without touching. Much preadolescent same-sex sexual behavior involves exploration and is short-lived.

LO4 Discuss the purposes and outcomes of sex education

Despite the increased availability of sex-education programs, friends remain a major source of sexual information. Adolescents actually talk to their parents about sex more frequently than commonly believed. Sex education has not been shown to increase the incidence of sexual behaviors among adolescents.

LO5 Define adolescence

Adolescence is bounded at its beginning by the advent of puberty and at its end by the capacity to take on adult responsibilities.

LO6 Describe the milestones of puberty

Puberty is ushered in by sex hormones. Puberty begins with the appearance of secondary sex characteristics and ends when the long bones make no further gains in length. Most major changes in primary sex characteristics occur within three years in girls and within four years in boys.

LO7 Describe sexual behaviors in adolescence

Masturbation is a major sexual outlet during adolescence. Many adolescents use petting as a way of achieving sexual gratification without becoming pregnant or ending their virginity. The incidence of premarital intercourse, especially for females, has increased dramatically since Kinsey's day. A minority of adolescents report sexual experience with people of the same sex, mostly with age-mates. Most of these sexual encounters are transitory. Adolescence is often more tumultuous for gay males and lesbians, largely because of stigmatization.

LO8 Discuss issues related to teenage pregnancy

About 700,000 adolescents in the United States become pregnant each year. Factors in teenage pregnancy include lack of closeness with parents, low interest and achievement in academics, and inconsistent use of contraceptives.

Test Your Learning

1. According to Kinsey, children first engage in behaviors that resemble orgasm
    (a) in infancy.
    (b) between the ages of 5 and 6.
    (c) between the ages of 6 and 11.
    (d) between the ages of 12 and adulthood.

2. It is *not* true that
    (a) teenage girls become pregnant despite using contraceptives.
    (b) pregnant teenagers obtain a good deal of support from their partner.
    (c) most teenage pregnancies are by choice.
    (d) babies of teenage mothers are healthier than babies of mothers in their 20s.

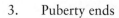

3. Puberty ends

   (a) with the appearance of primary sex characteristics.
   (b) with the appearance of secondary sex characteristics.
   (c) when people assume adult responsibilities.
   (d) when the long bones make no further gains in length.

4. Estrogen does *not* cause

   (a) growth of the uterus.
   (b) growth of fatty and supporting tissue in the breasts and buttocks.
   (c) growth of underarm and pubic hair.
   (d) thickening of the vaginal lining.

5. _____ encourage(s) teenagers to abstain from premarital sexual intercourse.

   (a) Curiosity about sex
   (b) High educational goals
   (c) Peer pressure
   (d) Poor communication with parents

6. According to the Guttmacher Institute, about _____% of teenage pregnancies in the United States end in abortion.

   (a) 10
   (b) 30
   (c) 50
   (d) 70

7. Sex games like "show" and "playing doctor" become common between the ages of

   (a) 1 and 2.
   (b) 3 and 7.
   (c) 8 and 10.
   (d) 11 and 15.

8. About how many U.S. adolescents become pregnant each year?

   (a) 7,000
   (b) 70,000
   (c) 700,000
   (d) 7,000,000

9. Research shows that teenaged girls are most likely to become pregnant in

   (a) New York State.
   (b) California.
   (c) New Hampshire.
   (d) Texas.

10. Teenage girls are most likely to talk to their parents about

    (a) how to say no to sex.
    (b) where to get birth control.
    (c) how to prevent HIV/AIDS.
    (d) how to use a condom.

Answers: 1. a; 2. d; 3. d; 4. c; 5. b; 6. b; 7. b; 8. c; 9. d; 10. a

My Life, My Sexuality

Talking with Your Children about Sex

*Explore this **My Life, My Sexuality** feature by scanning this QR code with your mobile device. If you don't already have one, you may download a free QR scanner for your device wherever smartphone apps are sold. You can also view this feature in MyDevelopmentLab, along with an accompanying critical thinking assignment.*

"Daddy, where do babies come from?"

"What are you asking me for? Go ask your mother."

Many children and adolescents do not find it easy to talk to their parents about sex. Yet most young children are curious about where babies come from, about how girls and boys differ, and so on. Parents who avoid discussing these matters convey their own uneasiness about sex and may teach children that sex is something to be ashamed of. Scan the code to learn more about how to provide your children with accurate information in a form they can understand.

14 Sexuality in Adulthood

Learning Objectives

BEING SINGLE

LO1 Describe the various motives and lifestyles of single people

LO2 Explain what is meant by "hooking up"

COHABITATION: "DARLING, WOULD YOU BE MY POSSLQ?"

LO3 Describe the incidence of cohabitation and public attitudes toward cohabitation

LO4 Discuss the relationships between cohabitation marriage

MARRIAGE: TYING THE KNOT

LO5 Discuss the changing incidence of marriage

LO6 Describe types of marriage

LO7 Discuss whom we marry

LO8 Discuss the rise of intermarriage in the United States

LO9 Discuss sex in marriage

LO10 Discuss factors in marital satisfaction

LO11 Discuss infidelity

DIVORCE: BREAKING BONDS

LO12 Discuss the incidence of divorce and issues connected with divorce

SEX IN THE LATER YEARS

LO13 Describe physical changes in the later years that affect sexual behavior

LO14 Discuss patterns of sexual activity in the later years

SEX AND DISABILITY

LO15 Discuss the relationships between physical disabilities and sexual behavior

LO16 Discuss the relationships between intellectual disabilities and sexual behavior

MY LIFE, MY SEXUALITY: MAKING DECISIONS ABOUT YOUR STYLE OF LIFE

Explore the video, **What's In It for Me?: The Dating Game,** by scanning this QR code with your mobile device. If you don't already have one, you may download a free QR scanner for your device wherever smartphone apps are sold. You can also view this video in MyDevelopmentLab. For more videos related to this chapter's content, log into MyDevelopmentLab to view the entire Human Sexuality Video Series.

TRUTH OR FICTION?

Which of the following statements are the truth, and which are fiction? Look for the Truth-or-Fiction icons on the pages that follow to find the answers.

1   Being single has become a more common U.S. lifestyle over the past few decades.   **T   F**?

2   Divorced people are more likely than never-married people to cohabit.   **T   F**?

3   Most of today's sophisticated young people see nothing wrong with an occasional extramarital fling.   **T   F**?

4   Few women can reach orgasm after the age of 70.   **T   F**?

5   People who are paralyzed because of spinal cord injuries cannot become sexually aroused or engage in sexual intercourse.   **T   F**?

mericans entering adulthood today face a wider range of sexual choices and lifestyles than those available to earlier generations. The sexual revolution loosened traditional constraints on sexual choices, especially for women. Couples experiment with lifestyles that would have been unthinkable in earlier generations. An increasing number of young people choose to remain single as a way of life, not merely as a way station preceding the arrival of Mr. or Ms. Right. Fifty years ago, a couple's living together without being married was dubbed "living in sin"; today many consider it to be a normal stage of courtship.

In this chapter, we discuss diverse forms of adult sexuality in the United States today, including being single, marriage, and alternative lifestyles such as cohabitation, open marriage, and group marriage. Let us begin as people begin—with being single.

Being Single

1

TRUTH OR **FICTION** REVISITED: Recent years have seen a sharp increase in the numbers of single young people in our society. Being single, not married, is now the most common lifestyle among people in their early 20s. Marriages may be made in heaven, but many Americans are saying heaven can wait. By 2000, one woman in four and three men in ten in the United States 15 years of age and older had never married. Half a century earlier, in 1950, one woman in five and about one man in four aged 15 and above had never been married. The rate of marriages had also fallen off. More than four men in five (84%) in the 20 to 24 age range were unmarried, up from 55% in 1970. By 2000, the number of single women in this age group had doubled to 73% from 36% in 1970 (U.S. Bureau of the Census, 2006).

Several factors contribute to the increased proportion of singles. For one thing, more people are postponing marriage to pursue educational and career goals. Many young people are deciding to "live together" (cohabit), at least for a while, rather than get married. Also, as you can see in Table 14.1, people are getting married later. The typical man in the United States gets married at about age 29 today, compared with age 23 just 50 years earlier (U.S. Bureau of the Census, 2006). The typical woman gets married today at 26 to 27; 50 years earlier, the typical woman married at age 20.

Single-mother family groups have doubled to more than one-quarter of all families as compared with three decades ago (U.S. Bureau of the Census, 2005). Some of these women started their families as single mothers, but the increased prevalence of divorce also swells the ranks.

Table 14.1

Median Age at First Marriage, by Gender: 1950 to 2011

Year	Males	Females
2011	28.7	26.5
2010	28.2	26.1
2000	26.8	25.1
1990	26.1	23.9
1980	24.7	22.0
1970	23.2	20.8
1960	22.8	20.3
1950	22.8	20.3

Source: U.S. Bureau of the Census. (2011). Table MS-2. Estimated median age at first marriage, by sex: 1890 to the present.

Singles. There is no single "singles scene." Although some singles meet in singles' bars, many meet in more casual settings, such as the neighborhood laundromat. Some singles advertise online or in newspapers or magazines.

Single people face less social stigma today. Although they are less likely today to be perceived as socially inadequate or as failures, some unmarried people still encounter stereotypes. Men who have never married may be suspected of being gay. Single women may feel that men perceive them as "loose." At least today, though, women over the age of 30 are unlikely to be regarded as "spinsters" (Edwards, 2000).

Many single people do not choose to be single. Some remain single because they have not yet found Mr. or Ms. Right. Yet, many young people see being single as an alternative, open-ended way of life—not a temporary stage that precedes marriage. As career options for women have expanded, women are not as financially dependent on men as their mothers and grandmothers were. A number of career women, like career-oriented men, choose to remain single (at least for a time) to focus on their careers.

Being single is not without its problems. Many single people are lonely. Some singles express concerns about a lack of a steady, meaningful social relationship. Others, usually women, worry about their physical safety. Some people living alone find it difficult to satisfy their needs for intimacy, companionship, sex, and emotional support. Despite these concerns, most singles are well adjusted and content. Singles who have a greater number of friends and a supportive social network tend to be more satisfied with their lifestyles.

There is no typical "singles scene." Single people differ in their sexual interests and lifestyles. Many achieve emotional and psychological security through a network of intimate relationships with friends. Most are sexually active and practice **serial monogamy.** Other singles have a primary sexual relationship with one steady partner but occasional brief flings. A few, even in this age of AIDS, are "swinging singles." That is, they pursue casual sexual encounters, or "one-night stands."

Some singles remain celibate, either by choice or due to lack of opportunity. People choose **celibacy** for a number of reasons. Nuns and priests do so for religious reasons. Others believe that celibacy allows them to focus their energies and attention on work or to commit themselves to an important cause. They see celibacy as a temporary accommodation to other pursuits. Others remain celibate because they view sex outside of marriage as immoral. Still others are celibate because they find the prospects of sexual activity aversive or unalluring, or because of fears of STIs.

CRITICAL THINKING

People face a variety of sources of pressure to get married. Which arguments for getting married or remaining single make sense to you? Why?

Serial monogamy A pattern of involvement in one exclusive relationship after another, as opposed to engaging in multiple sexual relationships at the same time.

Celibacy Complete sexual abstinence. (Sometimes used to describe the state of being unmarried, especially in the case of people who take vows to remain celibate.)

Using data from the National Survey of Family Growth, Laura Duberstein Lindberg and Susheela Singh (2008) analyzed the self-reported behavior of a nationally representative sample of 6,493 women. They found that 36% of the women aged 20 to 44 were single, and 9 in 10 of the single women had engaged in sexual intercourse. Seventy percent of the sexually initiated women were sexually active at the time of the study, and they had engaged in intercourse during 7 of the previous 12 months. A higher percentage of the single women (22%) than of married (2%) or cohabiting (9%) women reported having two or more sex partners during the past year.

DATING—HOOKING UP? HAVING FRIENDS WITH BENEFITS?

People are single prior to getting married, following divorce, and when widowed. Some people remain single for a lifetime. Throughout those years many of them date, although the term *dating* is not usually heard among people of high school or college age these days. We are more likely to hear of young people *seeing* one another, or in the case of an abrupt decision to engage in sexual activity without a mutual expectation of a romantic commitment, "hooking up." They meet in class, on campus, at sporting events, at parties, in cafeterias—wherever—and "hook up" (Felder & Carey, 2010). Going out on a date is likely to be something their parents did, or something you do if you hook up with somebody online.

A prospective study of 140 first-semester college students (109 women and 31 men) sought to determine whether assumed predictors of hooking up actually did so (Felder & Carey, 2010). Possible predictors included male gender, having divorced parents, having hooked up prior to college, the assumption that (nearly) everyone is doing it, less religiosity, permissive parental attitudes, permissive media messages, and drinking. Heavy drinking may lower sexual inhibitions, heighten susceptibility to social pressure, and boost one's confidence to approach a potential sex partner. The researchers also predicted that females who reported lower self-esteem, more stress, greater parental discouragement of relationships, more desire to be carefree in college, and more career-mindedness would be more likely to hook up. They found that one-third of the students had had hookups with oral sex during their first semester, and that such hookups could be predicted by drinking, precollege sexual behavior, and a conducive setting, such as a bar or a party where people danced slowly and groped one another (see Figure 14.1). Twenty-eight percent of the participants reported hookups with vaginal penetration. Men were more likely than women to engage in vaginal hookups, which were also predicted by precollege sexual behavior, drinking, and a conducive setting. Key additional findings were that women who had written early in the semester that they would refuse vaginal hookups in fact did so. Parental discouragement of relationships predicted more oral sex hookups. Hookups with vaginal penetration also increased the stress reported by women, but not men. The self-esteem of the men rose with their number of sexual hookups, while the reverse pattern was true for the women.

Single people sometimes engage in serial monogamy—a series of relationships that may or may not be long term, which may have the potential to turn into marriages. Some have casual relationships with **friends with benefits (FWBs)** that might coexist with other relationships (Bogle, 2008). Also known as *friends with privileges* or *cut friends,* these are people for casual sexual relationships. Friends with benefits are usually intended to meet singles'

CRITICAL THINKING

Why do you think the relationship between sexual hookups and self-esteem differed for college men and women in the Felder and Carey (2010) study? Why do you think that parental discouragements of relationships apparently contributed to hookups with oral sex for college women?

Friend with benefits (FWB) A friend with whom a person has a sexual but not a romantic relationship.

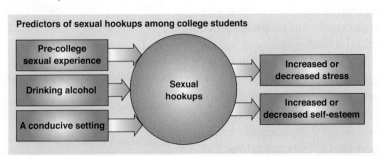

FIGURE 14.1 Contributors to Sexual Hookups among College Students and Possible Outcomes. How do the outcomes differ according to gender in the Felder and Carey (2010) study?

sexual needs rather than their romantic needs. Sometimes cut friends engage in sexual intercourse; sometimes they stay at second or third base, with mutual masturbation or oral sex. Relationships with FWBs are usually intended to be temporary and to end when either partner wishes it to, as when she or he finds Mr. or Ms. Right.

Divorced or widowed singles may be somewhat more formal in their dating practices for a number of reasons. One is that they come from an older cohort, perhaps one that was not as current with contemporary values (although many of them were a part of the sexual revolution!). They are likely to be concerned that they cannot make small talk about current pop stars and trends. (Neither can their peers, of course.) Another is that many of them have children for whom they are responsible, serious jobs, and mortgages, and consequently cannot afford to be as playful and adventurous as younger, less-burdened singles. They may also be more concerned about their bodies—more desirous of making love with the lights off, if a relationship develops to that point. Then, too, those who have been divorced may have been painfully "burned" by a former relationship, or former relationships, and not be ready to jump quickly. In these cases, dinner, nice clothing, a movie, even flowers—all the classic trappings—may be in order.

Divorced people, like other singles, go on dates. Some have been "burned" by a past relationship and are not ready to "hook up" quickly. They appreciate all the trappings of a real date—dinner, getting dressed up, a movie, and flowers.

Cohabitation: "Darling, Would You Be My POSSLQ?"

There is nothing I would not do
If you would be my POSSLQ
    —Charles Osgood

POSSLQ? POSSLQ is the unromantic abbreviation that was introduced by the U.S. Bureau of the Census to refer to **cohabitation**. It stands for "People of Opposite Sex Sharing Living Quarters" and applies to unmarried couples who live together.

The majority of Americans in their 20s and 30s cohabit at some point (Wilcox & Marquardt, 2011). We noted at the outset of the chapter that cohabitation has become part of the social mainstream. We rarely hear it referred to as "living in sin" or "shacking up" as we did in earlier generations. People today tend to refer to cohabitation with value-free expressions such as "living together." Does the current tolerance reflect society's adjustment to the numbers of cohabiting couples? Have numbers of cohabiting couples increased as a consequence of tolerance? Both views are probably correct.

The numbers of households consisting of an unmarried adult male and female couple living together in the United States has increased more than ten-fold since 1960, from fewer than half a million couples to nearly seven-and-a-half million couples today (Wilcox & Marquardt, 2011; see Figure 14.2). Another half million households consisted of same-sex partners.

Figure 14.3 shows that the number of cohabiting couples who are living with children has also mushroomed over the past 50 years. The children may be those of

Cohabitation. Cohabitation was once referred to as "living in sin," but it has become an increasingly common lifestyle. Some sociologists predict that cohabitation will replace marriage as the nation's most popular lifestyle sometime during this century.

Cohabitation Living together as though married but without legal sanction.

FIGURE 14.2 Number of Cohabiting, Unmarried Adult Couples of the Opposite Sex, by Year, United States

Source: U.S. Census Bureau.

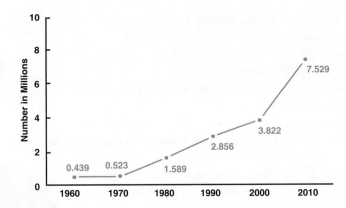

the cohabiting couple or children that the couple brings into the relationship from previous or other relationships (Kennedy & Bumpass, 2011).

More than half the marriages that take place are preceded by living together (Wilcox & Marquardt, 2011). There is a 75% probability that a cohabiting European American woman will marry her partner if the couple cohabits for five years (Bramlett & Mosher, 2002). The same study found that the probabilities drop to 61% for Latina women and 48% for African American women. Some social scientists suggest that cohabitation is a new stage of courtship for many couples. As you can see in Figure 14.4, more than half of today's high school seniors believe that it is a good idea for couples to live together before getting married to test their compatibility. Notice the dramatic rise since the more traditional days of the 1970s and the persistent gender difference: Boys are more likely than girls to say that living together before marriage is a good idea—although the gap has been narrowing. The gender difference might reflect gender differences in the perception of the value or importance of commitment in a sexual relationship. It might reflect felt differences in terms of social constraints. But a difference that was greater than ten percentage points in the 1970s through the 1980s is now five to six percentage points. In any event, trial marriages do not guarantee permanence. About 40% of couples who have cohabited and then gotten married get divorced later on.

People cohabit for many reasons. Cohabitation, like marriage, is an alternative to living alone. Partners may have deep feelings for each other but not be ready to get married. Some couples prefer cohabitation because it provides an abiding

FIGURE 14.3 Number of Cohabiting, Unmarried, Adult Couples of the Opposite Sex Living with One Child or More, by Year, United States

Source: U.S. Census Bureau.

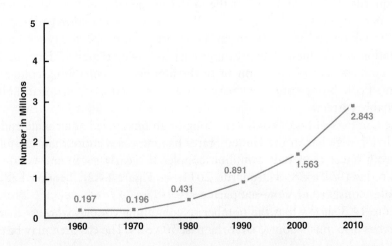

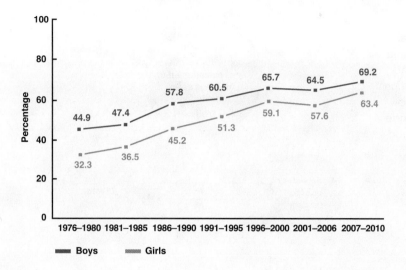

FIGURE 14.4 **Percentage of High School Seniors Who Agreed or Mostly Agreed with the Statement: "It is Usually a Good Idea for a Couple to Live Together Before Getting Married in Order to Find Out Whether They Really Get Along," by Period, United States**

Note: Number of respondents for each sex for each period is about 6,000.
Source: U.S. Census Bureau.

 2

relationship without the legal entanglements of marriage (Hussain, 2002; Marquis, 2003). And in some subcultures, cohabitation is the norm.

Willingness to cohabit is related to more liberal attitudes toward sexual behavior, less traditional views of marriage, and less traditional views of gender roles (Hsueh et al., 2009; Rhoades et al., 2009). **TRUTH** OR **FICTION** REVISITED: For example, divorced people are more likely than people who have never been married to cohabit. (Does the experience of divorce make some people more willing to share their lives than their bank accounts?) Cohabitants are less likely than noncohabitants to say that religion is very important to them (Bramlett & Mosher, 2002).

Many cohabitants are less committed to their relationships than married people are (Hsueh et al., 2009; Rhoades et al., 2009). It is more often the man who is unwilling to make a marital commitment (Peplau, 2003). Mark, a 44-year-old computer consultant, lives with Nancy and their 7-year-old daughter, Janet. Mark says, "We feel we are not primarily a couple but rather primarily individuals who happen to be a couple. It allows me to be a little more at arm's length. Men don't like committing, so maybe this is just some sort of excuse." David Popenoe of Rutgers University notes that many men cohabit because they get a "quasi-wife" without having to make a commitment (Hussain, 2002).

Economic factors also come into play. Partners may decide to cohabit because of the economic advantages of sharing household expenses. Cohabiting individuals who receive public assistance risk losing support if they get married. Some older couples cohabit rather than marry because of resistance from adult children. Some children fear that a parent will be victimized by a needy senior citizen. Others may not want their inheritances to come into question or may not want to decide where to bury the remaining parent. Younger couples may cohabit secretly to maintain parental support that they might lose if they were to get married or reveal their living arrangements.

COHABITATION AND LATER MARRIAGE: BENEFIT OR RISK?

Cohabiting couples may believe that cohabitation will strengthen eventual marriage by helping them iron out the kinks in their relationship. However, cohabitors who later marry also run a serious risk of getting divorced. According to Pamela Smock's (2000) survey at the Institute for Social Research at the University of Michigan, 40% of couples who cohabited before tying the knot got divorced later on. Cohabitors who marry may run a greater—not lesser—risk of divorce than noncohabitors. Some studies suggest that the likelihood of divorce within ten years of marriage is nearly twice as great among married couples who cohabited before marriage (Smock, 2000).

CRITICAL THINKING
Why might cohabiting couples run a greater risk of divorce than couples who did not cohabit prior to marriage? Do not assume that cohabitation causes divorce. We must always be cautious about drawing causal conclusions from correlational data. Note that none of the couples in these studies was randomly assigned to cohabitation or noncohabitation. Therefore, selection factors—the factors that lead some couples to cohabit and others not to cohabit—may explain the results (see Figure 14.5). Cohabitors tend to be more desirous of personal independence (Hsueh et al., 2009; Rhoades et al., 2009). They also tend to be less traditional and less religious than noncohabitors. All in all, people who cohabit prior to marriage tend to be less committed to the values and interests traditionally associated with the institution of marriage. The attitudes of cohabitors, not cohabitation itself, may account for their higher rates of marital dissolution.

FIGURE 14.5 Does Cohabitation Prior to Marriage Increase the Risk of Eventual Divorce? There is a correlational relationship between cohabitation prior to marriage and the risk of divorce later on. Does cohabitation increase the risk of divorce, or do other factors—such as a commitment to personal independence—contribute to both the likelihood of cohabitation and eventual divorce?

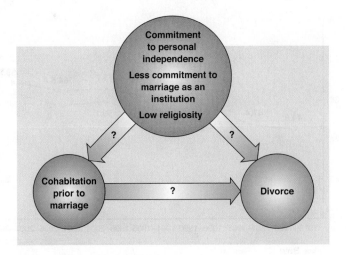

Marriage: Tying the Knot

Despite all the challenges to marriage, it remains the most common lifestyle in the United States. Figure 14.6 shows the marital status of 35- to 44-year-olds each decade from 1960, as compiled by the U.S. Bureau of the Census (Wilcox & Marquardt, 2011). This is the group of Americans who are mature enough to have completed graduate school or to have established themselves in careers. This is also a group that is young enough not to have generally suffered being widowed.

The overall percentage of American males aged 15 and above who are married declined from 69.3% in 1960 to 52.8% in 2010 (see Figure 14.7). For females the decline is from 65.9% in 1960 to 49.9% in 2010.[1] On the other hand, nearly two-thirds of American men and women ages 35 to 44 are married.

Marriage has a long and varied history. The ancient Hebrews, Greeks, and Romans lived in patriarchies in which men dominated most aspects of life. The wife was considered the husband's property: a chattel whose responsibilities consisted of childrearing and homemaking. Marriages were usually arranged by men, sometimes for financial or political gain. In classical Greece, men would turn to high-class prostitutes for sensual sex and sophisticated conversation.

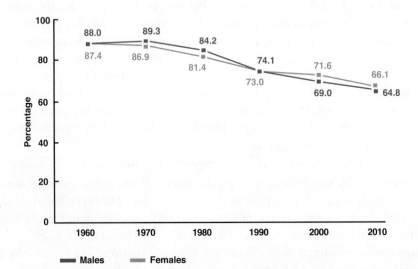

FIGURE 14.6 Percentages of Persons Age 35–44 Who Are Married, by Sex, 1960–2010, United States

Source: U.S. Census Bureau.

[1]U.S. Census Bureau, *Current Population Reports*, "America's Families and Living Arrangements" for 2010 (Table UC3), available online at www.census.gov/population/www/socdemo/hh-fam/cps2010.html.

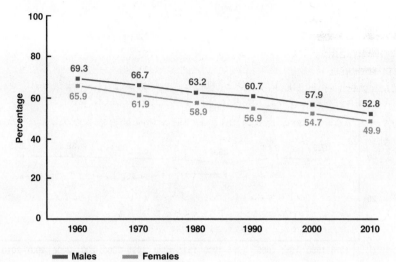

FIGURE 14.7 America's Families and Living Arrangements

Source: U.S. Census Bureau, *Current Population Reports,* "America's Families and Living Arrangements" for 2010 (Table UC3), available online at www.census.gov/population/www/socdemo/hh-fam/cps2010.html.

The Christian tradition also has a patriarchal foundation. Male dominance was legitimized by biblical scripture, as we can see in this passage from the New Testament: "Wives, submit to your own husbands, as unto the Lord. For the husband is the head of the wife, as Christ is the head of the church" (Ephesians 5:23–24).

Over time, women came to be viewed as loving companions rather than chattels. They became recognized as being capable of profiting from education. But the notion that a married woman might seek fulfillment through a career unrelated to her husband's needs is a recent development. The idea that women have a right to sexual fulfillment is also new. American couples today are more likely to share or even reverse marital roles than in the past.

A Closer Look
Is Marriage in Trouble?

So, who needs to be married? And why? After all, can't you just live together if you want to?

In the Western world, the answer would appear to be yes. You can do pretty much what you want to do. Even the bottom-line reasons for marriage are no longer as compelling as they once were. Many married people bring their own health plans into the marriage. And opinion polls are reflecting the more voluntary nature of marriage in modern times. For example, high school seniors have been asked whether they agree that people will have fuller and happier lives if they get married rather than live together or remain single. The results are shown in

Figure 14.8. About 40% of boys—but only 30% of girls!—agree with the statement. Girls have apparently been growing more skeptical over the past several decades. Could it be that many of their parents are divorced, or miserable in their marriages?

But now let us note some inconsistencies. The same high school seniors who do not necessarily agree that marriage will provide their lives with fulfillment nevertheless say that having a good marriage and family life is extremely important (see Figure 14.9).

Moreover, even though they have become more supportive of cohabitation and have some skepticism, they do not appear to take marriage lightly. Three out

of five female high school seniors (61.8%) and nearly as many males (56.3%) say that it is likely that once they will get married they will remain married (see Figure 14.10). The percentages have declined somewhat over the years for girls, perhaps because of the difficult and destroyed relationships many of them see around them. The numbers have remained more stable for boys. In any event, the majority of high school seniors still tend to see marriage as permanent. That doesn't mean that their marriages will in fact be permanent, but perhaps a marriage is more likely to endure when the couple does not enter into it as a temporary arrangement.

(continued on next page)

(continued from page 407)

FIGURE 14.8 Percentage of High School Seniors Who Agreed or Mostly Agreed that Most People Will Have Fuller and Happier Lives if They Choose Legal Marriage rather than Staying Single or Just Living with Someone, by Period, United States

Note: Number of respondents for each sex for each period is about 6,000.

Source: U.S. Census Bureau.

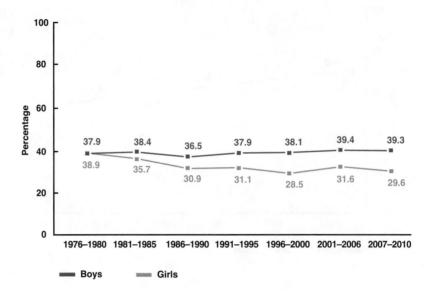

FIGURE 14.9 Percentage of High School Seniors Who Said Having a Good Marriage and Family Life is "Extremely Important," by Period, United States

Note: Number of respondents for each sex for each period is about 6,000.

Source: U.S. Census Breau.

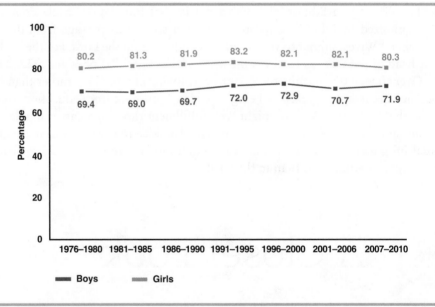

FIGURE 14.10 Percentage of High School Seniors Who Said It Is Likely They Will Stay Married to Same Person for Life, by Period, United States

Note: Number of respondents for each sex for each period is about 6,000.

Source: U.S. Census Bureau.

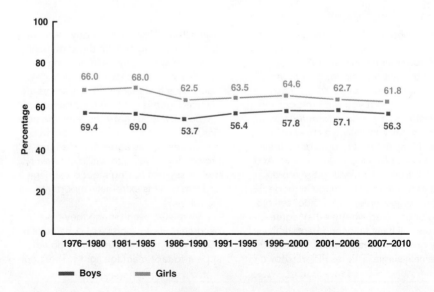
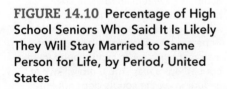

WHY DO PEOPLE GET MARRIED?

Even in this era of serial monogamy and cohabitation, people still get married. Why? Marriage meets a number of personal and cultural needs. For traditionalists—even the "traditional" polygamists we met at the beginning of the chapter—it legitimizes sexual relations. Marriage still provides a traditional institution in which children can be supported and socialized. Marriage (theoretically) restricts sexual relations so that a man can be assured—or at least assume—that his wife's children are his. Unless one has signed a prenuptial agreement to the contrary, marriage permits the orderly transmission of wealth from one family to another and from one generation to another. Notions such as romantic love, equality, and the radical concept that men as well as women would do well to aspire to the ideal of faithfulness are recent additions to the structure of marriage in Western society. Not until the nineteenth century did the notion of love as a basis for marriage become widespread in Western culture.

Today, because more people believe that premarital sex is acceptable between two people who feel affectionate toward each other, the desire for sex is less likely to motivate marriage. But marriage provides a sense of security and opportunities to share feelings, experiences, and ideas with someone with whom one forms a special attachment. Even younger people still buy into the notion that marriage is important for people who plan to spend the rest of their lives together (Wilcox & Marquardt, 2011).

Broadly speaking, many people in the United States today want to get married because they believe that they will be happier. A poll by the National Marriage Project (Wilcox & Marquardt, 2011) does suggest that they are likely to be happier (Figure 14.11) and less depressed (Figure 14.12) than people who are cohabiting or are single.

TYPES OF MARRIAGE

There are several types of marriage. Among male and female couples, we have two types: monogamy and polygamy. In **monogamy**, a husband and wife are wed only to each other. But let us not confuse monogamy, which is a form of matrimony, with sexual exclusivity. People who are monogamously wed often do have extramarital

Monogamy Marriage to one person.

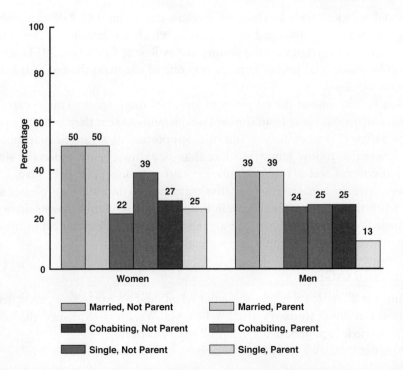

FIGURE 14.11 Predicted Probability of Being "Very Happy" with Life for 18- to 46-Year-Olds, by Marital Status and Parenthood

Source: W. Bradford Wilcox & Elizabeth Marquardt (Eds.) *The State of Our Unions: Marriage in America 2011.* Reprinted by permission of the National Marriage Project at the University of Virginia and the Institute for American Values. marriage@virginia.edu, Figure 1, p. 8.

FIGURE 14.12 Predicted Probability of Being Depressed among 24- to 28-Year-Olds, by Marital Staus and Parenthood

Source: W. Bradford Wilcox & Elizabeth Marquardt (Eds.) *The State of Our Unions: Marriage in America 2011.* Reprinted by permission of the National Marriage Project at the University of Virginia and the Institute for American Values. marriage@virginia.edu, Figure 2, p. 10.

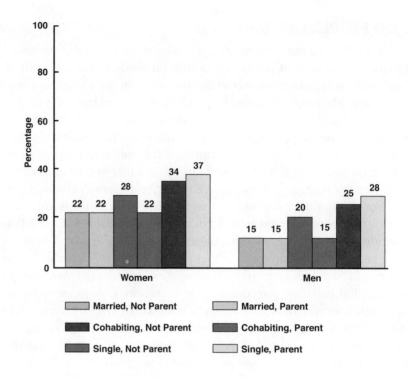

Singing the Song "Tradition." In the musical *Fiddler on the Roof,* the tradition of arranged marriage comes into conflict with the preferences of the younger generation.

Polygyny A form of marriage in which a man is married to more than one woman at the same time.

Polyandry A form of marriage in which a woman is married to more than one man at the same time.

affairs, as we shall see, but they are married to one person at a time. In polygamy, a person has more than one spouse (of the other sex) and is permitted sexual access to each of them. In gay marriage, an individual is married to someone of the same sex.

Polygyny has been the most prevalent form of polygamy among the world's preliterate societies (Ford & Beach, 1951; Frayser, 1985). **Polyandry** is relatively rare. In polygynous societies, including many Islamic societies, men are permitted to have multiple wives. Practically speaking, in many cases, only wealthy men can afford to support multiple wives and the children of these unions. But few societies have enough women to allow most men to have multiple wives.

ARRANGED MARRIAGE

Traditional societies such as those of modern-day India and Pakistan and olden Europe frequently use arranged marriages, in which the families of the bride and groom more or less arrange for the union (Stopes-Roe & Cochrane, 2011). Arranged marriage by traditional Jewish families was one of the main themes of the musical *Fiddler on the Roof.*

As in *Fiddler,* one of the purposes of arranged marriage is to make certain that the bride and groom come from similar backgrounds so that they will carry on their families' religious and cultural traditions. Supporters of arranged marriage argue that it is wiser to follow family wisdom than one's own heart, especially since the attraction couples feel is often infatuation and not a deep, abiding love. Couples also begin arranged marriages with low expectations and are then pleasantly surprised when things go reasonably well. Proponents also claim a lower divorce rate for arranged marriages than for "self-arranged marriages," but it must be noted that couples who enter arranged marriages are also more traditional.

GAY MARRIAGE

Mike and Sue Weinberg were out to dinner when their 6-year-old son, Jack, declared, "Mommy, I'm going to marry you." When Ms. Weinberg explained that she was already married, Jack persisted, "Then I'll marry Daddy."

"You can't marry Daddy," Ms. Weinberg said patiently, "He's a boy."

Gay Marriage. Several states and a number of countries around the world are allowing gay males and lesbians to get married or to enter civil unions that provide many of the benefits of marriage. Gay and lesbian couples are fitting into mainstream life in many locales across the United States.

"But Mark and Kevin are boys," replied Jack, logic that his mother could not refute.

Mark Demich and Kevin Hengst, the couple across the street, are not actually married. Still, in the seven years they have lived in this Chicago suburb they have become like the Buckinghams, the Therrons, the Siconolfis—just another young family in the neighborhood, socializing porch to porch on summer evenings.

Choosing the suburbs over the city, Mr. Demich and Mr. Hengst feared they would be "The Gay Couple." But even in Wheaton—the home of an evangelical Christian college that until recently prohibited drinking and dancing, the seat of a reliably Republican county—Mark and Kevin have found plenty of company. Sixty gay men and lesbians turned out for a wine-tasting a few weeks ago. About 30 played softball at a local park on a recent Saturday.

Thirty miles away, in the Chicago area known as Boystown, which officials say is the nation's first city-designated gay business district, business owners and residents say the influx of young heterosexual families has rendered the neighborhood's name an anachronism. The gay bookstore now sells more children's books than gay books.

In churches and in politics, the debate about homosexuality has focused recently on whether gays should be allowed to marry or whether gay sex should be legal. But in places like Wheaton and Boystown, people are sorting out more fundamental questions about everyday life. As gays live openly with straights, they are confronting stereotypes about one another and testing comfort zones, with varying degrees of conflict and cooperation.

And in many places today, as noted in Chapter 10, gay and lesbian couples are getting married. In many other places, where **gay marriage** is not allowed, gay and lesbian couples are entering civil unions that provide all or most of the advantages of married life.

OTHER WRINKLES IN MARRIAGE

Marriages are generally based on the expectation of sexual exclusivity. Alternative or nontraditional lifestyles, however, such as open marriages and group marriages, permit intimate relationships with people outside the marriage. Such alternative

CRITICAL THINKING
Some have suggested that the term *marriage* should be restricted to a religious ceremony and status, and that the term *civil union* should be restricted to a civil union and status. However, the religious status would also include the civil benefits. What do you think?

Gay marriage Marriage to a person of the same sex.

Although there are many—many!—exceptions, we tend to marry people who are similar to us in physical appeal and attitudes. We also tend to be similar in height and weight, intelligence, and even use of alcohol and other drugs.

lifestyles attracted a flurry of attention during the heyday of the sexual revolution in the 1960s and 1970s, but even then were more often talked about than practiced (Davis, 2010). Today, they find still fewer adherents.

Although the ideal of the traditional marriage remains strong in our culture, men are somewhat more likely than women to express an interest in sexual freedom (Davis, 2010). But even most of those who have tried lifestyles such as cohabitation, open marriage, or group marriage enter into traditional marriages at some time.

WHOM DO WE MARRY: ARE MARRIAGES MADE IN HEAVEN OR IN THE NEIGHBORHOOD?

In contemporary Western culture, mate selection is presumably free. Parents seldom arrange marriages, although they may still encourage their child to date that wonderful son or daughter of the solid churchgoing couple who lives down the street. Nevertheless, factors such as race, social class, religion, and level of education often—but clearly not always—determine the categories of people within which we seek mates. People in our culture tend to marry others from the same geographical area and social class (Schramm et al., 2012; Schwartz & Mare, 2012). Since neighborhoods are often made up of people from a similar social class, storybook marriages like Cinderella's are the exception to the rule.

Because we make choices, we tend to marry people who are similar to us in physical attractiveness and attitudes. As relationships progress through stages such as meeting, dating, perhaps cohabiting, and marriage, we tend to become more selective—that is, to narrow our choices to people yet more similar to us in background, attitudes, and interests (Schramm et al., 2012; Schwartz & Mare, 2012). We are more often than not similar to our mates in height, weight, personality traits, and intelligence, even on apparently minute matters such as use of alcohol and tobacco (Reynolds et al., 2006). We also tend to think about whether potential mates are likely to meet our material, sexual, and psychological needs.

The concept of "like marrying like" is termed **homogamy**. Most of the time, we also marry people of the same racial and ethnic background, educational level, and religion. Even so, more and more Americans are intermarrying because of love.

We also tend to follow *age homogamy*—to select a partner who falls in one's own age range (Michael et al., 1994). Age homogamy may reflect the tendency to marry early in adulthood. Persons who marry late or who remarry tend not to select partners so close in age. Bridegrooms tend to be two to five years older than their wives, on average, in European, North American, and South American countries (Buss, 1994).

Some marriages also show a mating gradient. The stereotype has been that an economically established older man would take an attractive, younger woman as his wife. But by and large, we are attracted to and marry the boy or girl (almost) next door or at the same office. Most marriages seem to be made not in heaven, but in the neighborhood.

All in all, keep in mind that we become attracted to people we meet and spend time with. You are a college student. If you are young and single—not a returning student, and not an online student—you may be meeting people who are more diverse in background and ethnicity than those who were nearby "at home." Therefore, you might find yourself becoming attracted to individuals who are in many ways more different from you than you would have anticipated in, say, high school. On the other hand, some students go to colleges that will have students who are yet more like them than were those at home, as in the case of students who enroll at Catholic colleges or Protestant evangelical colleges. They are seeking people who are yet more like them than they found at home, and they may set firm limits on whom they will consider as potential partners. Of course, if those relationships do not work out, and they are in a different city ten years later, ...

Homogamy The practice of marrying people who are similar in social background and standing. (From the Greek roots *homos*, meaning "same," and *gamos*, meaning "marriage.")

A WORLD OF DIVERSITY: THE RISE OF INTERMARRIAGE: "MARRYING OUT" VERSUS "MARRYING IN"[2]

There was a time when Americans tended to marry that "nice boy" or "nice girl" down the street, sitting behind them in 12th grade English, or going to the same church. That was then; this is now. People are getting married later, moving father from "home," and becoming more open in their attitudes and expectations. Let's get some insight into who is now marrying whom from the results of a Pew Research Center report (Wang, 2012) that is based largely on the Center's analysis of data from the U.S. Census Bureau's American Community Survey (ACS) in 2008–2010 and on findings from the Center's own nationwide telephone surveys that explore public attitudes toward intermarriage. The key findings of the report are as follows:

Intermarriage has become increasingly popular. About 15% of all new marriages in the United States in 2010 were between spouses of a different race or ethnicity from one another, more than double the share in 1980 (6.7%) (see Figure 14.13). Among all newlyweds in 2010, 9% of European Americans, 17% of African Americans, 26% of Latin

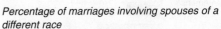
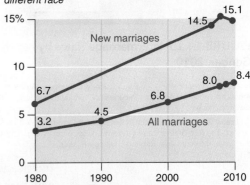

Percentage of marriages involving spouses of a different race

FIGURE 14.13 **Intermarriage Trend, 1980–2010**

Note: New marriages numbers are from 1980 Census and 2008–2010 American Community Survey (ACS). All marriages are from U.S. Decennial Census data and 2008–2010 ACS, IPUMS.

Source: © 2012 Pew Research Center, Social & Demographic Trends Project. *The Rise of Intermarriage.* www.pewsocialtrends.org/2012/02/16the-rise-of-intermarriage. Reprinted with permission.

---

[2]© 2012 Pew Research Center, Social & Demographic Trends Project. *The Rise of Intermarriage.* www.pewsocialtrends.org/2012/02/16the-rise-of-intermarriage. Reprinted with permission.

Percentage of newlyweds married to someone of a different race/ethnicity

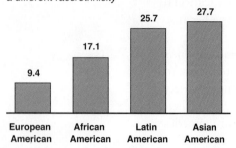

FIGURE 14.14 Intermarriage Rates, by Race and Ethnicity, 2010

Note: Asian American include Pacific Islanders. European American, African American and Asian American Include only non-Latin American. Latin American are of any Race.

Source: © 2012 Pew Research Center, Social & Demographic Trends Project. *The Rise of Intermarriage.* www.pewsocialtrends.org/2012/02/16 the-rise-of-intermarriage. Reprinted with permission.

Percentage of newlyweds married to someone of a different race/ethnicity

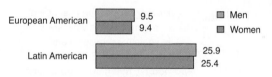

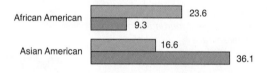

FIGURE 14.15 Intermarriage Rates by Newlyweds by Gender, 2010

Note: Asian American include Pacific Islanders. European American, African American and Asian American Inlcude only non-Latin American. Latin American are of any race.

Source: © 2012 Pew Research Center, Social & Demographic Trends Project. *The Rise of Intermarriage.* www.pewsocialtrends.org/2012/02/16 the-rise-of-intermarriage. Reprinted with permission.

Americans, and 28% of Asian Americans married out (Figure 14.14). Looking at all married couples in 2010, regardless of when they married, the share of intermarriages reached an all-time high of 8.4%. In 1980, that share was just 3.2% (see Figure 14.13).

Gender patterns in intermarriage vary widely. About 24% of all African American male newlyweds in 2010 married outside their race, compared with just 9% of African American female newlyweds (see Figure 14.15). Among Asian Americans, the gender pattern runs the other way. About 36% of Asian American female newlyweds married outside their race in 2010, compared with just 17% of Asian American male newlyweds. Intermarriage rates among European American and Latin American newlyweds do not vary by gender.

In some ways those who "married out" resembled those who "married in." In 2008–2010, the median combined annual earnings of both groups are similar—$56,711 for newlyweds who married out versus $55,000 for those who married in. In about one in five marriages for each group, both the husband and wife are college graduates. Spouses in the two groups also marry at similar ages (with a two-to three-year age gap between husband and wife), and an equal share are marrying for the first time.

However, these overall similarities mask sharp differences that emerge when the analysis looks in more detail at pairings by race and ethnicity. Some of these differences appear to reflect the overall characteristics of different groups in society at large, and some may be a result of a selection process. For example, in 2008–2010, European American/Asian American newlyweds had significantly higher median combined annual earnings ($70,952) than did any other pairing, including both European American/European American ($60,000) and Asian American/Asian American ($62,000) (see Figure 14.16). When it comes to educational characteristics, more than half of European American newlyweds who marry Asian Americans have a college degree, compared with roughly a third of European American newlyweds who married European Americans. Among Latin Americans and African Americans, newlyweds who married European Americans tend to have higher educational attainment than do those who married within their own racial or ethnic group.

The public has become more accepting of intermarriage. More than four in ten Americans (43%) say that more people of different races marrying each other has been a change for the better in our society, while 11% say it has been a change for the worse, and 44% say it has made no difference (see Figure 14.17). Minorities, younger adults, the college-educated, those who describe themselves as liberal, and those who live in the Northeast or the West are more disposed than others to see intermarriage in a positive light.

More than one-third of Americans (35%) say that a member of their immediate family or a close relative is currently married to someone of a different race.

Also, nearly two-thirds of Americans (63%) say it "would be fine" with them if a member of their own family were to marry someone outside their own racial or ethnic group. In 1986, the public was divided about this. Nearly three in ten Americans (28%) said people of different races marrying each other was not acceptable for anyone, and an additional 37% said this may be acceptable for others, but not for themselves. Again, in 1986, only one-third of the public (33%) viewed intermarriage as acceptable for everyone.

MARITAL SEX

Patterns of marital sexuality vary across cultures, yet anthropologists note common threads. Privacy for sexual relations is valued in almost all cultures. Most cultures also place restrictions on sex during menstruation, during some stages of pregnancy, and for a while after childbirth.

Until the sexual revolution of the 1960s and 1970s, Western culture could have been characterized as restrictive, even toward marital sex. We usually think of the sexual revolution in terms of the changes in sexual behaviors and attitudes that occurred among young, unmarried people. It also ushered in profound changes in marital sexuality, however. Compared to Kinsey's "pre-revolution" samples from the late 1930s and 1940s, married couples today engage in coitus more frequently, with greater variety, and for longer periods of time. They report greater sexual satisfaction. The sexual revolution helped dislodge the view that sexual pleasure is meant for men and that it is the duty of women to satisfy their husbands' sexual needs. Cable TV and downloads bring sexually explicit movies into suburban homes and cellphones.

Scientific findings were also liberalizing influences. Kinsey's and Masters and Johnson's findings that normal women were capable not only of orgasm but also of multiple orgasms punctured traditional beliefs that sexual gratification was the birthright of men alone. TV shows, films, and radio talk shows began to portray women as sexual initiators who enjoy sex. The affluence of the post–World War II years also encouraged more young people to pursue a college education and live away from home. College liberates not only through exposure to great books and scientific knowledge but also through interaction with students from different backgrounds.

The development of effective contraceptives separated sex from reproduction. Motives for sexual pleasure became more open. All these liberalizing forces have led to changes in the frequency of marital sex and in techniques of foreplay and coitus since Kinsey's day (Eisenberg et al., 2010).

Foreplay Married women in Kinsey's sample reported an average (median) length of foreplay of about 12 minutes. Kinsey found that men at lower educational levels engaged in briefer foreplay, generally lasting but a minute or two before penetration. The length of foreplay rose to 5 to 15 minutes among

Median combined annual earnings, in 2010 dollars

% both college educated

	Earnings	%
European American/Asian American	$70,952	41.2
Asian American/Asian American	$62,000	52.7
European American/European American	$60,000	23.3
European American/Latin American	$57,900	18.6
European American/African American	$53,187	14.5
African American/African American	$47,700	10.2
Latin American/Latin American	$35,578	5.4

FIGURE 14.16 Earnings and Education, Newlyweds in 2008–2010

Note: Asian American include Pacific Islanders, European American, African American and Asian American include only non-Latin American. Latin American are of any race.

Source: © 2012 Pew Research Center, Social & Demographic Trends Project. *The Rise of Intermarriage.* www.pewsocialtrends.org/2012/02/16 the-rise-of-intermarriage. Reprinted with permission.

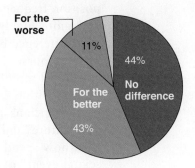

Percentage saying that more people of different races marrying each other has been a change...in our society.

For the worse 11%

No difference 44%

For the better 43%

FIGURE 14.17 For Better or for Worse?

Note: Mixed/Don't Know/Refused (3%) are shown but not labeled.

Source: © 2012 Pew Research Center, Social & Demographic Trends Project. *The Rise of Intermarriage.* www.pewsocialtrends.org/2012/02/16 the-rise-of-intermarriage. Reprinted with permission.

college-educated men. Marital foreplay has gained in duration and variety since Kinsey's day. Couples in more recent surveys report using a wider variety of foreplay techniques, including oral stimulation of the breasts and oral–genital contact (Laumann et al., 1994).

Frequency of Marital Coitus How frequently do married couples engage in coitus? Table 14.2 summarizes results from the Kinsey surveys. The frequency of coitus was negatively related to age. That is, older couples engaged in coitus less frequently.

As discussed in Chapter 9, married men and women in the National Survey of Family Growth reported engaging in sexual relations five to six times a month (Eisenberg et al., 2010). These figures are not notably different from Kinsey's.

The frequency of sexual relations declines with age, however (Eisenberg et al., 2010). At the ages of 50 to 59, for example, people reported an average of sexual relations four to five times per month (Laumann et al., 1994). Regardless of a couple's age, sexual frequency also appears to decline with years of marriage. There would thus appear to be a novelty effect.

Methods of Coitus In coitus, as in foreplay, the marital bed since Kinsey's day has become a stage on which the players act more varied roles. Today's couples use greater variety in positions.

As many as 70% of Kinsey's males used the male-superior position only (Kinsey et al., 1948). Perhaps three couples in ten used the female-superior position frequently. Approximately one in four or five used the lateral-entry position frequently, and about one in ten used the rear-entry position. Younger and more highly educated men showed greater variety, however. An important difference between Kinsey's and the NHSLS samples involves the length of intercourse. In Kinsey's time it was widely believed that the "virile" man ejaculated rapidly during intercourse. Kinsey estimated that most men reached orgasm within 2 minutes after penetration, many within 10 or 20 seconds. Yet some clinicians at the time were already asserting that a man's ejaculation was "premature" unless he delayed it until his partner was ready to reach orgasm. Men now spend more time on their partner's needs: The "duration of the last sexual event" of three out of four married couples was 15 minutes to an hour (Michael et al., 1994).

Table 14.2

Median Weekly Frequency of Marital Sexual Relations, Male and Female Estimates Combined, According to the Kinsey Surveys

Age	Frequency
16–25	2.45
26–35	1.95
36–45	1.40
46–55	0.85
55–60	0.50

Sources: A. C. Kinsey, W. B. Pomeroy, and C. E. Martin, (1948). *Sexual behavior in the human male.* Philadelphia: W. B. Saunders; A. C. Kinsey, W. B. Pomeroy, C. E. Martin, and P. H. Gebhard. (1953). *Sexual behavior in the human female.* Philadelphia: W. B. Saunders.

MARITAL SATISFACTION

Marital satisfaction is a complex phenomenon that includes the following (Wilcox & Marquardt, 2011):

- Commitment
- An adequate income (yes, money matters)
- Sharing in housework
- Generosity toward one's spouse (Dew & Wilcox, 2011)
- A match between the amount of work one wishes to have (none, part-time, or full-time employment) and the amount of work one has (U.S. Department of Labor, 2011)
- The support of one's family and friends (yes, in-laws can make a difference one way or the other)
- Agreement on attitudes toward having and raising children
- Sexual satisfaction (see Figure 14.18)
- For many couples, a belief in the religious or spiritual value of marriage

There are many ways to view the link between sexual satisfaction and marital satisfaction. Does marital satisfaction lead to feelings of attraction and sexual desire for one's spouse? Does "good sex" contribute to happiness with a marriage? It's likely that the answer to both questions is yes. When it comes to understanding human behavior and mental processes, it is often useful to look for an interaction between variables—in this case, marital satisfaction and sexual satisfaction—rather to think that one must directly cause the other. Then, too, in a cultural setting in which marriage partners (usually) choose one another, sexual attraction and sharing of important attitudes are likely to play key roles both in the selection process and the outcome.

Now let's think about belief in the spiritual value of marriage. There's little doubt about it: The data obtained by the National Marriage Project (Wilcox & Marquardt, 2011) do show that people who believe that their marriage fulfills a religious need or value and who attend church (or the synagogue or the mosque) regularly tend to be happier with their marriages and less prone toward getting divorced. But don't over-interpret this finding. It does not mean that you will be unhappily married and headed for divorce if you view marriage more in terms of personal commitment, a social contract, and a social setting for having and raising children—religion aside. Many people are happy with their marriages, and some are miserable, despite the

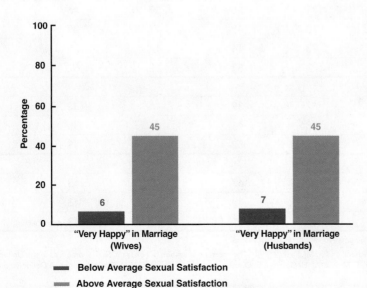

FIGURE 14.18 Marital Satisfaction 18- to 46-Year-Old Married Mothers and Fathers, by Sexual Satisfaction

Source: W. Bradford Wilcox & Elizabeth Marquardt (Eds.) (2011). *The State of Our Unions: Marriage in America 2011.* Reprinted by permission of the National Marriage Project at the University of Virginia and the Institute for American Values. marriage@virginia.edu, Figure 15, p. 37.

role they believe religion plays in their unions. Nor does this finding mean that you should look for or develop a spiritual value or role for your marriage if you don't believe in it. It's not something to fake. You can be truly and completely committed to your marriage—or not—regardless of your religious beliefs.

Now let's talk a bit more about sexual satisfaction. One index of sexual satisfaction is orgasmic consistency. Men tend to reach orgasm more consistently than women do. The NHSLS found that more than 90% of the men and about 70% of women reported reaching orgasm "always" or "usually" with their primary partner during the 12 months prior to the survey (Laumann et al., 1994; Michael et al., 1994) (see Table 14.3). Seventy-five percent of men and almost 29% of women reported reaching orgasm every time (not shown). Only 2% of the married women reported never reaching orgasm with their husbands during the past year (not shown).

Women in their 40s were somewhat more likely to reach orgasm than younger and older women. Women in their 40s have presumably have had more opportunity to learn about their sexuality and are more secure in their relationships than younger women are. Married women were most likely to reach orgasm consistently, followed by cohabiting women, then single women. Security apparently promotes orgasmic consistency. There do not seem to be notable racial or ethnic differences.

More recent analysis of the NHSLS data by Laura Carpenter and her colleagues (2009) found that among 1,053 heterosexual women and men aged 40 to 59, women were less likely to be sexually satisfied than men were. Interestingly, there was an apparent reversal of gender-role stereotypes among these people in midlife: Women's

Table 14.3

A World of Diversity: Demographic Factors and Sexual Satisfaction in Primary Relationship during the Past Year

Demographic Characteristics	Always or Usually Has an Orgasm with Partner		Has Been Extremely Physically Satisfied with Partner		Has Been Extremely Emotionally Satisfied with Partner	
	Men	Women	Men	Women	Men	Women
Age, Years						
18–24	92%	61%	44%	44%	41%	39%
25–29	94	71	50	39	46	40
30–39	97	70	45	41	39	38
40–49	97	78	44	42	38	42
50–59	91	73	53	32	52	32
Marital Status						
Single	94	62	39	40	32	31
Cohabiting	95	68	44	46	35	44
Married	95	75	52	41	49	42
Race/Ethnicity*						
European American	96	70	47	40	43	38
African American	90	72	43	44	43	38
Latin American	96	68	51	39	43	39

*The numbers of Asian Americans and Native Americans were too small to report reliable statistics.

Sources: Combined from E. O. Laumann, J. H. Gagnon, R. T. Michael, and S. Michaels, (1994). *The social organization of sexuality: Sexual practices in the United States.* Chicago: University of Chicago Press, Table 3.7, pp. 116–117; R. T. Michael, J. H. Gagnon, E. O. Laumann, and G. Kolata. (1994). *Sex in America: A Definitive Survey.* Boston: Little, Brown, Table 9, pp. 128–129.

Real Students, Real Questions

Q *How can I keep my partner interested in sex? We have been together for five years.*

A Do you have any "barriers" to sex? Kids running into the room? Incredibly stressful jobs? Impossibly long commutes? Fatigue? (Too much) alcohol? If so, you may want to consider reengineering your life in general. But if you've just got a little sexual boredom going, you may want to remember that the greatest known aphrodisiac, to quote from an earlier chapter, is variety. How about a new perfume or cologne? How about a change in hairstyle? Nightclothes or lingerie? How about a weekend away from things? How about trying something new sexually? A 75-year-old endocrinologist said he and his wife watched pornography while they were having sex. He said it was pretty much a yawner for her, but she appreciated what it did for him. In sum: Remove barriers. Create novelty. And if you happen to be a 75-year-old endocrinologist ...

emotional satisfaction was closely related to their "bodily sexual practices"—that is, to what sources of sexual stimulation they received—whereas the men's physical satisfaction was relatively more strongly related to factors in the relationship.

INFIDELITY

President Bill Clinton. Senator John Ensign, Senator John Edwards, Representative Newt Gingrich, Governor Elliot Spitzer. Senator David Vitter. Governor Mark Sanford. Governor David Paterson. What do these left-wing, right-wing, and "moderate" politicians have in common? They have all admittedly engaged in marital infidelity. We will see that they are not alone.

Some people engage in extramarital sex for variety (Peluso, 2008). Some have affairs to break the routine of a confining marriage (Allen & Atkins, 2005; Markman, 2005). Others enter affairs for reasons similar to the nonsexual reasons adolescents often have for sex: as a way of expressing hostility toward a spouse or retaliating for injustice. Husbands and wives who engage in affairs often report that they are not satisfied with or fulfilled by their marital relationships. Curiosity and desire for personal growth are often more prominent motives than marital dissatisfaction. Middle-aged people may have affairs to boost their self-esteem or to prove that they are still attractive.

Many times the sexual motive is less pressing than the desire for emotional closeness. Some women say they are seeking someone whom they can talk to or communicate with (Lamanna & Riedmann, 2005). There is a gender difference here (Petersen & Hyde, 2011). According to Janis Abrahms Spring, author of *After the Affair,* women are usually seeking "soul mates," whereas men are seeking "playmates." Women tend to justify affairs when they are for love, but men do so when the affair is *not* for love.

Women are less accepting of sex without emotional involvement (Petersen & Hyde, 2011). Men are more likely than women to distinguish between sex and love, whereas women see love and sex as going together so that falling in love justifies sex (Petersen & Hyde, 2011). But these are *group* differences. Many individual men are interested primarily in the extramarital relationship rather than the sex per se. Similarly, some women are out for the sex and not the relationship.

From an evolutionary perspective, infidelity can be seen as a short-term mating strategy—one that is more adaptive for men than women. Peter Jonason and his colleagues (2008) surveyed 224 people and found that a cluster of three characteristics, which the researchers term the *Dark Triad*, contributed to infidelity but not to enduring relationships: narcissism (vanity, or excessive self-love), psychopathy (amoral, antisocial behavior), and Machiavellianism (deception and expediency). This so-called Dark Triad facilitates exploitative, short-term relationships in men. But note that the researchers did not find that *all* unfaithful men can be characterized by the Dark Triad.

Patterns of Infidelity Let us begin with a few definitions. **Extramarital sex** is usually conducted without the spouse's knowledge or approval. Secret affairs are referred to as **conventional adultery**, infidelity, or simply "cheating." Conventional adultery runs the gamut from the "one-night stand" to the affair that persists for years. In **consensual adultery**, extramarital relationships are conducted openly—that is, with the knowledge and consent of the partner. In what is called **swinging**, or *mate-swapping*, the partner participates.

How many people "cheat" on their spouses? Viewers of TV talk shows may get the impression that everyone cheats, but reliable surveys paint a different picture. More than 90% of the married women and 75% of the married men in the NHSLS reported remaining loyal to their spouses (Laumann et al., 1994). The vast majority of people who were cohabiting also reported that they were sexually faithful to their partners. But results from the Laumann group reported more recently find that the lifetime rate of infidelity for men aged 60 and above increased to 28% in 2006, up from 20% in 1991 (Parker-Pope, 2008). For older women, the lifetime incidence rose to 15%, up from 5% in 1991. The researchers also found changes in newer marriages. About 20% of the men and 15% of the women under age 35 say they were unfaithful at some time, up from about 15% for men and 12% for women in 1991. A USA Today/Gallup Poll found that 54% of respondents said they personally knew someone who had been unfaithful (Blow, 2009).

Having presented the percentages of reported extramarital sex, we point out that these reports cannot be verified. People may be reluctant to reveal they have "cheated" even when they are assured of anonymity (Parker-Pope, 2008; Peluso, 2008). One study surveyed 4,884 married women, using both face-to-face interviews and anonymous computer questionnaires (Whisman & Snyder, 2007). Only 1% of women said they had been unfaithful during the previous year in the face-to-face interviews. However, 6% of the same sample admitted to infidelity on the computer questionnaire.

Attitudes Toward Infidelity Although Americans, especially younger Americans, may not see marriage as "very important" anymore, they still seem to value keeping one's promises. About nine out of ten Americans say that affairs are "always wrong" or "almost always wrong." Three out of four Americans say that infidelity is "always wrong" (Berke, 1997). Another one in seven say it is "almost always wrong." Only about 1% say that extramarital sex is "not at all wrong." Most married couples embrace monogamy as the cornerstone of their relationship.

3 Ⓣ/ꜰ   **TRUTH OR FICTION REVISITED:** It is not true that most of today's sophisticated young people see nothing wrong with an occasional extramarital fling. The sexual revolution never extended itself to infidelity—at least among the majority of married people.

Extramarital sex Sexual relations between a married person and someone other than his or her spouse.

Conventional adultery Extramarital sex that is kept hidden from one's spouse.

Consensual adultery Extramarital sex that is engaged in openly with the knowledge and consent of one's spouse.

Swinging A form of consensual adultery in which both spouses share extramarital sexual experiences. Also referred to as *mate-swapping*.

Real Students, Real Questions

Q *Is there any credibility to the "seven-year itch" idea—that partners will tend to stray every seven years?*

A The notion of the seven-year itch is presumably related to the fact that wool is one of the traditional seventh-year anniversary gifts (the other is copper) and hence, itchy. But the only credibility to the seven-year notion is that as time goes by, people become more accustomed to one another, and men especially may become more interested in looking for some sexual novelty.

Effects of Infidelity The discovery of infidelity can evoke a range of emotional responses. The spouse may be filled with anger, jealousy, and even shame. Feelings of inadequacy and doubts about one's attractiveness and desirability may surface. Infidelity may be seen by the betrayed spouse as a serious breach of trust and intimacy. Marriages that are not terminated in the wake of the disclosure may survive in a damaged condition.

The harm an affair does to a marriage may reflect the meaning of the affair to the individual and his or her spouse (Peluso, 2008). Deborah Lamberti (1997), director of a counseling and psychotherapy center in New York City, points again to women's traditional intertwining of sex with relationships and argues that "Men don't view [their own] sex with another person as a reason to leave a primary relationship" (pp. 131–132). Women may recognize this and be able to tell themselves that their husbands are sleeping with someone else just for physical reasons. But women are more concerned about remaining monogamous. Therefore, if a woman is sleeping with another man, she may already have a foot out the door. A wife's affair may be an unforgivable blow to the husband's ego or pride (Rasmussen & Kilborne, 2008). A woman may be more likely to see the transgression as a threat to the structure of her life (Allen & Atkins, 2005; Peluso, 2008).

If a person has an affair because the marriage is deeply troubled, the affair may be one more factor that speeds its dissolution. The effects on the marriage may depend on the nature of the affair. It may be easier to understand that a spouse has fallen prey to an isolated, unplanned encounter than to accept an extended affair (Rasmussen & Kilborne, 2008). In some cases the discovery of infidelity stimulates the couple to work to improve the relationship.

Divorce: Breaking Bonds

My wife and I were considering a divorce, but after pricing lawyers we decided to buy a new car instead.

　　—Henny Youngman

Whenever I date a guy, I think, is this the man I want my children to spend their weekends with?

　　—Rita Rudner

Some 40 to 50% of the Marriages in the United States end in divorce (Wilcox & Marquardt, 2010, 2011). The divorce rate in the United States rose steadily from 1960 to 1980, then declined gradually before leveling off in the 2000s (see Figure 14.19). Divorced women outnumber divorced men, in part because men are more likely to remarry.

Why did the incidence of divorce rise in the 1960s? Until the mid-1960s, adultery was the only legal grounds for divorce in most states. But no-fault divorce laws have been enacted in nearly every state, allowing a divorce to be granted without a finding of marital misconduct. The increased economic independence of women has also contributed to the divorce rate. More women today have the economic means of breaking away from a troubled marriage. Today, more people consider marriage an alterable condition than in prior generations.

People today also hold higher expectations of marriage than did their parents or grandparents. They expect marriage to be personally fulfilling as well as an institution for family life and rearing children. Most people want to be happy in marriage. Today, the most common reasons given by women for divorce are problems in communication and a lack of understanding. Key predictors of divorce today include husband's criticism, defensiveness, contempt, and stonewalling—not lack of financial support (Carrère et al., 2000; Mahoney & Knudson-Martin, 2009).

On the other hand, the following factors decrease the chances of getting divorced (Wilcox & Marquardt, 2011):

- Having an annual income above $50,000, as contrasted with an income below $25,000
- Having a baby seven months or more after getting married, as opposed to having a baby prior to getting married
- Getting married when you're over 25 years of age, as opposed to being a teenager
- Having an intact family of origin, rather than parents who are separated or divorced
- Having a religious affiliation
- Having a college education

But as is the case with martial satisfaction, starting to go to church or to try to believe in God (if you don't already) isn't going to save a troubled marriage. Nor has anyone ever shown that getting a college education in order to save a marriage works! These are all "selection factors"—meaning, in a nutshell, that if you belong

FIGURE 14.19 Number of Divorces per 1,000 Married Women Age 15 and Older, by Year, United States

Source: U.S. Census Bureau.

to one of these groups, your marriage has a better chance of surviving. But trying to join one of these groups to save a marriage makes no sense. Work on the marriage instead.

THE COST OF DIVORCE

Divorce is usually connected with financial and emotional problems. When a household splits, the resources often cannot maintain the earlier standard of living for each partner. Divorce hits women in the pocketbook harder than men. According to a Population Reference Bureau report, a woman's household income drops by about 24% (Bianchi & Spain, 1997). A man's income declines by about 6%. Women who have not pursued a career may have to struggle to compete with younger, more experienced workers. Divorced mothers often face the combined stress of having the sole responsibility for childrearing and the need to increase their incomes. Divorced fathers may find it difficult to pay alimony and child support while establishing a new lifestyle.

Divorce can also prompt feelings of failure as a spouse and parent, loneliness and uncertainty about the future, and depression. Married people appear to be better able to cope with the stresses and strains of life, perhaps because they can lend each other emotional support. Divorced and separated people have the highest rates of physical and mental illness (Levite & Cohen, 2012; Meadows, 2009). They also have high rates of suicide (Donald et al., 2006; Milner et al., 2012). On the other hand, divorce may permit personal growth and renewal—an opportunity to take stock of oneself and establish a new, more rewarding life.

Children are often the biggest losers when parents get a divorce, yet chronic marital conflict is also connected with psychological distress in children (Robbers et al., 2011). Boys have greater problems adjusting to conflict or divorce, such as having conduct problems at school and increased anxiety and dependence. The children of divorce are more likely to have psychological problems and conduct disorders, have lower self-esteem, abuse drugs and alcohol, and do more poorly in school (Amato, 2006; Fletcher & Sindelar, 2012). There are individual differences in all of this, and boys tend to fare worse than girls (Kim, 2011). But, by and large, the fallout for children is at its worst during the first year after the breakup. Children tend to rebound in a year or two.

Researchers attribute children's problems following divorce not only to the divorce itself but also to a consequent decline in the quality of parenting. Children's adjustment is enhanced when both parents maintain parenting responsibilities and set aside their differences long enough to agree on childrearing practices (Hetherington, 2006). Children of divorce also benefit when their parents avoid saying negative things about each other in the children's presence (Hetherington, 2006; Kim, 2011).

Despite the difficulties in adjustment, most divorced people eventually bounce back. Most remarry. Among older people, divorced men are more likely than divorced women to remarry—in part because men usually die earlier than women (and so fewer prospective husbands are available), and in part because older men tend to remarry younger women (Wilcox & Marquardt, 2011).

"ALL RIGHT, WE FIGHT—SHOULD WE REMAIN MARRIED 'FOR THE SAKE OF THE CHILDREN'?"

Let's have it out. We are going to address this issue from a scientific perspective only. Many readers believe—for moral reasons—that marriage must be permanent, no matter what. Readers will consider the moral aspects of divorce in the light of their own value systems.

So, from a purely scientific perspective, what should bickering parents do? The answer seems to depend largely on how they behave in front of the children. Research shows that parental bickering—especially severe fighting—is linked to the same kinds of problems for children that they experience when their parents get separated or divorced (Fabricius et al., 2012; Troxel & Matthews, 2004). Moreover, when children are exposed to marital conflict, they display a biological "alarm reaction": Their heart rate, blood pressure, and sweating rise sharply (El-Sheikh & Harger, 2001). The bodily response is even stronger when children blame themselves for parental conflict, as is common among younger children. These symptoms of stress also weaken the immune system and leave children more vulnerable to stress-related health problems.

One study analyzed data from 727 children aged 4 to 9 years from intact families and followed them 6 years later, when many of the families had undergone separation or divorce (Morrison & Coiro, 1999). Both separation and divorce were associated with increases in behavior problems in children, regardless of the amount of conflict between the parents. However, in the marriages that remained intact, high levels of marital conflict were associated with yet more behavior problems in the children. Message? Although separation and divorce are connected with adjustment problems in children, the outcome can be even worse for children when conflicted parents stay together. The problems caused by parents in conflict are further highlighted by studies that show that many psychological problems seen in the children of divorce were present prior to the breakup (Fabricius et al., 2012; Troxel & Matthews, 2004). Because of the stresses experienced by children caught up in marital conflict, child psychologists E. Mavis Hetherington and John Kelly (2003) suggest that divorce can be a positive response to destructive family functioning.

LIFE IN BLENDED FAMILIES: HIS, HERS, THEIRS, AND …

Because of the high incidence of divorce and remarriage, the stepfamily is becoming a more common family unit in the United States. Although many stepfamilies disband, often because of conflict over stepchildren (such as parental favoritism for their own [Golish, 2003; Hofferth & Anderson, 2003]), levels of happiness in others

Should They Remain Together "for the Sake of the Children"? The research seems to suggest that children may fare better when parents who are in regular conflict separate. The key issue appears to be how the parents interact in the presence of the children, not whether they get a divorce.

can be as high as they were in original marriages (Braithwaite et al., 2001). In any event, more than one in three American children will spend part of his or her childhood in a stepfamily (U.S. Bureau of the Census, 2005).

The rule of thumb about the effects of living in stepfamilies is that there is no rule of thumb. Living in a stepfamily may have no measurable psychological effects (Coleman et al., 2000). Stepparents may claim stepchildren as their own (Marsiglio, 2004). One study of the effects of stepparenting on middle schoolers found that good stepmother–stepchild relationships were linked with less aggressive behavior in both boys and girls and with higher self-esteem among stepdaughters (Anderson et al., 1999). But not everything comes up roses in stepfamilies. There are some risks. Infanticide (killing infants) is a rarity in the United States, but the crime occurs much more often in stepfamilies than in families with biological kinship (Daly & Wilson, 2003, 2005). There is also a significantly higher incidence of sexual abuse by stepparents than by natural parents.

Why do we find these risks in stepfamilies? According to evolutionary psychologists, people often behave as if they want their genes to flourish in the next generation. Thus, it could be that stepparents are less devoted to rearing the children of other people than their own. They may even see "foreign" children as competitors for resources with their own children. Or a stepfather may see a woman's possession of children by another man as lessening her capacity to bear and rear his children (Daly & Wilson, 2003, 2005).

Sex in the Later Years

What is the fastest growing segment of the U.S. population? People age 65 and above. The "graying" of the United States may have a profound effect on our views of the sexuality of older people. Many people think of sex as appropriate only for the young. This belief falls within a constellation of unfounded cultural myths about older people, which includes the notions that older people are sexless, older people with sexual urges are abnormal, and older men with sexual interests are "dirty old men."

Researchers find that sexual daydreaming, sex drive, and sexual activity tend to decline with age, whereas negative sexual attitudes tend to increase (Loe, 2012). However, research does not support the belief that people lose their sexuality as they age (Laumann et al., 2006). Most older people report that they like sex, and a majority report that orgasm is important to their sexual fulfillment. Sexual activity among older people, as among other groups, is influenced not only by physical structures and changes but also by psychological well-being, feelings of intimacy, and cultural expectations (Loe, 2012).

Sexuality in Late Adulthood. Are older people sexually active? If they are, are they abnormal or deviant? Although young people frequently find it difficult to imagine older people engaging in sexual activity, it is normal to retain sexual interest and activity for a lifetime.

PHYSICAL CHANGES

Although many older people retain the capacity to respond sexually, physical changes do occur as the years pass (see Table 14.4). If we are aware of them, we will not view them as abnormal or find ourselves unprepared to cope with them. Many potential problems can be averted by changing our expectations or making behavioral changes to accommodate aging.

Let's not start this section with a deeply biological focus on changes in cells, hormones, and the like. Let's

Table 14.4	
Changes in Sexual Response Connected with Aging	
Changes in the Female	**Changes in the Male**
Reduced muscle tension (myotonia)	Longer time to achieve erection and orgasm
Reduced lubrication	Need for more direct stimulation to achieve erection and orgasm
Reduced elasticity in the vaginal walls	Less semen emitted during ejaculation
Smaller increases in breast size during sexual arousal	Softer erections
Reduced intensity of spasms of orgasm	Testicles may not elevate as high prior to ejaculation
	Reduced intensity of spasms of orgasm
	Less need to ejaculate
	Longer refractory period

Source: Based on *The Kinsey Institute New Report on Sex*, 1990, p. 227. Reprinted by permission of The Kinsey Institute for Research in Sex, Gender, and Reproduction, Inc.

talk first about what happens when we look in the mirror. Many of us are dismayed by visible changes that occur as we age. We develop wrinkles. Our hair turns gray. Our muscle tone decreases. We tend to put on weight, especially if we do not exercise regularly. All in all, we are likely to feel less attractive than we did. And the fact is that our partners may find us to be less attractive. Nevertheless, in enduring intimate relationships, feelings of love, intimacy, and sharing life can outweigh those changes and feelings. But if we are single in our later years, perhaps because of divorce or becoming widowed, the future, including the sexual future, may look more bleak.

Yet, older people can also lead sexually fulfilling lives. If they fine-tune their expectations, they may find themselves leading some of the most sexually fulfilling years of their lives (Loe, 2012).

Changes in the Female Many of the physical changes in older women stem from decline in the production of estrogen. The vaginal walls lose much elasticity and the thick, corrugated texture of the childbearing years. The vaginal walls grow paler and thinner, perhaps making coitus irritating to the walls. Also, the thinning of the walls may place greater pressure against the bladder and urethra during sex, leading now and then to urinary urgency and burning urination. The condition may persist for days.

The vagina also shrinks. The labia majora lose much of their fatty deposits and thin. The introitus constricts, and penile entry may become difficult. On the other hand, increased friction between the penis and vaginal walls may heighten sexual sensations. Following menopause, women also produce less vaginal lubrication, and lubrication may take minutes, not seconds, to appear. Lack of adequate lubrication is a key reason for painful coitus.

Many of these changes may be slowed or reversed through estrogen-replacement therapy, although estrogen replacement has its hazards (see Chapter 3). Natural lubrication may be increased through more elaborate foreplay. Older men too will likely need more time to become aroused. An artificial lubricant can also ease problems in penile entry and thrusting.

Women's breasts show smaller increases in size with sexual arousal as they age, but the nipples still become erect. Because the muscle tone of the urethra and anal sphincters decreases, the spasms of orgasm become less powerful and fewer in number. Thus, orgasms may feel less intense, but the subjective experience of orgasm may remain satisfying. **TRUTH** OR **FICTION** REVISITED: Despite these changes, women

4 (T/F)

can retain their ability to reach orgasm well into their advanced years. Nevertheless, the uterine contractions that occur during orgasm may become discouragingly painful for some older women.

Changes in the Male Age-related changes tend to occur more gradually in men than in women and are not clearly connected with any one biological event (Loe, 2012). Male adolescents may achieve erection in seconds through sexual fantasy alone. After about age 50, men take progressively longer to achieve erection. Erections become less firm, perhaps because of lowered testosterone levels (Laumann et al., 2006). Older men may require prolonged direct stimulation of the penis to obtain an erection. Couples can adjust to these changes by extending the length and variety of foreplay.

Most men remain capable of erection throughout their lives. Erectile dysfunction is not inevitable with aging. Men generally require more time to reach orgasm as they age, however, which may again reflect lowered testosterone levels.

Testosterone production usually declines gradually from about age 40 to age 60, and then begins to level off. However, the decline is not inevitable and may be related to the man's general health. Sperm production tends to decline as the seminiferous tubules degenerate, but viable sperm may be produced by men in their 70s, 80s, and 90s.

Nocturnal erections tend to diminish in intensity, duration, and frequency as men age, but they do not normally disappear in healthy men (Loe, 2012). The refractory period tends to lengthen with age. An adolescent may require but a few minutes to regain erection and ejaculate again after a first orgasm, whereas a man in his 30s may require half an hour. Past age 50, the refractory period may increase to several hours.

Older men produce less ejaculate, and it may seep out rather than shoot out. The contractions of orgasm become weaker and fewer. Still, an older male may enjoy orgasm as thoroughly as he did at a younger age. Following orgasm, erection subsides more rapidly than in a younger man.

Real Students, Real Questions

Q *I caught my grandparents having sex. Now they will not talk to me, and they act differently toward me. What can I do?*

A Lesson for everyone: You gotta knock. Or you have to say "Anyone home?" or whatever, when entering someone's home. Your grandparents aren't talking to you? They're embarrassed, and for a number of reasons. One is that they were likely brought up in more traditional times. There is also the stereotype that sex is for young people. Why not drop them a handwritten note (without a return address so that they'll open it). Say you're sorry you didn't knock or whatever. Ask them to forgive you. And say something humorous like you wish your love life was as good as theirs. If you do that and they don't get over it, you tried. End of story.

PATTERNS OF SEXUAL ACTIVITY

Despite the decline in physical functions, older people can continue to lead a fulfilling sex life. Years of sexual experience may more than compensate for any diminution of physical response (Laumann et al., 2006; Loe, 2012). Coital frequency tends to decline with age (Laumann et al., 2006). Several factors play a role in declining activity, including physical problems, boredom, and cultural attitudes. Despite general trends, sexuality among older people is variable (Loe, 2012). Many older people engage in intercourse, oral sex, and masturbation as often (or more) as when they were younger; some become disgusted by sex; others simply lose interest.

Couples may accommodate the physical changes of aging by broadening their sexual repertoire to include more diverse forms of stimulation. Many older people report using oral–genital stimulation, sexual fantasy, pornography, anal stimulation, vibrators, and other techniques to offset problems in achieving lubrication or erection. Sexual satisfaction may be derived from manual or oral stimulation, cuddling, caressing, and tenderness, as well as intercourse to orgasm. The availability of a sexually interested and supportive partner may be the most important determinant of continued sexual activity (Laumann et al., 2006).

Sex and Disability

Like older people, people with disabilities (especially those whose physical disabilities render them dependent on others) are often seen as sexless and childlike. Such views are based on misconceptions about the sexual functioning of people with disabilities. Some of these myths and stereotypes may be eroding, however, in part because of the success of the civil and social rights movements, and in part because of the attention focused on the sexuality of people with disabilities in films such as *Born on the Fourth of July* and *My Left Foot*.

A person may have been born with or acquire a bodily impairment or may suffer a loss of function or a disfiguring change in appearance. Although the disability may require the person to make adjustments in order to perform sexually, most people with disabilities have the same sexual needs, feelings, and desires as people without disabilities. Their ability to express their sexual feelings and needs depends on the physical limitations imposed by their disabilities, their adjustment to their disabilities, and the availability of partners. The establishment of mature sexual relationships generally demands some distance from one's parents. Therefore, people with disabilities who are physically dependent on their parents may find it especially difficult to develop sexual relationships. Parents who acknowledge their children's sexual development can be helpful by facilitating dating. Far too often, parents become overprotective.

PHYSICAL DISABILITIES

According to Margaret A. Nosek (2011), sexual wellness, among the disabled, as among the population at large, involves

- Positive sexual self-concept; seeing oneself as valuable sexually and as a person
- Knowledge about sexuality
- Positive, productive relationships
- Coping with barriers to sexuality (social, environmental, physical, and emotional)
- Maintaining the best possible general and sexual health, given one's limitations

This model applies to all of us, of course. Let us now consider aspects of specific physical disabilities and human sexuality.

Multiple Sclerosis Multiple sclerosis (MS) is a chronic, unpredictable disease that affects the nervous system. The tissue called *myelin,* which surrounds and protects nerve cells, disintegrates and leaves scar tissue in its place. MS impairs sexual functioning, and people with MS report more sexual problems than people without the disorder (Forbes et al., 2006; McCabe, 2004). However, there is a good deal of individual difference, and the progression of the disorder, and its effects, do not follow a straight line. Many people with MS in good relationships enjoy fine sex lives for many years.

Cerebral Palsy Cerebral palsy and related disorders of the nervous system do not necessarily impair sexual interest, capacity for orgasm, or fertility. Depending on the nature and degree of muscle spasticity or lack of voluntary muscle control, however, afflicted people may be limited to certain types of sexual activities and coital positions (Cho et al., 2004).

People with disabilities such as cerebral palsy often suffer social rejection during adolescence and perceive themselves as unfit for or unworthy of intimate sexual relationships, especially with people who are not disabled. They are often socialized into an asexual role. Counseling can help them understand and accept their sexuality, promote a more positive body image, and provide the social skills to establish intimate relationships.

Spinal Cord Injuries People who suffer physical disabilities as the result of traumatic injuries or physical illness must not only learn to cope with their physical limitations but also to adjust to a world designed for nondisabled people. The majority of persons who suffer disabling spinal cord injuries are young, active males. Automobile or pedestrian accidents account for about half of these cases. Other common causes include stabbing or bullet wounds, sports injuries, and falls. Depending on the location of the injury to the spinal cord, a loss of voluntary control (paralysis) can occur in either the legs *(paraplegia)* or all four limbs *(quadriplegia)*. A loss of sensation may also occur in parts of the body that lie beneath the site of injury.

TRUTH OR FICTION REVISITED: Many people who are paralyzed due to spinal cord injuries usually can become sexually aroused and engage in coitus. The effect of spinal cord injuries on sexual response depends on the site and severity of the injury. Men have two erection centers in the spinal cord: a higher center in the lumbar region that controls psychogenic erections and a lower one in the sacral region that controls reflexive erections. When damage occurs at or above the level of the lumbar center, men lose the capacity for psychogenic erections—the kinds of erections that occur in response to mental stimulation alone, such as when viewing erotic films or fantasizing. They may still be able to achieve reflexive erections from direct stimulation of the penis, as these erections are controlled by the sacral erection center located in a lower portion of the spinal cord. However, they cannot feel any genital sensations because the nerve connections to the brain are severed. Men with damage to the sacral erection center lose the capacity for reflexive erections but can still achieve psychogenic erections so long as their upper spinal cord remains intact. Overall, researchers find that about three of four men with spinal cord injuries are able to achieve erections but only about one in ten continues to ejaculate naturally. Others can ejaculate with a vibrator. Their brains may help to fill in some of the missing sensations associated with coitus and even orgasm.

Although the frequency of sexual activity among spinal cord–injured men tends to decline following the injury, about one-third continue to engage in sexual intercourse (Hyde, 2005; Komisaruk & Whipple, 2005). Such men typically report increased interest in alternative sexual activities, especially those involving areas above the level of the spinal injury, such as the mouth, lips, neck, and ears.

Many spinal cord–injured men can obtain erections and many spinal cord–injured women can lubricate. Their ability to become sexually aroused—biologically—depends on the nature and extent of their injury. They may not be able to sense their own arousal or orgasm, but they can observe their partner's response and take psychological pleasure in it.

 5

Retention of sexual response in women depends on the site and severity of the spinal cord injury. Women may lose the ability to experience genital sensations or to lubricate normally during sexual stimulation (Hyde, 2005; Komisaruk & Whipple, 2005). However, sensations in the breasts may not be affected, making the breasts more erotogenic. Most women with spinal cord injuries can engage in coitus, become impregnated, and deliver vaginally. A survey of 68 spinal cord–injured women showed that about half were able to achieve orgasm as a result of audiovisual erotic material combined with manual genital stimulation (Sipski et al., 2001). Spinal cord–injured women can heighten their sexual pleasure by using sexual imagery and manual stimulation (Sipski et al., 2001).

Couples facing the challenge of spinal cord injury may expand their sexual repertoire to focus less on genital stimulation (except to attain the reflexes of erection and lubrication) and more on the parts of the body that retain sensation. Stimulation of some areas of the body, such as the ears, the neck, and the breasts (in both men and women), can yield pleasurable erotic sensations.

Sensory Disabilities Sensory disabilities, such as blindness and deafness, do not directly affect genital responsiveness. Still, sexuality may be affected in many ways. A person who has been blind since birth or early childhood may have difficulty understanding a partner's anatomy. Sex education curricula have been designed specifically to enable visually impaired people to learn about sexual anatomy via models. Anatomically correct dolls may be used to simulate positions of intercourse.

People who are deaf often lack knowledge about sex. Their ability to comprehend the social cues involved in forming and maintaining intimate relationships may also be impaired. Sex education programs based on sign language are helping many people with hearing impairments become more socially perceptive as well as more knowledgeable about the physical aspects of sex. People with visual and hearing impairments often lack self-esteem and self-confidence, problems that make it difficult for them to establish intimate relationships. Counseling may help them become more aware of their sexuality and develop social skills.

Other Physical Disabilities and Impairments Specific disabilities pose particular challenges to, and impose particular limitations on, sexual functioning. Arthritis may make it difficult or painful for affected individuals to bend their arms, knees, or hips during sexual activity. Coital positions that minimize discomfort and the application of moist heat to the joints before sexual relations may be helpful.

A male amputee may find that he is better balanced in the lateral-entry or female-superior position than in the male-superior position. A woman with limited hand function may find it difficult or impossible to insert a diaphragm and may need to request assistance from her partner or switch to another contraceptive. Sensitivity to each other's needs is as vital to couples in which one member has a disability as it is to nondisabled couples.

Speaking of sensitivity, let us now turn to other psychological issues.

INTELLECTUAL DISABILITIES

People with intellectual disabilities are often stereotyped as incapable of understanding or controlling their sexual impulses. They are sometimes assumed to maintain childlike innocence through their lives or to be devoid of sexuality. On the other hand, it is widely acknowledged that individuals with limited intellectual capacities are vulnerable to sexual abuse and may not be able to provide consent to sexual activity with others (Levy & Packman, 2004; Plaut, 2006; Servais, 2006).

Some stereotype people with intellectual disabilities in the opposite direction: as having stronger-than-normal sex drives and being incapable of controlling them. Some people with intellectual disabilities do act inappropriately—by masturbating publicly, for example. The stereotypes are exaggerated, however, and even many disabled people who act inappropriately can be trained to follow social rules.

Parents and caretakers often discourage people with intellectual disabilities from learning about their sexuality or teach them to deny or suppress their sexual feelings (Gross, 2006). Yet most of them have normal sexual needs and can be guided into rewarding and responsible intimate relationships (Gross, 2006).

One of the greatest impediments to sexual fulfillment among people with disabilities is difficulty in finding a loving and supportive partner. Some people engage in sexual relations with people with disabilities out of sympathy. By and large, however, the partners are other people with disabilities or nondisabled people who have overcome stereotypes that portray disabled people as undesirable. Many partners have had a prior positive relationship with a person with a disability, usually during childhood. Experience facilitates acceptance of the idea that a disabled person can be desirable. Depending on the nature of the disability, the nondisabled partner may need to be open to assuming a more active sexual role to compensate for the limitations of the partner with the disability. Two partners with disabilities need to be sensitive to each other's needs and physical limitations. People with disabilities and their partners may also need to expand their sexual repertoires to incorporate ways of pleasuring each other that are not fixated on genital stimulation.

The message of this chapter is simple: Sexuality can enrich the lives of nearly all adults at virtually any age and in most physical and mental conditions.

Real Students, Real Questions

Q *How do individuals who are mentally retarded ever truly consent to sexual activity?*

A Most mentally retarded individuals are mildly retarded, and of these, the great majority understand the concept of consenting to sexual activity. Many live in committed long-term relationships; some are married. But many mentally retarded people cannot provide consent, and laws in almost all states have been enacted to prevent others from sexually exploiting them.

Chapter Review   ✓•⊏Study and Review on MyDevelopmentLab

LO1 Describe the various motives and lifestyles of single people

Recent years have seen an increase in the numbers of single young people in our society. Reasons include increased permissiveness toward premarital sex and, particularly for women, the desire to become established in a career. Some people remain single or celibate for religious reasons.

LO2 Explain what is meant by "hooking up"

Hooking up involves abrupt decision to engage in sexual activity with another person without a mutual expectation of a romantic commitment.

LO3 Describe the incidence of cohabitation and public attitudes toward cohabitation

Since the 1960s, the numbers of inhabiting couples have mushroomed from about half a million to seven-and-a-half million. Cohabitation is more prevalent among less well educated and less affluent people. Some couples prefer cohabitation because it provides a consistent intimate relationship without the legal and economic entanglements of marriage. Some emotionally committed couples cohabit because of the economic advantages of sharing household expenses.

LO4 Discuss the relationships between cohabitation and marriage

Cohabitors who later marry may run a greater risk of divorce than noncohabitors, perhaps because cohabitors tend to be more liberal than people who do not live together before getting married.

LO5 Discuss the changing incidence of marriage

Fewer people in the United States are married than in the past; the number has decreased from about two-thirds to one-half over the past 50 years. (At the same time, more people are cohabiting than ever before.)

LO6 Describe types of marriage

The major male–female marriages consist of two types: monogamy and polygamy. Gay marriage is recognized in several Western nations and many states.

LO7 Discuss whom we marry

Americans tend to practice *homogamy*—that is, to marry partners similar to themselves. They often marry people from the same ethnic and religious background and the same geographical area. As they approach marriage, they also pay attention to personality traits and attitudes.

LO8 Discuss the rise of intermarriage in the United States

The incidence of intermarriage has been increasing and now accounts for 15% of new marriages and 8% of all marriages. African American men are more likely to intermarry than are African American women. Asian American women are more likely to intermarry than are Asian American men.

LO9 Discuss sex in marriage

Married couples today have sex more often and for longer durations of time than in Kinsey's day. Wives take more active sexual roles.

LO10 Discuss factors in marital satisfaction

Marital satisfaction involves factors such as commitment, adequate income, generosity, sharing of key attitudes, sexual satisfaction—and for those who are religious, belief in the spiritual value of marriage.

LO11 Discuss infidelity

People may have affairs for sexual variety, to punish their spouses, to achieve emotional closeness with someone, or to prove that they are attractive. In swinging, or mate-swapping, the partner participates. Extramarital sex continues to be viewed negatively by most people in our society.

LO12 Discuss the incidence of divorce and issues connected with divorce

Forty to fifty percent of the marriages in the United States end in divorce. Reasons for divorce include relaxed restrictions on divorce, greater financial independence among women, and the idea that marriages should be happy. Divorce is often associated with financial and emotional problems.

LO13 Describe physical changes in the later years that affect sexual behavior

Partners may become less attractive to one another. It becomes more difficult for males to attain and maintain erections, and for females to lubricate.

LO14 Discuss patterns of sexual activity in the later years

Older people engage in a variety of sexual behaviors, although not as frequently as younger people. Many potential sexual problems can be averted by changing expectations and making changes to accommodate aging.

LO15 **Discuss the relationships between physical disabilities and sexual behavior**
Cerebral palsy does not usually impair sexual interest, capacity for orgasm, or fertility, but afflicted people may be limited to certain types of sexual activities and coital positions. People with spinal cord injuries may be paralyzed and lose sensation below the waist but still respond reflexively to direct genital stimulation.

LO16 **Discuss the relationships between intellectual disabilities and sexual behavior**
Most people with mild intellectual disabilities can develop responsible intimate relationships.

Test Your Learning

1. All of the following are connected with getting married at later ages today *except*
   (a) living together first to test compatibility.
   (b) women's desire to focus on careers.
   (c) social pressure to remain single.
   (d) advanced education.

2. All of the following have contributed to the divorce rate in the United States *except*
   (a) higher expectations from marriage.
   (b) relaxation of legal restrictions on divorce.
   (c) increased economic independence of women.
   (d) sexual problems.

3. In late adulthood,
   (a) the testes increase slightly in size.
   (b) most men cannot obtain an erection.
   (c) most men still like sex.
   (d) testosterone production increases.

4. Which of the following is *not* true about first-year college students who "hook up"?
   (a) They have often been drinking.
   (b) They are firmly opposed to casual sexual relationships.
   (c) Hooking up may cause more distress in female than in male students.
   (d) They tend to place themselves in conducive settings.

5. A poll found that married people are more likely than single people to report they are happy. We should regard these results with skepticism because
   (a) of the selection factor.
   (b) they did not include gay marriages.
   (c) the definition of happiness was unclear.
   (d) the statistics were applied carelessly.

6. Polyandry is a form of marriage in which
   (a) one wife has more than one husband.
   (b) one husband has more than one wife.
   (c) there are multiple wives and husbands.
   (d) there is rapid divorce and remarriage.

7. About _____% of high school seniors say they expect to remain married to the same person for life.
   (a) 45   (b) 60
   (c) 75   (d) 90

8. About _____% of American marriages end in divorce.
   (a) 10–20   (b) 20–30
   (c) 30–40   (d) 40–50

9. The term *homogamy* refers to
   (a) like marrying like.   (b) gay marriage.
   (c) polygyny.   (d) polyandry.

10. _____ Americans are most likely to marry someone of a different race or ethnicity.
    (a) African   (b) Asian American
    (c) European   (d) Latin

Answers: 1. c; 2. b; 3. d; 4. b; 5. a; 6. a; 7. b; 8. d; 9. a; 10. b

My Life, My Sexuality

Making Decisions about Your Style of Life

*Explore this **My Life, My Sexuality** feature by scanning this QR code with your mobile device. If you don't already have one, you may download a free QR scanner for your device wherever smartphone apps are sold. You can also view this feature in MyDevelopmentLab, along with an accompanying critical thinking assignment.*

As a college student, you may well have some decisions to be made. Perhaps it's possible to look at some of the content of this chapter to see if it can be of help. For example, would you consider—or have you engaged in—one or more sexual hookups? What are the relationships between hookups, self-esteem, and stress for people of your gender? Are you cohabiting or would you consider cohabiting? Are you married, or do you plan on being married? Scan the code to learn more about the relationships between various lifestyles, your values, and your well-being.

15 Sexual Dysfunctions

Learning Objectives

TYPES OF SEXUAL DYSFUNCTIONS

LO1   Identify and define the various sexual dysfunctions

ORIGINS OF SEXUAL DYSFUNCTIONS: A BIOPSYCHOSOCIAL APPROACH

LO2   Discuss biological factors in sexual dysfunctions
LO3   Discuss psychosocial factors in sexual dysfunctions

TREATMENT OF SEXUAL DYSFUNCTIONS

LO4   Discuss the historic Masters and Johnson approach to sex therapy
LO5   Discuss the integration of sex therapy and psychotherapy
LO6   Discuss the treatment of specific sexual dysfunctions

MY LIFE, MY SEXUALITY: FINDING A QUALIFIED SEX THERAPIST

Explore the video, **Dr. Richard Carroll, Sex Therapist,** by scanning this QR code with your mobile device. If you don't already have one, you may download a free QR scanner for your device wherever smartphone apps are sold. You can also view this video in MyDevelopmentLab. For more videos related to this chapter's content, log into MyDevelopmentLab to view the entire Human Sexuality Video Series.

TRUTH OR FICTION?

Which of the following statements are the truth, and which are fiction? Look for the Truth-or-Fiction icons on the pages that follow to find the answers.

1 Sexual dysfunctions are rare.   **T   F?**

2 Only men can reach orgasm too early.   **T   F?**

3 The most common cause of painful intercourse in women is vaginal infection.   **T   F?**

4 Sex therapy teaches a man with erectile disorder how to "will" an erection.   **T   F?**

5 A doctor made a somewhat unusual presentation to a medical convention by dropping his pants to reveal an erection.   **T   F?**

6 Many sex therapists recommend masturbation as the treatment for women who have never been able to reach orgasm.   **T   F?**

7 A man can prevent ejaculation by squeezing his penis when he feels that he is about to ejaculate.   **T   F?**

Derek, 39, and his wife Pam, 37, had not attempted sexual intercourse for five years. Sexual relations had been limited to fondling, caressing, and occasional oral–genital contact. They had given up attempting intercourse because of Derek's difficulty in attaining and sustaining erections. But recently they had begun trying again. Some nights Derek would have an erection enabling him to penetrate, only to find that he quickly lost the erection. Many nights he was unable to perform at all. Each failure was another blow to his self-esteem. Pam worried that he could not perform because he was no longer attracted to her.

Terry, 24, has decided she is built differently from friends and women she reads about. They all reach orgasm, it seems, at the drop of a hat. But she has never managed "one of those things." Her husband David, also 24, is considerate, but Terry knows that he, too, is frustrated and feels guilty with every ejaculation. Why should he enjoy sex if Terry cannot? Terry and David anticipate sex with fear rather than pleasure, and David has been having

difficulty attaining erection. Terry wonders whether she should try to fake orgasm to hold on to him. But she fears she would not know how.

—The Authors' Files

Sexual dysfunctions Persistent or recurrent difficulties in becoming sexually aroused or reaching orgasm.

▶ **Watch the Video**
Dr. Richard Carroll, Sex Therapist
on **MyDevelopmentLab**

erek and Terry have sexual dysfunctions. **Sexual dysfunctions** are persistent or recurrent problems in becoming sexually aroused or reaching orgasm. Many of us have sexual problems from time to time. Men occasionally have difficulty obtaining an erection or ejaculate more quickly than they would like. Women occasionally have difficulty lubricating or reaching orgasm. But sexual dysfunctions, per se, are persistent and cause significant distress.

People with sexual dysfunctions may avoid sexual opportunities for fear of failure. They may anticipate that sex will result in frustration or pain rather than pleasure and gratification. Because our culture emphasizes sexual competence, people with sexual dysfunctions may feel inadequate or incompetent—feelings that diminish their self-esteem (Fishman & Mamo, 2001). They may also experience guilt, shame, frustration, depression, and anxiety.

Many people with sexual dysfunctions find it difficult to talk about them, even with spouses or helping professionals. A woman who cannot reach orgasm with her husband may not want to "make a fuss." A man may find it difficult to admit erectile problems to his physician during a physical exam. Many physicians are also uncomfortable talking about sex and may never ask about it.

We do not have precise figures on the occurrence of sexual dysfunctions. The most accurate information may be based on the report by Ronald Lewis and his colleagues (2010), which summarizes epidemiological data from surveys around the world (see Table 15.1). Although there is wide variation in the figures gleaned from the surveys, we can make a couple of generalizations:

- Women report a higher prevalence of sexual dysfunctions than men do.
- The prevalence of nearly every sexual dysfunction increases with age, with early ejaculation being a notable exception.
- The most prevalent sexual problems in women are low sexual desire and difficulty reaching orgasm.
- The least prevalent sexual dysfunctions are sexual pain disorders.
- Despite the stereotype that men are "always ready" to engage in sexual activity, many men report having low sexual desire. ◉

Table 15.1

Prevalence of Sexual Dysfunctions Based on Epidemiological Studies from around the World

	Women	Men
At least one sexual dysfunction	40–45%	20–30%
Low sexual desire	17–55%	8–25%
Arousal and lubrication problems; erectile dysfunction (ED) in males	8–28%	1–40%*
Orgasmic dysfunction**	16–25%***	12–19%
Early ejaculation		8–30%
Sexual pain disorders	1–27%	1–6%

Source: Lewis, R. W., Fugl-Meyer, K. S., Corona, G., Hayes, R. D., Laumann, E. O., Moreira, E. D., Jr., Rellini, A. H., & Segraves T. (2010). Definitions/Epidemiology/Risk Factors for Sexual Dysfunction. *Journal of Sexual Medicine, 7*, 1598–1607.

* The prevalence may double from the 40s to the 60s and again from the 60s to the 70s and above, with some studied showing rates much higher than those shown in the table.

** Difficulty reaching orgasm in women; "delayed ejaculation" in men.

*** Outliers put the percentage as high as 80% for older women.

TRUTH OR FICTION REVISITED: It is not true that sexual dysfunctions are rare. As noted in the study by Lewis and his colleagues (2010), about two women in five, and one-quarter of men, report experiencing at least one sexual dysfunction.

Types of Sexual Dysfunctions

The most widely used system of classification of sexual dysfunctions is based on the American Psychiatric Association's *Diagnostic and Statistical Manual of Mental Disorders (DSM)*. The *DSM* proposes four categories of sexual dysfunctions:

1. **Sexual desire disorders.** These generally involve lack of interest in sex or aversion to sexual contact. However, some professionals also include problems characterized by consuming too much time in sexual fantasies, urges, and behavior (a problem they term *hypersexual disorder*).
2. **Sexual arousal disorders.** Sexual arousal is mainly characterized by erection in the male and vaginal lubrication and swelling of the external genitalia in the female. In men, sexual arousal disorders involve difficulty in obtaining or sustaining erections sufficient to engage in sexual intercourse. In women, they typically involve insufficient lubrication.
3. **Orgasmic disorders.** Men or women may have difficulty reaching orgasm, or may reach orgasm more quickly than they would like. Women are more likely to encounter difficulties reaching orgasm. Men are more likely to reach orgasm too quickly (have early ejaculation).
4. **Sexual pain/penetration disorders.** Both men and women may suffer from **dyspareunia** (painful intercourse). Women may experience **vaginismus**, or involuntary contraction of muscles that surround the vaginal barrel, preventing penetration by the penis or making it painful.

Sexual dysfunctions are classified as lifelong or acquired. Acquired dysfunctions follow a period of normal functioning. Dysfunctions are also classified as generalized or situational. *Generalized* dysfunctions occur in all situations. *Situational* dysfunctions affect sexual functioning only in some situations, as during intercourse

 1

Sexual desire disorders Sexual dysfunctions in which people have persistent or recurrent lack of sexual desire or aversion to sexual contact.

Sexual arousal disorders Sexual dysfunctions in which people persistently or recurrently fail to become adequately sexually aroused to engage in or sustain sexual intercourse.

Orgasmic disorders Sexual dysfunctions in which people persistently or recurrently have difficulty reaching orgasm or reach orgasm more rapidly than they would like, despite attaining a level of sexual stimulation of sufficient intensity to normally result in orgasm.

Sexual pain disorders Sexual dysfunctions in which people persistently or recurrently experience pain during coitus.

Dyspareunia A sexual dysfunction characterized by persistent or recurrent pain during sexual intercourse.

Vaginismus A sexual dysfunction characterized by involuntary contraction of the muscles surrounding the vaginal barrel, preventing penile penetration or rendering penetration painful.

Real Students, Real Questions

Q *What does* prude *mean? Is this considered a sexual dysfunction?*

A The word *prude* has the same origin as the word *proud*, and it refers to being highly or evenly excessively proper or modest in one's own speech, behavior, and dress. In other words, prudes prefer not to curse, engage in behaviors such as serious kissing in public, or dress seductively. They also typically disapprove of such displays by others. What they do privately in a committed relationship might be quite different. In fact, they might enjoy sex a great deal, so there is no necessary connection between public prudery and sexual functioning or dysfunctioning. The origins of prudery are uncertain. Being reared strictly may have something to do with it, although many young people rebel, especially in open societies. And there might just be a genetic component.

but not masturbation, or with one partner but not another. If a man has never been able to obtain an erection during sexual relations with a partner but can do so during masturbation, his dysfunction is lifelong and situational.

SEXUAL DESIRE DISORDERS

Sexual desire disorders involve lack of sexual desire or aversion to genital sexual activity. People with little or no sexual interest or desire may be said to have *hypoactive sexual desire disorder*. They often report an absence of sexual fantasies. Lack of desire, as noted in Table 15.1, is more common among women than men.

Lack of sexual desire does not imply that a person is unable to achieve erection, lubricate adequately, or reach orgasm. Some people with low sexual desire can become sexually aroused and reach orgasm when stimulated adequately. Many enjoy sexual activity, even if they are unlikely to initiate it. Many appreciate the affection and closeness of physical intimacy, but have no interest in genital stimulation (Hackett, 2008).

Lack of sexual interest or desire is one of the most commonly diagnosed sexual dysfunctions, yet there is no clear consensus among clinicians and researchers concerning the definition of low sexual desire (Heiman, 2008). Lack of desire is usually considered a problem when couples recognize that their level of sexual interest has gotten so low that little remains (Heiman, 2008). Lack of desire is often limited to one partner. When one partner is more interested in sex than the other, sex therapists often recommend that couples compromise. They also try to resolve problems in the relationship that may dampen sexual ardor (Carvalho & Nobre, 2012).

When is lack of desire among women a dysfunction? The literature on sex differences strongly suggests that women, in general, are less interested in sex than men (Petersen & Hyde, 2011). This is not to suggest that there is anything wrong with women who experience strong, regular sexual urges.

CRITICAL THINKING
There is no consensus among clinicians and researchers concerning the definition of low sexual desire. How much sexual interest or desire would seem to be normal to you? Why?

SEXUAL AVERSION DISORDER

People with low sexual desire may have little or no interest in sex, but they are not repelled by genital contact. Some people, however, find sex disgusting or aversive and avoid such contact. A history of sexual trauma, such as rape or childhood sexual abuse or incest, often figures prominently in cases of sexual aversion, especially in women (Colangelo & Keefe-Cooperman, 2012).

SEXUAL AROUSAL DISORDERS

When we are sexually stimulated, our bodies normally respond with **vasocongestion**, which produces erection in the male and vaginal lubrication in the female. People with sexual arousal disorders fail to achieve or sustain the lubrication or erection necessary to enable sexual activity. Or they lack the feelings of sexual pleasure or excitement that normally accompany sexual arousal.

Problems of sexual arousal have sometimes been labeled *impotence* in the male and *frigidity* in the female. But these terms are pejorative, so many professionals prefer to use less threatening, more descriptive labels.

Erectile Disorder
Sexual arousal disorder in the male is called **male erectile disorder** or *erectile dysfunction*. It is characterized by persistent difficulty in achieving or maintaining an erection sufficient to allow the completion of sexual activity. In most cases the failure is limited to sexual activity with partners, or with some partners and not others. It can therefore be classified as *situational*. In some cases the dysfunction is found during any sexual activity, including masturbation. In these instances, it is considered *generalized dysfunction*. Some men with erectile disorder are unable to attain an erection with their partners. Others can achieve erection but not sustain it (or recover it) long enough for penetration and ejaculation (Becher & Bechara, 2011).

Erectile disorder usually develops after a period of normal functioning. Many men engage in years of successful coitus before the problem begins. Occasional problems in achieving or maintaining erection are quite common. 👁

Female Sexual Arousal Disorder
Women may encounter persistent difficulties becoming sexually excited or sufficiently lubricated in response to sexual stimulation. In some cases these difficulties are lifelong. In others, they develop after a period of normal functioning. In some cases difficulties are pervasive and occur during both masturbation and sex with a partner. More often they occur in certain

Vasocongestion Engorgement of blood vessels with blood, which swells the genitals and breasts during sexual arousal.

Erectile disorder Persistent difficulty achieving or maintaining an erection sufficient to allow the man to engage in or complete sexual intercourse. Also termed *erectile dysfunction*.

👁⃞**Watch** the **Video**
Men Seeking Medical Help
on **MyDevelopmentLab**

The Emotional Toll of Erectile Dysfunction. Male erectile disorder or erectile dysfunction is characterized by persistent difficulty in achieving or maintaining an erection sufficient to allow the completion of sexual activity. As many as 30 million men in the United States experience some degree of erectile dysfunction, and the incidence increases with age. Occasional erectile problems are common and may be caused by fatigue, alcohol, or anxiety about a new partner. However, fear of recurrence can create a vicious cycle, in which anxiety leads to failure, and failure heightens anxiety.

situations. For example, they occur with some partners and not with others, or during intercourse but not during oral sex or masturbation (Giraldi et al., 2012).

Female sexual arousal disorder often accompanies other sexual disorders such as hypoactive sexual desire disorder and orgasmic disorders. Despite problems in becoming sexually aroused, women with sexual arousal disorders can often engage in coitus. Vaginal dryness may produce discomfort.

Female sexual arousal disorder, like its male counterpart, may have physical causes. A thorough evaluation by a medical specialist is recommended. Any neurological, vascular, or hormonal problem that interferes with the lubrication or swelling response of the vagina to sexual stimulation may contribute to female sexual arousal disorder. For example, diabetes mellitus may damage the nerves and blood vessels servicing the clitoral region. Reduced estrogen production can result in vaginal dryness.

Another interesting line of research suggests that the skin of some women with sexual arousal problems is not as sensitive to touch as the skin of women who do not have such problems. In such cases, the woman might seek to increase sexual stimulation—psychological as well as physical.

Female sexual arousal disorder more commonly has psychological causes, however. In some cases, women harbor deep-seated anger and resentment toward their partners (McCabe et al., 2010). They therefore find it difficult to turn off these feelings when they go to bed. In other cases, sexual trauma is implicated. Survivors of sexual abuse often find it difficult to respond sexually to their partners. Childhood sexual abuse is especially prevalent in cases of female sexual arousal disorder (Colangelo & Keefe-Cooperman, 2012). Feelings of helplessness, anger, or guilt, or even flashbacks of the abuse, may surface when the woman begins sexual activity, dampening her ability to become aroused. Other psychosocial causes include anxiety or guilt about sex and ineffective stimulation by her partner (McCabe et al., 2010).

ORGASMIC DISORDERS

Orgasmic disorders include (1) female orgasmic disorder, (2) delayed ejaculation, and (3) early or premature ejaculation. In female or male orgasmic disorder, the woman or man is persistently delayed in reaching orgasm or does not reach orgasm

Real Students, Real Questions

Q *I was molested as a child, and the thought of sex does not interest me. What can I do about this?*

A We will offer you some generalizations, but we will also admit, right at the beginning, that we do not know enough about your particular situation to be more specific. We also suggest that you might want to talk it over with a helping professional who has expertise in the area. Having said that, you might begin by allowing a good relationship to develop with a decent, caring person. If you are comfortable in the relationship and are engaging in some cuddling and so on, you might find some interest in sex developing. If such a relationship does not stir sexual feelings, it still would not hurt to discuss the situation with a professional. Also consider that your history of being abused may not be the "cause" of your current lack of interest in sex. For the third time: Have a talk with a helping professional.

at all, despite achieving sexual stimulation of sufficient intensity to normally result in orgasm. The problem is more common among women than men. In some cases a person can reach orgasm without difficulty while engaging in sexual relations with one partner, but not with another.

Female Orgasmic Disorder Women with female orgasmic disorder are unable to reach orgasm or have difficulty reaching orgasm following what would usually be an adequate amount of sexual stimulation. Women who have never achieved orgasm through any means are sometimes labeled **anorgasmic** or *pre*orgasmic.

A woman who reaches orgasm through masturbation or oral sex may not necessarily reach orgasm during coitus with her partner. Penile thrusting during coitus may not provide sufficient clitoral stimulation to facilitate orgasm. An orgasmic disorder may be diagnosed, however, if orgasm during coitus was impaired by factors such as sexual guilt or performance anxiety. Women who try to force an orgasm may also find themselves unable to do so. They may assume a **spectator role** and observe rather than fully participate in their sexual encounters. "Spectatoring" may further decrease the likelihood of orgasm.

Delayed Ejaculation Male orgasmic disorder has also been termed *male orgasmic disorder, retarded ejaculation,* and *ejaculatory incompetence.* The problem may be lifelong or acquired, generalized or situational. There are very few cases of men who have never ejaculated. In most cases the disorder is limited to coitus. The man may be capable of ejaculating during masturbation or oral sex, but find it difficult, if not impossible—despite high levels of sexual excitement—to ejaculate during intercourse. One might think that female partners could possibly enjoy such a dysfunction because it would enable a man to last longer. But the experience can be frustrating for both partners (Althof, 2012). Male orgasmic disorder is relatively infrequent in the general population and in clinical practice, where it is among the least frequently diagnosed disorders.

Anorgasmic Never having reached orgasm.

Spectator role A role, usually taken on because of performance anxiety, in which people observe rather than fully participate in their sexual encounters.

Male orgasmic disorder may be caused by physical problems such as multiple sclerosis or neurological damage that interferes with neural control of ejaculation. It may also be a side effect of certain drugs. Various psychological factors may also play a role, including performance anxiety, sexual guilt, and hostility toward the partner. Emotional factors such as fears of pregnancy and anger toward one's partner can also play a role.

As with other sexual dysfunctions, men with orgasmic disorder and their partners may "try harder." But trying harder may worsen rather than help sexual problems. Sexual relations become a job to get done, a chore rather than an opportunity for pleasure and gratification.

Early Ejaculation A second type of male orgasmic disorder, early or premature or rapid ejaculation, is the most common male sexual dysfunction (see Table 15.1). Men with **early ejaculation** ejaculate too rapidly to permit their partners or themselves to fully enjoy sexual relations (Graziottin & Althof, 2011). The degree of prematurity or rapidity varies. Some men ejaculate during foreplay, even at the sight of their partner disrobing. But most ejaculate either just prior to or immediately upon penetration, or following a few coital thrusts. The point is that his partner—and he—would rather wait a while. In determining what is too rapid, some scholars argue that the focus should be on whether the couple is satisfied with the duration of coitus rather than on a specific time period. According to Ronald Lewis and his colleagues (2010), "premature ejaculation … always or nearly always occurs prior to or within about 1 minute of vaginal penetration, and the inability to delay ejaculation on all or nearly all vaginal penetrations, and negative personal consequences such as distress, bother, frustration, and/or the avoidance of sexual intimacy" (p. 1600).

Helen Singer Kaplan (1974) suggested that the label of early or premature ejaculation should be applied when men persistently or recurrently lack voluntary control over their ejaculations. This may sound like a contradiction in terms since ejaculation is a reflex, and reflexes need not involve thought or conscious control. Kaplan meant, however, that a man may control ejaculation by regulating the amount of sexual stimulation he experiences so that it remains low enough not to trigger the ejaculation reflex until the partners are ready.

Rapid Female Orgasm: Can Women Reach Orgasm Too Quickly? The female counterpart to early ejaculation, *rapid orgasm,* is so rarely recognized as a problem that it is generally ignored by clinicians and is not usually classified as a sexual

Early ejaculation A sexual dysfunction in which ejaculation occurs with minimal sexual stimulation and before the partners desire it.

Real Students, Real Questions

Q *Do women find a man ejaculating disgusting? Is that a dysfunction?*

A Some women find ejaculation disgusting. Others are turned on by it. Still others have no particular feelings about it. The reasons for these variations are unclear. Finding ejaculating disgusting is not in itself a sexual dysfunction. If it gives rise to a sexual aversion, it might be.

dysfunction. **TRUTH** OR FICTION REVISITED: Still, some women experience orgasm rapidly and show little interest in continuing sexual activity so that their partners can achieve gratification. Many women who reach orgasm rapidly are open to continued sexual stimulation and capable of experiencing successive orgasms, however.

SEXUAL PAIN/PENETRATION DISORDERS

For most of us, coitus is a source of pleasure. For some of us, however, coitus gives rise to pain and discomfort. And still others may experience pleasure, but pain is the price they pay for it.

Dyspareunia One sexual pain disorder, dyspareunia, or painful coitus, afflicts both men and women. Dyspareunia is a common sexual dysfunction and a common complaint of women seeking gynecological services.

Pain is usually a sign that something is physically wrong (Brauer et al., 2009). Dyspareunia may result from physical causes, emotional factors, or an interaction of the two.

TRUTH OR FICTION REVISITED: The most common cause of painful intercourse—or dyspareunia—in women is not vaginal infection. It is lack of adequate lubrication. In such a case, additional foreplay or artificial lubrication may help. The normal changes of aging may play a role among perimenopausal and post-menopausal women (Lewis et al., 2010). Vaginal infections or sexually transmitted infections (STIs) may also produce painful sex. Allergic reactions to spermicides, even the latex material in condoms, can give rise to painful sex. Pain during deep thrusting may indicate endometriosis, pelvic inflammatory disease (PID), or structural disorders of the reproductive organs.

Psychological factors such as unresolved guilt or anxiety about sex or the lingering effects of sexual trauma may also be involved. These factors may inhibit lubrication and cause involuntary contractions of the vaginal musculature, making penetration painful or uncomfortable.

Painful intercourse is less common in men and is generally associated with genital infections that cause burning or painful ejaculation. Smegma under the penile foreskin of uncircumcised men may also irritate the penile glans during sexual contact.

Vulvodynia The pain has lasted for months. You're so uncomfortable you can hardly sit. Having sex is unthinkable. Nothing alleviates the pain, burning and irritation, at least not for long. (Mayo Clinic, 2006)

This is the Mayo Clinic's description of the form of dyspareunia termed **vulvodynia**. Vulvodynia is a gynecological condition characterized by vulval pain, particularly chronic burning sensations, irritation, and soreness. Although vulvodynia and related conditions, such as vestibulitis, can give rise to painful intercourse, they are not in themselves considered sexual dysfunctions. Their causes are unknown, although a history of local infections, damage to local nerves, and allergies are among the suspects (van Lankveld et al., 2010). Cold compresses, local anesthetics, and topical creams with estrogen or cortisone may provide relief (Mayo Clinic, 2006). Consult your gynecologist about other possible treatments.

Vaginismus Another sexual pain disorder, vaginismus, involves involuntary contraction of the pelvic muscles that surround the outer third of the vaginal barrel. Vaginismus occurs reflexively during attempts at vaginal penetration, making entry by the penis painful or impossible. The muscle contractions are accompanied by fear of penetration. Some women with vaginismus are unable to tolerate penetration by any object, including a finger, tampon, or a physician's speculum. The prevalence of vaginismus is unknown.

Vulvodynia A gynecological condition characterized by vulva pain, burning sensations, irritation, and soreness.

The woman with vaginismus usually is not aware that she is contracting her vaginal muscles. In some cases, husbands of women with vaginismus develop erectile disorder after repeated failures at penetration.

Vaginismus is considered to be caused by psychological fear of penetration rather than physical injury or defect (Brauer et al., 2009; ter Kuile et al., 2009). Women with vaginismus often have histories of sexual trauma, rape, or botched abortions that resulted in vaginal injuries. They may desire sexual relations, and they may be capable of becoming sexually aroused and achieving orgasm. However, fear of penetration triggers an involuntary spasm of the vaginal musculature at the point of penile insertion. Vaginismus can also be a cause or an effect of dyspareunia. Women who experience painful coitus may develop a fear of penetration. Fear then leads to the development of involuntary vaginal contractions. Vaginismus and dyspareunia may also give rise to, or result from, erectile disorder in men. Feelings of failure and anxiety can overwhelm both partners.

Origins of Sexual Dysfunctions: A Biopsychosocial Approach

We human beings are complex, with complex bodies as well as complex mental processes. We are also reared in families within cultural settings. For these reasons, we need to consider possible biological, psychological, and social factors in sexual dysfunctions (Brown & Haaser, 2005). For example, biological and psychosocial factors—hormonal deficiencies, depression, dissatisfaction with one's relationship, and so on—contribute to lack of desire. Moreover, these factors can interact in a number of ways. Researchers refer to such an approach as a **biopsychosocial model**.

BIOLOGICAL FACTORS

Researchers find that health problems—especially cardiovascular disorders, hypertension, and obesity—can contribute to several kinds of sexual dysfunctions in men (Tan et al., 2012), but mostly to sexual pain in women (van Lankveld et al., 2010). Even when biological factors are involved in sexual dysfunctions, psychological factors such as anger and depression can prolong or worsen them (Tan et al., 2012).

Among the medical conditions that diminish sexual desire are testosterone deficiencies, thyroid overactivity or underactivity, and temporal lobe epilepsy. Sexual desire is stoked by testosterone, which is produced by men in the testes and both men and women in the adrenal glands (Buvat et al., 2010). Women may experience less sexual desire when their adrenal glands are surgically removed (Wierman et al., 2010). Low sexual interest, along with erectile difficulties, is also common among men with **hypogonadism**, which is treated with testosterone (Buvat et al., 2010).

The reduction in testosterone levels that occurs in middle and later life may in part explain a gradual decline in sexual desire among men (Buvat et al., 2010). But women's sexual desire may also decline with age, because of physical and psychological changes, as we will see (Wierman et al., 2010). Some medications, especially those used to control anxiety or hypertension, may also reduce desire. Changing medications or doses may reinstate the person's previous level of desire.

Fatigue may lead to erectile disorder and orgasmic disorder in men, and to inadequate lubrication and orgasmic disorder in women. But these will be isolated incidents unless the person attaches too much meaning to them and becomes concerned about future performances. Painful sex, however, often reflects underlying infections (van Lankveld et al., 2010). Medical conditions that affect sexual response include heart disease, diabetes mellitus, multiple sclerosis, spinal cord injuries,

Biopsychosocial model An approach to explaining dysfunctions that refers to the interactions of biological, psychological, and social/cultural factors.

Hypogonadism An endocrine disorder that reduces the output of testosterone.

complications from surgery (such as removal of the prostate in men), hormonal problems, and the use of some medicines, such as those used to treat hypertension and psychiatric disorders (Londoño et al., 2012).

HIV and Sexual Dysfunctions There is little doubt that HIV/AIDS is associated with sexual dysfunction in both men and women. Men with HIV are also more likely to have hypogonadism and erectile dysfunction, which are apparently worsened by antiretroviral therapy (Zona et al., 2012). Antiretroviral therapy is known to increase levels of estrogen in men. A study of 78 seropositive gay males found a host of sexual dysfunctions ranging from loss of interest in sex to delayed ejaculation and erectile disorder (Cove & Petrak, 2004). Because the men were more capable of obtaining and maintaining erections without condoms than with condoms, many of them used condoms inconsistently.

Fatigue and Sexual Dysfunction. They were tired and it didn't happen. Should they keep trying or wait until they have had a good night's sleep?

HIV-seropositive women, too, show various sexual dysfunctions, from lack of interest to sexual arousal disorders to orgasmic dysfunction (Florence et al., 2004). Researchers attribute the dysfunctions to psychological factors—anxiety, irritability, and depression—and to the effects of HIV.

Erectile Disorder Biological causes of erectile disorder affect the flow of blood to and through the penis—a problem that becomes more common as men age—or damage to nerves involved in erection (Eardley et al., 2010). Erectile problems can arise when clogged or narrow arteries leading to the penis deprive the penis of oxygen (Miner et al., 2011). For example, erectile disorder is common among men with diabetes mellitus, a disease that can damage blood vessels and nerves. Eric Rimm (2000) of the Harvard School of Public Health studied 2,000 men and found that erectile dysfunction was connected with a large waist, physical inactivity, and drinking too much alcohol (or not having any alcohol!). The common condition among these men may be **atherosclerosis,** or hardening of the arteries, which is related to high levels of "bad cholesterol" (LDL, or low-density lipoprotein). Atherosclerosis can impede the flow of blood to the penis just as it impedes the flow of blood to the heart. Exercise, weight loss, eating fewer animal fats, and use of medicines called statins (such as Zocor and Lipitor) help to lower cholesterol levels. However, statins may also contribute to erectile dysfunction (Trivedi et al., 2012). Ask your doctor.

Middle-aged and older men might try weight control and regular exercise. The findings of the Massachusetts Male Aging Study suggest that men who exercise regularly seem to ward off erectile dysfunction (Derby, 2000). Men who burn 200 calories or more a day in physical activity, an amount that be achieved by briskly walking for two miles, cut their risk of erectile dysfunction by about half. Exercise seems to prevent atherosclerosis, keeping the arteries clear for the flow of blood into the penis.

But men (and women!) need to think about one particular form of exercise—bicycling. Bicycling, done right, is not a problem. However, the use of standard narrow bicycle seats is a problem. Use of these seats exert continual pressure in the perineal area (which lies between the penis or vulva and the anus), causing vascular (blood-flow) problems and nerve damage (Sommer et al., 2010). Frank Sommer

Atherosclerosis Hardening and narrowing of the arteries; a condition caused by the buildup of a hard substance known as *plaque* on the inside walls of arteries.

Bicycles Can Provide Exercise, but Do Many Riders Do Themselves More Harm than Good? Narrow seats can place pressure against the perineal area, leading to vascular problems and nerve damage in the region—also impairing sexual response.

and his colleagues (2010) recommend use of a "properly fitted" bicycle, meaning a bicycle with a wide enough seat and a seat position which does not place pressure in the perineal area. Such seats are widely available for men, and women are advised to consider them as well.

Nerve damage resulting from prostate surgery may impair erectile response (Koehler et al., 2012). Erectile disorder may also result from multiple sclerosis (MS), a disease in which nerve cells lose the protective coatings that facilitate transmission of neural messages (Keller et al., 2012). MS has also been implicated in male orgasmic disorder.

The bacteria that cause syphilis, a sexually transmitted infection, can invade the spinal cord and affect the cells that control erections, resulting in erectile dysfunction. Chronic kidney disease, hypertension, cancer, emphysema, and heart disease can all impair erectile response, as can endocrine disorders that impair testosterone production (Buvat et al., 2010).

People with sexual dysfunctions are generally advised to undergo a physical examination to determine whether their problems are biologically based. Men with erectile disorder may be evaluated in a sleep center to determine whether they attain erections while asleep. The technique is termed nocturnal penile **tumescence** (NPT). Healthy men usually have erections during rapid-eye-movement (REM) sleep, which occurs every 90 to 100 minutes. Men with biologically based erectile disorder often do not have nocturnal erections.

Prescription drugs and illicit drugs account for many cases of erectile disorder. Antidepressant medication and antipsychotic drugs may impair erectile functioning and cause orgasmic disorders (Olfson et al., 2005; Taylor et al., 2005). Tranquilizers such as Valium and Xanax may cause orgasmic disorder in either men or women. Some drugs used to treat high blood pressure can impair erectile response. Switching to other blood pressure drugs or adjusting doses may help. Other drugs that can lead to erectile disorder include adrenergic blockers, diuretics, anti-convulsants, anti-Parkinson drugs, and dyspepsia and ulcer-healing drugs (Do et al., 2009).

People and physicians need to be very, very aware of the sexual side effects of some drugs used to treat depression. So-called selective serotonin reuptake inhibitors—SSRIs for short—are widely prescribed not only for depression but also for panic disorder, obsessive-compulsive disorder, anorexia nervosa, and other ills. Most physicians are aware that these drugs have "some" effect on sexual arousal in "some" patients. However, the fact of the matter is that they almost completely impair sexual arousal in many patients, especially older patients (Burri et al., 2012; Fabre et al., 2012). Moreover, even when the patients discontinue the drugs, sexual functioning does *not* necessarily bounce back.

Some drugs that are helpful with depression may not impair sexual functioning—at least in the short run. Bupropion, at least when used temporarily, *sometimes* improves sexual functioning and is prescribed along with an SSRI to help prevent sexual side effects. Ask your physician. ◉

Speaking of "pills," it should be noted that regular use of over-the-counter painkillers such as aspirin, acetaminophen (e.g., Tylenol), ibuprofen (e.g., Motrin), and naproxen (e.g., Aleve) are also connected with erectile dysfunction (Gleason et al., 2011). These drugs are also called "NSAIDs"—an abbreviation for

 Watch the **Video**
Aspirin and Sex Drive
on **MyDevelopmentLab**

Tumescence   Swelling; erection.

nonsteroidal anti-inflammatory agents. They have important uses and should not necessarily be completely avoided. For example, 81 mg of aspirin a day, which is a small dose, has been shown to help avert heart attacks. The thing to keep in minds is that even though you can buy these drugs with a prescription, they are serious medicines. As always, we advise checking with your doctor when there is a question about the use of medicines.

Central nervous system depressants such as alcohol, heroin, and methadone can reduce sexual desire and impair sexual arousal (Brown et al., 2005). Narcotics also depress testosterone production, thereby reducing sexual desire and leading to erectile failure. Marijuana use has been associated with reduced sexual desire and performance (Wilson et al., 2000).

Regular use of stimulants such as cocaine can cause erectile disorder or male orgasmic disorder and reduce sexual desire in both women and men (Ciccarone, 2011; Hart et al., 2012). Some people report increased sexual pleasure from initial use of cocaine, but repeated use can lead to dependency on the drug for sexual arousal. Long-term use may compromise the ability to experience sexual pleasure.

Despite the fact that alcohol can impair sexual arousal on a given occasion, Laumann and his colleagues (1999) found no general relationship between alcohol consumption and sexual dysfunctions. However, problems can arise when people misattribute the sexually dampening effects of depressants such as alcohol to causes within themselves. In other words, if you are unable to perform sexually when you have had a few drinks and do not know that alcohol can depress your performance, you may believe that something is wrong with you. This belief can create anxiety at your next sexual opportunity, and that anxiety can prevent normal functioning. A second failure may set off a vicious cycle in which self-doubts prompt anxiety, and anxiety results in repeated failure and more anxiety.

Finally, there is the question as to whether taking various kinds of pills together, whether they are prescription drugs or nonprescription drugs, is related to sexual erectile dysfunction. In brief, it is (Londoño et al., 2012). As men age, they tend to be prescribed more drugs, especially cholesterol-fighting drugs (statins, as discussed earlier), and drugs that fight high blood pressure (hypertension). Drugs that are taken for high blood pressure are known to be associated with erectile dysfunction, and statins have come under suspicion. A study of several thousand male patients at the Kaiser-Permanente clinics in California calculated the relationships between self-reported erectile problems of patients, their age, and the kinds and numbers of drugs used (Londoño et al., 2012). As expected, erectile problems were associated with aging: Older men were more likely to report having erectile disorder. Older men also use more drugs. However, older men who used, say, three or more different types of drugs were more likely to report erectile problems than men of the same age who used 0–2 types of drugs. The problems were also "dose-related"; that is, men who used higher doses of the same drugs reported erectile problems more frequently than men who used lower doses. It really didn't matter what the drugs were in this particular study. Again, check with your doctor about using drugs. Ask about their interactions with one another, their doses, and whether you have to stay on them indefinitely.

How do people get "trapped" into heavy drug use (and we're talking about prescribed drugs and over-the-counter drugs such as aspirin here)? One "problem" is that the drugs "work"—that is, the blood pressure medicines actually lower blood pressure, and statins actually lower blood levels of harmful cholesterol—and doctors are understandably reluctant to discontinue them. Patients can ask doctors about substitutes, but doctors often respond—accurately—that there are no substitutes.

Medication and Sexual Dysfunctions. The right drugs, especially the right drugs, can be healthful and even life-saving. However, research shows that taking many different drugs, including over-the-counter drugs, can lessen sexual response. Tell your physician about *all* the drugs you are taking and their doses.

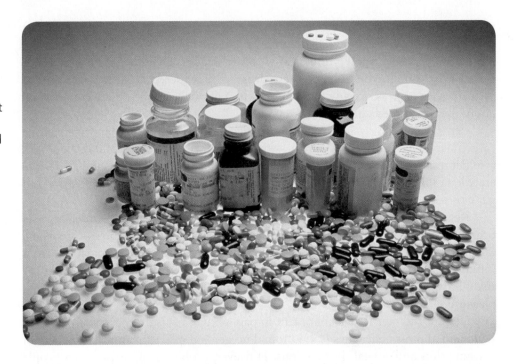

Another problem is that patients may have more than one doctor, perhaps a family doctor and one or two specialists, and they may all be prescribing something. A third problem is that patients may be mixing these drugs with NSAIDs, antihistamines (for allergies), and alcohol (which is a drug). It can be quite a brew. It can be wonderful and it can save lives. But there can also be problems. Patients need to inform their doctors about *everything* they are taking and they need to be frank if there are sexual problems.

Sexual Arousal in Women Aging can also affect the sexual response of women. Perimenopausal and postmenopausal women usually produce less vaginal lubrication than younger women and the vaginal walls become thin—changes that can render sex painful (van Lankveld et al., 2012). These physical changes, along with negative stereotypes of older women and men, can create performance anxiety and fumbling performances, and discourage both partners from attempting sexual activity (Brotto et al., 2012; McCabe et al., 2010). In such cases, artificial lubrication can help supplement the woman's own production, and estrogen replacement may halt or reverse some of the sexual changes of aging (Wierman et al., 2010). But partners also need to have realistic expectations and consider enjoyable sexual activities they can engage in without discomfort or high demands (Althof, 2010).

Women also develop vascular or nervous disorders that impair genital blood flow, reducing lubrication and sexual excitement, rendering intercourse painful, and reducing their ability to reach orgasm. As with men, these problems become more likely as women age.

PSYCHOSOCIAL FACTORS

Abrupt changes in sexual desire are more often explained by psychological and interpersonal factors such as depression, stress, and problems in the relationship (McCabe et al., 2010). Anxiety is the most commonly reported factor. It may dampen sexual desire, including performance anxiety (anxiety over being evaluated negatively), anxiety involving fears of pleasure or loss of control, and deeper sources of anxiety relating to fears of injury. Depression is also a common cause of lack of desire. A history of childhood sexual abuse or sexual assault has also been linked to low sexual desire (Colangelo & Keefe-Cooperman, 2012). ◉

Psychosocial factors connected with sexual dysfunctions include cultural influences, economic problems, psychosexual trauma, a gay sexual orientation, dissatisfaction with one's relationship, lack of sexual skills, irrational beliefs, and performance anxiety (McCabe et al., 2010).

Cultural Influences Children reared in sexually repressive cultural or home environments may learn to respond to sex with feelings of anxiety and shame, rather than anticipation and pleasure (Woo et al., 2011). People whose parents instilled in them a sense of guilt over touching their genitals may find it difficult to accept their sex organs as sources of pleasure (McCarthy et al., 2006).

In most cultures, sexual pleasure has traditionally been a male preserve. Young women may be reared to believe that sex is a duty to be performed for their husbands, not a source of personal pleasure. Although the traditional double standard has diminished in developed countries (Fugl-Meyer et al., 2006), some girls are still exposed to repressive attitudes. Women are more likely than men to be taught to suppress sexual desires (Nobre & Pinto-Gouveia, 2006). Self-control and vigilance—not sexual awareness and acceptance—become identified as feminine virtues. Women reared with such attitudes may not learn about their sexual potentials or express their erotic desires to their partners.

Many women who are exposed to negative attitudes about sex during childhood and adolescence find it difficult to suddenly view sex as a source of pleasure and satisfaction as adults. A lifetime of learning to turn themselves off sexually may impair sexual arousal and enjoyment when an acceptable opportunity arises (Woo et al., 2011).

Psychosexual Trauma Women and men who were sexually victimized in childhood are more likely to experience difficulty in becoming sexually aroused (Colangelo & Keefe-Cooperman, 2012; McCabe et al., 2010). Some learning theorists speak of conditioned anxiety in explaining sexual dysfunctions. Sexual stimuli come to elicit anxiety when they have been paired with traumatic experiences, such as rape, incest, or sexual molestation. Unresolved anger, misplaced guilt, and feelings of disgust also make it difficult for victims of sexual trauma to respond sexually, even years later and with loving partners.

Sexual Orientation Some gay males and lesbians test their sexual orientation by developing heterosexual relationships, even by entering heterosexual marriages and rearing children with their spouses. Others may wish to maintain the appearance of heterosexuality to avoid the social stigma attached to a gay male or lesbian sexual orientation. In such cases, problems with heterosexual partners can signify lack of heteroerotic interest (McCarthy et al., 2006).

Ineffective Sexual Techniques In some relationships, couples fall into a narrow sexual routine because one partner controls the timing and sequence of sexual techniques. A woman who remains unknowledgeable about the erotic importance of her clitoris may be unlikely to seek direct clitoral stimulation. A man who responds to one erectile failure by trying to force an erection may be unintentionally setting himself up for repeated failure. The couple who fail to communicate their sexual preferences or to experiment with new techniques may find themselves losing interest. Brevity of foreplay and coitus may contribute to female orgasmic disorder.

Emotional Factors Orgasm involves a sudden loss of voluntary control. Fear of losing control or "letting go" may block sexual arousal. Other emotional factors, especially depression, are often implicated in sexual dysfunctions (Carvalho &

◉ **Watch** the **Video**
Men Seeking Medical Help
on **MyDevelopmentLab**

CRITICAL THINKING
Are there any sexual attitudes common to people of your demographic background that can give rise to sexual problems or dysfunctions? What are the attitudes? Do you share these attitudes? Explain.

A Vicious Cycle? Conflict in the Relationship and Lack of Sexual Desire. Conflicts in a relationship may dampen sexual interest. Lack of sexual interest may then further strain the relationship.

Given our cultural values, why might it lead to a problem in a relationship if a woman were to exhibit sexual competence?

Nobre, 2010). Depression can contribute to lack of sexual desire. Stress can also interfere with sexual interest and response.

Problems in the Relationship Problems in the relationship are not easily left at the bedroom door (Brotto et al., 2010; Carvalho & Nobre, 2010). Heterosexual and homosexual couples alike usually find that sex is no better than other facets of their relationship (IsHak et al., 2010). Partners who have general trouble communicating may also be unable to communicate their sexual desires. Couples who harbor resentments may make sex their combat arena. They may fail to become aroused by their partners or "withhold" orgasm to make their partners feel guilty or inadequate (McCabe et al., 2010).

The following case highlights how sexual dysfunctions can develop against the backdrop of a troubled relationship:

> After living together for six months, Paul and Petula are contemplating marriage. But a problem has brought them to a sex therapy clinic. As Petula puts it, "For the last two months he hasn't been able to keep his erection after he enters me." Paul is 26, a lawyer; Petula, 24, is a buyer for a large department store. They both grew up in middle-class, suburban families, were introduced through mutual friends and began having intercourse, without difficulty, a few months into their relationship. At Petula's urging, Paul moved into her apartment, although he wasn't sure he was ready for such a step. A week later he began to have difficulty maintaining his erection during intercourse, although he felt strong desires for his partner. When his erection waned, he would try again, but would lose his desire and be unable to achieve another erection. After a few times like this, Petula would become so angry that she began striking Paul in the chest and screaming at him. Paul, who at 200 pounds weighed more than twice as much as Petula, would just walk away, which angered Petula even more.
>
> It became clear that sex was not the only trouble spot in their relationship. Petula complained that he preferred to be with his friends and go to baseball

games than to spend time with her. When they were together at home, he would become absorbed in watching sports events on television, and showed no interest in activities she enjoyed—attending the theater, visiting museums, etc. Since there was no evidence that the sexual difficulty was due to either organic problems or depression, a diagnosis of male erectile disorder was given. Neither Paul nor Petula was willing to discuss their nonsexual problems with a therapist. While the sexual problem was treated successfully with a form of sex therapy modeled after techniques developed by Masters and Johnson [see discussion later in the chapter] and the couple later married, Paul's ambivalence continued well into their marriage, and there were future recurrences of sexual problems as well. (Adapted from Spitzer et al., 1989, pp. 149–150)

Lack of Sexual Skills Sexual competency involves sexual knowledge and skills that are acquired through learning. We generally learn what makes us and others feel good through trial and error and by talking and reading about sex. Some people may not develop sexual competency because of a lack of opportunity to acquire knowledge and experience—even within a committed relationship. People with sexual dysfunctions may have been reared in families in which discussions of sexuality were off limits and early sexual experimentation was harshly punished.

Irrational Beliefs Irrational beliefs and attitudes may contribute to sexual dysfunctions. We cannot expect our partners to read our minds. We cannot assume that if they truly cared for us, they would know what we need, or want. Communication is one of the keys to sexual satisfaction.

Performance Anxiety Anxiety—especially **performance anxiety**—plays an important role in sexual dysfunctions (Althof & Needle, 2011; Althof, 2010). Performance anxiety occurs when a person becomes overly concerned with how well he or she performs a certain act or task. Performance anxiety may place a dysfunctional individual in a spectator rather than a performer role. Rather than focusing on erotic sensations and allowing reflexes like erection, lubrication, and orgasm to occur naturally, he or she focuses on self-doubts and thinks, "Will I be able to do it this time? Will this be another failure?"

In men, performance anxiety can inhibit erection while also triggering early ejaculation (Althof & Needle, 2011). Erection, mediated by the parasympathetic nervous system, can be blocked by activation of the sympathetic nervous system in the form of anxiety. Since ejaculation, like anxiety, is mediated by the sympathetic nervous system, arousal of this system in the form of anxiety can increase the level of stimulation and thereby heighten the potential for early ejaculation.

In women, performance anxiety can reduce vaginal lubrication and contribute to orgasmic disorder (Goldstein et al., 2006). Women with performance anxieties may try to force an orgasm, only to find that the harder they try, the more elusive it becomes. ◉

Treatment of Sexual Dysfunctions

When Kinsey conducted his surveys in the 1930s and 1940s, there was no effective treatment for sexual dysfunctions. At the time, the predominant model of therapy for sexual dysfunctions was long-term psychoanalysis. Psychoanalysts believed that the sexual problem would abate only if the presumed unconscious conflicts that lay at the root of the problem were resolved through long-term therapy.

◉ᴵ **Watch** the **Video**
In the Real World: Sexual Problems and Dysfunction on **MyDevelopmentLab**

Performance anxiety Anxiety concerning one's ability to perform behaviors, especially behaviors that may be evaluated by other people.

Evidence of the effectiveness of psychoanalysis in treating sexual dysfunctions is still lacking, however.

Since that time cognitive and behavioral models of short-term treatment, collectively called **sex therapy**, have emerged. Sex therapy aims to modify dysfunctional cognitions (beliefs and attitudes) and behavior as directly as possible. Sex therapists also recognize the roles of childhood conflicts and the quality of the partners' relationship. Therefore, they draw from various forms of therapy, as needed (Althof, 2010).

Although the particular approaches vary, sex therapies aim to do the following:

1. Change self-defeating beliefs and attitudes.
2. Enhance sexual knowledge.
3. Teach sexual skills.
4. Improve sexual communication.
5. Reduce performance anxiety.

Sex therapy usually involves both partners, although individual therapy is preferred in some cases. Therapists find that granting people "permission" to sexually experiment or discuss negative attitudes about sex helps many people overcome sexual problems without the need for more intensive therapy.

Today, biological treatments have also been emerging for various sexual dysfunctions. Most public attention has been focused on Viagra, a drug that is helpful in most cases of erectile dysfunction. But competitors to Viagra and biological treatments for early ejaculation, female orgasmic dysfunction, and lack of sexual desire are also emerging. Moreover, there are research findings to the effect that psychotherapy combined with Viagra or other medicines can be more effective than the medicine alone (Aubin et al., 2009).

In this section we explore psychological and behavioral approaches to the treatment of sexual dysfunctions. Let us begin with the pioneering work of Masters and Johnson.

THE MASTERS AND JOHNSON APPROACH

Masters and Johnson (1970) pioneered the use of direct cognitive-behavioral approaches to treating sexual dysfunctions. The couples they treated were heterosexual, and they used a female–male therapy team during a two-week residential program. Masters and Johnson considered the couple, not the individual, to be dysfunctional. A couple may describe the husband's erectile disorder as the problem, but this problem is likely to have led to problems in the relationship by the time they seek therapy. Similarly, a man whose wife has an orgasmic disorder is likely to be anxious about his ability to provide effective sexual stimulation.

The dual-therapist team permits each partner to discuss problems with someone of his or her own gender and allows each partner to hear concerns expressed by another member of the other gender. Anxieties and resentments are aired, but the focus of treatment is on behavioral change. Couples perform daily sexual homework assignments, such as **sensate focus exercises,** in the privacy of their own rooms.

Sensate focus sessions are carried out in the nude. Partners take turns giving and receiving stimulation in nongenital areas of the body. Without touching the breasts or genitals, the giver massages or fondles the receiving partner in order to provide pleasure under relaxing and nondemanding conditions. Since genital activity is restricted, there is no pressure to "perform." The giving partner is freed to engage in trial-and-error learning about the receiving partner's preferences. The receiving partner is also freed to enjoy the experience without feeling rushed to reciprocate

Sex therapy   A collective term for short-term behavioral models for treatment of sexual dysfunctions.

Sensate focus exercises Exercises in which sex partners take turns giving and receiving pleasurable stimulation in nongenital areas of the body.

A Closer Look

Sex Surrogates: Partners in Therapy or Prostitutes?

"Jane" is in her 30s, attractive but no supermodel. Even so, she is in demand by Los Angeles sex therapists and their clients. She is a sex surrogate, meaning that she helps male clients overcome their sexual dysfunctions by having sex with them. Over the past three years, she has worked with some 20 men (Alexander, 2009).

Jane charges $150 per hour. She has worked with trauma victims, depressed men, and men with erectile dysfunction. "My favorite clients are the 40-year-old virgins," she says. "Everybody is shocked, but there are a number of men out there who, for whatever reason, have not had many successful sexual experiences or none at all." She has had sexual intercourse with only two of them. After each session, she reports to the therapist.

Sex surrogates were once well known in the popular culture after Masters and Johnson revealed that they had arranged for some clients with sexual dysfunctions, but without regular partners, to meet with sex surrogates. Some men apparently developed sudden sexual dysfunctions and sought to work with "sex surrogates."

Many professionals wondered out loud whether sex surrogacy was a form of prostitution and whether therapists who prescribed them were, legally speaking, pimps. A sex surrogate in New York, Rita, argues that there are many differences between her line of work and prostitution. For example, she discusses her clients' dysfunctions with them at length. "I'll ask about his relationships, the attitudes toward sex when he was a child, his first sexual experience, whether he's on antidepressants." Some of her methods sound enjoyable but not necessarily as if they are forms of therapy: taking bubble baths with clients, foot massage, and "manual release." Rita advertises her services in the same outlets used by prostitutes.

Other sex surrogates are trained by the International Professional Surrogates Association (IPSA) and work closely with the therapists who recommend them, calling regularly to discuss clients' progress. Even so, the use of sex surrogates was never approved by the American Association of Sexuality Educators, Counselors, and Therapists (AASECT) (Conley, 2009). The Society for the Scientific Study of Sex (SSSS) has not been so adamantly opposed. A surrogate once served as the President of the San Francisco chapter of the SSSS. She says, "Apart from the humbling and amazingly rewarding experience of raising my wonderful children, nothing in my life has made me prouder than my work as a Surrogate Partner."

---

or obliged to perform by becoming sexually aroused. The receiving partner's only responsibility is to direct the giving partner as needed. In addition to these general sensate focus exercises, Masters and Johnson used specific assignments designed to help couples overcome particular sexual dysfunctions.

Masters and Johnson were pioneers in the development of sex therapy. Yet many sex therapists have departed from the Masters and Johnson format. For example, many do not treat clients in an intensive residential program. Many question the necessity of female–male therapist teams. Researchers find that one therapist is about as effective as two, regardless of her or his sex. Nor does it seem to matter whether sessions are conducted within a short period of time, as in the Masters and Johnson approach, or spaced over time.

INTEGRATION OF SEX THERAPY AND PSYCHOTHERAPY

Sex therapy, as noted, has cognitive components—for example, addressing self-defeating attitudes and expectations, and sex education. Few therapists use strict Masters and Johnson guidelines anymore, but many of their innovations are incorporated into their methods (Althof, 2010). Moreover, because sexual activity is so often embedded in relationships, many therapists (Althof, 2010) use psychotherapy and couple therapy to help couples learn how to share the power in relationships, how to improve sexual communication, and how to negotiate differences. The combination of sex therapy and couple therapy appears to be a powerful tool for enhancing relationships as well as sex lives.

Helen Singer Kaplan (1974) combined sex therapy with psychoanalytic methods. She saw sexual dysfunctions as having *immediate* causes and *remote* causes (conflicts that date to childhood). As a sex therapist, Kaplan focused on improving the couple's sexual communication, eliminating performance anxiety, and fostering sexual skills and knowledge. As a psychoanalyst, she used insight-oriented therapy when it appeared that remote causes impaired response to sex therapy. By so doing, she aimed to bring to awareness unconscious conflicts that might have stifled the person's sexual desire or response.

THE TREATMENT OF SPECIFIC SEXUAL DYSFUNCTIONS

Let us now consider some of the specific techniques that sex therapists have introduced in treating several of the major types of sexual dysfunction.

SEXUAL DESIRE DISORDERS

Some therapists help kindle the sexual appetites of people with hypoactive sexual desire by prescribing self-stimulation exercises combined with erotic fantasies (Knudson & Kingsberg, 2010). Sex therapists may also assist dysfunctional couples by prescribing sensate focus exercises, enhancing communication, and expanding the couple's repertoire of sexual skills. Sex therapists recognize that hypoactive sexual desire is often a complex problem that requires more intensive treatment than do problems of the arousal or orgasm phases. Counseling or psychotherapy may be helpful in the treatment of hypoactive sexual desire and sexual aversion to uncover and resolve psychological conflicts (Carvalho & Nobre, 2010).

Some cases of hypoactive sexual desire in men involve hormonal deficiencies, especially deficiencies in testosterone. Testosterone replacement therapy works with some men who have low testosterone levels (Buvat et al., 2010). Among women, as among men, lack of sexual desire can be connected with low levels of androgens. One study of postmenopausal women found that after using testosterone patches of various doses for 24 weeks, women taking 150-μg testosterone had a mean increase of 1.2 satisfying sexual episodes per four-week period, whereas women taking 300 μg testosterone had an increase of 2.1 episodes over the same period (Davis et al., 2008). Those using the patch also experienced heightened sexual desire.

Treatment of sexual aversion disorder may involve a multifaceted approach, including biological treatments such as the use of medications to reduce anxiety, and psychological treatments designed to help the individual overcome the underlying sexual phobia. Couples therapy may be used in cases in which sexual aversions arise from problems in relationships. Sensate focus exercises may be used to lessen anxiety about sexual contact. Fears may also need to be overcome through cognitive-behavioral exercises in which the client learns to manage the stimuli that evoke fears of sexual contact:

> Bridget, 26, and Bryan, 30, were married for four years but had never consummated their relationship because Bridget would panic whenever Bryan attempted coitus with her. While she enjoyed foreplay and was capable of achieving orgasm with clitoral stimulation, her fears of sexual contact were triggered by Bryan's attempts at vaginal penetration. The therapist employed a program of gradual exposure to the feared stimuli to allow Bridget the opportunity to overcome her fears in small, graduated steps. First she was instructed to view her genitals in a mirror when she was alone—this in order to violate her long-standing prohibition against looking at and enjoying her body. While this exercise initially made her feel anxious, with repeated exposure

she became comfortable performing it and then progressed to touching her genitals directly. When she became comfortable with this step, and reported experiencing pleasurable erotic sensations, she was instructed to insert a finger into the vagina. She encountered intense anxiety at this step and required daily practice for two weeks before she could tolerate inserting her finger into her vagina without discomfort. Her husband was then brought into the treatment process. The couple was instructed to have Bridget insert her own finger in her vagina while Bryan watched. When she was comfortable with this exercise, she then guided his finger into her vagina. Later he placed one and then two fingers into her vagina, while she controlled the depth, speed, and duration of penetration. When she felt ready, they proceeded to attempt penile penetration in the female superior position, which allowed her to maintain control over penetration. Over time, Bridget became more comfortable with penetration to the point that the couple developed a normal sexual relationship. (Adapted from Kaplan, 1987, pp. 102–103)

But we should note very clearly that many women do not want penetration by their partners' fingers. *No partner should ever attempt to convince a reluctant woman otherwise.*

SEXUAL AROUSAL DISORDERS

Sex therapists treat both male and female sexual arousal disorders.

Erectile Disorder Men with erectile disorder may ask their therapists to "teach" them or "show" them how to obtain an erection. Some of our clients have asked us to tell them what fantasies they should entertain to obtain an erection, or how they should touch their partners or be touched. Erection is a reflex, however, not a skill. A man need not learn how to have an erection any more than he need learn how to breathe.

In sex therapy, women who have trouble becoming lubricated and men with erectile problems learn that they don't need to "do" anything to become sexually aroused. As long as their problems are psychologically and not organically based, they need only receive sexual stimulation under relaxed circumstances, so that anxiety does not inhibit natural reflexes.

TRUTH OR **FICTION** REVISITED: It is not true that sex therapy teaches a man with erectile disorder how to "will" an erection. Men with erectile disorder are actually taught that it is not possible to "will" an erection. One can only set the stage for erection (or vaginal lubrication) to occur and then allow it to happen reflexively.

People with sexual arousal disorders frequently develop performance anxiety, which may be reduced by partners' initially engaging in nondemanding sexual contacts—contacts that do not demand lubrication or erection. They may start with nongenital sensate focus exercises in the style of Masters and Johnson. After a couple of sessions, sensate focus extends to the genitals. The position shown in Figure 15.1 allows the woman easy access to her partner's genitals. She repeatedly "teases" him to erection and allows the erection to subside. Thus she avoids creating performance anxiety that could lead to loss of erection. By repeatedly regaining his erection, the man loses the fear that loss of erection means it will not return. He learns also to focus on erotic sensations for their own sake. He experiences no demand to perform, as the couple is instructed to refrain from coitus.

When the dysfunctional partner can reliably achieve sexual excitement (denoted by erection in the male and lubrication in the female), the couple does not immediately attempt coitus, since this might rekindle performance anxiety. Rather, the

FIGURE 15.1 Behavioral Approach to Treatment of Erectile Disorder. In one part of a program designed to overcome erectile disorder, a man's partner repeatedly "teases" him to erection and allows the erection to subside. Thus, the partner avoids creating performance anxiety that could lead to loss of erection. Through repeated regaining of erection, the man loses the fear that loss of erection means it will not return.

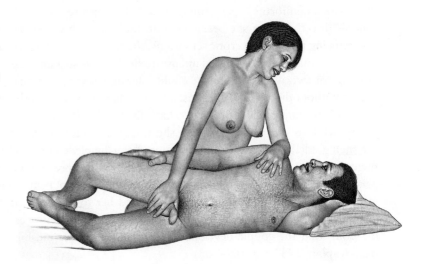

couple engages in a series of nondemanding, pleasurable sexual activities, eventually culminating in coitus.

In the Masters and Johnson approach, the couple begin coitus after about 10 days of treatment. The woman teases the man to erection while she is sitting above him, straddling his thighs. When he is erect, she inserts the penis—to avoid fumbling attempts at entry—and moves slowly back and forth in a *nondemanding way*. Neither attempts to reach orgasm. If erection is lost, teasing and coitus are repeated. Once the couple become confident that erection can be retained—or reinstated if lost—they may increase coital thrusting gradually to reach orgasm.

But note that problems in sexual arousal are frequently, and perhaps most often, biologically related. Let's consider biological treatment of erectile dysfunction.

Biological Approaches to Treatment of Erectile Disorder You have very likely heard the sales pitch "What happens in Las Vegas stays in Las Vegas." However, one event at the 1983 Las Vegas convention of the American Urological Association spread quickly beyond the borders of "sin city" into the consciousness of sexologists everywhere. **TRUTH** OR **FICTION** REVISITED: What happened, briefly, is that the British scientist Giles Brindley, who had been invited by the association to discuss the confusing issues surrounding male sexual response, dropped his pants to reveal a rather sizeable erection. He was demonstrating the effects of a chemical compound called *alprostadil*. The erection was not the result of sexual stimulation or sexual fantasies, but of an injection of alprostadil directly into his penis. Alprostadil is a vasodilator; it relaxes the muscles surrounding the arteries in the penis, allowing more blood to flow in, increasing vasocongestion and causing erection. Brindley was giving a "live" demonstration of a biological method of treating erectile disorder.

Biological and biomedical approaches are helpful in treating erectile disorder, especially when organic factors are involved. Many of these involve changes in lifestyle that have the "side effect" of improving the man's general health. Other treatments include surgery, medication, and vacuum pumps (see Table 15.2).

Lifestyle Changes When we consider the factors associated with erectile dysfunction, we find that men can modify their lives to remove or reduce their impact. Since erectile disorder is connected with obesity, men can lose weight by dieting and exercising in the effort to restore erectile functioning. Even if there is not complete

Table 15.2

Biological Treatments of Erectile Problems

Surgery	
Vascular surgery	Helps when blood vessels that supply the penis are blocked.
Penile implants	May be used when other treatments fail because of biological problems.
Medication	
Hormone therapy	Helps men (and women) with abnormally low levels of male sex hormones.
Injections	Muscle relaxants such as *alprostadil* and *phentolamine* are injected into the corpus cavernosum of the penis, relaxing the muscles that surround the arteries in the penis, allowing the vessels to dilate and blood to flow more freely.
Suppository	Alprostadil is inserted into the tip of the penis in gel form.
Oral medication	Oral forms of several compounds—sildenafil (Viagra), vardenafil (Levitra), and tadalafil (Cialis)—relax the muscles that surround the small blood vessels in the penis, allowing them to dilate so that blood can flow into them more freely. Apomorphine increases brain levels of the neurotransmitter dopamine. Called "Uprima," the drug is in clinical trials. Bremelanotide apparently acts directly on the central nervous system and, as the book goes to press, is also in clinical trials.
Vacuum Pump	
Vacuum pump	A *vacuum constriction device* creates a vacuum when it is held over the penis. The vacuum induces erection by increasing the flow of blood into the penis. Rubber bands around the base of the penis maintain the erection.

reversibility of the problem, there may be improvement. Men can also consider their use of drugs ranging from prescription drugs to alcohol to over-the-counter drugs such as pain killers, anti-inflammatory drugs, and anti-allergy drugs. It may be possible to avoid some of these drugs or to lower the dose (Londoño, et al., 2012). Men should *not* lower the doses of prescription drugs without medical advice, but they can inform their doctors that they would like to do so if it is safe, and they can lower their use of alcohol and other drugs. It may be that a drink a day is good for your heart, but two drinks a day is unnecessary for that purpose and may have overall depressive effects. Consider little things, such as getting a more sensible bicycle seat, that can have big effects (Sommer et al., 2010).

Surgery There are two main types of surgery: vascular surgery and the installation of penile implants. *Vascular surgery* can help in cases in which the blood vessels that supply the penis are blocked, or in which structural defects in the penis restrict blood flow. Arterial bypass surgery reroutes vessels around the blockage.

A *penile implant* may be used when other treatments fail. Implants are either malleable (semi-rigid) or inflatable (see Figure 15.2). The semi-rigid implant is made of rods that remain in a *permanent* semi-rigid position. It is rigid enough for intercourse but permits the penis to hang reasonably close to the body at other times. The inflatable type requires that cylinders be implanted in the penis. A fluid reservoir is placed near the bladder, and a tiny pump is inserted in the scrotum. To attain erection, the man squeezes the pump, releasing fluid into the cylinders. When the erection is no longer needed, a release valve returns the fluid to the reservoir, deflating the penis. The inflatable implant more closely duplicates the normal processes of tumescence and detumescence. Some adverse side effects of penile implants have been reported, including destruction of erectile tissue, impairing the man's ability to have normal erections. Penile implants do not affect sex drive, sexual sensations, or ejaculation.

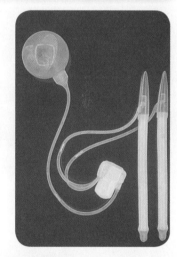

FIGURE 15.2 A Penile Implant. Penile implants provide erection when the man's cardiovascular system does not do the job. This implant consists of cylinders that are implanted in the penis. A fluid reservoir (top left) is placed near the bladder. A pump (lower middle) is typically inserted in the scrotum. Squeezing the pump forces fluid into the cylinders, inflating the penis. A release valve returns the fluid to the reservoir, deflating the penis.

Real Students, Real Questions

Q *I know that Viagra helps put more blood into the penis— but how does it do that? How does it actually work?*

A The answer is chemical and it applies to Levitra and Cialis as well as Viagra. The end point is to allow the arteries in the penis to dilate and fill up with blood to produce an erection. Chemically, what has to happen for arteries to dilate is that the brain sends a signal along a nerve fiber ending in a nonadrenergic–noncholinergic (NANC) cell in an artery; the NANC cell produces nitric oxide and injects it into the bloodstream and nearby cells. The nitric oxide causes a chemical called cyclic guanosine monophosphate (cGMP) to be produced, which relaxes the muscles that line an artery, increasing the flow of blood. However, a chemical called phosphodiesterase (PDE) deactivates cGMP. The specific type of PDE found in the penis is called PDE5.

Viagra, Levitra, and Cialis are all PDE5 inhibitors. That is, they work by deactivating PDE5. Step by step:

1. A man takes Viagra, Levitra, or Cialis.

2. The chemical in the pill circulates throughout his bloodstream.

3. The chemical attaches to PDE5 in his penis and deactivates most of it.

4. When he is sexually aroused, his brain sends the usual message to the cells in his penis, resulting in the output of nitric oxide.

5. In turn, the nitric oxide produces cGMP.

6. Because most PDE5 has been deactivated, cGMP builds up, allowing the arteries in the penis to dilate and produce a fuller erection.

Note: Although Viagra and its chemical cousins are marketed as PDE5 inhibitors, their effects are somewhat broader, which is why they sometimes produce migraines.

Implant surgery is irreversible. Therefore, the National Institutes of Health recommend that penile implants be used only when less invasive techniques, such as sex therapy and medication, are unsuccessful.

Medication There are several ways in which medication can be used to help men with erectile problems. For example, hormone (testosterone) treatments help restore the sex drive and erectile ability in many men with abnormally low levels of testosterone (Granata et al., 2011). Hormone therapy does not appear to help men with normal hormone levels.

The muscle relaxants *alprostadil* (brand names Caverject and Edex) and *phentolamine* (Invicorp) can be injected into the corpus cavernosum of the penis. These chemicals relax the muscles that surround the small blood vessels in the penis. The vessels dilate and allow blood to flow in more freely. Alprostadil erections last for an hour or more and occur whether or not there is sexual stimulation. A physician teaches the man how to inject himself. If phentolamine is used along with the protein VIP, erection occurs only when sexual stimulation is applied.

Penile injections may have side effects, including pain from the injection itself and prolonged, painful erections (*priapism*) (Ralph & McNicholas, 2000). Many men find the idea of penile injections distasteful (the "wince factor") and refuse them.

Alprostadil is also available as a suppository in gel form (brand name MUSE). It is then inserted into the tip of the penis by an applicator. The suppository helps men get around the "wince factor" that many experience with injections. "Putting a needle in your penis is not everybody's idea of foreplay," notes Dr. John Seely (in Kolata, 2000b).

Other medications are taken orally. For example, the oral form of sildenafil is sold as Viagra, and the oral form of vardenafil is sold as Levitra. The oral form of tadalafil (Cialis) lasts up to 36 hours. Users in France dubbed it "the weekend pill."

The drug apomorphine (Uprima) heightens brain levels of dopamine, a neurotransmitter that is involved in erection. Uprima is available in the United Kingdom and without prescription online, but it is advisable to consult your physician before using it. Researchers became aware of the potential benefits of dopamine-enhancing drugs through research with Parkinson's disease. Parkinson's is apparently caused by the loss of dopamine-producing cells, and is connected with loss of motor coordination and erectile dysfunction. L-dopa and other drugs that are used to treat Parkinson's raise dopamine levels and frequently have the "side effect" of erection (Senbel, 2011).

Vacuum Pumps Sounding like something from the "What will they think of next?" category, a *vacuum constriction device (VCD)* helps men achieve erections through vacuum pressure. The device (brand name ErecAid) consists of a cylinder that is connected to a hand-operated vacuum pump. It creates a vacuum when it is held over the limp penis. The vacuum induces erection by increasing the flow of blood into the penis. Rubber bands around the base of the penis can maintain the erection for as long as 30 minutes.

The device has been used successfully by men with both organically and psychologically based erectile failure. However, side effects such as pain and black-and-blue marks are common. The rubber bands prevent normal ejaculation, so semen remains trapped in the urethra until the bands are released. The quality of the erections produced by the device is also considered inferior to spontaneous erections.

Where Do We Go From Here? Oral medications (pills) have been the most popular biological treatment of erectile problems. They are helpful with most men and avoid the "wince factor." Viagra and Levitra have side effects, though, such as migraine headaches, flushing, and some others. The migraines are not surprising since they are related to increased blood flow, and these drugs are not precise enough to direct blood only to the genitals. Soon after Viagra was approved by the FDA, there were scattered reports of men with cardiovascular problems experiencing heart attacks. A carefully conducted study of the effects of Viagra on 14 older men with at least one severely constricted coronary artery suggests that Viagra by itself is not the problem (Herrmann et al., 2000). In this study, reported in the prestigious *New England Journal of Medicine,* Viagra was not shown to have adverse effects on the blood supply to the heart. As a matter of fact, Viagra, which dilates blood vessels, is being evaluated by some for use as a heart *medicine.*

Female Sexual Arousal Disorder Psychological treatments for female sexual arousal disorder parallel those for orgasmic disorder and are discussed in the following pages. They involve sex education (labeling the parts, discussing their functions, and explaining how to arouse them), searching out and coping with possible cognitive interference (such as negative sexual attitudes), creating nondemand situations in which sexual arousal may occur, and—when appropriate—working on problems in the relationship.

A Closer Look

Thinking Critically about Buying Viagra and Other Drugs Online

Viagra, Levitra, and Cialis are prescription drugs. Many men who might otherwise use them are reluctant to discuss erectile dysfunction with their physicians. The anonymity of doing things on the Internet is a lure—you don't have to admit your personal worries to your doctor face to face. Some men, unfortunately, do not even have a regular physician. What to do?

Many have discovered that by searching "Viagra" on the Net, they can find many websites where they can "consult" with online physicians, obtain a prescription, and order the drug for home delivery. Easy! A few questions and a fee—and they've got it. But is it wise? Perhaps, perhaps not.

Prescriptions are needed for various drugs because physicians are better equipped than most lay people to diagnose an individual's health problems, understand the chemical nature and side effects of the drugs that are available for treatment, and predict how the drugs will affect the individual patient. The physicians are also usually prepared to deal with the unexpected effects of the drugs, and there can be many.

So ask yourself what kind of physician will prescribe drugs online, without personally knowing the patient. Is it possible that some of them would have difficulty establishing private practices or getting jobs in hospitals? If you have a question about the drug once you use it, will you be able to get back to the prescriber easily for an answer, or will you wind up with an embarrassing call to your own physician or a trip to the emergency room?

You will find that many of the sites are online pharmacies that also advertise Propecia for treatment of hair loss, drugs that reverse the loss of pubic hair (yes, pubic hair), weight-control drugs that prevent the absorption of some of the fat in food (e.g., Xenical), herbal supplements, and so on. What you will tend to hit in your search are chemical armories of weapons that sound as if they can stop you from aging, or even reverse the aging process. It may sound as if they will help you remain (or return you to status as) a stud-muffin. But the fact is that medical science isn't there yet.

While surfing the Net, you will also come across sites that claim to have "natural" preparations, including a variety of herbs that are as effective as Viagra, but without the side effects, and without the need to get a prescription. Use some critical thinking: Are you convinced of the effectiveness and safety of these preparations? Since they are foods (sort of) rather than drugs, they escape the scrutiny of the Food and Drug Administration; the government is not watching over them. Be warned.

In sum, even if it is convenient to buy a drug online, you are well advised to get your prescription face to face—from a doctor you know and trust.

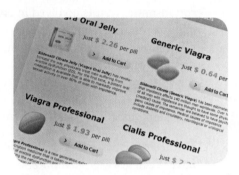

Should You Buy Viagra Online? Many websites enable men to consult with physicians and order Viagra online. Is it wise to purchase Viagra—or other prescription drugs—online? Prescriptions are needed for drugs when the person's diagnosis is in question and when the drugs have side effects. Physicians are better equipped than most laypeople to diagnose health problems, understand the chemical composition and effects of drugs, and predict how drugs will affect the individual.

Yet many cases of female sexual arousal disorder reflect impaired blood flow to the genitals, just as in erectile disorder. Female sexual arousal involves vaginal lubrication, which permits sexual intercourse without a great deal of pain-causing friction. Lubrication is made possible by vasocongestion—the flow of blood into the genitals. Lack of lubrication can reflect the physical effects of aging, menopause, and surgically induced menopause, as through surgery.

Sometimes all that is necessary to deal with lack of lubrication is an artificial lubricant such as K-Y Jelly. But lessened blood flow to the genitals can also sap sexual pleasure and, as a consequence, lessen a woman's desire for sex.

The development of treatments for women has lagged behind the development of treatments for men. Ironically, the treatments that are emerging are highly similar to those that help men with erectile disorder.

For example, drugs identical or similar to those used for men are being investigated for use with women (Leland, 2000). Many trials have been undertaken with Viagra for women (Nurnberg et al., 2008). Researchers are also developing alprostadil (the vasodilator) for use with women, largely in the form of creams that are inserted into the vagina to enhance the flow of blood and hence lubrication.

There is a perfect parallel in the area of lack of sexual desire for women who are low in sexual desire because of low levels of "male" sex hormones. As an aside, we might ask whether we should stop referring to estrogen as a female sex hormone and testosterone as a male sex hormone since they are both produced by both women and men—although in different quantities—and are both intricately involved with women's and men's health, sexual functioning, and other behavior. In any event, testosterone skin patches can be used by women who lack sexual desire because they lack adequate quantities of testosterone.

There is even a device—*Eros*—that is a parallel to the vacuum pump that is used by some men with erectile disorder. It is a clitoral device that is available by prescription. The clitoris swells during sexual arousal because of vasocongestion, and vasocongestion increases clitoral sexual sensations, thus moving somewhat in step with sexual interest and lubrication. The device creates gentle suction over the clitoris, increasing vasocongestion and sexual sensations (see Figure 15.3).

ORGASMIC DISORDERS

Because orgasmic disorders among men are relatively rare, our response will focus mainly on women. Women who have never experienced orgasm often harbor negative sexual attitudes that cause anxiety and inhibit sexual response. Treatment in such cases may first address these attitudes.

Masters and Johnson use a couples-oriented approach in treating anorgasmic women. They begin with sensate focus exercises. Then, during genital massage and later, during coitus, the woman guides her partner in the caresses and movements that she finds sexually exciting. Taking charge helps free the woman from the traditional role of the passive, subordinate female.

Masters and Johnson recommend a training position (see Figure 15.4) that gives the man access to his partner's breasts and genitals. She can guide his hands to show him the types of stimulation she enjoys. The genital play is *nondemanding*. The goals are to learn to provide and enjoy effective sexual stimulation, not to reach orgasm. The clitoris is not stimulated early, since doing so may produce a high level of stimulation, even hurt, before the woman is prepared.

After a number of occasions of genital play, the couple undertake coitus in the female-superior position (see Figure 15.5). This position allows the woman freedom of movement and control over her genital sensations. The couple engages in several sessions of deliberately slow thrusting to sensitize the woman to sensations produced by the penis and to break the common counterproductive pattern of desperate, rapid thrusting.

Orgasm cannot be willed or forced. When a woman receives effective stimulation, feels free to focus on erotic sensations, and feels that nothing is being demanded of her, she will generally reach orgasm. Once the woman is able to attain orgasm in the female-superior position, the couple may extend their sexual repertoire to other positions.

Masters and Johnson prefer working with the couple in cases of anorgasmia, but other sex therapists prefer to work with the woman individually through masturbation. **TRUTH OR FICTION** REVISITED: Many sex therapists do recommend masturbation as a treatment for women who have never been able to reach orgasm (Leiblum & Rosen, 2000). Masturbation allows people to get in touch with their sexual responses at their own pace. The sexual pleasure they experience helps counter

FIGURE 15.3 A Clitoral Device That Stimulates Genital Vasocongestion in Women by Creating (Gentle) Suction over the Clitoris

FIGURE 15.4 The Training Position for Nondemanding Stimulation of the Female Genitals. This position gives the woman's partner access to her breasts and genitals. The woman can guide her partner's hands to demonstrate the types of stimulation she enjoys.

FIGURE 15.5 The Female-Superior Position. In treatment of female orgasmic disorder, the couple undertakes coitus in the female-superior position after a number of occasions of genital play. This position allows the woman freedom of movement and control over her genital sensations. She is told to regard the penis as her "toy." The couple engages in several sessions of deliberately slow thrusting to sensitize the woman to sensations produced by the penis and to break the common counterproductive pattern of desperate, rapid thrusting.

lingering sexual anxieties. Although there is some variation among therapists, the following elements are commonly found in directed masturbation programs:

1. *Education.* The woman and her partner (if she has one) are educated about female sexuality.
2. *Self-exploration.* Self-exploration is encouraged as a way of increasing the woman's sense of body awareness. She may hold a mirror between her legs to locate her sexual anatomic features.
3. *Self-massage.* The woman creates a private, relaxing setting for self-massage. She begins to explore the sensitivity of her body to touch, discovering and repeating the caresses she finds pleasurable. Nonalcohol-based oils and lotions may be used to enhance the sensuous quality of the massage and to provide

lubrication for the external genitalia. To prevent performance anxiety, the woman does not attempt to reach orgasm during the first few occasions.

4. *Giving oneself permission.* The woman may be advised to challenge lingering guilt and anxiety about sex. For example, she might repeat to herself, "This is my body. I have a right to learn about my body and receive pleasure from it."

5. *Use of fantasy.* Arousal is heightened through the use of sexual images, fantasies, and fantasy aids, such as erotic written or visual materials.

6. *Use of a vibrator.* A vibrator may provide more intense stimulation.

7. *Involvement of the partner.* Once the woman is capable of regularly achieving orgasm through masturbation, the focus may shift to her sexual relationship with her partner. Nondemanding sensate focus exercises may be followed by nondemanding coitus. The female-superior position is often used so that the woman can control the depth, angle, and rate of thrusting. She thus ensures that she receives the kinds of stimulation she needs to reach orgasm.

Our focus has been on sexual techniques, but it is worth noting that a combination of approaches that focus on sexual techniques and underlying interpersonal problems may be more effective than focusing on sexual techniques alone—at least for couples whose relationships are troubled (Firestone et al., 2006).

Male Orgasmic Disorder Treatment of male orgasmic disorder generally focuses on increasing sexual stimulation and reducing performance anxiety (Althof, 2012). Masters and Johnson instruct the couple to practice sensate focus exercises for several days, during which the man makes no attempt to ejaculate. The couple is then instructed to bring the man to orgasm in any way it can, usually manually. Once the man can ejaculate in his partner's presence, she brings him to the point at which he is about to ejaculate. Then, in the female-superior position, she inserts the penis and thrusts vigorously to bring him to orgasm.

Early Ejaculation In the Masters and Johnson approach, sensate focus exercises are followed by practice in the training position shown in Figure 15.1 (refer to page 456). The woman teases her partner to erection and uses the **squeeze technique** when he indicates that he is about to ejaculate. She squeezes the tip of the penis, which temporarily prevents ejaculation. This process is repeated three or four times in a 15- to 20-minute session before the man purposely ejaculates.

TRUTH OR **FICTION** REVISITED: It is true that a man can be prevented from ejaculating by squeezing his penis when he feels that he is about to ejaculate. In using the squeeze technique, the partner holds the penis between the thumb and first two fingers of the same hand. The thumb presses against the frenulum. The fingers straddle the coronal ridge on the other side of the penis. Squeezing the thumb and forefingers together fairly hard for about 20 seconds (or until the man's urge to ejaculate passes) prevents ejaculation. The erect penis can withstand fairly strong pressure without discomfort, but erection may be partially lost.

After two or three days of these sessions, Masters and Johnson have the couple begin coitus in the female-superior position because it creates less pressure to ejaculate. The woman inserts the penis. At first she contains it without thrusting, allowing the man to get used to intravaginal sensations. If he signals that he is about to ejaculate, she lifts off and squeezes the penis. After some repetitions, she begins slowly to move backward and forward, lifting off and squeezing as needed. The man learns gradually to tolerate higher levels of sexual stimulation without ejaculating.

The "stop–start" method for treating early ejaculation was introduced formally by urologist James Semans (1956). However, many men with early ejaculation have thought to use stopping and starting on their own (Porst et al., 2007). Semans's

CRITICAL THINKING
Are there any sex therapy methods that seem "over the top" to you? Explain.

 7

Squeeze technique A method for treating early ejaculation whereby the tip of the penis is squeezed temporarily to prevent ejaculation.

A World of Diversity

Is Viagra for Women?

As women age, they, like men, also experience a reduced flow of blood to the genital region (Brotto et al., 2010). The clitoris becomes less engorged during sexual arousal and may be connected with feelings of lessened sexual arousal overall. Postmenopausal women experience vaginal dryness because of drop-off in estrogen (Wierman et al., 2010). Many older women say that they have lost interest in sex or have difficulty becoming aroused. Table 15.3 provides an overview of methods in use or under development.

Researchers have suspected that PDE5 inhibitors such as Viagra would increase vasocongestion in the genital region of women as it does with men. Shouldn't these drugs, then, enhance the sexual experiences of women as well as men? Meredith Chivers and Raymond Rosen (2010) report that the use of PDE5 does in fact increase women's vasocongestion. However, the women do not reliably report "feeling" more sexually aroused or enjoying sex more. Why? There is apparently a gender difference in the connection between vasocongestion and

the subjective sense of being sexually aroused. In men, the connection seems to be reliable, but in women, there is often either a minor connection or no connection between subjective feelings and physiological events in the genital region.

Put it another way. Use of a PDE5 inhibitor will usually increase vaginal lubrication in women, but that fact will not necessarily affect their sexual desire. The "medicalization" of sex therapy is unlikely to enhance the quality of a relationship. If people have serious problems with their partners, popping a pill is unlikely to erase them.

Table 15.3

Various Biological Treatments in Use or under Investigation to Help Women with Sexual Dysfunctions

Method	How Used	Effect	Current Status
Alprostadil	Gel, cream	May enhance arousal by improving blood flow to the clitoris	Studies under way
DHEA	Pill	May boost libido by increasing testosterone levels	Available by prescription; available as a dietary supplement, although experts caution against unsupervised use; studies under way
Eros (Figure 15.3)	Hand-held device that applies gentle suction to the clitoris	Promotes blood flow to the clitoris, enhancing arousal	Available by prescription
Estrogen	Pill, patch, gel, cream	Counters vaginal dryness	Available by prescription
PDE5 inhibitors	Pill	Enhances physiological aspects of sexual arousal by retaining blood in the genital region	PDE5 inhibitors such as Viagra and Cialis are available by prescription; studies under way for treating women's sexual problems
Testosterone	Pill, patch, gel, cream	May boost libido	Available by prescription; studies under way for treating women's sexual problems
VasoFem, Alista, FemProx	Viagra-like drugs	May improve blood flow to the clitoris, enhancing arousal	Studies under way for treating women's sexual problems
Yohimbine with nitric oxide	Pill	May improve blood flow to the clitoris enhancing arousal	Studies under way

approach can be applied to manual stimulation or coitus. For example, the man's partner can manually stimulate him until he is about to ejaculate. He then signals her to suspend sexual stimulation and allows his arousal to subside before stimulation is resumed. This process enables the man to recognize the cues that precede his point of ejaculatory inevitability, or "point of no return," and to tolerate longer periods of sexual stimulation. When the stop–start technique is applied to coitus, the couple begins with simple vaginal containment with no pelvic thrusting, preferably in the female-superior position. The man withdraws if he feels he is about to ejaculate. As the man's sense of control increases, thrusting can begin, along with variations in coital positions. The couple again stops when the man signals that he is approaching ejaculatory inevitability.

Biological Treatment of Early Ejaculation Some drugs that are usually used to treat psychological problems have been helpful in treating early ejaculation (McMahon, 2011). Clomipramine, which is used to treat people with obsessive-compulsive disorder or schizophrenia, can impair erectile response at high doses. But in a study with 15 couples, low doses helped men engage in coitus five times longer than usual without ejaculating (Althof, 1994). So-called anti-depressant drugs have also been helpful in treatment of early ejaculation, but are associated with erectile dysfunction (Waldinger, 2011). PDE5 inhibitors have also been tried for treatment of early ejaculation, especially when it is associated with erectile dysfunction. However, there is little experimental research into their effectiveness (Jannini et al., 2011).

Why do drugs used to treat psychological problems help with early ejaculation? The psychological problems are frequently connected with imbalances in body chemistry, such as neurotransmitters—the chemical messengers of the brain. Neurotransmitters are also involved in other bodily functions, including ejaculation. "Anti-depressant" drugs all work by increasing the action of the neurotransmitter serotonin. Serotonin, in turn, may inhibit the ejaculatory reflex (Waldinger, 2011). But note the cautions about using SSRIs expressed earlier in the chapter! It remains to be seen whether medications continue to show positive effects and compare their effectiveness with psychological sex therapy techniques.

SEXUAL PAIN DISORDERS

The two major sexual pain disorders are dyspareunia and vaginismus.

Dyspareunia Dyspareunia, or painful intercourse, generally calls for medical intervention to ascertain and treat any underlying physical problems, such as urinary tract genital infections, that might give rise to pain (van Lankveld et al., 2010). When dyspareunia is caused by vaginismus, treatment of vaginismus through a cognitive-behavioral approach, described below, may reduce pain.

Vaginismus Vaginismus is generally treated by "exposure"—that is, by insertion of fingers or vaginal dilators of increasing size under circumstances in which the woman remains relaxed (Reissing, 2012). In one study, for example, women with vaginismus performed vaginal penetration exercises in the company of a female therapist (ter Kuile et al., 2009). When the woman is able to tolerate dilators (or fingers) equivalent in thickness to the penis, the couple may try coitus, but the woman should control insertion. Circumstances should remain relaxed and nondemanding. The idea is to avoid resensitizing her to fears of penetration. Since vaginismus often occurs among women with a history of sexual trauma, such as rape or incest, treatment for the psychological effects of these experiences may also be in order.

CRITICAL THINKING

If you had a sexual dysfunction, do you think that you would be willing to participate in sex therapy? Explain. (And do you think women or men are likely to be more willing to have sex therapy? Why?)

Chapter Review ✓• ⌐**Study** and **Review** on **MyDevelopmentLab**

LO1 **Identify and define the various sexual dysfunctions**

Sexual dysfunctions are persistent or recurrent difficulties in becoming sexually aroused or reaching orgasm. Men are more likely to have rapid orgasm, and women are more likely to have lack of desire, difficulty reaching orgasm, and painful sex. In sexual desire disorders, the person experiences a lack of sexual desire or an aversion to genital sexual contact. In men, sexual arousal disorders involve recurrent difficulty in achieving or sustaining erections. In women, they typically involve failure to become sufficiently lubricated. Orgasmic disorders involve difficulty reaching orgasm or reaching orgasm too soon. Sexual pain disorders include dyspareunia, or painful sex, and vaginismus, in which involuntary contraction of vaginal muscles make penetration painful.

LO2 **Discuss biological factors in sexual dysfunctions**

Fatigue may lead to erectile disorder in men and to orgasmic disorder and dyspareunia in women. Dyspareunia may reflect vaginal infections and STIs. Biological factors are likely involved in most cases of erectile disorder. Medications for various health problems may impair sexual functioning. Aging can also impair sexual functioning.

LO3 **Discuss psychosocial factors in sexual dysfunctions**

Psychosocial factors connected with sexual dysfunctions include cultural influences (e.g., sexually repressive environments), psychosexual trauma, problems in the relationship, lack of sexual skills, irrational beliefs, and performance anxiety. Some people lack opportunity to acquire sexual knowledge and experience. Excessive needs for approval and perfection can contribute to sexual problems. Performance anxiety may place dysfunctional people in a spectator rather than performer role.

LO4 **Discuss the historic Masters and Johnson approach to sex therapy**

Sex therapy modifies dysfunctional behavior by changing self-defeating beliefs and attitudes, fostering sexual skills and knowledge, enhancing sexual communication, and using exercises that enhance sexual stimulation while reducing performance anxiety. Masters and Johnson employed an in-residence program that focused on the couple as the unit of treatment. Sensate focus exercises were used to enable the partners to give each other pleasure in a nondemanding situation.

LO5 **Discuss the integration of sex therapy and psychotherapy**

Other therapists combine sex therapy with couple therapy or, in the case of Helen Singer Kaplan, psychoanalytic therapy.

LO6 **Discuss the treatment of specific sexual dysfunctions**

Androgens heighten the sex drive in people with androgen deficiencies. Noninvasive biological treatments facilitate blood flow to the genitals or affect levels of neurotransmitters. Masters and Johnson used a couples approach in treating anorgasmic women. Other therapists prefer directed masturbation to enable women to learn about their own bodies at their own pace and free them of the need to rely on partners. Dyspareunia may be treated by tackling health problems, ensuring that the woman is adequately lubricated, or, among older women, using estrogen replacement. Vaginismus is generally treated with a series of dilators.

Test Your Learning

1. According to epidemiological studies, approximately _____ of men have experienced at least one sexual dysfunction.
   (a) 10–20%
   (b) 20–30%
   (c) 30–50%
   (d) 50–75%

2. Which of the following is most likely to have biological causes?
   (a) Dyspareunia
   (b) Vaginismus
   (c) Female orgasmic disorder
   (d) Performance anxiety

3. According to epidemiological studies, the most prevalent female sexual dysfunction is
   (a) dyspareunia.
   (b) low sexual desire.
   (c) rapid orgasm.
   (d) having trouble lubricating.

4. According to the text, _____ is most likely to be connected with a history of sexual trauma.
   (a) erectile disorder
   (b) early ejaculation
   (c) performance anxiety
   (d) vaginismus

5. Alprostadil is used in the treatment of
   (a) early ejaculation.
   (b) male erectile disorder.
   (c) female orgasmic disorder.
   (d) hypoactive sexual desire.

6. According to the text, a low level of _____ can lessen sexual desire.
   (a) testosterone
   (b) sildenafil
   (c) Depo-Provera
   (d) alprostadil

7. All of the following are sex therapy methods, with the exception of
   (a) penile implants.
   (b) improving sexual communication.
   (c) reducing performance anxiety.
   (d) sensate focus exercises.

8. _____ is sometimes treated with a series of rings of plastic dilators.
   (a) Dyspareunia
   (b) Female sexual arousal disorder
   (c) Vaginismus
   (d) Erectile disorder

9. Cialis is used to treat
   (a) erectile disorder.
   (b) female sexual arousal disorder.
   (c) dyspareunia.
   (d) early ejaculation.

10. Sex therapists are most likely to recommend masturbation as a treatment for
    (a) early ejaculation.
    (b) female orgasmic disorder.
    (c) vaginismus.
    (d) retarded ejaculation.

Answers: 1. b; 2. a; 3. b; 4. d; 5. b; 6. a; 7. a; 8. c; 9. a; 10. b

My Life, My Sexuality

Finding a Qualified Sex Therapist

Explore this *My Life, My Sexuality* feature by scanning this QR code with your mobile device. If you don't already have one, you may download a free QR scanner for your device wherever smartphone apps are sold. You can also view this feature in MyDevelopmentLab, along with an accompanying critical thinking assignment.

How would you find a qualified sex therapist if you had a sexual dysfunction? You might find advertisements for "sex therapists" in the Yellow Pages. But beware. Most states do not restrict usage of the term sex therapist to recognized professionals. In these states, anyone who wants to use the label may do so, including quacks and prostitutes. Scan the code to learn what you can do to locate a qualified professional.

16 Sexually Transmitted Infections

Learning Objectives

Explore the video, *Common Misconceptions About STDs: Michael Bailey,* by scanning this QR code with your mobile device. If you don't already have one, you may download a free QR scanner for your device wherever smartphone apps are sold. You can also view this video in MyDevelopmentLab. For more videos related to this chapter's content, log into MyDevelopmentLab to view the entire Human Sexuality Video Series.

TRUTH OR FICTION?

Which of the following statements are the truth, and which are fiction? Look for the Truth-or-Fiction icons on the pages that follow to find the answers.

1 Most women who contract gonorrhea do not develop symptoms. **T F?**

2 Christopher Columbus brought more than beads, blankets, and tobacco back to Europe from the New World: He also brought syphilis. **T F?**

3 Gonorrhea and syphilis can be contracted from toilet seats in public rest rooms. **T F?**

4 If a syphilitic sore goes away by itself, the infection does not require medical treatment. **T F?**

5 Men can develop vaginal infections. **T F?**

6 As you are reading this page, you are engaged in search-and-destroy missions against foreign agents within your body. **T F?**

7 Most people who are infected by HIV remain symptom-free and appear healthy for years. **T F?**

8 Genital herpes can be transmitted only during flare-ups of the infection. **T F?**

9 Pubic lice are of the same family of animals as crabs. **T F?**

arold and Carin, both 20, have been dating for several months. They feel strong sexual attraction toward each other but have hesitated to become sexually intimate because of fears about of HIV/AIDS and other sexually transmitted infections. Harold believes that using condoms is no guarantee against infection and wants the two of them to be tested for HIV, the virus that causes AIDS. Carin has resisted undergoing an HIV test, partly because she feels insulted that Harold fears that she may be infected, and frankly, partly in fear of the test results. She has heard that symptoms may not develop for years after infection. She wonders whether she might have been infected by one of the men with whom she had slept in the past.

Keisha has genital herpes. A 19-year-old pre-law student, she has had no recurrences since the initial outbreak two years earlier. But she knows that herpes is a lifelong infection and may recur periodically from time to time. She also knows that she may inadvertently pass the herpes virus along to her sex partners, even to the man she eventually marries. She has begun thinking seriously about Steve, a man she has been dating for the past month. She would like to tell him that she has herpes before they become sexually intimate. Yet she fears that telling him might scare him off.

José, 21, a math and computer science major, is planning a career in computer operations, hoping one day to run the computer systems for a large corporation. He lives off-campus with several of his buddies in a run-down house they've dubbed "The Nuclear Dumpsite." He has been dating Maria, a theater major, for several months. They have begun having sexual relations and have practiced "safer sex"— at least most of the time. During the past week he noticed a burning sensation while urinating. It seems to have passed now, so he figures that it was probably nothing to worry about. But he's not sure and wonders whether he should see a doctor.

◉▭Watch the Video
Common Misconceptions About STDs: Michael Bailey
on **MyDevelopmentLab**

arold, Carin, Keisha, and José express some of the fears and concerns of a generation of young people who are becoming sexually active at a time when the threat of HIV/AIDS and other **sexually transmitted infections (STIs)** hangs over every sexual decision. ◉

Epidemic!

Sexually transmitted infections are rampant. HIV/AIDS is indeed a scary thing—a very scary thing. But HIV/AIDS is only one of many STIs, and other STIs actually pose wider threats (STI trends, 2011):

- There are some 19 million new cases of STIs in the United States each year.
- The incidence of chlamydia has been increasing for the past 20 years, mostly undiagnosed.
- There are more than 700,000 new cases of gonorrhea each year, and the drug-resistant strains of gonorrhea are evolving.
- About one in six Americans is infected with *Herpes simplex* virus (HSV)-2.
- There are some 6 million new cases of human papilloma virus (HPV) each year, and more than 50% of some college populations are infected.
- There are about 50,000 new cases of HIV/AIDS in the United States each year (Grady, 2012).

College students have become reasonably well versed about HIV/AIDS. However, many are unaware that chlamydia can go undetected for years. Moreover, if it is left untreated, it can cause pelvic inflammation and infertility (Pelvic inflammatory disease, 2011). Many college students appear to be ignorant about HPV and its links to genital warts, cervical cancer, even cancer of the throat (Chaturvedi et al., 2011). But the Centers for Disease Control and Prevention estimates that as many as 6 million new cases of HPV infection occur each year in the United States—more than syphilis, genital herpes, and HIV/AIDS combined (STI trends, 2011). Whereas about 1 million Americans are thought to be infected with HIV, an estimated 50 to 60 million are infected with other STI-causing viruses, such as those causing herpes, hepatitis, and cervical cancer.

Sexually transmitted infections (STIs) Infections that can be communicated through sexual contact

Who Is at Risk? Evidence suggests that young people are more sexually active than ever before. Thus, it is as important as ever that they be aware of the risks involved and take responsibility for their sexual health.

Sexually transmitted infections are transmitted through sexual means, such as vaginal or anal intercourse or oral sex. They were formerly called *sexually transmitted diseases (STDs),* and before that, *venereal diseases (VDs)*—after Venus, the Roman goddess of love. We refer to them as sexually transmitted infections because a person can be infected before developing a disease. Human papilloma virus (HPV), for example, is an organism that infects people; genital warts and cancers are the kinds of diseases that can develop from infection.

Some STIs can be spread through nonsexual contact as well. For example, HIV/AIDS and viral hepatitis may be spread by sharing contaminated hypodermic syringes such as those used by people "shooting up" drugs. And a few STIs (such as the parasitic infection we sometimes refer to as "crabs") may be picked up from bedding or other objects, such as moist towels.

The United States is believed to have the highest rate of infection by STIs in the industrialized world. In a recent year, for example, 101 cases of gonorrhea were reported per 100,000 people in the United States (STI surveillance, 2010) as compared with 18.6 per 100,000 in Canada and 3 per 100,000 in Sweden.

At least one in four Americans is likely to contract an STI at some time. Two cases in three occur in people under the age of 25.

Do not read the remainder of this paragraph unless you are ready for the truth: Some of you readers have STIs and do not realize it. But ignorance is not bliss. Some STIs do not produce noticeable symptoms but can be harmful if left untreated. STIs can also be painful and—in the cases of HIV/AIDS, advanced syphilis, and the cervical cancer that can follow infection with HPV—lethal. Hundreds of thousands of women become infertile each year because of STIs that are spreading through their reproductive system (Pelvic inflammatory disease, 2011). Overall, STIs are believed to account for 15 to 30% of cases of infertility among women. In addition to their biological effects, STIs exact an emotional toll and strain relationships to the breaking point. 👁

Why the surge in the incidence of STIs? One is the increased number of young people who have sex. Many of them fail to use latex condoms consistently, if at all. Some people do not use condoms because the woman is on the pill or using another

CRITICAL THINKING
Why do you think the United States has the largest incidence of STIs in the industrialized world?

◉—Watch the Video
HIV as Result of Unsafe Sex
on **MyDevelopmentLab**

form of hormonal birth control (Morrison & Nanda, 2012). Although hormonal methods of birth control are reliable forms of contraception, they do not prevent STIs. Another reason is that people with some infections, such as chlamydia, are symptom-free. Therefore, they may unwittingly transmit them to others. Other risk factors include early sexual involvement and sex with multiple partners (Sex and infertility, 2011). Drug use is also associated with an increased risk of STIs (Staras et al., 2011). People who abuse drugs are more likely than others to engage in risky sexual practices. Moreover, certain forms of drug use, such as needle sharing, can directly transmit infectious organisms like HIV. Another risk factor, ironically, is the apparent success of new antiviral drugs in treating—but not curing!—HIV/AIDS. As a result, many individuals who had become more cautious in their sexual behavior have once again thrown caution to the wind (Grady, 2012; McNeil, 2012). 👁

◉⊣**Watch** the **Video**
Intimate Danger
on **MyDevelopmentLab**

Bacterial Infections

Bacteria are one-celled microorganisms, some that are essential to human life and some that are harmful. Bacteria play vital roles in our bodies' digestive systems. Bacteria are essential to fermentation. Without bacteria, there would be no wine. Unfortunately, bacteria also cause many diseases such as pneumonia, tuberculosis, and meningitis—along with the common STIs gonorrhea, syphilis, and chlamydia.

GONORRHEA

Gonorrhea—also known as "the clap" or "the drip"—was once the most widespread bacterial STI in the United States, but it has been replaced by chlamydia. The rate of infection declined 74% between 1975 and 1997, and 22% between 200 and 2010, possibly because of safer sex practices and use of antibiotics (STI surveillance, 2010; see Figure 16.1). It is estimated that there are about 700,000 new cases of

Bacteria One-celled microorganisms that have no chlorophyll and can give rise to many illnesses.

Gonorrhea An STI caused by the *Neisseria gonorrhoeae* bacterium and characterized by a discharge and burning urination.

FIGURE 16.1 Trends in Major Bacterial Sexually Transmitted Infections (STIs)

Source: STI surveillance, 2010. Centers for Disease Control and Prevention. (2010). 2010 Sexually transmitted diseases surveillance. http://www.cdc.gov/std/stats10/tables/trends-snapshot.htm (Accessed October 4, 2012).

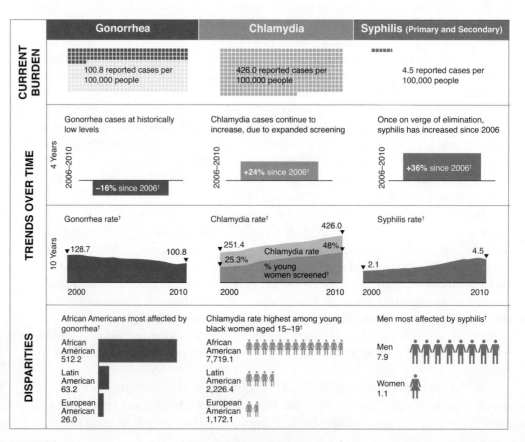

gonorrhea a year in the United States (Gonorrhea fact sheet, 2012). Most new cases are contracted by people between the ages of 20 and 24.

Gonorrhea is caused by the gonococcus bacterium (see Table 16.1). A penile discharge that was probably gonorrhea is described in ancient Egyptian and Chinese writings and is mentioned in the Old Testament (Leviticus 15). Ancient Jews and Greeks assumed that the discharge was an involuntary loss of seminal fluid. In about 400 BCE the Greek physician Hippocrates suggested that the loss stemmed from excessive sex or "worship" of Aphrodite (whom the Romans would later rename *Venus*). The term *gonorrhea* is credited to the Greek physician Galen, who lived in the second century CE. Albert L. S. Neisser identified the gonococcus bacterium that bears his name in 1879: *Neisseria gonorrhoeae*.

Table 16.1

Causes, Modes of Transmission, Symptoms, Diagnosis, and Treatment of Major STIs

STI and Pathogen	Modes of Transmission	Symptoms	Diagnosis	Treatment
Bacterial Infections				
Gonorrhea ("clap," "drip"): Gonococcus bacterium (*Neisseria gonorrhoeae*)	Transmitted by vaginal, oral, or anal sexual activity, or from mother to newborn during delivery	In men, yellowish, thick penile discharge, burning urination In women, increased vaginal discharge, burning urination, irregular menstrual bleeding (most women show no early symptoms)	Clinical inspection, culture of sample discharge	Antibiotics: ceftriaxone, ciprofloxin, cefixime, ofloxacin
Syphilis: *Treponema pallidum*	Transmitted by vaginal, oral, or anal sexual activity, or by touching an infectious chancre	In primary stage, a hard, round painless chancre or sore appears at site of infection within two to four weeks; may progress through secondary, latent, and tertiary stages if left untreated	Primary-stage syphilis is diagnosed by clinical examination and by examination of fluid from a chancre in a darkfield test; secondary-stage syphilis is diagnosed by blood test (the VDRL)	Penicillin, or doxycycline, tetracycline, or erythromycin for nonpregnant penicillin-allergic patients
Chlamydia and nongonococcal urethritis (NGU): *Chlamydia trachomatous* bacterium; NGU in men may also be caused by *Ureaplasma urealycticum* bacterium and other pathogens	Transmitted by vaginal, oral, or anal sexual activity; to the eye by touching one's eyes after touching the genitals of an infected partner, or to newborns passing through the birth canal of an infected mother	In women, frequent and painful urination, lower abdominal pain and inflammation, and vaginal discharge (but most women are symptom free) In men, symptoms are similar to but milder than those of gonorrhea: burning or painful urination, slight penile discharge (most men are also symptom free) Sore throat may indicate infection from oral-genital contact	The Abbott Testpack analyzes a cervical smear in women; in men, an extract of fluid from the penis is analyzed	Antibiotics: azithromycin, doxycycline, ofloxacin, amoxicillin

(continued)

Table 16.1

Causes, Modes of Transmission, Symptoms, Diagnosis, and Treatment of Major STIs *(continued)*

STI and Pathogen	Modes of Transmission	Symptoms	Diagnosis	Treatment
Vaginal Infections				
Bacterial vaginosis: *Gardnerella vaginalis* bacterium and others	Can arise by overgrowth of organisms in vagina, allergic reactions, etc.; also transmitted by sexual contact	In women, thin, foul-smelling vaginal discharge; irritation of genitals and mild pain during urination In men, inflammation of penile foreskin and glans, urethritis, and cystitis. May be symptom-free in both sexes	Culture and examination of bacterium	Metronidazole, clindamycin
Candidiasis (moniliasis, thrush, "yeast infection"): *Candida albicans*—a yeastlike fungus	Can arise by overgrowth of fungus in vagina; may also be transmitted by sexual contact or by sharing a washcloth with an infected person	In women, vulval itching; white, cheesy, foul-smelling discharge; soreness or swelling of vaginal and vulval tissues In men, itching and burning on urination, or a reddening of the penis	Diagnosis usually made on basis of symptoms	Single-dose oral fluconazole, or suppositories of miconazole, clotrimazole, or butaconazole; modification of use of other medicines and chemical agents; keep infected area dry
Trichomoniasis ("trich"): *Trichomonas vaginalis*—a protozoan (one-celled animal)	Almost always transmitted sexually	In women, foamy, yellowish, odorous vaginal discharge; itching or burning sensation in vulva; many women are symptom free In men, usually symptom free, but mild urethritis is possible	Microscopic examination of a smear of vaginal secretions or of culture of the sample (latter method preferred)	Metronidazole
Viral Infections				
Oral herpes: *Herpes simplex virus type 1 (or HSV-1)*	Touching, kissing, sexual contact with sores or blisters; sharing cups, towels, toilet seats	Cold sores or fever blisters on the lips, mouth, or throat; herpetic sores on the genitals	Usually, clinical inspection	OTC lip balms, cold sore medications; check with your physician, however
Genital herpes: *Herpes simplex virus type 2 (or HSV-2)*	Almost always by means of vaginal, oral, or anal sexual activity; most contagious during active outbreaks of the disease	Painful, reddish bumps around the genitals, thigh, or buttocks; in women, may also be in the vagina or on the cervix; bumps become blisters or sores that fill with pus and break, shedding viral particles; other possible symptoms: burning urination, fever, aches and pains, swollen glands; in women, vaginal discharge	Clinical inspection of sores; culture and examination of fluid drawn from the base of a genital sore	No cure, but the antiviral drugs acyclovir, famciclovir, and valacyclovir may provide relief and prompt healing; people with herpes often profit from counseling and group support

Table 16.1

Causes, Modes of Transmission, Symptoms, Diagnosis, and Treatment of Major STIs *(continued)*

Viral hepatitis: hepatitis A, B, C, and D type viruses	Sexual contact, especially involving the anus (especially hepatitis A); contact with infected fecal matter; transfusion of contaminated blood (especially hepatitis B and C)	Ranges from being symptom free to mild flulike symptoms and more severe symptoms, including fever, abdominal pain, vomiting, and "jaundiced" (yellowish) skin and eyes	Examination of blood for hepatitis antibodies; liver biopsy	Treatment usually involves bed rest, intake of fluids, and, sometimes, antibiotics to ward off bacterial infections that might take hold because of lowered resistance; alpha interferon is sometimes used in treating hepatitis C
HIV/AIDS	HIV is transmitted by sexual contact, by contaminated hypodermic syringes, by infusion with contaminated blood, from mother to fetus during pregnancy, or through childbirth or breastfeeding	Infected people may initially have no symptoms or develop mild flulike symptoms that may then disappear for many years prior to the development of "full-blown" AIDS; full-blown AIDS is symptomized by fever, weight loss, fatigue, diarrhea, and opportunistic infections such as rare forms of cancer (Kaposi's sarcoma) and pneumonia	Blood, saliva, or urine tests detect HIV antibodies; more expensive tests confirm the presence of the HIV virus itself; the diagnosis of HIV/AIDS is usually made on the basis of antibodies, a low count of CD4 cells, and/or the presence of indicator diseases	There is no cure for HIV infection or AIDS; treatment (HAART) is a "cocktail" of antiviral drugs including a protease inhibitor and nucleoside analogues such as zidovudine; new drugs such as fusion inhibitors are also coming online
Human Papilloma Virus (HPV)	Transmission is by sexual and other forms of contact, such as with infected towels or clothing	May cause painless warts, often resembling cauliflowers, on male and female genital organs. May eventually lead to cervical cancer in women and throat cancer in men who engage in cunnilingus with infected women.	Clinical inspection, Pap test, DNA test	Methods include cryotherapy (freezing), podophyllin, trichloroacetic acid or bichloroacetic acid, burning, surgical removal; a vaccine can protect most people from being infected with HPV
Ectoparasitic Infestations				
Pediculosis ("crabs"): *Pthirus pubis (public lice)*	Transmission by sexual contact or by contact with an infested towel, sheet, or toilet seat	Intense itching in pubic area and other hairy regions to which lice can attach	Clinical examination	Lindane (brand name Kwell)—a prescription shampoo; non-prescription medications containing pyrethrins or piperonal butoxide (brand names RID, Triple X)
Scabies: *Sarcoptes scabiei*	Transmission by sexual contact or by contact with infested clothing or bed linen, towels, and other fabrics	Intense itching; reddish lines on skin where mites have burrowed in; welts and pus-filled blisters in affected areas	Clinical inspection	Lindane (Kwell)

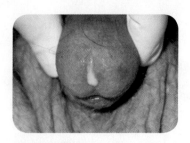

FIGURE 16.2 Gonorrheal Discharge. Gonorrhea in the male often causes a thick, yellowish, puslike discharge from the penis.

Transmission Gonococcal bacteria require a warm, moist environment, like that found along the mucous membranes of the urinary tract in both genders or the cervix in women. Outside the body, they die in about a minute. There is no evidence that gonorrhea can be picked up from public toilet seats or by touching dry objects. In rare cases, gonorrhea is contracted by contact with a moist, warm towel or sheet used immediately beforehand by an infected person. Gonorrhea is almost always transmitted by unprotected vaginal, oral, or anal sexual activity, or from mother to newborn during delivery.

A person who performs fellatio on an infected man may develop **pharyngeal gonorrhea**, which produces a throat infection. Mouth-to-mouth kissing and cunnilingus are less likely to spread gonorrhea. The eyes provide a good environment for the bacterium. Thus, a person whose hands come into contact with infected genitals and who inadvertently touches his or her eyes afterward may infect them. Babies have contracted gonorrhea of the eyes (**ophthalmia neonatorum**) when passing through the birth canals of infected mothers. This disorder may cause blindness but has become rare because the eyes of newborns are treated routinely with silver nitrate or penicillin ointment, which are toxic to gonococcal bacteria.

A gonorrheal infection may be spread from the penis to the partner's rectum during anal intercourse. A cervical gonorrheal infection can be spread to the rectum if an infected woman and her partner follow vaginal intercourse with anal intercourse. Gonorrhea is less likely to be spread by vaginal discharge than by penile discharge.

Gonorrhea is highly contagious. Women stand nearly a 50% chance of contracting gonorrhea after one exposure. Men have a 25% risk of infection (Hatcher et al., 2011). The risks to women are apparently greater because women retain infected semen in the vagina. The risk of infection increases with repeated exposure.

Symptoms Most men experience symptoms within two to five days after infection. Symptoms include a penile discharge that is clear at first (see Figure 16.2). Within a day it turns yellow to yellow-green, thickens, and becomes puslike. The urethra becomes inflamed, and urination is accompanied by a burning sensation. From 30% to 40% of males have swelling and tenderness in the lymph glands of the groin. Inflammation and other symptoms may become chronic if left untreated.

The initial symptoms of gonorrhea usually abate within a few weeks without treatment, leading people to think of gonorrhea as being no worse than a bad cold. However, the gonococcus bacterium will usually continue to damage the body internally.

The primary site of infection in women is the cervix, where it causes cervicitis. Cervicitis may cause a yellowish to yellow-green puslike discharge that irritates the vulva. If the infection spreads to the urethra, women may also note burning urination. **TRUTH** OR **FICTION** REVISITED: It is true that most women who contract gonorrhea do not have noticeable symptoms. *About 80% of the women who contract gonorrhea have no symptoms during the early stages of the infection.* Because many infected women do not seek treatment until symptoms develop, they may innocently infect another sex partner.

When gonorrhea is not treated early, it may spread through the urogenital systems in both genders and strike the internal reproductive organs. In men, it can lead to **epididymitis**, which can cause fertility problems. Swelling and feelings of tenderness or pain in the scrotum are the principal symptoms of epididymitis. Fever may also be present. Occasionally the kidneys are affected.

Pharyngeal gonorrhea A gonorrheal infection that is characterized by a sore throat.

1

Ophthalmia neonatorum A gonorrheal infection of the eyes of newborn children who contract the disease by passing through an infected birth canal.

Cervicitis Inflammation of the cervix.

Epididymitis Inflammation of the epididymis.

In women, the bacterium can spread through the cervix to the uterus, fallopian tubes, ovaries, and other parts of the abdominal cavity, causing **pelvic inflammatory disease (PID)**. Symptoms of PID include cramps, abdominal pain and tenderness, cervical tenderness and discharge, irregular menstrual cycles, coital pain, fever, nausea, and vomiting. PID may also occur without symptoms. Regardless of the presence or absence of symptoms, PID can cause scarring that blocks the fallopian tubes, leading to infertility. Pelvic inflammatory disease is a serious illness that requires aggressive treatment with antibiotics. Surgery may be needed to remove infected tissue. Unfortunately, many women become aware of a gonococcal infection only when they develop PID. These consequences are all the more unfortunate because gonorrhea, when diagnosed and treated early, clears up rapidly in over 90% of cases.

Diagnosis and Treatment Diagnosis of gonorrhea involves clinical inspection of the genitals by a physician (e.g., a family practitioner, urologist, or gynecologist) and the culturing and examination of a sample of genital discharge.

Antibiotics are the standard treatment for gonorrhea. Penicillin was once the favored antibiotic, but the rise of penicillin-resistant strains of *Neisseria gonorrhoeae* has required that alternative antibiotics be used (Multidrug-resistant gonorrhea, 2012). An injection of the antibiotic ceftriaxone is often recommended. Other antibiotics that are used to treat gonorrhea include ciprofloxacin and ofloxacin. Since gonorrhea and chlamydia often occur together, people who are infected with gonorrhea are usually also treated for chlamydia through the use of another antibiotic (Hatcher et al., 2011). Sex partners of people with gonorrhea should also be examined.

SYPHILIS

Nobody wanted to be associated with **syphilis**. In Naples they called it "the French disease." In France it was "the Neapolitan disease." Many Italians called it "the Spanish disease," but in Spain they called it "the disease of Española" (modern Haiti).

In 1530, the Italian physician Girolamo Fracastoro wrote a poem about a shepherd boy named Syphilus, who was afflicted with the disease as retribution for insulting the sun god Apollo.

Syphilis is caused by a bacterium isolated in 1905 by the German scientist Fritz Schaudinn: *Treponema pallidum* (*T. pallidum*, for short) (see Figure 16.3). The name contains roots meaning a "faintly colored (pallid) turning thread," describing the corkscrew-like shape of the microscopic organism. Because of the spiral shape, *T. pallidum* is also called a *spirochete*, from Greek roots meaning "spiral" and "hair."

The incidence of syphilis decreased in the United States with the introduction of penicillin (see Figure 16.4). Figure 16.5 shows that the rates of infection are highest in the south, Washington, DC, California, and New York. But despite the availability of penicillin, there has been a recent resurgence in rates of syphilis

CRITICAL THINKING
How do penicillin-resistant strains of a bacterial agent evolve?

Pelvic inflammatory disease (PID) Inflammation of the pelvic region; symptoms are abdominal pain, tenderness, nausea, fever, and irregular menstrual cycles; PID may lead to infertility.

Syphilis An STI that is caused by the *Treponema pallidum* bacterium, which may progress through several stages of development from a chancre to a rash to damage to vital body systems.

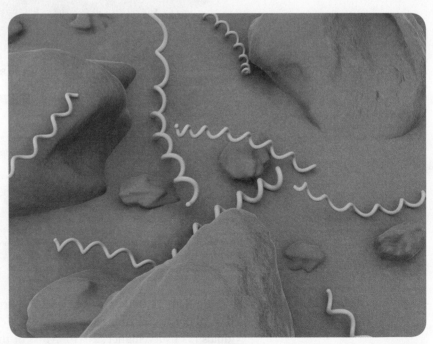

FIGURE 16.3 Treponema pallidum. *Treponema pallidum* is the bacterium that causes syphilis. Because of the spiral shape, *T. pallidum* is also called a spirochete.

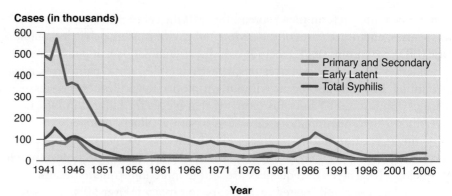

FIGURE 16.4 Reported Cases of Syphilis, According to Year and Stage of Infection. Due to frequent testing for syphilis, treatment with antibiotics, and preventive measures, the number of newly reported cases of syphilis has declined markedly since the 1940s.

Source: Centers for Disease Control and Prevention. (2011). 2010 Sexually transmitted diseases surveillance. Figure 34. Syphilis—Reported cases by stage of infection, United States, 1941–2010. http://www.cdc.gov/std/stats10/figures/34.htm (Accessed July 4, 2012).

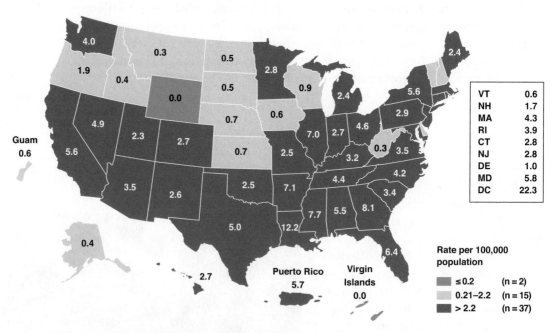

NOTE: The total rate of primary and secondary syphilis for the United States and outlying areas (Guam, Puerto Rico and Virgin Islands) was 4.5 per 100,000 population.

FIGURE 16.5 Rates of Primary and Secondary Syphilis Across the United States, 2010. Rates of syphilis are highest in the south, the District of Columbia, California, and New York State.

Source: Centers for Disease Control and Prevention. (2011). 2010 Sexually transmitted diseases surveillance. Figure 37. Primary and secondary syphilis—Rates by state, United States and outlying areas, 2010. http://www.cdc.gov/std/stats10/figures/37.htm (Accessed October 4, 2012).

to more than 11,000 cases per year, in part because the advent of effective drugs for HIV/AIDS has contributed to a new wave of risky sexual behavior among many individuals (STI surveillance, 2010). Most of the new cases were found in young African American men who have sex with men (Syphilis, 2012; Syphilis—reported cases, 2011). Even so, the rates among women and infants (due to **congenital syphilis**) have also risen.

Congenital syphilis A syphilis infection that is present at birth.

Depending on when syphilis is diagnosed and treated, its effects can range from negligible to harmful to lethal. They include heart disease, blindness, confusion, and death. Syphilis killed the painter Paul Gauguin.

The Origins of Syphilis The origins of syphilis are controversial. The Columbian theory holds that Christopher Columbus returned to Spain from his first voyage to the West Indies (1492–1493) with more than beads, blankets, and tobacco. Then, from Spain, Spanish mercenaries may have carried the disease to Naples when they were hired to protect that city from French invaders. Then the French army may have contracted syphilis from prostitutes, who also practiced their profession with the Spaniards and Neapolitans. Sailors may have eventually spread syphilis to the East.

It is generally accepted that Columbus exhibited symptoms of advanced syphilis when he died in 1506. **TRUTH OR FICTION** REVISITED: But it is unclear whether or not Columbus brought syphilis back to Europe from the New World.

Transmission **TRUTH OR FICTION** REVISITED: It is not true that gonorrhea and syphilis can be contracted from toilet seats in public rest rooms. Syphilis, like gonorrhea, is most often transmitted by vaginal or anal intercourse, or oral–genital or oral–anal contact with an infected person. The spirochete is usually transmitted when open lesions on an infected person come into contact with the mucous membranes or skin abrasions of the partner's body during sexual activity. Syphilis may also be contracted by touching an infectious **chancre**, but not from using the same toilet seat as an infected person.

Pregnant women may transmit syphilis to their fetuses, because the spirochete can cross the placental membrane. Miscarriage, stillbirth, or congenital syphilis may result. Congenital syphilis may impair vision and hearing or deform bones and teeth. Blood tests are administered routinely during pregnancy to diagnose syphilis in the mother so that congenital problems in the baby may be averted. The fetus will probably not be harmed if an infected mother is treated before the fourth month of pregnancy.

Symptoms and Course of Illness Syphilis develops through several stages. In the first or *primary stage* of syphilis, a painless chancre (a hard, round, ulcer-like lesion with raised edges) appears at the site of infection two to four weeks after contact. When women are infected, the chancre usually forms on the vaginal walls or the cervix. It may also form on the external genitalia, most often on the labia. When men are infected, the chancre usually forms on the penile glans. It may also form on the scrotum or penile shaft. If the mode of transmission is oral sex, the chancre may appear on the lips or tongue (see Figure 16.6). If the infection is spread by anal sex, the rectum may serve as the site of the chancre. The chancre disappears within a few weeks, but if the infection remains untreated, syphilis will continue to work within the body.

The *secondary stage* begins a few weeks to a few months later. A skin rash develops, consisting of painless, reddish, raised bumps that darken after a while and burst, oozing a discharge. Other symptoms include sores in the mouth, painful

Chancre A sore or ulcer.

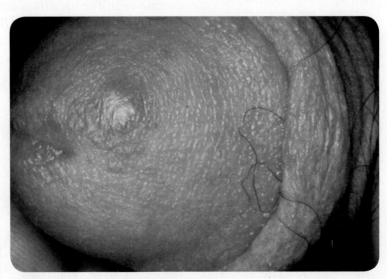

FIGURE 16.6 Syphilis Chancre. The first stage, or primary stage, of a syphilis infection is marked by the appearance of a painless sore or chancre at the site of the infection.

swelling of joints, a sore throat, headaches, and fever. A person with syphilis may thus wrongly assume that he or she has the flu.

These symptoms also disappear. Syphilis then enters the *latent stage* and may lie dormant for 1 to 40 years. But spirochetes continue to multiply and burrow into the circulatory system, central nervous system (brain and spinal cord), and bones. The person may no longer be contagious to sex partners after several years in the latent stage, but a pregnant woman may pass along the infection to her newborn at any time.

In many cases the disease eventually progresses to the late or *tertiary stage*. A large ulcer may form on the skin, muscle tissue, digestive organs, lungs, liver, or other organs. This destructive ulcer can often be successfully treated, but still more serious damage can occur as the infection attacks the central nervous system or the cardiovascular system (the heart and the major blood vessels). Either outcome can be fatal. **Neurosyphilis** can cause brain damage, resulting in paralysis or the mental illness called **general paresis**.

The primary and secondary symptoms of syphilis inevitably disappear. **TRUTH OR FICTION** REVISITED: But it is not true that the infection does not require medical treatment if a syphilitic chancre (sore) goes away by itself. The belief that medical treatment is unnecessary if the symptoms of an STI disappear by themselves is unfounded. Gonorrhea and syphilis, for example, both can damage the body even when their early symptoms have abated.

Diagnosis and Treatment Primary-stage syphilis is diagnosed by clinical examination. If a chancre is found, fluid drawn from it can be examined under a microscope. The spirochetes are usually quite visible. Blood tests are not definitive until the secondary stage begins. The most frequently used blood test is the **VDRL**, which tests for the presence of **antibodies** to *Treponema pallidum* in the blood.

Penicillin is the treatment of choice for syphilis, although for people allergic to penicillin, doxycycline, and some other antibiotics can be used (Hatcher et al., 2011). Sex partners of persons infected with syphilis should also be evaluated by a physician.

CHLAMYDIA

Chlamydia, another bacterial STI, is more common than gonorrhea and syphilis in the United States (STI surveillance, 2010). Chlamydia infections are caused by the *Chlamydia trachomatis* bacterium, a parasitic organism that can survive only within cells. The bacterium can cause several different types of infection, including *nongonococcal urethritis (NGU)* in men and women, *epididymitis* (infection of the epididymis) in men, and *cervicitis* (infection of the cervix), *endometritis* (infection of the endometrium), and PID in women (Pelvic inflammatory disease, 2011).

Neurosyphilis Syphilitic infection of the central nervous system, which can cause brain damage and death.

General paresis A progressive form of mental illness caused by neurosyphilis and characterized by gross confusion.

VDRL Named after the Venereal Disease Research Laboratory, a test for the presence of antibodies to *Treponema pallidum* in the blood.

Antibodies Specialized proteins that are produced by the white blood cells of the immune system in response to disease organisms and other toxic substances, and that recognize and attack the invading organisms or substances.

New cases of chlamydia, by age

Source: Centers for Disease Control and Prevention. (2009b, January 13). Trends in Reportable Sexually Transmitted Diseases in the United States, 2007: National Surveillance Data for Chlamydia, Gonorrhea, and Syphilis. http://www.cdc.gov/std/stats07/images/trends-chlamydia-700.gif.

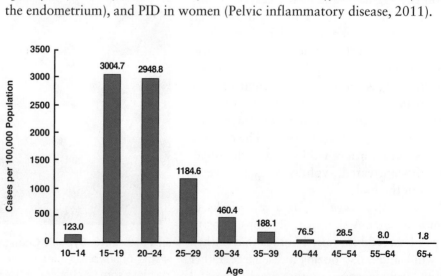

Although only 1 million to 1.5 million new cases of chlamydia are reported each year in the United States, the majority of cases go unreported (STI trends, 2011). The CDC estimates that there are actually about 3 million new chlamydia infections each year. The incidence of chlamydia infections is especially high among female teenagers and college students (Chlamydia statistics, 2012). The highest infection rates for women are found in the south and southwest, and also in Washington, DC and Illinois (see Figure 16.7).

Transmission *Chlamydia trachomatis* is usually transmitted through vaginal or anal sexual intercourse (Chlamydia—CDC fact sheet, 2012). *Chlamydia trachomatis* may also cause an eye infection if a person touches his or her eyes after handling the genitals of an infected partner. Oral sex with an infected partner can infect the throat. Newborns can acquire potentially serious chlamydia eye infections as they pass through the cervix of an infected mother during birth. Even newborns delivered by cesarean section may be infected if the amniotic sac breaks before delivery.

Symptoms Chlamydia infections usually produce symptoms that are similar to, but milder than, those of gonorrhea. In men, *Chlamydia trachomatis* can lead to nongonococcal urethritis (NGU). *Urethritis* is an inflammation of the urethra. NGU refers to forms of urethritis that are not caused by the gonococcal bacterium. (NGU is generally diagnosed only in men. In women, an inflammation of the urethra caused by *Chlamydia trachomatis* is called a chlamydia infection or simply chlamydia.) NGU was formerly called nonspecific urethritis or NSU. Many organisms can cause NGU. *Chlamydia trachomatis* accounts for about half of the cases among men (Hatcher et al., 2011).

Nongonococcal urethritis in men may produce a thin, whitish discharge from the penis and some burning or other pain during urination. These contrast with the yellow-green discharge and more intense pain produced by gonorrhea. There may be soreness in the scrotum and feelings of heaviness in the testes. NGU is about two to three times as prevalent among U.S. men as gonorrhea (Hatcher et al.,

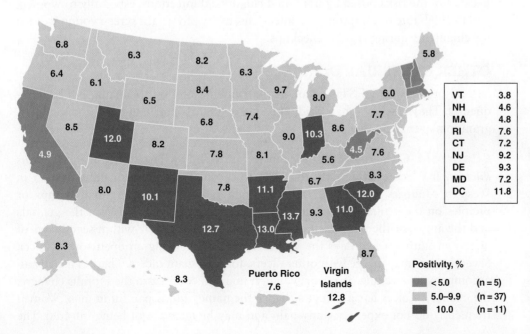

FIGURE 16.7 Percentage of Women Who Test Positive for Chlamydia across the United States, 2010

Source: Chlamydia positivity of women by state, 2010. Centers for Disease Control and Prevention. (2011). Sexually Transmitted Diseases (STDs). 2010 Sexually Transmitted Diseases Surveillance. http://www.cdc.gov/std/stats10/figures/11.htm (Accessed October 4, 2012).

2011). Young male adults are at the highest risk of contracting gonorrhea and NGU, presumably because of their high levels of sexual activity.

In women, chlamydial infections usually give rise to infections of the urethra or cervix (Chlamydia—CDC fact sheet, 2012). Women, like men, may experience burning when they urinate, genital irritation, and a mild (vaginal) discharge. Women are also likely to encounter pelvic pain and irregular menstrual cycles. The cervix may look swollen and inflamed. However, as many as 25% of men and 70% of women infected with chlamydia have no noticeable symptoms (Chlamydia—CDC fact sheet, 2012). For this reason, chlamydia has been dubbed the "silent disease." Symptom-free people may go untreated and unknowingly pass their infections to new partners. In women, an untreated chlamydial infection can spread throughout the reproductive system, leading to PID and scarring the fallopian tubes, resulting in infertility. About half of the more than 1 million annual cases of PID are attributed to chlamydia (Hatcher et al., 2011). Women exposed to *Chlamydia trachomatis* also stand a greater chance of incurring an ectopic (tubal) pregnancy.

Untreated chlamydial infections can also damage the internal reproductive organs of men. About 50% of cases of epididymitis are caused by chlamydial infections (Hatcher et al., 2011). Yet, only about 1 or 2% of men with untreated NGU caused by *Chlamydia trachomatis* go on to develop epididymitis. The long-term effects of untreated chlamydial infections in men remain undetermined.

Chlamydial infections also frequently occur together with other STIs, most often gonorrhea. Nearly half of the cases of gonorrhea involve coexisting chlamydial infections (Hatcher et al., 2011).

Diagnosis and Treatment Various tests are used in the laboratory or the physician's office to verify a diagnosis of chlamydia in women. The tests analyze a cervical smear and are highly reliable. In men, a swab may be inserted through the penile opening to extract fluid that is analyzed for the presence of *Chlamydia trachomatis*.

Antibiotics other than penicillin are highly effective in eradicating chlamydia infections. These include azithromycin, doxycycline, ofloxacin, and amoxicillin (Chlamydia—CDC fact sheet, 2012). Sex partners are treated when possible to prevent the infection from bouncing back and forth. Both partners may be unaware that they are infected and oblivious to the internal damage the infection is causing. Because of the risks posed by untreated chlamydial infections, especially to women, and the high rate of symptom-free infections, many physicians screen young women for chlamydia during regular checkups.

OTHER BACTERIAL DISEASES

Several other bacterial STIs occur in the United States and Canada, but less frequently. These include chancroid, shigellosis, granuloma inguinale, and lymphogranuloma venereum.

Chancroid **Chancroid,** or "soft chancre," is caused by the bacterium *Hemophilus ducreyi*. It is more commonly found in the tropics and Eastern nations than in Western countries. The chancroid sore consists of a cluster of small bumps or pimples on the genitals, perineum (the area of skin that lies between the genitals and the anus), or the anus itself. These lesions usually appear within seven days of infection. Within a few days the lesion ruptures, producing an open sore or ulcer. Several ulcers may merge with other ulcers, forming giant ulcers. There is usually an accompanying swelling of a nearby lymph node. In contrast to the syphilis chancre, the chancroid ulcer has a soft rim (hence the name) and is painful in men. Women frequently do not experience any pain and may be unaware of being infected. The

Chancroid An STI caused by the *Hemophilus ducreyi* bacterium. Also called *soft chancre.*

bacterium is typically transmitted through sexual or bodily contact with the lesion or its discharge. Diagnosis is usually confirmed by culturing the bacterium, which is found in pus from the sore, and examining it under a microscope. Antibiotics are usually effective in treating the disease (Hatcher et al., 2011).

Shigellosis Shigellosis is caused by the *Shigella* bacterium and is characterized by fever and severe abdominal symptoms, including diarrhea and inflammation of the large intestine. About 25,000 cases of shigellosis are reported each year in the United States. Shigellosis can result from food poisoning, but it is also often contracted by oral contact with infected fecal material, which may stem from oral–anal sex. Shigellosis often resolves itself, but people with the disease may become severely dehydrated from the diarrhea. Severe cases are usually treated with antibiotics.

Granuloma Inguinale Rare in the United States, **granuloma inguinale**, like chancroid, is more common in tropical regions. It is caused by the bacterium *Calymmatobacterium granulomatous* and is not as contagious as many other STIs. Primary symptoms are painless red bumps or sores in the groin area that ulcerate and spread. Like chancroid, it is usually spread by intimate bodily or sexual contact with a lesion or its discharge. Diagnosis is confirmed by microscopic examination of tissue of the rim of the sore. Numerous antibiotics are effective in treating this disease (Hatcher et al., 2011). If left untreated, however, it may lead to the development of fistulas (holes) in the rectum or bladder, destruction of infected tissues or organs, or scarring of skin tissue that results in a condition called **elephantiasis**, a condition that afflicted the so-called Elephant Man in the nineteenth century.

Lymphogranuloma Venereum (LGV) Another tropical STI that occurs only rarely in the United States and Canada is **lymphogranuloma venereum (LGV)**. Some U.S. soldiers returned home from Vietnam with cases of LGV. It is caused by several strains of the *Chlamydia trachomatis* bacterium. LGV usually enters the body through the penis, vulva, or cervix, where a small, painless sore may form. The sore may go unnoticed, but a nearby lymph gland in the groin swells and grows tender. Other symptoms mimic those of flu: chills, fever, and headache. Other possible symptoms include backache (especially in women) and arthritic complaints (painful joints). If LGV is untreated, growths and fistulas in the genitals and elephantiasis of the legs and genitals may occur. Diagnosis is made by skin tests and blood tests. Antibiotics are the usual treatment (Hatcher et al., 2011).

Vaginal Infections

A vaginal infection or inflammation is technically termed **vaginitis**. Vaginitis is typically symptomized by genital irritation or itching and burning during urination, but the most common symptom is an odious discharge.

Most cases of vaginitis are caused by organisms that reside in the vagina or by sexually transmitted organisms. Organisms that reside in the vagina may overgrow when the environmental balance of the vagina is upset by factors such as birth-control pills, antibiotics, dietary changes, excessive douching, or nylon underwear or pantyhose. (See Chapter 2 for ways to reduce the risk of vaginitis.) Still other cases are caused by sensitivities or allergic reactions to various chemicals.

The great majority of vaginal infections involve bacterial vaginosis (BV), candidiasis (commonly called a "yeast" infection), or trichomoniasis ("trich"). Bacterial vaginosis is the most common form of vaginitis, followed by candidiasis, then by trichomoniasis, but some cases involve combinations of the three.

Shigellosis An STI caused by the *Shigella* bacterium.

Granuloma inguinale A tropical STI caused by the *Calymmatobacterium granulomatous* bacterium.

Elephantiasis A disease characterized by enlargement of parts of the body, especially the legs and genitals, and by hardening and ulceration of the surrounding skin.

Lymphogranuloma venereum (LGV) A tropical STI caused by the *Chlamydia trachomatis* bacterium.

Vaginitis Any type of vaginal infection or inflammation.

The microbes causing vaginal infections in women can also infect the man's urethral tract. A "vaginal infection" can be passed back and forth between sex partners.

5

TRUTH OR FICTION REVISITED: Men can not literally develop vaginal infections. Only women have vaginas. However, the microbes that cause these infections in women may also cause problems for men.

BACTERIAL VAGINOSIS

Formerly called *nonspecific vaginitis*, **bacterial vaginosis** (BV) is most often caused by overgrowth of the bacterium *Gardnerella vaginalis* (Hatcher et al., 2011). The bacterium is mainly transmitted sexually. The most characteristic symptom in women is a thin, foul-smelling vaginal discharge, but infected women often have no symptoms. Diagnosis requires culturing the bacterium in the laboratory. Besides causing troublesome symptoms in some cases, BV may increase the risk of various gynecological problems, including infections of the reproductive tract (CDC, 2006). Oral treatment with metronidazole (brand name Flagyl) is recommended and is effective in most cases. Topical treatments with metronidazole or clindamycin are also effective. But recurrences are common.

Questions remain about whether a male partner should also be treated. The bacterium can usually be found in the urethra of a symptom-free male (Hatcher et al., 2011). Being symptom-free, the male may unknowingly pass the bacterium on to others.

CANDIDIASIS

Candidiasis is caused by a yeastlike fungus, *Candida albicans*. It is also known as *moniliasis, thrush,* or, more simply, a yeast infection. **Candidiasis** commonly produces soreness, inflammation, and intense (sometimes maddening!) itching around the vulva that is accompanied by a white, thick, curdlike vaginal discharge. Yeast generally produces no symptoms when the vaginal environment is normal. Yeast infections can also occur in the mouth in both men and women and in the penis in men.

Infections most often arise from changes in the vaginal environment that allow the fungus to overgrow. Factors such as the use of antibiotics, birth-control pills, intrauterine devices (IUDs), pregnancy, and diabetes may alter the vaginal balance, allowing the fungus that causes yeast infections to grow to infectious levels. Wearing nylon underwear and tight, restrictive, poorly ventilated clothing may also set the stage for a yeast infection.

Diet may play a role in recurrent yeast infections. Reducing intake of substances that produce excessive excretion of urinary sugars (such as dairy products, sugar, and artificial sweeteners) apparently reduces the frequency of recurrent yeast infections. Eating a pint of yogurt containing active bacterial (*Lactobacillus acidophilus*) cultures daily may reduce the rate of recurrent infections.

Candidiasis can be passed back and forth between sex partners through vaginal intercourse. It may also be passed back and forth between the mouth and the genitals through oral–genital contact and infect the anus through anal intercourse. However, most infections in women are believed to be caused by an overgrowth of "yeast" normally found in the vagina, not by sexual transmission. Still, it is advisable to evaluate partners simultaneously. Whereas most men with *Candida* have no symptoms, some may develop NGU or a genital thrush that is accompanied by itching and burning during urination or by reddening of the penis. Candidiasis may also be transmitted nonsexually, as between women who share a washcloth.

CRITICAL THINKING

Critical thinkers pay attention to definitions of terms. What does it mean to say that men have a vaginal infection?

Bacterial vaginosis A form of vaginitis usually caused by the *Gardnerella vaginalis* bacterium.

Candidiasis A form of vaginitis caused by a yeastlike fungus, *Candida albicans.*

At least half of adult women will experience at least one episode of candidiasis by their mid-20s (Hatcher et al., 2011). About 25% of these will have recurrent infections. A single dose of oral fluconazole, or vaginal suppositories or creams containing miconazole, clotrimazole, or butaconazole are recommended for treatment (Hatcher et al., 2011). Many of these treatments are sold over the counter. Ask the pharmacist which preparations contain these medicines (or read the labels). We advise women with vaginal complaints to consult their physicians before using any of these medications to ensure that they receive the proper diagnosis and treatment.

TRICHOMONIASIS

Trichomoniasis ("trich") is the most common STI. It is caused by *Trichomonas vaginalis,* a one-celled parasite. There are about 7.4 million new cases a year among women (and men) in the United States (STI trends, 2011). Symptoms include burning or itching in the vulva, mild pain during urination or coitus, and an odorous, foamy whitish to yellowish green discharge. Lower abdominal pain is reported by some infected women. Many women notice symptoms appearing or worsening during, or just following, their menstrual periods. Trichomoniasis facilitates the transmission of HIV and is linked to the development of tubal adhesions that can result in infertility. As with many other STIs, many infected women have no symptoms.

Candidiasis often reflects the overgrowth of organisms normally found in the vagina, but trich is almost always sexually transmitted. Because the parasite can survive for several hours on moist surfaces outside the body, trich can be communicated from contact with infected semen or vaginal discharges on towels, washcloths, and bedclothes. This parasite is one of the few disease agents that can be picked up from a toilet seat, but it would have to come into contact with the penis or vulva.

Trichomonas vaginalis can cause NGU in the male, which can be symptom-free or cause a slight penile discharge that is usually noticeable prior to first urination in the morning. There may be tingling, itching, and other irritating sensations in the urethral tract. But most infected men are symptom-free and can unwittingly transfer the organism to other sex partners. Diagnosis is frequently made by microscopic examination of a smear of a woman's vaginal fluids.

Except during the first three months of pregnancy, trichomoniasis is usually treated in both women and men with metronidazole (brand name Flagyl). If both partners are treated, the success rate approaches 100% (CDC, 2006; Hatcher et al., 2011).

Viral Infections

Viruses are tiny particles of DNA coated with a protein. They cannot reproduce on their own. When they invade a body cell, however, they can direct the cell's own reproductive machinery to spin off new viral particles that spread to other cells, causing infection. Our immune systems defeat many viruses, and many others are not lethal. In this section we discuss viral STIs, some of which are indeed deadly: HIV/AIDS, *Herpes simplex* virus, viral hepatitis, human papilloma virus (HPV), and molluscum contagiosum. 👁

HIV/AIDS

The **human immunodeficiency virus** (HIV) is the virus that causes **AIDS**, which stands for **acquired immunodeficiency syndrome**. HIV attacks and disables the immune system, the body's natural line of defense, stripping it of its ability to fend off disease-causing organisms. AIDS is considered fatal, although many people

◉—|**Watch** the **Video**
AIDS
on **MyDevelopmentLab**

Trichomoniasis   A form of vaginitis caused by the protozoan *Trichomonas vaginalis.*

Human immunodeficiency virus (HIV)   A sexually transmitted virus that destroys white blood cells in the immune system, leaving the body vulnerable to life-threatening diseases.

Acquired immunodeficiency syndrome (AIDS)   A condition caused by the human immunodeficiency virus (HIV) and characterized by destruction of the immune system so that the body is stripped of its ability to fend off life-threatening diseases.

Table 16.2

Estimated Numbers of People in the United States Living with HIV/AIDS by Race/Ethnicity

Race/Ethnicity	Number of Cases	Percentage of Total Number of People in United States Living with AIDS	Racial/Ethnic Group as Percentage of Population of United States
African American	473,229	42.5200	12.6
Asian American	8,759	00.0079	4.8
European American	429,804	38.6100	63.7
Latin American	197,449	17.7400	16.3
Native American	3,721	00.0033	1.1

Sources: HIV/AIDS surveillance, 2012HIV/AIDS surveillance, 2012. Centers for Disease Control and Prevention. (2012). Diagnoses of HIV infection and AIDS in the United States and dependent areas, 2010. *HIV surveillance report, Volume 22.* http://www.cdc.gov/hiv/surveillance/resources/reports/2010report/pdf/2010_HIV_Surveillance_Report_vol_22. pdf#Page=27 (Accessed October 4, 2012). Table 2a; U.S. Bureau of the Census. (2010). Table 1. Population by Hispanic or Latino Origin and by Race for the United States: 2010. http://www.census.gov/prod/cen2010/briefs/c2010br-02.pdf.

currently live with HIV/AIDS due to the development of powerful antiviral medications. For people in industrialized nations like the United States and Canada, Western European nations, Japan, and the like, HIV/AIDS may become a chronic but manageable condition, like diabetes. But for many millions in developing nations, where medications are too expensive or difficult to deliver, HIV/AIDS may remain a death sentence. ◉

Watch the **Video**
Dr. Richard Carroll, Sex Therapist on **MyDevelopmentLab**

Prevalence of HIV/AIDS   More than 1 million Americans are living with HIV/AIDS (HIV/AIDS surveillance, 2012). More than half a million Americans have died from it. The incidence of HIV/AIDS is highest people of color (see Table 16.2 and Figure 16.8), people who share needles when they inject drugs, and people who engage in unprotected, male–female sex.

Although half of those infected with HIV around the world are female, in the United States, HIV/AIDS is predominantly found among men who engage in sexual activity with other men or share needles when injecting drugs (Chandra et al., 2012; see Table 16.3). But male–female sex is the fasting-growing exposure category in the United States. Among women, male–female sexual contact accounts for more than half of the cases (see Table 16.3).

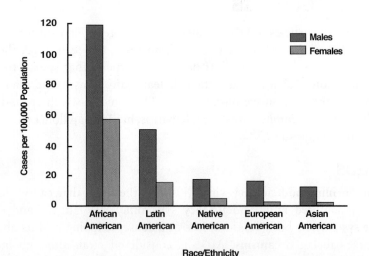

FIGURE 16.8 Rates of HIV Diagnosis for Various Ethnic Groups in the United States

Source: Centers for Disease Control and Prevention. (2008). HIV and AIDS in the United States: A Picture of Today's Epidemic. Accessed November 15, 2012. http://www.cdc.gov/HIV/topics/surveillance/united_states.htm.

Table 16.3

Cumulative Estimated Number of AIDS Diagnoses in the United States

Transmission Category	Adult and Adolescent Males	Adult and Adolescent Females	Total
Male-to-male sexual contact	529,908	–	529,908
Injection drug use	186,318	87,126	273,444
Male-to-male sexual contact and injection drug use	77,213	–	77,213
Heterosexual contact	72,183	126,637	198,820
Other*	12,744	7,032	19,776

*Includes hemophilia, blood transfusion, perinatal exposure, and risk not reported or not identified.

Source: Centers for Disease Control and Prevention. (2011). HIV/AIDS statistics and surveillance. AIDS diagnoses by transmission category. http://www.cdc.gov/hiv/topics/surveillance/basic.htm#exposure (Accessed October 4, 2012).

A World of Diversity

Does Use of Hormonal Methods of Contraception Increase a Woman's Risk of Being Infected with HIV?

In Africa, the answer to this question seems to be yes. A hormone injection given four times a year is the most popular contraceptive for women in eastern and southern Africa. Why? Hormone shots work, and in societies in which male dominance and prostitution are common, the woman need not argue with her partner about using condoms. In fact, it appears the hormone shots—or, more accurately—the sexual behavior that follows the shots, just about doubles the risk for women (Morrison & Nanda, 2012). Nor do the male partners necessarily "escape" infection. When the woman is infected with HIV but the man is not, use of the hormone shots also doubles the risks that women will transmit HIV to their partners.

The findings are of concern because hundreds of thousands of African women suffer injuries, bleeding, infections, even death in childbirth from unwanted pregnancies. Countries with the highest pregnancy rates also tend to be highest in transmission rates of HIV. Education and condoms may offer a way out—maybe.

Use of Hormonal Contraception Increases the Risk of HIV Transmission in Eastern and Southern Africa

Source: Morrison, C. S., & Nanda, K. (2011, October 4). Hormonal contraception and HIV: An unanswered question. *The Lancet Infectious Diseases.* Doi:10.1016/S1473-3099(11), 70254-7.

Greater H.I.V. Risk

A study found that an injected hormonal contraceptive widely used by women in Africa increases the risk of H.I.V. infection.

H.I.V. TRANSMISSION RATES
Annual incidence per 100 people

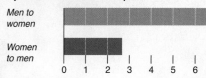

The Immune System and HIV/AIDS AIDS is caused by a virus that attacks the body's **immune system**—the body's natural line of defense against disease-causing organisms. The immune system combats disease in several ways. It produces white blood cells that envelop and kill **pathogens** such as bacteria, viruses, and funguses; worn-out body cells; and cancer cells. White blood cells are called **leukocytes**. Leukocytes engage in microscopic search-and-destroy missions. They identify and eradicate foreign agents and debilitated cells.

TRUTH OR **FICTION** REVISITED: It is true that as you read this page, you are engaged in search-and-destroy missions against foreign agents within your body. The white cells in your immune system continuously seek and destroy foreign pathogens within your body.

Leukocytes recognize foreign agents by their surface fragments. The surface fragments are termed **antigens** because the body reacts to their presence by developing specialized proteins, or antibodies. Antibodies attach themselves to the foreign bodies, inactivate them, and mark them for destruction. (Infection by HIV may be determined by examining the blood, saliva, or urine for the presence of antibodies.)

Rather than mark pathogens for destruction or war against them, special "memory lymphocytes" are held in reserve. Memory lymphocytes can remain in the bloodstream for years, and they form the basis for a quick immune response to an invader the second time around.

Another function of the immune system is to promote **inflammation**. When you suffer an injury, blood vessels in the region initially contract to check bleeding. Then they dilate. Dilation expands blood flow to the injured region, causing the redness and warmth that identify inflammation. The elevated blood supply also brings in an army of leukocytes to combat invading microscopic life forms, such as bacteria, that might otherwise use the local injury to establish a beachhead into the body.

Effects of HIV on the Immune System Spikes on the surface of HIV allow it to bind to sites on cells in the immune system. Like other viruses, HIV uses the cells it invades to spin off copies of itself. HIV uses the enzyme *reverse transcriptase* to cause the genes in the cells it attacks to make proteins that the virus needs in order to reproduce.

HIV attacks the immune system by destroying a type of lymphocyte called the *CD4 cell* (see Figure 16.9). The CD4 cell, also known as *T-cell* or *helper T-cell*, is the "quarterback" of the immune system. CD4 cells "recognize" invading pathogens and signal B-lymphocytes or B-cells—another kind of white blood cell—to produce antibodies that inactivate pathogens and mark them for annihilation. CD4 cells also signal another class of T-cells, called *killer T-cells*, to destroy infected cells. By attacking and destroying helper T-cells, HIV disables the very cells on which the body relies to fend off diseases. As HIV cripples the body's defenses, the individual develops infections that would not otherwise take hold. Cancer cells might also proliferate. Although the CD4 cells appear to be its main target, HIV also attacks other types of white blood cells.

The blood normally contains about 1,000 CD4 cells per cubic millimeter. The numbers of CD4 cells may remain at about this level for years following HIV infection. Many people show no symptoms and appear healthy while CD4 cells remain at this level. Then, for reasons that are not clearly understood, the levels of CD4 cells begin to drop off, although symptoms may not appear for a decade or more. As the numbers of CD4 cells decline, symptoms generally increase,

Immune system A term for the body's complex of mechanisms for protecting itself from disease-causing agents such as pathogens.

Pathogen An agent, especially a microorganism, that can cause a disease.

Leukocytes White blood cells that are essential to the body's defenses against infection.

Antigen A protein, toxin, or other substance to which the body reacts by producing antibodies.

Inflammation Redness and warmth that develop at the site of an injury, reflecting dilation of blood vessels that permits the expanded flow of leukocytes to the region.

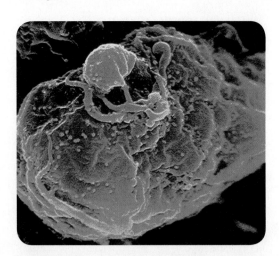

FIGURE 16.9 HIV (the AIDS Virus) Attacks a White Blood Cell. HIV progressively weakens the immune system, leaving the body vulnerable to infections and diseases that would otherwise be fended off.

and people fall prey to diseases that their weakened immune systems are unable to fight off. People become most vulnerable to opportunistic infections when the level of CD4 cells falls below 200 per cubic millimeter.

Progression of HIV/AIDS HIV follows a complex course once it enters the body. A recently infected individual may experience mild flulike symptoms—fatigue, fever, headaches, muscle pain, lack of appetite, nausea, swollen glands, and possibly a rash. Such symptoms usually disappear within a few weeks, and people may dismiss them as a case of the flu. People who enter this symptom-free or carrier state generally look and act well and do not realize that they are infectious. Thus, they can unwittingly pass the virus on to others.

　　TRUTH OR FICTION REVISITED: Most people who are infected with HIV remain symptom-free for years. Others enter a symptomatic state that is typically denoted by symptoms such as chronically swollen lymph nodes and intermittent weight loss, fever, fatigue, and diarrhea. This symptomatic state does not constitute full-blown AIDS, but shows that HIV is undermining the integrity of the immune system.

　　Even during the years when HIV appears to be dormant, billions of viral particles are being spun off. In a seesaw battle, the great majority of them are wiped out by the immune system. Eventually, in almost all cases, the balance tips in favor of HIV. Then the virus's numbers swell. Perhaps a decade or more after the person is infected with HIV, the virus begins to overtake the immune system. It obliterates the cells that house it and spreads to other immune-system cells. About half of the people with HIV develop AIDS within ten years of initial infection. For this reason, people who know that they are infected with HIV may feel that they are carrying time bombs within them.

　　AIDS is called a *syndrome* because it is characterized by a variety of different symptoms. The beginnings of full-blown cases of AIDS are often marked by such symptoms as swollen lymph nodes, fatigue, fever, night sweats, diarrhea, and weight loss (a "wasting syndrome") that cannot be attributed to dieting or exercise. AIDS is connected with the appearance of diseases such as pneumocystis carinii pneumonia (PCP); Kaposi's sarcoma (a form of cancer); toxoplasmosis of the brain (an infection of parasites); or *Herpes simplex* with chronic ulcers. These are termed **opportunistic diseases** because they are not likely to emerge unless a weakened immune system grants the opportunity.

　　About 10% of people with AIDS have the wasting syndrome. Wasting is the unintentional loss of more than 10% of a person's body weight and is connected with HIV/AIDS, some other infections, and cancer. As HIV/AIDS progresses, the individual becomes thinner and more fatigued. He or she becomes unable to perform ordinary life functions and falls prey to opportunistic infections. If left untreated, AIDS almost always results in death within a few years.

Transmission HIV can be transmitted by certain contaminated bodily fluids—blood, semen, vaginal secretions, or breast milk. The first three of these may enter the body through vaginal, anal, or oral–genital intercourse with an infected partner. An African study that followed seropositive mothers and their babies for two years found that the probability of transmission of HIV via breast milk was about 16.2% (1 in 6) (Nduati et al., 2000). Other avenues of infection include sharing a hypodermic needle with an infected person (as do many people who inject drugs), transfusion with contaminated blood, transplants of organs and tissues that have been infected with HIV, artificial insemination with infected semen, or being stuck by a needle used previously on an infected person. HIV may enter the body through tiny cuts or sores in the mucous lining of the vagina, the rectum, and even the mouth. These cuts or sores can be so tiny that you are not aware of them.

Opportunistic diseases
Diseases that take hold only when the immune system is weakened and unable to fend them off.

Transmission of HIV through kissing, even prolonged kissing or "French" kissing, is considered unlikely. When a person injects drugs, a small amount of his or her blood remains inside the needle and syringe. If the person is infected with HIV, the virus may be found in the blood remaining in the needle or syringe. Others who use the needle inject the infected blood into their bloodstream. HIV can also be spread by sharing needles used for other purposes, such as injecting steroids, ear piercing, or tattooing.

HIV can also be transmitted from mother to fetus during pregnancy or from mother to child through childbirth or breastfeeding. Transmission is most likely during childbirth.

Male-to-female transmission through vaginal intercourse is more than twice as likely as female-to-male transmission (see Table 16.3), partly because more of the virus is found in the ejaculate than in vaginal secretions. A man's ejaculate may also remain for many days in the vagina, providing greater opportunity for infection to occur. Male–female or male–male anal intercourse is especially risky since it often tears or abrades rectal tissue, facilitating entry of the virus into the bloodstream (Chandra et al., 2012).

Male–female transmission via sexual intercourse is the primary route of HIV infection in Africa, Latin America, and Asia. Worldwide, male–female sexual intercourse accounts for the majority of cases of HIV/AIDS (UNAIDS, 2006). In the United States, many cases of male–female transmission occur among people who inject drugs and their sex partners.

HIV may also be spread by donor semen, such as that used in artificial insemination. Cases have also been reported of women who have become infected with hepatitis B, gonorrhea, trichomoniasis, and chlamydia by donor semen.

Factors Affecting the Risk of Sexual Transmission of HIV Some people seem more likely to communicate HIV, and others seem to be especially vulnerable to infection. Several factors appear to affect the risk of HIV infection and development of AIDS:

- The probability of transmission rises with the number of sexual contacts with an infected partner.
- The probability of transmission is affected by the type of sexual activity. Anal intercourse provides a convenient port of entry for HIV because it abrades the rectal lining and rectal cells are particularly vulnerable.
- The viral load (the amount of virus in semen) peaks shortly after initial infection and when full-blown AIDS develops.
- STIs such as genital warts, gonorrhea, trichomoniasis, and chlamydia inflame the genital region, which heightens the risk of sexual transmission of other STIs. STIs that produce genital ulcers, such as syphilis and genital herpes, heighten vulnerability to HIV infection.
- Several studies run in Africa show that circumcision is associated with a lower risk of HIV infection in men who have sex with women (Gray et al., 2012; Gray & Wawer, 2012). Analysis of data from the African country of Uganda also found that circumcision lowered the risk of infection from HPV by 35%, and the risk from HSV-2, the virus that causes herpes, by 28% (Tobian et al., 2009).
- Genetic factors may also be at work. About 1% of people of Western European descent inherited a gene from both parents that prevents HIV from entering cells in the immune system and are therefore apparently immune to HIV infection. Perhaps 20% of individuals of Western European descent have inherited the gene from one parent; HIV disease appears to progress more slowly in them. Some prostitutes in Thailand and Africa, where HIV infection has run rampant, also appear to be immune to HIV infection (Shacklett & Ferre, 2011). Genetic factors may also affect the progression of HIV infection to AIDS.

How HIV is *not* Transmitted There is much misinformation about the transmission of HIV. Let us consider some of the ways in which HIV is not transmitted:

- HIV is not transmitted from donating blood. AIDS cannot be contracted by donating blood because needles are discarded after a single use.
- HIV is not transmitted through casual, everyday contact. There is no evidence of transmission of HIV through hugging someone; shaking hands; bumping into strangers on buses and trains; handling money, doorknobs, or other objects that have been touched by infected people; sharing drinking fountains, public telephones, public toilets, or swimming pools; or trying on clothing that has been worn by an infected person.
- HIV is not transmitted by insect bites or bites from other animals.
- HIV is not transmitted by airborne germs or contact with contaminated food.
- HIV is not transmitted through sharing work or home environments. No cases of HIV transmission have been documented based on nonsexual contact in schools or in the workplace.
- HIV is apparently not transmitted by kissing. But check out the nearby "A Closer Look."

The recently approved OraQuick home test for HIV uses a mouth swab to determine the presence of HIV antibodies within 20–40 minutes.

Diagnosis of HIV infection and AIDS The enzyme-linked immunosorbent assay (ELISA, or just EIA for short) is one widely used test for HIV. EIA does not directly detect HIV. Instead, it reveals HIV antibodies. The OraQuick home test indicates the presence of HIV antibodies within 20 minutes (McNeill, 2012). People may show an antibody response to HIV long before they develop symptoms of infection. A positive (**seropositive**) test result means that HIV antibodies were found. A negative (**seronegative**) outcome means that antibodies to HIV were not detected.

The EIA test can be performed on samples of blood, saliva, or urine. The new OraQuick test uses a mouth swab and is therefore less invasive than a blood test. A saliva test is not quite as accurate as a blood test, but it is less expensive, reasonably accurate, and might encourage people who avoid blood tests to be tested. Although HIV antibodies can be detected in saliva, HIV itself is not found in measurable quantities. This is why kissing is not considered an avenue of transmission of HIV. If HIV antibodies are found, health professionals may recommend testing for the presence of the virus itself can be confirmed by more expensive tests.

Biochemical Prevention of HIV/AIDS For many years, researchers were frustrated by failure in the effort to develop effective vaccines and treatments for HIV/AIDS. Potential HIV/AIDS vaccines are being tested on people and animals, but optimism seems to grow and then wane. As of this writing, there remains no safe, effective vaccine.

On the other hand, research has shown that taking a daily pill that has one or two antiviral HIV/AIDS aids drugs prevents many people from becoming infected with HIV (Grady, 2012; McNeill, 2011). The pill called Truvada contains a mix of tenofovir and emtricitabine and was shown in African studies to decrease the likelihood of infection by 63% to 73%. Another pill, Viread, contains tenofir only, and

Seropositive Having a pathogen or antibodies to that pathogen in the bloodstream.

Seronegative Lacking a pathogen or antibodies to that pathogen in the bloodstream.

lowered the probability of infection somewhat less, by 62%. The use of such pills is technically termed *pre-exposure prophylaxis*, or *PrEP*.

Yet these pills may not be all that they seem to be for "average" or "typical" users. Studies show that only 10% of users actually take the pill as directed—daily (Grady, 2012). That was not a misprint: 10%. Why? For one thing, those who would engage in risky sexual behavior might also take other risky behaviors, including using medicine haphazardly. There are also some side effects. Finally, the pills cost money or at least must be obtained. No further comment.

A Closer Look

Is Kissing Safe?

In a presentation on the safety of kissing that leaves us less than happy, the Centers for Disease Control and Prevention looks as though it comes close to speaking out of two sides of its mouth. But actually it doesn't. The following two quotations were downloaded on September 30, 2006, from www.cdc.gov/hiv/resources/factsheets/transmission.htm. Read them carefully. Then see our commentary below.

Kissing

Casual contact through closed-mouth or "social" kissing is not a risk for transmission of HIV. Because of the potential for contact with blood during "French" or open-mouth kissing, CDC recommends against engaging in this activity with a person known to be infected. However, the risk of acquiring HIV during open-mouth kissing is believed to be very low. CDC has investigated only one case of HIV infection that may be attributed to contact with blood during open-mouth kissing.

Saliva, Tears, and Sweat

HIV has been found in saliva and tears in very low quantities from some AIDS patients. It is important to understand that finding a small amount of HIV in a body fluid does not necessarily mean that HIV can be transmitted by that body fluid. HIV has not been recovered from the sweat of HIV-infected persons. Contact with saliva, tears, or sweat has never been shown to result in transmission of HIV.

Here's the skinny. If you engage in deep kissing—also known as open-mouthed kissing, tongue kissing, or French kissing—with a person who is infected with HIV, there is no evidence whatsoever that you will catch HIV from that person's *saliva*.

However, there is a remote chance you could be infected by sharing blood. How might that happen? One possibility is that the two of you might have brushed your teeth recently, creating tiny abrasions or cuts in your gums. Some blood from your kissing partner might make its way into your mouth and into one of those temporary ports of entry. It's an extremely slight risk, but that extremely slight risk does exist.

Here's our bottom line recommendation: If you really don't know your partner, don't engage in deep kissing. (Why would you deep kiss a stranger anyway?) If you have gotten to know your partner for a while and you have no reason to be suspicious that his or her sexual or injecting drug history places him or her at high risk of being infected with HIV, kiss away. (That does *not* mean you should also risk unprotected sex!)

Can Kissing Transmit HIV? HIV is a blood-borne virus that is transmitted via various bodily fluids, including blood, semen, and vaginal fluids. However, the Centers for Disease Control and Prevention (CDC) have not found that HIV occurs in infectious quantities in saliva.

Treatment of HIV/AIDS A combination, or "cocktail," of antiviral drugs has become the standard treatment for HIV/AIDS. This combination—referred to as **HAART** (for "highly active antiretroviral therapy")— decreases the likelihood that HIV will develop resistance to treatment. It has created hope that AIDS will become increasingly manageable, a chronic health problem as opposed to a terminal illness. However, HAART is expensive, and many people who could benefit from it cannot afford it. The side effects of these medicines can be unpleasant, including nausea and, in the case of protease inhibitors, unusual accumulations of fat, such as "buffalo humps" in the neck.

It is possible to obtain the benefits of HAART by taking a three-in-one pill, Atripla, whose sandwiched ingredients are released at different rates. Another combination pill, Quad, contains four antiviral drugs and appears to be somewhat more effective than Atripla, with a different constellation of side effects (DeJesus et al., 2012). Quad contains tenofovir and emtricitabine (the two ingredients in Truvada), elvitegravir, and cobicistat. After a year, 88% of the study participants taking Quad had no detectable virus in their bloodstreams, as compared with 84% of participants taking Atripla. However, having no detectable level of the virus in one's bloodstream does not mean that the individual is cured. Decades of research experience have shown that without continued use of antiviral drugs, blood levels of the virus will eventually rebound. Yet, 88% and 84% are both impressive numbers, especially when a person might continue to survive with a low detectable level of the virus. Physicians will therefore be comparing side effects, including ability to tolerate the drugs, and costs.

Speaking of costs, as this book goes to press, Atripla costs in the neighborhood of $22,000 per year in the United States. Quad, on the verge of being approved by the Food and Drug Administration, doesn't yet have a price tag. Viraday, a generic drug with Atripla's ingredients, is made by an Indian drug company, Cipla, for use with poor Indians. It costs $200 per year.

HAART has cut the U.S. death rate from HIV/AIDS-related causes by about 75% since the mid- to late-1990s (Sherer, 2012). Yet, HAART-resistant strains of HIV may evolve as HAART is being used. For this and other reasons, many HIV-infected people go on drug "vacations" after using HAART for a number of months or years. Promising results are also reported in treating the opportunistic infections such as PCP and fungal infections that take hold in people with weakened immune systems.

Despite the advent of HAART, nearly 10,000 people in the United States still die of HIV/AIDS each year. The Centers for Disease Control and Prevention attributes these deaths to lack of early testing and treatment for some people, failure of some people with HIV/AIDS to follow HAART treatment regimens, and, in some cases, treatment failure. People who assume that HIV/AIDS is no longer a deadly syndrome need to recognize that HAART does not help everyone with HIV/AIDS.

Unfortunately, the advances in treatment in the United States do not extend to everyone in the world, not even to everyone in the United States. Among women in the United States today, the risks of HIV/AIDS fall most heavily on poor women, mostly African American or Latina American, who live in urban areas. African American and Latina American women account for nearly three-quarters of women with HIV/AIDS in the United States, although they make up only about one-quarter of the female population (see Figure 16.8 on page 486).

GENITAL HERPES

Genital herpes is an STI caused by the *Herpes simplex* virus. The hysteria that surrounded the rapid spread of genital herpes in the 1970s and 1980s died down due to the advent of AIDS. Nevertheless, about one in six Americans aged 14 to 49 is infected with HSV-2, the form of the virus referred to commonly as genital herpes

HAART (pronounced *HEART*) The acronym for "highly active antiretroviral therapy," which refers to the combination or cocktail of drugs used to treat HIV/AIDS.

FIGURE 16.10 **Genital Herpes—Initial Visits to Physicians' Offices, United States, 1966–2010**

Source: Centers for Disease Control and Prevention. (2011). 2010 Sexually transmitted diseases surveillance. http://www.cdc.gov/std/stats10/figures/52.htm (Accessed October 4, 2012).

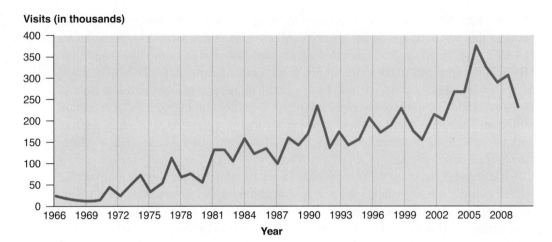

(STI trends, 2011). HSV-1, however, which causes fever blisters in the mouth and on the lips, may also affect the genital region (Genital herpes, 2012). Figure 16.10 shows that the incidence of doctors' visits for genital herpes has risen dramatically since the mid-1960s.

Once you get herpes, it's apparently yours for life. After the initial attack, it remains an unwelcomed guest in your body. It finds a cozy place to lie low until it stirs up trouble again. It causes recurrent outbreaks that often happen at the worst times, such as around final exams. This is because stress can depress the functioning of the immune system and heighten the likelihood of outbreaks.

You can also pass the infection along to sex partners for the rest of your life. Flare-ups may continue to recur, sometimes with annoying frequency. On the other hand, some people have no recurrences. Still others have mild, brief recurrences that become less frequent over time.

Different types of herpes are caused by variants of the *Herpes simplex* virus. The most common type, ***Herpes simplex* virus type 1 (HSV-1 virus)** causes oral herpes. Oral herpes, as noted, is characterized by cold sores or fever blisters on the lips or mouth. It can also be transferred to the genitals by the hands or by oral–genital contact. **Genital herpes** is caused by a related but distinct virus, the ***Herpes simplex* virus type 2 (HSV-2)**. This virus produces painful shallow sores and blisters on the genitals. HSV-2 can also be transferred to the mouth through oral–genital contact. Both types of herpes can be transmitted sexually.

Transmission Herpes can be transmitted through oral, anal, or vaginal sexual activity with an infected person. The herpes viruses can also survive for several hours on toilet seats or other objects, where they can be picked up by direct contact. Oral herpes is easily contracted by drinking from the same cup as an infected person, by kissing, even by sharing towels. But genital herpes is generally spread by coitus or by oral or anal sex.

One problem is that many people do not realize that they are infected. They can thus unknowingly transmit the virus through sexual contact. And many of the people who know they are infected don't realize that they can pass along the virus even when they have no noticeable outbreak. Although genital herpes is most contagious during active flare-ups, it can also be transmitted when an infected partner has no symptoms (genital sores or feelings of burning or itching in the genitals). Any intimate contact with an infected person carries some risk of transmission of the virus, even if the infected person never has another outbreak. People may also be infected with the virus and have no outbreaks, yet pass the virus along to others.

Herpes simplex **virus type 1 (HSV-1)** The virus that causes oral herpes, which is characterized by cold sores or fever blisters on the lips or mouth.

Genital herpes An STI caused by the *Herpes simplex* virus type 2 and characterized by painful shallow sores and blisters on the genitals.

Herpes simplex **virus type 2 (HSV-2)** The virus that causes genital herpes.

TRUTH OR **FICTION** REVISITED: It is not true that genital herpes can be transmitted only during flare-ups of the infection. Although people are most contagious during flare-ups, genital herpes can also be transmitted between them.

Herpes can also be spread from one part of the body to another by touching the infected area and then touching another body part. One potentially serious result is a herpes infection of the eye: **ocular herpes**. Thorough washing with soap and water after touching an infected area may reduce the risk of spreading the infection to other parts of the body. Still, it is best to avoid touching the infected area altogether, especially if there are active sores.

Women with genital herpes are more likely than the general population to have miscarriages. Passage through the birth canal of an infected mother can infect babies with genital herpes, damaging or killing them. Obstetricians therefore often perform cesarean sections if the mother has active lesions or **prodromal symptoms** at the time of delivery. Herpes can also place women at greater risk of genital cancers, such as cervical cancer. (All women, not just women with herpes, are advised to have regular pelvic examinations, including Pap tests for early detection of cervical cancer.)

Symptoms Genital lesions or sores appear about six to eight days after infection with genital herpes. At first they appear as reddish, painful bumps, or papules, along the penis or the vulva (see Figure 16.11). They may also appear on the thighs or buttocks, in the vagina, or on the cervix. These papules turn into groups of small blisters that are filled with fluid containing infectious viral particles. The blisters are attacked by the body's immune system (white blood cells). They fill with pus, burst, and become extremely painful, shallow sores or ulcers that are surrounded by a red ring. People are especially infectious during such outbreaks, as the ulcers shed millions of viral particles. Other symptoms may include headaches and muscle aches, swollen lymph glands, fever, burning urination, and a vaginal discharge. The blisters crust over and heal in one to three weeks. Internal sores in the vagina or on the cervix may take 10 days longer than external (labial) sores to heal. Physicians thus advise infected women to avoid unprotected intercourse for at least 10 days following the healing of external sores.

Although the symptoms disappear, the disease does not. The virus remains in the body, burrowing into nerve cells in the base of the spine, where it may lie dormant for years or a lifetime. The infected person is least contagious during this dormant stage. For reasons that remain unclear, the virus becomes reactivated and gives rise to recurrences in most cases.

Recurrences may be related to factors such as infections (as in a cold), stress, fatigue, depression, exposure to the sun, and hormonal changes, such as those that occur during pregnancy or menstruation. Recurrences tend to occur within 3 to 12 months of the initial episode and to affect the same part of the body.

Symptoms of oral herpes include sores or blisters on the lips, the inside of the mouth, the tongue, or the throat. Fever and feelings of sickness may occur. The gums may swell and redden. The sores heal over in about two weeks, and the virus retreats into nerve cells at the base of the neck, where it lies dormant between flare-ups. Most people with oral herpes experience recurrences.

Diagnosis and Treatment Genital herpes is first diagnosed by clinical inspection of herpetic sores or ulcers in the mouth or on the genitals. A sample of fluid may be taken from the base of a genital sore and cultured in the laboratory to detect the growth of the virus.

There is no safe, effective vaccine for genital herpes, but clinical trials of experimental vaccines are underway (National Institute of Allergy and Infective Diseases [NIAID], 2009). In earlier trials, one experimental vaccine showed some promise with women, but not with men (NIAID, 2009).

Ocular herpes A herpes infection of the eye, usually caused by touching an infected area of the body and then touching the eye.

Prodromal symptoms Warning symptoms that signal the onset of a disease.

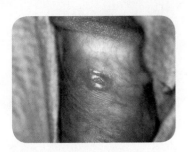

FIGURE 16.11 Herpes Lesions on the Male Genitals. Herpes lesions or sores can appear on the genitals in both men and women. In contrast to the syphilis chancre, they can be quite painful. Herpes is most likely to be transmitted during outbreaks of the disease (when the sores are present, that is), but it can be transmitted at other times as well. Stress increases the likelihood of outbreaks. Antiviral drugs tend to decrease the frequency, duration, and discomfort of outbreaks.

Viruses, unlike the bacteria that cause gonorrhea or syphilis, do not respond to antibiotics. Antiviral drugs such as acyclovir (brand name Zovirax), famciclovir, and valacyclovir can relieve pain, speed healing, and reduce the duration of viral shedding (Hatcher et al., 2011). Acyclovir can be applied directly to the sores in ointment form, but must be taken orally, in pill form, to help combat internal lesions in the vagina or on the cervix. Oral administration of antiviral drugs may reduce the severity of the initial episode and, if taken regularly, the frequency and duration of recurrent outbreaks (Hatcher et al., 2011). On the other hand, users may develop tolerance for these drugs, meaning that larger doses must be used to maintain effectiveness.

Warm baths, loose fitting clothing, aspirin, and cold, wet compresses may relieve pain during flare-ups. People with herpes are advised to maintain regular sleeping habits and to learn to manage stress.

Coping with Genital Herpes The psychological problems connected with herpes can be more distressing than the physical effects of the illness. The prospects of a lifetime of recurrences and concerns about infecting one's sex partners exacerbate the emotional impact of herpes. People with herpes often feel angry, especially toward those who transmitted the disease to them. They may feel anxious about making a long-term commitment or bearing children:

> After the first big episode of herpes, I felt distant from my body. When we began lovemaking again, I had a hard time having orgasms or trusting the rhythm of my responses. I shed some tears over that. I felt my body had been invaded. My body feels riddled with it; I'm somehow contaminated. And there is always that lingering anxiety: is my baby okay? It's unjust that the birth of my child may be affected. (Boston Women's Health Book Collective, 2005)

Most people with herpes learn to cope. Some are helped by support groups that share ways of living with the disease. A caring and trusting partner is important. Joanne, a 26-year-old securities analyst, kept her herpes a secret from Jonathan during the first month they were dating. But when they approached the point of becoming sexually intimate, she felt obligated to tell him that she carried the virus:

> *"I feared that telling him would scare him off. After all, who wants to have a relationship with someone who can give them herpes? After the first few dates I felt that this was the person I could spend the rest of my life with. I knew he also felt the same way. I had to tell him before things became too intense between us. Believe me, it wasn't easy blurting it out. He wasn't shocked or anything, although he did ask me all kinds of questions about it. I remember telling him that I got recurrences about once a year or so for about a week at a time. I told him that there was always the potential that I could infect him but that we would play it safe and avoid having sex whenever I had an outbreak. I also told him that even at other times I couldn't guarantee that it would be perfectly safe. He said at first that he needed some time to think about it. But later, that very night in fact, he called to tell me that he didn't want this to come between us and that we should try to make our relationship work."*
>
> *Joanne and Jonathan were married about six months later. A year after that their daughter Andrea was born. Jonathan remains uninfected. Joanne's occasional outbreaks are treated with acyclovir ointment and pass within a week or so.*
> —The Authors' Files

The attitudes of people with herpes also play a role in adjusting. People who view herpes as a manageable illness or problem, and not as a medical disaster or character deficit, seem to find it easier to cope.

HUMAN PAPILLOMA VIRUS

HPV is the world's most common STI, with signs of infection found in nearly half of the adult women in some countries (Genital HPV infection, 2012). Half or more of the sexually active college women in the United States are infected with HPV. The warts may appear in visible areas of the skin, but in most cases they appear in areas that cannot be seen, such as on the cervix in women or in the urethra in men. They occur most commonly among people in the 20- to 24-year-old age range (Genital HPV infection, 2012). Within a few months following infection, the warts are usually found in the genital and anal regions. Women are more susceptible to HPV infection because cells in the cervix divide swiftly, facilitating the multiplication of HPV. Women who initiate coitus prior to the age of 18 and who have many sex partners are particularly susceptible to infection. It is estimated that nearly half of the sexually active teenage women in some U.S. cities are infected with HPV (Genital HPV infection, 2012).

One study looked at 308 heterosexual college couples, all in newly formed relationships (Burchell et al., 2011). The researchers identified 179 pairs who were "discordant" for HPV infection; that is, one member of the couple was infected, and other one was not. However, six months later, HPV had been transmitted to 73 of the uninfected partners (41% of them). Fortunately, HPV infections clear up by themselves within two years in about 90% of cases.

Genital warts are one of the symptoms of infection by HPV, although many infected people either do not have the warts, or do not find them. **Genital warts** are similar to common plantar warts—itchy bumps that vary in size and shape. Genital warts are hard and yellow-gray when they form on dry skin. They take on pink, soft, cauliflower shapes in moist areas such as the lower vagina (see Figure 16.12). In men they appear on the penis, foreskin, and scrotum, and in the urethra. They appear on the vulva, along the vaginal wall, and on the cervix in women. They can also occur outside the genital area—for example, in the mouth; on the lips, eyelids, or nipples; around the anus; or in the rectum.

Genital warts may not cause any symptoms, but those that form on the urethra can cause bleeding or painful discharges. Genital warts are annoying but not deadly. However, HPV has been connected with cancer.

HPV has been implicated in cancers of the genital organs, particularly cervical cancer and penile cancer (Genital herpes, 2012). Nearly all cases of cervical cancer are linked to HPV. HPV has also been connected with throat cancer in people, mostly men, who engage in cunnilingus with HPV-infected women (Genital herpes, 2012). Men who have been circumcised are significantly less likely to carry HPV than men who have not been circumcised. All in all, it would seem wise for women to safeguard themselves from HPV-related cervical cancer by limiting their number of sex partners (to reduce their risk of exposure to HPV), thinking about the extracurricular sexual activities of their mates, and having regular Pap smears.

All sexually active individuals, female and male, should be regularly checked for the types of health problems that can develop from infection by HPV. On the other hand, the majority of cases of HPV infection clear on their own. That is, the

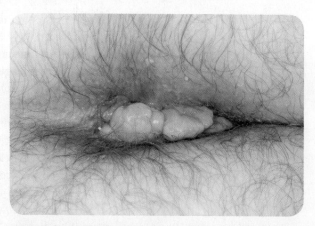

FIGURE 16.12 Genital Warts. Genital warts are caused by HPV and may have a cauliflower-like appearance. Many—perhaps most—cases occur where they can go visually undetected. HPV is implicated in cervical cancer, and women should be checked regularly for genital warts and other possibly "silent" STIs.

CRITICAL THINKING
What role is played by STIs in considering whether or not to have a male baby circumcised?

Human papilloma virus (HPV) The world's most common STI, which is linked to genital warts, cervical cancer in women, and throat cancer in men.

Genital warts An STI that is caused by the human papilloma virus and takes the form of warts that appear around the genitals and anus.

immune system eradicates HPV in most cases. But if you have been infected, or suspect that you have been infected, you need to be followed by a physician.

The human papilloma virus can be transmitted sexually through skin-to-skin contact during vaginal, anal, or oral sex. It can also be transmitted by other forms of contact, such as touching infected towels or clothing. The incubation period may vary from a few weeks to a couple of years.

Freezing a genital wart (*cryotherapy*) with liquid nitrogen is a preferred treatment for that particular problem. One alternative treatment involves painting or coating the warts over several days with podofilox solution or gel, imiquimod cream, trichloroacetic acid (TCA), or bichloroacetic acid (BCA) (Hatcher et al., 2011). An alcohol-based podophyllin solution causes the warts to dry up and fall off. Although the warts may be removed, treatment does not rid the body of the virus (Hatcher et al., 2011). There may be recurrences. Podophyllin is not recommended for use with pregnant women or for treatment of warts that form on the cervix. The warts can also be treated by a doctor with electrodes (burning) or surgery (by laser or surgical removal).

HPV Vaccines Vaccines are available for prevention of HPV infections. Cervarix and Gardasil protect girls and women against the types of HPV responsible for most cancers of the cervix. Gardasil also protects against genital warts, anal, vaginal, and vulvar cancers. Either vaccine is recommended for 11- and 12-year-old girls, although girls may receive them as early as age 9 and women may obtain them up to the age of 26 (Genital HPV infection, 2012). In our experience, these types of age frames can change rapidly; check with your physician. Gardasil also protects males against genital warts and anal cancer that is caused by HPV (Genital HPV infection, 2012). The vaccine is also apparently beneficial for men who have anal sex with other men (Palefsky et al., 2011). Ask your physician whether one of these vaccines would be helpful for you.

VIRAL HEPATITIS

Viral hepatitis refers to various types of liver infections (**hepatitis** is an inflammation of the liver) that are caused by viruses. The major types are *hepatitis A* (formerly called infectious hepatitis), *hepatitis B* (formerly called serum hepatitis), *hepatitis C* (formerly called hepatitis non-A, non-B), and *hepatitis D*.

Most people with hepatitis have no symptoms. When symptoms do appear, they often include **jaundice**, feelings of weakness and nausea, loss of appetite, abdominal discomfort, whitish bowel movements, and brownish or tea-colored urine. The symptoms of hepatitis B tend to be more severe and long-lasting than those of hepatitis A or C. In about 10% of cases, hepatitis B can lead to chronic liver disease. Hepatitis C tends to have milder symptoms but often leads to chronic liver disease

Hepatitis An inflammation of the liver.

Jaundice A yellowish discoloration of the skin and the whites of the eyes.

Real Students, Real Questions

Q *Do some infections just naturally go away?*

A Absolutely. Your immune system does clear some of them, and, fortunately, HPV can be one of those. Unfortunately, some of the worst ones, including HIV/AIDS, do not just disappear permanently on their own, even if they lie dormant for many years.

such as cirrhosis or cancer of the liver. Hepatitis D—also called *delta hepatitis* or *type D hepatitis*—occurs only in the presence of hepatitis B. Hepatitis D, which has symptoms similar to those of hepatitis B, can produce severe liver damage and often leads to death.

The hepatitis A virus is transmitted through contact with infected fecal matter found in contaminated food or water, and by oral contact with fecal matter, as through oral–anal sexual activity (licking or mouthing the partner's anus). (It is largely because of the risk of hepatitis A that restaurant employees are required to wash their hands after using the toilet.) Eating raw infested shellfish is also a common means of transmitting hepatitis A.

Hepatitis B can be transmitted sexually through anal, vaginal, or oral intercourse with an infected partner; through transfusion with contaminated blood supplies; by sharing contaminated needles or syringes; and by contact with contaminated saliva, menstrual blood, nasal mucus, or semen. Sharing razors, toothbrushes, or other personal articles with an infected person can also transmit hepatitis B. Hepatitis C and hepatitis D can also be transmitted sexually or through contact with contaminated blood. A person can transmit the viruses that cause hepatitis even if he or she is unaware of having any symptoms of the disease.

Hepatitis is usually diagnosed by testing blood samples for the presence of hepatitis antigens and antibodies. There is no cure for viral hepatitis. Bed rest and fluids are usually recommended until the acute stage of the infection subsides, generally in a few weeks. Full recovery may take months. A vaccine provides protection against hepatitis B and also against hepatitis D, since hepatitis D can occur only if hepatitis B is present (Hatcher et al., 2011).

MOLLUSCUM CONTAGIOSUM

Molluscum contagiosum is an STI that is characterized by painless raised lesions that appear on the genitals, buttocks, thighs, or lower abdomen and caused by a pox virus. Pinkish in appearance with a waxy or pearly top, the lesions usually appear within two or three months of infection. Most infected people have between 10 and 20 lesions, although the number of lesions can range from 1 to 100 or more. The lesions are generally not associated with serious complications and often disappear on their own within six months. Or they can be treated by squeezing them (like "popping" a blackhead) to exude the whitish center plug. Solutions of podophyllin, trichloroacetic acid (TCA), or silver nitrate are also used. Freezing with liquid nitrogen (*cryotherapy*) can also be used to remove the lesions. However, do not try to treat any lesions on your own. See your doctor.

Ectoparasitic Infestations

Ectoparasites, as opposed to endoparasites, live on the outer surfaces of animals (*ecto* means "outer"). *Trichomonas vaginalis* is an endoparasite (*endo* means "inner"). Ectoparasites are larger than the agents that cause other STIs. In this section we consider two types of STIs caused by ectoparasites: pediculosis and scabies.

PEDICULOSIS

Pediculosis is the name given to an infestation of a parasite whose proper Latin name, *Pthirus pubis* (pubic lice), sounds rather too dignified for these bothersome (dare we say ugly?) creatures that are better known as "crabs." **TRUTH OR FICTION REVISITED:** It is not true that pubic lice are of the same family of animals as crabs,

Molluscum contagiosum An STI that is caused by a pox virus that causes painless raised lesions to appear on the genitals, buttocks, thighs, or lower abdomen.

Ectoparasites Parasites that live on the outside of the host's body.

Pediculosis A parasitic infestation by pubic lice (*Pthirus pubis*) that causes itching.

FIGURE 16.13 Pubic Lice. Pediculosis is an infestation by pubic lice (*Phthirus pubis*). Pubic lice are commonly called "crabs" because of their appearance under a microscope.

CRITICAL THINKING

If pubic lice can be transmitted by contact with an infested toilet seat, why is it referred to as a sexually transmitted infection?

but when viewed under a microscope, they look similar to crabs (see Figure 16.13). They belong to a family of insects called *biting lice.* Another member of the family, the human head louse, is an annoying insect that clings to hair on the scalp and often spreads among schoolchildren.

In the adult stage, pubic lice are large enough to be seen with the naked eye. They are spread sexually but can also be transmitted by contact with an infested towel, sheet, or—yes—toilet seat. They can survive for only about 24 hours without a human host, but they may deposit eggs that can take up to seven days to hatch in bedding or towels. Therefore, all bedding, towels, and clothes that have been used by an infested person must be washed in hot water and dried on the hot cycle, or dry-cleaned to ensure that they are safe. Fingers may also transmit the lice from the genitals to other hair-covered parts of the body, including the scalp and armpits. Sexual contact should be avoided until the infestation is eradicated.

Itching, ranging from the mildly irritating to the intolerable, is the most prominent symptom of a pubic lice infestation. The itching is caused by the "crabs" attaching themselves to the pubic hair and piercing the skin to feed on the blood of their hosts. (Yecch!) The life span of these insects is only about one month, but they are prolific egg-layers and may spawn several generations before they die. An infestation can be treated effectively with a prescription medication, a 1% solution of lindane (brand name Kwell), which is available as a cream, lotion, or shampoo. Nonprescription medications containing pyrethrins or piperonyl butoxide (brand names RID, Triple X, and others) will also do the job. Kwell is not recommended for use by pregnant or lactating women. A careful reexamination of the body is necessary after several days of treatment to ensure that all lice and eggs were killed.

SCABIES

Scabies (short for *Sarcoptes scabiei*) is a parasitic infestation caused by a tiny mite that may be transmitted through sexual contact or contact with infested clothing, bed linen, towels, and other fabrics. The mites attach themselves to the base of pubic hair and burrow into the skin, where they lay eggs and subsist for the duration of their 30-day life span. Like pubic lice, scabies are often found in the genital region and cause itching and discomfort. They are also responsible for reddish lines (created by burrowing) and sores, welts, or blisters on the skin. Unlike lice, they are too tiny to be seen by the naked eye. Diagnosis is made by detecting the mite or its by-products on microscopic examination of scrapings from suspicious-looking areas of skin. Scabies are most often found on the hands and wrists, but they may also appear on the genitals, buttocks, armpits, and feet. They do not appear above the neck—thankfully!

Scabies, like pubic lice, may be treated effectively with 1% lindane (Kwell). The entire body from the neck down must be coated with a thin layer of the medication,

Scabies A parasitic infestation caused by a tiny mite (*Sarcoptes scabiei*) that causes itching.

which should not be washed off for eight hours. But lindane should not be used by women who are pregnant or lactating. To avoid reinfection, sex partners and others in close bodily contact with infected individuals should also be treated. Clothing and bed linen that the infected person has used must be washed and dried on the hot cycle or dry-cleaned. As with "crabs," sexual contact should be avoided until the infestation is eliminated.

Chapter Review ✔—⬛Study and Review on MyDevelopmentLab

LO1 Describe some of the features of the current epidemic of sexually transmitted infections

More than 19 million people in the United States contract an STI each year. Although public attention has been riveted on HIV/AIDS, other STIs such as chlamydia and HPV pose wider threats.

LO2 Discuss the transmission, effects, and treatment of gonorrhea

Gonorrhea is caused by the *gonococcus* bacterium. Men's symptoms include a penile discharge and burning urination. Most women are asymptomatic, but if untreated, gonorrhea can develop into pelvic inflammatory disease (PID).

LO3 Discuss the transmission, effects, and treatment of syphilis

Syphilis is caused by the *Treponema pallidum* bacterium. Syphilis undergoes several stages of development, beginning with a chancre. It can lie dormant for many years but eventually be lethal.

LO4 Discuss the transmission, effects, and treatment of chlamydia

Chlamydial infections are caused by *Chlamydia trachomatous*. Symptoms resemble those of gonorrhea but tend to be milder.

LO5 Discuss the transmission, effects, and treatment of other bacterial STIs

Other bacterial infections include chancroid, shigellosis, granuloma inguinale, and lymphogranuloma venereum. Bacterial infections are treated with antibiotics.

LO6 Discuss the transmission, effects, and treatment of various vaginal infections

Vaginitis is usually known by a foul-smelling discharge, genital irritation, and burning during urination. Most cases of vaginitis involve bacterial vaginosis, candidiasis (caused by a fungus), or trichomoniasis (caused by a protozoan). These microbes are normally found in the body but can "overgrow."

LO7 Discuss the transmission, effects, and treatment of HIV/AIDS

HIV causes AIDS by attacking the body's immune system, making the person vulnerable to opportunistic diseases—such as serious infections and cancers—that are normally held in check. HIV is found in the blood, semen, vaginal secretions, and breast milk. Common avenues of transmission include vaginal and anal intercourse, sharing hypodermic needles, childbirth, and breastfeeding. HIV infection can be diagnosed through tests of blood, saliva, or urine. The most effective form of treatment of HIV/AIDS is HAART, which uses a "cocktail" of antiviral agents.

LO8 Discuss the transmission, effects, and treatment of genital herpes

Genital herpes is caused by HSV-2, which produces painful shallow sores and blisters on the genitals. Antiviral drugs can relieve pain and speed healing during flare-ups.

LO9 Discuss the transmission, effects, and treatment of human papilloma virus

HPV causes genital warts and has been linked to cervical cancer in women and throat cancer in sex partners of infected women who engage in cunnilingus. Most cases of HPV infection clear by themselves, but those that do not can cause serious health problems.

LO10 Discuss the transmission, effects, and treatment of other viral STIs

The several types of hepatitis are caused by different viruses. Most cases are transmitted sexually or by contact with contaminated blood or fecal matter.

LO11 Discuss the transmission, effects, and treatment of ectoparasitic infestations

Pediculosis ("crabs") is caused by pubic lice (*Pthirus pubis*). Pubic lice attach themselves to pubic hair and feed on the blood of their hosts, which often causes itching. Infestations can be treated with lindane. Scabies (*Sarcoptes scabiei*) is caused by a tiny mite that causes itching and can be treated with lindane.

Test Your Learning

1. Which of the following is the most widespread STI?
   (a) Scabies
   (b) HIV/AIDS
   (c) Genital herpes
   (d) HPV

2. Treponema pallidum is the organism that causes
   (a) gonorrhea.
   (b) syphilis.
   (c) chlamydia.
   (d) genital herpes.

3. The Abbott Testpack is used to diagnose
   (a) trichomoniasis.
   (b) HIV infection.
   (c) chlamydia.
   (d) candidiasis.

4. Miconazole is used to treat
   (a) candidiasis.
   (b) hepatitis.
   (c) pediculosis.
   (d) syphilis.

5. HAART is used to treat
   (a) *Herpes simplex* virus, type 1.
   (b) HPV.
   (c) pthirus pubis.
   (d) HIV/AIDS.

6. General paresis may develop during the _____ stage of syphilis.
   (a) primary
   (b) secondary
   (c) tertiary
   (d) All of the above

7. As many as half of some populations of college women are infected with
   (a) gonorrhea.
   (b) genital herpes.
   (c) HPV.
   (d) HIV/AIDS.

8. HIV is *not* found in infectious amounts in
   (a) breast milk.
   (b) saliva.
   (c) blood.
   (d) semen.

9. _____ often reflects the overgrowth of organisms normally found in the vagina.
   (a) Gonorrhea
   (b) Candidiasis
   (c) Molluscum contagiosum
   (d) Chlamydia

10. Women infected with _____ are likely to encounter pelvic pain and irregular menstrual cycles.
    (a) hemophilus ducreyi
    (b) *Herpes simplex* virus, type 2
    (c) human papilloma virus
    (d) chlamydia trachomatis

Answers: 1. d; 2. b; 3. c; 4. a; 5. d; 6. c; 7. c; 8. b; 9. b; 10. d

My Life, My Sexuality

Talking with Your Partner about STIs

Explore this My Life, My Sexuality feature by scanning this QR code with your mobile device. If you don't already have one, you may download a free QR scanner for your device wherever smartphone apps are sold. You can also view this feature in MyDevelopmentLab, along with an accompanying critical thinking assignment.

Because talking about STIs with sex partners can be awkward, many people "wing it." They assume that their partners are free of STIs and hope for the best. Some people act as if not talking about HIV/AIDS and other STIs will cause them to go away. But the won't. Scan the code for advice on how to pursue a conversation with your partner abut STIs.

17 Atypical Sexual Variations

Learning Objectives

TRUTH OR FICTION?

Which of the following statements are the truth, and which are fiction? Look for the Truth-or-Fiction icons on the pages that follow to find the answers.

1 King Henry III of France insisted on being considered a woman and addressed as "Her Majesty." **T F?**

2 Female strippers are exhibitionists. **T F?**

3 People who enjoy watching their mates undress are voyeurs. **T F?**

4 Exhibitionists and voyeurs are never violent. **T F?**

5 It is considered normal to enjoy some mild forms of pain during sexual activity. **T F?**

6 Some people cannot become sexually aroused unless they are bound, flogged, or humiliated by their sex partners. **T F?**

7 There is a subculture in the United States in which sexual sadists and sexual masochists form liaisons to inflict and receive pain and humiliation during sexual activity. **T F?**

Jenna Caccaro, 22, a fashion student who lives in Brooklyn, said she was first flashed on the subway when she was 15. She thought it might have been because she was wearing her Catholic school uniform. "I thought that maybe I'd done something to attract him," she said, "but my family reassured me he was just a sleaze."

Sara Payne, 25, of Manhattan, who takes the No. 1 train to work for a jewelry company in the Bronx, said she has been flashed about six times on the subway in the eight years she has lived in New York. She said it happened more when she was a freshman in college than it does now.

"Maybe I'm a little more confident now," she said, "so people are less prone to try [to] intimidate me."

Vivian Lynch, 68, used to take the F train home to Queens. She shivered at the memory. "It happened to me in the 70s," she said. "Men used to touch women on the train and stand close to them and ruin their clothes."

In some ways, groping seems almost an accepted part of subway culture. Stephanie Vullo, 43, said she had dealt many times with men rubbing up against her or trying to touch her on crowded No. 4 or 5 trains in the morning when she takes her daughter to school. "It's worse in the

summer months when everyone is wearing less clothing," she said. "The first time I turned around and yelled at the guy, but with my daughter, I don't want to get her upset." (Hartocollis, 2006)

The trials of these women on the New York subway system—and on mass transportation systems around the world—raise a number of questions. For example, why is it that almost all perpetrators of crimes such as exhibitionism and mashing are male? Are the causes of such behavior psychological? Sociological? Could there be biological differences between people who engage in such deviant behavior and those who do not? What sort of satisfaction does a male obtain from exposing his genitals to a female stranger? How should a female victim respond? Why? If a perpetrator is apprehended by the law, how should he be treated?

Males who expose themselves to females usually seek sexual release by masturbating afterward, or, in the subways, by rubbing against females. Obtaining sexual satisfaction through exposing oneself or rubbing against a female stranger is considered abnormal. Just what is "normal" in sexual behavior and what is abnormal or deviant? In this chapter we explore a number of sexual and sexually related behaviors that deviate from the norm in one sense or another. Let us begin by exploring the question of normal versus deviant sexual behavior more deeply.

Normal versus Deviant Sexual Behavior

One common approach to defining normality is statistical (Laws & O'Donohue, 2012). From this perspective, rare or unusual sexual behaviors are considered abnormal or deviant. The statistical approach may seem value-free, since the yardstick of normality is based on the frequency of behavior, not on judgment of its social acceptability. But having sex while standing, or more than seven times a week, might be considered deviant by this yardstick.

Moreover, the choice of behaviors we subject to statistical comparison is not divorced from our underlying values. We tend to consider sexual behaviors abnormal or deviant, for example, when they run counter to our religious values, when they make most of us wince (as in sadism or masochism), or when they seem

CRITICAL THINKING

Why is statistical rarity an inadequate standard for considering a sexual practice to be normal or abnormal?

inexplicable (as in being turned on more by a woman's shoe than the woman herself) (A. D. Fisher et al., 2011; Laws & O'Donohue, 2012). Behaviors that run against someone's religious values may be common enough, but that individual might label them deviant because they deviate from what the person has been led to believe is normal (or "proper").

What is considered normal in one culture or at a particular time may be considered abnormal in other cultures and at other times. What is "normal" behavior for the female adolescent Trobriand Islander (see Chapter 1) might be considered deviant—even *nymphomaniacal*—by Western cultural standards.

In our own culture, sexual practices such as oral sex and masturbation were once considered to be deviant or abnormal. Today, however, they are practiced so widely that few people would label them as deviant. Concepts of "normalcy" and "deviance," then, reflect the mores and customs of a particular culture at a given time.

Another basis for determining sexual deviance is to classify sexual practices as deviant when they involve the persistent preference for nongenital sexual outlets (Laws & O'Donohue, 2012). If a man prefers fondling a woman's panties to engaging in sexual relations with her, or prefers to masturbate against her foot rather than engage in coitus, his behavior is likely to be labeled deviant. Such behaviors have a bizarre or "kinky" quality (A. D. Fisher et al., 2011).

Because of the confusing array of meanings of the terms *deviant* and *abnormal*, some professionals speak about unusual patterns of sexual arousal or behavior as "atypical variations" in sexual behavior rather than as "sexual deviations." Atypical patterns of sexual arousal or behavior that become problematic in the eyes of the individual or society are labeled *paraphilias* by the *Diagnostic and Statistical Manual of the American Psychiatric Association* (2012). Clinicians consider paraphilias to be mental disorders. But milder forms of these behaviors may be practiced by many people and fall within the normal spectrum of human sexuality.

The Paraphilias

Paraphilias involve sexual arousal in response to unusual stimuli such as children or other nonconsenting persons (such as unsuspecting people whom one watches or to whom one exposes one's genitals), nonhuman objects (such as shoes, leather, rubber, or undergarments), or pain or humiliation (A. D. Fisher et al., 2011). The psychiatric diagnosis of paraphilia requires that the person has acted on the urges or is distinctly distressed by them.

Paraphilia An atypical pattern of sexual arousal or behavior that becomes problematic in the eyes of the individual or society, such as fetishism or exhibitionism. The urges are recurrent and are either acted on or are distressing to the individual. (From Greek roots meaning "to the side of" [*para*-] and "loving" [*philos*].)

Real Students, Real Questions

Q *Is having sex underwater considered atypical? Can it cause infection?*

A It's not a paraphilia, and we hate to burst your bubble (pardon the pun), but it's not really all that unusual. You're unlikely to get anyone infected with salt water, although there can be some irritation. The same goes for the chlorine in a pool, but irritation is no fun, and the water is no lubricant. Remember to hold your breath or get scuba gear.

People with paraphilias usually feel that their urges are obsessional—insistent, demanding, or compulsory. They may describe themselves as overcome by them. People with paraphilias tend to experience their urges as beyond their control, as drug addicts or compulsive gamblers see themselves as helpless to avert irresistible urges. For these reasons theorists have speculated that paraphilias may represent a type of sexual compulsion or an addiction.

Paraphilias vary in severity. In some cases the person can function sexually in the absence of the unusual stimuli and seldom, if ever, acts on his or her deviant urges. In other cases the person resorts to paraphilic behavior only in times of stress. In more extreme forms the person repeatedly engages in paraphilic behavior and may become preoccupied with thoughts and fantasies about these experiences. In such cases the person may not be able to become sexually aroused without either fantasizing about the paraphilic stimulus or having it present. For some people paraphilic behavior is the only means of attaining sexual gratification (Lehne, 2009).

The person with a paraphilia typically replays the paraphilic act in sexual fantasies to stimulate arousal during masturbation or sexual relations. It is as if he or she is mentally replaying a videotape of the paraphilic scene. But the scene grows stale after a while, and the individual feels the urge to perform another paraphilic act to make a new "video."

Some paraphilias are mostly harmless and victimless, such as *fetishism* and cross-dressing to achieve sexual arousal (*transvestic fetishism*). Even being humiliated by one's partner may be relatively harmless if the partner consents. Other paraphilic behaviors, such as exposing oneself in public or enticing children into sexual relations, do have victims and may cause harm, sometimes severe physical or psychological harm. They are also against the law (Hart & Kropp, 2008). Sexual sadism, in which sexual arousal is connected to hurting or humiliating another person, can be a most harmful paraphilia when it is forced on a nonconsenting person. Some brutal rapes involve sexual sadism.

Except in the case of sexual masochism, paraphilias are believed to occur almost exclusively among men (Hucker, 2008; Logan, 2008). The prevalence of paraphilias in the general population remains unknown, because people are generally unwilling to talk about them. Much of what we have learned about paraphilias derives from the reported experiences of people who have been apprehended for performing illegal acts (such as exposing themselves in public) and the few who have voluntarily sought help. The characteristics of people who have not been identified or studied remain virtually unknown.

We discuss the major types of paraphilia in this chapter, beginning with fetishism. The one exception is *pedophilia*. In pedophilia, children become the objects of sexual arousal. Pedophilia often takes the form of sexual coercion of children, as in incest or sexual molestation (Lalumière, et al., 2005a; Seto, 2008). It is discussed in Chapter 18 as a form of sexual coercion.

FETISHISM

The roots of the word *fetish* come from the French *fétiche*, which is thought to derive from the Portuguese *feitico*, meaning "magic charm." The "magic" in this case lies in an object's ability to arouse a person sexually. In **fetishism**, an inanimate object elicits sexual arousal. Articles of clothing (for example, women's panties, bras, lingerie, stockings, gloves, shoes, or boots) and materials made of rubber, leather, silk, or fur are among the more common fetishistic objects (Kafka, 2010). Leather boots and high-heeled shoes are popular. There is a reported case of a diaper fetishist (Oguz & Uygur, 2005).

Fetishism   A paraphilia in which an inanimate object such as an article of clothing or items made of rubber, leather, or silk elicit sexual arousal.

Fetishism. In fetishism, inanimate objects such as leather shoes or boots, or parts of the body such as feet, elicit sexual arousal. Many fetishists cannot achieve sexual arousal without contact with the desired objects or without fantasizing about them. Women's undergarments and objects made of rubber, leather, silk, or fur are common fetishistic objects. Why is it that some men are more aroused by women's feet than by women's genitals?

The fetishist may act on the urges to engage in fetishistic behavior, such as by masturbating by stroking an object or while fantasizing about it, or he may be distressed about such urges or fantasies and not act on them (Kafka, 2010). In a related paraphilia, **partialism**, people are excessively aroused by a particular body part, such as the feet, breasts, or buttocks.

Most fetishes and partialisms are harmless. Fetishistic practices are almost always private and involve masturbation or are incorporated into sex with a willing partner (Darcangelo, 2008). Only rarely have fetishists coerced others into paraphilic activities. However, some partialists have touched parts of women's bodies in public. And some fetishists commit burglaries to acquire the fetishistic objects. Now and then we hear of someone who has stolen hundreds of pairs of women's shoes, for example.

TRANSVESTISM

Fetishism appears to include **transvestism**. Whereas other fetishists become sexually aroused by handling the fetishistic object while they masturbate, transvestites become excited by wearing articles of clothing—the fetishistic objects—of the other gender (Blanchard, 2010). A fetishist may find the object or gender involving the object to be erotically stimulating. For the transvestite, the object is sexually alluring only when it is worn. Transvestites are mostly males (Långström & Zucker, 2005). Transvestism has been described among both heterosexual and gay males (Taylor & Rupp, 2004; Wheeler et al., 2008). Many are in committed male–female relationships and otherwise stereotypically masculine in behavior.

TRUTH OR FICTION REVISITED: It is true that sixteenth-century King Henry III of France insisted on being considered a woman and addressed as "Her Majesty." But cross-dressing may occur in other cultures for reasons other than sexual arousal. In the case of Henry III, it appears that transsexualism, and not transvestism, was involved.

Transvestism differs markedly from transsexualism. It is true that some transvestites and some transsexuals appear to be motived by *autogynephilia*—a condition in which the individual is sexually stimulated by fantasies that his own body is female (Bailey, 2003b; Lawrence, 2004). However, transvestites are usually sexually gratified by cross-dressing and masturbating or having sex with others while cross-dressing.

Partialism A paraphilia related to fetishism in which sexual arousal is exaggeratedly associated with a particular body part, such as feet, breasts, or buttocks.

 1

Transvestism A paraphilia in which a person repeatedly cross-dresses to achieve sexual arousal or gratification, or is troubled by persistent, recurring urges to cross-dress.

They may also find it gratifying to masturbate while fantasizing about cross-dressing. But many transvestites have masculine gender identities and do not seek to change their anatomic sex. Transsexuals usually cross-dress because they are uncomfortable with the attire associated with their anatomic sex and truly wish to be members of the other gender. It is for this reason that many transsexuals seek gender reassignment.

Like fetishism in general, the origins of transvestism remain obscure. Evidence of biological hormonal and neurological abnormalities in transvestism is mixed (Bailey, 2003b). Långström and Zucker (2005) surveyed 2,450 Swedes and found transvestism in about 2.8% of men and 0.4% of women. A history of transvestism was associated with separation from parents, same-sex sexual experiences, use of pornography, high rates of masturbation, and other paraphilias—namely, sexual masochism, exhibitionism, and voyeurism.

A Closer Look

Archie: A Case of Transvestism

Many transvestites are in long-term, committed, male–female relationships and engage in sexual activity with their regular partners. Yet they seek additional sexual gratification through dressing as women, as in the case of Archie.

Archie, a 55-year-old plumber, had been cross-dressing for many years. There was a time when he would go out in public as a woman, but as his prominence in the community grew, he became more afraid of being discovered in public. His wife Myrna knew of his "peccadillo," especially since he borrowed many of her clothes. She urged him to stay at home, offering to help him with his "weirdness." For many years his paraphilia had been restricted to the home.

The couple came to the clinic at the urging of the wife. Myrna described how Archie had imposed his will on her for 20 years. Archie would wear her undergarments and masturbate while she told him how disgusting he was. (The couple also regularly engaged in "normal" sexual intercourse, which Myrna enjoyed.) The cross-dressing had come to a head because a teenage daughter had almost walked into the couple's bedroom while they were acting out Archie's fantasies.

With Myrna out of the consulting room, Archie explained how he grew up in a family with several older sisters. He described how underwear had been perpetually hanging to dry in the one

bathroom. As an adolescent, Archie experimented with rubbing against articles of underwear, then with trying them on. On one occasion a sister walked in while he was modeling panties before the mirror. She told him he was a "dredge to society," and he straightaway experienced unparalleled sexual excitement. He masturbated when she left the room, and his orgasm was the strongest of his young life.

Archie did not think that there was anything wrong with wearing women's undergarments and masturbating. He was not about to give it up, regardless of whether it destroyed his marriage. Myrna's main concern was finally separating herself from Archie's "sickness." She didn't care what he did anymore, so long as he did it by himself. "Enough is enough," she said.

That was the compromise the couple worked out. Archie would engage in his fantasies by himself. He would

do so when Myrna was not at home, and she would not be told of his activities. He would also be very, very careful to choose times when the children would not be around.

Six months later the couple were together and content. Archie had replaced Myrna's input into his fantasies with transvestic-sadomasochistic magazines. Myrna said, "I see no evil, hear no evil, smell no evil." They continued to have sexual intercourse. After a while, Myrna forgot to check to see which underwear had been used.

Some men cross-dress for reasons other than sexual arousal and so are not "true transvestites." Some men make a living by impersonating women like Marilyn Monroe and Madonna on stage and are not motivated by sexual arousal. Among some segments of the gay male community, it is fashionable to masquerade as women. Gay men do not usually cross-dress to become sexually stimulated, however.

Transvestic behaviors may range from wearing a single female garment when alone to sporting dresses, wigs, makeup, and feminine mannerisms at a transvestite club. Some transvestites become sexually aroused by masquerading as women and attracting the interest of unsuspecting males. They sometimes entice these men or string them along until they find some excuse to back out before their anatomic sex is revealed. The great majority of transvestites do not engage in anti-social or illegal behavior. Most practice their sexual predilection in private and would be horrified or embarrassed to be discovered by associates while dressed in female attire.

A study of male heterosexual cross-dressers in New England found that most of their wives were tolerant, but many who found out about their husbands' cross-dressing years into the marriage felt betrayed and angry (Reynolds & Caron, 2000). A common worry of the wives was that outsiders would learn about their husbands' behavior.

EXHIBITIONISM

If fetishism is often victimless, the same cannot be said for exhibitionism. **Exhibitionism** ("flashing") involves persistent, powerful urges and sexual fantasies involving exposing one's genitals to unsuspecting strangers for the purpose of achieving sexual arousal or gratification (Langstrom, 2010). The urges are either acted upon or are disturbing to the individual. Exhibitionists are almost always males, but there are some cases of female exhibitionists (Hugh-Jones et al., 2005).

What we know of exhibitionists, as with most other people with paraphilias, is almost entirely derived from studies of men who have been apprehended or treated by mental-health professionals (Langevin et al., 2004). Such knowledge may yield a biased picture because relatively few incidents result in apprehension and conviction. The characteristics of most perpetrators may thus differ from those of people who have been made available for study.

About 4% of the males in a national probability sample reported exposing their genitals to obtain sexual pleasure; the prevalence dropped to about 2% for women (Murphy & Page, 2008). A survey of college women at U.S. universities found exposure to exhibitionism to be widespread. About 32% to 39% report running into a "flasher" (Murphy & Page, 2008). A majority of the women had been approached for the first time (some had been approached more than once) by 16 years of age. Only 15 of the women had reported these incidents to the police. The clinical definition of exhibitionism involves exposure to a stranger, but about one-third (36%) of the incidents among the college women were committed by acquaintances, relatives, or "good friends."

The typical exhibitionist is young, either lonely or in an unhappy male–female relationship, and sexually repressed. An exhibitionist may claim that sex with his regular partner is reasonably satisfactory, but that he also experiences the compulsion to expose himself to strangers. Many exhibitionists are single, however. They typically have difficulties relating to women and have been unable to establish meaningful heterosexual relationships (Leue et al., 2004; Murphy & Page, 2008).

Exhibitionism usually begins before age 18 (American Psychiatric Association, 2012). The urge to exhibit oneself, if not the actual act, usually begins in early adolescence, generally between the ages of 13 and 16. The frequency of exhibitionism declines markedly after the age of 40 (American Psychiatric Association, 2012). The

Exhibitionism A paraphilia characterized by persistent, powerful urges and sexual fantasies involving exposing one's genitals to unsuspecting strangers for the purpose of achieving sexual arousal or gratification.

A Closer Look

Michael: A Case of Exhibitionism

Michael was a 26-year-old, handsome, boyish-looking married male with a 3-year-old daughter. He had spent about one-quarter of his life in reform schools and in prison. As an adolescent he had been a fire-setter. As a young adult, he had begun to expose himself. He came to the clinic without his wife's knowledge because he was exposing himself more and more often—up to three times a day—and he was afraid that he would eventually be arrested and thrown into prison again.

Michael said he liked sex with his wife, but it wasn't as exciting as exposing himself. He couldn't prevent his exhibitionism, especially now, when he was between jobs and worried about where the family's next month's rent was coming from. He loved his daughter more than anything and couldn't stand the thought of being separated from her.

Michael's method of operation was as follows: He would look for slender adolescent females, usually near the junior high school and the senior high school. He would take his penis out of his pants and play with it while he drove up to a girl or a small group of girls. He would lower the car window, continuing to play with himself, and ask them for directions. Sometimes the girls didn't see his penis. That was okay. Sometimes they saw it and didn't react. That was okay, too. When they saw it and became flustered and afraid, that was best of all. He would start to masturbate harder, and now and then he managed to ejaculate before the girls had departed.

Michael's history was unsettled. His father had left home before he was born, and his mother had drunk heavily. He was in and out of foster homes throughout his childhood—"all over" the capital district area of New York State. Before he was 10 years old he was involved in sexual activities with neighborhood boys. Now and then the boys also forced neighborhood girls into petting, and Michael had mixed feelings when the girls got upset. He felt bad for them, but he also enjoyed it. A couple of times girls seemed horrified at the sight of his penis, and it made him "really feel like a man. To see that look, you know, with a girl, not a woman, but a girl—a slender girl, that's what I'm after."

typical exhibitionist does not attempt further sexual contact with the victim. Thus, he does not usually pose a physical threat (American Psychiatric Association, 2012).

The police sometimes trivialize exhibitionism as a "nuisance crime," but the psychological consequences among victims, especially young children, indicate that exhibitionism is not victimless. For example, victims may feel violated and be bothered by recurrent images or nightmares; harbor misplaced guilt that they had unwittingly enticed the exhibitionist; blame themselves for reacting excessively or for failing to apprehend the perpetrator; and develop fears of venturing out on their own. Moreover, exhibitionists are highly likely to repeat their crimes, even if they spend time in prison for them (Langevin et al., 2004).

Some theorists see exhibitionism as a means of expressing hostility toward women (Murphy & Page, 2008). Exposure may be an attempt to strike back at women because of a belief that women have wronged him or damaged his self-esteem by failing to notice him or take him seriously. The direct expression of anger may be perceived as too risky, so the exhibitionist vents his rage by humiliating a defenseless stranger. The urge to expose oneself often occurs when the exhibitionist feels that his masculinity has been insulted. Are exhibitionists attempting to assert their masculinity by evoking a response from victims?

Other studies show exhibitionists to be shy, dependent, passive, lacking in sexual and social skills, even inhibited (Leue et al., 2004). They tend to have doubts about their masculinity, and to suffer from feelings of inadequacy and inferiority. Exhibitionists who are socially shy or inadequate may be using exhibitionism as a substitute for intimate relationships.

The preferred victims are typically girls or young women. The typical exhibitionist drives up to, or walks in front of, a stranger and exposes his penis. After his victim has registered fear, disgust, confusion, or surprise, an exhibitionist will typically cover himself and flee. He usually masturbates, either while exposing himself or shortly afterward while thinking about the act and the victim's response (American Psychiatric Association, 2012). Some exhibitionists ejaculate during the act.

Exhibitionists and some other people with paraphilias may find the risk of being caught to heighten their erotic response because it causes a rush of stress hormones that are chemically similar to testosterone (Haake et al., 2003). The exhibitionist may even purposefully increase the risk, as by exposing himself in the same location in his own easily identifiable car.

Courts tend to be hard on exhibitionists, partly because of evidence that shows that some exhibitionists progress to more serious crimes of sexual aggression (McLawsen et al., 2012). Still, most exhibitionists do not appear to become rapists or child molesters.

Definitions of exhibitionism also bring into focus the boundaries between normal and abnormal behavior (Hugh-Jones et al., 2005; Laws & O'Donohue, 2012). For example, people in intimate relationships may enjoy showing their bodies to their partners to sexually arouse them. That is normal. And we might ask, are exotic dancers (stripteasers) exhibitionists? After all, aren't they exposing themselves to strangers? **TRUTH** OR **FICTION** REVISITED: Yes they are, but it is not true that strippers are exhibitionists. They are more successful at their work if they sexually excite their audiences, but their audiences are not unsuspecting victims. They pay for the privilege of watching them. Their main motive is (usually) to earn a living (Philaretou, 2006).

It is also normal to become sexually excited while stripping before one's sex partner. Such stripping is done to sexually excite a willing partner, not to surprise or shock a stranger.

OBSCENE TELEPHONE CALLING AND CHAT-SCATOPHILIA

Like exhibitionists, obscene phone callers (almost all of whom are male) seek to become sexually aroused by shocking their victims (Briken et al., 2005; Pakhomou, 2006). Whereas an exhibitionist exposes his genitals to produce the desired response, the obscene phone caller "exposes" himself verbally by uttering obscenities and sexual provocations to a nonconsenting person. The *DSM* (American Psychiatric

Is she an exhibitionist, or is she putting food on the table?

Voyeurism. Voyeurs are turned on by watching unsuspecting strangers undressing or engaging in sexual behavior. They may show endless patience, waiting hours for a glimpse.

Association, 2012) labels this type of paraphilia **telephone scatologia**. People practicing "chat-scatophilia" are sexually aroused by sending obscene e-mails, instant messages, and chat-room messages (Abal et al., 2003; Quayle, 2008). These behaviors are sometimes considered a form of exhibitionism.

Relatively few obscene callers are women (Quayle, 2008). Women who are charged with such offenses are generally motivated by rage for some actual or fantasized rejection rather than the desire for sexual arousal. They use the phone to hurl sexual invectives against men whom they feel have wronged them. By contrast, male obscene phone callers are generally motivated by a desire for sexual excitement and usually choose their victims randomly from the phone book or by chance dialing. They typically masturbate during the phone call or shortly afterward. Most obscene telephone callers also engage in other paraphilic acts, especially voyeurism and exhibitionism (Heil & Simons, 2008).

There are many patterns of obscene phone calling. Some callers limit themselves to obscenities. Others make sexual overtures. Some just breathe heavily into the receiver. Others describe their masturbatory activity to their victims. Some profess to have previously met the victim at a social gathering or through a mutual acquaintance. Some even present themselves as "taking a sex survey" and ask a series of personally revealing questions.

The typical obscene phone caller is a socially inadequate heterosexual male who has had difficulty forming intimate relationships with women (Leue et al., 2004). The relative safety and anonymity of the telephone may shield him from the risk of rejection (Leue et al., 2004). A reaction of shock or fright from his victims may fill him with feelings of power and control that are lacking in his life, especially in his relationships with women. The obscenities may vent rage that he holds against women who have rejected him.

Obscene phone calls are illegal, but it has been difficult for authorities to track down perpetrators. Call tracing can help police track obscene or offending phone callers. Call tracing works in different ways in different locales. Caller ID shows the caller's telephone number on a display panel on the receiving party's telephone. In some locales, people can program their telephone service so that a caller who calls from a private number or one without caller ID received a message stating that the recipient accepts only calls from people who identify their phone numbers or names. These services may deter some obscene callers, but others may use public phones instead of their home phones. Check with your local telephone company if you are interested in these services.

What should a woman do if she receives an obscene phone call? Above all, women are advised to remain calm and not reveal shock or fright, since such reactions tend to reinforce the caller and increase the probability of repeat calls. Women may be best advised to say nothing at all and gently hang up the receiver. A woman might alternatively offer a brief response that alludes to the caller's problems before hanging up. She might say in a calm but strong voice, "It's unfortunate you have this problem. I think you should seek professional help." If she should receive repeated calls, the woman might request an unlisted number or contact the police. Many women list themselves only by their initials in the phone directory so as to disguise their gender. But since this practice is so widespread, obscene callers may assume that people listed by initials are women living alone.

Telephone scatologia A paraphilia characterized by the making of obscene telephone calls.

Voyeurism A paraphilia characterized by strong, repetitive urges and related sexual fantasies of observing unsuspecting strangers who are naked, disrobing, or engaged in sexual relations.

VOYEURISM

Voyeurism could be considered the flip side of the coin of exhibitionism. It involves strong, repetitive urges to observe unsuspecting strangers who are nude, undressing, or involved in sexual relations (Voyeuristic disorder, 2012). The voyeur becomes sexually aroused by watching and typically does not seek sexual relations with the "victim." Like fetishism and exhibitionism, voyeurism is found almost exclusively among males (Langstrom, 2010). It usually begins before age 15.

The voyeur may masturbate while peeping or afterward while replaying the incident in his mind. He may fantasize about sex with the observed person but have no intention of actually seeking sexual relations with her (Lavin, 2008).

Are people voyeurs who become sexually aroused by the sight of their lovers undressing? What about people who enjoy watching pornographic films or strip-teasers? No, no, and no. The people being observed are not unsuspecting strangers. The lover knows that his or her partner is watching. Porn actors and strippers know that others will be viewing them. They would not be performing if they did not expect or have an audience.

TRUTH OR **FICTION** REVISITED: It is not true that people who enjoy watching their mates undress are voyeurs. In such cases the person who is disrobing is knowingly and willingly observed, and the observer's enjoyment is normal (Montemurro et al., 2003). True voyeurs want to peep on *unsuspecting* strangers. Women who attend male strip clubs also enjoy "bonding" with their friends and other women at the clubs (Montemurro et al., 2003).

Voyeurs are also known as *peepers* and *peeping Toms*. Why "peeping Toms"? According to an old English legend, Lady Godiva asked the townspeople not to look at her while she rode horseback in the nude to protest the oppressive tax that her husband, a landowner, had imposed on them. A tailor named Tom of Coventry was the only townsperson not to grant her request.

Voyeurs often put themselves in risky situations in which they face the prospect of being caught. They may risk injury by perching themselves in trees or otherwise assuming precarious positions to catch a preferred view of their target. They will occupy rooftops and fire escapes in brutal winter weather. Peepers can be exceedingly patient. They may wait hour after hour, night after night, for a furtive glimpse of the target. One 25-year-old recently married man secreted himself in his mother-in-law's closet, waiting for her to disrobe. Part of the sexual excitement seems to stem from the risks voyeurs run. The need for risk may explain why voyeurs are not known to frequent nude beaches or nudist camps where it is acceptable to look (though not to stare) at nude people.

TRUTH OR **FICTION** REVISITED: It is fiction that exhibitionists and voyeurs are *never* violent. Exhibitionism and voyeurism per se are not violent in themselves, but some exhibitionists and voyeurs have been known to be violent; moreover, if provoked or angered, they may react violently (Lalumière et al., 2005a; Langevin, 2003). Voyeurs who break into and enter homes or buildings, or who tap at windows to gain the attention of victims, are among the more dangerous.

Compared to other types of sex offenders, voyeurs tend to be less sexually experienced and are less likely to be married (Lavin, 2008). Like many exhibitionists, voyeurs tend to harbor feelings of inadequacy and to lack social and sexual skills (Leue et al., 2004). They may thus have difficulty forming romantic relationships with women. For this shy and socially inadequate type of voyeur, "peeping" affords sexual gratification without the risk of rejection. Not all voyeurs are socially awkward and inept with women, however. 👁

SEXUAL MASOCHISM

TRUTH OR **FICTION** REVISITED: It is considered normal to enjoy some mild forms of pain during sexual activity. Love bites, hair pulls, and minor scratches are examples of sources of pain that are considered to fall within normal limits (Laws & O'Donohue, 2012).

Watch the **Video**
Video Voyeurism
on **MyDevelopmentLab**

Watch the **Video**
*DSM in Context: Speaking Out:
Jocelyn: Exploring Sadism and
Masochism Part 1*
on **MyDevelopmentLab**

But people who *prefer* or *require* having pain or humiliation inflicted on them by their sex partners are **sexual masochists**. A sexual masochist either acts on or is distressed by persistent urges and sexual fantasies involving the desire to be bound, flogged, humiliated, or made to suffer in some way by a sexual partner so as to achieve sexual excitement. **TRUTH** OR **FICTION** REVISITED: In some cases, the sexual masochist cannot become sexually aroused unless he or she is bound, flogged, or humiliated by his or her sex partner. Sexual masochism is the only paraphilia that is found among women with some frequency (Logan, 2008).

The word *masochism* derives from the name of the Austrian storyteller Leopold von Sacher-Masoch (1835–1895). He wrote tales of men who derived sexual satisfaction from having a female partner inflict pain on them, typically by flagellation (beating or whipping).

Sexual masochists may derive pleasure from various types of punishing experiences, including being restrained (a practice known as **bondage**), blindfolded (sensory bondage), spanked, whipped, or made to perform humiliating acts, such as walking around on all fours and licking the boots or shoes of the partner, or being subjected to vulgar insults. Some masochists have their partners urinate or defecate on them. Some masochists prefer a particular source of pain. Others seek an assortment. But we should not think that sexual masochists enjoy types of pain that do not involve sex. Sexual masochists are no more likely than anyone else to derive pleasure from the pain they experience when they stub their toe or touch a hot stove. Pain must be part of an elaborate sexual ritual to provide erotic gratification (Hucker, 2008).

Sexual masochists and **sexual sadists** often form sexual relationships to meet each other's needs (Yates et al., 2008). Some sexual masochists enlist the services of prostitutes or obtain the cooperation of their regular sexual partners to enact their masochistic fantasies.

It may seem contradictory for pain to become connected with sexual pleasure. The association of sexual arousal with mildly painful stimuli is actually quite common, however. Kinsey and his colleagues (1953) reported that perhaps as many as one person in four has experienced erotic sensations from being bitten during lovemaking. The eroticization of mild forms of pain (love bites, hair pulls, minor scratches) may fall within the normal range of sexual variation. Pain from these sources increases overall bodily arousal, which may enhance sexual excitement. Some of us become sexually excited when our partners "talk dirty" to us or call us vulgar names. When the urge for pain for purposes of sexual arousal becomes so persistent or strong that it overshadows other sources of sexual stimulation, or when the masochistic experience causes physical or psychological harm, we may say that the boundary between normality and abnormality has been breached.

Some theorists suggest that independent and responsible selfhood become burdensome or stressful at times (Knoll & Hazelwood, 2009). Sexual masochism provides a temporary reprieve from the responsibilities of independent selfhood. It is a blunting of one's ordinary level of self-awareness by focusing on immediate painful and pleasant sensations, and on the experience of being a sexual object.

Sexual masochism can range from relatively benign to potentially lethal practices, like **hypoxyphilia**. Hypoxyphiliacs put plastic bags over their heads, nooses around their necks, or pressure on their chests to temporarily deprive themselves of oxygen and enhance their sexual arousal. They usually fantasize that they are being strangled by a lover. They try to discontinue oxygen deprivation before they lose consciousness, but some miscalculations result in death by suffocation or strangulation (Behrendt et al., 2002; Santtila et al., 2002).

Sexual masochism A paraphilia characterized by the desire or need for pain or humiliation to enhance sexual arousal so that gratification may be attained.

Bondage Ritual restraint, as by shackles, as practiced by many sexual masochists.

Sexual sadists People who become sexually aroused by inflicting pain or humiliation on others.

Hypoxyphilia A practice in which a person seeks to enhance sexual arousal, usually during masturbation, by becoming deprived of oxygen.

Real Students, Real Questions

Q *Do people get genital piercings for sexual pleasure?*

A Some do, but the results are iffy at best and body piercings can carry dangers. Please check with your doctor before having any piercings. You will be surprised to hear that some are probably fine, but others are not fine. In any event, the kinds of piercings usually recommended for women who are looking to enhance their sexual pleasure are clitoral hood piercings, clitoral piercings, and labial piercings. Of these, clitoral piercings are the most dangerous since they pass through the most nerves and blood vessels. Piercings of nipples, male sex organs, and navels are usually for aesthetic purposes and have a subcultural message or appeal more than an aphrodisiacal effect. The really frightening thing here is how some people will allow anyone with a storefront to pierce their bodies—anywhere. Don't be one of them. If you decide to go in this direction, use a reputable piercing studio that employs only trained and licensed employees.

SEXUAL SADISM

Sexual sadism is the opposite of sexual masochism. Sadism is named after the infamous Marquis de Sade (1774–1814), a Frenchman who wrote tales of becoming sexually aroused by inflicting pain or humiliation on others. The virtuous Justine, the heroine of his best-known novel of the same name, endures terrible suffering at the hands of fiendish men. She is at one time bound and spread-eagled so that bloodhounds can savage her. She then seeks refuge with a surgeon who tries to dismember her. Later she falls into the clutches of a saber-wielding mass murderer, but Nature saves her with a timely thunderbolt.

Sexual sadism is characterized by persistent, powerful urges and sexual fantasies involving the inflicting of pain and suffering on others to achieve sexual excitement or gratification (Yates et al., 2008). The urges are acted on or are disturbing enough to cause personal distress. Some sexual sadists cannot become sexually aroused unless they make their sex partners suffer. Others can become sexually excited without such acts.

Some sadists hurt or humiliate willing partners, such as prostitutes or masochists. Others—a small minority—stalk and attack nonconsenting victims (Yates et al., 2008).

Sadomasochism Sadomasochism (S&M) involves *mutually gratifying sexual interactions* between *consenting partners*. Occasional S&M is quite common among the general population. Couples may incorporate mild or light forms of S&M in their lovemaking now and then, such as mild dominance and submission games or gentle physical restraint. It is also not uncommon for lovers to scratch or bite their partners to heighten their mutual arousal during coitus. They generally do not inflict severe pain or damage, however. ◉

Sexual sadism A paraphilia characterized by the desire or need to inflict pain or humiliation on others to enhance sexual arousal so that gratification is attained.

Sadomasochism (S&M) A mutually gratifying sexual interaction between consenting sex partners in which sexual arousal is associated with the infliction and receipt of pain or humiliation.

◉ **Watch** the **Video**
Commercial S&M
on **MyDevelopmentLab**

A Closer Look
Ron: A Case of Sexual Masochism

Ron's parents separated when he was 5 years old. However, his father continued to return to the house for visits until he was 9. During those visits his father would administer unjustified beatings with a belt on the children's bare buttocks, according to the order of his mother who said the children had to be punished for misbehavior. At about the age of 8 or 9, Ron experienced an erection during a beating, which shocked his father. His mother continued to spank him into his teens, and he would have erections during many of those times from age 12 on. It is possible that his father was a masochist and his mother was a sadist.

When Ron began to masturbate, he would spank himself to achieve erection and orgasm. His sexual fantasies were of women dominating him in various ways and punishing him, especially by spanking for his misbehavior. Ron did briefly marry, but could only become aroused for intercourse by having fantasies of being dominated

Ron could never save money or climb the ladder of success because of his investment in dominatrix prostitutes.

and punished by women. Although he could be highly successful in his work as a salesman, he was never able to accumulate money or be consistently successful because of the time and money he spent seeking out dominatrix prostitutes.

Source: Sex Offenders: Identification, Risk Assement, Treatment, and Legal Issue edited by Saleh et al (2009) 230w from Chp. "Phenomenology of Paraphilia: Lovemap Theory" by Lehne pp.12–26. By permission of Oxford University Press, USA.

Twenty-two percent of the men and 12% of the women surveyed by Kinsey and his colleagues (1953) reported at least some sexual response to sadomasochistic stories. Although mild sadomasochism may fall within the boundaries of normal sexual variation, sadomasochism becomes pathological when such fantasies are acted on in ways that become destructive, dangerous, or distressing to oneself or others, as we find in the following case example:

A 25-year-old female graduate student described a range of masochistic experiences. She reported feelings of sexual excitement during arguments with her husband when he would scream at her or hit her in a rage. She would sometimes taunt him to make love to her in a brutal fashion, as though she were being raped. She found the brutality and sense of being punished to be sexually stimulating. She had also begun having sex with strange men and enjoyed being physically punished by them during sex more than any other type of sexual stimulus. Being beaten or whipped produced the most intense sexual experiences she had ever had. Although she recognized the dangers posed by her sexual behavior, and felt somewhat ashamed about it, she was not sure that she wanted treatment for "it" because of the pleasure that it provided her. (Adapted from Spitzer et al., 1989, pp. 87–88)

7 **TRUTH OR FICTION REVISITED:** There is a subculture—the S&M subculture—in the United States in which sexual sadists and sexual masochists form liaisons

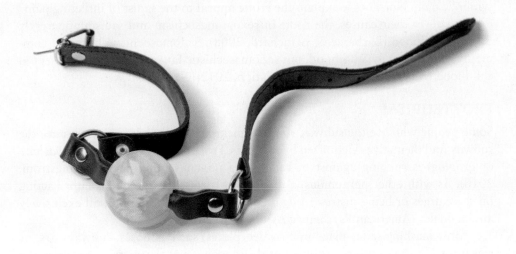

to inflict and receive pain and humiliation during sexual activity (Heil & Simons, 2008). It is catered to by sex shops that sell S&M paraphernalia and magazines. Paraphernalia includes leather restraints and leather face masks that resemble the ancient masks of executioners. People in the subculture seek one another out through mutual contacts, S&M social organizations, or personal ads in S&M magazines.

Participants in sadomasochism often engage in highly elaborate rituals involving dominance and submission. Rituals are staged, as if they were scenes in a play (Gross, 2006). In the "master and slave" game, the sadist leads the masochist around by a leash. The masochist performs degrading or menial acts. In bondage and discipline (B&D), the dominant partner restrains the submissive partner and flagellates (spanks or whips) or sexually stimulates her or him. The erotic appeal of bondage is connected with controlling or being controlled. ◉

Various sources of pain may be used during S&M encounters, but pain is not always employed. When it is, it is usually mild or moderate. Psychological pain, or humiliation, may be as common. Pain may also be symbolic, as in the case of a sadist who uses a harmless, soft rubber paddle to spank the masochist. Thus, the erotic appeal of pain for some S&M participants may derive from the ritual of control rather than pain itself. Extreme forms of pain, such as torture or severe beatings, are rarely reported by sadomasochists. Masochists may seek pain, but they usually avoid serious injury and dangerous partners (Gross, 2006).

S&M participants may be heterosexual, gay, or bisexual (Heil & Simons, 2008). They may assume either the masochistic or the sadistic role, or may alternate roles. People who seek sexual excitement by enacting both sadistic and masochistic roles are known as *sadomasochists*. In heterosexual relationships the partners may reverse traditional gender roles. The man may assume the submissive or masochistic role, and the woman may take the dominant or sadistic role (Gross, 2006). The majority of S&M participants are male, but a sizable minority are female (American Psychiatric Association, 2012). Most are in committed relationships.

The causes of sexual masochism and sadism, as of other paraphilias, are unclear, but pain might have biological links to pleasure (Grubin, 2008). Natural chemicals called *endorphins*, similar to opiates, are released in the brain in response to pain

◉ **Watch** the **Video**
Professional Dominatrix
on **MyDevelopmentLab**

and produce feelings of euphoria and well-being. Perhaps, then, pleasure is derived from pain because of the release or augmentation of endorphins. But this theory fails to explain the erotic appeal of sadomasochistic encounters that involve minimal or symbolic pain. Nor does it explain the erotic appeal to the sadist of inflicting pain.

Whatever their causes, the roots of sexual masochism and sadism apparently date to childhood (Barbaree & Blanchard, 2008). Sadomasochistic behavior commonly begins in early adulthood, but sadomasochistic fantasies are often present in childhood (American Psychiatric Association, 2012). ◉

◉⌐**Watch** the **Video**
DSM in Context: Speaking Out:
Jocelyn: Exploring Sadism and
Masochism Part 2
on **MyDevelopmentLab**

FROTTEURISM

Some people who use the subway run into pickpockets; some women who use the subway find themselves victimized by frotteurs. **Frotteurism** (also known as *mashing* or *groping*) is rubbing against or touching a nonconsenting person (Langstrom, 2010). As with other paraphilias, a diagnosis of frotteurism requires either acting on these urges or being distressed by them. Mashing has been reported exclusively among males (American Psychiatric Association, 2012).

Most mashing takes place in crowded places, such as buses, subway cars, or elevators. The man finds the rubbing or the touching, not the coercive nature of the act, to be sexually stimulating. While rubbing against a woman, he may fantasize a consensual, affectionate sexual relationship with her. Typically the man incorporates images of his mashing within his masturbation fantasies (Lussier & Piché, 2008). Mashing also incorporates a related practice, **toucherism**, which is fondling nonconsenting strangers.

Mashing may be so fleeting and furtive that the woman may not realize what has happened. Mashers therefore stand little chance of being caught. Consider the case of a man who victimized a thousand or so women within a decade but was arrested only twice:

> Charles, 45, was seen by a psychiatrist following his second arrest for rubbing against a woman in the subway. He would select as his target a woman in her 20s as she entered the subway station. He would then position himself behind her on the platform and wait for the train to arrive. He would then follow her into the subway car and when the doors closed would begin bumping his penis against her buttocks, while fantasizing that they were enjoying having intercourse in a loving and consensual manner. About half of the time he would ejaculate into a plastic bag that he had wrapped around his penis to prevent staining his pants. He would then continue on his way to work. Sometimes when he hadn't ejaculated he would change trains and seek another victim. While he felt guilty for a time after each episode, he would soon become preoccupied with thoughts about his next encounter. He never gave any thought to the feelings his victims might have about what he had done to them. While he was married to the same woman for 25 years, he appears to be rather socially inept and unassertive, especially with women. (Adapted from Spitzer et al., 1989, pp. 106–107)

Frotteurism A paraphilia characterized by recurrent, powerful sexual urges and related fantasies involving rubbing against or touching a nonconsenting person.

Toucherism A practice related to frotteurism and characterized by the persistent urge to fondle nonconsenting strangers.

Although this masher was married, many mashers have difficulties forming relationships with women and are handicapped by fears of rejection. Mashing provides sexual contact in a relatively nonthreatening context.

OTHER PARAPHILIAS

The paraphilias we have been discussing, fetishism through frotteurism, are the most common. But there are others, such as zoophilia.

Zoophilia   Zoophilia is one of the rarest paraphilias and is often associated with other disorders (Dittert et al., 2005; Lesjak et al., 2004). A person with **zoophilia** experiences repeated, intense urges and related fantasies involving sexual contact with animals. As with other paraphilias, the urges may be acted on or cause personal distress. A child or adolescent who shows some sexual response to an occasional episode of rough-and-tumble play with the family pet is not displaying zoophilia.

The term *bestiality* applies to actual sexual contact with an animal. Human sexual contact with animals, mythical and real, has a long history. Michelangelo's painting *Leda and the Swan* depicts the Greek god Zeus taking the form of a swan to mate with a woman, Leda. Zeus was also portrayed as taking the form of a bull or serpent to mate with humans. In the Old Testament, God is said to have put to death people who had sexual relations with animals. The Greek historian Herodotus notes that goats at the Egyptian temple at Mendes were trained to copulate with people.

Although the prevalence of zoophilia in the general population is unknown, Kinsey and his colleagues (1948, 1953) found that about 8% of the men and 3% to 4% of the women interviewed admitted to sexual contacts with animals. Men more often had sexual contact with farm animals, such as calves and sheep. Women more often reported sexual contacts with household pets. Men were more likely to masturbate or copulate with the animals. Women more often reported general body contact. Urban–rural differences emerged. Rates of bestiality were higher among boys reared on farms. Compared with only a few city boys, 17% of farm boys had reached orgasm at some time through sexual contact with dogs, cows, and goats. These contacts were generally restricted to adolescence, when human outlets were unavailable. Still, adults sometimes engage in sexual contacts with animals, generally because of curiosity or novelty or for a sexual release when human partners are unavailable. Zoophilia is often associated with problems such as alcoholism and intellectual deficiency (Lesjak et al. 2004).

Necrophilia   In **necrophilia**, a rare paraphilia, a person desires sex with corpses. Three types of necrophilia have been identified (Holmes & Holmes, 2002). In *regular necrophilia,* the person has sex with a deceased person. In *necrophilic homicide,* the person commits murder to obtain a corpse for sexual purposes. In *necrophilic fantasy,* the person fantasizes about sex with a corpse but does not actually carry out necrophilic acts. Necrophiles often obtain jobs that provide them with access to corpses, such as working in cemeteries, morgues, or funeral homes. The primary motivation for necrophilia appears to be the desire to sexually possess a completely unresisting and nonrejecting partner (Holmes & Holmes, 2002). Many necrophiles have serious psychological disorders.

Zoophilia   A paraphilia involving persistent or repeated sexual urges and related fantasies involving sexual contact with animals.

Necrophilia   A paraphilia characterized by desire for sexual activity with corpses.

Real Students, Real Questions

Q *Are there cultures that allow sex with animals/pets?*

A No modern cultures do, but ancient cave paintings and other artifacts suggest that sex with animals might have been allowed and sometimes incorporated into magical rituals before the advent of the so-called Abrahamic religions of Judaism, Christianity, and Islam. Many Egyptian gods were depicted as part animal, suggesting that sex with animals might have been included in some rituals. Goats and baboons might have been occasional sex partners in ancient Egypt.

A Closer Look

Cybersex Addiction: For Some, Sex Is Nothing but 'Net

Sex on the 'Net is like heroin. It grabs [people] and takes over their lives. And it's very difficult to treat because the people affected don't want to give it up.

—Mark Schwartz, Masters and Johnson Institute

It appears that at least one-third of Internet visits are directed to sexually oriented websites, with ample opportunity to contact potential sex partners—paid and amateur (Cooper et al., 2000, 2004). Of 9- to 17-year-olds who go online at least once a week, more than half have encountered online pornography, usually accidentally, and 38% have had pornographic advertisements pop up when they were doing something completely unrelated (Tsaliki, 2011). For most people these cybersex experiences are harmless enough, but the accessibility and anonymity of sex on the Internet are fueling what many health professionals have labeled a new form of addiction—*cybersex addiction*—that is spreading rapidly and bringing turmoil into the lives of those afflicted with it (Green et al., 2012). (The American Psychiatric Association added the broader category of *Internet addiction* to its list of disorders in 2013).

Is cybersex addiction a paraphilia? It shares certain characteristics: It tends to be repetitive and individuals with the problem have difficulty controlling it. Moreover, many cybersex users come to prefer their online images to the real people in their lives such that they sometimes develop problems in becoming sexually aroused by their flesh-and-blood partners. We might also ask whether cybersex addiction is truly an addiction. It depends on how one defines "addiction." Addiction to a substance such as alcohol or nicotine usually means that usage of the substance has changed the body so that having the substance in the body is the "new normal." But we speak more generally of being psychologically dependent on or addicted to something when it seems to be irresistible and interferes with vocational, academic, or social functioning.

Surveys show that many people, mostly men, now spend dozens of hours each week surfing pornographic and other sex-related websites (Cooper et al., 2004; Daneback et al., 2006). Nevertheless, they typically deny that they have a problem and refuse help unless their real relationships or jobs are in jeopardy. Those in relationships typically deny that cybersex excursions are cheating or infidelity (Jones & Hertlein, 2012; Schneider et al., 2012). Those most strongly hooked on online sex may spend hours a day masturbating to pornographic images or—less commonly—having "online sex" with someone who "popped up" online when visiting a pornographic website (Daneback et al., 2006).

Based on a survey of 9,265 men and women who admitted surfing the 'Net for sex, Cooper and his colleagues (1999, 2000) concluded that the 'Net is "the crack cocaine of sexual compulsivity," with at least 1% of respondents deeply addicted to online sex.

Cybersex compulsives are like drug addicts (Ayres & Haddock, 2009). They "use the Internet as an important part of their sexual acting out, much like a drug addict who has a drug of choice. [Especially vulnerable are those] whose sexuality may have been suppressed and limited all their lives [who] suddenly find an infinite supply of sexual opportunities" online (Cooper, cited in Brody, 2000). Although some studies find men who become addicted to online sex to have ample sexual opportunities in the real world, other studies find them to be lonelier than men with those opportunities (Yoder et al., 2005).

Physician Jennifer Schneider (2003, 2004) conducted a survey of 94 family members affected by cybersex addiction and found that it can arise even among people in good relationships and having an abundance of sexual opportunities. "Sex on the 'Net is just so seductive and it's so easy to stumble upon it [that] people who are vulnerable can get hooked before they know it" (cited in Brody, 2000).

Schneider (2005) defends the view that cybersex addiction is a true addiction, characterized by "loss of control, continuation of the behavior despite significant adverse consequences and preoccupation or obsession with obtaining the drug or pursuing the behavior."

As with other addictions, tolerance to cybersex stimulation can develop, prompting the addict to take more and more risks to recapture the initial high. Online viewing that began as a harmless recreation can become all-consuming and even lead to real sexual encounters with people met online. Cybersex compulsives sometimes ignore their partners and children and risk their jobs. Many companies monitor employees' online activities, and visits to sexual sites can cost employees their jobs. Other adverse consequences include broken relationships. Partners often report feeling betrayed, ignored, and unable to compete with the online fantasies.

A 34-year-old woman married 14 years to a minister told Schneider, "How can I compete with hundreds of anonymous others who are now in our bed, in his head? Our bed is crowded with countless faceless strangers, where once we were intimate" (cited in Brody, 2000). 👁

👁 **Watch** the **Video**
Facilitating an Addiction to Porn
on **MyDevelopmentLab**

Less Common Paraphilias   In **klismaphilia**, sexual arousal is derived from use of enemas. Klismaphiles generally prefer the receiving role to the giving role. Klismaphiles may have derived sexual pleasure in childhood from the anal stimulation provided by parents giving them enemas.

In **coprophilia**, sexual arousal is connected with feces. The person may desire to be defecated on or to defecate on a sex partner. The association of feces with sexual arousal may also be a throwback to childhood. Many children appear to obtain anal sexual pleasure by holding in and then purposefully expelling feces. It may also be that the incidental connection between erections or sexual arousal and soiled diapers during infancy eroticizes feces.

In **urophilia**, sexual arousal is associated with urine. As with coprophilia, the person may desire to be urinated on or to urinate on a sexual partner. Also like coprophilia, urophilia may have childhood origins. Stimulation of the urethral canal during urination may become associated with sexual pleasure. Or urine may have become eroticized by experiences in which erections occurred while the infant was clothed in a wet diaper.

Theoretical Perspectives

The paraphilias are fascinating and perplexing variations in sexual behavior. We may find it difficult to understand how people can become sexually excited by fondling an article of clothing or by cross-dressing. It may also be difficult to identify with people who feel compelled to exhibit their genitals or to rub their genitals against unsuspecting victims in crowded places. Perhaps we can recognize some voyeuristic tendencies in ourselves, but we cannot imagine peeping through binoculars while perched in a nearby tree or, for that matter, risking the social and legal consequences of being discovered in the act. Nor might we understand how people can become sexually turned on by inflicting or receiving pain. Let us consider explanations that have been advanced from various theoretical perspectives.

BIOLOGICAL PERSPECTIVES

Researchers are investigating whether there are biological factors in paraphilic behavior. The biological perspective looks into factors such as the endocrine system (hormones) and the nervous system in paraphilic behavior. The tendency of paraphilias to cluster within some families also raises the question as to whether genetic factors may be involved (Labelle et al., 2012).

Studies appear to confirm that many paraphilics have higher-than-normal sex drives (Jordan et al., 2011). A German study, for example, found that people with parahilias had shorter refractory periods after orgasm by masturbation than most men and experienced a higher frequency of sexual fantasies and urges (Haake et al., 2003). Kafka (2003) refers to this heightened sex drive as *hypersexual disorder*—the opposite of hypoactive sexual desire disorder (see Chapter 15). The psychiatric community is proposing that the "diagnosis" of **hypersexual disorder** may apply to many individuals with paraphilias and those with problems such as public masturbation, uncontrolled use of pornography, attendance at strip clubs, visiting prostitutes, and engaging in unprotected sex with multiple partners (Levine, 2012). Repetitive unsuccessful efforts to control the behavior are a key feature (Hypersexual disorder, 2012).

But these studies address the strength of the sex drive, not the direction it takes. Some studies have used the electroencephalograph (EEG) to investigate electrical responses in the brain among paraphilics and others who engage in impulsive behavior (e.g., W. Fisher et al., 2011). One study measured what is termed "evoked

Klismaphilia   A paraphilia in which sexual arousal is derived from use of enemas.

Coprophilia   A paraphilia in which sexual arousal is attained in connection with feces.

Urophilia   A paraphilia in which sexual arousal is associated with urine.

Hypersexual disorder   A new category of sexual disorders characterized by problematic sexual excesses and failed efforts to control them as expressed through paraphilias and other inappropriate sexual activities, such as public masturbation, uncontrolled use of Internet pornography, unprotected sex with multiple partners, finding of sex partners on the Internet, and so forth.

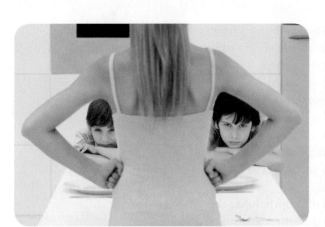

Psychoanalysts suggest that some cases of early punishment by the mother can lead to the development of aberrant sexual fantasies and deviant behavior.

electrical potentials" to erotic stimuli in a sample of 62 right-handed men, half of whom were considered to be normal in terms of their sexual fantasies and behaviors (the control subjects), and half of whom had been diagnosed as paraphilic (fetishistic and sadomasochistic) (Waismann et al., 2003). The men were shown three sets of 57 slides each in random order: 57 paraphilic slides that portrayed depicting fetishistic and sadomasochistic themes; 57 "normal" slides that depicted nude women, coitus, and oral sex: and 57 neutral slides of landscapes, street scenes, and the like. An electrical response labeled "P600" was determined to be the best indicator of sexual arousal in the men. It was found that the main site for evoking the P600 response to "normal" sexual stimuli was on the right side of the brain. The main site for paraphilic stimuli was the left, frontal part of the brain. Paraphilic men showed a significantly greater response than the control subjects in the P600 response in the left, frontal part of the brain. Moreover, control subjects were more likely to differentiate between paraphilic and normal stimuli on the right side of the brain.

Another neurological study may offer some insight into masochism. A research team from Massachusetts General Hospital found that the same neural circuits in the brain are often activated either by painful or by pleasurable stimuli (Becerra et al., 2001). The researchers discovered that a painfully hot (115°F) stimulus to the hand-activated areas of the brain believed to involve "reward" circuitry. The researchers had set out to find ways to help chronic pain patients and not to investigate sexual masochism, but their findings certainly have implications for masochism.

As time goes on, we may learn more about potential biological foundations of paraphilic behavior. Better understanding of these atypical patterns of sexual behavior may lead to the development of more effective treatments.

CRITICAL THINKING

If people with paraphilias have powerful urges to engage in deviant behavior due to biological forces or unconscious fears, can they be expected to control their behavior?

PSYCHOANALYTIC PERSPECTIVES

Psychoanalytic theory has attempted explanations of a number of sexual matters. Psychoanalytic theory suggests that paraphilias are psychological defenses, usually against unresolved castration anxiety dating to the Oedipus complex (Friedman & Downey, 2008). Perhaps the sight of a woman's vagina threatens to arouse castration anxiety in the transvestite, reminding him that women do not have penises and that he might suffer the same fate. Sequestering his penis beneath women's clothing symbolically asserts that women do have penises, which provides unconscious reassurance against his own fears of castration. By exposing his genitals, perhaps the exhibitionist unconsciously seeks reassurance that his penis is secure. It is as if he were asserting, "Look! I have a penis!" Shock or surprise on the victim's face confirms that his penis exists, temporarily relieving castration anxiety. Perhaps masturbation with an object such as a shoe allows the fetishist to gratify his sexual desires while keeping a safe distance from the dangers that he unconsciously associates with sexual contact with women. Or the fetishistic object itself—the shoe—may unconsciously symbolize the penis. Are sadists attempting to defend themselves against unconscious feelings of impotence by inflicting pain on others?

One psychoanalyst associates a type of male sexual masochism with a history of suppressed or repressed feelings of sexual guilt and shame (Schrut, 2005). As an adult, the male wants to be punished for feelings of wrongdoing at the same time he experiences sexual arousal. The pain or humiliation makes the experience "okay."

The paraphilias have provided a fertile ground for psychoanalytic theories. However, such evidence as there is consists of case studies and anecdotes, which are open to interpretation.

COGNITIVE-BEHAVIORAL PERSPECTIVES

Cognitive-behavioral theorists, like psychoanalytic theorists, believe that experience plays a role in the development of sexual preferences. Cognitive-behavioral theorists generally believe that fetishes and other paraphilias are learned through experience. An object may acquire sexually arousing properties through association with sexual arousal or orgasm. Alfred Kinsey and his colleagues (1953) wrote:

> Even some of the most extremely variant types of human sexual behavior may need no more explanation than is provided by our understanding of the processes of learning and conditioning. Behavior which may appear bizarre, perverse, or unthinkably unacceptable to some persons, and even to most persons, may have significance for other individuals because of the way in which they have been conditioned. (pp. 645–646)

Is Her Behavior Appropriate or Inappropriate? Many theorists suggest that early learning experiences contribute to the development of paraphilias. Is this woman's interaction with her young child of the sort that can lead to sexual problems as the child matures?

For example, a boy who glimpses his mother's stockings hanging on the towel rack while he is masturbating may develop a fetish for stockings. Orgasm in the presence of the object reinforces the erotic connection, especially if it is repeated.

Friedrich and Gerber (1994) studied five adolescent boys who practiced hypoxyphilia and found extensive early histories of choking in combination with physical or sexual abuse. The combination seems to have encouraged each of the boys to associate choking with sexual arousal.

Cognitive-behavioral explanations of sexual masochism focus on the pairing of sexual excitement with punishment. For example, a child may be punished when discovered masturbating. Or a boy may reflexively experience an erection if his penis accidentally rubs against the parent's body as he is being spanked. With repeated encounters like these, pain and pleasure may become linked.

Many exhibitionists, voyeurs, frotteurs, and other people with paraphilias have few interpersonal skills relating to women and may avoid "normal" social interactions with them for fear of rejection (Leue et al., 2004). Their furtive, paraphilic behaviors may provide sexual release without risk of rejection.

Observational learning may also play a role. Parents, for example, may inadvertently model exhibitionistic behavior to young sons, which can lead the sons to eroticize the act of exposing themselves. Young people may also read books or magazines or view films or TV programs with paraphilic content. Media may give them the idea of trying paraphilic behavior, and they may find it exciting, especially if acts such as exhibitionism or voyeurism provide a rush of adrenaline.

SOCIOLOGICAL PERSPECTIVES

The psychoanalytic and cognitive-behavioral perspectives are psychological; they focus on the behavior and mental processes of the individual. Sociological perspectives tend to focus on the effects of the group and of society in general on individual and group behavior. For example, although most people indulge paraphilias privately, sexual masochists and sadists require a partner. Most sadomasochists learn S&M rituals, make sexual contacts, acquire sexual paraphernalia, and confirm their sadomasochistic self-identities within what is termed an *S&M subculture*—a loosely connected network of S&M clubs, specialty shops, organizations, magazines, and so on. But the S&M subculture exists in the context of the larger society, and its rituals mirror widely based social and gender roles.

CRITICAL THINKING
Is it ethical for mental-health professionals to work with clients who do not want treatment?

Weinberg (1987) proposes a sociological model that focuses on the social context of sadomasochism. S&M rituals generally involve some form of dominance and submission. Weinberg attributes their erotic appeal to the opportunity to reverse the customary power relationships that exist between males and females and between social classes. Within the confines of the carefully scripted S&M encounter, the meek can be powerful and the powerful meek. People from lower social classes or in menial jobs may be drawn to S&M so they can enact a dominant role. Dominance and submission games allow people to accentuate or reverse the gender stereotypes that identify masculinity with dominance and femininity with submissiveness. Interviews with, and observations of, sadomasochists suggest that most often dominance–submission relationships tend to be consistent with traditional masculine and feminine gender roles in society (Damon, 2002; Santtila et al., 2002). Although there are many exceptions, men more often tend to be dominant and women to be submissive in S&M rituals.

AN INTEGRATED PERSPECTIVE: THE "LOVEMAP"

Like other sexual patterns, paraphilias may have complex biopsychosocial origins (Seligman & Hardenburg, 2000). Might our understanding of them thus be best approached from a theoretical framework that incorporates multiple perspectives? John Money (2003), for example, traces the origins of paraphilias to childhood. He believes that childhood experiences etch a pattern in the brain, called a **lovemap**. This lovemap determines the types of stimuli and activities that become sexually arousing to the individual. In the case of paraphilias, lovemaps become distorted or "vandalized" by early traumatic experiences, such as incest, anti-sexual upbringing, and abuse or neglect. As noted by Gregory K. Lehne, "A boy who is sexually abused may develop paraphilic fantasies involving sexual activity with a boy.... Being punished or embarrassed by being cross-dressed as a young boy may lead to some boys eroticizing the experience, which later is expressed as transvestism" (2009, p. 15). As a boy, Ron (see "A Closer Look" on page 518) was spanked repeatedly on his bare buttocks for "misbehavior" and began to experience sexual arousal during the experiences. He developed into a sexual masochist.

Research suggests that voyeurs and exhibitionists often were the victims of childhood sexual abuse (Barbaree & Blanchard, 2008). Not all children exposed to such influences develop paraphilic compulsions, however. For reasons that remain unknown, some children exposed to such influences appear to be more vulnerable to developing distorted lovemaps than are others. A genetic predisposition, hormonal factors, brain abnormalities, or a combination of these and other factors may play a role in determining one's vulnerability to vandalized lovemaps (Lehne, 2009).

Treatment of Paraphilias

The treatment of paraphilias raises a number of issues. First, many people with paraphilias do not want or seek treatment, at least not voluntarily. The Canadian criminologist Ron Langevin (2006), for example, followed nearly 800 sex offenders from the 1960s through the 2000s and found that only about half desired treatment and completed a course of treatment. But many offenders are seen by health-care providers (HCPs) only when they come into conflict with the law or at the urging of their family members or partners.

Second, HCPs may encounter ethical problems when they are asked to contribute to a judicial process by trying to persuade a sex offender that he (virtually all are male) *ought* to change his behavior. HCPs traditionally help clients clarify or meet their

Lovemap A representation in the mind and in the brain of the idealized lover and the idealized erotic activity with the lover.

own goals; it is not their role to impose societal goals on the individual. Many HCPs believe that the criminal justice system, not they, ought to enforce social standards.

The third issue is a treatment problem. Health-care providers realize that they are generally less successful with resistant or recalcitrant clients. Unless the motivation to change is present, therapeutic efforts are often wasted.

The fourth problem is the issue of perceived responsibility. Sex offenders typically claim that they cannot control their impulses, and accepting personal responsibility for one's actions is a prelude to change. Thus, if therapy is to be constructive, it is necessary to break through the client's personal mythology that he or she is powerless to control his or her behavior.

Despite these issues, many offenders are referred for treatment by the courts. Some seek therapy themselves because they have come to see how their behavior harms themselves or others (Langevin, 2006). We shall consider psychological and biological approaches to the treatment of people with paraphilias. Most sexual offender treatment programs use a combination of psychoanalytic psychotherapy, cognitive-behavioral treatment, and medication (Marvasti, 2004).

PSYCHOANALYTIC PSYCHOTHERAPY

Psychoanalysis focuses on resolving the unconscious conflicts that are believed to originate in childhood and to give rise in adulthood to pathological problems such as paraphilias. The aim of therapy is to help bring unconscious conflicts of childhood into conscious awareness so that they might be worked through in the light of the individual's adult personality (Laws & Marshall, 2003).

Although some favorable case results have been reported, psychoanalytic therapy of the paraphilias is rarely subjected to experimental analysis. Thus, we know little about whether successes are due to the psychoanalytic treatment itself or to other factors, such as spontaneous improvement or a client's willingness to change.

COGNITIVE-BEHAVIORAL THERAPY

Whereas traditional psychoanalysis tends to entail a lengthy process of exploration of the childhood origins of problem behaviors, **cognitive-behavioral therapy** is relatively briefer and focuses directly on changing behavior. Cognitive-behavioral therapy has spawned a number of techniques to help eliminate paraphilic behaviors and strengthen appropriate sexual behaviors: systematic desensitization, relapse prevention training, aversion therapy, empathy training, social skills training, anger management, covert sensitization, and orgasmic reconditioning, to name a few (Krueger & Kaplan, 2002; Marvasti, 2004).

Systematic desensitization attempts to break the link between the sexual stimulus (such as a fetishistic stimulus) and the inappropriate response (sexual arousal). The client is first taught to relax selected muscle groups in the body. Muscle relaxation is then paired repeatedly with each of a series of progressively more arousing paraphilic images or fantasies. Relaxation comes to replace sexual arousal in response to each of these stimuli, even the most provocative. In one case study, a fetishistic transvestite who had become attracted to his mother's lingerie at age 13 was taught to relax when presented with audiotaped scenes representing transvestite or fetishistic themes (Fensterheim & Kantor, 1980). He played such tapes daily while remaining relaxed. He later reported a complete absence of transvestite thoughts or activities.

In **aversion therapy**, the undesirable sexual behavior (for example, masturbation to fetishistic fantasies) is paired repeatedly with an aversive stimulus (such as a harmless but painful electric shock or a nausea-inducing chemical) in the hope that the client will develop a conditioned aversion toward the paraphilic behavior.

Cognitive-behavioral therapy Therapy that attempts to directly change the ways in which people view events and respond to them, relying frequently on principles of learning.

Systematic desensitization A method that uses muscle relaxation to break the connection between a stimulus (such as a fetishistic object) and an inappropriate response (sexual arousal).

Aversion therapy A method for terminating undesirable sexual behavior in which the behavior is repeatedly paired with an aversive stimulus such as electric shock to condition an aversion.

Covert sensitization is a variation of aversion therapy in which paraphilic fantasies are paired with an aversive stimulus in imagination. In one study of 38 **pedophiles** and 62 exhibitionists, more than half of whom were court-referred subjects, were treated by pairing imagined aversive odors with fantasies of the problem behavior (Maletzky, 1980). They were instructed to fantasize pedophiliac or exhibitionistic scenes. Then,

> At a point … when sexual pleasure is aroused, aversive images are presented. … Examples might include a pedophiliac fellating a child, but discovering a festering sore on the boy's penis, an exhibitionist exposing to a woman but suddenly being discovered by his wife or the police, or a pedophiliac laying a young boy down in a field, only to lie next to him in a pile of dog feces. (Maletzky, 1980, p. 308)

Maletzky used this treatment weekly for six months, then followed it with booster sessions every three months over a three-year period. The procedure resulted in at least a 75% reduction of the deviant activities and fantasies for over 80% of the study participants at follow-up periods of up to 36 months. At a 25-year follow-up of 7,275 sex offenders who received similar treatment, Maletzky and Steinhauser (2002) found that benefits were maintained for many of the exhibitionists but for fewer of the pedophiles. But fewer than 50% of the original participants could be contacted after this amount of time elapsed.

Social skills training focuses on helping the individual improve his ability to relate to the other gender. The therapist might first model a desired behavior, such as how to ask a woman out on a date or how to handle a rejection. The client might then role-play the behavior, with the therapist playing the part of the woman. Following the role-play enactment, the therapist would provide feedback and additional guidance and modeling to help the client improve his skills. This process would be repeated until the client mastered the skill.

Orgasmic reconditioning aims to increase sexual arousal to socially appropriate sexual stimuli by pairing culturally appropriate imagery with orgasmic pleasure. The person is instructed to become sexually aroused by masturbating to paraphilic images or fantasies. But as he approaches the point of orgasm, he switches to appropriate imagery and focuses on it during orgasm. In a case example, Davison (1977) reports reduction of sadistic fantasies in a 21-year-old college man. The client was instructed to attain an erection in any way he could, even through the use of the sadistic fantasies he wished to eliminate. But once erection was achieved, he was to masturbate while looking at photos of *Playboy* models. Orgasm was thus paired with nonsadistic images. These images and fantasies eventually acquire the capacity to elicit sexual arousal. Orgasmic reconditioning is often combined with other techniques, such as social skills training, so that more desirable social behaviors can be strengthened as well (Marvasti, 2004).

As we see next, in many ways the treatment of sexual problems is becoming more "medicalized" (Grubin, 2008).

MEDICAL APPROACHES

There may be no medical "cure" for paraphilias. No drug or surgical technique eliminates paraphilic ideas while leaving other cognitive functions intact. But some progress has been reported in using selective serotonin reuptake inhibitors (SSRIs), which are mainly used as anti-depressants, in treating exhibitionism, voyeurism, and fetishism (Grubin, 2008). Why anti-depressants? In addition to treating depression, SSRIs are often used to treat obsessive-compulsive disorder, a psychological

---

Covert sensitization A form of aversion therapy in which thoughts of engaging in undesirable behavior are paired repeatedly with imagined aversive stimuli.

Pedophiles Persons with a paraphilia involving sexual interest in children.

Social skills training Cognitive-behavioral therapy methods for building social skills that rely on a therapist's coaching and practice.

Orgasmic reconditioning A method for strengthening the connection between sexual arousal and appropriate sexual stimuli (such as fantasies about an adult of the other sex) by repeatedly pairing the desired stimuli with orgasm.

disorder involving recurrent obsessions (intrusive ideas) and/or compulsions (urges to repeat a certain behavior or thought). Paraphilic behavior has an obsessive-compulsive quality. People with paraphilias often experience intrusive, repetitive fantasies and urges (Saleh, 2009).

People who experience such intense urges that they are at risk of committing sexual offenses may be helped by drugs that reduce the level of testosterone in the bloodstream (Briken et al., 2011; Houts et al., 2011). Testosterone is closely linked to sex drive and interest. *Medroxyprogesterone acetate (MPA)* (trade name Depo-Provera), which is administered in weekly injections, is the antiandrogen that has been used most extensively in the treatment of sex offenders. In men, antiandrogen drugs reduce sexual desire and the frequencies of erections and ejaculations.

Depo-Provera suppresses the sexual appetite in men. It can lower the intensity of sex drive and erotic fantasies and urges so that the man may feel less compelled to act on them (Briken et al., 2011; Houts et al., 2011). Antiandrogens do not, however, eliminate all paraphilic urges or completely change a person's sexual behavior.

The use of antiandrogens is sometimes incorrectly referred to as *chemical castration*. Surgical castration, the surgical removal of the testes, has sometimes been performed on convicted rapists and violent sex offenders (del Busto & Harlow, 2011). Surgical castration eliminates testicular sources of testosterone. Antiandrogens suppress, but do not eliminate, testicular production of testosterone. Also, unlike surgical castration, the effects of antiandrogens can be reversed when the treatment is terminated.

Evidence suggests that antiandrogens help some people when they are used in conjunction with psychological treatment (Roesler & Witztum, 2000). The value of antiandrogens has been limited by high refusal and dropout rates, however (Roesler & Witztum, 2000). Questions also remain concerning side effects.

Although we have amassed a great deal of research on atypical variations in sexual behavior, our understanding of them and our treatment approaches to them remain less than satisfactory.

CRITICAL THINKING
Which methods of therapy aim to work by reducing the sex drive in general, and which aim to replace sexual response to socially inappropriate stimuli with sexual response to appropriate stimuli?

Anti-depressant medicines have been used to treat sexually compulsive behavior because they have shown promise in treating obsessions and compulsions.

Chapter Review ✓•⌐Study and Review on MyDevelopmentLab

LO1 Define normal and deviant sexual behavior
Sexual behaviors have been labeled deviant when they are statistically rare, run counter to our values, or—as in the case of the paraphilias—show a persistent preference for nongenital outlets.

LO2 Enumerate and define the paraphilias
Paraphilias involve sexual arousal in response to unusual stimuli such as children or other nonconsenting persons, certain objects, or pain or humiliation. The great majority of paraphilias occur among men. In fetishism, an inanimate object comes to elicit sexual arousal. In partialism, people are inordinately aroused by a particular body part, such as the feet. Transvestites become excited by wearing articles of clothing of the other sex. An exhibitionist experiences the compulsion to expose himself to strangers. Voyeurs become sexually aroused by watching, and usually do not seek sexual relations with the target. The obscene phone caller becomes sexually aroused by shocking his victim. Such callers typically masturbate during the phone call or shortly afterward. Sexual masochists associate the receipt of pain or humiliation with sexual arousal. Sexual sadism is characterized by persistent, powerful urges and sexual fantasies involving the inflicting of pain and suffering on others to achieve sexual excitement or gratification. Sexual sadists may be dangerous, especially when they seek nonconsenting "partners." Most frotteuristic acts—also known as mashing—take place in crowded places, such as buses, subway cars, or elevators. Zoophiles desire sexual contact with animals. Necrophiles desire sexual contact with dead bodies.

LO3 Discuss biological perspectives on the paraphilias
Many people with paraphilias have higher-than-normal sex drives. Their brains may also respond differently to deviant and normal sexual stimuli.

LO4 Discuss psychoanalytic perspectives on the paraphilias
Psychoanalytic theory suggests that paraphilias in males are defenses against castration anxiety.

LO5 Discuss cognitive-behavioral perspectives on the paraphilias
Some cognitive-behavioral theorists suggest that unusual stimuli may become sexually arousing through association with sexual arousal or orgasm.

LO6 Discuss sociological perspectives on the paraphilias
According to Weinberg's sociological model, the erotic appeal of S&M rituals may result from the opportunity to reverse the customary power relationships that exist between men and women and between social classes in society.

LO7 Discuss the "Lovemap"
John Money theorized that childhood experiences etch a "lovemap" in the brain that determines the types of stimuli that become sexually arousing. In paraphilias, lovemaps become distorted by early traumatic experiences.

LO8 Discuss the psychoanalytic treatment of the paraphilias
Psychoanalysis aims to bring unconscious conflicts that prompt paraphilic behavior into awareness so that they can be worked through in adulthood.

LO9 Discuss the cognitive-behavioral treatment of the paraphilias
Cognitive-behavioral therapy attempts to eliminate paraphilic behaviors through techniques such as systematic desensitization, aversion therapy, social skills training, covert sensitization, and orgasmic reconditioning.

LO10 Discuss medical treatment of the paraphilias
Selective serotonin reuptake inhibitors (SSRIs), which are usually used as anti-depressants, tend to curb compulsive behavior. Both SSRIs and anti-androgen drugs depress sexual response, which lessens sexual desire and helps individuals control sexual urges. Castration has also been used to curb sexual desire and response.

Test Your Learning

1. People who are excessively aroused by a particular body part, such as the feet, breasts, or buttocks, are said to have
   (a) voyeurism.
   (b) frotteurism.
   (c) partialism.
   (d) transvestism.

2. When cognitive-behavioral therapists work with people with paraphilias, they may use all of the following methods *except*
   (a) covert sensitization.
   (b) orgasmic reconditioning.
   (c) systematic desensitization.
   (d) antidepressant drugs.

3. According to psychoanalytic theory, the _____ is declaring, "Look, I have a penis!"
   (a) exhibitionist
   (b) voyeur
   (c) masher
   (d) sexual sadist

4. A "lovemap" is most likely to become distorted or "vandalized" by
   (a) alcohol.
   (b) physical abuse or neglect.
   (c) unconscious conflicts from the Oedipal period.
   (d) the sadomasochistic subculture.

5. Transvestism is considered to be most closely related to
   (a) fetishism.
   (b) exhibitionism.
   (c) mashing.
   (d) sadomasochism.

6. Which of the following are most likely to need to risk capture to heighten their sexual arousal?
   (a) sadomasochists
   (b) coprophiliacs
   (c) exhibitionists
   (d) mashers

7. Waismann and colleagues showed men slides and found that the main site for evoking the _____ response to "normal" sexual stimuli was on the right side of the brain.
   (a) P100
   (b) P300
   (c) P400
   (d) P600

8. Paraphilias are defined by
   (a) preference for deviant stimuli.
   (b) statistical rarity of the sexual interest.
   (c) sexual interests that deviate from the core values of a society.
   (d) a high sex drive.

9. All paraphilias
   (a) pose a physical threat to the victims.
   (b) are evidence that the perpetrator is out of touch with reality.
   (c) are more common among males.
   (d) can be treated by psychoanalysis.

10. The text states that it is normal to
    (a) expose one's genital organs to shock a stranger.
    (b) grope a nearby person in the subway,
    (c) enjoy exposing one's body to an intimate partner.
    (d) fantasize about sex with corpses.

Answers: 1. c; 2. d; 3. a; 4. b; 5. a; 6. c; 7. d; 8. c; 9. c; 10. c

---

My Life, My Sexuality

How to Respond to an Exhibitionist

Explore this **My Life, My Sexuality** *feature by scanning this QR code with your mobile device. If you don't already have one, you may download a free QR scanner for your device wherever smartphone apps are sold. You can also view this feature in MyDevelopmentLab, along with an accompanying critical thinking assignment.*

A woman who is exposed to an exhibitionist may react with surprise, shock, disgust, anger—and, in a few cases, indifference. But how should she behave? What should she say? Scan the code for some suggestions.

18 Sexual Coercion

Learning Objectives

RAPE: THE MOST INTIMATE CRIME OF VIOLENCE

LO1   Define rape

TYPES OF RAPE

LO2   Describe the various kinds of rape

SOCIAL ATTITUDES, MYTHS, AND CULTURAL FACTORS THAT ENCOURAGE RAPE

LO3   Explain how our culture encourages people to blame the victim of rape

PSYCHOLOGICAL CHARACTERISTICS OF RAPISTS: WHO ARE THEY?

LO4   Discuss the kinds of rapists and their personalities

ADJUSTMENT OF RAPE SURVIVORS

LO5   Discuss the effects of rape on victims

CHILDHOOD SEXUAL ABUSE

LO6   Discuss the origins and effects of sexual child abuse

TREATMENT OF RAPISTS AND CHILD MOLESTERS

LO7   Discuss the treatment options of treating rapists and child molesters, and their effectiveness

SEXUAL HARASSMENT

LO8   Define sexual harassment
LO9   Explain what victims of sexual harassment can do about it

MY LIFE, MY SEXUALITY: RAPE PREVENTION

Rape Is Not Sex

Explore the video, **Rape Is Not Sex,** by scanning this QR code with your mobile device. If you don't already have one, you may download a free QR scanner for your device wherever smartphone apps are sold. You can also view this video in MyDevelopmentLab. For more videos related to this chapter's content, log into MyDevelopmentLab to view the entire Human Sexuality Video Series.

TRUTH OR FICTION?

Which of the following statements are the truth, and which are fiction? Look for the Truth-or-Fiction icons on the pages that follow to find the answers.

1   Women are raped in the United States at a rate of more than one every minute.   **T F**?

2   The majority of rapes are committed by strangers in deserted neighborhoods or darkened alleyways.   **T F**?

3   Ten times as many women as men are raped in the United States.   **T F**?

4   Men who rape other men are gay.   **T F**?

5   Many women say no when they mean yes.   **T F**?

6   Most rapists are mentally ill.   **T F**?

7   Father–daughter incest is the most common type of incest.   **T F**?

"Penn State plans to renovate locker room and showers where Sandusky abused boys"

This message came across the "crawl" on a show airing July 16, 2012. About 15 years too late.

Jerry Sandusky, an assistant coach, was known to Penn State football fans. Perhaps he was also known to those who follow college football with a microscope. He was clearly known to the university vice president, Gary C. Schultz, who received complaints about Sandusky's behavior dating at least to 1998. He was known to the university president, Graham B. Spanier, since February of 2001, when the Penn State football head coach, Joe Paterno, told him that a graduate assistant had seen Sandusky raping a boy in the locker room. Who was Joe Paterno? Perhaps the best-known university football coach in the United States. When one thought of Penn State, or the football team—the Nittany Lions—one pictured Joe Paterno, the ageless leader who had brought the university countless wins and bowl appearances.

The president and vice president conferred with the university officials, including the athletic director and Paterno, but a couple of weeks later, they decided not to report the incident—or dozens of similar incidents—to police and to offer Sandusky "professional help" instead.

Why the reluctance to call in the police? In a word: scandal. The university's luminous reputation would be despoiled. Fanatical fans would be appalled. Alumni and sponsors of the team would be horrified. High school football stars, with a basketful of college offers before them, might choose to go elsewhere.

But in 2011–2012 it all unraveled. Sandusky's crimes came to the attention of the police and he was prosecuted for them. (In October of 2012, he was convicted of the crimes and sentences to 30 to 60 years in prison.) The cover-up finally came to the attention of the Board of Trustees, and the university president, the vice president, and, most shockingly, the apparently invulnerable Joe Paterno were fired. To put a coda on the drama, Paterno—not a young man—died a couple of months later.

Jerry Sandusky and Joe Paterno in better days

Here's a detail that borders on sounding silly. Karen B. Peetz, chairwoman of the Board of Trustees since January 2012, the month in which Paterno died, was asked if Paterno should continue to be venerated at Penn State. "The whole topic of Joe Paterno being honored or not being honored is a very sensitive topic," she said (cited in Perez-Pena, 2012). "This is something that will continue to be discussed with the entire university community."

Did she think that perhaps Paterno should still be revered? That's up to her to answer.

Another member of the Board of Trustees, Kenneth C. Frazier (cited in Perez-Pena, 2012), came closer to getting it right.

"We, the Penn State board of trustees, failed in our obligation to provide proper oversight of the university's operations," he said, "Our hearts remain heavy, and we are deeply ashamed."

The media are in a continuous feeding frenzy over sexual offenses involving minors, celebrities, highly placed politicians, and members of the armed services. In the 1990s, the spotlight was on the rape trial of boxer Mike Tyson and then on an affair between Bill Clinton and a White House intern named Monica Lewinsky. Many argued that their relationship comprised sexual harassment because of the disparity in their power, even though Lewinsky was a willing partner.

In the 2000s, there came the stories of American priests who sexually abused children. The Boston Archdiocese alone was reported to have received over 1,000 complaints of child sexual abuse over the past several decades and to have turned a blind eye to the charges (Finkelhor, 2003; Sex Abuse Victims, 2003). Some wondered aloud whether the church's requirement that priests remain celibate has contributed to the problem (Adams, 2003). 👁

👁︎**Watch** the **Video**
AP Exclusive: Abusive Priests Live Unmonitored
on **MyDevelopmentLab**

A Closer Look

The Penn State Scandal: Anatomy of Sexual Abuse and the Cover-Up[1]

In June of 2012, Jerry Sandusky, who had been a defensive coordinator for the vaunted Penn State football team, was convicted of the sexual assault of 10 boys. He was found guilty of 45 of the 48 counts against him. The conviction was one of the markers of the downfall not only of Sandusky but also of the football legendary coach Joe Paterno, the university president, and others who had participated in the cover-up. Although Paterno, caught up in the scandal, had announced his intention to retire at the end of the 2010–2011 season, the university Board of Trustees fired him. Sandusky's victims were from disadvantaged homes, befriended by Sandusky, then repeatedly abused by him. An outline of events follows:

1969

Jerry Sandusky, a defensive end at Penn State from 1963 to 1965, joins Paterno's staff as defensive line coach.

1994–1997

Victims 4, 5, 6, and 7 meet Sandusky at the ages of 7 to 12 through Sandusky's charity, Second Mile.

1996–1998

Sandusky showers with Victim 5, aged 8 to 10, in the Penn State locker rooms.

May 3, 1998

Victim 6 is violated in the Penn State locker rooms at the age of 11. His mother complains to the university police.

May 4–30, 1998

Penn State University vice president Gary C. Schultz is informed of the mother's complaint. His notes show that he wrote: "Behavior — at best inappropriate @ worst sexual improprieties." He asks, "Is this opening of pandora's box?" and "Other children?" University police listen in on a conversation between Victim 6's mother and Sandusky. Sandusky admits showering with the boy; he says: "I was wrong. I wish I could get forgiveness. I know I won't get it from you. I wish I were dead." The university police chief e-mails Schultz: "We're going to hold off on making any crime log entry. At this point I can justify that decision because of the lack of clear evidence of a crime." The university athletic director, Tim Curley, tells Schultz that he has informed Paterno of the incident. Later he e-mails: "Anything new in this department? Coach is anxious to know where it stands." Before his death in early 2012, Paterno insisted that he knew nothing of the incident.

June 1998

A university police detective and a state public welfare caseworker interview Sandusky, admits hugging Victim 6 in the shower to university police and a state welfare caseworker, but insists there was nothing "sexual about it." He admits to showering with other children, but the district attorney decides not to press criminal charges.

Summer, 1999

Tim Curley, university athletic director, reports that Paterno gave Sandusky the option to remain with the team as an assistant, but Sandusky chose, instead, to run a middle school football camp. The university agrees to "work collaboratively" with Sandusky on Second Mile, and gives him free lifetime use of a Penn State Locker Room.

July 1999–December 2001

Sandusky violates Victim 3 at Penn State and elsewhere "several times."

Fall 2000

A janitor observes Sandusky pinning Victim 8 against the wall of the showers and performing oral sex on him. Neither the janitor nor his supervisor, who was told of the incident, report it for fear of losing their jobs.

Feb. 9, 2001

A graduate assistant and hears "rhythmic, slapping sounds" in a Penn State locker room that sound like sexual activity. He later testifies, under oath, that Sandusky was raping a boy who looked to be about 10 years old.

Feb. 10, 2001

The graduate assistant tells Paterno what he witnessed the following morning. Paterno says, "You did what you had to do. It's my job now to figure out what we want to do." But before he died, Paterno denied that the assistant gave him any details of what he had witnessed, only that something inappropriate had happened between Sandusky and a child.

Feb. 11, 2001

Paterno reports the assistant's story to Schultz and the university president, Graham B. Spanier.

Feb. 27, 2001

The athletic director, Curley, informs his supervisors that he talked about the incident with Paterno. They decide to offer Sandusky "professional help" and advise him not to bring boys to the locker room rather than report the incident to police.

August 2001

Sandusky violates Victim 5 in the Penn State locker room.

Sept 21, 2001

Schultz praises Sandusky's work at Second Mile.

2005–2006

Sandusky meets Victim 1 through Second Mile at the age of 11 or 12.

Spring 2008

Victim 1 is now a freshman in high school. His mother informs school of a sexual assault, and Sandusky, a volunteer coach, is barred from the school district. The matter is reported to the authorities.

---

[1]Adapted from Justin Sablich, Ford Fessenden, & Alan McLean. (2012, July 13). Timeline: The Penn State Scandal, *The New York Times online*.

Early 2009

The Pennsylvania attorney general begins an investigation. Victim 1 reports that Sandusky inappropriately touched him repeatedly.

Winter 2011

A grand jury summons university officials and Paterno to testify. The university's Board of Trustees is not informed.

May 11, 2011

The Board of Trustees learns of the investigation on May 11 but takes no action.

Nov. 5, 2011

Sandusky is arrested on charges of childhood sexual abuse with eight boys. He is released on bail. Curley and Schultz are charged with failure to report the crimes and perjury.

Nov. 7, 2011

Curley and Schultz step down.

Nov. 9, 2011

Paterno announces his intended retirement, but the Board of Trustees fires him and the university president.

Nov. 14, 2011

In an interview with Bob Costas, Sandusky claims he is innocent and not a pedophile. He admits, "I shouldn't have showered with those kids."

Jan. 22, 2012

Paterno dies from lung cancer at the age of 85.

June 22, 2012

Jerry Sandusky is convicted of the sexual abuse of 10 boys.

July 12, 2012

Louis J. Freeh, former director of the FBI, releases a report on the scandal. He accuses Paterno, the university's former president, and other university officials of hiding the facts about Sandusky's sexual abuse of children.

At about the same time, it was charged that the Air Force Academy had "traditions" that encouraged or legitimized the sexual assault of female cadets. A number of women cadets left the academy, officers resigned, and policies were changed (Janofsky & Schemo, 2003).

Then there were the cases of Mary Kay LeTourneau, Pamela Rogers, and Debra LaFave—attractive women who were prosecuted for having sex with minor boys. While some men wondered whether these boys just "got lucky," David Finkelhor (2005a), director of the Crimes Against Children Research Center at the University

A Pair of Sex Offenders?
What do boxer Mike Tyson and teacher Debra LaFave have in common? Both were found guilty of sexual offenses. Tyson was convicted of the forcible rape of a woman who accompanied him to his hotel room. LaFave pleaded guilty to having sex with a minor boy. Tyson's crime was violent; LaFave's case involved statutory rape. In LaFave's case, although the boy was not forced into sex, at the age of 14 he was legally too young to provide consent.

of New Hampshire, notes that the bringing of these cases to court reflects a decline in the double standard that is applied to men and women. Finkelhor suggests that increasing numbers of female police and prosecutors are less likely to buy into the traditional idea that boys who have sex with older women have something to be thankful for.

All in all, a team of professional writers could not have developed more scandalous material, but the plots and the characters in these media series are very real. Many observers wince as they see aspects of themselves—either as aggressors or victims—laid bare before the public.

This chapter is about sexual coercion. Our topics include rape and other forms of sexual pressure, including sexual harassment. As we see in the cases involving minors, sexual coercion also includes *any* sexual activity between an adult and a child. Even when children cooperate, sexual relations with children are coercive because children are below the legal age of consent. ◉

Rape: The Most Intimate Crime of Violence

◉ Watch the Video
*South Korean Sex Workers Rally
Against Crackdown*
on **MyDevelopmentLab**

> During the school year, you talk to people it has happened to, even upperclassmen, and they all say the same thing. They tell you to expect getting raped, and if it doesn't happen to you, you're one of the rare ones. They say if you want a chance to stay [at the Air Force Academy], if you want to graduate, you don't tell. You just deal with it. (Sharon Fullilove, cited in Janofsky & Schemo, 2003)

The women at the Air Force Academy, like an estimated 1.3 million U.S. women each year (NISVS, 2011), were victimized by a most common crime of violence: rape. **Rape** has its sexual aspects but it is also the subjugation of women by men by force or threat of force (Ainsworth & Baumeister, 2012; Calhoun et al., 2012; Gillibrand, 2012).

For the first few thousand years of history, the only rapes that were punished were those that defiled virgins. These rapes were considered crimes against property (virgins being the property of their fathers)—not crimes against persons. In ancient Babylonia, rape laws applied to married women as well. Babylonian law required the assailant *and his victim* to be bound and thrown into a river. As the injured party (after all, *his* property had been damaged), the husband could choose to let his wife drown or save her. Blaming the victim of rape is thus an age-old tradition. The ancient Hebrews stoned to death a married woman who was raped, along with her assailant. In the ancient Babylonian and Hebrew cultures, the wife was seen as guilty of adultery. Virgins who were raped within the protection of the city gates would also be stoned by the Hebrews. It was thought that they could have maintained their purity by crying out.

The current definition of rape varies from state to state. **Forcible rape** is usually defined as sex with a nonconsenting person by the use of force or the threat of force. **Statutory rape** refers to sex with a person who is below the age of consent, even if the person cooperates.

Traditionally, a man could not be convicted for raping his wife, even though he might have forced her to submit to sexual activity by physical power or threats. This marital exclusion was derived from the English common law that held that a woman "gives herself over" to her husband when she becomes his wife and cannot retract her consent. Today, however, most states permit the prosecution of husbands who rape their wives.

CRITICAL THINKING
Why is rape a political issue as well as a crime?

Rape Sexual activity that takes place without consent. See *forcible rape* and *statutory rape*.

Forcible rape Sexual activity obtained by the use of force or the threat of force.

Statutory rape Sexual activity with a person below the age of consent, even when the victim cooperates.

Rape laws are now also applied to men who rape men and to women who coerce men into sexual activity or assist men in raping other women. Forcible rape is a form of **sexual assault**.

INCIDENCE OF RAPE

The numbers of women who have been raped are both inconsistent and staggering. First, the inconsistency. The FBI reported that 84,767 forcible rapes occurred in 2011(Rabin, 2011). However, the FBI tracked only those rapes that were reported to authorities. The National Intimate Partner and Sexual Violence Survey (NISVS, 2011), administered by the Centers for Disease Control and Prevention (CDC), is a continuing telephone survey of a nationally representative sample of some 16,500 adults. The CDC defined rape as completed forced penetration, forced penetration facilitated by alcohol or other substances, or attempted forced penetration. According to the results, 1% of the women surveyed reported being raped in the past year. That figure suggests that 1.3 million U.S. women are victimized by rape or attempted rape each year! And when we ask about lifetime incidence of sexual assault, nearly one woman in five reports being raped (NISVS, 2011). The same report found that about 1 man in 71 had been a rape victim at some time in his life, many earlier than the age of 11. Figure 18.1 shows the age of rape victims in the survey. Two out of three female rape victims are between the ages of 11 and 24.

1

How can we explain the discrepancy between the FBI's report and the CDC? The fact of the matter is that the vast majority of rapes that occur in the United States go unreported. **TRUTH** OR **FICTION** REVISITED: This means that two women in the United States are raped every minute on the average.

Why do most rape victims not report the assault to authorities? Many women choose not to report assaults because of concern that they will be humiliated by the criminal justice system. Others fear reprisal from their families or the rapist. Some simply assume that the offender will not be apprehended or prosecuted. Because Mexican American women live in a culture in which women are often expected to "suffer in silence," they are even more likely to remain quite about rape and sexual

Sexual assault Any sexual activity that involves the use of force or the threat of force.

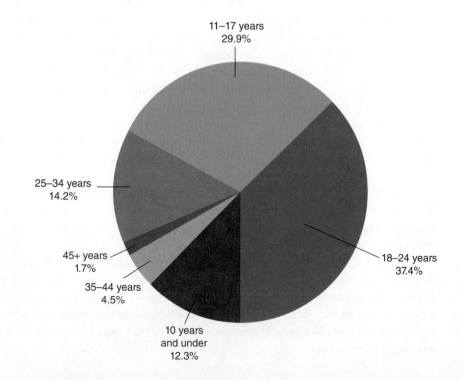

FIGURE 18.1 Age at Time of First Completed Rape Victimization More than three-quarters of female victims of completed rape (79.6%) were first raped before their 25th birthday, with 42.2% experiencing their first completed rape before the age of 18 (29.9% between 11–17 years old and 12.3% at or before age 10).
More than one-quarter of male victims of completed rape (27.8%) were first raped when they were 10 years old or younger (data not shown).

Source: NISVS. (2011, December 14). Centers for Disease Control and Prevention. The National Intimate Partner and Sexual Violence Survey (NISVS), Figure 2.2. http://www.cdc.gov/ViolencePrevention/NISVS/index.html (Accessed July 16, 2012).

A World of Diversity
Pakistan's War of Terror on Rape Victims

Pakistan's Hudood Ordinances make no distinction between rape and adultery and have created a war of terror against women. Particularly when there are few witnesses, a rape victim often ends up in prison when she "admits" to illicit intercourse, or *zina,* whether forced or not. Zina is male–female sexual intercourse between an unmarried couple (Critelli & Willett, 2012, 2006).

The law allows men or women who are found guilty of zina to be subjected to *Hadd,* which is carried out in the form of public stoning to death if the perpetrator is a Muslim. If the perpetrator is not a Muslim, then the perpetrator of zina can be given a public flogging of 100 lashes.

A report published by The Human Rights Commission of Pakistan (HRCP) stated that of the 6,000 women and children being held in prison in Pakistan, 80% were imprisoned because of the Hudood Ordinances.

The sin of rape is regarded as *zina-bil-jabr* and the sentence is the same, except that a non-Muslim can be sentenced to death as well as receiving 100 lashes. If a perpetrator (or victim of) zina-bil-jabr is a minor, the person can be given a sentence of five years, along with 30 lashes and a fine.

A man can be found guilty of rape only if he makes a confession or if at least four Muslim adult male eye-witnesses, held to be in good religious standing by the Court, provide testimony against him. Testimony by women, including the victim, is not admissible (Critelli & Willett, 2012). Thus, if a woman reports a rape,

she is therefore confessing to zina, and is liable to stoning. Fortunately, nobody has thus far been stoned to death under these rulings. The sentence of stoning to death has been given out, but so far, appeals to superior courts have reversed them.

The HRCP states that the fear of stoning prevents women from reporting rape. For example, five women from Larkana were gang-raped. They withdrew their accusations when threatened with being charged with Hudood. A woman called Majeeda Mujid was kidnapped by a gang of men and repeatedly raped over two months. When she went to the police, she was imprisoned, and her rapists were set free. HRCP states that the way most Hudood trials work, it is assumed that women are guilty until proven innocent.

---

abuse than European American women (Chen, 2012; Human Rights Watch, 2012). And as we see in the nearby diversity feature, women in traditional Islamic countries such as Pakistan are even more reluctant to report being raped.

There are other reasons that women do not report rape to authorities. Some women mistakenly believe that coercive sex is rape only when the rapist is a stranger. Some other women mistakenly assume that only forced vaginal penetration by the penis is defined as rape. But most states define rape more broadly, also considering nonconsensual anal and oral penetration by the penis or a finger or by a foreign object to be rape. And some count attempted rapes as rape.

The survey also asks respondents about violence by intimate partners. As you see in Figure 18.2, nearly 1 woman in 4 and 1 man in 7 have experienced severe physical violence at the hands of an intimate partner (NISVS, 2011).

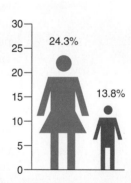

FIGURE 18.2 Violence by an Intimate Partner About 1 in 4 women (24.3%) and 1 in 7 men (13.8%) have experienced severe physical violence by an intimate partner (e.g., hit with a fist or something hard, beaten, slammed against something) at some point in their lifetime.

Source: NISVS. (2011, December 14). Centers for Disease Control and Prevention. The National Intimate Partner and Sexual Violence Survey (NISVS), Figure 2.2. http://www.cdc.gov/ViolencePrevention/NISVS/index.html (Accessed July 16, 2012).

Types of Rape

TRUTH OR FICTION REVISITED: It is not true that the majority of rapes are committed by strangers in deserted neighborhoods or darkened alleyways. Actually, most women are raped by men they know—often by men they have come to trust. Only 4% of the women in a national health and social life survey were "forced to do something sexual that they did not want to do" by a stranger (laumann et al., 1994). According to the U.S. Department of Justice (2006), about 83% of rapes are committed by acquaintances of the victim. The types of rape include stranger rape, acquaintance rape, partner rape, male rape, and rape by females.

STRANGER RAPE

Stranger rape refers to rape committed by an assailant (or assailants) who is not previously known to the person attacked. The stranger rapist often selects targets that seem vulnerable, such as women who live alone, who are older or mentally retarded, who are walking down deserted streets, or who are asleep or intoxicated. After choosing a target, the rapist may search for a safe time and place to commit the crime—a deserted, run-down part of town, a darkened street, a second-floor apartment without window bars or locks.

ACQUAINTANCE RAPE

Women are more likely to be raped by men they know, such as classmates, fellow office workers, and even their brothers' friends, than by strangers. **Acquaintance rapes** are less likely than stranger rapes to be reported to the police. One reason is that rape survivors may not perceive sexual assaults by acquaintances as rapes. Only about one-quarter of the women in a national college survey who had been sexually assaulted saw themselves as rape victims (Koss & Kilpatrick, 2001; Rozee & Koss, 2001). Let's repeat that: *Only about one-quarter of the women in a national college survey who had been sexually assaulted saw themselves as rape victims!* Despite increased public awareness of acquaintance rape, many still think of rapists as strangers lurking in shadows and that a woman should be able to resist a sexual advance unless the man uses a weapon. Acquaintance rapists tend to rationalize their behavior by believing in myths such as the traditional view that men are expected to assume a sexually aggressive role in dating and the belief that rapists are strangers (Bletzer & Koss, 2006). Even when acquaintance rapes are reported to police, they may be treated as "misunderstandings" or lovers' quarrels rather than violent crimes (Campbell, 2006; Logan et al., 2006).

DATE RAPE

Date rape is a form of acquaintance rape. Studies of college women show a consistent trend: as many as one college woman in four reports being forced into sexual intercourse by dates (McAnulty, 2012). Date rape is more likely to occur when the couple have too much to drink and then park in the man's car or goes back to his residence (McAnulty, 2012). The man tends to perceive his partner's willingness to return home with him as a signal of sexual interest, even if she resists his advances.

Date rapists may believe that acceptance of a date indicates willingness to have sexual relations. They may think that women should reciprocate with sex if they are taken to dinner. Other men assume that women who frequent places like singles bars are expressing tacit agreement to sex with men who show interest in them. Some date rapists believe that a woman who resists advances is just "protesting too much" so that she will not look "easy." They interpret resistance as coyness—a ploy in the cat-and-mouse game that typifies the so-called battle of the sexes. Date rapists may believe that when a woman says no, she means yes, especially when a sexual relationship has already been established (McAnulty, 2012). ◉

According to Roy Baumeister and his colleagues (2001), perpetrators and victims view sexual assaults in very different ways. Women see themselves as overpowered and deeply hurt. Men often focus on their own feelings, ignoring those

---

Stranger rape   Rape that is committed by an assailant previously unknown to the victim.

Acquaintance rape   Rape by an acquaintance of the victim.

◉ **Watch** the **Video**
Dating and Violence
on **MyDevelopmentLab**

A Closer Look

Anatomy of a Date Rape: Ann and Jim

ANN

I first met him at a party. He was really good looking and he had a great smile. I wanted to meet him but I wasn't sure how. I didn't want to appear too forward. Then he came over and introduced himself. We talked and found we had a lot in common. I really liked him. When he asked me over to his place for a drink, I thought it would be OK. He was such a good listener, and I wanted him to ask me out again.

When we got to his room, the only place to sit was on the bed. I didn't want him to get the wrong idea, but what else could I do? We talked for awhile and then he made his move. I was so startled. He started by kissing. I really liked him, so the kissing was nice. But then he pushed me down on the bed. I tried to get up and I told him to stop. He was so much bigger and stronger. I got scared and I started to cry. I froze and he raped me.

It took only a couple of minutes and it was terrible, he was so rough. When it was over he kept asking me what was wrong, like he didn't know. He had just forced himself on me and he thought that was OK. He drove me home and said he wanted to see me again. I'm so afraid to see him. I never thought it would happen to me.

JIM

I first met her at a party. She looked really hot, wearing a sexy dress that showed off her great body. We started talking right away. I knew that she liked me by the way she kept smiling and touching my arm while she was speaking. She seemed pretty relaxed so I asked her back to my place for a drink. When she said yes, I knew that I was going to be lucky!

When we got to my place, we sat on the bed kissing. At first, everything was great. Then, when I started to lay her down on the bed, she started twisting and saying she didn't want to. Most women don't like to appear too easy, so I knew that she was just going through the motions. When she stopped struggling, I knew that she would have to throw in some tears before we did it.

She was still very upset afterwards, and I just don't understand it! If she didn't want to have sex, why did she come back to the room with me? You could tell by the way she dressed and acted that she was no virgin, so why she had to put up such a big struggle I don't know.

of the victim, and act on their sexual frustration when the woman says it's time to call it quits. The more the man focuses on his own wants and ignores those of the woman, the more likely he is to commit rape (Bushman et al., 2003). In these cases, the motive may be largely sexual, but the man remains a violent criminal who refuses to take no for an answer.

The issue of consent lies at the heart of determining if a sexual act is rape. Unlike cases of stranger rape, date rape occurs within a context in which sexual relations could occur voluntarily. Thus, the issue of consent can become murky. Juries and judges are often faced with a woman plaintiff who alleges that the male defendant, who may

Taking Back the Night. Whose fault is it if a woman is raped when she goes out alone at night? Many women—and men who care about women—have marched to demonstrate their disgust for the men who might assault them if they were out walking by themselves, and toward a society that too often blames the victim for what happens to her.

appear neatly dressed and looking like the boy next door, forced her into a sexual act against her will. As in the Mike Tyson court appearances, the defendant may admit that sexual intercourse took place but claim that it was consensual. Judges and juries then have to distinguish shadings in meaning regarding "consent."

Cases of date rape often come down to his word against hers. Her word often becomes less persuasive in the eyes of the jury if it was clear that she had consented to acts beforehand, such as sharing dinner, attending the movies together, accompanying him to his home, sharing a drink alone, and perhaps kissing or petting (Maxwell et al., 2003; Osman, 2003). The issue becomes further clouded because some survivors of date rape continue their relationships, and even marry, the perpetrators.

The problem of date rape has been brought within closer public scrutiny in recent years. "Take Back the Night" marches have become a common form of student protest on college campuses against the sexual misconduct of men. Many colleges have mandated date rape seminars and workshops.

GANG RAPE

Exercise of power is a major motive behind gang rapes, although some attackers may also be expressing anger against women. Gang members often believe that once women engage in coitus they are "whores." Thus, each offending gang member may become more aggressive as he takes his turn. The Koss college survey showed that sexual assaults involving a group of assailants tend to be more vicious than individual assaults (Gidycz & Koss, 1990).

MALE RAPE

3 The prevalence of male rape is unknown because, as with female victimization, most assaults are not reported. **TRUTH** OR **FICTION** REVISITED: The U.S. Department of Justice (2006) estimates that one in ten rape survivors is a man. **4** **TRUTH** OR **FICTION** REVISITED: It is *not* true that men who rape other men are gay. Most are heterosexual. Their motives tend to include domination and control, revenge and retaliation, sadism and degradation, and (when the rape is carried out by a gang member) status and affiliation (Peterson et al., 2010).

Most rapes of men are carried out by other men (Peterson et al., 2010). Many male rapes occur in prison settings and in military service. Gay and bisexual men appear to be more likely to be victimized than heterosexual men. Males are more often attacked by multiple assailants, held captive longer, and reluctant to report the assault. After all, victimization does not fit the male stereotype of toughness. Men are expected to be not only strong but silent. But male rape survivors may suffer traumatic effects similar to those suffered by female survivors (Peterson et al., 2010).

PARTNER RAPE

Partner rapes are probably more common than date rapes because a sexual relationship has already been established (Monson et al., 2000; Osman, 2003). A "traditional" man may believe that it is his partner's duty to satisfy his sexual needs even when she is uninterested. However, men who are better educated and less rigid regarding stereotypes about sexual relationships are less likely to rape their partners (Basile, 2002).

Partner rape has been largely unreported and often unrecognized by survivors as actually being rape (Strebeigh, 2009). Women may also fail to report partner rape because of fear that no one will believe them.

Motives for partner rape vary. Sex is a motive, but some people use sex to dominate their partners. Others degrade their partners through sex, especially after

---

Real Students, Real Questions

Q *Can a prostitute be raped?*

A Absolutely! Sex workers consider rape to be one of the hazards of the job, but that certainly does not mean that they take it lightly. Rape causes physical harm, psychological disturbance, and, in the case of sex workers, job burnout.

---

arguments. Sexual coercion often occurs within a context of a pattern of violence and physical intimidation (Johnson, 2003). In some cases, though, violence is limited to the sexual relationship. Some men see sex as the solution to disputes. They think if they can force their partners into sex, "Everything will be OK."

Survivors of partner rape may be as fearful as survivors of stranger rape of serious injury or death. The long-term effects of partner rape on survivors are also similar to those experienced by survivors of stranger rape, including fear, depression, and sexual dysfunctions (Kaczmarek et al., 2006; Polusny & Arbisi, 2006). Moreover, the woman who is raped by her husband usually continues to live with her assailant and may fear repeated attacks.

RAPE BY WOMEN

Rape by women is rare. When it does occur, it often involves aiding or abetting men who are attacking another woman. Rape by women may occur in gang rape in which women follow male leaders to gain their approval. In such cases, a woman may be used to lure another woman to a reasonably safe place for the rape. Or the woman may hold the other woman down while she is assaulted.

But some men have been raped by women (Walker et al., 2005). Sarrel and Masters (1982) reported 11 such cases, including a 37-year-old man who was coerced into sexual intercourse by two women at gunpoint. In another case, a 27-year-old man fell asleep in his hotel room with a woman he had just met in a bar and then awakened to find that he was bound to his bed, gagged, and blindfolded. He was then forced into sexual intercourse with four different women, who threatened him with castration if he did not perform satisfactorily.

Social Attitudes, Myths, and Cultural Factors that Encourage Rape

Many people believe a number of myths about rape, such as "women say no when they mean yes," "all women like a man who is pushy and forceful," "the way women dress, they are just asking to be raped," and "rapists are crazed by sexual desire" (davies et al., 2012). Yet another myth is that deep down inside, women want to be overpowered and forced into sex by men. **TRUTH** OR **FICTION** REVISITED: But it is not true that women say no when they mean yes. This myth has the effect of encouraging rape.

CRITICAL THINKING
Check out the laws against marital rape (for example, see Strebeigh [2009]). Why do you think it was a political struggle to pass these laws?

 5

A Closer Look

Ten Cultural Myths That Create a Climate That Supports Rape

Myths about rape create a social climate that legitimizes rape. Although both men and women are susceptible to myths about rape, researchers find that college men show greater acceptance of rape myths than do college women (Davies et al., 2012). These myths tend to blame the victim rather than the rapist. Men also cling more stubbornly to myths about date rape than do women, even following date rape education classes designed to challenges these views. Such myths do not occur in a social vacuum. They are related to other social attitudes, including gender-role stereotyping, perception of sex as adversarial, and acceptance of violence in relationships. Here are some examples of myths about rape that help create a cultural climate that increases the likelihood of rape in the United States. Why not place a checkmark in front of those myths you believe—or did believe—before you read this Closer Look feature.

___Myth 1: That a woman who would go to a man's home or apartment on a first date is implying that she is willing to have sex. *A woman is free to be in a man's residence without expecting that she will be assaulted.*

___Myth 2: That many women would claim that they have been raped only to call attention to them-

selves. *Nonsense! One could be just as suspicious anytime anybody complained about anything, such as complaining about a painful toe.*

___Myth 3: That a healthy woman can resist a rapist if she sincerely wants to do so. The fact is that men are generally stronger than women and can overpower them. *The fact is that men are generally stronger than women and can overpower them.*

___Myth 4: That women who don't use bras or who wear short skirts and other sexually appealing clothing are asking for trouble. *Don't confuse the current style with a sexual invitation.*

___Myth 5: That most of the victims of rape are promiscuous or have a bad reputation. *It's not true, and even if it were, it wouldn't give men a license to commit rape.*

___Myth 6: That a girl who engages in necking or petting is letting things get out of hand, so you can't blame her partner it he forces sex on her. *Yes you can. A girl or woman has the right to say no at any time.*

___Myth 7: That women who are hitchhiking get what they deserve. *It may be a sign of poor judgment to hitchhike, but rape is not the appropriate "penalty."*

___Myth 8: That women who think they're too good to talk to men they pass on the street need to be taught a lesson. *This myth is a perfect example of hatred of women. Women walking on the street should not be victimized by catcalls, leering, and sexual invitations.*

___Myth 9: That many women have an unconscious desired to be raped. *Nonsense! Even if women, like men, occasionally entertain fantasies about rape, it does not mean they actually want to be raped and certainly doesn't give men an excuse to violently assault them.*

___Myth 10: That many women who report a rape are angry with them men they accuse and want to punish them, or they find themselves pregnant and don't want to be blamed. *Again, these are just excused for blaming the victim.*

CRITICAL THINKING

Agree or disagree with the following statement, and support your answer: A woman who walks in a dangerous neighborhood or talks to a stranger deserves what she gets.

Rape myths create a social climate that legitimizes rape. Although both men and women are susceptible to rape myths, researchers find that college men show greater acceptance of rape myths than do college women (Maxwell et al., 2003; Van Wie & Gross, 2001). Men also cling more stubbornly to myths about date rape than do women, even following date rape education classes designed to challenge these views (Maxwell et al., 2003). Such myths do not occur in a social vacuum. They are related to other social attitudes, including gender-role stereotyping, perception of sex as adversarial, and acceptance of violence in relationships (Yost & Zurbriggen, 2006). The nearby Closer Look feature will afford you insight as to whether you harbor myths that legitimize rape.

Many observers note that our society pushes males into socially and sexually dominant roles (Malamuth et al., 2005). Males are often reinforced from childhood for aggressive and competitive behavior. Gender typing may lead men to reject "feminine" traits such as tenderness and empathy that might restrain aggression (Davis & Liddell, 2002; Shultz et al., 2000).

Research with college students supports the connection between stereotypical masculine identification and tendencies to rape or condone rape. Studies have compared students who believed strictly in traditional gender roles with student holding less rigid attitudes. The traditionalists express a greater likelihood of committing rape, are more accepting of violence against women, are more likely to blame rape survivors, and are more aroused by depictions of rape (Malamuth et al., 2000; Raichle & Lambert, 2000). College men who identify with the traditional masculine gender role more often report pushing women verbally and by force (Steinfeldt & Steinfeldt, 2012; Yost & Zurbriggen, 2006).

Do the lessons learned in competitive sports predispose young American males to sexual violence (Steinfeldt & Steinfeldt, 2012)? Boys are often exposed to coaches who emphasize winning at all costs. They are taught to be dominant and to vanquish their opponents, even if winning means injuring or taking out the opposition (Steinfeldt & Steinfeldt, 2012). Does this philosophy carry over from the playing field into relationships with women?

Sexual behavior and sports in our culture are linked through common idioms. A young man may be taunted by his friends after a date with a woman with such questions as "Did you score?" or more bluntly, "Did you get it in?"

A Closer Look

"Rophies"—The Date Rape Drug

Rophies, roofies, R2, roofenol, roachies, la rocha, rope, or whatever you call it is dubbed the "date rape drug" because it has been slipped into the drinks of unsuspecting women with the effects of lowering their inhibitions, lessening their ability to resist a sexual assault, and, when mixed with alcohol, sometimes causing blackouts that prevent victims from remembering the assault. For this reason, Rohypnol has also been called "the forget pill," "trip-and-fall," and "mind-eraser." The drug has no taste or odor, so the victims don't realize what is happening when an assailant slips it into a drink. About 10 minutes after taking it, the woman may feel dizzy and disoriented, simultaneously too hot and too cold, or nauseated. She may have difficulty speaking and moving and then pass out. She may "black out" for 8 to 24 hours, with little or no memory of what happened.

Rohypnol is not manufactured or sold legally in the United States, but it is prescribed as a treatment for insomnia and as a sedative hypnotic in other countries. It is in the same class of drugs as the tranquilizer Valium, but about 10 times stronger.

Rohypnol is often used with other drugs, such as alcohol, to create a dramatic "high." Rohypnol intoxication is generally associated with impaired judgment, memory, and motor skills, and can make a victim unable to resist or recall a sexual attack. Effects begin within 30 minutes, peak within two hours, and can persist for eight hours or more.

Here are some ideas for avoiding problems with Rohypnol:

- Be wary about accepting drinks from anyone you don't know well or long enough to trust.
- Don't put your drink down and leave it unattended, even to go to the restroom.
- If you think that you have been a victim, notify authorities immediately.

Spiking a Drink with Rohypnol.

Psychological Characteristics of Rapists: Who Are They?

Although sexual aggressiveness may be embedded within our social fabric, not all men are equally vulnerable to these cultural influences. Personal factors, then, are also involved. Are rapists mentally disturbed? Intellectually deficient? Driven by insatiable sexual urges?

Most researchers acknowledge that sexual motivation plays a key role in rape (Bushman et al., 2003; Malamuth et al., 2005), but a generation ago some social scientists focused more on emotional and social factors. It was noted that rape can be in part motivated by anger, striving toward power, sadism, or some combination of the three. Anger usually motivates the rapist to use more force than needed to obtain compliance and to force the victim into degrading and humiliating acts. Those who are motivated by power seek to control and dominate the victim (Mardorossian, 2002). Sadistic rapists are most vicious; some torture or murder their victims.

Much of our knowledge of the psychological characteristics of rapists derives from studies of samples of incarcerated rapists. One conclusion that emerges is that there is no single type of rapist. Rapists vary in their psychological characteristics, family backgrounds, mental health, and criminal histories (Lalumière et al., 2005a).**TRUTH** OR **FICTION** REVISITED: It is not true that most rapists are mentally ill, even though their crimes might strike observers as being "sick." Generally speaking, rapists are no less intelligent or more mentally ill than other people. However, although many rapists do not show deep psychological disturbance, they do have an anti-social personality that enables them to violate their victims without guilt, shame, anxiety, or empathy (Lalumière et al., 2005a). Some anti-social rapists have long histories of violent behavior (Lalumière et al., 2005a, 2005b). The use of alcohol may also dampen self-restraint and spur sexual aggressiveness.

For some rapists violence and sexual arousal become enmeshed. Thus, they seek to combine sex and violence to enhance their sexual arousal (Lalumière et al., 2005a). Some rapists are more sexually aroused (as measured by the size of erections) by verbal descriptions, films, or audiotapes that portray themes of rape than are other people (Lalumière et al., 2005a, 2005b, 2005c). Other researchers, however, have failed to find deviant patterns of arousal in rapists (Lalumière et al., 2005a, 2005b, 2005c).

Studies of incarcerated rapists may be criticized on grounds that the samples may not represent the total population of rapists. To offset this methodological concern, researchers have turned to the survey method to study men who anonymously report that they have engaged in sexually coercive behaviors, including rape, but have not been identified by the criminal justice system (Locke & Mahalik, 2005; Yost & Zurbriggen, 2006). Sexually coercive men are more likely than other men to do the following:

- Condone rape and violence against women.
- Hold traditional gender-role attitudes.
- Be sexually experienced.
- Be hostile toward women.
- Engage in sexual activity in order to express social dominance.
- Be sexually aroused by depictions of rape.
- Be irresponsible and lack a social conscience.
- Have peer groups, such as fraternities, that pressure them into sexual activity.

Adjustment of Rape Survivors

Many survivors of stranger rape fear for their lives during the attack (Polusny & Arbisi, 2006). Whether or not weapons or threats are used, the experience of being dominated by an unpredictable and threatening assailant is terrifying. The woman does not know whether she will survive and may feel helpless to do anything about it.

Many survivors are in crisis in the days and weeks following the rape (Bryant-Davis, 2011). They have insomnia and cry frequently. They tend to report eating problems, cystitis, headaches, irritability, mood changes, anxiety and depression, and menstrual irregularity (Kaczmarek et al., 2006). They may become withdrawn, sullen, and mistrustful. People in the United States tend to believe that women who are raped are at least partly to blame for the assault (Boros et al., 2005); therefore, some survivors experience feelings of guilt and shame. Emotional distress tends to peak in severity by about three weeks following the assault and generally remains high before beginning to abate about a month or two later (Duke et al., 2008; Littleton & Henderson, 2009). Many survivors encounter more lasting problems. Victims' feelings of being powerless to affect their own fate can endure and change their personalities (Bryant-Davis, 2011). A study of women in the military who had survived rape and physical abuse revealed health problems a decade afterward (Sadler et al., 2000). Some survivors suffer physical injuries and STIs.

Survivors may also encounter problems at work, such as problems relating to co-workers or bosses or difficulties in concentrating. Relationships with spouses or partners may suffer. Disturbances in sexual functioning are common and may endure. Survivors often report a lack of sexual desire, fear of sex, and difficulty becoming aroused (Bryant-Davis, 2011).

Most women fail to report sexual assaults to police. Reasons include fears of retaliation, the social stigma attached to the survivors of rape, doubts that others will believe them, feelings that it would be hopeless to try to bring charges against the perpetrator, concerns about negative publicity, and fears about the emotional distress to which they would be subjected if the case were to go to trial (Bryant-Davis, 2011). 👁

◉ ▷ Watch the Video
Vets Sue Pentagon Over Sexual Abuse Cases
on **MyDevelopmentLab**

Real Students, Real Questions

Q *A friend of mine was raped at a party last semester. I took her to the hospital, but she refused to report it to the police. How can I convince her?*

A Good question. When one is at a party, and perhaps drinking and making out, one may not be sure where permission ended and rape began. There is also such a history of blaming the victim for sexual assault, or at least trotting out in public the victim's sexual history, that it is no surprise that your friend is reluctant to contact the criminal justice system. Perhaps she would talk it over first with a private attorney. But that takes money. She can also call the National Sexual Assault Hotline at 1-800-656-HOPE (4673). The call can be made 24/7. It's free, and all info will be kept confidential. But ultimately, your friend will have to decide for herself.

Many survivors of rape suffer from posttraumatic stress disorder.

RAPE AND PSYCHOLOGICAL DISORDERS

Rape survivors are at higher-than-average risk of developing anxiety disorders and depression, and of abusing alcohol and other substances. The vast majority of female rape victims report experiencing the anxiety disorder known as **posttraumatic stress disorder (PTSD)** (NISVS, 2011). PTSD is brought on by exposure to a traumatic event and is also often seen in soldiers who were in combat. People with PTSD may have flashbacks to the traumatic experience, disturbing dreams, emotional numbing, and nervousness. This disorder may persist for years. The person may also develop fears of situations connected with the traumatic event. For example, a woman who was raped on an elevator may develop a fear of riding elevators by herself. Researchers also report that women who blame themselves for the rape tend to suffer more severe depression and adjustment problems, including sexual problems (Kaczmarek et al., 2006; Vickerman & Margolina, 2009).

IF YOU ARE RAPED . . .

Here are some suggestions about what to do if you should be raped.

- Don't change anything about your body—don't wash, don't even comb your hair. Leave your clothes as they are. Otherwise you could destroy evidence.
- Strongly consider reporting the incident to police. You may prevent another woman from being assaulted, and you will be taking charge, starting on the path from victim to survivor.
- Ask a relative or friend to take you to a hospital if you can't get an ambulance or a police car. If you call the hospital, tell them why you're requesting an ambulance—the staff may be able to send someone trained to deal with rape cases.
- Seek help in an assertive way. Seek medical help. Injuries you are unaware of may be detected. Insist that a written or photographic record be made to document your condition. If you decide to file charges, the prosecutor may need this evidence to obtain a conviction.
- Question health professionals. Ask about your biological risks. Ask about prophylactic treatment against HIV infection. Ask what treatments are available. Ask for whatever will help make you comfortable. Call the shots. Demand confidentiality if that's what you want. Refuse what you don't want.

  If a rape crisis center or rape hotline is available in your area, you may wish to call for advice. A rape crisis volunteer may be available to accompany you to the hospital and help see you through the medical evaluation and police investigation if you report the attack. It is not unusual for rape survivors to try to erase the details of the rape from their minds. However, trying to remember details clearly will permit you to provide an accurate description of the rapist to the police, including his clothing, type of car, and so on. This information may help police apprehend the rapist and assist in the prosecution.

TREATMENT OF RAPE SURVIVORS

The treatment of survivors typically involves helping the woman (the vast majority are female) through the crisis following the attack and then helping to foster long-term adjustment (Bryant-Davis, 2011). Crisis intervention typically provides the survivor with support and information to help her express her feelings and develop strategies for coping with the trauma. Psychotherapy, involving group or individual approaches, can help the survivor cope with the emotional consequences of rape, avoid self-blame, improve self-esteem, validate the welter of feelings surrounding the experience, and help her establish or maintain loving relationships. Therapists

Posttraumatic stress disorder (PTSD) A type of stress reaction brought on by a traumatic event and characterized by flashbacks of the experience in the form of disturbing dreams or intrusive recollections, a sense of emotional numbing or restricted range of feelings, and heightened body arousal.

also recognize the importance of helping the rape survivor mobilize social support. Family, friends, religious leaders, and health-care specialists are all potential sources of help. However, women often find that those from whom they seek support, including family and clergy, blame them for the attack (Bryant-Davis, 2011). In major cities and many towns, concerned men and women have formed rape crisis centers and hotlines, peer counseling groups, and referral agencies geared to assessing and treating survivors' needs after the assault. Some counselors are specially trained to mediate between survivors of rape and their loved ones (husbands, lovers, and so on). These counselors help people to discuss and work through the often complex emotional legacy of rape. Phone numbers for these services can be obtained from feminist groups (for example, your local office of the National Organization for Women [NOW]), the police department, or the telephone directory.

A Closer Look

Is Rape Serious?

When a woman reports a rape, her body is a crime scene. She is typically asked to undress over a large sheet of white paper to collect hairs or fibers, and then her body is examined with an ultraviolet light, photographed and thoroughly swabbed for the rapist's DNA.

It's a grueling and invasive process that can last four to six hours and produces a "rape kit"—which, it turns out, often sits around for months or years, unopened and untested. Stunningly often, the rape kit isn't tested at all because it's not deemed a priority. If it is tested, this happens at such a lackadaisical pace that it may be a year or more before there are results (if expedited, results are technically possible in a week).

So while we have breakthrough DNA technologies to find culprits and exculpate innocent suspects, we aren't using them properly—and those who work in this field believe the reason is an underlying doubt about the seriousness of some rape cases. In short, this isn't justice; it's indifference.

A colleague of mine wrote about a 43-year-old legal secretary who was raped repeatedly in her home in Los Angeles as her son slept in another room. The attacker forced the woman to clean herself in an attempt to destroy the evidence. The detective on the case thought this

meant that the perpetrator was a habitual offender who would strike again. He rushed the rape kit to the crime lab but was told to expect a delay of more than one year. So he personally drove the kit 350 miles to deliver it to the state lab in Sacramento. Even there, the backlog resulted in a four-month delay—but then it produced a "cold hit," a match in a database of the DNA of previous offenders. Yet in the months while the rape kit sat on a shelf, the suspect had allegedly struck twice more. Police said he broke into the homes of a pregnant woman and a 17-year-old girl, sexually assaulting each of them.

"The criminal justice system is still ill equipped to deal with rape and not that good at moving rape cases forward," notes Sarah Tofte, who wrote a devastating report for Human Rights Watch about the rape-kit backlog. The report found that in Los Angeles County, there were at last count 12,669 rape kits sitting in police storage facilities. More than 450 of these kits had sat around for more than 10 years, and in many cases, the statute of limitations had expired. Since Human Rights Watch began its investigation, the department had resolved to test rape kits routinely—and as a result, cold hits have doubled.

Why don't police departments treat rape kits with urgency? One reason is

probably expense—each kit can cost up to $1,500 to test—but there also seems to be a broad distaste for rape cases as murky, ambiguous, and difficult to prosecute, particularly when they involve (as they often do) alcohol or acquaintance rape. "They talk about the victims' credibility in a way that they don't talk about the credibility of victims of other crimes," Ms. Tofte said.

While the backlog and desultory handling of rape kits are nationwide problems, there is one shining exception: New York City has made a concerted effort over the last decade to test every kit that comes in. The result has been at least 2,000 cold hits in rape cases, and the arrest rate for reported cases of rape in New York City rose from 40 percent to 70 percent, according to Human Rights Watch.

Some Americans used to argue that it was impossible to rape an unwilling woman. Few people say that today, or say publicly that a woman "asked for it" if she wore a short skirt. But the refusal to test rape kits seems a throwback to the same antediluvian skepticism about rape as a traumatic crime.

Source: Nicholas D. Kristof. (2009, April 30). Is rape serious? *The New York Times.*

A review of the effectiveness of various kinds of therapy for survivors of rape found that the treatment targets are most often post-traumatic stress disorder, depression, and anxiety (Vickerman & Margolina, 2009). The women in the reviewed studies most often experienced chronic (enduring) symptoms. The most effective forms of therapy were cognitive-behavioral (helping the victim view her assault in less self-defeating ways, such as encouraging her not to blame herself for the attack) and helping her approach rather than avoid the "scene of the crime" and other frightful factors so that she learns to cope with them.

Of course, if we *prevent* rape, we may not need to help as many survivors adjust. Check the chapter's "My Life, My Sexuality" feature.

Childhood Sexual Abuse

Many view sexual assaults on children—such as those committed by Jerry Sandusky—as among the most heinous of crimes. Children who are sexually assaulted often suffer social and emotional problems that impair their development and persist into adulthood, affecting their self-esteem and their ability to form intimate relationships.

No one knows how many children are sexually abused, although researcher David Finkelhor (2012) places the number at about 200,000 to 300,000 annually. (Finkelhor places the number of children who experience sexual harassment at close to 2 *million*.) Although most sexually abused children are girls, one-quarter to one-third—including Sandusky's victims—are boys (Edwards et al., 2003). An analysis of 65 studies in 22 countries concluded that 7 to 8% of boys and 19 to 20% of girls have been sexually abused (Pereda et al., 2009). The actual percentages might be higher because many people fail to report incidents due to faulty memory, shame, or embarrassment.

Sexual abuse of children ranges from exhibitionism, kissing, fondling, and sexual touching to oral sex and anal intercourse and, with girls, vaginal intercourse. Acts such as touching children's sexual organs while changing or bathing them, sleeping with children, or appearing nude before them are open to interpretation and often innocent. Sexual contact between an adult and a child is abusive, even if the child is willing, since children are legally incapable of consenting. Although the age of consent varies among the states, sexual relations between adults and children below the age of consent are a criminal offense in every state.

Sexual abuse also occurs over the Internet, with pornographic images and invitations to join XXX chat rooms, to interact with women who disrobe online, and to contact prostitutes and women who are (supposedly) seeking clandestine affairs "pop up." In 2010, 9% of children report receiving an unwanted sexual solicitation—a number which actually represents a decrease of about 50% since 2000 (Jones et al., 2012). About one in four children (23%) reported an unwanted exposure to pornography, down from one in three (34%) in 2000. Perhaps the Internet is becoming a safer place for children as parents apply filtering software; and browsers such as Safari and Windows have some filtering mechanisms of their own.

Voluntary sexual activity *between children* of similar ages is not sexual abuse. Children often engage in consensual sex play with peers or siblings, as in "playing doctor" or in mutual masturbation. Although such experiences may be recalled in adulthood with feelings of shame or guilt, they are not typically as harmful as experiences with adults. When the experience involves coercion, or when the other child is significantly older or in a position of power over the younger child, the sexual contact may be considered sexual abuse.

CRITICAL THINKING

Why do you think that most cases of child sexual abuse are not reported to the authorities?

PATTERNS OF ABUSE

Children from stable, middle-class families appear to be generally at lower risk of encountering sexual abuse than children from poorer, single parent, or stepfamilies (Amodeo et al., 2006; Turner et al., 2006). In most cases, children who are sexually abused are not accosted by the proverbial stranger lurking in the school yard. Most molesters are close to them: relatives, steprelatives, family friends, and neighbors (Turner et al., 2006).

Parents who discover that their child has been abused by a family member are often reluctant to notify authorities (Finkelhor et al., 2012). Some may feel that such problems are "family matters" that are best kept private. Others may be reluctant to notify authorities for fear that it may shame the family or that they may be held accountable for failing to protect the child. The decision to report abuse to the police depends largely on the relationship between the abuser and the person who discovers the abuse (Finkelhor et al., 2012). In a Finkelhor survey, none of the parents whose children were abused by family members notified authorities. By contrast, most parents whose children have been abused by strangers did so.

Typically, the child initially trusts the abuser. Physical force is seldom needed to gain compliance, largely because of the child's helplessness, gullibility, and submission to adult authority. Whereas most sexually abused children are abused only once, those who are abused by family members are more likely to suffer repeated abuse.

Genital fondling is the most common type of abuse (Edwards et al., 2003). In one sample of women who had been molested in childhood, most contacts involved genital fondling (38% of cases) or exhibitionism (20% of cases). Intercourse is rare. Repeated abuse by a family member, however, commonly follows a pattern that begins with fondling during preschool, progresses to oral sex or mutual masturbation during the early school years, and then to penetration (vaginal or anal intercourse) in preadolescence or adolescence.

Abused children rarely report the abuse, often because of fear of retaliation from the abuser or because they believe they will be blamed for it. Adults may suspect abuse if a child shows sudden personality changes or develops fears, problems in school, or eating or sleeping problems. A pediatrician may discover physical signs of abuse during a medical exam. The average age at which most children are first sexually abused ranges from 6 to 12 years for girls and 7 to 10 years for boys (Finkelhor et al., 2005b).

TYPES OF ABUSERS

The overwhelming majority of people who sexually abuse children (both boys and girls) are males (Turner et al., 2006). Although most child abusers are adults, some are adolescents. Male adolescent sex offenders are more likely than other adolescents to have been molested themselves as boys. Some adolescent sex offenders may be imitating their own victimization. Adolescent child molesters also tend to feel socially inadequate and to be fearful of social interactions with age-mates of the other gender.

Although the great majority of sexual abusers are male, the number of female sexual abusers may be greater than has been generally believed (Zernike, 2005). Many female sexual abusers may go undetected because society accords women a much freer range of physical contact with children than it does men. A woman who fondles a child might be seen as affectionate, or at worst seductive, whereas a man would be more likely to be perceived as a child molester.

Mark Foley. Foley abruptly resigned from the House of Representatives when it became known that he had sent seductive e-mails and instant messages to underage boys who served as pages in Congress.

Watch the **Video**
Anonymous: Pedophilia
on **MyDevelopmentLab**

Pedophilia A paraphilia that is defined by sexual attraction to children.

CRITICAL THINKING
Why is it assumed that sex between an adult woman and an adolescent boy is less damaging to the adolescent than sex between an adult man and an adolescent girl? What political issues are involved in attempting to decide whether or not sex between an adult woman and an adolescent boy be treated differently by the law than sex between an adult man and an adolescent girl?

What motivates a woman to sexually abuse children, even her own children? Some female abusers have histories of becoming dependent on, or rejected by, abusive males. Some appear to have been manipulated into engaging in sexual abuse by their husbands. Others appear to have unmet emotional needs and low self-esteem and may have been seeking acceptance, closeness, and attention though sexual acts with children (Zernike, 2005). Some, motivated by unresolved feelings of anger, revenge, powerlessness, or jealousy, may view their own and others' children as safe targets for venting these feelings. Some view their crimes as expressions of love.

Sexual interest in children may also be motivated by unusual patterns of sexual arousal. This brings us to pedophilia.

PEDOPHILIA

In 2006, Florida representative Mark Foley abruptly resigned from the House of Representatives when it became known that he had been pursuing congressional pages—predominantly boys aged 16 or so—for several years via e-mails and instant messages. His lawyer came out and stated that Foley was gay and a closet alcoholic. After resigning, Foley admitted himself somewhere for alcohol rehabilitation. Alcoholics quipped that Foley had given alcoholism a bad name, and gay males protested that the great majority of gay males did not seek relationships with underage boys. (We have not yet heard protests from closets.) In any event, Foley had admittedly pedophilic interests, although his lawyer protested he had never actually engaged in a pedophilic *act*.

Pedophilia is a paraphilia (see Chapter 17) in which an adult finds children to be the preferred and sometimes exclusive objects of sexual desire. The prevalence of pedophilia in the general population is unknown. Some pedophiles are so distressed by their urges that they never act on them. But many molest young children and adolescents, often repeatedly.

Although pedophiles are sometimes called child molesters, not all child molesters are pedophiles. Pedophilia involves persistent or recurrent sexual attraction to children. Some molesters, however, may seek sexual contacts only with children when they are under unusual stress or lack other sexual outlets. Thus, they do not meet the clinical definition of pedophilia.

Pedophiles are almost exclusively male (Finkelhor, 2005b), although some female pedophiles have been reported. Some pedophiles are sexually attracted only to children. Others are sexually attracted to adults as well. Some pedophiles limit their sexual interest in children to incestuous relationships with family members. Others abuse children to whom they are unrelated. Some pedophiles limit their sexual interest in children to looking at them or undressing them. Others fondle them or masturbate in their presence. Some manipulate children into penetration.

Children tend not to be worldly-wise. They can often be taken in by pedophiles who tell them that they would like to show them something, teach them something, or do something with them that they would like. Some pedophiles seek to gain the child's affection and discourage the child from disclosing the sexual activity by showering the child with attention and gifts. Others threaten the child or the child's family to prevent disclosure.

Although most pedophiles may not wear trench coats and hang around school yards, there is research evidence that many of them have personality disorders (Madsen et al., 2006). Research finds them to be emotionally unstable, disagreeable, angry, impulsive, and mistrustful.

Some pedophiles that are lacking in social skills may turn to children after failing to establish gratifying relationships with adult women. Yet psychological

A Closer Look

The Siren Song of Sex with Boys

When Sandra Beth Geisel, a former Catholic schoolteacher, was sentenced to six months in jail for having sex with a 16-year-old student, she received sympathy from a surprising source.

The judge, Stephen Herrick of Albany County Court in New York, told her she had "crossed the line" into "totally unacceptable" behavior. But, he added, the teenager was a victim in only the strictly legal sense. "He was certainly not victimized by you in any other sense of the word," the judge said. The prosecutor and a lawyer for the boy's family called the judge's comments outrageous. But is it possible that the 16-year-old wasn't really harmed?

The last few years have produced a spate of cases where women are prosecuted for having sex with boys: Debra LaFave of Florida, another teacher, was convicted of sleeping with a 14-year-old student; Lisa Lynette Clark of Georgia was impregnated by her son's 15-year-old friend, whom she married a day before she was arrested; Silvia Johnson of Colorado was sentenced to 30 years for having sex with teenagers and providing drugs and alcohol.

Certainly no one doubts that a teacher who has sex with her students should lose her job. Or that a 37-year-old mother should not find herself pregnant by her son's 15-year-old friend. Or that a 41-year-old mother who provides sex, drugs, and alcohol to teenagers so she can be cool among her daughter's friends is troubled.

But when the women face prison, questions are raised about where to set the age of consent. And because many of those named as victims refused to testify against the women in what they said were consensual relationships, not everyone agrees that the cases involve child abuse.

"We need to untangle the moral issues from the psychological issues from the legal issues," said Carol Tavris, the author of *The Mismeasure of Women* and a social psychologist. "That's the knot." She added: "You may not like something, but does that mean it should be illegal? If we have laws that are based on moral notions and developmental notions that are outdated, do we need to change the laws?"

Though it might seem that way from the headlines, women having sex with teenage boys is not new. A federal Department of Education study called "Educator Sexual Misconduct," released in 2004, found that 40 percent of the educators who had been reported for sexual misconduct with students were women.

Charol Shakeshaft, the author of the study and a professor of education at Hofstra University, said that even when the woman is not a teacher, the relationships are not healthy. "A 16-year-old is just not fully developed," she said. "Male brains tend to develop the part that can make decisions about whether it is a wise thing to do later."

Prosecutions of women have been rising slightly in the last several years, said David Finkelhor, director of the Crimes against Children Research Center at the University of New Hampshire. Mr. Finkelhor says he believes that the scandal involving sexual abuse by priests called more attention to cases with teachers and other authority figures. But the cases also reflect a decline in the double standard applied to men and women, brought on, he said, by increasing numbers of female prosecutors and police officers who may not buy into the traditional notion that a boy who has sex with an older woman just got lucky.

But several studies have raised questions about whether these cases should be filed under child sex abuse.

The most controversial study was published in 1998 in *Psychological Bulletin*. The article, a statistical reanalysis of 59 studies of college students who said they were sexually abused in childhood, concluded that the effects of such abuse "were neither pervasive nor typically intense, and that men reacted much less negatively than women."

The researchers questioned the practice, common in many studies, of lumping all sexual abuse together. They contended that treating all types equally presented problems that, they wrote, "are perhaps most apparent when contrasting cases such as the repeated rape of a 5-year-old girl by her father and the willing sexual involvement of a mature 15-year-old adolescent boy with an unrelated adult."

Pamela Rogers Turner. Pamela Rogers Turner was sentenced to nine months for having sex with a minor boy.

In the first case, serious harm may result, the article said, but the second case "may represent only a violation of social norms with no implication for personal harm."

They suggested substituting the term "adult–adolescent sex" for child abuse in some cases where the sex was consensual.

"*Abuse* implies harm in a scientific usage, and the term should not be in use if there is consent and no evidence of harm," said Bruce Rind, an author of the study and a psychology professor at Temple University.

This view could prove a hard sell, politically and legally. The article in *Psychological Bulletin* was roundly criticized by prominent conservatives and denounced in Congress, as was the judge in Ms. Geisel's case. Bruce Gaeta, a New Jersey judge, was reprimanded by the state's highest court for characterizing an encounter between a 43-year-old female teacher and a 13-year-old boy who had been a student as "just something between two people that clicked beyond the teacher–student relationship."

Pamela Rogers Turner, a Tennessee teacher, was sentenced to nine months in jail for sex with a 13-year-old boy.

Thirteen? Professor Rind and others agree that that is too low to set the age of consent, making 12 truly out of bounds— the age of Vili Fualaau when he began having sex with the most infamous of the teachers in sex scandals, Mary Kay LeTourneau. (The fact that a decade later the two are married and registered for china at Macy's has not changed anyone's mind.)

But Professor Rind and others point out that Canada and about half of Europe have set the age of consent at 14 after recommendations by national commissions. To set it much higher, as most states

do, they say, ignores the research, and the hormones.

Even those who argue for more protection of children agree that the laws in this country can be arbitrary. In Ms. Geisel's case, she was caught first with a 17-year-old student, but because he was of legal age, she was charged only after his 16-year-old friend came forward and said they had taken turns having sex. Can a few months make such a difference?

"I'm torn, I don't know," Professor Shakeshaft said. "Teachers are always wrong. And it would be my belief that people aren't formed by 16. On the other hand, my mother married my father at 16 and they were married 65 years."

Professor Finkelhor agrees that there is variability among cases and teenagers but says it's better to err on the side of safety.

investigation has found that many pedophiles distort reality in ways that enable them to pursue sexual activity with children (Marziano et al., 2006). Pedophiles often

- see children as sexual beings who want to have sex with adults.
- believe that sex does not harm children and may be beneficial.
- think of themselves as being so important that they are entitled to sex with whomever they want.
- see others are dangerous and controlling and think they must fight to gain control of their lives.
- believe they cannot control their impulses.

INCEST: BREAKING TABOOS

Incest involves people who are related, usually by blood, or *consanguineous.* Although a few societies have permitted incestuous pairings among royalty, most known cultures have an incest taboo (Argentieri, 2005).

Perspectives on the Incest Taboo Speculations about the origin of incest taboos abound. One explanation holds that the incest taboo developed because it was adaptive for ancient humans to prevent the harmful effects of inbreeding that may result when genetic defects or diseases are carried within family bloodlines (Ellis & Bjorklund, 2005). Our ancient ancestors lacked knowledge of genetics, but they may have observed that certain health problems tended to run in families. Evidence suggests that the offspring of close relatives bear an increased rate of genetic diseases, mental retardation, and other physical abnormalities. Inbreeding may also be counterproductive to survival because it reduces genetic variation in the gene pool. Therefore, it can reduce the ability of the population to adapt to changes in the environment.

The incest taboo may also play a part in maintaining stability in the family and establishing kinship ties within the larger group (Argentieri, 2005). The anthropologist Bronislaw Malinowski (1927), for example, argued that the incest taboo reduces sexual competition within the family. If left uncontrolled, competition would create rivalry and hostility such that the family might be unable to function as a unit. Since the family unit fosters survival of a society, the incest taboo may have developed as a means of keeping the family intact.

Types of Incest Most of our knowledge of incestuous relationships concerns father–daughter incest. Why? Most identified cases involve fathers who were eventually incarcerated.

Incest Marriage or sexual relations between people who are so closely related that sexual relations are prohibited and punishable by law.

About 1% of a sample of women in five American cities reported a sexual encounter with a father or stepfather (Anderson, 2006). **TRUTH** OR FICTION REVISITED: But brother–sister incest, not parent–child incest, is the most common type of incest (Caffaro & Conn-Caffaro, 2005). Brother–sister incest is also believed to be greatly underreported, possibly because it tends to be transient and is apparently less harmful than parent–child incest. Finkelhor (1990) found that 21% of the college men in his sample, and 39% of the college women, reported incestuous relationships with a sibling of the other sex. Only 4% reported an incestuous relationship with their fathers. Mother–daughter incest is the least common form of incest, but it does occur (Bartolo, 2005; Turton, 2005).

Let us further consider the two most common incest patterns: father–daughter incest and brother–sister incest.

Father–daughter incest often begins with affectionate cuddling or embraces and then progresses to teasing sexual play, lengthy caresses, hugs, kisses, and genital contact, even penetration. In some cases genital contact occurs more abruptly, usually when the father has been drinking or has been arguing with his wife. Force is not typically used to gain compliance, but daughters are sometimes physically overcome and injured by their fathers.

In sibling incest, the brother usually initiates sexual activity and assumes the dominant role. One study reported that penetration was more frequent in brother–sister incest (71%) than in stepfather–stepdaughter incest (27%) or father–daughter incest (35%) (Cyr et al., 2002). Some younger brothers and sisters may view their sexual activity as natural experimentation or play and not realize it is taboo.

Evidence on the effects of incest between brothers and sisters is mixed. In a study of college undergraduates, those who reported childhood incest with siblings did not reveal greater evidence of sexual adjustment problems than other undergraduates (Greenwald & Leitenberg, 1989). Sibling incest is most likely to be harmful when it is forced or when parental response is harsh (Adams, 2007).

Family Factors in Incest Incest frequently occurs within the context of general family disruption, as in families in which there is spouse abuse, a dysfunctional marriage, or alcoholic or physically abusive parents (Welldon, 2005). Stressful events in the father's life, such as the loss of a job or problems at work, often precede the initiation of incest.

Fathers who abuse older daughters tend to be domineering and authoritarian with their families (Waterman, 1986). Fathers who abuse younger, preschool daughters are more likely to be passive, dependent, and low in self-esteem. As Waterman (1986) notes:

> [The fathers] may need soothing and comforting, and may feel especially safe with preschool children: "I felt safe with her . . . . I didn't have to perform. She was so little that I knew she wouldn't and couldn't hurt me." (p. 215)

Marriages in incestuous families tend to be characterized by an uneven power relationship between the spouses. The abusive father is usually dominant. Another thread that frequently runs through incestuous families is a troubled sexual relationship between the spouses. The wife often rejects the husband sexually (Waterman, 1986).

In their classic research, Gebhard and his colleagues (1965) found that many fathers who committed incest with their daughters were religiously devout, fundamentalist, and moralistic. Perhaps such men, when sexually frustrated, are less likely to seek extramarital and extrafamilial sexual outlets or to turn to masturbation as a sexual release. He turns to a daughter as a wife surrogate, often when he has been drinking alcohol (Gebhard et al., 1965). The daughter may become, in her father's fantasies, the "woman of the house." This fantasy may become his justification for continuing the incestuous relationship. In some incestuous families, a role reversal occurs. The abused daughter assumes many of the mother's responsibilities for managing the household and caring for the younger children.

Incestuous abuse is often repeated from generation to generation. One study found that in 154 cases of children who were sexually abused within the family, more than one-third of the male offenders and about one-half of the mothers had either been abused themselves or were exposed to abuse as children (Faller, 1989).

EFFECTS OF SEXUAL ABUSE ON CHILDREN

The effects of sexual abuse are variable, and there is no single identifiable syndrome that emerges from sexual abuse (Anderson, 2006; Resick, 2003). Nevertheless, sexual abuse often inflicts great psychological harm on the child, whether perpetrated by a family member, acquaintance, or stranger. Children who are sexually abused may suffer from a litany of short- and long-term psychological complaints, including anger, depression, anxiety, eating disorders, inappropriate sexual behavior, aggressive behavior, self-destructive behavior, sexual promiscuity, drug abuse, suicide attempts, posttraumatic stress disorder, low self-esteem, sexual dysfunction, mistrust of others, and feelings of detachment (Edwards et al., 2003). Sexual abuse may also have physical effects such as genital injuries and cause psychosomatic problems such as stomach aches and headaches.

Abused children commonly "act out." Younger children have tantrums or display aggressive or antisocial behavior. Older children turn to substance abuse (Anderson, 2006; Herrera & McCloskey, 2003). Some abused children become withdrawn and retreat into fantasy or refuse to leave the house. Regressive behaviors, such as thumb sucking, fear of the dark, and fear of strangers, are also common among sexually abused children. On the heels of the assault and in the ensuing years, many survivors of childhood sexual abuse—like many rape survivors—show signs of posttraumatic stress disorder. They have flashbacks, nightmares, numbing of emotions, and feelings of estrangement from others (Herrera & McCloskey, 2003).

Sexual development of abused children may also become shaped in dysfunctional ways. The survivor may become prematurely sexually active or promiscuous in adolescence and adulthood (Anderson, 2006). Researchers find that adolescent girls who are sexually abused tend to have consensual sex at earlier ages than nonabused peers (Browning, 2002; Herrera & McCloskey, 2003).

Researchers generally find more similarities than differences between the sexes with respect to the effects of sexual abuse in childhood (Edwards et al., 2003). For example, both boys and girls tend to suffer fears and sleep disturbance. There are some sex differences, however. The most consistent sex difference appears to be that boys more often "externalize" their problems, perhaps by becoming more physically aggressive. Girls more often "internalize" their difficulties, as by becoming depressed (Anderson, 2006).

Late adolescence and early adulthood seem to pose especially difficult periods for survivors of childhood sexual abuse. Studies of women in these age groups reveal more psychological and social problems in abused women (Anderson, 2006; Herrera & McCloskey, 2003). Women who blame themselves for the abuse apparently have relatively lower self-esteem and more depression than those who do not (Edwards et al., 2003).

PREVENTION OF CHILDHOOD SEXUAL ABUSE

Many of us were taught by our parents never to accept a ride or an offer of candy from a stranger. However, many instances of sexual abuse are perpetrated by familiar adults, often a family member or friend (Zielbauer, 2000). Prevention programs

CRITICAL THINKING
Why do you think that boys and girls tend to react differently to childhood sexual abuse?

Real Students, Real Questions

Q *Does being sexually abused as a child mean someone will sexually abuse their children?*

A It puts a person in a higher-risk category for abusing his or her own children. However, when one is an adult, child abuse is a choice and not a necessity based on one's history. Anyone who feels in danger of harming a child can call 1-800-4-A-CHILD or another child abuse hotline for nonjudgmental help and support.

help children understand what sexual abuse is and how they can avoid it. In addition to learning to avoid strangers, children need to recognize the differences between acceptable touching, as in an affectionate embrace or pat on the head, and unacceptable or "bad" touching. Even elementary-school–age children can learn the distinction between "good touching and bad touching." School-based programs can help prepare children to handle an actual encounter with a molester. Children who receive training are more likely to use strategies such as running away, yelling, or saying no when they are threatened by an abuser. They are also more likely to report incidents to adults.

Researchers recognize that children can easily be intimidated or overpowered by adults or older children (Miller, 2005). Children may be unable to say no in a sexually abusive situation, even though they want to and know it is the right thing to do. Although children may not always be able to prevent abuse, they can be encouraged to tell someone about it. Most prevention programs emphasize teaching children messages such as "It's not your fault," "Never keep a bad or scary secret," and "Always tell your parents about this, especially if someone says you shouldn't tell them."

Children also need to be alerted to the types of threats they might receive for disclosing the abuse. They are more likely to resist threats if they are reassured that they will be believed if they disclose the abuse, that their parents will continue to love them, and that they and their families will be protected from the molester.

School-based prevention programs focus on protecting the child. In most states, teachers and helping professionals are required to report suspected abuse to authorities. Tighter controls and better screening are needed to monitor the hiring of day care employees. Administrators and teachers in preschool and day-care facilities also need to be educated to recognize the signs of sexual abuse and to report suspected cases. Treatment programs to help people who are sexually attracted to children *before* they commit abusive acts would also be of use.

TREATMENT OF SURVIVORS OF SEXUAL ABUSE

Because the majority of cases of sexual abuse go unreported during childhood, psychotherapy in adulthood can be the first opportunity for survivors to confront leftover feelings of pain, anger, and misplaced guilt (Finkelhor et al., 2005a). Group or individual therapy can help improve survivors' self-esteem and ability to develop intimate relationships. Social support is an important factor in helping survivors of childhood sexual abuse maintain their self-esteem and minimize the stress they experience (Hyman et al., 2003).

Sexual abuse of children is a devastating crime. How do we prevent it?

Many therapists recommend a comprehensive approach: individual therapy for the child, mother, and father; group therapy for the adolescent or even preadolescent survivor; art therapy or play therapy for the younger child (e.g., using drawings or puppets to express feelings); marital counseling for the parents; and family therapy for the entire family.

Treatment of Rapists and Child Molesters

Treating offenders? Just what does *treatment* mean? When a helping professional treats someone, the goal is usually to help that individual. When we speak of treating a sex offender, the goal is as likely, or more likely, to be to help society by eliminating the problem behavior.

Rapists and child molesters are criminals, not patients. Most convicted rapists and child molesters are incarcerated as a form of punishment, not treatment. They may receive psychological treatment or rehabilitation in prison to help prepare them for release and reentry into society, however. The most common form of treatment is group therapy, which is based on the belief that although offenders may fool counselors, they do not easily fool one another. Yet, most incarcerated sex offenders receive little or no treatment.

The results of prison-based treatment programs are mixed at best. Consider a Canadian study of 54 rapists who participated in a treatment program. Following release from prison, 28% were later convicted of a sexual offense, and 43% were convicted of a violent offense (Rice et al., 1990; Rice & Harris, 2011). Treatment also failed to curb recidivism among a sample of 136 child molesters (Rice & Harris, 2011).

More promising findings may result from programs incorporating cognitive-behavioral techniques such as empathy training and covert sensitization (Ho & Ross, 2012). Empathy training is intended to increase the offender's sensitivity to his victims. One empathy exercise had offenders write about their crimes from the perspective of the victim. Covert sensitization can be used to help offenders resist deviant sex fantasies, which often lead to deviant behavior. The offender would pair, in his imagination, scenes involving rape and molestation with aversive consequences. A child molester might fantasize about sexually approaching a child, only to find himself confronted by police officers. However, "the jury is out" on the effectiveness of cognitive-behavioral—or any other psychological—treatment of sex offenders (Ho & Ross, 2012).

CASTRATION—SURGICAL AND CHEMICAL

Pavel sought surgical castration; most others do not. But in a few places—including the state of Louisiana—it may be required by law for certain sex offenses. The Council of Europe's antitorture committee has called surgical castration "invasive, irreversible, and mutilating." Nevertheless, the Czech Republic has allowed some 94 sex offenders to be surgically castrated over the past decade, and is, for now, the only European country that uses the procedure. European countries are now debating use of chemical or surgical castration for some sex offenders (Bilefsky, 2009).

Castration reduces testosterone levels and, consequently, offenders' sex drives. Despite the case of Pavel, experts do not agree on whether castration helps sex offenders control their sexual urges (Rice & Harris, 2011). Many castrated rapists report lowered sex drives, as might be expected from the reductions in testosterone production that result from the removal of the testes. They may retain sexual interest and remain capable of erection, however. And some do repeat their crimes. Other researchers report lower recidivism rates among castrated offenders than among other offenders.

Surgical castration is an extreme measure. It raises ethical concerns because of its invasive character and irreversibility (Gooren, 2011). Anti-androgen drugs such as Depo-Provera chemically reduce testosterone levels (Thibaut, 2011). Unlike surgical castration, "chemical castration"—via anti-androgen drugs—is reversible (Thibaut, 2011). A typical study showed that anti-androgen drugs decreased pedophilic fantasies and masturbation to pedophilic fantasies in a group of incarcerated offenders (Schober et al., 2005). However, there was no reason to believe that the offenders would voluntarily use such drugs after their release.

Sexual Harassment

Sexual harassment occurs everywhere: in schools and colleges, in the workplace, in the military, and, of course, online (Barak, 2005; Chaiyavej & Morash, 2009; Sullivan, 2006). Even so, **sexual harassment** can be difficult to define. For legal purposes, sexual harassment in the workplace is usually defined as deliberate or repeated unwanted comments, gestures, or physical contact (Craig, 2005; Finkelman, 2005). Sexual harassment makes the workplace or other setting a hostile place. Examples range from unwelcome sexual jokes, overtures, suggestive comments, and sexual innuendos to outright sexual assault, and may include behaviors such as the following:

- Verbal harassment or abuse
- Subtle pressure for sexual activity
- Remarks about a person's clothing, body, or sexual activities
- Leering at or ogling a person's body
- Unwelcome touching, patting, or pinching
- Brushing against a person's body
- Demands for sexual favors accompanied by implied or overt threats concerning one's job or student status
- Physical assault

Men or women can both commit, and be subjected to, sexual harassment. However, an astonishing 99% of harassers are men (see Table 18.1; American Psychological Association, 1998). ◉

Charges of sexual harassment are often ignored or trivialized by co-workers and employers. The victim may hear, "Why make a big deal out of it? It's not like you were attacked in the street." Evidence shows, however, that persons subjected to sexual harassment do suffer from it. Some become physically ill (Rospenda et al., 2005). Others report anxiety, irritability, lowered self-esteem, and anger. Some find harassment on the job so unbearable that they resign (Sims et al., 2005). College women's grades suffer (Huerta et al., 2006). College women have dropped courses, switched majors, even medical residency programs to avoid sexual harassment (Huerta et al., 2006; Stratton et al., 2005).

One reason that sexual harassment is so stressful is that, as with so many other forms of sexual exploitation or coercion, the blame tends to fall on the victim. Some harassers seem to believe that charges of harassment were exaggerated or that the victim "overreacted" or "took me too seriously." In our society, women are expected to be "nice"—to be passive and not "make a scene." The woman who assertively protects her rights may be seen as "strange" and disturbing, or a "troublemaker." "Women are damned if they assert themselves and victimized if they don't" (Chaiyavej & Morash, 2009; Cortina & Wasti, 2005; Witkowska & Gådin, 2005).

◉ **Watch** the **Video**
More and More Men Claiming Sexual Harassment
on **MyDevelopmentLab**

Sexual harassment Deliberate or repeated unsolicited verbal comments, gestures, or physical contact of a sexual nature that is considered to be unwelcome by the recipient.

Table 18.1

Sexual Harassment: Myths and Realities

Myths	Realities
Sexual harassment is rare.	Sexual harassment is extremely widespread. It touches the lives of 40% to 60% of working women, and similar proportions of female students in colleges and universities.
The seriousness of sexual harassment has been exaggerated; most so-called harassment is really trivial and harmless flirtation.	Sexual harassment can be devastating. Studies indicate that most harassment has nothing to do with "flirtation" or sincere sexual or social interest. Rather, it is offensive, often frightening, and insulting to women. Research shows that women are often forced to leave school or jobs to avoid harassment; many experience serious psychological and health-related problems.
Many women make up and report stories of sexual harassment to get back at their employers or others who have angered them.	Research shows that fewer than 1% of complaints are false. Women rarely file false complaints. Women rarely file complaints even when they are justified in doing so.
Women who are sexually harassed generally provoke harassment by the way they look, dress, and behave.	Harassment does not occur because women dress provocatively or initiate sexual activity in the hope of getting promoted and advancing their careers. Studies have found that victims of sexual harassment vary in physical appearance, type of dress, age, and behavior. The only thing they have in common is that more than 99% of them are female.
If you ignore harassment, it will go away.	Harassment does not go away if it is ignored. Research has shown that simply ignoring the behavior is ineffective; harassers generally will not stop on their own. Ignoring such behavior may even be seen as agreement or encouragement.

Source: American Psychological Association, 1998.

Sexual harassment sometimes has more to do with the abuse of power than sexual desire (Chaiyavej & Morash, 2009). Relatively few cases of sexual harassment involve outright requests for sexual favors. Most involve the expression of power as a tactic to control or frighten someone, usually a woman. The harasser is usually in a dominant position and abuses that position by exploiting the victim's vulnerability. Sexual harassment may be used as a tactic of social control. It may be a means of keeping women "in their place." This is especially so in work settings that are traditional male preserves, such as the firehouse, the police department, the construction site, or the military academy—even in certain areas of medical practice, such as surgery (Stratton et al., 2005). Sexual harassment can be a way of expressing resentment and hostility toward women who venture beyond the boundaries of the traditional feminine role.

Sexual harassment is not confined to the workplace or the university. It may also occur between patients and doctors and between therapists and clients. Therapists may use their power and influence to pressure clients into sexual relations. The harassment may be disguised, expressed in terms of the "therapeutic benefits" of sexual activity.

SEXUAL HARASSMENT WITH VICTIMS FROM MINORITY GROUPS

A pair of Canadian studies shed light of different wrinkles and experiences in harassment. One study compared the experiences of white women, black women, and Filipina women. White women with full rights as citizens felt most at liberty to report the harassment to authorities. Black women and Filipinas felt that the term *sexual harassment* did not fully capture their experience—that their treatment also

CRITICAL THINKING

What would be the response of a critical thinker to the following argument: Because of all the publicity, people who are intolerant of normal sexual advances, or who want to punish their supervisors, are now crying sexual harassment.

had to do with the power that white men could exercise over blacks and, especially, live-in Filipina caregivers.

The second study was set in the workplace (Berdahl & Moore, 2006). It found that women experienced more sexual harassment than men, and in what the authors call double jeopardy, minority women encountered more harassment than white women.

SEXUAL HARASSMENT IN THE WORKPLACE

Harassers in the workplace can be employers, supervisors, co-workers, or clients of a company. In some cases clients make unwelcome sexual advances to employees that are ignored or approved of by the boss. If a worker asks a co-worker for a date and is refused, it is not sexual harassment. If the co-worker persists with unwelcome advances and does not take no for an answer, however, the behavior crosses the line and becomes harassment.

Perhaps the most severe form of sexual harassment, short of an outright assault, involves an employer or supervisor who demands sexual favors as a condition of employment or advancement (Stout, 2011). The definition of sexual harassment in the workplace includes any behavior of a sexual nature that interferes with an individual's work performance or creates a hostile, intimidating, or offensive work environment.

The U.S. Supreme Court has recognized sexual harassment as a form of sex discrimination under Title VII of the Civil Rights Act of 1964. It holds that employers can be held accountable if such behavior was deemed to create a hostile or abusive work environment or to interfere with an employee's work performance. A unanimous 1993 Supreme Court ruling held that a person need not suffer psychological damage to sue an employer on grounds of sexual harassment. Moreover, employers can be held responsible not only for their own actions but also for sexual harassment by their employees when they either knew *or should have known* that harassment was taking place and failed to eliminate it promptly (Resnik, 2011). To protect themselves, many companies and universities have developed programs to educate workers about sexual harassment, established mechanisms for dealing with complaints, and imposed sanctions against harassers.

Under the law, persons subjected to sexual harassment can obtain a court order to have the harassment stopped, have their jobs reinstated (when they have lost them by resisting sexual advances), receive back pay and lost benefits, and obtain monetary awards for the emotional strain imposed by the harassment. However, proving charges of sexual harassment is generally difficult because there are usually no corroborating witnesses or evidence. As a result, relatively few persons who encounter sexual harassment in the workplace file formal complaints or seek legal remedies. Like people subjected to other forms of sexual coercion, persons experiencing sexual harassment often do not report the offense for fear that they will not be believed or will be subjected to retaliation. Some fear that they will be branded as "troublemakers" and/or lose their jobs.

SEXUAL HARASSMENT ON CAMPUS

Estimates of the frequency of sexual harassment of college students vary widely across studies. Overall, 25 to 30% of students report at least one incident of sexual harassment in college, and males are overwhelmingly more likely than females to commit sexual harassment (Wright & Bonita, 2012). The federal law prohibiting sex discrimination in academic institutions permits students to sue their schools for monetary damages for sexual harassment.

Sexual harassment on campus usually involves the less severe forms of harassment, such as sexist comments and sexual remarks, as well as come-ons, suggestive looks, propositions, and light touching (Wright & Bonita, 2012). Relatively few acts involve the use of direct pressure for sexual intercourse. Most students who encounter sexual harassment do not report the incident. If they do, it is usually to a confidant and not a person in authority.

Most forms of harassment involve unequal power relationships between the harasser and the person harassed (Ainsworth & Baumeister, 2012). *Peer harassment* involves cases between people who are equal in power, as in the cases of repeated sexual taunts from fellow employees, students, or colleagues. In some cases, the harasser may even have less formal power than the person harassed. Women professors have been sexually harassed by students, but the traditional social dominance of the male may override the academic position of the woman—at least in the mind of the offender.

One common form of harassment by students, reported by nearly one-third of the female professors polled in one survey, involves sexist remarks (Wright & Bonita, 2012). Other common forms of harassment include obscene phone calls and undue attention.

Sexual harassment also occurs long before students get to college. Surveys of high school and junior high school students—even elementary school students!—find that many boys and girls had encountered harassment in the form of others grabbing or groping them or subjecting them to sexually explicit putdowns when walking through school hallways (Gådin, 2012; Rahimi & Liston, 2012). Sexual taunts and advances have become part of an unwelcome ritual for many students, especially girls, in trying to make their way through the hallways and stairwells of high schools. Many harassers and victims view harassment as "just part of school life" and "no big deal." Many girls who experience sexual harassment at school report that it made them feel that they didn't want to go to school. Some say it makes it more difficult to pay attention in class and lowers their grades.

HOW TO RESIST SEXUAL HARASSMENT

What would you do if you were sexually harassed by an employer or a professor? How would you handle it? Would you try to ignore it and hope that it would stop? Here are some suggestions that may be helpful. Recognize, however, that responsibility for sexual harassment always lies with the perpetrator and the organization that permits sexual harassment to take place, not with the victim.

- *Convey a professional attitude.* Harassment may be stopped cold by responding to the harasser with a businesslike, professional attitude.
- *Discourage harassing behavior, and encourage appropriate behavior.* Harassment may also be stopped cold by shaping the harasser's behavior. Your reactions to the harasser may encourage businesslike behavior and discourage flirtatious or suggestive behavior. If a harassing professor suggests that you come back after school to review your term paper so that the two of you will be undisturbed, set limits assertively. Tell the professor that you'd feel more comfortable discussing the paper during regular office hours. Remain task-oriented. Stick to business. The harasser should quickly get the message that you wish to maintain a strictly professional relationship. If the harasser persists, do not blame yourself. You are responsible only for your own actions. When the harasser persists, a more direct response may be appropriate: "Professor Jones, I'd like to keep our relationship on a purely professional basis, okay?"
- *Avoid being alone with the harasser.* If you are being harassed by your professor but need some advice about preparing your term paper, approach him or her after class when other students are milling about, not privately during office hours. Or bring a friend to wait outside the office while you consult the professor.

- *Maintain a record.* Keep a record of all incidents of harassment as documentation in the event you decide to lodge an official complaint. The record should include the following: (1) where the incident took place; (2) the date and time; (3) what happened, including the exact words that were used, if you can recall them; (4) how you felt; and (5) the names of witnesses. Some people who have been subjected to sexual harassment have carried a hidden tape recorder during contacts with the harasser. Such recordings may not be admissible in a court of law, but they are persuasive in organizational grievance procedures. A hidden tape recorder may be illegal in your state, however. It is thus advisable to check the law.

- *Talk with the harasser.* It may be uncomfortable to address the issue directly with a harasser, but doing so puts the offender on notice that you are aware of the harassment and want it to stop. It may be helpful to frame your approach in terms of a description of the specific offending actions (e.g., "When we were alone in the office, you repeatedly attempted to touch me or brush up against me"); your feelings about the offending behavior ("It made me feel like my privacy was being violated. I'm very upset about this and haven't been sleeping well"); and what you would like the offender to do ("So I'd like you to agree never to attempt to touch me again"). Having a talk with the harasser may stop the harassment. If the harasser denies the accusations, it may be necessary to take further action.

- *Write a letter to the harasser.* Set down on paper a record of the offending behavior, and put the harasser on notice that the harassment must stop. Your letter might (1) describe what happened ("Several times you have made sexist comments about my body"); (2) describe how you feel ("It made me feel like a sexual object when you talked to me that way"); and (3) describe what you would like the harasser to do ("I want you to stop making sexist comments to me").

- *Seek support.* Support from people you trust can help you through the often trying process of resisting sexual harassment. Talking with others allows you to express your feelings and receive emotional support, encouragement, and advice. In addition, it may strengthen your case if you have the opportunity to identify and talk with other people who have been harassed by the offender.

- *File a complaint.* Companies and organizations are required by law to respond reasonably to complaints of sexual harassment. In large organizations, a designated official (sometimes an ombudsman, affirmative action officer, or sexual harassment advisor) is usually charged to handle such complaints. Set up an appointment with this official to discuss your experiences. Ask about the grievance procedures in the organization and your right to confidentiality. Have available a record of the dates of the incidents, what happened, how you felt about it, and so on. The two major government agencies that handle charges of sexual harassment are the Equal Employment Opportunity Commission (look under the government section of your phone book for the telephone number of the nearest office) and your state's Human Rights Commission (listed in your phone book under state or municipal government). These agencies may offer advice on how you can protect your legal rights and proceed with a formal complaint.

- *Seek legal remedies.* Sexual harassment is illegal and actionable. If you are considering legal action, consult an attorney familiar with this area of law. You may be entitled to back pay (if you were fired for reasons arising from the sexual harassment), job reinstatement, and punitive damages.

In closing, we ask not what persons who suffer rape, incest, and sexual harassment will do to redress the harm that has been done to them. We ask what all of us will do to reshape our society so that sex is no longer used as an instrument of power, coercion, and violence.

Chapter Review

✓• ─[**Study** and **Review** on **MyDevelopmentLab**

LO1 Define rape
The perpetrator of forcible rape coerces a nonconsenting person into sex. Statutory rape involves sex with a willing person who is unable to provide consent, as in being too young.

LO2 Describe the various kinds of rape
Types of rapes include stranger rape, acquaintance rape, partner rape, gang rape, male rape, and rape by females. Women are more likely to be raped by men they know than by strangers.

LO3 Explain how our culture encourages people to blame the victim of rape
Social attitudes such as gender-role stereotyping, seeing sex as adversarial, and acceptance of violence in interpersonal relationships help create a climate that encourages rape. Social critics argue that our society breeds rapists by encouraging males to play socially dominant roles.

LO4 Discuss the kinds of rapists and their personalities
Sexually aggressive men are more likely than other men to condone rape and violence against women, have traditional gender-role attitudes, be hostile toward women, use sex as a way of expressing social dominance, lack empathy, and have peers that pressure them into sexual activity.

LO5 Discuss the effects of rape on victims
Rape survivors often experience crisis and stress disorders. Treatment of survivors typically involves supporting them through the crisis and then helping foster long-term adjustment.

LO6 Discuss the origins and effects of sexual child abuse
Any sexual contact between an adult and a child is abusive because children are legally incapable of providing consent. In most cases, molesters are close to the children they abuse—relatives, step-relatives, family friends, neighbors. Genital fondling is the most common type of abuse. Pedophiles are almost exclusively male. Father–daughter incest is most likely to be reported and prosecuted, but brother–sister incest is most common. Children who are sexually abused often suffer social and emotional problems, affecting their self-esteem and their formation of intimate relationships. Children need to be taught the difference between acceptable touching and "bad" touching.

LO7 Discuss the treatment options of treating rapists and child molesters, and their effectiveness
Methods include prison-based rehabilitation programs, often in the form of group therapy, and chemical castration (via anti-androgen drugs) or surgical castration.

LO8 Define sexual harassment
Sexual harassment involves unwanted sexual comments, gestures, or contact. It is often an expression of unequal power relationships. It may be used as a weapon to keep women "in their place," especially in work settings that are traditional male preserves.

LO9 Explain what victims of sexual harassment can do about it
Victims of sexual harassment can convey a professional attitude to the harasser, avoid being alone with him, keep a record of instances, write a letter to the harasser that outlines unwanted behaviors, file a complaint, and seek legal remedies.

Test Your Learning

1. All forms of sexual activity between adults and children are coercive because
   - (a) the children resist.
   - (b) the adults need to dominate the children.
   - (c) children are hurt by sexual activity.
   - (d) children are below the age of consent.

2. Which of the following is *not* a reason why the incidence of rape is underreported?
   - (a) Some women fear that they will be humiliated by the criminal justice system.
   - (b) Some women fear reprisal from their families or the rapist.
   - (c) Some women assume that the offender will not be caught or prosecuted.
   - (d) Some women are raped by strangers.

3. The most common type of rape is
   - (a) rape by an acquaintance.
   - (b) rape by a stranger.
   - (c) marital rape.
   - (d) rape by females.

4. Which one of the following is *not* a cultural myth that encourages rape?
   - (a) Women say no when they mean yes.
   - (b) The way women dress, they are asking to be raped.
   - (c) Women do not wish to be forced into sexual activity.
   - (d) Women want a truly masculine, sexually aggressive man.

5. Pedophiles often
   - (a) rape adult victims.
   - (b) seek treatment on their own.
   - (c) deny that sex is harmful to the child.
   - (d) come from liberal backgrounds.

6. Which of the following is the most common form of child sexual abuse?
   - (a) Exhibitionism
   - (b) Genital fondling
   - (c) Oral–genital sex
   - (d) Sexual intercourse

7. Pakistan's Hudood laws
   - (a) require male rapists to be excommunicated from the Islamic religion.
   - (b) consider female rape victims guilty of sex outside of marriage.
   - (c) allow only Islamic women to testify in court.
   - (d) consider the testimony of four women to be equal to the testimony of one man.

8. Rohypnol functions as a "date rape" drug because it
   - (a) can cause forgetfulness.
   - (b) is an aphrodisiac.
   - (c) multiplies the effects of testosterone.
   - (d) encourages women to recall consensual sex as an assault.

9. On-campus rape-prevention programs focus on increasing male students'
   - (a) academic interests.
   - (b) competitiveness.
   - (c) interest in sports.
   - (d) empathy.

10. Many pedophiles have
    - (a) long criminal records as rapists.
    - (b) interest in victims of both sexes and at all ages.
    - (c) personality disorders.
    - (d) gender identity disorders.

Answers: 1. d; 2. d; 3. c; 4. c; 5. c; 6. b; 7. b; 8. a; 9. d; 10. c

My Life, My Sexuality

Rape Prevention

Explore this **My Life, My Sexuality** *feature by scanning this QR code with your mobile device. If you don't already have one, you may download a free QR scanner for your device wherever smartphone apps are sold. You can also view this feature in MyDevelopmentLab, along with an accompanying critical thinking assignment.*

Rape prevention is a broad topic involving many issues and strategies. Generally speaking, there is a tendency to blame the victim: "She was 'dissing the guys on the street," "She was dressing like a slut." Or, "She could have avoided walking alone at night." These attitudes must be confronted. But until society changes its attitudes toward victims and toughens up on its treatment of rape as a crime of violence, you can scan the code to learn more about things you can do to prevent rape by strangers or acquaintance—including date rape.

19 Commercial Sex

Learning Objectives

PROSTITUTION

LO1 Define prostitution

LO2 Summarize what we know about female and male prostitutes, including their backgrounds

LO3 Discuss the relationship between prostitution and sexually transmitted infections (STIs)

PORNOGRAPHY AND OBSCENITY

LO4 Define pornography and obscenity

LO5 Describe the legal status of pornography and obscenity

LO6 Discuss the incidence and use of pornography

LO7 Discuss gender differences in response to pornography

LO8 Discuss possible relationships between pornography and sexual coercion

MY LIFE, MY SEXUALITY: DEVELOPING SELF-CONTROL TO AVOID USE OF COMMERCIAL SEX OUTLETS

TRUTH OR FICTION?

Which of the following statements are the truth, and which are fiction? Look for the Truth-or-Fiction icons on the pages that follow to find the answers.

1 Prostitution is illegal throughout the United States. **T F**?

2 The massage and escort services advertised in the Yellow Pages are fronts for prostitution. **T F**?

3 Most female prostitutes were sexually abused as children. **T F**?

4 Typical customers of prostitutes have difficulty forming sexual relationships with other women. **T F**?

5 Only males are sexually aroused by pornography. **T F**?

6 Pornography causes violence against women. **T F**?

The Secret Service is tasked with guarding the president of the United States, past presidents, and other high-ranking officials. If an assailant is attacking the president, they are supposed to leap in front of him and take the bullet.

In April of 2012, a number of Secret Service men did some leaping, and later on they took the bullet—that is, they lost their jobs.

But the *leaping* they did was in the Old English sense of the word—having sexual relations. And they carried out their personal tasks—not their professional tasks—with prostitutes in Cartagena, Columbia, where President Obama was visiting at the time.

"What they were thinking is beyond me," Congressperson Peter King, head of the House Homeland Security Committee, told NBC television's *Meet the Press.*

Well, what one of them was thinking about is clear enough: a prostitute named Dania. There are so-called tolerance zones in which prostitution is legal in Columbia. Many Cartagena brothels are situated in these zones. The matter came to the attention of authorities because Dania complained that she was not paid the agreed-upon tariff by the agent. She believed that deal was for several hundred dollars. He gave her less than $30.00.

The agents involved included explosives experts and snipers—the cream of the cream. Outraged U.S. officials said the agents could have been compromised and the president could have been in jeopardy. Senator Joe Lieberman, chairman of the Senate Homeland Security and Governmental Affairs Committee, told *Fox News Sunday* that "history is full of cases where enemies have compromised people and security or intelligence … with sex… . They were not acting like Secret Service agents," he continued. "They were acting like a bunch of college students [on spring break]." 👁

👁 **Watch** the **Video**
Escort
on **MyDevelopmentLab**

"Dania." The liaison of several Secret Service agents with Columbian prostitutes came to light because Dania complained that the agent with whom she had sexual relations had not paid her the agreed-upon price.

The Secret Service agents were not the only high-profile people to fall under the spell of prostitutes. In the spring of 2008, New York's governor Eliot Spitzer resigned his post, with a tearful Mrs. Spitzer at his side. It had come to light that Spitzer had recently spent some $80,000 on prostitutes. Worse yet, he could be prosecuted for violating the Mann Act, a rarely used century-old statute that makes transporting a prostitute across state lines a federal offense. Spitzer had arranged for prostitute Ashley Dupre to travel from New York to a $5,000 tryst in Washington, DC (Kornacki, 2008). One of the factors that led to his resignation was flagrant hypocrisy: Spitzer had vigorously prosecuted and stiffened the penalties against upscale prostitution rings and clients.

At about the same time, it also came to light that the name of Louisiana senator David Vitter had been found in the black book of the "DC Madam," who was about to go on trial. Vitter remains in his post. He acknowledged that he had committed "a very serious sin" and said that the matter was settled because he had "asked for and received forgiveness from God and my wife" (Roberts, 2008). Some wondered out loud exactly how Vitter knew God had forgiven him, but he rode out the storm—which lasted but a few days.

Although the Secret Service agents, Spitzer, and Vitter made headlines, they are clearly not unusual. Millions of men (and some women) have paid for sex through the ages. In the caverns of Wall Street, brokers and traders sell stocks and other financial instruments that drive the nation's commercial enterprises. On the floor of Chicago's Board of Trade, brokers trade commodities—soybeans, corn, wheat, and other

Eliot Spitzer resigns his governorship of the State of New York because of the uncovering of his use of prostitutes.

Ashley Dupre met Spitzer for a reported $5,000 tryst in Washington, DC.

goods. Prices go up, prices go down, responding to the law of supply and demand. On street corners a few short blocks from these financial institutions another sort of commerce takes place. In New York City and Chicago, as in Hollywood and in the nation's smaller towns and villages, prostitutes exchange sex for money or for goods such as drugs.

Sex as commerce runs the gamut from adult bookshops to strip clubs, sex toy shops, erotic hotels and motels, escort/outcall services, streetwalkers, some "massage parlors," some "tanning salons," cybersex (e.g., sex over the Internet), and the use of sex appeal in advertisements for products.

Prostitution

Eliot Spitzer and David Vitter ran afoul of the law because **prostitution**—the sale of sex for money—is illegal in New York and Washington, DC. **TRUTH OR FICTION REVISITED:** Prostitution is illegal everywhere in the United States except for some rural counties in Nevada, where it is restricted to state-licensed brothels. Although prostitutes and their clients can be male or female, most prostitutes are female and virtually all customers are male.

 1

Although soliciting a prostitute is also illegal in many states, police rarely crack down on customers or "johns." The few who are arrested are usually penalized with a small fine (Bennetts, 2011). Melissa Farley, who researches prostitution, reports that "for every john arrested for attempting to buy sex, there are up to 50 women in prostitution arrested." On occasion, the names of convicted johns are published in local newspapers to deter men who fear publicity.

Prostitution is often called "the world's oldest profession"—for good reason. (Norman Ramos [2012], director of the Coalition Against Trafficking in Women, who sees prostitution as the exploitation of women, comments that prostitution "is the world's oldest *oppression*.") Prostitution can be traced at least to ancient Mesopotamia, where temple prostitution flourished. The Greek historian Herodotus noted that all women in the city were expected to put in some time at the temple. They would offer their bodies to passers-by who would make a "religious" donation.

Prostitution flourished in medieval Europe and during the sexually repressive Victorian era. Then, as now, the major motive for the prostitutes was economic.

Prostitution The sale of sexual activity for money or goods of value, such as drugs.

Many poor women were—and are—drawn to prostitution as a means of survival. In Victorian England, it was widely held that women did not enjoy sex. Therefore, it was better for a man to visit a prostitute than "soil" his wife with his carnal passions.

In the nineteenth-century United States, married and unmarried men frequented prostitutes regularly. Use of prostitution cut across all economic and social boundaries. Prostitution most often occurred within two contexts, sexual initiation for males and regular brothel visitation.

Many prostitutes, along with many social commentators and researchers, have redefined prostitution as *sex work* (Jewkes et al., 2012). Conventional work has been widely studied, but "crime as work" has received less attention—especially when it involves women and sexual labor. Elite prostitutes—call girls and escorts—analyze their markets and their relationships with their customers and make career choices.

INCIDENCE OF PROSTITUTION IN THE UNITED STATES

There are hundreds of thousands of prostitutes or sex workers in the United States, but no one has an exact number. Sex workers are found in the streets, in brothels, in adult films, on the Internet, in the phone book, and in classified ads.

Almost two-thirds of the European American males in Kinsey's sample (Kinsey et al., 1948) reported visiting a prostitute at least once. About 15% to 20% did so regularly. The use of prostitutes varied with educational level, however. By age 20, about half of Kinsey's non-college-educated single males, but only one-fifth of his college-educated males, had visited a prostitute.

Kinsey's data foreshadowed a falling off of experience with prostitutes that seems linked to the decay of the sexual double standard. Young men in recent generations appear to be less likely to visit prostitutes because they are more likely to become sexually initiated with their girlfriends. Increased concern about STIs, especially HIV/AIDS, has also reduced the clientele of sex workers around the world (Kirby, 2008; Herbst et al., 2008). Nevertheless, prostitution continues to flourish.

FEMALE PROSTITUTES

Female prostitutes—commonly called *hookers, whores, working girls, masseuses* (although state-certified masseuses run legitimate businesses), or *escorts*—are usually classified according to the settings in which they work. The major types of prostitutes today are streetwalkers; brothel or "house" prostitutes, many of whom work in massage parlors; and "escorts" or call girls (Dodge, 2012). Many prostitutes today advertise their wares online at www.backpage.com or *The Village Voice*, in newspaper advertisements (where they often offer massage), or have their customers "let their fingers do the walking" through the Yellow Pages, where, in some cities, there are multiple pages of escort services and massage parlors.

Streetwalkers Although most prostitutes are **streetwalkers**, streetwalkers occupy the bottom rung in the hierarchy of prostitutes. They earn the lowest incomes and are usually considered to be the least desirable or attractive. They also incur the greatest risk of abuse by customers and **pimps.** Streetwalkers tend to come from poverty and to have had unhappy childhoods (Kristoff, 2009; Dodge, 2012). Many are survivors of rape, sexual abuse, or incest (Beech et al., 2009; Lloyd, 2012). Many are teenage runaways who turn to drugs and sex work to survive (Dodge, 2012).

Streetwalkers operate in the open. They are thus more likely than other prostitutes to draw attention to themselves and risk arrest (Kristof, 2009; McKeganey, 2006). To avoid arrest, streetwalkers may be indirect about their services. They may ask passers-by if they are interested in a "good time" or some "fun" rather than sex per se. In many cities, streetwalkers dress in revealing or provocative fashions.

Streetwalkers Prostitutes who solicit customers on the streets.

Pimps Men who serve as agents for prostitutes and live off their earnings.

Many cities throughout the United States, Europe, and elsewhere have "red light districts" or "tolerance zones" where prostitutes ply their trade with relatively little interference from police (Miller, 2012).

In most locales, penalties for prostitution involve small fines or short jail terms. Many police departments, besieged by crimes such as drug peddling and violent crimes, consider prostitution a "minor" or "nuisance" crime. Generally, prostitutes find the criminal justice system a revolving door. They pay the fine. They spend a night or two in jail. They return to the streets.

A bar prostitute is a variation of the streetwalker. She approaches men in a bar she frequents, rather than on the streets. Payoffs to bar owners or managers secure their cooperation, although the women are sometimes tolerated because they draw customers. Some streetwalkers work in X-rated, or "adult," movie houses and may service their patrons in their seats with manual or oral sex. Payoffs may secure the cooperation of the management.

Streetwalkers in Pattaya, Thailand.

About 40% of streetwalkers support a pimp (Norton-Hawk, 2004; Williamson & Cluse-Tolar, 2002). A pimp acts as lover-father-companion-master. He provides streetwalkers with protection, bail, and sometimes room and board, in exchange for a high percentage of their earnings. Still, prostitutes are often physically abused by their pimps, who may use threats and beatings as means of control (Nussbaum, 2012). Pimp-controlled prostitutes are more likely than their peers to come from dysfunctional families, to be poorly educated, never to have held legitimate jobs, and to come from racial minority groups (Nussbaum, 2012).

For many streetwalkers, "the life" is a round of sex, violence, disease, and drugs, including cocaine and heroin (Degenhardt et al., 2006; Romero-Daza et al., 2005). Many street prostitutes feel powerless to control their own fates, and are often talked into oral or vaginal sex without protection. Given these realities, streetwalkers do not stay in "the life" very long. Some make the transition to a more traditional life or get married. Others die young from drug abuse, disease, suicide, or physical abuse from pimps or customers (Lloyd, 2012). Those who survive become less marketable with age. Rachel Lloyd, who as a teenager worked as a prostitute in Germany, where prostitution is legal, writes that "Violence is inherent in the sex industry. Numerous studies show that between 70 percent and 90 percent of children and women who end up in commercial sex were sexually abused prior to entry. No other industry is dependent upon a regular supply of victims of trauma and abuse" (Lloyd, 2012).

Researchers also find a high level of psychological disturbance among prostitutes, especially female street sex workers (Brown, 2005; Raphael & Shapiro, 2005). Melissa Farley and her colleagues (2005) interviewed 100 prostitutes in Canada. They found that

- 82% had a history of childhood sexual abuse.
- 72% had a history of childhood physical abuse.
- 90% had been physically assaulted on the job.
- 78% had been raped on the job.
- 72% could be diagnosed with **posttraumatic stress disorder (PTSD)**.

Only 5% of the general population has posttraumatic stress disorder (PTSD), and only 20% to 30% of combat veterans has the disorder. The prostitutes also developed many health problems (other than STIs). From 90% to 95% said that they wanted to get out of "the life" (Farley et al., 2005). However, many who exit the life find themselves back in for financial and social reasons (Ramos, 2012).

Norma Ramos (2012), executive director of the Coalition Against Trafficking in Women, writes, "For the majority, prostitution has proved very hard to get out of, particularly since many women enter it at a very young age. To have been sexually

Posttraumatic stress disorder (PTSD) A stress reaction brought on by flashbacks in the form of disturbing dreams or intrusive recollections, emotional numbing or restricted range of feelings, and heightened vigilance.

A Closer Look

Girls on the Streets of Our Cities

Fourteen-year-old African American Jasmine Caldwell was selling sex on the streets of Atlanta, Georgia, when she thought she saw an opportunity to escape from her pimp: She was picked up by an undercover policeman. Her pimp "ran" 13 girls and took every penny they earned from their customers. If the policeman had taken Jasmine to Covenant House, a shelter for runaway teenagers, or a shelter for women who are victims of violence, perhaps she would have been able to resume her education and get her life back in some kind of order. But he didn't. He showed Jasmine his handcuffs and threatened to put her in prison. She was terrified and begged not to be imprisoned. Then the policeman offered to let her go in exchange for sex. Afterward, her pimp beat her for not collecting any payment.

Now 21, Jasmine said, "That happens a lot" (Kristof, 2009). "The cops sometimes just want to blackmail you into having sex."

Prostitution in the United States may not be as brutal as in India, Pakistan, Malaysia, and Cambodia, where young girls are frequently kidnapped and tortured by owners of brothels, and sometimes killed if they do not comply. Americans tend to envision forced prostitution as a problem for Asian or Mexican women who are brought into the United States and imprisoned in brothels. A greater scandal involves American teenagers. Streetwalkers in the United States encounter abuse and violence because the authorities seem to care little about 14-year-olds like Jasmine. When the occasional middle-class European American girl is missing, radio stations broadcast alerts, and cable TV broadcasts "missing beauty" updates (Kristof, 2009). But poor early teen African and Latina American girls vanish every day, and only pimps seem to be paying attention (Hallgrímsdóttir et al., 2008). These minority teens are typically runaways or "throwaways"—girls in conflict with parents or other "caregivers" who get kicked out.

Pimps are not father types or business partners. They exploit the girls they run by taking every cent they earn. They may force the girls to work seven days a week.

Occasionally they tattoo girls like ranchers brand cattle and horses. They beat girls who don't comply readily enough.

"If you don't earn enough money, you get beat," says Jasmine, "If you say something you're not supposed to, you get beat. If you stay too long with a customer, you get beat. And if you try to leave the pimp, you get beat."

Violence alone doesn't keep girls attached to their pimps. Jasmine had run away from a violent home at the age of 13, and she explained that she thought the pimp loved her. Drugs, gifts, a little bit of affection, and lack of an alternative keep most girls working. If a girl rebels, the pimp beats her and threatens to kill her.

According to *New York Times* columnist Nicholas Kristof (2009), "Solutions are complicated and involve broader efforts to overcome urban poverty, including improving schools and attempting to shore up the family structure. But a first step is to stop treating these teenagers as criminals and focusing instead on arresting the pimps and the customers—and the corrupt cops."

👁️ **Watch** the **Video**
America's Dirty Secret: Child Sex Trafficking
on **MyDevelopmentLab**

exploited since childhood is to have educational and other opportunities robbed of you. Women and girls in the sex industry are also routinely exposed to high levels of abuse" (Ramos, 2012). 👁️

Streetwalkers who work in hotels and conventions generally have higher status than those who work on the streets or bars. Clients are typically traveling conventioneers or businessmen. The hotel prostitute must be skilled in conveying subtle messages to potential clients without drawing the attention of hotel management or security. They usually provide sexual services in the client's hotel room. Some hotel managers will tolerate known prostitutes (usually for a payoff under the table), so long as the woman conducts herself discreetly.

Brothel Prostitution Many brothel prostitutes occupy a middle status in the hierarchy of prostitutes, between streetwalkers on one end and call girls on the other. They work in a brothel, or in a massage parlor (Parent & Bruckert, 2005).

The life of the brothel (or "house") prostitute is usually neither as lucrative as that of the call girl nor as degrading as that of the streetwalker. Some prostitutes in massage parlors or working for escort services may not consider themselves to be "real prostitutes" because they do not walk the streets and because they work for businesses that present a legitimate front. *Cathouse, bordello, cat wagon, parlor house, whorehouse, joy house, sport house, house of ill repute*—these are but a handful of the names given to houses in which prostitutes work. The heyday of the brothel may well be over in the United States. Formal brothels are rare, except in Nevada, where they are legal but regulated. Brothel prostitutes split their fees with management. In addition to their "split," they receive free room and board. They are on duty three weeks a month and on call 24 hours a day during that time. When a customer arrives, they step into the living room "lineup." After one has been chosen, they wait again, resting, reading, or watching television.

Barbara Brents, a sociology professor at the University of Nevada, has studied brothel prostitution in Nevada for 15 years. She writes, "In legal brothels, employees report that they feel safe, are free to come and go, and are bound only by their contract. Of the brothel workers we surveyed, 84 percent said that their job felt safe. Workers report that they felt safe largely because the police, employers and co-workers were there to protect them" (Brents, 2012).

Yet Stella Marr, founder of Survivors Connect, a network of survivors of prostitution and trafficking, offers a very different view of legal prostitution in Nevada: "Women who worked in Nevada's legal brothels said they were like prisons where you have to turn tricks. Rimmed with high-security fencing and an electronic gate, they can look like a detention camp. The women live in lockdown conditions and can't leave the premises unless they're accompanied by a male pimp. Living and working in cramped, dark rooms, they're on call 24 hours a day."

There is no doubt that some brothel prostitutes lead lives of degradation. Many poor Asian, East European, and African women are kidnapped or lured to the big city or to the West by promises of the good life (Kristof, 2006; Unigwe, 2012).

In *On Black Sisters Street*, Chika Unigwe (2011) describes the experiences of several African women who are trafficked to brothels in Western Europe. Dele, the trafficker, and the women are from Nigeria. Dele tells one of them, "Every month I send gals to Europe. Antwerp. Milan. Madrid. My gals dey there. Every month, four gals. Sometimes five or more," he boasts to Sisi when she first visits his office. "You be fine gal now. Abi, see your backside, kai! Who talk say na dat Jennifer Lopez get the finest *nyansh*? … As for those melons wey you carry for chest, omo, how you no go fin' work?" (Unigwe, 2011).

For his services, Dele charges 30,000 euros, which the women are indebted to pay off, and it is money that they really have little hope of repaying. The rent they will owe their madam in Antwerp will further eat at their ability to save money. Elsewhere, Unigwe had some apparently positive words for an Antwerp brothel,

Prostitution is legal in most counties in Nevada, as at the Chicken Ranch brothel.

Real Students, Real Questions

Q *What does the term fluffer mean?*

A A fluffer is a prostitute who works behind the scenes of porn films by sexually arousing male actors—usually by means of oral sex—prior to filming scenes where they need erections. The name may refer to the hair fluffing used by makeup artists to keep female starlets looking their best. For gay actors fluffers will be male, and for heterosexual actors, female. Sometimes straight actors work in gay films for more pay but rely on female fluffers. We've heard that the best fluffer in recent years has been Viagra.

Many workers in strip clubs limit their activity to removing their clothes, but some engage in various sexual activities with patrons, in the main stage areas or in 'VIP rooms.'

but given the frequent indebtedness of the women, for them such places of business are akin to prisons: "Antwerp has apparently one of the best bordellos in Europe, equipped with its own police station and high-tech sensors" (Unigwe, 2012). Thus the women are unlikely to be physically abused, and strangers will not be sneaking in at night. But leaving the life? For many women, it's only a dream.

The Massage Parlor Nature abhors a vacuum. "Massage parlors" have sprung up from coast to coast in the United States to fill the vacuum left by the decline of the brothels. Many massage parlors are legitimate establishments that provide massage and only massage. Masseuses and masseurs are licensed in many states, and laws prohibit them from offering sexual services. Many localities require that the masseuse keep certain parts of her or his body clothed (some masseuses in suburban Detroit wear a scarf or a garter to comply) and not touch the client's genitals.

Many massage parlors serve as fronts for prostitution, however (Lewis et al., 2005; Nemoto et al., 2004). They are often found in malls in middle-class suburbs, where there is ample parking. In these establishments, clients typically pay fees for a standard massage and then tip the workers for sexual extras.

Massage parlor prostitutes generally offer manual stimulation of the penis ("a local"), oral sex, or less frequently, sexual intercourse ("full service"). Some massage parlor prostitutes are better educated than streetwalkers and brothel workers and would not work in those other venues. But many massage parlor workers are Asians who are spirited from parlor to parlor, from city to city, and then back to Asia (Nemoto et al., 2004).

Strip Clubs Many sex workers in strip clubs limit their activity to dancing and doffing their clothes. Others do "lap dances" or "table dances" in which they contact customers as they dance (Rambo & Pruit, 2012). Customers may buy the dance from the club and then also be expected to tip the stripper (Frank, 2002, 2003). Some strip clubs have private shows, "VIP rooms," and the like, where strippers may be alone with their customers. What happens in these private shows may be tightly regulated by the club or depend on the size of the tip (Roach, 2011).

Escort Services Conventioneers and businessmen are more likely to turn to the listings for "massage" and "escort services" in the telephone directory, under personal ads in local newspapers, or online than to seek hotel prostitutes. Services that provide "outcall" send masseuses (or masseurs) or escorts to the hotel room.

 TRUTH OR FICTION REVISITED: Massage and escort services advertised in the Yellow Pages are typically, but not always, fronts for prostitution. Legitimate masseuses and masseurs often advertise that they are licensed by their states.

Escort services are found in every major U.S. city and present themselves as legitimate businesses providing escorts for men. Indeed, one will find female companionship for corporate functions and for unattached men traveling away from home under "escort services." Many escort services provide only prostitution, however, and clients of other escort services sometimes negotiate sexual services after formal escort duties are completed—or in their stead.

Prostitutes who work for escort services often come from middle-class backgrounds and are well educated—so much the better to help prepare them to hold their own in social conversation. Escort services may establish arrangements with legitimate companies to provide "escorts" for visiting customers or potential clients. Escort services also provide female escorts to "entertain" at conventions. Because of her high-society background, Sidney Biddle Barrow, the so-called Mayflower Madam, attracted a great deal of publicity when it was discovered that she ran an exclusive "escort service" in New York City.

Real Students, Real Questions

Q *I worked as a dancer and sometimes had sex for money. Should I tell my present boyfriend (whom I might marry), who does not know my past?*

A Our advice is that your past is your own and that your future belongs to the two of you, if you decide that you will in fact be a committed couple. Your boyfriend might not be able to live with the details of your past, and if you promise yourself to him, you are promising your future, not your history.

Call Girls Call **girls** occupy the highest status on the social ladder of female prostitution. Many of them overlap with escorts. Call girls tend to be the most attractive and well-educated prostitutes and tend to charge more for their services. Many come from middle-class backgrounds. Unlike other types of prostitutes, call girls usually work on their own. Thus, they need not split their income with a pimp, escort service, or massage parlor. Consequently, they can afford to lead a luxurious lifestyle when business is good, living in expensive neighborhoods and wearing stylish clothes, and to be more selective about the customers they will accept. They do, however, incur expenses for answering services and laundry services, and for payoffs to landlords, doormen, and sometimes to police to maintain their livelihood and avoid arrest.

Often, call girls escort their clients to dinner and social functions, and are expected not only to provide sex but also charming and gracious company and conversation. Call girls often give clients the feeling that they are important and attractive (Sanders, 2005). They may effectively simulate pleasure and orgasm and create the illusion that time does not matter. It does, of course. To the call girl, as to other entrepreneurs, time is money.

Call girls may receive clients in their apartments ("incalls") or make "outcalls" to clients' homes and hotels. Some call girls trade or sell "black books" that list clients and their sexual preferences. To protect themselves from police and abusive clients, call girls may insist on reviewing a client's business card or learning his home telephone number before personal contact is made. They may investigate whether the customer is who he claims to be.

Getting into "The Life" No single factor explains entry into female prostitution. **TRUTH OR FICTION REVISITED:** But poverty and sexual and/or physical abuse figure prominently in the backgrounds of the majority of female prostitutes (Carter & Dalla, 2006; Farley et al., 2005; Inciardi et al., 2006). They often come from conflict-ridden or single-parent homes in poor urban areas or rural farming communities.

 3

Max Waltman (2012) of Stockholm University writes that "most people in prostitution enter as children after being sexually abused. Lacking education and resources to survive, often destitute and homeless, they are easy prey to pimps and johns. Sexism and racism lock them in, as in the United States, where African American women and girls are overrepresented in prostitution, as are native Canadian women in Canada."

For young women of impoverished backgrounds and marginal skills, sex work may seem alluring. It is an alternative to the menial and dismal work that is otherwise available. Poverty accounts for the entry of young women into prostitution in many countries. In some Third World nations, such as Thailand and Cambodia,

Call girls Prostitutes who arrange for their sexual contacts by telephone. *Call* refers both to telephone calls and to being "on call."

many rural, impoverished parents in effect sell daughters to recruiters who place them in brothels in cities (Bamgbose, 2002; Gomes do Espirito & Etheredge, 2003; Kristof, 2006). Many of the women send home whatever money they can and also work hard to try to pay off the procurers and break free of their financial bonds.

In the United States and Canada, many initiates into prostitution are teenage runaways. Their family backgrounds vary in socioeconomic status; some come from middle-class or affluent homes, whereas others are reared in poverty. However, family discord and dysfunction frequently set the stage for entry into street life and prostitution (Carter & Dalla, 2006; Medrano et al., 2003). Many teenage runaways perceive life on the street to be the only possible escape from family strife and conflict, or from the physical, emotional, or sexual abuse they suffer at home. Despite its dangers, life on the streets appears more attractive than remaining in the troubled family environment.

Some teenagers who have endured sexual abuse or incest learn how to detach themselves emotionally from sex to survive unwanted sexual experiences (Sanders, 2005). The transition to sex work may represent an extension of this unfortunate learning experience.

"JOHNS"—THE CUSTOMERS OF FEMALE PROSTITUTES

Many prostitutes refer to their customers as "johns" or "tricks." Terms such as *patron, meatball, sucker,* and *beefbuyer* are also heard.

Men who use female prostitutes come from all walks of life and represent all socioeconomic and racial groups. Many, perhaps most, are married men of middle-class background (Bennetts, 2011).

Most patrons are *occasional johns*. Examples include traveling salesmen or military personnel who are stopping over in town without their regular sex partners. Men are more interested than women in sexual novelty or variety (Hill & Buss, 2008; Petersen & Hyde, 2011), and variety may provide a major motive, since most occasional johns have regular sex partners.

Habitual johns use prostitutes as their major or exclusive sexual outlet. Some habitual johns have never established an intimate sexual relationship. Some wealthy men who wish to avoid intimate relationships habitually patronize call girls.

Compulsive johns feel driven to prostitutes to meet some psychological or sexual need. They may repeatedly resolve to stop using prostitutes but feel unable to control their compulsions. Some compulsive johns engage in acts of fetishism or transvestism with prostitutes but would not inform their wives or girlfriends of their deviant interests. Some compulsive johns have a **whore–Madonna complex**. They see women as either sinners or saints. They can permit themselves to enjoy sex only with prostitutes, or would ask only prostitutes to engage in acts such as fellatio. They see marital coitus as a duty or obligation.

Motives for Using Prostitutes There appear to be six common motives for using prostitutes:

1. *Sex without negotiation.* A john cited in Bennetts (2011) remarks, "You can have a good time without the servitude." The research on gender differences suggests strongly that men have a stronger sex drive than women do (Petersen & Hyde, 2011). Sex work evens things up, making women available at the whim of the man. By turning to prostitutes, men need not spend the time, effort, and money to develop a relationship for the sake of sex.
2. *Sex without commitment.* Research on gender differences also shows that men are more willing to enter into sexual activity in the absence of a commitment (Petersen & Hyde, 2011). Sex workers require no commitment from the customer other than payment for services rendered.

Whore–Madonna complex
The rigid stereotyping of women as either sinners or saints.

3. *Sex for eroticism and variety.* Many sex workers offer "something extra" in the way of novel or kinky sex—for example, oral sex, use of costumes (e.g., leather), and S&M rituals (such as B&D). Men may desire such activity but not obtain it with their regular partners. They may even be afraid to mention the idea. Men are also more interested than women in sexual variety (Petersen & Hyde, 2011; Schmitt, 2003), and sex workers provide variety in partners.

4. *Prostitution as sociability.* In the nineteenth and early twentieth centuries, the brothel served not only as a place to obtain sex but also as a kind of "stopping off" place between home and work. Sex was secondary to the companionship and amiable conversation that men would find in brothels, especially in the days of the "bawdy houses" of the pioneer West. (Similarly, women who attend male strip clubs enjoy "bonding" with their friends at the clubs as well as the stripping itself [Montemurro et al., 2003].)

5. *Sex away from home.* The greatest contemporary use of prostitution occurs among male "road warriors"— traveling businessmen. It is also common among sports fans at out-of-town events. In these typical all-male preserves, peer pressure may encourage sexual adventures.

TRUTH OR **FICTION** REVISITED: It is not true that typical customers of prostitutes have difficulty forming sexual relationships with other women. Many men often turn to prostitutes for sexual variety or because they seek sexual activity when they are away from home.

6. *Problematical sex.* People who have physical disabilities or disfiguring conditions sometimes seek the services of prostitutes because of difficulty attracting other partners or because of fears of rejection. (One prostitute at a Nevada brothel said that she was a favorite of the management because she accepted johns with cerebral palsy.) Though some prostitutes are selective about their clients, others will accept anyone who will pay. Men with sexual dysfunctions may also turn to prostitutes who do not "demand" a certain quality of performance. Some men without partners may seek sex workers as substitutes.

MALE PROSTITUTES

Males also work as prostitutes. Some—especially those who work at strip clubs—have female clients. However, strippers, male and female, typically do not see themselves as prostitutes unless they also have sex with the clientele. Male prostitutes who service female clients—*gigolos*—are rare. Gigolos' clients are typically older, wealthy, unattached women. They may serve as escorts or as surrogate sons for the women, and may or may not offer sexual services. Many gigolos are struggling actors or models.

Most male prostitutes have male clients (Weitzer, 2012a). The overwhelming majority of male sex workers service gay men and are called **hustlers.** Their patrons are typically called **scores.** The average hustler is very young—17 to 18 years old— and was initiated into prostitution at age 14 or so. He typically has less than an 11-grade education and few, if any, marketable skills. The majority of hustlers come from working-class and lower-class backgrounds. Many male prostitutes, like many female prostitutes, come from families troubled by conflict, alcoholism, or physical or sexual abuse (Weitzer, 2012a).

Hustlers may be gay, bisexual, or heterosexual. In a large-scale Australian study, half of the male prostitutes surveyed described themselves as gay (Minichiello et al., 2001). About one-third (31%) said they were bisexual, and 5.5% said they were "straight."

A Norwegian study surveyed all adolescents aged 14 to 17 in public and private schools in Oslo, the capital of the country (Pedersen & Hegna, 2003). The response

CRITICAL THINKING
Agree or disagree with the following statement, and support your answer: Prostitution should be legalized throughout the United States.

Hustlers Males who engage in prostitution with male customers.

Scores Customers of hustlers.

Some men, as some women, earn an income by stripping. Audiences of male strippers are typically groups of women or gay males.

rate was 94%, or 10,828 students. About 1.4% of the sample had sold sexual favors, including three times as many boys as girls. Of these, half had done so more than 10 times. Prostitution was found to be connected with initiation of sexual intercourse at an early age, conduct problems, abuse of alcohol and other drugs, and physical and sexual abuse. The male prostitutes reported that many of their clients were gay or bisexual. The adolescents did not reliably use condoms, which placed them at risk of contracting HIV/AIDS and other STIs.

The major motive for male sex work, like female sex work, is money (Weitzer, 2012b). Running away from home typically serves as an entry point. Some males run away because of family problems; others are seeking adventure or independence. Some gay sex workers are literally thrown out because their families cannot accept their sexual orientation.

Most hustlers are part-timers who continue some form of educational or vocational activity as they support themselves through prostitution. Drug dealing and drug use are also common among hustlers (Weitzer, 2012b).

Hustlers typically are not attached to a pimp. They generally make contacts with clients in gay bars and social clubs, or by working the streets in areas frequented by gay men. They typically learn to hustle from watching other hustlers ply their trade. Various kinds of male sex workers have been identified (Minichiello et al., 2001):

- Strippers dance and strip. Patrons—female and male—may fondle them or sometimes have sex with them.
- Kept boys have relationships with older, economically secure men who keep them in an affluent lifestyle. The older male, or "sugar daddy," may assume a parental role.
- Call boys, like call girls, may work on their own or through an agency or escort service.
- "Punks" are prison inmates who service other inmates for protection or goods such as cigarettes or drugs.
- Drag prostitutes are transvestites or presurgical male-to-female transsexuals who impersonate females and have sex with men who may be unaware of their gender. Some of them conceal their gender and limit themselves to fellatio. Others take the passive role in anal sex.
- Male brothel prostitutes are rarer than their female counterparts.
- Bar hustlers and street hustlers, like their female counterparts, occupy the lowest status and ply their trade in gay bars or on streets frequented by gay passers-by. Street hustlers are the most common and typically the youngest subtype. They are also the most visible and consequently the ones most likely to draw the attention of the police.

By and large, hustling is an adolescent enterprise. The younger the hustler, the higher the fee he can command and the more tricks he can turn. By the time he reaches his mid-20s, he may be forced to engage in sexual activities he might have rejected when younger or seek clients in sleazier places.

SEXUALLY TRANSMITTED INFECTIONS (STIs) AND PROSTITUTION

Concerns about the spread of STIs by prostitution is nothing new. In the 1960s, two of three prostitutes surveyed by Gebhard (1969) had contracted gonorrhea or syphilis. Although prostitutes are still exposed to a heightened risk of contracting or spreading these and other STIs, such as chlamydia, the risk of HIV/AIDS poses a more deadly threat. The risk of HIV/AIDS has been linked to both male and female prostitution (Weitzer, 2012a). The risk of HIV/AIDS and other STIs is greater for

Q *Do women use male prostitutes at all? Do they use female prostitutes?*

A The best answer is sometimes, but certainly not as frequently as men do. When women visit strip clubs and toy with male dancers, they are in effect paying for sex. They may pay for sex (male strippers) at bachelorette parties. And now and then a woman uses a gigolo. As to whether women use female prostitutes, the best evidence we have is that heterosexual women sometimes get talked into using a female prostitute by their male companions—as a couple.

streetwalkers than brothel prostitutes (Weitzer, 2012a), and for women working illegally rather than women working legally (Leigh, 2012; Nussbaum, 2012).

Criminologist James Inciardi and his colleagues (2006) interviewed 586 streetwalkers in low-income sections of Miami, Florida. Their median age was 38 and they had been in "the life" for a median of 14 years. All women in the sample were heavily involved in alcohol and substance abuse, 42% were homeless, and half (51%) had engaged in unprotected vaginal sex with a customer in the past month. Their blood was tested for various STIs and it was found that:

- 22.4% tested positive for HIV.
- 53.4% tested positive for HBV (the hepatitis B virus).
- 29.7% tested positive for HCV (the hepatitis C virus).

We find another pocket of high infection rates among sex workers in California, and especially along the border with Mexico, where prostitution is legal. Many Californians visit Tijuana, Mexico, just south of the border, to find prostitutes (Strathdee et al., 2012). Similarly, the incidence of HIV infection is high in Ciudad Juarez, across the border from El Paso, Texas, and in that part of western Texas as well (Strathdee et al., 2010).

An analysis of 102 journal articles on the worldwide incidence of HIV infection among prostitutes confirmed the finding that the burden of disease is "disproportionately high" among prostitutes (Baral et al., 2012). Overall 11.8% of 99,878 female prostitutes were infected with HIV. That infection rate rose to 30.7% in countries with higher overall infection rates.

We have similar findings with men who have sex with male prostitutes (Jung et al., 2012). One study looked not only at infection with HIV but also at syphilis, chlamydia, and gonorrhea. High infection levels among the buyers were found among men with lower levels of education who had more sex partners, had anal sex—especially when they had unprotected anal sex—and among men who were more concerned about being infected with an STI. One might think that men who were more anxious about being infected would be more cautious; however, at least in this particular study, it would appear that men who were more anxious had good reason to feel anxious.

Sex with prostitutes is the most important factor in the male–female transmission of HIV in Africa, where HIV is spread mainly by male–female sexual intercourse. Prostitutes incur a greater risk of HIV transmission because they have sexual relations with many partners, often without protection (Surratt et al., 2005).

Moreover, many prostitutes and their clients and other sex partners inject drugs and share contaminated needles (Bobashev et al., 2009; Romero-Daza, et al., 2005). HIV/AIDS may be spread by unprotected sex from prostitutes to customers, then to the customers' wives or lovers.

SHOULD PROSTITUTION BE LEGALIZED?

As a counterpoint to the transmission of HIV/AIDS and other STIs by many street prostitutes, it can be noted that in the Netherlands and parts of Nevada, where prostitution is legal and carefully regulated by the state, transmission of STIs is extremely low (Wagenaar, 2006). In Nevada, condoms have been required since 1986, and prostitutes are tested for HIV and other infectious organisms regularly. Not one case of HIV/AIDS has been shown to be transmitted in a Nevada brothel (Mattson, 2011).

Legalization of prostitution has benefits beyond ensuring regular testing for STIs in licensed brothels (Weitzer, 2012a). It also turns prostitutes, other brothel employees, and brothel owners into taxpayers and provides safer venues for prostitution, both for prostitutes and their customers. Safer settings might help sever some of the links between prostitution and drug abuse. Moreover, brothel owners in legal setting are be required to obtain proof of age of sex workers.

Chika Unigwe, who wrote a novel about African women working in the red-light district of the Belgian city of Antwerp (Unigwe, 2011), supports legal status for prostitutes: "If prostitution is legalized, society gains income tax revenue that would have been otherwise lost. Granted, legalizing the profession might make it attractive for sex traffickers but the benefits outweigh this prospect" (Unigwe, 2012).

Opponents of legalization argue both on moral and practical grounds (Ramos, 2012). Many traditionalists and feminists alike find it morally reprehensible that civilized societies would legalize practices that degrade women and the value of the family. Moreover, given prostitutes' frequent histories of abuse and sexual exploitation, they wonder whether it can be claimed that prostitutes—even as adults—are ever truly making "free" decisions to enter the world's oldest profession.

On the other hand, Martha Nussbaum (2012), a professor of law and ethics at the University of Chicago, writes that "Feminist arguments about prostitution portray financial transactions in the area of female sexuality as demeaning to women. But all of us, with the exception of the independently wealthy and the unemployed, take money for the use of our bodies."

On a more practical level, many writers (e.g., Ramos, 2012) note that globalization and sex trafficking is likely to create a category of sex slaves regardless of whether or not prostitution is legalized or tolerated within a given country. Moreover, social class differences and prejudices are likely to remain such that less attractive prostitutes drawn from minority groups will remain on the streets, and unregulated, rather than finding their ways into the safer brothels.

Economics is to a large degree based on supply and demand. When the sexual

Amsterdam's Red-Light District. Amsterdam's red-light district is one of the city's tourist attractions. Prostitution is legal there and regulated. Condoms are a must. Tourists and locals stroll there by the canals and "window shop." Prim "blue rinse" grandmothers sometimes join the audiences at the live sex shows.

experiences desired by individuals are not supplied through personal intimate relationships, prostitution of some sort is likely to be in demand. Perhaps we'll give the final word on the matter to Carol Leigh (2012), director of the Bay Area Sex Workers Advocacy Network, which seeks legalization of prostitution in San Francisco: "Prostitution laws in the United States were developed from confused and contradictory impulses, to punish and help sex workers at the same time, reflecting our society's ambivalence and hypocrisy about sex, male desire and women's sexual autonomy."

Pornography and Obscenity

Sexually explicit materials are found nearly everywhere. In addition to the adult magazines and the DVD rentals, millions of people use Google or Yahoo! to search for pornography on the Internet or pay for pornographic films or channels from their cable or satellite dish services.

Pornography is indeed popular, but it is also highly controversial. Many are opposed to pornography on moral grounds. Feminists oppose pornography on the grounds that it portrays women in degrading and dehumanizing roles, as sex objects who are subservient to men's wishes, as sexually insatiable nymphomaniacs, or as sexual masochists who enjoy being raped and violated. Moreover, some feminists hold that depictions of women in sexually subordinate roles may encourage men to treat them as sex objects and increase the potential for rape (Itzin, 2002). On the other hand, many civil libertarians believe that the importance of freedom of speech overrides concerns about pornography.

WHAT IS PORNOGRAPHIC?

Webster's Deluxe Unabridged Dictionary defines **pornography** as "writing, pictures, etc., intended to arouse sexual desire." The inclusion of the word *intended* places the determination of what is pornographic in the mind of the person composing the work. Applying this definition makes it all but impossible to determine what is pornographic. If a film maker admits that he or she wanted to arouse the audience sexually, may we judge the work to be pornographic, even if no nudity or explicit sex scenes are

Pornography Sexually explicit material produced for purposes of eliciting or enhancing sexual arousal.

Prurient Tending to excite lust; lewd.

shown? On the other hand, explicit representations of people engaged in sexual activity would not be pornographic if the work was intended as an artistic expression, rather than created for its **prurient** value. Many works that were once prohibited in this country because of explicit sexual content—such as the novels *Tropic of Cancer* by Henry Miller, *Lady Chatterley's Lover* by D. H. Lawrence, and *Ulysses* by James Joyce—are now generally considered mainstream literature. Even Mark Twain's *Huckleberry Finn,* John Steinbeck's *The Grapes of Wrath,* and Ernest Hemingway's *For Whom the Bell Tolls* have been banned from place to place because local citizens found them to be offensive, obscene, or morally objectionable.

One alternative definition finds material pornographic when it is judged to be offensive by others. This definition, too, relies on the subjective judgment of the person exposed to the material. In other words, one person's pornography

Art, Religion, or Pornography? This statuary is found on a temple in India. There is a saying that one person's pornography is another person's art.

is another person's work of art. On the other hand, most people have no difficulty distinguishing between nudity that is art, nudity that is presented for information (such as illustrations presented in this textbook), and nudity that coincides with pornography.

Legislative bodies usually write laws about **obscenity** rather than pornography. In the case of *Miller v. California* (1973), Supreme Court Justice William Brennan wrote that obscenity is "incapable of definition with sufficient clarity to withstand attack on vagueness grounds." On the other hand, Justice Potter Stewart quipped that although he could not define obscenity, he knew it when he saw it. But even the Supreme Court has had trouble defining obscenity and determining where, if anywhere, laws against obscenity do not run afoul of the Bill of Rights' guarantee of free speech. Recall that *Huckleberry Finn* was once considered obscene.

Pornography is often classified as either *hard-core* (X-rated) or *soft-core* (R-rated). Hard-core pornography includes graphic and sexually explicit depictions of sex organs and sexual acts. Soft-core porn, as represented by R-rated films and *Playboy* photo spreads, features more stylized nude photos and suggested (or simulated) rather than explicit sex acts.

PORNOGRAPHY, LAW, AND POLITICS

Laws against obscenity provide the legal framework for outlawing the dissemination of pornography. Since the definition of obscenity relies on offending people or running afoul of community standards, that which is deemed obscene may vary from person to person and from culture to culture. Going topless on a public beach may be deemed obscene in some locales but not along beaches on the French Riviera or Rio de Janeiro, where this style of (un)dress is customary. The word *obscene* extends beyond sexual matters. One could judge TV violence or beer commercials to be obscene because they are personally offensive or are offensive to women, even if such depictions do not meet legal standards of obscenity.

In the United States, legal prohibition of pornography as a form of obscenity dates to the nineteenth century. In 1873, an anti-obscenity bill, the Comstock Act, was passed by Congress. One effect of the bill was to outlaw the dissemination of information about birth control. The Comstock Act and similar laws made it a felony to mail obscene books, pamphlets, photographs, drawings, or letters. But what is obscene?

A landmark case in 1957 helped establish the legal basis of obscenity in the United States. In *Roth v. United States*, the U.S. Supreme Court ruled that portrayal of sexual activity was protected under the First Amendment to the Constitution unless its dominant theme dealt with "sex in a manner appealing to prurient interest" (*Roth v. United States*, 1957, p. 487). In a 1973 case, *Miller v. California*, the U.S. Supreme Court held that obscenity is based on a determination of

(a) Whether the average person, applying contemporary community standards, would find that the work, taken as a whole, appeals to the prurient interest…;

(b) whether the work depicts or describes, in a patently offensive way, sexual conduct specifically defined by the applicable state law; and

(c) whether the work, taken as a whole, lacks serious literary, artistic, political, or scientific value. (*Miller v. California*, 1973, p. 24)

Courts have since had to grapple with the *Miller* standard in judging whether material is obscene. *Miller* recognizes that judgments of obscenity may vary with "community standards." As a result, the same material may be considered obscene in one community but not in another. The *Miller* standard raises some questions. For example, who is the "average person" who can speak for a community? Many of us live in ethnically, racially, and religiously diverse communities. Can one viewpoint

Obscenity That which offends people's feelings or goes beyond prevailing standards of decency or modesty.

in *any* community truly represent the community? Even in relatively homogeneous communities, a diversity of opinion may exist on particular issues. Moreover, what is a *community*? Is it one's neighborhood, police precinct, municipality, county, or a larger political unit? What does "patently" offensive mean? Who judges "serious" literary, artistic, political, or scientific value? An attempt to clarify this last question was made in a 1987 case, *Pope v. Illinois,* in which the Supreme Court held that

> The proper inquiry is not whether an ordinary member of any given community would find serious literary, artistic, political, or scientific value in allegedly obscene material, but whether a reasonable person would find such value in the material, taken as a whole. (*Pope v. Illinois*, p. 445)

In this ruling, the court held that sexually explicit material could not be declared obscene if many or most people in a particular community held it to lack serious literary, artistic, political, or scientific value, unless a "reasonable" person were to reach the same judgment. Whether the concept of a "reasonable" person will provide the courts with a clearer standard than that of an "average" or "ordinary" person for adjudicating obscenity cases remains to be seen.

Child pornography and violent, degrading, or dehumanizing pornography complicate matters further. People who do not find explicit depictions of consensual sex between adults to be obscene may regard child pornography or violent pornography as obscene. Child pornography is clearly psychologically harmful to the juvenile actors (McCabe, 2000; Quayle, 2012). Many people also object to sexually explicit material that portrays women as "sex objects," as existing to gratify men's sexual appetites.

Some footnotes: The U.S. Supreme Court ruled (in *Stanley v. Georgia,* 1969) that the possession of obscene material in one's home is not a criminal act. However, most states have criminalized the downloading and possession of child pornography. Police may seize suspects' computers and check them for the presence of child pornography.

Many individuals and communities have sought to ban pornography on the grounds that it discriminates against women (noted in Duggan, 2006a). In other words, pornography damages women's opportunities for equal rights by perpetuating stereotypes of women as subservient to men. ◉

The Regulation of Pornography If the First Amendment has protected people's rights to produce, act in, and possess pornography—with the exception of child pornography—it has not prevented various governing bodies from imposing some regulations on the industry. In sum, actors in adult films must be, in fact, adults, and, in many jurisdictions, they must be certified as free of certain sexually transmitted infections. As you can see in Figure 19.1, actors in southern California, where there are more than 200 adult movie studios, are required to receive monthly tests for HIV, chlamydia, and gonorrhea, and to be tested for other infections on other schedules (AIM Health Care Foundation, 2009). To avoid liability, most studios keep careful records of actors' proof of age and testing.

One might ask why actors are not required to wear condoms, as is common in the Brazilian adult film industry (Clendenning, 2004). The simple answer is that audiences prefer male actors to be "bareback." Very few American studios require actors to use condoms.

Feminists and Anti-Pornography Campaigns The sexual revolution liberated many in society from sexual inhibitions and prompted sexual exploration. As of the late 1960s, pornography became widespread. But many feminists found the proliferation of sexual imagery to be anything but liberating. Instead, it portrayed women as sex objects intended to be subservient to men.

◉ **Watch** the **Video**
Porn Industry Gearing Up for iPhone FaceTime
on **MyDevelopmentLab**

IF YOU'RE NEW TO THE ADULT FILM INDUSTRY THIS IS WHAT YOU NEED TO DO BEFORE YOU START WORKING:

1. *Get your blood tested for:
   - HIV (by "PCR DNA")
   - syphilis (an "RPR" test)

2. *Get your urine tested for:
   - gonorrhea (by "ultra-sensitive DNA amplification")
   - chlamydia (by "ultra-sensitive DNA amplification")

3. *View the "PORN 101" video which is available to take home and is also displayed in a condensed version at AIM Healthcare. Also pick up a copy of the "Responsibilities of Performers" list to help make your job easier.

4. *Every month get retested for gonorrhea, chlamydia, and HIV.

5. Get a genital exam:

   If you're a woman: Get a pelvic exam that includes an evaluation for herpes, genital warts, and the following tests:
   - PAP smear ("thin-prep with reflex HPV")
   - vaginal culture for bacterial vaginosis
   - vaginal culture for trichomonas

   If you're a man: Get a genital exam that includes an evaluation for herpes and genital warts.

6. Get your blood tested for Hepatitis A, B, and C.

   (If your test comes back negative, it is highly recommended that you get vaccinated for Hepatitis A and B. There is no vaccine for Hepatitis C.)

7. Get a skin test for tuberculosis.

8. Every six months:
   - women should have a genital exam with a PAP smear
   - men should have a genital exam
   - both men and women should be retested for syphilis

Note: *These items are recommended mandatory industry requirements to be done before your first shoot.

Source: Reprinted by permission of AIM Foundation/Dr. Sharon Mitchell.

FIGURE 19.1 AIM Health Care Foundation. The AIM Foundation helps actors in the adult film industry, especially "new talent," maintain their health and meet government-legislated testing requirements.

Some feminists joined with conservative Christian groups such as the Moral Majority to try to ban pornography, thereby aligning themselves with what amounted to a moral crusade (Duggan, 2006a). Their efforts ultimately failed, but it did spark conflict within the feminist movement and from some sexual minorities. Some groups claimed that banning pornography not only intrudes on First Amendment rights but also, by legislating what kinds of sexual themes may be portrayed, marginalizes people who derive sexual pleasure from pornography.

In 1980, Andrea Dworkin and Catherine MacKinnon (in MacKinnon, 2007) proposed legislation to the city of Minneapolis that would define pornography as

The graphic, sexually explicit subordination of women whether in pictures or in words that also includes one or more of the following: women are presented dehumanized as sexual objects … or women are presented as sexual objects who enjoy pain or humiliation; or women who experience pleasure in being raped… or women's body parts are exhibited, such that women are reduced to those parts; or women are presented in scenarios of degradation, … shown as filthy or inferior, bleeding, bruised or hurt in a context that makes these conditions sexual.

The proposed law included civil rather than criminal remedies for women affected by pornography. Women could sue makers, distributors, and sellers of pornography. The courts could also in effect remove pornography from the public, such that publishers and booksellers could be under scrutiny and surveillance.

Reactions Against Anti-Pornography Feminists Lisa Duggan (2006b) notes that feminist historians have criticized efforts to ban pornography and the political movements underlying it. One reason is the very fact that it leads to alliances with groups, such as the Moral Majority, whose agendas are otherwise opposed to "women's liberation." Another reason is the confusion over sexual explicitness, mistreatment of women, and violence. Pornography need not portray women as victims of men's lust. Nor, as discussed elsewhere in this chapter, has it been shown that pornography per se causes violence against women. Thus the battle against pornography misdirects resources that would be better directed against abuse of women and depictions of violence in the media.

Moreover, ordinances such as those offered by MacKinnon and Dworkin may be presented as ordinances to prevent gender discrimination, as recently in Indianapolis (Duggan, 2006a). However, they are clear censorship laws that would counter First Amendment rights (Duggan et al., 2006). The MacKinnon–Dworkin ordinance could have allowed for censorship of art, novels, plays, movies and other media that refer to sexuality and the female body. The price is unacceptable.

PREVALENCE AND USE OF EROTICA AND PORNOGRAPHY

Nearly all of us have been exposed to sexually explicit materials, whether in the form of a novel, a photo spread in *Penthouse* or *Club*, an X-rated film, or an adult website. The NHSLS found that about one man in four (23%) and one woman in ten (11%) had bought an X-rated movie or video within the past year (Michael et al., 1994). But today, adult websites have proliferated to the point where many students may be "burning the midnight oil" by surfing sex sites rather than professional journals. A study of 813 students (mean age = 20) from six colleges across the United States found that about 9 out of 10 (87%) men and one-third (31%) of women reported making use of pornography (Carroll et al., 2008). Viewing pornography wasn't associated with much stigma in this sample. Large percentages—two-thirds (67%) of the men and half (49%) of the women—responded that viewing pornography is acceptable.

When we are surfing the Internet, it is almost impossible to avoid all pornographic materials.

Figure 19.2 shows the states with the highest and lowest subscription rates to online pornography websites. With the exceptions of Hawaii and Florida, one might infer that the highest rates are in states with more-rural populations.

People in the United States are typically introduced to pornography by their high school years, often by peers. Females are more likely to have been exposed to pornography by boyfriends than the reverse. 👁

Pornography is typically used to elicit or enhance sexual arousal, often as a masturbation aid (Kingston et al., 2009; Owens et al., 2012). Couples may use pornographic materials to enliven their sexual appetite and enhance sexual arousal during lovemaking.

Researchers have found that both men and women are physiologically sexually aroused by sexually explicit pictures, movies, or audiotaped passages (Chivers & Timmers, 2012; Diamond & Dickenson, 2012). That is, both men and women respond to pornographic stimuli with vasocongestion of the genitals and myotonia (muscle tension). However, there is a difference between physiological response and subjective feelings of arousal in women. Despite what is happening within their bodies, women tend to rate romantic scenes as more sexually arousing than sexually

◉⊃ Watch the **Video**
Donna Rice Hughes: Teens and Technology
on **MyDevelopmentLab**

Highest Rates	Lowest Rates
Utah	Montana
Alaska	Idaho
Mississippi	Tennessee
Hawaii	Ohio
Oklahoma	Oregon
Arkansas	New Jersey
North Dakota	Delaware
Louisiana	Connecticut
Florida	Wyoming
West Virginia	Michigan

FIGURE 19.2 States with the Highest and Lowest Rates of Subscription to Online Pornography Websites.

Source: C. M. Blow. (2009, June 27). The prurient trap. The *New York Times.*

CRITICAL THINKING
How do you interpret the information in Figure 19.2?

explicit scenes (Chivers & Timmers, 2012). Women are less accepting than men of sex without emotional involvement (Petersen & Hyde, 2011). It is romance that encourages most women to follow the lead of genital arousal, when they do so. Even in the choice of erotic materials, women are much more likely than men to want the element of romance included (Petersen & Hyde, 2011).

Repeated exposure to the same pornographic materials progressively lessens the sexual response to them. People may become aroused by the familiar materials again if some time is allowed to go by. Novel materials are also likely to reactivate a sexual response (Hoffman et al., 2012).

GENDER DIFFERENCES IN RESPONSE TO PORNOGRAPHY

 5

TRUTH OR **FICTION** REVISITED: Both males and females can become physiologically aroused by erotic materials. Yet males and females do not necessarily share the same subjective response to them or level of interest in them. Most erotic visual materials are produced by men for men. Women may read erotic romance novels, but they show relatively less interest in erotic pictures, films, or websites (Petersen & Hyde, 2011). Many women find erotica a "turn-off" or disgusting, especially when it portrays women in unflattering roles, as "whorish," and subservient to men.

From the evolutionary perspective, could a basic evolutionary process be at work? Did ancestral men who were more sexually aroused by the sight of a passing female have reproductive advantages over their less arousable peers? Women, however, have fewer mating opportunities than men and must make the most of any reproductive opportunity by selecting the best possible mate and provider. To be sexually aroused by the sight of male genitalia might encourage random couplings, which would undermine their reproductive success.

PORNOGRAPHY AND SEXUAL COERCION

Pornography can be destructive to intimate relationships. Is it also a cause of sexual violence or other antisocial acts? Let us consider several sources of evidence in examining this highly charged question, beginning with history—the findings of a 1970 government commission impaneled to review the evidence that was available at the time.

The Commission on Obscenity and Pornography—A Political Agenda In the 1960s, Congress created the Commission on Obscenity and Pornography to study the effects of pornography. After reviewing the research, the commission (Abelson et al., 1970) concluded that there was no evidence that pornography led to crimes of violence or sexual offenses such as exhibitionism, voyeurism, or child molestation. Some people were sexually aroused by pornography and increased the frequency of their usual sexual activity, such as masturbation or sex with regular partners, following exposure. But they did not engage in antisocial behavior. These results have been replicated many times.

Finding pornography basically harmless, the commission recommended that "federal, state, and local legislation should not seek to interfere with the right of adults who wish to read, obtain, or view explicit sexual materials" (Abelson et al., 1970, p. 58). Congress and then-president Richard Nixon rejected the commission's findings and recommendation, however, on moral and political—not scientific—grounds.

The Meese Commission Report—Another Political Agenda In 1985, President Ronald Reagan appointed a committee headed by Attorney General Edwin Meese to reexamine the effects of pornography. In 1986, the U.S. Attorney General's Commission on Pornography, known as the Meese Commission, issued a report that reached very different conclusions from the 1970 commission. The Meese Commission claimed to find a causal link between sexual violence and exposure to violent pornography (U.S. Department of Justice, 1986). Moreover, the report concluded that exposure to pornography that portrayed women in degrading or subservient roles increased acceptability of rape in the minds of viewers. The commission found no evidence linking exposure to nonviolent, nondegrading pornography (consensual sexual activity between partners in equal roles) and sexual violence but noted that only a small fraction of the pornographic materials on the market was of this type.

Critics claim that the Meese Commission did not blatantly falsify the data, but it failed to distinguish between the effects of sexually explicit materials per se and the effects of violent materials (Sharp & Joslyn, 2008; Weizer, 2007b). Evidence of links between exposure to sexually explicit materials (without violent content) and sexual aggression is lacking.

Pornography and Sex Offenders Research comparing the experience of sex offenders and nonoffenders with pornographic materials has been mixed. A review of the research literature found little or no difference in the level of exposure to pornography between incarcerated sex offenders and comparison groups of felons who were incarcerated for nonsexual crimes (Marshall, 1989). Yet, more recent research finds that sexually aggressive individuals are more likely than others to use pornography (Alexy et al., 2009; Quayle, 2012). As many as one in three rapists and child molesters use pornography to become sexually aroused before they commit their crimes (Marshall, 1989). Even so, these studies are correlational and not experimental. It might be that desire to use pornography and commit sexually aggressive acts are both related to other factors, such as a general tendency to seek out sexual images and experiences that humiliate women. Moreover, only 38% of a male college sample reported acting out aggressive sexual fantasies (Williams et al., 2009), but one could argue that 38% is more than enough.

Experiments on the Effects of Violent Pornography Laboratory-based studies have shown that men exposed to violent pornography are more likely to become aggressive against females and to show less sensitivity toward women who have been sexually assaulted. In one classic study (Donnerstein, 1980), 120 college

Men who are exposed to violent pornography, or to pornography that degrades women, are more likely to be aggressive toward women in their own lives. But is it the sexual content or the violence that contributes to harmful behavior?

men interacted with a male or female confederate (accomplice) of the experimenter, who treated them in either a neutral or hostile manner. The subjects were then shown neutral, nonviolent pornographic films, or violent pornographic films. In the latter, a man forced himself into a woman's home and raped her. Subjects were then given the opportunity to deliver electric shock to the male or female confederate, presumably to assist the confederate in learning a task. The measure of aggression was the intensity of the shock chosen. No shock was actually delivered, but subjects did not know that the shock apparatus was fake. Unprovoked men who viewed violent pornographic films showed greater aggression toward the women than did unprovoked men who viewed nonviolent films, however. Provoked men who were shown violent pornography selected the highest shock levels of all. The film may have served as a model for retaliation.

In another study, aggression by males against female confederates following exposure to violent pornography (a rape scene) was increased by depictions of the woman being raped as either enjoying the experience or becoming sexually aroused during the rape (Donnerstein & Berkowitz, 1981). These findings suggest that depictions of women enjoying or becoming aroused by their victimization may legitimize violence against women in the viewer's mind, reinforcing the cultural myth that some women need to be dominated and are sexually aroused by an overpowering male.

Some research suggests that it is the violence in violent pornography, and not sexual explicitness, that hardens men's attitudes toward rape survivors. In one study (Donnerstein & Linz, 1987), college men were exposed to films consisting of either violent pornography, nonviolent pornography (a couple having consensual intercourse), or violence that was not sexually explicit. The violent pornographic and nonpornographic films both showed a woman being tied up and slapped at gunpoint, but the nonpornographic version contained no nudity or explicit sexual activity. The men had first been either angered or treated in a neutral manner by a female confederate of the experimenter. The results showed that, in comparison with nonviolent pornography, both violent pornographic films and violent *non*pornographic films produced greater acceptance of rape myths, increased reported willingness to force a woman into sexual activity, and greater reported likelihood of engaging in rape (if the man also knew that he could get away with it). These effects occurred regardless of whether the man was angered by the woman or not.

Research on the effects of pornography should be interpreted with caution, however (Sharp & Joslyn, 2008). Most of it has employed college students, whose behavior may or may not be typical of people in general or of people with propensities toward sexual violence. Another issue is that most studies in this area are laboratory-based experiments that involve simulated aggression or judgments of sympathy toward hypothetical women who have been portrayed as rape victims. None measured *actual* violence against women outside the lab. We still lack conclusive evidence that normal men have been, or would be, spurred to rape or to sexually violate women because of exposure to violent pornography.

In their comprehensive review of the research literature on pornography and sexual aggression, Neil Malamuth and his colleagues (2000) analyzed data from studies that found no reliable links between pornography and aggression, integrated the findings of multiple summaries of the experimental and naturalistic research literature, and analyzed questionnaire data obtained from a representative sample of 2,972 college men with a mean age of 21. Each method of analysis supported the existence of some reliable connections between the frequent use of pornography and sexually aggressive behavior—particularly in the cases of violent pornography and for men who were likely to engage in sexual aggression.

TRUTH OR **FICTION** REVISITED: Malamuth and his colleagues conclude not that pornography causes violence, but that relatively aggressive men react differently from nonviolent men to the same pornography. It is not so much that pornography makes men violent; instead, it seems to be more likely that pornography makes violent men more violent.

Experiments on the Effects of Nonviolent Pornography Nonviolent pornography may not contain scenes of sexual violence, but it typically portrays women in degrading or dehumanizing roles—as sexually promiscuous, insatiable, and subservient (Itzin et al., 2007). Might such portrayals of women reinforce traditional stereotypes of women as sex objects? Might they lead viewers to condone acts of rape by suggesting that women are essentially promiscuous? Might the depiction of women as readily sexually accessible inspire men to refuse to "take no for an answer"?

In classic research, Zillmann and Bryant (1984) exposed male and female subjects to six sessions of pornography over six consecutive weeks. Subjects were exposed to either a massive dose of pornography, consisting of six nonviolent pornographic films during each session; to an intermediate dose consisting of three pornographic and three neutral films each session; or to a no-dose control, consisting of six nonsexual films. When surveyed later, both males and females who received extended exposure to pornography, especially those receiving the massive dose, gave more lenient punishments to a rapist who was depicted in a newspaper article. Moreover, males became more callous in their attitudes toward women.

In a more recent study, 71 men watched one of three films: a film that was sexually explicit and degrading of women, a film that was sexually explicit but *not* degrading of women, and a nonsexual (control) film (Mulac et al., 2002). The men then worked in couples with women to solve problems. Men who watched the sexually explicit films behaved more dominantly toward their problem-solving partners than men who watched the control film. Moreover, men who watched the sexually explicit *and* degrading film showed more dominance than those who watched the sexually explicit but not degrading film.

Overall, it would appear that at least for some men, exposure to pornography can render attitudes toward women more negative and callous. Some men who view pornography may come to regard women as sexual playthings who are to be valued for their physical attributes and role in providing sexual release, and not as individuals (Kingston et al., 2009).

Another concern is the possible effect of nonviolent pornography on the viewer's sexual and family values. Nonviolent pornography typically features impromptu sexual encounters between new acquaintances. Does repeated exposure to nonviolent pornography loosen traditional sexual and family values? When compared to people who viewed nonsexual films, men and women who were exposed to weekly, hour-long sessions involving scenes of explicit sexual encounters between new acquaintances over a six-week period showed attitudinal changes including greater acceptance, in comparison to controls who viewed nonsexual films, of premarital and extramarital sex and of simultaneous sexual relationships with multiple partners (Zillman, 1989). They also reported desiring fewer children and were relatively less committed to marriage as an "essential institution."

Nonviolent pornography may loosen traditional family values by projecting an image of sexual enjoyment without responsibility or obligations (Carroll et al., 2008). Prolonged exposure may also foster dissatisfaction with the physical appearance and sexual performance of one's intimate partners (Brown, 2003).

CRITICAL THINKING
Which do you consider to be the greater danger—the danger of widely available pornography or the danger of censorship? Explain your point of view.

Chapter Review   ✓●⌐Study and Review on MyDevelopmentLab

LO1 Define prostitution

Prostitution or "sex work" is the sale of sex. Prostitution is illegal everywhere in the United States except rural counties in Nevada. Fewer young men in the United States use prostitutes than in Kinsey's day, apparently because of the sexual revolution.

LO2 Summarize what we know about female and male prostitutes, including their backgrounds

The major types of female prostitutes are streetwalkers, brothel prostitutes, "masseuses," "escorts," and call girls. Many prostitutes work in adult films and on adult websites. Poverty and child abuse figure in the backgrounds of many prostitutes. Teenage runaways are vulnerable to being drawn into prostitution. Most patrons of prostitutes are occasional johns with regular sex partners.

Most male prostitutes service male clients, but some male sex workers—for example, strippers— have female customers.

LO3 Discuss the relationship between prostitution and sexually transmitted infections (STIs)

Prostitutes are at greater risk of transmission of HIV and other STIs because they have sexual relations with many partners, often without protection. HIV may be spread by prostitutes to customers, then to the customers' regular partners.

LO4 Define pornography and obscenity

Pornography is "writing, pictures, etc., intended to arouse sexual desire." What is seen as pornographic or obscene varies from person to person and culture to culture. *Obscenity* refers to statements or materials that offend people or go beyond prevailing standards of decency or modesty.

LO5 Describe the legal status of pornography and obscenity

In *Miller v. California*, the U.S. Supreme Court held that obscenity is based on determination of "whether the average person, applying contemporary community standards, would find that the work ... appeals to the prurient interest ...; whether the work depicts [sexual behavior] in a patently offensive way; [and] whether the work, taken as a whole, lacks serious literary, artistic, political, or scientific value." The downloading or possession of child pornography has been criminalized throughout the United States.

LO6 Discuss the incidence and use of pornography

Americans are typically introduced to pornography by their high school years. Pornography is readily available on the Internet, in X-rated magazines, and in books.

LO7 Discuss gender differences in response to pornography

Although females and males can both be physiologically aroused by pornography, men are relatively more interested. Pornography is frequently used as a masturbation aid.

LO8 Discuss possible relationships between pornography and sexual coercion

A 1970 government commission found no harmful effects of pornographic material on normal people. A 1986 government commission reported that exposure to violent pornography is linked with sexual aggression, and exposure to degrading but nonviolent pornography is linked with increased acceptability of rape in the minds of viewers. Scientific experiments suggest that exposure to pornography may stimulate sexually deviant urges in men who are predisposed to commit crimes of sexual violence, and that violent pornography may stimulate college men to act more aggressively toward women.

Test Your Learning

1. _____ occupy the bottom rung in the hierarchy of prostitutes.
   (a) Streetwalkers
   (b) Brothel prostitutes
   (c) Massage parlor prostitutes
   (d) Call girls

2. Most patrons of prostitutes are "_____ johns."

   (a) habitual   (c) occasional
   (b) gay   (d) atypical

3. Female prostitutes differ from most women in that they do not require _____ from sex partners.

   (a) money   (c) condoms
   (b) commitment   (d) sexual activity

4. _____ are physiologically sexually aroused by pornography.

   (a) Men and women
   (b) Only men
   (c) Only women
   (d) Only gay males and lesbians

5. The Supreme Court decision in *Miller v. California* stated that _____ standards must be considered in defining obscenity.

   (a) biblical   (c) educational
   (b) community   (d) universal

6. Research appears to show that _____ pornography is connected with sexual aggression.

   (a) explicit   (c) violent
   (b) gay   (d) online

7. U.S. courts have held that the _____ Amendment to the Constitution guarantees freedom to use pornography.

   (a) First
   (b) Second
   (c) Fifth
   (d) Twenty-third

8. A study of 586 streetwalkers in Miami found that about _____ percent tested positive for HIV.

   (a) 22   (c) 62
   (b) 42   (d) 82

9. Farley and her colleagues interviewed 100 Canadian prostitutes and found that _____ percent reported a history of childhood sexual abuse.

   (a) 22   (c) 62
   (b) 42   (d) 82

10. What is true of the sexual orientation of hustlers?

    (a) They are straight.
    (b) They are gay.
    (c) They are bisexual.
    (d) They may have any sexual orientation.

Answers: 1. a; 2. c; 3. b; 4. a; 5. b; 6. c; 7. a; 8. a; 9. d; 10. d

My Life, My Sexuality

Developing Self-Control to Avoid Use of Commercial Sex Outlets

*Explore this **My Life, My Sexuality** feature by scanning this QR code with your mobile device. If you don't already have one, you may download a free QR scanner for your device wherever smartphone apps are sold. You can also view this feature in MyDevelopmentLab, along with an accompanying critical thinking assignment.*

A character in a play by Oscar Wilde says, "I can resist anything but temptation." How about you?

Prostitution and pornography are out there and are likely to remain out there. Therefore, if you are concerned with your own use—or urges to use—the commercial sex outlets of prostitutes and pornography, it is necessary to develop your own self-control. This My Life, My Sexuality feature employs so-called "cognitive-behavioral" methods of self-control to deal with urges to visit prostitutes or to use pornography. That is, it shows you how to use your thoughts, fantasies, and attitudes (the cognitive issues) and your actual behavior to build self-control.

Appendix

Scoring Keys for Self-Assessments

"WOULD YOU TELL AN INTERVIEWER THE TRUTH ON A SURVEY ABOUT YOUR SEXUAL BEHAVIOR? THE SOCIAL-DESIRABILITY SCALE" (Chapter 2, p. 42)

Place a check mark on the appropriate line of the scoring key each time your answer agrees with the one listed in the scoring key. Add the check marks and record the total number of check marks here.

1. T _____	12. F _____	23. F _____
2. T _____	13. T _____	24. T _____
3. F _____	14. F _____	25. T _____
4. T _____	15. F _____	26. T _____
5. F _____	16. T _____	27. T _____
6. F _____	17. T _____	28. F _____
7. T _____	18. T _____	29. T _____
8. T _____	19. F _____	30. F _____
9. F _____	20. T _____	31. T _____
10. F _____	21. T _____	32. F _____
11. F _____	22. F _____	33. T _____

INTERPRETING YOUR SCORE

Low Scorers (0–8 Points) About one respondent in six earns a score between 0 and 8 points. Such respondents answered in a socially *undesirable* direction much of the time. It may be that they are more willing than most people to respond to tests truthfully, even when their answers might meet with social disapproval.

Average Scorers (9–19 Points) About two respondents in three earn a score from 9 to 19 points. They tend to show an average degree of concern for the social desirability of their responses, and it may be that their general behavior represents an average degree of conformity to social rules and conventions.

High Scorers (20–33 Points) About one respondent in six earns a score between 20 and 33 points. These respondents may be highly concerned about social approval, and respond to test items in such as way as to avoid the disapproval of people who may read their responses. Their general behavior may show high conformity to social rules and conventions.

"DO YOU EXPERIENCE PMS OR PMDD?" (Chapter 3, p. 90)

There are no numerical answers to this self-assessment. Rather, ask yourself if you are experiencing any moderate to disabling psychological or physical symptoms of PMS or PMDD. We advise you to discuss any symptoms that are moderate or more severe with your physician, preferably a gynecologist. It is important for your health that you discuss any and all disabling symptoms with your gynecologist. Even if you have some mild symptoms, you may want to check them off and bring them to the attention of your gynecologist. Nothing is to be gained by suffering in silence.

"STERNBERG'S TRIANGULAR LOVE SCALE" (Chapter 7, p. 203)

Add your scores for the items on each of the three components—intimacy, passion, and commitment—and divide each total by 15. This procedure will yield an average rating for each subscale. An average rating of 5 points on a particular subscale indicates a moderate level of the component represented by the subscale. A higher rating indicates a greater level. A lower rating indicates a lower level. Examining your ratings on these components will give you an idea of the degree to which you perceive your love relationship to be characterized by these three components of love. For example, you might find that passion is stronger than commitment, a pattern that is common during the early stages of an intense romantic relationship. You might find it interesting to complete the questionnaire a few months or perhaps a year or so from now to see how your feelings about your relationship change over time. You might also ask your partner to complete the scale so that the two of you can compare your respective scores. Comparing your ratings for each component with those of your partner will give you an idea of the degree to which you and your partner see your relationship in a similar way.

Sternberg (1988) reports the results of administering the scale to a sample of 50 men and 51 women (average age, 31 years) from the New Haven, Connecticut, area who were either married or currently involved in a close relationship. Average scores for the three components were 7.39 points for intimacy, 6.51 points for passion, and 7.20 points for commitment. High scores (scores representing approximately the top 15% of scores) were 8.6 points for intimacy, 8.2 points for passion, and 8.7 points for commitment. Low scores, representing the bottom 15% of scores, were 6.2 points, 4.9 points, and 5.7 points for the three components, respectively. Because romantic ardor may be more difficult to maintain over time, the lower average scores for passion may reflect the length of the relationships in which the people in the sample were involved, which averaged 6.3 years. Although you may want to compare your scores with those from this sample, we caution that the Sternberg sample was small and most likely does not accurately represent the general population.

"PRO-CHOICE OR PRO-LIFE? WHERE DO YOU STAND?"
(Chapter 12, p. 362)

First, tally your scores for items 1, 3, 7, 8, 9, 11, 13, 14, 17, and 20. This score represents your support for a *pro-choice* point of view: _____.

Second, tally your scores for items 2, 4, 5, 6, 10, 12, 15, 16, 18, and 19. This score represents your support for a *pro-life* point of view: _____.

Next, subtract your pro-choice score from your pro-life score. Write the difference, including the sign ±, here: _____. A positive score indicates agreement with a pro-life philosophy. A negative score indicates agreement with a pro-choice philosophy. The higher your score, the more strongly you agree with the philosophy you endorsed. Scores may range from −40 to +40 points.

One sample of 230 undergraduate students (115 of each gender) obtained a mean score of −7.48 points and a median score of −13.33 points (Parsons et al., 1990). This indicates that the students tended to be pro-choice in their attitudes. Another sample of 38 graduate students (31 women and 7 men) obtained mean scores of −11 to −12 points and median scores of −17 to −18 points on two separate occasions. Scores for other samples may vary.

References

Aarts, H., & van Honk, J. (2009). Testosterone and unconscious positive priming increase human motivation separately. *NeuroReport, 20*(14), 1300–1303.

Abal, Y. N., Maríín, J. A. L., & Sánchez, S. R. (2003). A new paraphilia of the XXI century: Chat-scatophilia. *Archivos Hispanoamericanos de Sexologíía, 9*(1), 81–104.

Abell, J., Locke, A., Condor, S., Gibson, S., & Stevenson, C. (2006). Trying similarity, doing difference: The role of interviewer self-disclosure in interview talk with young people. *Qualitative Research, 6*(2), 221–244.

Abelson, H., et al. (1970). Public attitudes toward and experience with erotic materials. In *Technical reports of the commission on obscenity and pornography.* Vol. 6. Washington, DC: U.S. Government Printing Office.

Abma, J. C., et al. (2010). Teenagers in the United States: Sexual activity, contraceptive use, and childbearing. National Survey of Family Growth, 2006–2008. National Center for Health Statistics. *Vital and Health Statistics, 23*(30).

Ackerman, D. (1991). *The moon by whale light.* New York: Random House.

Ackerman, D. (2012, March 24). The brain on love. *New York Times* (Online).

ACOG (The American College of Obstetricians and Gynecologists). (2003, July 31). *Weighing the pros and cons of cesarean delivery.* ACOG news release. www.acog.com/from_home/publications/press_releases/nr07-31-03-3.cfm.

Adams, H. E., Wright, L. W., Jr., & Lohr, B. A. (1996). Is homophobia associated with homosexual arousal? *Journal of Abnormal Psychology, 105,* 440–445.

Adams, H., & Phillips, L. (2006). Experiences of two-spirit lesbian and gay Native Americans: An argument for standpoint theory in identity research. *Identity, 6*(3), 273–291.

Adams, K. M. (2003). Clergy sex abuse: A commentary on celibacy. *Sexual Addiction & Compulsivity: The Journal of Treatment and Prevention, 10*(2–3), 91–92.

Adams, N. (2006). Systemic therapy techniques for sexual difficulties. In J. Hiller et al. (Eds.), *Sex, mind, and emotion: Innovation in psychological theory and practice* (pp. 209–227). London, UK: Karnac Books.

Adams, R. A. (2007). College students' attribution of blame in father–daughter incest. *Family and Consumer Sciences Research Journal, 36*(1), 55–62.

Agrawal, A. (1997). Gendered bodies: The case of the "third gender" in India. *Contributions to Indian Sociology, 31,* 273–97.

AIM Health Care Foundation (2009). HIV/STD Testing. (Accessed November 6, 2009). http://www.aim-med.org/.

Ainsworth, S. E., & Baumeister, R. F. (2012). Theories of sexology: What have we learned from college students? In R. D. McAnulty (Ed.). *Sex in college: The things they don't write home about* (pp. 45–64). Santa Barbara, CA: ABC-CLIO.

Alemozaffar, M., et al. (2011). Prediction of erectile function following treatment for prostate cancer. *Journal of the American Medical Association, 306*(11), 1205–1214.

Alexander, B. (2009, March 26). "Sex surrogates" put personal touch on therapy: Despite dubious legality, some counselors still prescribe practice to patients. http://www.msnbc.msn.com/id/29881206/.

Alexander, G. M., Wilcox, T., & Woods, R. (2009). Sex differences in infants' visual interest in toys. *Archives of Sexual Behavior, 38*(3), 427–433.

Alexander, J. (2006). A critical introduction to queer theory. *Sexualities, 9*(1), 115–117.

Alexy, E. M., Burgess, A. W., & Prentky, R. A. (2009). Pornography use as a risk marker for an aggressive pattern of behavior among sexually reactive children and adolescents. *Journal of the American Psychiatric Nurses Association, 14*(6), 442–453.

Ali, M. M., & Dwyer, D. S. (2011). Estimating peer effects in sexual behavior among adolescents. *Journal of Adolescence, 34*(1), 183–190.

Allen, E. S., & Atkins, D. C. (2005). The multidimensional and developmental nature of infidelity: Practical applications. *Journal of Clinical Psychology, 61*(11), 1371–1382.

Allen, T. D., & de Tormes Eby, L. T. (2012). The study of interpersonal relationships: An introduction. In L. T. de Tormes Eby & T. D. Allen (Eds.). *Personal relationships* (pp. 3–14). New York: Routledge.

Allison, C. M., & Hyde, J. S. (2011). Early menarche: Confluence of biological and contextual factors. *Sex Roles.* DOI:10.1007/s11199-011-9993-5.

Aloi, J. A. (2009). Nursing the disenfranchised: Women who have relinquished an infant for adoption. *Journal of Psychiatric and Mental Health Nursing, 16*(1), 27–31.

Aloni, M., & Bernieri, F. J. (2004). Is love blind? The effects of experience and infatuation on the perception of love. *Journal of Nonverbal Behavior, 28*(4), 287–295.

Althof, S. E. (1994). Paper presented at the annual meeting of the American Urological Association, San Francisco, CA.

Althof, S. E. (2010). What's new in sex therapy? *Journal of Sexual Medicine, 7,* 5–13.

Althof, S. E. (2012). Psychological interventions for delayed ejaculation/orgasm. *International Journal of Impotence Research*, DOI:10.1038/ijir.2012.2.

Althof, S. E., & Needle, R. B. (2011). Sex therapy in male sexual dysfunction. *Current Clinical Urology, Part 5,* 731–738.

Altunkaynak, B. Z., et al. (2012). Effects of diabetes and ovariectomy on a rat hippocampus. *Gynecological Endocrinology, 28*(3), 228–233.

Alvarez, L., et al. (2012). The rate of change in Ca^{2+} concentration controls sperm chemotaxis. *The Journal of Cell Biology, 196*(5), 653–663.

Alzate, H., & Hoch, Z. (1986). The "G spot" and "female ejaculation": A current appraisal. *Journal of Sex and Marital Therapy, 12*(3), 211–220.

Amato, P. R. (2006). Marital discord, divorce, and children's well-being: Results from a 20-year longitudinal study of two generations. In A. Clarke-Stewart & J. Dunn (Eds.), *Families count: Effects on child and adolescent development* (pp. 179–202). The Jacobs Foundation series on adolescence. New York: Cambridge University Press.

Amato, P. R., & Afifi, T. D. (2006). Feeling caught between parents: Adult children's relations with parents and subjective wellbeing. *Journal of Marriage and Family, 68*(1), 222–235.

American Academy of Family Physicians. (2006). *Depo-Provera: An injectable contraceptive.* http://familydoctor.org/043.xml? printxml.

American Academy of Family Physicians. (2012, June 13). Family planning and contraception. http://www.aafp.org/afp/topicModules/viewTopicModule.htm?topicModuleId=71 (Accessed June 23, 2012).

American Academy of Pediatrics. (2005). Breastfeeding and the use of human milk. *Pediatrics, 115,* 496–506.

American Academy of Pediatrics Task Force on Circumcision. (2012, August 27). Male circumcision. *Pediatrics,* 2012-1990. DOI:10.1542/peds.

American Academy of Pediatrics. (2012, February 27). AAP Reaffirms breastfeeding guidelines. www.aap.org. (Accessed September 21, 2012).

American Cancer Society. (2006). *Cancer facts & figures 2006.* www.cancer.org/downloads/STT/CAFF2006f4PWSecured.pdf.

American Cancer Society. (2009). *Cancer facts & figures 2009.* http://www.cancer.org/downloads/STT/500809web.pdf.

American Cancer Society. (2012a). Breast cancer. http://www.cancer.org/Cancer/BreastCancer/index.

American Cancer Society. (2012b). Cervical cancer. http://www.cancer.org/Cancer/CervicalCancer/index.

American Cancer Society. (2012c). Endometrial cancer. http://www.cancer.org/Cancer/EndometrialCancer/index.

American Cancer Society. (2012d). Ovarian cancer. http://www.cancer.org/Cancer/OvarianCancer/index.

American Cancer Society. (2012e). Prostate cancer. http://www.cancer.org/Cancer/ProstateCancer/OverviewGuide/index.

American Cancer Society. (2012f). Testicular cancer. http://www.cancer.org/Cancer/TesticularCancer/index.

American Fertility Association. (2006, February). www.theafa.org.

American Fertility Association. (2012). Library: LGBT family building. http://www.theafa.org/library/lgbt-family-building/ (Accessed June 1, 2012).

American Psychiatric Association. (2000). *Diagnostic and statistical manual of mental disorders* (4th ed.). *DSM-IV-TR.* Washington, DC: Author.

American Psychiatric Association. (2012). DSM-5 development. http://www.dsm5.org/Pages/Default.aspx.

Amnesty International. (2012). Violence against women information. http://www.amnestyusa.org/our-work/issues/women-s-rights/violence-against-women/violence-against-women-information.

Amodeo, M., Griffin, M. K., Fassler, I. R., Clay, C. M., & Ellis, M. A. (2006). Childhood sexual abuse among black women and white women from two-parent families. *Child Maltreatment, 11*(3), 237–246.

Amodio, D. M., & Showers, C. J. (2005). "Similarity breeds liking" revisited: The moderating role of commitment. *Journal of Social and Personal Relationships, 22*(6), 817–836.

Andersen, M. L., Bignotto, M., & Tufik, S. (2003). The effect of apomorphine on genital reflexes in male rats deprived of paradoxical sleep. *Physiology & Behavior, 80*(2–3), 211–215.

Andersen, M. L., & Tufik, S. (2005). Effects of progesterone blockade over cocaine-induced genital reflexes of paradoxical sleep-deprived male rats. *Hormones and Behavior, 47*(4), 477–484.

Anderson, B. J., & Stein, M. D. (2011). A behavioral decision model testing the association of marijuana use and sexual risk in young adult women. *AIDS and Behavior, 15*(4), 875–884.

Anderson, E. R., Greene, S. M., Hetherington, E. M., & Clingempeel, W. G. (1999). Dynamics of parental remarriage: Adolescent, parent, and sibling influences. In E. M. Hetherington (Ed.), *Coping with divorce, single parenting, and remarriage: A risk and resiliency perspective* (pp. 295–319). Hillsdale, NJ: Erlbaum.

Anderson, G. L., et al. (2012). Conjugated equine oestrogen and breast cancer incidence and mortality in postmenopausal women with hysterectomy: Extended follow-up of the Women's Health Initiative randomised placebo-controlled trial. *Lancet Oncology, 13*(5). http://dx.doi.org/10.1016/S1470-2045(12)70075-X.

Anderson, K. M. (2006). Surviving incest: The art of resistance. *Families in Society, 87*(3), 409–416.

Anderson, M., Kunkel, A., & Dennis, M. R. (2011). "Let's (not) talk about that": Bridging the past sexual experiences taboo to build healthy romantic relationships. *Journal of Sex Research, 48*(4), 381–391.

Anderson, S. E., et al. (2003). Relative weight and race influence average age at menarche: Results from two nationally representative surveys of U.S. girls studied 25 years apart. *Pediatrics, 111*, 844–850.

Anderssen, N., Amlie, C., & Ytteroy, E. A. (2002). Outcomes for children with lesbian or gay parents: A review of studies from 1978 to 2000. *Scandinavian Journal of Psychology, 43*(4), 335–351.

Andreano, J. M., & Cahill, L. (2009). Sex influences on the neurobiology of learning and memory. *Learning and Memory, 16*, 248–266.

Andriole, G. L. (2009a March 24). In T. Parker-Pope, Screen or not? What those prostate studies mean. *The New York Times.*

Andriole, G. L., et al. (2009). Mortality results from a randomized prostate-cancer screening trial. *New England Journal of Medicine, 360*, 1310–1319.

Apperloo, M. J. A., et al. (2003). In the mood for sex: The value of androgens. *Journal of Sex & Marital Therapy, 29*(2), 87–102.

Argentieri, S. (2005). Incest yesterday and today: From conflict to ambiguity. In G. Ambrosio (Ed.), *On incest: Psychoanalytic perspectives* (pp. 17–49). London: Karnac Books.

Armstrong, E. A. (2009). Cited in P. L. Brown & C. Pogash. (2009, March 15). The pleasure principle. *The New York Times* (Online).

Aron, A., et al. (2008). Falling in love. In S. Sprecher, A. Wenzel, & J. Harvey (Eds.), *Handbook of relationship initiation* (pp. 315–336). New York: CRC Press.

Arriaga, X. B., & Rusbult, C. E. (1998). Standing in my partner's shoes: Partner perspective taking and reactions to accommodative dilemmas. *Personality & Social Psychology Bulletin, 24*(9), 927–948.

Arthur, B. I., Jr., et al. (1998). Sexual behaviour in *Drosophila* is irreversibly programmed during critical period. *Current Biology, 8*(21), 1187–1190.

Ascher, N. (2006, July 10.) *Fight ignorance before it's too late.* www.classicalvalues.com/archives/003848.html.

Ashley–Koch, A., Yang, Q., & Olney, R. S. (2000). Sickle hemoglobin (Hb S) allele and sickle cell disease. *American Journal of Epidemiology, 151*(9), 839–845.

Astley, S. J., & Clarren, S. K. (2001). Measuring the facial phenotype of individuals with prenatal alcohol exposure: Correlations with brain dysfunction. *Alcohol & Alcoholism, 36*(2), 147–159.

Aubin, S., Heiman, J. R., Berger, R. E., Murallo, A. V., & Yung-Wen, L. (2009). Comparing sildenafil alone vs. sildenafil plus brief couple sex therapy on erectile dysfunction and couples' sexual and marital quality of life. *Journal of Sex and Marital Therapy, 35*(2), 122–143.

"Australia scientists find flowers dupe lonely bees." (2000, June 16). Reuters News Agency online.

Auyeung, B., et al. (2009). Fetal testosterone predicts behavior in girls and in boys. *Psychological Science, 20*(2), 144–148.

Aveline, D. (2006). "Did I have blinders on or what?": Retrospective sense making by parents of gay sons recalling their sons' earlier years. *Journal of Family Issues, 27*(6), 777–802.

Avis, N. E. (2003). Depression during the menopausal transition. *Psychology of Women Quarterly, 27*(2), 91–100.

Avivi, Y. E., Laurenceau, J-P., & Carver, C. S. (2009). Linking relationship quality to perceived mutuality of relationship. *Journal of Social and Clinical Psychology, 28*(2), 137–164.

Ayres, M. M., & Haddock, S. A. (2009). Therapists' approaches in working with heterosexual couples struggling with male partners' online sexual behavior. *Sexual Addiction & Compulsivity, 16*(1), 55–78.

Bach, G., & Deutsch, R. M. (1970). *Pairing: How to achieve genuine intimacy.* New York: Avon Books.

Bäckström T., et al. (2003). The role of hormones and hormonal treatments in premenstrual syndrome. *CNS Drugs, 17*(5), 325–342.

Bader, M. (2003). *Arousal: The secret logic of sexual fantasies.* New York: Griffin Trade Paperback.

Bagley, C., & D'Augelli, A. R. (2000). Suicidal behaviour in gay, lesbian, and bisexual youth. *British Medical Journal, 320*, 1617–1618.

Bailes, E., et al. (2003). Hybrid origin of SIV in chimpanzees. *Science, 300*(5626), 1713.

Bailey, J. M. (1999). Homosexuality and mental illness. *Archives of General Psychiatry, 56*(10), 883–884.

Bailey, J. M. (2003a). Personal communication.

Bailey, J. M. (2003b). *The man who would be queen: The science of gender-bending and transsexualism.* Washington, DC: Joseph Henry Press.

Bailey, J. M., & Pillard, R. C. (1991). A genetic study of male sexual orientation. *Archives of General Psychiatry, 48*, 1089–1096.

Bailey, J. M., et al. (1999). A family history study of male sexual orientation using three independent samples. *Behavior Genetics, 29*(2), 79–86.

Bakalar, N. (2005, November 22). Premature births increase along with C-sections. *The New York Times*, p. F8.

Baker, J. L., et al. (2008). Breastfeeding reduces postpartum weight retention. *American Journal of Clinical Nutrition, 88*, 1553–1551.

Balsam, K. F., et al. (2004). Culture, trauma, and wellness: A comparison of heterosexual and lesbian, gay, bisexual, and two-spirit Native Americans. *Cultural Diversity & Ethnic Minority Psychology, 10*(3), 287–301.

Bamgbose, O. (2002). Teenage prostitution and the future of the female adolescent in Nigeria. *International Journal of Offender Therapy & Comparative Criminology, 46*(5), 569–585.

Bancroft, J. (Ed.). (2003). *Sexual development in childhood.* Bloomington: Indiana University Press.

Bancroft, J., Carnes, L., & Janssen, E. (2005a). Unprotected anal intercourse in HIV-positive and HIV-negative gay men: The relevance of sexual arousability, mood, sensation seeking, and erectile problems. *Archives of Sexual Behavior, 34*, 299–305.

Bancroft, J., Carnes, L., Janssen, E., Goodrich, D., & Long, J. S. (2005b). Erectile and ejaculatory problems in gay and heterosexual men. *Archives of Sexual Behavior, 34*(3), 285–297.

Bancroft, J., et al. (2005c). The relevance of the dual control model to male sexual dysfunction: The Kinsey Institute/BASRT collaborative project. *Sexual & Relationship Therapy, 20*, 13–30.

Bancroft, J., Long, J. S., & McCabe, J. (2011). Sexual well-being: A comparison of U.S. black and white women in heterosexual relationships. *Archives of Sexual Behavior, 40*(4), 725–740.

Banszegi, O., et al. (2010). Testosterone treatment of pregnant rabbits affects sexual development of their daughters. *Physiology and Behavior, 101*(4), 422–427.

Barak, A. (2005). Sexual harassment on the Internet. *Social Science Computer Review, 23*(1), 77–92.

Baral, S., et al. (2012). Burden of HIV among female sex workers in low-income and middle-income countries: a systematic review and meta-analysis. *The Lancet Infectious Diseases, 12*(7), 538–549.

Barbaree, H. E., & Blanchard, R. (2008). Sexual deviance over the lifespan. In D. R. Laws and W. T. O'Donohue (Eds.), *Sexual deviance: Theory, assessment, and treatment* (2nd ed., pp. 27–60). New York: Guilford Press.

Barelli, C., Heistermann, M., Boesch, C., & Reichard, U. H. (2008). Mating patterns and sexual swellings in pair-living and multiple groups of wild white-handed gibbons, *Hylobates lar. Animal Behaviour, 75*(3), 991–1001.

Barnard, N. D., Scialli, A. R., Hurlock, D., & Bertron, P. (2000). Diet and sex-hormone binding globulin, dysmenorrhea, and premenstrual symptoms. *Obstetrics & Gynecology, 95,* 245–250.

Barnett, J. E., & Dunning, C. (2003). Clinical perspectives on elderly sexuality. *Archives of Sexual Behavior, 32*(3), 295–296.

Barney, D., & Feenberg, A. (Eds.). (2004). *Community in the digital age: Philosophy and practice.* Lanham, MD: Rowman & Littlefield.

Barrett, M. B. (1990). *Invisible lives: The truth about millions of women-loving women.* New York: Harper & Row (Perennial Library).

Barrett, S. E., Chin, J. L., Comas–Diaz, L., Espin, O., Greene, B., & McGoldrick, M. (2005). Multicultural feminist therapy: Theory in context. *Women & Therapy, 28*(3–4), 27–61.

Barrionuevo, A. (2009, March 28). Amid abuse of girls in Brazil, abortion debate flares. *The New York Times.*

Barsky, J. L., Friedman, M. A., & Rosen, R. C. (2006). Sexual dysfunction and chronic illness: The role of flexibility in coping. *Journal of Sex & Marital Therapy, 32*(3), 235–253.

Bartels, R. M., & Gannon, T. A. (2011). Understanding the sexual fantasies of sex offenders and their correlates. *Aggression and Violent Behavior, 16*(6), 551–561.

Barth, R. P., et al. (2002). Methodological lessons from the National Survey of Child and Adolescent Well-Being: The first three years of the USA's first national probability study of children and families investigated for abuse and neglect. *Children & Youth Services Review, 24*(6–7), 513–541.

Bartolo, K. C. (2005). Mother–daughter incest: A guide for helping professionals. *Journal of Family Studies, 11*(2), 328–329.

Basile, K. C. (2002). Attitudes toward wife rape: Effects of social background and victim status. *Violence & Victims, 17*(3), 341–354.

Basow, S. A., & Rubenfeld, K. (2003). "Troubles talk": Effects of gender and gender-typing. *Sex Roles, 48*(3–4), 183–187.

Basson, B., Davis, S. R., & Rodenberg, C. (2009). Testosterone for low libido. *New England Journal of Medicine, 360*(7), 728–729.

Bastian, L. A., Smith, C. M., & Nanda, K. (2003). Is this woman perimenopausal? *Journal of the American Medical Association, 289,* 895–902.

Bauerle, S. Y., Amirkhan, J. H., & Hupka, R. B. (2002). An attribution theory analysis of romantic jealousy. *Motivation & Emotion, 26*(4), 297–319.

Bauland, C. G., et al. (2012). Similar risk for hemangiomas after amniocentesis and transabdominal chorionic villus sampling. *The Journal of Obstetrics and Gynecology Research, 38*(2), 371–375.

Baum, M. J., & Kelliher, K. R. (2009). Complementary roles of the main and accessory olfactory systems in mammalian mate recognition. *Annual Review of Physiology, 71,* 141–160.

Baumeister, R. F. (2000). Gender differences in erotic plasticity: The female sex drive as socially flexible and responsive. *Psychological Bulletin, 126*(3), 347–374.

Baumeister, R. F., Catanese, K. R., & Vohs, K. D. (2001). Is there a gender difference in strength of sex drive? Theoretical views, conceptual distinctions, and a review of relevant evidence. *Personality & Social Psychology Review, 5*(3), 242–273.

Bearak, B. (2006, July 9). The bride price. *The New York Times Magazine.* (Online).

Becerra, L., Breiter, H. C., Wise, R., Gonzalez, R. G., & Borsook, D. (2001). Reward circuitry activation by noxious thermal stimuli. *Neuron, 32*(5), 927–946.

Becher, E., & Bechara, A. (2011). Making the diagnosis of erectile dysfunction. *Contemporary Endocrinology,* 69–80.

Beckman, N., Waern, M., Gustafson, D., & Skoog, I. (2008). Secular trends in self reported sexual activity and satisfaction in Swedish 70 year olds: Cross sectional survey of four populations, 1971–2001. *British Medical Journal, 337,* a279.

Beech, A., et al. (2009). Evaluating rapists' distorted beliefs and deviant sexual fantasies: A preliminary study. *Journal of Aggression, Conflict, and Peace Research, 1*(1), 25–35.

Beech, A. R., Parrett, N., Ward, T., & Fisher, D. (2009). Assessing female sexual offenders' motivations and cognitions: an exploratory study. *Psychology, Crime & Law, 15*(2-3), 201–216.

Behrendt, N., Buhl, N., & Seidl, S. (2002). The lethal paraphiliac syndrome: Accidental autoerotic deaths in four women and a review of the literature. *International Journal of Legal Medicine, 116* (3). 148–152.

Belden, M. (2011). *Obstetrics & gynecology: A competency-based companion.* Philadelphia: Saunders.

Belgrave, F. Z., van Oss Marian, B., & Chambers, D. B. (2000). Cultural, contextual, and intrapersonal predictors of risky sexual attitudes among urban African American girls in early adolescence. *Cultural Diversity and Ethnic Minority Psychology, 6*(3), 309–322.

Belkin, L. (2009, April 5). Your old man. *The New York Times Magazine.*

Bell, A. P., & Weinberg, M. S. (1978). *Homosexualities: A study of diversity among men and women.* New York: Simon & Schuster.

Bell, A. P., Weinberg, M. S., & Hammersmith, S. K. (1981). *Sexual preference: Its development in men and women.* Bloomington, IN: University of Indiana Press.

Bellavia, G., & Murray, S. (2003). Did I do that? Self esteem-related differences in reactions to romantic partner's mood. *Personal Relationships, 10*(1), 77–95.

Belluck, P. (2006, February 6). Fugitive in gay bar attacks dies after shootout with Arkansas police. *The New York Times* (Online).

Bem, S. L. (1975). Sex role adaptability: One consequence of psychological androgyny. *Journal of Personality and Social Psychology, 31,* 634–643.

Bem, S. L. (1993). *The lenses of gender.* New Haven: Yale University Press.

Bem, S. L., Martyna, W., & Watson, C. (1976). Sex typing and androgyny: Further explorations of the expressive domain. *Journal of Personality and Social Psychology, 34,* 1016–1023.

Bengoa Vallejo, R. B., et al. (2008). Application of cantharidin and podophyllotoxin for the treatment of plantar warts. *Journal of the American Podiatric Medical Association, 98*(6), 445–450.

Bennets, L. (2011, July 18). The john next door. *Newsweek* magazine.

Benotsch, E. G., & Kalichman, S. C. (2002). Preventing HIV and AIDS. In L. A. Jason & D. S. Glenwick (Eds.), *Innovative strategies for promoting health and mental health across the life span* (pp. 205–226). New York: Springer.

Bentley, T. (2009, June 21). Harem envy. *The New York Times Magazine,* pp. 10–11.

Benvenuto, C., & Weeks, S. C. (2012). Intersexual conflict during mate guarding in an androdioecious crustacean. *Behavioral Ecology, 23*(1), 218–224.

Ben-Zur, H. (2003). Peer risk behavior and denial of HIV/AIDS among adolescents. *Sex Education, 3*(1), 75–85.

Berdahl, J. L., & Moore, C. (2006). Workplace harassment: Double jeopardy for minority women. *Journal of Applied Psychology, 91*(2), 426–436.

Berga, S., & Naftolin, F. (2012). Neuroendocrine control of ovulation. *Gynecological Endocrinology, 28*(S1), 9–13.

Berger, L. (2002, December 10). After long hiatus, new contraceptives emerge. *The New York Times.*

Bergner, D. (2009, January 22). What do women want? *The New York Times.*

Berke, R. L. (1997, June 15). Suddenly, the new politics of morality. *The New York Times,* p. E3.

Berke, R. L. (1998, August 2). Chasing the polls on gay rights. *The New York Times,* p. WK3.

Berman, J. R., & Berman, L. A., et al. (2001). Effect of sildenafil on subjective and physiologic parameters of the female sexual response in women with sexual arousal disorder. *Journal of Sex & Marital Therapy, 27*(5), 411–420.

Bernstein, I. M., et al. (2005). Maternal smoking and its association with birth weight. *Obstetrics & Gynecology, 106,* 986–991.

Bernstein, R. (2009). *The East, the West, and sex: A history of erotic encounters.* New York: Knopf.

Berry, D. A., et al. (2005). Effect of screening and adjuvant therapy on mortality from breast cancer. *The New England Journal of Medicine, 353,* 1784–1792.

Berscheid, E. (2003). On stepping on land mines. In R. J. Sternberg (Ed.), *Psychologists defying the crowd: Stories of those who battled the establishment and won* (pp. 33–44).

Washington, DC: American Psychological Association.

Berscheid, E. (2010). Love in the fourth dimension. *Annual Review of Psychology, 61*, 1–25.

Berscheid, E., & Walster, E. (1978). *Interpersonal attraction.* Reading, MA: Addison-Wesley.

Beutel, M. E., Stöbel-Richter, Y., & Brähler, E. (2008). Sexual desire and sexual activity of men and women across their lifespans: Results from a representative German community survey. *BJU International, 101*(1), 76–82.

Beyerlein, A., et al. (2011). The relationship between birth weight, smoking during pregnancy, and maternal weight gain. *American Journal of Epidemiology, 113*(5), 590–595.

Bhugra, D. (2004). Literature update: A critical review. *Sexual and Relationship Therapy, 19*(2), 201–208.

Bhugra, D. (2005). Queer theory. *Sexual and Relationship Therapy, 20*(4), 476.

Bhugra, D., Rahman, Q., & Bhintade, R. (2006). Sexual fantasy in gay men in India: A comparison with heterosexual men. *Sexual and Relationship Therapy, 21*(2), 197–207.

Bialy, M., & Sachs, B. D. (2002). Androgen implants in medial amygdala briefly maintain noncontact erection in castrated male rats. *Hormones & Behavior, 42*(3), 345–355.

Bianchi, S. M., & Spain, D. (1997). *Women, work and family in America.* Population Reference Bureau.

Bilefsky, D. (2009, March 11). Europeans debate castration of sex offenders. *The New York Times* (Online).

Billy, J. O. G., et al. (1993). The sexual behavior of men in the United States. *Family Planning Perspectives, 25*, 52–60.

Bimbi, D. S. (2007). Male prostitution: Pathology, paradigms and progress in research. *Journal of Homosexuality, 53*(1-2), 7–35.

Binik, Y. M. (2005). Should dyspareunia be retained as a sexual dysfunction in *DSM-V*? A painful classification decision. *Archives of Sexual Behavior, 34*(1), 11–21.

Birnie-Porter, C., & Lydon, J. E. (2012). A prototype approach to understanding sexual intimacy through its relationship to intimacy. *Personal Relationships.* DOI:10.1111/j.1475-6811.2012.01402.x.

Blackwell, D. L., & Lichter, D. T. (2004). Homogamy among dating, cohabiting, and married couples. *Sociological Quarterly, 45*(4), 719–737.

Blake, S. M., et al. (2003). Condom availability programs in Massachusetts high schools: Relationships with condom use and sexual behavior. *American Journal of Public Health, 93*, 955–962.

Blanchard, R. (1988). Nonhomosexual gender dysphoria. *Journal of Sex Research, 24*, 188–193.

Blanchard, R. (1989). The concept of autogynephilia and the typology of male gender dysphoria. *Journal of Nervous & Mental Disease, 177*(10), 616–623.

Blanchard, R. (2010). The DSM criteria for transvestic fetishism. *Archives of Sexual Behavior*, DOI 10.1007/s10508-009-9541-3.

Blanchard, R., Steiner, B. W., & Clemmensen, L. H. (1985). Gender dysphoria, gender reorientation, and the clinical management of transsexualism. *Journal of Consulting and Clinical Psychology, 53*, 295–304.

Blanker, M. H., et al. (2001). Erectile and ejaculatory dysfunction in a community-based sample of men 50 to 78 years old: Prevalence, concern, and relation to sexual activity. *Urology, 57*(4), 763–768.

Bletzer, K. V., & Koss, M. P. (2006). After rape among three populations in the southwest: A time of mourning, a time for recovery. *Violence Against Women, 12*(1), 5–29.

Blickstein, I., Goldman, R. D., & Mazkereth, R. (2000). Risk for one or two very low birth weight twins: A population study. *Obstetrics & Gynecology, 96*(3), 400–402.

Bloch, M., Rotenberg, N., Koren, D., & Ehud, K. (2006). Risk factors for early postpartum depressive symptoms. *General Hospital Psychiatry, 28*(1), 3–8.

Blow, A. J., & Hartnett, K. (2005). Infidelity in committed relationships II: A substantive review. *Journal of Family and Marital Therapy, 31*(2), 217–233.

Blow, C. M. (2009, June 27). The prurient trap. *The New York Times.*

Bobashev, G. V., Zule, W. A., Osilla, K. C., Kline, T. L., & Wechsberg, W. M. (2009). Transactional sex among men and women in the South at high risk for HIV and other STIs. (Accessed November 6, 2009). *Journal of Urban Health,* published online 10 June, 2009.

Bockting, W. O., & Fung, L. C. T. (2006). Genital reconstruction and gender identity disorders. In D. B. Sarwer (Ed.), *Psychological aspects of reconstructive and cosmetic plastic surgery: Clinical, empirical, and ethical perspectives* (pp. 207–229). New York: Lippincott Williams & Wilkins.

Bodurtha, J., & Strauss, J. F. (2012). Genomics and perinatal care. *The New England Journal of Medicine, 366*, 64–73.

Bogaert, A. F. (2006). Toward a conceptual understanding of asexuality. *Review of General Psychology, 10*(3), 241–250.

Bogin, G. Y. (2006). Out of the darkness: Male adolescents and the experience of sexual victimization. *School Social Work Journal, 30*(2), 1–21.

Bogle, K. (2008). *Hooking up: Sex, dating, and relationships on campus.* New York: New York University Press.

Bolton, J. M., Sareen, J., & Reiss, J. P. (2006). Genital anaesthesia persisting six years after sertraline discontinuation. *Journal of Sex & Marital Therapy, 32*(4), 327–330.

Born, L., Soares, C. N., Phillips, S., Jung, M., & Steiner, M. (2006). Women and reproductive-related trauma. In R. Yehuda (Ed.), *Psychobiology of posttraumatic stress disorders: A decade of progress* (Vol. 1071, pp. 491–494). New York: Blackwell.

Boros, S., Mateuca, A., & Matus, M. (2005). The role of social identity in attributions—Evaluating the guilt in rape assault. *Cognitie Creier Comportament, 9*(1), 35–57.

Bos, H. M. W., Sandfort, T. G. M., de Bruyn, E. H., & Hakvoort, E. M. (2008). Same-sex attraction, social relationships, psychosocial functioning, and school performance in early adolescence. *Developmental Psychology, 44*(1), 59–68.

Boss, S., & Maltz, W. (2001). *Private thoughts: Exploring the power of women's sexual fantasies.* New York: New World Library.

Boston Women's Health Book Collective. (2005). *Our bodies, ourselves: A new edition for a new era.* New York: Touchstone.

Bower, B. (2009). Infectious voyagers: DNA suggests Columbus took syphilis to Europe. *Science News, 173*(3), 38.

Bowes-Sperry, L., & O'Leary–Kelly, A. M. (2005). To act or not to act: The dilemma faced by sexual harassment observers. *Academy of Management Review, 30*(2), 288–306.

Bowlby, J. (1969). *Attachment and loss* (Vol. 1). New York: Basic Books.

Boxer, S. (2000, July 22). Truth or lies? In sex surveys, you never know. *The New York Times* (Online).

Boynton, P. (2008). A review of "G-strings and sympathy: Strip club regulars and male desire." *Journal of Sex & Marital Therapy, 34*(5), 457-459.

Bozell, B. (2005, December 30). Coming in 2006: Group marriage TV? www.townhall.com/opinion/columns/brentbozell/2005/12/30/180704.html.

Bradford, J. M. W. (1998). Treatment of men with paraphilia. *New England Journal of Medicine, 338*, 464–465.

Bradford, J. M. W. (2001). The neurobiology, neuropharmacology, and pharmacological treatment of the paraphilias and compulsive sexual behaviour. *Canadian Journal of Psychiatry, 46*(1), 26–34.

Bradley, S. J., Oliver, G. D., Chernick, A. B., & Zucker, K. J. (1998). Experiment of nurture: Ablatio penis at 2 months, sex reassignment at 7 months, and a psychosexual follow-up in young adulthood. *Pediatrics, 102*(1), e9.

Braithwaite, D. O., Olson, L. N., Golish, T. D., Soukup, C., & Turman, P. (2001). "Becoming a family": Developmental processes represented in blended family discourse. *Journal of Applied Communication Research, 29*(3), 221–247.

Bramlett, M. D., & Mosher, W. D. (2002). *Cohabitation, marriage, divorce, and remarriage.* National Center for Health Statistics, Vital Health Statistics, 23(22). www.cdc.gov/nchs/data/series/sr_23/sr23_022.pdf.

Brauer, M., ter Kuile, M. M., Laan, E., & Trimbos, B. (2009). Cognitive-affective correlates and predictors of superficial dyspareunia. *Journal of Sex & Marital Therapy, 35*(1), 1–24.

Brawley, O. (2009, March 24). In T. Parker-Pope, Screen or not? What those prostate studies mean. *The New York Times.*

Bray, P. F., et al. (2008). "Undesirable" lipid levels linked to HRT-related coronary events. *Inpharma, 1*, 20.

Breastfeeding. (2010). U.S. Department of Health and Human Services: http://www.womenshealth.gov/breastfeeding (Accessed September 21, 2012).

Brechin, S., & Bigrigg, A. (2006). Male and female sterilization. *Current Obstetrics & Gynaecology, 16*(1), 39–46.

Brents, B. G. (2012, April 19). Nevada's legal brothels make workers feel safer. The *New York Times* (Online).

Briken, P., Hill, A., & Berner, W. (2011). Pharmacotherapy of sexual offenders and men who are at risk of sexual offending. In D. P. Boer et al. (Eds.). *International Perspectives on the Assessment and*

Treatment of Sexual Offenders: Theory, Practice, and Research (pp. 419–431). Hoboken, NJ: Wiley.

Briken, P., Hill, A., Nika, E., & Berner, W. (2005). Obscene telephone calls—Relations to paraphilias, paraphilia related disorders and stalking. *Psychiatrische Praxis, 32*(6), 304–307.

Brin, D. J. (2004). The use of rituals in grieving for a miscarriage or stillbirth. *Women & Therapy, 27*(3–4), 123–132.

Brisch, K. H., et al. (2005). Effects of previous pregnancy loss on level of maternal anxiety after prenatal ultrasound screening for fetal malformation. *Journal of Loss & Trauma, 10*(2), 131–153.

Broder, M. S., Kanouse, D. E., Mittman, B. S., & Bernstein, S. J. (2000). The appropriateness of recommendations for hysterectomy. *Obstetrics & Gynecology, 95,* 199–206.

Brodkin, E. S., et al. (2002). Identification of quantitative trait loci that affect aggressive behavior in mice. *The Journal of Neuroscience, 22*(3), 1165–1170.

Brody, J. E. (1994, March 21). Notions of beauty transcend culture, new study suggests. *The New York Times,* p. A14.

Brody, J. E. (2000, May 16). Cybersex gives birth to a psychological disorder. *The New York Times,* pp. F7, F12.

Brody, J. E. (2012, February 27). Americans get reacquainted with IUDs. *New York Times* (online).

Brodzinsky, D. M., & Palacios, J. (2005). *Psychological issues in adoption: Research and practice.* Westport, CT: Praeger Publishers/Greenwood Publishing Group.

Bronner, E. (1998, February 1). "Just say maybe. No sexology, please. We're Americans." *The New York Times,* p. WK6.

Bross, D. C. (2005). Invited commentary: Minimizing risks to children when they access the World Wide Web. *Child Abuse & Neglect, 29*(7), 749–752.

Brotto L. A., Bitzer, J., Laan, E., Leiblum, S., & Luria, M. (2010). Women's sexual desire and arousal disorders. *Journal of Sexual Medicine, 7,* 586–614.

Broude, G. J., & Greene, S. J. (1976). Cross-cultural codes on twenty sexual attitudes and practices. *Ethnology, 15,* 409–429.

Brown, D. (2003). Pornography and erotica. In J. Bryant, D. Roskos–Ewoldsen, & J. Cantor (Eds.), *Communication and emotion: Essays in honor of Dolf Zillmann* (pp. 221–253). LEA's communication series. Hillsdale, NJ: Erlbaum.

Brown, G. R., & Haaser, R. C. (2005). Sexual disorders. In J. L. Levenson (Ed.), *The American psychiatric publishing textbook of psychosomatic medicine* (pp. 359–386). Washington, DC: American Psychiatric Publishing.

Brown, J., et al. (2009). Selective serotonin reuptake inhibitors for premenstrual syndrome. *Cochrane Database System Review, 15*(2), CD001396.

Brown, L. M., McNatt, P. S., & Cooper, G. D. (2003). Ingroup romantic preferences among Jewish and non-Jewish white undergraduates. *International Journal of Intercultural Relations, 27*(3), 335–354.

Brown, L. S. (2005). Prostitution, trafficking and traumatic stress. *Journal of Trauma & Dissociation, 6*(3), 143–145.

Brown, P. L., & Pogash, C. (2009, March 15). The pleasure principle. *The New York Times* (Online).

Brown, R., Balousek, S., Mundt, M., & Fleming, M. (2005). Methadone maintenance and male sexual dysfunction. *Journal of Addictive Diseases, 24*(2), 91–106.

Brown, S. L., & Manning, W. D. (2009). Family boundary ambiguity and the measurement of family structure: The significance of cohabitation. *Demography, 46*(1), 85–101.

Brown, T. (2002). A proposed model of bisexual identity development that elaborates on experiential differences of women and men. *Journal of Bisexuality, 2*(4), 67–91.

Browning, C. R. (2002). Trauma or transition: A life-course perspective on the link between childhood sexual experiences and men's adult well-being. *Social Science Research, 31*(4), 473–510.

Browning, D. S., Green, M. C., & Witte Jr., J. (Eds.). (2006). *Sex, marriage, and family in world religions.* New York: Columbia University Press.

Browning, J. R., Hatfield, E., Kessler, D., & Levine, T. (2000). Sexual motives, gender, and sexual behavior. *Archives of Sexual Behavior, 29*(2), 135–153.

Brun, C. C., et al. (2009). Sex differences in brain structure in auditory and cingulate regions. *NeuroReport: For Rapid Communication of Neuroscience Research, 20*(10), 930.

Brunet, P. M., & Schmidt, L. A. (2008). Are shy adults really bolder online? It depends on the context. *CyberPsychology & Behavior, 11*(6), 707–709.

Bryant-Davis, T. (Ed.). *Surviving sexual violence.* Lanham, MD: Rowman & Littlefield.

Bullough, V. L. (2002). Masturbation: A historical overview. *Journal of Psychology & Human Sexuality, 14*(2–3), 17–33.

Bunting, L., & McAuley, C. (2004). Teenage pregnancy and motherhood: The contribution of support. *Child & Family Social Work, 9*(2), 207–215.

Burch, B. (2008). Infidelity: Outlaws and in-laws and lesbian relationships. *Journal of Lesbian Studies, 12*(2-3), 145–159.

Burchell, A. N., et al. (2011). Genital transmission of human papillomavirus in recently formed heterosexual couples. *Journal of Infectious Disease, 204*(11), 1723–1729.

Burgess, A. W., & Morgenbesser, L. I. (2005). Sexual violence and seniors. *Brief Treatment and Crisis Intervention, 5*(2), 193–202.

Burke, T. J., & Young, V. J. (2012). Sexual transformations and intimate behaviors in romantic relationships. *Journal of Sex Research, 49*(5), 454–463.

Burri, A., Hysi, P., Clop, A., Rahman, Q., & Spector, T. D. (2012). A genome-wide association study of female sexual dysfunction. *PLoS ONE, 7*(4): e35041. DOI:10.1371/journal.pone.0035041.

Burt, M. R. (1980). Cultural myths and supports for rape. *Journal of Personality and Social Psychology, 38,* 217–230.

Bushman, B. J., Bonacci, A. M., van Dijk, M., & Baumeister, R. F. (2003). Narcissism, sexual refusal, and aggression: Testing a narcissistic reactance model of sexual coercion. *Journal of Personality and Social Psychology, 84*(5), 1027–1040.

Buss, D. M. (1994). *The evolution of desire: Strategies of human mating.* New York: Basic Books.

Buss, D. M. (2009). An evolutionary formulation of person–situation interactions. *Journal of Research in Personality, 43*(2), 241–242.

Buss, D. M. (2009). The great struggles of life: Darwin and the emergence of evolutionary psychology. *American Psychologist, 64*(2), 140–148.

Buss, D. M. (Ed.). (2005). *The handbook of evolutionary psychology.* Hoboken, NJ: Wiley.

Buss, D. M., & Schmitt, D. P. (2011). Evolutionary psychology and feminism. *Sex Roles, 64*(9–10), 768–787.

Butler, J. (1993). *Bodies that matter: On the discursive limits of sex.* New York: Routledge.

Butler, J. (2003). *Kritik der ethischen Gewalt.* Adorno lectures, 2002. Frankfurt am Main: Institut fur Sozialforschung an der Johann Wolfgang Goethe-Universitat.

Buvat, J., et al. (2010). Endocrine aspects of male sexual dysfunctions. *Journal of Sexual Medicine, 7,* 1627–1656.

Byerly, M. J., et al. (2006). Sexual dysfunction associated with second-generation antipsychotics in outpatients with schizophrenia or schizoaffective disorder: An empirical evaluation of olanzapine, risperidone, and quetiapine. *Schizophrenia Research, 86*(1–3), 244–250.

Byers, E. S., & Grenier, G. (2003). Premature or rapid ejaculation: Heterosexual couples' perceptions of men's ejaculatory behavior. *Archives of Sexual Behavior, 32*(3), 261–270.

Byrd, J., Hyde, J. S., DeLamater, J. D., & Plant, E. A. (1998). Sexuality during pregnancy and the year postpartum. *Journal of Family Practice, 47*(4), 305–308.

Cacioppo, J. T., Hawkley, L. C., & Bernston, G. G. (2003). The anatomy of loneliness. *Current Directions in Psychological Science, 12*(3), 71–74.

Cado, S., & Leitenberg, H. (1990). Guilt reactions to sexual fantasies during intercourse. *Archives of Sexual Behavior, 19,* 49–64.

Caffaro, J. V., & Conn-Caffaro, A. (2005). Treating sibling abuse families. *Aggression and Violent Behavior, 10*(5), 604–623.

Cai, R., Alexander, M., & Marson, L. (2008). Activation of somatosensory afferents elicit changes in vaginal blood flow and the urethrogenital reflex via autonomic efferents. *The Journal of Urology, 180*(3), 1167–1172.

Calhoun, K. S., Mouilso, E. R., & Edwards, K. M. (2012). Sexual assault among college students. In R. D. McAnulty (Ed.). *Sex in college: The things they don't write home about* (pp. 263–288). Santa Barbara, CA: ABC-CLIO.

Call, V., Sprecher, S., & Schwartz, P. (1995). The incidence and frequency of marital sex in a national sample. *Journal of Marriage and the Family, 57,* 639–652.

Callaway, E. (2012). Fathers bequeath more mutations as they age. *Nature, 488*(412), http://www.nature.com/news/fathers-bequeath-more-mutations-as-they-age-1.11247. (Accessed September 21, 2012).

Calmes, J., & Baker, P. (2012, May 10). Obama says same-sex marriage should be legal. *New York Times,* p. A1.

Campbell, R. (2006). Rape survivors' experiences with the legal and medical systems: Do rape victim advocates make a difference? *Violence Against Women, 12*(1), 30–45.

Campbell, R., & Wasco, S. M. (2005). Understanding rape and sexual assault: 20 years of progress and future directions. *Journal of Interpersonal Violence, 20*(1), 127–131.

Campbell, W. K., Foster, C. A., & Finkel, E. J. (2002). Does self-love lead to love for others? A story of narcissistic game playing. *Journal of Personality & Social Psychology, 83*(2), 340–354.

Cancer Statistics, 2008. In American Cancer Society. (2009). http://www.cancer.org/downloads/STT/Cancer_Statistics_2008.ppt#405,10,Cancer Sites in Men for Which African American Death Rates Exceed White Death Rates, US, 2000–2004.

Cantor, J. M. (2011). New MRI studies support the Blanchard typology of male-to-female transsexualism. *Archives of Sexual Behavior, 40*(5), 863–864.

Caporaletti, J. (2006, September 20). *Prostitution is a world-wide problem.* www.collegiatetimes.com.

Capron, C., Thérond, C., & Duyme, M. (2007). Brief report: Effect of menarcheal status and family structure on depressive symptoms and emotional/behavioural problems in young adolescent girls. *Journal of Adolescence, 30*(1), 175–179.

Carey, B. (2005, January 11). The secret lives of just about everybody. *The New York Times* (Online).

Carlson, N. (2007). *Physiology of behavior* (9th ed.). Boston: Allyn & Bacon.

Carpenter, L. M., Nathanson, C. A., & Kim, Y. J. (2009). Physical women, emotional men: Gender and sexual satisfaction in midlife. *Archives of Sexual Behavior, 38*(1), 87–107.

Carrère, S., Buehlman, K. T., Gottman, J. M., Coan, J. A., & Ruckstuhl, L. (2000). Predicting marital stability and divorce in newlywed couples. *Journal of Family Psychology, 14*(1), 42–58.

Carroll, J. S., et al. (2008). Generation XXX: Pornography acceptance and use among emerging adults. *Journal of Adolescent Research, 23*(1), 6–30.

Carter, D. J., & Dalla, R. L. (2006). Transactional analysis case report: Street-level prostituted women as mental health-care clients. *Sexual Addiction & Compulsivity, 13*(1), 95–119.

Carvalho, J., & Nobre, P. (2010). Gender issues and sexual desire: The role of emotional and relationship variables. *Journal of Sexual Medicine, 7*, 2469–2478.

Carvalho, J., & Nobre, P. (2010). Sexual desire in women: An integrative approach regarding psychological, medical, and relationship dimensions. *Journal of Sexual Medicine, 7*, 1807–1813.

Castellsague, X., et al. (2002). Male circumcision, penile human papillomavirus infection, and cervical cancer in female partners. *New England Journal of Medicine, 346*(15), 1105–1112.

Castellsague, X., et al. (2011). Intrauterine device use, cervical infection with human papillomavirus, and risk of cervical cancer: A pooled analysis of 26 epidemiological studies. *The Lancet Oncology, 12*(11), 1023–1031.

Caughlin, J. P., Hardesty, J. L., & Middleton, A. V. (2012). Conflict avoidance in families. In P. Noller & G. C. Karantzas (Eds.). *The Wiley-Blackwell handbook of couples and family relationships* (pp. 115–128). Chichester, West Sussex, UK: Wiley.

Cawley, J., Avery, R., & Eisenberg, M. (2011). The effect of advertising and deceptive advertising on consumption: The case of over-the-counter weight loss products. http://www.iza.org/conference_files/riskonomics2011/cawley_j6697.pdf

Ceci, S. J., Williams, W. M., & Barnett, S. R. (2009). Women's underrepresentation in science. *Psychological Bulletin, 135*(2), 218–261.

Celizic, M. (2009, March 10). With child porn charges being leveled, some say laws are behind the times. TODAYShow.com (contributor).

Center for Sexual Health Promotion. (2011). *National Survey of Sexual Health and Behavior (NSSHB).* Indiana University, Bloomington: School of Health, Physical Education, and Recreation. Accessed August 23, 2012, from http://www.nationalsexstudy.indiana.edu

Centers for Disease Control and Prevention (CDC). (2001, June). *Genital herpes.* National Center for HIV, STD and TB Prevention. Division of Sexually Transmitted Diseases. www.cdc.gov/nchstp/dstd/Fact_Sheets/facts_.Genital_Herpes.htm.

Centers for Disease Control and Prevention (CDC). (2002a). *Oral alternatives to cefixime for the treatment of uncomplicated* Neisseria gonorrhoeae *urogenital infections.* National Center for HIV, STD and TB Prevention. Division of Sexually Transmitted Diseases. www.cdc.gov/STD/treatment/Cefixime.htm.

Centers for Disease Control and Prevention (CDC). (2002b). *Laboratory guidelines screening tests to detect* Chlamydia trachomatis *and* Neisseria gonorrhoeae *infections.* National Center for HIV, STD and TB Prevention. Division of Sexually Transmitted Diseases. www.cdc.gov/STD/LabGuidelines/default.htm.

Centers for Disease Control and Prevention (CDC). (2003). *HIV/AIDS surveillance report: U.S. HIV and AIDS cases reported through December 2002, 14*(2).

Centers for Disease Control and Prevention (CDC). (2005a). *STD surveillance 2005.* www.cdc.gov/std/stats/toc2004.htm.

Centers for Disease Control and Prevention (CDC). (2005b). *DES Update: For Consumers.* www.cdc.gov/DES/consumers/index.html.

Centers for Disease Control and Prevention (CDC). (2006). *Sexually transmitted diseases.* Various fact sheets.

Centers for Disease Control and Prevention (CDC). (2008). HIV and AIDS in the United States: A picture of today's epidemic. Accessed December 22, 2008. http://www.cdc.gov/HIV/topics/surveillance/united_states.htm.

Centers for Disease Control and Prevention (CDC). (2009a, February 28). Cases of HIV infection and AIDS in the United States and dependent areas, 2007. http://www.cdc.gov/hiv/topics/surveillance/resources/reports/2007/report/table13.htm.

Centers for Disease Control and Prevention (CDC). (2009b, January 13). Trends in reportable sexually transmitted diseases in the United States, 2007: National surveillance data for chlamydia, gonorrhea, and syphilis. http://www.cdc.gov/std/stats07/trends.htm.

Chaiyavej, S., & Morash, M. (2009). Reasons for policewomen's assertive and passive reactions to sexual harassment. *Police Quarterly, 12*(1), 63–85.

Champion, D. R. (2006). Sexual harassment: Criminal justice and academia. *Criminal Justice Studies: A Critical Journal of Crime, Law & Society, 19*(2), 101–109.

Chance, S. E., Brown, R. T., Dabbs, J. M., Jr., & Casey, R. (2000). Testosterone, intelligence and behavior disorders in young boys. *Personality & Individual Differences, 28*(3), 437–445.

Chandler, C. H., & Zamudio, K. R. (2008). Reproductive success by large, closely related males facilitated by sperm storage in an aggregate breeding amphibian. *Molecular Ecology, 17*(6), 1564–1576.

Chandra, A., et al. (2008). Does watching sex on television predict teen pregnancy? Findings from a national longitudinal survey of youth. *Pediatrics, 122*(5), 1047–1054.

Chandra, A., et al. (2012). HIV risk-related behaviors in the United States household population aged 15–44 years: Data from the National Survey of Family Growth, 2002 and 2006–2110. *National Health Statistics Reports*, January 19, 2012, No. 46.

Chao, Q., Wang, P., & He, N. (2001). Comparative research on self-concept of middle school students from complete and divorced families. *Chinese Journal of Clinical Psychology, 9*(2), 143.

Chatham, M. L. (2008). Early predictors of disinhibited attachment behaviors among internationally adopted children. *Dissertation Abstracts International: Section B: The Sciences and Engineering, 69*(3-B), p. 1985.

Chaturvedi, A. K., et al. (2011). Human papillomavirus and rising oropharyngeal cancer incidence in the United States. *Journal of Clinical Oncology, 29*(32), 4294–4301.

Chavez, M. L., & Spitzer, M. F. (2002). Herbals and other dietary supplements for premenstrual syndrome and menopause. *Psychiatric Annals, 32*(1), 61–71.

Chen, M. (2012, May 27). Working with your rapist as your supervisor? The widespread sexual abuse of women in farm work. www.alternet.org. (Accessed July 16, 2012).

Cheng, H., & Furnham, A. (2002). Personality, peer relations, and self-confidence as predictors of happiness and loneliness. *Journal of Adolescence, 25*(3), 327–339.

Chesler, P. (2006, February 24). The failure of feminism. *Chronicle of Higher Education, 52*(25).

Cheyne, R. A. (2005). The sanctification of parenting and adoption among special needs adoptive parents. *Dissertation Abstracts International: Section B: The Sciences and Engineering, 66*(1-B), p. 545.

Chisholm, J., & Greene, B. (2008). Women of color: Perspectives on multiple identities in psychological theory, research, and practice. In F. L. Denmark & M. A. Paludi (Eds.),

Psychology of women (2nd ed., pp. 40–69). Westport, CT: Greenwood Publishing Group.

Chivers, M. L. (2010). A brief update on the specificity of sexual arousal. *Sexual and Relationship Therapy, 25*(4), 407–414.

Chivers, M. L., & Bailey, J. M. (2007). The sexual physiology of sexual orientation. In E. Janssen (Ed.), *The psychophysiology of sex. The Kinsey Institute series* (pp. 458–474). Bloomington: Indiana University Press.

Chivers, M. L., & Rosen, R. C. (2010). Phosphodiesterase Type 5 inhibitors and female sexual response: Faulty protocols or paradigms? *Journal of Sexual Medicine, 7*(2), 858–872.

Chivers, M. L., & Rosen, R. C. (2010). Phosphodiesterase type 5 inhibitors and female sexual response: Faulty protocols or paradigms? *The Journal of Sexual Medicine, 7*(2), 858–872.

Chivers, M. L., & Timmers, A. D. (2012). Effects of gender and relationship context in audio narratives on genital and subjective sexual response in heterosexual men and women. *Archives of Sexual Behavior, 41*(1), 185–197.

Chivers, M. L., Rieger, G., Latty, E., & Bailey, J. M. (2004). A sex difference in the specificity of sexual arousal. *Psychological Science, 15*(11), 736–744.

Chivers, M. L., Seto, M. C., & Blanchard, R. (2007). Gender and sexual orientation differences in sexual response to sexual activities versus gender of actors in sexual films. *Journal of Personality and Social Psychology, 93*(6), 1108–1121.

Chivers, M. L., Seto, M. C., Lalumiere, M. L., Laan, E., & Grimbos, T. (2010). Agreement of self-reported and genital measures of sexual arousal in men and women: A meta-analysis. *Archives of Sexual Behavior, 39*(1), 5–56.

Chivers, M., & Bailey, J. M. (2005). A sex difference in features that elicit genital response. *Biological Psychology, 70*(2), 115–120.

Chlamydia positivity of women by state, 2010. Centers for Disease Control and Prevention. (2011). Sexually Transmitted Diseases (STDs). 2010 Sexually Transmitted Diseases Surveillance. http://www.cdc.gov/std/stats10/figures/11.htm (Accessed October 4, 2012).

Chlamydia statistics, 2012. Centers for Disease Control and Prevention. (2012). Sexually Transmitted Diseases (STDs). Chlamydia statistics. http://www.cdc.gov/std/chlamydia/stats.htm (Accessed October 4, 2012).

Chlamydia—CDC fact sheet, 2012. Centers for Disease Control and Prevention. (2012). Sexually Transmitted Diseases (STDs). Chlamydia—CDC Fact Sheet. http://www.cdc.gov/std/chlamydia/STDFact-Chlamydia.htm (Accessed October 4, 2012).

Chlebowski, R, et al. (2003). Influence of estrogen plus progestin on breast cancer and mammography in healthy postmenopausal women: The Women's Health Initiative Randomized Trial. *Journal of the American Medical Association, 289*, 3243–3253.

Chlebowski, R., et al. (2009, May 30). HRT increases risk for death from non-small-cell lung cancer. American Society of Clinical Oncology, 45th Meeting.

Cho, S., Park, E. S., Park, C. I., & Na, S. (2004). Characteristics of psychosexual functioning in adults with cerebral palsy. *Clinical Rehabilitation, 18*(4), 423–429.

CIA (Central Intelligence Agency). (2012). The World Factbook. https://www.cia.gov/library/publications/the-world-factbook/fields/2018.html (Accessed June 23, 2012).

Ciccarone, D. (2011). Stimulant abuse: Pharmacology, cocaine, methamphetamine treatment, attempts at pharmacotherapy. *Primary Care: Clinics in Office Practice, 38*(1), 41–58.

Clay, R. A. (2006). Battling the self-blame of infertility. *Monitor on Psychology, 37*(8), 44–45.

Cleary Bradley, R. P., Friend, D. J., & Gottman, J. M. (2011). Supporting healthy relationships in low-income, violent couples: Reducing conflict and strengthening relationship skills and satisfaction. *Journal of Couple & Relationship Therapy: Innovations in Clinical and Educational Interventions, 10*(2), 97–116.

Cleland, K., Zhu, H., Goldstuck, N., Cheng, L., & Trussell, J. (2012). The efficacy of intrauterine devices for emergency contraception: A systematic review of 35 years of experience. *Human Reproduction, 27*(7), 1994–2000.

Clendenen, T. V., et al. (2009). Postmenopausal levels of endogenous sex hormones and risk of colorectal cancer. *Cancer Epidemiology Biomarkers & Prevention, 18*, 275.

Clendenning, A. (2004, April 29). *Yale global online.* www.yaleglobal.yale.edu.

Cnattingius, S. (2004). The epidemiology of smoking during pregnancy: Smoking prevalence, maternal characteristics, and pregnancy outcomes. *Nicotine & Tobacco Research, 6*(Suppl. 2), S125–S140.

Cnattingius, S., Bergstrom, R., Lipworth, L., & Kramer, M. S. (1998). Pre-pregnancy weight and the risk of adverse pregnancy outcomes. *New England Journal of Medicine, 338,* 147–152.

Cohen, A. B., & Tannenbaum, I. J. (2001). Lesbian and bisexual women's judgments of the attractiveness of different body types. *Journal of Sex Research, 38*(3), 226–232.

Cohen, D. L., & Belsky, J. (2008). Individual differences in female mate preferences as a function of attachment and hypothetical ecological conditions. *Journal of Evolutionary Psychology, 6*(1), 25–42.

Cohen, L. S., et al. (2006). Relapse of major depression during pregnancy in women who maintain or discontinue antidepressant treatment. *Journal of the American Medical Association, 295*(5), 499–507.

Cohen, M. S. (2000). Preventing sexual transmission of HIV: New ideas from sub-Saharan Africa. *The New England Journal of Medicine, 342*(13), 970–973.

Cohen-Bendahan, C. C. C., van de Beek, C., & Berenbaum, S. A. (2005). Prenatal sex hormone effects on child and adult sex-typed behavior: Methods and findings. *Neuroscience & Biobehavioral Reviews, 29*(2), 353–384.

Colangelo, J. J., & Keefe-Cooperman, K. (2012). Understanding the impact of childhood sexual abuse on women's sexuality. *Journal of Mental Health Counseling, 34*(1), 14–37.

Colapinto, J. (2000). *As nature made him: The boy who was raised as a girl.* New York: HarperCollins.

Colditz, G. A., & Rosner, B. A. (2000). Cumulative risk for breast cancer to age 70 years according to risk factor status. Data from the Nurses' Health Study. *American Journal of Epidemiology, 152*(10), 950–964.

Colditz, G. A., et al. (2004). Risk factors for breast cancer according to estrogen and progesterone receptor status. *Journal of the National Cancer Institute, 96,* 218–228.

Cole, F. S. (2000). Extremely preterm birth—Defining the limits of hope. *The New England Journal of Medicine, 343*(6).

Cole, T. B. (2006). Rape at US colleges often fueled by alcohol. *Journal of the American Medical Association, 296*(5), 504–505.

Coleman, E. (2002). Masturbation as a means of achieving sexual health. *Journal of Psychology & Human Sexuality, 14*(2–3), 5–16.

Coleman, M., Ganong, L. H., & Fine, M. (2000). Reinvestigating remarriage: Another decade of progress. *Journal of Marriage & the Family, 62*(4), 1288–1307.

Coles, L. S. (2010). The ethical basis for using human embryonic stem cells in the treatment of aging. *The Future of Aging, Part 1,* 63–86.

Collaer, M. L., & Hill, E. M. (2006). Large sex difference in adolescents on a timed line judgment task: Attentional contributors and task relationship to mathematics. *Perception, 35*(4), 561–572.

Collaer, M. L., & Hines, M. (1995). Human behavioral sex differences: A role for gonadal hormones during early development? *Psychological Bulletin, 118*(1), 55–107.

Collins, C., Harshbarger, C., Sawyer, R., & Hamdallah, M. (2006). The diffusion of effective behavioral interventions project: Development, implementation, and lessons learned. *AIDS Education and Prevention, 18*(Suppl. A), 5–20.

Collins, L. (2004). We are not gay. In K. K. Kumashiro (Ed.), *Restoried selves: Autobiographies of queer Asian/Pacific American activists* (pp. 13–17). New York: Harrington Park Press/The Haworth Press.

Collins, N. L., & Miller, L. C. (1994). Self-disclosure and liking: A meta-analytic review. *Psychological Bulletin, 116*(1), 457–475.

Collins, R. L., et al. (2004). Watching sex on television predicts adolescent initiation of sexual behavior. *Pediatrics, 114*(3), e280–e289.

Colson, M.-H., Lemaire, A., Pinton, P., Hamidi, K., & Klein, P. (2006). Sexual behaviors and mental perception, satisfaction and expectations of sex life in men and women in France. *Journal of Sexual Medicine, 3*(1), 121–131.

Conley, S. (2009, March 26). In B. Alexander, "Sex surrogates" put personal touch on therapy: Despite dubious legality, some counselors still prescribe practice to patients. http://www.msnbc.msn.com/id/29881206/.

Connolly, J., Craig, W., Goldberg, A., & Pepler, D. (2004). Mixed-gender groups, dating, and romantic relationships in early adolescence. *Journal of Research on Adolescence, 14*(2), 185–207.

Connor, E. M., et al. (1994). Reduction of maternal–infant transmission of human immunodeficiency virus type 1 with zidovudine treatment. *New England Journal of Medicine, 331,* 1173–1180.

Connor, P. D., Sampson, P. D., Streissguth, A. P., Bookstein, F. L., & Barr, H. M. (2006). Effects of prenatal alcohol exposure on fine motor coordination and balance: A study of two adult samples. *Neuropsychologia, 44*(5), 744–751.

Cooke, B. M., Breedlove, S. M., & Jordan, C. L. (2003). Both estrogen receptors and androgen receptors contribute to testosterone-induced changes in the morphology of the medial amygdala and sexual arousal in male rats. *Hormones & Behavior, 43*(2), 336–346.

Cooper, A. J., Galbreath, N., & Becker, M. A. (2004). Sex on the Internet: Furthering our understanding of men with online sexual problems. *Psychology of Addictive Behaviors, 18*(3), 223–230.

Cooper, A., Delmonico, D. L., & Burg, R. (2000). Cybersex users, abusers, and compulsives: New findings and implications. *Sexual Addiction & Compulsivity, 7*(1–2), 5–29.

Cooper, A., Delmonico, D. L., Griffin-Shelley, E., & Mathy, R. M. (2004). Online sexual activity: An examination of potentially problematic behaviors. *Sexual Addiction & Compulsivity, 11*(3), 129–143.

Cooper, S. M., Guthrie, B. J., Brown, C., & Metzger, I. (2011). Daily hassles and African American adolescent females' psychological functioning: Direct and interactive associations with gender role orientation. *Sex Roles, 65*(5–6), 397–409.

Corona, G., et al. (2009). The age-related decline of testosterone is associated with different specific symptoms and signs in patients with sexual dysfunction. *International Journal of Andrology,* 10.1111/j.1365-2605.2009.00952.

Cortina, L. M., & Wasti, S. A. (2005). Profiles in coping: Responses to sexual harassment across persons, organizations, and cultures. *Journal of Applied Psychology, 90*(1), 182–192.

Courtenay, W. H. (2000). Engendering health: A social constructionist examination of men's health beliefs and behaviors. *Psychology of Men & Masculinity, 1*(1), 4–15.

Cove, J., & Petrak, J. (2004). Factors associated with sexual problems in HIV-positive gay men. *International Journal of STD & AIDS, 15*(11), 732–736.

Cox, B., Sneyd, M. J., Paul, C., & Skegg, D. C. G. (2006). Risk factors for prostate cancer: A national case-control study. *International Journal of Cancer, 119*(7), 1690–1694.

Cox, D. J. (1988). Incidence and nature of male genital exposure behavior as reported by college women. *Journal of Sex Research, 24,* 227–234.

Cox, W. M., & Alm, R. (2005, February 25). Scientists are made, not born. *The New York Times* (Online).

Coyle, J. P. (2006). Treating difficult couples: Helping clients with coexisting mental and relationship disorders. *Family Relations: Interdisciplinary Journal of Applied Family Studies, 55*(1), 146–147.

Craig, R. J. (2005). Harassment. In R. J. Craig (Ed.), *Personality-guided forensic psychology. Personality-guided psychology* (pp. 155–167). Washington, DC: American Psychological Association.

Cramer, D. (2003). Facilitativeness, conflict, demand for approval, self-esteem, and satisfaction with romantic relationships. *Journal of Psychology, 137*(1), 85–98.

Crandall, C. J., et al. (2012). Breast tenderness and breast cancer risk in the estrogen plus progestin and estrogen-alone women's health initiative clinical trials. *Breast Cancer Research and Treatment, 132*(1), 275–285.

Crawford, T. V., Rawlins, J., McGrowder, D. A., & Adams, R. L. (2011). The Church's response to sexual reproductive health issues. *Journal of Religion and Health, 50*(1), 163–176.

Crepaz, N., Hart, T. A., & Marks, G. (2004). Highly active antiretroviral therapy and sexual risk behavior: A meta-analytic review. *Journal of the American Medical Association, 292*(2), 224–236.

Crews, D. (1994). Animal sexuality. *Scientific American, 270*(1), 108–114.

Critelli, F. M., & Willett, J. (2012). Struggle and hope: Challenging gender violence in Pakistan. *Critical Sociology,* DOI: 10.1177/0896920512438780.

Critelli, J. W., & Bivona, J. M. (2008). Women's erotic rape fantasies: An evaluation of theory and research. *Journal of Sex Research, 45*(1), 57–70.

Crofoot, M. C., & Wrangham, R. W. (2010). Intergroup aggression in primates and humans: The case for a unified theory. In P. M. Kappeler & J. B. Silk (Eds.), *Mind the gap: Tracing the origins of human universals* (pp. 171–195). New York: Springer.

Crosby, R., Yarber, W., Sanders, S., & Graham, C. (2005). Condom discomfort and associated problems with their use among university students. *Journal of American College Health 54*(3), 143–147.

Crowley, T., Richardson, D., Goldmeier, D., & BASHH Special Interest Group for Sexual Dysfunction. (2006). Recommendations for the management of vaginismus: BASHH Special Interest Group for Sexual Dysfunction. *International Journal of STD & AIDS, 17*(1), 14–18.

Crozier, I. (2012). Making up Koro: Multiplicity, psychiatry, culture, and penis-shrinking anxieties. *Journal of the History of Medicine and Allied Sciences, 67*(1), 36–70.

Crum, N. F., Furtek, K. J., Olson, P. E., Amling, C. L., & Wallace, M. R. (2005). A review of hypogonadism and erectile dysfunction among HIV-infected men during the pre-and post-HAART eras: Diagnosis, pathogenesis, and management. *AIDS Patient Care and STDs, 19*(10), 869–885.

Csoka, A. B., & Shipko, S. (2006). Persistent sexual side effects after SSRI discontinuation. *Psychotherapy and Psychosomatics, 75*(3), 187–188.

Cullen, K. J. (2011, October 4). In Grady, D., Study cites increase in cancers from HPV. *New York Times,* p. D5.

Cummings, S. R., et al. (1999). The effect of raloxifene on risk of breast cancer in postmenopausal women: Results from the MORE randomized trial. *Journal of the American Medical Association, 281,* 2189–2197.

Cunningham, A. L., et al. (2006). Prevalence of infection with herpes simplex virus types 1 and 2 in Australia: A nationwide population based survey. *Sexually Transmitted Infections, 82,* 164–168.

Cunningham, M. R., & Barbee, A. P. (2008). Prelude to a kiss: Nonverbal flirting, opening gambits, and other communication dynamics in the initiation of romantic relationships. In S. Sprecher, A. Wenzel, & J. Harvey (Eds.), *Handbook of relationship initiation* (pp. 97–120). New York: CRC Press.

Cunningham, M. R., et al. (1995). "Their ideas of beauty are, on the whole, the same as ours": Consistency and variability in the cross-cultural perception of female physical attractiveness. *Journal of Personality and Social Psychology, 68*(2), 261–279.

Curnoe, S., & Langevin, R. (2002). Personality and deviant sexual fantasies: An examination of the MMPIs. *Journal of Clinical Psychology, 58*(7), 803–815.

Cutler, W. B. (1999). Human sex-attractant hormones: Discovery, research, development, and application in sex therapy. *Psychiatric Annals, 29*(1), 54–59.

Cutler, W. B., Friedmann, E., & McCoy, N. L. (1998). Pheromonal influences on sociosexual behavior in men. *Archives of Sexual Behavior, 27*(1), 1–13.

Cuzin, B., et al. (2011). Guidelines for general practitioners for first-line management of erectile dysfunction. *Sexologies, 20*(1), 23–35.

Cyr, M., Wright, J., McDuff, P., & Perron, A. (2002). Intrafamilial sexual abuse: Brother–sister incest does not differ from father–daughter and stepfather–stepdaughter incest. *Child Abuse & Neglect, 26*(9), 957–973.

Czech, D. P., et al. (2012). The human testis-determining factor SRY localizes in midbrain dopamine neurons and regulates multiple components of catecholamine synthesis and metabolism. *Journal of Neurochemistry, 122*(2), 260–271.

D'Angelo, D., et al. (2007). Preconception and interconception health status of women who recently gave birth to a live-born infant—Pregnancy risk assessment monitoring system. *Morbidity and Mortality Weekly Report, 56*(SS10), 1–35.

Dabbs, J. M., Jr., & Morris, R. (1990). Testosterone, social class, and antisocial behavior in a sample of 4,462 men. *Psychological Science, 1,* 1–3.

Dahl, D. W., Sengupta, J., & Vohs, K. D. (2009, January 9). Sex in advertising: Gender differences and the role of relationship commitment, *Journal of Consumer Research,* published electronically.

Dake, J. A., Price, J. H., Maziarz, L., & Ward, B. (2012). Prevalence and correlates of sexting behavior in adolescents. *American Journal of Sexuality Education, 7*(1), 1–15.

Daley, A. (2009). Exercise and premenstrual symptomatology: A comprehensive review. *Journal of Women's Health, 18*(6), 895–899.

Dalla, R. L. (2006). "You can't hustle all your life": An exploratory investigation of the exit process among street-level prostituted women. *Psychology of Women Quarterly, 30*(3), 276–290.

Daly, M., & Wilson, M. (2003). Evolutionary psychology of lethal interpersonal violence. In W. Heitmeyer & J. Hagan (Eds.), *Handbook of research on violence* (pp. 709–734). New York: Westview.

Daly, M., & Wilson, M. (2005). Human behavior as animal behavior. In J. J. Bolhuis

& L. A Giraldeau (Eds.), *The behavior of animals. Mechanisms, function, and evolution* (pp. 393–408). Oxford: Blackwell.

Damon, W. (2002). Dominance, sexism, and inadequacy: Testing a compensatory conceptualization in a sample of heterosexual men involved in SM. *Journal of Psychology & Human Sexuality, 14*(4), 25–45.

Daneback, K., Ross, M. W., & Månsson, S. (2006). Characteristics and behaviors of sexual compulsives who use the Internet for sexual purposes. *Sexual Addiction & Compulsivity, 13*(1), 53–67.

Dantzker, M. L., & Eisenman, R. (2003). Sexual attitudes among Hispanic college students: Differences between males and females. *International Journal of Adolescence & Youth, 11*(1), 79–89.

Dao, J. (2011, September 19). Don't ask, don't tell ends this week with celebrations, revelations and questions. *New York Times* (online).

Darcangelo, S. (2008). Fetishism: Psychopathology and theory. In D. R. Laws and W. T. O'Donohue (Eds.), *Sexual deviance: Theory, assessment, and treatment* (2nd ed., pp. 76–107). New York: Guilford Press.

Darling, C. A., Davidson, J. K., & Jennings, D. A. (1991). The female sexual response revisited: Understanding the multiorgasmic experience in women. *Archives of Sexual Behavior, 20,* 527–540.

Das, A., et al. (2009). Frontiers of retrovirology: Complex retroviruses, retroelements and their hosts. Montpellier, France. 21-23 September 2009. *Retrovirology, 6*(Suppl 2), I24.

Dauwalder, B. (2011). The roles of *fruitless* and *doublesex* in the control of male courtship. In N. Atkinson (Ed.). *International Review of Neurobiology: Recent advances in the use of Drosophila in neurobiology and neurodegeneration, 99* (pp. 87–107). London: Academic Press.

Davidson, J. K., & Hoffman, L. E. (1986). Sexual fantasies and sexual satisfaction: An empirical analysis of erotic thought. *Journal of Sex Research, 22*(2), 184–205.

Davies, M. (2004). Correlates of negative attitudes toward gay men: Sexism, male role norms, and male sexuality. *Journal of Sex Research, 41*(3), 259–266.

Davies, M., Gilston, J., & Rogers, P. (2012). Examining the relationship between male rape myth acceptance, female rape myth acceptance, victim blame, homophobia, gender roles, and ambivalent sexism. *Journal of Interpersonal Violence, 27*(14), 2807–2823.

Davis, D., Shaver, P. R., & Vernon, M. L. (2003). Physical, emotional, and behavioral reactions to breaking up: The roles of gender, age, emotional involvement, and attachment style. *Personality & Social Psychology Bulletin, 29*(7), 871–884.

Davis, K. C. (2010). The influence of alcohol expectancies and intoxication on men's aggressive unprotected sexual intentions. *Experimental and Clinical Psychopharmacology, 18*(5), 418–428.

Davis, K. E., & Frieze, I. H., & Maiuro, R. D. (Eds.). (2002). *Stalking: Perspectives on victims and perpetrators* (pp. 212–236). New York: Springer.

Davis, R. L. (2010). *More perfect unions: The American search for marital bliss.* Cambridge, MA: Harvard University Press.

Davis, S. (2000). Testosterone and sexual desire in women. *Journal of Sex Education & Therapy, 25*(1), 25–32.

Davis, S. R., & Braunstein, G. D. (2012). Efficacy and safety of testosterone in the management of hypoactive sexual desire disorder in menopausal women. *The Journal of Sexual Medicine, 9*(4), 1134–1148.

Davis, S. R., et al. (2008). Testosterone for low libido in postmenopausal women not taking estrogen. *New England Journal of Medicine, 359,* 2005.

Davis, T. L., & Liddell, D. L. (2002). Getting inside the house: The effectiveness of a rape prevention program for college fraternity men. *Journal of College Student Development, 43*(1), 35–50.

Davison, G. C. (1977). Elimination of a sadistic fantasy by a client-controlled counter-conditioning technique. In J. Fischer & H. Gochios (Eds.), *Handbook of behavior therapy with sexual problems.* New York: Pergamon.

Dawood, K., Bailey, J. M., & Martin, N. G. (2009). Genetic and environmental influences on sexual orientation. In Y-K. Kim (Ed.), *Handbook of behavior genetics* (pp. 269–279). New York: Springer.

Dawson, S. J., Suschinsky, K. D., & Lalumiere, M. L. (2012). Sexual fantasies and viewing times across the menstrual cycle: A diary study. *Archives of Sexual Behavior, 41*(1), 173–183.

De Cuyper, M., de Bolle, M., & de Fruyt, F. (2012). Personality similarity, perceptual accuracy, and relationship satisfaction in dating and married couples. *Personal Relationships, 19*(1), 128–145.

De Graaf, H., & Rademakers, J. (2011). The psychological measurement of childhood sexual development in Western societies: Methodological challenges. *Journal of Sex Research, 48*(2–3), 118–129.

De Smet, O., Loeys, T., & Buysse, A. (2012). Post-breakup unwanted pursuit: A refined analysis of the role of romantic relationship characteristics. *Journal of Family Violence, 27*(5), 437–452.

De Vries, G. J., et al. (2002). A model system for study of sex chromosome effects on sexually dimorphic neural and behavioral traits. *Journal of Neuroscience, 22*(20), 9005–9014.

Deci, E. L., La Guardia, J. G., Moller, A. C., Scheiner, M. J., & Ryan, R. M. (2006). On the benefits of giving as well as receiving autonomy support: Mutuality in close friendships. *Personality and Social Psychology Bulletin, 32*(3), 313–327.

Degenhardt, L., Day, C., Conroy, E., & Gilmour, S. (2006). Examining links between cocaine use and street-based sex work in New South Wales, Australia. *Journal of Sex Research, 43*(2), 107–114.

DeJesus, E., et al. (2012). Co-formulated elvitegravir, cobicistat, emtricitabine, and tenofovir disoproxil fumarate versus ritonavir-boosted atazanavir plus co-formulated emtricitabine and tenofovir disoproxil fumarate for initial treatment of HIV-1 infection: a randomised, double-blind, phase 3, non-inferiority trial. *The Lancet, 379*(9835), 2429–2438.

Dekker, A., & Schmidt, G. (2002). Patterns of masturbatory behaviour: Changes between the sixties and the nineties. *Journal of Psychology & Human Sexuality, 14*(2–3), 35–48.

del Busto, E., & Harlow, M. C. (2011). American sex offender castration treatment and legislation. In D. P. Boer et al. (Eds.). *International Perspectives on the Assessment and Treatment of Sexual Offenders: Theory, Practice, and Research* (pp. 543–571). Hoboken, NJ: Wiley.

Del Rosso, J. (2011). The penis as public part: Embodiment and the performance of masculinity in public settings. *Sexualities, 14*(6), 704–724.

Delgado, A. R., & Prieto, G. (2004). Cognitive mediators and sex-related differences in mathematics. *Intelligence, 32*(1), 25–32.

Delgado, J. (1969). *Physical control of the mind.* New York: Harper & Row.

den Tonkelaar, I., & Oddens, B. J. (2000). Determinants of long-term hormone replacement therapy and reasons for early discontinuation. *Obstetrics & Gynecology, 95*(4), 507–512.

Denmark, F., Paludi, M. A., & Lott, B. (2008). *Psychology of women: A handbook of issues and theories.* Santa Barbara, CA: Greenwood Press.

Dennerstein, L., & Goldstein, I. (2005). Postmenopausal female sexual dysfunction: At a crossroads. *Journal of Sexual Medicine, 2*(Suppl. 3), 116–117.

Derby, C. A. (2000, October 2). Cited in Study finds exercise reduces the risk of impotence. The Associated Press.

Derlega, V. J., Winstead, B. A., & Greene, K. (2008). Self-disclosure and starting a close relationship. In S. Sprecher, A. Wenzel, & J. Harvey (Eds.), *Handbook of relationship initiation* (pp.153–174). New York: CRC Press.

Devereux, C. (2011). "Last night, I did a striptease for my husband." Erotic dance and the representation of "everyday" femininity. *Feminist media studies,* 10.1080/14680777.2011.615598.

Dew, J., & Wilcox, W. B. (2011, December 8). Give and you shall receive? Generosity, sacrifice, and marital quality. *National Marriage Project Working Paper* No. 11-1.

Dhar, N. B. (2006). Vasectomy men pose pregnancy risk. *British Journal of Urology International, 97,* 773–776.

Diamond, L. (2008). *Sexual fluidity: Understanding women's love and desire.* Cambridge, MA: Harvard University Press.

Diamond, L. M. (2000). Sexual identity, attractions, and behavior among young sexual-minority women over a 2-year period. *Developmental Psychology, 36*(2), 241–250.

Diamond, L. M. (2002). "Having a girlfriend without knowing it": Intimate friendships among adolescent sexual-minority women. *Journal of Lesbian Studies, 6*(1) 5–16.

Diamond, L. M. (2003a). Was it a phase? Young women's relinquishment of lesbian/bisexual identities over a 5-year period. *Journal of Personality & Social Psychology, 84*(2), 352–364.

Diamond, L. M. (2003b). What does sexual orientation orient? A biobehavioral model distinguishing romantic love and sexual desire. *Psychological Review, 110*(1), 173–192.

Diamond, L. M. (2008). Female bisexuality from adolescence to adulthood: Results from a 10-year longitudinal study. *Developmental Psychology, 44*(1), 5–14.

Diamond, L. M., & Dickenson, J. A. (2012). The neuroimaging of love and desire: Review and future directions. *Clinical Neuropsychiatry, 9*(1), 39–46.

Diamond, M. (1996). Prenatal predisposition and the clinical management of some pediatric conditions. *Journal of Sex & Marital Therapy, 22*(3), 139–147.

Diamond, M. (2011). Developmental, sexual and reproductive neuroendocrinology: Historical, clinical and ethical considerations. *Frontiers in Neuroendocrinology, 32*(2), 255–263.

DiDonato, M. D., & Berenbaum, S. A. (2011). The benefits and drawbacks of gender typing: How different dimensions are related to psychological adjustment. *Archives of Sexual Behavior, 40*(2), 457–463.

Dijkstra, P., & Buunk, B. P. (2002). Sex differences in the jealousy-evoking effect of rival characteristics. *European Journal of Social Psychology, 32*(6), 829–852.

Dilley, J. W., et al. (2003). Availability of combination therapy for HIV: Effects on sexual risk taking in a sample of high-risk gay and bisexual men. *AIDS Care, 15*(1), 27–37.

Dindia, K., & Allen, M. (1992). Sex differences in self-disclosure: A meta-analysis. *Psychological Bulletin, 112,* 106–124.

Dindia, K., & Timmerman, L. (2003). Accomplishing romantic relationships. In J. O. Greene & B. R. Burleson (Eds.), *Handbook of communication and social interaction skills* (pp. 685–721). Mahwah, NJ: Erlbaum.

Ding, Q. J., & Hesketh, T. (2006). Family size, fertility preferences, and sex ratio in China in the era of the one child family policy: Results from National Family Planning and Reproductive Health Survey. *British Medical Journal, 333*(7564), 371–373.

Dingfelder, S. F. (2011, April). Understanding orgasm. *Monitor on Psychology,* pp. 42–45.

Disney, E. R., Iacono, W., McGue, M., Tully, E., & Legrand, L. (2008). Strengthening the case: Prenatal alcohol exposure is associated with increased risk for conduct disorder. *Pediatrics, 122*(6), e1225–e1230.

Dittert, S., Seidl, O., & Soyka, M. (2005). Zoophilia as a special case of paraphilia. Presentation of three case reports and an Internet survey. *Nervenarzt, 76*(1), 61–67.

Dixson, B. J., Grimshaw, G. M., Linklater, W. L., & Dixson, A. F. (2011). Eye tracking of men's preferences for female breast size and areola pigmentation. *Archives of Sexual Behavior, 40*(1), 51–58.

Do, C., et al. (2009). Statins and erectile dysfunction: Results of a case/non-case study using the French Pharmacovigilance System Database. *Drug Safety, 32*(7), 591–597.

Dodge, M. (2012). Female prostitution. In C. D. Bryant (Ed.). *The Routledge handbook of deviant behavior* (pp. 371–377). New York: Routledge.

Donald, M., Dower, J., Correa-Velez, I., & Jones, M. (2006). Risk and protective factors for medically serious suicide attempts: A comparison of hospital-based with population-based samples of young adults.

Australian and New Zealand Journal of Psychiatry, 40(1), 87–96.

Donnerstein, E. (1980). Aggressive erotica and violence against women. *Journal of Personality and Social Psychology, 39,* 269–277.

Donnerstein, E. I., & Linz, D. G. (1987). *The question of pornography.* New York: The Free Press.

Donnerstein, E., & Berkowitz, L. (1981). Victim reactions in aggressive erotic films as a factor in violence against women. *Journal of Personality and Social Psychology, 41,* 710–724.

Downing, L., & Gillett, R. (2011). Viewing critical psychology through the lens of queer. *Psychology and Sexuality, 2*(1), 4–15.

Downs, M., & Nazario, B. (2003, February 11). *Aphrodisiacs through the ages.* WebMD Features. (Online).

Drews, C. D., et al. (April 1996). *Pediatrics.*

Drigotas, S. M., Rusbult, C. E., & Verette, J. (1999). Level of commitment, mutuality of commitment, and couple well-being. *Personal Relationships, 6*(3) 389–409.

Driver, J., Tabares, A., Shapiro, A., Nahm, E. Y., & Gottman, J. M. (2003). Interactional patterns in marital success and failure: Gottman laboratory studies. In F. Walsh (Ed.), *Normal family processes: Growing diversity and complexity* (3rd ed., pp. 493–513). New York: Guilford

Drucker, D. J. (2012). A most interesting chapter in the history of science: Intellectual responses to Alfred Kinsey's *Sexual behavior in the human male. History of the Human Sciences, 25*(1), 75–98.

Duenwald, M. (2002, July 16). Hormone therapy: One size, clearly, no longer fits all. *The New York Times.*

Duggan, L. (2006a). Censorship in the name of feminism. In L. Duggan & N. D. Hunter (Eds.), *Sex wars: Sexual dissent and political culture* (10th ed., pp. 29–39). Oxford, UK: Routledge/Taylor & Francis Group.

Duggan, L. (2006b). Feminist historians and antipornography campaigns: An overview. In L. Duggan & N. D. Hunter (Eds.), *Sex wars: Sexual dissent and political culture* (10th ed., pp. 65–69). Oxford, UK: Routledge/Taylor & Francis Group.

Duggan, L., Hunter, N. D., & Vance, C. S. (2006). False promises: Feminist antipornography legislation. In L. Duggan & N. D. Hunter (Eds.), *Sex wars: Sexual dissent and political culture* (10th ed., pp. 43–64). Oxford, UK: Routledge/Taylor & Francis Group.

Duggirala, M. K., et al. (2003). A human papillomavirus type 16 vaccine. *New England Journal of Medicine, 348,* 1402–1405.

Duke, L. A., Allen, D. N., Rozee, P. D., & Bommaritto, M. (2008). The sensitivity and specificity of flashbacks and nightmares to trauma. *Journal of Anxiety Disorders, 22*(2), 319–327.

Durante, K. M., Li, N. P., & Haselton, M. G. (2008). Changes in women's choice of dress across the ovulatory cycle: Naturalistic and laboratory task-based evidence. *Personality and Social Psychology Bulletin, 34*(11), 1451–1460.

Duru, C., Jha, S., & Lashen, H. (2012). Urodynamic outcomes after hysterectomy for

benign conditions: A systematic review and meta-analysis. *Obstetrical and Gynecological Survey, 67*(1), 45–54.

Dwyer, P. L. (2011). Skene's gland revisited: Function, dysfunction, and the G-spot. *International Urogynecology Journal, 23*(2), 135–137.

Dye, M. L., & Davis, K. E. (2003). Stalking and psychological abuse: Common factors and relationship-specific characteristics. *Violence & Victims, 18*(2), 163–180.

Dzokoto, V. A., & Adams, G. (2005). Understanding genital-shrinking epidemics in West Africa: Koro, juju, or mass psychogenic illness? *Culture, Medicine and Psychiatry, 29*(1), 53–78.

Eardley, I., et al. (2010). Pharmacotherapy for erectile dysfunction. *Journal of Sexual Medicine, 7,* 524–540.

Eason, E., & Feldman, P. (2000). Much ado about a little cut: Is episiotomy worthwhile? *Obstetrics & Gynecology, 95*(4), 616–618.

Eason, E., Labrecque, M., Wells, G., & Feldman, P. (2000). Preventing perineal trauma during childbirth: A systematic review. *Obstetrics & Gynecology, 95,* 464–471.

Eastwick, P. W., & Finkel, E. J. (2008). Sex differences in mate preferences revisited: Do people know what they initially desire in a romantic partner? *Journal of Personality and Social Psychology, 94*(2), 245–264.

Eastwick, P. W., & Finkel, E. J. (2008). Speed-dating: A powerful and flexible paradigm for stufying romantic relationship initiation. In S. Sprecher, A. Wenzel, & J. Harvey (Eds.), *Handbook of relationship initiation* (pp. 217–234). New York: CRC Press.

Eck, B. A. (2001). Nudity and framing: Classifying art, pornography, information, and ambiguity. *Sociological Forum, 16*(4), 603–632.

Ecuyer-Dab, I., & Robert, M. (2004). Have sex differences in spatial ability evolved from male competition for mating and female concern for survival? *Cognition, 91*(3), 221–257.

Edser, S. J., & Shea, J. D. (2002). An exploratory investigation of bisexual men in monogamous, heterosexual marriages. *Journal of Bisexuality, 2*(4), 5–29.

Edwards, T. M. (2000, August 28). Single by choice. *Time Magazine, 156*(9).

Edwards, V. J., Holden, G. W., Felitti, V. J., & Anda, R. F. (2003). Relationship between multiple forms of childhood maltreatment and adult mental health in community respondents: Results from the Adverse Childhood Experiences Study. *American Journal of Psychiatry, 160*(8), 1453–1460.

Egelman, P. C. (2011). *A history of the birth control movement in America.* Santa Barbara, CA: ABC-CLIO.

Eggers, D. (2000, May 7). Intimacies. *The New York Times Magazine,* 76–77.

Eisenberg, M. L., et al. (2010). Socioeconomic, anthropomorphic, and demographic predictors of adult sexual activity in the United States: Data from the National Survey of Family Growth. *Journal of Sexual Medicine, 7,* 50–58.

Eisenberg, M., Shindel, A. W., Smith, J. F., Breyer, B. N., & Lipshultz, L. I. (2010). Socioeconomic, anthropomorphic, and demographic predictors of adult sexual activity in the United States: Data from the national survey of family growth. *Journal of Sexual Medicine, 7,* 50–58.

El-Defrawi, M. H., Lotfy, G., Dandash, K. F., Refaat, A. H., & Eyada, M. (2001). Female genital mutilation and its psychosexual impact. *Journal of Sex & Marital Therapy, 27*(5), 465–473.

El-Gibaly, O., Ibrahim, B., Mensch, B. S., & Clark, W. H. (2002). The decline of female circumcision in Egypt: Evidence and interpretation. *Social Science & Medicine, 54*(2), 205–220.

Elliot, A. J., & Niesta, D. (2008). Romantic red: Red enhances men's attraction to women. *Journal of Personality and Social Psychology, 95*(5), 1150–1164.

Elliot, A. J., & Pazda, A. D. (2012). Dressed for sex: Red as a female sexual signal in humans. *PLoS ONE 7*(4): e34607. DOI:10.1371/journal.pone.0034607.

Elliot, A. J., et al. (2010). Red, rank, and romance in women viewing men. *Journal of Experimental Psychology: General, 139*(3), 399–417.

Ellis, B. J., & Bjorklund, D. F. (Eds.). (2005). *Origins of the social mind: Evolutionary psychology and child development.* New York: Guilford.

Ellis, L., & Ames, M. A. (1987). Neurohormonal functioning and sexual orientation: A theory of homosexuality–heterosexuality. *Psychological Bulletin, 101,* 233–258.

Else-Quest, N. M., & Grabe, S. (2012). The political is personal: Measurement and application of nation-level indicators of gender equity in psychological research. *Psychology of Women Quarterly, 36*(2), 131–144.

Else-Quest, N. M., Hyde, J. S., & Linn, M. C. (2010). Cross-national patterns of gender differences in mathematics: A meta-analysis. *Psychological Bulletin, 136*(1), 103–127.

El-Sheikh, M. & Harger, J. (2001). Appraisals of marital conflict and children's adjustment, health, and physiological reactivity. *Developmental Psychology, 37*(6), 875–885.

Eltahawy, M. (2003, January 9). Young Africans reject female genital mutilation. www.feminist.com/news/news141.html.

Emanuele, E., et al. (2006). Raised plasma nerve growth factor levels associated with early-stage romantic love. *Psychoneuroendocrinology, 31*(3), 288–294.

Emmanuele A., et al. (2011). The controversial role of phosphodiesterase type 5 inhibitors in the treatment of premature ejaculation. *The Journal of Sexual Medicine, 8*(8), 2135–2143.

Emmelot-Vonk, M. H., et al. (2009). Effect of testosterone supplementation on sexual functioning in aging men: A 6-month randomized controlled trial. *International Journal of Impotence Research, 21,* 129–138.

Engelhardt, A., Fischer, J., Neumann, C., Pfeifer, J., & Heistermann, M. (2012). Information content of female copulation calls in wild long-tailed macaques. *Behavioral Ecology and Sociobiology, 66*(1), 121–134.

Eriksson, C., Salander, K., & Hamberg, K. (2007). Men's experiences of intense fear related to childbirth investigated in a Swedish qualitative study. *The Journal of Men's Health & Gender, 4*(4), 409–418.

European Commission. Eurostat. (2009). Live births outside marriage. Accessed May 13, 2009.

Fabre, L. F., et al. (2012). The effect of gepirone-ER in the treatment of sexual dysfunction in depressed men. *Journal of Sexual Medicine, 9*(3), 821–829.

Fabricius, W. V., Sokol, K. R., Diaz, P., & Braver, S. L. (2012). Parenting time, parent conflict, parent–child relationships, and children's physical health. In K. Kuehnle, & L. Drozd. (Eds.). *Parenting plan evaluations: Applied research for the family court* (pp. 188–213). New York: Oxford University Press.

Fagot, B. I., Rodgers, C. S., & Leinbach, M. D. (2000). Theories of gender socialization. In T. Eckes & H. M. Trautner (Eds.), *The developmental social psychology of gender* (pp. 65–89). Mahwah, NJ: Erlbaum.

Faller, K. C. (1989). Why sexual abuse? An exploration of the intergenerational hypothesis. *Child Abuse and Neglect, 13,* 543–548.

Fang, A., & Hofmann, S. G. (2010). Relationship between social anxiety disorder and body dysmorphic disorder. *Clinical Psychology Review, 30*(8), 1040–1048.

Farley, M. Citied in Bennets, L. (2011, July 18). The john next door. *Newsweek* magazine.

Farley, M., Lynne, J., & Cotton, A. J. (2005). Prostitution in Vancouver: Violence and the colonization of First Nations Women. *Transcultural Psychiatry, 42*(2), 242–271.

Fausto-Sterling, A. (May/April 1993). The five sexes: Why male and female are not enough. *The Sciences,* 20–25.

Fava, N. M., & Bay-Cheng, L. Y. (2012). Young women's adolescent experiences of oral sex: Relation of age of initiation to sexual motivation, sexual coercion, and psychological functioning. *Journal of Adolescence, 35*(5), 1191–1201.

Feinberg, D. R., et al. (2006). Menstrual cycle, trait estrogen level, and masculinity preferences in the human voice. *Hormones and Behavior, 49*(2), 215–222.

Feingold, A. (1994). Gender differences in personality: A meta-analysis. *Psychological Bulletin, 116,* 429–456.

Felder, R. L., & Carey, M. P. (2010). Predictors and consequences of sexual "hookups" among college students: A short-term prospective study. *Archives of Sexual Behavior, 39,* 1105–1119.

Felson, R. B. (2002). *Violence and gender reexamined.* Washington, DC: American Psychological Association.

Fensterheim, H., & Kantor, J. S. (1980). Behavioral approach to sexual disorders. In B. Wolman & J. Money (Eds.), *Handbook of human sexuality.* Englewood Cliffs, NJ: Prentice-Hall.

Fenton, K., et al. (2008). Infectious syphilis in high-income settings in the 21st century. *The Lancet Infectious Diseases, 8*(4), 244–253.

Ferraro, G. (2004). *Cultural anthropology—An applied perspective* (5th ed.). Belmont, CA: Wadsworth.

Ferris, C. F., et al. (2004). Activation of neural pathways associated with sexual arousal in non-human primates. *Journal of Magnetic Resonance Imaging, 19*(2), 168–175.

Festa, E. D., et al. (2004). Sex differences in cocaine-induced behavioral responses,

pharmacokinetics, and monoamine levels. *Neuropharmacology, 46*(5), 672–687.

Festini, F., et al. (2006, August 22). The open problems of China's One-Child Family Policy: Men surplus and support of the elders. Available at www.bmj.com.

Fichner-Rathus, L. (2010). *Understanding art* (9th ed.). Belmont, CA: Thomson Learning/Wadsworth.

Finer, L. B., & Zolna, M. R. (2011). Unintended pregnancy in the United States: In cadence and disparities. *Contraception, 84*(5), 478–485.

Finkel, E. J., Eastwick, P., Karney, B., Reis, H. T., & Sprecher, S. (2012). Online dating: A critical analysis from the perspective of psychological science. *Psychological Science in the Public Interest,* 1–64. DOI:10.1177/1529100612436522.

Finkelhor, D. (1990). Early and long-term effects of child sexual abuse: An update. *Professional Psychology: Research and Practice, 21,* 325–330.

Finkelhor, D. (2003). The legacy of the clergy abuse scandal. *Child Abuse & Neglect, 27*(11), 1225–1229.

Finkelhor, D. (2011). Prevalence of child victimization, abuse, crime, and violence exposure. In J. W. White, M. P. Koss, & A. E. Kazdin (Eds.). *Violence against women and children, Vol 1: Mapping the terrain* (pp. 9–29). Washington, DC, US: American Psychological Association.

Finkelhor, D., Cross, T. P., & Cantor, E. N. (2005a). The justice system for juvenile victims: A comprehensive model of case flow. *Trauma, Violence, & Abuse, 6*(2), 83–102.

Finkelhor, D., Ormrod, R., Turner, H., & Hamby, S. (2012). *Child and Youth Victimization Known to Police, School, and Medical Authorities. National Survey of Children's Exposure to Violence.* Juvenile Justice Bulletin. Office of Juvenile Justice and Delinquency Prevention.

Finkelhor, D., Ormrod, R., Turner, H., & Hamby, S. L. (2005b). The victimization of children and youth: A comprehensive, national survey. *Child Maltreatment: Journal of the American Professional Society on the Abuse of Children, 10*(1), 5–25.

Finkelman, J. M. (2005). Sexual harassment: The organizational perspective. In A. Barnes (Ed.), *The handbook of women, psychology, and the law* (pp. 64–78). New York: Wiley.

Finkenauer, C., & Hazam, H. (2000). Disclosure and secrecy in marriage: Do both contribute to marital satisfaction? *Journal of Social & Personal Relationships, 17*(2), 245–263.

Firestone, R. W., Firestone, L. A., & Catlett, J. (2006a). *Sex and love in intimate relationships.* Washington, DC: American Psychological Association.

Firestone, R. W., Firestone, L. A., & Catlett, J. (2006b). Sexual withholding. In R. W. Firestone, L. A. Firestone, & J. Catlett (Eds.), *Sex and love in intimate relationships* (pp. 171–195). Washington, DC: American Psychological Association.

Fisher, A. D., Bandini, E., Casale, H., & Maggi, M. (2011). Paraphilic disorders: Diagnosis and treatment. In M. Maggi (Ed.). *Hormonal therapy for male sexual dysfunction* (pp. 94–110). Hoboken, NJ: Wiley.

Fisher, A. D., Bandini, E., Casale, H., & Maggi, M. (2012). Paraphilic disorders: Diagnosis and treatment. In M. Maggi (Ed.). *Hormonal therapy for male sexual dysfunction* (pp. 94–110). Hoboken, NJ: Wiley.

Fisher, B. S., Daigle, L. E., Cullen, F. T., & Turner, M. G. (2003). Reporting sexual victimization to the police and others: Results from a national-level study of college women. *Criminal Justice & Behavior, 30*(1), 6–38.

Fisher, H. E. (2000). Brains do it: Lust, attraction and attachment. *Cerebrum, 2,* 23–42.

Fisher, T. D., Moore, Z. T., & Pittenger, M. (2012). Sex on the brain? An examination of frequency of sexual cognitions as a function of gender, erotophilia, and social desirability. *Journal of Sex Research, 49*(1), 69–77.

Fisher, W. A., et al. (2005). Improving the sexual quality of life of couples affected by erectile dysfunction: A double-blind, randomized, placebo-controlled trial of vardenafil. *Journal of Sexual Medicine, 2*(5), 699–708.

Fisher, W., Ceballos, N., Matthews, D., & Ficher, L. (2011). Event-related potentials in impulsively aggressive juveniles: A retrospective chart-review study. *Psychiatry Research, 187*(3), 409–413.

Fishman, J. R., & Mamo, L. (2001). What's in a disorder: A cultural analysis of medical and pharmaceutical constructions of male and female sexual dysfunction. *Women & Therapy, 24*(1–2), 179–193.

Flaxman, S. M., & Sherman, P. W. (2000). Morning sickness: A mechanism for protecting mother and embryo. *The Quarterly Review of Biology, 75*(2), 113–148.

Fletcher, J. (1966). *Situation ethics.* Philadelphia: Westminster Press.

Fletcher, J. (1967). *Moral responsibility: Situation ethics at work.* Philadelphia: Westminster Press.

Fletcher, J. M., & Sindelar, J. L. (2012). The effects of family stressors on substance abuse initiation in adolescence. *Review of Economics of the Household, 10*(1), 99–114.

Fletcher, S. W., & Colditz, G. A. (2002). Failure of estrogen plus progestin therapy for prevention. *Journal of the American Medical Association, 288*(3).

Florence, E., et al. (2004). Prevalence and factors associated with sexual dysfunction among HIV-positive women in Europe. *AIDS Care, 16*(5), 550–557.

Floyd, R. L., O'Connor, M. J., Sokol, R. J., Bertrand, J., & Cordero, F. F. (2005). Recognition and prevention of fetal alcohol syndrome. *Obstetrics & Gynecology, 106,* 1059–1064.

Forbes, A., While, A., Mathes, L., & Griffiths, P. (2006). Health problems and health-related quality of life in people with multiple sclerosis. *Clinical Rehabilitation, 20*(1), 67–78.

Forbes, G. B., Adams-Curtis, L. E., Pakalka, A. H., & White, K. B. (2006). Dating aggression, sexual coercion, and aggression-supporting attitudes among college men as a function of participation in aggressive high school sports. *Violence Against Women, 12*(5), 441–455.

Ford, C. S., & Beach, F. A. (1951). *Patterns of sexual behavior.* New York: Harper & Row.

Forgas, J. P., Levinger, G., & Moylan, S. J. (1994). Feeling good and feeling close: Affective influences on the perception of intimate relationships. *Personal Relationships, 1*(2), 165–184.

Foubert, J. D., & Newberry, J. T. (2006). Effects of two versions of an empathy-based rape prevention program on fraternity men's survivor empathy, attitudes, and behavioral intent to commit rape or sexual assault. *Journal of College Student Development, 47*(2), 133–148.

Fox, N. S., et al. (2008). Physical and sexual activity during pregnancy and near delivery. *Journal of Women's Health, 17,* 1431.

Frank, K. (2002). *G-strings and sympathy: Strip club regulars and male desire.* Raleigh, NC: Duke University Press.

Frank, K. (2003). Just trying to relax: Masculinity, masculinizing practices, and strip club regulars. *The Journal of Sex Research, 40*(1), 61–75.

Frank, K. (2007). Thinking critically about strip club research. *Sexualities, 10*(4), 501–517.

Frayser, S. (1985). *Varieties of sexual experience: An anthropological perspective on human sexuality.* New Haven, CT: Human Relations Area Files Press.

Freud, S. (1922/1959). Analysis of a phobia in a 5-year-old boy. In A. J. Strachey (Ed., Trans.), *Collected papers* (Vol. 3). New York: Basic Books. [Original work published 1909].

Freudenmann, R. W., & Schönfeldt-Lecuona, C. (2005). The syndrome of genital retraction from a transcultural psychiatric point of view. Chinese suo yang, Indonesian koro and non-Asian forms (koro-like symptoms). *Nervenarzt, 76*(5), 569–580.

Frey, K. S., & Ruble, D. N. (1992). Gender constancy and the "cost" of sex-typed behavior: A test of the conflict hypothesis. *Developmental Psychology, 28,* 714–721.

Frick, K. D., Pugh, L. C., & Milligan, R. A. (2012). Costs related to promoting breastfeeding among urban low-income women. *Journal of Obstetric, Gynecologic, & Neonatal Nursing, 41*(1), 144–150.

Friday, N. (1973). *My secret garden.* New York: Trident.

Friday, N. (2008). *My secret garden: Women's sexual fantasies.* New York: Simon & Schuster.

Fried, P. A., & Smith, A. M. (2001) A literature review of the consequences of prenatal marihuana exposure: An emerging theme of a deficiency in aspects of executive function. *Neurotoxicology & Teratology, 23*(1), 1–11.

Friedman, R. C., & Downey, J. I. (2001). The Oedipus complex and male homosexuality. In P. Hartocollis (Ed.), *Mankind's Oedipal destiny: Libidinal and aggressive aspects of sexuality* (pp. 113–138). Madison, CT: International Universities Press.

Friedman, R. C., & Downey, J. I. (2008). Sexual differentiation of behavior: The foundation of a developmental model of psychosexuality. *Journal of the American Psychoanalytic Association, 56*(1), 147–175.

Friedrich, W., & Gerber, P. N. (1994). Autoerotic asphyxia: The development of a paraphilia. *Journal of the American Academy of Child and Adolescent Psychiatry, 33*(7), 970–974.

Friedrich, W., Fisher, J., Broughton, D., Houston, M., & Shafran, C. R. (1998). Normative sexual behavior in children: A contemporary sample. *Pediatrics, 101*(4), e9. (Online).

Frisch, R. E. (2002). *Female fertility and the body fat connection.* Chicago: University of Chicago Press.

Frohlich, P. F., & Meston, C. M. (2005). Tactile sensitivity in women with sexual arousal disorder. *Archives of Sexual Behavior, 34*(2), 207–217.

Frohmader, K. S., Bateman, K. L., Lehman, M. N., & Coolen, L. M. (2010). Effects of methamphetamine on sexual performance and compulsive sex behavior in male rats. *Psychopharmacology, 212*(1), 93–104.

Frost, J. J., & Frohwirth, L. A. (2005, July). *Family planning annual report: 2004 Summary.* The Alan Guttmacher Institute.

Fuentes-Afflick, E., & Hessol, N. A. (2000). Interpregnancy interval and the risk or premature infants. *Obstetrics & Gynecology, 95,* 383–390.

Fugl-Meyer, K. S., Öberg, K., Lundberg, P. O., Lewin, B., & Fugl-Meyer, A. (2006). On orgasm, sexual techniques, and erotic perceptions in 18- to 74-year-old Swedish women. *Journal of Sexual Medicine, 3*(1), 56–68.

Fulcher, M., Sutfin, E. L., & Patterson, C. J. (2008). Individual differences in gender development: Associations with parental sexual orientation, attitudes, and division of labor. *Sex Roles, 58*(5-6), 330–341.

Furnham, A. (2009). Sex differences in mate selection preferences. *Personality and Individual Differences, 47*(4), 262–267.

Furnham, A., Petrides, K. V., & Constantinides, A. (2005). The effects of body mass index and waist-to-hip ratio on ratings of female attractiveness, fecundity, and health. *Personality and Individual Differences, 38*(8), 1823–1834.

Furstenberg, F. F., & Kiernan, K. E. (2001). Delayed parental divorce: How much do children benefit? *Journal of Marriage & the Family, 63*(2), 446–457.

Gable, S. (2012). Approach and avoidance motivation. In P. Noller & G. C. Karantzas (Eds.). *The Wiley-Blackwell handbook of couples and family relationships* (pp. 193–206). Chichester, West Sussex, UK: Wiley.

Gabriel, T. (1995, June 12). A new generation seems ready to give bisexuality a place in the spectrum. *The New York Times,* p. A12.

Gådin, K. G. (2012). Sexual harassment of girls in elementary school. *Journal of Interpersonal Violence, 27*(9), 1762–1779.

Gagnon, J. H. (1977). *Human sexualities.* Glenview, IL: Scott, Foresman.

Gagnon, J. H., & Simon, W. (1973). *Sexual conduct: The social origins of human sexuality.* Chicago: Aldine.

Garcia-Falgueras, A., & Swaab, D. F. (2010). Sex hormones and the brain: An essential alliance for sexual identity and sexual orientation. In S. Loche et al. (Eds.), *Pediatric neuroendocrinology* (Vol. 17, pp. 22–35). Basel, Switzerland: Karger.

Garwood, S. G., et al. (1980). Beauty is only "name deep": The effect of first name in ratings of physical attraction. *Journal of Applied Social Psychology, 10,* 431–435.

Gass, M. L. S., et al. (2011). Patterns and predictors of sexual activity among women in the Hormone Therapy trials of the Women's Health Initiative. *Menopause, 18*(11), 1160–1171.

Gates, J. (2001). *Survivors of an open marriage.* KiwE Publishing.

Gavin, L., et al. (2009, July 17). Sexual and reproductive health of persons aged 10–24 years—United States, 2002–2007. *Morbidity and Mortality Weekly Report, 58*(27), 1–58. Available at http://www.cdc.gov/mmwr/preview/mmwrhtml/ss5806a1.htm

Gavin, N. I., et al. (2005). Perinatal depression: A systematic review of prevalence and incidence. *Obstetrics & Gynecology, 106,* 1071–1083.

Gebhard, P. H. (1969). Misconceptions about female prostitutes. *Medical Aspects of Human Sexuality, 3,* 24–26.

Gebhard, P. H., et al. (1965). *Sex offenders: An analysis of types.* New York: Harper & Row.

Geddes, L. (2008). Ultrasound nails location of the elusive G spot. *The New Scientist, 197*(2644), 6-7.

Genital herpes, 2012. Centers for Disease Control and Prevention. (2012). Sexually Transmitted Diseases (STDs). Genital herpes—CDC fact sheet. http://www.cdc.gov/std/Herpes/STDFact-Herpes.htm (Accessed October 4, 2012).

Genital HPV infection, 2012. Centers for Disease Control and Prevention. (2012). Sexually Transmitted Diseases (STDs). Genital HPV infection—Fact sheet. http://www.cdc.gov/std/HPV/STDFact-HPV.htm (Accessed October 4, 2012).

George, W. H., Stoner, S. A., Norris, J., Lopez, P. A., & Lehman, G. L. (2000). Alcohol expectancies and sexuality: A self-fulfilling prophecy analysis of dyadic perceptions and behavior. *Journal of Studies on Alcohol, 61*(1), 168–176.

Gidycz, C. A., & Koss, M. P. (1990). A comparison of group and individual sexual assault victims. *Psychology of Women Quarterly, 14,* 325–342.

Gidycz, C. A., Orchowski, L. M., & Berkowitz, A. D. (2011). Preventing sexual aggression among college men: An evaluation of a social norms and bystander intervention program. *Violence Against Women, 17*(6), 720–742.

Gidycz, C. A., Rich, C. L., Orchowski, L., King, C., & Miller, A. K. (2006). The evaluation of a sexual assault self-defense and risk-reduction program for college women: A prospective study. *Psychology of Women Quarterly, 30*(2), 173–186.

Gietzen, M. S. (2009). Cited in Monica Davey. (2009, June 7). Closed clinic leaves abortion protesters at a loss. *The New York Times.*

Gijs, L., & Gooren, L. (1996). Hormonal and psychopharmacological interventions in the treatment of paraphilias: An update. *Journal of Sex Research, 33,* 273–290.

Gillibrand, R. (2012). Sex, power and consent: Youth culture and the unwritten rules. *Sex Education: Sexuality, Society and Learning, 12*(1), 125–126.

Gillis, J. S., & Avis, W. E. (1980). The maletaller norm in mate selection. *Personality and Social Psychology Bulletin, 6,* 396–401.

Gillison, M. L. (2011, October 4). In Grady, D., Study cites increase in cancers from HPV. *New York Times,* p. D5.

Gillison, M. L., et al. (2012). Prevalence of Oral HPV Infection in the United States, 2009-2010. *Journal of the American Medical Association. 307*(7), 693–703.

Gilmore, K. (2008). Birth mother, adoptive mother, dying mother, dead mother. In E. L. Jurist et al. (Eds.), *Mind to mind: Infant research, neuroscience, and psychoanalysis* (pp. 373–397). New York: Other Press.

Gil-Rivas, V. (2012). Sexual risk taking among college students: Correlates and consequences. In R. D. McAnulty (Ed.). *Sex in college: The things they don't write home about.* Santa Barbara, CA: ABC-CLIO, LLC.

Ginzburg, E., et al. (2010). Long-term safety of testosterone and growth hormone supplementation: A retrospective study of metabolic, cardiovascular, and other outcomes. *Journal of Clinical Medicine and Research, 2*(4), 159–166.

Giotakos, O., Markianos, M., & Vaidakis, N. (2005). Aggression, impulsivity, and plasma sex hormone levels in a group of rapists, in relation to their history of childhood attention-deficit/hyperactivity disorder symptoms. *Journal of Forensic Psychiatry & Psychology, 16*(2), 423–433.

Giraldi, H. R., et al. (2012). Female sexual arousal disorders. *The Journal of Sexual Medicine,* DOI: 10.1111/j.1743-6109.2012.02820.x.

Glaesmer, H., et al. (2012). Gender differences in healthcare utilization. *Journal of Applied Social Psychology,* DOI:10.1111/j.1559-1816.2011.00888.x

Glasser, C. L., Robnett, B., & Feliciano, C. (2009). Internet daters' body type preferences: Race–ethnic and gender differences. *Sex Roles, 61*(1-2), 14–33.

Gleason, J. M., et al. (2011). Regular non-steroidal antiinflammatory drug use and erectile dysfunction. *Journal of Urology, 185,* 1388–1393.

Gnagy, S., Ming, E. E., Devesa, S. S., Hartge, P., & Whittemore, A. S. (2000). Declining ovarian cancer rates in U.S. women in relation to parity and oral contraceptive use. *Epidemiology, 11*(2), 102–105.

Goldberg, J., Holtz, D., Hyslop, T., & Tolosa, J. E. (2002). Has the use of routine episiotomy decreased? Examination of episiotomy rates from 1983 to 2000. *Obstetrics & Gynecology, 99*(3), 395–400.

Goldschmidt, L., Day, N. L., & Richardson, G. A. (2000). Effects of prenatal marijuana exposure on child behavior problems at age 10. *Neurotoxicology & Teratology, 22*(3), 325–336.

Goldstein, I. (2012). The hour lecture that changed sexual medicine—The Giles Brindley injection story. *Journal of Sexual Medicine, 9,* 337–342.

Goldstein, I., & Alexander, J. L. (2005). Practical aspects in the management of vaginal atrophy and sexual dysfunction in perimenopausal and postmenopausal women. *Journal of Sexual Medicine, 2*(Suppl. 3), 154–165.

Goldstein, I., et al. (1998). Oral sildenafil in the treatment of erectile dysfunction. *New England Journal of Medicine, 338,* 1397–1404.

Goldstein, I., Meston, C., Davis, S., & Traish, A. (Eds.). (2006). *Female sexual dysfunction.* New York: Parthenon.

Golish, T. D. (2003). Stepfamily communication strengths: Understanding the ties that bind. *Human Communication Research, 29*(1), 41–80.

Golombok, S., et al. (2008). Developmental trajectories of sex-typed behavior in boys and girls: A longitudinal general population study of children aged 2.5–8 Years. *Child Development, 79*(5), 1583–1593.

Gomes do Espirito, M. E., & Etheredge, G. D. (2003). HIV prevalence and sexual behaviour of male clients of brothels' prostitutes in Dakar, Senegal. *AIDS Care, 15*(1), 53–62.

Gonorrhea fact sheet, 2012. Centers for Disease Control and Prevention. (2012). Sexually Transmitted Diseases. Gonorrhea—CDC fact sheet. http://www.cdc.gov/std/gonorrhea/STDFact-gonorrhea.htm (Accessed October 4, 2012).

Gonzaga, G. C., Turner, R. A., Keltner, D., Campos, B., & Altemus, M. (2006). Romantic love and sexual desire in close relationships. *Emotion, 6*(2), 63–179.

Goodman, J. J. (2006). Becoming an involved father of an infant. *Journal of Obstetric, Gynecologic, & Neonatal Nursing, 34*(2), 190–200.

Goodson, P., McCormick, D., & Evans, A. (2001). Searching for sexually explicit materials on the Internet: An exploratory study of college students' behavior and attitudes. *Archives of Sexual Behavior, 30*(2), 101–118.

Goodwin, R. D., Canino, G., Ortega, A. N., & Bird, H. R. (2009). Maternal mental health and childhood asthma among Puerto Rican youth: The role of prenatal smoking. *Journal of Asthma, 46*(7), 726–730.

Gooren, L. J. (2011). Ethical and medical considerations of androgen deprivation treatment of sex offenders. *The Journal of Clinical endocrinology & Metabolism, 96*(12), 3626–3637.

Gordon, A. E., et al. (2002). Why is smoking a risk factor for sudden infant death syndrome? *Child: Care, Health & Development, 28*(Suppl. 1), 23–25.

Gorzalka, B. B., Hill, M. N., & Chang, S. C. H. (2011), Male–female differences in the effects of cannabinoids on sexual behavior and gonadal hormone function. *Hormones and Behavior, 58*(1), 91–99.

Gottman, J. M., & Gottman, J. S. (2008). Gottman method couple therapy. In A. S. Gurman (Ed.), *Clinical handbook of couple therapy* (pp. 138–164). New York: Guilford Press.

Gould, D. C., & Kirby, R. S. (2006). Testosterone replacement therapy for late onset hypogonadism: What is the risk of inducing prostate cancer? *Prostate Cancer and Prostatic Diseases, 9,* 14–18.

Goulet, J. (2006). The "berdache"/"two-spirit": A comparison of anthropological and native constructions of gendered identities among the Northern Athapaskans. *Journal of the Royal Anthropological Institute, 683*(19).

Gouveia, V. V., et al. (2009). Versão abreviada da Escala Triangular do Amor: Evidências de validade fatorial e consistência interna. *Estudos de Psicologia, 14*(1), 31–39.

Gow, J. L. (2008). The mating game: Do opposites really attract? *Molecular Ecology, 17*(6), 1399–1400.

Grace, D. M., David, B. J., & Ryan, M. K. (2008). Investigating preschoolers' categorical thinking about gender through imitation, attention, and the use of self-categories. *Child Development, 79*(6), 1928–1941.

Grady, D. (2012, May 14). Taking Truvada to prevent HIV also comes with risks. *The New York Times*, p. D5.

Graham, J. M. (2011). Measuring love in romantic relationships: A meta-analysis. *Journal of Social and Personal Relationships, 28*(6), 748–771.

Granata, A. R., et al. (2012). Hormonal regulation of male sexual desire: The role of testosterone, estrogen, prolactin, oxytocin, vasopressin and others. In M. Maggi (Ed.). *Hormonal therapy for male sexual dysfunction* (pp. 72–82). Hoboken, NJ: Wiley.

Granata, A. R., Pugni, V., Rochira, V., Zirilli, L., & Carani, C. (2012). Hormonal regulation of male sexual desire: The role of testosterone, estrogen, prolactin, oxytocin, and others. In M. Maggi (Ed.). *Hormonal therapy for male sexual dysfunction* (pp. 72–82). Hoboken, NJ: Wiley.

Gray, R. H., & Wawer, M. J. (2012). Probability of heterosexual HIV-1 transmission per coital act in sub-Saharan Africa. *Journal of Infectious Diseases, 205*(3), 351–352.

Gray, R. H., et al. (2012). The effectiveness of male circumcision for HIV prevention and effects on risk behavior in a post-trial follow-up study. *AIDS, 26*(5), 609–615.

Gray, R., et al. (2009). The role of genital ulcer disease in the efficacy of male circumcision for HIV prevention. Sixteenth Conference on Retroviruses and Opportunistic Diseases. http://www.retroconference.org/2009/PDFs/1063.pdf.

Graziano, W. G., & Bruce, J. W. (2008). Attraction and the initiation of relationships. In S. Sprecher, A. Wenzel, & J. Harvey (Eds.), *Handbook of relationship initiation* (pp. 269–296). New York: CRC Press.

Graziottin, A., & Althof, S. (2011). What does premature ejaculation mean to the man, the woman, and the couple? *The Journal of Sexual Medicine, 8*(Suppl s4), 304–309.

Graziottin, A., & Althof, S. E. (2011). What does premature ejaculation mean to the man, the woman, and the couple? *Journal of Sexual Medicine, 8*(Suppl. S4), 304–309.

Green, B. A., Carnes, S., & Carnes, P. J. (2012). Cybersex addiction patterns in a clinical sample of homosexual, heterosexual, and bisexual men and women. *Sexual Addiction and Compulsivity, 19*(1–2), 77–98.

Green, R. (2003). When therapists do not want their clients to be homosexual: A response to Rosik's article. *Journal of Marital & Family Therapy, 29*(1), 29–38.

Green, R. (2008). Childhood cross-gender behavior and adult homosexuality: Why the link? *Journal of Gay & Lesbian Mental Health, 12*(1), 17–28.

Greene, B. (2000). African American lesbian and bisexual women. *Journal of Social Issues, 56*(2), 239–249.

Greene, B. (2005). Psychology, diversity and social justice: Beyond heterosexism and across the cultural divide. *Counselling Psychology Quarterly, 18*(4), 295–306.

Greenwald, E., & Leitenberg, H. (1989). Long-term effects of sexual experiences with siblings and non-siblings during childhood. *Archives of Sexual Behavior, 18*, 389–399.

Grenz, S. (2006). Review of *The Politics of Prostitution. Women's Movements, Democratic States and the Globalisation of Sex Commerce* and *Not for Sale: Feminists Resisting Prostitution and Pornography. Sexualities, 9*(2), 256–259.

Griffith, K. H., & Hebl, M. R. (2002). The disclosure dilemma for gay men and lesbians: "Coming out" at work. *Journal of Applied Psychology, 87*(6), 1191–1199.

Grigoriadis, S., & Romans, S. (2006). Postpartum psychiatric disorders: What do we know and where do we go? *Current Psychiatry Reviews, 2*(1), 151–158.

Grodstein, F., Manson, J. E., & Stampfer, M. J. (2006). Hormone therapy and coronary heart disease: The role of time since menopause and age at hormone initiation. *The Journal of Women's Health, 15*(1), 35–44.

Gross, J. (2006, April 20). Learning to savor a full life, love life included. *The New York Times*.

Grov, C., Bimbi, D. S., Nanin, J. E., & Parsons, J. T. (2006). Race, ethnicity, gender, and generational factors associated with the coming-out process among gay, lesbian, and bisexual individuals. *The Journal of Sex Research, 43*(2), 115–121.

Grov, C., Parsons, J. T., & Bimbi, D. S. (2010). The association between penis size and sexual health among men who have sex with men. *Archives of Sexual Behavior, 39*(3), 788–797.

Grubb, A. R., & Harrower, J. (2009). Understanding attribution of blame in cases of rape: An analysis of participant gender, type of rape and perceived similarity to the victim. *Journal of Sexual Aggression, 15*(1), 63–81.

Grubin, D. (2008). Medical models and interventions in sexual deviance. In D. R. Laws and W. T. O'Donohue (Eds.), *Sexual deviance: Theory, assessment, and treatment* (2nd ed., pp. 594–610). New York: Guilford Press.

Grych, J. H., Fincham, F. D., Jouriles, E. N., & McDonald, R. (2000). Interparental conflict and child adjustment: Testing the mediational role of appraisals in the cognitive–contextual framework. *Child Development, 71*(6), 1648–1661.

Guay, A. T. (2001). Decreased testosterone in regularly menstruating women with decreased libido: A clinical observation. *Journal of Sex & Marital Therapy, 27*(5), 513–519.

Gueguen, N. (2012). Gait and menstrual cycle: Ovulating women use sexier gaits and walking slowly ahead of men. *Gait & Posture, 35*(4), 621–624.

Guerrero, L. K., Hannawa, A. F., & Babin, E. A. (2011). The Communicative Responses to Jealousy Scale: Revision, empirical validation, and associations with relational satisfaction. *Communication Methods and Measures, 5*(3), 223–249.

Gutmann, P. (2006). About confusions of the mind due to abnormal conditions of the sexual organs. *History of Psychiatry, 17*(1), 107–111.

Guttmacher Institute. (2009). Various fact sheets. (Accessed November 1, 2009). http://www.guttmacher.org/sections/adolescents.php.

Guttmacher Institute. (2011, August). Facts on induced abortion in the United States. http://www.guttmacher.org/pubs/fb_induced_abortion.html (Accessed June 23, 2012).

Guttmacher Institute. (2012). Facts on American teens' sources of information about sex. http://www.guttmacher.org/pubs/FB-Teen-Sex-Ed.html (Accessed September 23, 2012).

Guzick, D. S., & Hoeger, K. (2000). Sex, hormones, and hysterectomies. *The New England Journal of Medicine, 343*(10).

Haake, P., et al. (2003). Acute neuroendocrine response to sexual stimulation in sexual offenders. *Canadian Journal of Psychiatry, 48*(4), 265–271.

Haandrikman, K., Harmsen, C., van Wissen, L. J. G., & Hutter, I. (2008). Geography matters: Patterns of spatial homogamy in the Netherlands. *Population, Space, and Place, 14*, 387–405.

Hackett, G. I. (2008). Disorders of male sexual desire. In D. L. Rowland & L. Incrocci (Eds.), *Handbook of sexual and gender identity disorders*. Hoboken, NJ: Wiley.

Haldeman, D. C. (2002). Gay rights, patient rights: The implications of sexual orientation conversion therapy. *Professional Psychology: Research & Practice, 33*(3), 260–264.

Hall, G., Collins, A., Csemiczky, G., & Landgren, B. (2002). Lipoproteins and BMI: A comparison between women during transition to menopause and regularly menstruating healthy women. *Maturitas, 41*(3), 177–185.

Hallgrímsdóttir, H. K., Phillips, R., Benoit, C., & Walby, K. (2008). Sporting girls, streetwalkers, and inmates of houses of ill repute. *Sociological Perspectives, 51*(1), 119–138.

Halpern, D. F. (1997). Sex differences in intelligence: Implications for education. *American Psychologist, 52*, 1091–1102.

Halpern, D. F. (2003). Sex differences in cognitive abilities. *Applied Cognitive Psychology, 17*(3), 375–376.

Halpern, D. F., & LaMay, M. L. (2000). The smarter sex: A critical review of sex differences in intelligence. *Educational Psychology Review, 12*(2), 229–246.

Halpern, D. F., et al. (2007). The science of sex differences in science and mathematics. *Psychological Science in the Public Interest, 8*(1), 1–51.

Halpern-Felsher, B. (2008). Oral sexual behavior: Harm reduction or gateway behavior? *Journal of Adolescent Health, 43*(3), 207–208.

Hamann, S., Herman, R. A., Nolan, C. L., & Wallen, K. (2004). Men and women differ in amygdala response to visual sexual stimuli. *Nature Neuroscience, 7*(4), 411–416.

Hamer, D. H., et al. (1993, July 16). A linkage between DNA markers on the X chromosome and male sexual orientation. *Science, 261*, 321–327.

Hamilton, B. E., & Ventura, S. J. (2012). Birth rates for U.S. teenagers reach historic lows for all age and ethnic groups. NCHS data brief, No. 89. Hyattsville, MD. National Center for Health Statistics.

Hammack, P. L., & Cohler, B. J. (2009). *The story of sexual identity*. New York: Oxford University Press.

Hamplova, D. (2009). Educational homogamy among married and unmarried couples in Europe. *Journal of Family Issues, 30*(1), 28–52.

Harel, Z. (2008). Dysmenorrhea in adolescents. *Annals of the New York Academy of Sciences, 1135,* 185–195.

Harmon-Jones, E., Peterson, C. K., & Harris, C. R. (2009). Jealousy: Novel methods and neural correlates. *Emotion, 9*(1), 113–117.

Harris, G. (2011, October 6). U.S. panel advises against routine use of prostate test. *New York Times* (Online).

Hart, S. D., & Kropp, P. R. (2008). Sexual deviance and the law. In D. R. Laws and W. T. O'Donohue (Eds.), *Sexual deviance: Theory, assessment, and treatment* (2nd ed. pp. 557–570). New York: Guilford Press.

Hart, T. A., et al. (2012). The cumulative effects of medication use, drug use, and smoking on erectile dysfunctions among men who have sex with men. *Journal of sexual medicine, 9*(4), 1106–1113.

Hartley, H. (2006). The "pinking" of Viagra culture: Drug industry efforts to create and repackage sex drugs for women. *Sexualities, 9*(3), 363–378.

Hartocollis, A. (2006, June 24). Women have seen it all on subway, unwillingly. *The New York Times.*

Harvey, J., & Berry, J. (2009). Andropause in the aging male. *The Journal for Nurse Practitioners, 5*(3), 207–212.

Haselton, M. G., & Gildersleeve, K. (2011). Can Men Detect Ovulation? *Current Directions in Psychological Science, 20,* 87–92.

Haselton, M. G., Mortezaie, M., Pillsworth, E. G., Bleske-Rechek, A., & Frederick, D. A. (2007). Ovulatory shifts in human female ornamentation: Near ovulation, women dress to impress. *Hormones and Behavior, 51*(1), 40–45.

Hassebrauck, M. (2003). Romantische Männer und realistische Frauen: Geschlechtsunterschiede in Beziehungskognitionen. *Zeitschrift für Sozialpsychologie, 34*(1), 25–35.

Hassett, J. M., Siebert, E. R., & Wallen, K. (2008). Sex differences in rhesus monkey toy preferences parallel those of children. *Hormones and Behavior, 54*(3), 359–364.

Hatcher, R. A., et al. (2008). *Contraceptive technology,* 19th ed. New York: Ardent Media.

Hatcher, R. A., Trussell, J., Nelson, A. L., Cates, W., Kowal, D., & Policar, M. (Eds.). (2011). *Contraceptive Technology: Twentieth Revised Edition.* New York, NY: Ardent Media.

Hatfield, E., & Rapson, R. L. (2002). Passionate love and sexual desire: Cultural and historical perspectives. In A. L. Vangelisti, H. T. Reis, et al. (Eds.), *Stability and change in relationships. Advances in personal relationships* (pp. 306–324). New York: Cambridge University Press.

Hatfield, E., Bensman, L., & Rapson, R. L. (2012). A brief history of social scientists' attempts to measure passionate love. *Journal of Social and Personal Relationships, 29*(2), 143–164.

Hatfield, E., Pillemer, J. T., O'Brien, M. U., & Le, Y-C. L. (2008). The endurance of love: Passionate and companionate love in newlywed and long-term marriages. *Interpersona 2*(1), 35–64.

Hatzichristou, D. G., et al. (2000). Sildenafil versus intracavernous injection therapy: Efficacy and preference in patients on intracaverous injection for more than 1 year. *The Journal of Urology, 164,* 1197–1200.

Hatzichristou, D. G., et al. (2005). Vardenafil improves satisfaction rates, depressive symptomatology, and self-confidence in a broad population of men with erectile dysfunction. *Journal of Sexual Medicine, 2*(1), 109–116.

Haugaard, J. J. (2000). The challenge of defining child sexual abuse. *American Psychologist, 55*(9), 1036–1039.

Hawkley, L. C., Burleson, M. H., Berntson, G. G., & Cacioppo, J. T. (2003). Loneliness in everyday life: Cardiovascular activity, psychosocial context, and health behaviors. *Journal of Personality & Social Psychology, 85*(1), 105–120.

Hawkley, L. C., & Cacioppo, J. T. (2003). Loneliness and pathways to disease. *Brain, Behavior & Immunity, 17*(Suppl. 1), S98–S105.

Hay, D. F. et al. (2011). The emergence of gender differences in physical aggression in the context of conflict between young peers. *British Journal of Developmental Psychology, 29*(2), 158–175.

Haynes, A. (2012). Obscenity, sex education, and medical democracy in the antebellum United States. In E. Reis, (Ed.), *American sexual histories* (pp. 165–176). Chichester, West Sussex, UK: Wiley–Blackwell.

He, C., et al. (2009). Genome-wide association studies identify loci associated with age at menarche and age at natural menopause. *Nature Genetics, 41,* 724–728.

Health24.com. *The girl child.* (2006, February 10). www.health24.com/sex/sexuality_throughout_life.

Heath, R. (1972). Pleasure and brain activity in man. *Journal of Nervous and Mental Disease, 154,* 3–18.

Hegarty, P. (2011). Becoming curious: An invitation to the special issue on queer theory. *Psychology and Sexuality, 2*(1), 1–3.

Heil, P., & Simons, D. (2008). Multiple paraphilias: Prevalence, etiology, assessment, and treatment. In D. R. Laws and W. T. O'Donohue (Eds.), *Sexual deviance: Theory, assessment, and treatment* (2nd ed., pp. 527–556). New York: Guilford Press.

Heiman, J. (2000). The technology of orgasm: "Hysteria," the vibrator, and women's sexual satisfaction. *New England Journal of Medicine, 342*(25), 1925–1926.

Heiman, J. R. (2008). Treating low sexual desire—New findings for testosterone in women. *New England Journal of Medicine, 359*(19), 2047–2049.

Hellstrom, W. J. G., Nehra, A., Shabsigh, R., & Sharlip, I. D. (2006). Premature ejaculation: The most common male sexual dysfunction. *Journal of Sexual Medicine, 3*(Suppl. 1), 1–3.

Henderson, A. W., Lehavot, K., & Simoni, J. M. (2009). Ecological models of sexual satisfaction among lesbian/bisexual and heterosexual women. *Archives of Sexual Behavior, 38*(1), 50-65.

Hendrick, C., & Hendrick, S. S. (2003). Romantic love: Measuring Cupid's arrow. In S. Lopez & C. R. Snyder (Eds.), *Positive psychological assessment: A handbook of models and measures* (pp. 235–249). Washington, DC: American Psychological Association.

Hendrick, C., & Hendrick, S. S. (Eds.). (2000). *Close relationships: A sourcebook.* Thousand Oaks, CA: Sage.

Hendrick, C., Hendrick, S. S., & Reich, D. A. (2006). The Brief Sexual Attitudes Scale. *Journal of Sex Research, 43*(1), 76–86.

Hendrick, S. S., & Hendrick, C. (2002). Love. In C. R. Snyder & S. J. Lopez (Eds.), *Handbook of positive psychology* (pp. 472–484). London: Oxford University Press.

Henshaw, S. K. (2003, May 1). U.S. teenage pregnancy statistics with comparative statistics for women aged 20–24. www.guttmacher.org/pubs/teen_stats.html.

Henslin, J. H. (2007). *Sociology: A down-toearth approach* (8th ed.). Boston: Allyn & Bacon.

Herbenick, D., & Fortenberry, J. D. (2011). Exercise-induced orgasm and pleasure among women. *Sexual and Relationship Therapy, 26*(4), 373–388.

Herbenick, D., et al. (2009). Prevalence and characteristics of vibrator use by women in the United States: Results from a nationally representative study. *Journal of Sexual Medicine, 6,* 1857–1866.

Herbenick, D., et al. (2010a). Sexual behavior in the United States: Results from a national probability sample of males and females ages 14 to 94. *Journal of Sexual Medicine, 7*(suppl 5), 255–265.

Herbenick, D., et al. (2010b). Sexual behaviors, relationships, and perceived health among adult women in the United States: Results from a national probability sample. *Journal of Sexual Medicine, 7*(suppl 5), 277–290.

Herbenick, D., et al. (2010c). An event-level analysis of the sexual characteristics and composition among adults ages 18 to 59: Results from a national probability sample in the United States. *Journal of Sexual Medicine, 7*(suppl 5), 346–361.

Herbenick, D., et al. (2011). Beliefs about women's vibrator use: Results from a nationally representative probability survey in the United States. *Journal of Sex & Marital Therapy, 37*(5), 329–345.

Herbenick, D., Reece, M., Sanders, S. A., Schick, V., Dodge, B., & Fortenberry, J. D. (2010a). Sexual behavior in the United States: Results from a national probability sample of males and females ages 14 to 94. *Journal of Sexual Medicine, 7*(suppl 5), 255–265.

Herbenick, D., Reece, M., Schick, V., Sanders, S. A., Dodge, B., & Fortenberry, J. D. (2010b). Sexual behaviors, relationships, and perceived health among adult women in the United States: Results from a national probability sample. *Journal of Sexual Medicine, 7*(suppl 5), 277–290.

Herbenick, D., Reece, M., Schick, V., Sanders, S. A., Dodge, B., & Fortenberry, J. D. (2010c). An event-level analysis of the sexual characteristics and composition among adults ages 18 to 59: Results from a national probability sample in the United States. *Journal of Sexual Medicine, 7*(suppl 5), 346–361.

Herbst, J. H., et al. (2008). Estimating HIV prevalence and risk behaviors of transgender persons in the United States: A systematic review. *AIDS and Behavior, 12*(1), 1–17.

Herdt, G. (1990). Mistaken gender: 5-Alpha reductase hermaphroditism and biological reductionism in sexual identity reconsidered. *American Anthropologist, 92*(2), 433–446.

Herek, G. M., & Gonzalez–Rivera, M. (2006). Attitudes toward homosexuality among U.S. residents of Mexican descent. *Journal of Sex Research, 43*(2), 122–135.

Herek, G. M., Widaman, K. F., & Capitanio, J. P. (2005). When sex equals AIDS: Symbolic stigma and heterosexual adults' inaccurate beliefs about sexual transmission of AIDS. *Social Problems, 52*(1), 15–37.

Hergenhahn, B. R. (2013). *An introduction to the history of psychology* (7ᵗʰ ed.). Belmont, CA: Cengage.

Herrera, V. M., & McCloskey, L. A. (2003). Sexual abuse, family violence, and female delinquency: Findings from a longitudinal study. *Violence & Victims, 18*(3), 319–334.

Herrington, D. M., et al. (2000). Effects of estrogen replacement on the progression of coronary artery atherosclerosis. *The New England Journal of Medicine, 343*(8).

Herrmann, H. C., Chang, G., Klugherz, B. D., & Mahoney, P. D. (2000). Hemodynamic effects of sildenafil in men with severe coronary artery disease. *The New England Journal of Medicine, 342*(22), 1622–1626.

Hertlein, K. M., & Weeks, G. R. (2008). Toward a new paradigm in sex therapy. In K. M. Hertlein, G. R. Weeks, & N. Gambescia (pp. 44–61). *Systemic sex therapy*. New York: CRC Press.

Hertlein, K. M., Weeks, G. R., & Gambescia, N. (Eds.). (2009). *Systemic sex therapy*. New York: Routledge.

Hesketh, T., & Xing, Z. W. (2006). Abnormal sex ratios in human populations: Causes and consequences. *Proceedings of the National Academy of Sciences, 103*, 13271–13275.

Hester, J. D. (2005). Eunuchs and the postgender Jesus: Matthew 19:12 and transgressive sexualities. *Journal for the Study of the New Testament, 28*(1), 13–40.

Hetherington, E. M., & Kelly, J. (2003). For better or for worse: Divorce reconsidered. *American Journal of Psychiatry, 160*(3), 601–602.

Hicks, T. V., & Leitenberg, H. (2001). Sexual fantasies about one's partner versus someone else: Gender differences in incidence and frequency. *Journal of Sex Research, 38*(1), 43–50.

Hill, R. A., et al. (2009). Estrogen deficiency results in apoptosis in the frontal cortex of adult female aromatase knockout mice. *Molecular and Cellular Neuroscience, 41*(1), 1–7.

Hill, S. E., & Buss, D. M. (2008). The mere presence of opposite-sex others on judgments of sexual and romantic desirability. *Personality and Social Psychology Bulletin, 34*(5), 635–647.

Hines, D. A., & Saudino, K. J. (2003). Gender differences in psychological, physical, and sexual aggression among college students using the Revised Conflict Tactics Scales. *Violence & Victims, 18*(2), 197–217.

Hines, M. (2011). Prenatal endocrine influences on sexual orientation and on sexually differentiated childhood behavior. *Frontiers in Neuroendocrinology, 32*(2), 170–182.

Hines, M., Ahmed, S. F., & Hughes, I. A. (2003). Psychological outcomes and gender-related development in complete androgen insensitivity syndrome. *Archives of Sexual Behavior, 32*(2), 93–101.

Hines, T. M. (2001). The G-spot: A modern gynecological myth. *American Journal of Obstetrics and Gynecology, 185*(2), 359–362.

Hird, M. J. (2004). Naturally queer. *Feminist Theory, 5*(1), 85–89.

Hird, M. J. (2006). Sex diversity and evolutionary psychology. *The Psychologist, 19*(1), 30–32.

Hitt, J. (1998, January 18). Who will do abortions here? *The New York Times Magazine*, pp. 20–27, 42, 45–46, 54–55.

HIV/AIDS surveillance, 2012. Centers for Disease Control and Prevention. (2012). Diagnoses of HIV infection and AIDS in the United States and dependent areas, 2010. *HIV surveillance report, Volume 22*. http://www.cdc.gov/hiv/surveillance/resources/reports/2010report/index.htm (Accessed October 4, 2012).

Ho, D. K., & Ross, C. C. (2012). Cognitive behavior therapy for sex offenders. Too good to be true? *Criminal Behaviour and Mental Health, 22*(1), 1–6.

Hofferth, S. L., & Anderson, K. G. (2003). Are all dads equal? Biology versus marriage as a basis for paternal investment. *Journal of Marriage & Family, 65*(1), 213–232.

Hoffman, H., Peterson, K., & Garner, H. (2012). Field conditioning of sexual arousal in humans. *Socioaffective Neuroscience & Psychology, 2*, 17336 - DOI: 10.3402/snp.v2i0.17336.

Hogarth, H., & Ingham, R. (2009). Masturbation among young women and associations with sexual health: An exploratory study. *The Journal of Sex Research, 46*(1), 1559–8519.

Holman, T. B., & Jarvis, M. O. (2003). Hostile, volatile, avoiding, and validating couple-conflict types: An investigation of Gottman's couple-conflict types. *Personal Relationships, 10*(2), 267–282.

Holmberg, D., Blair, K. L., & Phillips, M. (2009). Women's sexual satisfaction as a predictor of well-being in same-sex versus mixed-sex relationships. *Journal of Sex Research*, 1559-8519.

Holmes, S. T., & Holmes, R. M. (2002). *Sex crimes*. Thousand Oaks, CA: Sage.

Holmstrom, A. J. (2009). Sex and gender similarities and differences in communication values in same-sex and cross-sex friendships. *Communication Quarterly, 57*(2), 224–238.

Honeycutt, J. M., & Cantrill, J. G. (2001). *Cognition, communication, and romantic relationships*. Mahwah, NJ: Erlbaum.

Hoover, K. C. (2010). Smell with inspiration: The evolutionary significance of olfaction. *American Journal of Physical Anthropology, 143*(Suppl 51), 63–74.

Horowitz, H. L. (2002). *Rereading sex: Battles over sexual knowledge and suppression in nineteenth-century America*. New York: Knopf.

Houts, F. W., Taller, I., Tucker, D. E., & Berlin, F. S. (2011). Sexual dysfunction. In R. Balon (Ed.). *Beyond the brain-body connection. Advances in Psychosomatic Medicine, Vol. 31*, 149–163. Basel: Karger.

Hsiao, M., Liu, C., Chen, K., & Hsieh, T. (2002). Characteristics of women seeking treatment for premenstrual syndrome in Taiwan. *Acta Psychiatrica Scandinavica, 106*(2), 150–155.

Hsueh, A. C., Morrison, K. R., & Doss, B. D. (2009). Qualitative reports of problems in cohabiting relationships: Comparisons to married and dating relationships. *Journal of Family Psychology, 23*(2), 236–246. http://caliber.ucpress.net/doi/abs/10.1525/ctx.2007.6.4.28 http://epp.eurostat.ec.europa.eu/portal/page/portal/eurostat/home/.

Hubbard, T. K. (2009). The paradox of "natural" heterosexuality with "unnatural" women. *Classical World, 102*(3), 249–258.

Huchard, E., et al. (2009). Studying shape in sexual signals: The case of primate sexual swellings. *Behavioral Ecology and Sociobiology, 63*(8), 1231–1242.

Hucker, S. J. (2008). Sexual masochism: Psychopathology and theory. In D. R. Laws and W. T. O'Donohue (Eds.), *Sexual deviance: Theory, assessment, and treatment* (2nd ed., pp. 250–263). New York: Guilford Press.

Huerta, M., Cortina, L. M., Pang, J. S., Torges, C. M., & Magley, V. J. (2006). Sex and power in the academy: Modeling sexual harassment in the lives of college women. *Personality and Social Psychology Bulletin, 32*(5), 616–628.

Hugh-Jones, S., Gough, B., & Littlewood, A. (2005). Sexual exhibitionism as "sexuality and individuality": A critique of psycho-medical discourse from the perspectives of women who exhibit. *Sexualities, 8*(3), 259–281.

Human Rights Watch. (2012, May). Cultivating fear: The vulnerability of immigrant farm workers in the U.S. to sexual violence and sexual harassment. http://www.hrw.org/sites/default/files/reports/us0512ForUpload_1.pdf (Accessed July 16, 2012).

Hummer, T. A., & McClintock, M. K. (2009). Putative human pheromone androstadienone attunes the mind specifically to emotional information. *Hormones and Behavior, 55*(4), 548–559.

Hunt, M. (1974). *Sexual behavior in the 1970's*. New York: Dell Books.

Hunt, S. A., & Kraus, S. W. (2009). Exploring the relationship between erotic disruption during the latency period and the use of sexually explicit material, online sexual behaviors, and sexual dysfunctions in young adulthood. *Sexual Addiction & Compulsivity, 16*(1), 79–100.

Hunter, M. S. (2011). Cortisol, hot flashes, and cardiovascular risk. *Menopause, 18*(3), 251–252.

Hussain, A. (2002, June 26) It's official. Men really are afraid of commitment.

Hutchings, J. (2004). Color in folklore and tradition—The principles. *Color Research and Application, 29*, 57–66.

Hutton, H. E. (2008, March 11). Gender differences in alcohol use and risky sexual behaviors and STDs among STD clinic patients. Chicago: 2008 National STD Prevention Conference,

Huxley, R. R. (2000). Nausea and vomiting in early pregnancy: Its role in placental development. *Obstetrics & Gynecology, 95*, 779–782.

Hyde, J. S. (Ed.) (2005). *Biological substrates of human sexuality*. Washington, DC: American Psychological Association.

Hyde, J. S., & Mertz, J. E. (2009). Gender, culture, and mathematics performance. *Proceedings of the National Academy of Sciences, 106,* 8801–8807.

Hyde, J. S., Fennema, E., & Lamon, S. J. (1990). Gender differences in mathematics performance: A meta-analysis. *Psychological Bulletin, 107,* 139–155.

Hyde, J. S., Lindberg, S. M., Linn, M. C., Ellis, A. B., & Williams, C. C. (2008). Gender similarities characterize math performance. *Science, 321,* 494–495.

Hyman, S. M., Gold, S. N., & Cott, M. A. (2003). Forms of social support that moderate PTSD in childhood sexual abuse survivors. *Journal of Family Violence, 18*(5), 295–300.

Hypersexual disorder. (2012). Hypersexual disorder. American Psychiatric Association. DSM-5 Development. http://www.dsm5.org/proposedrevision/pages/proposedrevision.aspx?rid=415.

Iemmola, F., & Ciani, A. C. (2009). New evidence of genetic factors influencing sexual orientation in men: Female fecundity increase in the maternal line. *Archives of Sexual Behavior, 38*(3), 393–399.

Illes, J. (October 2000). Beauty secrets of ancient Egypt: Nefertem, Ancient Lord of Perfume. *Tour Egypt Monthly, 5*(1).

Imperato-McGinley, J., et al. (1974). Steroid 5 reductase deficiency in man: An inherited form of male pseudohermaphroditism. *Science, 186,* 1213–1215.

Inciardi, J. A., Surratt, H. L., & Kurtz, S. P. (2006). HIV, HBV, and HCV infections among drug-involved, inner-city, street sex workers in Miami, Florida. *AIDS and Behavior, 10*(2), 139–147.

Intersex Society of North America. Accessed August 22, 2006. www.isna.org.

Irwin, T. W., Morgenstern, J., Parsons, J. T., Wainberg, M., & Labouvie, E. (2006). Alcohol and sexual HIV risk behavior among problem drinking men who have sex with men: An event level analysis of timeline followback data. *AIDS and Behavior, 10*(3), 299–307.

Isay, R. A. (1990). Psychoanalytic theory and the therapy of gay men. In D. P. McWhirter, S. A. Sanders, & J. M. Reinisch (Eds.), *Homosexuality/heterosexuality: Concepts of sexual orientation* (pp. 283–303). New York: Oxford University Press.

IsHak, W. W., Bokarius, A., Jeffrey, J. K., Davis, M. C., & Bakhta, Y. (2010). Disorders of orgasm in women: A literature review of etiology and current treatments. *Journal of Sexual Medicine, 7,* 3254–3268.

Itzin, C. (2002). Pornography and the construction of misogyny. *Journal of Sexual Aggression, 8*(3), 4–42.

Itzin, C., Taket, A., & Kelly, L. (2007). The evidence of harm to adults relating to exposure to extreme pornographic material: a rapid evidence assessment (REA). Ministry of Justice Research Series 11/07. http://webarchive.nationalarchives.gov.uk/+/http://www.justice.gov.uk/docs/280907.pdf

Jacob, S., & McClintock, M. K. (2000). Psychological state and mood effects of steroidal chemosignals in women and men. *Hormones and Behavior, 37*(1), 57–78.

Jacob, S., Hayreh, D. J. S., & McClintock, M. K. (2001). Context-dependent effects of steroid chemosignals on human physiology and mood. *Physiology & Behavior, 74*(1–2), 15–27.

Jaeger, F., Caflisch, M., & Hohlfeld, P. (2009). Female genital mutilation and its prevention: A challenge for paediatricians. *European Journal of Pediatrics, 168*(1), 27-33.

Jameson, M. (2000, June 12). Childbirth that's not so labor-intensive. *Los Angeles Times.*

Jannini, E. A., Blanchard, R., Camperio-Ciani, A., & Bancroft, J. (2010). Male homosexuality: Nature or culture. *Journal of Sexual Medicine, 7,* 3245–3253.

Jannini, E. A., McMahon, C., Chen, J., Aversa, A., & Perelman, M. (2011). The controversial role of PDE5 inhibitors in the treatment of premature ejaculation. *Journal of Sexual Medicine, 8,* 2135–2143.

Jannini, E. A., Whipple, B., Kingsberg, S. A., Buisson, O., Foldès, P., & Vardi, Y. (2010). Who's afraid of the G-spot? *Journal of Sexual Medicine, 7*(1), 25–34.

Jannini, E., et al. (2008). In vivo measurement of the human G-spot. *Sexologies, 17*(S1), S52-S53.

Janofsky, M., & Schemo, D. J. (2003, March 16). Women recount cadet life: Forced sex and fear. *The New York Times* (Online).

Janssen, E. (Ed.). (2006). *The psychophysiology of sex.* Bloomington, IN: Indiana University Press.

Janssen, E., & Bancroft, J. (2006). The dual-control model: The role of sexual inhibition & excitation in sexual arousal and behavior. In E. Janssen (Ed.), *The psychophysiology of sex.* Bloomington, IN: Indiana University Press.

Janssen, E., Prause, N., & Geer, J. (2006). The sexual response. In J. T. Cacioppo, L. G. Tassinary, & G. G. Berntson (Eds.), *Handbook of psychophysiology* (3rd ed.). New York: Cambridge University Press.

Jayaraman, S., & Mann, M. (2012). Male and female sterilization. *Obstetrics, Gynaecology, & Reproductive Medicine, 22*(4), 85–91.

Jayson, S. (2006, May 29). Poll: Boomers go easy on marriage. *USA Today.*

Jewkes, R., Morrell, R., Sikweyiya, Y., Dunckle, K., & Penn-Kekana, L. (2012). Transactional relationships and sex with a woman in prostitution: prevalence and patterns in a representative sample of South African men. *BMC Public Health, 12,* 325. http://www.biomedcentral.com/1471-2458/12/325 (Accessed July 18, 2012).

Johannes, C. B., et al. (2000). Incidence of erectile dysfunction in men 40 to 69 years old: Longitudinal results from the Massachusetts male aging study. *The Journal of Urology, 163,* 460.

Johanson, R. (2000). Perineal massage for prevention of perineal trauma in childbirth. *The Lancet, 355*(9200), 250–251.

Johnson, H. (2003). The cessation of assaults on wives. *Journal of Comparative Family Studies, 34*(1), 75–91.

Johnson, W., & Bouchard, T. J. Jr. (2007). Sex differences in mental abilities: *g* masks the dimensions on which they lie. *Intelligence, 35*(1), 23-39.

Johnson, W., & Bouchard, T. J. Jr. (2009). Linking abilities, interests, and sex via latent class analysis. *Journal of Career Assessment, 17*(1), 3–38.

Johnston, L. D., O'Malley, P. M., Bachman, J. G., & Schulenberg, J. E. (2005). *Monitoring the future national results on adolescent drug use: Overview of key findings, 2004.* NIH publication no. 05-5726. Bethesda, MD: National Institute on Drug Abuse.

Johnstone, S. J., et al. (2001). Obstetric risk factors for postnatal depression in urban and rural community samples. *Australian & New Zealand Journal of Psychiatry, 35*(1), 69–74.

Jonason, P. K., Li, N. P., Webster, G. D., & Schmitt, D. P. (2009). The dark triad: Facilitating a short-term mating strategy in men. *European Journal of Personality, 23*(1), 5–18.

Jones, B. E., & Hill, M. J. (2002). *Mental health issues in lesbian, gay, bisexual, and transgender communities: Review of Psychiatry* (Vol. 21). Washington, DC: American Psychiatric Publishing.

Jones, K. E., & Hertlein, K. M. (2012). Four key dimensions for distinguishing Internet infidelity from Internet and sex addiction: Concepts and clinical application. *The American Journal of Family Therapy, 40*(2), 115–125.

Jones, L. M., Mitchell, K. J., & Finkelhor, D. (2012). Trends in youth Internet victimization: Findings from three youth Internet safety surveys 2000–2010. *Journal of Adolescent Health, 50*(2), 179–186.

Jordan, K., Fromberger, P., Stolpmann, G., & Muller, J. L. (2011). The role of testosterone in sexuality and paraphilia—A neurobiological approach. *Sexual Medicine, 8*(11), 3008–3029.

Judge, A. M. (2012). "Sexting" among U.S. adolescents: Psychological and legal perspectives. *Harvard Review of Psychiatry, 20*(2), 86–96.

Jung, M., Lee, J., Kwon, D. D., & Park, B. (2012). Comparison of sexual risky factors of men who have sex with men and sex-buying men as groups vulnerable to sexually transmitted diseases. *Journal of Preventive Medicine & Public Health, 45*(3), 156–163.

Kaczmarek, P., LeVine, E., & Segal, A. F. (2006). Section 6. Civil and criminal trial matters. In P. Kaczmarek, E. LeVine, & A. F. Segal (Eds.), *Law & mental health professionals: New Mexico* (pp. 269–296). Washington, DC: American Psychological Association.

Kaestle, C. E., & Allen, K. R. (2011). The role of masturbation in healthy sexual development: Perceptions of young adults. *Archives of Sexual Behavior, 40*(5), 983–994.

Kafka, M. P. (2003). Sex offending and sexual appetite: The clinical and theoretical relevance of hypersexual desire. *International Journal of Offender Therapy & Comparative Criminology, 47*(4), 439–451.

Kafka, M. P. (2010). The DSM diagnostic criteria for fetishism. *Archives of Sexual Behavior,* DOI: 10.1007/s10508-009-9558-7.

Kaiser Family Foundation, Holt, T., Greene, L., & Davis, J. (2003). *National Survey of Adolescents and Young Adults: Sexual health knowledge, attitudes and experiences.* Menlo Park, CA: Henry J. Kaiser Family Foundation.

Kaler, A. (2005). Peer commentaries on Binik (2005): Classifying pain: What's at stake for women with dyspareunia. *Archives of Sexual Behavior, 34*(1), 34–36.

Kaplan, H. S. (1974). *The new sex therapy: Active treatment of sexual dysfunctions.* New York: Brunner/Mazel.

Kaplan, H. S. (1987). *Sexual aversion, sexual phobias, and panic disorder.* New York: Brunner/Mazel.

Karpman, E., Williams, D. H., & Lipshultz, L. I. (2006). Vasectomy reversal: New techniques and role in the era of intracytoplasmic sperm injection. *Canadian Journal of Urology, 13*(Suppl. 1), 22–27.

Katz, J., & Tirone, V. (2009). Women's sexual compliance with male dating partners: Associations with investment in ideal womanhood and romantic well-being. *Sex Roles, 60(5-6)*, 347–356.

Kayser, D. N., Elliot, A. J., & Feltman, R. (2010). Red and romantic behavior in men viewing women. *European Journal of Social Psychology, 40*(6), 901–908.

Keen, J. D., & Keen, J. E. (2009). What is the point: Will screening mammography save my life? *BMC Medical Informatics and Decision Making,* in press.

Keller, J. J., Liang, Y., & Lin, H. (2012). Association between multiple sclerosis and erectile dysfunction: A nationwide case-control study. *Journal of Sexual Medicine,* DOI: 10.1111/j.1743-6109.2012.02746.x.

Kelly, J. B. (2000). Children's adjustment in conflicted marriage and divorce: A decade review of research. *Journal of the American Academy of Child & Adolescent Psychiatry, 39*(8), 963–973.

Kendler, K. S., et al. (2000). Childhood sexual abuse and adult psychiatric and substance use disorders in women: An epidemiological and Cotwin control analysis. *Archives of General Psychiatry, 57*(10), 953–959.

Kennedy, N., & McDonough, M. (2002). Koro: A case in an eastern European asylum seeker in Ireland. *Irish Journal of Psychological Medicine, 19*(4), 130–131.

Kennedy, R. (2003). *Interracial intimacies: Sex, marriage, identity, and adoption.* New York: Knopf.

Kennedy, S. H., & Rizvi, S. (2009). Sexual dysfunction, depression, and the impact of antidepressants. *Journal of Clinical Psychopharmacology, 29*(2), 157–164.

Kennedy, S., & Bumpass, L. (2011, April 1). Cohabitation and trends in the structure and stability of children's family lives (paper presented at the Annual Meeting of the Population Association of America, Washington, DC, April 1, 2011).

Kenny, M. C., & Wurtele, S. K. (2012). Child sexual behavior inventory: A comparison between Latino and normative samples of preschoolers. *Journal of Sex Research.* DOI:10.1080/00224499.2011.652265.

Kersting, K. (2003). Cognitive sex differences: A "political minefield." *Monitor on Psychology, 34*(5).

Kessler, R. C. (2003). Epidemiology of women and depression. *Journal of Affective Disorders, 74*(1), 5–13.

Khoury, M. J., Burke, W., & Thomson, E. J. (Eds.). (2000). *Genetics and public health in the 21st century: Using genetic information to improve health and prevent disease.* New York: Oxford University Press.

Khurana, A., Cooksey, E. C., & Gavazzi, S. M. (2011). Juvenile delinquency and teenage pregnancy. *Psychology of Women Quarterly, 35*(2), 282–289.

Kilchevsky, A., Vardi, Y., Lowenstein, L., & Gruenwald, I. (2012). Is the female G-spot truly a distinct anatomic entity? *The Journal of Sexual Medicine, 9*(3), 719–726.

Kim, A. A., Kent, C. K., & Klausner, J. D. (2002). Increased risk of HIV and sexually transmitted disease transmission among gay or bisexual men who use Viagra, San Francisco 2000–2001. *AIDS, 16*(10), 1425–1428.

Kim, H. S. (2011). Consequences of parental divorce for child development. *American Sociological Review, 76*(3), 487–511.

Kimble, D. P. (1992). *Biological psychology* (2nd ed.). Fort Worth, TX: Harcourt Brace Jovanovich.

Kimmel, L. G., Miller, J. D., & Eccles, J. S. (2012). Do the paths to the STEMM professions differ by gender? *Peabody Journal of Education, 87*(1). doi:10.1080/01619 56X.2012.642276

King, J. A., De Oliveira, W. L., & Patel, N. (2005). Deficits in testosterone facilitate enhanced fear response. *Psychoneuroendocrinology, 30*(4), 333–340.

King, M. (2008). A systematic review of mental disorder, suicide, and deliberate self harm in lesbian, gay and bisexual people. *BMC Psychiatry, 8.* http://www.biomedcentral.com/1471244X/8/70. (Accessed October 15, 2009.)

Kingston, D. A., Malamuth, N. M., Fedoroff, P., & Marshall, W. L. (2009). The importance of individual differences in pornography use: Theoretical perspectives and implications for treating sexual offenders. *Journal of Sex Research, 46*(2-3), 216–232.

Kinsey, A. C., Pomeroy, W. B., & Martin, C. E. (1948). *Sexual behavior in the human male.* Philadelphia: W. B. Saunders.

Kinsey, A. C., Pomeroy, W. B., Martin, C. E., & Gebhard, P. H. (1953). *Sexual behavior in the human female.* Philadelphia: W. B. Saunders.

Kippax, S., & Smith, G. (2001). Anal intercourse and power in sex between men. *Sexualities, 4*(4), 413–434.

Kirby, D. (2008). Changes in sexual behaviour leading to the decline in the prevalence of HIV in Uganda: Confirmation from multiple sources of evidence. *Sexually Transmitted Infections, 84*(Suppl 2), ii35–ii41.

Kirby, D. (2011). *Sex education: Access and impact on sexual behavior of young people. United Nations expert group meeting on adolescents, youth and development.* Population Division. Department of Economic and Social Affairs. United Nations Secretariat. New York.

Kirby, D. B., Laris, B. A., & Rolleri, L. A. (2007). Sex and HIV education programs: Their impact on sexual behaviors of young people throughout the world. *Journal of Adolescent Health, 40*(3), 206–217.

Kirchheimer, S., & Smith, M. (2003, May 28). Condoms in schools don't boost teen sex: Key is making condom programs part of overall sex education, says one expert. *WebMD Medical News.* (Online).

Kirenskaya-Berus, A. V., & Tkachenko, A. A. (2003). Characteristic features of EEG spectral characteristics in persons with deviant sexual behavior. *Human Physiology, 29*(3), 278–287.

Kirkpatrick, R. C. (2000). The evolution of human homosexual behavior. *Current Anthropology, 41*(3), 385–413.

Kito, M. (2005). Self-disclosure in romantic relationships and friendships among American and Japanese college students. *Journal of Social Psychology, 145*(2), 127–140.

Kjerulff, K. H., et al. (2000). Effectiveness of hysterectomy. *Obstetrics & Gynecology, 95,* 319–326.

Klusmann, D. (2002). Sexual motivation and the duration of partnership. *Archives of Sexual Behavior, 31,* 275–287.

Klüver, H., & Bucy, P. C. (1939). Preliminary analysis of functions of the temporal lobes in monkeys. *Archives of Neurology and Psychiatry, 42,* 979.

Knaak, S. (2005). Breast-feeding, bottle-feeding and Dr. Spock: The shifting context of choice. *Canadian Review of Sociology and Anthropology, 42*(2), 197–216.

Knapp, M. L., & Vangelista, A. L. (2000). *Interpersonal communication and human relationships* (4th ed.). Boston: Allyn & Bacon.

Knickmeyer, R., et al. (2005). Gender-typed play and amniotic testosterone. *Developmental Psychology, 41,* 517–528.

Kniffin, K. M., & Wilson, D. S. (2004). The effect of nonphysical traits on the perception of physical attractiveness: Three naturalistic studies. *Evolution and Human Behavior, 25*(2), 88–101.

Knoll, J. L., & Hazelwood, R. R. (2009). Becoming the victim: Beyond sadism in serial sexual murderers. *Aggression and Violent Behavior, 14*(2), 106-114.

Knox, D., Schacht, C., & Zusman, M. E. (1999). Love relationships among college students. *College Student Journal, 33*(1), 149–151.

Knox, D., Gibson, L., Zusman, M., & Gallmeier, C. (1997). Why college students end relationships. *College Student Journal, 31*(4), 449–452.

Knox, D., & Schacht, C. (2002). *Choices in relationships—An introduction to marriage and the family* (7th ed.). Belmont, CA: Wadsworth.

Knudson, G. A., & Kingsberg, S. A. (2010). Hypoactive sexual desire disorder. *Journal of Sexual Medicine,* Virtual Issue Number 1.

Koblin, B. A., et al. (2006). Risk factors for HIV infection among men who have sex with men. *AIDS, 20*(5), 731–739.

Koehler, N., et al. (2012). Erectile dysfunction after radical prostatectomy: The impact of nerve-sparing status and surgical approach. *International Journal of Impotence Research,* DOI:10.1038/ijir.2012.8.

Kohlberg, L. (1966). A cognitive-developmental analysis of children's sex-role concepts and attitudes. In E. E. Maccoby (Ed.), *The development of sex differences.* Stanford, CA: Stanford University Press.

Kohtz, A. S., Paris, J. J., & Frye, C. A. (2010). Low doses of cocaine decrease, and high doses increase, anxiety-like behavior and brain progestogen levels among intact rats. *Hormones and Behavior, 57*(4–5), 474–480.

Kolata, G. (2000a, April 5). Estrogen tied to slight rise in heart attack. *The New York Times,* pp. A1, A20.

Kolata, G. (2000b, April 18). New name for impotence, and new drugs. *The New York Times,* pp. F6, F14.

Kolata, G. (2002, December 22). Chasing youth, many gamble on hormones. *The New York Times* (Online).

Kolata, G. (2005, October 27). Screening proves itself in breast cancer fight. *The New York Times* (Online).

Komisaruk, B. R., & Whipple, B. (2005). Brain activity imaging during sexual response in women with spinal cord injury. In J. S. Hyde (Ed.). *Biological substrates of human sexuality* (pp. 109–145). Washington, DC: American Psychological Association.

Komisaruk, B. R., et al. (2011). Women's clitoris, vagina, and cervix mapped on the sensory cortex: fMRI evidence. *Journal of Sexual Medicine, 8*(10), 2822–2830.

Korda, J. B., Goldstein, S. W., & Sommer, F. (2010). The history of female ejaculation. *Journal of Sexual Medicine, 7,* 1965–1975.

Koren, G., Pastuszak, A., & Ito, S. (1998). Drug therapy: Drugs in pregnancy. *New England Journal of Medicine, 338,* 1128–1137.

Kornacki, S. (2008, April 10). Spitzer and Vitter: Equal hypocrisy, unequal punishment.

Korobov, N., & Thorne, A. (2006). Intimacy and distancing: Young men's conversations about romantic relationships. *Journal of Adolescent Research, 21*(1), 27–55.

Koscik, T., O'Leary, D., Moser, D. J., Andreasen, N. C., & Nopoulos, P. (2009). Sex differences in parietal lobe morphology: Relationship to mental rotation performance. *Brain and Cognition, 69*(3), 451–459.

Koss, M. P., & Kilpatrick, D. G. (2001). Rape and sexual assault. In E. Gerrity et al. (Eds.), *The mental health consequences of torture. Plenum series on stress and coping* (pp. 177–193). Dordrecht, the Netherlands: Kluwer Academic Publishers.

Koss, M. P., Bailey, J. A., Yuan, N. P., Herrera, V. M., & Lichter, E. L. (2003). Depression and PTSD in survivors of male violence: Research and training initiatives to facilitate recovery. *Psychology of Women Quarterly, 27*(2), 130–142.

Koss, M. P., Figueredo, A. J., & Prince, R. J. (2002). Cognitive mediation of rape's mental, physical and social health impact: Tests of four models in cross-sectional data. *Journal of Consulting & Clinical Psychology, 70*(4), 926–941.

Kouros-Mehr, H., et al. (2001). Identification of non-functional human VNO receptor genes provides evidence for vestigiality of the human VNO. *Chemical Sciences, 26*(9), 1167–1174.

Kraft, J. M., Kulkarni, A., Hsia, J., Jamieson, D. J., & Warner, L. (2012). Sex education and adolescent sexual behavior: Do community characteristics matter? *Contraception, 86*(3), 276–280.

Krahe, B., Waizenhofer, E., & Moller, I. (2003). Women's sexual aggression against men: Prevalence and predictors. *Sex Roles, 49*(5–6), 219–232.

Kramer, M. S., et al. (2000). The contribution of mild and moderate preterm birth to infant mortality. *Journal of the American Medical Association, 284,* 843–849.

Kristof, N. D. (2004, January 24). Going home, with hope. *The New York Times*, p. A15.

Kristof, N. D. (2006, January 22). Slavery in our time. *The New York Times*, Section 4, p. 17.

Kristof, N. D. (2009, April 30). Is rape serious? *The New York Times*.

Kristof, N. D. (2009, May 7). Girls on our streets. *The New York Times*.

Krouse, A., et al. (2012). Bed-sharing influences, attitudes, and practices: Implications for promoting safe infant sleep. *Journal of Child Health Care.* DOI:10.1177/1367493511432300.

Krueger, R. B., & Kaplan, M. S. (2002). Behavioral and psychopharmacological treatment of the paraphilic and hypersexual disorders. *Journal of Psychiatric Practice, 8*(1), 21–32.

Kuehn, B. M. (2009). Sexually transmitted infections. *Journal of the American Medical Association, 301*(8), 817.

Kuhnle, U., Krob, G., & Maier, E. (2003). True hermaphroditism: Presentation, management, outcomes. *Endocrinologist, 13*(3), 214–218.

Kuiper, B., & Cohen–Kettenis, P. (1988). Sex reassignment surgery: A study of 141 Dutch transsexuals. *Archives of Sexual Behavior, 17,* 439–457.

Kulik, L. (2000). Gender identity, sex typing of occupations, and gender role ideology among adolescents: Are they related? *International Journal for the Advancement of Counselling, 22*(1), 43–56.

Kumashiro, K. K. (Ed.). (2004). *Restoried selves: Autobiographies of Queer Asian/Pacific American activists.* New York: Harrington Park Press/The Haworth Press.

Kurdek, L. A. (2005). What do we know about gay and lesbian couples? *Current Directions in Psychological Science, 14*(5), 251–254.

Kurdek, L. A. (2006). Differences between partners from heterosexual, gay, and lesbian cohabiting couples. *Journal of Marriage and Family, 68*(2), 509–528.

Kurutz, S. (2012, February 22). One is the quirkiest number: The freedom, and perils, of living alone. *New York Times,* D1.

Kurzban, R., & Weeden, J. (2005). HurryDate: Mate preferences in action. *Evolution and Human Behavior, 26*(3), 227–244.

La Rocque, C. L., & Cloe, J. (2011). An evaluation of the relationship between body image and sexual avoidance. *Journal of Sex Research, 48*(4), 397–408.

Laan, E. (2008). What makes women experience desire? *Feminism & Psychology, 18*(4), 505–514.

Labelle, A., Bourget, D., Bradford, J. M. W., Alda, M., & Tessier, P. (2012). Familial paraphilia: A pilot study with the construction of genograms. *ISRN Psychiatry, Volume 2012,* Article ID 692813, 9 pagesDOI:10.5402/2012/692813.

Ladas, A. K., Whipple, B., & Perry, J. D. (1982). *The G spot and other recent discoveries about human sexuality.* New York: Holt, Rinehart & Winston.

LaFraniere, S. (2009, April 11). Chinese bias for baby boys creates a gap of 32 million. *The New York Times.*

LaGasse, L. L., et al. (2012). Prenatal methamphetamine exposure and childhood behavior problems at 3 and 5 years of age. *Pediatrics, 129*(4), 681–688.

Lalumière, M. L., Harris, G. T., Quinsey, V. L., & Rice, M. E. (2005a). Introduction. In M. L. Lalumière, G. T. Harris, V. L. Quinsey, & M. E. Rice (Eds.), *The causes of rape: Understanding individual differences in male propensity for sexual aggression* (pp. 3–6).

Washington, DC: American Psychological Association.

Lalumière, M. L., Harris, G. T., Quinsey, V. L., & Rice, M. E. (2005b). Antisociality and mating effort. In M. L. Lalumière, G. T. Harris, V. L. Quinsey, & M. E. Rice (Eds.). *The causes of rape: Understanding individual differences in male propensity for sexual aggression* (pp. 61–103). Washington, DC: American Psychological Association.

Lalumière, M. L., Harris, G. T., Quinsey, V. L., & Rice, M. E. (2005c). Sexual interest in rape. In M. L. Lalumière, G. T. Harris, V. L. Quinsey, & M. E. Rice (Eds.), *The causes of rape: Understanding individual differences in male propensity for sexual aggression* (pp. 105–128). Washington, DC: American Psychological Association.

Lamanna, M. A., & Riedmann, A. (2005). *Marriages and families* (8th ed.). Belmont, CA: Wadsworth.

Lamaze, F. (1981). *Painless childbirth.* New York: Simon & Schuster.

Lamba, H., Goldmeier, D., Mackie, N. E., & Scullard, G. (2004). Antiretroviral therapy is associated with sexual dysfunction and with increased serum oestradiol levels in men. *International Journal of STD & AIDS, 15*(4), 234–237.

Lane, R., & Thayer, J. (2008). Sexual dysfunction and coronary artery disease. *The American Journal of Medicine, 121*(4), 256–257.

Lane, T., Pettifor, A., Pascoe, S., Fiamma, A., & Rees, H. (2006). Heterosexual anal intercourse increases risk of HIV infection among young South African men. *AIDS, 20*(1), 123–125.

Lang, C., & Kuhnle, U. (2008). Intersexuality and alternative gender categories in non-Western cultures. *Hormone Research in Paediatrics, 69*(4), 240–250.

Langevin, R. (2003). A study of the psychosexual characteristics of sex killers: Can we identify them before it is too late? *International Journal of Offender Therapy & Comparative Criminology, 47*(4), 366–382.

Langevin, R. (2006). Acceptance and completion of treatment among sex offenders. *International Journal of Offender Therapy and Comparative Criminology, 50*(4), 402–417.

Langevin, R., et al. (1979). Experimental studies of the etiology of genital exhibitionism. *Archives of Sexual Behavior, 8,* 307–332.

Langevin, R., et al. (2004). Lifetime sex offender recidivism: A 25-year follow-up study. *Canadian Journal of Criminology and Criminal Justice, 46*(5), 531–552.

Langhinrichsen-Rohling, J., Palarea, R. E., Cohen, J., & Rohlin, M. L. (2002). Breaking up is hard to do: Unwanted pursuit behaviors following the dissolution of a romantic relationship. In K. E. Davis, I. H. Frieze et al. (Eds.). *Stalking: Perspectives on victims and perpetrators* (pp. 212–236). New York: Springer.

Langille, D. B., & Curtis, L. (2002). Factors associated with sexual intercourse before age 15 among female adolescents in Nova Scotia. *Canadian Journal of Human Sexuality, 11*(3), 91–99.

Langlois, J. H., et al. (2000). Maxims or myths of beauty? A meta-analytic and theoretical review. *Psychological Bulletin, 126*(3), 390–423.

Langstrom, N. (2010). The DSM diagnostic criteria for exhibitionism, voyeurism, and frotteurism. *Archives of Sexual Behavior*, DOI 10.1007/s10508-009-9577-4.

Långström, N., & Zucker, K. J. (2005). Transvestic fetishism in the general population: Prevalence and correlates. *Journal of Sex & Marital Therapy, 31*(2), 87–95.

Laqueur, T. W. (2003). *Solitary sex: A cultural history of masturbation.* Zone Books. www.newzonebooks.com.

Larsson, I., & Svedin, C. (2002). Experiences in childhood: Young adults' recollections. *Archives of Sexual Behavior, 31*(3), 263–273.

LaSala, M. C. (2004). Monogamy of the heart: Extradyadic sex and gay male couples. *Journal of Gay & Lesbian Social Services: Issues in Practice, Policy & Research, 17*(3), 1–24.

Laturi, C. A., et al. (2010). Treatment of adolescent gynecomastia. *Journal of Pediatric Surgery, 45*(3), 650–654.

Lau, J. T. F., Siah, P. C., & Tsui, H. Y. (2002). A study of the STD/AIDS related attitudes and behaviors of men who have sex with men in Hong Kong. *Archives of Sexual Behavior, 31*(4), 367–373.

Lau, M., et al. (2009). Dating and sexual attitudes in Asian-American adolescents. *Journal of Adolescent Research, 24*(1), 91–113.

Laumann, E. O., et al. (2006). A cross-national study of subjective sexual well-being among older women and men: Findings from the global study of sexual attitudes and behaviors. *Archives of Sexual Behavior, 35*(2), 145–161.

Laumann, E. O., Gagnon, J. H., Michael, R. T., & Michaels, S. (1994). *The social organization of sexuality: Sexual practices in the United States.* Chicago: University of Chicago Press.

Laumann, E. O., Masi, C. M., & Zuckerman, E. W., et al. (1997, April 2). Circumcision in the United States: Prevalence, prophylactic effects, and sexual practice. *The Journal of the American Medical Association, 277,* 1052–1057.

Laumann, E. O., Paik, A., & Rosen, R. C. (1999). Sexual dysfunction in the United States. Prevalence and predictors. *Journal of the American Medical Association, 281*(6), 537–544.

Laurent, S. M., & Simons, A. D. (2009). Sexual dysfunction in depression and anxiety: Conceptualizing sexual dysfunction as part of an internalizing dimension. *Clinical Psychology Review,* in press.

Lavin, M. (2008). Voyeurism: Psychopathology and theory. In D. R. Laws and W. T. O'Donohue (Eds.), *Sexual deviance: Theory, assessment, and treatment* (2nd ed., pp. 305–319). New York: Guilford Press.

Lawrence, A. A. (2004). Autogynephilia: A paraphilic model of gender identity disorder. *Journal of Gay & Lesbian Psychotherapy, 8*(1–2), 69–87.

Lawrence, A. A. (2005). Sexuality before and after male-to-female sex reassignment surgery. *Archives of Sexual Behavior, 34*(2), 147–166.

Laws, D. R., & Marshall, W. L. (2003). A brief history of behavioral and cognitive behavioral approaches to sexual offenders: Part 1. Early developments. *Sexual Abuse: Journal of Research & Treatment, 15*(2), 75–92.

Laws, D. R., & O'Donohue, W. T. (2008). Introduction. *Sexual deviance: Theory, assessment, and treatment* (2nd ed., pp.1–20). New York: Guilford Press.

Leaper, C., & Bigler, R. S. (2011). In M. K. Underwood & L. H. Rosen (Eds.). *Social development* (pp. 289–315). New York: Guilford.

Leary, M. R., & Tangney, J. P. (2012). *Handbook of self and identity* (2nd ed.). New York: Guilford.

Lederman, M. M., & Valdez, H. (2000). Immune restoration with antiretroviral therapies: Implications for clinical management. *Journal of the American Medical Association, 284,* 223–228.

Lee, F. R. (2006, March 28). "Big love": Real polygamists look at HBO polygamists and find sex. *The New York Times.*

Lee, Y. (2006). *Man as the prayer: The origin and nature of humankind.* New York: Trafford.

Legate, N., Ryan, R. M., & Weinstein, N. (2012). Is coming out always a "good thing"? Exploring the relations of autonomy support, outness, and wellness for lesbian, gay, and bisexual individuals. *Social Psychology and Personality Science, 3*(2), 145–152.

Legato, M. J. (2000, May 12). Cited in "Study of children born without penises finds nature determines gender." The Associated Press online.

Lehne, G. K. (2009). Phenomenology of paraphilia: Lovemap theory. In F. M. Saleh et al. (Eds.), *Sex offenders: Identification, risk assessment, treatment, and legal issue* (pp. 12–26). New York: Oxford University Press.

Leiblum, S. R., & Rosen, R. C. (Ed.). (2000). *Principles and practice of sex therapy.* 3rd ed. New York: Guilford Press.

Leigh, C. (2012, April 19). Labor laws, not criminal laws, are the solution. The *New York Times* (Online).

Leinders-Zufall, T., et al. (2000). Ultrasensitive pheromone detection by mammalian vomeronasal neurons. *Nature, 405,* 792–796.

Leitenberg, H., & Henning, K. (1995). Sexual fantasy. *Psychological Bulletin, 117,* 469–496.

Leitenberg, H., Detzer, M. J., & Srebnik, D. (1993). Gender differences in masturbation and the relation of masturbation experience in preadolescence and/or early adolescence to sexual behavior and sexual adjustment in young adulthood. *Archives of Sexual Behavior, 22,* 87–98.

Leland, J. (2000, May 29). The science of women & sex. *Newsweek,* pp. 48–54.

Lesjak, B., Bogadi, M., & Tosic, G. (2004). Zoophilia in comorbidity with other psychiatric disorders. *Socijalna Psihijatrija, 32*(4), 160–164.

Leue, A., Borchard, B., & Hoyer, J. (2004). Mental disorders in a forensic sample of sexual offenders. *European Psychiatry, 19*(3), 123–130.

LeVay, S. (1991). A difference in hypothalamic structure between heterosexual and homosexual men. *Science, 253,* 1034–1037.

Lever, J., Frederick, D. A., & Peplau, L. A. (2006). Does size matter? Men's and women's views on penis size across the lifespan. *Psychology of Men & Masculinity, 7*(3), 129–143.

Levin, R. J. (2003). The G-spot: Reality or illusion? *Sexual and Relationship Therapy, 18*(1), 117–119.

Levin, R. J. (2005a). The mechanisms of human ejaculation—A critical analysis. *Sexual and Relationship Therapy, 20*(1), 123–131.

Levin, R. J. (2005b). The involvement of the human cervix in reproduction and sex. *Sexual and Relationship Therapy, 20*(2), 251–260.

Levin, R. J. (2006). The breast/nipple/areola complex and human sexuality. *Sexual and Relationship Therapy, 21*(2), 237–249.

Levine, D. (2000). Virtual attraction: What rocks your boat. *CyberPsychology & Behavior, 3*(4), 565–573.

Levine, M. P. (2012). Loneliness and eating disorders. *The Journal of Psychology: Interdisciplinary and Applied, 146*(1–2), 243–257.

Levine, S. B. (2012). Problematic sexual excesses. *Neuropsychiatry, 2*(1), 69–79.

Levite, A., & Cohen, O. (2012). The tango of loving hate: Dynamics in high-conflict divorce. *Clinical Social Work Journal, 40*(1), 46–55.

Levy, H., & Packman, W. (2004). Sexual abuse prevention for individuals with mental retardation: Considerations for genetic counselors. *Journal of Genetic Counseling, 13*(3), 189–205.

Lewin, T. (1998, January 17). Debate distant for many having abortions. *The New York Times,* pp. A1, A9.

Lewis, A. L., & White, J. (2009). The defense mechanisms of homophobia adolescent males. *Journal of Adolescence, 31*(2).

Lewis, J., Maticka-Tyndale, E., Shaver, F., & Schramm, H. (2005). Managing risk and safety on the job: The experiences of Canadian sex workers. *Journal of Psychology & Human Sexuality, 17*(1–2), 147–167.

Lewis, R. W., et al. (2010). Definitions/epidemiology/risk factors for sexual dysfunction. *Journal of Sexual Medicine, 7,* 1598–1607.

Ley, D. J. (2012). *The myth of sex addiction.* Lanham, MD: Rowman & Littlefield Publishers.

Li, N. P., & Kenrick, D. T. (2006). Sex similarities and differences in preferences for short-term mates: What, whether, and why. *Journal of Personality and Social Psychology, 90*(3), 468–489.

Lim, D. (2006, October 22). Mondo multiplex: The snuff film turns respectable. *The New York Times.*

Lindberg, L. D.,& Singh, S. (2008). Sexual behavior of single adult American women. *Perspectives on Sexual and Reproductive Health, 40*(1), 27–33.

Lindsay, R. (2011). Preventing osteoporosis with a tissue receptive estrogen complex containing bazedoxifene/conjugated estrogens. *Osteoporosis International, 22*(2), 447–451.

Lippa, R. (2001). On deconstructing and reconstructing masculinity–femininity. *Journal of Research in Personality, 35*(2), 168–207.

Lippa, R. (2008). The relation between childhood gender nonconformity and adult masculinity–femininity and anxiety in heterosexual and homosexual men and women. *Sex Roles, 59*, 684–693.

Lippa, R. A. (2012). Effects of sex and sexual orientation on self-reported attraction and viewing times to images of men and women: Testing for category specificity. *Archives of Sexual Behavior, 41*(1), 149–160.

Lippa, R., & Arad, S. (1997). The structure of sexual orientation and its relation to masculinity, femininity, and gender diagnosticity: Different for men and women. *Sex Roles, 37*(3–4), 187–208.

Liptak, A. (2003, January 23). Circumcision opponents use the legal system and legislatures. *The New York Times* (Online).

Lipworth, L., et al. (2008). Cancer among Scandinavian women with cosmetic breast implants: A pooled long-term follow-up study. *International Journal of Cancer, 124*(2), 490–493.

Lira, L. R., Koss, M. P., & Russo, N. F. (1999). Mexican American women's definitions of rape and sexual abuse. *Hispanic Journal of Behavioral Sciences, 21*(3), 236–265.

Little, A. C., Caldwell, C. A., Jones, B. C., & DeBruine, L. M. (2011). Effects of partner beauty on opposite-sex attractiveness judgments. *Archives of Sexual Behavior, 40*(6), 1119–1127.

Littleton, H., & Henderson, C. E. (2009). If she is not a victim, does that mean she was not traumatized? Evaluation of predictors of PTSD symptomatology among college rape victims. *Violence Against Women, 15*(2), 148–167.

Lloyd, R. (2012, April 19). Legality leads to more trafficking. The *New York Times* (Online).

Locke, B. D., & Mahalik, J. R. (2005). Examining masculinity norms, problem drinking, and athletic involvement as predictors of sexual aggression in college men. *Journal of Counseling Psychology, 52*(3), 279–283.

Locock, L., & Alexander, J. (2005). "Just a bystander"? Men's place in the process of fetal screening and diagnosis. *Social Science & Medicine, 62*(6), 1349–1359.

Loder, N. (2000). US science shocked by revelations of sexual discrimination. *Nature, 405*, 713–714.

Loe, M. (2012). Pleasure in old age. In L. M. Carpenter, & J. DeLamater (Eds.), *Sex for life* (pp. 278–298). New York: New York University Press.

Logan, C. (2008). Sexual deviance in females. In D. R. Laws and W. T. O'Donohue (Eds.), *Sexual deviance: Theory, assessment, and treatment* (2nd ed., pp. 486–507). New York: Guilford Press.

Logan, T. K., Walker, R., Jordan, C. E., & Leukefeld, C. G. (2006). Justice system options and responses. In T. K. Logan, R. Walker, C. E. Jordan, & C. G. Leukefeld (Eds.), *Women and victimization: Contributing factors, interventions, and implications* (pp. 161–194). Washington, DC: American Psychological Association.

Lohman, D. F., & Lakin, J. M. (2009). Consistencies in sex differences on the Cognitive Abilities Test across countries, grades, test forms, and cohorts. *British Journal of Educational Psychology, 79*(2), 389–407.

Lohmann, R. I. (2004). Sex and sensibility: Margaret Mead's descriptive and rhetorical ethnography. *Reviews in Anthropology, 33*(2), 111–130.

Londoño, D. C., et al. (2012). Population-based study of erectile dysfunction and polypharmacy. *BJUI, 110*(2), 254–259.

Long, C. R., Seburn, M., Averill, J. R., & More, T. A. (2003). Solitude experiences: Varieties, settings, and individual differences. *Personality & Social Psychology Bulletin, 29*(5), 578–583.

Lorant, V., et al. (2005). A European comparative study of marital status and socio-economic inequalities in suicide. *Social Science & Medicine, 60*(11), 2431–2441.

Lorenz, F. O., Wickrama, K. A. S., Conger, R. D., & Elder, G. H., Jr. (2006). The short-term and decade-long effects of divorce on women's midlife health. *Journal of Health and Social Behavior, 47*(2), 111–125.

Lotery, H. E., McClure, N., & Galask, R. P. (2004). Vulvodynia. *Lancet, 363*(9414), 1058–1060.

Lovaas, K. E., Elia, J. P., & Yep, G. A. (2007). Shifting ground(s): Surveying the contested terrain of LGBT studies and queer theory. *Journal of Homosexuality, 52*(1-2), 1–18.

Lucon, A. M., et al. (2006). Spontaneous recanalization after vasectomy. *TSW Urology, 1*, 71–74.

Luder, M., et al. (2011). Associations between online pornography and sexual behavior among adolescents: Myth or reality? *Archives of Sexual Behavior, 40*(5), 1027–1035.

Lue, T. F. (2000). Drug therapy: Erectile dysfunction. *The New England Journal of Medicine, 342*(24).

Lundström, J. N., & Marilyn Jones-Gotman, M. (2009). Romantic love modulates women's identification of men's body odors. *Hormones and Behavior, 55*(2), 280–284.

Lussier, P., & Piché, L. (2008). Frotteurism: Psychopathology and theory. In D. R. Laws and W. T. O'Donohue (Eds.), *Sexual deviance: Theory, assessment, and treatment* (2nd ed., pp. 131–149). New York: Guilford Press.

Lynn, B. M., McCord, J. L., & Halliwell, J. R. (2007). Effects of menstrual cycle and sex on progesterone hemodynamics. *American Journal of Physiology: Regulatory, Integrative, and Comparative Physiology, 292*, R1260–R1270.

Maaita, M. J., Bhaumik, J., & Davies, A. E. (2002). Sexual function after using tension-free vaginal tape for the surgical treatment of genuine stress incontinence. *British Journal of Urology International, 90*(6), 540.

Maartens, L. W. F., Knottnerus, J. A., & Pop, V. J. (2002). Menopausal transition and increased depressive symptomatology: A community based prospective study. *Maturitas, 42*(3), 195–200.

MacCallum, F., & Keeley, S. (2008). Embryo donation families: A follow-up in middle childhood. *Journal of Family Psychology, 22*(6), 799–808.

MacCulloch, D. (2011). *Christianity: The first three thousand years.* New York: Viking.

MacDonald, T. K., MacDonald, G., Zanna, M. P., & Fong, G. T. (2000). Alcohol, sexual arousal, and intentions to use condoms in young men: Applying alcohol myopia theory

to risky sexual behavior. *Health Psychology, 19*, 290–298.

MacGregor, E. (2009). Estrogen replacement and migraine. *Maturitas, 63*(1), 51–55.

Mackinnon, C. A. (2007). *Women's lives, men's laws.* Cambridge, MA: Harvard University Press.

Macy, R. J., Nurius, P. S., & Norris, J. (2006). Responding in their best interests: Contextualizing women's coping with acquaintance sexual aggression. *Violence Against Women, 12*(5), 478–500.

Madhyastha, T. M., Hamaker, E. L., & Gottman, J. M. (2011). Investigating spousal influence using moment-to-moment affect data from marital conflict. *Journal of Family Psychology, 25*(2), 292 –300.

Madsen, L., Parsons, S., & Grubin, D. (2006). The relationship between the five-factor model and *DSM* personality disorder in a sample of child molesters. *Personality and Individual Differences, 40*(2), 227–236.

Maggi, M. (2012). *Hormonal therapy for male sexual dysfunction.* Hoboken, NJ: Wiley.

Mahoney, A. R., & Knudson-Martin, C. (2009). *Couples, gender, and power.* New York: Springer.

Major, B., et al. (2000). Psychological responses of women after first-trimester abortion. *Archives of General Psychiatry, 57*, 777–784.

Major, B., Kaiser, C. R., & McCoy, S. K. (2003). It's not my fault: When and why attributions to prejudice protect self-esteem. *Personality & Social Psychology Bulletin, 29*(6), 772–781.

Malamuth, N. M., Addison, T., & Koss, M. (2000). Pornography and sexual aggression: Are there reliable effects and can we understand them? *Annual Review of Sex Research, 11*, 26–91.

Malamuth, N. M., Huppin, M., & Paul, B. (2005). Sexual coercion. In D. M. Buss (Ed.), *The handbook of evolutionary psychology* (pp. 394–418). Hoboken, NJ: Wiley.

Malaspina, D. (2009). Cited in L. Belkin (2009, April 5). Your old man. *The New York Times Magazine.*

Malec, K. (2003, Summer). The abortion–breast cancer link: How politics trumped science and informed consent. *Journal of American Physicians and Surgeons, 8*(2). www. abortionbreastcancer.com/jpands.pdf.

Maletzky, B. M. (1980). Assisted covert sensitization in the treatment of exhibitionism. *Journal of Consulting and Clinical Psychology, 48*(1), 306–312.

Maletzky, B. M., & Steinhauser, C. (2002). A 25-year follow-up of cognitive/behavioral therapy with 7,275 sexual offenders. *Behavior Modification, 26*(2), 123–147.

Malinowski, B. (1927). *Sex and repression in savage society.* London: Kegan Paul, Trench, Trubner & Co.

Malinowski, B. (1929). *The sexual life of savages in north-western Melanesia.* New York: Eugenics.

Man pays victim's husband in fondling case. (2000, June 2). Reuters News Agency. (Online).

Maner, J. K., Rouby, D. A., & Gonzaga, G. C. (2008). Automatic inattention to attractive alternatives: The evolved psychology of relationship maintenance. *Evolution and Human Behavior, 29*(5), 343–349.

Maniglio, R. (2011). The role of childhood trauma, psychological problems, and coping in the development of deviant sexual fantasies in sexual offenders. *Clinical Psychology Review, 31*(5), 748–756.

Mansergh, G., et al. (2008). Alcohol and drug use in the context of anal sex and other factors associated with sexually transmitted infections: Results from a multi-city study of high-risk men who have sex with men in the USA. *Sexually Transmitted Infections, 84,* 509–511.

Maranda, M. J., Han, C., & Rainone, G. A. (2004). Crack cocaine and sex. *Journal of Psychoactive Drugs, 36*(3), 315–322.

Marazziti, D. (2005). The neurobiology of love. *Current Psychiatry Reviews, 1*(3), 331–335.

Marchbanks, P. A., et al. (2002). Oral contraceptives and the risk of breast cancer. *New England Journal of Medicine, 346,* 2025–2032.

Marcus, D. K., & Miller, R. S. (2003). Sex differences in judgments of physical attractiveness: A social relations analysis. *Personality & Social Psychology Bulletin, 29*(3), 325–335.

Mardorossian, C. M. (2002). Toward a new feminist theory of rape. *Signs, 27*(3), 743–775.

Markman, H. J. (2005). The prevention of extramarital involvement: Steps toward "affair proofing" marriage. *Clinical Psychology: Science and Practice, 12*(2), 134–138.

Marquis, C. (2003, March 16). Living in sin. *The New York Times,* p. WK2.

Marr, S. (2012, April 20). Nevada's legal brothels are coercive too. The *New York Times* (Online).

Marrazzo, J. (2003). Vulvovaginal candidiasis: Over the counter treatment doesn't seem to lead to resistance. *British Medical Journal, 326,* 993–994.

Marshall, B. L. (2006). The new virility: Viagra, male aging and sexual function. *Sexualities, 9*(3), 345–362.

Marshall, W. L. (1989). Pornography and sex offenders. In D. Zillmann & J. Bryant (Eds.), *Pornography: Research advances and policy considerations* (pp. 185–214). Hillsdale, NJ: Erlbaum.

Marsiglio, W. (2004). When stepfathers claim stepchildren: A conceptual analysis. *Journal of Marriage & Family, 66*(1), 22–39.

Martin, J. A., et al. (2008). Annual summary of vital statistics: 2006. *Pediatrics, 121*(4), 788–801.

Martinez, G., Abma, J., & Copen, C. (2010). Educating teenagers about sex in the United States. NCHS data brief, no. 44. Hyattsville, MD: National Center for Health Statistics.

Martinez, G., Copen, C. E., & Abma, J. C. (2011). Teenagers in the United States: Sexual activity, contraceptive use, and childbearing, 2006–1010 National Survey of Family Growth. National Center for Health Statistics. *Vital Health Statistics, 23*(31).

Martino, S. C., et al. (2006). Exposure to degrading versus nondegrading music lyrics and sexual behavior among youth. *Pediatrics, 118,* e430–e441.

Martins, Y., Preti, G., Crabtree, C. R., Runyan, T., Vainius, A. A., & Wysocki, C. J. (2005). Preference for human body odors is influenced by gender and sexual orientation. *Psychological Science, 16*(9), 694.

Marvasti, J. A. (2004). Pharmacotherapy and surgical treatment of paraphiliacs and sexual offenders. In J. A. Marvasti (Ed.), *Psychiatric treatment of sexual offenders: Treating the past traumas in traumatizers. A bio-psychosocial perspective. American series in behavioral science and law* (pp. 97–115). Springfield, IL: Charles C. Thomas.

Marwick, C. (2000). Consensus panel considers osteoporosis. *Journal of the American Medical Association, 283*(16).

Marziano, V., Ward, T., Beech, A. R., & Pattison, P. (2006). Identification of five fundamental implicit theories underlying cognitive distortions in child abusers: A preliminary study. *Psychology, Crime & Law, 12*(1), 97–105.

Masheb, R. M., Lozano–Blanco, C., Kohorn, E. I., Minkin, M J., & Kerns, R. D. (2004). Assessing sexual function and dyspareunia with the female sexual function index (FSFI) in women with vulvodynia. *Journal of Sex & Marital Therapy, 30*(5), 315–324.

Masters, W. H., & Johnson, V. E. (1966). *Human sexual response.* Boston: Little, Brown.

Masters, W. H., & Johnson, V. E. (1970). *Human sexual inadequacy.* Boston: Little, Brown.

Masters, W. H., & Johnson, V. E. (1979). *Homosexuality in perspective.* Boston: Little, Brown.

Mathers, B. M., et al. (2008). Global epidemiology of injecting drug use and HIV among people who inject drugs: A systematic review. *The Lancet, 372*(9651), 1733–1745.

Matthews, A. K., Hughes, T. L., Tartaro, J., Omoto, A. M., & Kurtzman, H. S. (Eds.). (2006). *Sexual orientation and mental health: Examining identity and development in lesbian, gay, and bisexual people. Contemporary perspectives on lesbian, gay, and bisexual psychology.* Washington, DC: American Psychological Association.

Mattson, C. L., Bailey, R. C., Muga, R., Poulussen, R., & Onyango, T. (2005). Acceptability of male circumcision and predictors of circumcision preference among men and women in Nyanza Province, Kenya, *AIDS Care, 17*(2), 182–194.

Mattson, G. (2011). Sin in the suburbs: Nevada's changing brothel industry. *Journal of Sex Research, 48*(6), 599–601.

Maxson, S. C. (1998). Homologous genes, aggression, and animal models. *Developmental Neuropsychology, 14*(1), 143–156.

Maxwell, C. D., Robinson, A. L., & Post, L. A. (2003). The nature and predictors of sexual victimization and offending among adolescents. *Journal of Youth & Adolescence, 32*(6), 465–477.

Maybach, K. L., & Gold, S. R. (1994). Hyper-femininity and attraction to macho and non-macho men. *Journal of Sex Research, 31*(2), 91–98.

Mayo Clinic. (2006, October 10). Vulvodynia. www.mayoclinic.com/health/vulvodynia/DS00159.

Mayo Clinic. (2012a). Ectopic pregnancy. http://www.mayoclinic.com/health/ectopic-pregnancy/DS00622/DSECTION=risk-factors

Mazur, T. *The infant's developing sexuality.* Accessed February 10, 2006. www2.hu-berlin.de/sexology/GESUND/ARCHIV/SEN/CH07.HTM#b11-CHILDREN%20AND%20SEX.

McAndrew, F. T. (2009). The interacting roles of testosterone and challenges to status in human male aggression. *Aggression and Violent Behavior,* in press.

McAnulty, R. (2012). *Sex in college: The things they don't write home about.* Santa Barbara, CA: ABC-CLIO, LLC.

McAnulty, R. D. (Ed.). (2012). *Sex in college: The things they don't write home about* (pp. 263–288). Santa Barbara, CA: ABC-CLIO.

McBride, C. K., Paikoff, R. L., & Holmbeck, G. N. (2003). Individual and familial influences on the onset of sexual intercourse among urban African American adolescents. *Journal of Consulting and Clinical Psychology, 71*(1), 159–167.

McCabe M., et al. (2010). Psychological and interpersonal dimensions of sexual function and dysfunctions. *Journal of Sexual Medicine, 7,* 327–336.

McCabe, K. A. (2000). Child pornography and the Internet. *Social Science Computer Review, 18*(1), 73–76.

McCabe, M. P. (2004). Exacerbation of symptoms among people with multiple sclerosis: Impact on sexuality and relationships over time. *Archives of Sexual Behavior, 33*(6), 593–601.

McCabe, M. P. (2005). The role of performance anxiety in the development and maintenance of sexual dysfunction in men and women. *International Journal of Stress Management, 12*(4), 379–388.

McCabe, S. E., et al. (2005). Selection and socialization effects of fraternities and sororities on US college student substance use: A multi-cohort national longitudinal study. *Addiction, 100*(4), 512–524.

McCarthy, B. W., & Fucito, L. M. (2005). Integrating medication, realistic expectations, and therapeutic interventions in the treatment of male sexual dysfunction. *Journal of Sex & Marital Therapy, 31*(4), 319–328.

McCarthy, B. W., Bodnar, L. E., & Handal, M. (2004). Integrating sex therapy and couple therapy. In J. H. Harvey, A. Wenzel, & S. Sprecher (Eds.), *The handbook of sexuality in close relationships* (pp. 573–593). Erlbaum.

McCarthy, B. W., Ginsberg, R. L., & Fucito, L. M. (2006). Resilient sexual desire in heterosexual couples. *Family Journal: Counseling and Therapy for Couples and Families, 14*(1), 59–64.

McClamrock, H. D., Jones, H. W., & Adashi, E. Y. (2012). Ovarian stimulation and intrauterine insemination at the quarter centennial: Implications for the multiple births epidemic. *Fertility and Sterility, 97*(4), 802–809.

McCoy, N. L., & Pitino, L. (2002). Pheromonal influences on sociosexual behavior in young women. *Physiology & Behavior, 75*(3), 367–375.

McDonough, Y. Z. (1998, January 24). What Barbie really taught me. *The New York Times Magazine,* 70.

McElduff, A., & Beange, H. (2003). Men's health and well-being: Testosterone deficiency. *Journal of Intellectual & Developmental Disability, 28*(2), 211–213.

McEwan, S. L., de Man, A. F., & Simpson-Housley, P. (2005). Acquaintance rape, ego-identity achievement, and locus of control. *Social Behavior and Personality, 33*(6), 587–592.

McGue, M., Elkins, I., Walden, B., & Iacono, W. G. (2005). Perceptions of the parent–adolescent relationship: A longitudinal investigation. *Developmental Psychology, 41*(6), 971–984.

McHugh, M. C., & Hambaugh, J. (2010). She said, he said: Gender, language, and power. *Handbook of Gender Research in Psychology, 5,* 379–410.

McIntyre, S., Formichella, A., Osterhout, M. B., & Gresh, S. (1991). *Tell it like it is: Straight talk about sex.* New York: Avon Books (a division of HarperCollins).

McKeganey, N. (2006). Street prostitution in Scotland: The views of working women. *Drugs: Education, Prevention & Policy, 13*(2), 151–166.

McLawsen, J. E., Scalora, M. J., & Darrow, C. (2012). Civilly committed sex offenders: A description and interstate comparison of populations. Psychology, Public Policy, and Law. DOI: 10.1037/a0026116.

McLeod, J. D., & Knight, S. (2010). The association of socioemotional problems with early sexual initiation. *Perspectives on Sexual and Reproductive Health, 42*(2), 93–101.

McMahon, C. G. (2011). Premature ejaculation. *Journal of Sexual Medicine,* Virtual Issue Number 3.

McMillen, M. (2011, September 1). Circumcision rates are dropping in the U.S. CDC says circumcision is slightly less common today than a decade ago. WebMD Health News. http://www.webmd.com/parenting/baby/news/20110901/circumcision-rates-are-dropping-in-the-us

McNeil, D. G. (2011, July 13). Two studies show pills can prevent HIV infection. *The New York Times* (Online).

McNeil, D. G. (2012, July 3). AIDS: New Four-Drug Pill Taken Daily Tests Better Than Other Regimens. *The New York Times,* p. D6.

Mead, M. (1935). *Sex and temperament in three primitive societies.* New York: Dell.

Mead, M. (1935). *Sex and temperament in three primitive societies.* New York: William Morrow and Company.

Meadows, S. (2009). Family structure and fathers' well-being: Trajectories of mental health and self-rated health. *Journal of Health and Social Behavior, 50*(2), 115–131.

Medical News Today. (2008, January 17). Circumcision rates highest in Midwest, lowest in West. http://www.medicalnewstoday.com/articles/94200.php.

Medrano, M. A., Hatch, J. P., Zule, W. A., & Desmond, D. P. (2003). Childhood trauma and adult prostitution behavior in a multiethnic heterosexual drug-using population. *American Journal of Drug & Alcohol Abuse, 29*(2), 463–486.

Meissner, G. W., et al. (2011). Functional dissection of the neural substrates for sexual behaviors in *Drosophila melanogaster. Genetics, 189*(1), 195–211.

Menard, K. S., et al. (2003). Gender differences in sexual harassment and coercion in college students: Developmental, individual, and situational determinants. *Journal of Interpersonal Violence, 18*(10), 1222–1239.

Meston, C. M., & Frohlich, P. F. (2000). The neurobiology of sexual function. *Archives of General Psychiatry, 57*(11), 1012–1030.

Meston, C., & Buss, D. M. (2007). Why humans have sex. *Archives of Sexual Behavior, 36,* 477–507.

Meyer, I. H., Rossano, L., Ellis, J. M., & Bradford, J. (2002). A brief telephone interview to identify lesbian and bisexual women in random digit sampling. *Journal of Sex Research, 39*(2), 139–144.

Meyer, T. (1998, February 18). *AZT short treatment works.* The Associated Press. (Online).

Meyer-Bahlburg, H. F. L., et al. (1995). Prenatal estrogens and the development of homosexual orientation. *Developmental Psychology, 31*(1), 12–21.

Michael, R. T., Gagnon, J. H., Laumann, E. O., & Kolata, G. (1994). *Sex in America: A definitive survey.* Boston: Little, Brown.

Michel, A. & Pedinielli, J.-L. (2005). Vers une conceptualization du transsexualisme. *Annales Medico-Psychologiques, 163*(5), 379–386.

Mikach, S. M., & Bailey, J. M. (1999). What distinguishes women with unusually high numbers of sex partners? *Evolution & Human Behavior, 20*(3) 141–150.

Mill, J. S. (1983). *Utilitarianism.* Indianapolis: Hackett Publishing.

Miller, G., Tybur, J., & Jordan, B. D. (2007). *Evolution and Human Behavior, 28*(6), 375–381.

Miller, J. (2012). In C. D. Bryant (Ed.). *The Routledge handbook of deviant behavior* (pp. 383–389). New York: Routledge.

Miller, M. (1998, cited in Bronner, February 1). Just say maybe. No sexology, please. We're Americans. *The New York Times,* p. WK6.

Miller, R. (2005). Overcoming violence against women and girls: The international campaign to eradicate a worldwide problem. *Culture, Health & Sexuality, 7*(5), 519–521.

Miller, S. A., & Byers, E. S. (2004). Actual and desired duration of foreplay and intercourse: Discordance and misperceptions within heterosexual couples. *Journal of Sex Research, 41*(3), 301–309.

Miller, S. L., & Maner, J. K. (2009). Sex differences in response to sexual versus emotional infidelity: The moderating role of individual differences. *Personality and Individual Differences, 46*(3), 287-291.

Millett, G. A., et al. (2008). Circumcision status and risk of HIV and sexually transmitted infections among men who have sex with men: A meta-analysis. *Journal of the American Medical Association, 300*(14), 1674–1684.

Milner, A., McClure, R., & de Leo, D. (2012). Socio-economic determinants of suicide: An ecological analysis of 35 countries. *Social Psychiatry and Psychiatric Epidemiology, 47*(1), 19–27.

Miner, M. M. (2011). Erectile dysfunction and cardiovascular disease: A harbinger for cardiovascular events. *Journal of Sexual Medicine,* Virtual Issue Number 2.

Minichiello, V., et al. (2001). Male sex workers in three Australian cities: Socio-demographic and sex work characteristics. *Journal of Homosexuality, 42*(1), 29–51.

Mishra, G. D., Cooper, R., Tom, S. E., & Kuh, D. (2009). Early life circumstances and

their impact on menarche and menopause. *Women's Health, 5*(2), 175–190.

Missailidis, K., & Gebre–Medhin, M. (2000). Female genital mutilation in eastern Ethiopia. *The Lancet, 356,* 137–138.

Mitchell, K. J., Finkelhor, D., & Wolak, J. (2005). Protecting youth online: Family use of filtering and blocking software. *Child Abuse & Neglect, 29*(7), 753–765.

Mock, S. E., & Elbach, R. P. (2012). Stability and change in sexual orientation over a 10-year period in adulthood. *Archives of Sexual Behavior, 41*(3), 641–648.

Mofenson, L. M. (2000). Perinatal exposure to zidovudine—Benefits and risks. *The New England Journal of Medicine, 343*(11).

Mohan, R., & Bhugra, D. (2005). Literature update: A critical review. *Sexual and Relationship Therapy, 20*(1), 115–122.

Money, J. (1994). The concept of gender identity disorder in childhood and adolescence after 39 years. *Journal of Sex and Marital Therapy, 20*(3), 163–177.

Money, J. (2003). History, causality, and sexology. *Journal of Sex Research, 40*(3), 237–239.

Monson, C. M., Langhinrichsen-Rohling, J., & Binderup, T. (2000). Does "no" really mean "no" after you say "yes"? Attributions about date and marital rape. *Journal of Interpersonal Violence, 15*(11), 1156–1174.

Montano, D., Kasprzyk, D., von Haeften, I., & Fishbein, M. (2001). Toward an understanding of condom use behaviours: A theoretical and methodological overview of Project SAFER. *Psychology, Health & Medicine, 6*(2), 139–150.

Montemurro, B., Bloom, C., & Madell, K. (2003). Ladies night out: A typology of women patrons of a male strip club. *Deviant Behavior, 24*(4), 333–352.

Montgomery-Downs, H. E. (2008). Normal sleep development in infants and toddlers. In A. Ivanenko (Ed.), *Sleep and psychiatric disorders in children and adolescents* (pp. 11-21). London: informa healthcare.

Montoya, R. M., Horton, R. S., & Kirchner, J. (2008). Is actual similarity necessary for attraction? A meta-analysis of actual and perceived similarity. *Journal of Social and Personal Relationships, 25*(6), 889–922.

Moore, D. R., & Heiman, J. R. (2006). Women's sexuality in context: Relationship factors and female sexual functioning. In I. Goldstein, C. Meston, S. Davis, & A. Traish (Eds.), *Female sexual dysfunction.* New York: Parthenon.

Moore, M. M. (2010). Human nonverbal courtship behavior—A brief historical review. *Journal of Sex Research, 47,* 171–180.

Moore, S., & Leung, C. (2002). Young people's romantic attachment styles and their association with well-being. *Journal of Adolescence, 25*(2), 243–255.

Morley, J. E., & Perry, H. M., III. (2003). Androgens and women at the menopause and beyond. *Journals of Gerontology: Series A: Biological Sciences & Medical Sciences, 58A*(5), 409–416.

Morofushi, M., Shinohara, K., Funabashi, T., & Kimura, F. (2000). Positive relationship between menstrual synchrony and ability to smell 5alpha-androst-16-en-3alpha-ol. *Chemical Senses, 25*(4), 407–411.

Morris, L. B. (2000, June 25). For the partum blues, a question of whether to medicate. *The New York Times* (Online).

Morrison, C. S., & Nanda, K. (2012). Hormonal contraception and HIV: An unanswered question. *The Lancet Infectious Diseases, 12*(1), 2–3.

Morrison, D. R., & Coiro, M. J. (1999). Parental conflict and marital disruption: Do children benefit when high-conflict marriages are dissolved? *Journal of Marriage & the Family, 61*(3), 626–637.

Morrison, E. S., et al. (1980). *Growing up sexual.* New York: Van Nostrand Reinhold.

Morry, M. M. (2005). Allocentrism and friendship satisfaction: The mediating roles of disclosure and closeness. *Canadian Journal of Behavioural Science, 37*(3), 211–222.

Morry, M. M., & Gaines, S. O. (2005). Relationship satisfaction as a predictor of similarity ratings: A test of the attraction–similarity hypothesis. *Journal of Social and Personal Relationships, 22*(4), 561–584.

Morry, M. M., Kito, M., & Ortiz, L. (2011). The attraction–similarity model and dating couples. *Personal Relationships, 18*(1), 125–143.

Mortola, J. F. (1998). Premenstrual syndrome—Pathophysiologic considerations. *New England Journal of Medicine, 338,* 256–257.

Moser, C. (2010). Blanchard's autogynephilia theory: A critique. *Journal of Homosexuality, 57*(6), 790–809.

Moser, S. E., & Alken, L. S. (2011). Cognitive and emotional factors associated with elective breast augmentation among young women. *Psychology and Health, 26*(1), 41–60.

Mosher, W. D., Chandra, A., & Jones, J. (2005). *Sexual behavior and selected health measures: Men and women 15–44 years of age, United States, 2002. Advance data from vital and health statistics.* Centers for Disease Control and Prevention. National Center for Health Statistics, No. 362.

Mostafa, T., El Khouly, G., & Hassan, A. (2012). Pheromones in sex and reproduction: Do they have a role in humans? *Journal of Advanced Research, 3*(1), 1–9.

Mukherjee, S., et al. (2009). What is the effect of circumcision on risk of urinary tract infection in boys with posterior urethral valves? *Journal of Pediatric Surgery, 44*(2), 417–421.

Mulac, A., Jansma, L. L., & Linz, D. G. (2002). Men's behavior toward women after viewing sexually-explicit films: Degradation makes a difference. *Communication Monographs, 69*(4), 311–328.

Mulick, P. S., & Wright, L. W., Jr. (2002). Examining the existence of biphobia in the heterosexual and homosexual populations. *Journal of Bisexuality, 2*(4), 45–64.

Multidrug-resistant gonorrhea, 2012. Centers for Disease Control and Prevention. (2012). The growing threat of multidrug-resistant gonorrhea. http://www.cdc.gov/about/grand-rounds/archives/2012/May2012.htm (Accessed October 4, 2012).

Munarriz, R., et al. (2002). Androgen replacement therapy with dehydroepiandrosterone for androgen insufficiency and female sexual dysfunction: Androgen and questionnaire results. *Journal of Sex & Marital Therapy, 28*(Suppl. 1), 165–173.

Mundy, L. (2000, July 16). Sex and sensibility. *The Washington Post.* [Online].

Munro, V. E. (2006). Stopping traffic? A comparative study of responses to the trafficking in women for prostitution. *British Journal of Criminology, 46*(2), 318–333.

Murphy, S. M., Vallacher, R. R., Shackelford, T. K., Bjorklund, D. F., & Yunger, J. L. (2006). Relationship experience as a predictor of romantic jealousy. *Personality and Individual Differences, 40*(4), 761–769.

Murphy, W. D., & Page, I. J. (2008). Exhibitionism: Psychopathology and theory. In D. R. Laws and W. T. O'Donohue (Eds.), *Sexual deviance: Theory, assessment, and treatment* (2nd ed., pp. 61–75). New York: Guilford Press.

Murphy, W. D., & Page, I. J. (2012). Exhibitionism: Psychopathology and theory. I. D. R. Laws & W. T. O'Donohue (Eds.). *Sexual deviance: Theory, assessment, and treatment* (pp. 61–75). New York: Guilford Press.

Murray, S. H., & Milhausen, R. R. (2012). Sexual desire and relationship duration in young men and women. *Journal of Sex & Marital Therapy, 38*(1), 28–40.

Murray, S. L., & Holmes, J. G. (2000). Seeing the self through a partner's eyes: Why self-doubts turn into relationship insecurities. In A. Tesser, R. B. Felson, et al. (Eds.), *Psychological perspectives on self and identity* (pp. 173–197). Washington, DC: American Psychological Association.

Murray, S. L., Bellavia, G., Feeney, B., Holmes, J. G., & Rose, P. (2001). The contingencies of interpersonal acceptance: When romantic relationships function as a self-affirmational resource. *Motivation & Emotion, 25*(2), 163–189.

Murray, S. O., & Roscoe, W. (1997). *Islamic homosexualities: Culture, history, and literature.* New York: New York University Press.

Myers, J. E., Madathil, J., & Tingle, L. R. (2005). Marriage satisfaction and wellness in India and the United States: A preliminary comparison of arranged marriages and marriages of choice. *Journal of Counseling & Development, 83*(2), 183–190.

Myers, S. M. (2006). Religious homogamy and marital quality: Historical and generational patterns, 1980–1997. *Journal of Marriage and the Family, 68*(2), 292–304.

Myers, S. Myers, J. E., Madathil, J., & Tingle, L. R. (2005). Marriage satisfaction and wellness in India and the United States: A preliminary comparison of arranged marriages and marriages of choice. *Journal of Counseling & Development, 83*(2), 183–190.

Nagourney, A. (2009, April 29). Signs GOP is rethinking stance on gay marriage. *The New York Times,* p. A15.

Najman, J. M., Dunne, M. P., Purdie, D. M., Boyle, F. M., & Coxeter, P. D. (2005). Sexual abuse in childhood and sexual dysfunction in adulthood: An Australian population-based study. *Archives of Sexual Behavior, 34*(5), 517–526.

Nakaya, M. (2002). Fluvoxamine treatment of a Japanese patient with Koro. *Journal of Clinical Psychiatry, 63*(12), 1182–1183.

Nanda, S., & Warms, R. L. (2004). *Cultural anthropology* (8th ed.). Belmont, CA: Wadsworth.

Nappi, R. E., & Nappi, G. (2012). Neuroendocrine aspects of migraine in women. *Gynecological Endocrinology, 28*(1), 37–41.

Nappi, R. E., Wawra, K., & Schmitt, S. (2006). Hypoactive sexual desire disorder in postmenopausal women. *Gynecological Endocrinology, 22*(6), 318–323.

Narchi, H. (2003). Infantile masturbation mimicking paroxysmal disorders. *Journal of Pediatric Neurology, 1*(1), 43–45.

National Campaign to Prevent Teen and Unplanned Pregnancy. (2012). Counting it up: The public costs of teen childbearing: Key data. Washington, DC: The National Campaign to Prevent Teen and Unplanned Pregnancy. Available from http://www.thenationalcampaign.org/costs/pdf/counting-it-up/key-data.pdf (Accessed September 23, 2012).

National Campaign to Prevent Teen Pregnancy. (2003, September 30). *Teens say parents most influence their sexual decisions: New polling data and "Tips for Parents" released.* www.teenpregnancy.org/about/announcements/pr/2003/release9_30_03.asp.

National Cancer Institute. (2009). www.nci.nih.gov/.

National Cancer Institute. (2012). Breast cancer. http://www.cancer.gov/cancertopics/types/breast

National Cancer Institute. (2012). Prostate Cancer. Risk Factors. http://www.cancer.gov/cancertopics/wyntk/prostate/page4

National Center for Biotechnology Information (NCBI). (2006, February 1). National Institute of Health. [Online]. www.ncbi.nlm.nih.gov/entrez/query.fcgi?=CMD=Search&db=homologene&term=SRY.

National Institute of Alcohol Abuse and Alcoholism. (2005). Apparent per capita ethanol consumption for the United States, 1850–2002. [Gallons of ethanol, based on population age 15 and older prior to 1970 and on population age 14 and older thereafter]. www.niaaa.nih.gov/databases/consum01.htm.

National Institute of Allergy and Infectious Diseases. (2009, July 14). Herpevac trial for women. (Accessed November 2, 2009). http://www3.niaid.nih.gov/topics/genitalHerpes/research/herpevac/default.htm.

National Institute of Population and Social Security Research. Population statistics of Japan 2008. Accessed May 13, 2009. http://www.ipss.go.jp/indexe.html.

National Science Foundation. (2007). The General Social Survey. Arlington, VA: National Science Foundation. http://www.nsf.gov/pubs/2007/nsf0748/nsf0748.pdf.

Natsuaki, M. N., Leve, L. D., & Mendle, J. (2011). Going through the rites of passage: Timing and transition of menarche, childhood sexual abuse, and anxiety symptoms in girls. *Journal of Youth and Adolescence, 40*(10), 1357–1370.

Nduati, R., et al. (2000). Effect of breastfeeding and formula feeding on transmission of HIV-1. *Journal of the American Medical Association, 283,* 1167–1174.

Neerman-Arbez, M. (2003, June 4). Genes implicated in sexual differentiation. Geneva Foundation for Medical Education and Research. www.gfmer.ch/Endo/Lectures_10/Sexualdi.htm.

Nemoto, T., Iwamoto, M., Wong, S., Le, M. N., & Operario, D. (2004). Social factors related to risk for violence and sexually transmitted infections/HIV among Asian massage parlor workers in San Francisco. *AIDS and Behavior, 8*(4), 475–483.

Newman, G. A. (2006). Woman's place or women's spaces: Intertwining history, herstory, and Christianity. In C. K. Robertson (Ed.), *Religion & sexuality: Passionate debates* (pp. 65–76). New York: Peter Lang Publishing.

Newman, L. (2012). Questions about gender: Children with atypical gender development. *Disorders of Sex Development,* 31–39. DOI:10.1007/978-3-642-22964-0_4.

Newman, T. (2009). Cited in Monica Davey. (2009, June 7). Closed clinic leaves abortion protesters at a loss. *The New York Times.*

Nieto, J. J., Cogswell, D., Jesinger, D., & Hardiman, P. (2000). Lipid effects of hormone replacement therapy with sequential transdermal 17-beta-estradiol and oral dydrogesterone. *Obstetrics & Gynecology, 95,* 111–114.

NISVS. (2011, December 14). Centers for Disease Control and Prevention. The National Intimate Partner and Sexual Violence Survey (NISVS). http://www.cdc.gov/ViolencePrevention/NISVS/index.html (Accessed July 16, 2012).

Njus, D. M., & Bane, C. M. H. (2009). Religious identification as a moderator of evolved sexual strategies of men and women. *Journal of Sex Research,* DOI: 10.1080/00224490902867855.

Nobre, P. J., & Pinto-Gouveia, J. (2006). Dysfunctional sexual beliefs as vulnerability factors for sexual dysfunction. *Journal of Sex Research, 43*(1), 68–75.

Noller, P. (2012). Conflict in family relationships. In P. Noller & G. C. Karantzas (Eds.). *The Wiley-Blackwell handbook of couples and family relationships* (pp. 129–143). Chichester, West Sussex, UK: Wiley.

Norris, S. M., Huss, M. T., & Palarea, R. E. (2011). A pattern of violence: Analyzing the relationship between intimate partner violence and stalking. *Violence and Victims, 26*(1), 103–115.

Norton-Hawk, M. (2004). A comparison of pimp- and non-pimp-controlled women. *Violence Against Women, 10*(2), 189–194.

Nosek, M. A. (2005). Wellness in the context of disability. In J. E. Myers & T. J. Sweeney, (Eds.), *Counseling for wellness: Theory, research, and practice* (pp. 139–150). Alexandria, VA: American Counseling Association.

Nosek, M. A. (2011). The person with a disability. In D. R. Maki, & V. M. Tarvydas (Eds.). *The professional practice of rehabilitation counseling* (pp. 111–130). New York: Springer.

Nosek, M. A., et al. (2004). The meaning of health for women with physical disabilities: A qualitative analysis. *Family & Community Health, 27*(1), 6–21.

Nour, N. M. (2000). Female circumcision and genital mutilation: A practical and sensitive approach. *Contemporary OB/GYN, 45*(3), 50–55.

Novotny, R., et al. (2011). Puberty, body fat, and breast density in girls of several ethnic groups. *American Journal of Human Biology, 23*(3), 359–365.

Nurnberg, H. G., et al. (2008). Sildenafil treatment of women with antidepressant-associated sexual dysfunction: A randomized controlled trial. *Journal of the American Medical Association, 300*(4), 395–404.

Nussbaum, M. A. (2012, April 19). Ignore the stigma and focus on the need. The *New York Times* (Online).

Nuttbrock, L., et al. (2011). A further assessment of Blanchard's typology of homosexual versus non-homosexual or autogynephilic gender dysphoria. *Archives of Sexual Behavior, 40*(2), 247–257.

O'Dell, K. M. C., & Kaiser, K. (1997). Sexual behaviour: Secrets and flies. *Current Biology, 7*(6), R345–R347.

O'Doherty, J., et al. (2003). Beauty in a smile: The role of medial orbitofrontal cortex in facial attractiveness. *Neuropsychologia, 41*(2), 147–155.

O'Donnell, L., et al. (2003). Long-term influence of sexual norms and attitudes on timing of sexual initiation among urban minority youth. *Journal of School Health, 23*(2), 68–75.

O'Donohue, W., Yeater, E. A., & Fanetti, M. (2003). Rape prevention with college males: The roles of rape myth acceptance, victim empathy, and outcome expectancies. *Journal of Interpersonal Violence, 18*(5), 513–531.

O'Keeffe, M. J., et al. (2003). Learning, cognitive, and attentional problems in adolescents born small for gestational age. *Pediatrics, 112*(2), 301–307.

O'Sullivan, L. F. (2003). The development of romantic relationships in adolescence. *Archives of Sexual Behavior, 32*(3), 292–294.

Obald, F. P. (2012). Sigmund Freud and Otto Rank: Debates and confrontations about anxiety and birth. *The International Journal of Psychoanalysis, 93*(3), 449–471.

Ofer, D., & Weitzman, L. (Eds.). (1998). *Women in the Holocaust.* New Haven, CT: Yale University Press.

Oguz, N., & Uygur, N. (2005). A case of diaper fetishism. *Türk Psikiyatri Dergisi, 16*(2), 133–138.

Okami, P., Weisner, T., & Olmstead, R. (2002). Outcome correlates of parent–child bedsharing: An eighteen-year longitudinal study. *Journal of Developmental & Behavioral Pediatrics, 23*(4), 244–253.

Olds, J. (1956). Pleasure centers in the brain. *Scientific American, 193,* 105–116.

Olds, J., & Milner, P. (1954). Positive reinforcement produced by electrical stimulation of the septal area and other regions of the rat brain. *Journal of Comparative and Physiological Psychology, 47,* 419–427.

Oleksyk, T. K., et al. (2009, March 19). Extended IL10 haplotypes and their association with HIV progression to AIDS. *Genes and Immunity.* Advance online publication.

Olfson, M., Uttaro, T., Carson, W. H., & Tafesse, E. (2005). Male sexual dysfunction and quality of life in schizophrenia. *Journal of Clinical Psychiatry, 66*(3), 331–338.

Olshen, E., et al. (2006). Use of human immunodeficiency virus postexposure prophylaxis in adolescent sexual assault victims. *Archives of Pediatric Adolescent Medicine, 160,* 674–680.

Ompad, D. C., et al. (2006). Predictors of early initiation of vaginal and oral sex among urban young adults in Baltimore, Maryland. *Archives of Sexual Behavior, 35*(1), 53–65.

Orchowski, L. M., Mastroleo, N. R., & Borsari, B. (2012). Correlates of alcohol-related sex among college students. *Psychology of Addictive Behaviors.* DOI:10.1037/a0027840

Ortega, V., Ojeda, P., Sutil, F., & Sierra, J. C. (2005). Culpabilidad sexual en adolescentes: Estudio de algunos factores relacionados. *Anales de Psicología, 21*(2), 268–275.

Osman, S. L. (2003). Predicting men's rape perceptions based on the belief that "no" really means "yes." *Journal of Applied Social Psychology, 33*(4), 683–692.

Ostrzenski, A. (2011). Cosmetic gynecology in the view of evidence-based medicine and ACOG recommendations: A review. *Archives of Gynecology and Obstetrics, 284*(3), 61–630.

Osuch, J. R., et al. (2010). Association of age at menarche with adult leg length and trunk height: Speculations in relation to breast cancer risk. *Annals of Human Biology, 37*(1), 76–85.

Owens, E. W., Behun, R. J., Manning, J. C., & Reid, R. C. (2012). The impact of Internet pornography on adolescents: Review of the research. *Sexual Addiction & Compulsivity: The Journal of Treatment & Prevention, 19*(2), 99–122.

Paintner, A., Williams, A. D., & Burd, L. (2012). Fetal alcohol spectrum disorders—Implications for child neurology, Part 2: Diagnosis and management. *Journal of Child Neurology, 27*(3), 355–362.

Pakhomou, S. M. (2006). Methodological aspects of telephone scatologia: A case study. *International Journal of Law and Psychiatry, 29*(3), 178–185.

Palace, E. M. (1995). Modification of dysfunctional patterns of sexual arousal through autonomic arousal and false physiological feedback. *Journal of Consulting and Clinical Psychology, 63,* 604–615.

Palefsky, J. M., et al. (2011). HPV vaccine against anal HPV infection and anal intraepithelial neoplasia. *New England Journal of Medicine, 365,* 1576.

Parent, C., & Bruckert, C. (2005). Sex work in establishments offering erotic services: A form of marginalised work. *Déviance et Société, 29*(1), 33–53.

Parent, M. C., Moradi, B., Rummell, C. M., & Tokar, D. M. (2011). Evidence of construct distinctiveness for conformity to masculine norms. *Psychology of Men and Masculinity, 12*(4), 354–367.

Park, C. L., Edmonson, D., & Lee, J. (2012). Development of self-regulation abilities as predictors of psychological adjustment across the first year of college. *Journal of Adult Development, 19*(1), 40–49.

Park, N., Jin, B., & Jin, S. A. (2011). Effects of self-disclosure on relational intimacy in Facebook. *Computers in Human Behavior, 27*(5), 1974–1983.

Parker-Pope, T. (2008, February 5). No answers for men with prostate cancer. *The New York Times.*

Parker-Pope, T. (2008, October 27). Love, sex and the changing landscape of infidelity. *The New York Times.*

Parker-Pope, T. (2009, May 28). Study urges weight gain be curbed in pregnancy. *The New York Times.*

Parker-Pope, T. (2009a, March 24). Screen or not? What those prostate studies mean. *The New York Times.*

Parner, E. T., et al. (2012). Parental age and autism spectrum disorders. *Annals of Epidemiology, 22*(3), 143–150.

Parrott, D., Zeichner, A., & Hoover, R. (2006). Sexual prejudice and anger network activation: Mediating role of negative affect. *Aggressive Behavior, 32*(1), 7–16.

Parsons, N. K., Richards, H. C., & Kanter, G. D. (1990). Validation of a scale to measure reasoning about abortion. *Journal of Counseling Psychology, 37,* 107–112.

Pasupathy, D., & Smith, G. C. (2005). The analysis of factors predicting antepartum stillbirth. *Minerva Ginecology, 57*(4), 397–410.

Patrick, M. E., & Schulenberg, J. E. (2011). How trajectories of reasons for alcohol use relate to trajectories of binge drinking: National panel data spanning late adolescence to early adulthood. *Developmental Psychology, 47*(2), 311–317.

Paul, B., & Shim, J. W. (2008). Gender, sexual affect, and motivations for Internet pornography use. *International Journal of Sexual Health, 20*(3), 187–199.

Pauleta, J. R., Pereira, N. M., & Graca, L. M. (2010). Sexuality during pregnancy. *Journal of Sexual Medicine, 7,* 136–142.

Pause, B. M. (2012). Processing of body odor signals by the human brain. *Chemosensory Perception, 5*(1), 55–63.

Peaceman, A. M., et al. (2009). Previous preterm cesarean delivery and risk of subsequent uterine rupture. *Obstetric Anesthesia Digest, 29*(2), 69–70.

Pear, R. (2012, January 20). U.S. denies exemption sought by Church on coverage for contraceptives. *New York Times,* p. A17.

Pedersen, W., & Hegna, K. (2003). Children and adolescents who sell sex: A community study. *Social Science & Medicine, 56*(1), 135–147.

Peluso, P. R. (Ed.). (2008). *Infidelity.* Danvers, MA: CRC Press.

Pelvic inflammatory disease, 2011. Centers for Disease Control and Prevention. (2011). Sexually transmitted diseases. Pelvic inflammatory disease (PID)—CDC fact sheet. http://www.cdc.gov/std/PID/STDFact-PID. htm (Accessed October 4, 2012).

Peplau, L. A. (2003). Human sexuality: How do men and women differ? *Current Directions in Psychological Science, 12*(2), 37–40.

Pereda, N., Guilera, G., Forns, M., & Gómez-Benito, J. (2009). The prevalence of child sexual abuse in community and student samples: A meta-analysis. *Clinical Psychology Review, 29,* 328–338.

Perelman, M. A., & Rowland, D. L. (2008). Retarded and inhibited ejaculation. In D. L. Rowland & L. Incrocci (Eds.), *Handbook of sexual and gender identity disorders* (pp. 100–121). Hoboken, NJ: Wiley.

Perez-Pena, R. (2012, July 12). In report, failures at every level of hierarchy. The New York Times, p. B12.

Peris, A. (2006, February 8). *Fertilitext: At the pharmacy: OTC.* www.fertilitext.org/ p3_pharmacy/OTCproducts.html.

Perlman, D., & Sprecher, S. (2012). Sex, intimacy, and dating. In R. D. McAnulty (Ed.). *Sex in college: The things they don't write home about* (pp. 91–118). Santa Barbara, CA: ABC-CLIO, LLC.

Perrin, M. C., Brown, A. S., & Malaspina, D. (2007, August 21). Aberrant epigenetic regulation could explain the relationship of paternal age to schizophrenia. *Schizophrenia Bulletin online.* http://schizophreniabulletin. oxfordjournals.org/cgi/content/abstract/ sbm093v1.

Perry, J. D., & Whipple, B. (1981). Pelvic muscle strength of female ejaculation: Evidence in support of a new theory of orgasm. *Journal of Sex Research, 17,* 22–39.

Perry, P. J., et al. (2001). Bioavailable testosterone as a correlate of cognition, psychological status, quality of life, and sexual function in aging males: Implications for testosterone replacement therapy. *Annals of Clinical Psychiatry, 13*(2), 75–80.

Petersen, J. L., & Hyde, J. S. (2011). Gender differences in sexual attitudes and behaviors: A review of meta-analytic results and large datasets. *Journal of Sex Research, 48*(2–3), 149–165.

Petersen, J., & Hyde, J. S. (2010). Gender differences in sexuality. *Handbook of Gender Research in Psychology, 6,* 471–491.

Peterson, C. K., & Harmon-Jones, E. (2011). Anger and testosterone: Evidence that situationally-induced anger related to situationally-induced testosterone. *Emotion,* DOI:10.1037/a0025300

Peterson, Z. D., Voller, E. K., Polusny, M. A., & Murdoch, M. (2010). Prevalence and consequences of adult sexual assault of men: Review of empirical findings and state of the literature. *Clinical Psychology Review, 31,* 1–24.

Philaretou, A. G. (2006). Female exotic dancers: Intrapersonal and interpersonal perspectives. *Sexual Addiction & Compulsivity, 13*(1), 41–52.

Phillips, K. (2009, November 18). Sebelius on mammograms: Don't change what you're doing. *The New York Times (Online).*

Phipps, A. I., et al. (2011). Long-term use of continuous-combined estrogen-progestin hormone therapy and the risk of endometrial cancer. *Cancer Causes and Control, 22*(2), 1639–1646.

Phoenix, C. H. (2009). Organizing action of prenatally administered testosterone propionate on the tissues mediating mating behavior in the female guinea pig. *Hormones and Behavior, 55*(5), 566.

Pierce, A., Miller, G., Arden, R., & Gottfredson, L. S. (2009). Why is intelligence correlated with semen quality? *Communicative and Integrative Biology, 2*(5), 1–3.

Pike, L. B. (2005, July 1). *Sexuality and your child.* MU Extension, University of Missouri–Columbia.

Pinkerton, S. D., Bogart, L. M., Cecil, H., & Abramson, P. R. (2002). Factors associated with masturbation in collegiate sample. *Journal of Psychology & Human Sexuality, 14*(2–3), 103–121.

Planned Parenthood Federation of America. (2006). www.plannedparenthood.org/pp2/ portal.

Plant, E. A., Hyde, J. S., Keltner, D., & Devine, P. G. (2000). The gender stereotyping of emotions. *Psychology of Women Quarterly, 24*(1), 81–92.

Plante, R. F. (2006). The rise of Viagra: How the little blue pill changed sex in America. *Sexualities, 9*(3), 379–380.

Plaut, S. M. (2006). Consent to sexual relations. *Archives of Sexual Behavior, 35*(1), 101–103.

Plomin, R., & Asbury, K. (2005). Nature and nurture: Genetic and environmental influences on behavior. *Annals of the American Academy of Political and Social Science, 600,* 86–98.

Polansky, D. C. (2006). The big book of masturbation: From angst to zeal. *Journal of Sex & Marital Therapy, 32*(1), 75–78.

Poll shows decline in sex by high school students. (1998, September 18). *The New York Times,* p. A26.

Pollack, A. (2009, April 14). Promising test for Dendreon's prostate cancer drug. *The New York Times.*

Pollack, H. A. (2001). Sudden infant death syndrome, maternal smoking during pregnancy, and the cost-effectiveness of smoking cessation intervention. *American Journal of Public Health, 91*(3), 432–436.

Polusny, M. A., & Arbisi, P. A. (2006). Assessment of psychological distress and disability after sexual assault in adults. In G. Young et al. (Eds.), *Psychological knowledge in court: PTSD, pain, and TBI* (pp. 97–125). Springer Science + Business Media.

Pommier, C. D., et al. (2008). Improved breast cancer survival among hormone replacement therapy users is durable after 5 years of additional follow-up. *American Journal of Surgery, 196,* 505–511.

Poppen, P. J., et al. (2005). Serostatus disclosure, seroconcordance, partner relationship, and unprotected anal intercourse among HIV-positive Latino men who have sex with men. *AIDS Education and Prevention, 17*(3), 227–237.

Porst, H., et al. (2008). The Premature Ejaculation Prevalence and Attitudes (PEPA) Survey: Prevalence, comorbidities, and professional help-seeking. *European Urology, 51*(3), 816–824.

Potosky, A. L., et al. (2000). Health outcomes after prostatectomy or radiotherapy for prostate cancer: Results from the Prostate Cancer Outcomes Study. *Journal of the National Cancer Institute, 92,* 1582–1592.

Potter, S. J., et al. (2009). Empowering bystanders to prevent campus violence against women. *Violence Against Women, 15*(1), 106–121.

Potts, A., Grace, V. M., Vares, T., & Gavey, N. (2006). "Sex for life?" Men's counter-stories on "erectile dysfunction," male sexuality and ageing. *Sociology of Health & Illness, 28*(3), 306–329.

Potts, M. (2006). China's one child policy. *British Medical Journal, 333,* 361–362.

Powell, E. (1991). *Talking back to sexual pressure.* Minneapolis: CompCare Publishers.

Pradhan, D. S., et al. (2010). Aggressive interactions rapidly increase androgen synthesis in the brain during the non-breeding season. *Hormones and Behavior, 57*(4–5), 381–389.

Prakash, J., et al. (2010). Does androgyny have psychoprotective attributes? A cross-sectional community-based study. *Industrial Psychiatry Journal, 19*(2), 119–124.

Premberg, A., & Lundgren, I. (2006). Fathers' experiences of childbirth education. *Journal of Perinatal Education, 15*(2), 21–28.

Prentice, R. L., et al. (2006). Low-fat dietary pattern and risk of invasive breast cancer: The Women's Health Initiative Randomized Controlled Dietary Modification Trial. *Journal of the American Medical Association, 295,* 629–642.

Preterm J., & Valkenburg, P. M. (2011). The use of sexually explicit Internet material and its antecedents: a longitudinal comparison of adolescents and adults. *Archives of Sexual Behavior, 40*(5), 1015–1025.

Preti, G., et al. (1986). Human axillary secretions influence women's menstrual cycles: The role of donor extract of females. *Hormones and Behavior, 20,* 474–482.

Preti, G., Wysocki, C. J., Barnhart, K. T., Sondheimer, S. J., & Leyden, J. J. (2003). Male axillary extracts contain pheromones that affect pulsatile secretion of luteinizing hormone and mood in women recipients. *Biology of Reproduction, 68*(6), 2107–2113.

Price, M., Kafka, M. P., Commons, M. L., Gutheil, T. G., & Simpson, W. (2002). Telephone scatologia: Comorbidity with other paraphilias and paraphilia-related disorders. *International Journal of Law & Psychiatry, 25*(1), 37–49.

Proctor, F., Wagner, N., & Butler, J. (1974). The differentiation of male and female orgasm: An experimental study. In N. Wagner (Ed.), *Perspectives on human sexuality.* New York: Behavioral Publications.

Psychology Today. (2006, July 25.) www. psychologytoday.com/images/.PT_MediaKit_Health_2006.pdf.

Public Policy Polling. (2012, February 10). Our polling on the birth control issue. http://www.publicpolicypolling.com/main/2012/02/our-polling-on-the-birth-control-issue.html. (Accessed June 23, 2012).

Puente, S., & Cohen, D. (2003). Jealousy and the meaning (or nonmeaning) of violence. *Personality & Social Psychology Bulletin, 29*(4), 449–460.

Punyanunt-Carter, N. M. (2006). An analysis of college students' self-disclosure behaviors on the Internet. *College Student Journal, 40*(2), 329–331.

Purdie, M. P., et al. (2011). The effects of acute alcohol intoxication, partner risk level, and general intention to have unprotected sex on women's sexual decision making with a new partner. *Experimental and Clinical Psychopharmacology, 19*(5), 378–388.

Puri, S., & Nachtigall, R. D. (2009). The ethics of sex selection: A comparison of the attitudes and experiences of primary care physicians and physician providers of clinical sex selection services. *Fertility and Sterility,* in press.

Puts, D. A., Welling, L. L. M., Burriss, R. P., & Dawood, K. (2011). Men's masculinity and attractiveness predict their female partners' reported orgasm frequency and timing. *Evolution and Human Behavior, 33*(1), 1.

Quartaro, G. K., & Spier, T. E. (2002). We'd like to ask you some questions, but we have to find you first: Internet-based study of lesbian clients in therapy with lesbian feminist therapists. *Journal of Technology in Human Services, 19*(2–3), 109–118.

Quayle, E. (2008). Online sex offending: Psychopathology and theory. In D. R. Laws and W. T. O'Donohue (Eds.), *Sexual deviance: Theory, assessment, and treatment* (2nd ed., pp. 439–458). New York: Guilford Press.

Quayle, E. (2012). Pedophilia, child porn, and cyberpredators. In C. D. Bryant (Ed.). *The Routledge handbook of deviant behavior* (pp. 390–396). New York: Routledge.

Quayle, E., Taylor, M. (2002). Child pornography and the Internet: Perpetuating a cycle of abuse. *Deviant Behavior, 23*(4), 331–362.

Quayle, E., Taylor, M. (2003). Model of problematic Internet use in people with sexual interest in children. *CyberPsychology & Behavior, 6*(1), 93–106.

Quinsey, V. L., Harris, G. T., Rice, M. E., & Cormier, C. A. (2006). Sex offenders. In V. L. Quinsey, G. T. Harris, M. E. Rice, & C. A. Cormier (Eds.), *Violent offenders: Appraising and managing risk. The law and public policy* (2nd ed.. pp. 131–151). Washington, DC: American Psychological Association.

Rabin, R. (2006, January 31). Rethinking hormones, again. *The New York Times* (Online).

Rabin, R. C. (2011, August 22). Circumcise or don't? Quandary for parents. *New York Times,* p. D5.

Rabin, R. C. (2011, December 14). Nearly 1 in 5 women in U.S. survey say they have been sexually assaulted. *The New York Times,* p. A32.

Ragsdale, K., et al. (2012). High-risk drinking among female college drinkers at two reporting intervals: Comparing Spring Break to the 30 days prior. *Sexuality Research and Social Policy, 9*(1), 31–40.

Rahimi, R., & Liston, D. D. (2012). *Pervasive vulnerabilities: Sexual harassment in school.* New York: Peter Lang.

Raichle, K., & Lambert, A. J. (2000). The role of political ideology in mediating judgments of blame in rape victims and their assailants: A test of the just world, personal responsibility, and legitimization hypotheses. *Personality & Social Psychology Bulletin, 26*(7), 853–863.

Rakic, Z., Starcevic, V., Starcevic, V. P., & Marinkovic, J. (1997). Testosterone treatment in men with erectile disorder and low levels of total testosterone in serum. *Archives of Sexual Behavior, 26*(5), 495–504.

Rako, S. (2003). *No more periods? The risks of menstrual suppression and other cutting-edge issues about hormones and women's health.* New York: Crown.

Ralph, D., & McNicholas, T. (2000). UK management guidelines for erectile dysfunction. *British Medical Journal, 321,* 499–503.

Rambo, C., & Pruit, J. (2012). In C. D. Bryant (Ed.). *The Routledge handbook of deviant behavior* (pp. 397–402). New York: Routledge.

Ramos, N. (2012, April 19). Such oppression can never be safe. The *New York Times* (Online).

Randolph, M. E., et al. (2009). Alcohol use and sexual risk behavior among college students. *The American Journal of Drug and Alcohol Abues, 35*(2), 80–84.

Raphael, J., & Shapiro, D. L. (2005). Reply to Weitzer. *Violence Against Women, 11*(7), 965–970.

Rasmussen, K. M., et al. (2009, May 27). Institute of Medicine report. In T. Parker-Pope, Study urges weight gain be curbed in pregnancy. *The New York Times,* May 28.

Rasmussen, P. R., & Kilborne, K. J. (2008). Sex in intimate relationships: Variations and challenges. In

Rathus, S. A. (2011). *Childhood and Adolescence: Voyages in development.* (4th ed.) Belmont, CA: Cengage.

Rathus, S. A. (2014). *Childhood and adolescence: Voyages in development* (5th ed.). Belmont, CA: Cengage.

Ratnayake, H. (2011, April 29). Co-sleeping with infants can be risky, experts say. *USA Today.*

Rawson, R. A., Washton, A., Domier, C. P., & Reiber, C. (2002). Drugs and sexual effects: Role of drug type and gender. *Journal of Substance Abuse Treatment, 22*(2), 103–108.

Reddy, D. M., et al. (2002). Effect of mandatory parental notification on adolescent girls' use of sexual health care services. *Journal of the American Medical Association, 288,* 710–714.

Reece, M., et al. (2009). Prevalence and characteristics of vibrator use by men in the United States. *Journal of Sexual Medicine, 6*(7), 1867–1874.

Reece, M., et al. (2010). Background and considerations on the National Survey of Sexual Health and Behavior (NSSHB) from the investigators. *Journal of Sexual Medicine, 7*(suppl 5), 243–245.

Reece, M., et al. (2010). Sexual behaviors, relationships, and perceived health among adult men in the United States: Results from a national probability sample. *Journal of Sexual Medicine, 7*(suppl 5), 291–304.

Reece, M., Herbenick, D., Schick, V., Sanders, S. A., Dodge, B., & Fortenberry, J. D. (2010). Sexual behaviors, relationships, and perceived health among adult men in the United States: Results from a national probability sample. *Journal of Sexual Medicine, 7*(suppl 5), 291–304.

Reed, M., & Lampe, M. S. (2003). *Margaret Sanger: Her life in her words.* Barricade Books.

Reed, S. C., Levin, F. R., & Evans, S. M. (2008). Changes in mood, cognitive performance and appetite in the late luteal and follicular phases of the menstrual cycle in women with and without PMDD (premenstrual dysphoric disorder). *Hormones and Behavior, 54*(1), 185–193.

Regnerus, M. (2012). How different are the adult children of parents who have same-sex relationships? Findings from the New Family Structures Study. *Social Science Research, 41*(4), 752–770.

Reichenberg, A., et al. (2006). Advancing paternal age and autism. *Archives of General Psychiatry, 63*(9), 1026–1032.

Reiner, W. G. (2000). Cited in Study of children born without penises finds nature determines gender. Associated Press. (Online).

Reinisch, J. M. (1990). *The Kinsey Institute new report on sex: What you must know to be sexually literate.* New York: St. Martin's Press.

Reis, H. T., & Aron, A. (2008). Love: What is it, why does it matter, and how does it operate? *Perspectives on Psychological Science, 3*(1), 80–86.

Reis, H. T., Maniaci, M. R., Caprariello, P. A., Eastwick, P. W., & Finkel, E. L. (2011). Familiarity does indeed promote attraction in live interaction. *Journal of Personality and Social Psychology, 101*(3), 557–570.

Reissing, E. D. (2012). Consultation and treatment history and causal attributions in an online sample of women with lifelong and acquired vaginismus. *Journal of Sexual Medicine, 9*(1), 251–258.

Renk, K., Liljequist, L., Simpson, J. E., & Phares, V. (2005). Gender and age differences in the topics of parent–adolescent conflict. *Family Journal: Counseling and Therapy for Couples and Families, 13*(2), 139–149.

Rerks-Ngarm, S., et al. (2009). Vaccination with ALVAC and AIDSVAX to prevent HIV-1 infection in Thailand. *New England Journal of Medicine online.* www.nejm.org October 20, 2009 (10.1056/NEJMoa0908492)

Resick, P. A. (2003). Post hoc reasoning in possible cases of child sexual abuse: Just say no. *Clinical Psychology: Science & Practice, 10*(3), 349–351.

Resnik, J. (2011). Cited in Stout, H. (2011, November 6). Less "He Said, She Said" in Sex Harassment Cases. *The New York Times,* p. B10.

Reynolds, A., & Caron, S. L. (2000). How intimate relationships are impacted when heterosexual men crossdress. *Journal of Psychology & Human Sexuality, 12*(3), 63–77.

Reynolds, C. A., Barlow, T., & Pedersen, N. L. (2006). Alcohol, tobacco and caffeine use: Spouse similarity processes. *Behavior Genetics, 36*(2), 201–215.

Reynolds, S. J., et al. (2004). Male circumcision and risk of HIV-1 and other sexually transmitted infections in India. *The Lancet, 363*(9414), 1039.

Rhoades, G. K., Kamp Dush, C. M., Atkins, D. C., Stanley, S. M., & Markman, H. J. (2011). Breaking up is hard to do: The impact of unmarried relationship dissolution on mental health and life satisfaction. *Journal of Family Psychology, 25*(3), 366–374.

Rhoades, G. K., Stanley, S. M., & Markman, H. J. (2009). Couples' reasons for cohabitation. *Journal of Family Issues, 30*(2), 233–258.

Ricci, E., Parazzini, F, & Pardi, G. (2000). Caesarean section and antiretroviral treatment. *The Lancet, 355*(9202), 496–502.

Rice, M. E., & Harris, G. T. (2011). Is androgen deprivation therapy effective in the treatment of sex offenders? *Psychology, Public Policy, and Law, 17*(2), 315–332.

Rice, M. E., Harris, G. T., & Quinsey, V. L. (1990). A follow-up of rapists assessed in a maximum-security psychiatric facility. *Journal of Interpersonal Violence, 5,* 435–448.

Rice, M. E., Quinsey, V. L., & Harris, G. T. (1991). Sexual recidivism among child molesters released from a maximum security psychiatric institution. *Journal of Consulting and Clinical Psychology, 59,* 381–386.

Rich, F. (2009, June 28). 40 years later, still second-class Americans. *The New York Times,* p. WK 8.

Richters, J., Hendry, O., & Kippax, S. (2003). When safe sex isn't safe. *Culture, Health & Sexuality, 5*(1), 37–52.

Rickwood, A. M. K., Kenny, S. E., & Donnell, S. C. (2000). Towards evidence based circumcision of English boys: Survey of trends in practice. *British Medical Journal, 321,* 792–793.

Rieger, G., Linsenmeier, J. A. W., Gygax, L., & Bailey, J. M. (2008). Sexual orientation and childhood gender nonconformity: Evidence from home videos. *Developmental Psychology, 44*(1), 46–58.

Riggio, R. E., & Woll, S. B. (1984). The role of nonverbal cues and physical attractiveness in the selection of dating partners. *Journal of Social and Personal Relationships, 1,* 347–357.

Rimm, E. (May 2000). *Lifestyle may play role in potential for impotence.* Presented at the annual meeting of the American Urological Association, Atlanta, GA.

Rincon, M., & Lam, B. T. (2011). The perspectives of Latina mothers on Latina lesbian families. *Journal of Human Behavior in the Social Environment, 21*(4), 334–349.

Ring-Cassidy, E., & Gentles, I. (2002). *Women's health after abortion: The medical and psychological evidence.* Toronto, Ontario: The deVeber Institute.

Ritner, C., & Roth, J. (1993). *Different voices: Women and the Holocaust.* New York: Paragon House.

Roach, C. M. (2011). *Stripping, sex, and popular culture.* London: Berg Publishers.

Roan, S. (2006, July 22). Newer contraceptives put an end to "the period." *Los Angeles Times.* (Online).

Robbers, S. C. C., et al. (2011). Pre-divorce problems in 3-year-olds. *Social Psychiatry and Psychiatric Epidemiology, 46*(4), 311–319.

Robbins, C. L., et al. (2011). Prevalence, frequency, and associations of masturbation with partnered sexual behaviors among U.S. adolescents. *Archives of Pediatrics & Adolescent Medicine, 165*(12), 1087–1093.

Robert-McComb, J. J. (2008). The female athletic triad: Disordered eating, amenorrhea, and osteoporosis. In Robert-McComb, J. J., Norman, R., & Zumwalt, M. (Eds.), *The active female: Health issues throughout the lifespan* (pp. 81–92). Totowa, NJ: Humana Press.

Roberts, S. (2006, October 15). It's official: To be married means to be outnumbered. *The New York Times* (Online).

Roberts, S. (2008, March 20). Podcast: Oh, these government affairs. http://cityroom.blogs.nytimes.com/2008/03/20/podcast-oh-these-government-affairs/?scp=5&sq=Spitzer% 20Vitter&st=cse

Robinson, J. D., & Parks, C. W. (2003). Lesbian and bisexual women's sexual fantasies, psychological adjustment, and close relationship functioning. *Journal of Psychology & Human Sexuality, 15*(4), 185–203.

Roddy, R. E., et al. (1998). A controlled trial of nonoxynol 9 film to reduce male-to-female transmission of sexually transmitted diseases. *New England Journal of Medicine, 339,* 504–510.

Rodriguez, I., Greer, C. A., Mok, M. Y., & Mombaerts, P. (2000). A putative pheromone receptor gene expressed in human olfactory mucosa. *Nature Genetics, 26*(1), 18–19.

Roesler, A., & Witztum, E. (2000). Pharmacotherapy of paraphilias in the next millennium. *Behavioral Sciences & the Law, 18*(1), 43–56.

Rojewski, J. W. (2005). A typical American family? How adoptive families acknowledge and incorporate Chinese cultural heritage in their lives. *Child & Adolescent Social Work Journal, 22*(2), 133–164.

Romero-Daza, N., Weeks, M., & Singer, M. (2005). Conceptualizing the impact of indirect violence on HIV risk among women involved in street-level prostitution. *Aggression and Violent Behavior, 10*(2), 153–170.

Rosario, M., Schrimshaw, E. E., Hunter, J., & Levy-Warren, A. (2009). The coming-out process of young lesbian and bisexual women: Are there butch/femme differences in sexual identity development? *Archives of Sexual Behavior, 38*(1), 34–49.

Roscoe, W. (2000). *Changing ones: Third and fourth genders in native North America.* Palgrave: Macmillan.

Rosen, R. C., & Laumann, E. O. (2003). The prevalence of sexual problems in women: How valid are comparisons across studies? Commentary on Bancroft, Loftus, and Long's (2003) "Distress about sex: A national survey of women in heterosexual relationships." *Archives of Sexual Behavior, 32*(3), 209–211.

Rosenbaum, J. E. (2006). Reborn a virgin: Adolescents' retracting of virginity pledges and sexual histories. *American Journal of Public Health, 96,* 1098–1103.

Rosenblatt, P. C., & Rieks, S. J. (2009). No compromise: Couples dealing with issues for which they do not see a compromise. *The American Journal of Family Therapy, 37*(3), 196–208.

Rosenthal, A. M., Sylva, D., Safron, A., & Bailey, J. M. (2012). The male bisexuality debate revisited: Some bisexual men have bisexual arousal patterns. *Archives of Sexual Behavior, 41*(1), 135–147.

Rosik, C. H. (2003). Motivational, ethical, and epistemological foundations in the treatment of unwanted homoerotic attraction. *Journal of Marital & Family Therapy, 29*(1), 13–28.

Rosky, C. J. (2009). Like father, like son: Homosexuality, parenthood, and the gender of homophobia. *Yale Journal of Law & Feminism, 20,* 257.

Rospenda, K. M., Richman, J. A., Ehmke, J. L. Z., & Zlatoper, K. W. (2005). Is workplace harassment hazardous to your health? *Journal of Business and Psychology, 20*(1), 95–110.

Ross, J. L., Roeltgen, D., Feuillan, P., Kushner, H., & Cutler, W. B. (2000). Use of estrogen in young girls with Turner syndrome: Effects on memory. *Neurology, 54*(1), 164–170.

Rothrauff, T., Middlemiss, W., & Jacobson, L. (2004). Comparison of American and Austrian infants' and toddlers' sleep habits: A retrospective, exploratory study. *North American Journal of Psychology, 6*(1), 125–144.

Roughgarden, J. (2004). *Evolution's rainbow: Diversity, gender, and sexuality in nature and people.* University of California Press.

Rowland, D. L., & Incrocci, L. (2008). *Handbook of sexual and gender identity disorders.* Hoboken, NJ: Wiley.

Royce, R. A., Seña, A., Cates, W., Jr., & Cohen, M. S. (1997). Sexual transmission of HIV. *New England Journal of Medicine, 336,* 1072–1078.

Rozee, P. D., & Koss, M. P. (2001). Rape: A century of resistance. *Psychology of Women Quarterly, 25*(4), 295–311.

Rubenson, B., Hanh, L. T., Höjer, B., & Johansson, E. (2005). Young sex-workers in Ho Chi Minh City telling their life stories. *Childhood: A Global Journal of Child Research, 12*(3), 391–411.

Rubin, H., & Campbell, L. (2012). Day-to-day changes in intimacy predict heightened relationship passion, sexual occurrence, and sexual satisfaction: A dyadic diary analysis. *Social Psychological and Personality Science, 3*(2), 224–231.

Rule, N. O., Ambady, N., & Hallett, K. C. (2009). Female sexual orientation is perceived accurately, rapidly, and automatically from the face and its features. *Journal of Experimental Social Psychology, 45,* 1245–1251.

Rule, N. O., Ishii, K., Ambady, N., Rosen, K. S., & Hallett, K. C. (2011). Found in translation: Cross-cultural consensus in the accurate categorization of male sexual orientation. *Personality and Social Psychology Bulletin, 37,* 1499–1507.

Rupp, H. A., & Wallen, K. (2009). Sex-specific content preferences for visual sexual stimuli. *Archives of Sexual Behavior, 38*(3), 417–426.

Rupp, H., et al. (2009). Neural activation in women in response to masculinized male faces: Mediation by hormones and psychosexual factors. *Evolution and Human Behavior, 30*(1), 1–10.

Ruppel, H. (2009, March 26). In B. Alexander, "Sex surrogates" put personal touch on therapy: Despite dubious legality, some counselors still prescribe practice to patients. http://www.msnbc.msn.com/id/29881206/.

Rusbult, C. E., & Van Lange, P. A. M. (2003). Interdependence, interaction and relationships. *Annual Review of Psychology, 54,* 351–375.

Rusbult, C. E., Abnew, C. R., & Arriaga, X. B. (2012). The investment model of commitment processes. In P. A. M. Van Lange, et al. (Eds.), *Handbook of theories of social psychology, Vol. 2* (pp. 218–231). Thousand Oaks, CA: Sage.

Rusbult, C. E., Martz, J. M., & Agnew, C. R. (1998). The Investment Model Scale: Measuring commitment level, satisfaction level, quality of alternatives, and investment size. *Personal Relationships, 5*(4), 357–391.

Rush, G., & Schapiro, R. (2009, April 19). Slain masseuse Julissa Brisman once worked for madam Kristin Davis. *Daily News.*

Russell, S. T., van Campen, K. S., & Muraco, J. A. (2012). Sexuality development in adolescence. In L. M. Carpenter, & J. DeLamater (Eds.), *Sex for life* (pp. 70–87). New York: New York University Press.

Russo, N. F., Pirlott, A. G., & Cohen, A. B. (2012). The psychology of women and gender in international perspective: Issues and challenges. *International and Cultural Psychology,* 157–178. DOI:10.1007/978-1-4614-0073-8_8.

Ryan, R. M., & Ryan, W. S. (2012, April 27). Homophobic: Maybe you're gay. *New York Times,* SR12.

Saad, L. (2009, May 15). More Americans "prolife" than "pro-choice" for first time. *The New York Times.*

Saad, L. (2012, May 23). Pro-choice Americans at record-low 41%. http://www.gallup.com/poll/154838/pro-choice-americans-record-low.aspx (Accessed June 23, 2012).

Sadalla, E. K., Kenrick, D. T., & Vershure, B. (1987). Dominance and heterosexual attraction. *Journal of Personality and Social Psychology, 52,* 730–738.

Sadker, M., & Sadker, D. (1994). *How America's schools cheat girls.* New York: Scribners.

Sadler, A. G., Booth, B. M., Nielson, D., & Doebbeling, B. N. (2000). Health-related consequences of physical and sexual violence: Women in the military. *Obstetrics & Gynecology, 96*(3), 473–480.

Sagan, C., & Dryan, A. (1990, April 22). The question of abortion: A search for answers. *Parade Magazine,* pp. 4–8.

Sagarin, B. J., Becker, D. V., Guadagno, R. E., Nicastle, L. D., & Millevoi, A. (2003). Sex differences (and similarities) in jealousy: The moderating influence of infidelity experience and sexual orientation of the infidelity. *Evolution & Human Behavior, 24*(1), 17–23.

Sagarin, B. J., et al. (2012). Sex differences in jealousy: A meta-analytic examination. *Evolution and Human Behavior.* Retrieved from http://dx.doi.org/10.1016/j.evolhumbehav.2012.02.006 (Accessed September 15, 2012).

Saigal, S., et al. (2006). Transition of extremely low-birth-weight infants from adolescence to young adulthood. *Journal of the American Medical Association, 295,* 667–675.

Saks, B. R. (2008). Common issues in female sexual dysfunction. *Psychiatric Times, 25*(5), 2.

Saleh, F. M. (2009). Pharmacological treatment of paraphilic sex offenders. In In F. M. Saleh et al. (Eds.), *Sex offenders: Identification, risk assessment, treatment, and legal issue* (pp. 189–210). New York: Oxford University Press.

Salska, I., et al. (2008). Conditional mate preferences: Factors influencing preferences for height. *Personality and Individual Differences, 44*(1), 203–215.

Sanders, S. A., Yarber, W. L., Kaufman, E. L., Crosby, R. A., Graham, C.A., & Milhausen, R. R. (2012). Condom use errors and problems: A global view. *Sexual Health, 9*(1), 81–95.

Sanders, T. (2005). "It's just acting": Sex workers' strategies for capitalizing on sexuality. *Gender, Work & Organization, 12*(4), 319–342.

Sandin, S., et al. (2012). Advancing maternal age is associated with increasing risk for autism: A review and meta-analysis. *Journal of the American Academy of Child & Adolescent Psychiatry, 51*(5), 477–486.

Sanger, M. (1938). *Margaret Sanger: An autobiography.* New York: Norton.

Sangrador, J. L., & Yela, C. (2000). "What is beautiful is loved": Physical attractiveness in love relationships in a representative sample. *Social Behavior & Personality, 28*(3) 207–218.

Santelli, J. S., et al. (2003). Reproductive health in school-based health centers: Findings from the 1998–99 census of school-based health centers. *Journal of Adolescent Health, 32*(6), 443–451.

Santtila, P., Sandnabba, N. K., Alison, L., & Nordling, N. (2002). Investigating the underlying structure in sadomasochistically oriented behavior. *Archives of Sexual Behavior, 31*(2), 185–196.

Sarrel, P., & Masters, W. (1982). Sexual molestation of men by women. *Archives of Sexual Behavior, 11,* 117–131.

Sartorius, G. A., & Nieschlag, E. (2009). Paternal age and reproduction. *Human Reproduction Update,* DOI:10.1093/humupd/dmp027.

Sasaki, E., et al. (2008). Adverse birth outcomes associated with maternal smoking and polymorphisms in the N-nitrosamine-metabolizing enzyme genes NQ01 and CYP2E1. *American Journal of Epidemiology,* DOI: 10.1093/aje/kwm360.

Saul, J. M. (2003). *Feminism: Issues & arguments.* Oxford: Oxford University Press.

Save the Children. (2008). Annual report. www.savethechildren.org.

Save the Children. (2008). *State of the world's mothers 2008.* www.savethechildren.org/publications/mothers/2008/SOWM-2008-full-report.pdf.

Save the Children. (2011). *State of the World's Mothers 2011.* Westport, CT: Save the Children. www.savethechildren.org

Savic, I., & Lindström, P. (2008). PET and MRI show differences in cerebral asymmetry and functional connectivity between homo- and heterosexual subjects. Published online on June 16, 2008. *Proceedings of the National Academy of Sciences.* USA, 10.1073/pnas.0801566105.

Savic, I., Berglund, H., & Lindström, P. (2005). Brain response to putative pheromones in homosexual men. *Proceedings of the National Association of Sciences, 102,* 7356–7361.

Savic, I., Garcia-Falgueras, A., & Swaab, D. F. (2010). Sexual differentiation of the human brain in relation to gender identity and sexual orientation. In I. Savic (Ed.), *Sex differences in the human brain, Their underpinnings and implications. Progress in Brain Research, 186* (pp. 41–64). New York: Elsevier.

Savic, I., Garcia-Falgueras, A., & Swaab, D. F. (2010). Sexual differentiation of the human brain in relation to gender identity and sexual orientation. In I. Savic. (Ed.), *Progress in brain research: Sex differences in the human brain, their underpinnings and implications, 186,* 41–64. Amsterdam: Elsevier.

Savin-Williams, R. C. (2006). Who's gay? Does it matter? *Current Directions in Psychological Science, 15*(1), 40–44.

Savin-Williams, R. C., & Diamond, L. M. (2000). Sexual identity trajectories among sexual-minority youths: Gender comparisons. *Archives of Sexual Behavior, 29*(6), 607–627.

Savin-Williams, R., Joyner, K., & Rieger, G. (2012). Prevalence and stability of self-reported sexual orientation identity during young adulthood. *Archives of Sexual Behavior, 41*(1), 103–110.

Sax, L. (2002). How common is intersex? A response to Anne Fausto-Sterling. *Journal of Sex Research, 39,* 174–179.

Saywitz, K. J., Mannarino, A. P., Berliner, L., & Cohen, J. A. (2000). Treatment for sexually abused children and adolescents. *American Psychologist, 55*(9), 1040–1049.

Schaller, S., & Træen, B. (2008).Attitudes toward pornography, self-esteem and feelings about sex in a longitudinal sample of Norwegian adolescents. *Sexologies, 17*(Suppl. 1), S148.

Schieve, L. A., et al. (1999). Live-birth rates and multiple-birth risk using in vitro fertilization. *Journal of the American Medical Association, 282*, 1832–1838.

Schlichter, A. (2004). *Contesting "straights," "lesbians," "queer heterosexuals," and the critique of heteronormativity.* Binghamton, NY: Haworth.

Schmidt, P. J., et al. (1998). Differential behavioral effects of gonadal steroids in women with and in those without premenstrual syndrome. *New England Journal of Medicine, 338*, 209–216.

Schmidt, S. R., Bonner, B. L., & Chaffin, M. (2012). Understanding and treating adolescents with illegal sexual behavior. In P. Goodyear-Brown (Ed.). *Handbook of child sexual abuse: Identification, assessment, and treatment* (pp. 469–485). Hoboken, NJ: Wiley.

Schmitt, D. (2008). An evolutionary perspective on mate choice and relationship initiation. In S. Sprecher, A. Wenzel, & J. Harvey (Eds.), *Handbook of relationship initiation* (pp. 55–74). New York: CRC Press.

Schmitt, D. P. (2003). Universal sex differences in the desire for sexual variety: Tests from 52 nations, 6 continents, and 13 islands. *Journal of Personality and Social Psychology, 85*(1), 85–104.

Schmitt, D. P., et al. (2012). A reexamination of sex differences in sexuality: New studies reveal old truths. *Current Directions in Psychological Science, 21*(2), 135–139.

Schmitt, D., Jonason, P. K., Byerley, G. J., Flores, S. D., Illbeck, B. E., O'Leary, K. N., & Qudrat, A. (2012). A reexamination of sex differences in sexuality: New studies reveal old truths. *Current Directions in Psychological Science, 21*(2), 135–139.

Schmitt, M. T., Branscombe, N. R., & Postmes, T. (2003). Women's emotional responses to the pervasiveness of gender discrimination. *European Journal of Social Psychology, 33*(3), 297–312.

Schneider, J. P. (2003). The impact of compulsive cybersex behaviours on the family. *Sexual and Relationship Therapy, 18*(3), 329–354.

Schneider, J. P. (2004). Editorial: Sexual addiction & compulsivity: Twenty years of the field, ten years of the journal. *Sexual Addiction & Compulsivity, 11*(1–2), 3–5.

Schneider, J. P. (2005). Addiction is addiction is addiction. *Sexual Addiction & Compulsivity, 12*(2/3), 75–77.

Schneider, J. P., Weiss, R., & Samenow, C. (2012). Really cheating? Understanding the emotional reactions and clinical treatment of spouses and partners affected by cybersex infidelity. *Sexual Addiction and Compulsivity, 19*(1–2), 123–139.

Schneidewind-Skibbe, A., Hayes, R. D., Koochaki, P. E., Meyer, J., & Dennerstein, L. (2007). The frequency of sexual intercourse reported by women: A Review of community-based studies and factors limiting their conclusions. *Journal of Sexual Medicine, 5*(2), 301–335.

Schober, J. M., et al. (2005). Leuprolide acetate suppresses pedophilic urges and arousability. *Archives of Sexual Behavior, 34*(6), 691–705.

Schramm, D. G., Marshall, J. P., Harris, V. W., & Lee, T. R. (2012). Religiosity, homogamy, and marital adjustment. *Journal of Family Issues, 33*(2), 246–268.

Schröder, F. H., et al. (2009). Screening and prostate-cancer mortality in a randomized European study. *New England Journal of Medicine, 360*, 1320–328.

Schroeder–Printzen, I., et al. (2000). Surgical therapy in infertile men with ejaculatory duct obstruction: Technique and outcome of a standardized surgical approach. *Human Reproduction, 15*, 1364–1368.

Schrut, A. (2005). A psychodynamic (nonoedipal) and brain function hypothesis regarding a type of male sexual masochism. *Journal of the American Academy of Psychoanalysis and Dynamic Psychiatry, 33*(2), 333–349.

Schtscherbyna, A., Soares, E., de Oliveira, F., & Ribeiro, B. (2009). Female athlete triad in elite swimmers of the city of Rio de Janeiro, Brazil. *Nutrition, 25*(6), 634–639.

Schultz, W. W., et al. (2005). Women's sexual pain and its management. *Journal of Sexual Medicine, 2*(3), 301–316.

Schwam-Harris, M. (2008). Achieving permanency in public agency adoptions: Secondary analyses of the national survey of child and adolescent well-being data. *Dissertation Abstracts International Section A: Humanities and Social Sciences, 68*(9-A), 4073.

Schwartz, C. R., & Mare, R. D. (2012). The proximate determinants of educational homogamy. *Demography, 49*(2), 629–650.

Schwartz, P., & Young, L. (2009). Sexuality Sexual satisfaction in committed relationships. *Research and Social Policy: Journal of NSRC, 6*(1), 1–17.

Sciolino, E., & Mekhennet, S. (2008, June 11). In Europe, debate over Islam and virginity. *The New York Times.*

Scott, B. E., Weiss, H. A., & Viljoen, J. I. (2005). The acceptability of male circumcision as an HIV intervention among a rural Zulu population, KwaZulu-Natal, South Africa. *AIDS Care, 17*(3), 304–313.

Scott-Sheldon, L. A. J., Carey, M. P., & Carey, K. B. (2010). Alcohol and risky sexual behavior among heavy drinking college students. *AIDS and Behavior, 14*(4), 845–853.

Secker-Walker, R. H., & Vacek, P. M. (2003). Relationships between cigarette smoking during pregnancy, gestational age, maternal weight gain, and infant birthweight. *Addictive Behaviors, 28*(1), 55–66.

Segrin, C., Powell, H. L., Givertz, M., & Brackin, A. (2003). Symptoms of depression, relational quality, and loneliness in dating relationships. *Personal Relationships, 10*(1), 25–36.

Seidman, S. M. (2003). The aging male: Androgens, erectile dysfunction, and depression. *Journal of Clinical Psychiatry, 64*(Suppl. 10), 31–37.

Seifert-Klauss V., et al. (2005). Bone metabolism, bone density and estrogen levels in perimenopause: A prospective 2-year study. *Zentralbl Gynakol., 127*(3), 132–139.

Seiffge-Krenke, I., & Kuehnemund, M. (2001). Relationship experiences during adolescence: How important are they for predicting romantic outcomes in young adulthood? *Zeitschrift für Entwicklungspsychologie und Paedagogische Psychologie, 33*(2), 112–123.

Seligman, L., & Hardenburg, S. A. (2000). Assessment and treatment of paraphilias. *Journal of Counseling & Development, 78*(1), 107–113.

Semans, J. (1956). Premature ejaculation: A new approach. *Southern Medical Journal, 49*, 353–358.

Semp, D. (2011). Questioning heteronormativity: Using queer theory to inform research and practice with mental health services. *Psychology and Sexuality, 2*(1), 69–86.

Semple, S. J., Patterson, T. L., & Grant, I. (2003). HIV-positive gay and bisexual men: Predictors of unsafe sex. *AIDS Care, 15*(1), 3–15.

Senbel, A. M. (2011). Interaction between nitric oxide and dopaminergic transmission in the peripheral control of penile erection. *Fundamental and Clinical Pharmacology, 25*(1), 63–71.

Servais, L. (2006). Sexual health care in persons with intellectual disabilities. *Mental Retardation and Developmental Disabilities Research Reviews, 12*(1), 48–56.

Servin, A., Nordenström, A., Larsson, A., & Bohlin, G. (2003). Prenatal androgens and gender-typed behavior: A study of girls with mild and severe forms of congenital adrenal hyperplasia. *Developmental Psychology, 39*(3), 440–450.

Seto, M. C. (2008). Pedophilia: Psychopathology and theory. In D. R. Laws and W. T. O'Donohue (Eds.), *Sexual deviance: Theory, assessment, and treatment* (2nd ed., pp. 164–182). New York: Guilford Press.

Seward, R. R. (2005). Family and community in Ireland. *Journal of Comparative Family Studies, 36*(2), 343–344.

Sex & Tech. (2009). A survey commissioned by The National Campaign to Prevent Teen and Unplanned Pregnancy and *CosmoGirl.com.*

Sex abuse victims in Boston Church estimated at over 1,000. (2003). *The New York Times* (Online).

Shackelford, T. K., & Goetz, A. T. (2012). *The Oxford handbook of sexual conflict in humans.* New York: Oxford University Press.

Shackelford, T. K., Goetz, A. T., Buss, D. M., Euler, H. A., & Hoier, S. (2005). When we hurt the ones we love: Predicting violence against women from men's mate retention. *Personal Relationships, 12*(4), 447–463.

Shacklett, B. L., & Ferre, A. L. (2011). Mucosal immunity in HIV controllers: The right place at the right time. *Current Opinion in HIV & AIDS, 6*(3), 202–207.

Sharp, D. (2002). Telling the truth about sex. *Lancet, 359*(9312), 1084.

Sharp, E. B., & Joslyn, M. (2008). Individual and contextual effects on attributions about pornography. *The Journal of Politics, 63*, 501–519.

Shaywitz, B. A., et al. (1995). Sex differences in the functional organization of the brain for language. *Nature, 373*, 607–609.

Sheffield, J. S., & Cunningham, F. G. (2005). Urinary tract infection in women. *Obstetrics & Gynecology, 106,* 1085–1092.

Sherer, R. (2012). The future of HIV care in the USA. *Sexually Transmitted Infections, 88,* 106–111.

Sherwin, B. B. (2012). Estrogen and cognitive functioning in women: Lessons we have learned. *Behavioral Neuroscience, 126*(1), 123–127.

Sherwin, B. B., Gelfand, M. M., & Brender, W. (1985). Androgen enhances sexual motivation in females: A prospective, crossover study of sex steroid administration in the surgical menopause. *Psychosomatic Medicine, 47,* 339–351.

Shevell, T., et al. (2005). Assisted reproductive technology and pregnancy outcome. *Obstetrics & Gynecology, 106,* 1039–1045.

Shick, V., et al. (2011). Prevalence and characteristics of vibrator use among women who have sex with women. *Journal of Sexual Medicine, 8*(12), 3306–3315.

Shields, S. A., & Dicicco, E. C. (2011). The social psychology of sex and gender. *Psychology of Women Quarterly, 35*(3), 491–499.

Shifren, J. L., et al. (2000). Transdermal testosterone treatment in women with impaired sexual function after oophorectomy. *The New England Journal of Medicine, 343*(10), 682–688.

Shifren, J. L., et al. (2008). Sexual problems and distress in United States women: Prevalence and correlates. *Obstetrics & Gynecology, 112,* 970–978.

Shipko, S. (2000, February 7). *Antidepressants linked to sexual side effects.* WebMD/Healtheon. (Online).

Shlipak, M. G., et al. (2000). Estrogen and progestin, lipoprotein(a), and the risk of recurrent coronary heart disease events after menopause. *Journal of the American Medical Association, 283,*1845–1852.

Shoveller, J. A., Johnson, J. L., & Savoy, D. M. (2006). Preventing sexually transmitted infections among adolescents: An assessment of ecological approaches and study methods. *Sex Education, 6*(2), 163–183.

Shultz, S. K., Scherman, A., & Marshall, L. J. (2000). Evaluation of a university-based date rape prevention program: Effect on attitudes and behavior related to rape. *Journal of College Student Development, 41*(2), 193–201.

Shuster, S. M., & Sassaman, C. (1997). Genetic interaction between male mating strategy and sex ratio in a marine isopod. *Nature, 388*(6640), 373–377.

Siegel-Hinson, R. I., & McKeever, W. F. (2002). Hemispheric specialisation, spatial activity experience, and sex differences on tests of mental rotation ability. *Laterality: Asymmetries of Body, Brain and Cognition, 7*(1), 59–74.

Silva, P. (2005). The state of affairs. *Sexual and Relationship Therapy, 20*(2), 261–262.

Simon, S. (2011). Report: Breast cancer death rates decline, but more slowly among poor. American Cancer Society. http://www.cancer.org/Cancer/news/News/report-breast-cancer-death-rates-decline-but-more-slowly-among-poor

Simpson, J. L. (2000, June 1). Invasive diagnostic procedures for prenatal genetic diagnosis. *Journal Watch Women's Health.*

Sims, C. S., Drasgow, F., & Fitzgerald, L. F. (2005). The effects of sexual harassment on turnover in the military: Time-dependent modeling. *Journal of Applied Psychology, 90*(6), 1141–1152.

Singer, J., & Singer, I. (1972). Types of female orgasm. *Journal of Sex Research, 8,* 255–267.

Singh, D., Vidaurri, M., Zambrano, R. J., & Dabbs, J. M., Jr. (1999). Lesbian erotic role identification: Behavioral, morphological, and hormonal correlates. *Journal of Personality & Social Psychology, 76*(6), 1035–1039.

Sipski, M. L., Alexander, C. J., & Rosen, R. (2001). Sexual arousal and orgasm in women. *Annals of Neurology, 49*(1), 35–44.

Skopek, J., Schulz, F., & Blossfeld, H. (2011). Who contacts whom? Educational homophily in online mate selection. *European Sociological Review, 27*(2), 180–195.

Slackman, M. (2007, September 20). In Egypt, a rising push against genital cutting. *The New York Times.*

Slovenko, R. (2001). Aphrodisiacs—then and now. *Journal of Psychiatry & Law, 29*(1), 103–116.

Smart, C. (2006). The state of affairs: Explorations in infidelity and commitment. *Sexualities, 9*(2), 259–262.

Smith, C. A., & Konik, J. (2011). Feminism and evolutionary psychology: Allies, adversaries, or both? *Sex Roles, 64*(9–10), 595–602.

Smith, D. K., et al. (2010). Male circumcision in the United States for the prevention of HIV infection and other adverse health outcomes: Report from a CDC consultation. *Public Health Reports, 125*(Suppl 1), 72–82.

Smith, Y. L. S., Van Goozen, S. H. M., Kuiper, A. J., & Cohen–Kettenis, P. T. (2005). Sex reassignment: Outcomes and predictors of treatment for adolescent and adult transsexuals. *Psychological Medicine, 35*(1), 89–99.

Smock, P. J. (2000, February 15). Cited in E. Nagourney, *Annual Review of Sociology.* Study finds families bypassing marriage. *The New York Times,* p. F8.

Soble, A. (2009). A history of erotic philosophy. *Journal of Sex Research, 46*(2), 104–120.

Sommer, F., Goldstein, I., & Korda, J. B. (2010). Bicycle riding and erectile dysfunction: A review. *Journal of Sexual Medicine, 7,* 2346–2358.

Sommerfeld, J. (2000, April 18). *Lifting the curse: Should monthly periods be optional?* MSNBC. (Online).

Song, A. V., & Halpern-Felsher, B. L. (2011). Predictive relationship between adolescent oral and vaginal sex: Results from a prospective, longitudinal study. *Archives of Pediatrics & Adolescent Medicine, 165*(3), 243–249.

Special, W. P., & Li-Barber, K. T. (2012). Self-disclosure and student satisfaction with Facebook. *Computers in Human Behavior, 28*(2), 624–630.

Spehr, M., et al. (2003). Identification of a testicular odorant receptor mediating human sperm chemotaxis. *Science, 299*(5615).

Spehr, M., Schwane, K., Riffell, J. A., Zimmer, R. K., & Hatt, H. (2006). Odorant receptors and olfactory-like signaling mechanisms

in mammalian sperm. *Molecular and Cell Endocrinology, 250*(1-2), 128–136.

Spencer, A. L., & Bonnema, R. (2011). Health issues in oral contraception: Risks, side effects, and health benefits. *Expert Review of Obstetrics & Gynecology, 6*(5), 551–557.

Spencer, N. (2006). Explaining the social gradient in smoking in pregnancy: Early life course accumulation and cross-sectional clustering of social risk exposures in the 1958 British national cohort. *Social Science & Medicine, 62*(5),, 1250–1259.

Spencer, T., Biederman, J., & Mick, E. (2006). Attention-deficit/hyperactivity disorder: Diagnosis, lifespan, comorbidities, and neurobiology. *Ambulatory Pediatrics, 7*(1), 73–81.

Spiegel, D. (2001). Breast cancer: Society shapes and epidemic. *New England Journal of Medicine, 334,* 1337–1338.

Spiro, M. E. (1965). *Children of the kibbutz.* New York: Schocken Books.

Spitzer, R. L. (2005). Peer commentaries on Binik: A more radical proposal: Dyspareunia is not a mental disorder. *Archives of Sexual Behavior, 34*(1), 48.

Spitzer, R. L., et al. (1989). *DSM-III-R casebook.* Washington, DC: American Psychiatric Association.

Sprecher, S. (1998). Insiders' perspectives on reasons for attraction to a close other. *Social Psychology Quarterly, 61*(4), 287–300.

Sprecher, S., & Fehr, B. (2011). Dispositional attachment and relationship-specific attachment as predictors of compassionate love for a partner. *Journal of Social and Personal Relationships, 28*(4), 558–574.

Sprecher, S., Barbee, A., & Schwartz, P. (1995). "Was it good for you, too?" Gender differences in first sexual intercourse experiences. *The Journal of Sex Research, 32,* 3–15.

Sprecher, S., Sullivan, Q., & Hatfield, E. (1994). Mate selection preferences: Gender differences examined in a national sample. *Journal of Personality and Social Psychology, 66*(6), 1074–1080.

Squeglia, L. M., et al. (2012). Binge drinking differentially affects adolescent male and female brain morphometry. *Psychopharmacology, 220*(3), 529–539.

Squier, S., & Littlefield, M. M. (Eds). (2004). Feminist theory and/of science: Feminist Theory special issue. *Feminist Theory, 5*(2), 123–126.

Stake, J. E., & Hoffman, F. L. (2001). Changes in student social attitudes, activism, and personal confidence in higher education: The role of women's studies. *American Educational Research Journal, 38*(2), 411–436.

Stamback, A., & Miriam, D. (2005). Feminist theory and educational policy: How gender has been "involved" in family school choice debates. *Signs, 30*(2), 1633–1658.

Staras, S., Tobler, A. L., Maldonado-Molina, M., & Cook, R. (2011). Riskier sexual partners contribute to the increased rate of sexually transmitted diseases among youth with substance abuse disorders. *Sexually Transmitted Diseases, 38*(5), 413–418.

Starr, K. E., & Aron, L. (2011). Women on the couch: Genital stimulation and the birth of psychoanalysis. *Psychoanalytic Dialogues:*

The International Journal of Relational Perspectives, 21(4), 373–392.

Stead, L., et al. (2009).Triple negative breast cancers are increased in Black Women regardless of age or body mass index. *Breast Cancer Research, 11*(2), R18.

Stearns, V., Beebe, K. L., Iyengar, M., & Dube, E. (2003). Paroxetine controlled release in the treatment of menopausal hot flashes. *Journal of the American Medical Association, 289*, 2827–2834.

Steele, C. M., & Josephs, R. A. (1990). Alcohol myopia: Its prized and dangerous effects. *American Psychologist, 45*, 921–933.

Stefanick, M. L., et al. (2006). Effects of conjugated equine estrogens on breast cancer and mammography screening in postmenopausal women with hysterectomy. *Journal of the American Medical Association, 295*, 1647–1657.

Stein, C. J., & Colditz, G. A. (2004). Modifiable risk factors for cancer. *Journal of Breast Cancer, 90*(2), 299–303.

Stein, D. J., Black, D. W., Shapira, N. A., & Spitzer, R. L. (2001). Hypersexual disorder and preoccupation with Internet pornography. *American Journal of Psychiatry, 158*(10), 1590–1594.

Stein, Z., & Susser, M. (2000). The risks of having children in later life. *British Medical Journal, 320*(7251), 1681–1682.

Steinemann, S., & Steinemann, M. (2005). Retroelements: Tools for sex chromosome evolution. *Cytogenetic and Genome Research, 110*, 134–143.

Steinfeldt, M., & Steinfeldt, J. A. (2012). Athletic identity and conformity to masculine norms among college football players. *Journal of Applied Sport Psychology, 24*(2), 115–128.

Stengers, J., Van Neck, A., & Hoffmann, K. (2001). *Masturbation: The history of a great terror.* New York: St. Martin's Press.

Stephanou, G. (2012). Romantic relationships in emerging adulthood: Perception-partner ideal discrepancies, attributions, and expectations. *Psychology, 3*(2), 150–160.

Stephenson, J. (2000). Widely used spermicide may increase, not decrease, risk of HIV transmission. *Journal of the American Medical Association, 284*(8). (Online).

Stephenson, K. R., Rellini, A. H., & Meston, C. M. (2012). Relationship satisfaction as a predictor of treatment response during cognitive behavioral sex therapy. *Archives of Sexual Behavior.* DOI:10.1007/s10508-012-9961-3.

Sternberg, R. J. (1988). *The triangle of love: Intimacy, passion, commitment.* New York: Basic Books.

Sternberg, R. J. (2004). A triangular theory of love. In H. T. Reis & C. E. Rusbult (Eds.), *Close relationships: Key readings* (pp. 213–227). London: Taylor & Francis.

Sternberg, R. J. (2007). Triangulating love. In T. J. Oord (Ed.), *The altruism reader* (pp. 331–374). West Conshohocken, PA: Templeton Press.

Stewart, S. M., Lee, P. W. H., & Tao, R. (2010). Psychiatric disorders in the Chinese. In M. H. Bond (Ed.), *The Oxford handbook of Chinese psychology.* Oxford, UK: Oxford University Press, pp. 367–382.

STI surveillance, 2010. Centers for Disease Control and Prevention. (2010). 2010 Sexually transmitted diseases surveillance. http://www.cdc.gov/std/stats10/tables/trends-snapshot.htm (Accessed October 4, 2012).

STI trends, 2011. Centers for Disease Control and Prevention. (2011). STD Trends in the United States: 2010 National data for gonorrhea, chlamydia, and syphilis. http://www.cdc.gov/std/stats10/trends.htm (Accessed October 4, 2012).

STIs and infertility, 2011. Centers for Disease Control and Prevention. (2011). Sexually transmitted diseases (STDs). STDs and infertility. http://www.cdc.gov/std/infertility (Accessed October 4, 2012).

STIs, 2011. Centers for Disease Control and Prevention. (2011). Sexually Transmitted Diseases (STDs). HIV/AIDS and STDs treatment: Guidelines, research, and updates. http://www.cdc.gov/std/hiv/treatment.htm (Accessed October 4, 2012).

Stockett, M. K. (2005). On the importance of difference: Re-envisioning sex and gender in ancient Mesoamerica, *World Archaeology, 37*(4), 566–578.

Stone, B. (2009, May 13). Under pressure, Craigslist to remove "erotic" ads. *The New York Times.*

Stopes-Roe, M., & Cochrane, R. (2011). Marriage in two cultures. *British Journal of Social Psychology, 27*(2), 159–169.

Storms, M. D. (1980). Theories of sexual orientation. *Journal of Personality and Social Psychology, 38*, 783–792.

Stout, H. (2011, November 6). Less "he said, she said" in sex harassment cases. *The New York Times,* p. B10.

Strassberg, D. S., & Holty, S. (2003). An experimental study of women's Internet personal ads. *Archives of Sexual Behavior, 32*(3), 253–260.

Strathdee, S. A., Magis-Rodriguez, C., Mays, V. M., Jiminez, R., & Patterson, T. L. (2012). The emerging HIV epidemic on the Mexico-U.S. Border: An international case study characterizing the role of epidemiology in surveillance and response. *Annals of Epidemiology, 22*(6), 426–438.

Stratton, T. D., McLaughlin, M. A., Witte, F. M., Fosson, S. E., & Nora, L. M. (2005). Does students' exposure to gender discrimination and sexual harassment in medical school affect specialty choice and residency program selection? *Academic Medicine, 80*(4), 400–408.

Strebeigh, F. (2009). *Equal: Women reshape American law.* New York: Norton.

Studd, J. (2009). Estrogens as first-choice therapy for osteoporosis prevention and treatment in women under 60. *Climacteric, 12*(3), 206–209.

Studd, J., & Nappi, R. E. (2012). Reproductive depression. *Gynecological Endocrinology, 28*(S1), 42–45.

Stulhofer, A. (2006). How (un)important is penis size for women with heterosexual experience? *Archives of Sexual Behavior, 35*(1), 5–6.

Sulak, P. J., et al. (2000). Hormone withdrawal symptoms in oral contraceptive users. *Obstetrics & Gynecology, 95*, 261–266.

Sullivan, C. (2006). Women and men in management. *Gender, Work & Organization, 13*(1), 96–98.

Sullum, J. (2007, January 25). 10 million missing Chinese girls reason online. Available at http://www.reason.com/blog/show/118311.html.

Sun, A., & Ren, J. (2012). Estrogen replacement therapy and cardiac function under metabolic syndrome. *Hypertension, 59*, 552–554.

Surratt, H. L., Kurtz, S. P., Weaver, J. C., & Inciardi, J. A. (2005). The connections of mental health problems, violent life experiences, and the social milieu of the "stroll" with the HIV risk behaviors of female street sex workers. *Journal of Psychology & Human Sexuality, 17*(1–2), 23–44.

Sutcliffe, C. G., et al. (2009). Incidence of HIV and sexually transmitted infections and risk factors for acquisition among young methamphetamine users in Northern Thailand. *Sexually Transmitted Diseases, 36*(5), 284–289.

Symons, D. (1995, Cited in Goleman, D., June 14). Sex fantasy research said to neglect women. *The New York Times,* p. C14.

Syphilis—reported cases, 2011. Centers for Disease Control and Prevention. (2011). 2010 Sexually transmitted diseases surveillance. Figure 34. Syphilis—Reported cases by stage of infection, United States, 1941–2010. http://www.cdc.gov/std/stats10/figures/34.htm (Accessed October 4, 2012).

Syphilis, 2012. Centers for Disease Control and Prevention. (2012). Sexually transmitted diseases (STDs). Syphilis. http://www.cdc.gov/std/syphilis/default.htm (Accessed October 4, 2012).

Szabo, R., & Short, R. V. (2000). How does male circumcision protect against HIV infection? *British Medical Journal, 320*, 1592–1594.

Tabak, J. A., & Zayas, V. (2012). The Roles of featural and configural face processing in snap judgments of sexual orientation. *PLoS ONE, 7*(5), e36671. DOI:10.1371/journal.pone.0036671.

Taha, E. T., et al. (2003). Short postexposure prophylaxis in newborn babies to reduce mother-to-child transmission of HIV-1: NVAZ randomised clinical trial. *The Lancet, 362*(9391), 1171–1177.

Tamimi, R. M., Hankinson, S. E., Chen, W. Y., Rosner, B., & Colditz, G. A. (2006). Combined estrogen and testosterone use and risk of breast cancer in postmenopausal women. *Archives of Internal Medicine, 166*, 1483–1489.

Tan, H. M., Tong, S. F., & Ho, C. C. K. (2012). Men's health: Sexual dysfunction, physical, and psychological health—Is there a link? *Journal of Sexual Medicine, 9*(3), 663–671.

Tan, R. S. (2002). Managing the andropause in aging men. *Clinical Geriatrics.* www.mmhc.com/cg/articles/CG9907/Tan.html.

Tan, R. S., & Culberson, J. W. (2003). An integrative review on current evidence of testosterone replacement therapy for the andropause. *Maturitas, 45*(1), 15–27.

Tanfer, K., Grady, W. R., Klepinger, D. H., & Billy, J. O. G. (1993). Condom use among U.S. men, 1991. *Family Planning Perspectives, 25*, 61–66.

Tang, C. S., Yeung, D. Y., & Lee, A. M. (2003). Psychosocial correlates of emotional responses to menarche among Chinese adolescent girls. *Journal of Adolescent Health, 33*(3), 193–201.

Tang, M. C., Weiss, N. S., & Malone, K. E. (2000). Induced abortion in relation to breast cancer among parous women: A birth certificate registry study. *Epidemiology, 11*(2), 177–180.

Tashiro, T., & Frazier, P. (2003). "I'll never be in a relationship like that again": Personal growth following romantic relationship breakups. *Personal Relationships, 10*(1), 113–128.

Taylor, M. J., Rudkin, L., & Hawton, K. (2005). Strategies for managing antidepressant-induced sexual dysfunction: Systematic review of randomised controlled trials. *Journal of Affective Disorders, 88*(3), 241–254.

Taylor, V., & Rupp, L. J. (2004). Chicks with dicks, men in dresses: What it means to be a drag queen. *Journal of Homosexuality, 46*(3–4), 113–133.

Teen Pregnancy Prevention and United States Students. (2011, July 12). Centers for Disease Control and Prevention. http://www.cdc.gov/healthyyouth/yrbs/pdf/us_pregnancy_combo.pdf (Accessed September 23, 2012).

Telushkin, J. (1991). *Jewish literacy*. New York: HarperCollins.

Temple, J. R., et al. (2012). Teen sexting and its association with sexual behaviors. *Archives of Pediatric & Adolescent Medicine, 166*(9), 828–833.

Templeton, A., & Grimes, D. A. (2011). A request for abortion. *The New England Journal of Medicine, 365*, 2198–2204.

Teo, F. H., Oliveira, R. T. D., Mamoni, R. L., Coelho, O. R., & Blotta, M. H. S. L. (2009). I 009 Quantification and Characterization of CD4$^+$CD28^{null} and CD4$^+$CD28$^+$ T Cells in Patients with Chronic Coronary Artery Disease and Healthy Subjects. *Atherosclerosis Supplements, 10*(3), 30.

ter Kuile, M. M., Both., S., & van Lankveld, J. J. D. M. (2012). Sexual dysfunctions in women. In P. Sturmey, & M. Hersen (Eds.). *Handbook of evidence-based practice in clinical psychology, adult disorders* (pp. 413–436). Hoboken, NJ: Wiley.

ter Kuile, M. M., et al. (2009). Therapist-aided exposure for women with lifelong vaginismus: A replicated single-case design. *Journal of Consulting and Clinical Psychology, 77*, 149–159.

Terasawa, E., et al. (2012). Body weight impact on puberty: Effects of high-calorie diet on puberty onset in female rhesus monkeys. *Endocrinology, 153*(4), 1696–1705.

Thachil, A., & Bhugra, D. (2006). Literature update: A critical review. *Sexual and Relationship Therapy, 21*(2), 229–235.

Thapar, A., Cooper, M., Jefferies, R., & Stergiakoull, E. (2010). What causes attention deficit hyperactivity disorder? *Archives of Disease in Childhood, 97*, 260–265.

The New York Observer. http://www.observer.com/2008/equal-hypocrisy-unequal-punishment.

The New York Times/CBS News Poll, April 22–26, 2009. (2009, April 27). http://graphics8.nytimes.com/packages/images/nytint/docs/new-york-times-cbs-news-poll-obamas-100th-day-in-office/original.pdf.

Thibaut, F. (2011). Pharmacological treatment of sex offenders. *Sexologies, 20*(3),166–168.

Thigpen, T. W. (2009). Early sexual behavior in a sample of low-income, African American children. *Journal of Sex Research, 46*(1), 67–79.

Thomas, N. L., & Coughtrie, M. W. H. (2003). Sulfation of apomorphine by human sulfotransferases: Evidence of a major role for the polymorphic phenol sulfotransferase, SULT1A1. *Xenobiotica, 33*(11), 1139–1148.

Thomas, R. M., & Murray, T. R. (2009). *Sex and the American teenager: Seeing through the myths and confronting the issues.* Lanham, MD: L & R Publishers.

Thompson, A. E., & O'Sullivan, L. F. (2011). Gender differences in associations of sexual and romantic stimuli. *Archives of Sexual Behavior, 41*(4), 949–957.

Thompson, A. E., & O'Sullivan, L. F. (2011). Gender differences in associations of sexual and romantic stimuli: Do young men really prefer sex over romance? *Archives of Sexual Behavior,* DOI:10.1007/s10508-011-9794-5

Thompson, B., & Borrello, G. M. (2008). Different views of love: Deductive and inductive lines of inquiry. *Current Directions in Psychological Science, 1*(5), 154–156.

Thompson, E. M., & Morgan, E. M. (2008). "Mostly straight" young women: Variations in sexual behavior and identity. *Developmental Psychology, 44*(1), 15–21.

Thompson, I. M., et al. (2005). Erectile dysfunction and subsequent cardiovascular disease. *Journal of the American Medical Association, 294*(23), 2996–3002.

Thompson, J. K., & Tantleff, S. (1992). Female and male ratings of upper torso: Actual, ideal, and stereotypical conceptions. *Journal of Social Behavior and Personality, 7*, 345–354.

Tobian, A. A. R, et al. (2009). Male circumcision for the prevention of HSV-2 and HPV infections and syphilis. *New England Journal of Medicine, 360*, 1298–1309.

Tobian, A. A. R., & Gray, R. H. (2011). The medical benefits of male circumcision. *Journal of the American Medical Association, 306*(13), 1479–1480.

Totman, R. (2004). *The third sex: Kathoey: Thailand's ladyboys.* London: Souvenir Press.

Touhara, K., & Vosshall, L. B. (2009). Sensing odorants and pheromones with chemosensory receptors. *Annual Review of Physiology, 71*, 307–332.

Traish, A. M., Goldstein, I., Munarriz, R., & Guay, A. (2006). Roles of androgens in women's sexual function & dysfunction: What have we learned in sex decades? *Current Women's Health Reviews, 2*(1), 75–86.

Trivedi, D., et al. (2012). Can simvastatin improve erectile function and health-related quality of life in men aged ≥40 years with erectile dysfunction? Results of the Erectile Dysfunction and Statins Trial. *BJUI*, DOI: 10.1111/j.1464-410X.2012.11241.x.

Troxel, W. M., & Matthews, K. A. (2004). What are the costs of marital conflict and dissolution to children's physical health? *Clinical Child & Family Psychology Review, 7*(1), 29–57.

Trudel, G., Turgeon, L., & Piche, L. (2000). Marital and sexual aspects of old age. *Sexual & Relationship Therapy, 15*(4), 381–406.

Trulsson, O., & Rådestad, I. (2004). The silent child—Mothers' experiences before, during, and after stillbirth. *Birth: Issues in Perinatal Care, 31*(3), 189–195.

Tsaliki, L. (2011). Playing with porn: Greek children's explorations in pornography. *Sex Education: Sexuality, Society and Learning, 11*(3), 293–302.

Tucker, J., & Poston, D. L. (Eds.). (2009). *Gender policy and HIV in China: Catalyzing policy change.* Amsterdam: Springer.

Tunariu, A. D., & Reavey, P. (2003). Men in love: Living with sexual boredom. *Sexual & Relationship Therapy, 18*(1), 63–94.

Tuomikoski, P., et al. (2009). Evidence for a role for hot flushes in vascular function in recently postmenopausal women. *Obstetrics and Gynecology, 113*(4), 902–908.

Turner, H. A., Finkelhor, D., & Ormrod, R. (2006). The effect of lifetime victimization on the mental health of children and adolescents. *Social Science & Medicine, 62*(1), 13–27.

Turton, J. (2005). Perspectives on female sex offending: A culture of denial. *Sexualities, 8*(5), 632–633.

Turton, P., et al. (2006). Psychological impact of stillbirth on fathers in the subsequent pregnancy and puerperium. *British Journal of Psychiatry, 188*(2), 165–172.

Tyler, M. (2009). No means yes? Perpetuating myths in the sexological construction of women's desire. *Women & Therapy, 32*(1), 40–50.

U.S. Abortion Statistics. (2012, May 24). Facts and figures relating to the frequency of abortion in the United States. http://www.abort73.com/abortion_facts/us_abortion_statistics (Accessed June 23, 2012).

U.S. Bureau of the Census. (2005). *Statistical abstract of the United States* (125th ed.). Washington, DC: U.S. Government Printing Office.

U.S. Bureau of the Census. (2006). U.S. Bureau of the Census, current population reports, estimated median age at first marriage, by sex: 1890–present. www.census.gov/population/socdemo/hh-fam/ms2.pdf.

U.S. Bureau of the Census. (2011). *Families and living arrangements.* Retrieved from http://www.census.gov/population/www/socdemo/hh-fam.html

U.S. Census Bureau, ,"America's Families and Living Arrangements" for 2010 (Table UC3). *Current Population Reports.* Available online at www.census.gov/population/www/socdemo/hh-fam/cps2010.html

U.S. Census Bureau. (2011). *America's families and living arrangements for 2010.* (Current Population Reports, Table UC3). Retrieved from www.census.gov/population/www/socdemo/hh-fam/cps2010.html

U.S. Department of Justice. (1986). *Attorney general's commission on pornography: Final report.* Washington, DC: U.S. Government Printing Office.

U.S. Department of Justice. *Criminal victimization in the United States. Statistical tables, 2003.* Office of Justice Programs. Bureau of Justice Statistics. Accessed February 15, 2006. www.ojp.usdoj.gov/bjs/abstract/cvus/rape_sexual_assault.htm.

U.S. Department of Labor, Bureau of Labor Statistics, Economic News Release. (September 2011). Employment situation. Employment status of the civilian population 25 years and over by educational attainment (Table A-4). Available at http://www.bls.gov/news.release/empsit.t04.htm

U.S. National Library of Medicine. (2006). *Androgen insensitivity syndrome*. National Institutes of Health. http://ghr.nlm.nih.gov/condition-androgeninsensitivitysyndrome.

U.S. Preventive Services Task Force. (2009). Screening for breast cancer: U.S. Preventive Services Task Force recommendation statement. *Annals of Internal Medicine, 151*(10), 716–726.

Udry, J. R. (2001). Feminist critics uncover determinism, positivism, and antiquated theory. *American Sociological Review, 66*(4), 611–618.

Ullman, S. E., Filipas, H. H., Townsend, S. M., & Starzynski, L. L. (2006). The role of victim–offender relationship in women's sexual assault experiences. *Journal of Interpersonal Violence, 21*(6), 798–819.

UNAIDS. (2006). *Report on the global AIDS epidemic: Executive summary*. Joint United Nations Programme on HIV/AIDS (UNAIDS). Geneva: UNAIDS.

UNICEF. (2012). HIV and Infant Feeding. http://www.unicef.org/programme/breastfeeding/hiv.htm (Accessed September 21, 2012).

Unigwe, C. (2011). *On Black Sisters Street*. New York: Random House.

Unigwe, C. (2012, April 19). Legality brings protection and better care. The *New York Times* (Online).

United Nations Special Session on AIDS. (2001, June 25–27). *Preventing HIV/AIDS among young people*. New York: United Nations.

University of Maryland Medical Center. (2011). Cervical cancer—Prognosis. http://www.umm.edu/patiented/articles/how_serious_cervical_cancer_000046_5.htm

University of Michigan. (2009). *Masturbation*. http://www.med.umich.edu/yourchild/topics/masturb.htm (Accessed September 23, 2012).

Utian, W. H. (2012). Recent developments in pharmacotherapy for vasomotor symptoms. *Current Obstetrics and Gynecology Reports*, DOI:10.1007/s13669-012-0009-4

Uysal., A., Lin, H. L., Knee, C. R., & Bush, A. L. (2012). The association between self-concealment from one's partner and relationship well-being. *Personality and Social Psychology Bulletin, 38*(1), 39–51.

Vaculík, M., & Hudecek, T. (2005). Development of close relationships in the Internet environment. *Ceskoslovenská Psychologie, 49*(2), 157–174.

Valkenburg, P. M., Sumter, S. R., & Peter, J. (2011). Gender differences in online and offline self-disclosure in pre-adolescence and adolescence. *British Journal of Developmental Psychology, 29*(2), 253–269.

Valocchi, S. (2005). Not yet queer enough: The lessons of queer theory for the sociology of gender and sexuality. *Gender & Society, 19*(6), 750–770.

van de Beek, C., van Goozen, S. H. M., Buitelaar, J. K., & Cohen-Kettenis, P. T. (2009). Prenatal sex hormones (maternal and amniotic fluid) and gender-related play behavior in 13-month-old infants. *Archives of Sexual Behavior, 38*(1), 6–15.

van den Bree, M. B. M., & Pickworth, W. B. (2005). Risk factors predicting changes in marijuana involvement in teenagers. *Archives of General Psychiatry, 62*(3), 311–319.

van der Made, F., et al. (2008). Childhood sexual abuse, selective attention for sexual cues and the effects of testosterone with or without vardenafil on physiological sexual arousal in women with sexual dysfunction: A pilot study. *Journal of Sexual Medicine, 6*(2), 429–439.

Van Lange, P. A. M., & Rusbult, C. E. (2012). Interdependence theory. In P. A. M. Van Lange et al. (Eds.). *Handbook of theories of social psychology, Vol. 2* (pp. 251–272). Thousand Oaks, CA: Sage.

Van Lange, P. A. M., et al. (1997). Willingness to sacrifice in close relationships. *Journal of Personality & Social Psychology, 72*(6), 1373–1395.

van Lankveld, J. (2008). Problems with sexual interest and desire in women. In D. L. Rowland & L. Incrocci (Eds.), *Handbook of sexual and gender identity disorders*. Hoboken, NJ: Wiley.

van Lankveld, J. (2009). Self-help therapies for sexual dysfunction. *Journal of Sex Research, 46*(2), 143–155.

van Lankveld, J. J. D. M., et al. (2010). Women's sexual pain disorders. *Journal of Sexual Medicine, 7*, 615–631.

van Oort, J. (2012). Augustine and the books of the Manichaeans. In M. Vessey (Ed.). *A companion to Augustine* (pp. 188–199). Chichester, West Sussex, UK: Wiley-Blackwell.

van Straaten, I., Engels, R. C. M. E., Finkenauer, C., & Holland, R. W. (2009). Meeting your match: How attractiveness similarity affects approach behavior in mixed-sex dyads. *Personality and Social Psychology Bulletin, 35*(6), 685–697.

Van Wie, V. E., & Gross, A. M. (2001). The role of woman's explanations for refusal on men's ability to discriminate unwanted sexual behavior in a date rape scenario. *Journal of Family Violence, 16*(4), 331–344.

Ventura, S. J. (2009, May). Changing patterns of nonmarital childbearing in the United States. NCHS data brief number 18. Hyattsville, MD: National Center for Health Statistics. Accessed May 13, 2009. http://www.cdc.gov/nchs/data/databriefs/db18.htm.

Vickerman, K. A., & Margolina, G. (2009). Rape treatment outcome research: Empirical findings and state of the literature. *Clinical Psychology Review, 29*, 431–448.

Villar, F., Villamizar, D. J., & López–Chivrall, S. (2005). Components of loving experience in old age: Older people and long-term relationships. *Revista Espanola de Geriatria y Gerontologia, 40*(3), 166–177.

Vladutiu, C. J., Martin, S. L., & Macy, R. J. (2011). College- or university-based sexual assault prevention programs: A review of program outcomes, characteristics, and recommendations. *Trauma, Violence, Abuse, 12*(2), 67–86.

Vohs, K. D., & Baumeister, R. F. (2004). Sexual passion, intimacy, and gender. In D. J. Mashek & A. P. Aron (Eds.), *Handbook of closeness and intimacy* (pp. 189–199). Hillsdale, NJ: Erlbaum.

Vorauer, J. D., Cameron, J. J., Holmes, J. G., & Pearce, D. G. (2003). Invisible overtures: Fears of rejection and the signal amplification bias. *Journal of Personality & Social Psychology, 84*(4), 793–812.

Voyeuristic disorder. (2012). U 07 Voyeuristic disorder. American Psychiatric Association. DSM-5 Development. http://www.dsm5.org/proposedrevision/pages/proposedrevision.aspx?rid=190.

Vrangalova, Z., & Savin-Williams, R. (2012). Mostly heterosexual and mostly gay/lesbian: Evidence for new sexual orientation identities. *Archives of Sexual Behavior, 41*(1), 85–101.

Wack, E. R., & Tantleff-Dunn, S. (2008). Cyber sexy: Electronic game play and perceptions of attractiveness among college-aged men. *Body Image, 5*(4), 365–374.

Wade, T. J., Butrie, L. K., & Hoffman, K. M. (2009). Women's direct opening lines are perceived as most effective. *Personality and Individual Differences, 47*(2), 145–149.

Wagenaar, H. (2006). Democracy and prostitution: Deliberating the legalization of brothels in the Netherlands. *Administration & Society, 38*(2), 98–235.

Waismann, R., Fenwick, P. B. C., Wilson, G. D., Hewett, T. D., & Lumsden, J. (2003). EEG responses to visual erotic stimuli in men with normal and paraphilic interests. *Archives of Sexual Behavior, 32*(2), 135–144.

Wald, A. (2005, November 22). Investigational HPV vaccine shows 100% efficacy. *Journal Watch Women's Health*.

Waldinger, M. D. (2011). The management of premature ejaculation. *Current Clinical Urology, Part 5*, 709–720.

Waldinger, M. D., et al. (2002). The selective serotonin re-uptake inhibitors fluvoxamine and paroxetine differ in sexual inhibitory effects after chronic treatment. *Psychopharmacology, 160*(3), 283–289.

Waldinger, M. D., Zwinderman, A. H., & Olivier, B. (2001). Antidepressants and ejaculation: A double-blind, randomized, placebo-controlled, fixed-dose study with paroxetine, sertraline and nefazodone. *Journal of Clinical Psychopharmacology, 21*(3), 293–297.

Walker, A. (2010). Breast milk as the gold standard for protective nutrients. *Journal of Pediatrics, 156*(Suppl. 2), S3–S7.

Walker, J., Archer, J., & Davies, M. (2005). Effects of rape on men: A descriptive analysis. *Archives of Sexual Behavior, 34*(1), 69–80.

Wallen, K., & Hassett, J. M. (2009). Sexual differentiation of behaviour in monkeys: Role of prenatal hormones. *Journal of Neuroendocrinology, 21*(4), 421–426.

Walther, C. S., & Poston, D. L., Jr. (2004). Patterns of gay and lesbian partnering in the larger metropolitan areas of the United States. *Journal of Sex Research, 41*(2), 201–214.

Waltman, M. (2012, April 20). Criminalize only the buying of sex. The *New York Times* (Online).

Wambach, K. A., et al. (2011). A randomized controlled trial of breastfeeding support and education for adolescent mothers. *Western Journal of Nursing Research, 33*(4), 486–505.

Wang, W. (2012, February 16). *The Rise of Intermarriage: Rates, Characteristics Vary by Race and Gender*. http://www.pewsocialtrends.org/2012/02/16/the-rise-of-intermarriage/1/ (Accessed June 24, 2012).

Ward, T., & Gannon, T. A. (2006). Rehabilitation, etiology, and self-regulation: The comprehensive good lives model of treatment for sexual offenders. *Aggression and Violent Behavior, 11*(1), 77–94.

Waterman, J. (1986). Overview of treatment issues. In K. MacFarlane et al. (Eds.), *Sexual abuse of young children: Evaluation and treatment* (pp. 197–203). New York: Guilford.

Watts, C., & Zimmerman, C. (2002). Violence against women: Global scope and magnitude. *Lancet, 359*(9313), 1232–1237.

Waylen, A. E., et al. (2010). Romantic and sexual behavior in young adolescents: Repeated surveys in a population-based cohort. *Journal of Early Adolescence, 30*(3), 432–443.

Weaver, L. (2012). A short history of infant feeding and growth. *Early Human Development, 88*(Suppl. 1), S57–S 59.

Weeden, J., & Sabini, J. (2005). Physical attractiveness and health in Western societies: A review. *Psychological Bulletin, 131*(5), 635–653.

Weinberg, T. S. (1987). Sadomasochism in the United States: A review of recent sociological literature. *Journal of Sex Research, 23*, 50–69.

Weinrich, J. D., & Klein, F. (2002). Bi-gay, bi-straight, and bi-bi: Three bisexual subgroups identified using cluster analysis of the Klein Sexual Orientation Grid. *Journal of Bisexuality, 2*(4), 109–139.

Weinstein, N., Ryan, W. S., DeHaan, C. R., Przybylski, A. K., Legate, N., & Ryan, R. M. (2012). Parental autonomy support and discrepancies between implicit and explicit sexual identities: Dynamics of self-acceptance and defense. *Journal of Personality and Social Psychology, 102*(4), 815–832.

Weiss, H. A., Wasserheit, J. N., Barnabas, R. V., Hayes, R. J., & Abu-Raddad, L. J. (2008). Persisting with prevention: The importance of adherence for HIV prevention. *Emerging Themes in Epidemiology, 5*, 8.

Weitzer, R. (2007a). Prostitution: Facts and fictions. *Contexts, 6*(4), 28–33.

Weitzer, R. (2012a). *Legalizing prostitution: From illicit vice to lawful business.* New York: New York University Press.

Weitzer, R. (2012b). Male prostitution. In C. D. Bryant (Ed.). *The Routledge handbook of deviant behavior* (pp. 378–382). New York: Routledge.

Weizer, R. (2007b). The social construction of sex trafficking: Ideology and institutionalization of a moral crusade. *Politics & Society, 35*(3), 447–475.

Welldon, E. V. (2005). Incest: A therapeutic challenge. In G. Ambrosio (Ed.), *On incest: Psychoanalytic perspectives* (pp. 81–100). London: Karnac Books.

West, S. L., et al. (2008). Prevalence of low sexual desire and hypoactive sexual desire disorder in a nationally representative sample of US women. *Archives of Internal Medicine, 168*(13), 1441–1449.

Western Resistance. (2006, May 25). Pakistan: "Hudood" ordinances (Islamic rape/ adultery laws) may be repealed. www. westernresistance.com/blog/archives/002215. html.

Wheeler, J., Newring, K. A. B., & Draper, C. (2008). Transvestic fetishism: Psychopathology and theory. In D. R. Laws and W. T. O'Donohue (Eds.), *Sexual deviance: Theory, assessment, and treatment* (2nd ed., pp. 272–284). New York: Guilford Press.

Whipple, B., & Komisaruk, B. R. (1988). Analgesia produced in women by genital self-stimulation. *Journal of Sex Research, 24*, 130–140.

Whisman, M. A., & Snyder, D. K. (2007). Sexual infidelity in a national survey of American women: differences in prevalence and correlates as a function of method of assessment. *The Journal of Family Psychology, 21*(2),147–154.

White, R. G., et al. (2008). Male circumcision for HIV prevention in sub-Saharan Africa: Who, what and when? *AIDS, 22*(14), 1841–1850.

Whitehead, B. D., & Popenoe, D. (2006). The state of our unions: The social health of marriage in America 2006. New Brunswick, NJ: Rutgers University.

Whitley, B. E., Jr. (1983). Sex role orientation and self-esteem: A critical meta-analysis. *Journal of Personality and Social Psychology, 44,* 765–788.

Wierman, M. E., et al. (2010). Endocrine aspects of women's sexual function. *Journal of Sexual Medicine, 7,* 561–585.

Wieselquist, J., Rusbult, C. E., Foster, C. A., & Agnew, C. R. (1999). Commitment, pro-relationship behavior, and trust in close relationships. *Journal of Personality & Social Psychology, 77*(5), 942–966.

Wilcox, A. J., Dunson, D., & Baird, D. D. (2000). The timing of the "fertile window" in the menstrual cycle: Day specific estimates from a prospective study. *British Medical Journal, 321*, 1259–1262.

Wilcox, W. B., & Marquardt, E. (Eds.). (2010). *When marriage disappears: The new middle America.* Charlottesville, VA: National Marriage Project/Institute for American Values.

Wilcox, W. B., & Marquardt, E. (Eds.). (2011). *The state of our unions: Marriage in America 2011.* Charlottesville, VA: The National Marriage Project/Institute for American Values.

Willetts, M. C. (2006). Union quality comparisons between long-term heterosexual cohabitation and legal marriage. *Journal of Family Issues, 27*(1), 110–127.

Williams, D. E., & D'Alessandro, J. D. (1994). A comparison of three measures of androgyny and their relationship to psychological adjustment. *Journal of Social Behavior and Personality, 9*(3), 469–480.

Williams, J. E., & Best, D. L. (1994). Cross-cultural views of women and men. In W. J. Lonner & R. Malpass (Eds.), *Psychology and culture.* Boston: Allyn & Bacon.

Williams, K. M., Cooper, B. S., Howell, T. M., Yuille, J. C., & Paulhus, D. L. (2009). Inferring sexually deviant behavior from corresponding fantasies: The role of personality and pornography consumption. *Criminal Justice and Behavior, 36*(2), 198–222.

Williams, M. E. (Ed.). (2001). *Abortion: Opposing viewpoints.* Greenhaven Press.

Williams, S. L. (2011). Gender research then and now: Complexity, intersectionality, and scientific rigor. *Sex Roles, 65*(5–6), 435–437.

Williamson, C., & Cluse–Tolar, T. (2002). Pimp-controlled prostitution: Still an integral part of street life. *Violence Against Women, 8*(9), 1074–1092.

Wilson, J. M. B., Tripp, D. A., & Boland, F. J. (2005). The relative contributions of waist-to-hip ratio and body mass index to judgments of attractiveness. *Sexualities, Evolution & Gender, 7*(3), 245–267.

Wilson, W., et al. (2000). Brain morphological changes and early marijuana use: A magnetic resonance and positron emission tomography study. *Journal of Addictive Diseases, 19*(1), 1–22.

Wing, R. R., et al. (2010). Effects of weight loss intervention on erectile function in older men with type 2 diabetes in the look AHEAD trial. *Journal of Sexual Medicine, 7,* 156–165.

Winter, S. (2003). *Research and discussion paper: Language and identity in transgender: Gender wars and the case of the Thai kathoey.* Paper presented at the Hawaii conference on Social Sciences. Waikiki, HI.

Wismer Fries, A. B., Shirtcliff, E. A., & Pollak, S. D. (2008). Neuroendocrine dysregulation following early social deprivation in children. *Developmental Psychobiology, 50*(6), 588–599.

Witkowska, E., & Gådin, K. G. (2005). Have you been sexually harassed in school? What female high school students regard as harassment. *International Journal of Adolescent Medicine and Health, 17*(4), 391–406.

Womenshealth.gov. (2009, December). Female genital cutting fact sheet. http:// www.womenshealth.gov/publications/our-publications/fact-sheet/female-genital-cutting. cfm

Wong, C. F., Kipke, M. D., & Weiss, G. (2008). Risk factors for alcohol use, frequent use, and binge drinking among young men who have sex with men. *Addictive Behaviors, 33*(8), 1012–1020.

Wong, D. (2012). Doing gender, doing culture: Division of labour among lesbians in Hong Kong. *Women's Studies International Forum, 35*(4), 266–275.

Wong, W. I., Pasterski, V., Hindmarsh, P. C., Geffner, M. E., & Hines, M. (2012). Are there parental socialization effects on the sex-typed behavior of individuals with congenital adrenal hyperplasia? *Archives of Sexual Behavior.* DOI:10.1007/s10508-012-9997-4.

Woo, J. S. T., Brotto, L. A., & Gorzalka, B. B. (2011). The role of sex guilt in the relationship between culture and women's sexual desire. *Archives of Sexual Behavior, 40*(2), 385–394.

Wood, J. T. (2005). *Gendered lives: Communication, gender, and culture* (6th ed.). Belmont, CA: Wadsworth.

Wood, N. S., et al. (2000). Neurologic and developmental disability after extremely preterm birth. *The New England Journal of Medicine, 343*(6).

Wooster, R., & Weber, B. L. (2003). Genomic medicine: Breast and ovarian cancer. *New England Journal of Medicine, 348*, 2339–2347.

Wooten, J. M. (2008). Drug-induced sexual problems. *Southern Medical Journal, 101*(11), 1092–1093.

World Health Organization. (2012, February). Female genital mutilation. Fact sheet N 241. http://www.who.int/mediacentre/factsheets/ fs241/en/

Wortman, C. B., et al. (1976). Self-disclosure: An attributional perspective. *Journal of Personality and Social Psychology, 33,* 184–191.

Wright, J. L., Lin, D. W., & Stanford, J. L. (2012). Circumcision and the risk of prostate cancer. *Cancer,* DOI: 10.1002/cncr.26653

Wright, L. W., & Bonita, A. G. (2012). A negative campus climate: Sexual harassment and homophobia. In R. D. McAnulty (Ed.). *Sex in college: The things they don't write home about* (pp. 189–210). Santa Barbara, CA: ABC-CLIO.

Wyatt, G. E. (1985). The sexual abuse of Afro-American and white American women in childhood. *Child Abuse and Neglect, 9,* 507–519.

Wyatt, G. E. (1989). Reexamining factors predicting Afro-American and white American women's age at first coitus. *Archives of Sexual Behavior, 18,* 271–298.

Wyatt, G. E., Williams, J. K., & Myers, H. F. (2008). African-American sexuality and HIV/AIDS. *Journal of the National Medical Association, 100*(1), 44–51.

Wyatt, G. E., Williams, J. K., Henderson, T., & Sumner, L. (2009). On the outside looking in: Promoting HIV/AIDS research initiated by African American investigators. *American Journal of Public Health, 99*(S1), S48–S53.

Wyatt, T. (2003). *Pheromones and animal behaviour: Communication by smell and taste.* Cambridge, UK: Cambridge University Press.

Wyatt, T. D. (2009). *Fifty years of pheromones.* Nature, 457, 262–263.

Xu, J., Burgoyne, P. S., & Arnold, A. P. (2002). Sex differences in sex chromosome gene expression in mouse brain. *Human Molecular Genetics, 11*(12), 1409–1419.

Yamaguchi, K., et al. (2011). Assessment of possible effects for testosterone replacement therapy in men with symptomatic late-onset hypogonadism. *Andrologia, 43*(1), 52–56.

Yarber, W. L., Torabi, M. R., & Veenker, C. H. (1989). Development of a three-component sexually transmitted diseases attitude scale. *Journal of Sex Education & Therapy, 15,* 36–49.

Yates, P. M., Hucker, S. J., & Kingston, D. A. (2008). Sexual sadism: Psychopathology and theory. In D. R. Laws and W. T. O'Donohue (Eds.), *Sexual deviance: Theory, assessment, and treatment* (2nd ed., pp. 213–230). New York: Guilford Press.

Yazzie, A. (2010). Visual-spatial thinking and academic achievement: A concurrent and predictive validity study. *Dissertation Abstracts International: Section A, Humanities and Social Sciences, 70*(8-A), 2897.

Yeap, B. B. (2009). Testosterone and ill-health in aging men. *Nature Clinical Practice Endocrinology & Metabolism, 5,* 113–121.

Yeh, K-Y., Pu, H-F., Wu, C-H., Tai, M-Y., & Tsai, Y-F. (2009). Different subregions of the medial preoptic area are separately involved in the regulation of copulation and sexual incentive motivation in male rats: A behavioral and morphological study. *Behavioural Brain Research, 205*(1), 219–225.

Yela, C. (2000). Predictors of and factors related to loving and sexual satisfaction for men and women. *European Review of Applied Psychology, 50*(1), 235–243.

Yela, C. (2006). The evaluation of love: Simplified version of the scales for Yela's tetrangular model based on Sternberg's model. *European Journal of Psychological Assessment, 22*(1), 21–27.

Yoder, V. C., Virden, T. B., III, & Amin, K. (2005). Internet pornography and loneliness: An association? *Sexual Addiction & Compulsivity, 12*(1), 19–44.

Yoshimoto, D., et al. (2006). Nonverbal communication coding systems of committed couples. In *The new handbook of methods in nonverbal behavior research* (pp. 369–397). New York: Oxford University Press.

Yost, M. R., & Thomas, G. D. (2011). Gender and binegativity: Men's and women's attitudes toward male and female bisexuals. *Archives of Sexual Behavior.* doi:10.1007/s10508-011-9767-8

Yost, M. R., & Zurbriggen, E. L. (2006). Gender differences in the enactment of sociosexuality: An examination of implicit social motives, sexual fantasies, coercive sexual attitudes, and aggressive sexual behavior. *The Journal of Sex Research, 43*(2), 163–173.

Young, K. S. (2008). Internet sex addiction: Risk factors, stages of development, and treatment. *American Behavioral Scientist, 52*(1), 21–37.

Zablotska, I. B., et al. (2009). Gay men's current practice of HIV seroconcordant unprotected anal intercourse. *AIDS Care: Psychological and Socio-medical Aspects of AIDS/HIV, 21*(4), 501–510.

Zaidi, A. U., & Shuraydi, M. (2002). Perceptions of arranged marriages by young Pakistani Muslim women living in a Western society. *Journal of Comparative Family Studies, 33*(4), 495–514.

Zaviacic, M., & Whipple, B. (1993). Update on the female prostate and the phenomenon of female ejaculation. *Journal of Sex Research, 30,* 148–151.

Zaviacic, M., et al. (1988a). Concentrations of fructose in female ejaculate and urine: A comparative biochemical study. *Journal of Sex Research, 24,* 319–325.

Zaviacic, M., et al. (1988b). Female urethral expulsions evoked by local digital stimulation of the G-spot: Differences in the response patterns. *Journal of Sex Research, 24,* 311–318.

Zeichner, A., Parrott, D. J., & Frey, F. C. (2003). Gender differences in laboratory aggression under response choice conditions. *Aggressive Behavior, 29*(2), 95–106.

Zelenski, J. M., Rusting, C. L., & Larsen, R. J. (2003). Consistency in the time of experimental participation and personality correlates. *Personality & Individual Differences, 34*(4), 547–558.

Zernike, K. (2005, December 11). The siren song of sex with boys. *The New York Times* (Online).

Zerubavel, E. (2006). *The elephant in the room: Silence and denial in everyday life.* New York: Oxford University Press.

Zezima, K. (2006, February 3). Teenager attacks three men at gay bar in Massachusetts. *The New York Times* (Online).

Zhang, H., Ho, P. S. Y., & Ylp, P. S. F. (2011). Does similarity breed marital and sexual satisfaction. *Journal of Sex Research.* DOI:10.1080/00224499.2011.574240.

Zhang, J., Pang, X., Zhang, L., Medina, A., & Rozelle, S. (2012, May). Gender inequality in education in China: A meta-regression analysis. Working paper 239. www.reapchina.org/reap.stanford.edu (Accessed June 23, 2012).

Zhou, Q., Zhang, K., Li, Z., Liu, D., & Zhou, X. (2002). Personality of 133 male commercial sex service providers and acceptors. *Chinese Mental Health Journal, 16*(1), 48.

Zhu, B., et al. (2011). Transition from paroxysmal disorder in infancy to the masturbatory orgasm in childhood. *International Journal of Sexual Health, 23*(4), 278–281.

Zielbauer, P. (2000, May 22). Sex offender listings on Web set off debate. *The New York Times* (Online).

Zilbergeld, B. (1999). *The new male sexuality* (rev. ed.). New York: Bantam Doubleday Dell.

Zillmann, D. (1989). Effects of prolonged consumption of pornography. In D. Zillmann & J. Bryant (Eds.), *Pornography: Research advances and policy considerations* (pp. 127–157). Hillsdale, NJ: Erlbaum.

Zillmann, D., & Bryant, J. (1984). Effects of massive exposure to pornography. In N. M. Malamuth & E Donnerstein (Eds.), *Pornography and sexual aggression* (pp. 115–138). New York: Academic Press.

Zona, S., et al. (2012). Erectile dysfunction is more common in young to middle-aged HIV-infected men than in HIV-uninfected men. *The Journal of Sexual Medicine.* DOI: 10.1111/j.1743-6109.2012.02750.x.

Zosuls, K. M., et al. (2009). The acquisition of gender labels in infancy: Implications for gender-typed play. *Developmental Psychology, 45*(3), 688–701

Zubeidat, l., Ortega, V., & Sierra, J. C. (2004). Assessment of some determinant factors of sexual desire: Emotional state, sexual attitudes and sexual fantasies. *Análisis y Modificación de Conducta, 30*(129), 105–128.

Zucker, K. J. (2005a). Gender identity disorder in children and adolescents. *Annual Review of Clinical Psychology, 1*(1), 467–492.

Zucker, K. J. (2005b). Gender identity disorder in girls. In D. J. Bell, S. L. Foster, & E. J. Mash (Eds.), *Handbook of behavioral and emotional problems in girls. Issues in clinical child psychology* (pp. 285–319). Kluwer Academic/Plenum Publishers.

Zuckerman, P. (2012). *Faith no more: Why people reject religion.* New York: Oxford University Press.

Photo Credits

Chapter 1: p. xxvi top: Hill Street Studios/Blend Images/Getty Images; p. xxvi bottom: Radius Images/Alamy; p. 1 bottom right: Image Source Photography/Veer; p. 2 bottom: Chad Ehlers/Alamy; p. 3 bottom: RubberBall/SuperStock; p. 6: Medioimages/Photodisc/Getty Images; p. 7: Hola Images/Getty Images; p. 11: BeBa/Iberfoto/The Image Works; p. 13: Scala/Art Resource, NY; p. 15: JFB/The Art Archive at Art Resource, NY; p. 17 right: Alexander Bassano/Stringer/Hulton Royals Collection/Getty Images; p. 19: Fred W. McDarrah/Contributor/Premium Archive/Getty Images; p. 20: Hill Street Studios/Blend Images/Getty Images; p. 23: Photo Researchers/Alamy; p. 24 bottom left: Johannes Eisele/Staff/DDP/AFP/Getty Images; p. 25 bottom right: Radius Images/Alamy; p. 27: RubberBall/SuperStock. **Chapter 2:** p. 30 top: Linda Lewis/FLPA/Age Fotostock; p. 30 bottom: Eric Audras/Alamy; p. 30 bottom: fuzzbones/Fotolia; p. 31 bottom right: Image Source Photography/Veer; p. 32: Spencer Grant/PhotoEdit; p. 34: Linda Lewis/FLPA/Age Fotostock; p. 35: Eric Audras/PhotoAlto/Alamy; p. 37: Wallace Kirkland/Time & Life Pictures/Getty Images; p. 38: RubberBall/SuperStock; p. 44 top right: Fotosearch/Archive Photos/Getty Images; p. 44 bottom left: Rebecca Henry, Mirabel Studios, 2006, Courtesy of Kate Frank; p. 45 top right: Behavioral Technology, Inc., Salt Lake City, UT; p. 46: Behavioral Technology, Inc., Salt Lake City, UT; p. 51 bottom left: National Archives and Records Administration; p. 51 bottom center: National Archives and Records Administration. **Chapter 3:** p. 54 center left: Jim Cummins/Taxi/Getty Images; p. 54 top left: Stockbroker/SuperStock; p. 54 bottom: www.hiped.com/Fotolia; p. 55 bottom right: PhotoAlto Photography/Veer; p. 56: ULRIKE KOTERMANN/EPA/Newscom; p. 57: Jose Luis Pelaez, Inc/Blend Images/Getty Images; p. 58 center: Custom Medical Stock Photo; p. 58 left: Science Photo Library/Custom Medical Stock Photo; p. 58 right: Keith/Custom Medical Stock; p. 60: reprinted courtesy of the John Money Collections at the Kinsey Institute for Research in Sex, Gender, and Reproduction, Inc; p. 69 top right: Thierry Berrod, Mona Lisa Production/Photo Researchers, Inc.; p. 73 left: Chris Rout/Alamy; p. 73 center: Chris Rout/Alamy; p. 73 right: Chris Rout/Alamy; p. 74 top left: John Birdsall/Age Fotostock; p. 76 bottom: CHASSENET/BSIP/Age Fotostock; p. 85: Oote Boe 1/Alamy; p. 91 top right: Getty Images; p. 91 bottom: Jim Cummins/Taxi/Getty Images. **Chapter 4:** p. 94 top left: Dr. David Phillips/Visuals Unlimited/Getty Images; p. 94 center left: rubberball/Glow Images; p. 94 bottom: www.hiped.com/Fotolia; p. 95: Roger Antrobus/Taxi/Getty Images; p. 99 left: Custom Medical Stock Photo; p. 99 center: John Henderson/Alamy; p. 99 right: Custom Medical Stock Photo; p. 103: Dr. David Phillips/Visuals Unlimited/Getty Images; p. 105: Jose Luis Pelaez, Inc/Blend Images/Getty Images; p. 112: rubberball/Glow Images; p. 114: J.B Nicholas/Splash News/Newscom. **Chapter 5:** p. 122 top left: Comstock/Thinkstock; p. 122 center left: Michael Austen/Alamy; p. 122 bottom: Hamik/Fotolia; p. 123: Beyond/Superstock; p. 124: Martin Fowler/Shutterstock; p. 127: Comstock/Thinkstock; p. 128 bottom left: SuperStock; p. 129 bottom right: Katrina Brown/Fotolia; p. 130 top right: Veer; p. 134: Michael Austen/Alamy; p. 137: Dmitry Melnikov/Shutterstock; p. 142: Artpose Adam Borkowski/Shutterstock; p. 145: Yuri Arcurs/Shutterstock; p. 147: Andres Rodriguez/Fotolia. **Chapter 6:** p. 152 top left: Buena Vista Images/The Image Bank/Getty Images; p. 152 bottom left: Adam Gault/Alamy; p. 152 bottom: Modella/Shutterstock; p. 153: Rubberball/Mike Kemp/Getty Images; p. 154: Tom Grill/Spirit/Corbis; p. 159 top right: reprinted courtesy of the John Money Collections at the Kinsey Institute for Research in Sex, Gender, and Reproduction, Inc; p. 161 bottom right: Roger de la Harpe/Gallo Images/Getty Images; p. 162: Stockbroker/SuperStock; p. 163: REUTERS/Str Old; p. 164: Mirek Towski/Contributor/Time & Life Pictures/Getty Images; p. 165: RubberBall/SuperStock; p. 168: Peter Treanor/Alamy; p. 169: Taxi/Getty Images; p. 171 bottom right: Adam Gault/Alamy; p. 175 top right: Buena Vista Images/The Image Bank/Getty Images; p. 176: RubberBall/SuperStock; p. 179 top right: Tony Freeman/PhotoEdit, Inc. **Chapter 7:** p. 184 top: Pictorial Press Ltd/Alamy; p. 184 center: Sam Bloomberg-Rissman/Blend Images/Alamy; p. 184 bottom: xpixel/Shutterstock; p. 185: RubberBall/Superstock; p. 186: Fancy/Alamy; p. 189 left: Ingram Publishing/Alamy; p. 189 center: Gazimal/Getty Images; p. 189 right: blickwinkel/Alamy; p. 190 bottom: Elliot, A. J., & Niesta, D. (2008). Romantic red: Red enhances men's attraction to women. Journal of Personality and Social Psychology, 95(5), 1150–1164; p. 191 bottom left: Pictorial Press Ltd/Alamy; p. 191 bottom left: Leah-Anne Thompson/Shutterstock.com; p. 191 bottom right: Comstock/Jupiterimages/Thinkstock; p. 191 bottom right: Celebrity Spotlight/Alamy; p. 192: Apollofoto/Shutterstock; p. 193: StockLite/Shutterstock; p. 194 bottom left: Shannon J Hager/Flickr/Getty Images; p. 194 bottom right: Sam Bloomberg-Rissman/Blend Images/Alamy; p. 197: Alila/Fotolia; p. 197 bottom left: Kazuhiro Nogi/AFP/Getty Images/Newscom; p. 201: Odua Images/Shutterstock; p. 205: Flashon Studio/Shutterstock. **Chapter 8:** p. 208 top: Corinne Malet/PhotoAlto Agency/Getty Images; p. 208 center: irabel8/Shutterstock; p. 208: Arcady/Fotolia; p. 209: Jose Luis Pelaez Inc/Blend Images/Getty Images; p. 210 top left: Véronique Durruty/Le Desk/Alamy; p. 212: Peter Scholey/Photographer's Choice/Getty Images; p. 213 top right: Mika/zefa/Corbis; p. 214: Corinne Malet/PhotoAlto Agency/Getty Images; p. 215: Spencer Rathus; p. 220 top right: PhotoAlto Photography/Veer; p. 221 bottom left: Digital Vision/Getty Images; p. 222: Dan Burn-Forti/Getty Images; p. 223 top: irabel8/Shutterstock; p. 224: Corbis/SuperStock; p. 227 top right: Custom Medical Stock Photo/Alamy. **Chapter 9:** p. 230 top: Sanjay Deva/Fotolia; p. 230 center: Alloy Photography/VEER; p. 230 bottom: Pavel Losevsky/Fotolia; p. 231: Dominique Douieb/ PhotoAlto Agency RF Collections/Getty Images; p. 232: Public Domain/Pearson; p. 235: Sandro Botticelli/The Bridgeman Art Library/Getty Images; p. 239: John Henderson/Alamy; p. 241 bottom right: Sanjay Deva/Fotolia; p. 242 top left: Alloy Photography/VEER. **Chapter 10:** p. 258 top: Focus Films/Everett Collection; p. 258 center: Ryan McVay/Photodisc/Getty Images; p. 258 bottom: Paulista/Fotolia; p. 259 bottom right: Blend Images/Veer; p. 260 top right: Focus Films/Everett Collection; p. 262: Ingram Publishing/SuperStock; p. 269 top right: Michael Dwyer/Alamy; p. 272 top left: I. Savic, and P. Lindström. (2008). PET and MRI show differences in cerebral asymmetry and functional connectivity between homo- and heterosexual subjects. Published online on June 16, 2008. Proceedings of the National Academy of Sciences. USA, 10.1073/pnas.0801566105; p. 277 top right: Mike Kemp/Glow Images; p. 281 bottom: Jim West/Alamy; p. 283 top right: The Standard-Times, Peter Pereira/AP images; p. 287 top: Ryan McVay/Getty Images. **Chapter 11:** p. 290 top: DAVID PHILLIPS/PRI/Photo Researchers/Getty Images; p. 290 center: Exactostock/SuperStock; p. 290 bottom: Simon/Fotolia; p. 291: Blend Images/SuperStock; p. 292: Comstock/Thinkstock; p. 293 top right: DAVID PHILLIPS/PRI/ Photo Researchers/Getty Images; p. 295: BSIP SA/Alamy; p. 299 top right: Phanie/SuperStock; p. 300 top left: "Junko Kimura/Getty Images Entertainment/Getty Images"; p. 303: Blend Images/veer; p. 305: Exactostock/SuperStock; p. 315: Jaqui Farrow/Bubbles Photolibrary/Alamy; p. 317: Bettmann/Corbis; p. 318: Courtesy of Jeff Nevid; p. 320: Illene MacDonald/PhotoEdit; p. 327: reflektastudios/Fotolia; p. 328 top left: Nancy Ostertag/Getty Images; p. 328: Adrian Weinbrecht/DK Images. **Chapter 12:** p. 334 bottom: AP Photo/File; p. 334 center: Upi/Landov; p. 334 bottom: vectormart/Fotolia; p. 335 bottom right: image100 Photography/Veer; p. 336 top right: AP Photo/File; p. 342 top left: Ocean Photography/Veer; p. 343 top right: Upi/Landov; p. 345 top: Michael Newman/PhotoEdit; p. 350 top left: Science Source/Photo Researchers; p. 351 top right: Comstock/Thinkstock; p. 353: Ruth Jenkinson/ Dorling Kindersley/Getty Images; p. 358: Michael Newman/PhotoEdit; p. 361: Yang Liu/Flirt/Corbis; p. 365: Steve Herbert/ The New York Times/Redux. **Chapter 13:** p. 372 top right: Blend Images/Veer; p. 372 center: Sean Justice/Riser/Getty Images; p. 372: Alice/Fotolia; p. 373: Rubberball/Getty Images; p. 375: Robert Brenner/PhotoEdit; p. 375: shalunishka/Shutterstock; p. 380: Igor Mojzes/Fotolia; p. 382: Blend Images/Veer; p. 384: Sean Justice/Riser/Getty Images; p. 386: Rubberball/Glow Images; p. 387: Peter Mason/ Stone/Getty Images. **Chapter 14:** p. 398 center left: Corbis Photography/Veer; p. 398 center left: Ariel Skelley/Glow Images, Inc.; p. 398 bottom: Alice/Fotolia; p. 399: George Doyle/Stockbyte/Getty Images; p. 401: Corbis Photography/Veer; p. 403 top: Tim Pannell/Cardinal/Corbis; p. 403 bottom: auremar/Shutterstock.com; p. 410: Frank Micelotta/Getty Images; p. 411: Zach Goldberg/Queerstock, Inc./Alamy; p. 412: Christine Reilly/Solus/Corbis; p. 424: Corbis Photography/Veer; p. 425: Ariel Skelley/Glow Images, Inc.; p. 429: Imagesource/Getty Images. **Chapter 15:** p. 434 top left: Don Hammond/Design Pics Inc./Alamy; p. 434 center left: BananaStock/Jupiter Images; p. 434 bottom: StudioAraminta/Fotolia; p. 435: PhotoAlto Photography/Veer; p. 436: Ryan McVay/Digital Vision/Getty Images; p. 440: Don Hammond/Design Pics Inc./Alamy; p. 445: Corbis Photography/Veer; p. 446: RubberBall/Alamy; p. 448: PhotoLink/Photodisc/Getty Images; p. 450: BananaStock/Jupiter Images; p. 457: G. Thomas Bishop/Custom Medical Stock Photo/Newscom; p. 458: RubberBall/SuperStock; p. 460: David Kilpatrick/Alamy; p. 461: PRNewsFoto/UroMetrics, Inc./AP Photos. **Chapter 16:** p. 468 top: Oliver Eltinger/Blink/Corbis; p. 468 center left: AISPIX by Image Source/Shutterstock; p. 468 bottom: vinz89/Fotolia; p. 469: Ocean Photography/Veer; p. 471: Oliver Eltinger/Blink/Corbis; p. 476: Dr. P. Marazzi/Photo Researchers; p. 477: Sebastian Kaulitzki/Shutterstock; p. 479: UIG via Getty Images; p. 488: Scott Camazine/Photo Researchers, Inc.; p. 491: CHUCK ZOVKO/EPA/Newscom; p. 492: AISPIX by Image Source/Shutterstock; p. 496: Custom Medical Stock; p. 497: Marazzi/Photo Researchers, Inc.; p. 500 top left: E. Gray/Photo Researchers, Inc. **Chapter 17:** p. 504 top left: Rainer Elstermann/Fancy/Alamy; p. 504 center left: Olinchuk/Shutterstock; p. 504 bottom: Ellie Nator/Fotolia; p. 505: Sarah Ashun/Dorling Kindersley/Getty Images; p. 506 top: Digital Vision/Getty Images; p. 509: Rainer Elstermann/Fancy/Alamy; p. 510: Corbis Cusp/Alamy; p. 513: Warrick Page/Getty Images; p. 514: fStop/Alamy; p. 518: Blend Images/Veer; p. 519 top: Olinchuk/Shutterstock; p. 524 top: PhotoAlto Photography/Veer; p. 525: philipus/Alamy; p. 529: Darrin Klimek/ Photonica/Getty Images. **Chapter 18:** p. 532 top: WpN/Photoshot; p. 532 center left: ChameleonsEye/Shutterstock; p. 532 bottom: Viktoria/Shutterstock; p. 533: RubberBall Photography/Veer; p. 534 top: Paul Vathis/AP images; p. 536 left: Ben Wyeth/Alamy; p. 536 right: Tim Boyles/Stringer/Getty Images News/Getty Images; p. 541 bottom: WpN/Photoshot; p. 545: Rommel Canlas/Shutterstock; p. 548: ChameleonsEye/Shutterstock; p. 552: WireImage/Getty Images; p. 553: Warren County Police/ZUMA Press/Newscom; p. 557: Balqis Amran/Shutterstock. **Chapter 19:** p. 566 center left: Mike McQueen/Impact/HIP/The Image Works; p. 566 center left: mtkang/Shutterstock; p. 566 bottom: Lee Avison Photography/Shutterstock; p. 567 center right: Tom Stoddart/Getty Images; p. 568 top right: Redaccion eltiempo.com/El Tiempo de Colombia/Newscom; p. 569 top left: Stephen Chernin/AP Images; p. 569 top right: Carlo Allegri/Reuters/Landov; p. 571 top right: Sean Sprague/The Image Works; p. 573 top right: Bloomberg via Getty Images; p. 574 top left: Daevid/Fotolia; p. 578 top left: Wallenrock/Shutterstock.com; p. 580 bottom left: Mike McQueen/Impact/HIP/The Image Works; p. 581 bottom right: davidevison/Fotolia; p. 585 center right: mtkang/Shutterstock; p. 588 top left: Miriam Doerr/Shutterstock.

Name Index

Subject Index

(continued)

(*continued*)

(*continued*)

A Sexual History Time Line

The world of human sexuality has been marked by many influential historical events. To illustrate we journey back over 150 years of significant events that have changed our views of human sexuality.

1846
U.S. patent issued for first diaphragm contraceptive device (5)

1873
Congress passes Comstock Act outlawing distribution of contraception information and devices (5)

1874
Women's Christian Temperance Union founded to oppose men's drinking of alcohol and engaging in "immoral acts" (15)

1897
Havelock Ellis publishes first of six-volume, *Studies in the Psychology of Sex*; advocating sex as pleasurable, central function in life (6)

1909
Sigmund Freud lectures at Clark University in Massachusetts; introduces U.S. to his theories of sex as primary driving force in human nature (1)

1916
Margaret Sanger arrested and jailed for opening first birth control clinic in Brooklyn signaling change in sexual norms; marks separation of sex from reproduction for women (5)

1920s
Widespread introduction of automobile offers privacy and independence for dating couples (4)

1923
John Kellogg becomes president of Battle Creek Sanitarium; promotes plain foods such as corn flakes in order to prevent sexual feelings and discourage masturbation (6)

1953
Hugh Hefner publishes first issue of *Playboy Magazine* (15)

1953
Christine Jorgensen is among first to undergo male-to-female "sex change" operation (10)

1953
Publication of *Kinsey Institute's Sexual Behavior of the Human Female*; sells 250,000 copies (1, 6)

1966
Publication of *Human Sexual Response* by Masters and Johnson revolutionizes public understanding of sexual physiology (3, 6, 7)

1969
Huge rock concert at Woodstock marks culmination of "hippie free love" movement (6)

1975
U.S. Civil Service Administration lifts ban on hiring gays and lesbians (11)

1976
The Hite Report is published detailing sexual fantasies and behaviors of women (1, 6)

1950 | **1960** | **1970** | **1980**

1934
Catholic Church forms "Legion of Decency" to evaluate and rate films; Hollywood responds by reducing sexual content of movies (15)

1934
Appeals court overturns ruling of James Joyce's *Ulysses* as obscene, signaling liberalization of obscenity laws (15)

1936
U.S. Federal Court overturns Comstock Act's anti-contraception laws (5)

1942
Planned Parenthood Federation of America founded: advocates family planning and sexual satisfaction in marriage (5)

1950
Existence of "zone of erogenous feeling" on wall of vagina suggested by Ernst Grafenberg (now known as the G-Spot) (2)

1960
Feminine Mystique by Betty Friedan published; signals beginning of feminist movement (10)

1960 Food and Drug Administration approves first oral contraceptive: trade name: "Enovid" (5)

1948
Publication of *Kinsey Institute's Sexual Behavior and the Human Male*; sold 200,000 copies and was on *The New York Times* bestseller list for 27 weeks (1, 6)

1969
Police clash violently with patrons of Stonewall Inn, a gay bar in New York's Greenwich Village; marks beginning of gay rights movement (11)

1970
Feature film *The Boys in the Band* first wide-release movie with openly gay plot and characters (11)

1972
Rocky Horror Picture Show shakes up gender stereotypes (10)

1973
The American Psychiatric Association (APA) votes to remove homosexuality from list of psychological disorders (11)

1973
U.S. Supreme Court, in landmark decision in case of *Roe vs. Wade*; declares a woman's right to an abortion is protected by her constitutional right to privacy, effectively legalizing abortion (5, 9)

1978
Birth of Louise Brown, first infant conceived through in vitro fertilization, dubbed "test tube baby" by media (9)

1979
California first state to classify forced sex by husband on wife as rape (13)

(Numbers in parentheses indicate text chapters for additional information)

MyDevelopmentLab

MyDevelopmentLab for Human Sexuality combines proven learning applications with powerful assessment to engage students, assess their learning, and help them succeed.

- **An individualized study plan for each student**, based on performance on chapter pre-tests, helps students focus on the specific topics where they need the most support. The personalized study plan arranges content from less complex thinking, like remembering and understanding—to more complex critical thinking skills—like applying and analyzing and is based on Bloom's taxonomy. Every level of the study plan provides a formative assessment quiz.

- **The NEW MyDevelopmentLab Video Series for Human Sexuality** engages students and brings course material to life through a wide range of videos, featuring over 125 carefully selected clips.

- **Media Assignments** for each chapter—including videos with assignable questions—feed directly into the gradebook, enabling instructors to track student progress automatically.

- **The Pearson eText** lets students access their textbook anytime and anywhere, and any way they want, including listening online. With assessment tied to every chapter, students get immediate feedback, and instructors can see what their students know with just a few clicks. Instructors can also personalize MyDevelopmentLab to meet the needs of their students.

The NEW MyDevelopmentLab Video Series for Human Sexuality engages students and brings course material to life through a wide range of videos, featuring over 125 carefully selected clips. Drawn from a variety of sources including the Associated Press, ABC News, and Science Central, this video series contains the most recent research, science, and applications in human sexuality. Many of the videos are accompanied by media assignments in MyDevelopmentLab that allow instructors to assess student comprehension. For maximum flexibility, the videos are also available for viewing on iPad and iPhone.

For additional information please visit **www.mydevelopmentlab.com**